The
Cherry Red
Non-League Newsdesk
Annual 2007

by
James Wright

CONTENTS

PUBLISHED BY
James Wright
Non-League Newsdesk
6 Harp Chase
Taunton
Somerset TA1 3RY
(Tel: 07786 636659 Fax: 0871 994 3274)
Email: james@nlnewsdesk.co.uk

DESIGNED AND SET BY
Nigel Davis
Broomhouse Farmhouse
George Nympton
South Molton
Devon EX36 4JF
(Tel: 01769 572257/ 07768 204784)
Email: NigelDavis@aol.com or NLNAnnual@aol.com

PRINTED BY
Antony Rowe Ltd
Bumpers Farm
Chippenham
Wiltshire SN14 6LH
(Tel: 01249 659 705 Fax: 01249 443 103)

ISBN 978-0-9539198-7-1

FRONT COVER

Taunton Town's Shane Hobbs (left) battles with Toby Redwood of Lymington & New
Milton during a British Gas Business Southern League fixture at Wordsworth Drive
Photo: Somerset County Gazette

EDITORIAL

Without doubt the great positive of the 2006-07 season was Non-League's return to Wembley Stadium. The Trophy and Vase finals were memorable occasions, not least because they were in a way unexpected bonuses, the availability of the new venue not being confirmed until quite late in the day. The attendances of both games were of course boosted by general sports followers eager to take an early, affordable look at the new facilities.

The Trophy and Vase have done well to survive the years in exile. Without the lure of Wembley, crowds in latter rounds in recent times have been alarmingly low. I believe it was no coincidence that, whilst the FA Trophy final was almost an exclusive preserve of Conference clubs during the 1990s, five out of the seven finals in the non-Wembley years featured teams from outside the top flight. Hopefully, now the Trophy and Vase have come home, the crowds will come flooding back and the top clubs will treat the competitions with the utmost seriousness.

I say "hopefully" because the nature of the pyramid has changed considerably since the last Wembley finals in 2000. Many smaller clubs are now being required to travel far greater distances week in, week out for league games, so the novelty value of occasional long Trophy or Vase away days may be somewhat diminished. It remains to be seen.

I hope you enjoy this eighth edition of our Annual. Production has not been without its "excitements", not least the shock closure in June of our long-time printers Bath Press Ltd. Thankfully CPI Anthony Rowe of Chippenham have been able to take on the job at short notice. Our sincere thanks, and best wishes for the future, go to Jeremy Hancock and his Bath Press team both for facilitating this transfer and all their help in recent years.

My thanks also go to Iain McNay of Cherry Red Records for his generous sponsorship, to Nigel Davis for over-seeing technical matters, to Mark Broom for revamping the website, to Dave Boyle of Supporters Direct for his interesting introduction piece, and of course the vast army of contributors who feed me scores and snippets throughout the season. As ever, I've tried to list all contributors below.

WWW.NLNEWSDESK.CO.UK

JAMES WRIGHT

CONTRIBUTORS

John Adamson, Roy Ainge, Roger Allen, Martin Bayliss, Jim Bean, Chris Berezai, Gary Berwick, Jeremy Biggs, Paul Birkitt, Dave Boyle, Daniel Braddock, Chris Bridges, Ron Bridges, Mark Broom, Martin Bryant, Ann Camm, Steve Clark, Tom Clark, Alan Constable, John Cooper, Greg Cunningham, Peter Danzey, William Davies, Ed Davis, Richard Durrant, Rolant Ellis, Denis Emery, Margaret Errington, Robert Errington, Bob Flight, Alun Foulkes, Peter Francis, Bill Gardner, Peter Godfrey, Arthur Green, James Greenwood, Tony Griffiths, Rob Grillo, Gary Hall, Ian Hallett, Phil Hiscox, Stephen Hosmer, Nick House, Frank Hunt, David Jarrett, Geoff Jenkins, Adam Jeskins, Dennis Johnson, Neil Johnson, Graham Jones, Neil Juggins, Brian King, Phil Lewis, David Lumley, David Marsay, Dave McCann, Danny McConnell, Chris McCullough, Mark McIntyre, Warren McMahon, Mervyn Miles, Jim Milner, Phil Mitcham, Andrew Moffat, John Mugridge, David Munday, Jane Phillips, Michael Piatek, Phil Platt, Stephen Poole, Derrick Procter, Brian Redmond, Hilary Redmond, Philip Rhodes, Paul Rivers, Mark Rozzier, Richard Rundle, Mike Sampson, Del Saunders, Trevor Scorah, John Shenton, Bob Sinclair, Brenda Sprules, Mike Stokes, Rob Sutherland, Trevor Syms, Mel Thomas, Peter Toft, Chris Ward, David Ward, Alan Watkins, Nigel West, Jim Wicks, Chris Wight, David Wilcox, Mike Williams, John Wilson, Mike Wilson, Nigel Wood, Jeff Worrall

THINKING BIG,
THINKING BETTER

I'm honoured to have been asked to write this introduction. My own involvement with non-League football began when I was a student in Lancaster, and I often used to watch the Dolly Blues in far happier times than they are currently experiencing. I used to live near the Giant Axe, so the club bar, the Dolly Blue Tavern, was my local. With entry to matches priced at a highly competitive £2, it was affordable and located in the heart of the community. The trouble was, not enough of the community came to watch, even though the club was at the time pushing for a place in the Conference.

The failure of local people to get behind their clubs in good times is something with which many in the non-League scene will immediately identify. Unfortunately, many will also know all about the implosion of a club over a season, and Lancaster's sad year is not the first and nor will it be the last.

The last five years as an AFC Wimbledon fan have seen me immersed in non-League football. Up to then, I thought of non-League in much the same way as many who have not fully experienced it. Corinthian amateurs playing for the love of it, fans united in pursuit of survival rather than unrealistic dreams of global domination, officials motivated by simple service rather than power-brokering and politicking.

There is much of the non-League story about which English football can be justly proud. The depth of competitive football across the country is something that truly marks it out from many, many other countries and that is in no small part thanks to the unpaid hours put in by supporters all over the country. The culture of personal sacrifice, or pitching in for the greater good with no reward other than just making sure a team can take the park and the punters can pay over the turnstile.

But there is another side to the game which is less than admirable. I consider myself a friend of non-League football, and occasionally, friends have to tell people some home truths that might seem harsh. Like friends in our personal lives, I hope that people understand they are motivated by a desire to see the game improve and become what it could so easily be.

It is important to recognise at the start the obstacles many clubs have to deal with. They are trying to compete against people with better resources, better access to the media and more pull with unaffiliated football fans. There is a justified sense of resentment at the way in which the better appointed within the game seem to go out of their way to make life difficult, such as with the scheduling of European matches. But the idea that if some things from 'big football' simply disappeared life would become good is both untrue and dangerous. It stops the microscope being turned inwards to see what problems lie there.

For starters, there is a simple reason why non-League topics do not get coverage on national and regional TV or newspapers. Clubs outside the top six in the Premiership can make the same claim, and with more people watching the Football League clubs each year than the Premiership, it is a justified grievance. But below the bottom tier of the Football League, the lack of coverage reflects the reality of the audience's interests, not a bias against the non-League game.

Take midweek matches. There is absolutely no chance of the bigger clubs having a moratorium on week night fixtures. Therefore smaller clubs would be as better advised to try to work out why people happily forego watching them in the ground for their sofas and TV than vainly hoping for the European Cup to revert to its old knock-out format.

Now, I'm sure that some would cite a chicken and egg argument here. The lack of coverage the non-League game gets undoubtedly does contribute to the lack of profile,

numbers and everything else the top flight gets for free in every daily newspaper. But regardless of what came first, the top flight is not going to forego coverage, and nor are the newspapers about to radically re-appraise their policy. Change is going to have to come from below. And part of that change might be the 'exclusive' atmosphere that some clubs cultivate. Make no bones about it – following non-League sides is a labour of love. To keep the faith in the face of the rival fayre on offer, the facilities provided, the length of journeys involved requires an uncommon sense of attachment. But maybe this virtue is also a potential problem?

Let me explain. If football fandom is obsessional, to extend the metaphor non-League starts to be a little kinky. It is an acquired taste, and like stilton, black olives and real ale, things that need effort to be acquired will always be minority pursuits in competition to the blandness of the mass-market cheddars and lagers.

But in an environment where the very existence of the club is permanently in doubt, what tastes are people being invited to acquire? When some Manchester United fans intimated they were thinking of starting their own team, many in non-League criticised them. Why did they not all start watching Altrincham or Droylsden? The point is that the whole reason they wanted to start again was because they were annoyed at having someone steal their club. The last thing they wanted to do was do the same to others.

More cynically, officials of one club effectively offered to sell FC United their league place in the Conference as long as they played in that town, an offer the FC United Board were lightning quick to refuse. At AFC Wimbledon, some long-standing officials of Kingstonian intimated that a merger between the two clubs would make most sense. Sadly, the fans of both FC United and Wimbledon continue to be on the end of grumpy letters in the Non-League Paper and on various internet forums. The main crime they appear to have committed though is to be new. They have not got the battle scars of when the club flirted with extinction, nor the enamel badges of the glorious FA Trophy run to the semi-finals way back in the day.

Through my day job I have been lucky enough to travel the country working with fans at the 45 non-League clubs who now have a Supporters' Trust, and through Wimbledon I have seen a lot more clubs. At many there is something there that looks like a siege mentality. There seems to be a lingering passive-aggressive sense that everyone is being measured by how much – or how little – they are doing for the cause. Are they a real fan? Do they do enough?

Let's imagine you have moved to an area with a small non-League club. You don't want to go to the professional club up the road; you like the idea of non-League football and you're attracted to a place without the exploitative attitude prevalent higher up the leagues.

You'll find that the price to get in will more than likely be over £10, which surprises you, as the place looks and feels ramshackle. The toilets are pretty basic and you might see fixtures and fittings well past their useful life, victims of one-too-many cutbacks on year-end maintenance having to be shelved through lack of funds.

You'll be asked to add to your spending for a burger that is often unedifying and potentially unhealthy. There is the commemorative badge to buy, the collection of old programmes to peruse, the Race Night to go to, the end of season fundraiser to turn out for. There is an all-pervading sense of this club having to practically suck money out of people over and above the basics of a match ticket and a cup of tea.

So you contribute but wonder why, despite this, the club seems to be living hand-to-mouth and whether things could perhaps be improved on the cost control side of things, with every bill a crisis waiting to explode. You are told – like an article of faith – that the board and the officials are tremendous chaps who work ever so hard and have done for years. The fact that the benefits of their efforts are not particularly clear is neither here nor there.

The Supporters Club often do not seem interested as there is a raffle to organise, and ultimately one would not want to annoy the directors by asking difficult questions. What if they stop the players attending the end-of-the-season function organised by the Supporters Club? The whole thing feels like a fund-raising scheme that occasionally plays a match and you would be forgiven for deciding that it is not for you.

Best keep to oneself darker thoughts about rampant egos of many of the people who have become owners or Chairman of non-League clubs, musings about why people are prepared to get involved in this level, about the status of the loans the board makes, and whether the ground is being lined up for redevelopment.

It has been going on so long that many simply accept this as the natural order of things. Every few years, the budgets get blasted apart, a crisis ensues, and new local worthies come forward. They run the club the same way as their predecessors, the debts build up and there is a crisis again a bit later leading to a new set of worthies coming forward. Repeat again and again, with a ground sale and new stadium thrown in every generation or so.

Except each time, a little bit more of the club dies. A few more supporters disappear, and a few other potential fans walk away. And a strategy for success that seems to be based on importing the worst features of the professional game will never resolve it.

There is a palpable sense that so many clubs are so desperate for success, so desperate for an end to the incessant work and fund-raising that they will be grateful for any benefactor in a storm, who often as not will leave a few years hence. To paraphrase the Life of Brian, fans say "you're the saviour of the club, and we should know, since we've followed a few!"

The days when non-League football could regularly get five-figure crowds have gone, as have the clubs who were best placed to get those types of crowds, most of them having become league clubs over the last 40 years.

The only path to success for non-League clubs is to truly re-orientate themselves as community clubs, owned by their communities and run by them, not by an assorted collection of businessmen of dubious strategic vision, nor giants of the local football scene who have been doing it their way for so long that they have forgotten that new ideas are always needed. All of this is of course dependent on a volunteer army of well-meaning fans who have for too long acted as though it is tantamount to treason to ask that their love and loyalty be rewarded with a meaningful stake in the club, and a say in how it is run.

Non-League football – away from the hype and greed of the professional game – is well placed to enjoy a renaissance as people want to see their local club and be filled with pride and being able to identify as a supporter of it. As fans of AFC Wimbledon and FC United of Manchester have shown, people who have enjoyed the Premiership can find a lot more to cherish further down.

But for it to happen, the current generation have to change the vibe. There are good times waiting to happen across the country if supporters can grasp the opportunity to make it happen and take on real involvement themselves. Time to get the party started!

DAVE BOYLE, Deputy Chief Executive *Supporters Direct*

(The opinions expressed in this article are those of Dave Boyle, and do not necessarily reflect those of Supporters Direct nor the Cherry Red Non-League Newsdesk Annual)

WWW.CHERRYRED.CO.UK

SOME CONVENTIONS USED WITHIN THIS BOOK

Results grids
W-L: Points awarded to home side
L-W: Points awarded to away side
n/a: Game not scheduled, or not played due to one side having withdrawn
M: Scoreline awarded by management committee
(e.g. 0M0 denotes a goalless draw awarded for an unplayed game)

Some standard abbreviations
aet: after extra time
Corries: Corinthians
INT: Intermediate
INV: Invitation
OB: Old Boys
PF: Playing Field or Playing Fields
Res.: Reserves
Rgrs: Rangers
scr.: Scratched (in cup competitions)
Utd: United
w/o: Walkover (in cup competitions)
Wdrs: Wanderers

Inter-league movement
Promoted/relegated clubs are listed in alphabetical preference with abbreviations showing the origin of the move:-
(E) – Expelled; (F) – Folded; (P) – Promoted; (R) – Relegated; (S) – Switched;
(W) – Withdrew after season ended;
(WN) – Withdrew playing no games;
(WS) – Withdrew during the course of the season

League tables
All tables are final.
Total points and goal adjustments (eg -2g) are shown before the playing record.

Order of entries
The leagues in this book appear alphabetically.

Cup competitions
Penalty shoot-out scores are indicated in parentheses,
the first listed side's score preceding the second listed side.
So (3-4p) means the second listed side won 4-3 on penalties.
Some Welsh cup results are only recorded after penalties and are denoted as such.

Sponsors
For alphabetical ease of reference, and historical continuity sponsors names have been dropped from league titles.
Non-League football is indebted to its many sponsors,
and their generosity is recognised in the strap line at the top of each pages for major leagues, and in parentheses under the title for minor leagues.
The listed sponsors are those in place during 2006-07 unless they have been subsequently replaced

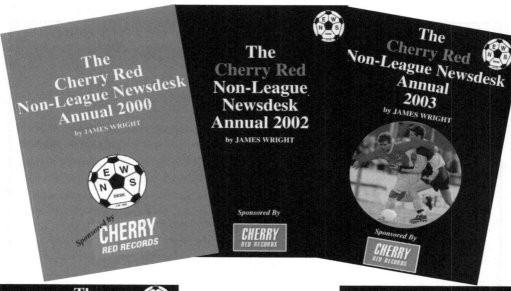

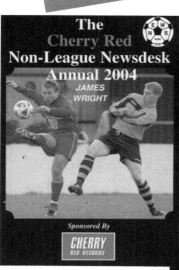

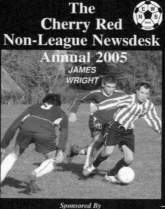

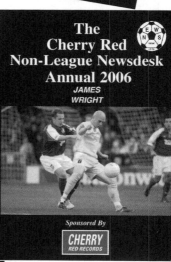

CAPITAL COUNTIES FEEDER LEAGUES TROPHY

For Isthmian feeder clubs not entered in the FA Vase
Sponsored by Anagram Records – part of Cherry Red

FIRST ROUND

MK Scot 4 Bedmond Sports & Social 0
Metropolitan Police Bushey 2 **Frenford Senior** 3 *aet*
Sport London E Benfica 3 Barnston 0
Stony Stratford Town 1 Manford Way 0 *aet*

SECOND ROUND

Brache Sparta 2 **Hadley** 4 *aet*
Bushey Rangers 0 **White Ensign** 1
Epping 1 Bedfont Sports 0
Hatfield Town 2 MK Scot 0
Hertford Heath 4 Winslow United 0
Kent Athletic 2 Hinton 1
Kings Meadow 2 **Knebworth** 3
Sandridge Rovers 3 Elliott Star 2
Sheerwater 3 **Canning Town** 4 *aet*
Spelthorne Sports 0 **Frenford Senior** 2
Sport London E Benfica 1 Farleigh Rovers 0
Stony Straford Town 4 Wormley Rovers 1
Takeley 4 Standon & Puckeridge 2
The 61 FC 3 White Notley 0
Walthamstow Avenue & Pennant (scr.) v **London Lions** (w/o)
Whitewebbs 2 Codicote 1 *aet*

THIRD ROUND

Epping 1 **Stony Stratford Town** 3
Hatfield Town 5 London Lions 2 *aet*
Hertford Heath 2 Hadley 2 *aet* (3-1p)
Knebworth 0 **Frenford Senior** 1 *aet*
Sandridge Rovers 3 Kent Athletic 2 *aet*
Sport London E Benfica 3 **Canning Town** 4 *aet*
The 61 FC 5 Takeley 1
Whitewebbs v White Ensign

QUARTER-FINALS

Hatfield Town 1 Frenford Senior 1 *aet* (5-3p)
Hertford Heath v Whitewebbs/White Ensign
Sandridge Rovers 1 **The 61 FC** 2 *aet*
Stony Stratford Town 2 Canning Town 1

SEMI-FINALS

Hertford Heath/Whitewebbs/White Ensign v The 61 FC
Stony Stratford Town v Hatfield Town

COMPETITION TO BE COMPLETED IN PRE-SEASON 2007-08

AMATEUR FOOTBALL ALLIANCE

AMATEUR COMBINATION

	Albanian	Bealonians	Honourable Artillery Company	Old Aloysians	Old Hamptonians	Old Meadonians	Old Parmiterians	Parkfield	Southgate County	UCL Academicals
Albanian		2-7	1-2	5-2	1-2	0-7	1-2	3-1	2-1	3-5
Bealonians	1-1	P	2-0	2-1	1-1	1-3	1-2	5-1	4-0	1-1
Honourable Artillery Co.	3-0	1-2	R	2-2	2-0	3-1	3-4	4-2	1-1	5-3
Old Aloysians	1-0	1-1	3-4	E	2-1	2-2	0-2	5-2	2-1	1-2
Old Hamptonians	1-2	1-3	5-2	1-1	M	1-2	2-0	6-2	7-3	0-1
Old Meadonians	3-0	3-2	3-1	0-0	3-2		1-0	4-2	5-1	5-0
Old Parmiterians	1-1	2-2	4-3	0-2	1-5	1-10	D	3-1	3-1	2-0
Parkfield	1-2	1-4	1-4	0-3	1-6	0-6	0-3	I	3-2	1-2
Southgate County	1-4	0-3	2-0	1-1	0-3	4-6	6-4	4-1	V	1-6
UCL Academicals	2-0	2-3	2-3	0-1	0-3	1-3	0-1	2-3	2-1	

Premier Division	P	W	D	L	F	A	Pts
Old Meadonians	18	15	2	1	67	21	47
Bealonians	18	10	5	3	45	23	35
Old Parmiterians	18	10	2	6	35	39	32
Old Hamptonians	18	9	2	7	47	27	29
Honourable Artillery Company	18	9	2	7	43	38	29
Old Aloysians	18	7	6	5	30	26	27
UCL Academicals	18	7	1	10	31	37	22
Albanian	18	6	2	10	28	43	20
Southgate County	18	3	2	13	30	57	11
Parkfield	18	2	0	16	23	68	6

Senior Division One		P	W	D	L	F	A	Pts
Enfield Old Grammarians		20	13	1	6	48	23	40
Hale End Athletic		20	12	4	4	52	36	40
Old Ignatian		20	12	3	5	50	24	39
Old Salvatorians		20	11	3	6	53	33	36
Sinjuns Grammarians	-1	20	10	2	8	43	37	31
Old Challoners		20	10	1	9	46	43	31
Glyn Old Boys		20	10	1	9	35	40	31
Economicals		20	8	3	9	29	34	27
Old Tiffinians		20	7	2	11	31	49	23
Old Danes		20	4	1	15	20	61	13
Wood Green Old Boys		20	1	3	16	37	64	6

Senior Division Two		P	W	D	L	F	A	Pts
Old Meadonians Res.		20	14	4	2	60	18	46
Old Suttonians		20	13	6	1	64	18	45
Clapham Old Xaverians		20	13	4	3	53	31	43
Old Paulines		20	10	4	6	57	43	34
Old Vaughanians		20	10	1	9	47	46	31
Shene Old Grammarians		20	8	3	9	70	52	27
Kings Old Boys		20	8	2	10	54	48	26
Old Aloysians Res.		20	7	3	10	37	50	24
Albanian Res.		20	6	0	14	33	73	18
Old Salvatorians Res.	-4	20	4	3	13	32	50	11
Wandsworth Borough		20	1	2	17	22	100	5

Senior Division Three North	P	W	D	L	F	A	Pts
Mill Hill Village	20	15	2	3	75	30	47
Old Minchendenians	20	14	4	2	71	26	46
Old Meadonians 'A'	20	13	3	4	66	21	42
UCL Academicals Res.	20	10	2	8	42	34	32
Old Isleworthians	20	9	1	10	39	50	28
Old Manorians	20	7	5	8	48	54	26
Brent	20	8	2	10	46	60	26
Latymer Old Boys	20	5	4	11	45	53	19
Hale End Athletic Res.	20	6	1	13	34	57	19
Parkfield Res.	20	4	4	12	34	62	16
Southgate County Res.	20	4	2	14	30	83	14

Senior Division Three South		P	W	D	L	F	A	Pts
Old Belgravians		20	13	3	4	54	37	42
Hon. Artillery Co. Res.		20	13	2	5	62	24	41
Old Dorkinians		20	11	5	4	52	33	38
Marsh		20	11	2	7	59	40	35
Old Tenisonians		20	9	2	9	45	47	29
Old Guildfordians		20	8	5	7	32	34	29
Hampstead Heathens	-1	20	8	4	8	34	38	27
Old Hamptonians Res.		20	7	5	8	36	31	26
Fitzwilliam Old Boys		20	7	3	10	37	49	24
John Fisher Old Boys		20	1	7	12	27	62	10
Nat. Westminster Bank		20	1	4	15	26	69	7

(Lower divisions in "Other Leagues" section – page 237)

WWW.CHERRYRED.CO.UK

ARTHURIAN LEAGUE

Note – Old Reptonians withdrew during the course of the season Their results are expunged from the league table	Lancing Old Boys	Old Brentwoods	Old Carthusians	Old Cholmeleians	Old Etonians	Old Foresters	Old Harrovians	Old Reptonians	Old Salopians	Old Westminsters
Lancing Old Boys		0-2	0-3	2-0	3-2	0-0	1-1	2-0	5-4	4-1
Old Brentwoods	0-2	P	2-2	5-2	2-0	1-0	3-3	9-1	4-3	9-2
Old Carthusians	2-0	2-2	R	0-2	2-2	1-0	6-0	n/a	3-1	1-0
Old Cholmeleians	1-2	0-6	0-2	E	3-0	1-3	3-1	4-0	3-2	1-2
Old Etonians	0-0	0-1	3-3	2-1	M	5-1	3-2	10-0	3-4	5-2
Old Foresters	4-0	0-1	2-2	1-0	4-4		3-1	14-1	2-1	3-2
Old Harrovians	3-3	2-1	2-2	4-1	2-0	3-5	D	14-1	W-L	1-1
Old Reptonians	n/a	0-8	n/a	1-1	n/a	0-3	1-5	I	0-5	0-5
Old Salopians	1-9	0-5	1-3	2-0	2-6	1-4	0-4	3-1	V	2-4
Old Westminsters	2-5	0-2	2-6	2-2	4-3	4-0	2-5	n/a	3-2	

Premier Division	P	W	D	L	F	A	Pts
Old Brentwoods	16	11	3	2	46	18	36
Old Carthusians	16	9	6	1	40	19	33
Lancing Old Boys	16	8	4	4	36	26	28
Old Foresters	16	8	3	5	32	27	27
Old Harrovians	16	6	5	5	34	34	23
Old Etonians	16	5	4	7	38	36	19
Old Westminsters	16	5	2	9	33	51	17
Old Cholmeleians	16	4	1	11	20	36	13
Old Salopians	16	2	0	14	26	58	6

Old Reptonians – record expunged

Division One		P	W	D	L	F	A	Pts
Old Bradfieldians		16	12	2	2	45	21	38
Old Tonbridgians		16	11	0	5	50	33	33
Old Aldenhamians		16	7	3	6	38	38	24
Old Wykehamists		16	7	2	7	40	39	23
Old Malvernians		16	6	3	7	39	34	21
Old Radleians		16	6	3	7	31	29	21
Old Haileyburians		16	5	3	8	29	43	18
King's Wimbledon OB		16	5	2	9	27	43	17
Old Chigwellians		16	3	2	11	21	43	11

Division Two		P	W	D	L	F	A	Pts
Old Chigwellians Res.		16	13	1	2	42	15	40
Old Foresters Res.	-3	16	9	1	6	44	35	25
Old Carthusians Res.		16	8	0	8	47	40	24
Old Haberdashers		16	7	2	7	44	37	23
Old Etonians Res.		16	6	4	6	30	32	22
Old Brentwoods Res.		16	6	3	7	25	38	21
Old Westminsters Res.	-6	16	7	2	7	31	32	17
Old Salopians Res.	-3	16	4	3	9	27	42	12
Old Etonians 'A'		16	3	2	11	28	47	11

Division Three		P	W	D	L	F	A	Pts
Old Aldenhamians Res.		14	10	3	1	34	23	33
Old King's Scholars		14	6	3	5	34	26	21
Old Oundelians		14	5	3	6	29	28	18
Old Bradfieldians Res.		14	5	3	6	27	29	18
Old Wellingtonians		14	5	2	7	29	36	17
Old Chigwellians 'A'	-3	14	5	4	5	22	23	16
Old Carthusians 'A'		14	4	3	7	24	28	15
Old Cholmeleians Res.	-3	14	5	1	8	31	37	13

Division Four		P	W	D	L	F	A	Pts
Old Foresters 'A'		14	10	2	2	33	18	32
Old Harrovians Res.		14	8	3	3	37	23	27
Old Westminsters 'A'	-3	14	8	1	5	33	24	22
Old Malvernians Res.		14	6	2	6	26	18	20
Old Brentwoods 'B'		14	6	1	7	24	24	19
Lancing Old Boys Res.		14	4	3	7	17	22	15
Old Brentwoods 'A'		14	4	2	8	18	37	14
Old Eastbournians	-3	14	2	2	10	19	41	5

Division Five		P	W	D	L	F	A	Pts
Old Foresters 'B'		14	9	2	3	29	16	29
Old Berkhamstedians		14	9	1	4	36	18	28
Old Wykehamists Res.	-6	14	10	0	4	37	26	24
Old Cholmeleians 'A'		14	6	1	7	43	31	19
Old Chigwellians 'B'	-3	14	7	0	7	32	23	18
Old Harrovians 'A'	-3	14	6	2	6	30	35	17
Old Amplefordians		14	3	1	10	15	50	10
Old Cholmeleians 'B'	-3	14	2	1	11	24	47	4

ARTHUR DUNN CUP

SEMI-FINALS

Lancing Old Boys 0 **Old Bradfieldians** 1

Old Salopians 2 **Old Harrovians** 3

FINAL

(April 21st at Imperial University, Teddington)

Old Harrovians 1 Old Bradfieldians 0

WWW.NLNEWSDESK.CO.UK

SOUTHERN AMATEUR LEAGUE

	Alleyn Old Boys	Broomfield	Civil Service	East Barnet O. Gram.	Nottsborough	Old Lyonians	Old Owens	Old Salesians	Old Wilsonians	West Wickham	Winchmore Hill
Alleyn Old Boys	S	2-1	4-2	2-2	1-5	3-0	2-3	4-2	0-2	1-1	0-1
Broomfield	0-0	E	3-2	0-2	3-4	4-0	2-3	4-1	0-3	1-0	3-1
Civil Service	3-0	2-4	N	1-0	1-3	5-0	0-4	3-1	0-3	0-1	2-4
East Barnet Old Grammarians	2-4	3-4	2-3	I	1-3	2-2	2-6	0-3	0-4	1-1	0-7
Nottsborough	5-1	1-2	3-2	3-0	O	4-3	1-1	2-0	2-1	3-1	2-3
Old Lyonians	0-2	3-2	1-3	1-0	0-7	R	0-6	1-2	0-3	2-6	0-4
Old Owens	3-1	1-0	2-2	1-0	0-3	4-0		7-1	1-2	1-2	3-1
Old Salesians	4-1	2-3	0-2	4-2	2-2	2-0	1-2		0-3	0-2	1-1
Old Wilsonians	2-0	4-1	2-1	5-0	2-3	2-0	3-2	2-3	O	0-2	2-1
West Wickham	1-1	4-0	3-0	5-0	0-4	3-0	3-2	1-1	0-0	N	3-0
Winchmore Hill	3-0	2-1	3-0	4-1	0-5	6-0	2-1	0-0	1-0	0-2	E

Senior Division One

	P	W	D	L	F	A	Pts
Nottsborough	20	16	2	2	65	24	50
Old Wilsonians	20	14	1	5	45	17	43
West Wickham	20	12	5	3	41	17	41
Old Owens	20	12	2	6	53	28	38
Winchmore Hill	20	12	2	6	44	26	38
Broomfield	20	9	1	10	38	40	28
Civil Service	20	7	1	12	34	43	22
Old Salesians	20	6	4	10	30	42	22
Alleyn Old Boys	20	6	4	10	29	42	22
Old Lyonians	20	2	1	17	13	70	7
E. Barnet Old Grammarians	20	1	3	16	20	63	6

Senior Division Two

	P	W	D	L	F	A	Pts
Polytechnic	20	14	3	3	60	22	45
Old Actonians Association	20	12	3	5	52	34	39
Carshalton	20	11	4	5	42	29	37
Weirside Rangers	20	11	3	6	45	39	36
HSBC	20	10	4	6	50	41	34
Old Esthameians	20	10	0	10	38	41	30
Norsemen	20	8	3	9	32	31	27
Merton	20	6	3	11	33	44	21
BB Eagles	20	4	5	11	39	52	17
Bank of England	20	4	5	11	29	45	17
Ibis	20	2	3	15	35	77	9

Senior Division Three

	P	W	D	L	F	A	Pts
South Bank Cuaco	20	15	2	3	64	34	47
Kew Association	20	13	4	3	61	38	43
Old Westminster Citizens	20	12	4	4	56	34	40
Crouch End Vampires	20	9	7	4	46	25	34
Old Parkonians	20	9	5	6	42	34	32
Old Finchleians	20	9	3	8	55	34	30
Old Latymerians	20	9	1	10	38	46	28
Southgate Olympic	20	4	6	10	41	57	18
Old Stationers	20	5	3	12	34	57	18
Lloyds TSB Bank	20	3	2	15	31	76	11
Alexandra Park	20	2	3	15	30	63	9

Intermediate Division One

	P	W	D	L	F	A	Pts
West Wickham Res.	20	13	5	2	48	17	44
Civil Service Res.	20	12	3	5	41	21	39
Nottsborough Res.	20	11	4	5	42	26	37
Winchmore Hill Res.	20	8	6	6	27	23	30
Old Wilsonians Res.	20	8	6	6	31	31	30
HSBC Res.	20	9	2	9	41	41	29
Old Actonians A. Res. -2	20	7	5	8	32	39	24
Old Owens Res.	20	6	4	10	40	34	22
East Barnet Old Gram. Res.	20	7	1	12	38	39	22
Old Finchleians Res.	20	6	2	12	32	55	20
Polytechnic Res.	20	2	4	14	19	65	10

Intermediate Division Two

	P	W	D	L	F	A	Pts
Carshalton Res.	20	14	3	3	73	31	45
Old Esthameians Res.	20	14	3	3	57	28	45
Weirside Rangers Res.	20	11	4	5	59	30	37
Merton Res.	20	8	7	5	30	33	31
Alleyn Old Boys Res.	20	9	3	8	43	39	30
BB Eagles Res.	20	8	3	9	48	49	27
Old Salesians Res.	20	8	3	9	33	39	27
Bank of England Res.	20	8	2	10	29	49	26
Norsemen Res. -3	20	6	3	11	52	61	18
Old Westminster C. Res.	20	2	5	13	39	68	11
Broomfield Res.	20	3	2	15	26	62	11

Intermediate Division Three

	P	W	D	L	F	A	Pts
Crouch End Vampires Res.	20	12	4	4	59	32	40
Old Latymerians Res.	20	12	3	5	49	42	39
Old Parkonians Res.	20	12	2	6	52	34	38
Southgate Olympic Res.	20	11	4	5	50	24	37
South Bank Cuaco Res.	20	10	6	4	60	34	36
Kew Association Res.	20	10	5	5	42	32	35
Ibis Res.	20	9	1	10	39	31	28
Alexandra Park Res.	20	6	4	10	39	42	22
Old Lyonians Res.	20	4	4	12	37	62	16
Lloyds TSB Bank Res.	20	2	3	15	26	83	9
Old Stationers Res. -2	20	1	6	13	23	60	7

(Lower divisions in "Other Leagues" section – page 257)

AMATEUR FOOTBALL ALLIANCE SENIOR CUP

FIRST ROUND

Albanian 3 **Ibis** 4

Alleyn Old Boys 2 Enfield Old Grammarians 1

Bank of England 1 **Old Buckwellians** 3

Bealonians 6 Old Woodhouseians 0

Brent 1 **HSBC** 7

Cardinal Manning Old Boys 5 Parkfield 3

Carshalton 2 Old Minchendenians 1

Fulham Compton Old Boys 2

Old Vaughanians 2 *aet* (3-4p)

Lancing Old Boys 1 **Hale End Athletic** 2

Lloyds TSB Bank 3 Wandsworth Borough 2 *aet*

Marsh 1 **Honourable Artillery Company** 3

Merton 4 Southgate Olympic 0

Mill Hill County Old Boys 4 **Old Malvernians** 5

Old Actonians Association 3 Glyn Old Boys 2

Old Belgravians 3 **Old Westminster Citizens** 4

Old Brentwoods 2 Old Challoners 0

Old Cholmeleians 4 BB Eagles 0

Old Finchleians 2 **Alexandra Park** 3

Old Foresters 3 **Mill Hill Village** 7

Old Isleworthians 2 **Old Tenisonians** 7

Old Latymerians 8 The Comets

(New Scotland Yard) 1

Old Lyonians 0 **Clapham Old Xaverians** 2

Old Manorians 1 Old Chigwellians 0

Old Parkonians 0 **Old Carthusians** 3

Old Paulines 2 **Hampstead Hthns** 2 *aet* (3-4p)

Old Reptonians (w/o) v Old Wokingians (scr.)

Old Salopians 7 Pegasus 2

Old Sedcopians 2 **Sinjuns Grammarians** 6

Old Tiffinians 3 **Old Suttonians** 4

Queen Mary College Old Boys 0 **Nottsborough** 9

UCL Academicals 5 Old Salvatorians 0

SECOND ROUND

Alexandra Park 5 Old Esthameians 4

Bromleian Sports 1 Wake Green Amateurs 0

Cardinal Manning Old Boys 2 Old Manorians 0

Carshalton 4 Hampstead Heathens 2

Clapham Old Xaverians 1 **Crouch End Vampires** 2

East Barnet Old Gramm. 3 **West Wickham** 9

HSBC 9 Old Bradfieldians 0

Latymer Old Boys 4 **Old Edmontonians** 5

Lloyds TSB Bank 2 **Kew Association** 5

Merton 4 Old Cholmeleians 2

Mill Hill Village 0 **UCL Academicals** 2

National Westminster Bank 0 **Old Ignatians** 4

Norsemen 0 **Honourable Artillery Company** 1

Nottsborough 3 Old Meadonians 1

Old Aloysians 1 **Ibis** 2

Old Brentwoods 0 **Old Actonians Association** 2

Old Carthusians 1

Old Guildfordians 1 *aet* (3-2p)

Old Danes 2 Old Buckwellians 0

Old Owens 5 Old Latymerians 2

Old Reptonians 0 **Old Hamptonians** 6

Old Salopians 4 Old Stationers 1

Old Suttonians 0 **Civil Service** 2

Old Vaughanians 8 Old Malvernians 1

Old Westminster Citizens 1 **Old Salesians** 3

Old Wilsonians 1 **Alleyn Old Boys** 2 *aet*

Polytechnic 7 Old Tenisonians 2

Sinjuns Grammarians 3 Hale End Athletic 0

Southgate County 0 **Bealonians** 3

Weirside Rangers 3 London Welsh 0

William Fitt 5 **South Bank Cuaco** 5 *aet* (3-4p)

Winchmore Hill 7 Old Camdenians 0

Wood Green Old Boys 3 **Broomfield** 4

THIRD ROUND

Alexandra Park 1 **UCL Academicals** 3

Alleyn Old Boys 2 **Nottsborough** 4

Cardinal Manning Old Boys 3 Ibis 2

Civil Service 3 Old Ignatians 1

Crouch End Vampires 0 **Old Owens** 3

Honourable Artillery Company 6 Old Danes 1

Kew Association 3 **Sinjuns Grammarians** 4 *aet*

Merton 4 Old Salopians 3

Old Actonians Association 1 **Winchmore Hill** 2

Old Carthusians 2 HSBC 0

Old Edmontonians 3 Old Vaughanians 1

Old Hamptonians 3 South Bank Cuaco 2

Old Salesians 1 **Carshalton** 2

Polytechnic 3 Broomfield 0

Weirside Rangers 0 **Bealonians** 2

West Wickham 1 Bromleian Sports 0

FOURTH ROUND

Cardinal Manning Old Boys 0 **UCL Academicals** 1

Carshalton 1 **Civil Service** 2

Honourable Artillery Company 4 Bealonians 1

Merton 2 **Old Carthusians** 4

Old Hamptonians 3 Old Owens 2

Polytechnic 6 Old Edmontonians 0

Sinjuns Grammarians 1 **Nottsborough** 4

West Wickham 1 Winchmore Hill 0

QUARTER-FINALS

Old Carthusians 0 **Old Hamptonians** 1

Polytechnic 1 **Hon. Artillery Co.** 1 *aet* (3-4p)

UCL Academicals 1 **Nottsborough** 3

West Wickham 2 Civil Service 1

SEMI-FINALS

(both at UCL Academicals)

Old Hamptonians 2 Honourable Artillery Company 1

West Wickham 2 Nottsborough 0

FINAL

(April 14th at Old Parkonians)

West Wickham 4 Old Hamptonians 0

ANGLIAN COMBINATION

	Acle United	Attleborough Town	Beccles Town	Blofield United	Brandon Town	Cromer Town	Dersingham Rovers	Halvergate United	Lowestoft Town Res.	Mattishall	North Walsham Town	Norwich Union	Sheringham	Sprowston Athletic	St Andrews	Wroxham Res.
Acle United	P	3-1	2-0	2-3	1-3	3-3	7-1	1-2	2-0	1-1	5-0	2-2	1-2	3-3	3-1	6-2
Attleborough Town	1-6	R	1-3	2-2	0-4	1-3	3-3	3-1	1-2	1-2	1-0	3-1	1-2	1-1	5-2	2-0
Beccles Town	3-1	4-1	E	2-4	0-3	3-1	0-1	3-0	2-3	2-1	4-2	1-1	0-3	2-0	1-0	3-3
Blofield United	2-1	3-1	5-0	M	4-2	3-2	0-2	2-1	5-1	1-0	1-0	1-0	1-1	2-1	4-1	2-1
Brandon Town	2-1	4-1	3-0	4-1	I	3-2	1-2	3-0	1-0	5-1	1-1	4-2	1-0	1-4	3-0	3-3
Cromer Town	7-2	4-1	2-1	1-1	2-1	E	5-2	0-2	4-1	3-1	3-3	2-0	2-1	2-2	5-2	3-0
Dersingham Rovers	4-2	6-1	1-1	0-0	1-2	1-2	R	2-3	1-1	0-0	5-1	4-1	2-1	4-2	3-3	3-0
Halvergate United	0-1	5-0	2-0	1-5	0-1	3-2	2-3		3-1	2-0	5-1	6-1	0-1	1-2	3-1	0-3
Lowestoft Town Res.	2-1	3-0	0-5	4-3	2-2	1-4	3-0	1-0	D	0-1	2-0	0-1	0-2	1-1	0-1	2-1
Mattishall	2-0	4-0	2-1	0-4	2-4	1-3	1-1	0-1	3-1	I	5-1	1-0	1-4	0-0	5-0	1-2
North Walsham Town	2-1	2-0	1-5	1-1	1-2	2-4	2-0	2-0	0-0	0-2	V	0-0	0-4	1-0	1-0	3-3
Norwich Union	0-1	2-0	1-0	0-4	2-3	0-1	0-6	2-3	2-2	1-0	1-0	I	1-4	2-5	3-1	1-3
Sheringham	3-0	3-0	2-1	2-2	1-2	0-0	1-0	2-1	3-5	3-0	0-1	2-1	S	0-1	1-1	1-3
Sprowston Athletic	3-2	2-1	1-6	1-1	1-0	1-4	4-0	2-2	1-1	1-0	5-1	2-5	2-2	I	1-1	1-3
St Andrews	0-1	2-1	0-1	1-2	4-1	0-2	1-2	2-1	0-1	1-2	1-3	1-0	0-1	2-2	O	0-1
Wroxham Res.	2-1	3-2	3-1	2-0	5-1	1-1	3-0	4-1	0-1	3-1	0-0	5-0	2-1	1-1	4-0	N

Premier Division		P	W	D	L	F	A	Pts
Blofield United		30	19	7	4	69	37	64
Brandon Town		30	20	3	7	70	44	63
Sheringham		30	17	6	7	54	28	57
Cromer Town		30	17	5	8	76	47	56
Wroxham Res.		30	16	7	7	64	42	55
Dersingham Rovers		30	13	7	10	60	53	46
Sprowston Athletic		30	11	11	8	53	51	44
Beccles Town		30	13	3	14	55	50	42
Lowestoft Town Res.		30	12	6	12	41	50	42
Acle United		30	11	4	15	63	57	37
Halvergate United	-3	30	13	1	16	51	51	37
Mattishall		30	11	4	15	40	46	37
North Walsham Town		30	8	7	15	32	61	31
Norwich Union		30	8	4	18	36	67	28
St Andrews		30	5	4	21	29	63	19
Attleborough Town		30	5	3	22	36	82	18

MUMMERY CUP
(Premier and Division One teams)

FIRST ROUND

Acle United 2 **Sprowston Athletic** 3
Attleborough Town 1 **Dereham Town Res.** 3
Beccles Town 1 **Lowestoft Town Res.** 3
Blofield United 2 Sprowston Wanderers 0
Brandon Town 2 Mundford 1
Cromer Town 0 **North Walsham Town** 1
Dersingham Rovers 4 Hindringham 0
Halvergate United 2 Stalham Town 1
Hempnall 3 Long Stratton 0
Holt United 0 **Aylsham Wanderers** 3
Loddon United 3 Southwold Town 1
Norwich Union 0 St Andrews 0 *aet* (4-3p)
Sheringham 2 **Wroxham Res.** 3
Watton United 1 **Scole United** 2
Wells Town 0 **Gayton United** 5
Wymondham Town 1 Mattishall 0

ANGLIAN COMBINATION PREMIER DIVISION CONSTITUTION 2007-08

ACLE UNITED . . . . Bridewell Lane, Acle, Norwich NR13 3RA 01493 751379
BECCLES TOWN . . . . College Meadow, Beccles NR34 7FA 07729 782817
BLOFIELD UNITED . . . . Old Yarmouth Road, Blofield, Norwich NR13 4LE 01603 712576
BRANDON TOWN . . . . Remembrance Playing Field, Church Road, Brandon IP27 0JB. 01842 813177
CROMER TOWN. . . . . Cabbell Park, Mill Road, Cromer NR27 0AD 01263 512185
DERSINGHAM ROVERS . . . . . . Behind Feathers Hotel, Manor Road, Dersingham, King's Lynn PE31 6LN. 01485 542707
HALVERGATE UNITED. . . . . Playing Field, Wickhampton Road, Halvergate NR13 3BQ. 01493 700349
HEMPNALL. . . . . Bungay Road, Hempnall, Norwich NR15 2NG. 01508 498086
HINDRINGHAM. . . . . Wells Road, Hindringham, Fakenham NR21 0PL . . . . None
LOWESTOFT TOWN RESERVES. . . . . Crown Meadow, Love Road, Lowestoft NR32 2PA 01502 573818
MATTISHALL . . . . Mattishall Playing Fields, South Green, Mattishall, Norwich NR20 3JY 01362 850246
NORTH WALSHAM TOWN . . . . Sports Centre, Greens Road, North Walsham NR28 0HW 01692 406888
NORWICH UNION . . . . Pinebanks, White Farm Lane, Thorpe NR7 0BP. 01603 434457
SHERINGHAM . . . . Weybourne Road, Sheringham NR26 8WD 01263 824804
SPROWSTON ATHLETIC. . . Sprowston Sports & Social Club, Blue Boar Lane, Sprowston, Norwich NR7 8RJ 01603 427688
WROXHAM RESERVES . . . . Trafford Park, Skinners Lane, Wroxham NR12 8SJ 01603 783538
IN: Hempnall (P), Hindringham (P)
OUT: Attleborough Town (R), St Andrews (R)

	Aylsham Wanderers	Dereham Town Res.	Gayton United	Hempnall	Hindringham	Holt United	Loddon United	Long Stratton	Mundford	Scole United	Southwold Town	Sprowston Wanderers	Stalham Town	Watton United	Wells Town	Wymondham Town
Aylsham Wanderers		1-3	0-2	1-3	1-1	0-1	4-3	4-0	2-3	5-1	0-1	1-2	3-4	2-2	1-3	2-1
Dereham Town Res.	5-0		4-1	1-4	1-3	2-0	1-3	0-0	4-2	4-3	4-0	3-1	3-1	1-1	3-0	4-1
Gayton United	0-1	6-2	D	2-0	2-6	3-1	6-3	2-3	3-1	1-1	2-1	2-0	7-2	3-5	1-1	1-1
Hempnall	3-0	2-2	3-1	I	0-1	5-2	6-0	3-3	5-0	2-2	4-1	3-2	2-1	5-1	6-2	0-0
Hindringham	5-1	1-5	2-5	2-2	V	1-0	1-0	3-0	4-1	3-3	4-1	4-1	1-1	1-4	1-2	2-0
Holt United	4-3	1-2	1-2	1-0	0-1	I	0-1	2-0	1-1	2-1	4-2	4-2	3-1	4-3	1-1	0-0
Loddon United	2-5	3-2	2-2	1-1	2-0	2-0	S	1-2	4-2	0-1	1-1	5-2	3-1	4-3		3-0
Long Stratton	3-2	0-0	3-2	2-2	0-1	3-2	2-2	I	2-2	1-0	0-2	0-2	1-0	3-0	3-0	3-0
Mundford	1-0	2-1	0-3	2-4	0-2	0-1	0-3	3-0	O	0-5	1-4	2-3	1-2	3-3	1-3	1-3
Scole United	0-3	0-2	3-2	0-1	0-1	3-1	0-2	1-0	1-2	N	3-2	2-2	2-1	3-2	3-0	2-4
Southwold Town	1-6	2-3	0-1	1-1	0-1	4-1	0-5	5-3	4-0	3-0		3-0	2-2	2-0	3-0	0-4
Sprowston Wanderers	3-1	1-6	1-3	0-4	0-1	2-3	0-4	3-2	2-1	0-0	2-1	O	1-2	0-3	1-1	4-1
Stalham Town	0-0	2-0	1-1	0-3	2-2	0-2	2-3	1-2	4-0	1-1	2-5	2-1	N	3-2	2-0	0-1
Watton United	1-0	1-2	3-2	0-3	1-3	2-0	1-4	4-5	0-1	3-2	2-0	5-1	3-2	E	0-3	4-0
Wells Town	2-2	0-0	1-0	0-0	0-1	2-1	1-3	1-4	1-1	1-1	0-1	2-2	4-3	3-2		2-1
Wymondham Town	2-0	1-1	4-5	1-6	1-1	0-0	1-6	4-0	1-2	2-1	2-0	3-2	2-2	3-2	5-1	

SECOND ROUND
Aylsham Wanderers 0 **Scole United** 3
Dersingham Rovers 5 Lowestoft Town Res. 0
Gayton United 4 Wroxham Res. 1
Halvergate United 4 Norwich Union 0
Loddon United 3 **Dereham Town Res.** 4
North Walsham Town 1 Hempnall 0
Sprowston Athletic 2 **Blofield United** 3
Wymondham Town 2 **Brandon Town** 2 *aet* (2-4p)
QUARTER-FINALS
Brandon Town 1 **Blofield United** 5
Dereham Town Res. 0 **Gayton United** 5
North Walsham Town 2 **Dersingham Rovers** 3
Scole United 1 **Halvergate United** 2
SEMI-FINALS
Blofield United 3 **Gayton United** 5
Halvergate United 3 **Dersingham Rovers** 4 *aet*
(at Dersingham Rovers)
FINAL
(April 11th at Holt United)
Gayton United 1 Dersingham Rovers 0

Division One		P	W	D	L	F	A	Pts
Hempnall		30	18	9	3	83	32	63
Hindringham		30	19	6	5	60	36	63
Loddon United		30	19	4	7	48		61
Dereham Town Res.		30	17	6	7	71	43	57
Gayton United		30	15	5	10	73	56	50
Long Stratton		30	12	6	12	49	55	42
Southwold Town		30	13	2	15	52	57	41
Holt United		30	12	4	14	43	49	40
Watton United		30	11	4	15	59	64	37
Wells Town		30	9	9	12	41	57	36
Wymondham Town	-6	30	11	7	12	49	57	34
Scole United		30	8	7	15	46	57	31
Stalham Town		30	7	8	15	45	62	29
Sprowston Wanderers		30	8	5	17	42	70	29
Aylsham Wanderers		30	8	4	18	51	62	28
Mundford		30	8	4	18	36	72	28

DON FROST MEMORIAL CUP
(Premier Division champions v Mummery Cup holders)
(August 19th at Norwich United)
Cromer Town 2 **Brandon Town** 3

WWW.NLNEWSDESK.CO.UK

ANGLIAN COMBINATION DIVISION ONE CONSTITUTION 2007-08

ATTLEBOROUGH TOWN........... Recreation Ground, Station Road, Attleborough NR17 2AS 01953 455365
DEREHAM TOWN RESERVES.......... Aldiss Park, Norwich Road, Dereham NR20 3AL 01362 690460/693677
FAKENHAM TOWN RESERVES .... Clipbush Park, Clipbush Lane, Fakenham NR21 8SW 01328 856222/855859
GAYTON UNITED........................ Lime Kiln Road, Gayton, King's Lynn PE32 1QB .... None
HOLT UNITED .... Sports Centre, Kelling Road, Holt NR25 7DU 01263 711217
KIRKLEY & PAKEFIELD RESERVES .. Kirkley Rec Ground, Walmer Road, Lowestoft NR33 8HZ........................ 01502 513549
LODDON UNITED .... George Lane Playing Fields, Loddon, Norwich NR14 6NB....................... 01508 528497
LONG STRATTON .... Manor Road Playing Fields, Long Stratton, Norwich NR15 2XR .... None
SCOLE UNITED .... Ransome Avenue Playing Field, Scole, Diss IP21 4EA............................ 01379 741204
SOLE BAY.......................... Southwold Common, Southwold. .... None
SPROWSTON WANDERERS .... Sprowston Cricket Club, Barkers Lane, Sprowston, Norwich NR7 8QZ 01603 404042
ST ANDREWS.............. Thorpe Recreation Ground, Laundry Lane, Thorpe St Andrew, Thorpe NR7 0XQ 01603 300316
STALHAM TOWN................. Rivers Park, Stepping Stone Lane, Stalham, Norwich NR12 9EP .... None
WATTON UNITED .... Watton Playing Field, Dereham Road, Watton, Thetford IP25 6EZ 01953 881281
WELLS TOWN .... Beach Road, Wells-next-the-Sea NR23 1DR 01328 710907
WYMONDHAM TOWN .... Kings Head Meadow, Wymondham NR18 0LB 01953 607326
IN: Attleborough Town (R), Fakenham Town Reserves (P), Kirkley & Pakefield (formerly Kirkley Reserves) (P), St Andrews (R)
OUT: Aylsham Wanderers (R), Hempnall (P), Hindringham (P), Mundford (R)
Southwold Town become Sole Bay

	Anglian Windows	Bungay Town	Caister United	Corton	Downham Town Res.	Fakenham Town Res.	Great Yarmouth Town Res.	Horsford United	Kirkley Res.	Norwich CEYMS	Norwich St Johns	Norwich United Res.	Poringland Wanderers	Reepham Town	Thorpe Rovers	Wortwell
Anglian Windows		2-1	2-2	6-3	1-5	1-11	3-1	3-0	1-5	3-1	5-3	2-1	0-7	1-2	0-2	2-3
Bungay Town	3-1		3-5	3-1	6-1	0-3	1-2	2-0	2-1	2-2	1-1	3-0	1-0	3-0	2-1	1-1
Caister United	8-2	5-0	D	0-4	10-1	3-5	5-2	4-0	0-1	2-1	1-2	2-1	2-1	3-1	3-2	3-2
Corton	1-3	1-1	1-2	I	2-1	3-0	2-0	1-2	2-1	1-0	1-2	1-1	0-4	1-0	5-0	1-1
Downham Town Res.	2-2	3-1	3-3	1-3	V	3-2	4-0	2-2	1-1	3-1	2-3	1-1	0-3	2-0	4-0	5-1
Fakenham Town Res.	2-1	3-0	0-2	1-1	4-1	I	5-1	1-0	4-1	2-0	4-2	1-2	0-0	7-2	2-0	
Great Yarmouth Town Res.	2-1	3-1	1-4	2-0	1-1	0-5	S	2-3	2-2	2-1	1-5	2-2	0-1	2-0	2-0	2-2
Horsford United	1-2	5-1	1-5	2-1	1-0	1-1	3-3	I	0-5	2-2	0-4	1-4	3-0	1-3	1-0	0-2
Kirkley Res.	4-0	1-0	1-0	3-0	4-0	0-1	1-0	2-0	O	6-0	3-1	0-2	2-2	3-1	5-3	1-2
Norwich CEYMS	2-2	3-3	0-3	3-0	4-0	2-7	2-3	3-1	4-0	N	2-5	0-2	0-2	3-1	1-2	1-4
Norwich St Johns	2-1	1-3	5-2	3-2	2-1	0-2	1-0	2-0	1-4	1-1		0-0	1-2	1-3	3-0	0-1
Norwich United Res.	2-0	1-2	3-2	3-0	0-0	2-2	0-1	4-0	0-0	3-0	4-1	T	2-0	2-1	5-2	2-1
Poringland Wanderers	2-4	2-1	3-1	3-0	2-2	5-3	1-1	6-0	1-2	1-2	0-0	2-2	W	4-0	5-2	0-0
Reepham Town	2-0	0-2	4-3	3-1	2-2	1-1	3-1	5-0	0-5	6-2	1-2	2-2	1-5	O	5-1	2-2
Thorpe Rovers	0-3	2-2	0-5	0-0	2-0	1-1	1-2	1-2	4-6	2-2	1-2	2-1	1-2	2-4		2-1
Wortwell	4-1	0-0	1-1	1-0	7-1	2-4	4-0	2-1	1-4	2-1	1-2	3-1	1-1	1-3	2-0	

Division Two	P	W	D	L	F	A	Pts
Kirkley Res.	30	19	4	7	74	35	61
Fakenham Town Res.	30	18	6	6	84	39	60
Caister United	30	18	3	9	91	53	57
Poringland Wanderers	30	16	7	7	69	35	55
Norwich St Johns	30	17	4	9	58	45	55
Norwich United Res.	30	13	9	8	55	37	48
Wortwell	30	13	8	9	55	44	47
Bungay Town	30	12	7	11	51	51	43
Reepham Town	30	12	5	13	56	58	41
Anglian Windows	30	11	3	16	55	84	36
Great Yarmouth Town Res.	30	9	7	14	40	64	34
Downham Town Res.	30	8	9	13	52	71	33
Corton	30	9	5	16	39	52	32
Horsford United	30	8	4	18	33	73	28
Norwich CEYMS	30	6	7	17	46	72	25
Thorpe Rovers	30	5	4	21	38	83	19

CYRIL BALLYN CUP

(Division Two, Three, Four, Five and Six first teams and external league reserve sides)

FIRST ROUND
Corton 8 Harleston Town 1
Freethorpe 1 **Great Yarmouth Town Res.** 3
Great Ryburgh 1 **Fakenham Town Res.** 2
Necton SSC 1 **Swaffham Town Res.** 3
Newton Flotman 3 Thetford Rovers 1
Oulton Broad & Notleys 1 **Wortwell** 2

SECOND ROUND
Anglian Windows 1 **West Lynn SSC** 2
Beccles Caxton 3 Horsford United 1
Bradenham Wanderers 1 **Norwich United Res.** 7
Corton 3 Easton 1 *aet*
East Harling 4 Caister United 2
Foulsham 2 Poringland Wanderers 1
Hoveton Wherrymen 1 **Fakenham Town Res.** 3
Kirkley Res. 1 **Norwich St Johns** 3
Marlingford 2 Downham Town Res. 0
Morley Village 1 **Bungay Town** 2 *aet*
Newton Flotman 4 Hellesdon 0
Norwich CEYMS 0 **Great Yarmouth Town Res.** 3

ANGLIAN COMBINATION DIVISION TWO CONSTITUTION 2007-08

ANGLIAN WINDOWS.................Horsford Manor, Cromer Road, Norwich NR5 8AP 01603 404723
AYLSHAM WANDERERS ....Sir Williams Lane, Aylsham, Norwich NR11 6AN .... None
BECCLES CAXTON....................Caxton Meadow, Adj. Beccles Station, Beccles NR34 9QH........... 01502 712829
BUNGAY TOWN......................Maltings Meadow, Ditchingham, Bungay............................... 01986 894028
CAISTER.........................Caister Playing Fields, off Allendale Road, Caister-on-Sea NR30 5ES .... None
CORTON...........................Village Playing Field, Long Lane, Corton, Lowestoft NR32 5HE.................. None
DOWNHAM TOWN RESERVES ... Memorial Playing Field, Lynn Road, Downham Market PE38 9QG........... 01366 388424
GREAT YARMOUTH TOWN RESERVES .. Wellesley Road Rec Ground, Sandown Road, Great Yarmouth NR30 1EY........ 01493 843373
HORSFORD UNITED...................Holt Road, Horsford NR10 3DN...................................... None
MUNDFORD........................The Glebe, Mundford, Thetford IP26 5EJ............................. None
NORWICH ST JOHNS ....Cringleford Recreation Ground, Oakfields Road, Cringleford NR4 6XE.................. None
NORWICH UNITED RESERVES ... Plantation Park, off Plantation Road, Blofield, Norwich NR13 4PL........... 01603 716963
PORINGLAND WANDERERS .. Poringland Memorial Field, The Footpath, Poringland, Norwich NR14 7RF 01508 495198
REEPHAM TOWN......................Stimpsons Piece Rec Ground, Reepham, Norwich........................ None
WEST LYNN SSC ....West Lynn Sports & Social Club, St Peters Road, West Lynn PE34 3LB 01553 761646
WORTWELL .... Wortwell Playing Field, opposite Bell PH, High Road, Wortwell, Harleston IP20 0HH .... None
IN: *Aylsham Wanderers (R), Beccles Caxton (P), Mundford (R), West Lynn SSC (P)*
OUT: *Fakenham Town Reserves (P), Kirkley & Pakefield (formerly Kirkley) Reserves (P), Norwich CEYMS (R), Thorpe Rovers (R)*
Caister United become Caister

	Acle United Res.	Beccles Caxton	Beccles Town Res.	Brandon Town Res.	City of Norwich SOBU	Hellesdon	Hempnall Res.	Martham	Mattishall Res.	Morley Village	Oulton Broad & Notleys	South Walsham	Sprowston Athletic Res.	Swaffham Town Res.	Thorpe Village	West Lynn SSC
Acle United Res.		1-4	5-3	7-4	3-3	2-0	3-0	6-0	3-0	3-0	1-2	3-0	8-3	3-1	2-3	0-4
Beccles Caxton	3-2	D	4-1	10-2	4-2	2-0	2-1	3-2	3-3	4-1	2-0	1-0	6-3	3-1	3-1	0-2
Beccles Town Res.	1-6	1-7	I	4-0	1-1	1-6	0-3	3-4	3-2	5-2	0-5	0-0	1-2	1-0	1-3	3-4
Brandon Town Res.	2-2	1-7	3-2	V	3-1	1-2	0-3	2-4	2-1	0-1	0-5	3-6	3-4	2-3	2-1	0-10
City of Norwich SOBU	1-2	1-2	0-0	1-2	I	2-5	2-0	1-2	3-3	3-3	1-3	2-3	2-5	2-3	0-1	1-8
Hellesdon	1-4	1-2	0-4	5-1	2-2	S	0-0	2-2	1-2	2-2	2-1	4-4	5-0	3-3	4-1	0-4
Hempnall Res.	0-1	0-0	1-2	2-1	2-2	2-2	I	1-1	1-0	5-2	0-2	2-2	2-0	1-0	1-1	0-5
Martham	3-2	1-3	4-5	5-0	7-3	3-2	2-1	O	2-1	3-1	4-5	5-0	1-2	3-5	5-1	4-0
Mattishall Res.	4-2	2-3	6-0	5-2	3-0	3-1	5-2	2-1	N	1-1	1-0	6-0	3-0	4-2	4-0	4-0
Morley Village	2-5	2-1	2-3	2-2	3-1	0-0	3-0	3-2	1-3		2-3	2-0	1-2	1-2	3-2	1-3
Oulton Broad & Notleys	1-1	0-2	5-0	4-0	7-2	4-4	1-0	2-0	0-1	5-2	T	3-0	3-1	2-5	2-2	1-7
South Walsham	2-8	0-3	2-1	1-0	1-0	2-4	2-0	1-5	0-4	2-0	0-3	H	2-1	2-6	0-5	2-4
Sprowston Athletic Res.	0-5	2-1	0-6	0-1	1-1	2-4	3-3	2-3	2-6	3-3	2-4	2-2	R	3-1	1-4	1-4
Swaffham Town Res.	1-2	2-0	6-1	0-2	8-3	3-2	2-0	1-1	3-2	1-2	2-5	2-1	3-2	E	4-1	1-1
Thorpe Village	2-5	0-3	4-2	6-0	8-2	1-1	0-2	1-2	2-2	3-2	1-4	1-0	1-2	2-2	E	1-2
West Lynn SSC	3-2	1-1	10-0	3-0	7-1	3-2	3-1	4-2	4-0	4-1	1-2	4-0	4-5	4-0	3-1	

Reepham Town 3 City of Norwich SOBU 0
South Walsham 1 **Martham** 7
Thorpe Rovers 3 **Swaffham Town Res. 4** *aet*
Thorpe Village 0 **Wortwell** 1
THIRD ROUND
Fakenham Town Res. 1 **Bungay Town** 2
Marlingford 4 Reepham Town 2
Martham 2 **Foulsham** 5
Newton Flotman 2 **Swaffham Town Res.** 3
Norwich St Johns 5 **Beccles Caxton** 6
Norwich United Res. 0 **Corton** 2
West Lynn SSC (w/o) v Great Yarmouth Town Res.
(scr.)
Wortwell 1 **East Harling** 2
QUARTER-FINALS
Beccles Caxton 1 **Marlingford** 2
Corton 3 Bungay Town 2
Foulsham 3 East Harling 1
Swaffham Town Res. 0 **West Lynn SSC** 2
SEMI-FINALS
Foulsham 0 **Marlingford** 1
West Lynn SSC 1 **Corton** 2
FINAL
(May 7th at Wroxham)
Marlingford 2 Corton 1

Division Three

		P	W	D	L	F	A	Pts
West Lynn SSC		30	24	2	4	116	37	74
Beccles Caxton		30	23	3	4	89	36	72
Oulton Broad & Notleys		30	20	3	7	84	46	63
Acle United Res.		30	19	3	8	99	53	60
Mattishall Res.		30	18	4	8	83	44	58
Martham		30	16	3	11	83	65	51
Swaffham Town Res.		30	15	4	11	74	61	49
Hellesdon		30	9	10	11	67	63	37
Thorpe Village		30	10	5	15	60	66	35
Sprowston Athletic Res.		30	9	4	17	56	94	31
Hempnall Res.	-3	30	8	8	14	36	49	29
South Walsham		30	8	4	18	37	84	28
Morley Village	-3	30	8	6	16	51	73	27
Beccles Town Res.	-3	30	9	3	18	55	97	27
Brandon Town Res.		30	7	2	21	41	107	23
City of Norwich SOBU		30	1	8	21	46	102	11

WWW.NLNEWSDESK.CO.UK

ANGLIAN COMBINATION DIVISION THREE CONSTITUTION 2007-08
ACLE UNITED RESERVES . . . . Bridewell Lane, Acle, Norwich NR13 3RA 01493 751379
BECCLES TOWN RESERVES . . . . College Meadow, Beccles NR34 7FA 07729 782817
CAISTER RESERVES . . . . Caister Playing Fields, off Allendale Road, Caister-on-Sea NR30 5ES . . . . None
HELLESDON . . . . Hellesdon Community Centre, Wood View Road, Hellesdon, Norwich NR6 5QB 01603 427675
HEMPNALL RESERVES . . . . Bungay Road, Hempnall, Norwich NR15 2NG 01508 498086
MARTHAM . . . . Coronation Recreation Ground, Rollesby Road, Martham, Great Yarmouth NR29 4SP 01493 740252
MATTISHALL RESERVES . . . . . . Mattishall Playing Fields, South Green, Mattishall, Norwich NR20 3JY 01362 850246
MORLEY VILLAGE . . . . Golf Links Road, Morley St Peter, Wymondham NR18 9SU . . . . None
NORWICH CEYMS . . . . Hilltops Sports Centre, Main Road, Swardeston, Norwich NR14 8DU 01508 578826
OULTON BROAD & NOTLEYS . . . . Kirkley Recreation Ground, Walmer Road, Lowestoft NR33 8HZ . . . . None
SOUTH WALSHAM . . . . The Playing Field, South Walsham . . . . None
SPROWSTON ATHLETIC RESERVES . . Sprowston S&S, Blue Boar Lane, Sprowston, Norwich NR7 8RJ 01603 427688
SWAFFHAM TOWN RESERVES . . . . Shoemakers Lane, off Cley Road, Swaffham PE37 7NT 01760 722700
THETFORD ROVERS . . . . Euston Park, Euston, near Thetford IP24 2QP. . . . . None
THORPE ROVERS . . . . Dussindale Park, Pound Lane, Thorpe NR7 0SR . . . . None
THORPE VILLAGE . . . . Thorpe Recreation Ground, Laundry Lane, Thorpe St Andrew, Norwich NR7 0XQ 01603 300316
IN: Caister Reserves (formerly Caister United Reserves) (P), Norwich CEYMS (R), Thetford Rovers (P), Thorpe Rovers (R)
OUT: Beccles Caxton (P), Brandon Town Reserves (R), City of Norwich SOBU (R), West Lynn SSC (P)

	Blofield United Res.	Bradenham Wanderers	Bungay Town Res.	Caister United Res.	Cromer Town Res.	Halvergate United Res.	Harleston Town	Hindringham Res.	Loddon United Res.	Necton SSC	Norwich St Johns Res.	Norwich Union Res.	St Andrews Res.	Thetford Rovers	Wells Town Res.	Wymondham Town Res.
Blofield United Res.		1-3	1-1	1-1	10-1	6-1	7-0	4-0	1-1	2-1	1-0	4-2	2-0	2-1	3-2	3-2
Bradenham Wanderers	0-2	D	2-2	0-3	4-2	3-2	2-2	2-3	1-2	7-0	2-4	0-2	0-1	3-7	3-1	1-2
Bungay Town Res.	1-3	0-1	I	1-3	7-2	3-2	6-3	3-0	4-1	6-0	2-1	1-2	0-1	2-4	2-0	1-0
Caister United Res.	3-2	2-3	4-0	V	0-6	12-3	6-0	4-2	5-0	7-1	4-2	0-2	5-2	4-2	6-1	6-2
Cromer Town Res.	2-5	3-0	1-2	1-11	I	4-3	2-2	3-4	2-7	2-1	2-3	0-2	0-3	2-2	2-0	1-3
Halvergate United Res.	1-10	0-0	1-3	1-9	2-7	S	1-7	2-5	3-9	1-1	0-5	1-1	1-5	1-6	0-3	0-7
Harleston Town	2-7	2-2	0-2	3-4	5-1	8-0	I	1-4	1-2	1-1	3-2	2-4	1-3	0-5	5-3	1-6
Hindringham Res.	0-3	5-2	3-2	3-0	2-2	12-1	2-1	O	2-2	3-0	5-1	1-1	3-4	0-2	4-2	6-0
Loddon United Res.	3-1	3-1	3-4	1-2	0-0	7-0	3-0	3-0	N	6-0	3-1	1-1	0-3	0-0	2-2	2-1
Necton SSC	1-2	2-4	1-1	2-6	3-1	2-1	4-4	1-1	1-5		0-2	2-2	2-4	2-9	4-0	0-2
Norwich St Johns Res.	4-2	4-2	5-5	1-1	6-0	3-0	3-1	0-0	1-1	4-2		1-1	4-0	0-0	2-0	1-1
Norwich Union Res.	2-2	3-0	2-0	1-2	5-0	13-0	3-0	0-0	3-2	2-0	2-1	F	1-1	2-1	1-3	3-1
St Andrews Res.	1-1	3-1	5-1	0-2	3-1	8-0	5-0	3-1	0-2	0-7	2-0	2-1	O	0-2	2-4	2-2
Thetford Rovers	2-2	3-0	4-2	6-1	3-2	14-0	11-2	2-1	0-1	3-0	1-0	5-3	1-4	U	2-2	0-2
Wells Town Res.	0-4	4-2	2-2	0-10	2-1	5-1	0-1	0-0	0-1	3-1	1-2	0-0	2-3	2-4	R	4-0
Wymondham Town Res.	2-1	2-0	2-1	2-5	1-3	4-1	2-2	1-1	2-0	3-2	0-3	1-1	0-3	3-3	2-0	

WWW.CHERRYRED.CO.UK

Division Four

		P	W	D	L	F	A	Pts
Caister United Res.		30	23	2	5	128	51	71
Thetford Rovers		30	19	6	5	107	43	63
Blofield United Res.		30	19	6	5	95	40	63
St Andrews Res.		30	19	3	8	73	47	60
Norwich Union Res.		30	16	9	5	78	33	57
Loddon United Res.		30	16	7	7	73	42	55
Norwich St Johns Res.		30	14	8	8	69	45	50
Hindringham Res.		30	13	8	9	73	52	47
Bungay Town Res.		30	12	6	12	67	60	42
Wymondham T. Res.	-3	30	12	7	11	58	59	40
Bradenham Wders	-3	30	8	4	18	51	72	25
Wells Town Res.	-3	30	8	4	18	46	72	25
Cromer Town Res.		30	7	4	19	56	101	25
Harleston Town		30	6	6	18	60	103	24
Necton SSC		30	5	5	20	49	95	20
Halvergate Utd Res.	-3	30	0	1	29	31	199	-2

Division Five

		P	W	D	L	F	A	Pts
East Harling		30	24	3	3	101	29	75
Easton		30	22	2	6	86	45	68
North Walsham T. Res.		30	20	4	6	85	47	64
Foulsham		30	19	5	6	93	52	62
Watton United Res.		30	19	3	8	71	48	60
Newton Flotman		30	14	6	10	70	54	48
Norwich CEYMS Res.		30	13	3	14	65	65	42
Sheringham Res.		30	12	4	14	77	66	40
Dersingham Rov. Res.	-6	30	13	7	10	59	60	40
Attleborough T. Res.	-3	30	12	3	15	70	67	36
Sprowston Wdrs Res.	-3	30	11	2	17	53	66	32
Stalham Town Res.		30	8	2	20	49	98	26
Mundford Res.		30	7	4	19	41	84	25
Aylsham Wdrs Res.		30	7	4	19	48	106	25
Thorpe Village Res.		30	5	3	22	36	81	18
Scole United Res.	-3	30	5	3	22	38	74	15

Division Six

		P	W	D	L	F	A	Pts
Freethorpe		28	24	3	1	137	25	75
Marlingford		28	23	3	2	108	24	72
Great Ryburgh		28	20	4	4	110	48	64
Hoveton Wherrymen	-3	28	18	5	5	101	49	56
Long Stratton Res.		28	13	6	9	78	60	45
Reepham Town Res.		28	14	2	12	63	65	44
Hellesdon Res.		28	13	2	13	49	65	41
Gayton United Res.	-9	28	12	5	11	67	72	32
Horsford United Res.		28	9	5	14	42	56	32
Poringland Wdrs Res.		28	6	7	15	41	73	25
Martham Res.		28	7	4	17	63	100	25
City of Norw. SOBU Res.		28	6	4	18	49	121	22
Wortwell Res.	-6	28	7	6	15	40	66	21
Holt United Res.	-9	28	8	1	19	57	83	16
Easton Res.	-3	28	1	1	26	26	124	1

C S MORLEY

(Anglian Combination club reserve teams)

FINAL

(April 9th at Wroxham)

Norwich Union Res. 1 Acle United Res. 0

ANGLIAN COMBINATION DIVISION FOUR CONSTITUTION 2007-08

BLOFIELD UNITED RESERVES.......... Old Yarmouth Road, Blofield, Norwich NR13 4LE........................... 01603 712576
BRADENHAM WANDERERS .... Hale Road, Bradenham, Thetford IP25 7RA........................... None
BRANDON TOWN RESERVES ...... Remembrance Playing Field, Church Road, Brandon IP27 0JB...................... 01842 813177
BUNGAY TOWN RESERVES .... Maltings Meadow, Ditchingham, Bungay........................... 01986 894028
CITY OF NORWICH SOBU .... Britannia Barracks, Mousehold, Norwich .... None
CROMER TOWN RESERVES .... Cabbell Park, Mill Road, Cromer NR27 0AD 01263 512185
EAST HARLING........................... Memorial Fields, Church Street, East Harling........................... 01953 718251
EASTON .... Easton College, Bawburgh Road, Norwich NR9 5DX 01603 731208
HARLESTON TOWN........... Rec & Memorial Leisure Centre, Wilderness Lane, Harleston IP20 9DD........ 01379 854519
HINDRINGHAM RESERVES .... Wells Road, Hindringham, Fakenham NR21 0PL .... None
LODDON UNITED RESERVES .... George Lane Playing Fields, Loddon, Norwich NR14 6NB 01508 528497
NORWICH ST JOHNS RESERVES .. Cringleford Recreation Ground, Oakfields Road, Cringleford NR4 6XE........................... None
NORWICH UNION RESERVES ...... Pinebanks, White Farm Lane, Harvey Lane, Thorpe NR7 0BP........................... 01603 434457
ST ANDREWS RESERVES.. Thorpe Recreation Ground, Laundry Lane, Thorpe St Andrew, Thorpe NR7 0XQ 01603 300316
WELLS TOWN RESERVES .... Beach Road, Wells-next-the-Sea NR23 1DR........................... 01328 710907
WYMONDHAM TOWN RESERVES .... Kings Head Meadow, Wymondham NR18 0LB 01953 607326

IN: Brandon Town Reserves (R), City of Norwich SOBU (R), East Harling (P), Easton (P)
OUT: Caister Reserves (formerly Caister United Reserves) (P), Halvergate United Reserves (F), Necton SSC (R), Thetford Rovers (P)

BEDFORDSHIRE LEAGUE

	AFC Kempston Town	Bedford SA	Blunham	Caldecote	Campton	Goldington Lions	Henlow	Ickwell & Old Warden	Luton Borough	Oakley Sports	Riseley Sports	Sandy	Sharnbrook	Turvey	Westoning Recreation Club	Wilhamstead
AFC Kempston Town	P	4-1	3-4	3-3	3-0	4-1	2-2	1-5	1-0	3-1	6-1	5-0	4-1	9-1	1-2	3-2
Bedford SA	1-6	R	0-3	3-1	3-3	3-0	0-1	1-1	3-8	0-3	1-2	1-2	2-3	1-5	0-8	1-5
Blunham	0-3	4-1	E	1-2	1-1	1-1	2-0	1-2	3-1	2-0	5-0	4-2	3-2	4-0	2-1	2-0
Caldecote	0-0	3-1	6-1	M	4-4	2-3	2-1	2-2	0-4	0-0	1-0	0-4	3-0	5-0	3-0	2-2
Campton	0-1	3-1	3-1	3-4	I	5-1	2-2	3-1	2-3	0-1	5-0	3-1	6-1	1-0	0-0	3-3
Goldington Lions	2-0	2-2	0-3	3-4	2-3	E	2-1	2-7	1-3	1-7	3-2	2-4	4-3	1-3	5-0	2-4
Henlow	2-3	4-0	0-2	4-1	0-2	1-1	R	4-0	1-1	2-1	1-2	1-2	4-0	2-0	0-1	3-2
Ickwell & Old Warden	2-2	4-2	2-2	3-0	3-1	4-2	1-1		2-3	5-1	0-0	2-0	3-1	11-0	0-2	7-1
Luton Borough	1-2	6-0	1-1	0-2	1-3	3-1	2-2	1-2	D	8-3	1-2	1-2	3-1	3-1	2-5	2-2
Oakley Sports	3-0	1-2	1-5	0-0	1-5	2-0	1-2	2-0	2-2	I	4-6	1-1	2-1	1-1	2-6	1-1
Riseley Sports	2-3	0-3	1-3	2-2	1-4	3-1	1-6	1-3	2-2	5-0	V	1-4	3-0	1-0	1-2	3-1
Sandy	4-1	5-1	0-1	3-0	1-3	3-1	2-1	2-2	3-2	3-2	2-0	I	2-1	2-2	1-3	1-1
Sharnbrook	1-1	3-0	2-0	1-2	0-5	1-0	2-1	1-0	1-5	1-3	1-2	0-7	S	5-0	0-2	2-0
Turvey	1-3	2-3	0-3	0-6	0-3	0-1	0-3	1-6	3-2	2-1	4-3	0-6	0-4	I	1-5	0-4
Westoning Recreation Club	1-3	3-1	4-0	3-2	1-2	2-1	3-1	2-0	4-3	4-0	3-1	1-0	2-0	3-0	O	1-3
Wilhamstead	2-3	3-1	3-0	0-1	2-1	5-1	1-1	3-2	3-1	3-4	3-3	1-1	7-1	1-1	1-1	N

Premier Division	P	W	D	L	F	A	Pts
Westoning Rec. Club	30	22	2	6	75	36	68
AFC Kempston Town	30	19	5	6	83	46	62
Blunham	30	18	4	8	64	42	58
Campton	30	17	6	7	79	43	57
Sandy	30	17	5	8	70	44	56
Ickwell & Old Warden	30	15	7	8	82	45	52
Caldecote	30	14	8	8	63	51	50
Wilhamstead	30	11	10	9	69	55	43
Henlow	30	11	8	11	54	40	41
Luton Borough	30	11	6	13	75	60	39
Oakley Sports	30	9	6	15	50	70	33
Riseley Sports	30	9	5	16	51	75	32
Sharnbrook	30	9	1	20	40	76	28
Goldington Lions	30	7	3	20	47	85	24
Bedford SA	30	5	3	22	39	98	18
Turvey	30	5	3	22	28	103	18

BEDFORDSHIRE LEAGUE PREMIER DIVISION CONSTITUTION 2007-08

AFC KEMPSTON TOWN . . . . Hillgrounds Road, Kempston, Bedford MK42 8QU 01234 852346
BLUNHAM . . . . The Playing Fields, Blunham Road, Moggerhanger, Sandy MK44 3RG . . . . None
CALDECOTE . . . . Harvey Close, Upper Caldecote, Biggleswade SG18 9BQ . . . . None
CAMPTON . . . . The Recreation Ground, Church Road, Campton SG17 5BN . . . . None
ICKWELL & OLD WARDEN . . . . Ickwell Green, Ickwell, Biggleswade SG18 9EF . . . . None
LUTON BOROUGH . . . . Luton Regional Sports Centre, St Thomas's Road, Stopsley, Luton LU2 7XP 01582 453919
MELTIS CORINTHIANS . . . . Meltis Sports Club, Miller Road, Bedford MK42 9NY 01234 352872
OAKLEY SPORTS . . . . Oakley Village Sports Centre, Oakley, Bedford MK43 7RG . . . . None
RENHOLD UNITED . . . . Renhold Playing Fields, Renhold, Bedford. . . . . None
RISELEY SPORTS . . . . Gold Street, Riseley MK44 1EG . . . . None
SANDY . . . . Recreation Ground, Bedford Road, Sandy SG19 1BW . . . . None
SHARNBROOK . . . . Playing Fields, Lodge Road, Sharnbrook MK44 1JP . . . . None
WESTONING RECREATION CLUB . . Recreation Ground, Greenfield Road, Westoning MK45 5JP . . . . None
WILHAMSTEAD. . . . . Jubilee Playing Fields, Bedford Road, Wilshamstead MK45 3HN . . . . None
WOBURN . . . . Crawley Road, Woburn MK17 9QD . . . . None

IN: Meltis Corinthians (P), Renhold United (N), Woburn (P)
OUT: Bedford SA (R), Goldington Lions (F), Henlow (R), Turvey (R)

BRITANNIA CUP
(Bedfordshire League Premier Division teams)

FIRST ROUND
Bedford SA 2 **Blunham** 3
Campton 5 AFC Kempston Town 2
Henlow 2 Riseley Sports 0
Ickwell & Old Warden 4 Sharnbrook 1
Luton Borough 6 Turvey 1
Oakley Sports 2 Goldington Lions 1
Sandy 2 **Caldecote** *aet* (4-5p)
Wilshamstead 0 **Westoning Recreation Club** 1

QUARTER-FINALS
Caldecote 2 **Luton Borough** 1 *(Caldecote expelled)*
Campton 1 **Ickwell & Old Warden** 2
Henlow 1 **Oakley Sports** 2
Westoning Recreation Club 3 Blunham 2

SEMI-FINALS
Luton Borough 0 **Westoning Recreation Club** 1
Oakley Sports 1 Ickwell & Old Warden 1 *aet* (9-8p)

FINAL
(May 12th at Biggleswade United)
Westoning Recreation Club 3 Oakley Sports 2

Division One		P	W	D	L	F	A	Pts
Meltis Corinthians		28	25	2	1	139	33	77
Woburn		28	22	2	4	99	31	68
Flitwick Town		28	16	5	7	87	52	53
Reddings Wood		28	16	3	9	75	47	51
AFC Kempston Town Res.	-3	28	15	5	8	71	48	47
Caldecote Reserves	-3	28	15	4	9	77	56	46
Campton Reserves		28	13	6	9	65	44	45
Stevington		28	11	5	12	65	67	38
Kempston		28	9	4	15	58	87	31
Blunham Village	-3	28	10	3	15	57	72	30
Royal Oak Kempston		28	7	6	15	45	64	27
Elstow Abbey		28	8	2	18	40	75	26
Marston Social		28	6	2	20	37	93	20
Saffron	-3	28	6	3	19	43	91	18
Meppershall Jurassic		28	3	4	21	28	126	13

Division Two		P	W	D	L	F	A	Pts
Westoning Recreation Club Res.		28	19	7	2	100	34	64
Sandy Res.		28	19	5	4	76	24	62
Meppershall Jurassic Res.	-2	28	17	7	4	103	41	56
Woburn Res.		28	15	7	6	85	55	52
Great Barford		28	13	8	7	55	39	47
Blunham Res.		28	13	6	9	83	70	45
Marston Shelton Rovers		28	12	7	9	76	49	43
Potton Wanderers	-3	28	12	4	12	83	82	37
Lidlington United Sports		28	10	6	12	67	84	36
Newnham Athletic		28	9	8	11	51	58	35
Mulberry Bush		28	10	5	13	62	85	35
Bedford Albion		28	8	2	18	61	78	26
Russell Park United		28	8	2	18	62	82	26
Twinwoods Thistle	-3	28	5	5	18	49	104	17
Exel United		28	0	1	27	44	172	1

CENTENARY CUP
FINAL *(May 11th at Biggleswade United)*
Meltis Corinthians 4 Flitwick Town 3 *aet*

JUBILEE CUP
FINAL *(May 9th at Biggleswade United)*
Westoning Recreation Club Res. 1 Woburn Res. 0

Division Three	P	W	D	L	F	A	Pts
Ickwell & Old Warden Res.	28	22	2	4	91	28	68
Oakley Sports Res.	28	21	4	3	83	34	67
Henlow Res.	28	20	3	5	98	37	63
Putnoe United	28	17	7	4	94	43	58
Clifton	28	15	7	6	107	51	52
Kings AFC	28	14	3	11	85	74	45
Sandy 'A'	28	12	3	13	57	64	39
Meltis Corinthians Res.	28	10	8	10	53	53	38
Caldecote 'A'	28	11	5	12	64	66	38
Marsh Leys	28	9	4	15	62	76	31
Wilshamstead Res.	28	9	4	15	49	64	31
Flitwick Town Res.	28	8	2	18	38	84	26
Blue Chip	27	5	3	19	36	97	18
Riseley Sports Res.	28	3	3	22	48	97	12
Lidlington Utd Sports Res.	-6	27	3	2	22	30	127	5

Lidlington United Sports Res. v Blue Chip not played

WATSON SHIELD
FINAL *(May 7th at Biggleswade United)*
Clifton 6 Henlow Res. 1

CAMBRIDGESHIRE COUNTY LEAGUE

	Cambridge University Press	Cottenham United	Eaton Socon	Fordham	Great Paxton	Great Shelford	Histon 'A'	Linton Granta	Littleport Town	Needingworth United	Newmarket Town Res.	Over Sports	Sawston United	Somersham Town	Waterbeach	Wickhambrook
Cambridge University Press	P	2-2	3-0	3-2	6-1	1-1	3-0	4-0	1-1	5-2	3-3	4-4	6-0	8-2	5-4	2-1
Cottenham United	2-1	R	2-1	3-2	3-1	1-4	0-2	2-1	1-2	5-3	2-0	5-1	1-3	1-0	2-3	2-1
Eaton Socon	3-2	2-0	E	2-2	1-4	2-3	3-2	3-1	1-6	6-1	6-2	2-3	3-2	4-1	2-0	1-2
Fordham	0-1	2-1	5-1	M	2-0	3-4	3-2	3-0	2-2	0-2	2-4	2-2	1-3	1-0	4-1	3-1
Great Paxton	1-5	1-1	2-6	1-4	I	0-3	1-4	1-1	1-4	5-3	1-0	0-4	1-1	3-1	1-4	0-3
Great Shelford	1-1	2-4	1-0	6-1	7-1	E	3-2	8-0	3-0	4-0	8-1	1-0	4-0	2-0	4-3	2-1
Histon 'A'	2-1	5-2	2-0	3-3	2-0	1-2	R	3-0	2-1	2-4	2-4	4-3	2-0	1-0	5-0	4-2
Linton Granta	0-4	1-7	3-1	3-3	3-0	0-1	0-1		0-3	2-4	1-5	1-2	1-4	4-1	0-1	5-3
Littleport Town	3-1	2-1	3-2	0-3	3-2	0-5	2-3	3-0	D	1-0	2-1	1-2	2-2	2-0	2-3	1-1
Needingworth United	2-2	4-0	3-1	1-2	1-2	0-2	1-3	4-1	2-3	I	3-1	0-1	4-2	4-0	2-4	0-2
Newmarket Town Res.	6-1	2-2	4-2	0-2	1-1	1-2	2-2	5-2	2-0	1-1	V	0-4	1-3	3-1	1-2	4-0
Over Sports	4-0	1-0	3-1	0-3	4-2	0-1	2-1	4-0	3-2	5-1	0-1	I	1-0	3-1	5-1	5-2
Sawston United	1-3	1-2	4-1	3-4	1-3	2-1	0-6	7-3	1-8	2-4	1-2	1-3	S	2-2	1-1	3-2
Somersham Town	1-2	0-6	1-2	4-4	2-1	1-2	4-2	3-2	1-4	1-2	0-1	1-5	1-4	I	2-0	0-4
Waterbeach	2-2	1-2	2-0	4-2	0-0	2-5	6-1	1-1	0-1	4-1	4-1	1-2	10-0	3-1	O	2-2
Wickhambrook	1-5	1-1	3-0	2-3	3-2	2-4	1-0	4-1	0-4	2-1	2-2	1-5	3-1	2-1	0-3	N

Premier Division	P	W	D	L	F	A	Pts
Great Shelford	30	26	2	2	96	30	80
Over Sports	30	22	2	6	82	39	68
Cambridge Univ. Press	30	16	8	6	87	52	56
Littleport Town	30	17	4	9	68	46	55
Histon 'A'	30	17	2	11	71	53	53
Cottenham United	30	15	4	11	63	53	49
Fordham	30	14	6	10	71	62	48
Waterbeach	30	14	5	11	71	55	47
Newmarket Town Res.	30	12	6	12	61	62	42
Wickhambrook	30	12	4	14	56	67	40
Needingworth United	30	11	2	17	60	71	35
Eaton Socon	30	11	1	18	58	70	34
Sawston United	30	9	4	17	55	86	31
Great Paxton	30	6	5	19	39	83	23
Linton Granta	30	4	3	23	37	95	15
Somersham Town	30	4	2	24	33	84	14

PREMIER DIVISION CUP

FIRST ROUND
Cambridge University Press 1 **Eaton Socon** 2
Great Paxton 0 **Fordham** 1
Histon 'A' 0 Waterbeach 0 *aet* (5-4p)
Linton Granta 0 **Somersham Town** 2
Littleport Town 2 Great Shelford 0
Needingworth United 3 Sawston United 2
Newmarket Town Res. 3 **Cottenham United** 7
Wickhambrook 2 Over Sports 1

QUARTER-FINALS
Eaton Socon 1 **Cottenham United** 2
Fordham 2 **Littleport Town** 2 *aet* (5-6p)
Histon 'A' 7 Somersham Town 0
Needingworth United 1 **Wickhambrook** 2
(Wickhambrook expelled)

SEMI-FINALS
Cottenham United 1 **Histon 'A'** 3
Needingworth United 0 **Littleport Town** 3

FINAL
(May 7th at Cambridge City)
Histon 'A' 3 Littleport Town 2

CAMBRIDGESHIRE COUNTY LEAGUE PREMIER DIVISION CONSTITUTION 2007-08

CAMBRIDGE UNIVERSITY PRESS .. CUP Sports Ground, Shaftesbury Road, Cambridge CB2 2BS .... None
COTTENHAM UNITED .... Lambs Lane, Cottenham, Cambridge CB4 8TA 01954 250873
EATON SOCON .... River Road, Eaton Ford, St Neots PE19 7AU .... None
ELY CITY RESERVES .... The Unwin Ground, Downham Road, Ely CB6 2SH 01353 662035
FORDHAM......................... Recreational Ground, Carter Street, Fordham, Ely CB7 5JT........................ None
GREAT PAXTON .... Recreation Ground, High Street, Great Paxton, St Neots PE19 6RG................ None
GREAT SHELFORD .... Recreation Ground, Woollards Lane, Great Shelford CB2 5LZ................ 01223 842590
HISTON 'A' .... The Glassworld Stadium, Bridge Road, Impington, Cambridge CB4 9PH 01223 237373
HUNDON............................... North Street, Hundon CO10 8EE .... None
LITTLEPORT TOWN .... Sports Centre, Camel Road, Littleport, Ely CB6 1EW................ None
NEEDINGWORTH UNITED .... Mill Field, Holywell Road, Needingworth PE27 4TF .... None
NEWMARKET TOWN RESERVES .. Cricket Field Road, off New Cheveley Road, Newmarket CB8 8BG................ 01638 663637
OVER SPORTS .... Over Recreation Ground, The Doles, Over CB4 5NW................ None
SAWSTON UNITED................. Spicers Sports Ground, New Road, Sawston CB2 4BN .... None
WATERBEACH.................... Recreation Ground, Waterbeach .... None
WICKHAMBROOK................... Recreation Ground, Cemetery Hill, Wickhambrook................ None
IN: Ely City Reserves (P), Hundon (P)
OUT: Linton Granta (R), Somersham Town (R)

	Bluntisham Rangers	Brampton	Ely City Res.	Foxton	Fulbourn Institute	Gamlingay United	Girton United	Grampian	Hardwick	Hemingford United	Hundon	Lakenheath	Mildenhall Town Res.	Soham Town Rangers Res.	West Wratting	Wisbech Town Res.
Bluntisham Rangers		0-1	1-8	0-4	2-3	3-0	1-2	3-1	1-1	1-4	0-9	2-4	1-1	0-3	1-3	1-2
Brampton	1-0		0-6	0-4	0-0	2-0	2-1	3-1	5-4	2-3	0-4	3-1	0-2	2-1	2-0	1-2
Ely City Res.	6-0	3-0	*S*	2-1	2-1	3-0	4-1	2-0	3-0	3-1	1-3	1-2	3-1	4-0	2-0	3-1
Foxton	4-0	2-0	0-5	*E*	0-2	3-0	0-1	2-1	6-1	4-0	1-2	3-2	4-1	1-3	1-0	1-0
Fulbourn Institute	4-0	3-0	1-1	0-1	*N*	0-1	0-1	7-2	1-1	1-0	2-0	1-1	7-3	1-3	0-2	1-2
Gamlingay United	4-4	2-2	2-3	0-3	3-1	*I*	1-0	1-3	1-2	2-2	2-4	4-0	3-3	2-4	1-5	3-1
Girton United	3-1	2-3	0-3	1-3	1-2	2-0	*O*	5-0	3-0	0-1	2-4	4-0	2-2	0-1	1-0	0-1
Grampian	2-0	0-5	2-2	2-5	2-4	4-1	2-3	*R*	1-1	0-1	1-3	3-1	1-0	1-3	1-3	1-3
Hardwick	1-0	2-3	0-3	0-0	2-1	3-4	1-3	1-0		2-3	1-1	3-1	1-0	2-1	3-0	2-3
Hemingford United	3-0	3-1	1-4	3-0	0-2	3-1	4-0	4-2		*D*	2-0	9-0	0-0	1-3	1-1	1-2
Hundon	3-1	3-0	1-3	0-0	3-0	6-2	2-2	4-1	4-0	3-1	*I*	5-2	4-1	4-2	4-1	1-0
Lakenheath	3-1	2-2	1-4	2-4	0-0	1-1	4-1	2-7	3-3	1-1	1-2	*V*	3-1	1-4	2-4	1-4
Mildenhall Town Res.	2-0	0-5	0-2	3-0	2-0	5-0	3-1	4-0	1-1	2-0	3-0	5-4		1-2	5-0	1-1
Soham Town Rangers Res.	3-2	7-2	1-2	1-1	1-4	3-1	4-0	6-1	4-1	5-0	2-2	2-1	0-0	*A*	0-1	2-3
West Wratting	4-0	5-0	0-3	1-4	0-1	5-1	0-0	3-1	2-2	2-1	1-2	1-2	2-3	2-1		4-2
Wisbech Town Res.	5-1	2-1	0-0	2-1	5-1	7-0	3-1	2-0	1-2	4-0	0-0	10-0	2-2	2-1	1-1	

Senior Division A

		P	W	D	L	F	A	Pts
Ely City Res.		30	25	3	2	91	20	78
Hundon		30	22	5	3	83	32	71
Wisbech Town Res.		30	18	6	6	73	35	60
Foxton		30	18	3	9	63	35	57
Soham Town Rgrs Res.		30	17	3	10	73	45	54
Fulbourn Institute		30	13	5	12	51	41	44
Mildenhall Town Res.		30	12	8	10	57	49	44
West Wratting		30	13	4	13	53	48	43
Brampton		30	13	3	14	48	65	42
Girton United		30	12	4	14	43	45	40
Hemingford United		30	11	6	13	50	52	39
Hardwick		30	9	8	13	45	63	35
Lakenheath		30	6	6	18	48	95	24
Gamlingay United	-3	30	6	5	19	44	87	20
Grampian	-3	30	6	2	22	41	84	17
Bluntisham Rangers		30	2	3	25	27	94	9

WILLIAM COCKELL CUP

FIRST ROUND

Bluntisham Rangers 2 **Girton United** 3
Foxton 3 Fulbourn Institute 2
Gamlingay United 1 **Ely City Res.** 4
Grampian 1 **Mildenhall Town Res.** 4
Hardwick 3 Lakenheath 0
Hemingford United 1 **West Wratting** 5
Soham Town Rangers Res. 3 **Brampton** 3 *aet* (3-4p)
Wisbech Town Res. 1 **Hundon** 2

QUARTER-FINALS

Ely City Res. 2 Brampton 0
Foxton 1 Mildenhall Town Res. 0
Hundon 2 **Girton United** 4
West Wratting 3 Hardwick 2

SEMI-FINALS

Girton United 0 Ely City Res. 2 *(Ely City Res. expelled)*
West Wratting 1 **Foxton** 2

FINAL

(May 7th at Cambridge City)
Foxton 1 Girton United 0

CAMBRIDGESHIRE COUNTY LEAGUE SENIOR DIVISION A CONSTITUTION 2007-08

BRAMPTON . . . . Thrapston Road Playing Fields, Brampton, Huntingdon PE28 4NL . . . . None
COMBERTON UNITED . . . . Recreation Ground, Hines Lane, Comberton CB3 7BZ . . . . None
DEBDEN . . . . Recreation Ground, High Street, Debden, Saffron Walden CB11 3LE . . . . None
FOXTON . . . . Recreation Ground, Foxton. . . . . None
FULBOURN INSTITUTE. . . . . Fulbourn Recreation, Home End, Fulbourn CB1 5BS. . . . . None
GIRTON UNITED . . . . Girton Recreation, Cambridge Road, Girton CB3 0FH . . . . None
HARDWICK . . . . Egremont Road, Hardwick, Cambridge CB3 7XR . . . . None
HEMINGFORD UNITED . . . Memorial Playing Fields, Manor Road, Hemingford Grey, Huntingdon PE28 9BX. . . . . None
LAKENHEATH . . . . The Nest, Wings Road, Lakenheath IP27 9HW. . . . . None
LINTON GRANTA . . . . Recreation Ground, Meadow Lane, Linton, Cambridge CB1 6HX . . . . None
MILDENHALL TOWN RESERVES. . . . . Recreation Way, Mildenhall, Bury St Edmunds IP28 7EL 01638 713449
SOHAM TOWN RANGERS RESERVES . . . . . . Julius Martin Lane, Soham, Ely CB7 5EQ 01353 720732/722158
SOMERSHAM TOWN . . . . West End Ground, St Ives Road, Somersham, Huntingdon PE28 3ET. 01487 843384
WEST WRATTING . . . . Recreation Ground, Bull Lane, West Wratting CB1 5NJ. . . . . None
WHITTLESFORD UNITED . . . . The Lawn, Whittlesford CB2 4NG. . . . . None
WISBECH TOWN RESERVES . . . . Fenland Park, Lerowe Road, Wisbech PE13 3QL 01945 584176
IN: Comberton United (P), Debden (P), Linton Granta (R), Somersham Town (R), Whittlesford United (P)
OUT: Bluntisham Rangers (R), Ely City Reserves (P), Gamlingay United (R – Division Two A), Grampian (R), Hundon (P)

	Barton Mills	Castle Camps	Cherry Hinton	Comberton United	Debden	Haddenham Rovers	J M Sports	Milton	Outwell Swifts	Soham United	Swavesey Institute	West Row Gunners	West Wratting Res.	Whittlesford United	Willingham
Barton Mills		3-1	2-1	0-3	1-2	1-5	4-3	0-8	1-4	0-1	2-1	3-1	1-6	2-2	
Castle Camps	4-0		4-0	0-2	0-3	3-3	4-2	1-3	2-2	2-2	4-0	4-2	2-0	6-0	2-4
Cherry Hinton	1-4	3-3	S	3-0	1-3	1-2	4-2	2-1	1-0	4-3	2-0	3-1	3-2	2-6	3-2
Comberton United	4-1	10-1	3-0	E	0-2	3-1	1-1	1-0	1-1	3-0	2-0	4-1	2-1	4-4	1-1
Debden	8-0	2-0	4-0	4-1	N	3-0	5-2	2-1	2-2	2-0	4-1	4-1	5-1	0-1	5-2
Haddenham Rovers	6-0	4-4	1-1	0-4	1-3	I	4-1	3-5	0-1	2-0	3-2	3-3	3-1	1-4	3-2
J M Sports	6-4	2-0	3-0	0-2	2-2	1-6	O	0-2	2-0	1-4	1-0	1-1	2-2	2-2	1-2
Milton	3-0	6-3	3-2	1-2	4-3	2-4	7-0	R	2-3	3-1	1-0	6-0	4-2	2-2	3-3
Outwell Swifts	11-0	3-2	3-2	1-4	1-1	2-6	2-1	1-1		1-3	2-1	1-2	3-5	3-0	3-0
Soham United	2-4	2-3	1-3	0-5	2-7	3-4	3-4	2-1	3-3	D	1-2	6-3	3-0	4-9	1-2
Swavesey Institute	1-0	0-3	2-1	0-4	1-1	0-0	0-0	1-1	0-5	2-0	I	2-2	3-2	1-3	1-2
West Row Gunners	2-0	2-1	4-2	1-2	0-5	1-1	4-3	0-2	1-1	0-4	4-1	V	6-3	1-2	1-0
West Wratting Res.	2-3	4-2	2-4	1-2	1-3	7-1	0-2	6-3	0-4	0-1	1-4	5-0		0-6	2-4
Whittlesford United	6-1	4-2	3-0	1-0	4-1	2-0	3-1	1-4	2-1	2-1	2-1	2-2	3-3	B	4-0
Willingham	5-0	0-1	1-2	1-4	0-6	3-0	0-2	2-3	0-6	1-1	2-4	4-3	0-3	0-4	

Senior Division B		P	W	D	L	F	A	Pts
Whittlesford United		28	20	5	3	88	44	65
Debden	-3	28	21	4	3	92	30	64
Comberton United		28	20	4	4	74	27	64
Milton		28	16	4	8	82	47	52
Outwell Swifts		28	13	7	8	74	44	46
Haddenham Rovers		28	12	6	10	67	63	42
Cherry Hinton		28	12	2	14	51	65	38
Castle Camps		28	10	5	13	64	68	35
Swavesey Institute	+2	28	8	5	15	31	53	31
West Row Gunners		28	8	6	14	49	74	30
Willingham		28	8	4	16	45	71	28
Soham United		28	8	3	17	57	74	27
J M Sports	-4	28	8	6	14	48	68	26
Barton Mills		28	8	1	19	37	107	25
West Wratting Res.		28	6	2	20	57	81	20

PERCY OLDHAM CUP

FIRST ROUND
Barton Mills 0 **Comberton United** 7
Debden 2 Castle Camps 0
Ely Crusaders (scr.) v **Cherry Hinton** (w/o)
JM Sports 1 **Whittlesford United** 2
Soham United 1 **Milton** 3
West Row Gunners 4 **Haddenham Rovers** 2
West Wratting Res. 1 Swavesey Institute 0
Willingham 5 Outwell Swifts 5 *aet* (2-4p)

QUARTER-FINALS
Cherry Hinton 0 **Debden** 1
Outwell Swifts 4 West Row Gunners 3
West Wratting Res. 0 **Milton** 4
Whittlesford United 0 **Comberton United** 2

SEMI-FINALS
Debden 2 Outwell Swifts 0
Milton 3 Comberton United 0

FINAL
(May 9th at Cambridge City)
Milton 3 Debden 2 *aet*

WWW.NLNEWSDESK.CO.UK

CAMBRIDGESHIRE COUNTY LEAGUE SENIOR DIVISION B CONSTITUTION 2007-08

BLUNTISHAM RANGERS . . . . Mill Lane, Bluntisham, Huntingdon PE28 3LR . . . . None
CASTLE CAMPS . . . . Recreation Ground, Bumpstead Road, Castle Camps, Cambridge . . . . None
CHERRY HINTON. . . . . Recreation Ground, Cherry Hinton, Cambridge . . . . None
GRAMPIAN . . . . Sports Ground, Grampian Foods, Little Wratting CB9 7TD . . . . None
GREAT CHESTERFORD. . . . Great Chesterford Rec Ground, Newmarket Road, Great Chesterford CB10 1NS . . . . None
HADDENHAM ROVERS. . . . . Hop Row, Haddenham, Ely CB6 3SR. . . . . None
HELIONS BUMPSTEAD . . The New Shed Recreation Ground, Church Hill Road, Helions Bumpstead, Haverhill . . . . None
HUNTINGDON UNITED RGE . . Sapley Park Playing Fields, Sapley Road, Hartford, Huntingdon PE18 7PT. None
LITTLEPORT TOWN RESERVES . . . . . . Sports Centre, Camel Road, Littleport, Ely CB6 1EW. . . . . None
MILTON. . . . . Milton Recreation Ground, The Sycamores, Milton, Cambridge CB4 6ZN 01706 53339
OUTWELL SWIFTS. . . . . The Nest, Wisbech Road, Outwell PE14 8PE. . . . . None
SAFFRON CROCUS. . . . . Ickleton Recreation Ground, Frogge Street, Ickleton CB10 1NS . . . . None
SOHAM UNITED . . . . Qua Fen Common, Soham, Ely CB7 5DH . . . . None
SWAVESEY INSTITUTE . . . . The Green, High Street, Swavesey CB4 5QU. . . . . None
WEST ROW GUNNERS. . . . . Chapel Row, West Row, Bury St Edmunds IP28 8PA . . . . None
WILLINGHAM . . . . Recreation Ground, West Fen Road, Willingham, Cambridge. . . . . None
IN: Bluntisham Rangers (R), Grampian (R), Great Chesterford (P – Division One A), Helions Bumpstead (P – Division One A), Huntingdon United RGE (P – Division One B), Littleport Town Reserves (P – Division One B), Saffron Crocus (P – Division One A)
OUT: Barton Mills (R – Division One B), Comberton United (P), Debden (P), Ely Crusaders (WN), J M Sports (R – Division One A), West Wratting Reserves (R – Division One A), Whittlesford United (P)

Division One A	P	W	D	L	F	A	Pts
Saffron Crocus	26	21	3	2	77	21	66
Helions Bumpstead	26	19	3	4	93	33	60
Great Chesterford	26	17	3	6	70	49	54
Camden United	26	16	4	6	73	44	52
Girton United Res.	26	15	2	9	57	38	47
Steeple Bumpstead	26	12	2	12	57	62	38
Barrington	26	11	3	12	66	70	36
Great Shelford Res.	26	11	1	14	51	65	34
Fulbourn Institute Res.	26	9	4	13	51	57	31
Sawston Rovers	26	8	4	14	39	53	28
Litlington Athletic	26	7	5	14	53	74	26
Sawston United Res.	26	6	4	16	48	78	22
Fowlmere	26	4	5	17	43	78	17
Linton Granta Res.	26	4	1	21	29	85	13

Division One B		P	W	D	L	F	A	Pts
Huntingdon Utd RGE		26	20	3	3	74	27	63
Littleport Town Res.		26	18	2	6	81	46	56
St Ives Rangers		26	15	1	10	50	45	46
Cottenham United Res.		26	13	3	10	58	50	42
Eaton Socon Res.		26	11	4	11	51	45	37
Tuddenham Rovers	-3	26	11	6	9	66	44	36
Fenstanton		26	11	3	12	47	77	36
Bottisham Sports		26	10	5	11	51	55	35
Waterbeach Res.		26	10	1	15	45	60	31
Gransden Chequers		26	8	6	12	29	50	30
Great Paxton Res.		26	9	2	15	56	75	29
Buckden		26	8	3	15	42	54	27
March T. Utd Res.	-6	26	9	2	15	43	52	23
Godmanchester Res.	-3	26	6	5	15	33	46	20

DIVISION ONE CHAMPIONSHIP PLAY-OFF *(May 12th at Huntingdon Utd RGE)* Huntingdon Utd RGE 1 **Saffron Crocus** 3

Division Two A		P	W	D	L	F	A	Pts
Duxford United		26	18	5	3	81	15	59
Comberton United Res.		26	16	8	2	61	24	56
Cambourne Rovers		26	17	4	5	89	33	55
Camb. Univ. Press Res.		26	16	5	5	72	33	53
Melbourn		26	13	4	9	69	51	43
Hardwick Res.		26	13	4	9	69	63	43
Balsham		26	11	6	9	56	53	39
Grampian Res.		26	11	5	10	46	59	38
Thaxted		26	11	4	11	77	78	37
Mott MacDonald		26	8	4	14	47	72	28
Camden United Res.		26	7	2	17	34	97	23
Gamlingay United Res.		26	4	4	18	47	95	16
Papworth		26	5	0	21	51	86	15
Foxton Res.	-3	26	3	3	20	47	87	9

Division Two B	P	W	D	L	F	A	Pts
Longstanton	26	19	4	3	102	41	61
Wisbech St Mary	26	18	6	2	91	39	60
Ely City 'A'	26	19	3	4	81	44	60
Sutton United	26	17	1	8	95	51	52
Newmarket White Lion	26	15	4	7	94	55	49
Witchford	26	14	3	9	73	52	45
Needingworth Utd Res.	26	10	4	12	62	58	34
Over Sports Res.	26	10	3	13	54	58	33
Hemingford United Res.	26	8	7	11	63	67	31
Lode	26	8	4	14	47	100	28
Milton Res.	26	7	1	18	47	75	22
Stretham Hotspurs	26	6	4	16	48	76	22
Isleham United	26	3	6	17	27	86	15
Bluntisham Rangers Res.	26	2	2	22	36	118	8

DIVISION TWO CHAMPIONSHIP PLAY-OFF *(May 15th at Longstanton)* Longstanton 2 **Duxford United** 3
CREAKE CHARITY SHIELD FINAL *(May 8th at Cambridge City)* **Littleport Town Res.** 1 Wisbech St Mary 0

Division Three A		P	W	D	L	F	A	Pts
Elsworth Sports		26	22	2	2	118	38	68
Whittlesford United Res.		26	20	1	5	92	33	61
Great Chishill		26	17	3	6	75	34	54
Wilbraham		26	14	1	11	68	60	43
Abington United		26	13	4	9	70	79	43
Ashdon Villa		26	12	2	12	60	62	38
Bassingbourn		26	10	7	9	57	48	37
Steeple Morden		26	11	2	13	53	47	35
Hempstead United		26	10	2	14	62	87	32
Great Chesterford Res.		26	8	7	11	58	81	31
Eaton Socon 'A'		26	8	3	15	54	68	27
Harston		26	8	2	16	52	77	26
Withersfield	-3	26	8	3	15	45	90	18
Orwell		26	1	5	20	28	88	8

Division Three B	P	W	D	L	F	A	Pts
The Vine	26	19	6	1	85	37	63
Somersham Town Res.	26	19	5	2	86	31	62
Wisbech St Mary Res.	26	19	2	5	111	35	59
Pymoor	26	19	1	6	109	62	58
Lakenheath Res.	26	15	3	8	84	50	48
Fordham Res.	26	12	4	10	71	67	40
Soham United Res.	26	10	3	13	64	88	33
Hunt'gdon Utd RGE Res.	26	8	5	13	31	55	29
Dullingham	26	9	1	16	64	110	28
St Ives Town 'A'	26	8	3	15	47	62	27
Cottenham United 'A'	26	7	3	16	47	82	24
Little Downham Swifts	26	6	4	16	48	61	22
Brampton Res.	26	6	4	16	47	89	22
Hemingford United 'A'	26	2	2	22	35	100	8

DIVISION THREE CHAMPIONSHIP PLAY-OFF *(May 12th at Elsworth Sports)* **Elsworth Sports** 4 The Vine 1
JOHN ABLETT CUP *(May 10th at Cambridge City)* **Newmarket Town 'A'** 2 Elsworth Sports 0

Division Four A	P	W	D	L	F	A	Pts
Newmarket Town 'A'	26	20	2	4	121	28	62
Fulbourn S & S Club	26	20	1	5	90	33	61
Camb. Univ. Press 'A'	26	18	4	4	94	33	58
J M Sports Res.	26	14	5	7	85	62	47
Litlington Athletic Res.	26	15	2	9	79	69	47
Hundon Res.	26	14	2	10	97	68	44
Saffron Crocus Res.	26	13	3	10	79	69	42
Figleaves	26	10	3	13	64	68	33
Linton Granta 'A'	26	10	1	15	47	74	31
Sawston Rovers Res.	26	8	2	16	47	75	26
Hardwick 'A'	26	8	2	16	55	97	26
Sawston United 'A'	26	7	2	17	48	89	23
Steeple Bumpstead Res.	26	6	4	16	40	89	22
Fowlmere Res.	26	2	1	23	28	120	7

Division Four B	P	W	D	L	F	A	Pts
Mepal Sports	26	15	6	5	60	25	51
March Rangers	26	17	0	9	88	56	51
Ely Crusaders	26	14	3	9	76	52	45
Wisbech St Mary 'A'	26	14	1	11	62	47	43
Haddenham Rovers Res.	26	14	1	11	63	88	43
Burwell Swifts	26	11	9	6	63	41	42
Exning Athletic	26	12	4	10	54	54	40
Sutton United Res.	26	10	5	11	45	51	35
Barton Mills Res.	26	8	8	10	46	65	32
West Row Gunners Res.	26	8	4	14	56	59	28
Willingham Res.	26	8	4	14	53	67	28
Swavesey Institute Res.	26	9	1	16	50	78	28
Milton 'A'	26	7	5	14	58	75	26
Earith United	26	4	1	21	48	64	25

DIVISION FOUR CHAMPIONSHIP PLAY-OFF *(May 15th at Newmarket Town)* **Newmarket Town 'A'** 5 Mepal Sports 0

Division Five A	P	W	D	L	F	A	Pts
Saffron Rangers	28	21	3	4	103	30	66
City Life	28	19	3	6	91	47	60
Barton	28	18	3	7	84	57	57
Great Shelford 'A'	28	17	2	9	86	51	53
Dalehead United	28	15	7	6	82	49	52
Duxford United Res.	28	15	7	6	85	53	52
Gransden Chequers Res.	28	16	3	9	71	48	51
Haslingfield	28	14	4	10	65	77	46
Bottisham Sports Res.	28	10	3	15	62	91	33
Hundon 'A'	28	6	8	14	63	78	26
Comberton United 'A'	28	8	2	18	52	71	26
Melbourn Res.	28	7	4	17	70	94	25
Barrington Res.	28	6	4	18	41	80	22
Steeple Morden Res.	28	4	3	21	40	90	15
Newport Veterans	28	3	5	20	24	103	14

Division Five B	P	W	D	L	F	A	Pts
Fenstanton Res.	28	20	4	4	101	50	64
Outwell Swifts Res.	28	20	4	4	85	45	64
The Vine Res.	28	16	6	6	72	42	54
Cottenham United 'B'	28	16	4	8	76	61	52
Littleport Town 'A'	28	15	6	7	84	52	51
Wicken Amateurs	28	14	5	9	82	61	47
Burwell Swifts Res.	28	13	5	10	65	63	44
Walsoken United	28	13	2	13	91	56	41
Lode Res.	28	11	5	12	73	70	38
March Rangers Res.	28	9	6	13	50	78	33
Isleham United Res.	28	9	2	17	58	76	29
Longstanton Res.	28	5	7	16	58	68	22
L. Downham Swifts Res.	28	6	3	19	66	116	21
Dataracks Elite	28	6	2	20	58	101	18
Coldham United	28	3	6	19	32	112	15

DIVISION FIVE CHAMPIONSHIP PLAY-OFF *(May 17th at Fenstanton)* **Fenstanton Res.** 1 Saffron Rangers 0
REG HAIGH/ALEX PECK CUP *(May 11th at Cambridge City)* **Great Shelford 'A'** 5 Dalehead United 3

WWW.CHERRYRED.CO.UK

CENTRAL MIDLANDS LEAGUE

	Appleby Frod'ham	Askern Welfare	Barton Town OB	Bilborough Pelican	Blackwell MW	Bottesford Town	Clipstone Welfare	Dunkirk	Gedling MW	Graham St. Prims	Greenwood Mdws	Heanor Town	Holbrook MW	Kimberley Town	Nettleham	Radcliffe Olympic	Radford	Rainworth MW	Rolls Royce Leisure	Southwell City
Appleby Frodingham		1-1	0-3	4-3	4-1	1-4	1-2	0-5	1-1	3-3	2-1	1-4	6-3	3-1	3-2	1-1	1-1	0-1	0-4	1-3
Askern Welfare	5-0		2-1	6-1	5-2	0-0	3-0	2-1	1-0	1-0	2-1	2-4	1-1	3-2	4-0	2-2	5-1	1-0	1-4	1-4
Barton Town Old Boys	7-3	4-1	S	6-4	6-1	0-1	3-0	2-1	3-0	4-1	7-0	3-0	1-0	14-0	10-0	1-0	4-1	0-0	3-1	4-0
Bilborough Pelican	6-5	1-2	0-2	U	0-1	1-4	2-1	0-1	7-0	15-3	2-0	5-0	2-1	6-1	2-2	0-3	1-1	1-7	0-0	1-0
Blackwell Miners Welfare	0-2	2-2	3-5	1-4	P	2-4	4-1	1-0	5-1	6-1	2-0	3-2	1-3	2-1	5-1	0-0	0-2	1-5	2-1	4-2
Bottesford Town	2-3	2-1	0-1	3-0	0-1	R	5-1	4-1	3-1	2-2	6-0	3-1	3-0	3-2	7-0	3-0	3-0	1-2	2-0	3-0
Clipstone Welfare	5-0	0-0	1-1	3-1	2-1	0-2	E	1-3	3-2	4-2	6-3	2-0	2-3	5-2	3-0	2-1	2-0	1-3	2-1	4-1
Dunkirk	3-0	2-3	4-3	0-0	1-1	1-1	0-5	M	2-1	3-5	7-0	3-1	0-3	3-2	3-1	3-2	3-0	3-1	1-0	3-0
Gedling Miners Welfare	7-0	0-4	1-2	0-1	1-2	1-4	1-1	2-2	E	2-0	1-0	3-0	0-0	2-3	5-0	2-1	3-3	1-1	1-5	0-2
Graham Street Prims	0-1	2-1	1-6	0-4	2-0	0-6	2-3	0-2	1-0		4-1	1-6	3-2	4-0	6-2	1-1	2-3	2-3	0-3	2-4
Greenwood Meadows	1-4	0-5	1-3	0-6	2-1	0-6	2-3	3-2	2-1	3-0	D	3-1	1-2	2-3	3-5	1-1	0-1	1-2	1-3	2-3
Heanor Town	2-2	0-0	1-4	0-4	2-1	0-6	2-5	1-1	1-0	5-2	4-0	I	2-1	1-1	2-1	1-2	0-1	1-1	1-1	1-2
Holbrook Miners Welfare	0-0	2-0	0-4	1-1	0-0	2-1	2-3	1-2	0-4	1-0	2-0	1-3	V	3-0	5-3	3-5	1-0	0-2	3-6	0-0
Kimberley Town	1-5	0-6	1-4	0-6	1-4	1-3	0-6	2-5	1-1	2-6	0-2	2-3	0-1	I	0-2	0-1	0-3	0-2	0-2	1-3
Nettleham	1-3	0-1	0-0	1-9	0-3	0-3	0-2	0-1	1-0	3-2	2-1	3-3	1-4	3-1	S	1-2	0-1	0-2	1-4	0-4
Radcliffe Olympic	2-0	2-0	2-0	3-0	1-1	1-3	0-1	1-0	0-2	1-3	3-2	2-0	6-2	2-0	2-0	I	2-0	0-2	2-2	0-3
Radford	1-3	2-2	1-1	0-0	2-3	1-3	2-0	1-3	3-1	3-1	1-1	3-2	3-2	0-2	0-2	0-2	O	0-0	3-1	2-1
Rainworth Miners Welfare	4-2	2-1	1-1	2-1	0-0	1-2	0-2	5-0	1-0	6-0	6-0	2-2	3-1	5-1	1-0	4-1	3-0	N	0-0	3-2
Rolls Royce Leisure	2-2	1-3	2-4	0-0	1-0	0-4	1-3	3-1	2-1	3-0	2-2	2-1	2-0	3-1	1-1	1-2	1-0	0-0		0-0
Southwell City	3-0	0-4	1-1	3-1	2-1	0-4	3-3	2-1	0-3	2-4	1-3	0-0	3-0	1-0	7-2	4-1	3-0	0-0	2-1	

Supreme Division		P	W	D	L	F	A	Pts
Bottesford Town		38	30	3	5	118	28	93
Barton Town Old Boys		38	28	6	4	128	36	90
Rainworth Miners Welfare		38	26	8	4	88	30	86
Askern Welfare		38	22	8	8	86	47	74
Clipstone Welfare		38	23	4	11	91	59	73
Dunkirk		38	22	5	11	80	58	71
Radcliffe Olympic		38	20	6	12	66	51	66
Southwell City		38	18	7	13	74	57	61
Rolls Royce Leisure		38	16	11	11	65	49	59
Bilborough Pelican		38	16	7	15	98	67	55
Blackwell Miners Welfare		38	16	5	17	68	71	53
Radford		38	14	9	15	51	59	51
Appleby Frodingham		38	13	8	17	68	96	47
Heanor Town		38	12	8	18	63	81	44
Holbrook Miners Welfare	-3	38	13	7	18	55	67	43
Gedling Miners Welfare		38	8	8	22	51	70	32
Graham Street Prims		38	9	3	26	67	123	30
Nettleham		38	5	5	28	36	114	20
Greenwood Meadows		38	5	4	29	38	123	19
Kimberley Town		38	2	2	34	35	140	8

Reserve Premier Division		P	W	D	L	F	A	Pts
Arnold Town Res.		30	21	1	8	77	41	64
Rainworth MW Res.		30	18	9	3	71	32	63
Holbrook MW Res.		30	19	5	6	76	45	62
Retford United Res.		30	16	6	8	70	41	54
Appleby Frod'gham Res.		30	16	5	9	85	57	53
Linc. Moorlands Res.	-5	30	16	5	9	77	36	48
Welbeck Welfare Res.		30	14	6	10	70	57	48
Dunkirk Res.	-3	30	14	6	10	52	47	45
Clipstone Welfare Res.		30	13	2	15	66	61	41
Heanor Town Res.		30	10	3	17	50	77	33
Forest Town Res.		30	9	5	16	52	75	32
Southwell City Res.		30	9	5	16	53	78	32
Radford Res.		30	8	5	17	47	66	29
Blackwell MW Res.		30	7	3	20	35	93	24
Bilborough Pelican Res.		30	6	5	19	62	103	23
Nettleham Res.		30	5	7	18	49	83	22

WWW.NLNEWSDESK.CO.UK

CENTRAL MIDLANDS LEAGUE SUPREME DIVISION CONSTITUTION 2007-08

APPLEBY FRODINGHAM ..... Brumby Hall Corus Sports Ground, Ashby Road, Scunthorpe DN16 1AA 01724 843024
ASKERN WELFARE .... Welfare Sports Ground, Manor Way, Askern, Doncaster DN6 0AL 01302 700957
BENTLEY COLLIERY .... Bentley Miners Welfare, The Avenue, Bentley, Doncaster DN5 0NP 01302 874420
BLACKWELL MINERS WELFARE .. Welfare Ground, Primrose Hill, Blackwell, Alfreton DE55 5JF 01773 811295
CLIPSTONE WELFARE .... Lido Ground, Clipstone Road East, Clipstone, Mansfield NG21 9AZ 01623 477978
DUNKIRK .... Ron Steel Sports Ground, Lenton Lane, Clifton Bridge, Nottingham NG7 2SA 0115 985 0803
FOREST TOWN .... Forest Town Academy, Clipstone Road West, Forest Town, Mansfield NG19 0EE 01623 626478
GEDLING MINERS WELFARE.... Plains Social Club, Plains Road, Mapperley, Nottingham NG3 5RH 0115 926 6300
GRAHAM STREET PRIMS ...... Asterdale Sports Centre, Borrowash Road, Spondon, Derby DE21 7PH 01332 668653
GREENWOOD MEADOWS............... Lenton Lane, Clifton Bridge, Nottingham NG7 2AX 0115 986 5913
GRIMSBY BOROUGH .... Brigg Town FC, The Hawthorns, Hawthorn Avenue, Brigg DN20 8PG 01652 651605
HATFIELD MAIN .... Dunscroft Welfare Ground, Broadway, Dunscroft, Doncaster DN7 4HD 01302 841326
HEANOR TOWN .... The Town Ground, Mayfield Avenue, Heanor DE75 7EN 01773 713742
HOLBROOK MINERS WELFARE .... Welfare Ground, Shaw Lane, Holbrook DE56 0TG 01332 880259
NETTLEHAM .... Mulsanne Park, Field Close, Nettleham, Lincoln LN2 2RX. 01522 750007
PINXTON .... Welfare Ground, Wharf Road, Pinxton NG16 6NY 07989 324249
RADCLIFFE OLYMPIC ..... Recreational Ground, Wharf Lane, Radcliffe-on-Trent, Nottingham NG12 2AN............ 0115 942 3250
RADFORD .... Selhurst Street, Off Radford Road, Radford, Nottingham NG7 5EH 0115 942 3250
ROLLS ROYCE LEISURE .... Rolls Royce Sports & Social, Watnall Road, Hucknall NG15 6EU 0115 963 2380
SOUTHWELL CITY............. War Memorial Recreation Ground, Bishops Drive, Southwell NG25 0JP. 01636 814386
IN: Bentley Colliery (P), Forest Town (P), Grimsby Borough (P), Hatfield Main (P), Pinxton (P)
OUT: Barton Town Old Boys (P – Northern Counties East League Division One), Bilborough Pelican (W – Notts Senior League Senior Division), Bottesford Town (P – Northern Counties East League Division One), Kimberley Town (R), Rainworth Miners Welfare (P – Northern Counties East League Division One)

	Bentley Colliery	Blidworth Welfare	Bolsover Town	Calverton MW	Forest Town	Grimsby Borough	Harworth Colliery I.	Hatfield Main	Kiveton Park	Louth United	Newark Flowserve	Newark Town	Ollerton Town	Pinxton	Sandiacre Town	Thoresby CW	Thorne Colliery	Welbeck Welfare	Yorkshire Main
Bentley Colliery		5-1	2-0	0-1	5-1	2-2	3-2	2-3	4-0	3-0	2-1	1-2	2-1	1-2	6-0	8-1	9-1	0-1	3-1
Blidworth Welfare	1-2	*P*	1-2	1-2	0-1	3-3	1-1	0-1	1-4	2-0	1-3	2-2	2-2	0-3	2-2	2-0	2-1	3-0	2-2
Bolsover Town	1-1	2-3	*R*	2-2	1-2	1-1	2-1	0-2	1-0	0-0	0-0	0-2	1-2	1-2	1-0	4-2	2-2	1-3	2-0
Calverton Miners Welfare	2-0	2-3	1-1	*E*	1-0	1-4	3-0	0-1	1-1	5-0	0-1	0-1	1-2	0-0	5-2	2-1	1-0	4-2	5-1
Forest Town	2-3	3-0	0-0	2-1	*M*	0-3	2-0	2-3	1-5	1-0	3-0	3-0	2-1	2-2	4-1	3-0	3-0	2-0	3-2
Grimsby Borough	1-4	2-0	3-2	2-0	0-1	*I*	5-0	1-2	4-0	5-0	3-1	3-1	5-3	3-1	2-1	2-0	4-1	3-0	4-1
Harworth Colliery Institute	2-5	0-0	3-1	0-1	0-4	0-4	*E*	1-7	2-1	1-0	3-0	1-0	2-2	0-1	1-3	2-1	0-1	2-1	0-2
Hatfield Main	3-3	1-1	1-1	2-0	4-0	1-2	3-2	*R*	2-0	1-0	3-0	3-1	2-1	2-3	1-3	3-1	6-1	9-1	2-1
Kiveton Park	2-2	2-2	1-1	3-2	1-2	2-5	4-0	4-2		5-2	1-3	2-0	2-1	1-3	1-0	1-1	1-0	2-4	3-1
Louth United	0-2	1-3	2-0	3-1	0-4	0-4	2-3	1-4	0-1	*D*	4-1	0-1	1-4	0-2	0-5	9-0	2-2	2-6	3-1
Newark Flowserve	0-2	0-0	3-1	0-0	2-0	3-1	3-1	3-0	0-0	2-1	*I*	1-1	0-0	2-1	2-0	2-1	0-2	0-1	1-1
Newark Town	1-1	0-1	6-1	3-2	1-1	0-1	4-4	0-0	1-2	2-2	0-1	*V*	2-2	3-1	4-0	0-2	1-4	1-0	1-5
Ollerton Town	2-4	4-4	0-1	3-2	0-3	1-0	4-0	1-3	2-1	2-0	1-0	0-1	*I*	0-1	4-1	0-3	0-0	3-1	1-1
Pinxton	0-0	2-1	2-2	2-2	1-4	4-2	1-4	4-2	0-2	7-1	3-2	2-1	6-0	*S*	2-1	6-0	3-6	2-0	4-2
Sandiacre Town	1-5	0-1	3-4	1-5	0-4	1-2	0-3	0-5	2-2	2-2	1-4	1-2	0-2	0-3	*I*	3-3	1-1	3-1	1-1
Thoresby Colliery Welfare	1-2	1-4	0-2	1-2	0-5	1-6	0-0	0-5	2-1	2-3	3-4	0-0	1-1	2-1	4-1	*O*	2-1	1-3	1-1
Thorne Colliery	0-4	0-0	1-3	0-3	2-3	0-1	1-2	1-2	1-1	3-0	2-3	1-1	4-0	2-3	1-1	4-0	*N*	5-9	1-3
Welbeck Welfare	1-3	3-2	5-4	1-3	0-3	4-0	6-3	1-2	3-2	0-4	1-1	0-1	3-1	5-3	4-2	3-1	2-2		6-5
Yorkshire Main	2-1	0-1	0-4	2-1	4-0	2-2	2-3	2-4	3-0	3-2	3-3	0-3	4-2	0-1	2-4	1-3	1-1	4-1	

Premier Division

Team		P	W	D	L	F	A	Pts
Hatfield Main	-3	36	28	4	4	101	38	85
Grimsby Borough		36	26	4	6	97	41	82
Bentley Colliery		36	23	6	7	102	42	75
Forest Town		36	23	4	9	74	44	73
Pinxton		36	20	6	10	74	55	66
Newark Flowserve		36	18	10	8	54	42	64
Calverton Miners Welfare		36	17	7	12	66	46	58
Welbeck Welfare		36	17	2	17	83	89	53
Kiveton Park		36	15	7	14	64	62	52
Blidworth Welfare		36	11	12	13	53	59	45
Newark Town		36	12	9	15	47	55	45
Bolsover Town		36	11	11	14	52	59	44
Ollerton Town		36	10	10	16	58	66	40
Yorkshire Main		36	10	8	18	66	79	38
Harworth Colliery Institute		36	10	6	20	47	84	36
Louth United		36	8	4	24	48	83	28
Thoresby Colliery Welfare		36	7	7	22	42	97	28
Thorne Colliery		36	6	8	22	50	85	26
Sandiacre Town		36	4	7	25	46	98	19

Reserve Division One

Team		P	W	D	L	F	A	Pts
Radcliffe Olympic Res.		22	16	2	4	60	28	50
Calverton Miners W. Res.		22	15	3	4	68	26	48
Blidworth Welfare Res.		22	14	2	6	57	38	44
Sandiacre Town Res.		22	12	6	4	60	35	42
Pinxton Res.		22	9	6	7	46	47	33
Bilborough Pelican 'A'		22	8	4	10	41	43	28
Ollerton Town Res.	-3	22	9	3	10	37	49	27
Graham Street Prims Res.		22	7	4	11	46	54	25
Newark Town Res.		22	7	2	13	39	60	23
Thoresby Colliery W. Res.		22	6	4	12	28	48	22
Blackwell Miners W 'A'		22	4	3	15	37	58	15
Kimberley Town Res.		22	3	5	14	34	67	14

RESERVES CUP FINAL

FINAL
(April 11th at Radford)
Arnold Town Res. 3 Heanor Town Res. 1

CENTRAL MIDLANDS LEAGUE PREMIER DIVISION CONSTITUTION 2007-08

ARMTHORPE .... Armthorpe Welfare FC, Church Street, Armthorpe, Doncaster DN3 3AG 01302 831247
BLIDWORTH WELFARE ... Blidworth Recreation Centre, Mansfield Road, Blidworth, Mansfield NG21 0LR 01623 793361
BOLSOVER TOWN .... Bolsover Town Sports & Social Club, Moor Lane, Bolsover, Chesterfield S44 6EW 01246 822449
CALVERTON MINERS WELFARE ..... Calverton MW, Hollinwood Lane, Calverton NG14 6NR 0115 965 4390
HARWORTH COLLIERY INSTITUTE .... Scrooby Road, Bircotes, Doncaster DN11 8JT 01302 750614
KIMBERLEY TOWN .... The Stag Ground, Nottingham Road, Kimberley NG16 2ND 0115 938 2769
KINSLEY BOYS .... Kinsley Playing Fields, Wakefield Road, Kinsley WF9 5EH 07883 373232
KIVETON PARK.................. Kiveton Park MW, Hard Lane, Kiveton Park, Sheffield S26 6NB 07763 467979
LOUTH TOWN .... Park Avenue, Louth LN11 8BY 07712 653791
NEWARK FLOWSERVE .... Lowfields Works, Hawton Lane, New Balderton, Newark NG24 3EH 01636 494780
NEWARK TOWN .... Collingham FC, Station Road, Collingham NG23 7RA 01636 892303
OLLERTON TOWN .... The Lane, Walesby Lane, New Ollerton, Newark NG22 9UX .... None
PARKHOUSE.................... Mill Lane Ground, Mill Lane, Clay Cross, Chesterfield 07816 758778
PHOENIX SPORTS & SOCIAL .. Phoenix Sports Complex, Bawtry Road, Brinsworth, Rotherham S60 5PA 01709 363864
STANTON ILKESTON .. South Normanton Ath. FC, ExChem Spts Ground, Lees Lane, South Normanton DE55 2AD 01773 581491
SUTTON TOWN .... The Fieldings, Huthwaite Road, Sutton-in-Ashfield NG17 2HB 01623 552376
THORESBY COLLIERY WELFARE ... Thoresby Colliery Sports Ground, Fourth Avenue, Edwinstowe NG21 9NS ... 07802 417987
THORNE COLLIERY .... Moorends Welfare, Grange Road, Moorends, Thorne, Doncaster DN8 4LU 07855 545221
WELBECK WELFARE .... Colliery Ground, Elkesley Road, Meden Vale, Warsop, Mansfield NG20 9PS... 07863 568576/01623 842267
YORKSHIRE MAIN .... Edlington Lane, Edlington, Doncaster DN12 1DA 07775 714558

IN: Armthorpe (N), Kimberley Town (R), Kinsley Boys (P – Doncaster Senior League Premier Division), Parkhouse (P – Midland Regional Alliance Division Two), Phoenix Sports & Social (P – Sheffield & Hallamshire County Senior League Division Two), Stanton Ilkeston (P – Notts Amateur Alliance Premier League), Sutton Town (W – Northern Counties East League Premier Division)
OUT: Bentley Colliery (P), Forest Town (P), Grimsby Borough (P), Hatfield Main (P), Matlock United (WN), Pinxton (P), Sandiacre Town (R – Midland Regional Alliance Premier Division)
Louth United become Louth Town

LEAGUE CUP

PRELIMINARY ROUND
Bentley Colliery 3 Rainworth Miners Welfare 1
Bottesford Town 0 **Barton Town Old Boys** 3
Dunkirk 0 Forest Town 0
Forest Town 0 **Dunkirk** 4 *replay*
Harworth Colliery Institute 0 **Kiveton Park** 2
Heanor Town 6 Gedling Miners Welfare 0
Louth United 2 Thoresby Colliery Welfare 1
Pinxton 2 Holbrook Miners Welfare 1
Radford 0 **Rolls Royce Leisure** 1

FIRST ROUND
Appleby Frodingham 5 Bilborough Pelican 4
Blidworth Welfare 0 **Southwell City** 3
Calverton Miners Welfare 3 Nettleham 3
Nettleham 2 Calverton Miners Welfare 1 *replay*
Dunkirk 1 Barton Town Old Boys 1
Barton Town Old Boys 8 Dunkirk 2 *replay*
Graham St Prims 0 **Heanor Town** 5
Greenwood Meadows 2 **Hatfield Main** 3
Kiveton Park 0 **Askern Welfare** 2
Matlock United (scr.) v **Ollerton Town** (w/o)
Newark Flowserve 0 **Bentley Colliery** 2
Newark Town 2 Blackwell Miners Welfare 1
Pinxton 1 Clipstone Welfare 1
Clipstone Welfare 1 **Pinxton** 2 *replay*
Radcliffe Olympic 3 Rolls Royce Leisure 0
Sandiacre Town 0 **Louth United** 2
Thorne Colliery 1 **Grimsby Borough** 4

Welbeck Welfare 4 Bolsover Town 0
Yorkshire Main 1 **Kimberley Town** 2

SECOND ROUND
Askern Welfare 1 Grimsby Borough 1
Grimsby Borough 0 **Askern Welfare** 2 *replay*
Barton Town Old Boys 3 Radcliffe Olympic 2 *aet*
Heanor Town 2 Nettleham 0
Louth United 2 Hatfield Main 2
Hatfield Main 2 Louth United 0 *replay*
Newark Town 4 Southwell City 2
Ollerton Town 0 Kimberley Town 0
Kimberley Town 1 **Ollerton Town** 4 *replay*
Pinxton 0 **Bentley Colliery** 2
Welbeck Welfare 5 Appleby Frodingham 3

QUARTER-FINALS
Bentley Colliery 4 Newark Town 0
Heanor Town 2 Askern Welfare 1
Ollerton Town 3 Hatfield Main 1
Welbeck Welfare 4 Barton Town Old Boys 3

SEMI-FINALS
Ollerton Town 2 Welbeck Welfare 1
(at Blidworth Welfare)

FINAL
(May 6th at Alfreton Town)
Heanor Town 5 Ollerton Town 3

FLOODLIGHT TROPHY

FIRST ROUND
Bottesford Town 2 **Dunkirk** 3
Clipstone Welfare 9 Nettleham 1
Gedling Miners Welfare 3 Louth United 2
Harworth Colliery Institute 3 Greenwood Meadows 2
Hatfield Main 2 Graham Street Prims 0
Heanor Town 1 **Bilborough Pelican** 2
Holbrook Miners Welfare 3 Rainworth
Miners Welfare 3
Rainworth Miners Welfare 3 Holbrook Miners
Welfare 2 *replay*
Newark Town 2 Blidworth Welfare 2
Blidworth Welfare 0 Newark Town 1 *replay*
(Newark Town expelled)
Radcliffe Olympic 2 Askern Welfare 1
Radford 2 Rolls Royce Leisure 0
Southwell City 2 Calverton
Miners Welfare 0

SECOND ROUND
Appleby Frodingham 4 Gedling Miners Welfare 1
Blidworth Welfare 6 Radford 1
Clipstone Welfare 3 Rainworth Miners Welfare 1
Dunkirk 2 Blackwell Miners Welfare 1
Harworth Colliery Institute 2 **Bilborough Pelican** 3

Hatfield Main 0 **Barton Town Old Boys** 1
Radcliffe Olympic 1 Southwell City 0
Sandiacre Town 1 **Kimberley Town** 2

QUARTER-FINALS
Appleby Frodingham 4 Blidworth Welfare 0
Barton Town Old Boys 3 Radcliffe Olympic 1
Dunkirk 2 Bilborough Pelican 0
Kimberley Town 0 **Clipstone Welfare** 1

SEMI-FINALS
(played over two legs)
Appleby Frodingham 1 Barton Town Old Boys 6,
Barton Town Old Boys 5 Appleby Frodingham 1
Dunkirk 0 Clipstone Welfare 3,
Clipstone Welfare 2 Dunkirk 1

FINAL
(April 19th at Southwell City)
Clipstone Welfare 3 Barton Town Old Boys 1

CLWYD LEAGUE

Note – Rhyl Youth withdrew during the course of the season. Their results are shown herein but are expunged from the league table	Aston Park Rangers	Bro Cernyw	Flint Town United Res.	Halkyn United Res.	Llandyrnog United Res.	Llansannan	Mochdre Sports	Penmaenmawr Phoenix	Prestatyn Town Res.	Rhuddlan Town	Rhyl Nomads	Rhyl Youth
Aston Park Rangers	P	3-0	2-1	3-0	1-2	4-2	2-2	1-4	1-1	8-0	6-4	1-4
Bro Cernyw	1-1	R	1-2	1-3	2-5	0-1	0-1	2-1	5-5	3-3	2-2	4-3
Flint Town Utd Res.	3-0	1-1	E	7-1	5-2	3-0	1-2	4-3	4-3	3-2	3-3	n/a
Halkyn United Res.	1-2	2-2	1-1	M	0-0	2-3	1-0	2-1	0-5	2-8	2-5	0-4
Llandyrnog Utd Res.	0-1	2-2	3-2	3-0	I	3-1	8-1	2-1	1-1	2-0	3-2	1-0
Llansannan	3-2	4-2	3-5	2-1	3-4	E	2-0	2-3	0-3	4-2	3-1	1-4
Mochdre Sports	2-3	2-0	1-2	4-1	1-5	2-1	R	1-0	0-1	1-4	1-4	1-1
Penmaenmawr Pho.	2-5	3-0	1-5	6-1	2-1	3-3	0-0		2-3	2-2	0-0	0-1
Prestatyn Town Res.	4-3	5-0	7-1	2-3	5-1	6-0	4-0	3-1		6-1	3-1	1-4
Rhuddlan Town	2-1	0-0	2-3	2-2	1-5	2-2	4-0	3-4	0-0	D	2-5	2-0
Rhyl Nomads	4-2	1-0	3-2	7-0	2-2	5-0	4-1	2-2	1-0	1-1	I	1-1
Rhyl Youth	n/a	3-3	2-1	n/a	n/a	3-0	3-1	0-2	1-5	4-0	1-6	V

PREMIER CUP

FIRST ROUND
Llansannan 3 Rhyl Nomads 2
Penmaenmawr Phoenix 0 **Aston Park Rangers** 3
Prestatyn Town Res. 3 Llandyrnog Res. 2
Rhuddlan Town 6 Bro Cernyw 3
QUARTER-FINALS
Aston Park Rangers (w/o) v Rhyl Youth (scr.)
Halkyn United Res. 0 **Flint Town United Res.** 1
Prestatyn Town Res. 1 Mochdre Sports 0
Rhuddlan Town 1 Llansannan 0
SEMI-FINALS
Aston Park Rgrs 3 Prestatyn Town Res. 0
Flint Town United Res. 1 **Rhuddlan Town** 1
aet (3-5p)
FINAL
(April 26th at Halkyn United)
Aston Park Rangers 4 Rhuddlan Town 0

Premier Division		P	W	D	L	F	A	Pts
Prestatyn Town Res.		20	13	4	3	67	25	43
Llandyrnog United Res.		20	12	4	4	54	33	40
Flint Town United Res.		20	12	3	5	58	41	39
Rhyl Nomads		20	10	6	4	57	35	36
Aston Park Rangers		20	10	3	7	51	38	33
Llansannan		20	8	2	10	39	53	26
Penmaenmawr Phoenix		20	6	5	9	41	42	23
Rhuddlan Town		20	4	7	9	41	54	19
Mochdre Sports	-3	20	6	2	12	22	47	17
Halkyn United Res.		20	4	4	12	25	64	16
Bro Cernyw		20	1	8	11	24	47	11

Rhyl Youth – record expunged

CLWYD LEAGUE PREMIER DIVISION CONSTITUTION 2007-08

ASTON PARK RANGERS . . . . 33 Club, Shotton Lane, Shotton, Deeside . . . . None
DENBIGH TOWN RESERVES . . . . Central Park, Park Street, Denbigh LL16 3DD 01745 812505
FLINT TOWN UNITED RESERVES . . . . Cae Y Castell, March Lane, Flint CH6 5PJ 01352 730982
HALKYN UNITED RESERVES . . . . Pant Newydd, Halkyn 01352 780576
LLANDYRNOG UNITED RESERVES . . . . . . Swyn Y Nant, Llandyrnog, Denbigh LL16 4HB . . . . None
LLANSANNAN . . . . Cae Chwareuon, Maes Gogor, Llansannan, Conwy . . . . None
MOCHDRE SPORTS . . . . Mochdre Sports Club, Swan Road, Mochdre, Colwyn Bay LL28 5HA 01492 546661
PENMAENMAWR PHOENIX . . . . Cae Sling, Conwy Road, Penmaenmawr, Conwy LL34 6BL . . . . None
PRESTATYN TOWN . . . . Bastion Road, Prestatyn LL17 7ET 01745 856905
RHUDDLAN TOWN RESERVES . . . . Pengwyn College, Rhuddlan . . . . None
RHYL NOMADS . . . . Coronation Gardens, Rhyl . . . . None
TREFNANT VILLAGE . . . . Village Hall, Denbigh Road, Trefnant . . . . None
IN: Denbigh Town Reserves (P), Trefnant Village (P)
OUT: Bro Cernyw (R), Rhyl Youth (WS)

Division One		P	W	D	L	F	A	Pts
Abergele Rovers		18	14	2	2	70	21	44
Denbigh Town Res.		18	12	1	5	41	34	37
Trefnant Village		18	10	3	5	40	32	33
Mochdre Sports Res.		18	7	6	5	43	39	27
Point of Ayr		18	7	5	6	43	38	26
Greenfield		18	6	3	9	41	48	21
Brynford United	-3	18	8	0	10	49	70	21
Mostyn		18	6	2	10	45	44	20
Cerrigydrudion		18	4	3	11	36	49	15
Caerwys Res.		18	3	1	14	29	62	10

Division Two	P	W	D	L	F	A	Pts
Glan Conwy Res.	20	13	5	2	56	26	44
Aztec Sports	20	11	5	4	48	33	38
Sychdyn	20	11	3	6	47	44	36
Rhuddlan Town Res.	20	11	2	7	44	36	35
Abergele Rovers Res.	20	10	1	9	50	33	31
Northop Hall	20	8	4	8	53	47	28
Y Glannau	20	8	3	9	31	32	27
Aston Park Rangers Res.	20	7	5	8	44	45	26
Rhos United	20	8	1	11	37	37	25
Wepre Rangers	20	3	4	13	32	58	13
St Asaph	20	3	1	16	33	84	10

WWW.CHERRYRED.CO.UK

R.E.M. JONES CUP *(Div One teams)*
FINAL *(April 7th at Denbigh Town)*
Greenfield 2 Abergele Rovers 1

HALKYN CUP *(Div Two teams)*
FINAL *(May 17th at Rhuddlan Town)*
Aztec Sports 1 Rhuddlan Town Res. 0

PRESIDENT'S CUP *(All teams)*
FINAL *(May 10th at Halkyn United)*
Rhuddlan Town 1 Llandyrnog United Res. 0

COMBINED COUNTIES LEAGUE

	Ash United	Banstead Athletic	Bedfont	Bedfont Green	Bookham	Camberley Town	Chertsey Town	Chessington & Hook Utd	Chipstead	Cobham	Colliers Wood United	Cove	Dorking	Egham Town	Epsom & Ewell	Guildford City	Merstham	North Greenford United	Raynes Park Vale	Reading Town	Sandhurst Town	Wembley
Ash United		1-3	6-1	3-0	6-0	0-0	3-0	2-0	0-0	2-0	2-1	1-1	0-1	3-0	3-0	2-0	0-0	4-1	4-3	3-5	2-0	1-2
Banstead Athletic	1-2		4-2	1-0	2-2	0-4	2-4	2-0	2-1	0-7	2-1	1-3	1-2	1-1	0-0	2-1	3-0	2-2	4-3	3-0		4-2
Bedfont	0-2	1-5		0-2	0-1	1-2	1-4	0-1	0-1	1-2	2-3	0-0	1-3	0-2	1-2	4-0	0-5	1-4	1-3	3-2	2-0	0-2
Bedfont Green	0-2	1-3	1-1	*P*	2-3	1-1	1-1	2-2	0-3	0-0	2-1	0-2	0-3	1-1	2-0	3-2	0-1	0-1	1-1	1-0	2-2	0-1
Bookham	1-4	3-4	1-1	1-3	*R*	2-1	0-2	0-2	3-4	1-0	1-0	1-0	1-2	1-0	0-3	5-2	0-2	2-3	2-2	3-3	2-3	2-1
Camberley Town	1-0	1-1	2-3	1-0	3-1	*E*	1-0	0-3	1-3	1-2	2-1	1-0	0-1	2-1	1-0	0-4	5-2	1-0	1-0	1-0	0-0	0-0
Chertsey Town	1-1	1-1	3-0	2-1	2-0	0-5	*M*	1-0	0-2	2-1	2-1	5-1	1-0	1-1	2-0	4-1	1-4	3-5	1-1	1-1	1-0	0-0
Chessington & Hook United	0-4	2-2	2-0	2-3	5-1	2-1	4-2	*I*	0-4	1-1	1-0	4-3	4-2	3-7	1-1	3-1	0-1	0-0	2-1	3-0	1-1	2-2
Chipstead	5-0	3-0	2-0	1-0	2-0	1-0	4-2	4-1	*E*	5-2	3-0	4-2	4-2	4-3	6-3	1-0	1-2	4-1	3-0	5-1	2-0	2-1
Cobham	0-1	2-3	2-2	1-1	1-0	2-2	3-0	1-0	1-3	*R*	0-1	2-1	3-0	2-1	3-0	0-1	3-2	2-4	1-0	2-1	2-0	2-1
Colliers Wood United	1-1	1-0	5-3	2-0	2-0	0-1	3-0	1-0	1-2	1-0		3-4	1-0	1-1	3-0	2-2	0-1	3-3	4-2	1-2	0-2	2-3
Cove	1-1	0-2	1-0	1-0	3-1	0-1	3-1	2-1	2-6	0-1	2-3	*D*	0-3	2-1	2-2	1-0	1-2	1-5	0-1	1-1	1-1	1-1
Dorking	1-4	1-2	1-2	1-0	3-1	1-0	0-1	2-2	3-1	1-2	2-1	3-1	*I*	2-1	2-2	1-2	2-2	2-2	2-1	1-0	1-0	0-1
Egham Town	2-0	0-2	3-0	2-0	2-2	2-3	0-2	1-1	0-3	3-0	2-4	4-2	4-1	*V*	0-0	6-0	0-3	2-2	4-0	3-1	3-1	2-2
Epsom & Ewell	0-3	0-0	1-0	1-1	1-1	1-2	2-1	0-2	0-2	0-2	4-2	0-2	1-6	1-0	*I*	2-0	0-3	0-0	4-4	0-1	2-1	2-3
Guildford City	0-2	0-5	4-1	0-1	5-2	0-1	2-1	2-0	0-2	1-4	1-2	3-2	4-1	0-4	4-0	*S*	1-3	1-1	1-2	0-0	0-0	0-4
Merstham	4-3	1-1	3-0	5-2	6-1	4-0	2-3	5-1	0-1	3-0	2-0	6-0	3-0	0-1	2-1	3-1	*I*	3-1	2-1	3-0	6-1	0-4
North Greenford United	0-1	2-1	4-1	1-1	2-3	2-2	2-2	0-1	1-0	4-1	5-0	4-4	1-1	2-1	4-3	1-0	3-1	*O*	3-0	0-2	0-1	0-4
Raynes Park Vale	0-2	1-0	1-2	0-2	0-3	3-2	3-3	4-1	3-2	2-1	1-0	2-5	1-0	1-2	1-0	1-2	2-3	2-2	*N*	3-2	4-2	1-4
Reading Town	0-2	3-1	3-0	1-0	7-0	1-0	3-4	1-1	1-1	3-1	0-0	4-1	2-3	2-1	1-0	0-2	1-0	0-2	0-3		3-0	6-0
Sandhurst Town	1-1	2-1	3-1	1-1	3-0	0-0	1-2	1-3	4-3	3-3	2-1	2-1	2-2	2-1	4-2	0-2	2-2	3-1	2-0			0-1
Wembley	0-2	1-5	2-1	5-1	5-3	5-0	2-0	3-0	2-0	3-0	5-1	4-1	1-0	5-0	6-0	1-0	1-1	1-0	0-2	1-0	1-5	

Premier Division		P	W	D	L	F	A	Pts
Chipstead		42	32	3	7	114	48	99
Merstham		42	31	2	9	100	35	95
Wembley		42	27	8	7	95	45	89
Ash United		42	26	8	8	86	37	86
North Greenford United		42	21	12	9	90	62	75
Banstead Athletic		42	20	10	12	76	64	70
Camberley Town		42	21	7	14	60	59	70
Chertsey Town		42	20	7	15	72	71	67
Reading Town		42	18	6	18	72	64	60
Egham Town		42	16	10	16	80	59	58
Chessington & Hook United		42	15	12	15	63	72	57
Sandhurst Town		42	15	10	17	61	67	55
Colliers Wood United	-3	42	17	6	19	69	62	54
Cobham		42	16	6	20	56	64	54
Raynes Park Vale		42	15	8	19	69	85	53
Dorking	-6	42	16	7	19	65	73	49
Epsom & Ewell		42	10	10	22	44	78	40
Cove	-1	42	11	7	24	56	96	39
Bedfont Green		42	9	10	23	38	62	37
Bookham		42	10	6	26	54	105	36
Guildford City		42	8	4	30	46	96	28
Bedfont		42	6	5	31	41	103	23

Reserve Premier Division	P	W	D	L	F	A	Pts
Colliers Wood Utd Res.	20	14	2	4	42	19	44
Ash United Res.	20	13	4	3	42	19	43
Cobham Res.	20	11	7	2	40	16	40
Westfield Res.	20	11	4	5	39	25	37
Cove Res.	20	10	5	5	38	23	35
Farnham Town Res.	20	9	3	8	43	38	30
Chessington & Hook Res.	20	9	3	8	29	25	30
Bedfont Green Res.	20	7	3	10	28	26	24
Frimley Green Res.	20	5	1	14	22	42	16
Guildford City Res.	20	3	1	16	16	58	10
Hartley Wintney Res.	20	1	1	18	15	63	4

Reserve Division One	P	W	D	L	F	A	Pts
Warlingham Res.	22	15	3	4	72	20	48
Staines Lammas Res.	22	14	5	3	59	23	47
CB Hounslow United Res.	22	13	6	3	32	17	45
Hanworth Villa Res.	22	12	5	5	56	29	41
Crescent Rovers Res.	22	12	3	7	51	40	39
Bookham Res.	22	11	4	7	51	38	37
Farleigh Rovers Res.	22	10	2	10	34	41	32
Coney Hall Res.	22	7	4	11	44	52	25
Worcester Park Res.	22	8	1	13	40	52	25
Merrow Res.	22	5	2	15	35	64	17
Sheerwater Res.	22	5	1	16	34	72	16
Chobham Res.	22	2	0	20	21	81	6

COMBINED COUNTIES LEAGUE PREMIER DIVISION CONSTITUTION 2007-08

ASH UNITED .... Youngs Drive, Shawfield Road, Ash, near Aldershot GU12 6RE 01252 345757
BANSTEAD ATHLETIC...................... Merland Rise, Tadworth KT20 5JG 01737 350982
BEDFONT............................ The Orchard, Hatton Road, Bedfont TW14 9QT 020 8890 7264
BEDFONT GREEN .... Avenue Park, Western Avenue, Greenford UB6 8GA 020 8578 2706
BOOKHAM .... Dorking FC, Meadowbank, Mill Lane, Dorking RH4 1DX 01306 884112
CAMBERLEY TOWN .... Krooner Park, Wilton Road, off Frimley Road, Camberley GU15 2QP 01276 65392
CHERTSEY TOWN .... Alwyns Lane, Chertsey KT16 9DW......................... 01932 561774/571792
CHESSINGTON & HOOK UNITED .... Chalky Lane, Chessington KT9 2PW.......................... 01372 745777
COBHAM .... Leg O'Mutton Field, Anvil Lane, Downsbridge Road, Cobham KT11 3BD 01932 865959
COLLIERS WOOD UNITED...... Wibbandune Sports Ground, Robin Hood Way, Kingston SW20 0AA 020 8942 8062
COVE............................. Oak Farm, 7 Squirrel Lane, Cove, Farnborough GU14 8PB 01252 543615
DORKING .... Meadowbank, Mill Lane, Dorking RH4 1DX 01306 884112
EGHAM TOWN .... Runnymede Stadium, Tempest Road, Egham TW20 8HX 01784 435226/436466
EPSOM & EWELL................... Banstead Athletic FC, Merland Rise, Tadworth KT20 5JG 01737 350982
GUILDFORD CITY .... Spectrum Leisure Centre, Parkway, Guildford GU1 1UP 01483 443132
HORLEY TOWN.................... The New Defence, Court Lodge Road, Horley RH6 8RS................... 01293 822000
MERSTHAM.................. Merstham Recreation Ground, Weldon Way, Merstham RH1 3PF 01737 644046
NORTH GREENFORD UNITED .... Berkeley Fields, Berkeley Avenue, Greenford UB6 0NZ 020 8422 8923
RAYNES PARK VALE.......... Princes Georges Playing Field, Grand Drive, Raynes Park SW20 9LN 020 8540 8843
READING TOWN........................... Scours Lane, Tilehurst, Reading RG30 6AY 0118 945 3555
SANDHURST TOWN.......... Bottom Meadow, Memorial Park, Yorktown Road, Sandhurst GU47 9BJ 01252 878768
WEMBLEY........................ Vale Farm, Watford Road, Sudbury, Wembley HA0 4UR........... 020 8904 8169/020 8908 5461

IN: Horley Town (P)
OUT: Chipstead (P – Isthmian League Division One South)

LEAGUE CUP

FIRST ROUND
Ash United 3 Bedfont 0
Cobham 2 Worcester Park 0
Coulsdon Town 0 **Cove** 6
Crescent Rovers 1 **Chessington & Hook United** 4
Egham Town 0 **Bookham** 3
Farleigh Rovers 1 **Hartley Wintney** 3
Horley Town 4 Reading Town 2
Merrow 2 **Chertsey Town** 4
Salfords 2 Frimley Green 1
South Park 2 Bedfont Green 1
Staines Lammas 0 **Wembley** 1
SECOND ROUND
Ash United 1 Guildford City 0
CB Hounslow United 2 Epsom & Ewell 1
Chertsey Town 3 Sheerwater 1
Chessington & Hook United 4 Sandhurst Town 3 *aet*
Chipstead 2 **Raynes Park Vale** 3
Chobham 0 **Camberley Town** 3
Cobham 4 Cove 1
Colliers Wood United 1 Westfield 0 *aet*
Coney Hall 0 **Horley Town** 2
Dorking 3 Bookham 1
Farnham Town 1 **Hartley Wintney** 3
Feltham 1 **Merstham** 3

Hanworth Villa 2 Warlingham 1
North Greenford United 4 South Park 0
Tongham 0 **Banstead Athletic** 3 *(at Banstead Athletic)*
Wembley 9 Salfords 1
THIRD ROUND
Ash United 0 **Chertsey Town** 2
Banstead Athletic 1 Chessington & Hook United 0 *aet*
Camberley Town 3 **North Greenford United** 5 *aet*
Colliers Wood United 5 Hartley Wintney 1
Dorking 0 **Horley Town** 2
Merstham 3 CB Hounslow United 1
Raynes Park Vale 2 Hanworth Villa 1
Wembley 3 Cobham 1
QUARTER-FINALS
Banstead Athletic 3 Raynes Park Vale 2
Horley Town 2 **Chertsey Town** 4
Merstham 1 Wembley 1 *aet (4-2p)*
North Greenford United 3 Colliers Wood United 1
SEMI-FINALS
Banstead Athletic 1 **Merstham** 3 *aet*
Chertsey Town 1 **North Greenford United** 3
FINAL
(April 20th at Woking)
Merstham 4 North Greenford United 1

PREMIER RESERVE CUP

FINAL
(April 25th at North Greenford United)
Cobham Res. 2 Colliers Wood United Res. 1

RESERVE DIVISION ONE CUP

FINAL
(May 8th at Cobham)
Staines Lammas Res. 4 Warlingham Res. 3

RESERVES SHIELD

FINAL
(May 15th at Banstead Athletic)
Staines Lammas Res. 2 Warlingham Res. 2 *aet (5-4p)*

	CB Hounslow United	Chobham	Coney Hall	Coulsdon Town	Crescent Rovers	Farleigh Rovers	Farnham Town	Feltham	Frimley Green	Hanworth Villa	Hartley Wintney	Horley Town	Merrow	Salfords	Sheerwater	South Park	Staines Lammas	Tongham	Warlingham	Westfield	Worcester Park
CB Hounslow United		3-1	0-2	5-0	0-1	1-1	1-1	2-2	3-5	0-3	1-3	1-6	5-0	4-1	4-4	2-1	1-1	2-2	0-1	3-2	0-3
Chobham	1-3		1-3	4-2	4-1	1-6	1-2	2-3	4-0	0-5	0-1	0-4	4-3	7-1	0-2	1-2	2-1	4-1	1-0	2-2	2-3
Coney Hall	2-4	6-0		5-2	6-1	2-2	0-2	4-3	2-3	3-0	1-5	1-3	4-2	2-1	0-5	3-1	3-3	3-4	2-2	0-2	0-2
Coulsdon Town	0-3	5-5	3-3		1-4	3-0	1-3	2-3	2-0	3-5	2-4	1-4	2-3	4-2	3-2	0-7	2-5	2-2	3-2	2-4	1-3
Crescent Rovers	2-5	2-2	1-1	6-3	D	3-4	0-3	0-2	2-0	0-4	0-1	3-0	3-1	5-1	1-2	1-3	1-2	7-1	0-1	2-3	0-2
Farleigh Rovers	1-0	3-2	0-0	2-0	2-2	I	0-0	1-1	1-0	3-1	2-0	1-1	0-0	1-0	1-2	0-0	2-3	2-1	0-1	1-3	0-2
Farnham Town	1-4	3-1	6-0	7-2	5-0	1-1	V	1-0	2-0	2-0	2-1	1-2	1-1	2-0	4-1	1-0	2-2	3-1	1-0	2-0	1-0
Feltham	2-0	1-3	0-3	8-2	5-0	3-3	2-1	I	3-2	2-6	4-1	1-4	1-0	1-3	1-3	2-0	0-1	4-0	0-3	2-1	4-0
Frimley Green	1-3	0-3	1-1	1-3	1-2	2-0	1-5	2-1	S	2-0	2-6	2-3	1-3	7-1	1-1	6-1	2-1	2-2	3-3	0-1	5-1
Hanworth Villa	3-1	6-0	W-L	W-L	0-0	2-0	2-3	3-0	2-0	I	8-0	1-1	5-1	9-1	1-1	3-2	1-1	4-3	0-0	1-1	1-3
Hartley Wintney	1-3	0-5	3-1	8-0	3-0	1-2	1-2	2-1	1-1	3-3	O	2-4	4-1	2-0	1-1	1-2	1-2	2-2	1-3	2-2	1-3
Horley Town	1-0	3-0	8-0	1-0	3-3	1-0	1-3	1-1	1-0	1-0	6-1	N	4-0	6-0	2-2	3-2	3-3	5-0	3-0	1-0	0-0
Merrow	4-4	1-3	0-1	3-1	2-1	1-1	0-2	1-2	3-1	0-3	2-4	0-5		1-0	2-0	2-3	0-4	3-3	1-2	2-0	1-6
Salfords	2-1	1-0	2-0	5-2	1-4	1-2	1-2	1-0	1-2	0-2	1-0	0-7	1-0		2-3	1-0	1-0	4-4	1-4	0-6	0-3
Sheerwater	4-2	1-2	2-2	5-1	2-1	1-2	1-3	2-0	2-6	2-3	1-3	7-1	1-1	O	2-3	5-3	3-3	3-1	0-11	3-1	1-1
South Park	3-0	0-1	1-0	3-0	L-W	1-0	0-2	3-1	2-1	0-0	3-1	1-0	4-3	1-1	5-3	N	1-1	3-0	0-3	2-2	3-5
Staines Lammas	4-0	3-1	1-0	5-0	2-3	5-0	0-0	7-0	5-0	2-1	3-0	1-1	9-0	1-0	1-1	3-3	E	3-0	1-0	5-1	2-2
Tongham	0-1	3-4	1-5	3-2	3-2	1-7	0-0	2-3	2-4	1-3	2-2	5-3	6-0	4-1	1-0	0-2		2-2	3-0	1-2	
Warlingham	2-1	10-3	1-1	4-0	1-0	1-2	2-2	2-0	1-3	2-1	6-1	2-0	W-L	2-1	4-2	2-1	3-3	11-2		1-0	1-1
Westfield	4-1	1-3	3-1	12-0	1-0	3-0	1-2	0-2	1-1	2-3	4-1	1-0	2-0	6-1	2-2	1-1	1-2	3-0	1-1		2-4
Worcester Park	1-0	4-3	2-1	3-1	3-2	3-2	2-1	2-2	3-1	1-3	1-3	2-1	3-0	1-1	4-0	3-2	2-0	12-0	2-3	1-1	

Division One	P	W	D	L	F	A	Pts
Farnham Town	40	27	8	5	84	33	89
Horley Town	40	27	7	6	104	31	88
Worcester Park	40	27	7	6	100	53	88
Warlingham	40	25	8	7	97	42	83
Staines Lammas	40	23	11	6	104	45	80
Hanworth Villa	-3	40	25	7	8	101	44	79
South Park	40	18	7	15	75	61	61
Farleigh Rovers	40	15	12	13	58	56	57
Feltham	40	17	4	19	73	78	55
Westfield	40	15	9	16	82	62	54
Sheerwater	40	14	12	14	88	93	54
CB Hounslow United	40	14	7	19	74	79	49
Frimley Green	40	14	7	19	70	76	49
Coney Hall	-2	40	14	9	17	75	82	49
Chobham	40	15	3	22	82	104	48
Hartley Wintney	40	13	7	20	71	92	46
Crescent Rovers	40	12	5	23	66	86	41
Salfords	40	10	3	27	42	108	33
Tongham	40	7	9	24	67	130	30
Merrow	-3	40	7	5	28	49	116	23
Coulsdon Town	40	6	3	31	63	154	21

DIVISION ONE CUP

FIRST ROUND
Chobham 2 Coulsdon Town 0
Farnham Town 2 Westfield 0
Hartley Wintney 0 **Hanworth Villa** 1
Staines Lammas 4 Horley Town 2
Warlingham 2 Frimley Green 1
Tongham 0 **Sheerwater** 2 *(at Cove)*
Warlingham 2 CB Hounslow United 1

SECOND ROUND
Chobham 3 Feltham 1
Crescent Rovers 4 Farleigh Rovers 3
Hanworth Villa 4 Farnham Town 0
Merrow 1 Salfords 1 *aet (4-5p)*
South Park 2 Coney Hall 4
Staines Lammas 4 Worcester Park 0

QUARTER-FINALS
Chobham 0 **Sheerwater** 2
Crescent Rovers 1 **Staines Lammas** 4
Salfords 1 **Coney Hall** 3
Warlingham 0 **Hanworth Villa** 3

SEMI-FINALS
Hanworth Villa 2 Staines Lammas 1
Sheerwater 2 **Coney Hall** 6

FINAL
(May 2nd at Tooting & Mitcham Utd)
Hanworth Villa 2 Coney Hall 1

COMBINED COUNTIES LEAGUE DIVISION ONE CONSTITUTION 2007-08

CB HOUNSLOW UNITED . . . . Osterley Sports Club, Tentelow Lane, Osterley, Southall UB2 4LW 020 8574 3774
CHOBHAM . . . . Chobham Recreation Ground, Station Road, Chobham GU24 8AZ 01276 857876
COULSDON UNITED . . . . Woodplace Lane, Coulsdon CR5 1NB 01737 557509
CRESCENT ROVERS . . . . Wallington Sports/Social Club, Mollison Drive, Wallington SM6 9BY 020 8647 2558
FARLEIGH ROVERS . . . . Parsonage Field, Harrow Road, Farleigh, Warlingham CR6 9EY 01884 626483
FARNHAM TOWN . . . . Memorial Ground, West Street, Farnham GU9 7DY 01252 715305
FELTHAM . . . . Hampton & Richmond Borough FC, Beaver Close, Station Road, Hampton TW12 2BX 020 8941 2838/436466
FRIMLEY GREEN . . . . . . Frimley Green Rec. Ground, Frimley Green Road, Frimley Green, Camberley GU16 6LL 01252 835089
HANWORTH VILLA . . . . Rectory Meadow, Park Road, Hounslow Road, Hanworth 020 8831 9391
HARTLEY WINTNEY . . . . Memorial Playing Fields, Green Lane, Hartley Wintney RG27 8HD 01252 843586
KNAPHILL . . . . Brookwood Country Park, Lower Guildford Road, Knaphill, Woking GU21 2AY . . . . None
MERROW . . . . The Urnfield, Downside Road, Guildford GU4 8PH. . . . . None
NEASDEN FOUNDATION . . . . Avenue Park, Western Avenue, Greenford UB6 8GA 020 8578 2706
SHEERWATER . . . . Blackmore Crescent, Sheerwater Estate, Woking GU21 5NW . . . . None
SOUTH PARK . . . . Whitehall Lane, South Park, Reigate RH2 8LG . . . . None
STAINES LAMMAS . . . . Laleham Recreation Ground, The Broadway, Laleham, Staines TW18 1RX 01784 465204
TONGHAM . . . . Recreation Ground, Poyle Road, Tongham GU10 1BS . . . . None
WARLINGHAM . . . . Warlingham Sports Club, Church Road, Warlingham CR6 9PR 01883 622943
WESTFIELD . . . . Woking Park, off Elmbridge Lane, Kingfield, Woking GU2279AA 01483 771106
WORCESTER PARK . . . . Skinners Field, Green Lane, Worcester Park KT4 8AJ 020 8337 4995

IN: Knaphill (P – Surrey Intermediate League (West) Premier Division), Neasden Foundation (P – Middlesex County League Premier Division)
OUT: Coney Hall (S – Kent County League Premier Division), Horley Town (P)
Coulsdon Town and Salfords haved merged to become Coulsdon United

CORNWALL COMBINATION

Note – Truro City Reserves failed to fulfil their fixtures. Their results are shown herein but are expunged from the league table

	Falmouth Tn Res.	Hayle	Helston Athletic	Holmans SC	Illogan RBL	Ludgvan	Mousehole	Mullion	Newquay Res.	Penryn Ath. Res.	Penzance Res.	Perranporth	Perranwell	RNAS Culdrose	St Agnes	St Day	St Ives Town	St Just	Truro City Res.	Wendron CC Utd
Falmouth Town Res.		0-1	2-0	2-1	0-4	3-1	0-4	4-1	2-4	1-2	0-1	0-1	1-4	1-1	3-1	0-5	2-1	3-1	1-2	0-2
Hayle	1-0		2-1	5-1	0-2	4-0	4-0	4-1	5-0	2-1	4-1	1-1	2-2	2-1	1-0	3-1	1-1	4-2	1-7	1-3
Helston Athletic	2-2	1-1		4-1	0-5	4-0	2-3	1-4	7-0	2-2	3-0	1-2	2-2	1-4	2-1	0-3	3-1	2-1	1-4	6-2
Holmans Sports Club	2-1	1-2	1-3		1-1	2-1	0-0	6-2	2-4	1-3	5-2	0-1	1-3	1-1	1-2	1-5	2-2	1-4	1-6	1-0
Illogan RBL	3-2	3-2	2-0	4-0		6-1	1-0	7-2	1-0	1-1	0-0	4-1	5-1	5-0	1-0	1-2	3-1	2-0	1-4	5-1
Ludgvan	1-4	0-0	1-2	0-6	1-3		0-2	1-5	2-3	0-6	1-7	2-2	1-3	0-2	2-1	0-4	1-5	1-4	1-3	
Mousehole	2-0	1-1	3-1	1-1	0-1	6-0		3-1	4-0	1-1	2-2	1-0	2-0	5-2	3-0	1-2	2-1	2-0	1-3	1-3
Mullion	0-1	1-1	0-2	0-2	1-6	3-0	2-1		13-2	1-4	1-4	1-1	0-3	4-3	1-2	1-4	2-3	1-2	0-6	1-3
Newquay Res.	4-1	0-0	0-8	0-4	1-3	1-0	3-2	3-0		0-3	4-1	2-0	3-3	1-2	2-1	3-0	0-1	1-1		
Penryn Athletic Res.	3-0	3-0	2-0	2-2	2-1	1-1	1-5	1-0	4-1		8-0	2-4	1-0	5-1	3-1	1-0	1-1	3-0	3-3	1-1
Penzance Res.	1-1	0-3	3-4	0-1	1-2	0-2	0-2	9-1	1-0	1-2		1-1	0-2	3-2	4-2	3-0	2-0	1-2	1-2	0-5
Perranporth	1-1	1-0	0-2	0-4	0-3	1-1	4-2	2-0	0-3	2-3	4-0		2-2	4-2	1-3	3-2	6-2	1-1	1-1	1-0
Perranwell	0-2	2-1	2-1	1-0	2-1	1-1	0-2	2-1	10-1	3-3	4-2	2-0		2-2	4-2	1-3	3-2	6-2	1-1	1-1
RNAS Culdrose	2-4	0-2	3-3	1-1	2-3	2-2	2-3	2-0	6-1	0-6	2-3	4-1	2-1		2-4	3-3	1-0	3-2	6-3	0-0
St Agnes	3-1	3-2	1-4	1-1	2-1	4-0	3-2	5-1	3-1	1-5	3-1	3-4	1-1	2-4		0-1	1-0	2-0	2-0	3-2
St Day	6-1	0-4	1-3	2-5	1-1	2-3	6-2	3-0	2-1	1-3	2-1	4-2	5-3		3-2		3-4	3-2	1-4	
St Ives Town	1-2	0-0	5-0	2-0	0-2	1-0	0-3	0-3	5-2	1-1	2-2	0-0	0-3	2-1	1-3	1-0		4-2	3-1	0-3
St Just	2-4	3-7	2-1	2-1	1-2	2-5	0-4	1-2	1-1	1-1	1-2	1-1	0-2	0-3	3-2	3-2	2-2		1-2	2-1
Truro City Res.	3-0	0-1	n/a	4-1	1-1	11-0	0-3	6-3	1-1	3-3	2-1	2-0	1-4	n/a	6-3	0-1	2-1	2-6		0-2
Wendron CC United	5-2	0-1	2-0	3-2	1-1	5-0	1-2	3-3	2-1	4-1	1-1	2-0	3-2	0-2	0-4	2-4	1-2	3-2	3-0	

	P	W	D	L	F	A	Pts
Illogan RBL	36	27	5	4	96	30	86
Mousehole	36	24	5	7	84	40	77
Penryn Ath Res.	36	21	10	5	90	42	73
Hayle	36	20	9	7	74	37	69
St Day	36	20	3	13	83	65	63
Perranwell	36	17	8	11	76	55	59
St Agnes	36	18	1	17	76	71	55
Wendron CCU -1	36	16	7	13	72	58	54
Helston Athletic	36	16	5	15	78	66	53
Perranporth	36	13	10	13	51	57	49
RNAS Culdrose	36	12	9	15	74	83	45
Holmans Spts Club	36	12	7	17	63	67	43
Falmouth T. Res.	36	13	4	19	53	74	43
Newquay Res.	36	12	5	19	50	102	41
Penzance Res.	36	11	6	19	60	79	39
St Ives Town -1	36	10	9	17	50	59	38
St Just	36	11	5	20	60	84	38
Mullion	36	7	3	26	62	106	24
Ludgvan	36	3	7	26	31	108	16

Truro City Res. – record expunged

GEORGE EVELY CUP
(Cornwall Combination Cup winners v East Cornwall League Cup winners)
(May 10th at St Blazey)
Penryn Athletic Res. 2 Godolphin Atlantic 1

LEAGUE CUP

PRELIMINARY ROUND
Falmouth Town Res. 0 **Penryn Athletic Res.** 1
Holmans SC 3 Truro City Res. 0
Mullion 1 Newquay Res. 1
Newquay Res. 3 Mullion 1 *replay*
Penzance Res. 1 **Perranporth** 3

FIRST ROUND
Helston Athletic 0 **Hayle** 1
Mousehole 5 St Agnes 1
Newquay Res. 0 **RNAS Culdrose** 2
Perranporth 0 **Illogan RBL** 1
Perranwell 0 **Penryn Ath. Res.** 2
St Day 2 Holmans Sports Club 0
St Ives Town 4 Ludgvan 0
Wendron CC United 0 St Just 0
St Just 1 **Wendron CCU** 4 *replay*

QUARTER-FINALS
Mousehole 5 Hayle 2
Penryn Athletic Res. 1 Wendron CC United 1
Wendron CC United 3 **Penryn Athletic Res.** 4 *aet replay*
RNAS Culdrose 1 **St Ives Town** 2
St Day 2 Illogan RBL 1

SEMI-FINALS
Mousehole 2 St Ives Town 0
(at Hayle)
Penryn Athletic Res. 6 St Day 0
(at Mullion)

FINAL
(April 8th at Illogan RBL)
Penryn Athletic Res. 1
Mousehole 1 *aet (4-3p)*

SUPPLEMENTARY CUP

(Teams eliminated in the Preliminary and First Round of the League Cup)

PRELIMINARY ROUND
Falmouth Town Res. 4 Penzance Res. 2
Perranporth 2 Mullion 1
St Agnes 4 Newquay Res. 0
Truro Res. 3 Holmans SC 1

QUARTER-FINALS
Ludgvan 4 **Helston Athletic** 6 *aet*
Perranporth 2 St Just 1
St Agnes 1 Perranwell 0
Truro City Res. 3 Falmouth Town Res. 1

SEMI-FINALS
St Agnes 2 Perranporth 1 *(at Newquay)*
Helston 3 Truro Res. 2 *(at Wendron CC United)*

FINAL *(May 20th at Falmouth)*
St Agnes 5 Helston Athletic 2

CORNWALL COMBINATION CONSTITUTION 2007-08

FALMOUTH TOWN RESERVES ...... Bickland Park, Bickland Water Road, Falmouth TR11 4PB 01326 377736
HAYLE RESERVES ...... Trevassack Park, Viaduct Hill, Hayle TR27 4HT 01736 757157
HELSTON ATHLETIC ...... Kellaway Parc, Clodgy Lane, Helston TR13 8BN 01326 573742
HOLMANS SPORTS CLUB ...... Blaythorne Mem. Sports Ground, Pendarves, Camborne TR14 7QG 01209 713631
ILLOGAN RBL ...... Oxland Park, Richards Lane, Illogan, Redruth TR16 4HA 01209 216488
LUDGVAN ...... Ludgvan Community Centre, Fairfield, Ludgvan TR20 8ES 01736 740774
MULLION ...... Clifden Parc, Clifden Close, Mullion, Helston TR12 7EQ 01326 240676
NEWQUAY RESERVES ...... Mount Wise, Clevedon Road, Newquay TR7 2BU 01637 872935
PENRYN ATHLETIC RESERVES ...... Kernick, Kernick Road, Penryn TR10 8NT 01326 375182
PENZANCE RESERVES ...... Penlee Park, Alexandra Place, Penzance TR18 4NE 01736 361964
PERRANPORTH ...... Budnick Estate, Perranporth TR6 0DB 01872 575000
PERRANWELL ...... King George V Playing Field, School Hill, Perranwell Station TR3 7LA 01872 870202
PORTHLEVEN RESERVES ...... Gala Parc, Mill Lane, Porthleven TR13 9LQ 01326 574754
RNAS CULDROSE ...... Sports Field, RNAS Culdrose, Helston TR12 7RH 01326 574121x7167
ST AGNES ...... Enys Park, West Polperro, St Agnes TR5 0SS 01872 553673
ST DAY ...... Vogue, St Day, Redruth TR16 5NP ...... None
ST IVES TOWN ...... The Saltings, Lelant TR26 3DL ...... None
ST JUST ...... Lafrowda Park, St Just, Penzance TR19 7RY 01736 788503
TRURO CITY RESERVES ...... Treyew Road, Truro TR1 2TH 01872 278853
WENDRON CC UNITED RESERVES ...... Underlane, Carnkie, Wendron, Helston TR13 0EH 01209 860946

IN: Hayle Reserves, Porthleven Reserves, Wendron CC United Reserves (all P – Falmouth-Helston League Division One)
OUT: Hayle, Mousehole, Wendron CC United (all P – South West Peninsula League Division One West)

CYMRU ALLIANCE

	Bala Town	Bodedern	Buckley Town	Flint Town United	Glantraeth	Gresford Athletic	Guilsfield	Holyhead Hotspur	Lex XI	Llandudno Town	Llandyrnog United	Llanfairpwll	Llangefni Town	Mynydd Isa	Penrhyncoch	Prestatyn Town	Queens Park	Ruthin Town
Bala Town		3-0	0-2	2-2	1-2	4-1	2-3	1-2	6-0	0-0	1-1	3-0	0-0	3-1	4-1	4-2	3-0	3-0
Bodedern	2-1		1-4	3-6	1-2	1-2	0-0	0-3	1-1	1-1	3-2	1-2	0-1	1-0	4-0	0-4	7-0	0-3
Buckley Town	2-4	0-2		1-2	0-0	0-1	2-0	3-2	3-1	2-2	3-3	1-3	1-1	2-0	1-3	1-1	5-1	3-1
Flint Town United	1-1	0-0	0-0		2-0	2-1	3-0	1-0	1-1	4-2	2-0	2-0	0-2	0-2	4-1	3-1	2-0	1-0
Glantraeth	1-4	2-1	1-1	3-3		1-4	1-0	1-2	9-1	1-4	5-3	4-2	0-3	2-3	3-1	3-6	7-1	3-2
Gresford Athletic	0-2	1-0	1-2	0-2	0-2		0-1	3-1	2-3	2-1	0-2	1-2	1-3	3-1	5-1	1-0	2-0	1-1
Guilsfield	0-4	3-0	2-3	0-2	4-3	1-3		3-0	4-0	1-2	2-4	2-0	1-4	4-0	1-1	1-4	3-3	3-0
Holyhead Hotspur	0-0	5-2	3-3	2-2	2-0	1-1	0-2		6-2	1-3	3-2	3-1	2-1	1-3	2-0	2-1	3-0	3-1
Lex XI	1-5	1-2	5-0	0-2	2-5	2-1	1-2	0-4		4-2	2-3	4-2	1-1	1-1	2-2	1-8	6-1	0-1
Llandudno Town	2-3	0-4	3-1	2-1	1-1	4-1	1-1	2-0	1-2		4-2	4-4	0-2	1-2	2-1	1-2	3-1	1-2
Llandyrnog United	0-2	0-3	1-3	2-4	0-3	3-1	3-0	3-1	2-1	0-5		1-1	1-1	1-3	1-3		4-1	1-3
Llanfairpwll	0-1	2-1	0-2	2-1	1-1	3-1	8-1	2-1	2-0	2-6	4-1		1-1	2-0	2-0	3-3	3-1	4-1
Llangefni Town	3-0	1-1	5-0	2-1	1-4	3-1	4-1	1-1	3-0	3-1	3-0	3-1		1-0	3-2	2-0	3-0	1-0
Mynydd Isa	1-1	2-1	3-0	2-1	1-1	5-2	3-2	2-0	2-2	2-1	2-2	0-1	1-1		1-2	0-1	6-1	2-0
Penrhyncoch	0-1	1-2	0-0	1-5	3-4	7-2	1-1	3-4	4-0	2-1	0-0	1-5	2-2	0-4		3-1	13-0	3-2
Prestatyn Town	0-1	7-2	1-1	2-0	4-1	1-0	1-2	0-3	5-0	2-0	1-3	5-1	6-1	1-0	2-2		11-1	2-3
Queens Park	0-6	1-2	1-2	0-5	3-4	1-1	1-2	0-2	1-0	2-3	3-3	1-2	3-2	1-2	5-5	1-7		2-3
Ruthin Town	1-4	1-0	0-1	1-3	2-3	1-4	0-5	2-1	2-2	0-1	3-3	1-1	0-1	2-2	2-1	0-3	2-3	

		P	W	D	L	F	A	Pts
Llangefni Town		34	21	9	4	69	33	72
Bala Town		34	21	7	6	80	31	70
Prestatyn Town		34	20	4	10	98	46	64
Flint Town United	-3	34	20	7	7	70	36	64
Glantraeth		34	17	6	11	83	69	57
Llanfairpwll		34	17	6	11	69	59	57
Holyhead Hotspur		34	16	5	13	63	51	53
Mynydd Isa		34	15	8	11	57	45	53
Buckley Town		34	14	10	10	55	54	52
Llandudno Town		34	14	6	14	67	59	48
Guilsfield		34	14	5	15	58	64	47
Gresford Athletic		34	12	3	19	50	64	39
Penrhyncoch		34	10	8	16	70	75	38
Bodedern		34	11	5	18	49	62	38
Llandyrnog United		34	9	9	16	58	77	36
Ruthin Town		34	8	5	21	41	71	29
Lex XI		34	7	7	20	49	96	28
Queens Park	-3	34	3	4	27	40	134	10

LEAGUE CUP

PRELIMINARY ROUND
Buckley Town 0 **Bala Town** 4
Mynydd Isa 3 Bodedern 0

FIRST ROUND
Bala Town 5 Penrhyncoch 0
Flint Town United 5
Llandyrnog United 2 *aet*
(Flint Town United expelled)
Glantraeth 5 Guilsfield 3 *aet*
Holyhead Hotspur 4 Ruthin
Town 1
Lex XI 1 **Prestatyn Town** 7
Llandudno Town 2 Mynydd
Isa 0
Llangefni 4 Llanfairpwll 1
Queens Park 1 **Gresford** 3

QUARTER-FINALS
Bala Town 2 Gresford Ath. 0
Glantraeth 3 Llandyrnog
United 2
Llangefni Town 0 **Holyhead
Hotspur** 1
Prestatyn Town 3 Llandudno 2

SEMI-FINALS
Bala Town 3 Prestatyn Town 0
(at Buckley Town)
Glantraeth 0 **Holyhead
Hotspur** 1 *(at Llangefni Town)*

FINAL
(May 12th at Llandudno Town)
Bala Town 2 Holyhead
Hotspur 1

CYMRU ALLIANCE CONSTITUTION 2007-08

BALA TOWN ... Maes Tegid, Castle Street, Bala LL23 7YB ... None
BODEDERN ... Cae r Ysgol, Holyhead Road, Bodedern LL65 3SU ... None
BUCKLEY TOWN ... Globe Way, Liverpool Way, Buckley CH7 3LL ... None
DENBIGH TOWN ... Central Park, Park Street, Denbigh LL16 3DD ... 01745 812505
FLINT TOWN UNITED ... Cae Y Castell, March Lane, Flint CH6 5PJ ... 01352 730982
GLANTRAETH ... Trefdraeth, Bodorgan, LL62 5EU ... 01407 840401
GRESFORD ATHLETIC ... Clapper Lane, Gresford, Wrexham LL12 8RW ... None
GUILSFIELD ... Community Centre, Guilsfield, Welshpool SY21 9ND ... None
HOLYHEAD HOTSPUR ... New Oval, Leisure Centre, Kingsland, Holyhead LL65 2YE ... 01407 764111
LEX XI ... Stansty Park, Summerhill, Wrexham LL11 4YG ... 01978 261148
LLANDUDNO TOWN ... Maesdu Park, Builder Street, Llandudno LL30 1HH ... 01492 860945
LLANDYRNOG UNITED ... Swyn Y Nant, Llandyrnog, Denbigh LL16 4HB ... None
LLANFAIRPWLL ... Rear of Post Office, Ffordd Caergybi, Llanfairpwllgwyngyll LL61 5YG ... None
MYNYDD ISA ... Argoed Sports Field, Snowden Avenue, Bryn-y-Baal, Mold CH7 6SZ ... None
PENRHYNCOCH ... Cae Baker, Penrhyncoch, Aberystwyth SY23 3XH ... 01970 828992
PRESTATYN TOWN ... Bastion Road, Prestatyn LL17 7ET ... 01745 856905
QUEENS PARK ... Queensway Athletics Stadium, Montgomery Road, Wrexham LL13 8UH ... 01978 261182
RUTHIN TOWN ... Memorial Playing Fields, Park Road, Ruthin LL15 1NB ... None
IN: Denbigh Town (P – Welsh Alliance)
OUT: Llangefni Town (P – Welsh Premier League)

WWW.NLNEWSDESK.CO.UK

DEVON COUNTY LEAGUE

	Alphington	Appledore	Buckland Athletic	Budleigh Salterton	Crediton United	Cullompton Rangers	Dartmouth	Elburton Villa	Holsworthy	Ivybridge Town	Newton Abbot	Newton Abbot Spurs	Ottery St Mary	Plymstock United	Stoke Gabriel	Teignmouth	Totnes & Dartington	University of Exeter	Vospers Oak Villa	Witheridge
Alphington		0-1	2-0	1-4	1-2	2-3	1-4	0-1	2-4	0-3	1-2	2-2	1-1	1-2	7-3	3-0	5-2	2-1	2-1	5-0
Appledore	1-0		1-3	0-4	1-1	0-0	2-2	1-3	3-2	1-0	1-1	1-3	2-2	0-1	3-0	3-0	1-2	0-5	3-0	3-2
Buckland Athletic	5-4	0-1		3-3	2-0	1-3	0-4	1-4	3-1	2-1	0-1	2-2	0-2	4-0	2-2	0-1	2-1	0-2	0-1	0-2
Budleigh Salterton	1-1	4-1	0-0		0-1	4-3	0-2	3-0	1-2	2-2	2-3	2-0	3-0	6-1	1-0	4-0	1-0	3-1	3-0	6-2
Crediton United	2-1	2-1	0-3	1-3		1-0	1-0	1-2	0-4	1-3	0-1	0-0	1-4	0-1	1-4	2-1	6-1	0-3	3-1	1-0
Cullompton Rangers	3-3	2-1	2-4	1-3	2-1		1-4	0-1	0-2	4-1	1-0	2-0	2-1	5-3	0-5	4-0	1-4	2-0	1-2	7-1
Dartmouth	2-1	2-1	3-0	0-1	4-0	5-3		3-2	3-1	3-0	1-0	2-1	3-0	2-0	4-2	5-0	5-1	2-2	4-0	1-2
Elburton Villa	2-1	3-1	2-3	3-1	5-2	1-4	1-1		7-1	3-3	0-0	2-3	1-0	2-0	2-0	5-1	2-1	2-1	2-0	2-1
Holsworthy	2-1	2-0	4-1	3-2	3-2	2-1	2-2	4-1		3-2	2-3	3-3	3-0	1-0	2-0	4-1	4-4	4-0	4-1	2-0
Ivybridge Town	3-1	5-1	2-0	2-2	4-1	4-2	1-2	0-2	5-1		3-1	2-2	0-2	1-1	2-2	8-0	2-1	2-4	4-0	1-0
Newton Abbot	3-1	4-2	4-0	1-1	3-1	1-1	1-0	4-1	4-0	1-1		2-0	2-2	5-1	4-0	3-1	6-0	1-2	3-1	1-0
Newton Abbot Spurs	1-0	0-1	3-1	3-2	0-0	0-5	2-0	2-1	2-2	2-1	0-1		2-1	3-1	1-4	3-1	5-1	2-4	3-0	1-1
Ottery St Mary	4-2	3-1	1-3	0-1	0-4	3-4	1-4	0-1	3-0	2-0	3-2	0-3		2-1	7-0	4-1	0-0	2-4	2-1	1-1
Plymstock United	0-1	1-2	2-0	2-3	2-1	4-2	1-3	1-3	1-1	0-1	0-1	3-3	1-3		3-1	3-1	0-1	0-3	2-0	0-1
Stoke Gabriel	2-1	1-2	0-2	1-3	1-3	1-5	1-7	1-1	1-2	0-4	1-0	0-3	1-3	0-4		3-0	0-2	0-3	1-0	0-1
Teignmouth	1-2	2-1	0-5	2-3	2-0	0-2	2-5	0-3	1-4	0-9	1-5	1-1	0-3	0-2	3-5		2-3	3-3	4-3	0-2
Totnes & Dartington SC	0-1	2-2	5-2	4-0	1-1	1-2	1-1	0-1	4-1	0-5	0-6	1-1	2-2	5-4	3-0	10-1		2-3	3-3	2-2
University of Exeter	3-2	0-0	1-0	1-2	4-0	0-2	0-0	2-2	3-1	1-3	7-0	0-4	0-2	3-0	4-1	6-0	0-0		3-0	2-1
Vospers Oak Villa	2-2	3-1	1-0	0-1	3-2	2-6	1-3	0-3	1-0	1-0	2-1	1-1	0-2	2-1	1-3	1-0	0-1	1-1		3-1
Witheridge	3-1	2-2	3-3	0-2	2-2	0-3	0-2	1-4	3-3	1-1	1-3	1-2	2-1	3-3	4-2	7-1	5-1	2-0	4-2	

	P	W	D	L	F	A	Pts
Dartmouth	38	27	6	5	100	36	87
Newton Abbot	38	25	6	7	85	39	81
Elburton Villa	38	25	5	8	83	48	80
Budleigh Salterton	38	24	6	8	87	47	78
Holsworthy	38	21	6	11	86	71	69
University of Exeter	38	20	7	11	83	51	67
Cullompton Rangers	38	21	3	14	91	68	66
Ivybridge Town	38	18	9	11	94	52	63
Newton Abbot Spurs	38	17	12	9	70	55	63
Ottery St Mary	38	16	7	15	68	61	55
Witheridge	38	12	9	17	64	78	45
Buckland Athletic	38	13	5	20	57	71	44
Appledore	38	12	8	18	49	69	44
Totnes & Dartington Sports Club	38	11	10	17	73	87	43
Crediton United	38	12	5	21	47	73	41
Plymstock United	38	11	4	23	52	78	37
Vospers Oak Villa	38	10	6	22	46	80	36
Alphington	38	10	5	23	64	76	35
Stoke Gabriel	38	8	3	27	43	99	27
Teignmouth	38	5	2	31	37	140	17

CHARITY SHIELD

(League Champions v League Cup holders)

(August 6th at Elburton Villa)

Ivybridge Town 4 Plymstock United 0

THE DEVON COUNTY LEAGUE HAS MERGED WITH THE SOUTH WESTERN LEAGUE. SEE PAGE 171 FOR CLUB DETAILS

LEAGUE CUP

FIRST ROUND
Alphington 0 **Totnes & Dartington SC** 3
Ottery St Mary 0 **Budleigh Salterton** 1
Plymstock United 1 **University of Exeter** 2
Witheridge 4 Stoke Gabriel 2
SECOND ROUND
Appledore 0 **Cullompton Rangers** 2 *aet*
Budleigh Salterton 1 Buckland Athletic 0
Crediton United 1 **Dartmouth** 3
Ivybridge Town 0 **Newton Abbot Spurs** 2
Teignmouth 0 **Newton Abbot** 4
Totnes & Dartington SC 2 Witheridge 0
University of Exeter 2 Elburton Villa 1

Vospers Oak Villa 4 Holsworthy 2 *aet*
QUARTER-FINALS
Cullompton Rangers 3 Dartmouth 0
Newton Abbot 3 Budleigh Salterton 1 *(at Budleigh Salterton)*
University of Exeter 4 Newton Abbot Spurs 1 *aet*
Vospers Oak Villa 1 **Totnes & Dartington SC** 2
SEMI-FINALS
Cullompton 0 University of Exeter 0 *aet (5-4p) (at Ottery)*
Newton Abbot 4 Totnes & Dartington SC 2 *(at Buckland)*
FINAL
(April 9th at Newton Abbot Spurs)
Newton Abbot 2 Cullompton Rangers 2 *aet (5-4p)*

DEVON & EXETER LEAGUE

Note – St Loyes withdrew during the course of the season. Their results are shown herein but are expunged from the league table	Axminster Town	Beer Albion	Clyst Valley	Cullompton Rangers Res.	Exeter Civil Service	Exmouth Town	Feniton	Hatherleigh Town	Heavitree Social United	Okehampton Argyle	Pinhoe	Sidmouth Town	St Loyes	St Martins	Thorverton	University of Exeter Res.
Axminster Town	P	2-1	1-1	9-0	3-0	1-2	1-0	5-0	1-0	1-0	5-2	1-1	n/a	1-1	1-0	0-0
Beer Albion	5-0	R	3-2	2-4	1-0	0-0	3-5	3-0	1-0	2-0	3-1	3-2	n/a	3-3	2-1	2-4
Clyst Valley	2-3	3-0	E	3-1	5-2	1-2	2-0	3-3	2-2	1-1	4-1	0-2	n/a	1-2	1-1	3-1
Cullompton Rangers Res.	0-3	0-3	0-3	M	1-3	1-4	1-5	2-2	2-1	0-7	0-2	1-2	n/a	1-3	0-0	1-1
Exeter Civil Service	1-4	2-4	3-3	3-1	I	1-1	4-2	5-4	0-2	2-1	3-0	5-2	n/a	2-4	2-2	4-2
Exmouth Town	0-2	2-1	5-1	3-0	3-1	E	1-3	1-1	3-1	3-3	1-1	0-1	1-1	1-1	4-0	3-3
Feniton	0-3	0-1	0-1	1-0	1-0	1-5	R	6-1	3-3	3-2	2-0	7-2	n/a	1-2	1-3	2-0
Hatherleigh Town	1-3	2-2	0-1	4-0	7-2	1-5	4-1		2-1	1-3	0-0	4-2	n/a	1-2	1-0	2-5
Heavitree Social United	3-6	6-0	0-2	11-1	2-1	1-6	0-0	4-1	D	3-1	6-3	10-1	n/a	6-1	2-2	2-2
Okehampton Argyle	1-3	4-2	4-2	9-0	0-3	6-0	7-0	2-1	7-3	I	2-0	4-1	n/a	1-4	2-1	1-0
Pinhoe	0-3	3-1	1-2	2-1	2-5	1-2	1-3	1-3	1-5	3-1	V	2-2	n/a	0-8	0-3	3-2
Sidmouth Town	2-2	2-1	2-3	3-1	5-3	0-7	2-3	0-1	0-2	3-3	1-2	I	2-0	1-1	2-1	0-3
St Loyes	0-2	n/a	1-1	n/a	n/a	n/a	n/a	n/a	n/a	n/a	n/a	n/a	S	n/a	2-4	n/a
St Martins	2-1	2-1	2-1	4-0	3-2	2-0	1-0	2-1	3-1	2-3	1-2	4-2	n/a	I	1-1	4-0
Thorverton	1-3	3-1	2-1	2-2	3-1	0-2	2-2	2-2	0-3	1-3	4-3	3-4	n/a	n/a	O	5-2
University of Exeter Res.	2-2	0-1	1-2	1-0	2-2	0-2	4-1	3-1	1-3	1-1	5-1	1-1	n/a	1-1	2-1	N

Premier Division		P	W	D	L	F	A	Pts
Axminster Town		28	19	6	3	70	28	63
St Martins		28	18	7	3	67	36	61
Exmouth Town		28	16	7	5	68	35	55
Okehampton Argyle		28	15	4	9	79	46	49
Clyst Valley		28	13	6	9	56	45	45
Heavitree Social United		28	13	5	10	83	53	44
Beer Albion		28	13	3	12	52	53	42
Feniton		28	12	3	13	53	56	39
University of Exeter Res.		28	8	9	11	49	51	33
Exeter Civil Service	-2	28	10	4	14	62	70	32
Hatherleigh Town		28	8	6	14	51	66	30
Sidmouth Town		28	8	6	14	48	78	30
Thorverton	-1	28	7	9	12	45	51	29
Pinhoe		28	7	3	18	38	78	24
Cullompton Rangers Res.		28	2	4	22	21	96	10

St Loyes – record expunged

Senior Division One	P	W	D	L	F	A	Pts
Heavitree Harriers	26	17	6	3	62	30	57
Wellington Town Res.	26	16	5	5	77	31	53
Topsham Town	26	15	6	5	60	40	51
Bickleigh	26	14	8	4	69	32	50
Seaton Town	26	14	6	6	67	35	48
Culm United	26	13	6	7	54	54	45
Newtown	26	10	6	10	61	51	36
Exeter St Thomas	26	10	2	14	51	55	32
Broadclyst Social Club	26	6	8	12	48	57	26
Westexe Rovers	26	4	14	8	35	44	26
Exmouth Amateurs	26	7	4	15	45	56	25
North Tawton	26	7	3	16	43	86	24
Exeter Civil Service Res.	26	4	4	18	30	95	16
Halwill	26	2	8	16	29	65	14

DEVON & EXETER LEAGUE PREMIER DIVISION CONSTITUTION 2007-08

BEER ALBION.......................Furzebrake, Stovar Long Lane, Beer EX12 3DY.................None
BICKLEIGH........................Happy Meadow, Bickleigh, Tiverton.....................None
CLYST VALLEY....................Winslade Park, Exmouth Road, Clyst St Mary....................None
CULLOMPTON RANGERS RESERVES..Speeds Meadow, Duke Street, Cullompton EX15 1DW........01884 33090
EXETER CIVIL SERVICE................Foxhayes, Exwick, Exeter EX4 2BQ.....................01392 273976
FENITON.....................Station Road, Feniton, Honiton EX14 3DF.................01404 850835
HATHERLEIGH TOWN..........The Sportsfield, Okehampton Road, Hatherleigh, Okehampton.......01837 810346
HEAVITREE HARRIERS.....Withycombe Common Archery Club, Raleigh Common, Exmouth EX8 5EE...01395 442421
HEAVITREE SOCIAL UNITED.........Wingfield Park, East Wonford Hill, Exeter EX1 3BS.........01392 273020
PINHOE.........................Station Road, Pinhoe, Exeter EX1 3SA.................None
SIDMOUTH TOWN.........Manstone Recreation Ground, Manstone Lane, Sidmouth EX10 9TS.......01395 577087
ST MARTINS.................Minster Park, Exminster Hospital, Exminster...............01392 823909
THORVERTON..................Recreation Playing Field, Riaddon Road, Thorverton, Exeter..........None
TOPSHAM TOWN..............Coronation Field, Exeter Road, Topsham.................01392 873678
UNIVERSITY OF EXETER RESERVES......University Sports Ground, Topsham EX4 4QJ.............01392 264452
WELLINGTON TOWN RESERVES....Wellington Playing Field, North Street, Wellington TA1 8NA...01823 664810
IN: Bickleigh (P), Heavitree Harriers (P), Topsham Town (P), Wellington Town Res. (P)
OUT: Axminster Town, Exmouth Town, Okehampton Argyle (all P – South West Peninsular League Division One East), St Loyes (WS)

EAST DEVON SENIOR CUP

SEMI-FINALS	**FINAL**
Culm United 3 Okehampton Argyle 1	*(May 6th at Tiverton Town)*
Wellington Town Res. 2 Clyst Valley 1	**Wellington Town Res.** 2 Culm United 1

Senior Division Two

Team		P	W	D	L	F	A	Pts
University of Exeter 'A'		26	20	2	4	81	27	62
East Budleigh		26	19	4	3	66	31	61
Willand Rovers Res.		26	19	3	4	66	26	60
Alphington Res.		26	15	5	6	51	30	50
Budleigh Salterton Res.		26	13	4	9	56	40	43
Otterton		26	13	2	11	61	47	41
Elmore Res.	-1	26	13	2	11	57	52	40
Barnstaple T. Res.	-1	26	11	1	14	55	56	33
Honiton Town		26	9	1	16	53	52	28
Lympstone		26	8	4	14	41	53	28
Sidmouth Town Res.		26	8	1	17	37	71	25
Sandford		26	7	3	16	40	79	24
Kentisbeare		26	5	3	18	30	74	18
Lapford		26	4	1	21	33	89	13

Senior Division Three

Team		P	W	D	L	F	A	Pts
Bow AAC		26	19	2	5	93	28	59
Dawlish Town Res.	-2	26	18	4	4	76	37	56
Univ. of Exeter 'B'	-4	26	17	3	6	78	36	50
Newtown Res.		26	15	3	8	65	43	48
Sidbury United		26	13	6	7	56	34	45
Upottery		26	12	5	9	47	38	41
St Loyes Res.		26	12	2	12	43	61	38
Heavitree Soc. Utd Res.		26	12	1	13	45	50	37
Motel Rgrs & Offwell		26	9	5	12	38	53	32
Seaton Town Res.		26	9	3	14	34	53	30
Colyton		26	9	1	16	47	59	28
Newton St Cyres		26	5	5	16	47	72	20
Tedburn St Mary	-1	26	5	2	19	48	99	16
Topsham Town Res.	-2	26	5	2	19	37	91	15

Senior Division Four

Team		P	W	D	L	F	A	Pts
Beacon Knights		26	21	2	3	101	26	65
Pinhoe Res.		26	19	3	4	75	54	60
South Zeal United		26	16	5	5	82	39	53
Winkleigh		26	16	2	8	69	38	50
Morchard Bishop		26	15	3	8	85	43	48
Tipton St John		26	14	3	9	74	55	45
Uplowman Athletic		26	13	5	8	73	53	44
Bampton		26	10	7	9	50	41	37
Dunkeswell Rovers		26	9	5	12	69	75	32
Westexe Rovers Res.		26	7	6	13	55	63	27
Crescent	-1	26	7	3	16	54	63	23
Sampford Peverell		26	5	5	16	38	55	20
Exmouth Amats Res.	-4	26	4	3	19	44	82	11
Newton Town	-2	26	0	0	26	8	190	-2

Senior Division Five

Team		P	W	D	L	F	A	Pts
Newtown 'A'		26	16	8	2	66	24	56
Witheridge Res.		26	14	9	3	69	35	51
Clyst Valley Res.		26	15	4	7	65	47	49
Axminster Town Res.		26	13	9	4	80	29	48
Woodbury		26	12	3	11	52	61	39
Crediton United Res.		26	11	5	10	70	65	38
Kentisbeare Res.		26	11	3	12	59	69	36
Oakwood		26	10	5	11	47	56	35
Thorverton Res.		26	9	7	10	56	61	34
St Martins Res.		26	9	5	12	59	74	32
Broadclyst SC Res.		26	6	8	12	45	60	26
Bickleigh Res.		26	7	2	17	53	68	23
Exmouth Town Res.		26	6	3	17	47	80	21
Alphington 'A'	-1	26	7	1	18	46	85	21

Intermediate Division One

Team		P	W	D	L	F	A	Pts
Phoenix Club		26	20	3	3	92	32	63
Colaton Raleigh		26	20	1	5	86	30	61
Dawlish United		26	16	6	4	96	49	54
Legends		26	16	4	6	88	40	52
Sidbury United Res.	-2	26	13	7	6	55	41	44
Lord's XI		26	13	2	11	72	77	41
Feniton Res.		26	13	1	12	58	54	40
Okehampton A. Res.	-1	26	11	3	12	71	56	35
Dawlish Town 'A'		26	9	4	13	78	77	31
Cullompton Rgrs 'A'		26	8	5	13	65	72	29
Up & Under	-1	26	9	2	15	48	77	28
Lympstone Res.		26	7	3	16	61	97	24
North Tawton Res.	-2	26	2	6	18	37	87	10
Exmouth Amats 'A'		26	1	1	24	22	140	4

Intermediate Division Two

Team		P	W	D	L	F	A	Pts
Countess Wear D'moes		24	16	3	5	71	38	51
Heavitree Harriers Res.		24	14	4	6	66	49	46
Culm United Res.		24	13	5	6	56	48	44
Culmstock		24	13	3	8	75	55	42
Axmouth United		24	12	1	11	53	53	37
Awliscombe United		24	10	5	9	46	46	35
Northlew		24	11	1	12	74	63	34
Honiton Town Res.		24	9	7	8	53	50	34
Uplowman Res.		24	10	3	11	54	60	33
Axminster Town 'A'		24	9	5	10	43	50	32
Cheriton Fitzpaine	-5	24	9	4	11	51	69	26
Silverton	-1	24	6	2	16	45	71	19
Met Office		24	1	3	20	23	58	6

Flying Horse – record expunged

Intermediate Division Three

Team		P	W	D	L	F	A	Pts
Beer Albion Res.		26	20	3	3	68	35	63
AFC Sidford		26	18	4	4	83	37	58
Hatherleigh T. Res.	-1	26	17	7	2	80	25	57
Newton St Cyres Res.		26	15	6	5	83	38	51
East Budleigh Res.		26	16	3	7	63	31	51
Bow AAC Res.		26	13	4	9	64	50	43
Priory		26	12	5	9	93	61	41
Tedburn St M. Res.		26	8	5	13	61	90	29
Colyton Res.	-4	26	8	4	14	39	60	24
Follygate/Inwardleigh		26	7	2	17	59	82	23
Wingfield Park		26	6	4	16	40	67	22
Seaton Town 'A'		26	5	3	18	36	99	18
Lapford Res.		26	5	2	19	36	81	17
Bradninch		26	5	2	19	35	84	17

Intermediate Division Four

Team		P	W	D	L	F	A	Pts
Halwill Res.		24	19	2	3	74	33	59
Clyst Valley 'A'		24	17	3	4	83	43	54
Crediton United 'A'		24	17	2	5	96	35	53
Amory Argyle		24	16	2	6	99	45	50
Winkleigh Res.		24	16	1	7	74	39	49
Langdon Res.		24	13	2	9	97	64	41
Bampton Res.		24	7	7	10	53	60	28
Okehampton A. 'A'	-9	24	12	1	11	66	78	28
Otterton Res.		24	7	5	12	43	66	26
Motel & Offwell Res.		24	6	3	15	50	99	21
Feniton 'A'		24	4	5	15	54	78	17
Sandford Res.		24	3	0	21	37	114	9
Awliscombe United Res.		24	2	1	21	31	103	7

Exeter Civil Service 'A' – record expunged

DORSET COUNTY LEAGUE

Note – Weymouth Spartans withdrew during the course of the season. Their results are shown herein but are expunged from the league table	Allendale	Chickerell United	Easton United	Moreton	Okeford United	Stalbridge	Tintinhull	Wareham Rangers	Weymouth Spartans	Weymouth Sports	Wincanton Town	Witchampton United
Allendale	S	1-0	6-0	0-2	1-1	2-0	4-1	1-2	n/a	0-1	0-2	1-1
Chickerell United	1-1	E	7-1	5-1	4-0	3-0	5-0		n/a	1-1	0-0	2-2
Easton United	1-1	0-3	N	1-0	1-2	0-4	0-2	1-1	n/a	0-3	0-6	0-3
Moreton	2-2	1-4	5-0	I	1-2	2-4	1-0	1-4	3-2	2-5	1-5	0-2
Okeford United	1-1	3-2	4-4	2-2	O	0-2	1-2		n/a	0-2	0-2	3-0
Stalbridge	1-6	1-4	2-2	2-1	1-1	R	1-1	0-1	n/a	1-2	1-4	1-1
Tintinhull	1-6	1-2	0-2	0-2	4-2	2-3		1-1	n/a	1-6	0-3	2-1
Wareham Rangers	2-0	4-2	7-2	3-3	3-1	5-0	6-4		n/a	1-2	0-1	0-2
Weymouth Spartans	n/a	n/a	1-3	3-0	n/a	n/a	n/a	n/a		n/a	n/a	n/a
Weymouth Sports	4-1	0-3	5-0	3-0	4-0	3-2	0-2	1-3	3-0	D	1-2	1-0
Wincanton Town	3-2	2-1	2-2	4-1	4-0	3-1	4-1	5-0	n/a	5-0	I	0-2
Witchampton United	0-2	0-0	3-0	2-1	0-3	2-1	0-0	1-0	n/a	2-0	2-4	V

Senior Division	P	W	D	L	F	A	Pts
Wincanton Town	20	16	2	2	57	17	50
Weymouth Sports	20	13	1	6	44	26	40
Wareham Rangers	20	12	3	5	47	30	39
Chickerell United	20	11	5	4	54	19	38
Witchampton United	20	9	5	6	26	21	32
Allendale	20	7	6	7	38	26	27
Okeford United	20	5	5	10	26	42	20
Stalbridge	20	5	4	11	28	45	19
Tintinhull	20	5	3	12	25	49	18
Moreton	20	4	3	13	29	50	15
Easton United	20	2	5	13	17	66	11

Weymouth Spartans – record expunged

DORSET COUNTY LEAGUE SENIOR DIVISION CONSTITUTION 2007-08

AC MATRAVERS . . . . Lytchett Matravers Recreation Ground, Lytchett Matravers . . . . None
ALLENDALE . . . . Redcotts Recreation Ground, School Lane, Wimborne BH21 1HQ . . . . None
BOURNEMOUTH UNIVERSITY . . Bournemouth Sports Club, Chapel Gate, East Parley, Christchurch BH23 6BD. 01202 581933
BROADMAYNE . . . . Thomas Hardye Leisure Centre, Coburg Road, Dorchester DT1 2HR 01305 266772
CHICKERELL UNITED . . . . Weymouth College, Cranford Avenue, Weymouth DT4 7LQ 01305 208892
EASTON UNITED. . . . . Grove Road Playing Field, Easton, Portland. . . . . None
KANGAROOS . . . . Thomas Hardye Leisure Centre, Coburg Road, Dorchester DT1 2HR 01305 266772
MORETON. . . . . Recreation Field, Dick o'the Banks Road, Crossways DT2 8BJ . . . . None
OKEFORD UNITED. . . . . Recreation Ground, Okeford Fitzpaine, Blandford Forum . . . . None
STALBRIDGE . . . . The Park, Park Grove, Stalbridge DT10 2RA . . . . None
TINTINHULL . . . . The Village Green, Tintinhull, Yeovil . . . . None
WAREHAM RANGERS . . . . Purbeck Sports Centre, Worgret Road, Wareham BH20 4PH 01929 556454
WEYMOUTH SPORTS . . . . The Marsh (Main Pitch), Weymouth . . . . None
WITCHAMPTON UNITED . . . . Crichel Park, Witchampton. 01258 840986

IN: AC Matravers (P), Bournemouth University (N), Broadmayne (P), Kangaroos (P)
OUT: Weymouth Spartans (WS), Wincanton Town (P – Dorset Premier League)

WWW.NLNEWSDESK.CO.UK

Reserve Division		P	W	D	L	F	A	Pts
Portland United Res.		22	17	4	1	66	19	55
Blandford United Res.		22	15	5	2	53	20	50
Chickerell United Res.		22	10	8	4	54	31	38
Sturminster Newton United Res.		22	11	4	7	32	28	37
Bournemouth Sports CM Res.		22	10	3	9	44	40	33
Sherborne Town Res.	-3	22	10	5	7	56	34	32
Holt United Res.		22	9	2	11	47	56	29
Wincanton Town Res.		22	6	7	9	42	39	25
Poole Borough Res.	-3	22	7	3	12	45	49	21
Gillingham Town Res.	-3	22	6	2	14	37	70	17
Shaftesbury Res.		22	3	4	15	32	61	13
Cobham Sports Res.		22	2	5	15	22	83	11

Division One		P	W	D	L	F	A	Pts
Kangaroos		24	17	3	4	59	31	54
AC Matravers	-3	24	16	3	5	75	34	48
Wareham Rangers Res.		24	13	4	7	48	36	43
Broadmayne		24	13	3	8	56	46	42
Bishop's Caundle		24	13	2	9	66	47	41
Purbeck Panthers		24	12	3	9	48	39	39
Ferndown Sports	-3	24	11	3	10	47	55	33
Lytchett Red Triangle		24	9	4	11	41	34	31
Cranborne Res.		24	8	4	12	47	52	28
Corfe Castle		24	7	3	14	43	58	24
Easton United Res.		24	6	2	16	32	73	20
Bere Regis		24	4	7	13	40	70	19
AFC Bluebird	-1	24	5	3	16	30	57	17

Division Two		P	W	D	L	F	A	Pts
Swanage Town & Herston Res.		24	17	2	5	60	32	53
Barwick & Stoford		24	16	4	4	78	36	52
Stourpaine Res.		24	13	6	5	65	36	45
Piddletrenthide United		24	13	5	6	58	50	44
Poundbury		24	13	2	9	74	46	41
Linthorpe		24	11	4	9	63	60	37
The Balti House		24	9	5	10	56	50	32
Child Okeford		24	8	4	12	48	64	28
Stalbridge Res.		24	9	1	14	51	79	28
Sturminster Marshall Res.		24	6	4	14	39	60	22
Wyke Regis Social Club		24	6	4	14	53	78	22
Gillingham Town 'A'		24	6	3	15	34	61	21
Handley Sports		24	6	2	16	33	60	20

Division Three		P	W	D	L	F	A	Pts
Upwey & Broadwey		26	24	1	1	122	28	73
Crossways		26	20	2	4	90	38	62
Antelope Hotel Wareham		26	19	1	6	101	49	58
Chickerell United 'A'		26	17	1	8	92	53	52
Witchampton United Res.		26	14	4	8	73	48	46
Puddletown		26	13	6	7	48	41	45
Stickland United		26	11	2	13	62	70	35
Railway Tavern, Weymouth		26	8	3	15	46	79	27
Donhead United		26	7	4	15	44	81	25
AC Matravers Res.		26	7	3	16	61	66	24
Maiden Newton & Cattistock		26	4	9	13	46	66	21
Piddlehinton United		26	6	3	17	59	90	21
Shaftesbury 'A'		26	4	6	16	49	106	18
Lytchett Red Triangle Res.		26	4	3	19	35	113	15

Division Four		P	W	D	L	F	A	Pts
Kingston Lacy		22	21	1	0	151	4	64
FC Windowman		22	17	0	5	86	45	51
Harbour View Developments		22	16	1	5	130	26	49
Swanage Town & Herston 'A'		22	15	2	5	78	44	47
Sturminster Newton United 'A'		22	13	3	6	70	32	42
Okeford United Res.		22	8	3	11	49	64	27
Purbeck Panthers Res.	-1	22	8	2	12	37	78	25
Granby Rovers	-5	22	8	1	13	47	77	20
Milborne St Andrew		22	5	4	13	42	92	19
Quayside		22	6	1	15	49	100	19
Handley Sports Res.		22	3	1	18	23	111	10
Athletico Chickerell		22	2	1	19	28	117	7

NO DIVISIONAL CUP COMPETITIONS IN 2006-07

DORSET PREMIER LEAGUE

Note – Dorchester United and Stourpaine withdrew during the course of the season. Their results are shown herein but are expunged from the league table

	Blandford United	Bournemouth Spts CM	Bridport Res.	Cobham Sports	Cranborne	Dorchester Town Res.	Dorchester United	Gillingham Town	Hamworthy Recreation	Hamworthy United Res.	Holt United	Poole Borough	Portland United	Stourpaine	Sturminster Marshall	Sturminster Newton Utd	Swanage T. & Herston	Westland Sports
Blandford United		2-2	4-0	1-2	3-5	1-0	n/a	1-2	0-6	3-1	4-5	1-1	0-5	n/a	1-3	2-1	3-3	1-2
Bournemouth Sports CM	3-2		4-5	0-2	0-1	0-0	n/a	2-5	1-6	2-3	1-3	4-5	4-1	n/a	1-4	2-1	0-2	1-2
Bridport Res.	1-1	6-1		2-1	3-1	2-2	n/a	1-2	3-3	0-3	4-3	0-1	1-0	n/a	4-3	0-1	2-1	0-2
Cobham Sports	2-2	5-2	3-3		3-3	5-3	2-1	4-2	1-1	1-2	0-2	1-1	0-0	14-0	3-1	1-0	4-3	1-4
Cranborne	1-2	2-1	2-1	1-2		1-1	n/a	3-1	1-2	2-2	0-2	2-1	2-1	n/a	3-5	4-1	2-1	2-5
Dorchester Town Res.	2-2	3-2	0-2	3-0	3-2		n/a	1-0	0-3	3-0	3-4	1-1	1-3	n/a	1-1	1-2	0-1	1-1
Dorchester United	n/a	n/a	n/a	n/a	n/a	n/a		n/a	1-3	n/a	n/a	n/a	n/a	1-3	n/a	n/a	n/a	n/a
Gillingham Town	2-1	1-2	4-1	1-1	2-3	3-2	n/a		2-1	2-1	0-0	0-1	1-8	n/a	2-1	1-1	1-1	0-3
Hamworthy Recreation	0-0	3-1	5-0	3-0	3-1	1-3	n/a	5-2		1-1	4-1	2-2		n/a	3-2	0-2	4-0	1-1
Hamworthy United Res.	1-3	4-1	2-1	5-1	4-2	0-5	n/a	5-1	0-4		1-5	2-7	1-1	n/a	2-2	0-3	1-1	0-1
Holt United	3-1	6-0	3-2	6-1	1-0	4-0	6-0	2-0	3-0	4-1		2-1	2-2	n/a	1-0	1-1	2-0	1-2
Poole Borough	1-0	2-1	3-3	2-3	4-0	1-1	n/a	1-1	0-3	1-2	0-3		1-2	n/a	2-2	1-2	1-1	1-2
Portland United	3-1	2-0	7-1	3-3	3-0	3-3	1-1	4-2	3-1	2-1	5-0			n/a	3-2	2-1	2-0	0-3
Stourpaine	0-7	n/a	n/a	n/a	2-5	n/a	n/a	n/a	n/a	n/a	n/a	n/a	n/a		n/a	n/a	n/a	n/a
Sturminster Marshall	2-0	1-2	5-1	4-2	1-2	1-1	n/a	4-0	1-2	3-1	1-3	2-0	2-2	n/a		3-3	5-1	0-4
Sturminster Newton Utd	1-1	6-3	2-0	0-1	1-2	2-2	n/a	1-1	1-2	4-0	0-1	1-1	2-0	n/a	0-0		2-1	0-1
Swanage Town & Herston	1-3	3-2	6-0	2-1	4-0	5-2	3-1	1-1	2-0	4-0	1-1	0-3		n/a	2-1	1-4		0-3
Westland Sports	4-0	6-1	6-2	2-0	1-0	0-1	n/a	3-1	3-1	5-0	1-1	2-4	4-2	n/a	3-1	4-0	3-2	

Team		P	W	D	L	F	A	Pts
Westland Sports		30	25	3	2	83	25	78
Holt United		30	23	4	3	79	28	73
Portland United		30	18	6	6	76	41	60
Hamworthy Recreation		30	17	5	8	72	39	56
Sturminster Newton United		30	11	8	11	46	39	41
Cobham Sports		30	11	8	11	54	64	41
Sturminster Marshall		30	11	7	12	62	51	40
Cranborne		30	12	3	15	50	64	39
Gillingham Town		30	10	7	13	43	62	37
Swanage Town & Herston		30	10	6	14	50	56	36
Dorchester Town Res.	-6	30	8	11	11	49	53	29
Poole Borough	-3	30	7	11	12	50	56	29
Blandford United		30	7	8	15	46	65	29
Hamworthy Uited Res.	-3	30	8	6	16	46	79	27
Bridport Res.	-6	30	7	5	18	48	84	20
Bournemouth Sports CM	-3	30	5	2	23	46	94	14

Dorchester United and Stourpaine – records expunged

EDGAR MAIDMENT CHARITY SHIELD

(League Champions v League Cup holders)

(Not contested as Holt United won both trophies in 2005-06)

LEAGUE CUP

FIRST ROUND
Dorchester Town Res. 2 **Swanage T. & Herston** 3 aet
SECOND ROUND
Bournemouth Sports CM 2 Bridport Res. 2 aet
Bridport Res. 0 **Bournemouth Sports CM** 3 replay
Dorchester United (scr.) v **Blandford United** (w/o)
Hamworthy Recreation 4 Cranborne 1
Hamworthy United Res. 1 **Sturminster Marshall** 4
Poole Borough 3 Cobham Sports 2
Portland United 2 Holt United 1
Swanage Town & Herston 3 Sturminster Newton 3 aet
Sturminster Newton Utd 2 **Swanage T. & H.** 3 replay
Westland Sports 1 Gillingham Town 0
QUARTER-FINALS
Blandford United 6 Sturminster Marshall 5 aet
Hamworthy Recreation 6 Bournemouth Sports CM 0
Poole Borough 2 **Swanage Town & Herston** 3 aet
Portland United 2 Westland Sports 1
SEMI-FINALS
Blandford United 0 Portland United 0 aet
Portland United 4 Blandford United 0 replay
Hamworthy Recreation 3 Swanage Town & Herston 1
FINAL
(May 3rd at Dorchester Town)
Hamworthy Recreation 1 Portland United 1 aet (4-2p)

DORSET PREMIER LEAGUE CONSTITUTION 2007-08

BLANDFORD UNITED.............. Recreation Ground, Park Road, Blandford Forum DT11 7BX .... None
BRIDPORT RESERVES .... St Marys Field, Skilling Hill Road, Bridport DT6 5LN 01308 423834
COBHAM SPORTS .... Merley Park, Merley Lane, Wimborne BH21 .... 01202 885773
CRANBORNE .... Recreation Ground, Penny's Lane, Cranborne, Wimborne BH21 5QE..................... None
GILLINGHAM TOWN .... Hardings Lane, Gillingham SP8 4HX 01747 823673
HAMWORTHY RECREATION .. Hamworthy Recreation Club, Magna Road, Canford Magna, Wimborne BH21 3AP......... 01202 881922
HAMWORTHY UNITED RESERVES .. The County Ground, Blandford Close, Hamworthy, Poole BH15 4BF 01202 674974
HOLT UNITED .... Gaunts Common, Holt, Wimborne BH21 4JR 01258 840379
POOLE BOROUGH .... Turlin Moor Recreation Ground, Blandford Moor, Hamworthy, Poole BH15 5XX ... Club Office: 01202 674973)
PORTLAND UNITED .... New Grove Corner, Grove Road, Portland DT5 1DP 01305 861489
STURMINSTER MARSHALL............. Churchill Close, Sturminster Marshall BH21 4BQ .... None
STURMINSTER NEWTON UTD.... Barnetts Field, Honeymead Lane, Sturminster Newton DT10 7EW 01258 471406
SWANAGE TOWN & HERSTON .... Day's Park, off De Moulham Road, Swanage BH19 2JW 01929 424673
WESTLAND SPORTS .... Alvington Lane, Yeovil BA22 8UX .... None
WINCANTON TOWN .... Wincanton Sports Ground, Moor Lane, Wincanton BA9 9EJ 01963 31815

IN: Wincanton Town (P – Dorset League Senior Division)
OUT: Bournemouth Sports CM (F), Dorchester Town Res. (W), Dorchester United (WS), Stourpaine (WS)

DURHAM ALLIANCE

Note – Fatfield withdrew during the course of the season. Their results are shown herein but are expunged from the league table

	Ashbrooke Belford	Birtley Town Res.	Blackhall	Brandon Prince Bishop	Ebchester Consett	Fatfield	Ferryhill Athletic	Hartlepool Town	Herrington Colliery Welfare	Newton Aycliffe	Ryton Res.	Seaham Town Community	Shildon Railway	Silksworth CC	Simonside Social Club	Thornley	Wheatley Hill WMC	Whitehill
Ashbrooke Belford		3-2	1-2	6-1	4-1	6-1	2-2	2-1	7-0	2-2	10-0	4-1	8-0	4-1	1-0	2-0	2-3	2-2
Birtley Town Res.	1-6		3-5	2-2	2-1	n/a	1-1	7-2	2-0	1-3	2-3	6-2	6-0	2-5	3-1	1-3	5-2	3-4
Blackhall	3-5	1-0		3-3	2-2	4-0	4-1	4-0	1-2	0-2	4-3	6-1	2-2	3-1	7-5	6-0	4-1	1-0
Brandon Prince Bishop	1-4	5-1	4-2		6-3	n/a	1-4	2-2	2-2	0-4	5-1	1-0	4-1	3-1	8-1	1-1	3-2	2-4
Ebchester Consett	1-4	2-1	3-0	0-1		n/a	2-2	1-1	2-1	1-1	0-2	4-1	2-1	2-2	2-3	5-4	1-2	
Fatfield	n/a	n/a	n/a	n/a	n/a		1-3	2-6	n/a	n/a	1-5	0-8	n/a	n/a	4-2	n/a	n/a	1-2
Ferryhill Athletic	3-2	1-2	0-3	3-0	5-4	n/a		4-2	4-0	0-0	3-2	3-0	2-0	2-1	2-3	1-1	6-1	1-2
Hartlepool Town	0-1	2-3	3-4	3-1	1-1	1-8	4-2		0-3	1-1	1-1	1-6	2-2	1-1	1-4	8-4		0-2
Herrington Colliery Welfare	2-6	2-3	0-3	2-2	0-2	n/a	0-0	2-3		0-0	3-4	2-6	0-3	1-2	1-1	1-4	8-4	1-1
Newton Aycliffe	4-1	1-1	3-3	3-0	1-1	n/a	3-2	3-4	2-5		4-5	1-2	1-3	3-1	4-4	0-1	4-1	3-6
Ryton Res.	1-4	2-1	3-4	3-4	0-3	n/a	3-3	1-3	0-3	3-10		5-0	2-3	7-3	5-3	1-7	4-4	3-4
Seaham Town Community	1-2	0-2	1-2	4-4	3-4	n/a	2-0	4-0	3-1	5-1	4-1		4-3	1-1	7-0	1-5	3-1	1-3
Shildon Railway	1-2	2-5	1-3	3-1	4-3	n/a	0-3	3-3	3-5	2-2	2-2	2-5		7-0	1-5	3-1	3-3	1-4
Silksworth CC	5-4	2-0	2-2	1-2	1-2	n/a	6-1	4-1	4-0	1-3	3-1	0-2	7-2		7-3	3-6	2-1	1-3
Simonside Social Club	1-2	2-1	1-4	5-3	2-2	n/a	1-3	2-5	2-2	1-4	5-0	4-1	5-0	3-1		5-3	5-3	0-3
Thornley	4-1	1-4	1-4	4-4	2-0	6-2	3-1	3-4	3-1	2-4	8-4	2-0	6-2	0-1	3-2		3-2	2-4
Wheatley Hill WMC	0-7	4-4	1-5	3-5	2-2	n/a	0-4	2-2	2-1	2-0	7-2	4-1	7-1	2-2	1-5	5-2		3-1
Whitehill	2-1	1-0	0-2	7-1	3-0	n/a	0-1	1-2	5-0	8-0	4-2	4-3	0-0	2-0	6-4	1-1	6-1	

Division Two		P	W	D	L	F	A	Pts
Whitehill		32	23	4	5	97	42	73
Blackhall		32	22	5	5	99	55	71
Ashbrooke Belford		32	22	3	7	112	48	69
Thornley		32	17	4	11	87	73	55
Newton Aycliffe		32	14	8	10	80	68	50
Brandon Pce Bishop		32	13	8	11	82	85	47
Ferryhill Athletic	-9	32	16	7	9	75	52	46
Simonside Soc. Club		32	13	5	14	87	89	44
Birtley Town Res.		32	13	4	15	77	71	43
Silksworth CC		32	13	4	15	76	75	43
Hartlepool Town		32	10	9	13	69	88	39
Seaham Town Comm.		32	11	3	18	66	82	36
Ebchester Consett		32	9	8	15	59	73	35
Shildon Railway		32	8	6	18	65	106	30
Wheatley Hill WMC	-6	32	9	6	17	82	110	30
Ryton Res.		32	7	5	20	75	125	26
Herrington Colliery W.		32	5	5	22	43	89	20

Fatfield – record expunged

DURHAM ALLIANCE CONSTITUTION 2007-08

BIRTLEY TOWN RESERVES .. Birtley Sports Complex, Durham Road, Birtley, Chester-le-Street DH3 2TB .... None
BLACKHALL HARDWICK .... Welfare Park, Blackhall TS27 4LX .... None
BRANDON BRITISH LEGION .... Community Centre, Brandon Lane, Brandon DH7 8PU .... None
CORNFORTH UNITED ...... West Cornforth Community Centre, Station Road, West Cornforth DL17 9JQ .... None
EBCHESTER CONSETT .... Crookhall, Delves Lane, Consett DH8 7LR 01740 654628
FERRYHILL ATHLETIC .... Mainsforth Complex, Ferryhill DL17 0AG .... None
HARTLEPOOL TOWN .... Grayfields Enclosure, Jesmond Road, Hartlepool TS26 0HN .... None
HERRINGTON COLLIERY WELFARE .. Welfare Park, New Herrington, Houghton-le-Spring DH4 4LR .... None
JARROW TOWN .... Perth Green Community Assoc., Inverness Road, Jarrow NE32 4AQ .... None
NEWTON AYCLIFFE .... Newton Aycliffe Sports Club, Moore Lane, Newton Aycliffe DL5 5AG ... 0191 489 3743
RYTON RESERVES .... Clara Vale Recreation Ground, Ryton NE40 3SW 01325 300324
SEAHAM TOWN COMMUNITY .... Dawdon Welfare Park, Green Drive, Dawdon, Seaham SR7 7XL .... None
SHILDON RAILWAY .... Shildon Railway Sports & Social, Hackworth Street, Shildon DL4 1XL .... None
SIMONSIDE SOCIAL CLUB .. Boldon Community Association, New Road, Boldon Colliery NE35 9DS ...... 0191 536 4180 (Cricket Club)
THORNLEY .... Thornley Colliery Welfare, Ashfield Grove, Thornley .... None
WASHINGTON RESERVES .... Albany Park, Spout Lane, Concord, Washington N37 2AB .... None
WHEATLEY HILL WMC .... Old Fire Station, Quetlaw Road, Wheatley Hill DH6 3SB 0191 417 7779
WHITEHILL .... Riverside Ground, Chester-le-Street .... None

IN: Cornforth United (N), Jarrow Town (N), Washington Reserves (N)
OUT: Ashbrooke Belford (now Belford House) (P – Wearside League), Fatfield (WS), Silksworth CC (P – Wearside League)
Blackhall become Blackhall Hardwick, Brandon Prince Bishop become Brandon British Legion

LEAGUE CUP

PRELIMINARY ROUND
Ashbrooke Belford 6 Wheatley Hill WMC 2
Ebchester Consett 1 **Simonside Social Club** 5
FIRST ROUND
Ashbrooke Belford 1 **Brandon Prince Bishop** 2
Birtley Town Res. (w/o) v Fatfield (scr.)
Blackhall 5 Ryton Res. 2
Ferryhill Athletic 3 Thornley 1
Hartlepool Town 2 **Whitehill** 3
Herrington Colliery Welfare 3 Simonside
Social Club 1
Newton Aycliffe 3 **Shildon Railway** 5
Silksworth CC 2 Seaham Town Community 1

QUARTER-FINALS
Birtley Town Res. 10 Shildon Railway 4
Blackhall 3 Silksworth CC 2
Herrington Colliery Welfare 1 **Ferryhill Athletic** 4
Whitehill 3 Brandon
Prince Bishop 0
SEMI-FINALS
Blackhall 1 **Ferryhill Athletic** 2
Whitehill 2 Birtley Town Res. 1
FINAL
(April 23rd at Chester-le-Street Town)
Ferryhill Athletic 3 Whitehill 2

CLEM SMITH BOWL

PRELIMINARY ROUND
Birtley Town Res. 1 **Whitehill** 2
Newton Aycliffe 3 Ebchester Consett 0
FIRST ROUND
Ashbrooke Belford 7 Newton Aycliffe 2
Brandon Prince Bishop 3 Ryton Res. 2
Herrington Colliery Welfare 1 **Shildon**
Railway 7
Silksworth CC 2 Ferryhill Athletic 0
Simonside Social Club 5 Hartlepool Town 1
Thornley 0 **Seaham Town Community** 1
Wheatley Hill WMC 1 **Blackhall** 4
Whitehill (w/o) v Fatfield (scr.)

QUARTER-FINALS
Ashbrooke Belford 7 Shildon Railway 1
Blackhall 7 Seaham Town Community 0
Brandon Prince Bishop 7 Simonside Social Club 3
Silksworth CC 0 **Whitehill** 1
SEMI-FINALS
Ashbrooke Belford 4 Whitehill 0
Blackhall 3 Brandon Prince Bishop 1
FINAL
(March 12th at Chester-le-Street Town)
Ashbrooke Belford 2 Blackhall 1

WASHINGTON AGED PEOPLE'S CUP

PRELIMINARY ROUND
Ryton Res. 6 Simonside
Social Club 4
FIRST ROUND
Birtley Town Res. 2 **Whitehill** 3
Blackhall 2 Seaham Town Community 1
Brandon Prince Bishop 5 Shildon Railway 1
Ferryhill Athletic 6 Wheatley Hill WMC 0
Hartlepool Town 7 Newton Aycliffe 1
Herrington Colliery Welfare 0 **Ashbrooke Belford** 5
Ryton Res. 7 Ebchester Consett 3
Silksworth CC 2 **Thornley** 3

QUARTER-FINALS
Ashbrooke Belford 6 Ferryhill Athletic 0
Blackhall 5 Whitehill 4
Brandon Prince Bishop 3 Thornley 2
Ryton Res. 3 Hartlepool Town 1
SEMI-FINALS
Ashbrooke Belford 3 Brandon Prince Bishop 1
Ryton Res. 0 **Blackhall** 2
FINAL
(March 19th at Chester-le-Street Town)
Blackhall 6 Ashbrook Belford 5

MARK BLAKE MEMORIAL TROPHY

FIRST ROUND
Newton Aycliffe 3 **Birtley Town Res.** 5
Shildon Railway 7 Hartlepool Town 5
Simonside Social Club 5 Ebchester Consett 3
Wheatley WMC 8 Herrington
Colliery Welfare 5

SEMI-FINALS
Shildon Railway 3 Birtley Town Res. 3 *aet* (3-0p)
Simonside SC 4 **Wheatley Hill WMC** 4 *aet* (1-3p)
FINAL
(March 26th at Chester-le-Street Town)
Wheatley Hill WMC 0 **Shildon Railway** 2

EAST CORNWALL LEAGUE

Note – St Dennis withdrew during the course of the season Their results are shown herein but are expunged from the league table	Bodmin Town Res.	Camelford	Dobwalls	Foxhole Stars	Godolphin Atlantic	Launceston Res.	Liskeard Athletic Res.	Padstow United	Probus	Saltash United Res.	St Dennis	Sticker	Torpoint Athletic Res.	Wadebridge Town Res
Bodmin Town Res.		2-6	2-6	1-2	1-5	1-3	3-4	0-0	2-1	1-0	n/a	2-3	1-3	2-0
Camelford	2-2	P	1-1	1-4	4-1	2-3	3-0	2-0	1-3	1-2	n/a	1-2	4-5	1-2
Dobwalls	5-0	3-2	R	2-4	2-1	3-0	2-1	7-1	1-0	1-1	n/a	1-0	5-3	2-2
Foxhole Stars	2-0	2-0	2-2	E	0-1	2-0	5-0	3-1	2-0	1-1	n/a	3-1	4-1	2-0
Godolphin Atlantic	6-2	0-1	1-5	0-2	M	3-1	2-1	7-1	1-1	4-0	10-0	6-1	6-2	3-1
Launceston Res.	6-0	3-0	2-2	1-1	0-0	I	0-0	4-2	0-2	1-1	n/a	1-1	1-0	0-0
Liskeard Athletic Res.	2-2	0-2	1-2	2-2	2-2	1-1	E	5-2	5-1	1-0	n/a	2-4	4-1	1-1
Padstow United	1-1	0-3	0-5	0-5	1-2	2-0	4-2	R	0-7	2-2	n/a	1-2	0-1	1-1
Probus	1-2	0-0	3-1	3-3	1-3	0-3	0-3	2-1		1-0	n/a	4-1	2-1	1-0
Saltash United Res.	1-1	2-3	0-0	1-3	1-3	0-1	1-0	2-2	2-0		n/a	1-3	1-0	3-2
St Dennis	n/a	0-9	n/a	n/a	1-3	1-3	0-2	0-1	0-1	n/a	D	1-3	n/a	n/a
Sticker	2-1	1-1	1-4	2-1	3-1	0-0	1-0	3-1	1-2	7-0	n/a	I	5-2	4-0
Torpoint Athletic Res.	1-0	0-0	0-1	1-1	5-3	1-0	1-0	1-3	2-2	4-2	n/a	2-1	V	2-1
Wadebridge Town Res.	2-0	3-0	3-1	0-3	3-1	3-2	1-1	0-2	5-0	0-2	n/a	0-2	1-1	

LEAGUE CUP

QUARTER-FINALS
Lanreath 2 Dobwalls 3 *aet*
(Dobwalls expelled)
St Blazey Res. 1 **Foxhole Stars** 4
Tamarside 2 **Godolphin Atlantic** 3
aet
Wadebridge Town Res. 2
Launceston Res. 3

SEMI-FINALS
Godolphin Atlantic 1 Foxhole
Stars 0
Lanreath 1 **Launceston Res.** 2

FINAL
(May 6th at Nanpean Rovers)
Launceston Res. 1 **Godolphin Atlantic** 1 *aet* (4-5p)

Premier Division	P	W	D	L	F	A	Pts
Foxhole Stars	24	16	6	2	59	21	54
Dobwalls	24	15	6	3	64	31	51
Sticker	24	14	3	7	51	37	45
Godolphin Atlantic	24	13	3	8	63	42	42
Probus	24	11	4	9	40	37	37
Torpoint Athletic Res.	24	10	4	10	40	48	34
Launceston Res.	24	8	9	7	33	27	33
Camelford	24	8	5	11	41	41	29
Wadebridge Town Res.	24	8	5	11	31	36	29
Saltash United Res.	24	6	7	11	26	42	25
Liskeard Athletic Res.	24	5	5	12	36	47	22
Bodmin Town Res.	24	4	5	15	29	64	17
Padstow United	24	4	4	16	27	67	16

St Dennis – record expunged

Division One	P	W	D	L	F	A	Pts
Tamarside	26	24	2	0	103	22	74
Morwenstow	26	22	0	4	89	39	66
Biscovey	26	18	2	6	78	40	56
Lanreath	26	14	5	7	56	35	47
St Blazey Res.	26	14	2	10	61	54	44
St Columb Major	26	11	1	14	62	72	34
Lifton	26	10	2	14	41	55	32
Callington Town Res.	26	8	6	12	46	55	30
Bude Town	26	8	4	14	48	69	28
Tavistock Res.	26	8	4	14	50	82	28
Nanpean Rovers	26	8	2	16	42	64	26
Roche	26	7	4	15	36	48	25
St Stephen	26	5	3	18	42	75	18
Holsworthy Res.	26	5	3	18	29	73	18

WWW.CHERRYRED.CO.UK

EAST CORNWALL LEAGUE PREMIER DIVISION CONSTITUTION 2007-08

BISCOVEY .... Par Athletics Track, Moorland Road, Par, St Austell PL24 2PB .... None
BODMIN TOWN RESERVES .... Priory Park, Bodmin PL31 2PP 01208 78165
GODOLPHIN ATLANTIC .... Godolphin Way, Newquay TR7 3BU .... None
LANREATH .... Rally Park, Lanreath Village Hall, Lanreath .... None
LAUNCESTON RESERVES .... Pennygillam, Pennygillam Industrial Estate, Launceston PL15 7ED 01566 773279
LISKEARD ATHLETIC RESERVES .... Lux Park, Coldstyle Lane, Liskeard PL14 3HZ 01579 342665
MORWENSTOW .... Playing Field, Shop, Morwenstow, Bude EX23 9SQ .... None
PADSTOW UNITED .... Wadebridge Road, Padstow .... None
PROBUS .... Recreation Ground, Probus .... None
SALTASH UNITED RESERVES .... Kimberley Stadium, Callington Road, Saltash PL12 6DX 01752 845746
STICKER .... Burngallow Park, Burngallow Lane, Sticker, St Austell PL26 7EN 01726 71003
TAMARSIDE .... Parkway Sports & Social Club, Ernesettle Lane, Ernesettle, Plymouth PL5 2EY .... None
TORPOINT ATHLETIC RESERVES .... The Mill, Mill Lane, Torpoint PL11 2RE 01752 812889
WADEBRIDGE TOWN RESERVES .... Bodieve Park, Bodieve Road, Wadebridge PL27 6EA 01208 812537
IN: Biscovey (P), Lanreath (P), Morwenstow (P), Tamarside (P)
OUT: Camelford, Dobwalls, Foxhole Stars (all P – South West Peninsula League Division One West), St Dennis (WS)

EAST CORNWALL LEAGUE DIVISION ONE CONSTITUTION 2007-08

BERE ALSTON UNITED .... Recreation Field, The Down, Bere Alston .... None
BUDE TOWN .... Broadclose, Bude EX23 8DR .... None
CALLINGTON TOWN RESERVES . Ginsters Marshfield Stadium, Callington CC, Launceston Rd, Callington PL17 7DR 01579 382647
CAMELFORD RESERVES .... Trefrew Park, Trefrew, Camelford PL32 9TS .... None
HOLSWORTHY RESERVES .... Upcott Field, North Road, Holsworthy EX22 6HF 01409 254295
LIFTON .... Recreation Ground, Lifton .... None
NANPEAN ROVERS .... Victoria Park, Victoria Bottoms, Nanpean PL26 7YE 01726 823435
POLPERRO .... Killigarth, Polperro, Looe .... None
ROCHE .... Trezaise Road, Roche, St Austell PL26 8HD 01726 890718
ST BLAZEY RESERVES .... Blaise Park, Station Road, St Blazey PL24 2ND 01726 814110
ST COLUMB MAJOR .... Recreation Ground, St Columb Major TR9 6RP .... None
ST NEWLYN EAST .... Cargoll Road, St Newlyn East, Newquay TR8 5LB .... None
ST STEPHEN .... Trethosa Road, St Stephen, St Austell PL26 7PZ .... None
TAVISTOCK RESERVES .... Langsford Park, Crowndale Road, Tavistock PL19 8DD 01822 614447
IN: Bere Alston United (P – Duchy League Premier Division), Camelford Reserves (P – South West Peninsula League Division Two), Polperro (P – Duchy League Premier Division), St Newlyn East (P – Duchy League Premier Division)
OUT: Biscovey (P), Lanreath (P), Morwenstow (P), Tamarside (P)

EASTERN COUNTIES LEAGUE

	CRC	Clacton Town	Dereham T.	Diss Town	Felixstowe	Halstead T.	Harwich & P.	Histon Res.	Ipswich Wdrs	K. Lynn Res.	Kirkley	Leiston	Lowestoft T.	Mildenhall T.	Needham Mkt	Newmarket	Norwich Utd	Soham TR	Stanway Rov.	Wisbech Town	Woodbridge T.	Wroxham
CRC		3-0	2-1	2-0	2-0	1-0	2-6	1-2	1-4	2-0	3-4	1-4	1-1	1-2	2-0	1-2	1-1	1-2	3-0	0-2	1-1	1-3
Clacton Town	1-0		1-6	3-2	1-5	2-2	0-1	5-2	2-2	1-1	3-2	1-2	1-2	0-6	0-4	3-1	2-3	5-4	4-1	2-1	1-3	0-4
Dereham Town	3-2	0-1		4-2	8-4	4-0	2-2	5-1	2-5	4-1	3-2	3-3	2-1	4-3	1-0	2-2	5-1	5-1	1-0	0-4	0-5	0-2
Diss Town	1-2	2-1	0-3	*P*	2-4	1-3	2-2	2-0	0-2	1-1	1-1	2-3	0-3	2-3	0-1	4-1	0-1	2-2	2-0	0-1	2-2	0-2
Felixstowe & Walton United	5-2	2-1	0-3	2-0	*R*	3-1	1-2	3-3	0-0	0-0	0-4	0-6	1-4	1-2	0-3	1-0	1-0	2-0	1-2	1-2	1-2	0-6
Halstead Town	2-2	4-0	0-1	1-3	4-1	*E*	2-1	0-0	3-1	2-2	0-1	0-4	0-2	2-1	0-0	0-1	0-0	3-3	2-3			0-4
Harwich & Parkeston	1-3	7-0	1-1	2-4	1-2	1-0	*M*	0-2	1-8	3-0	0-0	0-3	0-5	0-4	3-4	2-0	2-1	3-4	1-3	1-2	3-0	0-1
Histon Res.	2-0	2-0	2-2	1-1	2-3	6-2	2-1	*I*	0-2	5-2	0-2	0-1	1-1	2-3	2-0	2-0	0-1	0-1	2-2	2-1	4-2	1-3
Ipswich Wanderers	2-0	2-0	1-1	2-0	5-1	2-0	4-0	2-0	*E*	1-2	3-3	0-0	1-2	3-3	0-0	0-2	1-0	1-0	1-0	1-2	2-2	0-1
King's Lynn Res.	1-2	5-1	4-0	1-2	3-4	0-2	1-2	5-1	5-2	*R*	2-2	1-1	0-2	0-2	2-3	2-1	2-2	0-2	1-3	0-2	1-2	2-2
Kirkley	1-0	3-0	1-0	1-2	1-0	3-1	0-3	1-0	3-1	2-1		4-1	1-3	1-2	0-0	1-0	3-0	3-2	1-0	3-1	0-3	0-3
Leiston	1-0	7-0	3-4	0-3	3-1	3-1	3-2	1-2	2-1	0-0		*D*	5-0	4-2	5-2	4-2	3-2	0-1	3-1	3-1	2-2	0-0
Lowestoft Town	4-1	0-1	0-1	1-0	3-0	2-2	7-0	4-2	4-1	2-0	2-2	3-1	*I*	5-0	1-0	2-0	1-0	2-0	0-3	3-3	4-2	1-1
Mildenhall Town	3-3	2-2	4-1	2-3	4-1	2-0	1-1	3-1	2-0	5-0	2-1	1-2	6-0	*V*	1-0	2-0	1-0	2-0	0-3	3-2	4-2	3-2
Needham Market	3-2	5-3	3-0	6-1	2-1	1-2	3-1	2-0	0-0	2-1	1-3	3-2		3-1	*I*	3-1	1-1	2-3	2-3	1-4	3-2	1-6
Newmarket Town	2-1	2-4	3-2	1-0	3-0	5-1	1-0	0-5	0-2	2-1	2-4	2-2	2-0	0-0		*S*	2-0	3-3	3-1	1-4	3-2	1-6
Norwich United	2-2	1-3	0-0	2-1	4-0	0-3	1-0	1-0	1-1	1-4	2-0	0-3	1-3	1-2	1-3		*I*	1-1	2-2	1-1	0-0	1-2
Soham Town Rangers	3-1	3-1	2-3	1-2	1-0	3-3	2-1	3-1	3-1	0-1	0-0	5-0	4-1	0-2	2-0	2-1	3-0	*O*	3-2	2-3	1-0	2-2
Stanway Rovers	1-2	1-0	1-2	4-1	2-1	2-1	2-3	1-1	0-1	0-0	4-0	2-3	0-5	0-1	1-0	1-0	3-2	1-5	*N*	2-2	1-2	1-1
Wisbech Town	3-2	1-1	1-1	5-1	3-1	2-1	4-4	3-1	0-1	1-4	1-1	2-3	1-2	2-3	1-2	2-3	0-3	2-2			2-3	0-2
Woodbridge Town	2-1	4-2	1-6	5-3	2-2	2-2	4-2	6-0	3-0	2-1	1-1	1-3	5-5	3-4	0-5	3-2	3-0	0-2	0-2	0-0		0-0
Wroxham	1-0	6-1	1-0	3-1	4-3	4-1	1-0	3-1	1-1	1-1	3-1	2-0	2-0	8-0	2-0	3-1	4-0	2-0				

Premier Division	P	W	D	L	F	A	Pts
Wroxham	42	31	9	2	107	27	102
Mildenhall Town	42	31	4	7	105	56	97
Lowestoft Town	42	26	10	6	103	51	88
Needham Market	42	25	6	11	85	51	81
Leiston	42	24	7	11	98	71	79
Dereham Town	42	22	8	12	97	73	74
Kirkley	42	21	11	10	65	46	74
Soham Town Rangers	42	21	6	15	81	62	69
Woodbridge Town	42	17	11	14	83	80	62
Ipswich Wanderers	42	17	7	18	71	58	58
Wisbech Town	42	14	9	19	71	71	51
Newmarket Town	42	14	4	24	57	82	46
Felixstowe & Walton United	42	14	4	24	61	99	46
Stanway Rovers	42	12	9	21	56	76	45
Histon Res.	42	12	9	21	61	82	45
Norwich United	42	10	14	18	44	72	44
CRC	42	12	6	24	60	79	42
Harwich & Parkeston	42	12	6	24	67	96	42
King's Lynn Res.	42	10	11	21	60	76	41
Diss Town	42	11	6	25	58	87	39
Clacton Town	42	11	5	26	60	119	38
Halstead Town	42	9	10	23	53	83	37

EASTERN COUNTIES LEAGUE PREMIER DIVISION CONSTITUTION 2007-08

CRC . . . . Abbey Stadium, Newmarket Road, Cambridge CB5 8LN 01223 566500
DEREHAM TOWN. . . . . Aldiss Park, Norwich Road, Dereham NR20 3AL 01362 690460/693677
FELIXSTOWE & WALTON UNITED . . . . Town Ground, Dellwood Avenue, Felixstowe IP11 9HT 01394 282917
HARWICH & PARKESTON . . . . Royal Oak, Main Road, Dovercourt, Harwich CO12 4AX 01255 503643
HAVERHILL ROVERS . . . . Hamlet Croft, Hamlet Road, Haverhill CB9 8LH. 01440 712396
HISTON RESERVES . . . . The Glassworld Stadium, Bridge Road, Impington, Cambridge CB4 9PH 01223 237373
IPSWICH WANDERERS. . . . . SEH Sports Centre, Humberdoucy Lane, Ipswich IP4 3PB 01473 728581
KING'S LYNN RESERVES . . . . The Walks Stadium, Tennyson Road, King's Lynn PE30 5LL 01553 760060
KIRKLEY & PAKEFIELD . . . . Kirkley Recreation Ground, Walmer Road, Lowestoft NR33 8HZ 01502 513549
LEISTON . . . . LTAA, Victory Road, Leiston IP16 4DQ 01728 830308
LOWESTOFT TOWN. . . . . Crown Meadow, Love Road, Lowestoft NR32 2PA 01502 573818
MILDENHALL TOWN. . . . . Recreation Way, Mildenhall, Bury St Edmunds IP28 7EL 01638 713449
NEEDHAM MARKET . . . . Bloomfields, Quinton Road, Needham Market IP6 8DA 01638 663637
NEWMARKET TOWN . . . . Cricket Field Road, off New Cheveley Road, Newmarket CB8 8BG 01638 663637
NORWICH UNITED . . . . Plantation Park, off Plantation Road, Blofield, Norwich NR13 4PL 01603 716963
SOHAM TOWN RANGERS . . . . Julius Martin Lane, Soham, Ely CB7 5EQ 01353 720732/722139
STANWAY ROVERS . . . . Hawthorns, New Farm Road, Stanway, Colchester CO3 0PG 01206 578187
SWAFFHAM TOWN. . . . . Shoemakers Lane, off Cley Road, Swaffham PE37 7NT 01760 722700
WALSHAM-LE-WILLOWS . . . . . . Walsham Sports Club, Summer Road, Walsham-le-Willows IP31 3AH 01359 259298
WISBECH TOWN. . . . . Fenland Park, Lerowe Road, Wisbech PE13 3QL 01945 584176
WOODBRIDGE TOWN . . . . Notcutts Park, Fynn Road, off Seckford Hall Lane, Woodbridge IP12 4DA 01394 385308
WROXHAM . . . . Trafford Park, Skinners Lane, Wroxham NR12 8SJ 01603 783538
IN: Haverhill Rovers (P), Swaffham Town (P), Walsham-le-Willows (P)
OUT: Diss Town (R), FC Clacton (formerly Clacton Town) (R), Halstead Town (R)
Kirkley become Kirkley & Pakefield

WWW.NLNEWSDESK.CO.UK

	Cornard United	Debenham Leis. Centre	Downham Town	Ely City	Fakenham Town	Godmanchester Rovers	Gorleston	Great Yarmouth Town	Hadleigh United	Haverhill Rovers	Long Melford	March Town United	Saffron Walden Town	Stowmarket Town	Swaffham Town	Thetford Town	Tiptree United	Walsham-le-Willows	Whitton United
Cornard United		1-2	2-2	2-3	1-2	2-1	1-0	2-2	2-1	0-1	1-4	1-1	1-2	1-2	2-1	1-3	1-0	1-2	
Debenham Leisure Centre	2-1		6-0	2-2	2-0	5-1	5-6	6-0	0-0	1-1	3-1	5-1	3-2	4-2	3-2	2-1	3-2	0-2	2-2
Downham Town	3-0	0-0		2-3	1-2	1-3	1-2	1-2	1-0	0-3	3-1	0-3	1-1	0-0	3-3	0-3	1-1	0-2	0-2
Ely City	6-1	2-3	5-0	D	3-0	2-0	6-0	2-0	1-3	1-1	7-0	7-2	0-0	2-0	2-1	2-0	3-0	1-2	1-0
Fakenham Town	0-3	3-2	2-1	0-3	I	4-0	1-0	6-0	0-2	1-1	4-1	3-1	2-1	4-0	2-2	0-2	1-4	0-1	3-3
Godmanchester Rovers	1-5	0-3	2-2	1-2	1-0	V	2-1	0-4	1-2	0-1	0-6	2-1	1-0	0-1	0-1	1-1	2-2	0-4	1-4
Gorleston	5-1	2-5	5-1	0-2	0-3	5-1	I	3-1	2-2	0-0	1-4	2-0	2-2	0-3	1-3	1-0	1-2	1-2	3-4
Great Yarmouth Town	2-1	2-1	2-0	0-2	0-2	1-0	0-1	S	0-0	0-3	7-1	2-1	1-2	0-1	0-1	1-2	1-5	0-0	0-1
Hadleigh United	2-1	2-2	2-0	1-1	2-1	2-0	4-0	2-1	I	0-2	2-1	3-0	2-4	1-3	0-4	2-1	0-0	0-1	0-3
Haverhill Rovers	9-0	1-1	4-0	2-2	3-0	2-1	5-0	2-2	1-0	O	4-1	3-2	0-0	4-0	1-0	3-3	2-1	1-2	2-3
Long Melford	1-1	3-3	2-0	1-1	1-5	1-1	3-2	0-1	2-3	2-3	N	1-1	1-2	1-0	0-4	4-1	1-8	0-1	1-4
March Town United	1-1	1-1	2-0	1-2	1-1	0-2	1-2	1-3	2-0	0-4	2-1		0-1	0-2	0-3	0-2	1-3	1-2	1-3
Saffron Walden Town	4-0	0-0	2-1	4-1	2-0	3-0	5-0	1-0	2-0	2-1	1-0	1-0		2-1	0-0	3-1	0-0	0-1	3-2
Stowmarket Town	2-1	1-3	3-1	0-5	2-2	4-1	2-2	1-1	3-3	0-3	4-0	2-2	2-2	O	2-3	2-0	2-4	1-3	1-4
Swaffham Town	3-1	2-3	1-0	1-2	1-1	3-1	4-0	3-0	1-1	0-0	7-0	3-1	4-1	1-0	N	3-0	3-1	2-2	2-1
Thetford Town	0-1	0-4	2-2	0-2	1-0	1-0	3-0	2-3	0-1	0-3	2-1	2-1	0-1	2-1	1-2	E	0-2	0-2	3-2
Tiptree United	5-0	1-2	7-1	1-1	2-2	3-2	10-3	4-1	0-1	2-4	2-1	3-1	4-2	3-1	2-2	2-1		3-1	1-1
Walsham-le-Willows	2-0	1-0	4-2	4-3	1-1	5-0	1-0	4-0	4-0	0-0	4-1	3-0	0-2	3-0	1-2	0-0	1-2		2-1
Whitton United	1-1	2-0	1-2	1-0	3-0	1-0	6-0	3-0	0-0	0-6	6-2	3-1	0-0	3-1	0-1	1-2	2-2	1-0	

Division One	P	W	D	L	F	A	Pts
Walsham-le-Willows	36	25	5	6	68	26	80
Haverhill Rovers	36	22	11	3	86	27	77
Swaffham Town	36	23	8	5	80	34	77
Ely City	36	23	7	6	90	36	76
Debenham Leisure Centre	36	20	10	6	89	50	70
Saffron Walden Town	36	20	10	6	59	32	70
Tiptree United	36	20	9	7	97	52	69
Whitton United	36	20	7	9	76	45	67
Hadleigh United	36	15	9	12	46	47	54
Fakenham Town	36	14	8	14	58	54	50
Thetford Town	36	12	4	20	40	57	40
Stowmarket Town	36	11	7	18	52	72	40
Great Yarmouth Town	36	11	5	20	40	67	38
Gorleston	36	10	4	22	53	96	34
Cornard United	36	8	6	22	42	80	30
Long Melford	36	7	5	24	51	101	26
Godmanchester Rovers	36	6	4	26	29	85	22
Downham Town	36	4	8	24	33	85	20
March Town United	36	4	7	25	35	78	19

EASTERN COUNTIES LEAGUE DIVISION ONE CONSTITUTION 2007-08

CORNARD UNITED . . . . Blackhouse Lane Sport Ground, Great Cornard, Sudbury CO10 0NL 01787 376719
DEBENHAM LEISURE CENTRE . . . . Gracechurch Street, Debenham, Stowmarket IP14 6BY 01728 861101
DISS TOWN . . . . Brewers Green Lane, Diss IP22 4DQ 01379 651223
DOWNHAM TOWN . . . . Memorial Playing Field, Lynn Road, Downham Market PE38 9QG 01366 388424
ELY CITY . . . . The Unwin Ground, Downham Road, Ely CB6 2SH 01353 662035
FC CLACTON . . . . Rush Green Bowl, Rush Green Road, Clacton-on-Sea CO16 7BQ 01255 432590
FAKENHAM TOWN . . . . Clipbush Park, Clipbush Lane, Fakenham NR21 8SW 01328 856222/855859
GODMANCHESTER ROVERS . . . . Bearscroft Lane, Godmanchester PE29 2LQ. 07950 367417
GORLESTON . . . . Emerald Park, Wood Farm Lane, Gorleston NR31 9AQ. 01493 602802
GREAT YARMOUTH TOWN . . . Wellesley Road Rec Ground, Sandown Road, Great Yarmouth NR30 1EY 01493 843373
HADLEIGH UNITED . . . . Millfield, Tinkers Lane, off Duke Street, Hadleigh IP7 5NG 01473 822165
HALSTEAD TOWN . . . . Rosemary Lane, Broton Industrial Estate, Halstead CO9 1HR 01787 472082
LONG MELFORD . . . . Stoneylands Stadium, New Road, Long Melford CO10 9JY 01787 312187
MARCH TOWN UNITED . . . . GER Sports Ground, Robin Goodfellows Lane, March PE15 8HS. 01354 653073
SAFFRON WALDEN TOWN . . . . Catons Lane, Saffron Walden CB10 2DU 01799 522789
STOWMARKET TOWN . . . . Greens Meadow, Bury Road, Stowmarket IP14 1JQ 01449 612533
THETFORD TOWN . . . . Recreation Ground, Mundford Road, Thetford IP24 1NB 01842 766120
TIPTREE UNITED . . . . Chapel Road, Tiptree, near Colchester CO5 0RA 01621 815213
WHITTON UNITED . . . . King George V Playing Fields, Old Norwich Road, Ipswich IP6 6LE 01473 464030
IN: Diss Town (R), FC Clacton (formerly Clacton Town) (R), Halstead Town (R)
OUT: Haverhill Rovers (P), Swaffham Town (P), Walsham-le-Willows (P)

LEAGUE CUP

PRELIMINARY ROUND

Clacton Town 8 Cornard United 2
Dereham Town 4 Great Yarmouth Town 1
Downham Town 0 **King's Lynn Res.** 6
Gorleston 0 **Lowestoft Town** 5
Leiston 1 **Woodbridge Town** 6
Newmarket Town 1 CRC 0
Stowmarket Town 1 **Debenham Leisure Centre** 3
Tiptree United 3 Haverhill Rovers 2
Wisbech Town 0 **Histon Res.** 4

FIRST ROUND

Clacton Town 4 Stanway Rovers 0
Ely City 7 Godmanchester Rovers 0
Fakenham Town 4 Norwich United 1
Hadleigh United 0 **Halstead Town** 3
Harwich & Parkeston 1 **Ipswich Wanderers** 3
King's Lynn Res. 3 Dereham Town 0
Lowestoft Town 2 Wroxham 1
March Town United 0 **Histon Res.** 6
Mildenhall Town 3 Saffron Walden Town 2
Newmarket Town 1 **Soham Town Rangers** 3
Swaffham Town 2 Kirkley 0
Thetford Town 2 Diss Town 0
Tiptree United 4 Long Melford 2
Walsham-le-Willows 0 **Needham Market** 1

Whitton United 0 **Debenham Leisure Centre** 1
Woodbridge Town 2 **Felixstowe & Walton United** 3

SECOND ROUND

Debenham Leisure Centre 3 Thetford Town 0
Ely City 2 King's Lynn Res. 1
Felixstowe & Walton United 0 **Needham Market** 3
Halstead Town 2 **Clacton Town** 4
Ipswich Wanderers 6 Tiptree United 1
Lowestoft Town 3 Histon Res. 0
Soham Town Rangers 2 Mildenhall Town 1
Swaffham Town 0 **Fakenham Town** 1

QUARTER-FINALS

Debenham Leisure Centre 3 Clacton Town 2
Ipswich Wanderers 1 Needham Market 0 *aet*
Lowestoft Town 4 Ely City 0
Soham Town Rangers 4 Fakenham Town 1

SEMI-FINALS

Lowestoft Town 3 Debenham Leisure Centre 2
Soham Town Rangers 0 **Ipswich Wanderers** 1

FINAL

(May 7th at Diss Town)
Lowestoft Town 3 Ipswich Wanderers 0

DIVISION ONE CUP

PRELIMINARY ROUND

Cornard United 0 **Long Melford** 1
Gorleston 1 **Fakenham Town** 2
Stowmarket Town 1 Debenham Leisure Centre 0

FIRST ROUND

Ely City 1 **Haverhill Rovers** 2
Fakenham Town 3 Downham Town 1
Long Melford 0 **Hadleigh United** 2
March Town United 2 **Godmanchester Rovers** 2
Swaffham Town 2 Great Yarmouth Town 1
Thetford Town 0 **Walsham-le-Willows** 3
Tiptree United 1 **Saffron Walden Town** 3

Whitton United 3 Stowmarket Town 0

QUARTER-FINALS

Fakenham Town 2 Walsham-le-Willows 1
Haverhill Rovers 1 Whitton United 0
Saffron Walden Town 2 Hadleigh United 0
Swaffham Town 2 Godmanchester Rovers 0

SEMI-FINALS

Haverhill Rovers 4 Fakenham Town 0
Swaffham Town 1 **Saffron Walden Town** 2

FINAL

(April 25th at Mildenhall Town)
Haverhill Rovers 3 Saffron Walden Town 1

RESERVES CUP

FINAL *(March 27th at Hadleigh United)*
Witham Town Res. 3 Haverhill Rovers Res. 0

RESERVES TROPHY

FINAL *(April 21st at Bury Town)*
Wroxham Res. 2 Tiptree United Res. 1

Reserve Division (North)	P	W	D	L	F	A	Pts
Bury Town Res.	22	17	1	4	77	21	52
Diss Town Res.	22	13	4	5	39	34	43
Felixstowe & Walton Res.	22	13	2	7	58	32	41
Whitton United Res.	22	12	3	7	46	31	39
Walsham-le-Willows Res.	22	10	4	8	43	35	34
Woodbridge Town Res.	22	8	4	10	41	42	28
Ipswich Wanderers Res.	22	7	6	9	36	49	27
Debenham Leis. Centre Res.	22	7	5	10	41	46	26
Stowmarket Town Res.	22	8	1	13	33	51	25
Leiston Res.	22	6	5	11	32	47	23
Needham Market Res.	22	6	4	12	28	46	22
Thetford Town Res.	22	4	3	15	26	67	15

Reserve Division (South)		P	W	D	L	F	A	Pts
Stanway Rovers Res.		22	16	3	3	59	25	51
Witham Town Res.		22	13	5	4	59	25	44
Haverhill Rovers Res.		22	14	2	6	67	43	44
Wivenhoe Town Res.		22	13	5	4	44	22	44
AFC Sudbury Res.		22	11	3	8	42	37	36
Halstead Town Res.	-1	22	10	4	8	47	45	33
Braintree Town Res.		22	9	4	9	50	41	31
Clacton Town Res.		22	7	5	10	31	39	26
Harwich & Parkeston Res.		22	6	4	12	39	69	22
Tiptree United Res.		22	5	5	12	37	37	20
Long Melford Res.		22	3	2	17	18	59	11
Hadleigh United Res.		22	2	4	16	18	69	10

RESERVES CHAMPIONSHIP

(Reserve Division (North) champions v Reserve Division (South) champions)

(May 8th at Cornard United)
Bury Town Res. 2 **Stanway Rovers Res.** 3

ESSEX OLYMPIAN LEAGUE

	Bishop's Stortford Swifts	Canning Town	Epping	Frenford Senior	Galleywood	Harold Wood Athletic	Kelvedon Hatch	Manford Way	Mountnessing	Roydon	Takeley	White Ensign	White Notley
Bishop's Stortford Swifts	D	0-2	0-2	1-4	1-0	0-0	3-1	4-0	0-2	5-0	2-2	0-1	3-1
Canning Town	0-3	I	2-1	2-2	0-2	2-3	1-0	1-1	3-2	2-1	2-2	3-1	5-1
Epping	3-0	0-3	V	1-3	2-2	0-1	3-2	1-0	1-3	3-1	0-3	3-0	0-1
Frenford Senior	1-2	0-2	1-1	I	2-0	2-0	1-5	2-1	1-2	3-0	2-2	1-2	2-0
Galleywood	1-2	0-2	1-0	1-1	S	0-1	0-0	2-2	2-0	3-0	3-0	1-1	
Harold Wood Athletic	4-0	4-0	0-3	4-0	0-1	I	2-4	0-1	2-3	3-0	0-1	2-0	2-3
Kelvedon Hatch	2-1	2-1	2-0	0-0	3-0	0-1	O	4-3	2-1	2-1	4-1	5-2	4-2
Manford Way	2-1	0-0	0-1	1-1	2-0	0-0	2-3	N	2-0	5-1	2-0	1-1	2-0
Mountnessing	3-0	4-1	1-0	2-1	0-2	1-1	1-3	2-1		8-1	2-3	2-5	1-5
Roydon	2-1	0-4	0-1	2-1	1-2	1-2	1-0	0-3	1-7		1-2	0-2	1-3
Takeley	1-1	4-2	2-1	2-1	3-2	0-1	2-4	3-1	2-4	2-2	O	0-5	4-3
White Ensign	1-2	1-0	2-1	3-0	3-2	3-2	5-2	3-1	3-2	3-0	5-1	N	3-0
White Notley	0-0	1-1	1-1	0-0	1-2	4-0	1-2	2-2	2-3	4-0	1-3	2-4	E

WWW.CHERRYRED.CO.UK

Division One

	P	W	D	L	F	A	Pts
White Ensign	24	17	1	6	58	35	52
Kelvedon Hatch	24	16	2	6	57	36	50
Takeley	24	12	5	7	48	50	41
Mountnessing	24	12	2	10	56	45	38
Canning Town	24	11	5	8	41	35	38
Harold Wood Athletic	24	10	3	11	34	31	33
Galleywood	24	9	6	9	31	30	33
Manford Way	24	8	8	8	33	29	32
Bishop's Stortford Swifts	24	9	4	11	32	35	31
Epping	24	8	4	12	28	31	28
Frenford Senior	24	7	7	10	32	36	28
White Notley	24	7	6	11	40	44	27
Roydon	24	3	1	20	17	70	10

SENIOR CHALLENGE CUP
(Division One champions v Senior Cup holders)

(September 2nd at Frenford Senior)
Harold Wood Athletic 0 **Frenford Senior** 2

ESSEX OLYMPIAN LEAGUE PREMIER DIVISION (FORMERLY DIVISION ONE) CONSTITUTION 2007-08

BENFLEET . . . . The Club House, Woodside Extension, Manor Road, Benfleet, Rayleigh SS7 4BG 01268 743957
BISHOP'S STORTFORD SWIFTS . . Silver Leys, Hadham Road (A1250), Bishop's Stortford CM23 2QE 01279 658941
CANNING TOWN . . . . Gooseleys Playing Fields, St Albans Avenue, East Ham E6 6HQ . . . . None
EPPING . . . . Stonards Hill Rec Ground, Tidy's Lane, Epping CM16 6SP . . . . None
FRENFORD SENIOR . . . . Oakfields Sports Ground, Forest Road, Barkingside IG6 3HD 020 8500 1998
GALLEYWOOD . . . . Clarkes Field, Slades Lane, Galleywood, Chelmsford CM2 8RW 01245 352975
HAROLD WOOD ATHLETIC . . . . Harold Wood Recreation Park, Harold View, Harold Wood RM3 0LX 01708 348827
KELVEDON HATCH . . . . New Hall, School Road, Kelvedon Hatch, Brentwood CM15 0DH 01277 372153
MANFORD WAY . . . . London Marathon Sports Ground, Forest Road, Hainault IG6 3HJ 020 8500 3486
MOUNTNESSING . . . . The Football Academy, Sports Pavilion, Langston Road, Loughton IG10 3TQ 0870 084 2111
SHELL CLUB CORRINGHAM . . . . Shell Club, Springhouse Road, Corringham SS17 7QT 01375 673100
TAKELEY . . . . Station Rd (adjacent to rail bridge), Takeley, Bishop's Stortford CM22 6SG 01279 870404
WHITE ENSIGN . . . . Borough Football Comb. HQ, Eastwoodbury Lane, Southend-on-Sea SS2 6XG . . . . None
IN: Benfleet (P), Shell Club Corringham (P)
OUT: Roydon (P), White Notley (S – Essex & Suffolk Border League Division One)

Reserve Division One

	P	W	D	L	F	A	Pts
Harold Wood Ath. Res.	24	15	6	3	74	33	51
Frenford Senior Res.	24	16	3	5	68	31	51
Canning Town Res.	24	15	5	4	48	22	50
Manford Way Res.	24	13	7	4	50	25	46
Epping Res.	24	10	8	6	54	35	38
White Ensign Res.	24	12	0	12	44	48	36
Rayleigh Town Res.	24	10	3	11	38	40	33
B. Stortf'd Swifts Res.	24	9	4	11	39	55	31
Galleywood Res.	24	7	5	12	33	53	26
Old Chelmsf'd Res. +3	24	7	1	16	35	55	25
Ryan Res.	24	7	3	14	25	56	24
Shenfield Assoc. Res.	24	5	2	17	34	64	17
Kelvedon Hatch Res. -3	24	5	3	16	32	57	15

Reserve Division Two

	P	W	D	L	F	A	Pts
Shell Club C'ham Res.	22	15	5	2	64	20	50
Runwell Hospital Res.	22	14	3	5	44	23	45
Faces Res.	22	14	2	6	49	41	44
Herongate Ath. Res.	22	14	1	7	52	29	43
Takeley Res.	22	12	1	9	43	38	37
Hutton Res.	22	9	6	7	37	27	33
Hannakins Farm Res.	22	7	5	10	34	38	26
White Notley Res.	22	7	5	10	36	43	26
Ramsden Res.	22	5	5	12	28	45	20
Metpol Chigwell Res.	22	5	4	13	27	52	19
Sandon Royals Res.	22	5	2	15	27	57	17
Roydon Res.	22	4	3	15	28	56	15

Reserve Division Three

	P	W	D	L	F	A	Pts
M & B Club Res.	22	17	4	1	59	24	55
Basildon Town Res.	22	14	3	5	44	16	45
Potter Street Res.	22	13	1	8	63	45	40
Mountnessing Res.	22	11	3	8	39	41	36
Writtle Res.	22	10	2	10	41	47	32
Westhamians Res. +3	22	8	3	11	33	39	30
Leigh Ramblers Res. -3	22	9	4	9	44	46	28
Benfleet Res.	22	8	3	11	35	39	27
Broomfield Res.	22	6	7	9	35	39	25
Leytonstone Utd Res.	22	6	4	12	35	45	22
Springfield Res.	22	6	2	14	35	60	20
Barnston Res.	22	6	0	16	32	54	18

	Benfleet	Faces	Herongate	Leigh Ramb.	O. C'fordians	Ongar Town	Rayleigh Town	Ryan	Sandon Royals	Shell Club	Shenfield Ass.	Springfield	Stambridge U.	Upminster
Benfleet		1-2	1-1	5-2	3-1	2-1	2-2	5-1	3-0	2-0	6-1	6-0	3-0	3-0
Faces	1-2	D	1-1	2-0	4-1	2-1	3-0	1-3	4-2	1-4	2-2	3-2	4-2	9-2
Herongate Athletic	1-1	0-2	I	0-1	1-0	2-2	3-1	3-5	1-1	1-2	2-1	1-2	2-1	2-1
Leigh Ramblers	0-6	1-7	2-3	V	5-3	0-3	1-1	3-4	4-0	2-2	4-0	1-0	1-2	9-1
Old Chelmsfordians	0-2	0-3	2-1	4-1	I	1-2	2-3	1-2	0-1	2-0	2-2	1-1	W-L	
Ongar Town	1-2	3-0	4-2	4-3	1-0	S	3-1	2-2	4-0	2-1	3-0	4-3	1-2	W-L
Rayleigh Town	0-10	1-2	3-2	2-2	1-2	4-3	I	1-2	1-2	2-3	1-1	2-0	0-2	3-0
Ryan	0-1	1-3	3-0	0-1	1-2	1-5	2-4	O	0-2	2-1	2-3	W-L		2-1
Sandon Royals	0-2	2-4	0-1	3-1	1-5	0-1	2-1	W-L	N	0-0	2-0	2-1	1-1	2-1
Shell Corringham	1-1	7-2	4-0	3-0	3-1	4-2	3-0	1-0	2-0		7-0	6-1	2-1	4-1
Shenfield Association	1-2	1-1	2-1	1-2	0-2	0-2	1-3	2-1	2-3	0-3	T	2-0	2-2	3-2
Springfield	1-4	2-2	3-6	3-0	5-3	1-0	4-0	1-3	1-0	1-6	2-0	W	0-0	4-3
Stambridge United	0-1	1-3	1-0	0-2	2-3	0-3	2-2	4-1	2-1	0-3	1-1	2-0	O	3-2
Upminster	1-5	2-6	0-7	2-2	1-0	2-4	0-1	3-6	1-1	0-4	1-5	1-2	0-0	

Division One	P	W	D	L	F	A	Pts
Benfleet	26	21	4	1	81	18	67
Shell Club Corringham	26	21	3	2	77	20	66
Ongar Town	26	17	2	7	61	35	53
Faces	26	17	4	5	74	44	52
Old Chelmsfordians	26	10	2	14	39	46	35
Ryan	26	11	1	14	47	51	34
Stambridge United	26	9	6	11	33	39	33
Springfield	26	10	3	13	44	61	33
Herongate Athletic	26	9	5	12	44	46	32
Sandon Royals	26	9	4	13	27	44	31
Rayleigh Town	26	8	5	13	40	59	29
Leigh Ramblers	26	8	4	14	49	62	28
Shenfield Association	26	5	5	16	29	62	20
Upminster	26	1	4	21	28	86	7

ESSEX OLYMPIAN LEAGUE DIVISION ONE (FORMERLY DIVISION TWO) CONSTITUTION 2007-08

FACES .... Ford Sports & Social Club, Aldbrough Road South, Newbury Park, Ilford IG3 8HG 020 8590 3797
HERONGATE ATHLETIC........ Adjacent to 77 Billericay Road, Herongate, Brentwood CM13 3PU 01277 811260
LEIGH RAMBLERS................ Belfairs Park, Eastwood Road North, Leigh-on-Sea SS9 4LR. 01702 421077
LEYTONSTONE UNITED.....:........ Ilford Wanderers RFC, Forest Road, Hainault IG6 3HJ 020 8500 4622
M & B CLUB .... M & B Sports & Social Club, Dagenham Road, Dagenham RM10 .... 020 8919 2427
OLD CHELMSFORDIANS .... Lawford Lane, Roxwell Road, Chelmsford CM1 2NS............................. 01245 420442
ONGAR TOWN........................ Love Lane, High Street, Ongar CM5 9BL................................... 01277 363838
POTTER STREET.................... Minton Lane, Church Langley Country Park, Harlow .... None
RAYLEIGH TOWN.............. Rayleigh Town Sports/Soc. Club, London Road, Rayleigh SS6 9HR................. 01268 784001
ROYDON .... Roydon Playing Fields, Harlow Road, Roydon, Harlow CM19 5HE .... None
RYAN .... Old Parmiters Sports Ground, 102a Nelson Road, Chingford E4 9AS .... None
SANDON ROYALS .... Sandon Sports Club, Rectory Chase, Sandon, Chelmsford CM2 7SQ 01245 476626
SPRINGFIELD .... Springfield Hall Park, Arun Close, Springfield, Chelmsford CM1 7QE .... None
STAMBRIDGE UNITED .. Stambridge Recreation Ground, Rochford Rd, Great Stambridge, Rochford SS4 2AX 01702 258988
IN: Leytonstone United (P), M & B Club (P), Potter Street (P), Roydon (R)
OUT: Benfleet (P), Shell Club Corringham (P), Shenfield Association (R), Upminster (R)

SENIOR CUP

(All teams from Divisions One, Two and Three)

FIRST ROUND

Frenford Senior 5 Leytonstone Utd 3 aet
Linford Wanderers 0 **Kelvedon Hatch** 12
Manford Way 1 **Mountnessing** 2
Ongar Town 4 Broomfield 0
Ramsden 1 **Old Chelmsfordians** 3
Roydon 0 **Potter Street** 1
Runwell Hospital 0 **Harold Wood Ath.** 6
Takeley 3 Metropolitan Police Chigwell 0
Westhamians 3 **Hutton** 4
White Ensign 3 Herongate Athletic 2

SECOND ROUND

Bishop's Stortford Swifts 3 **Upminster** 4
Canning Town 0 **Potter Street** 4
Galleywood 1 **Harold Wood Athletic** 4
Great Baddow 1 **Barnston** 2
Hannakins Farm 0 **Ryan** 2

Mountnessing 4 Basildon Town 4 (3-1p)
Old Chelmsfordians 0 **Frenford Senior** 4
Ongar Town 3 **Kelvedon Hatch** 4
Rayleigh Town 1 **White Notley** 3
Sandon Royals 2 Benfleet 1
Shell Club Corringham 0 **Epping** 2
Shenfield Association 3 **M & B Club** 4
Springfield 0 **Hutton** 1
Stambridge United 0 **White Ensign** 1
Takeley 5 Faces 2
Writtle 5 Leigh Ramblers 0

Potter Street 3 Epping 1
Ryan 9 Upminster 0
Takeley 3 **White Notley** 4
White Ensign 2 Sandon Royals 1 aet

THIRD ROUND

Barnston 3 Writtle 2
Frenford Senior 0 **Kelvedon Hatch** 2
Hutton 1 **Harold Wood Athletic** 3
Mountnessing 3 M & B Club 0

QUARTER-FINALS

Barnston 0 **White Ensign** 6
Potter Street 2 Harold Wood Athletic 1
Ryan 0 **Kelvedon Hatch** 1
White Notley 0 **Mountnessing** 2

SEMI-FINALS

Mountnessing 2 **White Ensign** 4
Potter Street 0 **Kelvedon Hatch** 2

FINAL

(May 15th at Billericay Town)
Kelvedon Hatch 2 White Ensign 0

	Barnston	Basildon Town	Broomfield	Great Baddow	Hannakins Farm	Hutton	Leytonstone United	Linford Wanderers	M & B Club	Met. Police Chigwell	Potter Street	Ramsden	Runwell Hospital	Westhamians	Writtle
Barnston	D	0-4	2-2	4-1	3-5	1-1	1-3	3-1	1-4	0-3	1-3	5-2	2-4	1-3	3-1
Basildon Town	1-2	I	1-2	7-1	2-1	3-3	1-2	4-0	1-7	2-2	1-2	1-4	3-1	4-2	2-2
Broomfield	3-0	3-0	V	1-1	3-1	2-3	0-1	4-2	0-8	4-0	1-2	1-3	4-2	1-1	1-4
Great Baddow	3-0	3-2	2-2	I	1-0	1-1	1-0	7-0	2-9	0-2	1-2	2-1	7-1	2-1	0-2
Hannakins Farm	3-2	2-1	5-1	1-2	S	1-2	1-2	8-1	3-1	0-0	2-4	2-1	9-1	2-4	3-3
Hutton	1-1	0-2	3-0	2-0	3-3	I	3-1	5-0	2-2	1-3	1-2	0-2	3-2	W-L	2-3
Leytonstone United	4-0	0-6	W-L	3-2	1-3		O	3-1	1-0	0-2	1-1	0-2	1-1	3-2	3-0
Linford Wanderers	1-6	0-5	1-4	1-6	2-2	0-5	2-3	N	1-10	1-2	0-6	1-5	3-3	1-4	1-3
M & B Club	5-1	2-3	4-1	3-4	5-0	2-1	2-1	6-4		3-3	W-L	1-2	1-2	2-2	2-3
Met. Police Chigwell	3-1	2-1	1-0	4-1	4-2	0-5	2-0	5-1	1-2		3-1	3-1	7-2	3-2	1-3
Potter Street	2-0	2-3	4-0	4-0	1-0	0-0	2-2	6-1	2-6	6-1	T	5-0	11-1	4-3	4-0
Ramsden	1-1	2-2	1-0	2-2	4-2	2-2	4-4	8-1	2-3	3-2	3-2	H	2-1	4-3	1-4
Runwell Hospital	0-3	1-4	2-3	4-0	1-2	0-4	0-5	2-1	2-3	1-5	0-3	1-4	R	1-0	3-4
Westhamians	3-2	1-3	2-4	1-2	1-4	2-4	0-1	5-2	1-3	2-2	0-3	1-2	1-6	E	0-3
Writtle	2-0	1-2	3-1	1-1	0-5	3-2	0-2	2-0	1-1	4-1	1-5	1-2	0-2	6-1	E

Division Three		P	W	D	L	F	A	Pts
Potter Street		28	21	2	5	90	31	65
M & B Club		28	17	4	7	98	48	55
Leytonstone United		28	17	4	7	57	40	55
Met. Police Chigwell	+3	28	16	4	8	65	50	52
Ramsden		28	15	6	7	69	54	51
Hutton		28	13	8	7	62	39	47
Basildon Town		28	14	4	10	71	50	46
Writtle	-3	28	15	4	9	60	51	46
Great Baddow		28	12	5	11	55	61	41
Hannakins Farm		28	11	5	12	72	58	38
Broomfield		28	10	4	14	48	59	34
Barnston		28	7	4	17	46	69	25
Runwell Hospital		28	7	1	20	48	97	22
Westhamians		28	5	3	20	47	74	18
Linford Wanderers		28	0	2	26	29	136	2

ESSEX OLYMPIAN LEAGUE DIVISION TWO (FORMERLY DIVISION THREE) CONSTITUTION 2007-08

BARNSTON............................High Easter Road, Barnston, Dunmow CM6 1LZ.............................01371 876364
BASILDON TOWN.....GEC Avionics Sports Ground, Gardiners Lane South, Gardiners Way, Basildon SS14 3AP..........01268 883128
BROOMFIELD..................The Angel Meadow, Main Road, Broomfield, Chelmsford CM1 7AH.....................01245 443819
GREAT BADDOW...........Great Baddow Rec, Baddow Road, Great Baddow, Chelmsford CM2 9RL.....................01245 475899
HANNAKINS FARM..................Hannakins Farm, Rosebay Avenue, Billicay CM12 0SY.....................01277 630851
HUTTON...................Polo Fields, Hall Green Lane, Hutton, Brentwood CM13 2QT.....................01277 262257
LINFORD WANDERERS....................Lakeside Pitches, Thurrock RM20 2ZL.................................None
METROPOLITAN POLICE CHIGWELL..Met Police Sports Club, High Road, Chigwell IG7 6BD.............020 8500 1017/2735
NEWHAM UNITED................Southern Road Playing Fields, Cave Road, Plaistow E13 0HZ.....................07939 788048
RAMSDEN...............Nursery Sports Ground, Downham Road, Ramsden Heath, Billericay CM11 1PU.............01268 711502
RUNWELL HOSPITAL...............Runwell Hospital, Runwell Chase, Wickford SS11 7QE.....................01268 562967
SHENFIELD ASSOCIATION................The Drive, Warley, Brentwood CM13 3BH.............................None
UPMINSTER...............Hall Lane Playing Fields, Hall Lane, Upminster, Romford RM14 1AU.............01708 220320
WESTHAMIANS....................Fairlop Oak Playing Fields, Forest Road, Hainault IG6 3HT.....................None
WRITTLE....................Paradise Road Playing Fields, Writtle, Chelmsford CM1 3HW.............01245 420332
IN: Newham United (P – Essex Business Houses League Premier Division), Shenfield Association (R), Upminster (R)
OUT: Leytonstone United (P), M & B Club (P), Potter Street (P)

DENNY KING MEMORIAL CUP
(All teams eliminated from Rounds One and Two of the Senior Cup)

FIRST ROUND   *(The 2006-07 competition was then abandoned*
Ramsden 4 Roydon 2   *due to the wet weather)*

RESERVE DIVISIONS CHALLENGE CUP
(Reserve Div One champions v Reserve Div Cup holders)

(September 16th at Harold Wood Athletic)
Frenford Senior Res. 2 Harold Wood Athletic Res. 1

RESERVE DIVISIONS CUP
(All Reserve Division teams)

(May 8th at Billericay Town)
Shell Club Res. 2 Harold Wood Athletic Res. 2 *aet* (5-4p)

ESSEX SENIOR LEAGUE

	Barking	Barkingside	Basildon United	Beaumont Athletic	Bowers & Pitsea	Brentwood Town	Burnham Ramblers	Clapton	Concord Rangers	Eton Manor	Hullbridge Sports	London APSA	Romford	Sawbridgeworth Town	Southend Manor	Stansted
Barking		1-4	2-3	6-1	2-1	1-2	3-0	1-0	4-1	3-2	0-1	2-0	4-4	1-1	2-1	5-0
Barkingside	2-0		0-0	4-1	1-2	1-1	1-1	3-1	2-1	2-0	3-0	1-0	1-2	1-1	3-0	8-1
Basildon United	1-2	1-1		2-0	0-1	0-0	2-1	2-1	1-0	2-1	5-0	3-0	1-3	0-5	1-2	0-0
Beaumont Athletic	2-4	3-6	2-4		0-4	0-5	2-5	3-1	2-6	1-1	2-0	3-4	1-8	1-8	0-5	1-1
Bowers & Pitsea	2-2	1-0	0-0	5-1		2-4	0-0	3-1	0-2	3-0	0-0	5-2	1-1	2-1	1-1	14-1
Brentwood Town	0-0	2-1	3-0	7-1	2-1		1-1	1-0	4-0	5-1	5-2	3-1	1-4	1-0	2-1	3-1
Burnham Ramblers	3-1	2-1	1-0	11-0	1-3	0-2		1-2	2-1	2-1	1-0	5-0	1-0	2-0	1-0	3-0
Clapton	0-2	2-2	0-0	2-3	1-2	0-6	2-0		0-3	1-2	0-1	1-1	1-2	1-2	1-2	4-2
Concord Rangers	4-1	1-2	3-2	7-1	0-0	1-1	2-1	2-0		4-2	3-3	2-0	1-0	1-0	1-1	4-2
Eton Manor	1-1	0-2	2-3	6-2	0-1	1-1	0-4	4-3	3-3		1-4	4-0	1-0	1-2	0-0	4-1
Hullbridge Sports	1-4	0-0	0-2	2-2	1-4	0-3	0-2	0-1	0-1	2-1		1-1	0-2	1-1	2-2	0-1
London APSA	1-2	1-2	1-1	3-1	0-2	0-2	1-2	1-1	0-4	1-6	2-0		0-2	0-4	2-0	3-2
Romford	2-2	3-1	3-2	3-0	2-0	1-0	1-1	3-1	3-2	2-2	6-1	5-2		2-0	1-3	1-0
Sawbridgeworth Town	2-2	0-2	2-2	8-1	3-2	0-2	1-0	1-0	2-2	0-1	4-1	1-0	1-2		3-0	4-1
Southend Manor	0-1	0-3	2-1	2-0	2-0	0-1	2-1	1-1	3-1	1-3	2-0	1-1	1-1	3-1		3-0
Stansted	1-4	0-1	0-3	2-4	2-3	0-4	0-4	1-5	0-4	1-1	0-2	1-1	0-6	0-2	0-4	

	P	W	D	L	F	A	Pts
Brentwood Town	30	22	6	2	74	21	72
Romford	30	20	6	4	75	32	66
Barkingside	30	17	7	6	61	28	58
Bowers & Pitsea	30	16	7	7	65	33	55
Burnham Ramblers	30	17	4	9	59	29	55
Barking	30	16	7	7	65	43	55
Concord Rangers	30	16	6	8	67	42	54
Sawbridgeworth Town	30	14	6	10	60	35	48
Southend Manor	30	13	7	10	45	35	46
Basildon United	30	11	9	10	44	40	42
Eton Manor	30	9	7	14	52	57	34
Hullbridge Sports	30	5	8	17	27	61	23
London APSA	30	5	6	19	29	69	21
Clapton	30	5	5	20	34	56	20
Beaumont Athletic	30	4	3	23	41	132	15
Stansted	30	1	4	25	20	105	7

ESSEX SENIOR LEAGUE CONSTITUTION 2007-08

BARKING.........................Mayesbrook Park, Lodge Avenue, Dagenham RM8 2JY.........................020 8595 6511
BARKINGSIDE.............Redbridge FC, Oakside Stadium, Station Road, Barkingside, Ilford IG6 1NB...............020 8550 3611
BASILDON UNITED............The Stadium, Gardiners Close, Gardiners Lane, Basildon SS14 3AN...................01268 520268
BEAUMONT ATHLETIC........Mile End Stadium, Rhodeswell Road, Burdett Road, Poplar E14 7TW...................020 8980 1885
BOWERS & PITSEA..........Ken Salmon Stadium, Crown Avenue, off Kenneth Road, Pitsea, Basildon SS14 2BE...........01268 452068
BURNHAM RAMBLERS...........Leslie Field, Springfield Road, Burnham-on-Crouch CM0 8TE.......................01621 784383
CLAPTON.........................Old Spotted Dog Ground, Upton Lane, Forest Gate E7 9NP...................020 8472 0822/9426
CONCORD RANGERS............Thames Road Stadium, Thames Road, Canvey Island SS8 0HH......................01268 691780
ENFIELD.....................Ware FC, Wodson Park, Wadesmill Road, Ware SG12 0HZ.........................01920 463247
ETON MANOR.....................Tilbury FC, Chadfields, St Chad's Road, Tilbury RM18 8NL......................01375 843093
HULLBRIDGE SPORTS.....................Lower Road, Hullbridge, Hockley SS5 6BJ.............................01702 230420
LONDON APSA...........Terence McMillan Stadium, 281 Prince Regent Lane, Plaistow E13 8SD.................01708 349597
MAURITIUS SPORTS & PENNANT.......Aveley FC, Mill Field, Mill Road, Aveley RM15 4SJ.....................01708 865940
ROMFORD.............Ford Sports & Social Club, Rush Green Road, Rush Green, Romford RM7 0LU...............01708 737457
SAWBRIDGEWORTH TOWN..........Crofters End, West Road, Sawbridgeworth CM21 0DE.........................01279 722039
SOUTHEND MANOR.........Southchurch Park Arena, Lifstan Way, Southend-on-Sea SS1 2TH.....................01702 615577
STANSTED.........................Hargrave Park, Cambridge Road, Stansted CM24 8DL.........................01279 812897
IN: Enfield (W – Isthmian League Division One North), Mauritius Sports & Pennant (an amalgamation of Mauritius Sports CMB and Walthamstow Avenue & Pennant) (P – Middlesex County League Premier Division)
OUT: Brentwood Town (P – Isthmian League Division One North)

LEAGUE CUP

GROUP A

	P	W	D	L	F	A	Pts
Barking	6	5	0	1	21	5	15
Clapton	6	4	0	2	17	7	12
Basildon United	6	2	0	4	8	9	6
Beaumont Athletic	6	1	0	5	7	32	3

Barking 1 Basildon United 0
Barking 13 Beaumont Athletic 0
Barking 0 Clapton 2
Basildon United 1 Barking 2
Basildon United 5 Beaumont Athletic 0
Basildon United 2 Clapton 1
Beaumont Athletic 1 Barking 2
Beaumont Athletic 4 Basildon United 0
Beaumont Athletic 1 Clapton 6
Clapton 1 Barking 3
Clapton 1 Basildon United 0
Clapton 6 Beaumont Athletic 1

GROUP B

	P	W	D	L	F	A	Pts
London APSA	6	5	0	1	14	9	15
Bowers & Pitsea	6	3	1	2	11	7	10
Barkingside	6	2	1	3	8	7	7
Stansted	6	0	2	4	8	18	2

Barkingside 1 Bowers & Pitsea 0
Barkingside 1 London APSA 2
Barkingside 2 Stansted 2
Bowers & Pitsea 2 Barkingside 1
Bowers & Pitsea 3 London APSA 1
Bowers & Pitsea 4 Stansted 1
London APSA 1 Barkingside 0
London APSA 2 Bowers & Pitsea 1
London APSA 5 Stansted 3
Stansted 0 Barkingside 3
Stansted 1 Bowers & Pitsea 1
Stansted 1 London APSA 3

GROUP C

	P	W	D	L	F	A	Pts
Romford	6	5	0	1	16	6	15
Concord Rangers	6	4	0	2	8	5	12
Hullbridge Sports	6	2	0	4	4	10	6
Eton Manor	6	1	0	5	6	13	3

Concord Rangers 1 Eton Manor 0
Concord Rangers 2 Hullbridge Sports 0
Concord Rangers 0 Romford 1
Eton Manor 0 Concord Rangers 1
Eton Manor 1 Hullbridge Sports 2
Eton Manor 1 Romford 3
Hullbridge Sports 1 Concord Rangers 2
Hullbridge Sports 0 Eton Manor 2
Hullbridge Sports 1 Romford 0
Romford 3 Concord Rangers 2
Romford 6 Eton Manor 2
Romford 3 Hullbridge Sports 0

GROUP D

	P	W	D	L	F	A	Pts
Brentwood Town	6	3	2	1	12	6	11
Burnham Ramblers	6	2	1	3	7	8	7
Southend Manor	6	1	4	1	4	5	7
Sawbridgeworth Town	6	1	3	2	4	8	6

Brentwood Town 1 Burnham Ramblers 3
Brentwood Town 3 Sawbridgeworth Town 0
Brentwood Town 1 Southend Manor 1
Burnham Ramblers 1 Brentwood Town 3
Burnham Ramblers 0 Sawbridgeworth Town 2
Burnham Ramblers 0 Southend Manor 1
Sawbridgeworth Town 0 Brentwood Town 3
Sawbridgeworth Town 1 Burnham Ramblers 1
Sawbridgeworth Town 1 Southend Manor 1
Southend Manor 1 Brentwood Town 1
Southend Manor 0 Burnham Ramblers 2
Southend Manor 0 Sawbridgeworth Town 0

Top two teams from each group qualify for knockout stage

QUARTER-FINALS
(played over two legs)
Bowers & Pitsea 3 Barking 3, **Barking** 1 Bowers & Pitsea 0
Brentwood Town 2 Concord Rangers 1, Concord Rangers 0 **Brentwood Town** 1
Burnham Ramblers 3 London APSA 0, London APSA 1 **Burnham Ramblers** 4
Clapton 1 Romford 2, **Romford** 3 Clapton 0

SEMI-FINALS
(played over two legs)
Barking 0 Romford 1, **Romford** 4 Barking 3
Brentwood Town 0 Burnham Ramblers 0, Burnham Ramblers 0 **Brentwood Town** 1

FINAL
(May 7th at Barkingside)
Brentwood Town 1 Romford 1 *aet* (5-4p)

GORDON BRASTED MEMORIAL TROPHY

FIRST ROUND
Barking 1 Burnham Ramblers 0 *aet*
Basildon United 0 **Romford** 1
Brentwood Town 5 Beaumont Athletic 0
Clapton 1 **Barkingside** 2
Eton Manor 4 Hullbridge Sports 1
London APSA 2 Bowers & Pitsea 1
Sawbridgeworth Town 2 **Stansted** 2 *aet* (3-4p)
Southend Manor 1 **Concord Rangers** 1
aet (4-5p)

QUARTER-FINALS
Barkingside 4 Eton Manor 2
Brentwood Town 4 Romford 0
Concord Rangers 1 **Barking** 2
London APSA 2 **Stansted** 2 *aet* (2-4p)

SEMI-FINALS
Barking 0 **Barkingside** 1
Brentwood Town 4 Stansted 0

FINAL *(April 7th at Burnham Ramblers)*
Barkingside 0 **Brentwood Town** 4

ESSEX & SUFFOLK BORDER LEAGUE

	Alresford Colne Rangers	Coggeshall Town	Dedham Old Boys	Earls Colne	Gas Recreation	Great Bentley	Hatfield Peverel	Lawford Lads	Little Oakley	Mistley United	St Osyth	Tiptree Heath	University of Essex	Walton Town	Weeley Athletic	West Bergholt
Alresford Colne Rangers	P	2-0	3-1	1-4	0-2	1-1	3-0	1-1	0-0	2-1	8-0	3-0	0-1	3-0	2-2	1-3
Coggeshall Town	2-2	R	1-2	2-2	2-4	2-0	1-0	5-1	0-1	4-0	5-0	1-0	4-1	4-1	1-1	0-4
Dedham Old Boys	2-2	1-2	E	9-0	1-3	3-2	2-0	4-0	3-0	5-0	3-4	6-1	2-4	1-0	1-2	6-1
Earls Colne	2-2	1-0	1-2	M	1-5	4-2	1-1	2-3	4-3	1-2	W-L	2-0	2-1	3-0	2-3	1-0
Gas Recreation	0-2	5-2	4-3	5-0	I	6-1	5-0	5-2	4-0	8-0	4-1	3-0	3-1	6-0	2-2	4-3
Great Bentley	2-3	1-1	1-0	2-1	0-2	E	0-0	3-0	3-0	3-0	3-1	2-0	0-4	0-1	3-3	2-0
Hatfield Peverel	3-2	0-4	0-1	2-2	0-0	1-2	R	3-0	3-3	3-1	2-0	1-3	1-1	1-1	1-3	0-1
Lawford Lads	0-1	1-1	1-2	2-3	0-5	1-1	1-1		1-2	0-1	4-0	4-3	2-0	2-3	1-1	0-1
Little Oakley	3-8	3-5	0-2	2-1	0-6	2-2	3-0	1-2	D	2-1	4-1	2-2	2-3	4-3	2-0	2-2
Mistley United	0-3	1-1	0-2	2-1	0-3	2-2	2-1	0-4	0-4	I	W-L	1-3	0-5	1-0	0-1	2-3
St Osyth	0-5	3-5	1-1	2-5	0-8	1-1	0-5	3-2	1-3	0-4	V	2-1	3-0	1-2	0-2	3-2
Tiptree Heath	2-1	0-1	2-2	0-1	2-3	1-1	4-1	2-3	1-1	1-4	3-0	I	1-2	3-0	1-0	1-4
University of Essex	2-3	5-1	4-2	3-1	4-4	2-3	5-0	4-1	4-0	5-0	8-0	7-1	S	3-1	6-0	4-5
Walton Town	0-0	1-1	4-2	1-2	0-12	2-3	1-0	1-4	1-0	2-1	3-1	1-1	1-3	I	3-1	0-7
Weeley Athletic	0-2	2-0	4-1	4-1	1-3	4-1	0-1	1-2	1-1	2-2	2-0	0-3	3-2	2-0	O	3-3
West Bergholt	6-0	2-2	3-0	3-1	1-2	1-0	0-1	3-2	2-2	5-0	5-0	6-0	3-2	3-0	5-1	N

Premier Division		P	W	D	L	F	A	Pts
Gas Recreation		30	26	3	1	126	29	81
West Bergholt		30	19	4	7	87	42	61
University of Essex		30	18	2	10	96	49	56
Alresford Colne Rangers		30	15	8	7	66	40	53
Dedham Old Boys		30	15	3	12	72	50	48
Coggeshall Town		30	13	8	9	60	47	47
Weeley Athletic		30	12	8	10	51	52	44
Earls Colne		30	13	4	13	52	64	43
Great Bentley	+2	30	10	10	10	47	51	42
Little Oakley		30	10	7	13	52	67	37
Lawford Lads		30	9	5	16	47	63	32
Tiptree Heath		30	9	5	16	45	65	32
Walton Town		30	9	4	17	33	75	31
Hatfield Peverel		30	7	8	15	32	52	29
Mistley United		30	8	3	19	28	76	27
St Osyth	-1	30	5	2	23	28	100	16

A V LEE MEMORIAL TROPHY
(Premier Division champions v League Cup holders)
(Not contested in 2006-07 due to the previous season's League Cup final being delayed)

ESSEX & SUFFOLK BORDER LEAGUE PREMIER DIVISION CONSTITUTION 2007-08

ALRESFORD COLNE RANGERS . . . . Ford Lane, Alresford, Colchester CO7 8AY 07796 036467
BRIGHTLINGSEA REGENT . . . . North Road, Brightlingsea, Colchester CO7 0PL 01206 304199
COGGESHALL TOWN . . . . The Crops, West Street, Coggeshall CO6 1NS 01376 562843
DEDHAM OLD BOYS . . . . The Old Grammar School, Royal Square, Dedham, Colchester CO7 6AA 01206 322302
EARLS COLNE . . . . Green Farm Meadow, Halstead Road, Earls Colne, Colchester CO6 2NG 01787 223584
GAS RECREATION . . . . Bromley Road, Colchester CO4 3JF 01206 860383
GREAT BENTLEY . . . . The Green, Great Bentley, Colchester CO7 8LX 01206 251532
HATFIELD PEVEREL . . . . Strutt Memorial Field, Maldon Road, Hatfield Peverel CM3 2JP . . . . None
LAWFORD LADS . . . . School Lane, Lawford, Manningtree CO11 2JA 01206 397211
LITTLE OAKLEY . . . . War Memorial Club Ground, Harwich Road, Little Oakley, Harwich CO12 5EB 01255 880370
TEAM BURY . . . . Out Risbygate, Bury St Edmunds IP33 3RL 01284 701301
TIPTREE HEATH . . . . Colchester Road, Tiptree CO5 0EX 07889 463004
UNIVERSITY OF ESSEX . . . . Wivenhoe Town FC, Broad Lane Sports Ground, Wivenhoe CO7 7HA 01206 825380
WALTON TOWN . . . . Frinton Playing Fields, Jubilee Way, Frinton-on-Sea CO13 0AP . . . . None
WEELEY ATHLETIC . . . . Weeley Playing Fields, Clacton Road, Weeley, Clacton-on-Sea CO16 9DH . . . . None
WEST BERGHOLT . . . . Lorkin Daniel Field, Lexden Road, West Bergholt, Colchester CO6 3BW 01206 241525

IN: Brightlingsea Regent (P), Team Bury (formerly West Suffolk College) (P)
OUT: Mistley United (R), St Osyth (R)

	Alresford Colne Rgrs Res.	Boxted Lodgers	Bradfield Rovers	Brightlingsea Regent	Bures United	Coggeshall Town Res.	Dedham Old Boys Res.	Gas Recreation Res.	Glemsford/Cavendish Utd	Gosfield United	Kelvedon Social	Mersea Island	Mistley United Res.	Weeley Athletic Res.	West Bergholt Res.	West Suffolk College
Alresford Colne Rangers Res.		1-2	4-4	1-1	3-2	3-4	2-0	2-2	3-1	0-2	3-1	2-0	W-L	8-0	4-3	3-0
Boxted Lodgers	2-0		3-2	0-1	2-1	3-0	2-1	3-2	1-0	1-0	3-2	1-2	2-2	1-2	2-2	2-0
Bradfield Rovers	5-5	2-3	D	2-4	1-1	2-2	5-2	2-0	1-4	2-0	3-5	2-4	2-1	3-3	1-3	
Brightlingsea Regent	4-2	1-2	7-1	I	3-0	2-1	2-0	8-1	4-2	1-1	W-L	2-0	6-0	2-4	1-0	1-4
Bures United	7-0	0-0	2-1	2-6	V	1-1	0-4	1-1	2-2	2-4	4-1	0-1	2-1	3-0	5-1	4-1
Coggeshall Town Res.	2-0	0-7	0-0	1-5	0-2	I	2-0	4-4	3-2	1-2	2-4	2-1	4-1	1-1	1-1	0-5
Dedham Old Boys Res.	1-3	4-2	3-4	1-3	1-2	6-0	S	0-3	4-0	1-2	0-1	3-2	3-2	4-0	1-1	3-3
Gas Recreation Res.	4-3	2-3	4-2	3-2	2-2	0-2	5-2	I	2-4	4-4	2-2	3-2	4-1	5-1	2-1	0-5
Glemsford & Cavendish United	1-4	1-3	3-4	1-2	4-1	1-1	0-3	1-2	O	1-6	1-3	1-4	2-3	4-2	3-3	1-3
Gosfield United	4-1	2-2	4-3	1-2	3-2	2-3	0-2	2-1	2-1	N	5-3	5-1	4-2	2-2	2-2	1-2
Kelvedon Social	5-1	2-3	2-1	1-1	0-4	1-2	2-1	1-4	1-1	1-3		4-1	1-1	7-0	1-2	1-2
Mersea Island	2-1	2-3	2-1	2-2	4-1	1-1	2-0	3-2	6-0	0-3	1-4	O	1-4	W-L	1-5	1-1
Mistley United Res.	2-2	1-2	5-0	1-2	2-2	4-1	4-2	1-2	6-1	4-3	5-2	6-0	N	5-1	2-2	2-3
Weeley Athletic Res.	1-2	2-1	3-2	0-7	2-2	0-4	0-2	3-0	2-3	0-9	2-1	0-3	1-2	E	1-5	0-2
West Bergholt Res.	0-0	1-1	1-3	3-2	3-0	3-1	3-0	3-2	1-1	1-2	2-3	4-2	4-3	2-2		2-1
West Suffolk College	4-1	6-1	7-2	1-0	4-1	2-2	1-2	W-L	2-0	3-1	7-2	3-3	1-1	6-2	4-0	

WWW.CHERRYRED.CO.UK

Division One	P	W	D	L	F	A	Pts
W. Suffolk Col. +3	30	20	5	5	86	40	68
Bright'sea Regent	30	20	4	6	84	38	64
Boxted Lodgers -4	30	19	5	6	63	44	58
Gosfield United	30	17	5	8	85	54	56
W. B'holt Res. +2	30	11	11	8	64	56	46
Gas Rec. Res.	30	13	6	11	71	70	45
Mersea Island	30	13	4	13	58	67	43
Mistley Utd Res.	30	12	6	12	77	60	42
Alresford CR Res.	30	12	6	12	64	66	42
Coggeshall T. Res.	30	11	8	11	52	67	41
Bures United	30	10	8	12	58	58	38
Kelvedon Social	30	10	4	16	57	65	34
Dedham Res. -3	30	11	2	17	55	58	32
Bradfield Rovers	30	7	6	17	65	89	27
Weeley A. Res. +3	30	6	3	21	35	100	24
Glemsford & CU	30	4	5	21	43	85	17

FIRST ROUND
Alresford Colne Rangers 5 Bradfield Rovers 1
Boxted Lodgers 1 **Little Oakley** 2
Bures United 1 **Foxash Social** 2
Dedham Old Boys 1 Brightlingsea Regent 0
Gosfield United 1 **West Suffolk College** 2
Great Bradfords 2 Kelvedon Social 0
Hedinghams 4 Mistley United 3
Holland 4 Glemsford & Cavendish United 1
Lawford Lads 8 Mersea Island 1
Sudbury Athletic 0 **Weeley Athletic** 4
Tiptree Heath 4 St Osyth 1
University of Essex 4 Hatfield Peverel 1
Walton Town 2 Earls Colne 1
West Bergholt 2 Gas Recreation 0

SECOND ROUND
Alresford CR 3 Little Oakley 2
Dedham OB 2 Tiptree Heath 1
Great Bentley 5 Holland 3 *aet*
Great Bradfords 0 **Coggeshall** 1
Mistley United 2 Lawford Lads 0
University of Essex 7 Foxash 1
Walton Town 2 Weeley Athletic 1
West Suffolk College 2 **West Bergholt** 4

QUARTER-FINALS
Alresford CR 2 West Bergholt 1
Dedham Old Boys 7 Mistley 2
Gt Bentley 1 **Univ. of Essex** 2
Walton Town 1 **Coggeshall** 3

SEMI-FINALS
Dedham OB 6 Coggeshall 2
University of Essex 3 Alresford Colne Rangers 1

FINAL
(April 18th at AFC Sudbury)
Univ. of Essex 2 Dedham OB 1

LEAGUE CUP

ESSEX & SUFFOLK BORDER LEAGUE DIVISION ONE CONSTITUTION 2007-08

BOXTED LODGERS . . . . The Playing Field, Cage Lane, Boxted, Colchester CO4 5RE 01206 271969
BRADFIELD ROVERS . . . . The Playing Field, The Street, Bradfield, Manningtree CO11 2UU . . . . None
BURES UNITED . . . . Recreation Ground, Nayland Road, Bures CO8 5BX . . . . None
FOXASH SOCIAL . . . . Foxash Playing Field, Harwich Road, Lawford, Manningtree CO11 2LP 01206 231309
GLEMSFORD & CAVENDISH UTD . . . . . . Memorial Hall, Melford Road, Cavendish CO10 8AA . . . . None
GOSFIELD UNITED . . . . The Playing Field, Gosfield, Halstead . . . . None
GREAT BRADFORDS . . . . Notley Sports Centre, Notley Road, Braintree CM7 1WX 01376 323873
HEDINGHAMS UNITED . . . . Lawn Meadow, Yeldham Road, Sible Hedingham, Halstead CO9 3QJ . . . . None
HOLLAND . . . . Eastcliff Sports Ground, Dulwich Road, Holland-on-Sea CO15 5HR 01255 814874
KELVEDON SOCIAL . . . . The Chase, High Street, Kelvedon, Colchester CO5 9JD 01376 572240
MERSEA ISLAND . . . . The Glebe, Colchester Road, West Mersea CO5 8JZ 01206 385216
MISTLEY UNITED . . . . Furze Hill, Shrubland Road, Mistley CO11 1HS 01206 392714
ROWHEDGE . . . . Rectory Road, Rowhedge CO5 7HP 01206 728022
ST OSYTH . . . . Cowley Park, Mill Street, St Osyth, Clacton-on-Sea CO16 8EJ . . . . None
SUDBURY ATHLETIC . . . . Lucas Social Club, Alexandra Road, Sudbury CO10 2XH 01787 881143
WHITE NOTLEY . . . . Oak Farm, Faulkbourne, Witham CM8 1ST 01376 519864

IN: Foxash Social (P), Great Bradfords (P), Hedinghams United (P), Holland (P), Mistley United (R), Rowhedge (N), St Osyth (R), Sudbury Athletic (P), White Notley (S – Essex Olympian League Division One)
OUT: Alresford Colne Rangers Reserves (R – Reserve Premier Division), Brightlingsea Regent (P), Coggeshall Town Reserves (R – Reserve Premier Division), Dedham Old Boys Reserves (R – Reserve Premier Division), Gas Recreation Reserves (R – Reserve Premier Division), Mistley United Reserves (R – Reserve Premier Division), Team Bury (formerly West Suffolk College) (P), Weeley Athletic Reserves (R – Reserve Premier Division), West Bergholt Reserves (R – Reserve Premier Division)

Note – Walton Town Reserves withdrew during the course of the season Their results are shown herein but are expunged from the league table	Boxted Lodgers Res.	Brightlingsea Regent Res.	Bures United Res.	Earls Colne Res.	Foxash Social	Great Bentley Res.	Great Bradfords	Hatfield Peverel Res.	Hedinghams United	Holland	Kelvedon Social Res.	Lawford Lads Res.	Little Oakley Res.	Mersea Island Res.	Sudbury Athletic	Walton Town Res.
Boxted Lodgers Res.		1-2	2-0	0-6	0-8	1-1	0-3	0-1	3-7	2-6	2-3	1-2	0-6	3-0	2-1	n/a
Brightlingsea Reg. Res.	1-0		1-0	0-1	1-0	0-0	2-3	3-1	1-2	1-2	2-1	2-0	0-4	2-2	1-4	1-1
Bures United Res.	2-2	0-5	D	1-6	0-7	1-4	1-2	3-5	L-W	L-W	5-3	2-7	0-3	2-0	1-9	n/a
Earls Colne Res.	2-1	3-1	4-0	I	0-4	1-1	6-1	1-2	1-4	0-6	2-1	2-3	0-3	2-0	2-5	3-0
Foxash Social	3-1	1-0	1-0	1-0	V	0-0	1-2	4-0	1-1	1-0	6-0	3-0	4-0	1-0	1-1	5-1
Great Bentley Res.	4-0	1-1	W-L	1-2	1-2	I	0-1	2-2	1-3	0-2	3-0	1-5	0-5	W-L	0-5	1-0
Great Bradfords	5-2	2-0	5-2	2-0	3-1	3-0	S	4-0	3-0	1-1	7-1	4-0	2-1	2-2	2-3	6-2
Hatfield Peverel Res.	2-1	1-3	1-1	0-0	0-4	1-2	0-3	I	1-3	2-5	6-2	0-2	2-3	2-1	1-3	n/a
Hedinghams United	3-2	3-2	4-1	2-1	4-2	1-2	4-3	3-0	O	0-3	7-4	1-0	2-4	7-0	1-2	3-1
Holland	8-0	3-1	2-0	0-2	1-1	3-2	4-1	2-0	8-0	N	10-0	6-2	0-0	3-1	0-0	5-2
Kelvedon Social Res.	3-5	3-2	1-2	0-0	0-5	2-3	0-4	0-4	1-4	0-14		1-1	2-2	7-4	1-4	n/a
Lawford Lads Res.	0-0	2-1	4-0	0-3	1-4	3-0	2-7	2-1	2-5	1-6	2-2	T	1-4	0-0	0-2	W-L
Little Oakley Res.	4-1	1-0	W-L	3-1	2-2	4-3	1-5	4-0	2-1	5-2	8-1	4-0	W	9-0	1-1	n/a
Mersea Island Res.	0-7	0-3	W-L	3-1	1-2	0-7	0-3	1-2	0-3	0-7	2-1	1-1	3-5	O	0-3	n/a
Sudbury Athletic	7-1	1-0	5-1	2-0	0-2	6-1	1-1	4-1	5-1	4-3	4-2	2-3	0-0	3-2		4-1
Walton Town Res.	n/a	n/a	5-1	n/a	n/a	n/a	2-9	n/a	n/a	n/a	n/a	n/a	n/a	n/a	2-9	

Division Two	P	W	D	L	F	A	Pts
Great Bradfords	28	21	3	4	84	35	66
Sudbury Athletic	28	20	5	3	87	31	65
Little Oakley Res.	28	20	5	3	88	33	65
Holland	28	20	4	4	107	27	64
Foxash Social	28	19	5	4	72	19	62
Hedinghams United	28	19	1	8	76	55	58
Earls Colne Res.	28	12	3	13	49	47	39
Lawford Lads Res.	28	10	5	13	46	65	35
Great Bentley Res.	28	9	6	13	40	54	33
Brigh'sea Reg. Res. -3	28	10	3	15	38	42	30
Hatfield Peverel Res.	28	8	3	17	38	66	27
Boxted Lodgers Res.	28	5	3	20	40	90	18
Kelvedon Soc. Res. +3	28	3	4	21	42	120	16
Mersea Island Res.	28	3	4	21	23	88	13
Bures United Res.	28	3	2	23	25	83	11

Walton Town Res. – record expunged

RESERVES CUP

FINAL *(April 25th at Wivenhoe Town)*
Gas Recreation Res. 4 Alresford CR Res. 1

TOMMY THOMPSON CUP
(Division Two teams)

FIRST ROUND
Foxash Social 0 **Sudbury Athletic** 3
Great Bentley Res. 3 Holland 3 *aet* (1-3p)
Great Bradfords 5 Boxted Lodgers Res. 1
Hatfield Peverel Res. 1 **Brightlingsea Regent Res.** 2
Hedinghams United 4 Walton Town Res. 2
Kelvedon Social Res. 2 Bures United Res. 1
Little Oakley Res. 2 Earls Colne Res. 0
Mersea Island Res. 1 **Lawford Lads Res.** 10
QUARTER-FINALS
Brightlingsea Regent Res. 2 Hedinghams United 1 *aet*
Holland 2 Sudbury Athletic 0
Kelvedon Social Res. 0 **Little Oakley Res.** 13
Lawford Lads Res. 0 **Great Bradfords** 11
SEMI-FINALS
Great Bradfords 1 **Brightlingsea Regent Res.** 1 *aet* (2-4p)
Little Oakley Res. 0 **Holland** 2
FINAL
(May 7th at Little Oakley)
Holland 4 Brightlingsea Regent Res. 0

ESSEX & SUFFOLK BORDER LEAGUE DIVISION TWO
OUT: Boxted Lodgers Reserves (R – Reserve Division One), Brightlingsea Regent Reserves (R – Reserve Division One), Bures United Reserves (R – Reserve Division One), Earls Colne Reserves (R – Reserve Premier Division), Foxash Social (P), Great Bentley Reserves (R – Reserve Division One), Great Bradfords (P), Hatfield Peverel Reserves (R – Reserve Division One), Hedinghams United (P), Holland (P), Kelvedon Social Reserves (R – Reserve Division One), Lawford Lads Reserves (R – Reserve Division One), Little Oakley Reserves (R – Reserve Division One), Mersea Island Reserves (R – Reserve Division One), Sudbury Athletic (P), Walton Town Reserves (WS)

THIS DIVISION
HAS
BEEN
DISBANDED

FOOTBALL CONFERENCE

WWW.CHERRYRED.CO.UK

Results grid — column/row legend:
1 Aldershot Town, 2 Altrincham, 3 Burton Albion, 4 Cambridge United, 5 Crawley Town, 6 Dagenham & Redbridge, 7 Exeter City, 8 Forest Green Rovers, 9 Gravesend & Northfleet, 10 Grays Athletic, 11 Halifax Town, 12 Kidderminster Harriers, 13 Morecambe, 14 Northwich Victoria, 15 Oxford United, 16 Rushden & Diamonds, 17 Southport, 18 St Albans City, 19 Stafford Rangers, 20 Stevenage Borough, 21 Tamworth, 22 Weymouth, 23 Woking, 24 York City

(The diagonal cells spell **FOOTBALL CONFERENCE**.)

	1	2	3	4	5	6	7	8	9	10	11	12	13	14	15	16	17	18	19	20	21	22	23	24
1 Aldershot Town		0-0	3-2	0-1	0-2	1-1	3-2	2-1	3-2	1-0	1-0	4-2	0-1	1-3	1-1	2-2	2-2	2-0	4-2	4-0	3-3	1-0	2-2	0-2
2 Altrincham	0-0		2-3	5-0	1-1	0-5	1-1	2-2	0-2	1-0	1-0	0-1	0-2	3-0	0-3	2-1	2-1	2-0	0-1	2-1	2-0	0-0	2-3	0-4
3 Burton Albion	1-3	2-1	F	2-1	2-1	0-2	1-0	1-0	0-1	3-0	1-0	1-1	2-1	2-0	1-2	1-2	0-1	1-0	0-0	2-1	1-0	1-1	2-1	1-2
4 Cambridge United	2-0	2-2	1-2	O	1-2	4-2	1-3	1-1	3-0	2-0	1-2	1-1	1-3	0-1	0-3	0-1	2-2	0-2	0-1	1-2	3-0	1-0	7-0	0-5
5 Crawley Town	1-2	1-1	1-0	1-1	O	0-0	0-3	3-1	1-1	0-1	2-0	0-0	4-0	0-2	0-1	1-0	2-1	2-1	1-2	3-0	1-0	0-3	0-0	0-1
6 Dagenham & Redbridge	2-1	4-1	3-0	2-0	2-1	T	4-1	1-1	2-1	0-0	1-3	2-1	5-0	1-1	1-2	1-0	0-0	4-2	1-1	2-0	4-0	4-1	3-2	2-1
7 Exeter City	0-0	2-1	3-0	2-0	1-1	3-2	B	1-0	1-3	2-1	4-1	1-1	1-0	1-1	2-1	0-0	2-1	4-2	1-2	1-1	1-1	4-0	1-0	1-1
8 Forest Green Rovers	3-0	2-2	1-0	1-1	1-0	0-1	2-1	A	0-0	2-0	2-1	1-3	2-1	1-5	0-2	1-2	2-2	1-2	4-4	2-0	3-2	2-3		0-1
9 Gravesend & Northfleet	1-1	3-1	0-0	2-0	1-0	0-0	2-1	2-1	L	2-0	1-3	2-1	3-0	1-0	1-0	0-4	3-2	1-4	1-1	4-1	1-3	1-0	0-1	
10 Grays Athletic	1-2	1-1	0-1	1-1	0-0	0-1	2-2	1-1	0-2	L	1-0	3-0	0-1	1-0	2-2	3-1	4-0	2-1	1-1	0-2	1-0	2-2	3-0	0-0
11 Halifax Town	1-1	1-1	1-2	1-0	2-1	1-3	2-1	1-1	0-2	1-0		2-0	1-1	0-1	1-0	0-1	1-1	4-1	3-1	2-1	3-1	4-1	3-0	1-0
12 Kidderminster Harriers	0-0	3-2	0-0	1-0	0-1	1-4	0-2	2-2	1-2	2-1	2-1		0-1	0-1	0-0	0-0	2-0	1-3	2-0	1-2	0-2	0-1	0-1	2-1
13 Morecambe	2-1	0-1	0-1	2-2	1-0	1-1	2-2	1-1	1-0	1-0	4-0	0-1	C	2-1	0-3	1-0	0-0	2-0	1-0	3-3	0-0	2-0	2-0	1-3
14 Northwich Victoria	1-3	1-1	0-3	0-4	2-1	2-0	1-0	2-0	1-2	0-3	3-2	0-2	0-2	O	1-0	4-1	3-1	0-3	4-0	0-0	0-1	0-1	0-2	1-2
15 Oxford United	2-0	1-1	0-0	1-1	1-1	1-2	1-0	0-2	1-0	0-1	0-1	0-0	1-0	5-1	N	2-2	2-1	2-0	2-0	2-1	4-1	0-0	2-0	0-1
16 Rushden & Diamonds	0-1	3-0	1-2	3-1	1-1	2-3	3-0	2-0	0-0	1-3	0-1	0-1	2-2	1-0	1-0	F	2-3	1-0	2-1	2-2	1-1	4-1	2-0	0-1
17 Southport	1-0	2-1	3-1	1-2	3-1	1-4	0-1	1-2	2-2	3-1	1-1	0-1	1-2	1-2	0-1	1-2	E	1-1	5-1	1-2	1-0	1-0	0-1	0-1
18 St Albans City	3-5	1-5	0-1	0-0	2-2	1-2	1-2	0-0	2-3	0-6	3-2	1-1	0-2	1-3	0-2	3-2	2-2	R	0-3	2-3	1-0	1-0	0-1	4-2
19 Stafford Rangers	0-3	1-0	1-1	1-2	0-1	1-2	0-1	3-1	4-2	2-3	1-2	1-3	2-0	0-1	1-1	1-0	2-2	1-3	E	1-2	6-0	3-0	1-0	0-0
20 Stevenage Borough	3-2	0-1	2-1	4-1	2-3	1-2	0-0	3-3	3-0	1-0	2-1	1-2	3-3	0-2	2-2	1-0	3-1	1-2	6-0	N	3-0	1-0	3-2	1-2
21 Tamworth	2-0	1-0	0-1	0-1	0-2	1-0	1-1	2-1	4-2	1-0	0-0	0-1	1-3	1-4	1-1	1-1	0-0	2-1	1-1	1-0	C	1-3	3-1	2-2
22 Weymouth	1-0	1-2	1-1	2-3	3-2	1-1	2-1	1-0	2-1	3-2	1-0	1-1	2-1	1-1	1-1	1-1	2-0	2-1	1-2	0-1	3-1	E	2-3	1-2
23 Woking	2-0	2-0	0-0	0-1	1-2	2-2	0-2	3-3	2-2	1-0	2-2	3-0	1-3	3-2	1-0	3-0	1-1	1-1	1-1	0-1	0-2	4-0		1-2
24 York City	1-0	1-0	3-2	1-2	5-0	2-3	0-0	0-0	2-2	2-0	1-0	2-3	2-1	2-2	0-0	0-0	3-1	2-2	0-0	0-0	1-0	0-1		

League Table

		HOME					AWAY					TOTAL					
	P	W	D	L	F	A	W	D	L	F	A	W	D	L	F	A	Pts
Dagenham & Redbridge	46	16	4	3	50	20	12	7	4	43	28	28	11	7	93	48	95
Oxford United	46	11	9	3	33	16	11	6	6	33	17	22	15	9	66	33	81
Morecambe	46	11	7	5	29	20	12	5	6	35	26	23	12	11	64	46	81
York City	46	10	6	7	29	22	13	5	5	36	23	23	11	12	65	45	80
Exeter City	46	14	7	2	39	19	8	5	10	28	29	22	12	12	67	48	78
Burton Albion	46	13	3	7	28	21	9	6	8	24	26	22	9	15	52	47	75
Gravesend & Northfleet	46	12	6	5	33	25	9	5	9	30	31	21	11	14	63	56	74
Stevenage Borough	46	12	4	7	46	30	8	6	9	30	36	20	10	16	76	66	70
Aldershot Town	46	11	7	5	40	31	7	4	12	24	31	18	11	17	64	62	65
Kidderminster Harriers	46	7	5	11	19	26	10	7	6	24	24	17	12	17	43	50	63
Weymouth	46	12	6	5	35	26	6	3	14	21	47	18	9	19	56	73	63
Rushden & Diamonds	46	10	6	8	34	24	7	6	10	24	30	17	11	18	58	54	62
Northwich Victoria	46	9	2	12	26	33	9	2	12	25	36	18	4	24	51	69	58
Forest Green Rovers	46	10	5	8	34	33	3	13	7	25	31	13	18	15	59	64	57
Woking	46	8	8	7	34	26	7	4	12	22	35	15	12	19	56	61	57
Halifax Town	46	12	8	3	40	22	3	2	18	15	40	15	10	21	55	62	55
Cambridge United	46	8	4	11	34	33	7	6	10	23	33	15	10	21	57	66	55
Crawley Town *-10*	46	10	6	7	27	20	7	7	9	25	32	17	12	17	52	52	53
Grays Athletic	46	8	9	6	29	21	5	4	14	27	34	13	13	20	56	55	52
Stafford Rangers	46	7	4	12	25	33	7	6	10	24	38	14	10	22	49	71	52
Altrincham	46	9	4	10	28	32	4	8	11	25	35	13	12	21	53	67	51
Tamworth	46	8	6	9	24	27	5	3	15	19	34	13	9	24	43	61	48
Southport	46	7	4	12	29	30	4	10	9	28	37	11	14	21	57	67	47
St Albans City	46	5	5	13	28	49	5	5	13	29	40	10	10	26	57	89	40

PLAY-OFFS

SEMI-FINALS (1st leg)
(May 4th) Exeter City 0 Oxford United 1 *Att* 8,659
(May 4th) York City 0 Morecambe 0 *Att* 6,660

SEMI-FINALS (2nd leg)
(May 7th) **Morecambe** 2 York City 1 *Att* 5,567
(May 8th) Oxford Utd 1 **Exeter City** 2 *aet (3-4p) Att* 10,691

FINAL (May 20th at Wembley Stadium)
Exeter City 1 **Morecambe** 2 *Att* 40,043

DATES & GATES

Home \ Away	York City	Woking	Weymouth	Tamworth	Stevenage Borough	Stafford Rangers	St Albans City	Southport	Rushden & Diamonds	Oxford United	Northwich Victoria	Morecambe	Kidderminster Harriers	Halifax Town	Grays Athletic	Gravesend & Northfleet	Forest Green Rovers	Exeter City	Dagenham & Redbridge	Crawley Town	Cambridge United	Burton United	Altrincham	Aldershot Town
Aldershot Town	10 Mar 2,435	13 Mar 2,739	27 Mar 2,224	3 Oct 2,084	12 Sep 2,371	9 Apr 1,734	31 Mar 1,749	18 Nov 2,290	24 Feb 2,189	10 Feb 3,621	16 Sep 2,588	21 Oct 2,394	14 Oct 2,182	2 Sep 2,330	6 Feb 1,924	12 Aug 2,487	26 Dec 2,216	3 Apr 2,250	26 Aug 2,657	13 Jan 2,349	21 Apr 3,068	27 Jan 1,970	30 Sep 2,433	—
Altrincham	10 Feb 1,327	16 Sep 886	7 Oct 1,214	23 Sep 882	12 Aug 1,035	1 Jan 1,150	20 Jan 890	21 Oct 1,336	6 Jan 1,111	17 Mar 1,497	23 Sep 2,330	24 Mar 1,085	27 Jan 1,116	27 Jan 1,036	20 Mar 829	9 Apr 990	18 Nov 912	31 Mar 1,100	3 Sep 951	18 Nov 1,033	6 Mar 891	2 Dec 1,212	—	28 Apr 2,005
Burton Albion	13 Mar 2,718	10 Mar 1,603	9 Sep 1,523	20 Feb 1,953	3 Nov 1,907	1 Jan 2,570	2 Dec 2,131	28 Apr 2,910	24 Dec 3,000	20 Oct 4,002	12 Aug 2,506	18 Nov 3,142	12 Sep 1,860	17 Apr 2,056	10 Feb 2,842	11 Nov 1,933	27 Feb 2,127	1 Sep 2,335	17 Feb 1,809	3 Oct 1,768	19 Sep 1,612	—	9 Dec 1,441	9 Dec 1,876
Cambridge United	13 Mar 2,428	27 Jan 2,206	31 Mar 2,698	28 Apr 6,021	16 Sep 2,696	13 Jan 2,056	2 Dec 2,131	24 Feb 3,444	26 Dec 2,910	18 Sep 5,244	12 Aug 2,506	26 Sep 2,148	14 Apr 1,865	27 Feb 4,294	1 Sep 2,568	2 Sep 861	3 Feb 2,033	30 Sep 2,344	20 Feb 1,383	14 Oct 2,590	—	17 Mar 1,177	3 Oct 3,375	22 Sep 2,535
Crawley Town	24 Feb 932	9 Apr 1,098	10 Oct 1,218	9 Dec 957	31 Mar 1,258	4 Nov 929	4 Nov 840	12 Jan 1,152	12 Aug 1,088	18 Sep 2,102	12 Apr 778	7 Oct 890	28 Apr 1,664	25 Nov 1,062	23 Sep 974	3 Jan 816	3 Feb 1,076	9 Apr 1,562	1 Jan 1,486	—	13 Mar 1,766	6 Mar 663	17 Feb 1,180	3 Mar 1,737
Dagenham & Redbridge	24 Feb 2,252	31 Mar 1,389	23 Sep 1,602	19 Aug 947	20 Mar 1,984	6 Mar 1,710	21 Apr 1,508	2 Dec 1,285	10 Feb 1,817	15 Apr 2,022	7 Oct 1,235	7 Oct 1,237	21 Oct 1,874	30 Dec 1,261	26 Dec 1,855	28 Apr 3,021	17 Mar 1,800	27 Jan 1,816	—	17 Feb 1,711	28 Jan 1,539	18 Aug 1,581	14 Apr 1,473	7 Apr 4,044
Exeter City	16 Aug 4,410	16 Aug 3,363	23 Jan 3,474	18 Apr 4,180	23 Sep 3,194	2 Dec 3,977	19 Sep 3,082	6 Dec 6,670	6 Jan 3,135	1 Jan 4,720	10 Oct 2,928	17 Mar 3,114	3 Nov 3,083	7 Oct 3,114	6 Mar 2,894	20 Jan 3,287	15 Aug 3,527	—	17 Mar 3,403	23 Mar 3,475	14 Apr 4,364	18 Aug 3,475	19 Aug 3,345	9 Sep 3,933
Forest Green Rovers	2 Dec 1,125	16 Sep 1,116	6 Mar 1,245	20 Jan 1,049	9 Apr 969	30 Sep 945	11 Nov 1,003	9 Dec 1,090	31 Mar 762	6 Oct 3,021	18 Nov 860	30 Sep 1,056	10 Feb 1,211	21 Apr 1,664	3 Apr 782	26 Aug 881	—	27 Mar 1,691	26 Aug 757	27 Jan 1,067	9 Sep 1,139	10 Dec 888	19 Sep 910	23 Jan 951
Gravesend & Northfleet	19 Aug 1,036	9 Apr 1,479	2 Sep 1,333	15 Aug 936	17 Feb 1,552	21 Oct 1,049	12 Aug 1,035	9 Sep 1,024	27 Mar 1,110	18 Nov 2,019	4 Nov 776	28 Aug 1,909	3 Oct 1,438	30 Sep 1,458	19 Aug 1,589	—	7 Apr 1,063	16 Sep 1,691	11 Apr 757	21 Apr 2,561	7 Apr 1,942	7 Oct 1,612	1 Jan 725	23 Mar 1,103
Grays Athletic	9 Dec 1,139	2 Dec 1,536	3 Mar 1,003	13 Mar 779	17 Feb 1,409	21 Oct 1,373	25 Nov 1,584	23 Jan 1,484	1 Sep 1,850	18 Nov 2,314	27 Feb 1,621	21 Apr 1,654	3 Oct 1,160	30 Dec 1,860	—	9 Sep 1,641	23 Sep 1,561	10 Mar 1,591	20 Feb 1,383	26 Dec 1,561	1 Jan 1,844	21 Oct 1,367	9 Feb 900	19 Sep 1,215
Halifax Town	23 Jan 2,308	1 Sep 1,228	1 Jan 1,245	14 Oct 1,014	10 Oct 1,010	31 Mar 1,012	12 Apr 1,806	19 Sep 1,258	13 Mar 1,314	21 Mar 1,473	31 Mar 1,621	21 Apr 1,909	3 Oct 1,438	—	7 Oct 1,316	9 Sep 1,508	4 Nov 1,661	10 Mar 2,033	20 Feb 1,383	16 Sep 1,163	1 Jan 1,922	21 Oct 1,177	9 Dec 1,455	17 Apr 1,215
Kidderminster Harriers	20 Jan 2,073	20 Jan 1,208	26 Aug 1,753	9 Sep 1,646	25 Nov 1,584	9 Dec 1,573	12 Aug 1,806	19 Aug 1,258	30 Dec 1,252	20 Jan 2,264	26 Sep 1,059	26 Dec 1,804	—	27 Mar 1,409	7 Oct 1,316	3 Mar 1,508	4 Nov 1,661	17 Apr 1,834	14 Apr 1,578	14 Apr 1,834	17 Feb 1,766	6 Feb 1,635	13 Mar 1,403	20 Mar 1,165
Morecambe	1 Jan 2,203	1 Jan 1,466	3 Mar 874	3 Mar 1,070	25 Apr 1,524	3 Mar 1,373	24 Jan 1,415	23 Jan 1,484	27 Mar 1,252	27 Mar 2,314	27 Feb 1,315	—	21 Apr 1,654	6 Mar 890	28 Apr 2,303	28 Apr 1,429	4 Nov 1,561	20 Mar 1,582	20 Jan 1,374	10 Mar 1,374	17 Feb 1,493	21 Apr 1,907	20 Feb 1,403	20 Jan 1,165
Northwich Victoria	3 Oct 1,021	30 Sep 990	4 Nov 1,056	3 Mar 1,070	25 Apr 515	19 Sep 971	25 Apr 717	1 Jan 1,056	14 Oct 853	18 Nov 1,759	—	15 Aug 1,346	15 Aug 1,496	4 Nov 1,150	28 Aug 874	25 Nov 813	15 Aug 773	20 Mar 784	11 Apr 706	14 Apr 967	25 Mar 1,156	10 Oct 1,218	20 Feb 1,290	20 Jan 890
Oxford United	30 Sep 6,602	21 Apr 1,922	9 Dec 5,582	26 Dec 6,614	23 Sep 6,410	21 Apr 7,007	6 Jan 6,190	3 Oct 5,844	29 Jan 5,654	—	26 Dec 5,364	28 Aug 5,489	3 Oct 4,542	28 Aug 1,909	19 Aug 6,504	17 Feb 5,615	23 Sep 6,157	12 Sep 6,083	26 Mar 6,836	23 Mar 6,368	3 Feb 5,613	21 Oct 6,187	15 Aug 5,938	4 Nov 8,185
Rushden & Diamonds	21 Apr 2,416	21 Apr 1,305	3 Apr 1,624	1 Jan 1,872	6 Oct 2,309	20 Jan 1,837	1 Jan 2,488	7 Apr 2,122	—	9 Dec 3,270	23 Apr 1,533	6 Mar 1,701	14 Apr 1,925	30 Dec 1,016	28 Apr 2,015	19 Sep 1,879	19 Aug 1,693	3 Mar 2,344	4 Nov 2,039	23 Mar 2,239	23 Jan 2,239	23 Jan 1,493	9 Sep 1,680	25 Nov 2,128
Southport	21 Apr 3,206	21 Apr 1,305	17 Mar 918	4 Nov 1,014	10 Oct 1,010	31 Mar 1,012	30 Sep 1,005	—	26 Aug 1,083	6 Mar 1,054	26 Feb 1,059	16 Dec 1,804	30 Dec 1,016	27 Mar 936	6 Jan 810	2 Sep 861	4 Nov 1,104	30 Sep 1,206	13 Mar 1,655	16 Sep 1,025	25 Nov 1,106	21 Oct 1,370	3 Feb 1,145	17 Feb 1,160
St Albans City	14 Oct 1,237	14 Oct 1,018	28 Apr 734	4 Nov 1,184	26 Dec 2,878	31 Mar 1,012	—	1 Jan 1,005	14 Oct 853	14 Apr 1,713	31 Mar 1,059	6 Jan 613	24 Mar 821	27 Jan 1,009	21 Oct 1,045	20 Feb 861	2 Sep 806	30 Dec 1,314	13 Mar 734	3 Jan 857	15 Aug 1,916	15 Apr 680	20 Feb 680	19 Aug 1,373
Stafford Rangers	14 Apr 1,293	14 Oct 1,033	4 Nov 1,884	10 Mar 1,303	20 Feb 653	—	25 Nov 1,030	3 Oct 948	26 Aug 1,083	31 Mar 1,012	17 Apr 1,049	7 Apr 957	24 Mar 821	6 Mar 890	28 Jan 865	13 Mar 524	15 Aug 773	20 Mar 970	3 Oct 1,143	23 Mar 967	3 Mar 1,096	6 Mar 1,554	15 Apr 1,410	28 Apr 1,720
Stevenage Borough	15 Aug 2,306	26 Dec 990	19 Sep 1,674	14 Apr 2,202	—	9 Sep 1,708	6 Jan 1,190	3 Oct 2,309	17 Apr 1,715	26 Dec 5,244	21 Oct 1,773	7 Apr 1,845	3 Nov 3,083	30 Sep 1,907	18 Nov 2,207	9 Dec 2,014	28 Aug 1,905	12 Sep 3,058	26 Dec 2,362	19 Aug 1,751	20 Jan 2,759	24 Nov 2,154	24 Nov 1,913	1 Jan 2,683
Tamworth	21 Oct 1,311	26 Dec 11,065	12 Aug 1,409	—	2 Sep 1,034	7 Oct 1,249	23 Jan 2,141	7 Jan 2,122	12 Sep 1,105	24 Feb 2,089	21 Oct 1,006	7 Apr 1,029	20 Mar 1,115	17 Mar 1,337	10 Oct 907	27 Mar 1,044	19 Aug 1,215	21 Apr 1,242	14 Oct 1,269	27 Jan 1,101	30 Dec 1,234	30 Sep 2,029	24 Jun 2,411	6 Mar 1,086
Weymouth	16 Sep 1,774	20 Mar 1,257	—	24 Mar 1,369	6 Mar 1,407	17 Mar 1,294	1 Jan 2,178	24 Mar 2,084	23 Sep 2,148	23 Sep 2,228	27 Jan 1,451	14 Apr 1,222	20 Mar 1,206	16 Sep 1,676	2 Dec 1,451	20 Feb 2,153	14 Apr 1,568	26 Dec 4,294	21 Apr 1,655	13 Mar 1,310	19 Aug 1,766	30 Dec 1,370	17 Feb 1,503	15 Aug 3,583
Woking	19 Sep 1,907	—	25 Nov 1,884	17 Feb 1,411	6 Mar 1,407	17 Mar 1,294	1 Jan 2,178	24 Jan 2,276	23 Sep 2,084	23 Sep 2,228	6 Mar 1,753	16 Sep 1,222	20 Feb 1,544	9 Sep 1,724	7 Apr 1,834	20 Feb 851	14 Apr 1,578	9 Sep 2,590	3 Mar 1,655	15 Sep 1,750	25 Nov 1,886	6 Oct 1,651	14 Apr 1,612	9 Oct 3,725
York City	16 Sep 1,907	29 Dec 3,173	17 Feb 2,767	3 Feb 2,477	27 Mar 2,969	1 Sep 2,955	1 Jan 2,927	23 Sep 2,446	10 Apr 2,955	28 Apr 5,378	6 Mar 2,132	16 Sep 2,233	16 Sep 2,181	23 Dec 3,588	27 Jan 2,689	31 Mar 2,709	3 Mar 2,923	12 Aug 2,789	25 Nov 3,050	6 Jan 2,590	10 Oct 2,614	25 Aug 2,812	5 Nov 2,726	6 Oct 2,679

FOOTBALL CONFERENCE PREM. DIV. CONSTITUTION 2007-08

ALDERSHOT TOWN
Recreation Ground, High Street, Aldershot, Hampshire GU11 1TW
Tel: 01252 337065   Fax: 01252 324347
Manager: Gary Waddock   www.theshots.co.uk   Colours: Red

ALTRINCHAM
Moss Lane, Altrincham, Cheshire WA15 8AP
Tel: 0161 928 1045   Fax: 0161 926 9934
Manager: Graham Heathcote   www.altrinchamfc.com   Colours: Red, white & black

BURTON ALBION
Pirelli Stadium, Princess Way, Burton-on-Trent, Staffordshire DE13 0AR
Tel: 0870 190 0060   Fax: 01283 523199
Manager: Nigel Clough   www.burtonalbionfc.co.uk   Colours: Yellow & black

CAMBRIDGE UNITED
Abbey Stadium, Newmarket Road, Cambridge, Cambridgeshire CB5 8LN
Tel: 01223 566500   Fax: 01223 566502
Manager: Jimmy Quinn   www.cambridge-united.co.uk   Colours: Amber & black

CRAWLEY TOWN
Broadfield Stadium, Brighton Road, Crawley, West Sussex RH11 9RX
Tel: 01293 410000   Club: 01293 410001   Fax: 01293 410002
Manager: Steve Evans   www.ctfc.net   Colours: Red

DROYLSDEN
Butchers Arms, Market Street, Droylsden, Manchester M43 7AY
Tel: 0161 370 1426   Club: 0161 301 1352   Fax: 0161 370 8341
Manager: David Pace   www.droylsdenfc.co.uk   Colours: Red & black

EBBSFLEET UNITED
Stonebridge Road, Northfleet, Gravesend, Kent DA11 9GN
Tel: 01474 533796   Fax: 01474 327754
Manager: Liam Diaish   www.ebbsfleetunited.co.uk   Colours: Red & white

EXETER CITY
St James Park, Stadium Way, Exeter, Devon EX4 6PX
Tel: 01392 411243   Fax: 01392 413959
Manager: Paul Tisdale   www.exetercityfc.co.uk   Colours: Red, white & black

FARSLEY CELTIC
Throstle Nest, Newlands, Farsley, Pudsey, Leeds, West Yorkshire LS28 5BE
Tel: 0113 255 7292   Fax: 0113 257 1058
Manager: Lee Sinnott   www.farsleyceltic.co.uk   Colours: Blue

FOREST GREEN ROVERS
Nympsfield Road, Forest Green, Nailsworth, Gloucestershire GL6 0ET
Tel: 01453 834860   Fax: 01453 835291
Manager: Jim Harvey   www.fgrfc.co.uk   Colours: Black & white

GRAYS ATHLETIC
Recreation Ground, Bridge Road, Grays, Essex RM17 6BZ
Tel: 01375 377753   Club: 01375 391649   Fax: 01375 377753
Manager: Justin Edinburgh   www.graysathletic.co.uk   Colours: Sky blue

HALIFAX TOWN
The Shay Stadium, Shaw Hill, Halifax, West Yorkshire HX1 2YS
Tel: 01422 341222   Ticket Office: 01422 353423   Fax: 01422 349487
Manager: Chris Wilder   www.halifaxafc.co.uk   Colours: Blue & white

HISTON
The Glassworld Stadium, Bridge Road, Impington, Cambridge, Cambs CB4 9PH
Tel: 01223 237373   Fax: 01223 872246
Manager: Steve Fallon   www.histonfc.co.uk   Colours: Red & black

KIDDERMINSTER HARRIERS
Aggborough Stadium, Hoo Road, Kidderminster, Worcestershire DY10 1NB
Tel: 01562 823931   Fax: 01562 827329
Manager: Mark Yates   www.harriers.co.uk   Colours: Red & white

NORTHWICH VICTORIA
Victoria Stadium, Wincham Avenue, Wincham, Northwich, Cheshire CW9 6GB
Tel: 01606 41450   Fax: 01606 330577
Manager: Neil Redfearn   www.nvfc.co.uk   Colours: Green & white

OXFORD UNITED
The Kassam Stadium, Grenoble Road, Oxford, Oxfordshire OX4 4XP
Tel: 01865 337500   Fax: 01865 337555
Manager: Jim Smith   www.oufc.co.uk   Colours: Yellow & navy blue

RUSHDEN & DIAMONDS
Nene Park, Diamond Way, Irthlingborough, Northants NN9 5QF
Tel: 01933 652000   Fax: 01933 650418
Manager: Garry Hill   www.thediamondsfc.com   Colours: Red

SALISBURY CITY
Raymond McEnhill Stadium, Partidge Way, Old Sarum, Salisbury, Wilts SP4 6PU
Tel: 01722 326454   www.salisburyjournal.co.uk/sport/salisburycityfc   Fax: 01722 323100
Manager: Nick Holmes   Colours: White & black

STAFFORD RANGERS
Marston Road, Stafford, Staffordshire ST16 3BX
Tel: 01785 602430   Fax: 01785 602431
Manager: Phil Robinson   www.staffordrangers.co.uk   Colours: Black & white

STEVENAGE BOROUGH
Broadhall Way Stadium, Broadhall Way, Stevenage, Herts SG2 8RH
Tel: 01438 223223   Fax: 01438 743666
Manager: Mark Stimson   www.stevenageborofc.com   Colours: White & red

TORQUAY UNITED
Plainmoor Ground, Torquay, Devon TQ1 3PS
Tel: 01803 328666   Fax: 01803 323976
Manager: Paul Buckle   www.torquayunited.com   Colours: Yellow & blue

WEYMOUTH
Wessex Stadium, Radipole Lane, Weymouth, Dorset DT4 9XJ
Tel: 01305 785558   Fax: 01305 766658
Manager: Jason Tindall   www.theterras.co.uk   Colours: Claret, blue & white

WOKING
Kingfield, Kingfield Road, Woking, Surrey GU22 9AA
Tel: 01483 772470   Fax: 01483 888423
Manager: Frank Gray   www.wokingfc.co.uk   Colours: Red, white & black

YORK CITY
Kit Kat Crescent, Grosvenor Road, York, North Yorkshire YO30 7AQ
Tel: 01904 624447   Fax: 01904 631457
Manager: Billy McEwan   www.ycfc.net   Colours: Red & white

IN: Droylsden (P – Football Conference North), Farsley Celtic (P – Football Conference North), Histon (P – Football Conference South), Salisbury City (P – Football Conference South), Torquay United (R – Football League Division Two)
OUT: Dagenham & Redbridge (P – Football League Division Two), Morecambe (P – Football League Division Two), Southport (R – Football Conference North), St Albans City (R – Football Conference South), Tamworth (R – Football Conference North)
Gravesend & Northfleet become Ebbsfleet United

	Alfreton Town	Barrow	Blyth Spartans	Droylsden	Farsley Celtic	Gainsborough Trinity	Harrogate Town	Hinckley United	Hucknall Town	Hyde United	Kettering Town	Lancaster City	Leigh RMI	Moor Green	Nuneaton Borough	Redditch United	Scarborough	Stalybridge Celtic	Vauxhall Motors	Worcester City	Workington	Worksop Town
Alfreton Town		1-0	0-1	1-3	0-1	3-1	0-0	0-1	2-1	2-2	1-1	2-1	1-0	3-0	0-0	1-1	1-2	2-0	0-2	1-1	1-1	3-0
Barrow	1-1		0-2	2-1	2-2	3-0	2-3	1-0	1-0	1-2	0-1	3-0	1-1	0-1	0-4	1-1	2-1	0-0	0-1	0-0	0-1	1-2
Blyth Spartans	3-0	1-0		0-3	4-1	2-0	0-0	3-1	2-2	0-0	2-2	3-0	1-0	0-1	1-2	1-2	2-0	1-0	1-2	2-2	0-2	2-0
Droylsden	1-1	2-1	0-0	C	4-1	2-1	2-0	3-1	5-3	4-2	1-1	6-1	2-2	1-0	4-2	2-1	1-3	6-1	1-0	2-1	2-1	3-2
Farsley Celtic	1-1	2-2	3-0	0-3	O	1-0	1-0	0-2	1-0	1-1	2-1	3-1	1-1	0-1	0-1	4-0	0-2	1-1	3-2	1-0	1-2	1-0
Gainsborough Trinity	4-0	1-0	0-2	3-2	0-0	N	1-3	1-0	2-3	2-3	2-3	1-0	0-0	1-0	1-1	2-2	3-1	2-0	1-2	1-3	1-0	1-1
Harrogate Town	0-1	1-1	1-2	1-1	1-0	1-1	F	2-0	1-1	1-2	2-3	3-0	2-1	1-1	1-1	2-2	0-1	0-0	1-0	1-0	4-0	1-0
Hinckley United	2-2	1-1	2-1	2-1	1-1	0-1	0-1	E	1-1	2-0	3-1	5-0	3-1	2-0	2-2	3-1	1-1	2-3	1-1	3-3	2-1	0-1
Hucknall Town	0-2	1-3	1-2	2-2	0-1	3-3	0-3	1-2	R	4-2	1-2	5-0	1-3	3-2	2-1	2-2	0-1	2-1	2-2	4-2	2-1	4-0
Hyde United	2-1	1-1	5-1	2-1	3-4	3-0	4-0	2-0	1-0	E	3-5	5-0	2-0	4-1	3-2	0-2	1-1	3-1	1-1	0-0	1-1	1-2
Kettering Town	0-1	3-2	1-1	1-0	3-2	4-2	3-1	1-2	0-0	1-0	N	3-3	4-0	1-1	3-2	3-1	2-1	0-1	1-1	2-3	2-2	3-1
Lancaster City	0-2	0-2	0-2	1-2	1-2	0-1	0-2	1-4	0-1	2-3	0-1	C	0-0	0-3	0-4	1-2	1-5	0-1	2-2	0-2	1-5	0-3
Leigh RMI	2-0	0-3	3-1	2-2	1-3	2-0	1-3	2-3	4-3	2-0	1-2	0-1	E	2-2	1-0	0-0	1-1	1-3	0-3	2-1	2-0	2-1
Moor Green	2-0	0-0	0-2	5-2	1-1	2-1	0-1	0-1	1-2	1-1	1-2	3-1	0-0		1-1	1-1	1-2	2-1	5-2	3-1	1-0	0-1
Nuneaton Borough	1-0	3-0	1-1	1-0	1-1	0-1	0-0	0-1	2-1	0-0	2-1	1-0	0-1	1-0	N	1-0	1-1	3-2	1-1	1-1	0-0	0-0
Redditch United	3-2	1-1	0-2	0-0	1-4	1-1	2-1	1-3	1-2	2-1	4-4	2-2	2-1	0-1	2-0	O	1-1	1-2	3-3	1-2	4-1	0-1
Scarborough	0-1	1-1	0-1	1-0	0-0	0-0	1-1	3-0	1-2	1-2	1-1	1-1	3-0	1-3	3-2	0-1	R	0-1	0-1	1-0	0-1	2-1
Stalybridge Celtic	3-2	0-4	3-2	1-2	0-2	0-2	0-2	2-2	3-7	0-0	3-1	2-1	2-3	4-3	3-2	3-2	1-0	T	3-3	1-1	1-2	3-0
Vauxhall Motors	1-2	0-1	2-0	2-3	1-2	0-1	1-5	2-2	1-2	1-0	1-1	4-1	2-1	1-1	1-3	1-1	1-1	2-2	H	2-0	1-2	2-0
Worcester City	0-0	3-0	3-2	3-1	0-1	1-1	2-3	3-1	2-0	2-2	2-0	4-1	1-2	0-1	3-3	1-1	3-2	1-1	3-3		2-2	2-1
Workington	1-1	1-1	3-0	0-0	3-0	1-2	3-2	1-1	1-0	3-1	2-0	1-1	0-1	3-2	2-0	1-0	0-1	2-1	2-0	0-1		3-2
Worksop Town	2-0	2-0	1-1	0-2	2-2	1-2	0-0	1-1	1-3	3-1	0-2	3-1	2-0	0-1	0-0	2-3	0-0	2-1	1-4	0-2	1-3	

WWW.CHERRYRED.CO.UK

Conference North

		HOME					AWAY					TOTAL					
	P	W	D	L	F	A	W	D	L	F	A	W	D	L	F	A	Pts
Droylsden	42	16	4	1	54	25	7	5	9	31	30	23	9	10	85	55	78
Kettering Town	42	11	6	4	41	27	9	7	5	34	31	20	13	9	75	58	73
Workington	42	12	5	4	33	17	8	5	8	28	29	20	10	12	61	46	70
Hinckley United	42	10	8	3	40	24	9	4	8	28	30	19	12	11	68	54	69
Farsley Celtic	42	10	5	6	27	21	9	6	6	31	30	19	11	12	58	51	68
Harrogate Town	42	8	8	5	27	18	10	5	6	31	23	18	13	11	58	41	67
Blyth Spartans	42	10	5	6	31	20	9	4	8	26	29	19	9	14	57	49	66
Hyde United	42	12	5	4	47	24	6	6	9	32	38	18	11	13	79	62	65
Worcester City	42	9	8	4	41	28	7	6	8	26	26	16	14	12	67	54	62
Nuneaton Borough	42	8	9	4	19	13	7	6	8	35	32	15	15	12	54	45	60
Moor Green	42	8	6	7	30	23	8	5	8	23	28	16	11	15	53	51	59
Gainsborough Trinity	42	9	5	7	30	26	6	6	9	21	31	15	11	16	51	57	56
Hucknall Town	42	8	4	9	40	37	7	5	9	29	32	15	9	18	69	69	54
Alfreton Town	42	8	6	7	24	21	6	6	9	20	29	14	12	16	44	50	54
Vauxhall Motors	42	6	6	9	29	31	6	9	6	33	33	12	15	15	62	64	51
Barrow	42	7	6	8	23	23	5	8	8	24	25	12	14	16	47	48	50
Leigh RMI	42	9	4	8	31	32	4	6	11	16	29	13	10	19	47	61	49
Stalybridge Celtic	42	7	6	8	38	45	6	4	11	26	36	13	10	19	64	81	49
Redditch United	42	6	7	8	32	35	5	8	8	29	33	11	15	16	61	68	48
Scarborough *-10*	42	6	6	9	21	21	7	10	4	29	24	13	16	13	50	45	45
Worksop Town	42	6	6	9	24	29	6	3	12	20	33	12	9	21	44	62	45
Lancaster City *-10*	42	0	2	19	10	49	2	3	16	17	61	2	5	35	27	110	1

PLAY-OFFS

SEMI-FINALS *(1st leg)*
(May 2nd) Hinckley United 0 **Workington** 0 *Att* 1,092
(May 2nd) **Farsley Celtic** 1 Kettering 1 *Att* 1,621

SEMI-FINALS *(2nd leg)*
(May 5th) Workington 1 **Hinckley United** 2 *Att* 1,519
(May 5th) Kettering 0 **Farsley Celtic** 0 *aet* (2-4p) *Att* 2,033

FINAL
(May 14th at Burton Albion)
Farsley Celtic 4 Hinckley United 4 *Att* 2,495

DATES & GATES

DATES & GATES	Alfreton Town	Barrow	Blyth Spartans	Droylsden	Farsley Celtic	Gainsborough Trinity	Harrogate Town	Hinckley United	Hucknall Town	Hyde United	Kettering Town	Lancaster City	Leigh RMI	Moor Green	Nuneaton Borough	Redditch United	Scarborough	Stalybridge Celtic	Vauxhall Motors	Worcester City	Workington	Worksop Town
Alfreton Town		18 Nov *310*	17 Mar *265*	6 Jan *314*	10 Mar *243*	14 Nov *254*	1 Sep *325*	31 Mar *286*	26 Dec *519*	22 Aug *267*	6 Oct *539*	12 Aug *279*	27 Jan *231*	16 Sep *241*	9 Dec *333*	21 Apr *272*	20 Mar *236*	3 Feb *279*	17 Feb *246*	9 Apr *246*	26 Aug *253*	13 Feb *261*
Barrow	10 Feb *696*		31 Mar *759*	26 Aug *738*	24 Feb *703*	13 Jan *758*	22 Aug *820*	17 Apr *690*	17 Mar *742*	9 Apr *670*	13 Feb *805*	26 Dec *959*	4 Nov *921*	7 Oct *820*	21 Apr *735*	9 Sep *816*	3 Mar *852*	23 Sep *819*	20 Jan *717*	12 Aug *986*	12 Sep *935*	2 Dec *763*
Blyth Spartans	19 Aug *561*	15 Aug *745*		16 Sep *872*	28 Aug *631*	18 Nov *551*	30 Dec *652*	28 Apr *836*	6 Jan *652*	28 Oct *574*	9 Dec *599*	21 Oct *566*	2 Sep *573*	16 Dec *561*	3 Feb *651*	24 Mar *612*	26 Dec *903*	7 Apr *705*	14 Apr *551*	27 Jan *675*	17 Feb *716*	10 Mar *662*
Droylsden	9 Sep *372*	7 Apr *652*	13 Jan *457*		24 Mar *501*	9 Dec *316*	21 Apr *1,027*	26 Feb *582*	18 Nov *367*	7 Oct *709*	23 Sep *517*	17 Feb *460*	3 Feb *431*	14 Apr *394*	19 Aug *470*	14 Aug *443*	4 Nov *467*	18 Sep *909*	1 Jan *329*	3 Mar *474*	20 Jan *394*	28 Aug *323*
Farsley Celtic	4 Nov *275*	9 Dec *275*	9 Apr *326*	12 Aug *342*		17 Feb *381*	26 Dec *573*	17 Mar *339*	16 Sep *326*	26 Aug *267*	18 Nov *349*	22 Aug *305*	31 Mar *347*	2 Sep *275*	27 Jan *459*	7 Oct *275*	30 Dec *634*	3 Mar *401*	3 Feb *291*	6 Jan *349*	21 Apr *765*	17 Apr *427*
Gainsborough Trinity	3 Mar *429*	16 Sep *379*	17 Apr *338*	24 Feb *370*	2 Dec *375*		6 Mar *386*	12 Aug *377*	30 Dec *367*	6 Jan *381*	4 Nov *602*	3 Feb *371*	9 Apr *361*	27 Jan *379*	3 Sep *415*	5 Dec *238*	31 Mar *671*	28 Apr *555*	21 Oct *358*	26 Aug *408*	22 Aug *373*	26 Dec *719*
Harrogate Town	20 Feb *360*	14 Apr *453*	12 Sep *454*	21 Oct *639*	6 Feb *444*	20 Jan *424*		27 Mar *849*	10 Mar *473*	14 Nov *384*	28 Aug *616*	13 Jan *468*	18 Nov *383*	24 Mar *483*	17 Feb *714*	7 Apr *505*	3 Feb *1,058*	19 Aug *502*	23 Sep *376*	28 Apr *526*	9 Dec *515*	15 Aug *523*
Hinckley United	14 Aug *546*	3 Feb *479*	7 Oct *853*	2 Sep *609*	19 Aug *484*	24 Mar *511*	6 Jan *607*		9 Dec *635*	21 Apr *691*	14 Apr *1,405*	23 Apr *629*	30 Oct *564*	30 Dec *594*	26 Dec *2,889*	28 Aug *587*	17 Feb *583*	18 Nov *731*	7 Apr *508*	6 Mar *482*	4 Nov *860*	27 Jan *581*
Hucknall Town	1 Jan *731*	19 Aug *385*	9 Sep *445*	20 Mar *272*	13 Jan *371*	12 Sep *240*	4 Nov *382*	24 Feb *450*		11 Nov *329*	15 Aug *700*	20 Jan *357*	3 Mar *292*	2 Dec *348*	28 Aug *522*	14 Apr *383*	28 Apr *646*	24 Mar *308*	23 Jan *254*	21 Oct *428*	23 Sep *626*	16 Dec *479*
Hyde United	14 Apr *355*	28 Aug *456*	20 Jan *413*	28 Apr *656*	6 Apr *502*	9 Sep *311*	3 Mar *401*	21 Oct *364*	3 Feb *402*		25 Mar *826*	22 Jan *301*	16 Feb *334*	18 Sep *334*	18 Nov *413*	23 Sep *342*	9 Dec *388*	26 Dec *917*	23 Oct *415*	4 Nov *401*	13 Jan *362*	19 Aug *349*
Kettering Town	28 Apr *1,204*	2 Sep *1,011*	24 Feb *1,193*	27 Jan *2,352*	3 Apr *1,025*	10 Mar *1,125*	9 Apr *1,651*	22 Aug *1,055*	31 Mar *1,340*	12 Aug *1,208*		26 Aug *977*	6 Jan *1,009*	6 Mar *809*	30 Dec *1,469*	2 Dec *1,080*	16 Sep *1,235*	21 Oct *1,252*	21 Nov *736*	26 Dec *1,597*	17 Mar *1,514*	9 Jan *1,023*
Lancaster City	24 Mar *216*	1 Jan *463*	21 Apr *353*	2 Dec *283*	14 Apr *175*	19 Aug *254*	16 Sep *247*	28 Oct *238*	27 Mar *159*	10 Oct *251*	7 Apr *321*		3 Apr *198*	10 Feb *169*	6 Jan *273*	10 Mar *196*	27 Jan *317*	15 Aug *267*	28 Aug *233*	11 Nov *194*	7 Oct *339*	17 Mar *173*
Leigh RMI	23 Sep *157*	10 Mar *251*	13 Mar *145*	11 Nov *209*	15 Aug *151*	28 Aug *165*	10 Feb *155*	20 Feb *125*	5 Dec *140*	1 Dec *151*	9 Sep *251*	12 Sep *156*		7 Apr *131*	14 Apr *191*	19 Aug *155*	21 Oct *215*	20 Jan *216*	23 Mar *201*	24 Feb *175*	2 Jan *207*	28 Apr *325*
Moor Green	13 Jan *224*	28 Apr *245*	3 Mar *229*	22 Aug *141*	20 Feb *102*	23 Sep *192*	12 Aug *221*	5 Dec *160*	17 Feb *226*	31 Mar *250*	20 Jan *431*	18 Nov *164*	26 Aug *217*		4 Nov *504*	1 Jan *343*	9 Apr *250*	9 Sep *234*	9 Dec *141*	17 Mar *351*	3 Feb *186*	21 Oct *194*
Nuneaton Borough	27 Mar *553*	21 Oct *771*	11 Nov *892*	17 Mar *652*	23 Sep *893*	27 Feb *705*	2 Dec *779*	1 Jan *1,333*	9 Apr *652*	20 Mar *511*	12 Sep *1,202*	9 Sep *881*	22 Aug *843*	10 Mar *671*		20 Jan *823*	26 Aug *873*	13 Feb *728*	28 Apr *2,077*	31 Mar *775*	12 Aug *1,073*	28 Oct *813*
Redditch United	21 Oct *380*	13 Mar *445*	12 Aug *538*	31 Mar *635*	28 Apr *514*	24 Apr *374*	26 Aug *326*	11 Nov *533*	22 Aug *346*	27 Jan *440*	17 Feb *670*	4 Nov *424*	17 Mar *443*	26 Dec *482*	6 Mar *476*		2 Sep *472*	9 Dec *195*	18 Nov *364*	20 Feb *603*	28 Oct *358*	16 Sep *426*
Scarborough	20 Jan *977*	14 Nov *679*	1 Jan *1,239*	10 Mar *836*	12 Sep *640*	15 Aug *1,095*	11 Nov *1,031*	2 Dec *796*	7 Oct *833*	24 Feb *748*	30 Jan *915*	23 Sep *986*	21 Apr *1,196*	28 Aug *770*	7 Apr *1,077*	12 Dec *759*		14 Apr *1,043*	19 Aug *789*	10 Feb *756*	9 Sep *902*	23 Mar *1,089*
Stalybridge Celtic	11 Nov *404*	27 Jan *683*	26 Aug *431*	30 Dec *813*	15 Nov *280*	7 Oct *430*	17 Mar *457*	3 Apr *365*	12 Aug *430*	1 Jan *761*	21 Apr *615*	31 Mar *443*	6 Mar *397*	6 Jan *395*	17 Oct *308*	24 Feb *441*	22 Aug *401*		28 Oct *388*	2 Dec *520*	9 Apr *457*	2 Sep *446*
Vauxhall Motors	2 Dec *197*	6 Mar *179*	22 Aug *180*	26 Dec *209*	12 Dec *99*	21 Apr *164*	27 Jan *201*	26 Aug *154*	2 Sep *184*	30 Dec *201*	3 Mar *235*	9 Apr *173*	12 Aug *180*	24 Feb *145*	6 Oct *242*	17 Apr *190*	17 Mar *301*	4 Nov *251*		16 Sep *237*	31 Mar *290*	13 Jan *175*
Worcester City	28 Aug *1,103*	23 Mar *775*	23 Sep *952*	13 Nov *865*	9 Sep *864*	7 Apr *818*	6 Oct *883*	20 Jan *1,150*	21 Apr *835*	10 Mar *935*	1 Jan *1,190*	26 Feb *725*	9 Dec *973*	19 Aug *888*	14 Aug *1,189*	11 Sep *1,098*	18 Nov *1,053*	17 Feb *910*	12 Feb *849*		8 Jan *827*	14 Apr *689*
Workington	7 Apr *705*	30 Dec *891*	2 Dec *718*	24 Apr *567*	21 Oct *562*	14 Apr *609*	24 Feb *524*	10 Mar *537*	27 Jan *562*	16 Sep *519*	19 Aug *588*	28 Apr *523*	26 Dec *663*	11 Nov *462*	23 Mar *804*	14 Oct *685*	6 Jan *577*	28 Aug *635*	5 Sep *494*	1 Sep *569*		10 Feb *346*
Worksop Town	12 Sep *411*	17 Feb *384*	4 Nov *449*	9 Apr *393*	20 Jan *321*	1 Jan *499*	31 Mar *353*	23 Sep *447*	26 Aug *387*	14 Oct *339*	20 Mar *372*	9 Dec *322*	7 Oct *277*	21 Apr *768*	3 Mar *452*	27 Mar *273*	12 Aug *610*	13 Mar *338*	9 Sep *249*	22 Aug *347*	18 Nov *423*	

FOOTBALL CONFERENCE NORTH CONSTITUTION 2007-08

AFC TELFORD UNITED
New Bucks Head Stadium, Watling Street, Wellington, Telford, Shropshire TF1 2TU
Tel: 01952 640064
Fax: 01952 640021
Manager: Rob Smith
www.telfordunited.com
Colours: White & black

ALFRETON TOWN
Impact Arena, North Street, Alfreton, Derbyshire DE55 7FZ
Tel: 01773 830277
Club: 01773 832819
Fax: 01773 836164
Manager: Nicky Law
www.alfretontownfc.com
Colours: Red

BARROW
Holker Street Stadium, Wilkie Road, Barrow-in-Furness, Cumbria LA14 5UW
Tel: 01229 820346
Fax: 01229 820346
Manager: Phil Wilson
www.barrowafc.com
Colours: Blue & white

BLYTH SPARTANS
Croft Park, Plessey Road, Blyth, Northumberland NE24 3JE
Tel: 01670 352373
Club: 01670 354818
Fax: 01670 545592
Manager: Harry Dunn
www.blythspartansafc.co.uk
Colours: Green & white

BOSTON UNITED
York Street Ground, York Street, Boston, Lincolnshire
Tel: 01205 365525/364406
Club: 01205 362967
Fax: 01205 354063
Manager: Tommy Taylor
www.bufc.co.uk
Colours: Amber & black

BURSCOUGH
Victoria Park, Mart Lane, Burscough, Ormskirk, Lancashire L40 0SD
Tel: 01704 893237
Fax: 01704 893237
Manager: Liam Watson
www.burscoughfc.co.uk
Colours: Green & white

GAINSBOROUGH TRINITY
The Northolme, North Street, Gainsborough, Lincolnshire DN21 2QN
Tel: 01427 613295
Club: 01427 615625
Fax: 01427 613295
Manager: Paul Mitchell
www.gainsboroughtrinity.com
Colours: Blue & white

HARROGATE TOWN
Wetherby Road, Harrogate, North Yorkshire HG2 7SA
Tel: 01423 880675
Fax: 01423 880675
Manager: Neil Aspin
www.harrogatetown.com
Colours: Yellow & black

HINCKLEY UNITED
The Marstons Stadium, Leicester Road, Hinckley, Leicestershire LE10 3DR
Tel: 01455 840088
Fax: 01455 840088
Manager: Dean Thomas
www.hinckleyunitedfc.org
Colours: Red & blue

HUCKNALL TOWN
Watnall Road, Hucknall, Nottinghamshire NG15 6EY
Tel: 0115 963 0206
Club: 0115 956 1253
Fax: 0115 963 0716
Manager: Andy Legg
www.hucknalltownfc.com
Colours: Yellow & black

HYDE UNITED
Tameside Stadium, Ewens Fields, Walker Lane, Hyde, Cheshire SK14 2SB
Tel: 0161 368 1031
Club: 0161 368 1621
Fax: 0161 367 7273
Manager: Steve Waywell
www.hydeunited.co.uk
Colours: Red & white

KETTERING TOWN
Rockingham Road, Kettering, Northants NN16 9AW
Tel: 01536 483028
Clubhouse: 01536 410962
Fax: 01536 412273
Manager: Mark Cooper
www.ketteringtownfc.co.uk
Colours: Red & black

WWW.CHERRYRED.CO.UK

LEIGH RMI
Hilton Park, Kirkhall Lane, Leigh, Lancashire WN7 1RN
Tel: 01942 743743   Fax: 01942 719266
Manager: Stuart Humphreys   www.leighrmi-mad.co.uk   Colours: Red & white

NUNEATON BOROUGH
Liberty Way Stadium, Liberty Way, Nuneaton, Warwickshire CV11 6RR
Tel: 024 7638 3206   Fax: 024 7639 3925
Manager: Kevin Wilkin   www.nbafc.net   Colours: White & blue

REDDITCH UNITED
Valley Stadium, Bromsgrove Road, Redditch, Worcestershire B97 4RN
Tel: 01527 67450   Fax: 01527 60611
Manager: Gary Whild   www.redditchunited.moonfruit.co.uk   Colours: Red

SOLIHULL MOORS
Damson Park, Damson Parkway, Solihull, West Midlands B91 2PP
Tel: 0121 705 6770   Fax: 0121 711 4045
Manager: Bob Faulkner   www.solihullmoorsfc.co.uk   Colours: Amber & black

SOUTHPORT
Haig Avenue, Southport, Merseyside PR8 6JZ
Tel: 01704 533422   Club: 01704 530182   Fax: 01704 533455
Manager: Peter Davenport   www.southportfc.net   Colours: Yellow & black

STALYBRIDGE CELTIC
Bower Fold, Mottram Road, Stalybridge, Cheshire SK15 2RT
Tel: 0161 338 2828   Club: 0161 338 8443   Fax: 0161 338 8256
Manager: Steve Burr   www.stalybridgeceltic.co.uk   Colours: Blue & white

TAMWORTH
The Lamb Ground, Kettlebrook, Tamworth, Staffordshire B77 1AA
Tel: 01827 65798   Fax: 01827 62236
Manager: Gary Mills   www.thelambs.co.uk   Colours: Red

VAUXHALL MOTORS
Vauxhall Sports Ground, Rivacre Rd, Hooton, Ellesmere Port, South Wirral CH66 1NJ
Tel: 0151 328 1114   Club: 0151 327 2294   Fax: 0151 328 1114
Manager: Chris Macauley   www.vmfc.com   Colours: White & navy blue

WORCESTER CITY
St George's Lane, Barbourne, Worcester, Worcestershire WR1 1QT
Tel: 01905 23003   Fax: 01905 26668
Manager: Andy Preece   www.worcestercityfc.co.uk   Colours: Blue & white

WORKINGTON
Borough Park, Workington, Cumbria CA14 2DT
Tel: 01900 602871   Fax: 01900 67432
Manager: Tommy Cassidy   www.workingtonreds.co.uk   Colours: Red

IN: AFC Telford United (P – Northern Premier League Premier Division), Boston United (R – Football League Division Two), Burscough (P – Northern Premier League Premier Division), Southport (R), Tamworth (R)
OUT: Droylsden (P), Farsley Celtic (P), Lancaster City (R – Northern Premier League Division One), Scarborough (F), Worksop Town (R)
Moor Green have merged with Southern League Division One Midlands side Solihull Borough to form Solihull Moors

WWW.NLNEWSDESK.CO.UK

	Basingstoke Town	Bedford Town	Bishop's Stortford	Bognor Regis Town	Braintree Town	Cambridge City	Dorchester Town	Eastbourne Borough	Eastleigh	Farnborough Town	Fisher Athletic	Havant & Waterlooville	Hayes	Histon	Lewes	Newport County	Salisbury City	Sutton United	Thurrock	Welling United	Weston-super-Mare	Yeading
Basingstoke Town		0-1	1-0	4-0	1-2	0-0	2-2	0-1	0-1	0-2	2-1	2-1	1-1	1-2	0-0	0-1	1-1	0-2	1-1	1-3	0-1	1-3
Bedford Town	0-0		3-1	2-3	1-2	0-1	1-1	1-1	1-1	0-2	1-4	2-1	1-2	0-2	0-2	0-2	1-2	2-0	3-1	2-2	2-1	2-5
Bishop's Stortford	3-1	2-2		0-1	0-2	2-1	4-3	1-0	1-1	2-1	2-2	1-0	3-1	0-0	2-2	1-1	3-2	2-1	1-3	2-2	1-1	2-0
Bognor Regis Town	1-2	1-0	2-4	*C*	1-2	0-1	3-0	1-1	0-0	1-1	1-1	0-0	5-1	0-0	1-1	1-1	1-1	0-4	3-0	1-1	3-1	3-1
Braintree Town	1-0	2-0	3-1	1-2	*O*	2-1	3-1	1-1	1-1	2-1	2-2	0-0	0-1	1-1	1-1	2-1	0-0	0-1	0-1	2-1	0-1	3-1
Cambridge City	0-1	0-0	0-1	2-0	1-0	*N*	1-0	2-0	1-1	0-0	3-0	2-2	0-1	1-1	2-3	2-3	0-1	2-3	3-0	1-0	2-0	0-0
Dorchester Town	1-2	1-3	0-1	0-1	0-0	3-1	*F*	0-0	1-0	4-1	1-3	1-3	0-2	1-2	1-5	0-4	0-3	5-4	3-1	0-1	1-5	3-2
Eastbourne Borough	1-1	0-3	2-1	2-0	1-2	2-1	1-1	*E*	0-0	0-0	3-1	1-1	0-0	1-1	2-1	2-1	1-0	2-0	3-1	0-0	3-0	2-0
Eastleigh	3-1	2-0	1-1	0-4	0-3	0-1	1-1	1-1	*R*	3-1	4-0	0-1	2-1	1-0	0-0	3-1	0-1	1-0	1-1	1-3	1-1	1-4
Farnborough Town	1-1	3-2	3-1	3-1	2-1	2-1	1-1	1-0	0-0	*E*	2-1	1-3	2-3	1-1	1-0	0-1	4-0	2-1	2-1	0-0	2-1	2-1
Fisher Athletic	3-3	3-0	0-1	3-0	3-0	3-0	1-1	0-3	3-1	3-0	*N*	3-3	3-0	1-4	5-1	3-3	1-4	2-1	3-5	2-1	1-1	3-1
Havant & Waterlooville	1-0	4-0	5-4	2-2	1-1	2-3	2-0	2-1	1-1	2-0	1-3	*C*	6-0	2-1	1-1	3-1	3-1	1-0	3-0	4-0	2-1	4-0
Hayes	1-1	3-1	1-2	2-3	2-3	0-1	4-0	1-1	2-1	1-1	4-3	0-1	*E*	1-3	1-4	0-1	0-4	0-4	1-1	1-1	0-1	1-0
Histon	4-2	1-0	0-2	2-1	2-0	2-1	3-0	1-2	1-0	2-1	2-1	4-0	5-0		3-2	1-0	4-2	2-1	3-1	1-0	3-2	1-2
Lewes	2-2	5-1	2-3	1-1	0-1	1-1	2-2	1-1	0-3	1-0	2-0	1-1	2-0	3-1	*S*	2-0	1-0	3-1	1-1	4-2	4-2	3-2
Newport County	3-0	2-0	4-1	3-1	0-1	1-2	0-1	4-0	3-1	3-4	4-2	1-0	2-0	5-1	1-0	*O*	4-3	3-1	1-3	3-1	1-0	4-1
Salisbury City	0-0	3-1	3-1	0-1	0-1	2-0	1-1	1-2	1-0	0-1	3-0	1-1	0-0	0-3	1-1	1-0	*U*	1-0	0-0	1-0	0-0	4-0
Sutton United	3-3	3-1	1-1	3-2	0-0	2-2	0-0	3-1	2-2	1-0	2-2	0-1	1-0	1-0	0-2	1-1	0-1	*T*	2-1	1-2	3-1	1-3
Thurrock	2-2	2-1	0-3	1-1	0-1	1-0	2-3	2-4	1-1	1-4	5-1	1-1	0-1	0-4	3-2	2-2	1-5	3-0	*H*	1-2	2-1	1-0
Welling United	0-2	5-0	2-3	3-0	4-1	1-0	1-2	1-0	2-1	0-0	2-0	1-1	1-1	2-4	0-0	2-3	1-2	1-0	1-2		1-0	5-1
Weston-super-Mare	1-3	2-1	1-2	1-3	0-0	0-1	1-2	2-4	3-3	2-1	0-1	1-5	0-5	1-2	1-1	3-4	1-1	0-2	2-1	1-2		2-1
Yeading	1-1	2-1	1-1	2-0	0-1	5-0	0-0	2-5	1-4	2-1	1-1	1-1	1-1	1-3	1-0	1-1	1-3	2-2	2-1	0-1	0-0	

Conference South

	P	HOME					AWAY					TOTAL					Pts
		W	D	L	F	A	W	D	L	F	A	W	D	L	F	A	
Histon	42	18	0	3	47	20	12	4	5	38	24	30	4	8	85	44	94
Salisbury City	42	10	7	4	26	14	11	5	5	39	23	21	12	9	65	37	75
Braintree Town	42	9	7	5	27	19	12	4	5	24	19	21	11	10	51	38	74
Havant & Waterlooville	42	15	4	2	52	20	5	9	7	23	26	20	13	9	75	46	73
Bishop's Stortford	42	11	7	3	37	26	10	3	8	35	35	21	10	11	72	61	73
Newport County	42	15	1	5	52	24	6	6	9	31	33	21	7	14	83	57	70
Eastbourne Borough	42	11	8	2	29	15	7	7	7	29	27	18	15	9	58	42	69
Welling United	42	11	3	7	37	23	10	3	8	28	28	21	6	15	65	51	69
Lewes	42	11	7	3	41	25	4	10	7	26	27	15	17	10	67	52	62
Fisher Athletic	42	11	5	5	49	33	4	6	11	28	44	15	11	16	77	77	56
Farnborough Town *-10*	42	14	4	3	36	20	5	4	12	23	32	19	8	15	59	52	55
Bognor Regis Town	42	6	10	5	29	23	7	3	11	27	39	13	13	16	56	62	52
Cambridge City	42	8	4	9	25	21	7	3	11	19	31	15	7	20	44	52	52
Sutton United	42	8	8	5	30	26	6	1	14	28	37	14	9	19	58	63	51
Eastleigh	42	8	6	7	26	26	3	9	9	22	27	11	15	16	48	53	48
Yeading	42	6	9	6	27	28	6	0	15	29	50	12	9	21	56	78	45
Dorchester Town	42	6	2	13	26	44	5	10	6	23	33	11	12	19	49	77	45
Thurrock	42	6	6	9	31	40	5	5	11	27	39	11	11	20	58	79	44
Basingstoke Town	42	4	6	11	18	26	5	10	6	28	32	9	16	17	46	58	43
Hayes	42	5	4	12	25	37	6	6	9	22	36	11	10	21	47	73	43
Weston-super-Mare	42	4	4	13	25	45	4	7	10	24	32	8	11	23	49	77	35
Bedford Town	42	5	5	11	25	36	3	2	16	18	46	8	7	27	43	82	31

PLAY-OFFS

SEMI-FINALS (1st leg)

(May 2nd) Bishop's Stortford 1 Salisbury City 1
Att 1,049

(May 2nd) Havant & Waterlooville 1 Braintree Town 1
Att 1,011

SEMI-FINALS (2nd leg)

(May 5th) **Braintree Town** 1 Havant & Waterlooville 1
aet (4-2p) *Att* 1,519

(May 5th) **Salisbury City** 3 Bishop's Stortford 1 *aet*
Att 1,920

FINAL

(May 13th at Stevenage Borough)
Braintree Town 0 **Salisbury City** 1 *Att* 3,167

WWW.CHERRYRED.CO.UK

DATES & GATES

WWW.NLNEWSDESK.CO.UK

Only the values that could be read with confidence are reproduced below; cells left blank could not be read reliably from the source image.

Home \ Away	Basingstoke Town	Bedford Town	Bishop's Stortford	Bognor Regis Town	Braintree Town	Cambridge City	Dorchester Town	Eastbourne Borough	Eastleigh	Farnborough Town	Fisher Athletic	Havant & Waterlooville	Hayes	Histon	Lewes	Newport County	Salisbury City	Sutton United	Thurrock	Welling United	Weston-super-Mare	Yeading
Basingstoke Town	—	2 Sep / 310	9 Apr / 265	27 Jan / 314	5 Dec / 243	26 Aug / 254	16 Jan / 325	21 Apr / 286	1 Jan / 731	27 Mar / 267	10 Mar / 539	13 Jan / 279	10 Feb / 231	24 Feb / 241	3 Apr / 333	31 Mar / 272	7 Oct / 236	17 Mar / 279	12 Aug / 246	23 Sep / 246	22 Aug / 253	12 Sep / 261
Bedford Town	13 Feb / 696	—	22 Aug / 759																			
Bishop's Stortford	28 Aug / 561	14 Apr / 745	—																			
Bognor Regis Town	16 Sep / 372	3 Feb / 652		—																		
Braintree Town	3 Mar / 275	12 Sep / 275			—																	
Cambridge City	7 Apr / 429	26 Dec / 379				—																
Dorchester Town	17 Feb / 360	23 Sep / 453					—															
Eastbourne Borough	21 Oct / 546	23 Sep / 679						—														
Eastleigh	1 Jan / 731	14 Apr / 385							—													
Farnborough Town	6 Mar / 355	18 Nov / 456								—												
Fisher Athletic	4 Nov / 1,204	9 Dec / 1,011									—											
Havant & Waterlooville	3 Feb / 216	19 Feb / 463										—										
Hayes	18 Nov / 157	3 Apr / 679											—									
Histon	9 Dec / 224	16 Aug / 245												—								
Lewes	9 Sep / 553	17 Feb / 771													—							
Newport County	16 Aug / 380	7 Apr / 445														—						
Salisbury City	28 Apr / 977	27 Jan / 679															—					
Sutton United	19 Aug / 404	10 Mar / 683																—				
Thurrock	23 Mar / 197	28 Oct / 179																	—			
Welling United	17 Apr / 1,103	21 Oct / 775																		—		
Weston-super-Mare	14 Apr / 705	10 Aug / 891																			—	
Yeading	20 Jan / 411	19 Aug / 384																				—

FOOTBALL CONFERENCE SOUTH CONSTITUTION 2007-08

BASINGSTOKE TOWN
The Camrose Ground, Western Way, Basingstoke, Hampshire RG22 6EZ
Tel: 01256 327575   Boardroom: 01256 325063   Fax: 01256 869997
Manager: Francis Vines   www.btfc.co.uk   Colours: Blue & yellow

BATH CITY
Twerton Park, Twerton, Bath, North Somerset BA2 1DB
Tel: 01225 423087   Club: 01225 313247   Fax: 01225 481391
Manager: John Relish   www.bathcityfc.com   Colours: Black & white

BISHOP'S STORTFORD
Woodside Park, Dunmow Road, Bishop's Stortford, Hertfordshire CM23 5RG
Tel: 08700 339930   Fax: 08700 339931
Manager: Martin Hayes   www.bsfc.co.uk   Colours: Blue & white

BOGNOR REGIS TOWN
Nyewood Lane, Bognor Regis, West Sussex PO21 2TY
Tel: 01243 822325   Fax: 01243 866151
Manager: Jack Pearce   www.therocks.co.uk   Colours: White & green

BRAINTREE TOWN
Cressing Road Stadium, Clockhouse Way, Braintree, Essex CM7 6RD
Tel: 01376 345617   Fax: 01376 323369
Manager: George Borg   www.braintreetownfc.org.uk   Colours: Yellow

BROMLEY
The Clive Christian Stadium, Hayes Lane, Bromley, Kent BR2 9EF
Tel: 020 8313 3992   Boardroom: 020 8460 5291
Manager: Mark Goldberg   www.bromleyfc.net   Colours: White & black

CAMBRIDGE CITY
City Ground, Milton Road, Cambridge, Cambridgeshire CB4 1UY
Tel: 01223 357973   Fax: 01223 351582
Manager: Gary Roberts   www.cambridgecityfc.com   Colours: White & black

DORCHESTER TOWN
The Avenue Stadium, Weymouth Avenue, Dorchester, Dorset DT1 2RY
Tel: 01305 262451   Fax: 01305 267623
Manager: Shaun Brooks   www.dorchestertownfc.co.uk   Colours: Black & white

EASTBOURNE BOROUGH
Langney Sports Club, Priory Lane, Eastbourne, East Sussex BN23 7QH
Tel: 01323 743561   Fax: 01323 743561
Manager: Garry Wilson   www.eastbourneboroughfc.co.uk   Colours: Red & black

EASTLEIGH
Silverlake Stadium, Ten Acres, Stoneham Lane, North Stoneham, Eastleigh SO50 9HT
Tel: 023 8061 3361   Fax: 023 8061 2379
Manager: Paul Dowsell   www.eastleigh-fc.co.uk   Colours: White & navy blue

FISHER ATHLETIC
Dulwich Hamlet FC, Champion Hill Stadium, Dog Kennel Hill, East Dulwich SE22 8BD
Tel: 020 7274 2707
Manager: Wayne Burnett   www.fisherathletic.co.uk   Colours: Black & white

HAMPTON & RICHMOND BOROUGH
Beveree Stadium, Beaver Close, Station Road, Hampton, Middlesex TW12 2BX
Tel: 020 8941 2838   Boardroom: 020 8941 4936   Fax/Club: 020 8979 2456
Manager: Alan Devonshire   www.hamptonfc.com   Colours: Red & blue

HAVANT & WATERLOOVILLE
Westleigh Park, Martin Road, Havant, Hampshire PO9 5TH
Tel: 023 9278 7822   Club: 023 9278 7855   Fax: 023 9226 2367
Manager: Ian Baird   www.havantandwaterlooville.net   Colours: White

HAYES & YEADING UNITED
Townfield House, Church Road, Hayes, Middlesex UB3 2LE
Tel: 020 8573 2075   Fax: 020 8573 2075
Manager: Garry Haylock   www.hyufc.net   Colours: Red, white & black

LEWES
The Dripping Pan, Mountfield Road, Lewes, East Sussex BN7 1XN
Tel: 01273 472100   Fax: 01273 472100
Manager: Steve King   www.lewesfc.com   Colours: Red & black

MAIDENHEAD UNITED
York Road, Maidenhead, Berkshire SL6 1SQ
Tel: 01628 636314   Club: 01628 624739
Manager: Johnson Hippolyte   www.maidenheadunitedfc.co.uk   Colours: Black & white

NEWPORT COUNTY
Newport Stadium, Langland Way, Spytty Park, Newport, Gwent NP19 4PT
Tel: 01633 662262   Stadium: 01633 671815   Fax: 01633 666107
Manager: Peter Beadle   www.newport-county.co.uk   Colours: Amber & black

ST ALBANS CITY
Clarence Park, York Road, St Albans, Hertfordshire AL1 4PL
Tel: 01727 864296   Club: 01727 866819   Fax: 01727 866235
Manager: Ritchie Hanlon   www.sacfc.co.uk   Colours: Yellow & blue

SUTTON UNITED
Borough Sports Ground, Gander Green Lane, Sutton, Surrey SM1 2EY
Tel: 020 8644 4440   Fax: 020 8644 5120
Manager: Ian Hazel   www.suttonunited.net   Colours: Chocolate & amber

THURROCK
Thurrock Hotel, Ship Lane, Grays, Essex RM19 1YN
Tel: 01708 865492   Club: 01708 865492   Fax: 01708 868863
Manager: Hakan Hayrettin   www.thurrockfc.co.uk   Colours: Yellow & green

WELLING UNITED
Park View Road, Welling, Kent DA16 1SY
Tel: 020 8301 1196   Fax: 020 8301 5676
Manager: Neil Smith   www.wellingunited.com   Colours: Red & white

WESTON-SUPER-MARE
Winterstoke Road, Weston-super-Mare, North Somerset BS24 9AA
Tel: 01934 621618   Fax: 01934 622704
Manager: Tony Ricketts   www.westonsupermareafc.co.uk   Colours: White & blue

IN: Bath City (P – Southern League Premier Division), Bromley (P – Isthmian League Premier Division), Hampton & Richmond Borough (P – Isthmian League Premier Division), Maidenhead United (P – Southern League Premier Division), St Albans City (R)
OUT: Bedford Town (R – Southern League Premier Division), Farnborough (formerly Farnborough Town) (R – Southern League Division One South), Histon (P), Salisbury City (P)
Hayes and Yeading haved merged to form Hayes & Yeading United

WWW.NLNEWSDESK.CO.UK

THE BEST BET FOR NON-LEAGUE FOOTBALL

GLOUCESTERSHIRE COUNTY LEAGUE

	AXA	Berkeley Town	DRG Stapleton	Ellwood	Hanham Athletic	Hardwicke	Henbury Old Boys	Highridge United	Kings Stanley	Patchway Town	Pucklechurch	RG St George	Sea Mills Park	Taverners	Thornbury Town	Totterdown PB	Wotton Rovers	Yate Town Res.
AXA		5-2	1-1	5-0	1-1	0-0	0-2	2-3	0-2	3-2	8-3	1-3	2-1	0-1	2-0	3-2	0-0	0-0
Berkeley Town	2-1		0-2	0-2	0-2	1-4	2-1	1-1	0-2	3-3	3-1	0-1	2-1	0-3	2-1	2-2	2-2	0-3
DRG Stapleton	3-3	0-1		1-0	3-2	2-1	1-3	0-2	1-2	2-4	1-0	2-2	0-1	2-4	1-1	4-2	1-1	1-2
Ellwood	1-2	3-2	0-1		W-L	3-2	0-2	3-2	3-0	0-3	3-1	1-1	3-0	1-0	5-0	1-2	3-1	0-4
Hanham Athletic	2-2	2-1	2-0	3-0		2-3	0-1	2-2	4-0	0-0	5-1	0-2	0-0	0-0	1-0	1-0	1-0	2-1
Hardwicke	2-2	2-4	2-3	2-0	1-0		2-1	0-6	2-0	0-2	4-0	0-0	2-3	1-1	1-1	0-2	2-1	1-0
Henbury Old Boys	2-2	6-1	1-0	2-1	3-1	0-2		2-3	3-0		1-2	1-5	2-1	0-3	3-1	2-1	4-0	2-5
Highridge United	7-1	3-2	2-0	2-0	0-1	2-1	5-2		1-0	0-1	1-1	0-2	3-2	1-0	2-1	1-4	2-2	1-1
Kings Stanley	1-2	1-0	2-0	1-1	4-0	0-3	0-7	0-2		3-0	0-1	2-5	2-1	0-0	2-1	3-2	5-0	1-4
Patchway Town	3-0	1-0	4-0	3-2	2-1	2-0	0-3	1-0	1-1		6-0	1-1	2-2	1-0	3-0	2-1	0-0	2-1
Pucklechurch Sports	0-1	4-2	0-1	1-2	0-2	2-1	1-2	0-4	0-4	1-4		0-1	1-1	0-1	1-1	0-0	0-0	1-3
Roman Glass St George	2-1	1-1	3-0	1-2	2-0	2-0	1-1	1-2	3-1	1-3	4-0		2-1	4-0	4-1	3-3	4-2	3-3
Sea Mills Park	4-2	0-0	2-2	0-1	1-4	3-1	2-2	2-1	2-0	2-1	0-0	1-2		0-3	4-2	1-5	4-2	2-1
Taverners	2-1	0-1	3-1	2-0	2-2	3-0	0-1	1-3	3-0	2-3	1-0	1-2	1-0		1-0	1-4	2-1	2-1
Thornbury Town	1-1	2-1	2-4	1-2	0-0	0-1	1-2	0-2	1-3	4-0	2-2	0-2	3-1	1-1		0-2	2-2	1-0
Totterdown Port of Bristol	0-0	1-4	3-1	1-6	0-3	4-1	2-4	1-1	0-2	0-2	2-1	1-3	8-0	0-1	2-1		4-0	1-3
Wotton Rovers	1-3	1-1	4-1	1-4	0-0	0-2	4-2	0-3	3-0	1-1	3-0	0-7	0-2	0-1	1-4	3-0		0-5
Yate Town Res.	5-0	1-1	5-0	5-0	7-0	1-2	1-0	3-2	1-1	1-1	3-1	0-1	5-0	0-1	3-1	3-0	5-2	

	P	W	D	L	F	A	Pts
Roman Glass St George	34	22	8	4	77	36	74
Patchway Town	34	21	8	5	66	36	71
Highridge United	34	20	6	8	72	40	66
Henbury Old Boys	34	20	4	10	75	47	64
Yate Town Res.	34	19	6	9	86	34	63
Taverners	34	19	5	10	46	30	62
Ellwood	34	17	2	15	53	54	53
Hanham Athletic *-3*	34	14	9	11	46	39	48
Hardwicke	34	14	5	15	48	53	47
Kings Stanley	34	14	4	16	45	57	46
AXA	34	11	11	12	57	61	44
Totterdown Port of Bristol	34	13	4	17	63	63	43
Sea Mills Park	34	11	7	16	48	67	40
DRG Stapleton	34	10	6	18	42	67	36
Berkeley Town	34	9	8	17	44	65	35
Wotton Rovers *-1*	34	5	10	19	37	76	24
Thornbury Town	34	5	8	21	37	64	23
Pucklechurch Sports	34	3	7	24	25	78	16

LES JAMES MEMORIAL CUP

PRELIMINARY ROUND
DRG Stapleton 3 Kings Stanley 2
Thornbury Town 2 Sea Mills Park 0
FIRST ROUND
Berkeley Town 0 **Totterdown Port of Bristol** 0 (3-4p)
Hanham Athletic 1 AXA 1 (4-3p)
Henbury Old Boys 1 **Roman Glass St George** 3
Highridge United 3 DRG Stapleton 1 (at DRG Stapleton)
Patchway Town 4 Ellwood 0
Taverners 6 Hardwicke 2
Wotton Rovers 2 Pucklechurch Sports 0
Yate Town Res. 3 Thornbury Town 0
QUARTER-FINALS
Hanham Athletic 1 Highridge United 0
Roman Glass St George 1 **Taverners** 3
Totterdown Port of Bristol 1 **Patchway Town** 4
Wotton Rovers 1 **Yate Town Res.** 4 (at Yate Town)
SEMI-FINALS
Patchway Town 2 Taverners 1 (at Yate Town)
Yate Res. 1 Hanham 1 (3-5p) (at Yate) (Hanham expelled)
FINAL
(April 25th at Yate Town)
Patchway Town 1 Yate Town Res. 0

WWW.NLNEWSDESK.CO.UK

GLOUCESTERSHIRE COUNTY LEAGUE CONSTITUTION 2007-08
AXA . . . . Cribbs Causeway, Bristol BS10 7TT 0117 950 2303
BERKELEY TOWN . . . . Station Road, Berkeley GL13 9AJ . . . . None
DRG STAPLETON . . . . Frenchay Park Road, Frenchay, Bristol BS16 1HY . . . . None
ELLWOOD . . . . Bromley Road, Ellwood, Coleford GL16 7LZ 01594 832927
HANHAM ATHLETIC . . . . Vicarage Road Playing Fields, Hanham, Bristol BS15 3AH . . . . None
HARDWICKE . . . . Green Lane, Hardwicke, Gloucester GL2 4QA 01452 720587
HENBURY OLD BOYS . . . . Lorain Walk, Henbury, Bristol BS10 7AS 0117 959 0475
HIGHRIDGE UNITED . . . . Lakemead Grove, Highridge, Bristol BS13 8EA 0117 978 4878
KINGS STANLEY . . . . Marling Close, Kings Stanley GL5 5AQ 01453 828975
PATCHWAY TOWN . . . . Scott Park, Coniston Road, Patchway, Bristol BS34 5JR 0117 949 3952
PUCKLECHURCH SPORTS . . Pucklechurch Rec Ground, St Aldams Drive, Pucklechurch, Bristol BS16 9QQ 0117 937 2102
SEA MILLS PARK . . . . Napier Miles Road, Lawrence Weston, Bristol BS11 0UU . . . . None
TAVERNERS . . . . Highwood School, Spring Hill, Nailsworth GL6 0LU . . . . None
THORNBURY TOWN . . . . Mundy Playing Fields, Kington Lane, Thornbury BS35 1NB . . . . None
TOTTERDOWN PORT OF BRISTOL . . City & Port of Bristol SC, Nibley Road, Shirehampton, Bristol BS11 9XW 0117 982 3927
TUFFLEY ROVERS . . . . Glevum Park, Lower Tuffley Lane, Gloucester GL2 6DT 01452 423402
WOTTON ROVERS . . . . Synwell Playing Fields, Synwell Lane, Wotton-under-Edge GL12 7HQ 01453 842929
YATE TOWN RESERVES . . . . Lodge Road, Yate, Bristol BS17 5LE 01454 228103
IN: Tuffley Rovers (P – Gloucestershire Northern Senior League Division One)
OUT: Roman Glass St George (P – Western League Division One)

GLOUCESTERSHIRE NORTHERN SENIOR LEAGUE

	Bishops Cleeve Res.	Bourton Rovers	Brimscombe & Thrupp	Broadwell Amateurs	Brockworth Albion	Cam Bulldogs	Cheltenham Civil Service	Huntley	Kingswood	Longlevens	Lydbrook Athletic	Sharpness	Shortwood United Res.	Tetbury Town	Tuffley Rovers	Viney St Swithins
Bishops Cleeve Res.		4-1	1-1	2-2	1-0	1-1	4-1	5-0	0-1	2-0	1-0	1-0	4-0	3-0	0-2	4-0
Bourton Rovers	0-5		0-1	1-2	1-1	4-0	1-0	6-3	1-2	0-1	1-3	2-2	2-0	1-2	2-5	4-0
Brimscombe & Thrupp	1-2	1-3	D	0-1	3-0	0-0	6-2	3-5	3-1	0-3	1-3	2-1	2-3	1-0	1-3	3-3
Broadwell Amateurs	1-3	2-1	2-4	I	4-1	3-0	0-2	5-1	2-1	5-2	2-1	1-1	4-0	6-0	0-1	2-0
Brockworth Albion	2-6	0-3	0-2	0-0	V	2-0	3-2	3-1	1-0	0-2	2-1	1-1	2-0	3-1	0-3	2-1
Cam Bulldogs	2-1	4-1	3-0	2-4	1-0	I	3-0	1-2	2-1	5-2	1-2	0-2	2-1	2-1	1-5	4-0
Cheltenham Civil Service	2-1	1-1	2-1	1-2	2-3	2-1	S	8-2	1-1	2-4	1-2	6-1	1-3	1-2	2-5	5-1
Huntley	1-4	1-3	1-3	0-9	1-1	2-0	1-3	I	0-6	2-5	1-1	3-3	3-3	1-5	1-1	5-2
Kingswood	2-0	2-1	2-0	0-5	1-2	2-1	3-4	2-1	O	0-0	3-5	0-4	4-3	2-1	2-4	5-0
Longlevens	1-2	1-0	1-3	3-0	1-1	1-0	0-5	5-1	2-3	N	2-4	2-0	5-1	1-6	0-2	2-0
Lydbrook Athletic	2-0	2-2	2-2	1-4	4-1	2-1	2-0	3-1	5-0	2-1		1-1	2-2	4-2	2-0	6-0
Sharpness	1-4	4-0	2-2	1-3	0-2	2-1	4-2	1-0	4-2	3-1	3-0	O	2-3	1-4	3-1	6-0
Shortwood United Res.	1-1	3-0	0-2	1-2	3-1	0-2	4-2	2-1	4-2	4-3	0-1	1-4	N	3-3	1-5	4-0
Tetbury Town	2-1	2-1	0-0	1-0	0-0	0-0	4-4	1-1	1-6	4-0	2-1	0-3	3-2	E	0-3	5-0
Tuffley Rovers	3-0	1-1	2-2	3-2	3-2	3-1	2-0	6-0	1-1	2-2	2-0	1-1	2-1	5-1		2-0
Viney St Swithins	0-3	1-6	0-5	0-3	1-2	0-3	0-1	0-3	1-2	1-4	0-2	0-0	2-3	0-0	1-5	

Division One	P	W	D	L	F	A	Pts
Tuffley Rovers	30	22	6	2	83	28	72
Broadwell Amateurs	30	20	3	7	78	34	63
Lydbrook Athletic	30	18	5	7	66	39	59
Bishops Cleeve Res.	30	18	4	8	66	30	58
Sharpness	30	13	8	9	61	46	47
Kingswood	30	14	3	13	59	59	45
Brimscombe & Thrupp	30	12	7	11	55	48	43
Tetbury Town	30	12	7	11	53	56	43
Longlevens	30	13	3	14	57	60	42
Brockworth Albion	30	12	6	12	37	49	42
Cam Bulldogs	30	12	3	15	43	45	39
Shortwood United Res.	30	11	4	15	56	69	37
Cheltenham Civil Service	30	11	3	16	65	68	36
Bourton Rovers	30	9	5	16	50	56	32
Huntley	30	5	6	19	45	100	21
Viney St Swithins	30	0	3	27	14	101	3

WWW.CHERRYRED.CO.UK

REG DAVIS MEMORIAL CUP

FIRST ROUND

Ashton Keynes 1 **Tetbury Town** 5
Bishops Cleeve Res. (scr.) v **Cam Bulldogs** (w/o)
Bourton Rovers 5 Brockworth Albion 2
Broadwell Amateurs 10 Huntley 1
Chalford 0 **Sharpness** 9
Charfield 1 **Brimscombe & Thrupp** 1 (2-3p)
Gala Wilton 1 Cheltenham Civil Service 0
Harrow Hill Res. 4 Longford 0
Longlevens 4 Stonehouse Freeway 2
Mitcheldean 1 **Lydbrook Athletic** 1 (0-3p)
Mushet & Coalway 1 **Bredon** 1 (4-5p)
Shortwood United Res. 4 Dursley Town 1
Slimbridge Res. 3 Kingswood 1
Smiths Athletic 0 **Newton Heath** 5
Staunton & Corse 1 **Viney St Swithins** 2
Tuffley Rovers 6 Star 0

GLOUCESTERSHIRE NORTHERN SENIOR LEAGUE DIVISION ONE CONSTITUTION 2007-08

BISHOPS CLEEVE RESERVES . . . . Kayte Lane, Bishops Cleeve, Cheltenham GL52 3PD 07866 077291
BOURTON ROVERS . . . . Rissington Road, Bourton-on-the-Water, Cheltenham GL54 2DZ. 01451 821977
BRIMSCOMBE & THRUPP . . . . The Meadow, London Road, Brimscombe, Stroud GL5 2QE. 01453 885039
BROADWELL AMATEURS . . . . The Hawthornes, Poolway Road, Broadwell, Coleford GL16 7BE. 01594 837347
BROCKWORTH ALBION . . . . Parton Road, Churchdown GL3 2JH. . . . . None
CAM BULLDOGS . . . . Recreation Ground, Everlands, Cam, Dursley GL11 5NL 01453 546736
CHELTENHAM CIVIL SERVICE . . Civil Service Sports Ground, Tewkesbury Road, Uckington, Cheltenham GL51 9SX 01242 680424
KINGSWOOD . . . . Wickwar Road, Kingswood, Wotton-under-Edge GL12 8RF 07836 734020
LONGLEVENS . . . . Longford Lane, Longlevens, Gloucester GL2 9EU 01452 530388
LYDBROOK ATHLETIC . . . . Reeds Sports Ground, Lydbrook. . . . . None
NEWTON HEATH . . . . Whaddon Road Recreation Ground, Whaddon Road, Cheltenham GL52 5NS . . . . None
SHARPNESS. . . . . Berkeley Vale Community School, Sharpness. . . . . None
SHORTWOOD UNITED RESERVES . . . . Meadowbank, Shortwood, Nailsworth, Stroud GL6 0SJ. 01453 833936
SLIMBRIDGE . . . . Wisloe Road, Cambridge GL2 7AF 01453 890361
STAR . . . . Kayte Lane, Bishops Cleeve, Cheltenham GL52 3PD . . . . None
TETBURY TOWN. . . . . Preston Park, Cirencester Road, Tetbury GL8 8EZ. . . . . None

IN: Newton Heath (P), Slimbridge (W – Hellenic League Premier Division), Star (P)
OUT: Huntley (R), Tuffley Rovers (P – Gloucestershire County League), Viney St Swithins (R)

	AK	Bre	Cha	Chf	Dur	Gal	Har	Lon	Mit	Mus	New	Sli	Smi	Sta	S&C	Sto
Ashton Keynes		0-0	1-2	4-1	1-0	2-8	0-3	1-0	1-1	3-1	0-1	1-0	0-6	1-0	4-1	4-1
Bredon	2-1		2-2	2-2	2-1	3-1	5-0	1-2	3-1	4-0	0-1	2-3	0-0	1-4	3-0	4-0
Chalford	1-0	1-1	D	1-1	0-3	0-12	1-7	3-0	1-1	1-0	0-1	0-9	0-2	0-5	2-1	2-4
Charfield	3-4	1-2	1-5	I	4-2	1-4	1-3	2-2	3-2	3-1	3-0	0-2	1-2	2-4	4-1	2-1
Dursley Town	2-0	2-0	8-0	5-1	V	2-3	1-0	4-2	2-1	1-0	1-4	2-4	2-1	3-3	4-3	4-1
Gala Wilton	4-2	3-1	4-2	5-1	2-1	I	2-5	3-1	1-1	2-0	0-2	1-4	2-3	1-2	5-0	3-2
Harrow Hill Res.	3-1	2-0	3-1	1-6	2-0	3-5	S	2-2	0-1	1-1	2-3	0-3	0-1	2-4	10-2	4-0
Longford	4-0	1-0	1-0	1-2	0-4	1-4	2-2	I	1-1	4-0	3-2	0-1	0-4	0-0	0-4	1-3
Mitcheldean	6-3	0-2	1-2	4-1	1-3	0-6	0-0	1-1	O	5-3	4-3	0-5	1-0	0-3	1-0	5-1
Mushet & Coalway	2-3	1-3	0-1	3-1	3-1	0-1	0-4	3-1	1-1	N	1-2	0-5	1-2	0-5	4-2	3-0
Newton Heath	3-0	1-1	2-1	2-0	3-1	3-1	0-1	0-4	3-2	3-2		0-3	5-0	1-1	2-1	3-0
Slimbridge Res.	2-0	1-0	3-0	1-0	5-0	3-2	6-1	6-0	9-0	2-0	5-0	T	3-1	1-0	7-0	5-1
Smiths Athletic	5-2	2-1	6-0	3-3	0-4	3-1	2-2	1-0	4-1	7-1	1-0	1-4	W	2-1	3-0	5-0
Star	0-1	2-1	1-0	3-0	2-1	2-2	1-2	5-5	3-1	3-0	1-1	0-2	1-0	O	4-0	4-1
Staunton & Corse	1-4	0-6	1-3	2-4	1-4	1-8	1-4	0-1	0-1	1-0	1-3	0-6	0-2	1-8		1-5
Stonehouse Freeway	0-1	2-3	5-0	0-2	1-2	3-4	2-0	3-2	1-2	4-4	4-2	0-7	3-2	0-2	4-1	

SECOND ROUND

Brimscombe & Thrupp 0 **Slimbridge Res.** 7
Broadwell Amateurs 6 Harrow Hill Res. 0
Cam Bulldogs 1 **Tuffley Rovers** 4
(at Tuffley Rovers)
Gala Wilton 1 **Bourton Rovers** 2
Longlevens 3 **Bredon** 3 (3-4p)
Sharpness 3 Tetbury Town 1
Shortwood United Res. 4 Newton Heath 2
(at Newton Heath)
Viney St Swithins 0 **Lydbrook Athletic** 4

QUARTER-FINALS

Bourton Rovers 3 Shortwood United Res. 0
Lydbrook Athletic 2 Bredon 0
Sharpness 2 **Slimbridge Res.** 5
Tuffley Rovers 8 Broadwell Amateurs 3

SEMI-FINALS

Slimbridge Res. 5 Bourton Rovers 2
Tuffley Rovers 2 Lydbrook Athletic 1

FINAL

(October 4th at Bishops Cleeve)
Tuffley Rovers 0 **Slimbridge Res.** 2

Division Two	P	W	D	L	F	A	Pts
Slimbridge Res.	30	30	0	0	124	12	90
Star	30	20	5	5	84	31	65
Newton Heath	30	20	4	6	57	38	64
Gala Wilton	30	19	2	9	100	54	59
Smiths Athletic	30	17	4	9	57	40	59
Dursley Town	30	17	1	12	70	50	52
Bredon	30	13	6	11	55	37	45
Harrow Hill Res.	30	13	5	12	68	56	44
Ashton Keynes	30	12	2	16	42	66	38
Mitcheldean	30	10	7	13	45	68	37
Charfield	30	10	4	16	56	72	34
Longford	30	9	6	15	45	62	33
Chalford	30	9	4	17	32	86	31
Stonehouse Freeway	30	8	1	21	49	80	25
Mushet & Coalway	30	5	3	22	37	75	18
Staunton & Corse	30	1	0	29	23	117	3

WWW.NLNEWSDESK.CO.UK

GLOUCESTERSHIRE NORTHERN LEAGUE DIVISION TWO CONSTITUTION 2007-08

ASHTON KEYNES .... Bradstone Sports Ground, Rixon Gate, Ashton Keynes, Swindon SN6 6PH .... None
BREDON .... Main Road, Bredon, Tewkesbury GL20 7EG 01684 773152
CHALFORD .... Chalford Sports & Social Club, Chalford Hill, Stroud GL6 8BD 01453 884214
CHARFIELD................................ Charfield Memorial Hall, Charfield 01454 260204
DURSLEY TOWN .... Memorial Ground, Kingshill Road, Dursley GL11 4BJ 01453 546122
GALA WILTON................... Gala Club, Fairmile Gardens, Longford, Gloucester GL2 9EB .... None
HARROW HILL RESERVES .... Larksfield Road, Harrow Hill, Drybrook GL17 9JP 01594 543873
HATHERLEY RANGERS..................... The Newlands, Bishops Cleeve .... None
HUNTLEY............................. Recreation Ground, Huntley .... None
LONGFORD .... Playing Field, Longford Lane, Gloucester GL2 9EU .... None
MITCHELDEAN .... Townsend Playing Fields, Mitcheldean GL17 0BA .... None
RAMBLERS .... Wagon Works Sports & Social, Tuffley Park, Tuffley Avenue, Gloucester GL1 5NS 01452 524621
SMITHS ATHLETIC........ Dowty Rotol Sports Ground, Hatherley Lane, Staverton, Cheltenham GL51 4NF 01242 525515
STONEHOUSE TOWN .... Oldends Lane, Stonehouse GL10 2DG .... None
TIDENHAM .... Tidenham Recreation Ground, Tidenham .... None
VINEY ST SWITHINS .... Viney Sports & Social Club, Viney Hill, Lydney GL15 4NF 01594 510658

IN: Hatherley Rangers (P – Cheltenham Association League Division One), Huntley (R), Ramblers (P – Stroud & District League Division One), Viney St Swithins (R), Tidenham (P – North Gloucestershire League)
OUT: Mushet & Coalway (R), Newton Heath (P), Slimbridge Reserves (F), Star (P), Staunton & Corse (R)
Stonehouse Freeway become Stonehouse Town

GWENT COUNTY LEAGUE

	Abercarn United	Albion Rovers	Blaenavon Blues	Clydach Wasps	Coed Eva Athletic	Cwmffrwdoer Sports	Mardy	Monmouth Town	Newport Civil Service	Panteg	Spencer Youth & Boys	Treowen Stars	Trinant	Undy Athletic	West Pontnewydd
Abercarn United		5-3	3-1	1-1	0-2	3-1	2-0	0-4	1-1	4-1	2-0	1-3	1-1	1-3	3-2
Albion Rovers	2-1	D	3-1	2-1	4-4	1-3	5-0	1-1	0-2	1-1	4-0	0-2	2-2	1-4	0-1
Blaenavon Blues	2-3	1-0	I	2-0	1-1	0-2	1-1	2-1	1-2	1-0	1-0	0-2	4-1	4-4	6-1
Clydach Wasps	2-1	3-3	1-3	V	5-1	2-4	1-3	2-0	4-1	3-1	2-2	3-2	2-1	2-3	4-2
Coed Eva Athletic	4-1	3-6	1-4	2-2	I	2-3	1-2	0-5	0-2	6-2	3-3	0-4	4-0	2-3	7-3
Cwmffrwdoer Sports	4-1	1-4	2-5	1-2	0-1	S	6-3	7-1	1-1	0-0	4-0	2-2	3-0	2-3	3-0
Mardy	2-4	3-0	1-3	0-5	1-0	3-0	I	2-2	0-1	2-1	2-0	1-3	2-1	2-5	1-0
Monmouth Town	2-0	2-1	3-2	4-0	0-2	3-0	3-1	O	5-1	7-0	4-5	2-2	5-0	4-3	7-1
Newport Civil Service	2-0	2-0	4-3	2-1	4-1	5-0	6-1	3-2	N	5-2	1-1	2-1	2-1	3-2	5-0
Panteg	5-3	0-2	1-1	1-1	1-1	0-2	1-4	1-3	0-1		4-4	2-2	2-2	1-1	3-2
Spencer Youth & Boys	5-1	0-1	0-1	0-2	7-0	2-1	4-0	0-2	2-1	1-2		2-2	0-0	2-3	2-4
Treowen Stars	1-0	3-1	1-0	1-1	2-5	2-0	1-0	1-1	1-0	1-1	3-3	O	2-2	0-0	0-2
Trinant	2-2	2-4	4-2	0-3	1-1	4-2	0-3	0-0	1-2	3-2	2-5	1-1	N	2-3	5-1
Undy Athletic	0-0	2-4	1-0	3-3	2-1	1-1	3-2	0-4	2-1	1-3	0-3	1-1	4-2	E	5-1
West Pontnewydd	2-3	2-5	3-3	1-2	3-4	0-2	1-5	1-5	0-6	2-3	1-5	1-3	3-1	0-1	

Division One	P	W	D	L	F	A	Pts
Newport Civil Serve	28	20	3	5	68	33	63
Monmouth Town	28	17	5	6	82	38	56
Undy Athletic	28	14	7	7	61	52	49
Treowen Stars	28	12	12	4	49	34	48
Clydach Wasps	28	13	7	8	60	47	46
Blaenavon Blues	28	12	5	11	55	46	41
Albion Rovers	28	12	5	11	60	52	41
Cwmffrwdoer Sports	28	12	4	12	57	51	40
Mardy	28	12	2	14	47	60	38
Abercarn United	28	10	5	13	47	58	35
Spencer Youth & Boys	28	9	7	12	58	53	34
Coed Eva Athletic	28	9	6	13	59	71	33
Panteg	28	5	10	13	41	66	25
Trinant	28	5	9	14	39	65	24
West Pontnewydd	28	4	1	23	40	97	13

WWW.CHERRYRED.CO.UK

LEAGUE CUP

FIRST ROUND
Albion Rovers 2 New Inn 0
Cefn Fforest 1 RTB Ebbw Vale 0
FC Dugout 1 **AC Pontymister** 2
Lliswerry 1 Abertillery 0
Mardy 4 Blaenavon Blues 2
Newport Civil Service 2 **Cwmffrwdoer Sports** 3
Panteg 1 Crusaders 0
Pentwynmawr Athletic 3 Crickhowell 2
Race 1 **Lucas Cwmbran** 6
Rogerstone Welfare 2 **Trethomas Bluebirds** 4
Thornwell Red & White 0 **Sebastopol** 5
Treowen Stars 5 Abercarn United 2
West Pontnewydd 1 **Spencer Youth & Boys** 3
Whiteheads 0 **Caldicot Castle** 6
SECOND ROUND
AC Pontymister 2 **Underwood Social Club** 3
Albion Rovers 8 Abergavenny Thursdays 1
Caldicot Castle 1 **Cromwell Youth** 3
Cefn Fforest 2 **Abertillery Bluebirds** 5
Clydach Wasps 6 Coed Eva Athletic 1
Cwmffrwdoer Sports 8 Christchurch Hamdden 2
Fairfield United 1 **Spencer Youth & Boys** 2
Llanhilleth Athletic 5 Garnlydan Athletic 1

GWENT COUNTY LEAGUE DIVISION ONE CONSTITUTION 2007-08

ABERCARN UNITED.................Welfare Ground, Abercarn, Blackwood NP12 3XX.................01495 243047
ABERTILLERY BLUEBIRDS..........Cwmnantygroes Field, Six Bells, Abertillery NP13 2PR.................01495 213999
ALBION ROVERS......................Kimberley Park, Malpas Road, Newport NP20 6WE.................None
BLAENAVON BLUES...........Recreation Ground, Coed Cae Road, Blaenavon, Pontypool NP4 9PP.................None
CEFN FFOREST..............Welfare Ground, Ty Isha Terrace, Cefn Fforest, Blackwood NP12 1ER.................None
CHEPSTOW TOWN............Larkfield Ground, Newport Road, Chepstow NP16 5PR.................01291 629220
CLYDACH WASPS.................Recreation Ground, Clydach.................None
COED EVA ATHLETIC................Cwmbran Park, Wesley Street, Cwmbran NP44 3LX.................01633 485491
CWMFFRWDOER SPORTS....Cwmffrwdoer Sports Ground, Gwenhallt Industrial Estate, Cwmffrwdoer.................None
MARDY.................Mardy Playing Field, Mardy.................None
NEWPORT CIVIL SERVICE........Civil Service Sports Ground, Shannon Road, Bettws NP20 7LX.................01633 855576
PANTEG.................Panteg House, Greenhill Road, Griffithstown NP4 5BE.................01495 763605
SPENCER YOUTH & BOYS.................Ringland Park, Newport NP18 2TA.................None
TREOWEN STARS.................Bush Park, Newbridge.................01495 248249
UNDY ATHLETIC.................Undy Playing Fields, The Causeway, Undy, Caldicot NP26 3EN.................01633 881352
IN: Abertillery Bluebirds (P), Cefn Fforest (P), Chepstow Town (Welsh League Division Three)
OUT: Monmouth Town (Welsh League Division Three), Trinant (R), West Pontnewydd (R)

	Abertillery	Abertillery Bluebirds	Cefn Fforest	Cromwell Youth	FC Dugout	Llanhilleth Athletic	Lliswerry	Lucas Cwmbran	Newport Corinthians	Pentwynmawr Athletic	RTB Ebbw Vale	Race	Rogerstone Welfare	Tranch	Trethomas Bluebirds
Abertillery		0-5	1-3	1-1	2-1	2-4	1-5	0-7	2-4	2-4	2-3	0-3	1-5	3-4	2-1
Abertillery Bluebirds	3-3	D	6-1	5-0	4-0	1-0	2-1	3-2	4-2	2-0	12-0	2-1	3-1	4-4	4-3
Cefn Fforest	2-1	2-3	I	8-3	3-1	0-1	2-0	2-1	0-0	0-1	1-0	4-1	1-0	2-1	4-4
Cromwell Youth	3-0	3-3	1-2	V	4-0	1-3	5-3	4-0	3-0	9-0	3-5	3-1	1-1	3-3	0-6
FC Dugout	1-0	1-1	1-3	1-1	I	3-1	0-0	3-2	3-2	2-2	2-2	2-0	1-1	5-1	0-1
Llanhilleth Athletic	2-0	0-3	2-1	3-1	0-1	S	2-0	3-0	4-2	3-0	3-1	1-3	3-2	3-2	3-2
Lliswerry	3-2	3-2	1-1	4-1	1-2	2-0	I	1-0	0-0	4-1	0-1	3-1	3-3	1-2	3-1
Lucas Cwmbran	2-3	1-3	5-5	3-3	5м0	4-0	3-4	O	2-3	12-2	4-2	2-5	3-4	4-2	2-3
Newport Corinthians	0-0	1-1	2-3	3-7	0-0	1-2	1-1	3-2	N	2-2	2-0	0-4	2-1	2-1	1-4
Pentwynmawr Athletic	4-3	0-10	2-1	2-2	2-1	0-2	3-1	1-0	4-2		1-3	3-2	2-5	2-5	3-7
RTB Ebbw Vale	4-2	1-1	0-2	2-1	0-2	2-0	4-1	1-3	3-2	4-2		2-0	1-2	3-1	2-2
Race	5-0	2-4	2-4	2-2	2-3	4-1	1-3	1-2	3-4	3-2		T	3-5	1-2	1-0
Rogerstone Welfare	6-2	1-2	6-2	2-3	1-1	0-8	3-4	6-3	1-2	2-5	4-2	1-5	W	3-1	5-2
Tranch	4-2	0-1	2-3	3-2	0-2	4-0	1-6	0-2	1-1	2-2	1-2	1-1	3-1	O	6-3
Trethomas Bluebirds	4-2	4-1	2-2	2-2	4-0	1-4	1-1	3-1	8-0	8-2	1-2	3-2	4-0	2-1	

Lucas Cwmbran 6 Trinant 2
Newport Corinthians 2 Lliswerry 1
Panteg 0 **Treowen Stars** 2
Pentwynmawr Athletic 5 **Sebastopol** 8
PILCS 2 **Tranch** 3
Sudbrook Cricket Club 7 Malpas Gladiator 5
Trethomas Bluebirds 1 **Monmouth Town** 3
Undy Athletic 0 **Mardy** 3
THIRD ROUND
Clydach Wasps 4 Underwood Social Club 1
Cromwell Youth 1 **Monmouth Town** 3
Cwmffrwdoer Sports 3 **Abertillery Bluebirds** 4
Lucas Cwmbran 2 **Albion Rovers** 5
Mardy 2 Llanhilleth Athletic 1
Newport Corinthians 0 **Sudbrook Cricket Club** 3
Spencer Youth & Boys 6 Sebastopol 4
Tranch 0 **Treowen Stars** 1
QUARTER-FINALS
Abertillery Bluebirds 3 Spencer Youth & Boys 2
Clydach Wasps 4 Monmouth Town 3
Mardy 2 **Sudbrook Cricket Club** 4
Treowen Stars 1 **Albion Rovers** 2
SEMI-FINALS
Abertillery Bluebirds 4 Sudbrook Cricket Club 1 *(at Mardy)*
Clydach Wasps 1 **Albion Rovers** 2 *(at Undy Athletic)*
FINAL
(May 4th at Abergavenny Thursdays)
Abertillery Bluebirds 2 Albion Rovers 1 *aet*

Division Two		P	W	D	L	F	A	Pts
Abertillery Bluebirds		28	20	6	2	96	37	66
Cefn Fforest		28	16	5	7	64	50	53
Llanhilleth Athletic		28	17	1	10	57	43	52
Trethomas Bluebirds		28	14	5	9	86	56	47
RTB Ebbw Vale		28	14	3	11	53	60	45
Lliswerry		28	12	7	9	59	49	43
Rogerstone Welfare		28	12	4	12	73	71	40
Pentwynmawr Athletic		28	11	4	13	58	100	37
FC Dugout	-3	28	10	9	9	38	45	36
Cromwell Youth		28	9	8	11	70	69	35
Lucas Cwmbran		28	10	2	16	80	67	32
Tranch		28	9	5	14	58	66	32
Newport Corinthians		28	8	8	12	40	63	32
Race		28	9	2	17	60	62	29
Abertillery		28	3	3	22	39	93	12

WWW.NLNEWSDESK.CO.UK

GWENT COUNTY LEAGUE DIVISION TWO CONSTITUTION 2007-08

CROMWELL YOUTH. . . . . Hartridge Comprehensive School, Ringland Way, Newport NP18 2TA. . . . . None
FAIRFIELD UNITED . . . . Garndiffaith Ravine, Pontypool 01495 773745
LLANHILLETH ATHLETIC. . . . . Llanhilleth Park, Llanhilleth 01495 217840
LLISWERRY . . . . Spytty Park, Newport NP9 0RH. 01633 281087
LUCAS CWMBRAN. . . . . Lucas Sports Ground, Cwmbran 01633 861624
MALPAS GLADIATOR. . . . . Westfield, Darwin Drive, Malpas, Newport NP20 6FR. . . . . None
NEWPORT CORINTHIANS . . . . Coronation Park, Stephenson Street, Newport NP19 0RB 01633 274717
PENTWYNMAWR ATHLETIC. . . . . Welfare Ground, Pentwynmawr, Newbridge, Newport 01495 243403
RTB EBBW VALE . . . . Eugene Cross Park, Pontygof, Ebbw Vale NP23 5AZ. 01495 302995
ROGERSTONE WELFARE. . . . . Welfare Ground, Rogerstone, Newport . . . . None
TRANCH. . . . . Tranch Playing Fields, Tranch . . . . None
TRETHOMAS BLUEBIRDS . . . . Llanfabon Drive, Trethomas, Caerphilly CF83 8GJ. None
TRINANT. . . . . Trinant Recreation, Trinant, Caerphilly . . . . None
WEST PONTNEWYDD . . . . The Birches, West Pontnewydd, Pontypool. . . . . None
IN: *Fairfield United (P), Malpas Gladiator (P), Trinant (R), West Pontnewydd (R)*
OUT: *Abertillery (W), Abertillery Bluebirds (P), Cefn Fforest (P), FC Dugout (R – North Gwent League Premier Division), Race (R)*

	AC Pontymister	Abergavenny Thursdays	Caldicot Castle	Christchurch Hamdden	Crickhowell	Crusaders	Fairfield United	Garnlydan Athletic	Malpas Gladiator	New Inn	PILCS	Sebastopol	Sudbrook Cricket Club	Thornwell Red & White	Underwood Social Club	Whiteheads
AC Pontymister		5-1	1-1	2-3	3-1	1-0	2-1	4-2	4-0	2-2	3-1	4-2	0-3	n/a	3-0	7-1
Abergavenny Thursdays	0-3	D	2-1	1-5	1-3	3-1	0-0	3-1	0-3	3-4	0-3	2-4	4-3	n/a	1-3	2-0
Caldicot Castle	3-4	1-3	I	1-7	2-1	2-3	1-5	0-1	1-3	2-1	2-3	0-4	1-2	n/a	3-2	2-1
Christchurch Hamdden	4-2	3-2	6-1	V	4-4	8-1	2-2	5M0	0-0	5-1	3-1	0-5	4-3	5-1	7-5	1-2
Crickhowell	1-6	2-4	3-0	1-1	I	5-1	2-4	1-1	1-2	1-1	0-2	5-3	1-3	n/a	4-3	5-1
Crusaders	0-2	1-0	0-0	4-2	3-3	S	0-2	4-1	3-3	3-1	0-2	1-6	3-1	n/a	3-4	1-2
Fairfield United	1-0	6-1	4-2	2-1	2-1	1-0	I	3-2	1-1	5-1	2-2	4-0	1-0	n/a	3-1	3-1
Garnlydan Athletic	1-6	3-5	1-3	2-6	6-4	2-2	0-5	O	1-3	4-2	3-3	2-6	1-7	2-2	2-8	0-2
Malpas Gladiator	5-2	4-3	4-1	2-1	1-0	7-2	1-0	3-1	N	6-2	1-0	9-1	1-0	n/a	4-1	3-2
New Inn	2-3	2-3	1-1	0-2	0-1	3-0	0-3	4-0	0-2		1-2	3-3	1-8	n/a	3-2	3-2
PILCS	2-1	7-0	3-1	0-2	2-2	1-3	1-2	3-3	0-2	4-0	T	2-1	1-3	n/a	2-2	4-3
Sebastopol	0-2	2-5	0-1	2-2	3-0	0-1	1-5	5-0	0-4	1-1	1-2	H	1-9	n/a	2-0	2-2
Sudbrook Cricket Club	0-1	3-1	4-2	5-2	6-1	6-0	2-3	4-2	2-1	7-1	1-2	3-0	R	9-0	6-1	1-0
Thornwell Red & White	1-7	1-0	1-2	n/a	2-4	3-3	0-1	n/a	n/a	n/a	n/a	1-4	n/a	E	n/a	n/a
Underwood Social Club	4-0	0-4	3-3	3-2	3-2	6-3	0-2	4-0	3-1	1-0	2-3	3-3	2-2	n/a	E	2-4
Whiteheads	0-4	6-3	2-0	3-5	2-8	1-2	0-5	5-2	2-2	2-1	1-5	2-2	0-2	n/a	0-3	

Note – Thornwell Red & White withdrew during the course of the season
Their results are shown above but are expunged from the league table

Division Three	P	W	D	L	F	A	Pts
Fairfield United	28	21	4	3	73	25	67
Malpas Gladiator	28	21	4	3	78	34	67
AC Pontymister	28	19	2	7	77	41	59
Sudbrook Cricket Club	28	19	1	8	96	38	58
Christchurch Hamdden	28	16	5	7	93	57	53
PILCS	28	15	5	8	63	45	50
Underwood Social Club	28	11	4	13	71	72	37
Crickhowell	28	10	5	13	66	66	35
Abergavenny Thursdays	28	11	1	16	57	79	34
Crusaders	28	9	4	15	45	75	31
Sebastopol	28	8	6	14	60	74	30
Whiteheads	28	8	3	17	49	80	27
Caldicot Castle	28	6	4	18	38	74	22
New Inn	28	5	5	18	41	78	20
Garnlydan Athletic	28	3	3	22	44	113	12

Thornwell Red & White – record expunged

GWENT COUNTY LEAGUE DIVISION THREE CONSTITUTION 2007-08

AC PONTYMISTER . . . . Pontymister Recreation Ground, Pontymister, Caerphilly NP11 6LT . . . . None

ABERGAVENNY THURSDAYS . . . . Penypound Stadium, Pen-Y-Pound, Abergavenny 01873 854405

CALDICOT CASTLE . . . . Caldicot Castle Grounds, Caldicot NP26 4HU 01291 431581

CHRISTCHURCH HAMDDEN . . . . Glebelands Sports Stadium, Bank Street, Newport NP19 7HF . . . . None

CRICKHOWELL . . . . Elvicta Estate, Brecon Road, Crickhowell NP8 1DG . . . . None

CRUSADERS. . . . . Fields Park, Newbridge, Newport NP11 3NQ . . . . None

GOVILON . . . . Crickhowell FC, Elvicta Estate, Brecon Road, Crickhowell NP8 1DG . . . . None

NEW INN . . . . Woodfield Road Arena, New Inn, Pontypool NP4 0PS. 01495 755169

PILCS. . . . . PILCS Sports & Social Club, New Road, Griffithstown, Pontypool NP4 0TL 01495 762039

RACE . . . . Pontypool College, Blaendare Road, Pontypool NP4 5YE 01495 763656

SEBASTOPOL . . . . The Ruffetts, Pontnewynydd, Sebastopol, Pontypool 01495 763719

SUDBROOK CRICKET CLUB . . . . Deepweir, Caldicot NP26 5JG. . . . . None

UNDERWOOD SOCIAL CLUB . . . . Larch Grove, Newport NP20 6JB . . . . None

WHITEHEADS . . . . Whiteheads Sports Ground, Park View, Bassaleg NP10 8LA 01633 893227

IN: Govilon (P – Gwent Central League Division One), Race (R)

OUT: Farfield United (P), Garnlydan Athletic (R – North Gwent League Premier Division), Malpas Gladiator (P), Thornwell Red & White (WS)

GWYNEDD LEAGUE

	Amlwch Town	Barmouth & Dyffryn United	Beaumaris Town	Bethel	Blaenau Ffestiniog Amateurs	Bontnewydd	Cemaes Bay	Gaerwen	Holyhead Hotspurs Res.	Llanfairfechan Town	Llangefni Town Res.	Llanllyfni	Nantlle Vale	Porthmadog Res.	Real Llandudno	University of Bangor
Amlwch Town		0-5	5-0	4-0	5-1	6-0	10-0	5-1	4-3	2-2	2-1	4-1	2-3	5-0	2-1	4-1
Barmouth & Dyffryn United	3-1		4-1	3-2	5-1	8-0	15-0	5-1	4-1	7-4	3-1	3-0	6-1	3-2	9-2	2-0
Beaumaris Town	0-1	5-3		5-2	2-4	4-1	5-0	6-5	3-2	3-4	4-2	5-1	3-2	3-2	3-2	7-1
Bethel	2-3	2-3	0-4		6-4	2-3	1-0	3-6	2-2	10-2	2-3	3-0	1-1	1-3	3-1	2-0
Blaenau Ffestiniog Amateurs	2-1	0-2	1-0	5-1		0-1	4-0	2-2	4-3	5-0	5-4	1-1	1-2	2-0	5-1	4-1
Bontnewydd	2-4	1-3	3-2	2-0	1-4		14-0	4-4	1-4	2-2	4-5	3-3	1-2	2-1	1-3	3-0
Cemaes Bay	0-4	0-7	0-2	2-6	1-11	0-4		1-7	0-10	1-7	0-4	0-12	1-2	0-4	0-3	1-3
Gaerwen	3-3	0-5	1-4	3-1	2-7	1-1	10-0		4-0	2-2	2-8	1-1	1-2	1-4	4-3	1-1
Holyhead Hotspurs Res.	4-4	5-2	2-2	2-1	3-1	3-2	4-1	3-2		6-1	2-1	7-2	2-5	5-1	2-1	4-1
Llanfairfechan Town	4-3	1-5	2-3	1-4	4-2	1-3	5-0	2-0	4-0		1-2	1-2	2-2	1-2	3-3	4-2
Llangefni Town Res.	3-3	0-2	2-2	2-2	8-0	0-2	8-0	1-1	5-3	6-0		2-1	1-3	1-4	1-0	3-0
Llanllyfni	3-4	2-2	1-8	3-2	2-1	5-2	3-1	3-3	4-1	4-2	1-1		1-3	3-0	2-2	2-3
Nantlle Vale	0-1	2-1	3-1	1-3	3-3	4-2	4-0	5-0	2-1	4-2	4-1			3-2	8-1	1-2
Porthmadog Res.	1-3	4-1	2-1	2-2	2-5	2-0	6-1	4-1	0-1	4-0	1-3	8-1	2-1		7-2	3-0
Real Llandudno	0-1	1-1	0-3	0-2	3-3	0-1	5-0	1-1	1-2	2-2	2-3	3-1	1-3	0-6		1-1
University of Bangor	3-4	0-2	1-4	2-2	1-3	2-0	2-1	0-5	1-1	3-3	0-6	2-2	2-4	0-8	1-2	

	P	W	D	L	F	A	Pts
Barmouth & Dyffryn United	30	24	2	4	124	40	74
Amlwch Town	30	21	4	5	100	49	67
Nantlle Vale	30	19	5	6	92	49	62
Beaumaris Town	30	19	2	9	95	59	59
Holyhead Hotspurs Res.	30	16	5	9	89	66	53
Porthmadog Res.	30	17	1	12	87	54	52
Blaenau Ffestiniog Amateurs	30	16	4	10	91	67	52
Llangefni Town Res.	30	15	5	10	92	57	50
Bontnewydd	30	11	4	15	66	75	37
Bethel	30	10	5	15	70	72	35
Llanllyfni	30	9	8	13	60	82	35
Gaerwen	30	7	11	12	76	87	32
Llanfairfechan Town	30	8	7	15	71	93	31
Real Llandudno	30	5	7	18	47	81	22
University of Bangor	30	5	6	19	36	89	21
Cemaes Bay	30	0	0	30	12	188	0

GWYNEDD CUP
(All teams)
FINAL *(May 11th at Porthmadog)*
Beaumaris Town 2 Llanllyfni 0

PRESIDENT'S CUP
(Previous season's top eight teams)
FINAL *(May 21st at Porthmadog)*
Nantlle Vale 1 Barmouth & Dyffryn United 0 *aet*

ERYI SHIELD
(All teams)
FINAL *(May 30th at Caernarfon Town)*
Porthmadog Res. 4 Holyhead Hotspur Res. 0

WWW.NLNEWSDESK.CO.UK

GWYNEDD LEAGUE CONSTITUTION 2007-08

BARMOUTH & DYFFRYN UNITED .... Wern Mynach, Park Road, Barmouth LL42 1PL.................................... None
BEAUMARIS TOWN .... The Green, Beaumaris .... None
BETHEL .... Ysgol Brynrefail, Llanrug, Caernarfon LL55 4AD .... None
BLAENAU FFESTINIOG AMATEURS...... Cae Clyd, Manod, Blaenau Ffestiniog LL41 4BA.................................... None
BODEDERN RESERVES .... Cae r Ysgol, Holyhead Road, Bodedern LL65 3SU .... None
BONTNEWYDD............................ Cae Stanley, Bontnewydd. .... None
CEMAES BAY .... School Lane Stadium, School Lane, Cemaes Bay, Anglesey LL67 0LB.................... 01407 710600
GAERWEN .... Lon Groes, Gaerwen, Anglesey LL60 6DD .... None
HOLYHEAD HOTSPUR RESERVES... New Oval, Leisure Centre, Kingsland, Holyhead LL65 2YE 01407 764111
LLANFAIRFECHAN TOWN .... Recreation Ground, Station Road, Llanfairfechan LL33 0BD .... None
LLANGEFNI TOWN RESERVES .... Cae Bob Parry, Talwrn Road, Llangefni LL77 7LP.................................... None
LLANLLYFNI .... St Georges Field, Llanllyfni............................ None
LLANYSTUMDWY .... Parc Dwyfor, Llanystumdwy, Criccieth .... None
PORTHMADOG RESERVES..................... Y Traeth, Porthmadog LL49 9PP 01766 514687
REAL LLANDUDNO............................ The Oval, Llandudno.................................. None
UNIVERSITY OF BANGOR.......... Maes Glas Sports Field, Ffriddoedd Road, Bangor LL57 2EH 01248 382571
IN: Bodedern Reserves (P – Anglesey League), Llanystumdwy (P – Caernarfon & District League)
OUT: Amlwch Town (P – Welsh Alliance), Nantlle Vale (P – Welsh Alliance)

HAMPSHIRE LEAGUE

	AFC Wolversdene	Broughton	Durley	East Lodge	Fair Oak	Four Marks	Ludgershall Sports	Ludwig Leis. Basingstoke	Lyndhurst STJs	Michelmersh & Timsbury	Mottisfont	Netley Central Sports	Over Wallop	Sporting BTC	Upham	Winchester Castle
AFC Wolversdene		1-2	0-2	W-L	4-2	1-4	2-0	0-0	2-2	0-4	0-3	0-1	3-3	2-2	5-2	1-3
Broughton	8-2		2-1	3-2	4-4	3-6	2-2	0-2	0-1	2-0	1-6	W-L	12-0	3-3	4-2	2-2
Durley	6-2	2-2		1-1	1-3	3-0	1-1	1-0	3-1	1-1	0-4	1-0	3-4	3-1	0-2	0-4
East Lodge	3-1	W-L	3-2		4-2	1-3	1-1	0-1	1-1	2-1	1-1	1-3	3-1	3-1	1-3	2-2
Fair Oak	1-0	1-1	1-2	1-4		4-2	1-5	0-4	2-1	1-2	0-6	0-5	6-1	0-2	0-6	0-5
Four Marks	0-1	4-0	5-0	2-1	1-0		7-2	1-1	5-2	4-0	0-2	1-0	4-0	1-1	3-1	2-2
Ludgershall Sports	3-1	2-1	1-3	1-1	1-3	0-0		1-3	1-2	0-1	0-2	0-4	2-0	1-1	0-4	2-8
Ludwig Leisure Basingstoke	5-1	1-2	2-2	2-2	2-5	1-1	4-0		4-0	3-0	1-2	1-3	5-0	2-0	4-2	2-2
Lyndhurst STJs	3-1	3-1	2-0	3-1	4-1	3-5	1-1	2-2		1-2	0-3	1-0	W-L	1-2	2-1	1-4
Michelmersh & Timsbury	0-1	1-1	3-0	2-1	2-0	2-6	3-1	0-2	1-1		0-3	1-4	3-0	1-1	1-2	1-3
Mottisfont	3-0	4-1	5-0	0-0	2-0	5-1	7-0	3-0	0-0	2-1		1-0	6-0	0-3	5-0	3-0
Netley Central Sports	3-1	4-2	8-0	3-1	4-1	3-0	4-0	1-0	1-0	3-1	0-1		4-1	2-0	5-0	2-1
Over Wallop	2-3	0-2	1-4	2-5	4-0	1-5	0-3	1-2	1-6	1-3	2-3			2-4	0-7	2-2
Sporting BTC	0-1	1-1	2-2	3-0	3-0	3-2	3-1	1-0	1-2	1-0	1-2	0-1	4-1		1-3	4-0
Upham	8-1	4-0	3-0	5-1	1-2	3-0	4-1	2-1	1-0	1-1	2-2	0-3	2-6	4-2		2-2
Winchester Castle	2-4	7-2	0-3	5-2	1-5	0-3	5-0	2-0	3-1	3-0	2-2	1-0	5-2	3-1	3-0	

		P	W	D	L	F	A	Pts
Mottisfont		30	25	5	0	89	13	80
Netley Central Sports		30	23	0	7	73	21	69
Four Marks		30	17	5	8	78	46	56
Winchester Castle		30	16	7	7	81	51	55
Upham		30	16	4	10	78	56	52
Ludwig Leisure B'stoke		30	13	7	10	56	36	46
Sporting BTC		30	12	7	11	52	45	43
Lyndhurst STJs		30	11	7	12	49	49	40
Durley		30	11	6	13	47	64	39
Broughton	-3	30	10	8	12	64	68	35
East Lodge		30	9	8	13	48	56	35
Michelmersh/Timsbury		30	9	6	15	38	52	33
AFC Wolversdene		30	9	4	17	41	77	31
Fair Oak		30	9	2	19	46	84	29
Ludgershall Sports		30	5	6	19	33	81	21
Over Wallop		30	3	2	25	39	113	11

WWW.CHERRYRED.CO.UK

LEAGUE CUP

FIRST ROUND
Durley 4 Ludwig Leisure Basingstoke 3
East Lodge 4 Broughton 2
Ludgershall Sports 3 **Winchester Castle** 4
Lyndhurst STJs 3 AFC Wolversdene 2
Michelmersh & Timsbury 3 **Four Marks** 7
Mottisfont 5 Over Wallop 0
Netley Central Sports 2 Fair Oak 1
Upham 1 **Sporting BTC** 3
QUARTER-FINALS
Durley 1 **East Lodge** 4
Lyndhurst STJs 1 Netley Central Sports 0 *aet*
Mottisfont 3 Four Marks 2
Sporting BTC 2 Winchester Castle 1
SEMI-FINALS
East Lodge 1 **Mottisfont** 1 *aet* (2-4p)
Lyndhurst STJs 1 **Sporting BTC** 2
FINAL
(May 2nd at Hamble ASSC)
Sporting BTC 2 Mottisfont 1

HAMPSHIRE LEAGUE CONSTITUTION 2007-08

AFC WOLVERSDENE . . . . Charlton Sports & Leisure Centre, West Portway, Andover SP10 3LF 07712 924103
ACADEMICALS . . . . Wide Lane, Eastleigh SO50 5PE. 02380 592832
BROUGHTON . . . . The Sportsfield, Buckholt Road, Broughton, Stockbridge SO20 8DA 01794 301150
CRUSADERS . . . . Worthies Sports & Social Club, Eversley Park, Kings Worthy, Winchester SO23 7NJ 01962 880457
DENMEAD & PURBROOK . . King George V Playing Field, Southwick Rd, Denmead, Waterlooville PO7 6XT. . . . . None
DURLEY . . . . Kytes Lane, Durley, Southampton SO32 2AE 07837 786381
EAST LODGE . . . . Langstone Harbour Spts Ground, Eastern Road, Portsmouth 023 9282 4798
FAIR OAK. . . . . Lapstone Park, Pavilion Close, Botley Road, Fair Oak, Eastleigh SO50 7AN 07775 826091
FOUR MARKS. . . . . The Recreation Ground, Upland Lane, Four Marks, Alton GU34 5AF. 07793 450208
LUDGERSHALL SPORTS . . . . Astor Crescent, Ludgershall, Andover SP11 9RG 01264 398200
MICHELMERSH & TIMSBURY . Timsbury Rec. Trust, Mannyngham Way, Timsbury, Romsey SO51 0NJ. 01794 368955
MOTTISFONT . . . . Bengers Lane, Mottisfont, Romsey SO51 0LR . . . . None
NETLEY CENTRAL SPORTS . . Netley Rec. Ground, Station Road, Netley Abbey, Southampton SO21 5AF 023 8045 2267
TWYFORD . . . . Hunters Park, Park Lane, Twyford, Winchester SO21 1QT 07956 445290
IN: Academicals (S – Southampton League Premier Division), Crusaders (P – Winchester & District League Division One), Denmead &
Purbrook (N), Twyford (P – Winchester & District League Division One)
OUT: Ludwig Leisure Basingstoke (P – Hampshire Premier League), Lyndhurst STJs (P – Hampshire Premier League), Over Wallop (W), Sporting
BTC (P – Hampshire Premier League), Upham (W), Winchester Castle (P – Hampshire Premier League)

HELLENIC LEAGUE

Note – Chipping Norton Town and Hounslow Borough withdrew during the course of the season. Their results shown here are expunged	AFC Wall'ford	Abingdon T.	Almondsb'y T.	Ardley United	Bicester Town	Carterton	C. Norton T.	Fairford Town	Harrow Hill	Highworth T.	Hounslow B.	Hungerford T.	Kidlington	Milton United	North Leigh	Pegasus Juniors	Shortwood Utd	Shrivenham	Slimbridge	Thame United	Wantage Town	Witney United
AFC Wallingford		2-0	1-1	0-0	5-4	1-2	3-2	0-5	0-2	1-7	6-1	0-4	0-1	1-2	0-1	1-0	0-2	2-2	0-1	1-0	0-3	2-0
Abingdon Town	1-1		1-2	2-2	1-2	0-2	n/a	0-0	2-3	0-2	2-4	1-1	0-0	0-1	1-2	1-1	1-0	1-3	0-5	3-1	3-3	0-3
Almondsbury Town	5-0	1-1		1-2	5-1	0-2	0-0	5-0	2-2	2-0	n/a	2-0	2-0	4-2	0-2	3-2	1-1	4-0	1-0	1-0	2-1	2-3
Ardley United	1-1	5-2	1-1	P	1-2	6-0	4-3	2-2	2-0	n/a	1-4	5-0	1-0	0-5	2-2	6-4	0-1	1-2	6-3	3-1	1-1	
Bicester Town	0-0	0-1	1-1	2-1	R	3-0	n/a	1-1	3-0	1-1	3-2	1-1	2-1	0-5	2-2	1-2	2-3	1-2	1-4	4-0	0-0	1-5
Carterton	1-2	1-3	3-2	0-1	1-1	E	2-2	0-0	3-3	1-2	7-0	0-1	4-0	1-4	1-1	2-2	2-1	2-0	0-1	6-0	1-1	1-2
Chipping Norton Town	n/a	n/a	n/a	n/a	n/a	0-3	M	1-1	4-2	n/a	2-3	3-2	n/a	n/a	2-1	2-1	3-2	n/a	0-2	1-0	0-2	1-5
Fairford Town	3-2	3-3	0-2	0-0	0-0	2-0	n/a	I	0-2	3-0	0-0	L-W	1-1	3-1	1-0	0-1	1-3	1-4	3-3	3-0	1-0	0-3
Harrow Hill	1-2	0-3	2-3	2-0	0-2	0-3	2-2	0-4	E	1-1	1-3	4-2	0-0	1-3	0-1	0-1	0-5	1-3	0-1	1-2	0-1	1-1
Highworth Town	2-0	0-0	0-1	4-4	2-2	1-1	5-2	1-1	3-2	R	2-0	0-3	0-1	2-3	0-1	3-2	3-0	1-3	3-2	0-1	1-1	2-0
Hounslow Borough	0-2	n/a	2-3	1-3	2-1	0-1	n/a	n/a	n/a	n/a		2-2	1-2	n/a	n/a	1-4	n/a	0-6	2-3	2-3	2-3	n/a
Hungerford Town	3-0	4-0	2-0	3-0	1-1	4-2	3-0	1-2	1-1	2-1	1-1	D	1-0	1-2	1-2	3-1	2-0	1-2	0-1	6-1	1-3	1-0
Kidlington	1-2	4-0	0-2	1-2	1-0	1-3	n/a	3-2	2-1	2-2	n/a	2-1	I	1-1	2-0	1-2	3-2	1-1	0-0	1-0	2-2	2-0
Milton United	2-4	2-1	0-3	2-0	0-7	2-1	n/a	4-1	3-0	3-1	3-0	1-6	2-2	V	0-1	4-0	1-1	2-1	1-6	2-1	1-2	0-1
North Leigh	1-0	0-0	2-2	0-0	4-1	4-1	3-2	0-0	1-1	1-1	5-1	4-4	4-0	4-4	I	5-0	2-1	1-0	3-1	2-1	2-1	0-1
Pegasus Juniors	3-1	1-0	4-2	0-3	3-1	1-2	2-1	0-1	1-1	1-2	1-4	2-2	1-0	0-2	0-3	S	0-4	0-1	2-3	1-2	1-4	1-1
Shortwood United	0-0	5-2	2-1	0-3	0-0	1-1	n/a	3-1	4-2	n/a	n/a	0-3	2-3	1-4	2-3	5-3	I	3-3	1-5	3-2	5-1	2-1
Shrivenham	2-0	5-2	2-1	3-1	3-3	0-2	n/a	2-5	6-0	2-1	2-2	1-2	0-1	1-1	1-3	5-1	2-2	O	0-1	3-2	1-0	0-2
Slimbridge	4-0	5-1	2-0	2-1	2-1	3-0	n/a	2-2	11-1	1-1	1-1	2-1	0-1	3-0	2-2	2-0	2-2	2-0	N	3-0	4-0	0-2
Thame United	0-2	1-2	1-1	2-2	1-4	n/a	3-2	5-2	1-1	5-0	n/a	0-3	1-2	2-4	2-2	3-0	2-1	4-0			2-6	0-7
Wantage Town	2-2	1-3	0-4	0-4	2-1	3-1	5-0	4-2	2-0	0-0	1-3	0-1	2-1	1-2	1-2	1-1	5-2	1-1	1-2	2-2		0-1
Witney United	2-1	6-1	1-1	2-2	3-3	1-1	n/a	3-1	0-0	1-0	2-1	1-2	3-2	0-2	3-4	3-0	1-1	0-5	1-1	0-3		

Premier Division		P	W	D	L	F	A	Pts
Slimbridge		38	27	7	4	93	29	88
North Leigh		38	25	10	3	77	33	85
Hungerford Town		38	21	8	9	77	40	71
Ardley United		38	19	10	9	78	54	67
Almondsbury Town		38	19	9	10	73	44	66
Witney United		38	16	13	9	67	49	61
Milton United		38	18	6	14	73	70	60
Shortwood United		38	15	9	14	76	72	54
Kidlington		38	14	11	13	47	52	53
Shrivenham	-4	38	16	8	14	67	59	52
Wantage Town		38	13	11	14	62	60	50
Carterton		38	13	9	16	58	61	48
Fairford Town		38	12	10	16	56	61	46
Bicester Town		38	10	15	13	59	64	45
Highworth Town		38	10	14	14	54	55	44
AFC Wallingford		38	10	8	20	37	71	38
Pegasus Juniors		38	9	7	22	45	85	34
Abingdon Town		38	6	12	20	42	80	30
Harrow Hill		38	5	9	24	36	82	24
Thame United		38	6	6	26	45	101	24

Chipping Norton Town and Hounslow Borough – records expunged

Reserve Division One	P	W	D	L	F	A	Pts
Kidlington Res.	32	25	3	4	92	28	78
Carterton Res.	32	21	5	6	92	43	68
Fairford Town Res.	32	19	9	4	77	37	66
Bisley Res.	32	18	7	7	75	55	61
North Leigh Res.	32	15	6	11	68	50	51
Binfield Res.	32	14	6	12	55	50	48
Wantage Town Res.	32	13	6	13	54	49	45
Didcot Town Res.	32	11	10	11	65	50	43
Wootton Bassett Town Res.	32	11	9	12	52	59	42
Finchampstead Res.	32	12	6	14	55	72	42
Hungerford Town Res.	32	11	6	15	43	54	39
Abingdon United Res.	32	10	5	17	54	64	35
Milton United Res.	32	9	8	15	47	66	35
Cheltenham Saracens Res.	32	8	7	17	46	80	31
Henley Town Res.	32	8	4	20	46	69	28
Badshot Lea Res.	32	7	7	18	49	82	28
Cirencester United Res.	32	5	6	21	27	89	21

HELLENIC LEAGUE PREMIER DIVISION CONSTITUTION 2007-08

AFC WALLINGFORD . . . . Wallingford Sports Park, Hithercroft Road, Wallingford OX10 9RB 01491 835044
ABINGDON TOWN . . . . Culham Road, Abingdon OX14 3HP 01235 521684
ALMONDSBURY TOWN . . . . Oakland Park, Gloucester Road, Almondsbury, Bristol BS32 4AG 01454 612220
ARDLEY UNITED . . . . The Playing Field, Fritwell Road, Ardley, Bicester OX27 7NS 01869 345597
BADSHOT LEA . . . . Farnborough FC, Cherrywood Road, Farnborough GU14 8UD 01252 541469
BICESTER TOWN . . . . Sports Ground, Oxford Road, Bicester OX26 2AD 01869 241036
CARTERTON . . . . Kilkenny Lane, Swinbrook Road, Carterton OX18 1DP 01993 842410
FAIRFORD TOWN . . . . Cinder Lane, London Road, Fairford GL7 4AX 01285 712071
FLACKWELL HEATH . . . . Wilks Park, Magpie Lane, Flackwell Heath, High Wycombe HP10 9EA 01628 523892
HARROW HILL . . . . Larksfield Road, Harrow Hill, Drybrook GL17 9JP 01594 543873
HIGHWORTH TOWN . . . . The Elms Recreation Grnd, Highworth, Swindon SN6 7HU 01793 766263
HOOK NORTON . . . . The Playfields, The Bourne, Hook Norton OX15 5PB 01608 737132
HUNGERFORD TOWN . . . . War Memorial Ground, Bulpit Lane, Hungerford RG17 0AY 01488 682939
KIDLINGTON . . . . Yarnton Road, Kidlington OX5 1AT 01865 841526
LYDNEY TOWN . . . . Recreation Trust Ground, Lydney 01594 844523
MILTON UNITED . . . . The Sports Field, Potash Lane, Milton Heights, Abingdon OX13 6AG 01235 832999
NORTH LEIGH . . . . Eynsham Park, Woodstock Road, North Leigh, Witney OX8 6PW 01993 881427
PEGASUS JUNIORS . . . . Old School Lane, Hereford HR1 1QE 07970 556580
SHORTWOOD UNITED . . . . Meadowbank, Shortwood, Nailsworth, Stroud GL6 0SJ 01453 833936
SHRIVENHAM . . . . Recreation Ground, Highworth Road, Shrivenham, Swindon SN6 8BJ 01793 784453
WANTAGE TOWN . . . . Alfredian Park, Manor Road, Wantage OX12 8DW 01235 764781
WITNEY UNITED . . . . Marriotts Stadium, Downs Road, Culbridge, Witney OX29 7WT 01993 488558

IN: Badshot Lea (P – Division One East), Flackwell Heath (R – Isthmian League Division One North), Hook Norton (P – Division One West), Lydney Town (P – Division One West)
OUT: Chipping Norton Town (WS), Hounslow Borough (WS), Slimbridge (W – Gloucestershire Northern Senior League Division One), Thame United (R – Division One East)

	Badshot Lea	Binfield	Bisley Sports	Chalfont Wasps	Chinnor	Englefield Green Rovers	Eton Wick	Finchampstead	Headington Amateurs	Henley Town	Holyport	Kintbury Rangers	Marlow United	Oxford Quarry Nomads	Penn & Tylers Green	Prestwood	Rayners Lane	Wokingham & Emmbrook
Badshot Lea	D	1-1	1-3	2-1	2-1	0-0	12-0	5-1	3-2	2-1	6-1	0-1	3-1	3-1	8-0	4-0	1-1	3-0
Binfield	2-1	I	2-3	1-4	0-1	0-1	5-0	1-2	2-0	2-0	1-3	2-3	0-1	W-L	1-1	3-0	2-2	2-2
Bisley Sports	1-2	5-0	V	2-1	3-0	3-0	9-0	2-0	2-0	8-0	1-3	0-0	7-0	5-0	3-3	4-0	5-2	6-0
Chalfont Wasps	2-4	1-0	1-1	I	4-0	2-3	5-1	3-2	3-0	5-0	4-3	2-0	2-1	5-1	4-0	4-0	3-0	1-0
Chinnor	1-2	1-2	0-1	1-1	S	1-1	5-1	2-3	1-1	1-1	2-3	1-3	0-3	3-0	0-1	4-1	0-0	2-1
Englefield Green Rovers	0-2	2-1	1-1	0-4	2-3	I	3-1	2-1	1-0	2-0	2-0	1-3	1-0	3-2	1-0	2-0	0-2	0-1
Eton Wick	2-4	1-2	0-4	2-8	2-4	0-0	O	0-2	0-1	0-5	0-4	0-7	0-2	1-2	1-8	0-2		
Finchampstead	0-1	1-0	0-3	0-5	1-1	2-2	7-0	N	2-2	3-2	2-2	0-4	3-0	0-3	3-1	1-1	3-0	
Headington Amateurs	3-3	3-5	0-2	0-2	1-1	2-1	7-1	1-0		2-2	3-1	1-3	1-0	2-2	1-1	4-0	1-3	1-2
Henley Town	1-0	0-2	0-8	0-4	2-1	1-1	0-3	3-1	1-2	O	0-6	1-3	1-2	3-2	1-0	5-0	1-2	0-1
Holyport	2-4	3-1	1-2	1-4	1-2	4-0	3-2	3-2	1-1	0-6	N	1-0	0-1	3-1	2-0	0-2	2-4	2-0
Kintbury Rangers	0-2	2-1	1-2	0-4	2-0	3-1	3-0	3-0	2-1	4-0	2-2	E	3-2	9-0	4-1	7-1	1-3	7-1
Marlow United	1-3	4-1	1-1	1-2	2-0	0-0	0-5	6-0	3-2	7-0	2-1	2-4		0-1	3-3	3-0	1-1	1-1
Oxford Quarry Nomads	0-5	4-1	2-5	6-1	2-1	2-1	3-0	5-0	2-3	5-1	1-0	2-3	2-2	(E)	2-5	1-0	1-3	0-2
Penn & Tylers Green	3-0	2-2	1-6	0-3	0-3	7-0	13-2	1-2	1-3	0-4	2-0	0-5	1-1	2-3	A	2-0	1-4	4-0
Prestwood	0-4	1-2	0-2	1-2	1-1	0-4	4-0	0-3	1-2	3-2	1-4	0-2	1-3	3-1	1-1	S	1-4	0-1
Rayners Lane	1-3	2-0	0-4	3-0	6-0	1-2	9-0	1-1	2-0	1-0	4-1	2-4	4-1	1-3	2-0	1-4	T)	0-1
Wokingham & Emmbrook	3-2	0-5	0-7	0-1	2-0	3-8	7-1	1-1	0-0	1-2	3-2	4-3	2-1	1-0	0-3	2-0	6-3	

Division One (East)

	P	W	D	L	F	A	Pts
Bisley Sports	34	27	5	2	121	22	86
Chalfont Wasps	34	25	2	7	96	37	77
Badshot Lea	34	24	4	6	98	37	76
Kintbury Rangers	34	24	3	7	92	38	75
Rayners Lane	34	19	8	7	86	46	65
Englefield Green Rovers	34	16	6	12	53	52	54
Marlow United	34	15	6	13	65	52	51
Wokingham/Emmbrook	34	15	4	15	49	73	49
Holyport	34	15	3	16	65	64	48
Headington Amateurs	34	11	9	14	57	62	42
Binfield	34	12	5	17	52	57	41
Oxford Quarry Nomads	34	13	2	19	64	79	41
Penn & Tylers Green	34	11	7	16	65	73	40
Finchampstead	34	11	7	16	51	65	40
Chinnor	34	9	9	16	45	58	36
Henley Town	34	9	4	21	43	80	31
Prestwood	34	5	3	26	25	87	18
Eton Wick	34	1	1	32	23	168	4

Reserve Division Two (East)

	P	W	D	L	F	A	Pts
Rayners Lane Res.	20	16	3	1	68	13	51
Chalfont Wasps Res.	20	13	3	4	65	28	42
Holyport Res.	20	12	0	8	48	30	36
Penn & Tylers Green Res.	20	10	4	6	57	30	34
Wokingham/Emmbrook Res.	20	9	5	6	65	28	32
Chinnor Res.	20	9	4	7	29	26	31
Englefield Green Rovers Res.	20	9	1	10	34	25	28
Kintbury Rangers Res.	20	7	5	8	39	41	26
Thame United Res.	20	7	3	10	39	52	24
Prestwood Res.	20	1	5	14	15	55	8
Eton Wick Res.	20	0	1	19	3	134	1

ANNUAL CHALLENGE MATCH

(Not contested in 2006-07 due to the inclement weather)

HELLENIC LEAGUE DIVISION ONE EAST CONSTITUTION 2007-08

ASCOT UNITED . . . . Ascot Race Course, Winkfield Road, Ascot SL5 7LJ . . . . None
BINFIELD . . . . Stubbs Hill, Binfield, Bracknell RG42 4NN 01344 860822
BISLEY SPORTS . . . . Lion Park, Church Lane, Bisley GU24 9ED . . . . None
CHALFONT WASPS . . . . Playing Fields, Bowstridge Lane, Chalfont St Giles HP8 4DF 01494 875050
CHINNOR . . . . Station Road, Chinnor OX39 4QQ . . . . None
ENGLEFIELD GREEN ROVERS . . Coopers Hill Sports Ground, Coopers Hill Lane, Englefield Green TW20 0JX 01784 435666
ETON WICK . . . . Haywards Mead, Eton Wick, Windsor SL4 6JN 01753 852749
FINCHAMPSTEAD . . . . Memorial Ground, Finchampstead Park, Finchampstead RG11 4JR 0118 973 2890
HENLEY TOWN . . . . Triangle Ground, Mill Lane, Henley-on-Thames RG9 4HB 01491 411083
HOLYPORT . . . . Braywick Sports Centre, Braywick Road, Maidenhead SL6 1BN . . . . None
KINTBURY RANGERS . . . . Inkpen Road, Kintbury, Hungerford RG17 9UA 01488 657001
MARLOW UNITED . . . . Flackwell Heath FC, Wilks Park, Magpie Lane, Flackwell Heath, High Wycombe HP10 9EA 01628 523892
PENN & TYLERS GREEN . . . . French School Meadows, Elm Road, Penn HP10 8LG 01494 815346
PRESTWOOD . . . . Prestwood Sports Centre, Honor End Lane, Prestwood, Great Missenden HP16 9HG 01494 865946
RAYNERS LANE . . . . Tithe Farm Social Club, 151 Rayners Lane, South Harrow HA2 0XH 020 8868 8724
THAME UNITED . . . . AFC Wallingford, Wallingford Sports Park, Hithercroft Road, Wallingford OX10 9RB 01491 835044
WOKINGHAM & EMMBROOK . . . . Emmbrook Sports Ground, Lowther Road, Emmbrook, Wokingham RG41 1JB 01189 780209

IN: Ascot United (P – Reading League Senior Division), Thame United (R)
OUT: Badshot Lea (P), Headington Amateurs (S – Division One West), Oxford City Nomads (formerly Oxford Quarry Nomads) (S – Division One West)

	Banbury United Res.	Cheltenham Saracens	Cirencester United	Clanfield	Cricklade Town	Easington Sports	Hook Norton	Letcombe	Lydney Town	Malmesbury Victoria	Old Woodstock Town	Pewsey Vale	Purton	Ross Town	Trowbridge Town	Tytherington Rocks	Winterbourne United	Wootton Bassett Town
Banbury United Res.	D	0-1	4-0	1-0	0-2	1-5	0-3	4-0	1-2	0-2	5-4	1-0	3-2	7-0	2-2	0-3	2-2	5-3
Cheltenham Saracens	3-2	I	1-1	1-0	3-0	0-1	2-0	0-1	1-2	0-1	1-1	1-2	2-2	2-0	1-0	2-2	1-1	6-0
Cirencester United	1-1	4-4	V	1-0	0-1	3-2	0-3	0-0	0-2	0-2	2-2	2-1	6-1	3-0	3-1	1-4	3-2	1-0
Clanfield	1-2	0-1	1-4	I	0-1	1-1	1-4	2-1	0-3	0-1	2-1	1-2	0-2	2-2	1-2	2-3	3-0	0-2
Cricklade Town	0-2	2-2	0-3	2-0	S	3-2	0-3	0-2	1-2	2-1	0-2	3-1	4-1	3-2	1-1	2-3	0-2	3-2
Easington Sports	2-1	0-1	4-1	2-2	3-1	I	1-3	0-1	1-1	5-5	1-1	3-1	5-1	6-1	0-3	3-1	6-0	4-2
Hook Norton	3-0	1-1	2-1	3-2	1-0	2-1	O	3-2	0-2	2-2	2-0	0-0	1-0	3-2	2-1	3-2	0-1	3-0
Letcombe	0-0	1-3	1-3	2-2	4-0	3-0	4-0	N	1-0	2-2	3-5	2-0	0-1	2-2	1-3	1-4	4-1	1-2
Lydney Town	3-0	0-0	3-1	4-0	1-0	4-1	3-1	2-1		0-1	1-0	1-1	8-3	4-0	2-1	0-0	0-2	2-1
Malmesbury Victoria	3-1	3-5	1-0	3-0	0-1	6-1	1-1	0-1	1-2	O	1-1	0-1	2-0	3-2	2-2	4-2	1-1	3-3
Old Woodstock Town	2-0	0-4	1-1	2-2	3-3	2-1	2-2	5-3	0-5	0-1	N	1-1	0-0	6-0	2-3	1-0	1-1	2-1
Pewsey Vale	3-2	2-2	3-1	1-1	1-1	1-1	0-0	1-2	1-2	1-1	0-2	E	1-1	3-2	0-3	2-3	3-4	0-0
Purton	1-1	3-1	2-2	2-2	0-2	3-2	1-4	1-2	2-3	0-1	0-0	1-1		3-0	1-2	3-3	1-4	0-3
Ross Town	1-3	1-2	0-1	2-1	1-7	4-4	2-3	1-4	1-2	1-5	0-2	1-2	0-6	W	0-11	2-2	1-4	1-5
Trowbridge Town	1-0	3-1	2-2	4-2	1-2	4-0	1-0	5-0	3-1	0-0	2-0	2-0	4-1	W-L	E	1-1	1-1	1-1
Tytherington Rocks	1-1	6-1	2-0	4-0	3-0	1-1	4-0	4-0	1-3	2-0	2-1	1-1	2-1	4-4	0-3	S	0-0	1-2
Winterbourne United	3-1	2-1	2-3	0-1	1-3	9-0	3-2	3-3	1-1	1-1	1-2	2-3	3-3	4-2	1-0	2-0	T	2-2
Wootton Bassett Town	3-2	1-0	3-2	4-0	3-1	1-1	0-2	1-0	1-2	1-1	2-3	1-2	5-1	4-0	1-3	0-1	4-2	

Division One (West)

	P	W	D	L	F	A	Pts
Lydney Town	34	24	6	4	72	29	78
Trowbridge Town	34	21	7	6	76	31	70
Hook Norton	34	20	6	8	62	42	66
Malmesbury Victoria	34	16	11	7	62	38	59
Tytherington Rocks	34	15	10	9	71	48	55
Cheltenham Saracens	34	14	10	10	57	45	52
Old Woodstock Town	34	12	13	9	58	54	49
Cricklade Town	34	15	4	15	51	56	49
Pewsey Vale	34	12	12	10	47	46	48
Winterbourne United	34	12	11	11	64	59	47
Wootton Bassett Town	34	14	5	15	64	62	47
Cirencester United	34	13	8	13	56	58	47
Easington Sports	34	12	9	13	72	74	45
Banbury United Res.	34	11	6	17	55	62	39
Letcombe	34	11	6	17	54	63	39
Purton	34	6	10	18	50	79	28
Clanfield	34	4	7	23	32	70	19
Ross Town	34	1	5	28	36	123	8

Reserve Division Two (West)

	P	W	D	L	F	A	Pts
Headington Amateurs Res.	24	18	2	4	88	40	56
Abingdon Town Res.	24	16	3	5	67	44	51
Highworth Town Res.	24	16	2	6	74	31	50
Oxford Quarry Nomads 'A'	24	15	0	9	93	62	45
Ardley United Res.	24	12	5	7	44	28	41
Shrivenham Res.	24	12	2	10	59	47	38
Bicester Town Res. -1	24	10	3	11	49	70	32
Old Woodstock Town Res.	24	9	4	11	40	60	31
Letcombe Res.	24	9	3	12	45	45	30
Hook Norton Res.	24	6	5	13	35	60	23
Witney United Res.	24	7	1	16	38	70	22
Cricklade Town Res.	24	5	2	17	30	69	17
Clanfield Res.	24	3	4	17	29	65	13

RESERVES CUP

FINAL

(May 2nd at Bicester Town)

Fairford Town Res. 3 Rayners Lane Res. 2

HELLENIC LEAGUE DIVISION ONE WEST CONSTITUTION 2007-08

BANBURY UNITED RESERVES .... Spencer Stadium, Station Approach, Banbury OX16 5TA 01295 263354/261899
CHELTENHAM SARACENS .... Petersfield Park, Tewkesbury Road, Gloucester GL51 8JL 01242 584134
CIRENCESTER UNITED.... Cirencester Town FC, Corinium Stadium, Kingshill Lane, Cirencester GL7 1XG 01285 654543
CLANFIELD .... Radcot Road, Clanfield, Faringdon SN7 8DT 01367 810314
CRICKLADE TOWN .... Cricklade Leisure Centre, Stones Lane, Cricklade SN6 6JW 01793 750011
EASINGTON SPORTS.................. Addison Road, Easington Estate, Banbury OX16 9DH 01295 257006
HEADINGTON AMATEURS .... Recreation Ground, Barton, Oxford OX3 9LA................................ 01865 760489
LAUNTON SPORTS .... Launton Sports & Social Club, Bicester Road, Bicester OX26 5DP 01869 242007
LETCOMBE .... Bassett Road, Letcombe Regis, Wantage OX12 9LJ.......................... 01235 768685
MALMESBURY VICTORIA .... Flying Monk Ground, Gloucester Road, Malmesbury SN16 0AJ 01666 822141
OLD WOODSTOCK TOWN .... New Road, Woodstock OX20 1PD................................... None
OXFORD CITY NOMADS .... Oxford City FC, Court Place Farm, Marsh Lane, Marston OX3 0NQ 01865 744493/742492
PEWSEY VALE .... Recreation Ground, Kings Corner, Ball Road, Pewsey SN9 5GF 01672 562990
PURTON................................ The Red House, Church Street, Purton SN5 4DT............................. 01793 770262
TROWBRIDGE TOWN.................... Woodmarsh, North Bradley, Trowbridge BA14 0SA .... None
TYTHERINGTON ROCKS .. Hardwicke Playing Fields, Woodlands Road, Tytherington, Wotton-under-Edge GL12 8UU .... None
WINTERBOURNE UNITED .... The Rec, Parkside Avenue, Winterbourne, Bristol BS36 1LZ.................... 01454 850059
WOOTTON BASSETT TOWN... Gerard Buxton Sports Ground, Rylands Way, Wootton Bassett SN4 8AY 01793 853880

IN: Headington Amateurs (S – Division One West), Launton Sports (P – Oxfordshire Senior League Premier Division), Oxford City Nomads (formerly Oxford Quarry Nomads) (S – Division One West)
OUT: Hook Norton (P), Lydney Town (P), Ross Town (R – Herefordshire League Premier Division)

LEAGUE CUP
(All teams in league)

PRELIMINARY ROUND

AFC Wallingford 3 Abingdon Town 2
Banbury United Res. 3 Wokingham & Emmbrook 2
Bicester Town 0 Kidlington 0 *aet* (4-3p)
Binfield 1 Prestwood 0
Carterton 1 **Almondsbury Town** 2
Chalfont Wasps 5 Eton Wick 0
Chinnor 1 **Thame United** 3
Cirencester United 3 Winterbourne Utd 1
Clanfield 1 Chipping Norton Town 0 *aet*
Cricklade Town 1 **Pegasus Juniors** 6
Englefield Green Rovers 2 Hounslow Borough 2 *aet* (4-1p)
Fairford Town 2 Highworth Town 0
Harrow Hill 0 **Trowbridge Town** 2
Henley Town 0 **Bisley Sports** 5
Hungerford 3 Penn & Tylers Green 1
Letcombe 1 **Easington Sports** 5
Malmesbury Victoria 2 **Witney United** 3
Marlow United 1 **Holyport** 2
Milton United 2 **Shortwood United** 3
Pewsey Vale 3 Lydney Town 0
Purton 0 **Cheltenham Saracens** 4
Rayners Lane 6 Oxford Quarry Nomads 4
Ross Town 0 **Old Woodstock Town** 3
Shrivenham 4 Hook Norton 2
Wantage Town 4 Badshot Lea 3
Wootton Bassett Town 4 Headington Amateurs 2

FIRST ROUND

AFC Wallingford 0 **Finchampstead** 1
Bisley Sports 2 Ardley United 1
Chalfont Wasps 5 Holyport 1
Cirencester United 4 Cheltenham Saracens 3 *aet*
Fairford Town 0 **Easington Sports** 2
Hungerford Town 3 Englefield Green Rovers 0

Kintbury Rangers 1 **Banbury United Res.** 3
Pegasus Juniors 2 **North Leigh** 4
Pewsey Vale 2 **Old Woodstock Town** 9
Rayners Lane 3 Thame United 2
Shortwood United 3 Binfield 1
Shrivenham 1 Trowbridge Town 1 *aet* (4-1p)
Tytherington Rocks 0 **Almondsbury Town** 3
Wantage Town 6 Bicester Town 1
Witney United 5 Clanfield 1
Wootton Bassett Town 1 **Slimbridge** 4

SECOND ROUND

Almondsbury Town 2 Bisley Sports 0
Banbury United Res. 0 **North Leigh** 2
Cirencester United 1 **Shortwood United** 3
Hungerford Town 5 Easington Sports 1
Rayners Lane 2 Old Woodstock Town 0
Shrivenham 0 **Chalfont Wasps** 1
Slimbridge 4 Finchampstead 0
Witney United 1 Wantage Town 0

QUARTER-FINALS

Almondsbury Town 1 **Chalfont Wasps** 3
Hungerford Town 2 North Leigh 0
Rayners Lane 2 **Witney United** 4
Slimbridge 4 **Shortwood United** 5 *aet*

SEMI-FINALS

(played over two legs)

Chalfont Wasps 1 Witney United 1,
Witney United 2 Chalfont Wasps 1
Hungerford Town 1 Shortwood United 0
Shortwood United 1 **Hungerford Town** 3

FINAL

(May 5th at Milton United)

Hungerford Town 2 Witney United 1

HELLENIC GROUND HOP VENUES 2007

Sunday 26th Aug	*Tytherington Rocks v Winterboourne United*	11:00
Sunday 26th Aug	*Shortwood United v Lydney Town*	14:30
Sunday 26th Aug	*Fairford Town v Highworth Town*	18:30
Monday 27th Aug	*Wantage Town v Hungerford Town*	11:00
Monday 27th Aug	*Henley Town v Marlow United*	14:30
Monday 27th Aug	*Eton Wick v Binfield*	18:30

Full details can be obtained at www.groundhopuk.co.uk

SUPPLEMENTARY CUP
(League Cup Preliminary and First Round losers)

PRELIMINARY ROUND
AFC Wallingford 3 Abingdon Town 1
Ardley United 8 Eton Wick 0
Cheltenham Saracens 3 Pegasus Juniors 0
Lydney Town 3 **Highworth Town** 4
Marlow United 1 **Headington Amateurs** 3
Milton United 4 Hounslow Borough 0
Purton 1 **Harrow Hill** 2
Ross Town 1 **Hook Norton** 4 *(at Hook Norton)*
Oxford Quarry Nomads 1 **Badshot Lea** 2
Winterbourne United (w/o) v Chipping Norton (scr.)

FIRST ROUND
Bicester Town 0 **Penn & Tylers Green** 2
Binfield 5 Headington Amateurs 2
Clanfield 0 **Tytherington Rocks** 5
Cricklade Town 1 **Fairford Town** 3 *aet*
Englefield Green Rovers 0 **Holyport** 2
Harrow Hill 1 Cheltenham Saracens 0
Henley Town 1 **Wokingham & Emmbrook** 2
Hook Norton 6 Winterbourne United 2
Kintbury Rangers 3 **Badshot Lea** 4
Malmesbury Victoria 3 Letcombe 3 *aet* (2-1p)
Milton United 0 **Ardley United** 3
Pewsey Vale 4 Highworth Town 1
Prestwood 1 **Chinnor** 3
Thame United 2 **AFC Wallingford** 4
Trowbridge Town 3 Kidlington 1
Wootton Bassett Town 1 **Carterton** 3

SECOND ROUND
AFC Wallingford 2 Wokingham & Emmbrook 1
Ardley United 3 Penn & Tylers Green 1
Badshot Lea 4 Chinnor 1 *aet*
Holyport 3 Binfield 2
Hook Norton 1 Carterton 1 *aet* (8-7p)
Malmesbury Victoria 0 **Fairford Town** 2
Pewsey Vale 2 Harrow Hill 1
Tytherington Rocks 1 **Trowbridge Town** 2

QUARTER-FINALS
AFC Wallingford 2 Hook Norton 1
Ardley United 2 Pewsey Vale 0
Fairford Town 3 Trowbridge Town 0
Holyport 1 Badshot Lea 1 *aet* (5-4p)

SEMI-FINALS
(played over two legs)
AFC Wallingford 2 Holyport 2,
Holyport 1 **AFC Wallingford** 4
Fairford Town 2 Ardley United,
Ardley United 4 Fairford Town 0

FINAL
(May 5th at Milton United)
Ardley United 3 AFC Wallingford 0

NORMAN MATTHEWS FLOODLIGHT CUP

PRELIMINARY ROUND
Abingdon Town 2 **Penn & Tylers Green** 2 *aet* (4-5p)
Harrow Hill 0 **Slimbridge** 1
Highworth Town 1 **Witney United** 4
FIRST ROUND
Almondsbury Town 0 **Witney United** 1
Ardley United 4 Banbury United Res. 0
Bicester Town 2 Kidlington 1 *aet*
Carterton 0 **Penn & Tylers Green** 1
Cheltenham Saracens 0 **Fairford Town** 3
Cirencester United 2 Pegasus Juniors 1
Didcot Town 0 **Kintbury Rangers** 3
Finchampstead 2 Badshot Lea 1
Henley Town 1 **Abingdon United** 4
Malmesbury Victoria 0 **Wantage Town** 6
Milton United 0 **Hungerford Town** 1
Oxford Quarry Nomads 3 Chipping Norton Town 2 *aet*
Pewsey Vale 1 **Bishops Cleeve** 5
Shrivenham 3 North Leigh 2
Slimbridge 2 Wootton Bassett Town 0
SECOND ROUND
Abingdon United 1 Bishops Cleeve 2
(Bishops Cleeve expelled)
Ardley United 3 Bicester Town 0
Cirencester United 1 **Penn & Tylers Green** 2

Fairford Town 2 **Hungerford Town** 3
Kintbury Rangers 3 Shrivenham 2
Oxford Quarry Nomads 1 **Slimbridge** 4
Wantage Town 3 Finchampstead 1
Witney United 5 Shortwood United 1

QUARTER-FINALS
Abingdon United 1 **Wantage Town** 3
Ardley United 5 Penn & Tylers Green 1
Kintbury Rangers 4 Hungerford Town 1
Witney United 1 **Slimbridge** 2

SEMI-FINALS
(played over two legs)
Kintbury Rangers 2 Ardley United 2,
Ardley United 2 Kintbury Rangers 0
Wantage Town 0 Slimbridge 1,
Slimbridge 2 Wantage Town 0

FINAL
(played over two legs)
(April 6th)
Slimbridge 0 Ardley United 0
(April 13th)
Ardley United 1 **Slimbridge** 3

HERTS SENIOR COUNTY LEAGUE

	Bedmond	Buntingf'd	Bushey R.	Codicote	Elliott Star	Hadley	Hatfield T.	Hertford H.	Hinton	Knebworth	L. Lions	MP Bushey	Sandridge	Standon	Whitewebbs	Wormley
Bedmond Sports & Social	P	0-2	2-0	1-0	2-1	0-4	0-5	0-0	0-3	1-4	3-0	1-4	0-3	3-2	1-1	1-0
Buntingford Town	3-2	R	3-0	1-0	8-0	1-1	2-1	3-2	0-1	2-2	8-1	4-1	3-0	4-2	2-1	10-0
Bushey Rangers	0-2	1-1	E	1-3	2-0	0-5	0-5	2-3	2-0	3-1	1-1	2-2	0-0	3-0	1-2	2-1
Codicote	3-1	2-3	0-3	M	0-2	0-4	1-0	1-0	1-0	2-1	3-2	3-2	1-3	4-1	0-3	2-1
Elliott Star	1-3	0-2	5-0	1-2	I	0-1	1-2	1-4	2-3	2-1	0-1	1-2	3-2	0-3	0-3	2-1
Hadley	4-0	1-0	2-0	1-1	3-2	E	0-1	4-0	0-0	5-2	3-0	2-2	1-0	1-1	1-0	4-0
Hatfield Town	4-1	1-3	5-1	8-3	3-2	4-2	R	W-L	2-4	1-4	2-3	3-2	0-2	3-2	1-2	4-2
Hertford Heath	2-0	1-1	1-1	1-1	5-0	0-4	0-6		4-1	3-0	5-1	1-3	1-1	3-1	3-2	
Hinton	2-3	2-3	0-1	1-2	1-2	0-2	2-2	1-1	D	0-1	3-1	1-1	3-6	5-3	1-3	3-4
Knebworth	1-2	1-2	7-1	4-1	2-2	1-2	1-4	2-0	2-0	I	2-3	2-2	2-2	1-3	1-4	0-1
London Lions	3-0	0-1	2-4	0-3	1-2	3-3	1-3	1-4	2-2	2-1	V	4-0	0-1	3-0	0-1	6-0
Metropolitan Police Bushey	2-1	1-5	3-0	4-1	4-0	1-2	2-1	3-2	7-2	3-4	0-1	I	3-1	6-1	0-2	4-1
Sandridge Rovers	4-3	1-9	5-1	3-0	1-1	2-1	1-1	3-1	3-1	0-0	0-5	0-0	S	5-1	2-2	2-0
Standon & Puckeridge	1-1	1-5	2-1	0-0	4-3	2-1	2-2	2-4	4-1	3-2	2-1	2-5	0-4	I	0-4	0-2
Whitewebbs	5-3	0-0	7-2	3-0	W-L	1-1	3-2	0-1	3-1	5-0	2-1	3-1	3-0	2-2	O	4-0
Wormley Rovers	3-1	2-0	1-1	2-3	0-0	1-3	1-6	0-3	2-1	4-1	0-2	2-3	2-1	0-1	2-3	N

Premier Division

		P	W	D	L	F	A	Pts
Whitewebbs		30	21	5	4	73	29	68
Hadley		30	20	7	3	70	25	67
Buntingford Town	-6	30	22	5	3	91	28	65
Sandridge Rovers	+3	30	15	7	8	60	48	55
Hatfield Town		30	17	3	10	82	50	54
Met. Police Bushey	+3	30	14	5	11	71	59	50
Hertford Heath		30	13	7	10	55	45	46
Codicote		30	14	3	13	43	57	45
London Lions		30	11	3	16	50	57	36
Bedmond Sports & Social		30	10	3	17	37	65	33
Standon & Puckeridge		30	8	6	16	48	79	30
Bushey Rangers		30	8	6	16	36	71	30
Knebworth		30	8	5	17	52	65	29
Wormley Rovers		30	8	2	20	37	76	26
Hinton		30	6	6	18	44	65	24
Elliott Star		30	7	3	20	36	66	24

Reserve Division One

	P	W	D	L	F	A	Pts
Hadley Res.	24	21	2	1	93	26	65
Hatfield Town Res.	24	17	4	3	74	42	55
Buntingford Town Res.	24	14	4	6	61	34	46
Bovingdon Res.	24	15	1	8	58	43	46
Standon & Puckeridge Res.	24	13	3	8	50	41	42
Codicote Res.	24	10	5	9	67	48	35
London Lions Res.	24	10	1	13	47	49	31
Hinton Res.	24	9	4	11	46	54	31
Knebworth Res.	24	10	1	13	41	55	31
Bedmond Sports & Social Res.	24	8	2	14	44	58	26
Buckhurst Hill Res.	24	5	1	18	34	60	16
Lemsford Res.	24	4	4	16	36	76	16
Elliott Star Res.	24	3	2	19	29	94	11

Reserve Division Two

	P	W	D	L	F	A	Pts
Sarratt Res.	24	17	3	4	88	22	54
Evergreen Res.	24	15	6	3	56	32	51
Met. Police Bushey Res.	24	16	2	6	89	41	50
Whitewebbs Res.	24	15	4	5	68	45	49
Sandridge Rovers Res.	24	12	4	8	47	51	40
North Mymms Res.	24	12	3	9	44	37	39
Croxley Guild Res.	24	10	3	11	48	50	33
Bushey Rangers Res.	24	10	2	12	65	63	32
Wormley Rovers Res.	24	7	3	14	33	54	24
Old Parmiterians Res.	24	6	4	14	47	85	22
Mill End Sports Res.	24	5	3	16	32	60	18
Cuffley Res.	24	4	6	14	43	80	18
Chipperfield Corinthians Res.	24	4	3	17	36	76	15

RESERVES CUP

FINAL

(May 6th at Buntingford Town)

Buntingford Town 5 Buckhurst Hill 1

HERTS SENIOR COUNTY LEAGUE PREMIER DIVISION CONSTITUTION 2007-08

BEDMOND SPORTS & SOCIAL . . Toms Lane Rec Ground, Toms Lane, Bedmond, Abbots Langley WD5 0RA 01923 267991
BOVINGDON. . . . . Green Lane, Bovingdon, Hemel Hempstead HP3 0LB. 01442 832628
BUNTINGFORD TOWN. . . . . Sainsburys Depot Sports Ground, London Road, Buntingford SG9 9JR . . . . None
BUSHEY RANGERS . . . . Moatfield, Bournehall Lane, Bushey WD23 3JU 020 8386 1875
CODICOTE . . . . John Clements Memorial Ground, Bury Lane, Codicote SG4 8XX 01438 821072
EVERGREEN . . . . South Way, Kings Langley, Abbots Langley WD5 0JL 01923 267812
HATFIELD TOWN . . . . Birchwood Leisure Centre, Longmead, Birchwood, Hatfield AL10 0AS 01707 270772
HERTFORD HEATH . . . . The Playing Field, Trinity Road, Hertford Heath SG13 7QR . . . . None
KNEBWORTH . . . . The Recreation Ground, Watton Road, Knebworth, Stevenage SG3 6AH. . . . . None
LONDON LIONS. . . . . Laing Sports, Rowley Lane, Barnet EN5 3HW 020 8441 6051
METROPOLITAN POLICE BUSHEY . . . . Aldenham Road, Bushey, Watford WD2 3TR 01923 243947
PARK STREET VILLAGE . . Park Street Recreation Ground, Park Street Lane, Park Street, St Albans AL2 2JB . . . . None
SANDRIDGE ROVERS . . . . Spencer Recreation Ground, Sandridge, St Albans AL4 9BZ. 01727 835506
STANDON & PUCKERIDGE . . . . Station Road, Standon, near Ware SG11 1QW. 01920 823460
WHITEWEBBS . . . . The Whitewebbs Centre, Whitewebbs Lane, Enfield EN2 9HH. 01992 760716
WORMLEY ROVERS . . . . Wormley Sports Club, Church Lane, Wormley EN10 7QF. 01992 460650

IN: Bovingdon (P), Evergreen (P), Park Street Village (P)
OUT: Elliott Star (W), Hadley (W – West Herts League Premier Division), Hinton (R)

	Allenburys Sports	Bovingdon	Buckhurst Hill	Chipperfield Corinthians	Croxley Guild	Cuffley	Evergreen	Lemsford	Little Munden	Loughton	Mill End Sports	North Mymms	Old Parmiterians	Park Street Village	Sarratt	St Peters	Wodson Park
Allenburys Sports		4-3	2-2	1-1	2-1	5-1	3-1	2-1	6-1	1-2	3-2	2-1	3-0	1-4	1-0	1-4	1-2
Bovingdon	4-2		3-3	1-0	2-2	5-4	1-3	2-1	0-3	7-1	2-0	1-0	2-1	4-1	3-0	3-2	1-2
Buckhurst Hill	4-2	4-2	D	W-L	1-0	4-1	1-1	2-2	2-3	1-0	1-2	1-3	3-0	0-1	4-0	3-0	1-2
Chipperfield Corinthians	5-1	1-2	4-1	I	6-3	3-1	1-1	2-1	1-7	7-0	1-3	6-1	0-2	4-3	2-2	3-2	
Croxley Guild	0-1	1-3	2-0	3-1	V	1-0	1-2	1-1	1-1	W-L	0-1	2-1	3-3	0-3	1-2	3-0	2-2
Cuffley	3-1	2-3	1-0	0-4	3-2	I	5-1	1-5	0-3	4-2	2-4	1-1	3-1	0-5	1-0	3-3	1-1
Evergreen	2-0	1-3	1-3	2-4	2-0	8-2	S	2-0	1-0	W-L	1-0	2-2	2-1	1-1	2-1	3-1	5-1
Lemsford	0-2	1-0	1-1	6-4	1-5	2-3	4-6	I	3-3	10-0		3-5	3-2	2-0	1-1	3-1	2-1
Little Munden	3-4	2-2	2-4	4-1	5-2	2-2	1-2	1-2	O	1-1	0-2	2-4	6-0	0-2	1-2	1-1	3-0
Loughton	L-W	0-2	0-2	1-5	3-3	1-5	0-1	1-1	1-5	N	1-3	0-5	3-1	L-W	0-4	L-W	3-4
Mill End Sports	4-3	1-1	1-6	0-3	0-2	3-2	2-2	1-3	2-0	2-1		3-1	2-2	2-0	0-3	1-1	2-1
North Mymms	4-0	1-0	2-5	2-1	1-0	3-1	0-1	3-1	2-1	2-1	3-1		3-4	1-3	1-1	3-1	4-2
Old Parmiterians	1-3	1-9	1-2	0-4	0-7	1-5	1-4	0-8	1-1	W-L	4-1	2-4	O	1-7	2-3	0-0	4-2
Park Street Village	1-0	0-0	6-0	2-2	5-0	1-0	5-0	2-0	3-1	8-0	2-2	3-1		N	2-0	0-1	2-0
Sarratt	3-2	1-2	W-L	1-2	2-1	1-1	1-1	0-2	2-0	W-L	3-1	0-3	2-1	3-0		2-2	5-1
St Peters	0-1	1-1	3-3	1-2	2-1	1-1	3-1	1-2	2-5	11-1	1-0	1-0	W-L	2-0	3-3	E	3-0
Wodson Park	4-0	0-2	3-0	4-1	2-1	4-3	0-2	2-1	2-3	3-1	3-2	5-0	5-2	0-1	3-3		

Division One	P	W	D	L	F	A	Pts
Park Street Village	32	23	3	6	74	22	72
Bovingdon	32	19	6	7	76	46	63
Evergreen	32	18	5	9	62	49	59
Chipperfield Cor.	32	17	4	11	88	60	55
North Mymms	32	17	3	12	66	53	54
Sarratt	32	15	7	10	50	45	52
Buckhurst Hill	32	15	6	11	64	51	51
Allenburys Sports	32	16	2	14	60	64	50
Wodson Park	32	15	4	13	65	67	49
Mill End Sports +3	32	13	7	12	50	55	49
Lemsford	32	13	7	12	73	57	46
St Peters	32	11	9	12	58	57	42
Little Munden	32	11	7	14	72	60	40
Cuffley	32	10	6	16	62	81	36
Croxley Guild +2	32	9	6	17	51	58	35
O. Parmiterians -4	32	4	3	25	38	110	11
Loughton	32	2	3	27	24	98	9

AUBREY CUP

FIRST ROUND
Mill End Sports 2 **Hatfield Town** 6

SECOND ROUND
Bedmond 0 **Chipperfield Cor.** 2
Buckhurst Hill 6 Allenburys Sports 5
Bushey Rgrs 2 Little Munden 1
Codicote 0 **Hadley** 1
Croxley Guild 0 **Whitewebbs** 2
Elliott Star 4 Lemsford 2
Hatfield Town 6 Hertford Heath 0
London Lions 1 **Park Street Village** 1 aet (2-4p)
Loughton 1 **Bovingdon** 5
Metropolitan Police Bushey 7 Evergreen 4 aet
North Mymms 4 Standon & Puckeridge 1
Sandridge Rovers 0 **Hinton** 2
Sarratt 1 Old Parmiterians 0
St Peters 1 **Buntingford Town** 6
Wodson Park 4 **Cuffley** 7 aet
Wormley Rovers 2 Knebworth 2 aet (5-3p)

SECOND ROUND
Buntingford Town 4 Elliott Star 2
Bushey Rangers 1 **Hadley** 5
Chipperfield Corinthians 0 **Park Street Village** 1 aet
Cuffley 1 **Hinton** 2
Hatfield Town 1 **Whitewebbs** 2
Metropolitan Police Bushey 4 North Mymms 1
Sarratt 1 **Buckhurst Hill** 2
Wormley Rovers 3 Bovingdon 1

QUARTER-FINALS
Hadley 2 Buntingford Town 1
Metropolitan Police Bushey 2 Hinton 0
Whitewebbs 4 Park St Village 1
Wormley Rovers 3 Buckhurst Hill 1

SEMI-FINALS
Hadley 2 Metropolitan Police Bushey 1
Wormley Rovers 0 **Whitewebbs** 4

FINAL
(at HCFA, Letchworth)
Whitewebbs 2 Hadley 0

HERTS SENIOR COUNTY LEAGUE DIVISION ONE CONSTITUTION 2007-08

ALLENBURYS SPORTS .... Glaxo Smith Kline, Westfield, Park Road, Ware SG12 0DP .... None
BALDOCK TOWN .... Norton Road, Baldock SG7 5AU 01462 895449
BEDWELL RANGERS .... Meadway Park, Gunnelswood Road, Stevenage SG1 2EF .... None
BUCKHURST HILL.................... Roding Lane, Buckhurst Hill IG9 5BJ.................. 020 8504 1189
CHIPPERFIELD CORINTHIANS........ Queens Street, Chipperfield, Kings Langley WD4 9BT 01923 269554
CROXLEY GUILD .... Croxley Guild of Sport, The Green, Croxley Green, Rickmansworth WD3 3HT 01923 770534
CUFFLEY .... King George's Playing Fields, Northaw Road East, Cuffley EN6 4LL 07815 174434
DEBDEN SPORTS .... Chigwell Lane, Loughton, Ilford IG10 3TP....................... 020 8508 9392
HINTON .... Holtwhites Sports & Social, Kirkland Drive, Enfield EN2 0RU 020 8363 4449
LEMSFORD .... Gosling Sports Park, Stanborough Road, Welwyn Garden City AL8 6XE 01707 331056
MILL END SPORTS ...... King George V Playing Fields, Shepherds Lane, Mill End, Rickmansworth WD3 8JN 01923 776392
NORTH MYMMS .... Welham Green Recreation, Dellsome Lane, North Mymms, Hatfield AL9 7DY ... 01707 266972/260338
OLD PARMITERIANS .... Parmiters School, High Elms Lane, Garston, Watford WD25 0JU..................... 01923 682805
SARRATT .... King George V Playing Fields, King Georges Avenue, Sarratt .... None
ST PETERS .... William Bird Playing Fields, Toulmin Drive, St Albans AL3 6DX.................... 01727 852401
WODSON PARK .... Wodson Park Spts & Rec. Centre, Wadesmill Road, Ware SG12 0UQ 01920 487091

IN: Baldock Town (P – North & Mid Herts League Premier Division), Bedwell Rangers (P – North & Mid Herts League Division One North), Debden Sports (P – Ilford & District League Premier Division)
OUT: Bovingdon (P), Evergreen (P), Little Munden (W), Loughton (W), Park Street Village (P)

HUMBER PREMIER LEAGUE

Note – Bridlington Town Reserves withdrew during the course of the season. Their results shown here are expunged	Barton Town OB Res.	Beverley Town	Bridlington Town Res.	Easington United	Hedon Rangers	Hedon United	Hessle Rangers	Hornsea Town	Hutton Cranswick United	North Ferriby Utd Res.	Pocklington Town	Reckitts	Sculcoates Amateurs	Westella & Willerby	Withernsea
Barton Town OB Res.		2-5	n/a	1-1	4-4	5-4	2-0	1-2	3-3	1-2	0-1	0-4	1-1	0-3	5-2
Beverley Town	2-1		n/a	0-1	0-0	2-3	4-3	2-2	0-2	2-1	2-0	1-1	1-4	1-0	1-2
Bridlington Town Res.	3-2	2-4	P	n/a	n/a	n/a	n/a	n/a	n/a	3-4	1-1	n/a	2-1	3-6	n/a
Easington United	4-0	2-1	1-1	R	0-2	3-0	1-1	3-4	3-3	4-1	1-6	0-2	1-1	1-0	
Hedon Rangers	1-4	0-3	n/a	0-4	E	2-3	1-2	0-1	3-6	3-0	2-1	0-4	0-1	2-7	4-1
Hedon United	3-3	1-6	1-3	0-3	0-2	M	0-2	0-7	0-5	5-9	2-0	1-5	0-3	2-2	0-5
Hessle Rangers	2-3	1-9	n/a	0-4	1-1	2-4	I	1-3	2-0	0-2	2-1	0-2	0-2	0-1	2-2
Hornsea Town	3-0	3-1	n/a	1-4	3-0	5-1	4-2	E	2-1	2-3	0-3	1-3	1-2	3-4	2-0
Hutton Cranswick United	3-2	2-0	8-0	3-2	6-2	5-0	8-1	0-1	R	2-0	2-0	1-2	0-1	0-2	8-0
North Ferriby Utd Res.	3-5	4-0	10-1	3-2	1-1	4-1	1-0	3-2	0-2		1-1	2-2	1-3	1-4	2-0
Pocklington Town	0-0	0-2	n/a	2-1	2-0	5-2	5-1	3-1	1-0	0-0	D	0-2	2-3	1-1	4-0
Reckitts	1-2	1-1	4-0	2-2	2-2	8-1	1-0	2-3	1-3	1-5	3-1	I	1-1	0-0	6-0
Sculcoates Amateurs	2-1	1-1	5-1	6-1	9-0	9-3	3-1	3-0	2-1	0-0	1-1	1-1	V	2-0	6-0
Westella & Willerby	2-3	7-1	10-2	1-3	2-1	4-0	4-1	3-1	3-0	0-2	0-1	1-1	1-5		3-1
Withernsea	0-3	3-2	2-5	1-3	4-3	2-5	0-3	2-7	1-3	1-4	1-2	0-7	1-8	2-4	

Note – Bridlington Town Reserves withdrew during the course of the season
Their results are shown above but are expunged from the league table

Premier Division		P	W	D	L	F	A	Pts
Sculcoates Amateurs		26	20	6	0	81	19	66
Westella & Willerby		26	15	6	5	62	32	51
Hutton Cranswick United		26	16	1	9	70	34	49
Reckitts		26	13	9	4	69	30	48
North Ferriby United Res.		26	13	6	7	55	42	45
Hornsea Town		26	14	2	10	61	45	44
Easington United		26	13	5	8	57	41	44
Beverley Town		26	10	5	11	50	47	35
Pocklington Town		26	10	4	12	36	35	34
Barton Town Old Boy Res.	-6	26	9	6	11	52	58	27
Hedon Rangers		26	5	5	16	36	71	20
Hessle Rangers		26	5	2	19	29	70	17
Hedon United		26	5	2	19	41	108	17
Withernsea		26	4	1	21	31	98	13

Bridlington Town Reserves – record expunged

HUMBER PREMIER LEAGUE PREMIER DIVISION CONSTITUTION 2007-08

BARTON TOWN OLD BOYS RESERVES .. The Euronics Ground, Marsh Lane, Barton-on-Humber DN15 5HB 07900 105204
BEVERLEY TOWN .... Recreation Ground, Norwood, Beverley HU17 9HW 01482 862520
EASINGTON UNITED .... Low Farm, Beck Street, Easington, Hull HU12 0TT............................ None
HEDON RANGERS..................... Destiny Fitness, Staithes Road, Hedon, Hull HU12 8DX 01482 896113
HESSLE RANGERS .... Blackburn Leisure, Prescott Avenue, Brough HU15 1BB .... None
HORNSEA TOWN .... Hollis Recreation Ground, Atwick Road, Hornsea HU18 1EL .... None
HUTTON CRANSWICK UNITED .... Rotsea Lane, Hutton Cranswick, Driffield YO25 9QG....................... 01377 270357
LSS LUCARLY'S .... Wilton Road, Humberston, Grimsby DN36 4AW.......................... 01472 812936
MALET LAMBERT YC .... Malet Lambert School, James Reckitt Avenue, Hull HU8 0JD 01482 374211
NORTH FERRIBY UNITED RESERVES .. Grange Lane, Church Road, North Ferriby HU14 3AA 01482 634601
POCKLINGTON TOWN...................... The Balk, Pocklington, York YO42 2NZ 01759 303638
RECKITTS .... Humberside Police Spts Ground, Inglemire Lane, Hull HU6 8JG 01482 326111x2317
SCULCOATES AMATEURS ..... Hull & East Riding Spts Ground, Chanterlands Avenue, Hull HU5 4ED 01482 342156
SMITH & NEPHEW. .... Hull University, Inglemire Lane, Hull .... None
WESTELLA & WILLERBY .... Hull YPI, Chanterlands Avenue, Hull HU5 4EF .... None
WITHERNSEA .... Hull Road, Withernsea HU19 2EG.................................. None

IN: LSS Lucarly's (P), Malet Lambert YC (P), Smith & Nephew (P)
OUT: Bridlington Town Reserves (WS), Hedon United (W)

Note – Anlaby United withdrew during the course of the season. Their results shown here are expunged	Anlaby United	Brandesburton	Bransholme Athletic	Discount Carpets	East Hull Amateurs	Hall Road Rangers Res.	LSS Lucarly's	Long Riston	Malet Lambert YC	North Cave	Pinefleet Wolfreton	Smith & Nephew	St Andrews Police Club
Anlaby United	D	1-6	n/a	n/a	n/a	n/a	n/a	n/a	n/a	n/a	n/a	0-1	n/a
Brandesburton	n/a	I	1-1	5-3	3-1	1-1	2-1	1-1	0-3	2-1	1-1	0-6	1-2
Bransholme Athletic	1-1	2-3	V	2-2	4-1	1-4	1-2	0-3	1-3	0-1	0-2	0-2	0-1
Discount Carpets	n/a	1-1	6-2	I	6-0	2-4	2-2	0-0	0-2	2-4	1-3	0-4	4-3
East Hull Amateurs	n/a	2-3	0-1	3-7	S	0-2	0-2	3-3	1-2	1-2	1-2	1-5	0-7
Hall Road Rangers Res.	3-1	0-3	1-2	2-2	2-0	I	2-2	2-2	2-10	0-1	1-1	0-1	2-2
LSS Lucarly's	3-2	4-0	0-1	5-1	6-3	9-0	O	1-0	3-2	3-1	3-2	0-2	2-1
Long Riston	2-3	2-1	1-2	2-2	2-0	1-5	1-4	N	1-2	1-1	0-6	0-4	0-3
Malet Lambert YC	3-1	1-1	4-0	4-2	3-1	7-0	1-0	1-0		5-0	0-2	0-2	6-1
North Cave	n/a	2-2	2-1	0-3	2-1	2-2	4-3	1-0	2-0		4-2	0-5	3-3
Pinefleet Wolfreton	2-1	2-3	2-0	4-2	1-4	4-1	2-6	2-2	2-4	1-3	O	1-4	1-1
Smith & Nephew	n/a	4-0	9-0	3-1	6-1	4-2	3-0	0-1	2-0	5-1	2-1	N	2-1
St Andrews Police Club	0-3	2-2	5-5	4-2	0-2	0-2	2-4	1-1	0-1	2-0	2-2	2-4	E

Division One	P	W	D	L	F	A	Pts
Smith & Nephew	22	21	0	1	79	12	63
Malet Lambert YC	22	16	1	5	61	23	49
LSS Lucarly's	22	14	2	6	62	33	44
North Cave	22	11	4	7	38	44	37
Brandesburton	22	8	8	6	36	43	32
Pinefleet Wolfreton	22	8	5	9	46	45	29
St Andrews Police Club	22	6	7	9	45	46	25
Hall Road Rangers Res.	22	6	7	9	37	58	25
Discount Carpets	22	5	6	11	51	59	21
Long Riston	22	4	8	10	24	42	20
Bransholme Athletic	22	5	3	14	26	55	18
East Hull Amateurs	22	2	1	19	26	71	7

Anlaby United – record expunged

HUMBER PREMIER LEAGUE DIVISION ONE CONSTITUTION 2007-08

BRANDESBURTON........ Brandesburton Playing Fields, Catwick Lane, Brandesburton, Driffield YO25 8SB .... None
BRANSHOLME ATHLETIC .... Hull University, Inglemire Lane, Hull 01482 466000
DISCOUNT CARPETS .... Brooklands Park, Chamberlain Road, Hull 01482 794193
HALL ROAD RANGERS RESERVES .. Dene Park, Dene Close, Beverley Rd, Dunswell, Hull HU6 0AB 01482 850101
HESSLE SPORTING CLUB .... South Hunsley School, Melton, North Ferriby HU14 3HS 01482 631208
KINNERSLEY .... Brooklands Park, Chamberlain Road, Hull 01482 794193
LONG RISTON .... Long Riston Playing Fields, Long Riston. .... None
MILL LANE UNITED .... Broadgates Playing Fields, Walkington, Beverley. .... None
NORTH CAVE .... North Cave Playing Field, North Cave, Brough .... None
PINEFLEET WOLFRETON........ Marist RU Club, Cranbrook Ave., Cottingham Rd, Hull HU6 7TT 01482 859216
SELBY TOWN RESERVES .... Flaxley Road Ground, Richard Street, Scott Road, Selby YO8 0BS 01757 210900
ST ANDREWS POLICE CLUB .... East Mount Rec, Waverley Road, Hull. .... None
IN: Hessle Sporting Club (P – East Riding Amateur League Premier Division), Kinnersley (P – East Riding Amateur League Premier Division), Mill Lane United (P – Sunday football), Selby Town Reserves (N)
OUT: AFC Charleston (WN), Anlaby United (WS), East Hull Amateurs (W), LSS Lucarly's (P), Malet Lambert YC (P), Smith & Nephew (P)

WWW.NLNEWSDESK.CO.UK

LEAGUE CUP

FIRST ROUND
Anlaby United 5 East Hull Amateurs 0
Barton Town Old Boys Res. 1 **Pinefleet Wolfreton** 3
Beverley Town 4 Bransholme Athletic 2
Discount Carpets 0 **Bridlington Town Res.** 2
Easington Utd 1 North Ferriby Res. 0
Hessle Rangers 4 Hedon United 2
Hutton Cranswick 1 **Hornsea Town** 2
Reckitts (w/o) v St Andrews Police Club (scr.)
Sculcoates Amateurs 5 Hall Road Res. 1
Smith & Nephew (w/o) v North Cave (scr.)

Westella & Willerby 3 Brandesburton 0
Withernsea 2 **Hedon Rangers** 4
SECOND ROUND
Anlaby United (scr.) v **Hessle Rangers** (w/o)
Beverley Town 2 **Pocklington Town** 2 aet (2-3p)
Bridlington Town Res. (scr.) v **Sculcoates Amateurs** (w/o)
Hedon Rangers 0 **Smith & Nephew** 9
Hornsea Town 2 Easington United 1
Malet Lambert YC 4 LSS Lucarly's 2 aet
Reckitts 3 Pinefleet Wolfreton 2
Westella & Willerby 6 Long Riston 1

QUARTER-FINALS
Hessle Rangers 0 **Hornsea Town** 3
Pocklington Town 4 Reckitts 2
Sculcoates Amateurs 1 Westella & Willerby 0
Smith & Nephew 3 Malet Lambert YC 0
SEMI-FINALS
Pocklington Town 0 **Sculcoates Amateurs** 2 *(at Hutton Cranswick Utd)*
Smith & Nephew 3 Hornsea Town 1 aet *(at Hutton Cranswick United)*
FINAL
(May 4th at North Ferriby United)
Sculcoates Amateurs 1
Smith & Nephew 0

ISTHMIAN LEAGUE

	AFC Wimbledon	Ashford Town (Middx)	Billericay Town	Boreham Wood	Bromley	Carshalton Athletic	Chelmsford City	East Thurrock United	Folkestone Invicta	Hampton/Richmond Boro'	Harrow Borough	Hendon	Heybridge Swifts	Horsham	Leyton	Margate	Ramsgate	Slough Town	Staines Town	Tonbridge Angels	Walton & Hersham	Worthing
AFC Wimbledon		2-1	3-2	1-1	3-2	2-0	1-2	4-0	4-0	0-1	4-2	3-0	1-1	0-0	1-0	0-0	0-0	9-0	1-1	2-3	3-1	1-1
Ashford Town (Middx)	1-2		0-1	1-1	2-0	2-2	2-3	0-2	2-1	1-2	1-0	2-0	3-2	1-2	2-2	1-1	4-1	1-1	1-1	1-2	3-0	3-0
Billericay Town	3-0	5-0		0-0	0-0	0-0	2-1	2-1	1-1	1-0	3-0	2-1	0-0	1-0	2-0	3-2	0-1	5-0	1-0	3-0	3-1	3-1
Boreham Wood	0-0	5-4	1-1	P	0-2	0-0	2-0	1-2	1-2	0-2	1-1	3-2	2-1	1-2	1-1	6-1	1-2	6-0	2-1	1-3	1-0	3-2
Bromley	1-3	5-1	1-0	1-1	R	2-1	2-1	2-0	1-2	3-2	3-2	1-1	0-1	0-3	4-1	1-3	1-0	4-0	2-1	3-0	4-2	3-3
Carshalton Athletic	1-2	1-1	3-2	1-0	1-1	E	0-3	1-1	1-1	0-1	3-1	1-3	0-2	1-3	2-0	2-1	4-0	5-1	0-4	1-0	3-0	1-1
Chelmsford City	0-3	2-1	2-2	2-0	1-1	5-1	M	2-1	3-0	4-0	3-2	1-0	1-1	5-0	2-2	1-3	4-0	5-0	7-3	3-2	7-0	3-1
East Thurrock United	0-4	3-0	0-4	2-0	1-5	0-0	1-1	I	0-3	0-2	0-2	1-2	1-3	0-2	3-0	0-3	0-1	4-1	4-1	0-1	1-0	1-2
Folkestone Invicta	0-1	3-1	3-3	1-4	0-0	2-4	1-0	3-2	E	1-1	0-1	1-0	0-0	0-1	1-3	1-5	0-2	0-0	1-2	0-2	4-3	1-0
Hampton/Richmond Borough	2-0	1-1	0-0	2-5	0-4	1-1	1-3	3-0	1-0	R	1-0	3-1	2-2	1-1	2-0	3-2	1-4	4-2	3-2	2-2	2-0	4-2
Harrow Borough	0-1	2-0	5-2	2-3	2-1	1-2	0-3	5-4	0-2	1-2		1-2	2-0	2-0	1-1	4-4	1-3	0-2	1-2	0-1	1-0	1-0
Hendon	3-1	0-0	0-1	1-2	0-2	3-5	0-3	2-1	1-0	0-2	1-1	D	1-1	2-0	1-2	1-0	2-4	2-0	1-1	0-1	3-0	2-1
Heybridge Swifts	0-1	0-2	1-2	1-1	0-1	0-1	1-1	0-0	2-0	2-2	2-1	0-0	I	1-1	3-0	1-0	2-0	2-3	1-0	2-1	2-0	3-1
Horsham	1-1	1-1	3-1	0-2	1-1	1-1	2-1	1-1	2-2	1-2	4-1	1-1	1-1	V	2-1	0-4	4-1	4-0	1-1	4-3	4-0	1-1
Leyton	2-5	1-1	3-2	0-1	0-0	3-0	3-2	0-3	0-0	0-3	2-1	1-4	1-6	1-3	I	0-4	4-1	1-0	4-2	0-1	3-0	1-1
Margate	0-0	1-1	0-0	0-2	0-0	1-0	3-0	1-1	1-0	2-0	4-1	4-1	0-1	1-1	5-1	S	1-0	2-1	2-4	1-2	3-0	2-1
Ramsgate	1-1	2-1	2-0	1-1	1-3	2-1	1-1	3-0	3-0	1-3	2-0	3-0	2-0	0-2	0-3	1-1	I	2-1	1-0	2-3	1-0	4-3
Slough Town	0-0	0-2	2-0	0-4	0-8	0-2	0-4	0-5	0-2	0-3	0-5	0-1	0-2	1-3	0-1	2-2	0-3	O	0-2	2-3	0-5	1-1
Staines Town	1-1	2-2	0-1	2-1	1-4	3-1	1-1	2-3	1-0	2-2	1-1	1-3	2-1	0-0	1-1	1-0	3-1	1-2	N	2-0	2-0	2-2
Tonbridge Angels	1-3	4-1	1-2	1-1	1-2	2-0	1-3	1-1	3-3	1-3	0-1	3-1	2-3	1-4	2-5	1-2	3-2	3-2	3-1		0-0	6-1
Walton & Hersham	1-1	2-3	2-2	1-2	0-0	1-0	2-0	0-2	3-1	0-4	2-2	0-2	1-0	5-1	0-0	0-2	1-0	3-0	0-2	2-1		0-6
Worthing	1-1	3-1	1-3	0-1	1-2	0-0	0-2	0-2	1-2	1-1	1-2	1-2	0-3	3-2	2-1	2-5	3-2	2-2	1-2	1-1	2-0	

Premier Division

		HOME					AWAY					TOTAL					
	P	W	D	L	F	A	W	D	L	F	A	W	D	L	F	A	Pts
Hampton & Richmond Boro'	42	11	6	4	39	32	13	4	4	38	21	24	10	8	77	53	82
Bromley	42	13	3	5	44	28	10	8	3	39	15	23	11	8	83	43	80
Chelmsford City	42	15	4	2	63	23	8	4	9	33	28	23	8	11	96	51	77
Billericay Town	42	15	5	1	40	9	7	6	8	31	33	22	11	9	71	42	77
AFC Wimbledon -3	42	11	7	3	45	18	10	8	3	31	19	21	15	6	76	37	75
Margate	42	11	6	4	34	17	9	5	7	45	31	20	11	11	79	48	71
Boreham Wood	42	9	5	7	38	29	10	7	4	33	20	19	12	11	71	49	69
Horsham	42	8	9	4	39	30	10	5	6	31	27	18	14	10	70	57	68
Ramsgate	42	12	4	5	35	24	8	1	12	28	39	20	5	17	63	63	65
Heybridge Swifts	42	9	6	6	26	18	8	7	6	31	22	17	13	12	57	40	64
Tonbridge Angels	42	9	3	9	43	40	11	1	9	31	32	20	4	18	74	72	64
Staines Town	42	8	8	5	31	27	7	4	10	33	37	15	12	15	64	64	57
Carshalton Athletic	42	9	5	7	32	28	5	7	9	22	31	14	12	16	54	59	54
Hendon	42	8	4	9	26	28	8	2	11	27	36	16	6	20	53	64	54
Leyton	42	8	4	9	30	40	5	6	10	25	37	13	10	19	55	77	49
East Thurrock United	42	6	2	13	22	37	8	4	9	34	33	14	6	22	56	70	48
Ashford Town (Middx)	42	8	6	7	34	26	3	7	11	25	45	11	13	18	59	71	46
Folkestone Invicta	42	6	5	10	23	35	6	5	10	22	31	12	10	20	45	66	46
Harrow Borough	42	8	2	11	32	35	5	4	12	29	36	13	6	23	61	71	45
Worthing	42	6	4	11	26	36	2	7	12	31	46	8	11	23	57	82	35
Walton & Hersham	42	8	5	8	26	31	1	1	19	12	52	9	6	27	38	83	33
Slough Town	42	1	3	17	8	58	3	3	15	18	65	4	6	32	26	123	18

PLAY-OFFS

SEMI-FINALS
(April 30th) Chelmsford City 1 **Billericay Town** 1 *aet* (3-5p) *Att* 2,025
(May 1st) **Bromley** 1 AFC Wimbledon 0 *Att* 3,289

FINAL
(May 5th at Bromley)
Bromley 1 Billericay Town 1 *aet* (4-2p) *Att* 3,012

DATES & GATES

	AFC Wimbledon	Ashford Town (Middx)	Billericay Town	Boreham Wood	Bromley	Carshalton Athletic	Chelmsford City	East Thurrock United	Folkestone Invicta	Hampton & Richmond	Harrow Borough	Hendon	Heybridge Swifts	Horsham	Leyton	Margate	Ramsgate	Slough Town	Staines Town	Tonbridge Angels	Walton & Hersham	Worthing
AFC Wimbledon		21 Nov / 1,939	24 Apr / 2,620	26 Aug / 2,356	10 Feb / 3,034	6 Mar / 2,143	9 Jan / 2,471	30 Jan / 2,092	2 Sep / 2,165	7 Oct / 2,529	27 Jan / 2,481	9 Sep / 2,273	21 Apr / 3,377	2 Dec / 2,707	17 Oct / 1,960	3 Mar / 2,768	22 Aug / 2,290	31 Mar / 2,754	9 Apr / 3,002	18 Nov / 2,534	30 Dec / 2,808	17 Mar / 2,456
Ashford Town (Middx)	26 Sep / 922		24 Mar / 217	2 Sep / 137	10 Mar / 250	10 Feb / 190	22 Aug / 322	26 Aug / 127	18 Nov / 189	20 Jan / 267	2 Dec / 157	31 Mar / 154	23 Sep / 147	31 Oct / 235	11 Nov / 149	24 Feb / 194		9 Apr / 279	20 Mar / 249	17 Apr / 181	13 Jan / 181	28 Apr / 230
Billericay Town	9 Dec / 923	7 Oct / 351		13 Jan / 555	23 Dec / 543	2 Sep / 403	30 Dec / 1,508	9 Apr / 782	22 Aug / 385	9 Sep / 382	21 Nov / 200	3 Mar / 585	9 Jan / 415	27 Jan / 548	28 Apr / 761	17 Oct / 358	31 Mar / 661	17 Mar / 532	26 Aug / 397	12 Dec / 340	3 Feb / 523	17 Feb / 576
Boreham Wood	7 Apr / 1,103	14 Apr / 134	19 Aug / 212		28 Apr / 385	18 Nov / 190	27 Jan / 337	17 Mar / 152	24 Feb / 207	21 Nov / 120	28 Aug / 166	7 Oct / 240	6 Jan / 187	5 Sep / 172	26 Dec / 100	9 Sep / 248	10 Feb / 196	28 Oct / 230	2 Dec / 181	17 Oct / 188	17 Oct / 119	3 Mar / 161
Bromley	3 Jan / 1,639	9 Sep / 512	21 Apr / 1,460	16 Dec / 577		9 Apr / 822	13 Jan / 911	7 Oct / 800	31 Mar / 602	3 Mar / 913	17 Oct / 436	17 Mar / 707	17 Feb / 631	28 Nov / 499	3 Feb / 540	21 Nov / 618	26 Aug / 454	2 Sep / 507	22 Aug / 411	27 Jan / 924	23 Dec / 469	30 Dec / 655
Carshalton Athletic	19 Aug / 1,797	23 Jan / 132	14 Apr / 384	3 Feb / 248	26 Dec / 548		17 Oct / 258	3 Mar / 200	28 Apr / 372	28 Aug / 283	23 Dec / 271	9 Dec / 285	5 Sep / 210	13 Feb / 261	17 Mar / 215	17 Feb / 355	11 Nov / 224	9 Jan / 181	20 Jan / 301	7 Apr / 323	9 Sep / 234	7 Oct / 251
Chelmsford City	20 Jan / 1,686	6 Jan / 817	28 Aug / 1,268	4 Nov / 678	19 Aug / 777	26 Feb / 1,011		25 Nov / 682	13 Nov / 576	6 Apr / 2,008	28 Apr / 1,405	3 Feb / 1,005	26 Dec / 1,236	10 Mar / 1,231	4 Sep / 675	14 Apr / 1,194	23 Sep / 804	23 Dec / 722	24 Mar / 1,010	25 Sep / 681	17 Feb / 818	28 Oct / 734
East Thurrock United	28 Apr / 1,187	7 Apr / 105	26 Dec / 257	14 Oct / 107	24 Mar / 219	23 Sep / 119	13 Mar / 418		26 Sep / 109	19 Aug / 132	5 Sep / 123	27 Jan / 127	28 Aug / 144	20 Mar / 65	14 Apr / 75	23 Jan / 142	10 Mar / 144	24 Feb / 178	18 Nov / 117	9 Jan / 75	23 Dec / 114	28 Oct / 107
Folkestone Invicta	14 Apr / 1,082	3 Feb / 237	6 Jan / 364	9 Dec / 313	4 Sep / 284	16 Dec / 312	17 Mar / 524	20 Nov / 235		17 Feb / 367	17 Apr / 306	16 Oct / 303	24 Apr / 524	21 Apr / 388	9 Sep / 255	28 Aug / 445	18 Nov / 485	28 Apr / 377	2 Sep / 307	14 Nov / 474	7 Oct / 285	25 Nov / 274
Hampton & Richmond	24 Mar / 1,802	17 Feb / 326	10 Mar / 466	26 Sep / 170	20 Mar / 357	30 Dec / 356	26 Aug / 340	13 Jan / 274	2 Dec / 275		17 Apr / 435	22 Aug / 178	24 Apr / 632	13 Mar / 290	23 Dec / 255	27 Jan / 445	20 Jan / 251	3 Mar / 282	13 Jan / 378	14 Nov / 573	21 Nov / 233	10 Apr / 377
Harrow Borough	11 Nov / 790	17 Feb / 185	23 Sep / 205	24 Mar / 168	4 Dec / 200	21 Apr / 177	28 Apr / 1,405	5 Sep / 123	17 Apr / 306	26 Dec / 191		9 Apr / 226	14 Apr / 178	18 Nov / 314	20 Mar / 306	14 Oct / 161	26 Feb / 247	22 Aug / 202	10 Mar / 201	23 Sep / 207	26 Aug / 156	26 Aug / 89
Hendon	10 Mar / 859	4 Sep / 177	27 Mar / 385	30 Dec / 168	2 Dec / 376	9 Dec / 285	3 Feb / 1,005	16 Oct / 235	16 Oct / 303	22 Aug / 178	9 Apr / 226		14 Apr / 150	20 Mar / 198	16 Jan / 167	16 Jan / 265	25 Sep / 196	27 Jan / 202	28 Nov / 201	19 Aug / 207	20 Jan / 156	13 Jan / 608
Heybridge Swifts	23 Dec / 614	3 Mar / 216	2 Dec / 205	9 Dec / 313	23 Sep / 357	5 Sep / 210	26 Dec / 1,236	28 Aug / 144	24 Apr / 524	24 Apr / 632	14 Apr / 178	6 Mar / 150		14 Apr / 246	19 Aug / 246	11 Nov / 248	9 Dec / 456	26 Sep / 521	23 Jan / 71	26 Sep / 195	26 Dec / 183	9 Sep / 180
Horsham	17 Feb / 1,486	17 Mar / 357	11 Nov / 462	31 Mar / 334	20 Jan / 166	13 Feb / 261	10 Mar / 1,231	20 Mar / 65	21 Apr / 388	13 Mar / 290	18 Nov / 314	14 Apr / 260	28 Aug / 343		19 Aug / 246	9 Dec / 258	16 Dec / 167	3 Mar / 282	9 Dec / 378	17 Mar / 255	11 Nov / 233	3 Feb / 285
Leyton	27 Jan / 510	27 Jan / 40	16 Dec / 166	19 Mar / 94	18 Nov / 147	17 Mar / 215	4 Sep / 675	14 Apr / 75	9 Sep / 255	23 Dec / 255	16 Jan / 167	9 Dec / 171	7 Oct / 443	3 Mar / 356		28 Oct / 122	2 Dec / 66	13 Jan / 96	24 Feb / 49	10 Mar / 201	7 Apr / 423	21 Nov / 146
Margate	23 Sep / 1,385	28 Aug / 429	4 Sep / 645	14 Dec / 286	26 Sep / 603	17 Feb / 355	14 Apr / 1,194	23 Jan / 142	28 Aug / 445	27 Jan / 445	14 Oct / 161	16 Jan / 265	28 Apr / 417	26 Feb / —	28 Oct / 122		9 Apr / 1,676	26 Aug / 709	28 Nov / 588	20 Feb / 430	31 Mar / 575	22 Aug / 407
Ramsgate	6 Jan / 631	9 Dec / 312	5 Sep / 386	20 Jan / 376	6 Apr / 483	27 Jan / 322	23 Sep / 804	10 Mar / 144	18 Nov / 485	20 Jan / 251	13 Feb / 215	25 Sep / 196	9 Dec / 456	26 Sep / 167	2 Dec / 66	26 Dec / 1,762		7 Oct / 285	23 Dec / 282	16 Dec / 320	7 Apr / 270	27 Jan / 143
Slough Town	5 Sep / 839	26 Dec / 253	14 Oct / 295	19 Mar / 267	14 Apr / 286	26 Sep / 212	23 Dec / 722	6 Feb / 179	4 Sep / 496	9 Dec / 282	19 Aug / 246	9 Dec / 255	23 Jan / 208	26 Sep / 167	13 Jan / 378	26 Aug / 709	7 Oct / 285		17 Oct / 291	27 Mar / 140	5 Sep / 195	18 Nov / 395
Staines Town	26 Dec / 1,984	9 Jan / 195	28 Aug / 429	17 Feb / 261	20 Feb / 238	28 Oct / 215	24 Mar / 1,010	2 Sep / 52	3 Feb / 178	13 Jan / 378	24 Apr / 178	28 Nov / 201	5 Sep / 208	24 Apr / 178	24 Feb / 49	28 Nov / 588	23 Dec / 253	17 Oct / 291		5 Sep / 257	3 Mar / 268	26 Sep / 228
Tonbridge Angels	3 Feb / 1,320	23 Sep / 195	9 Dec / 342	23 Sep / 362	16 Jan / 266	23 Jan / 463	25 Sep / 681	22 Aug / 702	14 Apr / 404	14 Nov / 573	17 Mar / 377	13 Jan / 258	9 Dec / 162	16 Dec / 456	13 Jan / 89	20 Feb / 430	6 Feb / 320	31 Mar / 367	31 Mar / 367		2 Sep / 533	22 Aug / 407
Walton & Hersham	28 Aug / 1,220	19 Aug / 135	20 Jan / 508	23 Sep / 100	28 Aug / 450	24 Mar / 397	17 Feb / 818	10 Feb / 103	5 Sep / 543	21 Nov / 311	7 Apr / 130	3 Mar / 377	26 Dec / 167	26 Dec / 431	7 Apr / 423	31 Mar / 575	28 Aug / 283	27 Mar / 140	3 Mar / 268	2 Sep / 533		11 Nov / 373
Worthing	16 Jan / 1,104	30 Jan / 321	30 Jan / 397	23 Sep / 362	10 Feb / 190	28 Apr / 215	28 Oct / 734	16 Dec / 300	26 Dec / 431	21 Apr / 347	14 Apr / 130	21 Apr / 347	10 Mar / 393	19 Dec / 445	7 Apr / 423	19 Aug / 445	27 Feb / 233	18 Nov / 395	26 Sep / 228	6 Jan / 351	11 Nov / 373	

WWW.NLNEWSDESK.CO.UK

ISTHMIAN LEAGUE PREMIER DIVISION CONSTITUTION 2007-08

AFC HORNCHURCH
Hornchurch Stadium, Bridge Avenue, Upminster, Essex RM14 2LX
Tel: 01708 220080
Manager: Colin McBride   www.hornchurchfc.com   Colours: Red, white & black

AFC WIMBLEDON
Kingsmeadow Stadium, Kingston Road, Kingston-upon-Thames, Surrey KT1 3PB
Tel: 020 8547 3528
Manager: Terry Brown   www.afcwimbledon.co.uk   Colours: Blue

ASHFORD TOWN (MIDDX)
Short Lane Stadium, Short Lane, Stanwell, Staines, Middlesex TW19 7BH
Tel: 01784 245908   www.ashfordtownmiddlesexfc.co.uk
Manager: Mark Butler   Colours: Tangerine, white & black

BILLERICAY TOWN
New Lodge, Blunts Wall Road, Billericay, Essex CM12 9SA
Tel: 01277 655177   Club: 01277 652188
Manager: Matt Jones   www.billericaytownfc.co.uk   Colours: Blue & white

BOREHAM WOOD
Meadow Park, Broughinge Road, Boreham Wood, Hertfordshire WD6 5AL
Tel: 020 8953 5097   Club: 020 8207 7982   Fax: 020 8207 7982
Manager: Steve Cook   www.web-teams.co.uk/borehamwoodfc   Colours: White & black

CARSHALTON ATHLETIC
War Memorial Sports Ground, Colston Avenue, Carshalton, Surrey SM5 2PW
Tel: 020 8642 8658   Fax: 020 8643 0999
Manager: Dave Garland   www.carshaltonathletic.org   Colours: White & maroon

CHELMSFORD CITY
Melbourne Stadium, Salerno Way, Chelmsford, Essex CM1 2EH
Tel: 01245 290959
Manager: Jeff King   www.chelmsfordcityfc.com   Colours: Claret

EAST THURROCK UNITED
Rookery Hill, Corringham, Stanford-le-Hope, Essex SS17 9LB
Tel: 01375 382999   Boardroom: 01375 641009   Fax: 01375 641009
Manager: Lee Patterson   www.eastthurrockunited.co.uk   Colours: Amber & black

FOLKESTONE INVICTA
The Buzzlines Stadium, Cheriton Road Sports Ground, Folkestone, Kent CT20 5JU
Tel: 01303 257461   Fax: 01303 255541
Manager: Neil Cugley   www.folkestoneinvicta.co.uk   Colours: Black & amber

HARLOW TOWN
Barrows Farm Stadium, Elizabeth Way, The Pinnacles, Harlow, Essex CM19 5BL
Tel: 01279 445319
Manager: Ryan Kirby   www.harlowtownfc.co.uk   Colours: Red & white

HARROW BOROUGH
Earlsmead Stadium, Carlyon Avenue, South Harrow, Middlesex HA2 8SS
Tel: 0870 609 1959   Fax: 020 8423 0159
Manager: David Howell   www.harrowboro.com   Colours: Red

HASTINGS UNITED
The Pilot Field, Elphinstone Road, Hastings, East Sussex TN34 2AX
Tel: 01424 444635   Club: 01424 430517   Fax: 01424 729068
Manager: Nigel Kane   www.hastingsunitedfc.co.uk   Colours: Claret & blue

HENDON
Claremont Road, Brent Cross, London NW2 1AE
Tel: 020 8201 9494   Club: 020 8455 9185   Fax: 020 8905 5966
Manager: Gary McCann   www.hendonfc.net   Colours: White & green

HEYBRIDGE SWIFTS
Scraley Road, Heybridge, Maldon, Essex CM9 8JA
Tel: 01621 852978   Club: 01621 852978
Manager: Brian Statham   www.heybridgeswifts.com   Colours: Black & white

HORSHAM
Queen Street, Horsham, West Sussex RH12 5AD
Tel: 01403 252310   Boardroom: 01403 255787
Manager: John Maggs   www.horshamfc.co.uk   Colours: Amber & green

LEYTON
Leyton Stadium, 282 Lea Bridge Road, Leyton, London E10 7LD
Tel: 020 8988 7642   Club: 020 8988 7642
Manager: Roy Parkin   www.leytonfc.co.uk   Colours: Blue & white

MAIDSTONE UNITED
Sittingbourne FC, Eurolink Industrial Estate, Church Road, Sittingbourne, Kent ME10 3SB
Tel: 01795 435077   www.maidstoneunited.co.uk
Manager: Lloyd Hume / Alan Walker   Colours: Amber & black

MARGATE
Hartsdown Park, Hartsdown Road, Margate, Kent CT9 5QZ
Tel: 01843 221769   Fax: 01843 221769
Manager: Robin Trott   www.margate-fc.com   Colours: Royal blue & white

RAMSGATE
Southwood Stadium, Prices Avenue, Ramsgate, Kent CT11 0AN
Tel: 01843 591662
Manager: Jim Ward   www.ramsgate-fc.co.uk   Colours: Red

STAINES TOWN
Wheatsheaf Park, Wheatsheaf Lane, Staines, Middlesex TW18 2PD
Tel: 01784 225943
Manager: Steve Cordery   www.stainesmassive.co.uk   Colours: Old gold & blue

TONBRIDGE ANGELS
Longmead Stadium, Darenth Avenue, Tonbridge, Kent TN10 3JW
Tel: 01732 352477   Club: 01732 352417
Manager: Tony Dolby   www.tonbridgeangels.co.uk   Colours: Black & white

WEALDSTONE
Northwood FC, Northwood Park, Chestnut Avenue, Northwood, Middlesex HA6 1HR
Tel: 01923 827148
Manager: Gordon Bartlett   www.come-to-wealdstonefc.co.uk   Colours: Blue & white

WWW.NLNEWSDESK.CO.UK

IN: AFC Hornchurch (P – Division One North), Harlow Town (P – Division One North), Hastings United (P – Division One South), Maidstone United (P – Division One South), Wealdstone (S – Southern League Premier Division) OUT: Bromley (P – Football Conference South), Hampton & Richmond Borough (P – Football Conference South), Slough Town (R – Southern League Division One South), Walton & Hersham (R – Division One South), Worthing (R – Division One South)

	AFC Hornchurch	AFC Sudbury	Arlesey Town	Aveley	Bury Town	Canvey Island	Enfield	Enfield Town	Flackwell Heath	Great Wakering Rovers	Harlow Town	Ilford	Maldon Town	Potters Bar Town	Redbridge	Tilbury	Waltham Abbey	Waltham Forest	Ware	Wingate & Finchley	Witham Town	Wivenhoe Town
AFC Hornchurch		2-1	2-2	5-0	1-2	2-1	3-1	2-1	5-0	0-0	3-0	1-2	2-0	2-1	2-0	1-1	0-0	2-1	1-1	2-1	7-1	2-0
AFC Sudbury	1-1		1-2	2-0	3-0	1-2	2-1	1-1	1-1	4-0	1-2	6-3	0-1	2-1	2-0	2-0	2-2	1-1	5-0	1-2	1-1	1-1
Arlesey Town	0-2	1-2	D	1-1	1-1	3-1	0-3	1-4	1-1	0-1	0-2	1-0	1-0	2-1	1-0	2-1	2-1	1-1	0-3	2-1	2-0	1-1
Aveley	0-1	2-0	0-1	I	5-3	1-2	1-1	0-0	3-0	0-0	1-0	1-1	2-3	1-0	1-0	3-1	1-1	3-0	1-2	0-2	0-1	
Bury Town	1-2	1-4	1-3	3-0	V	3-0	4-3	1-2	1-1	2-5	2-2	1-0	1-1	2-1	1-2	2-2	0-1	1-1	2-1	1-0	1-0	2-1
Canvey Island	1-2	2-2	1-0	0-1	2-2	I	4-3	3-1	4-0	1-4	0-0	6-1	2-0	2-0	2-1	0-2	1-1	2-2	1-1	2-0	3-0	1-3
Enfield	1-3	0-2	1-0	3-2	3-1	1-0	S	2-3	3-0	3-3	1-0	3-1	1-3	1-2	0-2	1-1	1-1	2-2	1-2	1-1	5-0	1-0
Enfield Town	1-2	1-1	2-0	3-1	3-0	1-0	0-2	I	5-0	1-0	1-0	4-1	0-1	1-2	4-0	1-0	0-0	1-0	2-1	2-1	2-1	2-0
Flackwell Heath	0-1	0-0	2-0	1-2	0-0	0-2	1-3	0-2	O	0-2	1-2	0-1	0-1	2-1	0-0	2-1	0-3	2-1	2-5	1-2	1-1	0-2
Great Wakering Rovers	1-3	1-0	2-1	2-1	2-1	1-3	1-2	3-3	3-1	N	0-1	3-0	0-2	0-1	1-0	1-1	1-1	2-0	0-4	3-0	0-2	0-0
Harlow Town	2-0	2-1	0-0	0-2	3-0	0-2	2-0	0-1	7-0	1-0		2-2	0-0	2-2	4-1	2-1	5-1	2-0	0-0	6-3	3-1	1-1
Ilford	1-6	0-1	2-2	0-1	1-1	0-2	0-3	3-2	1-3	1-1	0-2	O	0-4	1-0	0-3	0-3	2-1	1-0	2-6	1-0	1-3	2-1
Maldon Town	0-1	2-2	4-1	2-0	2-1	2-0	1-0	0-2	1-1	2-1	1-3	1-0	N	0-4	1-0	1-1	0-0	2-2	1-1	1-0	1-0	0-1
Potters Bar Town	0-1	0-1	1-1	0-2	0-1	2-2	0-1	2-1	3-1	4-2	0-2	1-3	1-2	E	3-1	3-1	2-2	1-1	1-3	2-2	2-1	3-0
Redbridge	1-3	0-1	5-0	0-1	0-1	0-0	2-1	2-1	2-1	2-2	1-2	1-2	2-0	0-1		0-1	1-0	1-3	2-0	1-0	1-0	0-1
Tilbury	0-4	0-1	0-2	2-0	0-3	2-1	2-1	0-4	2-1	0-1	1-3	1-1	2-1	1-2	0-0	N	0-2	0-2	1-1	2-2	4-4	0-2
Waltham Abbey	0-2	0-0	3-1	3-3	3-3	0-1	1-3	0-2	4-3	2-3	0-0	2-0	2-0	1-1	2-3	2-0	O	3-1	3-0	2-0	4-1	3-0
Waltham Forest	0-2	1-2	2-1	3-2	2-1	0-0	3-0	2-0	2-3	3-1	1-0	1-0	0-0	0-0	2-1	2-1	1-1	R	2-1	0-0	3-1	1-4
Ware	1-2	1-1	3-3	0-0	2-1	2-1	2-1	0-4	5-0	2-2	1-0	2-0	1-1	1-0	1-0	4-0	1-1	1-3	T	2-0	2-1	0-1
Wingate & Finchley	1-1	3-0	2-0	1-0	1-0	0-0	2-0	1-1	4-0	2-1	1-3	5-1	3-0	3-3	3-0	2-3	1-4	1-2	2-2	H	2-0	0-1
Witham Town	0-7	0-3	1-0	0-1	1-0	0-2	1-0	2-4	0-3	2-0	1-2	5-0	1-1	3-3	2-1	1-1	0-1	7-3	1-4	1-2		1-3
Wivenhoe Town	0-1	0-2	1-1	5-1	2-2	0-3	1-1	0-0	2-2	0-1	1-2	3-1	1-2	2-1	1-0	2-3	1-0	1-3	0-1	2-1	1-1	

Division One North

	P	HOME					AWAY					TOTAL					
		W	D	L	F	A	W	D	L	F	A	W	D	L	F	A	Pts
AFC Hornchurch	42	14	5	2	49	15	18	2	1	47	12	32	7	3	96	27	103
Harlow Town	42	13	5	3	45	16	11	5	5	26	15	24	10	8	71	31	82
Enfield Town	42	14	2	5	35	14	10	5	6	39	25	24	7	11	74	39	79
Maldon Town	42	10	6	5	25	21	10	5	6	25	21	20	11	11	50	42	71
AFC Sudbury	42	9	7	5	40	22	10	6	5	27	19	19	13	10	67	41	70
Canvey Island	42	10	6	5	40	26	9	4	8	25	21	19	10	13	65	47	67
Ware	42	11	6	4	34	22	8	4	9	36	34	19	10	13	70	56	67
Waltham Forest	42	12	4	5	30	21	5	10	6	30	35	17	14	11	60	56	65
Wingate & Finchley	42	12	5	4	41	20	4	6	11	17	29	16	11	15	58	49	59
Waltham Abbey	42	10	5	6	40	27	5	8	8	25	24	15	13	14	65	51	58
Wivenhoe Town	42	6	6	9	26	29	10	3	8	24	23	16	9	17	50	52	57
Great Wakering Rovers	42	9	4	8	27	27	7	5	9	30	37	16	9	17	57	64	57
Enfield	42	9	4	8	35	30	7	2	12	30	33	16	6	20	65	63	54
Potters Bar Town	42	7	5	9	31	31	7	4	10	29	31	14	9	19	60	62	51
Aveley	42	8	6	7	26	19	6	3	12	21	38	14	9	19	47	57	51
Redbridge	42	10	2	9	26	21	5	3	13	16	27	15	5	22	42	48	50
Bury Town	42	9	5	7	33	32	4	6	11	24	37	13	11	18	57	69	50
Arlesey Town	42	9	5	7	23	27	4	6	11	21	36	13	11	18	44	63	50
Tilbury	42	5	5	11	20	38	6	5	10	23	34	11	10	21	43	72	43
Witham Town	42	7	3	11	30	41	3	4	14	22	49	10	7	25	52	90	37
Ilford	42	6	3	12	19	45	3	2	16	17	52	9	5	28	36	97	32
Flackwell Heath	42	4	4	13	15	32	3	5	13	22	58	7	9	26	37	90	30

PLAY-OFFS

SEMI-FINAL (May 1st)
Enfield Town 2 **AFC Sudbury** 4 *Att* 414
(Maldon Town excluded due to ground grading)

FINAL
(May 5th at Harlow Town)
Harlow Town 2 AFC Sudbury 2 *aet* (5-3p) *Att* 948

DATES & GATES

WWW.NLNEWSDESK.CO.UK

The following grid lists, for each fixture, the date and the attendance (gate). Rows are the home teams; columns are the away teams. A blank cell on the diagonal marks where a club would meet itself.

	AFC Hornchurch	AFC Sudbury	Arlesey Town	Aveley	Bury Town	Canvey Island	Enfield	Enfield Town	Flackwell Heath	Gt Wakering Rovers	Harlow Town	Ilford	Maldon Town	Potters Bar Town	Redbridge	Tilbury	Waltham Abbey	Waltham Forest	Ware	Wingate & Finchley	Witham Town	Wivenhoe Town
AFC Hornchurch		24 Mar / 444	10 Mar / 423	30 Mar / 444	9 Sep / 509	9 Apr / 751	2 Dec / 416	13 Jan / 613	31 Jan / 315	22 Aug / 410	27 Jan / 509	28 Apr / 552	18 Nov / 406	28 Nov / 311	31 Mar / 402	23 Sep / 416	24 Feb / 416	20 Feb / 287	23 Dec / 437	20 Mar / 240	6 Mar / 244	26 Aug / 424
AFC Sudbury	2 Jan / 327																				17 Mar / 289	13 Mar / 277
Arlesey Town	14 Nov / 129	2 Dec / 271																			3 Mar / 95	31 Mar / 84
Aveley	28 Aug / 278	11 Nov / 150	17 Mar / 71																		21 Apr / 114	17 Feb / 106
Bury Town	14 Apr / 257	26 Dec / 474	6 Apr / 126	28 Apr / 186																	19 Sep / 106	3 Feb / 175
Canvey Island	26 Dec / 702	14 Apr / 392	30 Apr / 406	30 Sep / 355	28 Oct / 305																11 Nov / 175	17 Oct / 272
Enfield	17 Feb / 166	9 Dec / 121	11 Nov / 101	9 Sep / 125	26 Aug / 249	28 Aug / 246															30 Sep / 94	21 Nov / 86
Enfield Town	19 Aug / 371	19 Aug / 257	26 Dec / 237	17 Oct / 54	17 Mar / 208	20 Mar / 242	28 Aug / 542														14 Apr / 285	28 Oct / 247
Flackwell Heath	21 Nov / 88	3 Nov / 102	3 Nov / 50	21 Mar / 51	21 Oct / 77	13 Jan / 161	21 Apr / 81	16 Dec / 135													28 Oct / 55	30 Sep / 60
Gt Wakering Rovers	13 Mar / 129	24 Apr / 178	18 Nov / 83	20 Mar / 67	3 Apr / 94	14 Oct / 106	19 Aug / 103	2 Jan / 171	7 Apr / 98												16 Jan / 80	16 Jan / 104
Harlow Town	11 Nov / 360	23 Sep / 192	23 Dec / 192	2 Dec / 196	22 Nov / 306	20 Jan / 145	20 Jan / 349	21 Apr / 81	6 Jan / 178	21 Feb / 167											19 Aug / 110	4 Apr / 143
Ilford	16 Dec / 192	9 Jan / 235	23 Sep / 97	21 Oct / 51	24 Oct / 66	14 Feb / 106	14 Oct / 72	14 Nov / 113	21 Mar / 37	9 Sep / 57	30 Dec / 103										2 Dec / 44	13 Jan / 62
Maldon Town	3 Feb / 171	3 Mar / 333	23 Sep / 183	22 Aug / 121	31 Mar / 67	24 Mar / 156	24 Mar / 131	26 Aug / 152	23 Sep / 58	9 Apr / 74	26 Aug / 117	28 Aug / 128									7 Apr / 68	21 Apr / 105
Potters Bar Town	9 Dec / 159	20 Feb / 195	20 Jan / 110	17 Oct / 94	4 Nov / 77	18 Nov / 111	11 Nov / 187	3 Feb / 201	26 Dec / 57	13 Feb / 71	13 Mar / 89	28 Aug / 58	10 Feb / 44								18 Nov / 61	12 Dec / 68
Redbridge	20 Jan / 129	22 Aug / 288	21 Nov / 54	3 Mar / 71	17 Oct / 77	23 Dec / 151	6 Mar / 81	23 Sep / 73	14 Apr / 51	11 Nov / 82	14 Oct / 89	26 Dec / 58	14 Oct / 132	2 Dec / 72					28 Oct / 57		24 Mar / 71	16 Dec / 50
Tilbury	19 Sep / 177	17 Apr / 264	27 Mar / 178	31 Dec / 165	3 Apr / 94	31 Mar / 135	27 Mar / 72	23 Sep / 89	21 Mar / 98	9 Apr / 57	10 Mar / 117	23 Jan / 65	9 Sep / 86	27 Jan / 61	28 Oct / 59		10 Mar / 69	17 Feb / 132	13 Jan / 71	14 Oct / 98	21 Apr / 86	7 Oct / 38
Waltham Abbey	24 Apr / 108	28 Apr / 112	13 Jan / 71	13 Jan / 90	22 Aug / 67	4 Nov / 198	24 Mar / 113	27 Mar / 62	23 Sep / 63	9 Apr / 74	26 Aug / 117	3 Feb / 53	27 Jan / 101	9 Sep / 86	30 Sep / 65	10 Mar / 69		26 Aug / 61	31 Mar / 106	14 Oct / 73	20 Feb / 62	30 Jan / 93
Waltham Forest	9 Dec / 159	31 Oct / 102	3 Apr / 64	21 Nov / 60	20 Oct / 77	31 Mar / 151	27 Mar / 62	6 Mar / 81	26 Dec / 45	13 Jan / 101	16 Dec / 87	3 Mar / 59	28 Oct / 64	24 Feb / 82	30 Sep / 61	21 Apr / 72	9 Dec / 72		28 Oct / 57	19 Sep / 56	13 Feb / 51	17 Mar / 44
Ware	21 Apr / 108	16 Jan / 102	23 Sep / 50	18 Nov / 61	17 Apr / 66	31 Oct / 111	14 Oct / 72	26 Dec / 247	2 Dec / 58	23 Sep / 82	20 Mar / 143	21 Nov / 124	14 Apr / 132	7 Nov / 63	4 Nov / 130	28 Oct / 57	19 Sep / 92	24 Mar / 153		10 Mar / 153	24 Feb / 123	27 Jan / 152
Wingate & Finchley	23 Jan / 85	23 Jan / 148	10 Feb / 55	18 Aug / 168	16 Dec / 169	23 Sep / 156	13 Feb / 71	17 Feb / 71	23 Sep / 154	9 Apr / 57	9 Sep / 177	3 Feb / 53	28 Dec / 64	7 Oct / 75	9 Apr / 55	9 Dec / 53	30 Sep / 66	31 Mar / 64	30 Sep / 66		21 Nov / 30	9 Apr / 65
Witham Town	25 Nov / 133	28 Aug / 428	19 Sep / 87	19 Sep / 101	18 Dec / 141	27 Mar / 135	24 Mar / 204	24 Jan / 204	20 Jan / 72	9 Apr / 98	23 Sep / 110	19 Jan / 132	13 Feb / 103	10 Mar / 84	23 Jan / 76	23 Jan / 49	10 Feb / 108	14 Oct / 103	11 Nov / 111	14 Apr / 77		26 Dec / 97
Wivenhoe Town	7 Apr / 245																					

	Ashford Town	Burgess Hill Town	Chatham Town	Corinthian-Casuals	Cray Wanderers	Croydon Athletic	Dartford	Dover Athletic	Dulwich Hamlet	Fleet Town	Godalming Town	Hastings United	Horsham YMCA	Kingstonian	Leatherhead	Maidstone United	Metropolitan Police	Molesey	Sittingbourne	Tooting & Mitcham Utd	Walton Casuals	Whyteleafe
Ashford Town		3-1	1-1	2-2	0-1	0-1	0-0	0-3	1-0	1-2	2-1	2-3	1-1	2-1	1-1	1-1	2-1	0-4	3-3	0-1	0-1	0-0
Burgess Hill Town	0-2		2-1	1-4	2-1	2-0	1-6	1-4	3-2	2-2	1-0	2-3	0-4	1-1	4-1	1-1	1-1	0-2	2-2	0-1	1-1	2-1
Chatham Town	1-0	1-1	D	2-2	2-1	1-1	2-3	1-2	0-3	0-0	1-0	5-1	0-1	1-1	2-0	1-1	3-0	3-1	1-3	2-0	0-4	0-1
Corinthian-Casuals	0-3	2-2	1-4	I	1-4	4-0	1-3	0-5	2-1	0-2	0-4	1-2	0-1	0-0	3-1	1-2	2-3	1-1	1-4	0-3	3-3	3-4
Cray Wanderers	0-4	6-2	3-2	2-4	V	1-1	4-0	1-2	4-3	0-4	2-2	1-1	2-0	1-1	0-2	1-2	2-1	2-0	2-1	0-0	0-2	0-0
Croydon Athletic	1-1	1-2	2-2	1-0	1-2	I	0-1	0-2	1-0	4-4	4-3	3-2	0-2	2-0	1-3	1-4	0-2	1-2	1-2	0-4	3-1	1-0
Dartford	4-3	7-2	1-3	4-0	0-0	3-0	S	1-1	1-1	1-2	3-1	0-2	4-2	1-0	1-2	2-1	2-2	2-2	1-2	2-2	0-0	4-2
Dover Athletic	4-0	2-1	5-0	1-0	1-0	3-0	2-2	I	3-1	0-1	2-1	2-1	5-0	2-2	2-1	2-4	0-1	1-2	2-0	1-1	0-2	1-1
Dulwich Hamlet	3-3	2-1	2-0	2-2	1-0	2-2	3-2	3-1	O	1-1	8-1	3-3	4-1	1-0	3-0	0-0	0-0	1-3	3-1	0-2	0-1	5-0
Fleet Town	2-1	1-1	1-1	1-0	2-2	3-0	0-3	1-0	4-1	N	2-1	2-3	1-0	2-1	1-0	0-1	1-4	1-1	1-0	0-2	2-1	2-1
Godalming Town	3-0	3-2	0-0	0-4	3-1	1-1	1-3	1-1	0-2	1-2		0-4	0-2	0-1	2-1	0-1	1-2	1-1	2-2	1-1	2-1	2-0
Hastings United	0-1	0-1	2-1	0-0	2-2	4-0	1-2	1-1	4-2	3-1	1-0	O	2-2	3-1	1-1	0-2	3-0	2-0	5-2	1-0	2-1	1-0
Horsham YMCA	2-1	0-3	3-1	4-1	2-4	0-1	3-2	0-0	0-1	0-0	3-1	1-2	N	2-3	0-3	2-2	0-2	2-1	3-4	0-3	2-1	3-2
Kingstonian	2-1	5-0	1-0	1-1	2-4	1-3	1-1	1-3	2-5	1-2	4-0	1-1	1-2	E	2-3	0-3	3-1	2-0	1-1	3-3	3-1	0-3
Leatherhead	3-3	2-1	1-0	1-0	2-2	1-2	0-1	0-0	0-4	2-1	3-0	1-1	1-3	0-1		0-3	2-1	2-0	2-3	2-0	2-0	
Maidstone United	3-2	1-0	1-2	6-0	1-0	0-0	4-1	0-0	2-3	3-2	2-1	3-1	1-0	2-1	4-2	S	1-0	0-1	2-2	2-3	2-2	2-3
Metropolitan Police	2-1	0-0	4-0	0-0	1-1	1-0	4-3	2-0	0-2	4-1	0-0	1-1	1-1	1-1	2-2	1-0	O	2-1	3-3	1-1	0-0	5-2
Molesey	1-2	0-2	1-1	0-3	5-3	3-0	2-1	0-3	1-1	1-3	1-0	3-2	1-1	0-2	2-2	1-3	0-0	U	1-5	2-0	1-1	1-2
Sittingbourne	0-0	1-4	3-1	1-0	0-1	3-1	1-2	1-2	0-0	0-0	3-0	1-2	2-0	1-1	1-1	1-2	3-1	2-1	T	1-0	1-0	3-1
Tooting & Mitcham United	3-0	0-2	1-0	3-2	3-1	3-1	2-1	4-1	1-1	3-1	1-0	1-0	1-2	1-1	3-1	3-1	3-1	0-0	2-2	H	2-2	0-2
Walton Casuals	1-1	1-1	1-3	1-2	2-1	2-1	2-2	1-4	1-3	1-2	0-4	1-3	4-2	1-2	0-3	1-2	2-1	2-1	2-1	3-1		3-3
Whyteleafe	1-1	3-0	2-0	3-0	2-2	0-1	1-3	1-1	1-1	2-2	2-3	0-1	1-2	0-0	2-2	0-2	0-2	0-0	1-1	0-1	0-1	

Division One South

	P	HOME					AWAY					TOTAL					
		W	D	L	F	A	W	D	L	F	A	W	D	L	F	A	Pts
Maidstone United	42	12	4	5	42	26	11	7	3	37	21	23	11	8	79	47	80
Tooting & Mitcham United	42	13	5	3	40	22	9	8	4	30	19	22	13	7	70	41	79
Dover Athletic	42	12	4	5	41	21	10	7	4	36	20	22	11	9	77	41	77
Hastings United	42	12	5	4	38	20	10	5	6	41	36	22	10	10	79	56	76
Fleet Town	42	12	5	5	30	22	9	7	5	35	30	21	12	9	65	52	75
Metropolitan Police	42	9	11	1	35	20	9	4	8	30	28	18	15	9	65	48	69
Dartford	42	9	7	5	44	30	10	4	7	42	35	19	11	12	86	65	68
Dulwich Hamlet	42	10	8	3	46	25	8	5	8	37	31	18	13	11	83	56	67
Horsham YMCA	42	8	3	10	31	38	9	4	8	28	31	17	7	18	59	69	58
Sittingbourne	42	8	7	6	27	21	6	8	7	41	42	14	15	13	68	63	57
Leatherhead	42	9	4	8	28	28	6	6	9	30	35	15	10	17	58	63	55
Cray Wanderers	42	8	6	7	34	34	6	6	9	33	35	14	12	16	67	69	54
Kingstonian	42	7	5	9	37	38	6	8	7	23	25	13	13	16	60	63	52
Burgess Hill Town	42	7	6	8	29	40	6	6	9	29	41	13	12	17	58	81	51
Molesey	42	6	6	9	27	37	6	7	8	25	26	12	13	17	52	63	49
Chatham Town	42	8	6	7	29	26	4	5	12	23	36	12	11	19	52	62	47
Walton Casuals	42	6	5	10	31	43	5	8	8	26	28	11	13	18	57	71	46
Ashford Town	42	5	8	8	22	29	5	6	10	30	36	10	14	18	52	65	44
Croydon Athletic	42	7	3	11	28	39	5	5	11	16	38	12	8	22	44	77	44
Whyteleafe	42	3	11	7	24	25	6	4	11	28	40	9	15	18	52	65	42
Corinthian-Casuals	42	3	4	14	26	52	5	6	10	27	36	8	10	24	53	88	34
Godalming Town	42	6	6	9	24	32	2	3	16	21	44	8	9	25	45	76	33

PLAY-OFFS

SEMI-FINALS *(May 1st)*

Dover Athletic 0 **Hastings United** 2 *Att* 1,018

Tooting & Mitcham United 2 Fleet Town 1 *Att* 424

FINAL

(May 5th at Tooting & Mitcham United)

Tooting & Mitcham Utd 0 **Hastings United** 2 *Att* 1,132

DATES & GATES

	Whyteleafe	Walton Casuals	Tooting & Mitcham Utd	Sittingbourne	Molesey	Metropolitan Police	Maidstone United	Leatherhead	Kingstonian	Horsham YMCA	Hastings United	Godalming Town	Fleet Town	Dulwich Hamlet	Dover Athletic	Dartford	Croydon Athletic	Cray Wanderers	Corinthian-Casuals	Chatham Town	Burgess Hill Town	Ashford Town
Ashford Town	9 Apr / 196	24 Mar / 200	28 Apr / 437	31 Mar / 245	26 Aug / 133	27 Jan / 144	24 Apr / 811	6 Feb / 121	4 Nov / 207	20 Feb / 83	13 Mar / 294	10 Mar / 175	9 Dec / 133	23 Dec / 210	3 Feb / 557	20 Mar / 221	23 Sep / 178	22 Aug / 190	21 Feb / 148	17 Feb / 213	9 Sep / 143	
Burgess Hill Town	23 Sep / 156	20 Feb / 109	7 Apr / 242	9 Dec / 182	6 Mar / 118	24 Mar / 170	19 Sep / 178	25 Nov / 254	16 Dec / 264	26 Dec / 213	20 Jan / 224	28 Aug / 181	31 Oct / 170	3 Feb / 185	21 Apr / 301	19 Aug / 232	14 Oct / 175	17 Feb / 151	17 Apr / 124	10 Mar / 149		30 Sep / 151
Chatham Town	13 Mar / 121	24 Feb / 136	18 Nov / 211	28 Oct / 275	28 Apr / 141	4 Nov / 123	28 Aug / 790	14 Apr / 129	3 Mar / 204	23 Dec / 150	17 Oct / 150	7 Apr / 123	27 Jan / 131	21 Nov / 136	19 Sep / 373	26 Dec / 353	19 Aug / 174	17 Mar / 151	6 Jan / 138		10 Mar / 149	30 Sep / 137
Corinthian-Casuals	4 Nov / 107	13 Feb / 86	5 Apr / 216	17 Mar / 107	2 Jan / 80	10 Apr / 102	23 Jan / 186	28 Apr / 146	31 Mar / 287	30 Sep / 108	23 Dec / 124	18 Nov / 130	9 Sep / 117	13 Jan / 162	24 Apr / 207	28 Oct / 167	27 Jan / 91	26 Aug / 119		22 Aug / 112	16 Sep / 101	21 Nov / 70
Cray Wanderers	24 Mar / 158	6 Feb / 86	28 Aug / 230	11 Nov / 127	20 Jan / 172	10 Mar / 118	16 Jan / 297	23 Dec / 169	10 Feb / 235	19 Aug / 128	24 Feb / 223	27 Mar / 110	23 Sep / 124	28 Apr / 264	14 Apr / 248	18 Nov / 257	26 Dec / 181		7 Apr / 102	14 Oct / 146	2 Dec / 132	11 Apr / 137
Croydon Athletic	28 Mar / 132	18 Nov / 106	30 Jan / 175	9 Sep / 77	17 Oct / 136	31 Mar / 76	24 Feb / 306	20 Jan / 129	22 Aug / 191	28 Oct / 103	26 Aug / 146	20 Mar / 99	23 Dec / 128	30 Dec / 159	21 Nov / 193	30 Sep / 195		9 Apr / 60	11 Nov / 116	13 Jan / 102	17 Mar / 116	3 Apr / 51
Dartford	30 Dec / 1,265	21 Apr / 1,309	27 Feb / 1,117	25 Apr / 1,047	21 Aug / 263	16 Dec / 245	25 Sep / 547	30 Oct / 268	26 Aug / 336	11 Nov / 4,100	9 Sep / 281	14 Oct / 262	17 Feb / 1,661	31 Mar / 1,409	9 Dec / 1,652		16 Jan / 1,342	3 Feb / 1,590	24 Mar / 1,274	9 Apr / 1,223	13 Jan / 1,168	20 Jan / 1,470
Dover Athletic	27 Jan / 725	14 Apr / 634	13 Mar / 820	16 Dec / 852	11 Nov / 725	2 Dec / 858	23 Jan / 1,527	27 Feb / 428	7 Oct / 855	28 Apr / 1,009	9 Apr / 1,007	24 Mar / 675	26 Aug / 706	22 Aug / 802		24 Feb / 1,273	16 Jan / 566	9 Sep / 801	23 Sep / 715	31 Mar / 724	23 Dec / 696	18 Nov / 792
Dulwich Hamlet	14 Oct / 317	14 Apr / 264	19 Dec / 414	13 Dec / 305	28 Oct / 316	10 Feb / 330	20 Feb / 611	10 Mar / 338	2 Dec / 381	7 Apr / 237	24 Feb / 404	26 Sep / 226	3 Apr / 246		24 Apr / 518	19 Sep / 300	28 Aug / 305	16 Dec / 286	19 Aug / 256	31 Oct / 218	28 Nov / 226	21 Apr / 280
Fleet Town	18 Nov / 149	28 Aug / 142	11 Nov / 159	13 Nov / 140	21 Nov / 129	6 Feb / 102	20 Feb / 281	19 Aug / 205	17 Mar / 224	20 Mar / 75	28 Nov / 183	26 Dec / 201		30 Sep / 146	7 Apr / 314	2 Dec / 210	21 Apr / 131	3 Mar / 140	14 Apr / 138	11 Nov / 186	21 Nov / 117	18 Apr / 134
Godalming Town	31 Mar / 102	27 Jan / 112	23 Jan / 230	9 Apr / 127	30 Sep / 129	30 Dec / 118	18 Nov / 236	9 Dec / 220	9 Sep / 231	17 Feb / 106	28 Apr / 191		9 Apr / 201	3 Mar / 146	4 Nov / 250	17 Mar / 230	7 Apr / 76	17 Oct / 84	3 Feb / 135	26 Aug / 90	13 Feb / 117	30 Sep / 89
Hastings United	31 Oct / 382	23 Sep / 270	11 Nov / 404	23 Aug / 425	21 Nov / 129	12 Dec / 245	19 Aug / 721	29 Aug / 485	27 Jan / 410	19 Sep / 292		3 Apr / 273	10 Mar / 554	25 Sep / 291	26 Dec / 631	14 Apr / 656	7 Apr / 499	9 Dec / 311	21 Apr / 535	21 Apr / 279	4 Nov / 314	28 Aug / 316
Horsham YMCA	24 Feb / 171	3 Apr / 77	24 Mar / 147	17 Oct / 201	8 Sep / 120	18 Nov / 113	14 Oct / 356	23 Sep / 168	6 Feb / 157		31 Mar / 165	2 Dec / 124	4 Nov / 104	26 Dec / 153	16 Dec / 197	27 Jan / 246	24 Mar / 122	13 Jan / 121	10 Mar / 123	21 Apr / 163	9 Apr / 164	27 Mar / 110
Kingstonian	26 Feb / 258	10 Mar / 258	24 Mar / 444	26 Aug / 274	9 Dec / 289	29 Jan / 257	23 Dec / 421	26 Dec / 343		28 Aug / 279	11 Nov / 280	24 Feb / 233	14 Oct / 294	17 Feb / 391	7 Apr / 518	7 Jan / 388	6 Jan / 248	22 Jan / 254	19 Aug / 289	23 Sep / 264	28 Apr / 346	19 Aug / 305
Leatherhead	7 Apr / 166	14 Apr / 100	3 Apr / 220	9 Apr / 167	31 Mar / 187	30 Dec / 164	18 Nov / 410		21 Apr / 603	3 Mar / 210	16 Jan / 191	20 Jan / 223	7 Nov / 105	7 Nov / 234	30 Jan / 271	21 Nov / 191	14 Mar / 378	21 Apr / 149	16 Dec / 222	9 Sep / 216	27 Jan / 173	17 Mar / 171
Maidstone United	10 Mar / 320	16 Dec / 290	11 Nov / 404	9 Apr / 682	30 Sep / 347	9 Sep / 397		3 Feb / 385	21 Apr / 603	17 Mar / 464	17 Mar / 382	3 Apr / 352	21 Aug / 335	23 Dec / 382	25 Nov / 719	14 Apr / 814	14 Mar / 378	22 Nov / 222	17 Feb / 467	18 Mar / 384	31 Mar / 405	18 Oct / 326
Metropolitan Police	8 Sep / 170	7 Apr / 100	13 Oct / 204	17 Oct / 102	3 Mar / 158		14 Apr / 395	17 Apr / 123	18 Nov / 193	24 Apr / 117	18 Nov / 115	7 Nov / 105	19 Aug / 168	28 Aug / 105	25 Nov / 172	23 Jan / 145	19 Sep / 55	14 Mar / 72	27 Dec / 142	27 Feb / 111	28 Oct / 114	11 Nov / 114
Molesey	17 Apr / 124	26 Dec / 162	13 Oct / 204	21 Apr / 80		23 Sep / 117	3 Mar / 158	31 Mar / 187	9 Dec / 289	8 Sep / 120	3 Mar / 210	30 Sep / 129	21 Nov / 129	28 Oct / 316	11 Nov / 725	21 Aug / 263	17 Oct / 136	20 Jan / 172	2 Jan / 80	28 Apr / 141	6 Mar / 118	26 Aug / 133
Sittingbourne	10 Dec / 133	23 Dec / 270	13 Oct / 80		17 Oct / 102	21 Apr / 80	18 Nov / 410	9 Apr / 167	26 Aug / 274	17 Oct / 201	23 Aug / 425	3 Apr / 102	13 Nov / 140	16 Dec / 140	28 Oct / 275	19 Sep / 300	27 Mar / 77	22 Nov / 127	16 Dec / 167	9 Sep / 157	17 Oct / 102	21 Apr / 80
Tooting & Mitcham United	23 Sep / 230	17 Apr / 292		13 Oct / 204	16 Feb / 306	13 Oct / 204	11 Nov / 404	27 Mar / 256	13 Jan / 266	24 Apr / 185	18 Nov / 137	21 Apr / 335	7 Nov / 105	17 Oct / 140	18 Oct / 172	27 Jan / 315	27 Mar / 140	22 Nov / 149	16 Sep / 222	23 Sep / 264	28 Apr / 272	23 Sep / 230
Walton Casuals	19 Aug / 108		13 Jan / 118	21 Nov / 64	9 Apr / 81	21 Apr / 61	28 Apr / 586	20 Mar / 134	30 Sep / 201	17 Oct / 45	3 Mar / 102	19 Sep / 141	7 Nov / 93	23 Dec / 132	17 Mar / 140	28 Aug / 217	27 Mar / 64	31 Mar / 62	20 Jan / 84	31 Mar / 57	22 Aug / 47	28 Oct / 47
Whyteleafe		19 Aug / 108	14 Apr / 273	10 Oct / 133	17 Apr / 124	21 Apr / 138	6 Apr / 561	20 Mar / 142	17 Oct / 161	9 Dec / 242	21 Nov / 133	19 Sep / 103	3 Mar / 165	17 Nov / 264	11 Nov / 272	28 Aug / 217	16 Dec / 141	7 Oct / 128	20 Jan / 145	9 Jan / 122	3 Mar / 172	26 Dec / 129

ISTHMIAN LEAGUE DIV. ONE NORTH CONSTITUTION 2007-08

AFC SUDBURY
Colours: Yellow & blue
Kingsmarsh Stadium, Brundon Lane,
Sudbury, Suffolk CO10 6XR
Tel: 01787 376213

ARLESEY TOWN
Colours: Navy & sky blue
Hitchin Road, Arlesey, Bedfordshire SG15 6RS
Tel: 01462 734504
Boardroom: 01462 734512

AVELEY
Colours: Blue
Mill Field, Mill Road, Aveley, Essex RM15 4SJ
Tel: 01708 865940 Fax: 01708 680995

BRENTWOOD TOWN
Colours: Blue & white stripes
The Arena, Brentwood Centre, Doddinghurst
Road, Brentwood, Essex CM15 9NN
Tel: 01277 215151 Ext.713

BURY TOWN
Colours: Blue
Ram Meadow, Cotton Lane,
Bury St Edmonds, Suffolk IP33 1XP
Tel: 01284 754721

CANVEY ISLAND
Colours: Yellow, blue & white
Park Lane, Canvey Island, Essex SS8 7PX
Tel: 01268 682991 Fax: 01268 698586

DARTFORD
Colours: White & black
Princes Park, Grassbanks, Darenth Road,
Dartford, Kent DA1 1RT
Tel: 01322 299990 Fax: 01322 299996

EDGWARE TOWN
Colours: Green & white
Harrow Borough FC, Earlsmead Stadium,
Carlyon Avenue, South Harrow TW12 2BX
Tel: 0870 609 1959 Fax: 020 8433 0159

ENFIELD TOWN
Colours: White & blue
Brimsdown Rovers FC, Goldsdown Road,
Enfield, Middlesex EN3 7RP
Tel: 020 8804 5491

GREAT WAKERING ROVERS
Colours: Green & white
Burroughs Park, Little Wakering Hall Lane, Great
Wakering, Southend-on-Sea, Essex SS3 0HH
Tel: 01702 217812

ILFORD
Colours: Royal blue & white hoops
Cricklefield Stadium, 486 High Road,
Seven Kings, Ilford, Essex IG1 1UB
Tel: 020 8514 8352

MALDON TOWN
Colours: Blue & white
Wallace Binder Ground, Park Drive,
Maldon, Essex CM9 5XX
Tel: 01621 853762

NORTHWOOD
Colours: Red
Northwood Park, Chestnut Avenue,
Northwood, Middlesex HA6 1HR
Tel: 01923 827148 Fax: 020 8428 1533

POTTERS BAR TOWN
Colours: Red & royal blue
Parkfield, Watkins Rise, The Walk,
Potters Bar, Hertfordshire EN6 1QN
Tel: 01707 654833

REDBRIDGE
Colours: Blue
Oakside Stadium, Station Road,
Barkingside, Ilford, Essex IG6 1NA
Tel: 020 8550 3611

TILBURY
Colours: Black & white
Chadfields, St Chad's Road, Tilbury, Essex RM18 8NL
Tel: 01375 843093

WALTHAM ABBEY
Colours: White & green
Capershotts, Sewardstone Road,
Waltham Abbey, Essex EN9 1LU
Tel: 01992 711287

WALTHAM FOREST
Colours: White & navy blue
Wadham Lodge Sports Ground, Kitchener Road,
Walthamstow, London E17 4JP
Tel: 020 8527 2444

WARE
Colours: Blue & white
Wodson Park, Wadesmill Road,
Ware, Hertfordshire SG12 0HZ
Tel: 01920 463247

WINGATE & FINCHLEY
Colours: Blue & white
The Abrahams Stadium, Summers Lane,
Finchley, London N12 0PD
Tel: 020 8446 2217 Fax: 020 8343 8194

WITHAM TOWN
Colours: Red, black & white
Spa Road, Witham, Essex CM8 1UN
Tel: 01376 511198 Fax: 01376 520996

WIVENHOE TOWN
Colours: Blue & yellow
Broad Lane Sports Ground, Elmstead Road,
Wivenhoe, Essex CO7 7HA
Tel: 01206 825380

WWW.CHERRYRED.CO.UK

IN: Brentwood Town (P – Essex Senior League), Dartford (S – Division One South), Edgware Town (P – Spartan South Midlands Premier Division), Northwood (R – Southern League Premier Division)

OUT: AFC Hornchurch (P), Harlow Town (P), Enfield (W – Essex Senior League), Flackwell Heath (R – Hellenic League Premier Division)

ISTHMIAN LEAGUE DIV. ONE SOUTH CONSTITUTION 2007-08

ASHFORD TOWN
Colours: Green & navy blue
The Homelands, Ashford Road, Kingsnorth,
Ashford, Kent TN26 1NJ
Tel: 01233 611838 Fax: 01233 662510

BURGESS HILL TOWN
Colours: Yellow & black
Leylands Park, Maple Drive, Burgess Hill,
West Sussex RH15 8DL
Tel: 01444 242429

CHATHAM TOWN
Colours: Red & black
Sports Ground, Maidstone Road, Bourneville Avenue,
Chatham, Kent ME4 6EJ
Tel: 01634 812194 Fax: 01634 812194

CHIPSTEAD
Colours: Green, white & black
High Road, Chipstead, Surrey CR5 3SF
Tel: 01737 553250

CORINTHIAN CASUALS
Colours: Chocolate, pink & sky blue
King Georges Field, Queen Mary Close,
Tolworth, Surrey KT6 7NA
Tel: 020 8397 3368

CRAY WANDERERS
Colours: Amber & black
Bromley FC, Hayes Lane, Bromley, Kent BR2 9EF
Tel: 020 8460 5291

CROYDON ATHLETIC
Colours: Maroon & white
Mayfields, Mayfield Road, Thornton
Heath, Surrey CR7 6DN
Tel: 020 8664 8343 Fax: 020 8664 8343

DOVER ATHLETIC
Colours: White & Black
Crabble Athletic Ground, Lewisham Road,
River, Dover, Kent CT17 0PB
Tel: 01304 822373 Fax: 01304 240041

DULWICH HAMLET
Colours: Navy blue & pink
Champion Hill Stadium, Edgar Kail Way, Dog Kennel
Hill, East Dulwich, London SE22 8BD
Tel: 020 7274 8707/7501 9323 Fax: 020 7501 9255

EASTBOURNE TOWN
Colours: Yellow & blue
The Saffrons Sports Club, Compton Place Road,
Eastbourne, East Sussex BN21 1EA
Tel: 01323 723734

HORSHAM YMCA
Colours: White & black
Gorings Mead, off Queen Street,
Horsham, West Sussex RH13 5BP
Tel: 01403 252689

KINGSTONIAN
Colours: Red & white
AFC Wimbledon, Kingsmeadow, 422a Kingston Road,
Kingston-upon-Thames, Surrey KT1 3PM
Tel: 020 8547 3528

LEATHERHEAD
Colours: Green & white
Fetcham Grove, Guildford Road,
Leatherhead, Surrey KT22 9AS
Tel: 01372 360151 Fax: 01372 362705

METROPOLITAN POLICE
Colours: Blue
Imber Court Sports Club, Ember
Lane, East Molesey, Surrey KT8 0BT
Tel: 020 8398 7358

MOLESEY
Colours: Black & white
412 Walton Road, West Molesey, Surrey KT8 2JG
Tel: 020 8979 4823/8941 7989 Fax: 020 8979 9103

SITTINGBOURNE
Colours: Red & black
Central Park Stadium, Church Road, Eurolink,
Sittingbourne, Kent ME10 3SB
Tel: 01795 435077

TOOTING & MITCHAM UNITED
Colours: White & black
Imperial Fields, Bishopsford Road,
Morden, Surrey SM4 6BF
Tel: 020 8648 3248 Boardroom: 020 8685 9229

WALTON CASUALS
Colours: Tangerine & black
Franklyn Road Sports Ground, Waterside Drive,
Walton-on-Thames, Surrey KT12 2JP
Tel: 01932 787749

WALTON & HERSHAM
Colours: Red
Sports Ground, Stompond Lane,
Walton-on-Thames, Surrey KT12 1HF
Tel: 01932 244967/245363 Fax: 01932 885814

WHITSTABLE TOWN
Colours: Red & white
Belmont Road, Whitstable, Kent CT5 1QP
Tel: 01227 266012

WHYTELEAFE
Colours: Green & white
15 Church Road, Whyteleafe, Surrey CR3 0AR
Tel: 020 8660 5491/8645 0422
Fax: 020 8645 0422

WORTHING
Colours: Red
Woodside Road, Worthing, West Sussex BN14 7HQ
Tel: 01903 239575 Fax: 01903 239575

WWW.NLNEWSDESK.CO.UK

IN: Chipstead (P – Combined Counties Division One), Eastbourne Town (P – Sussex County League Division One), Walton & Hersham (R), Whitstable Town (P – Kent League Premir Division), Worthing (R)

OUT: Dartford (S – Division One North), Fleet Town (S – Southern League Division One South), Godalming Town (S – Southern League Division One South), Hastings United (P), Maidstone United (P)

LEAGUE CUP

FIRST ROUND
Metropolitan Police 4 Godalming Town 1
Tilbury 2 **Wivenhoe Town** 3

SECOND ROUND
AFC Hornchurch 4 Canvey Island 0
AFC Wimbledon 2 Hastings United 1
Arlesey Town 1 **Slough Town** 3
Ashford Town 2 Bromley 0
Aveley 2 **AFC Sudbury** 3
Boreham Wood 4 Enfield Town 3
Carshalton Athletic 1 **Horsham** 3
Chatham Town 0 **Dover Athletic** 1 *aet*
Chelmsford City 1 Wivenhoe Town 0
Cray Wanderers 3 Whyteleafe 1
Croydon Athletic 4 Sittingbourne 1
Dartford 2 Folkestone Invicta 2 *aet* (5-3p)
East Thurrock United 1 Billericay Town 0
Flackwell Heath 3 **Hendon** 4
Great Wakering Rovers 0 **Redbridge** 1
Harrow Borough 0 **Enfield** 1
Heybridge Swifts 4 Ilford 0
Kingstonian 3 Hampton & Richmond
Borough 2
Leatherhead 4 Molesey 0
Leyton 2 Witham Town 1
Maldon Town 2 Bury Town 1
Ramsgate 2 Margate 0
Staines Town 3 Potters Bar Town 2 *aet*
Tonbridge Angels 4 Maidstone United 0
Tooting & Mitcham United 1 Corinthian
Casuals 1 *aet* (8-7p)
Waltham Abbey 0 **Harlow Town** 1
Waltham Forest 0 **Fleet Town** 5
Walton & Hersham 0 **Metropolitan
Police** 2
Walton Casuals 4 Dulwich Hamlet 1
Ware 0 **Ashford Town (Middx)** 1
Wingate & Finchley 2 **Burgess Hill
Town** 4 *aet*
Worthing 3 Horsham YMCA 2

THIRD ROUND
AFC Sudbury 2 Chelmsford City 1

Ashford Town 2 **Cray Wanderers** 4
Boreham Wood 3 Harlow Town 1
Burgess Hill Town 2 **AFC Wimbledon** 3
Croydon Athletic 1 **Tooting & Mitcham
United** 1 *aet* (3-4p)
Fleet Town 3 **Enfield** 4 *aet*
Hendon 1 **Staines Town** 2
Heybridge Swifts 3 AFC Hornchurch 2
Horsham 3 **Walton Casuals** 5 *aet*
Leatherhead 1 Worthing 0
Leyton 1 Maldon Town 0
Metropolitan Police 4 Kingstonian 1
Ramsgate 1 **Dover Athletic** 1 *aet* (7-8p)
Redbridge 1 **East Thurrock United** 3
Slough Town 0 **Ashford Town (Middx)** 4
Tonbridge Angels 1 **Dartford** 3

FOURTH ROUND
AFC Sudbury 2 Metropolitan Police 1
Ashford Town (Middx) 2 Enfield 1
Dartford 0 **Boreham Wood** 3
Dover Athletic 1 East Thurrock United 0
Leyton 2 **Leatherhead** 3
Staines Town 2 Heybridge Swifts 1
Tooting & Mitcham United 1 AFC
Wimbledon 0
Walton Casuals 1 **Cray Wanderers** 2

QUARTER-FINALS
Boreham Wood 1 **Cray Wanderers** 2
Dover Athletic 2 Leatherhead 1
Staines Town 3 AFC Sudbury 1
Tooting & Mitcham United 1 **Ashford
Town (Middx)** 3

SEMI-FINALS
Dover Athletic 4 Cray Wanderers 3
Staines Town 2 **Ashford Town (Middx)** 3

FINAL
(April 4th at Bromley)
Ashford Town (Middx) 4 Dover Athletic 1

KENT COUNTY LEAGUE

	Bearsted	Bromley Green	Cray Valley Paper Mills	Crockenhill	Fleet Leisure	Hollands & Blair	Holmesdale	Lewisham Borough	Milton Athletic	Norton Sports	Old Roan	Rusthall	Sheerness East	Snodland	Stansfeld Oxford/Bermondsey
Bearsted		1-3	0-0	1-0	5-1	1-1	0-1	0-3	1-1	3-0	2-0	1-2	2-0	4-0	2-4
Bromley Green	3-0		2-1	5-0	0-3	4-0	2-2	4-1	1-0	2-2	1-2	6-0	3-1	8-0	0-2
Cray Valley Paper Mills	2-1	3-5	P	3-1	0-0	1-3	1-2	2-1	2-1	2-0	0-0	0-1	4-1	4-0	2-1
Crockenhill	0-0	1-3	3-2	R	0-1	1-3	0-4	2-0	2-1	1-1	0-2	0-1	1-2	3-2	1-0
Fleet Leisure	2-2	0-6	2-1	2-0	E	2-0	1-0	1-3	0-1	0-1	1-0	1-3	3-0		2-1
Hollands & Blair	2-2	1-1	1-2	2-0	0-2	M	0-0	2-3	1-3	0-3	6-0	2-0	2-1	1-2	1-0
Holmesdale	0-2	4-0	2-1	2-0	5-0	3-0	I	1-1	3-1	1-2	8-0	2-2	3-1	1-0	5-1
Lewisham Borough	0-2	1-3	0-0	0-1	1-0	2-0	3-2	E	0-1	1-3	3-0	1-1	0-1	1-2	
Milton Athletic	1-1	1-6	3-5	5-1	0-2	1-3	2-4	1-1	R	0-3	3-1	4-4	3-3	1-2	2-2
Norton Sports	4-1	1-2	3-0	4-0	2-1	1-3	3-2	3-3	0-2		5-1	2-2	4-3	2-0	2-5
Old Roan	4-2	0-3	4-4	1-1	1-1	3-1	1-3	1-2	1-1	0-3	D	0-2	1-1	1-3	1-3
Rusthall	0-3	3-2	0-3	1-1	1-0	1-2	1-3	0-0	3-1	1-1	1-1	I	0-0	2-2	1-1
Sheerness East	1-2	1-0	1-1	3-0	0-3	2-0	1-5	4-4	1-0	3-3	1-0	3-2	V	3-1	0-2
Snodland	0-8	0-5	1-0	0-0	0-1	2-2	1-4	1-2	1-1	3-1	1-3	1-2	1-0		2-3
Stansfeld Oxford & Bermondsey Club	3-1	5-5	2-0	4-0	5-0	0-2	2-2	0-2	2-0	2-1	3-0	0-0	0-1	2-2	

CHAMPIONS TROPHY
(Prem Div champions v Inter-Regional Challenge Cup holders)
(August 30th at Sevenoaks Town)
Lewisham Borough 1 Norton Sports 2

WWW.NLNEWSDESK.CO.UK

Premier Division

	P	W	D	L	F	A	Pts
Holmesdale	28	18	6	4	73	28	60
Bromley Green	28	18	4	6	85	36	58
Norton Sports	28	14	6	8	60	44	48
Stansfeld O & B Club	28	14	5	9	57	39	47
Fleet Leisure	28	13	4	11	32	39	43
Bearsted	28	11	7	10	50	38	40
Cray Valley Paper Mills	28	11	6	11	44	38	39
Hollands & Blair	28	11	5	12	42	43	38
Lewisham Borough	28	10	7	11	39	38	37
Sheerness East	28	10	7	11	42	49	37
Rusthall	28	9	10	9	34	44	37
Milton Athletic	28	6	8	14	40	55	26
Snodland	28	7	5	16	29	67	26
Old Roan	28	6	7	15	30	64	25
Crockenhill	28	6	5	17	20	55	23

Reserve Division East

	P	W	D	L	F	A	Pts
Bearsted Res.	24	19	1	4	67	23	58
Kennington Res.	24	18	2	4	57	21	56
University of Kent Res.	24	16	2	6	60	30	50
Bromley Green Res.	24	12	5	7	58	37	41
Otford United Res.	24	12	5	7	49	37	41
Oakwood Res.	24	12	4	8	56	39	40
New Romney Res.	24	11	3	10	48	38	36
Lydd Town Res.	24	10	4	10	49	45	34
Borden Village Res.	24	6	4	14	47	85	22
Chipstead Res.	24	5	5	14	38	63	20
Larkfield & New Hythe Wdrs Res.	24	4	4	16	34	71	16
APM Mears Res.	24	4	3	17	40	81	15
Putlands Athletic Res.	24	2	8	14	20	53	14

Reserve Division West

		P	W	D	L	F	A	Pts
Stansfeld O & B Club Res.		24	20	1	3	80	29	61
Holmesdale Res.		24	20	0	4	98	21	60
Orpington Res.	-3	24	18	4	4	85	25	53
Fleet Leisure Res.		24	12	4	8	50	46	40
Greenways Res.		24	12	2	10	60	34	38
Bly Spartans Res.		24	10	3	11	46	58	33
Bromleians Sports Res.		24	10	2	12	46	54	32
Westerham Res.		24	9	4	11	46	50	31
Belvedere Res.		24	8	4	12	49	60	28
Fleetdown United Res.		24	6	2	16	33	87	20
Wickham Park Res.		24	5	4	15	22	60	19
Halls Res.		24	5	2	17	27	75	17
Borough United Res.		24	4	4	16	24	67	16

KENT COUNTY LEAGUE PREMIER DIVISION CONSTITUTION 2007-08

BEARSTED . . . . Otham Sports Ground, Honey Lane, Otham, Maidstone ME15 8RG 07831 251657
BROMLEY GREEN . . . . The Swan Centre, Cudworth Road, South Willesborough, Ashford TN24 0BB 01233 645982
CONEY HALL . . . . Tie Pigs Lane, Coney Hall, West Wickham BR4 9BT 020 8462 9103
CRAY VALLEY PAPER MILLS . . . . . Badgers Sports Ground, Middle Park Avenue, Eltham SE9 5HT. 020 8850 4273
CROCKENHILL. . . . . Wested, Eynsford Road, Crockenhill, Swanley BR8 8EH 01322 662067
FLEET LEISURE . . . . Beauwater Leisure Sports Club, Nelson Road, Northfleet DA11 7EE 01474 359222
HOLLANDS & BLAIR . . . . Rochagas Sports & Social, Star Meadow, Dartford Avenue, Gillingham ME7 3AN 01634 573839
LEWISHAM BOROUGH . . . . Ladywell Arena, Doggett Road, Catford SE6 4QX. 020 8314 1986
MILTON ATHLETIC . . . . UK Paper Sports Ground, Gore Court Road, Sittingbourne ME10 1QN 01795 564213
NORTON SPORTS. . . . . Norton Park, Provender Lane, Norton, Faversham ME9 9JU 07989 581062
ORPINGTON. . . . . Westcombe Park & Orpington SC, Goddington Lane, Orpington BR6 9SH 01689 834902
RUSTHALL . . . . Jockey Farm, Nellington Lane, Rusthall, Tunbridge Wells TN4 8SH 07940 277138
SHEERNESS EAST . . . . . . Sheerness East WMC, 47 Queensborough Road, Halfway, Sheerness ME12 3BZ 01795 662049
SNODLAND . . . . Potyn's Field, Paddlesworth Road, Snodland ME6 5DL. 01634 243961
TYLER HILL. . . . . Hersden Recreation Ground, The Avenue, Hersden, Canterbury CT3 4HY. 07930 100034

IN: Coney Hall (S – Combined Counties League Division One), Orpington (P – Division One West), Tyler Hill (P – Division One East)
OUT: Holmesdale (P – Kent League Premier Division), Old Roan (W), Stansfeld Oxford & Bermondsey Club (R – Division One West)

Division One East

	Ashford Borough	Betteshanger W.	Borden Village	Kennington	Lydd Town	New Romney	Oakwood	Sheppey United	St Margarets	Staplehurst	Tyler Hill	Uniflo	Univ. of Kent
Ashford Borough	D	1-3	6-1	4-3	0-3	3-2	2-5	4-0	8-1	2-2	4-3	4-5	1-5
Betteshanger Welfare	1-1	I	5-0	4-1	1-1	1-2	6-1	2-1	3-1	2-3	0-3	1-1	1-5
Borden Village	1-3	2-3	V	1-1	0-3	1-3	1-1	0-1	0-4	1-1	2-2		1-5
Kennington	2-1	1-4	5-0		2-3	1-3	0-1	1-3	4-0	3-0	0-1	0-2	1-2
Lydd Town	7-1	2-1	3-1	2-1	O	2-0	0-1	3-0	2-1	1-2	1-0	0-0	0-2
New Romney	1-3	2-1	3-1	0-1	2-3	N	1-2	5-3	1-1	0-2	2-1		4-3
Oakwood	4-2	3-1	2-3	2-1	3-0	1-3	E	1-1	6-1	2-0	2-3	3-4	4-2
Sheppey United	1-1	1-3	1-3	0-3	3-0	5-3	1-1		4-1	3-0	3-0	3-1	2-1
St Margarets	3-0	0-1	0-0	2-1	1-4	2-2	1-4	1-1	E	6-0	0-2	2-2	2-1
Staplehurst/Monarchs	1-1	2-1	4-1	4-1	1-0	2-2	3-3	5-1	1-2	A	2-3	1-1	1-1
Tyler Hill	2-0	2-0	3-2	3-1	4-1	0-1	3-2	3-1	2-2	1-2	S	5-3	1-1
Uniflo	2-4	1-0	1-1	3-2	0-4	2-4	1-1	2-2	2-0	2-2	1-4	T	1-2
University of Kent	3-4	0-0	1-4	1-1	2-1	1-0	2-3	1-4	0-1	3-1	2-3	0-0	

Division One East	P	W	D	L	F	A	Pts
Tyler Hill	24	16	3	5	54	32	51
Oakwood	24	14	4	6	62	42	46
Lydd Town	24	14	2	8	51	46	44
Staplehurst & Mon.	24	12	1	11	46	43	37
Betteshanger Welfare	24	10	5	9	45	33	35
University of Kent	24	10	5	9	44	34	35
Ashford Borough	24	10	4	10	44	61	34
Sheppey United	24	9	5	10	40	46	32
Uniflo	24	7	6	11	34	51	27
St Margarets	24	6	8	10	36	55	26
Kennington	24	6	1	17	23	46	19
Borden Village	24	2	6	16		68	12

University of Kent −1

KENT COUNTY LEAGUE DIVISION ONE EAST CONSTITUTION 2007-08

ASHFORD BOROUGH . . . . Sandyacres Sports & Social, Sandyhurst Lane, Ashford TN25 4NT 01233 627373
BETTESHANGER WELFARE . . . . Welfare Ground, Cavell Square, Mill Hill, Deal CT14 9HR 01304 372080
BLY SPARTANS . . . . Bly Spartans Sports Ground, Rede Court Road, Strood ME2 3TU 01634 710577
GURU NANAK . . . . AEI Henley Sports Club, Dunkirk Close, Gravesend DA12 5NN . . . . None
KENNINGTON . . . . Kennington Cricket Club, Ulley Road, Kennington, Ashford TN24 9HY 07887 995219
LYDD TOWN . . . . The Lindsey Field, Dengemarsh Road, Lydd, Romney Marsh TN29 9JH 01797 321904
NEW ROMNEY . . . . The Maud Pavilion, Station Road, New Romney TN28 8SR 01797 364858
OAKWOOD . . . . Honey Lane, Otham, Maidstone ME15 8RG. 07745 383328
SHEPPEY UNITED . . . . Medway Ports Authority Ground, Holm Place, Halfway, Sheerness ME12 3AT 01795 668054
ST MARGARETS . . . . Alexander Field, Kingsdown Rd, St Margarets-at-Cliffe, Dover CT15 6BD 01304 852386
STAPLEHURST & MONARCHS UTD . . The Old County Ground, Norman Road, West Malling ME19 6RL. . . . . None
UNIFLO . . . . The Oast House, Park Wood Road, Giles Lane, University of Kent, Canterbury CT2 7SY . . 01227 827430
UNIVERSITY OF KENT . The Oast House, Park Wood Road, Giles Lane, University of Kent, Canterbury CT2 7SY . . 01227 827430

IN: Bly Spartans (S – Division One West), Guru Nanak (P – Division Two East)
OUT: Borden Village (R – Division Two East), Tyler Hill (P)

Division One West

	Belvedere	Bly Spartans	Bridon Ropes	Bromleians Spts	Fleetdown United	Greenways	Halls	Larkfield/NHW	Metrogas	Orpington	Phoenix Sports	Samuel Montagu	Westerham
Belvedere	D	2-2	2-3	1-1	1-1	0-2	0-1	5-0	1-1	3-4	1-0	0-1	0-0
Bly Spartans	2-1	I	3-2	0-1	4-0	2-0	3-1	4-0	2-1	1-0	1-2	5-2	3-0
Bridon Ropes	2-3	0-3	V	1-3	5-2	1-4	2-0	5-0	0-4	0-0	2-3	5-2	0-4
Bromleians Sports	1-1	0-5	5-3		3-2	3-1	2-1	3-0	1-6	1-0	1-1		2-1
Fleetdown United	3-1	2-2	0-3	0-3	O	2-1	1-1	2-1	2-4	2-3	0-1	2-3	1-3
Greenways	2-2	0-1	4-0	0-1	3-0	N	4-2	1-1	0-3	2-5	3-4		2-1
Halls	0-1	0-6	2-1	1-4	0-5	0-0	E	1-0	0-2	1-5	0-4	2-0	2-0
Larkfield & New HW	0-0	1-5	0-3	1-7	0-2	1-6	1-2		2-7	1-6	0-3	1-0	2-8
Metrogas	2-1	0-2	0-1	3-0	1-2	1-3	2-1	6-1	W	1-3	2-1	3-0	1-2
Orpington	3-1	1-0	4-3	2-1	3-0	2-0	6-3	18-0	1-3	E	3-0	4-0	1-1
Phoenix Sports	3-2	2-2	2-2	1-1	3-0	1-4	3-3	3-5	3-0	1-4	S	1-0	2-1
Samuel Montagu YC	3-1	2-1	2-3	1-2	2-1	2-2	0-4	4-1	3-1	1-1	1-1	T	2-2
Westerham	1-1	0-2	3-2	2-1	6-2	1-5	3-1	1-0	1-2	0-1	0-2	4-1	

Division One West	P	W	D	L	F	A	Pts
Orpington	24	20	2	2	85	25	62
Bly Spartans	24	17	3	4	58	20	54
Bromleians Sports	24	15	4	5	49	32	49
Metrogas	24	13	1	10	51	33	40
Phoenix Sports	24	11	7	6	47	38	40
Westerham	24	10	7	7	50	36	37
Greenways	24	9	7	8	49	39	34
Bridon Ropes	24	8	5	11	39	55	29
Samuel Montagu YC	24	6	11	7	34	52	29
Belvedere	24	5	6	13	27	31	21
Fleetdown United	24	5	6	13	19	57	21
Halls	24	5	4	15		59	19
Larkfield & New HW	24	2	2	20		102	8

KENT COUNTY LEAGUE DIVISION ONE WEST CONSTITUTION 2007-08

BELVEDERE . . . . Memorial Ground, 101a Woolwich Road, Abbey Wood SE2 0DY 01322 436724
BRIDON ROPES. . . . . Meridian Sports Club, Charlton Park Road, Charlton SE7 8QS. 020 8856 1923
BROMLEIANS SPORTS . . . . Scrubbs Farm, Lower Gravel Road, Bromley BR2 8LL 020 8462 5068
FLEETDOWN UNITED . . . . Heath Lane Open Space, Heath Lane (Lower), Dartford BA1 2QD 01322 273848
GREENWAYS . . . . Fleet Leisure & Sports Club, Nelson Road, Northfleet DA11 7EE 01474 359222
METROGAS . . . . Marathon Playing Fields, Forty Foot Way, New Eltham SE9 2HL 020 8859 1579
PHOENIX SPORTS . . . . Phoenix Sports Club, Mayplace Road East, Bexleyheath DA7 6JT 01322 526159
SAMUEL MONTAGU YOUTH CLUB . . . . Samuel Montagu YC, Broadwalk, Kidbrooke SE3 8ND 020 8856 1126
STANSFELD O & B CLUB . . . . . . Greenwich University Sports Club, Kidbrooke Lane, Eltham SE9 6TA. 020 8850 0210
SUTTON ATHLETIC . . . . The Roaches, Parsonage Lane, Sutton-at-Hone, Dartford DA4 9HD. 01322 280507
TONBRIDGE INVICTA . . . . Swanmead Sports Ground, Swanmead Way, off Cannon Lane, Tonbridge TN9 1PP 01732 350473
TUDOR SPORTS . . . . 31 Eltham Road, Lee Green SE12 8ES . . . . None
WESTERHAM . . . . Westerham Sports Association, King George V PF, Costells Meadow, Westerham TN16 1BL 01959 561106

IN: Stansfeld O & B Club (R), Sutton Athletic (P – Division Two East), Tonbridge Invicta (P – Division Two West), Tudor Sports (P – Division Two West)
OUT: Bly Spartans (S – Division One East), Halls (R – Division Two West), Larkfield & New Hythe Wanderers (R – Division Two East), Orpington (P)

Division Two East — Results Grid 2006-07

	APM Mears	Atcost	Guru Nanak	Lanes End	Otford United	Pembury	Platt United	Putlands Athletic	Saga Sports & S.	Sutton Athletic	Tenterden Town	UK Paper	Woodstock Park
APM Mears	D	5-0	0-4	5-1	2-3	7-1	2-1	3-0	3-3	2-3	7-1	2-1	2-2
Atcost	2-1	I	1-2	3-1	3-0	2-0	5-1	2-0	3-3	2-0	7-2	1-3	3-0
Guru Nanak	2-1	3-3	V	2-1	0-0	5-0	10-1	2-2	2-1	1-1	7-1	4-0	6-0
Lanes End	0-3	0-4	6-5		1-3	1-2	2-0	L-W	1-2	0-4	3-0	0-1	0-1
Otford United	6-0	1-0	0-3	0-1	T	3-2	4-0	1-1	4-1	2-0	3-0	2-0	2-3
Pembury	3-1	2-1	0-4	1-4	1-3	W	3-3	3-1	2-2	3-1	4-2	5-3	1-2
Platt United	0-3	1-1	0-6	1-5	2-4	3-4	O	3-6	1-2	0-7	1-3	1-2	0-3
Putlands Athletic	2-1	3-0	0-3	1-3	2-4	1-1	6-2		5-3	5-0	7-1	1-4	2-1
Saga Sports & Social	0-2	1-1	0-4	1-0	2-2	1-1	5-0	2-5	E	1-9	5-0	5-4	0-1
Sutton Athletic	3-1	3-0	0-1	5-0	3-0	2-0	6-2	5-2	7-0	A	2-1	4-5	0-1
Tenterden Town	0-4	0-3	0-1	2-0	0-1	2-4	3-2	1-1	2-0	1-5	S	1-5	0-0
UK Paper	4-0	3-1	2-1	4-1	2-0	3-1	8-2	0-2	4-2	0-4	2-0	T	1-2
Woodstock Park	0-1	1-2	0-4	2-2	0-3	6-2	4-2	3-1	1-1	6-6	1-6	6-2	

Division Two East — final table (positions 1–13, P W D L F A Pts):

Pos	P	W	D	L	F	A	Pts
1	24	18	4	2	82	20	58
2	24	17	1	6	85	29	52
3	24	15	3	6	51	47	48
4	24	15	0	9	62	46	45
5	24	12	3	9	45	42	39
6	24	11	5	8	58	39	38
7	24	11	4	9	46	51	37
8	24	9	4	11	51	63	31
9	24	8	3	13	46	64	27
10	24	7	4	13	45	48	25
11	24	4	2	18	36	80	14
13	24	0	2	22	29	104	2

Division Two East (rotated team-name column): Guru Nanak, Sutton Athletic, Otford United, UK Paper, Woodstock Park, APM Mears, Putlands Athletic, Pembury, Saga Sports & Social, Lanes End, Tenterden Town, Platt United

KENT COUNTY LEAGUE DIVISION TWO EAST CONSTITUTION 2007-08

APM MEARS . . . . Cobdown Sports & Social Club, Ditton Corner, Station Road, Aylesford ME20 6AU 01622 716824
ATCOST . . . . Pippin Road, Bramley Gardens, East Peckham, Tonbridge TN12 5BT 07932 792188
BORDEN VILLAGE . . . . Borden Playstool, Wises Lane, Borden, Sittingbourne ME9 8LP 07903 016794
CANTERBURY CITY . . . . Bridge Recreation Ground, Patrixbourne Road, Bridge, Canterbury CT4 5BL . . . . None
LANES END . . . . Waller Park, Wood Lane, Darenth, Dartford DA2 7LR 01322 221006
LARKFIELD & NEW HYTHE WDRS . . Larkfield Sports Ground, New Hythe Lane, Larkfield, Aylesford ME20 6PU 01732 873310
OTFORD UNITED . . . . Otford Recreation Ground, High Street, Otford, Sevenoaks TN14 5PG 01959 524405
PEMBURY . . . . Woodside Recreation Ground, Henwoods Mount, Woodside Road, Pembury TN2 4BH 07970 026628
PUTLANDS ATHLETIC . . . . Putlands Sports Centre, Mascalls Road, Paddock Wood TN12 6NZ 01892 838290
SAGA SPORTS & SOCIAL . . . . . . Canteen Meadow, The Street, Bishopsbourne, Canterbury CT4 5HX . . . . None
TENTERDEN TOWN. . . . . Recreation Ground Road, High Street, Tenterden TN30 6RA 07786 932151
UK PAPER . . . . UK Paper Sports Ground, Gore Court Road, Sittingbourne ME10 1QN 01795 477047
WOODSTOCK PARK . . . . Sittingbourne Research Centre, Broadoak Road, Sittingbourne ME9 8AG 07774 654912
IN: Borden Village (R – Division One East), Canterbury City (N), Larkfield & New Hythe Wanderers (R – Division One West)
OUT: Guru Nanak (P – Division One East), Platt United (W), Sutton Athletic (P – Division One West)

Division Two West — Results Grid 2006-07

	Borough United	Chipstead	Chislehurst	Cray W & NB	Eltham Palace	Erith '147	Farnboro. OBG	Meridian Sports	Old Addeyans	Old Bexleians	Tonbridge Inv.	Tudor Sports	Wickham Park
Borough United	D	2-3	4-1	3-1	2-0	5-1	1-1	1-4	1-0	4-2	0-2	1-2	2-4
Chipstead	4-1	I	4-2	2-4	2-1	5-3	0-3	10-1	3-3	3-1	0-1	1-3	2-3
Chislehurst	2-1	2-3	V	0-2	1-6	2-2	0-1	2-1	2-0	3-1	1-2	1-2	0-1
Cray W & NB	1-0	2-2	4-0		4-5	1-2	4-5	5-0	0-0	1-1	1-4	1-5	1-0
Eltham Palace	1-1	2-1	3-0	1-1	T	3-0	1-1	6-4	4-2	0-0	3-5	3-1	
Erith '147	1-2	2-1	1-1	3-2	2-1	W	0-3	5-0	5-2	3-0	2-2	1-1	2-3
Farnborough OBG	3-2	1-0	3-1	8-1	2-2	0-2	O	0-2	3-0	4-0	1-1	1-4	1-1
Meridian Sports	2-1	0-5	1-2	0-1	3-4	2-5	0-0		3-3	3-6	1-4	0-2	1-2
Old Addeyans	2-1	0-4	1-5	0-4	1-1	1-4	1-0	0-0	W	2-0	0-6	1-3	1-7
Old Bexleians	1-1	2-1	2-1	0-7	0-1	0-1	1-1	1-2	1-2	E	2-4	0-6	3-3
Tonbridge Invicta	3-0	3-1	5-2	1-0	4-1	6-0	3-1	2-0	4-0	3-2	S	3-2	1-4
Tudor Sports	7-2	4-1	1-0	3-1	1-1	4-1	1-1	2-1	7-2	2-0	5-2	T	1-4
Wickham Park	2-1	1-3	3-0	0-4	5-1	0-3	4-0	7-3	1-0	0-5	1-4		

Division Two West — final table (P W D L F A Pts):

Team	P	W	D	L	F	A	Pts
Tudor Sports	24	20	3	1	78	32	63
Tonbridge Invicta	24	17	4	3	67	25	55
Wickham Park	24	14	7	7	59	45	42
Farnborough OB Guild	24	11	7	6	46	26	40
Eltham Palace	24	11	7	6	57	47	40
Chipstead	24	11	2	10	53	54	35
Erith '147	24	10	3	9	54	42	33
Cray W & NB	24	8	3	13	40	49	27
Borough United	24	7	2	16	31	51	23
Chislehurst	24	4	3	16	26	51	15
Old Addeyans	24	3	5	16	34	77	14
Meridian Sports	24	2	5	17	26	66	11
Old Bexleians	24						

KENT COUNTY LEAGUE DIVISION TWO WEST CONSTITUTION 2007-08

BOROUGH UNITED . . . . Princes Golf & Leisure Club, Darenth Road, Dartford DA1 1LZ 01322 276565
CHIPSTEAD . . . . Chipstead Rec, Chevening Road, Chipstead, Sevenoaks TN13 2RZ 07753 603944
CHISLEHURST . . . . Coldharbour Leisure Centre, Chaple Farm Road, New Eltham SE9 3LX 020 8851 8692
CRAY W & NB . . . . Coney Hall Recreation Ground, Church Drive, West Wickham, Bromley BR4 9JJ . . . . None
ELTHAM PALACE . . . . Beaverwood Lodge, Beaverwood Road, Chislehurst BR7 6HF 020 8300 1385
ERITH '147 . . . . STC Sports Ground, Ivor Grove, New Eltham SE9 2AJ . . . . None
FARNBOROUGH OLD BOYS GUILD . . Farnborough (Kent) Sports Club, High Street, Farnborough BR6 7BA 01689 826949
HALLS . . . . Bexley Park S & S Club, Calvert Drive, Bexley DA2 7GU . . . . None
HAWKHURST UNITED . . . . King George V Playing Field, Moor Hill, Hawkhurst, Cranbrook TN18 4QB . . . . None
MERIDIAN SPORTS . . . . Meridian Sports & Social, 110 Charlton Park Lane, Charlton SE7 8QS 020 8856 1923
OLD ADDEYANS . . . . Blackheath Park, Blackheath SE3 0HB . . . . None
OLD BEXLEIANS . . . . Seven Acre Sports Club, Church Manor Avenue, Abbey Wood SE2 0HY . . . . None
WICKHAM PARK . . . . . . Wickham Park Sports Club, 228-230 Pickhurst Rise, West Wickham, Bromley BR4 0AQ 020 8777 2550
IN: Halls (R – Division One West), Hawkhurst United (P – East Sussex League Premier Division)
OUT: Tonbridge Invicta (P – Division One West), Tudor Sports (P – Division One West)

WWW.NLNEWSDESK.CO.UK

BILL MANKELOW INTER-REGIONAL CHALLENGE CUP
(All clubs in league)

FIRST ROUND EAST
Borden Village 1 **Lydd Town** 3
New Romney 0 **St Margarets** 2
Sheppey United 4 Ashford Borough 1
FIRST ROUND WEST
Bridon Ropes 2 Orpington 1
Bromleians Sports 1 Westerham 1 *aet* (3-1p)
Cray Valley Paper Mills 4 Lewisham Borough 1
Crockenhill 3 **Holmesdale** 7
Fleet Leisure 3 Larkfield & New Hythe Wanderers 3 *aet* (6-5p)
Fleetdown United 3 **Greenways** 4
SECOND ROUND EAST
Bearsted (w/o) v Hollands & Blair (scr.)
Betteshanger Welfare 4 Tyler Hill 3 *aet*
Bromley Green 1 **Oakwood** 3
Kennington 5 Uniflo 3 *aet*
Milton Athletic 2 Sheppey United 1

Norton Sports 1 **Lydd Town** 2
Sheerness East 2 Staplehurst & Monarchs United 0
St Margarets 1 University of Kent 0
SECOND ROUND WEST
Belvedere 1 **Halls** 2
Bly Spartans 1 Fleet Leisure 1 *aet* (3-2p)
Bridon Ropes 7 Greenways 4 *aet*
Holmesdale 2 Bromleians Sports 1
Old Roan 2 Snodland 1
Rusthall 0 **Metrogas** 2
Samuel Montagu YC 1 **Phoenix Sports** 2
Stansfeld O & B Club 3 Cray Valley Paper Mills 0
THIRD ROUND EAST
Betteshanger Welfare 0 **Bearsted** 5
Lydd Town 2 Oakwood 0
Milton Athletic 6 St Margarets 1
Sheerness East 4 **Kennington** 4 *aet* (4-5p)

THIRD ROUND WEST
Bly Spartans 3 Phoenix Sports 0
Halls 3 **Metrogas** 5
Holmesdale 0 **Bridon Ropes** 3
Stansfeld O & B Club 3 Old Roan 0
QUARTER-FINALS
Bearsted 6 Milton Athletic 0
Bly Spartans 2 Kennington 0
Lydd Town 1 **Bridon Ropes** 2
Metrogas 1 **Stansfeld O & B Club** 2 *aet*
SEMI-FINALS
Bly Spartans 1 Bridon Ropes 0
Stansfeld O & B Club 2 **Bearsted** 3
FINAL
(April 26th at Chatham Town)
Bly Spartans 2 Bearsted 1

LES LECKIE CUP *(Eastern region clubs from outside the Premier Division)*

FIRST ROUND
APM Mears 0 **Guru Nanak** 2
Kennington 6 Tenterden Town 0
Lanes End 3 Pembury 0
Lydd Town 3 Woodstock Park 0
Oakwood 5 Uniflo 0
Putlands Athletic 2 **New Romney** 6
Saga Sports & Social 2 Otford United 1
Sheppey United 4 **UK Paper** 4 *aet* (3-4p)
St Margarets 1 **Betteshanger Welfare** 3
Staplehurst & Monarchs United 3 Tyler Hill 1
SECOND ROUND
Ashford Borough 6 Lydd Town 0
Atcost 0 **Sutton Athletic** 4
Kennington 2 Guru Nanak 1

Lanes End 1 Saga Sports & Social 0
Oakwood 3 University of Kent 1
Platt United 0 **Betteshanger Welfare** 8
Staplehurst & Monarchs United 5 Borden Village 0
UK Paper 3 New Romney 2
QUARTER-FINALS
Ashford Borough 4 Betteshanger Welfare 2
Kennington 1 **UK Paper** 2
Oakwood 5 Sutton Athletic 1
Staplehurst & Monarchs United 6 Lanes End 0
SEMI-FINALS
Ashford Borough 3 UK Paper 1
Staplehurst & Monarchs United 0 **Oakwood** 3
FINAL *(April 17th at Lordswood)*
Oakwood 1 **Ashford Borough** 2

WEST KENT CHALLENGE SHIELD *(Western region clubs from outside the Premier Division)*

FIRST ROUND
Borough United 0 **Bromleians Sports** 7
Bridon Ropes 5 Greenways 3
Farnborough Old Boys Guild 1 Fleetdown United 0
Halls 0 **Eltham Palace** 3
Meridian Sports 1 **Cray W & NB** 1 *aet* (2-4p)
Old Addeyans 3 **Phoenix Sports** 6 *aet*
Orpington 1 Tonbridge Invicta 0
Samuel Montagu Youth Club 1 **Erith '147** 3
Tudor Sports 6 Chipstead 1
Westerham 4 Old Bexleians 0
SECOND ROUND
Belvedere 0 **Bly Spartans** 2
Bridon Ropes 2 Wickham Park 1
Bromleians Sports 0 **Metrogas** 2

Erith '147 2 **Cray W & NB** 3
Farnborough Old Boys Guild 2 Phoenix Sports 0
Larkfield & New Hythe Wdrs 2 **Eltham Palace** 7
Tudor Sports 2 Chislehurst 1
Westerham 1 **Orpington** 2
QUARTER-FINALS
Cray W & NB 3 Bridon Ropes 2
Metrogas 3 Eltham Palace 2 *aet*
Orpington 1 Bly Spartans 0
Tudor Sports 4 Farnborough Old Boys Guild 2
SEMI-FINALS
Metrogas 1 **Cray W & NB** 2
Orpington 3 Tudor Sports 0
FINAL *(May 3rd at Sevenoaks Town)*
Orpington 3 Cray W & NB 2

FLOODLIGHT CUP
(All Eastern teams from Premier Division and selected teams from Div One East – all games played at Faversham Tn)

FIRST ROUND
Ashford Borough 6 Kennington 2
Crockenhill 1 **Bly Spartans** 2

Hollands & Blair 1 **Sheerness East** 2
Norton Sports 2 Lydd Town 2 *aet* (7-6p)
Staplehurst & Monarchs United 2 **New Romney** 5

Uniflo 2 **Borden Village** 4 *aet*
(Competition held over until 2007-08 due to the inclement weather)

RESERVES CUP
FINAL *(May 1st at Corinthian)*
Holmesdale Res. 5 Bly Spartans Res. 0

KENT LEAGUE

	Beckenham Town	Croydon	Deal Town	Erith Town	Erith & Belvedere	Faversham Town	Greenwich Borough	Herne Bay	Hythe Town	Lordswood	Sevenoaks Town	Slade Green	Sporting Bengal United	Thamesmead Town	Tunbridge Wells	VCD Athletic	Whitstable Town
Beckenham Town	P	2-3	2-1	2-1	1-2	1-2	2-1	2-1	3-1	4-1	1-4	4-2	9-0	1-1	1-0	1-2	3-3
Croydon	0-4	R	2-1	1-0	2-0	5-1	1-2	1-1	0-0	1-1	3-0	4-0	1-1	3-1	3-1	1-1	
Deal Town	1-4	2-4	E	6-2	1-1	2-2	0-2	0-0	1-1	1-2	3-1	2-1	7-0	1-3	2-2	2-2	4-5
Erith Town	1-0	0-1	2-3	M	2-2	0-1	2-3	1-3	1-2	5-1	0-1	1-0	7-1	0-3	2-1	0-1	0-4
Erith & Belvedere	3-2	2-0	0-1	1-0	I	2-0	1-1	2-1	2-2	3-4	3-2	4-2	5-0	1-1	2-3	2-0	2-0
Faversham Town	2-1	0-2	0-1	0-1	2-0	E	1-6	0-3	0-0	1-0	2-0	2-1	2-3	3-2	0-0	0-3	0-1
Greenwich Borough	1-0	0-2	0-2	5-0	3-1	1-2	R	1-2	2-0	3-2	3-2	1-1	2-1	2-0	3-2	1-2	2-2
Herne Bay	2-1	1-2	1-2	1-1	0-2	3-2	1-3		3-1	4-0	2-0	0-0	2-1	4-0	1-0	1-1	0-1
Hythe Town	2-1	0-1	4-1	1-0	2-2	3-0	1-1	2-1		1-0	0-1	3-0	7-0	1-1	4-3	2-0	1-1
Lordswood	3-2	0-0	0-2	3-0	1-2	1-1	0-4	3-3	0-4	D	1-1	2-1	2-0	1-2	2-1	1-3	1-2
Sevenoaks Town	1-0	1-1	2-0	1-0	3-4	2-0	1-1	4-3	1-2	3-1	I	3-3	3-2	1-2	1-0	0-0	1-3
Slade Green	1-1	0-3	0-1	2-3	0-4	3-1	1-1	1-0	0-4	4-1	2-2	V	2-0	0-4	0-2	2-2	0-4
Sporting Bengal United	0-0	1-2	0-8	3-1	0-5	0-5	2-3	1-1	0-2	0-3	2-3	1-1	I	0-2	1-1	0-3	1-5
Thamesmead Town	3-1	5-0	1-3	1-1	2-2	3-1	3-1	4-3	1-0	3-1	1-2		10-3	S	0-3	3-1	2-2
Tunbridge Wells	2-6	3-4	1-2	1-2	1-3	2-2	0-1	0-0	1-2	3-2	0-3	2-1	3-3	0-3	I	1-1	1-3
VCD Athletic	3-2	2-2	3-1	3-0	3-3	2-0	1-2	0-2	4-3	3-0	6-0	4-2	8-1	4-2	2-0	O	4-0
Whitstable Town	2-0	1-0	5-4	1-0	4-2	1-1	0-1	2-1	3-1	1-1	4-1	2-1	6-1	2-0	4-1	1-2	N

Premier Division	P	W	D	L	F	A	Pts
Whitstable Town	32	21	7	4	76	40	70
VCD Athletic	32	20	7	5	79	38	67
Croydon	32	20	7	5	58	34	67
Thamesmead Town	32	19	6	7	75	44	63
Greenwich Borough	32	19	6	7	63	38	63
Hythe Town	32	16	8	8	59	35	56
Erith & Belvedere	32	16	8	8	68	50	56
Deal Town	32	14	6	12	68	55	48
Herne Bay	32	12	8	12	51	41	44
Sevenoaks Town	32	12	6	14	50	57	42
Beckenham Town	32	12	4	16	64	52	40
Faversham Town	32	10	6	16	36	55	36
Lordswood	32	8	5	19	40	68	29
Erith Town	32	7	3	22	35	60	24
Tunbridge Wells	32	5	8	19	39	66	23
Slade Green	32	5	8	19	36	68	23
Sporting Bengal United	32	2	5	25	28	124	11

KENT LEAGUE PREMIER DIVISION CONSTITUTION 2007-08

BECKENHAM TOWN .... Eden Park Avenue, Beckenham BR3 3JJ 020 8650 1066
CROYDON .... Croydon Sports Arena, Albert Road, South Norwood SE25 4QL 020 8654 8555/3462
DEAL TOWN .... Charles Sports Ground, St Leonards Road, Deal CT14 9BB 01304 375623
ERITH TOWN .... Erith Sports Centre, Avenue Road, Erith DA8 3AJ 01322 350271
ERITH & BELVEDERE .... Welling United FC, Park View Road, Welling DA16 1SY 020 8304 0333
FAVERSHAM TOWN .... Salter Lane, Faversham ME13 8ND .... None
GREENWICH BOROUGH .... Harrow Meadow, Eltham Green Road, Eltham SE9 6BA 020 8859 5788
HERNE BAY .... Winchs Field, Stanley Gardens, Herne Bay CT6 5SG 01227 374156
HOLMESDALE .... Holmesdale Sports & Social, Oakley Road, Bromley Common BR9 8HG ... 020 8462 4440
HYTHE TOWN .... Reachfields Stadium, Fort Road, Hythe CT21 6JS 01303 264932
LORDSWOOD .... Martyn Grove, Northdane Way, Walderslade ME5 8YE 01634 669138
SEVENOAKS TOWN .... Greatness Park, Seal Road (on main A25), Sevenoaks TN14 5BL 01732 741987
SLADE GREEN .... The Small Glenn, 35 Moat Lane, Slade Green, Erith BA8 2ND 01322 351077
SPORTING BENGAL UNITED ... Mile End Stadium, Rhodeswell Road, Burdett Road, Poplar E14 7TW ... 020 8980 1885
THAMESMEAD TOWN .... Bayliss Avenue, Thamesmead SE28 8NJ 020 8311 4211
TUNBRIDGE WELLS .... Culverden Stadium, Culverden Down, Tunbridge Wells TN4 9SH 01892 520517
VCD ATHLETIC .... Oakwood, Old Road, Crayford DA1 4DN 01322 524262

IN: Holmesdale (P – Kent County League Premier Division)
OUT: Whitstable Town (P – Isthmian League Division One South)

CHALLENGE SHIELD *(Premier Division champions v League Cup holders)*
Beckenham Town qualify as league runners-up as Maidstone United won both in 2005-06

(August 5th at Maidstone United) Maidstone United 1 **Beckenham Town** 2

PREMIER DIVISION CUP

GROUP A

	P	W	D	L	F	A	Pts
Herne Bay	8	5	2	1	18	9	17
Hythe Town	8	5	1	2	14	7	16
VCD Athletic	8	4	2	2	15	11	14
Slade Green	8	1	2	5	3	12	5
Lordswood	8	1	1	6	7	18	4

Herne Bay 1 Hythe Town 1
Herne Bay 5 Lordswood 0
Herne Bay 3 Slade Green 0
Herne Bay 3 VCD Athletic 1
Hythe Town 1 Herne Bay 3
Hythe Town 3 Lordswood 0
Hythe Town 2 Slade Green 0
Hythe Town 0 VCD Athletic 2
Lordswood 4 Herne Bay 0
Lordswood 0 Hythe Town 3
Lordswood 0 Slade Green 1
Lordswood 1 VCD Athletic 2
Slade Green 0 Herne Bay 1
Slade Green 0 Hythe Town 1
Slade Green 1 Lordswood 1
Slade Green 0 VCD Athletic 0
VCD Athletic 2 Herne Bay 2
VCD Athletic 1 Hythe Town 3
VCD Athletic 3 Lordswood 1
VCD Athletic 4 Slade Green 1

GROUP B

	P	W	D	L	F	A	Pts
Erith & Belvedere	6	3	2	1	9	5	11
Faversham Town	6	3	1	2	9	8	10
Deal Town	6	2	2	2	12	9	8
Sevenoaks Town	6	1	1	4	2	10	4

Deal Town 2 Erith & Belvedere 2
Deal Town 2 Faversham Town 3
Deal Town 4 Sevenoaks Town 0
Erith & Belvedere 2 Deal Town 2
Erith & Belvedere 2 Faversham Town 0
Erith & Belvedere 1 Sevenoaks Town 0
Faversham Town 2 Deal Town 1
Faversham Town 0 Erith & Belvedere 2
Faversham Town 1 Sevenoaks Town 1
Sevenoaks Town 0 Deal Town 1
Sevenoaks Town 1 Erith & Belvedere 0
Sevenoaks Town 0 Faversham Town 3

GROUP C

	P	W	D	L	F	A	Pts
Whitstable Town	6	2	4	0	16	8	10
Croydon	6	2	3	1	12	8	9
Greenwich Borough	6	2	3	1	10	9	9
Sporting Bengal United	6	1	0	5	4	17	3

Croydon 3 Greenwich Borough 0
Croydon 3 Sporting Bengal United 0
Croydon 2 Whitstable Town 2
Greenwich Borough 2 Croydon 2
Greenwich Borough 1 Sporting Bengal United 0
Greenwich Borough 1 Whitstable Town 1
Sporting Bengal United 3 Croydon 1
Sporting Bengal United 0 Greenwich Borough 3
Sporting Bengal United 0 Whitstable Town 7
Whitstable Town 1 Croydon 1
Whitstable Town 3 Greenwich Borough 3
Whitstable Town 2 Sporting Bengal United 1

GROUP D

	P	W	D	L	F	A	Pts
Beckenham Town	6	4	2	0	17	7	14
Thamesmead Town	6	3	1	2	17	10	10
Tunbridge Wells	6	2	0	4	6	12	6
Erith Town	6	1	1	4	6	13	4

Beckenham Town 1 Erith Town 1
Beckenham Town 5 Thamesmead Town 1
Beckenham Town 2 Tunbridge Wells 1
Erith Town 0 Beckenham Town 3
Erith Town 2 Thamesmead Town 1
Erith Town 1 Tunbridge Wells 2
Thamesmead Town 4 Beckenham Town 4
Thamesmead Town 4 Erith Town 2
Thamesmead Town 2 Tunbridge Wells 0
Tunbridge Wells 0 Beckenham Town 2
Tunbridge Wells 2 Erith Town 0
Tunbridge Wells 1 Thamesmead Town 5

QUARTER-FINALS

Beckenham Town 1 **Hythe Town** 2
Erith & Belvedere 2 **Thamesmead Town** 5
Herne Bay 3 Croydon 2
Whitstable Town 3 Faversham Town 0

SEMI-FINALS (played over two legs)

Thamesmead 0 Herne Bay 2, Herne Bay 0 **Thamesmead** 3
Whitstable 2 Hythe 2, Hythe Town 1 **Whitstable Town** 2 aet

FINAL (May 5th at Folkestone Invicta)

Thamesmead Town 3 Whitstable Town 0

Division One	P	W	D	L	F	A	Pts
Thamesmead Town Res.	22	16	3	3	55	21	51
Bromley Res.	22	15	3	4	58	27	48
Whitstable Town Res.	22	14	4	4	49	24	46
Maidstone United Res.	22	11	4	7	45	25	37
Dartford Res.	22	10	3	9	31	34	33
Erith & Belvedere Res.	22	10	2	10	37	34	32
Folkestone Invicta Res.	22	8	5	9	31	28	29
Erith Town Res.	22	8	1	13	32	42	25
Ramsgate Res.	22	7	4	11	31	45	25
Cray Wanderers Res. -1	22	6	5	11	38	57	22
Sevenoaks Town Res.	22	4	7	11	27	33	19
Ashford Town Res.	22	1	3	18	14	78	6

Division Two	P	W	D	L	F	A	Pts
Chatham Town Res.	24	17	6	1	61	24	57
Margate Res.	24	15	4	5	54	29	49
VCD Athletic Res.	24	12	5	7	46	36	41
Dover Athletic Res.	24	11	6	7	55	36	39
Hythe Town Res.	24	11	2	11	55	48	35
Greenwich Borough Res.	24	10	5	9	48	42	35
Herne Bay Res.	24	9	6	9	33	47	33
Faversham Town Res.	24	8	8	8	50	44	32
Deal Town Res.	24	9	5	10	36	46	32
Sittingbourne Res.	24	8	6	10	48	49	30
Lordswood Res.	24	6	5	13	46	65	23
Tilbury Res.	24	4	4	16	45	70	16
Tunbridge Wells Res.	24	3	4	17	32	73	13

WWW.CHERRYRED.CO.UK

DIVISION ONE/TWO CUP

FINAL
(May 1st at Lordswood)
Thamesmead Town Res. 2 Deal Town Res. 1

LEICESTERSHIRE SENIOR LEAGUE

	Anstey Nomads	Aylestone Park Old Boys	Bardon Hill Sports	Barrow Town	Birstall United	Blaby & Whetstone Athletic	Downes Sports	Ellistown	Highfield Rangers	Holwell Sports	Ibstock United	Kirby Muxloe SC	Ratby Sports	Rothley Imperial	St Andrews SC	Stapenhill	Thurmaston Town	Thurnby Rangers
Anstey Nomads		3-2	1-2	2-3	2-3	2-3	5-2	0-2	2-1	1-2	4-1	1-1	1-1	1-0	2-1	1-1	2-1	4-2
Aylestone Park Old Boys	4-1	P	0-2	1-3	3-0	2-3	1-2	1-1	3-1	0-1	1-7	1-3	1-1	1-1	2-4	0-3	0-3	0-3
Bardon Hill Sports	2-3	2-1	R	4-2	0-1	2-0	4-0	1-2	5-0	1-2	0-0	0-1	5-5	4-0	4-2	0-1	0-1	2-2
Barrow Town	2-0	4-1	4-1	E	3-1	2-0	3-0	2-1	5-1	1-2	2-3	2-2	4-3	3-2	0-0	2-1	4-3	1-8
Birstall United	4-1	3-2	0-1	0-3	M	4-0	0-2	0-1	1-2	1-2	0-1	0-5	3-1	5-1	2-0	0-0	2-0	1-4
Blaby & Whetstone Athletic	4-1	2-3	2-0	1-2	0-1	I	2-0	3-1	4-1	0-1	0-3	2-1	3-1	2-2	2-2	0-3	1-0	1-4
Downes Sports	4-1	1-2	1-6	1-4	2-5	0-1	E	0-3	1-2	1-1	2-3	0-1	2-3	2-0	3-0	1-3	5-4	0-6
Ellistown	4-0	1-2	1-3	0-4	2-1	2-1	0-1	R	3-1	3-0	0-0	3-0	1-0	1-1	0-0	1-1	1-3	1-5
Highfield Rangers	1-3	1-3	2-3	1-2	1-2	3-1	1-1	0-1		0-0	0-3	1-2	1-3	9-0	1-2	0-3	3-2	2-3
Holwell Sports	1-3	1-1	2-1	0-2	1-2	0-2	2-1	3-4	0-1	D	4-0	0-3	1-1	5-0	1-0	0-1	3-2	2-1
Ibstock United	2-0	3-2	3-3	1-2	1-1	3-1	3-0	2-1	0-0	3-0	I	1-3	3-2	2-1	3-1	0-2	4-1	1-3
Kirby Muxloe SC	1-0	4-1	5-1	5-3	3-0	3-1	1-0	3-2	0-0	1-2	0-3	V	3-2	5-1	2-0	0-4	2-0	1-3
Ratby Sports	1-4	1-4	0-2	1-3	2-4	2-1	0-0	0-3	0-0	0-1	1-1	0-3	I	5-1	1-3	3-5	2-2	4-2
Rothley Imperial	1-4	1-2	0-4	3-1	1-2	3-1	0-3	4-2	1-4	1-2	1-3	0-2	1-3	S	0-2	0-1	0-5	1-3
St Andrews SC	6-1	0-3	4-2	1-1	2-2	4-1	8-0	3-1	3-3	1-0	0-2	1-6	2-0	6-0	I	2-2	1-2	2-2
Stapenhill	6-2	2-0	2-4	6-0	1-0	0-0	2-0	4-3	0-1	5-2	1-0	0-1	2-1	3-2	3-3	O	3-0	2-0
Thurmaston Town	1-1	0-1	2-2	0-2	3-0	2-1	3-0	2-3	4-2	2-1	2-3	1-2	3-0	1-0	2-0	0-3	N	1-4
Thurnby Rangers	7-1	4-2	2-0	2-4	1-1	1-1	2-1	1-0	1-0	1-1	0-2	2-3	2-1	3-1	6-2	3-0	1-2	

Premier Division		P	W	D	L	F	A	Pts
Stapenhill		34	25	5	4	78	29	80
Kirby Muxloe SC		34	24	3	7	77	39	75
Barrow Town		34	24	3	7	85	58	75
Ibstock United		34	21	7	6	72	41	70
Thurnby Rangers	-3	34	20	4	10	95	52	61
Holwell Sports		34	17	4	13	49	46	55
Bardon Hill Sports		34	16	5	13	73	54	53
Ellistown	-3	34	16	4	14	56	48	49
Birstall United		34	15	4	15	52	54	49
St Andrews SC		34	12	9	13	66	59	45
Anstey Nomads		34	13	4	17	60	79	43
Thurmaston Town		34	13	3	18	60	64	42
Blaby & Whetstone Athletic		34	13	3	18	48	61	42
Aylestone Park Old Boys		34	11	4	19	53	72	37
Highfield Rangers		34	8	7	19	47	68	31
Ratby Sports		34	6	9	19	51	77	27
Downes Sports		34	8	3	23	38	81	27
Rothley Imperial	-3	34	2	3	29	29	107	6

LEICESTERSHIRE SENIOR LEAGUE PREMIER DIVISION CONSTITUTION 2007-08

ANSTEY NOMADS . . . . Cropston Road, Anstey LE7 7BY 0116 236 4868
AYLESTONE PARK . . . . Dorset Avenue, Wigston, Leicester LE18 4WB 0116 277 5307
BARDON HILL SPORTS . . . . Bardon Close, Coalville LE67 4BS 01530 815569
BARROW TOWN . . . . Riverside Park, Meynell, Barrow Road, Quorn, Loughborough LE12 8PJ 01509 620650
BIRSTALL UNITED . . . . Meadow Lane, Birstall LE4 4FN 0116 267 1230
BLABY & WHETSTONE ATHLETIC . . Blaby & Whetstone BC, Warwick Road, Whetstone LE8 6LW 0116 286 4852
ELLISTOWN . . . . 1 Terrace Road, Ellistown, Coalville LE67 1GD 01530 230159
HINCKLEY DOWNES . . . . . . Hinckley United FC, The Marstons Stadium, Leicester Road, Hinckley LE10 3DR. 01455 840088
HIGHFIELD RANGERS . . . . 443 Gleneagles Avenue, Rushey Mead, Leicester LE4 7YJ 0116 266 0009
HOLWELL SPORTS . . . . Welby Road, Asfordby Hill, Melton Mowbray LE14 3RD 01664 812715
IBSTOCK UNITED . . . . The Welfare, Leicester Road, Ibstock LE67 6HN. 01530 260656
KIRBY MUXLOE SC . . . . Ratby Lane, Kirby Muxloe, Leicester LE9 9AQ 0116 239 3201
RATBY SPORTS . . . . Desford Lane, Ratby, Leicester LE6 0LF. 0116 239 2474
ROTHLEY IMPERIAL . . . . Loughborough Road, Mountsorrell, Leicester LE12 7AU. 0116 237 4003
SAFFRON DYNAMO . . . . Cambridge Road, Whetstone LE8 2LH 0116 284 9695
ST ANDREWS SC . . . . Canal Street, Aylestone, Leicester LE2 8LX 0116 283 9298
THURMASTON TOWN . . . . Elizabeth Park, Checkland Road, Thurmaston, Leicester LE4 8FN 0116 260 2519
THURNBY RANGERS . . . . Dakyn Road, Thurnby Lodge Estate, Leicester LE5 2ED 0116 243 3698
IN: Saffron Dynamo (P)
OUT: Stapenhill (P – Midland Alliance)
Downes Sports become Hinckley Downes

Note – Syston Fosse Sports withdrew during the course of the season. Their results are shown herein but are expunged from the league table

Key to columns: AT = Anstey Town, AA = Asfordby Amateurs, AI = Ashby Ivanhoe, CA = Cottesmore Amateurs, ESA = Earl Shilton Albion, FBV = FC Braunstone Victoria, Hat = Hathern, HSS = Huncote Sports & Social, LC = Leics Constabulary, LA = Lutterworth Athletic, LT = Lutterworth Town, NL = Narborough & Littlethorpe, Rav = Ravenstone, SD = Saffron Dynamo, ST = Sileby Town, SFS = Syston Fosse Sports

	AT	AA	AI	CA	ESA	FBV	Hat	HSS	LC	LA	LT	NL	Rav	SD	ST	SFS
Anstey Town		3-0	3-1	4-2	3-3	3-0	2-2	2-0	2-4	4-1	4-1	4-0	2-2	0-1	0-1	n/a
Asfordby Amateurs	0-2		2-0	1-1	1-5	1-1	1-0	0-2	2-2	2-2	4-1	4-1	4-0	0-1	0-1	n/a
Ashby Ivanhoe	0-3	1-3	*D*	6-4	1-2	4-0	2-2	3-2	4-1	1-4	2-3	4-0	1-0	1-2	3-5	n/a
Cottesmore Amateurs	0-0	1-0	1-5	*I*	3-2	1-4	1-2	4-1	0-1	0-2	1-2	1-1	1-1	0-1	0-1	n/a
Earl Shilton Albion	1-3	0-1	1-0	5-0	*V*	0-5	1-4	1-2	0-2	2-0	5-1	1-1	4-2	1-4	2-5	9-1
FC Braunstone Victoria	2-3	3-0	7-1	4-1	5-4	*I*	2-3	3-0	5-4	4-4	4-2	1-1	3-0	0-2	3-3	n/a
Hathern	0-1	1-3	0-1	4-0	1-1	4-2	*S*	2-1	1-2	0-2	3-4	5-1	2-1	3-0	0-1	n/a
Huncote Sports & Social	0-7	1-1	0-3	3-1	0-2	4-5	0-0	*I*	0-1	2-1	1-4	0-3	4-3	2-3	1-3	n/a
Leics Constabulary	0-2	1-3	2-1	2-3	1-1	4-0	2-3	0-4	*O*	1-2	4-1	0-1	1-0	0-3	0-2	1-0
Lutterworth Athletic	1-4	3-2	2-0	4-1	2-3	0-0	1-2	1-2	4-1	*N*	2-2	0-3	6-0	2-1	3-2	n/a
Lutterworth Town	1-2	2-1	0-2	2-1	2-0	2-2	0-1	0-0	4-2	2-2		5-0	3-0	0-5	0-2	n/a
Narborough & Littlethorpe	0-0	2-5	2-2	3-3	1-4	2-2	2-3	1-1	2-0	1-0	0-0	*O*	1-2	1-7	1-4	n/a
Ravenstone	2-4	3-2	0-1	1-0	2-3	0-2	2-6	0-3	1-0	0-0	3-3	1-2	*N*	1-3	0-3	n/a
Saffron Dynamo	0-1	2-3	0-3	1-0	5-0	2-4	3-1	3-1	2-2	2-1	1-2	2-0	5-1	*E*	3-4	n/a
Sileby Town	0-2	1-1	1-4	4-1	1-0	3-0	5-2	2-2	3-1	2-0	1-1	1-1	7-0	3-2		3-0
Syston Fosse Sports	n/a	n/a	n/a	1-1	n/a	n/a	1-5	n/a	n/a	1-5	n/a	n/a	n/a	n/a	n/a	

Division One		P	W	D	L	F	A	Pts
Anstey Town		28	20	6	2	72	26	66
Sileby Town		28	19	6	3	72	35	63
Saffron Dynamo	-3	28	17	1	10	65	39	49
FC Braunstone Victoria		28	13	8	7	76	58	47
Hathern		28	14	3	11	55	45	45
Lutterworth Athletic		28	12	6	10	53	43	42
Ashby Ivanhoe		28	13	2	13	57	52	41
Asfordby Amateurs		28	11	6	11	47	43	39
Lutterworth Town		28	10	7	11	46	56	37
Earl Shilton Albion		28	11	3	14	53	59	36
Huncote Sports & Social		28	10	6	12	45	51	36
Leics Constabulary		28	8	3	17	37	56	27
Narborough & Littlethorpe	-3	28	6	10	12	35	64	25
Cottesmore Amateurs		28	4	5	19	30	68	17
Ravenstone		28	4	4	20	26	75	16

Syston Fosse Sports – record expunged

LEICESTERSHIRE SENIOR LEAGUE DIVISION ONE CONSTITUTION 2007-08

ANSTEY TOWN . . . . Leicester Road, Thurcaston, Leicester LE7 7JH. 0116 236 8231
ASFORDBY AMATEURS . . . . Hoby Road Sports Ground, Hoby Road, Asfordby, Melton Mowbray LE14 3TL 01664 434545
ASHBY IVANHOE . . . . Hood Park, North Street, Ashby-de-la-Zouch LE65 1HU . . . . None
COTTESMORE AMATEURS . . . . Rogues Park, Main Street, Cottesmore, Oakham LE15 4DH 01572 813486
DUNTON & BROUGHTON RANGERS . . . . Station Road, Dunton Bassett LE17 5LF 01455 284998
EARL SHILTON ALBION . . . . Stoneycroft Park, New Street, Earl Shilton LE9 7FR 01455 844277
FC BRAUNSTONE VICTORIA . . . . Braunstone Park, Hinckley Road, Leicester LE3 1HX. . . . . None
FC KHALSA . . . . Judgemeadow Community College, Marydene Drive, Evington, Leicester LE5 6HP 0116 2417580
HATHERN . . . . Pasture Lane, Hathern, Loughborough LE12 5LJ . . . . None
HUNCOTE SPORTS & SOCIAL. . . . . Enderby Lane, Thurlaston LE9 7TF 01455 888430
LEICS CONSTABULARY . . . . Police Headquarters, St Johns, Enderby. . . . . 0116 248 2198(matchdays only)
LUTTERWORTH ATHLETIC . . . . Dunley Way, Lutterworth LE17 4NA. . . . . None
LUTTERWORTH TOWN . . . . Hall Lane, Bitteswell, Lutterworth LE17 4LN 01455 554046
NARBOROUGH & LITTLETHORPE. . . . . Leicester Road, Narborough LE19 2DG 0116 275 1855
RAVENSTONE . . . . Ravenslea, Ravenstone, Coalville LE67 2AW . . . . None
SILEBY TOWN. . . . . Memorial Park, Seagrave Road, Sileby, Loughborough LE12 7TP 01509 816104

IN: Dunton & Broughton Rangers (P – Leicester & District League Premier Division), FC Khalsa (P – Leicester City League Premier Division)
OUT: Saffron Dynamo (P), Syston Fosse Sports (WS)

LEAGUE CUP

PREMIER DIVISION SECTION
PRELIMINARY ROUND
Anstey Nomads 2 Birstall United 0
Thurnby Rangers 2 Downes Sports 1
FIRST ROUND
Bardon Hill Sports 1 Aylestone Park Old Boys 0
Barrow Town 2 Kirby Muxloe SC 0
Holwell Sports 1 **Rothley Imperial** 1 (2-4p)
Ratby Sports 1 **Ibstock United** 3
St Andrews SC 1 Anstey Nomads 0
Stapenhill 4 Ellistown 3
Thurmaston Town 1 **Highfield Rangers** 3
Thurnby Rangers 9 Blaby & Whetstone Athletic 1
SECOND ROUND
Bardon Hill Sports 3 **Rothley Imperial** 4
Ibstock United 3 Barrow Town 2
St Andrews SC 2 **Thurnby Rangers** 5
Stapenhill 1 **Highfield Rangers** 2

DIVISION ONE SECTION
FIRST ROUND
Anstey Town 1 **Saffron Dynamo** 1 (2-4p)
Ashby Ivanhoe 4 Ravenstone 2
Asfordby Amateurs 5 Cottesmore Amateurs 2
Hathern 1 **Leics Constabulary** 2
Huncote Sports & Social 2 Narborough & Littlethorpe 2 (2-3p)
Lutterworth Athletic 2 Earl Shilton Albion 0
Lutterworth Town 1 **Sileby Town** 1 (7-8p)
Syston Fosse Sports 0 **FC Braunstone Victoria** 8
SECOND ROUND
Asfordby Amateurs 2 FC Braunstone Victoria 2 (5-4p)
Leics Constabulary 0 **Saffron Dynamo** 2
Lutterworth Athletic 1 Ashby Ivanhoe 0
Sileby Town 7 Huncote Sports & Social 0

QUARTER-FINALS
Highfield Rangers 2 Sileby Town 0
Ibstock United 3 Lutterworth Athletic 0
Rothley Imperial 0 **Asfordby Amateurs** 2
Thurnby Rangers 2 **Saffron Dynamo** 3

SEMI-FINALS
Ibstock United 1 **Highfield Rangers** 2
Saffron Dynamo 3 Asfordby Amateurs 0

FINAL
(May 1st at Barrow Town)
Saffron Dynamo 3 Highfield Rangers 0

Combination One		P	W	D	L	F	A	Pts
Barrow Town Res.		30	22	5	3	111	39	71
Ibstock United Res.		30	20	3	7	70	41	63
Birstall United Res.		30	19	4	7	67	28	61
Thurmaston Town Res.		30	18	6	6	64	36	60
Anstey Town Res.		30	17	4	9	61	42	55
Kirby Muxloe SC Res.		30	14	6	10	71	58	48
Highfield Rangers Res.		30	13	8	9	59	44	47
Sileby Town Res.		30	14	5	11	63	50	47
Blaby & Whetstone Athletic Res.		30	11	6	13	57	52	39
St Andrews SC Res.		30	9	8	13	49	57	35
Rothley Imperial Res.	*-1*	30	9	5	16	38	73	31
Ratby Sports Res.	*-1*	30	9	3	18	51	85	29
Leics Constabulary Res.		30	6	9	15	49	74	27
Downes Sports Res.		30	7	4	19	41	79	25
Aylestone Park Old Boys Res.		30	6	2	22	42	81	20
Lutterworth Athletic Res.		30	4	6	20	33	87	18
Combination Two		P	W	D	L	F	A	Pts
Earl Shilton Albion Res.		24	17	2	5	68	27	53
FC Braunstone Victoria Res.		24	15	4	5	73	41	49
Holwell Sports Res.		24	13	7	4	64	32	46
Narborough & Littlethorpe Res.		24	13	4	7	55	36	43
Ellistown Res.		24	11	7	6	52	36	40
Lutterworth Town Res.		24	11	4	9	48	35	37
Ashby Ivanhoe Res.		24	11	2	11	43	56	35
Hathern Res.		24	9	5	10	38	43	32
Bardon Hill Sports Res.		24	8	5	11	44	44	29
Anstey Nomads Res.		24	6	6	12	44	56	24
Saffron Dynamo Res.		24	7	3	14	43	69	24
Huncote Sports & Social Res.		24	4	4	16	39	84	16
Cottesmore Amateurs Res.		24	3	3	18	21	73	12

PRESIDENT'S CUP

FINAL
(May 10th at Ibstock United)
Ellistown Res. 0 Anstey Town Res. 0 *aet* (5-3p)

LINCOLNSHIRE LEAGUE

	Boston Colts	CGB Humb.	Caistor Rvrs	Grim. B Res.	Horncastle	Hykeham T.	Keelby Utd	L'carly Res.	Linc. U. Res.	Louth Res.	Ruston Spts	Skegness T.
Boston Town Colts		1-3	3-0	3-1	0-7	2-2	5-0	3-0	0-3	W-L	1-1	L-W
CGB Humbertherm	3-0		3-1	2-0	0-0	1-6	2-2	2-1	2-3	4-2	2-0	2-0
Caistor Rovers	4-0	0-0		3-3	2-0	0-2	2-1	5-1	5-0	2-0	2-2	0-2
Grimsby Boro. Res.	1-1	2-0	0-3		2-3	1-2	1-2	2-3	2-1	12-0	2-1	0-2
Horncastle Town	3-0	1-3	5-1	2-1		2-3	2-0	5-0	12-3	1-1	0-0	
Hykeham Town	1-1	4-0	2-0	2-1	0-1		7-1	5-0	4-0	6-1	1-0	1-1
Keelby United	0-1	2-4	0-4	2-4	1-2	0-5		3-1	0-8	2-1	0-3	1-4
LSS Lucarly's Res.	0-0	1-3	1-1	0-1	4-0	0-5	2-5		2-2	4-0	1-2	0-2
Lincoln United Res.	0-1	3-1	1-3	1-4	3-3	2-1	5-0	0-1		4-1	0-4	2-4
Louth United Res.	5-1	2-5	0-7	1-0	1-7	2-3	5-2	1-0	1-2		2-4	0-5
Ruston Sports	5-1	1-0	3-1	0-1	2-0	0-4	2-0	3-1	1-1	5-0		2-1
Skegness Town	2-0	0-0	2-1	3-1	1-0	5-2	6-1	2-1	3-2	7-0	3-0	

		P	W	D	L	F	A	Pts
Skegness Town		22	17	3	2	55	16	54
Hykeham Town		22	16	3	3	68	21	51
Horncastle Town		22	12	4	6	58	28	40
Ruston Sports		22	12	4	6	42	25	40
CGB Humbertherm		22	12	4	6	42	32	40
Caistor Rovers		22	11	4	7	48	28	37
Lincoln United Res.		22	8	3	11	43	45	27
Grimsby Borough Res.	-3	22	8	2	12	42	37	23
Boston Town Colts		22	6	5	11	21	42	23
Keelby United		22	4	1	17	25	76	13
LSS Lucarly's Res.	-3	22	4	3	15	24	52	12
Louth United Res.		22	4	0	18	28	94	12

LINCOLNSHIRE LEAGUE CONSTITUTION 2007-08

BOSTON TOWN RESERVES .... The Stadium, Tattershall Road, Boston PE21 9LR 01205 365470
CGB HUMBERTHERM. .... The Playing Fields, Fulstow, Louth. .... None
CAISTOR ROVERS .... Brigg Road, Caistor, Market Rasen LN7 6RX .... None
COLSTERWORTH UNITED .. Colsterworth S&S Club, Old Post Lane, Colsterworth, Grantham NG33 5PG. .... None
GRANTHAM TOWN RESERVES .. South Kesteven Sports Stadium, Trent Road, Grantham NG31 7XQ 01476 402224/402225
GRIMSBY SOCCER SCHOOL .... Novartis Sports & Social, Moody Lane, Pyewipe, Grimsby. .... None
HARROWBY UNITED .... Dickens Road, Grantham. .... None
HORNCASTLE TOWN .... The Wong, Boston Road, Horncastle LE9 6EY. .... None
HYKEHAM TOWN. .... Memorial Hall Ground, Newark Road, North Hykeham, Lincoln LN6 9RJ. 01522 880035
KEELBY UNITED .... Keelby Village Green, Keelby, Grimsby. .... None
LSS LUCARLY'S RESERVES .... Wilton Road, Humberston, Grimsby DN36 4AW. 01472 812936
LINCOLN MOORLANDS RAILWAY RESERVES .. Moorlands Sports Ground, Newark Road, Lincoln LN6 8RT...... 01522 520184/874111
LINCOLN UNITED RESERVES .... Ashby Avenue, Hartsholme, Lincoln LN6 0DY 01522 696400/690674
LOUTH UNITED .... The Playing Fields, Grainthorpe, Louth. .... None
RUSTON SPORTS .... Ruston Marconi Sports Club, Newark Road, Lincoln. 01522 882111
SKEGNESS TOWN .... Burgh Road, Skegness PE25 2RJ 01754 612654
SLEAFORD TOWN RESERVES. .... Eslaforde Park, Boston Road, Sleaford NG34 9GH. .... None

IN: Colsterworth United (N), Grantham Town Reserves (N), Grimsby Soccer School (N), Harrowby United (P – Grantham League), Lincoln Moorlands Railway Reserves (N), Sleaford Town Reserves (P – Boston League Premier Division)
OUT: Grimsby Borough Reserves (W)
Louth United Reserves become Louth United

WWW.CHERRYRED.CO.UK

LEAGUE CUP

FIRST ROUND
Grimsby Borough Res. 1 **Lincoln United Res. 4**
Horncastle Town 1 Hykeham Town 0
Ruston Sports 3 Caistor Rovers 1
Skegness 0 **Boston Town Colts** 1 *aet*

QUARTER-FINALS
Boston Colts 1 **Lincoln United Res.** 2 *aet*
Keelby United 1 **Ruston Sports** 5
Louth United Res. 1 **Horncastle Town** 6
LSS Lucarly's Res. 2 **CGB Humb'thm** 1
aet (LSS Lucarly's Res. expelled)

SEMI-FINALS
Horncastle 2 CGB Humbertherm 0
Ruston Sports 3 **Lincoln United Res.** 4
FINAL
(April 12th at Lincoln United)
Horncastle Town 0 **Lincoln Utd Res.** 1

SUPPLEMENTARY CUP

PRELIMINARY ROUND
Boston Colts 2 LSS Lucarly's Res. 0
Caistor Rovers 3 Keelby United 0
Louth United Res. 1 **CGB Humbertherm** 5
Skegness Town 0 **Ruston Sports** 1

QUARTER-FINALS
Boston Town Colts Res. 0 **Hykeham** 2
CGB Humbertherm 1 **Caistor Rovers** 3
Grimsby Borough Res. 2 **Horncastle Town** 3 *aet*
Lincoln United Res. 3 Ruston Sports 0

SEMI-FINALS
Caistor Rovers 2 **Horncastle** 2 *aet (2-4p)*
Hykeham Town 4 Lincoln United Res. 2
FINAL
(April 5th at Lincoln Moorlands)
Horncastle Town 2 Hykeham Town 1

LIVERPOOL COUNTY PREMIER LEAGUE

	Birchfield	Collegiate OB	Croxteth Red Rum	East Villa	Ford Motors	Lucas Sports	Mackets	NELTC	Old Xaverians	Penlake	Roma	South Sefton Boro.	Speke	St Aloysius	St Dominics	Waterloo Dock
Birchfield	P	3-1	1-2	0-2	3-2	6-1	2-0	1-3	1-3	1-1	2-1	2-4	2-2	0-2	1-2	0-2
Collegiate Old Boys	1-1	R	2-8	0-4	4-1	1-1	1-1	2-3	2-1	2-1	0-4	2-1	3-3	3-5	0-3	0-3
Croxteth Red Rum	4-0	4-2	E	0-0	2-1	6-2	W-L	1-3	6-0	2-4	1-0	0-3	W-L	0-2	2-2	2-4
East Villa	5-1	3-0	3-3	M	7-2	1-1	3-0	3-1	1-2	2-2	2-1	2-4	2-0	1-1	1-1	3-3
Ford Motors	2-0	3-0	3-3	3-1	I	4-3	1-2	2-7	0-1	0-3	5-1	4-2	1-0	2-17	1-1	1-3
Lucas Sports	2-3	2-6	4-1	0-1	1-2	E	1-0	2-0	4-1	3-3	4-0	4-1	0-1	5-2	2-0	2-3
Mackets	2-2	2-0	0-5	0-3	4-2	2-2	R	0-2	0-1	2-3	1-3	1-4	0-4	3-4	1-2	5-5
NELTC	2-2	0-2	4-3	2-3	6-1	1-1	1-0		3-1	3-1	2-2	2-1	3-0	2-1	0-0	0-2
Old Xaverians	2-3	1-2	1-3	0-0	2-1	1-3	5-0	2-0	D	2-1	3-0	3-1	1-6	1-3	1-2	0-9
Penlake	6-3	3-3	0-4	0-0	1-2	2-4	2-1	2-1	1-1	I	1-0	0-1	2-3	1-3	0-2	0-3
Roma	3-1	2-1	0-2	0-3	3-0	0-4	2-0	0-4	2-2	0-1	V	1-2	2-1	2-1	1-2	3-3
South Sefton Borough	3-2	1-1	4-2	0-1	8-0	1-2	5-0	0-1	1-0	2-1	8-1	I	3-0	0-2	0-6	1-4
Speke	0-1	1-0	2-3	1-4	1-1	2-4	5-1	2-0	3-0	1-5	6-1	1-3	S	3-6	0-3	1-4
St Aloysius	3-2	1-0	1-2	0-1	4-0	5-2	5-1	1-0	2-0	1-0	3-2	6-4	2-0	I	2-1	0-1
St Dominics	2-1	4-0	2-5	1-3	4-4	2-3	5-3	1-2	3-1	4-0	5-1	0-1	0-2	1-4	O	1-3
Waterloo Dock	8-0	6-2	4-1	1-3	3-1	6-1	6-1	2-0	1-1	3-1	4-0	2-1	0-2	W-L	4-2	N

Premier Division		P	W	D	L	F	A	Pts
Waterloo Dock		30	24	4	2	102	35	76
East Villa		30	18	9	3	68	30	63
St Aloysius	-6	30	22	1	7	88	39	61
Croxteth Red Rum		30	17	4	9	77	54	55
NELTC		30	16	4	10	58	41	52
South Sefton Borough		30	16	1	13	72	55	49
Lucas Sports		30	14	5	11	70	64	47
St Dominics		30	13	6	11	64	51	45
Old Xaverians		30	10	4	16	40	64	34
Speke	-3	30	10	4	16	52	56	31
Penlake		30	8	7	15	49	61	31
Ford Motors		30	9	4	17	52	97	31
Roma		30	9	3	18	39	73	30
Birchfield		30	8	5	17	47	73	29
Collegiate Old Boys		30	7	7	16	43	75	28
Mackets	-6	30	3	4	23	33	86	7

ZINGARI CHALLENGE CUP

FIRST ROUND
Collegiate Old Boys 3 Penlake 2
Croxteth Red Rum 3 Mackets 1
East Villa 3 Ford Motors 1
Lucas Sports 1 **South Sefton Borough** 6
(at South Sefton Borough)
Old Xaverians 2 NELTC 1
Roma 0 **St Aloysius** 7 *(at St Aloysius)*
Speke 1 **Waterloo Dock** 4
St Dominics 0 **Birchfield** 4

QUARTER-FINALS
Collegiate Old Boys 0 **East Villa** 3
Croxteth Red Rum 0 **Waterloo Dock** 1
South Sefton Borough 1 **Old Xaverians** 2
St Aloysius 1 Birchfield 1 *aet* (3-1p)

SEMI-FINALS
East Villa 2 St Aloysius 0
Waterloo Dock 2 Old Xaverians 1

FINAL
(May 16th at Civil Service, Thornton)
East Villa 1 Waterloo Dock 0

LIVERPOOL COUNTY PREMIER LEAGUE PREMIER DIVISION CONSTITUTION 2007-08

BRNESC... Melling Road, Aintree, Liverpool L9 0LQ.. None
BIRCHFIELD........................... Edge Hill College, St Helens Road, Ormskirk L39 4QP................... 01695 584745
EAST VILLA................... MYA Jeffreys Humble, Long Lane, Walton, Liverpool L9 9AQ............................... None
FORD MOTORS........... Ford Sports & Social Club, Cronton Lane, Widnes WA8 5AJ............. 0151 424 7078
LUCAS SPORTS........... William Collins Memorial Ground, Commercial Road, Liverpool............................ None
NELTC................................ Edinburgh Park, Townsend Lane, Liverpool L13 9DY............................... None
OLD XAVERIANS............... St Francis Xaviers College, Beconsfield Road, Liverpool L25 6EG......... 0151 288 1000
PENLAKE........................... Edge Hill College, St Helens Road, Ormskirk L39 4QP................... 01695 584745
RED RUM............... Croxteth Community Comprehensive School, Parkstile Lane, Liverpool L11 0PB........ 0151 546 4168
ROMA....................... Kirkby Sports Centre, Valley Road, Kirkby L20 9PQ................... 0151 443 4404
SOUTH LIVERPOOL.................... Jericho Lane, Aigburth, Liverpool L17 5AR....................................... None
SOUTH SEFTON BOROUGH.................... Mill Dam Field, Bridges Lane, Sefton................................... None
SPEKE........................... Speke Hall Avenue, Speke, Liverpool L24 1YD................... 0151 486 1588
ST ALOYSIUS............ King George V Sports Complex, Long View Lane, Huyton, Liverpool L36 7UN....... 0151 443 5712
ST DOMINICS...................... St Dominics School, Lordens Road, Huyton L14 8UD................ 0151 489 8279
WATERLOO DOCK................... Edinburgh Park, Townsend Lane, Liverpool L6 0BB................ 0151 263 5267
IN: BRNESC (P), South Liverpool (P)
OUT: Collegiate Old Boys (R), Mackets Grenadier (formerly Mackets) (R)
Croxteth Red Rum become Red Rum

Note – St Ambrose withdrew during the course of the season. Their results are shown herein but are expunged from the league table

	APH	AOB	BRN	CHL	COP	HIL	KIN	NAL	MHA	PAG	QBO	SLV	STA	STO	VIS	WAR
Aigburth PH		5-4	2-2	2-2	4-1	6-0	3-2	1-3	4-3	1-1	4-3	1-4	2-2	4-2	2-4	4-5
Alsop Old Boys	1-3		0-8	1-2	2-5	3-3	5-0	0-3	2-1	5-4	0-5	n/a	2-2	3-4	2-4	
BRNESC	2-2	3-0	D	2-1	4-0	12-0	2-1	3-1	1-0	1-2	2-1	5-0	n/a	1-1	5-2	4-2
Cheshire Lines	10-0	5-0	0-1	I	4-2	6-1	1-0	1-3	2-1	0-3	3-1	1-3	0-3	0-3	2-2	0-0
Copperas Hill	2-0	2-1	0-2	0-1	V	4-1	2-2	1-2	2-2	0-2	1-2	1-2	4-4	3-5	2-0	2-0
Hill Athletic	2-1	2-2	0-6	1-1	3-1	I	2-4	4-1	1-1	0-3	0-2	n/a	3-5	3-6	0-0	
Kingsley United	5-5	6-1	0-8	2-6	2-1	4-2	S	4-0	0-1	0-1	2-3	1-6	2-4	1-2	4-4	3-2
Liverp'l NALGO	0-3	1-1	2-9	0-0	2-2	8-4	1-2	I	0-3	1-5	1-0	0-2	1-6	1-2	6-2	1-0
Mossley Hill Ath.	2-1	6-1	2-3	4-2	0-5	1-3	0-3	3-0	O	3-2	1-2	0-3	4-0	5-3	0-0	2-2
Page Celtic	2-2	5-0	4-0	3-1	4-0	1-0	0-3	3-2	3-2	N	7-1	0-0	1-1	3-2	3-3	5-0
Quarry Bank OB	0-1	0-0	3-4	1-0	5-4	1-4	3-1	3-1	0-9	0-2		0-3	0-2	0-4	1-3	4-3
South Liverpool	5-1	12-0	4-1	3-0	1-0	10-0	3-1	1-0	2-2	3-2	0-2	O	3-2	6-2	6-0	2-2
St Ambrose	4-2	2-2	1-1	6-2	n/a	3-0	n/a	1-1	2-0	2-4	n/a	1-0	N	4-0	n/a	2-2
Stoneycroft	4-3	3-2	2-3	4-1	3-0	2-0	3-1	1-1	3-3	1-4	2-3	0-3	1-2	E	2-3	W-L
Vision	2-1	5-4	5-2	1-0	1-1	3-2	7-3	3-3	0-4	4-2	3-1	0-5	0-1	3-5		2-4
Warbreck	3-0	4-3	2-6	2-0	1-3	2-1	0-0	2-0	1-1	2-5	5-4	1-5	1-3	2-4	3-1	

Division One		P	W	D	L	F	A	Pts
South Liverpool		28	23	2	3	103		71
BRNESC		28	21	3	4	102	39	66
Page Celtic		28	20	4	4	79	33	64
Mossley Hill Athletic		28	15	6	7	70	35	51
Vision	-3	28	14	6	8	75	77	45
Stoneycroft	-9	28	14	4	10	70	62	37
Cheshire Lines		28	10	5	13	52	46	35
Warbreck	-3	28	10	5	13	53	64	32
Copperas Hill		28	8	5	15	44	61	29
Liverpool NALGO		28	8	5	15	44	65	29
Quarry Bank OB	-3	28	10	1	17	47	77	28
Kingsley United	-7	28	8	4	16	54	77	21
Aigburth P. Hall	-18	28	10	6	12	66	77	18
Hill Athletic	-3	28	4	5	19	41	102	14
Alsop Old Boys	-3	28	3	5	21	44	106	8

St Ambrose – record expunged

ROY WADE CUP

FIRST ROUND
Hill Athletic 2 Stoneycroft 3
Kingsley United 4 Cheshire Lines 6
Mossley Hill Athletic 7 Liverpool NALGO 1
Page Celtic 3 Copperas Hill 0
(at Copperas Hill)
Quarry Bank Old Boys 2 BRNESC 5
St Ambrose 0 South Liverpool 4
Vision 5 Alsop Old Boys 1
Warbreck 4 Aigburth People's Hall 7
aet

QUARTER-FINALS
BRNESC 4 Page Celtic 3 *aet*
Cheshire Lines 0 Mossley Hill Athletic 4
South Liverpool 5 Stoneycroft 3
Vision 2 Aigburth People's Hall 4

SEMI-FINALS
BRNESC 3 Aigburth People's Hall 4 *aet*
Mossley Hill Athletic 1 South Liverpool 1 *aet (4-3p)*
(at South Liverpool)

FINAL
(May 16th at LCFA, Walton Hall Avenue)
Aigburth People's Hall 3
Mossley Hill Athletic 1

PETER COYNE / GEORGE MAHON CUP
(All teams in league)

FIRST ROUND
Aigburth People's Hall (w/o) v Old Holts (scr.)
Alsop Old Boys 3 Copperas Hill 6 *aet*
Blueline 5 Rockville Wallasey 2
Edge Hill BCOB 0 **Cheshire Lines** 2
Essemmay Old Boys 0 **Sacre Coeur FP** 1
Finn Harps 6 Eli Lilly 5
Hill Athletic 1 Quarry Bank Old Boys 0
Kingsley United 5 Lydiate Weld 1
Liobians 2 **Albany Athletic** 4
Liverpool NALGO 4 Leyfield 2
Mossley Hill Athletic 4 BRNESC 3
Redgate Rovers 2 Jubilee Triangle 0
REMYCA United 1 **St Aloysius** 4
South Liverpool 2 **Rolls Royce** 3 *aet*
Stoneycroft 1 **St Ambrose** 2 *aet*
Vision 2 **Page Celtic** 5
Warbreck 7 Leisure Sports Orchard 0

SECOND ROUND
Birchfield 1 **Aigburth People's Hall** 2
Blueline 1 **South Sefton Borough** 3
Collegiate Old Boys 3 Hill Athletic 0
Copperas Hill 4 **Albany Athletic** 4 *aet (2-3p)*
Ford Motors 9 Finn Harps 1
Lucas Sports 0 **Croxteth Red Rum** 3
Mackets 5 Penlake 1, NELTC 1 **Speke** 2
Old Xaverians 2 Rolls Royce 0
Page Celtic 0 **Mossley Hill Athletic** 3
Redgate Rovers 5 Liverpool NALGO 2
Roma 1 **East Villa** 4
Sacre Coeur Former Pupil 1 **Cheshire Lines** 3
St Dominics 7 Warbreck 0
Waterloo Dock 3 St Aloysius 1

THIRD ROUND
Mackets 1 **East Villa** 4 *(at East Villa)*

Mossley Hill 1 Collegiate Old Boys 1 *aet (4-3p)*
Old Xaverians 1 Aigburth People's Hall 0
Redgate Rovers 0 **Albany Athletic** 1 *(at Albany)*
Speke 3 South Sefton Borough 2
St Ambrose 3 Cheshire Lines 1
St Dominics 4 Croxteth Red Rum 0
Waterloo Dock 3 Ford Motors 2

QUARTER-FINALS
Albany Athletic 2 Mossley Hill Athletic 1
East Villa 4 St Ambrose 2
Speke 1 **St Dominics** 3
Waterloo Dock 4 Old Xaverians 1

SEMI-FINALS
East Villa 6 Albany Athletic 2
Waterloo Dock 3 St Dominics 0 *aet*

FINAL
(May 18th at LCFA, Walton Hall Avenue)
East Villa 1 Waterloo Dock 1 *aet (3-2p)*

LIVERPOOL COUNTY PREMIER LEAGUE DIVISION ONE CONSTITUTION 2007-08

AIGBURTH PEOPLE'S HALL....... MYA Jeffreys Humble, Long Lane, Walton, Liverpool L9 9AQ............................None
ALBANY ATHLETIC....................Millbank College, Bankfield Road, Liverpool L13 0BQ............................None
ALDER....................Alder Road Sports Club, Alder Road, West Derby, Liverpool L12 2BA............................None
ANGUS VILLAGE....................Lower Breck Road Playing Flds, Lower Breck Road, Liverpool L6 0AQ............................None
CHESHIRE LINES....................Southmead Road, Allerton, Liverpool L19 5NB............................0151 427 7176
COLLEGIATE OLD BOYS......Holly Lodge Playing Fields, Mill Lane, West Derby, Liverpool L13 0DQ............................None
COPPERAS HILL....................Breckside Park, Liverpool............................None
KINGSLEY UNITED....................Edinburgh Park, Townsend Lane, Liverpool L6 0BB............................0151 263 5267
MACKETS GRENADIER....................Great Lakes, Lower Road, Halebank, Widnes WA8 8NT............................None
NORTH SEFTON....................Litherland Park Sports Centre, Liverpool L21 7LA............................0151 288 6288
PAGE CELTIC....................King George V Sports Complex, Long View Lane, Huyton, Liverpool L36 7UN............................0151 443 5712
QUARRY BANK OLD BOYS....................Greenhill Road, Liverpool............................None
REMYCA UNITED....................Playfootball.com, Drummond Road, Thornton L20 6DX............................None
STONEYCROFT....................Maiden Lane Playing Fields, Maiden Lane, Liverpool L13 9AN............................None
TELECOMS....................Litherland Park Sports Centre, Liverpool L21 7LA............................None
WARBRECK....................Playfootball.com, Drummond Road, Thornton L20 6DX............................None
IN: Albany Athletic (P), Collegiate Old Boys (R), Mackets Grenadier (formerly Mackets) (R), REMYCA Utd (P), Telecoms (formerly Rolls Royce) (P)
OUT: Alsop Old Boys (W), BRNESC (P), Mossley Hill Athletic (S – West Cheshire League Division Three), South Liverpool (P), St Ambrose (WS)
Hill Athletic become North Sefton, Liverpool NALGO become Alder, Vision become Angus Village

	Albany Athletic	Blueline	Edge Hill BCOB	Eli Lilly	Essemay Old Boys	Finn Harps	Jubilee Triangle	Leisure Sports Orchard	Leyfield	Liobians	Lydiate Weld	Old Holts	REMYCA United	Redgate Rovers	Rockville Wallesey	Rolls Royce	Sacre Coeur Former P.
Albany Athletic		3-1	3-1	5-1	2-0	2-1	9-0	2-0	2-0	2-2	4-3	3-2	3-2	3-0	3-1	3-0	3-1
Blueline	1-3		4-4	2-2	2-2	4-1	4-2	5-0	1-4	3-1	0-5	4-0	0-3	3-1	0-1	2-2	1-5
Edge Hill BCOB	0m0	0-0	*D*	3-2	3-2	1-1	7-1	1-0	2-1	1-1	2-3	1-1	3-3	6-3	0-1	5-1	5-0
Eli Lilly	3-1	7-2	1-3	*I*	2-3	3-1	6-0	4-1	7-2	0-1	5-3	2-0	0-1	1-1	2-2	0-1	2-1
Essemay Old Boys	0-0	0-2	0-1	0-1	*V*	1-2	6-0	2-1	0-2	4-1	1-2	0-0	2-5	1-4	2-1	3-3	4-2
Finn Harps	1-2	2-3	1-7	0-2	2-2	*I*	3-0	3-1	0-2	3-4	3-7	3-3	3-5	0-1	2-4	0-2	0-3
Jubilee Triangle	0-4	1-4	0-6	0-2	1-3	3-0	*S*	1-1	2-3	0-7	2-2	1-2	0-6	1-4	3-3	0-6	0-4
Leisure Sports Orchard	0-4	2-5	2-3	1-7	1-3	1-2	1-3	*I*	3-2	1-5	2-3	0-1	2-4	1-0	2-1	2-5	2-5
Leyfield	4-2	1-2	2-1	1-1	3-4	6-2	7-1	5-3	*O*	4-3	W-L	1-2	4-0	6-0	0-2	2-3	2-3
Liobians	1-1	1-2	0-2	5-1	2-2	6-3	2-0	1-1	1-1	*N*	3-2	5-2	0-4	5-0	4-1	1-1	3-2
Lydiate Weld	0-2	2-1	2-1	2-2	1-2	2-1	5-4	4-1	2-4	2-2		5-4	2-4	8-3	3-2	0-4	0m0
Old Holts	2-4	5-5	2-3	1-3	1-1	2-4	1-2	0-0	0-1	3-2	5-2		1-9	2-1	6-1	1-2	L-W
REMYCA United	1-2	6-3	2-2	6-0	4-0	4-1	4-0	5-1	0-0	3-1	5-2	6-1	*T*	0-9	2-3	3-2	3-1
Redgate Rovers	1-1	2-2	1-1	0-5	2-0	0-4	1-1	2-1	1-3	1-2	3-6	3-3	1-6	*W*	0-1	2-3	1-3
Rockville Wallesey	1-3	2-4	1-5	3-0	2-1	0-3	3-1	1-2	0-3	1-2	0-3	1-2	0-1	3-2	*O*	0-2	2-4
Rolls Royce	2-4	4-2	2-1	6-2	2-0	2-0	9-1	4-0	3-2	4-0	2-1	3-2	2-3	5-2	4-0		2-0
Sacre Coeur Former Pupils	0-1	4-2	2-5	3-4	4-5	5-3	3-1	4-1	2-3	3-3	4-2	2-4	L-W	5-0	5-3	2-3	

Division Two		P	W	D	L	F	A	Pts
REMYCA United		32	27	2	3	120	41	83
Albany Athletic		32	25	5	2	86	32	80
Rolls Royce	-4	32	24	3	5	94	41	71
Edge Hill BCOB		32	19	8	5	88	43	65
Leyfield		32	18	3	11	79	53	57
Eli Lilly		32	16	5	11	80	61	53
Liobians		32	14	9	9	77	60	51
Blueline		32	13	7	12	76	78	46
Sacre Coeur F. Pupils	-3	32	15	2	15	82	70	44
Lydiate Weld	-6	32	14	5	13	84	79	41
Essemay Old Boys		32	11	7	14	56	61	40
Old Holts	-7	32	9	6	17	61	80	26
Rockville Wallesey		32	7	2	23	43	92	23
Finn Harps	-3	32	7	3	22	55	90	21
Redgate Rovers	-6	32	6	6	20	41	86	18
Leisure Sports Orchard	-3	32	4	3	25	37	97	12
Jubilee Triangle	-3	32	3	4	25	32	127	10

LORD WAVERTREE CUP

FIRST ROUND
Leisure Sports Orchard 2 **REMYCA United** 3
SECOND ROUND
Albany Athletic 1 **REMYCA United** 3
Blueline 0 **Liobians** 3
Edge Hill BCOB 14 Jubilee Triangle 1
Essemay Old Boys 6 Redgate Rovers 2
Finn Harps 4 Eli Lilly 3
Rockville Wallasey 1 **Lydiate Weld** 1 *aet* (1-3p)
(at Lydiate Weld)
Rolls Royce 2 Leyfield 1
Sacre Coeur FP 4 Old Holts 4 *aet* (4-1p) *(at Old Holts)*
QUARTER-FINALS
Essemay Old Boys 1 **Sacre Coeur FP** 1 *aet* (3-4p)
Lydiate Weld 3 Finn Harps 1
REMYCA United 3 **Edge Hill BCOB** 4
Rolls Royce 4 Liobians 3
SEMI-FINALS
Edge Hill BCOB 7 Rolls Royce 1
Sacre Coeur Former Pupils 1 Lydiate Weld 0
FINAL
(May 8th at Civil Service, Thornton)
Edge Hill BCOB 3 Sacre Coeur Former Pupils 2

WWW.NLNEWSDESK.CO.UK

LIVERPOOL COUNTY PREMIER LEAGUE DIVISION TWO CONSTITUTION 2007-08

ACTIVE SEFTON . . . . Litherland Sports Park, Moss Lane, Litherland, Liverpool L21 7LE 0151 288 6288
BANKFIELD OLD BOYS . . . . Lower Breck Road, Anfield, Liverpool L6 4BZ. . . . . None
BLUELINE. . . . . Buckley Hill Playing Fields, Buckley Hill Lane, Netherton, Bootle L29 1YB. . . . . None
EDGE HILL BCOB . . . . Simpson Ground, Hillfoot Road, Liverpool L25 0NB. 0151 486 3166
ELI LILLY . . . . Thomas Lane Playing Fields, Thomas Lane, Liverpool L14 5NR . . . . None
ESSEMAY OLD BOYS . . . . Jericho Lane Recreation Playing Field, Jericho Lane, Liverpool L17 5AR . . . . None
FINN HARPS . . . . Thomas Lane Playing Fields, Thomas Lane, Liverpool L14 5NR . . . . None
JUBILEE TRIANGLE . . . . Buckley Hill Playing Fields, Buckley Hill Lane, Netherton, Bootle L29 1YB. . . . . None
LEISURE SPORTS ORCHARD . . . . . Clarence House School, West Lane, Formby, Liverpool L37 7AZ. . . . . None
LEYFIELD. . . . . Thomas Lane Playing Fields, Thomas Lane, Liverpool . . . . None
LIOBIANS . . . . Mersey Road, Aigburth, Liverpool L17 6AG. . . . . None
LYDIATE WELD. . . . . Sandy Lane Playing Fields, Sandy Lane, Lydiate, Liverpool L31 2LB . . . . None
OLD HOLTS. . . . . Simpson Ground, Hillfoot Road, Liverpool L25 0ND. 0151 486 3166
ROCKVILLE WALLESEY . . . . Belvidere Recreation Ground, Belvidere Road, Liscard, Wallesey CH45 4RY . . . . None
SACRE COEUR FORMER PUPILS . . . . Playfootball.com, Drummond Road, Thornton L20 6DX. . . . . None

IN: Active Sefton (N), Bankfield Old Boys (P – Liverpool Old Boys League Division One)
OUT: Albany Athletic (P), REMYCA United (P), Redgate Rovers (W), Telecoms (formerly Rolls Royce) (P)

MANCHESTER LEAGUE

	AFC Blackley	Atherton T.	Avro	Breightmet	Dukinfield	E. M'chester	Gregorians	Hindsford	Hollinwood	Irlam	Leigh Athletic	Monton Arms	Prestwich H.	Rochdale SH	Royton Town	Springhead	Stockport G.	Whitworth V.	Wythenshawe
AFC Blackley		3-2	2-0	1-1	5-2	1-0	2-3	2-0	1-1	4-1	3-0	2-1	2-4	7-2	4-5	2-2	2-2	4-0	2-1
Atherton Town	1-2	P	3-1	2-2	2-0	0-1	2-0	2-2	2-4	0-3	3-0	2-1	1-2	2-2	3-1	2-1	0-1	2-2	0-0
Avro	1-1	4-3	R	4-1	1-2	0-2	1-1	2-1	2-5	1-2	5-0	3-0	1-3	1-2	2-4	4-0	2-1	2-3	2-0
Breightmet United	0-3	1-2	1-2	E	3-4	2-2	3-0	2-0	2-2	2-1	3-3	2-0	2-0	1-2	4-2	2-3	2-3	3-1	2-3
Dukinfield Town	2-2	0-3	3-1	2-1	M	0-2	0-0	5-1	4-1	0-4	1-1	5-3	0-4	4-3	1-3	0-2	0-1	2-1	2-3
East Manchester	0-1	3-2	0-0	3-0	3-0	I	1-2	1-2	2-1	W-L	1-1	4-1	0-1	2-5	2-0	4-1	2-2	3-3	1-2
Gregorians	1-0	1-2	3-1	2-4	2-6	0-1	E	4-5	4-1	2-0	0-5	1-2	0-0	3-3	0-1	0-2	2-1	0-2	0-1
Hindsford	1-3	1-1	3-0	3-1	3-3	3-2	1-1	R	4-2	0-1	4-4	4-2	0-3	2-0	3-5	3-1	1-2	0-1	1-2
Hollinwood	4-4	0-5	3-4	4-3	6-2	0-4	3-2	4-2		3-3	2-5	0-3	1-5	6-2	3-1	0-2	5-2	4-2	1-1
Irlam	3-0	0-2	6-1	0-1	4-0	2-2	5-0	1-1	0-1		3-2	2-1	1-4	4-3	5-0	3-0	0-1	2-1	1-1
Leigh Athletic	3-1	2-2	5-0	2-1	3-0	2-3	1-2	0-3	5-1	2-2	D	2-1	1-2	2-3	1-0	5-3	3-2	2-2	2-2
Monton Amateurs	3-2	2-1	0-2	1-1	1-0	2-1	0-1	1-5	4-1	2-2	1-4	I	1-1	0-1	4-0	0-0	1-2	0-0	1-0
Prestwich Heys	1-1	2-1	1-0	2-1	1-1	4-0	3-2	1-0	2-1	4-0	2-2	4-0	V	4-1	2-0	3-0	3-0	1-1	4-0
Rochdale Sacred Heart	1-4	1-1	2-2	2-1	2-2	2-1	1-1	2-0	4-1	2-3	2-2	2-1	1-2	I	1-0	4-3	2-3	1-4	2-2
Royton Town	1-2	0-1	2-0	2-2	2-1	1-2	2-3	0-1	3-3	1-2	3-2	3-3	1-3	3-1	S	3-4	2-1	0-2	0-5
Springhead	1-2	3-3	2-3	0-0	6-1	0-3	0-2	0-1	4-5	0-0	1-1	2-1	0-2	3-0	2-2	I	2-4	2-1	0-1
Stockport Georgians	1-0	1-2	1-0	2-0	4-4	3-0	2-2	3-0	2-2	3-0	1-1	1-0	0-0	2-2	1-1	1-1	O	1-0	0-1
Whitworth Valley	0-1	0-1	5-4	0-1	4-0	0-3	2-1	1-2	1-2	1-0	4-0	4-0	3-0	2-2	1-1	2-2	1-1	N	0-0
Wythenshawe Amateur	6-2	1-3	4-1	3-2	5-1	4-2	2-4	2-1	2-0	3-1	0-1	2-2	2-2	3-1	1-4	0-1	2-1	0-5	

Premier Division		P	W	D	L	F	A	Pts
Prestwich Heys		36	26	8	2	82	29	86
AFC Blackley		36	19	8	9	80	57	65
Wythenshawe Amateurs		36	18	9	9	68	55	63
Stockport Georgians		36	16	11	9	59	48	59
Irlam		36	17	7	12	69	52	58
Atherton Town		36	16	9	11	66	50	57
East Manchester		36	17	6	13	63	50	57
Whitworth Valley		36	13	10	13	61	50	49
Hollinwood		36	13	7	16	82	98	46
Rochdale Sacred Heart		36	12	10	14	69	84	46
Leigh Athletic	-6	36	13	12	11	79	66	45
Gregorians		36	12	7	17	52	68	43
Springhead		36	10	10	16	57	69	40
Hindsford	-6	36	13	6	17	63	68	39
Royton Town		36	11	6	19	59	78	39
Breightmet United		36	10	8	18	60	68	38
Dukinfield Town		36	10	7	19	60	93	37
Monton Amateurs		36	10	7	19	50	66	37
Avro		36	10	4	22	53	83	34

GILGRYST CUP

PRELIMINARY ROUND
AFC Blackley 4 Springhead 3
Gregorians 1 **Dukinfield Town** 3
Windsford 1 **Prestwich Heys** 2
FIRST ROUND
Atherton Town 3 AFC Blackley 1
Dukinfield Town 2 **Avro** 3 *aet*
Irlam 2 Breightmet United 1
Prestwich Heys 1 Monton Amateurs 0
Rochdale Sacred Heart 1 **East Manchester** 2
Royton Town 3 Hollinwood 2
Whitworth Valley 3 Stockport Georgians 0
Wythenshawe Amateurs 1 **Leigh Athletic** 4
QUARTER-FINALS
East Manchester 2 **Atherton Town** 3
Irlam 4 Whitworth Valley 1
Prestwich Heys 0 **Leigh Athletic** 3
Royton Town 2 **Avro** 4
SEMI-FINALS
Atherton Town 3 Leigh Athletic 0
Avro 1 Irlam 0
FINAL
(May 9th at Trafford)
Atherton Town 2 Avro 1

MANCHESTER LEAGUE PREMIER DIVISION CONSTITUTION 2007-08
AFC BLACKLEY . . . . White House Social Club, Middleton Road, Crumpsall M8 4JZ . . . . None
ATHERTON TOWN . . . . Howe Bridge Sports Centre, Leigh Road, Atherton M46 0PJ 01942 884882
BREIGHTMET UNITED . . . . Moss Park, Bury Road, Breightmet, Bolton BL2 6QB 01204 533930
EAST MANCHESTER . . . . Longsight Sports & Social, Kirkmanshulme Lane, Gorton M12 4WB 0161 224 3213
GREGORIANS . . . . MCFC, Platt Lane Complex, Yew Tree Road, Fallowfield M14 7UU . . . . None
HINDSFORD . . . . Squires Lane, Tyldesley M29 8JH . . . . None
HOLLINWOOD . . . . Lime Lane, Hollinwood, Oldham OL8 3TB 0161 681 3385
IRLAM . . . . Silver Street, Irlam M44 6JL . . . . None
LEIGH ATHLETIC . . . . Leigh Harriers AC, Madley Park, Charles Street, Leigh WN7 1BG 01942 673500
PENNINGTON . . . . Jubilee Park, Leigh Road, Atherton M46 0RN . . . . None
PRESTWICH HEYS . . . . Sandgate Road, Prestwich Heys M45 6WG 0161 773 8888
ROCHDALE SACRED HEART . . . . Fox Park, Belfield Mill Lane, Rochdale OL16 2UB . . . . None
ROYTON TOWN . . . . Crompton Cricket Club Complex, Glebe Street, Shaw, Oldham OL2 7SF 01706 847421
SPRINGHEAD . . . . St John Street, Lees, Oldham OL4 4DB 0161 627 0260
STOCKPORT GEORGIANS . . . . Cromley Road, Woodsmoor, Stockport SK6 8BP 0161 483 6581
WALSHAW SPORTS CLUB . . . . Walshaw Sports Club, Sycamore Road, Tottington, Bury BL8 3EG 01204 882448
WHITWORTH VALLEY . . . . Rawston Street Stadium, Whitworth, Rochdale OL12 8BA . . . . None
WIGAN ROBIN PARK . . . . Robin Park, Newton (adj Wigan Athletic FC), Wigan WN5 0UZ . . . . None
WYTHENSHAWE AMATEUR . . . . Longley Lane, Northenden, Wythenshawe M22 4LA 0161 998 7268
IN: Pennington (P), Walshaw Sports (P), Wigan Robin Park (P)
OUT: Avro (R), Dukinfield Town (R), Monton Amateurs (R)

	Chapel Town	Elton Vale	Fives Athletic	Heywood St James	Manchester Juniors	Manchester Titans	Milton	Pennington	Salford Victoria	Stand Athletic	Tintwistle Villa	Walshaw Sports	West Didsbury & C.	Wigan Robin Park	Wilmslow Albion	Wythenshawe Town
Chapel Town	W-L	0-2	1-5	0-1	2-2	7-0	3-1	1-0	0-2	1-7	0-5	1-2	2-0	1-2		
Elton Vale	4-3		1-1	4-3	1-1	7-1	9-0	1-2	3-3	2-0	3-0	1-2	3-1	1-1	9-0	1-3
Fives Athletic	1-1	1-2	D	2-4	1-1	W-L	4-0	1-2	1-2	3-1	1-1	1-3	1-3	3-5	W-L	3-2
Heywood St Jms	1-4	0-5	9-3	I	2-4	W-L	11-3	4-5	4-1	3-3	4-2	2-3	6-3	1-3	2-3	7-2
Manchester Jnrs	4-0	3-2	2-2	3-1	V	4-0	3-0	2-4	4-4	3-2	0-0	1-1	2-3	1-0	2-1	1-3
Manchester Titans	3-5	1-7	1-1	W-L	0-1	I	2-6	W-L	0-7	2-1	1-3	W-L	W-L	0-4	1-4	2-3
Milton	2-7	0-5	2-3	1-3	1-5	W-L	S	2-3	2-2	1-4	0-5	1-6	0-2	0-2	4-1	1-8
Pennington	4-1	4-1	0-0	1-1	2-1	6-1		I	3-3	3-0	2-0	0-2	0-0	2-1	6-2	5-0
Salford Victoria	0-3	4-3	3-3	4-0	0-0	W-L	4-1	3-2	O	3-4	1-6	0-4	6-3	2-3	6-5	0-1
Stand Athletic	2-3	1-4	1-2	2-3	0-5	W-L	3-1	3-1	4-5	N	2-5	1-5	2-3	0-5	2-2	1-10
Tintwistle Villa	1-5	1-5	3-1	W-L	2-1	W-L	1-0	0-2	1-2	3-1		1-1	2-3	3-3	5-0	2-0
Walshaw Sports	1-0	4-0	3-1	8-1	2-1	3-0	8-1	3-2	3-3	6-0	4-0	O	6-1	2-2	8-0	
W. Didsb'y & C.	2-4	1-2	2-0	4-2	0-1	W-L	5-1	0-1	0-0	2-1	0-1	0-4	N	3-4	2-2	1-6
Wigan Robin Pk	3-0	2-1	4-1	1-2	0-0	W-L	4-1	2-0	2-1	1-1	6-0	2-2	7-1	E	7-1	6-3
Wilmslow Albion	0-6	0-8	0-7	0-3	1-2	3-4	7-1	0-9	0-1	1-7	1-2	1-4	1-5	1-7		3-0
Wythenshawe T.	2-1	1-2	3-4	4-2	2-0	W-L	2-0	1-2	0-1	0-1	2-3	2-0	2-1	1-3	4-1	

Division One

Division One	P	W	D	L	F	A	Pts
Walshaw Sports	30	24	5	1	109	28	77
Wigan Robin Park	30	21	6	3	92	35	69
Pennington	30	20	4	6	73	38	64
Elton Vale	30	17	4	9	97	44	55
Manchester Juniors	30	15	8	7	39	37	53
Tintwistle Villa	30	16	4	10	55	51	52
Wythenshawe Town	30	16	0	14	69	63	48
Salford Victoria	30	13	8	9	72	68	47
Heywood St James	30	14	2	14	86	79	44
Chapel Town	30	14	2	14	65	59	44
West Didsbury & Chorlton	30	13	3	14	56	67	42
Fives Athletic	30	10	8	12	54	61	38
Stand Athletic	30	7	3	20	50	88	24
Wilmslow Albion	30	4	2	24	43	122	14
Milton	30	3	1	26	33	132	10
Manchester Titans	30	2	2	26	20	61	8

MURRAY SHIELD

FIRST ROUND
Chapel Town 0 **Salford Victoria** 1
Elton Vale 9 Milton 2
Fives Athletic 5 Wythenshawe Town 5 *aet* (4-2p)
Manchester Juniors 4 Stand Athletic 1
Manchester Titans 1 **West Didsbury & Chorlton** 4
Pennington 3 Heywood St James 1
Wigan Robin Park 1 **Tintwistle Villa** 2
Wilmslow Albion 1 **Walshaw Sports** 3

QUARTER-FINALS
Elton Vale 7 Salford Victoria 1
Manchester Juniors 1 **Pennington** 2
Tintwistle Villa 0 **Fives Athletic** 3
West Didsbury/Chorlton 1 **Walshaw** 2

SEMI-FINALS
Elton Vale 2 Fives Athletic 1
Pennington 2 Walshaw SC 2 *aet* (3-4p)

FINAL
(April 28th at Wigan Robin Park)
Walshaw Sports 5 Elton Vale 0

OPEN TROPHY

FINAL
(May 7th at West Didsbury & Chorlton)
Prestwich Hey Res. 2 Leigh Athletic Res. 1

LEAGUE CUP

FINAL
(May 12th at Salford Victoria)
Salford Victoria 'B' 0 **Irlam Res.** 2

MANCHESTER LEAGUE DIVISION ONE CONSTITUTION 2007-08

AVRO . . . . Lancaster Club, Broadway, Failsworth, Oldham M35 0DX 0161 681 3083
CHAPEL TOWN . . . . Rowton Ground, Willow Drive, Chapel-en-le-Frith, High Peak SK23 0ND . . . . None
DUKINFIELD TOWN . . . . Blocksages Playing Fields, Birch Lane, Dukinfield SK16 5AP 0161 343 4529
ELTON VALE . . . . Elton Vale Road, Bury BL8 2RZ 0161 762 0666
FIVES ATHLETIC . . . . Harriet Street, Walkden, Worsley M28 3QA . . . . None
HEYWOOD ST JAMES . . . . Phoenix Ground, Heywood OL10 2JG . . . . None
MANCHESTER JUNIORS . . . . Ford Lane, Northenden M22 4NQ . . . . None
MILTON . . . . Springfield Park, Rochdale . . . . None
MONTON AMATEURS . . . . Granary Lane, Worsley M28 2PH . . . . None
OLD ALTRINCHAMIANS . . . . Crossford Bridge PF, Meadow Road, Sale 0161 767 9233
SALFORD VICTORIA . . . . Salford Sports Village, Littleton Road, Salford. . . . . None
STAND ATHLETIC . . . . The Elms, Whitefield, Manchester M45 7FD. . . . . None
WEST DIDSBURY . . . . Brookburn Road, Chorlton-cum-Hardy M21 8EH . . . . None
WILMSLOW ALBION . . . . Oakwood Farm, Styal Road, Wilmslow SK9 4HP 01625 535823
WYTHENSHAWE TOWN . . . . Ericstan Park, Timpson Road, Baguley M23 9LL 0161 998 5076

IN: Avro (R), Dukinfield Town (R), Monton Amateurs (R), Old Altrinchamians (P – Altrincham & District Amateur League Division Two)
OUT: Manchester Titans (W), Pennington (P), Salford AFC (WN), Tintwistle Villa (W), Walshaw Sports (P), Wigan Robin Park (P)
West Didsbury & Chorlton become West Didsbury

Division Two

Division Two		P	W	D	L	F	A	Pts
Prestwich Heys Res.		30	25	3	2	91	32	78
East Manchester Res.		30	22	4	4	102	32	70
Leigh Athletic Res.		30	20	4	6	70	37	64
Stock. Georgians Res.		30	17	3	10	70	54	54
Wythenshawe A. Res.		30	15	6	9	86	60	51
Gregorians Res.		30	15	4	11	68	53	49
AVRO Res.		30	14	5	11	72	63	47
Dukinfield T. Res.	-3	30	15	3	12	75	61	45
Elton Vale Res.		30	14	1	15	77	67	43
Springhead Res.		30	10	8	12	54	50	38
Monton Amats Res.		30	11	4	15	57	51	37
Walshaw SClub Res.		30	10	1	19	63	83	31
Breightmet Utd Res.		30	9	3	18	54	75	30
WD & Chorlton Res.		30	6	5	19	59	101	23
Hindsford Res.		30	6	3	21	44	89	21
Salford Victoria Res.		30	2	1	27	24	158	7

Division Three

Division Three		P	W	D	L	F	A	Pts
Whitworth Valley Res.		24	19	3	2	78	23	60
Irlam Res.		24	18	2	4	105	25	56
Gregorians 'A'		24	18	1	5	61	31	55
Wythenshawe T. Res.		24	16	4	4	96	36	52
Stand Athletic Res.		24	15	0	9	59	60	45
Rochdale S. Heart Res.		24	12	2	10	70	64	38
Atherton Town Res.		24	8	8	8	36	43	32
Leigh Athletic 'A'		24	9	2	13	43	53	29
Hollinwood Res.		24	6	2	16	39	70	20
Springhead 'A'		24	5	2	17	40	85	17
Dukinfield Town 'A'		24	4	3	17	42	70	15
WD & Chorlton 'A'		24	5	0	19	34	93	15
Milton Res.	-6	24	5	3	16	45	95	12

Division Four

Division Four	P	W	D	L	F	A	Pts
Chapel Town Res.	22	14	6	2	59	35	48
Royton Town Res.	22	14	3	5	51	32	45
Walshaw Sports 'A'	22	13	3	6	67	45	42
Stockport Georg. 'A'	22	11	6	5	48	25	39
Irlam 'A'	22	10	8	4	54	34	38
AFC Blackley Res.	22	9	3	10	48	51	30
Pennington Res.	22	7	3	12	44	50	24
Gregorians 'B'	22	7	2	13	37	63	23
Fives Athletic Res.	22	5	7	10	35	50	22
West Did. & C. 'B'	22	5	4	13	62	83	19
Wilmslow Alb. Res.	22	4	7	11	48	70	19
Salford Victoria 'B'	22	4	6	12	41	56	18

WWW.NLNEWSDESK.CO.UK

MID-CHESHIRE LEAGUE
(now CHESHIRE LEAGUE)

	Barnton	Crosfields	Daten	Gamesley	Garswood United	Greenalls Padgate St Oswalds	Knutsford	Linotype & Cheadle HN	Middlewich Town	Pilkington	Poynton	Rylands	Styal	Trafford Res.	Witton Albion Res.	Woodley Sports Res.
Barnton		2-1	2-0	4-2	4-3	1-1	0-3	1-2	0-2	1-1	3-2	3-2	2-0	2-2	0-0	4-1
Crosfields	1-1		3-0	2-3	1-0	0-1	0-1	0-1	0-2	0-2	3-2	1-0	0-0	4-1	2-1	0-1
Daten	1-3	0-0	D	0-2	0-3	3-6	1-3	2-3	1-5	3-4	3-0	1-2	4-1	0-1	3-1	1-4
Gamesley	3-1	0-1	1-0	I	3-0	1-1	1-3	2-2	3-4	5-0	5-0	1-1	3-1	1-1	1-1	1-1
Garswood United	2-1	2-0	2-0	1-1	V	0-1	0-2	2-0	1-3	2-0	3-4	1-3	0-2	0-1	1-1	1-2
Greenalls Padgate St Oswalds	2-1	1-1	2-0	4-2	1-2	I	1-0	3-1	3-1	2-2	3-2	4-1	1-3	2-0	1-1	5-1
Knutsford	1-1	1-0	1-0	2-1	3-1	3-1	S	2-1	0-2	1-3	3-2	0-2	0-2	3-0	2-0	2-0
Linotype & Cheadle HN	0-3	1-1	3-0	4-1	2-2	2-0	0-3	I	0-4	2-4	0-0	1-2	0-0	0-4	3-1	2-0
Middlewich Town	1-0	4-0	3-0	3-0	4-0	2-0	3-1	2-0	O	2-0	5-2	3-0	2-2	3-0	5-1	2-0
Pilkington	3-2	2-3	3-1	2-1	1-4	3-1	0-0	1-1	1-1	N	3-1	4-0	4-2	1-4	1-0	0-1
Poynton	1-1	3-2	2-0	3-1	1-1	0-2	0-3	1-5	0-2	1-1		1-4	1-4	1-4	1-0	0-1
Rylands	0-2	0-3	1-1	1-1	0-2	0-3	1-2	0-1	2-3	0-2	1-1	O	0-2	0-3	0-3	2-2
Styal	1-0	1-2	3-0	2-0	2-2	4-1	2-3	2-0	2-0	2-2	2-3	2-0	N	1-1	1-4	1-0
Trafford Res.	3-1	0-2	1-5	3-1	4-1	0-2	2-1	1-0	0-3	5-0	2-0	0-3	2-0	E	1-2	2-0
Witton Albion Res.	2-5	0-0	5-0	4-2	1-3	1-2	3-4	1-1	0-2	0-0	0-0	0-3	1-3	1-3		2-4
Woodley Sports Res.	1-0	3-5	3-0	3-0	3-1	0-4	2-4	1-3	0-3	3-5	1-1	2-2	2-0	1-0	2-0	

Division One		P	W	D	L	F	A	Pts
Middlewich Town		30	25	2	3	78	20	77
Knutsford		30	20	3	7	55	32	63
Greenalls P'gate St Oswalds		30	18	5	7	61	38	59
Styal		30	16	7	7	53	34	55
Pilkington		30	16	7	7	59	45	55
Trafford Res.		30	16	4	10	48	37	52
Crosfields		30	12	6	12	38	36	42
Woodley Sports Res.		30	12	6	12	48	54	42
Barnton		30	11	8	11	52	45	41
Linotype & Cheadle HN		30	11	6	13	41	47	39
Garswood United		30	10	5	15	43	51	35
Gamesley		30	9	6	15	53	57	33
Poynton		30	6	8	16	39	71	26
Witton Albion Res.		30	6	6	18	39	59	24
Rylands	-3	30	4	7	19	24	62	16
Daten		30	4	2	24	30	73	14

CHESHIRE (FORMERLY MID-CHESHIRE LEAGUE) DIVISION ONE CONSTITUTION 2007-08

BARNTON...................................... Townfield, Townfield Lane, Barnton, Northwich CW8 4LH .... None
CROSFIELDS.............. Crosfields Recreation Ground, Hood Lane, Warrington WA5 1ES............. 01925 411730
CURZON ASHTON RESERVES .. The Tameside Stadium, Richmond Street, Ashton-under-Lyne OL7 9HG 0161 330 6033
GAMESLEY .... Melandra Park, Melandra Castle Road, Gamesley, Glossop SK13 6UQ .... None
GARSWOOD UNITED .. The Wooders, Simms Lane End, Garswood Road, Garswood, Ashton-in-Makerfield WN4 0XF 01744 892258
GREENALLS PADGATE ST OSWALDS .... Walkers Club, Long Lane, Warrington WA2 8PU 01925 634971
KNUTSFORD............................. Manchester Road, Knutsford WA16 0NU... None
LINOTYPE & CHEADLE HN .. The Heath, Norbreck Avenue, Norbreck Avenue, Cheadle, Stockport SK8 2ET 0161 282 6574
MIDDLEWICH TOWN .... Seddon Street, Middlewich CW10 9DT.. 01606 835842
PILKINGTON.......................... Ruskin Drive, Dentons Green, St Helens WA10 6RP 01744 22893
POYNTON............................ London Road North, Poynton, Stockport SK12 1AG 01625 875765
RYLANDS .... Rylands Recreation Club, Gorsey Lane, Warrington WA2 7RZ 01925 625700
STALYBRIDGE CELTIC RESERVES ..... Bower Fold, Mottram Road, Stalybridge SK15 2RT 0161 338 2828/8443
STYAL................................ Altrincham Road, Styal, Wilmslow SK9 4JE 01625 529303
TRAFFORD RESERVES .... Shawe View, Pennybridge Lane, Flixton, Urmston M41 5DL 0161 747 1727/749 8217
WITTON ALBION RESERVES .... Moss Farm Leisure Complex, Moss Road, Winnington, Northwich 01606 783835
WOODLEY SPORTS RESERVES .... Ridgeway Road, Timperley, Altrincham WA15 7EY 0161 283 1376
IN: Curzon Ashton Reserves (P), Stalybridge Celtic Reserves (P)
OUT: Daten (R)

	Billinge	Broadheath Central	Club AZ	Congleton Town Res.	Crewe	Curzon Ashton Res.	Eagle Sports	Fearnhead	Golborne Sports	Lostock Gralam	Maine Road Res.	Malpas	Monk Sports	Stalybridge C. Res.	Tarporley Victoria	Warrington T. Res.	Whitchurch Alport
Billinge		2-1	0-4	5-2	1-5	2-2	0-2	2-7	0-0	2-0	1-0	2-1	0-0	2-4	0-3	0-3	1-2
Broadheath Central	4-0	D	5-1	5-0	2-3	2-2	1-3	n/a	1-3	2-0	5-5	2-2	5-2	1-3	6-0	0-0	3-0
Club AZ	1-0	0-3	I	3-1	1-3	5-4	4-2	3-0	1-0	3-0	1-1	6-0	0-1	2-1	3-0	2-0	1-0
Congleton Town Res.	2-1	1-2	2-2	V	2-3	0-3	0-0	6-2	1-0	1-2	1-3	2-5	2-4	0-1	1-0	1-3	1-4
Crewe	2-0	0-6	1-2	2-2	I	1-4	1-2	3-0	1-3	1-0	4-0	2-1	2-0	0-4	2-3	2-6	3-2
Curzon Ashton Res.	5-0	3-3	2-3	3-0	2-2	S	3-0	6-1	1-0	4-0	2-0	3-0	4-1	3-2	2-1	2-2	4-3
Eagle Sports	1-1	1-3	0-4	2-0	0-2	2-3	I	1-9	7-0	1-2	2-1	3-0	2-0	1-3	1-5	1-0	
Fearnhead	1-2	1-7	0-6	3-0	1-3	n/a	1-2	O	5-1	0-3	n/a	2-1	7-3	3-4	n/a	1-2	n/a
Golborne Sports	4-1	1-5	3-1	3-0	2-1	2-1	4-0	7-2	N	2-1	2-3	6-0	8-1	1-1	2-2	3-3	2-1
Lostock Gralam	4-2	1-1	0-1	1-5	1-3	2-1	3-1	n/a	2-2		2-2	2-3	3-0	2-3	2-2	2-1	0-1
Maine Road Res.	2-1	1-0	1-1	1-2	4-3	1-2	2-4	n/a	4-2	2-1		2-2	2-2	2-4	2-1	2-1	2-1
Malpas	3-3	2-3	1-2	3-3	1-1	0-3	2-3	2-0	2-9	1-1	2-2		2-1	0-5	3-3	1-3	0-1
Monk Sports	2-1	3-3	1-3	5-4	4-2	1-0	2-1	n/a	1-5	3-1	2-1	2-2		3-1	3-2	0-2	0-4
Stalyb'dge Celtic Res.	7-0	2-0	1-1	2-1	1-1	2-2	2-1	13-1	3-1	4-2	3-2	4-0		T	3-0		5-2
Tarporley Victoria	3-0	2-2	2-2	0-0	1-1	1-2	1-1	3-0	3-2	3-0	2-1	1-2	0-1	1-1	W	0-0	5-2
Warrington T. Res.	2-1	1-3	1-1	5-0	2-1	0-0	1-0	n/a	2-0	1-0	3-1	0-0	2-1	1-1	1-0	O	4-1
Whitchurch Alport	2-3	1-4	3-1	2-1	0-4	0-2	1-0	1-0	1-2	0-2	0-3	3-0	3-1	1-2	2-1	0-1	

Note – Fearnhead withdrew during the course of the season
Their results are shown above but are expunged from the league table

Division Two	P	W	D	L	F	A	Pts
Curzon Ashton Res.	30	18	7	5	74	38	61
Stalybridge Celtic Res.	30	18	7	5	74	38	61
Club AZ	30	18	6	6	62	39	60
Warrington Town Res.	30	16	8	6	58	32	56
Broadheath Central	30	15	8	7	83	45	53
Golborne Sports	30	16	5	9	83	45	53
Crewe	30	13	5	12	59	59	44
Monk Sports	30	13	4	13	48	70	43
Maine Road Res.	30	11	7	12	53	62	40
Eagle Sports	30	12	4	14	47	59	40
Tarporley Victoria	30	9	10	11	47	47	37
Whitchurch Alport	30	11	1	18	43	54	34
Lostock Gralam	30	6	6	18	34	63	24
Billinge	30	6	5	19	32	73	23
Malpas	30	4	10	16	45	81	22
Congleton Town Res.	30	5	5	20	38	75	20

Fearnhead – record expunged

CHAMPIONSHIP PLAY-OFF

(May 14th at Stalybridge Celtic)
Stalybridge Celtic Res. 2 Curzon Ashton Res. 2 *aet* (5-4p)

CHESHIRE (FORMERLY MID-CHESHIRE LEAGUE) DIVISION TWO CONSTITUTION 2007-08

BILLINGE . . . . John Eddleston Sports Ground, Rainford Road, Billinge WN5 7PF 07742 418591
BROADHEATH CENTRAL . . . . Silver Wings, Clay Lane, Timperley, Altrincham WA15 7AB 0161 980 7354/3658
CLUB AZ . . . . Mulberries Sports Centre, Astra Zeneca (off 34), Macclesfield SK10 4TF 01625 514040
CONGLETON TOWN RESERVES . . . Booth Street Ground, off Crescent Road, Congleton CW12 4DG 01260 274460
CREWE . . . . Cumberland Arena, Thomas Street, Crewe CW1 2BD 01270 537913
DATEN . . . . Culcheth Sports Club, Charnock Road, Culcheth, Warrington WA3 5SH 01925 763096
EAGLE SPORTS . . . . Eagle Sports Club, Thornton Road, Great Sankey, Warrington WA5 1RB 01925 632926
FC UNITED OF MANCHESTER RESERVES . . Abbey Hey FC, Goredale Ave., Gorton M18 7HD 0161 231 7147
GOLBORNE SPORTS . . . . Simpson Playing Fields, Stone Cross Road, Lowton WA3 2FL 01942 510161
GRAPPENHALL SPORTS . . . Grappenhall Sports Club, Stockton Lane, Grappenhall, Warrington WA4 3HQ . . . . None
LOSTOCK GRALAM . . . . The Park Stadium, Manchester Road, Lostock Gralam CW9 7PJ 01606 42148
MAINE ROAD RESERVES . . . Manchester FA Ground, Branthingham Road, Chorlton-cum-Hardy M21 0TT 0161 881 0299
MALPAS . . . . Malpas & District Sports Club, Oxheys, Wrexham Road, Malpas SY14 7EJ 01948 860662
MONK SPORTS . . . . Hillock Lane, Woolston, Warrington WA1 4QL 01925 812320
TARPORLEY VICTORIA . . . . Tattenhall Recreation Club, Field Lane, Tattenhall CH3 9QF 01829 770710
WARRINGTON TOWN RESERVES . . . . . Cantilever Park, Common Lane, Warrington WA4 2RS 01925 631932
WHITCHURCH ALPORT . . . . Yockings Park, Blackpark Road, Whitchurch SY13 1PG 01948 667415
IN: Daten (R), FC United of Manchester Reserves (N), Grappenhall Sports (P – Warrington & District League Division One)
OUT: Curzon Ashton Reserves (P), Fearnhead (WS), Stalybridge Celtic Reserves (P)

J B PARKER DIVISION ONE CUP

FIRST ROUND
Barnton 3 **Knutsford** 3 *aet* (3-4p)
Daten 1 **Styal** 2
Middlewich Town 3 Woodley Sports Res. 1
Pilkington 3 Crosfields 2
Poynton 0 **Greenalls Padgate St Oswalds** 1
Rylands 0 **Linotype & Cheadle HN** 2
Trafford Res. 3 **Gamesley** 5
Witton Albion Res. 0 **Garswood United** 1

QUARTER-FINALS
Gamesley 2 Knutsford 1

Garswood 0 **Middlewich** 1
Pilkington 4 Linotype & Cheadle HN 2
Styal 0 **Greenalls Padgate St Oswalds** 1

SEMI-FINALS
Middlewich Town 3 Greenalls Pad. St Oswalds 2
Pilkington 3 Gamesley 2

FINAL
(March 14th at Trafford)
Middlewich Town 3 Pilkington 0

DIVISION TWO CUP

PRELIMINARY ROUND
Curzon Ashton Res. 3 **Broadheath
Central** 6

FIRST ROUND
Broadheath Central 3 Crewe 0
Club AZ 2 Fearnhead 1
Congleton Town Res. 4 **Eagle Sports** 3
Golborne Sports 2 **Billinge** 3
Lostock Gralam 0 **Warrington Town Res.** 2
Maine Road Res. 5 Monk Sports 3
Malpas 3 Whitchurch Alport 1
Tarporley Victoria 1 **Stalybridge Celtic Res.** 2

QUARTER-FINALS
Billinge 3 Maine Road Res. 1
Broadheath Central 3 Congleton Town Res. 0
Malpas 0 **Warrington Town Res.** 1
Stalybridge Celtic Res. 3 Club AZ 1

SEMI-FINALS
Billinge 0 **Warrington Town Res.** 1
Stalybridge Celtic Res. 2 **Broadheath Central** 6

FINAL
(March 7th at Trafford)
Broadheath Central 2 Warrington Town Res. 0

PRESIDENT'S CUP
(First Round losers from Division One, Two and Reserve Cups)

PRELIMINARY ROUND
Crewe 1 Daten 1 *aet* (5-4p)
Crosfields 1 Garswood United Res. 0
Lostock Gralam 4 Styal Res. 3
Pilkington Res. 3 Poynton 2
Rylands 2 **Woodley Sports Res.** 4
Whitchurch Alport 2 Barnton 2
aet (6-5p)
Witton Res. 5 Eagle Sports Res. 0
FIRST ROUND
Crosfields Res. (Scr.) v **Pilkington Res.**
(w/o)

Eagle Sports 0 **Golborne Sports** 4
Fearnhead 0 **Greenalls Padgate St
Oswalds Res.** 2
Tarporley Victoria 1 Lostock Gralam 0
Trafford Res. 0 **Crosfields** 1
Whitchurch Alport 2 Crewe 1
Witton Albion Res. 2 Curzon Ashton
Res. 0
Woodley Sports Res. 2 Monk Sports 0
QUARTER-FINALS
Pilkington Res. 2 Golborne Sports 1
Tarporley Vics 1 **Crosfields** 1 *aet* (3-4p)

Whitchurch Alport 5 Greenalls Padgate
St Oswalds Res. 4
Woodley Sports Res. 2 Witton Albion
Res. 1
SEMI-FINALS
Whitchurch Alport 0 **Crosfields** 2
Woodley Sports Res. 1 Pilkington
Res. 0
FINAL
(May 5th at Trafford)
Crosfields 2 Woodley Sports Res. 0

Reserve Division	P	W	D	L	F	A	Pts
Golborne Sports Res.	24	15	3	6	54	21	48
Pilkington Res.	24	14	5	5	72	36	47
Middlewich Town Res.	24	12	6	6	69	36	42
Poynton Res.	24	11	8	5	38	25	41
Linotype/Cheadle HN Res.	24	11	7	6	47	32	40
Greenalls Padgate SO Res.	24	10	4	10	42	51	34
Daten Res.	24	10	3	11	52	50	33
Styal Res.	24	8	8	8	44	38	32
Garswood United Res.	24	8	5	11	34	41	29
Broadheath Central Res.	24	8	2	14	41	50	26
Gamesley Res.	24	7	4	13	36	50	25
Billinge Res.	24	6	4	14	28	75	22
Eagle Sports Res.	24	4	5	15	26	78	17

RESERVES CUP
FINAL
(April 4th at Trafford)
Poynton Res. 2 Golborne Sports Res. 1

MEMORIAL CUP
(Division One champions v J B Parker Cup holders)
(August 8th at Middlewich Town)
Middlewich Town 1 **Garswood United** 4

MID-WALES LEAGUE

	Aberystwyth Town Res.	Berriew	Caersws Res.	Carno	Four Crosses	Kerry	Knighton Town	Llanfyllin Town	Llanidloes Town	Llanrhaeadr	Newbridge	Newtown Res.	Presteigne St Andrews	The New Saints Res.	Tywyn & Bryncrug	UW Aberystwyth	Waterloo Rovers
Aberystwyth Town Res.		2-1	1-3	1-0	5-0	4-3	0-2	2-1	3-0	1-1	1-0	1-1	0-0	3-3	0-0	4-1	7-0
Berriew	3-2		0-0	4-0	3-1	1-1	3-1	4-0	2-0	0-0	2-3	2-0	0-1	0-0	2-1	0-1	
Caersws Res.	1-0	1-0		2-1	2-0	0-1	0-0	1-1	4-2	1-1	3-1	3-1	3-2	1-1	1-0	2-0	1-1
Carno	1-2	1-2	1-1		2-0	2-2	5-1	1-2	2-0	1-2	2-1	0-4	1-6	1-5	0-5	3-2	1-1
Four Crosses	1-0	1-1	0-2	2-1		2-0	4-4	1-1	5-0	0-1	1-4	2-4	2-1	0-3	1-2	0-2	
Kerry	5-1	1-1	1-2	1-0	0-1		2-0	3-4	0-0	0-0	1-0	0-1	1-2	1-2	2-3	1-2	2-2
Knighton Town	2-1	0-1	1-1	1-1	3-2	1-1		3-1	3-0	0-0	1-1	0-0	1-3	1-0	0-4	3-2	1-1
Llanfyllin Town	1-2	4-1	2-2	4-1	5-1	2-1	10-2		6-0	1-3	1-1	2-1	2-3	4-4	2-1	3-1	3-0
Llanidloes Town	0-7	2-1	0-3	1-2	4-4	0-3	1-0	2-3		0-6	2-0	0-6	1-4	0-6	0-4	0-4	4-2
Llanrhaeadr	2-3	4-4	0-2	5-1	2-4	2-1	1-2	1-1	4-1		5-1	2-2	1-1	0-2	2-3	3-3	3-1
Newbridge	2-4	0-1	1-1	5-0	2-0	1-0	3-0	3-5	5-2	3-1		1-0	0-1	0-3	0-1	3-1	5-2
Newtown Res.	1-3	3-2	1-1	2-0	4-0	2-2	3-1	0-1	4-0	2-2	0-2		1-1	1-1	3-0	4-2	6-3
Presteigne St Andrews	4-0	1-1	0-0	1-0	4-1	4-0	1-0	0-2	7-1	3-1	3-1	1-1		2-1	1-4	4-0	2-1
The New Saints Res.	4-1	1-0	1-2	3-0	5-1	4-2	4-0	1-1	1-1	3-3	2-0	2-1	0-1		3-1	1-2	1-1
Tywyn & Bryncrug	2-4	4-0	1-1	1-0	1-1	4-1	0-1	3-0	3-0	2-2	3-1	2-0	0-2	0-2		4-0	5-1
UW Aberystwyth	1-4	2-4	4-1	1-0	1-1	3-0	1-0	2-1	2-1	0-2	3-1	6-4	3-6	0-5	1-3		4-2
Waterloo Rovers	0-3	1-0	0-2	0-7	3-1	1-1	3-1	3-1	2-1	1-2	2-0	1-0	1-6	0-2	0-3	1-4	

	P	W	D	L	F	A	Pts
Presteigne St Andrews	32	22	6	4	80	33	72
Caersws Res.	32	18	12	2	50	25	66
Tywyn & Bryncrug	32	19	5	8	70	31	62
Aberystwyth T. Res.	32	18	5	9	72	46	59
The New Saints Res. -3	32	17	9	6	74	33	57
Llanfyllin Town	32	16	7	9	78	53	55
Newtown Res.	32	12	9	11	63	48	45
Llanrhaeadr	32	11	12	9	64	52	45
UW Aberystwyth	32	14	2	16	61	74	44
Berriew	32	11	10	11	45	40	43
Knighton Town	32	10	9	13	37	57	39
Newbridge	32	11	5	16	46	51	38
Waterloo Rovers	32	9	5	18	39	79	32
Four Crosses	32	8	6	18	44	71	30
Kerry	32	6	9	17	40	54	27
Carno	32	7	4	21	38	70	25
Llanidloes Town	32	4	3	25	26	110	15

LEAGUE CUP

FIRST ROUND
Kerry 0 **Berriew** 3
SECOND ROUND
Aberystwyth Town Res. 4 Knighton Town 0
Berriew 2 Tywyn & Bryncrug 1 *aet*
Carno 2 Waterloo Rovers 2 *aet* (4-3p)
Four Crosses 0 **Newbridge** 4
Llanidloes Town 0 **Caersws Res.** 1
Presteigne St Andrews 3 **Llanrhaeadr** 2
The New Saints Res. 2 Newtown Res. 1
UW Aberystwyth 5 Llanfyllin Town 2
QUARTER-FINAL
Carno 1 **Presteigne St Andrews** 3
Newbridge 0 **Aberystwyth Town Res.** 2
The New Saints Res. 0 **Caersws Res.** 1
UW Aberystwyth 4 Berriew 1
SEMI-FINALS
Aberystwyth Town Res. 3 UW Aberystwyth 1
Caersws Res. 1 Presteigne St Andrews 1 *aet* (4-2p)
FINAL
(May 16th at Rhayader Town)
Caersws Res. 2 Aberystwyth Town Res. 1

MID-WALES LEAGUE CONSTITUTION 2007-08

ABERYSTWYTH TOWN RESERVES.... Park Avenue, Maesgogerddan, Aberystwyth SY23 2EY 01970 617939
BERRIEW .... Recreation Ground, Berriew .... None
BOW STREET.......................... Rhydypennau Playing Field, Bow Street .... None
CAERSWS RESERVES............. Recreation Ground, Bridge Street, Caersws SY17 5DT 01686 688753
CARNO .... Recreation Ground, Carno .... None
FOUR CROSSES .... Foxen Manor, Four Crosses, Llanymynech .... None
KERRY .... Dolforgan Park, Glanmule, Kerry 01686 670637
KNIGHTON TOWN .... The Showground, Bryn-Y-Castell, Ludlow Road, Knighton LD7 1HP 01547 528999
LLANFYLLIN TOWN............................. High School, Llanfyllin .... None
LLANIDLOES TOWN .... Victoria Park, Victoria, Llanidloes.................................... 01686 412196
LLANRHAEADR .... The Recreation Park, Llanrhaeadr.. None
NEWBRIDGE .... Penbont Field, Newbridge-on-Wye. .... None
NEWTOWN RESERVES .... Latham Park, Park Lane, Newtown SY1 6XX 01686 623120/622666/626159
PRESTEIGNE ST ANDREWS .... Llanandras Park, Clatterbrune, Presteigne 01544 267838
THE NEW SAINTS RESERVES .... Recreation Park, Treflan, Llansantffraid SY22 6AE 01691 8281122
TYWYN & BRYNCRUG .... Cae Chwarae Bryncrug, (Bryncrug Recreation Ground), Bryncrug, Tywyn .... None
UW ABERYSTWYTH .... Vicarage Fields, Llanbadarn, Aberystwyth 01970 623036
WATERLOO ROVERS .... Maesydre Extension, Welshpool SY21 7SU .... None
N: Bow Street (P – Aberystwyth & District League Division One)

MIDDLESEX COUNTY LEAGUE

Note – Ealing withdrew during the course of the season. Their results are shown herein but are expunged from the league table

	Bedfont Sports	Bison	Brazilian Sports Club	Ealing	FC Deportivo Galicia	Kings Meadow	Marsh Rangers	Mauritius Sports (CMB)	Neasden Foundation	Parkfield Youth Old Boys	Southall	Spelthorne Sports	Sport London E Benfica	Walthamstow Avenue & P.	Willesden Constantine	Wraysbury
Bedfont Sports	P	1-3	2-3	2-1	4-0	7-0	1-0	5-2	3-4	5-0	4-0	2-3	0-1	5-1	5-1	5-1
Bison	3-6	R	3-4	n/a	4-1	3-1	1-3	3-4	0-8	4-2	5-4	1-1	1-3	1-3	0-2	2-2
Brazilian Sports Club	0-5	1-0	E	n/a	2-2	4-1	1-2	2-0	1-2	2-0	1-3	1-1	2-1	4-2	3-2	2-3
Ealing	n/a	2-1	n/a	M	L-W	0-2	1-0	1-4	n/a	0-1	n/a	n/a	n/a	n/a	n/a	0-5
FC Deportivo Galicia	1-7	2-2	0-2	4-0	I	0-3	1-3	1-0	1-3	0-0	2-2	0-3	0-0	1-1	1-2	2-4
Kings Meadow	2-2	4-1	0-1	n/a	3-1	E	3-0	2-2	2-5	2-2	1-1	2-2	1-3	2-0	2-0	2-1
Marsh Rangers	2-10	0-1	3-4	5-0	2-2	1-4	R	0-3	1-6	4-2	3-1	2-5	1-4	1-5	1-0	1-3
Mauritius Sports (CMB)	2-2	0-1	2-3	n/a	2-1	1-1	1-2		2-4	2-1	1-3	2-1	0-2	4-4	0-0	1-3
Neasden Foundation	2-2	4-1	2-0	n/a	1-1	4-1	3-3	5-0	D	1-1	L-W	0-2	3-3	W-L	3-1	2-3
Parkfield Youth Old Boys	3-3	4-1	2-0	n/a	2-3	2-1	4-0	5-1	2-3	I	1-1	2-1	1-1	0-1	2-0	3-3
Southall	L-W	2-1	1-2	2-1	3-2	4-2	L-W	1-0	1-9	2-1	V	3-2	0-2	L-W	1-1	W-L
Spelthorne Sports	0-2	2-0	0-0	4-1	1-0	1-2	1-1	1-2	1-0	1-4	3-1	I	1-3	0-3	1-1	3-1
Sport London E Benfica	4-2	3-1	2-1	2-1	4-0	0-0	5-2	W-L	1-1	3-1	4-1	1-5	S	2-1	2-0	4-0
Walthamstow Avenue & Pennant	1-5	4-2	0-0	n/a	0-3	0-0	2-2	1-1	0-0	1-1	4-0	0-0	0-0	I	1-3	1-0
Willesden Constantine	0-6	5-3	0-3	1-1	2-1	0-1	3-1	1-3	W-L	0-4	2-4	3-0	0-2	3-2	O	2-1
Wraysbury	1-7	0-0	3-2	n/a	4-1	6-4	3-0	8-4	3-4	3-4	5-1	2-0	1-3	1-3	W-L	N

Premier Division		P	W	D	L	F	A	Pts
Sport London E Benfica		28	19	6	3	67	30	63
Neasden Foundation		28	18	6	4	79	34	60
Bedfont Sports		28	17	4	7	104	41	55
Brazilian Sports Club		28	15	5	8	53	44	50
Parkfield Youth OB		28	11	8	9	59	48	41
Walthamstow A & P	-3	28	11	10	7	39	29	40
Wraysbury	-3	28	12	4	12	64	63	37
Spelthorne Sports		28	10	7	11	44	49	37
Kings Meadow		28	10	7	11	51	59	37
Will'den Constantine	-3	28	10	2	16	38	59	29
Southall	-9	28	11	4	13	39	55	28
Bison		28	7	4	17	48	76	25
Marsh Rangers		28	7	3	18	34	79	24
Mauritius (CMB)	-6	28	8	5	15	44	57	23
FC Deportivo Galicia		28	3	7	18	28	68	16

Ealing – record expunged

ALEC SMITH CUP

FIRST ROUND
Brazilian Sports Club 4 Parkfield Youth Old Boys 0
Kings Meadow 2 Marsh Rangers 0
Neasden Foundation 4 FC Deportivo Galicia 1
Southall 4 Bedfont Sports 0
Sport London E Benfica 0 **Spelthorne Sports** 2
Walthamstow Avenue & Pennant 0 **Mauritius Sports (CMB)** 3
Willesden Constantine 2 Bison 0
Wraysbury 7 Ealing 1
QUARTER-FINALS
Brazilian Sport Club 1 **Southall** 4 *aet*
Kings Meadow 0 **Neasden Foundation** 3
Spelthorne Sports 1 **Wraysbury** 2
Willesden Constantine 3 Mautitius Sports (CMB) 1
SEMI-FINALS
Neasden Foundation 4 **Wraysbury** 5 *aet*
Willesden Constantine 0 **Southall** 1
FINAL
(April 21st at Yeading)
Wraysbury (w/o) v Southall (scr.)

MIDDLESEX COUNY LEAGUE PREMIER DIVISION CONSTITUTION 2007-08

BARNET TOWN . . . . *t.b.a. – either Hemel hempstead Town or Haringey Borough FC* . . . . None
BEDFONT SPORTS . . . . Bedfont Sports Club, Hatton Road, Bedfont, Feltham TW14 9NP . . . . None
BETHNAL GREEN UNITED . . . . Meath Gardens, Smart Street, off Roman Road, Mile End . . . . None
BRAZILIAN SPORTS CLUB . . Waltham Forest FC, Wadham Lodge, Kitchener Road, Walthamstow E17 4JP 020 8527 2444
FC DEPORTIVO GALICIA . . . . Osterley Sports Club, Tentelow Lane, Osterley, Southall UB2 4LW 020 8574 3774
INDIAN GYMKHANA . . . . Indian Gymkhana Club, Thornbury Avenue, Osterley TW7 4NQ 020 8568 4005
KINGS MEADOW . . . . Chertsey Town FC, Alwyns Lane, Chertsey KT16 9DN 01932 561774
MARSH RANGERS . . . . Stockley Park, Chestnut Avenue, West Drayton UB7 8BT . . . . None
NEASDEN . . . . Conquest Sports & Social Club, Wood Lane, Isleworth TW7 5EJ 020 8560 2892
SIGNCRAFT . . . . Richings Park Sports & Social, Wellesley Ave., Richings Park, Iver SL0 9BN 01753 651320
SOUTH KILBURN . . . . Sudbury Court, East Lane, Wembley . . . . None
SUTTON COMMON ROVERS . . Mole Valley Predators, River Lane, off Randalls Rd, Leatherhead KT22 0AU . . . . None
WALTHAMSTOW AVENUE . . . . Town Mead Leisure Park, Brooker Road, Waltham Abbey . . . . None
WILLESDEN CONSTANTINE . . . . Alperton Sports Ground, Alperton Lane, Wembley HA0 1JH 020 8997 9905
WRAYSBURY . . . . Memorial Ground, The Green, Wraysbury, Staines TW19 5NA 01784 482155
IN: Barnet Town (N), Bethnal Green United (N), Indian Gymkhana (N), Neasden (N), Signcraft (P), South Kilburn (P), Sutton Common Rovers (P – Surrey South Eastern Combination Intermediate Division One), Walthamstow Avenue (N)
OUT: Bison (W), Ealing (WS), Mauritius Sports (P – Essex Senior League having merged with Walthamstow Avenue & Pennant), Neasden Foundation (P – Combined Counties LeagueDivision One), Parkfield Youth Old Boys (W), Southall (R – Division One Central & East), Spelthorne Sports (S – Surrey Intermediate League (West) Premier Division), Sport London E Benfica (P – Spartans South Midlands League Division One), Walthamstow Avenue & Pennant (P – Essex Senior League having merged with Mauritius Sports)

Division One		P	W	D	L	F	A	Pts
South Kilburn		24	15	5	4	48	26	50
Signcraft		24	14	4	6	78	55	46
Nth Greenford Utd Soc.		24	13	5	6	56	37	44
Hayes United	-9	24	14	6	4	59	28	39
Woodberry Downs	-3	24	10	9	5	52	29	36
Hounslow Wanderers		24	10	6	8	38	39	36
Stonewall		24	8	9	7	48	43	33
FC Assyria		24	9	4	11	41	52	31
Bridge Rovers		24	7	6	11	37	48	27
North Hayes Academicals		24	6	7	11	35	47	25
Haref'ld Ex-Serv'mens	-6	24	7	6	11	25	35	21
The Wilberforce Wdrs		24	2	8	14	26	58	14
St John's Athletic	-3	24	1	5	18	27	73	5

JIM ROGERS DIVISION ONE PRESIDENT'S CUP FINAL
(May 11th at Yeading)
Signcraft 3 North Greenford United Social 2

Division Two		P	W	D	L	F	A	Pts
London Utd Football Acad.		24	17	4	3	54	26	55
Imperial College Old Boys		24	15	4	5	60	31	49
South Acton		24	14	5	5	68	41	47
Brentham		24	12	6	6	46	34	42
LPOSSA	-3	24	12	2	10	52	43	35
Harrow St Mary's YOB		24	11	1	12	49	40	34
Haringey Town	-3	24	10	5	9	45	45	32
Harefield Wednesday		24	8	5	11	20	30	29
Blue Marlin		24	8	5	11	38	59	29
Puma 2000		24	7	5	12	34	44	26
Hillingdon & Barnhill		24	7	5	12	36	53	26
AGBLC of Hackney	-3	24	7	3	14	42	43	21
Kentish Town Res.	-9	24	3	0	21	23	78	0

SIR JOHN SALMOND DIVISION TWO CUP FINAL
(April 28th at Yeading)
Imperial College Old Boys 3 Blue Marlin 1

Senior Reserve Division		P	W	D	L	F	A	Pts
Spelthorne Sports Res.		24	21	2	1	103	20	65
CB Hounslow United 'A'		24	18	2	4	85	26	56
Nth Greenford US Res.		24	16	4	4	65	29	52
North Hayes Acad. Res.	+3	24	13	1	10	66	49	37
Imperial Coll. OB Res.		24	10	2	12	35	37	32
Hounslow Wdrs Res.		24	8	6	10	40	44	30
Brentham Res.	-3	24	8	8	8	41	40	29
Cockfosters 'A'	-3	24	9	5	10	53	54	29
Harefield Wed. Res.		24	7	2	15	50	83	23
FC Tilburg Reg. Res.		24	6	2	16	31	84	20
South Acton Res.	-6	24	8	1	15	27	57	19
Harrow Club Res.	-12	24	8	3	13	44	59	15
Stonewall Res.	-3	24	2	6	16	33	91	9

JEFF NARDIN JUNIOR RESERVE DIVISION TROPHY FINAL
(April 7th at Yeading)
Cockfosters 'A' 3 North Hayes Academicals Res. 1

Division Three East		P	W	D	L	F	A	Pts
FC Baresi		14	12	1	1	79	15	37
Samba Street Soccer		14	11	1	2	40	15	34
FC Tilburg Regents		14	8	2	4	41	34	26
New Life Assembly	-3	14	9	0	5	44	23	24
Renegades	-6	14	5	1	8	32	37	10
Acton Town	-3	14	4	1	9	32	50	10
Warren		14	2	2	10	22	40	8
Freezywater	-3	14	1	0	13	16	92	0

P D MARDON DIVISION THREE CUP FINAL
(April 14th at Yeading)
Brunswick 4 Greens United 1

LEAGUE OPEN CUP

THIRD ROUND

AGBLC of Hackney 4 Bison 2
Blue Marlin (w/o) v Ealing (scr.)
Brazilian Sports Club 0 **Willesden Constantine** 1
Brentham 1 **Brunswick** 3
Cockfosters 'A' 1 **Bedfont Sports** 8
Hariney Town 1 **Parkfield Youth Old Boys** 5
Hayes United (scr.) v **Neasden Foundation** (w/o)
Hounslow Wanderers Res. (w/o) v Kentish Town (scr.)
Imperial College Old Boys 0 **Sport London E Benfica** 2
Kings Meadow 7 Barn Elms 1
North Hayes Academicals (w/o) v Kentish Town Res. (scr.)
Signcraft 3 **LPOSSA** 4
Spelthorne Sports 3 Brunel University 1
Walthamstow Avenue & Pennant 2 Wraysbury 0
Wilberforce Wanderers 1 **South Kilburn** 2
Woodberry Downs 2 Junior All Stars 2 *aet* (4-1p)

FOURTH ROUND

Bedfont Sports 3 Parkfield Youth Old Boys 1
Blue Marlin 0 **Kings Meadow** 3
Brunswick 3 Willesden Constantine 1
Hounslow Wanderers Res. (scr.) v **AGBLC of Hackney** (w/o)
LPOSSA 2 **North Hayes Academicals** 3
Spethorne Sports 7 Sport London E Benfica 0
Walthamstow Avenue & Pennant 3 South Kilburn 1
Woodberry Downs 2 Neasden Foundation 1

QUARTER-FINALS

AGBLC of Hackney 2 Spelthorne Sports 1
Bedfont Sports 2 Woodberry Downs 1
North Hayes Academicals 1 **Kings Meadow** 2
Walthamstow Avenue & Pennant 4 **Brunswick** 4 *aet* (3-4p)

SEMI-FINALS

Bedfont Sports 6 Brunswick 3
Kings Meadow 1 **AGBLC of Hackney** 1 *aet* (11-12p)

FINAL

(May 5th at Yeading)
Bedfont Sports 3 AGBLC of Hackney 1

Division Three West		P	W	D	L	F	A	Pts
Brunswick		18	16	0	2	111	32	48
Greens United		18	14	1	3	70	37	43
Junior All Stars		18	11	3	4	44	29	36
Stedfast United		18	10	2	6	64	54	32
The Wanderers		18	7	0	11	34	55	21
Barn Elms	-3	18	7	1	10	42	61	19
Brunel University	-6	18	7	2	9	62	55	17
Harrow Club	-6	18	7	2	9	49	42	17
Phoenix Rovers		18	2	0	16	25	79	6
ACA	-3	18	2	3	13	38	95	6

MIDLAND ALLIANCE

	Alvechurch	Atherstone	Barwell	Biddulph	Boldmere	Causeway	Coalville	Cradley T.	Friar Lane	Leamington	Loughboro.	M.Drayton	Oadby T.	Oldbury U.	Quorn	R Warwick	Rocester	Romulus	Stratford	Studley	Tipton T.	Westfields
Alvechurch		3-4	2-2	3-0	1-0	3-1	2-1	0-0	4-0	3-3	0-0	1-0	2-3	0-1	0-0	1-3	1-1	2-2	1-0	2-3	3-2	6-0
Atherstone Town	0-1		2-2	3-1	2-1	2-1	2-1	5-0	4-0	0-0	3-0	5-1	0-1	1-1	1-1	0-1	2-3	1-1	0-3	6-1	1-3	0-1
Barwell	0-2	2-2		3-0	4-2	3-1	3-1	3-1	0-1	0-3	6-0	2-3	3-1	0-0	2-0	2-0	1-1	3-1	3-2	2-3	2-3	2-0
Biddulph Victoria	0-1	0-0	1-2		1-4	0-2	0-4	8-0	1-5	2-1	0-5	2-1	3-2	0-0	1-4	4-0	1-2	0-1	1-2	0-0	0-2	2-2
Boldmere St Michaels	1-1	1-1	1-3	3-1		3-1	3-0	5-0	0-2	1-3	2-1	1-2	1-1	1-3	1-1	3-0	2-2	1-1	2-1	1-0	3-1	
Causeway United	0-1	2-3	2-3	0-2	2-1		2-0	6-0	3-3	0-2	0-1	2-0	1-3	2-3	1-2	3-0	0-3	0-1	0-2	1-3	1-2	4-0
Coalville Town	2-1	1-2	3-4	0-4	0-3	2-2		1-0	2-2	0-3	1-4	1-2	1-0	0-2	1-0	3-2	0-4	1-4	2-1	0-1	2-0	
Cradley Town	1-1	2-2	1-2	1-3	1-3	0-5	2-1		2-2	0-4	1-3	2-1	1-5	0-5	2-3	0-3	0-2	0-1	0-3	3-4		
Friar Lane & Epworth	3-3	0-1	3-2	1-0	2-1	2-5	5-4		0-2	1-2	2-2	0-3	1-3	4-4	1-2	1-1	2-3	2-1	3-1	1-1		
Leamington	2-1	1-0	3-2	2-0	1-3	5-1	4-0	3-0	4-0		5-0	4-2	1-0	4-1	1-1	3-0	3-0	4-3	0-0	3-0	3-1	3-2
Loughborough Dynamo	3-1	1-1	4-2	2-2	2-1	0-1	1-2	3-5	0-1	3-4		1-1	2-2	0-3	3-1	4-5	2-1	1-0	3-3	2-3	2-0	0-1
Market Drayton Town	0-1	2-3	2-1	1-1	0-2	0-0	3-0	5-0	3-2	1-1	1-1		2-2	2-2	0-2	2-0	4-1	3-2	0-2	3-0	0-2	1-1
Oadby Town	2-0	1-2	2-0	2-2	2-1	2-0	1-0	0-1	5-1	2-0	2-4	0-1		1-1	3-2	1-0	0-1	0-1	2-1	3-1	5-1	
Oldbury United	1-3	0-0	1-3	2-0	0-1	0-0	1-3	1-0	1-1	0-1	0-3	2-1			3-0	2-2	0-1	1-2	3-1	0-2	0-3	3-1
Quorn	4-1	1-1	1-2	2-3	1-0	0-1	5-0	4-1	0-4	1-2	0-0	1-0	3-0			2-0	3-0	4-0	5-0	1-0	0-2	0-1
Racing Club Warwick	5-1	2-2	3-5	4-0	0-1	2-1	2-1	4-1	1-4	0-3	0-2	1-1	0-1	0-1	0-0		1-1	1-4	1-4	4-2	0-2	4-3
Rocester	1-0	0-1	3-2	1-0	2-1	0-5	3-1	0-0	3-2	0-1	1-1	0-1	1-0	3-1	1-3	0-3		1-2	0-4	0-0	0-1	
Romulus	1-1	1-1	4-3	4-0	3-1	5-0	2-0	9-1	1-1	0-1	2-1	3-0	3-1	2-0	2-0	4-0	3-1		3-1	2-2	4-0	2-0
Stratford Town	3-1	1-1	2-0	1-0	1-2	1-2	5-0	1-0	2-3	1-1	4-2	1-1	3-0	2-1	3-1	3-2			2-1	0-1	0-0	
Studley	1-3	3-2	2-1	2-3	3-2	2-1	1-3	2-0	1-2	2-3	0-1	1-3	1-2	4-2	2-3	3-0	1-1	1-3	2-6		2-0	0-2
Tipton Town	0-0	1-0	0-1	6-1	1-2	4-1	2-0	3-0	2-4	0-1	2-4	0-1	5-1	0-2	5-1	3-0	2-0	2-1	3-0			4-4
Westfields	1-2	3-2	1-2	1-1	1-3	2-3	1-3	1-1	2-4	0-1	3-1	2-0	1-2	0-1	2-1	0-2	1-2	2-5	0-0	0-0	1-0	

	P	W	D	L	F	A	Pts
Leamington	42	33	4	5	105	36	103
Romulus	42	25	11	6	102	47	86
Quorn	42	25	7	10	82	40	82
Stratford Town	42	25	7	10	81	47	82
Tipton Town	42	22	8	12	71	48	74
Barwell	42	22	5	15	88	68	71
Boldmere St Mich.	42	20	6	16	73	56	66
Atherstone Town	42	16	16	10	71	50	64
Loughborough Dyn.	42	19	7	16	73	70	64
Alvechurch	42	17	12	13	66	57	63
Oadby Town	42	19	5	18	68	59	62
Rocester	42	16	7	19	45	66	55
Market Drayton T.	42	14	11	17	61	62	53
Oldbury United -1	42	13	13	16	48	57	51
Friar Lane & E'wth	42	12	12	18	66	86	48
Westfields	42	13	9	20	57	78	48
Causeway United	42	14	5	23	63	72	47
Coalville Town	42	15	2	25	51	83	47
Racing Warwick	42	10	8	24	57	88	38
Studley	42	11	5	26	55	86	38
Biddulph Victoria	42	10	8	24	51	84	38
Cradley Town	42	4	6	32	35	129	18

LEAGUE CUP

FIRST ROUND
Alvechurch 1 Stratf'd 1 *aet* (5-4p)
Boldmere St Michaels 0 **Studley** 1
Causeway Utd 1 **RC Warwick** 4
Leamington 3 Barwell 1
Market Drayton 4 Cradley 1
Tipton Town 4 Oadby Town 1

SECOND ROUND
Alvechurch 1 **Rocester** 2 *aet*
Atherstone Town 4 Studley 3
Biddulph Victoria 2 Friar Lane 1
Leamington 2 Westfields 0
Loughborough D. 4 Romulus 1
Oldbury Utd 1 **Market Drayton** 2
Quorn 0 **Coalville Town** 2
Tipton Town 2 RC Warwick 1

QUARTER-FINALS
Atherstone Town 2
Loughborough Dynamo 1
Biddulph Victoria 0
Leamington 2
Market Drayton 2 Rocester 1
Tipton Town 4 Coalville Town 0

SEMI-FINALS
(played over two legs)
Leamington 3 Atherstone Town 1,
Atherstone Town 3 **Leamington** 2
Tipton 1 Market Drayton Town 0,
Market Drayton 0 **Tipton Town** 0

FINAL
(May 3rd at Walsall)
Leamington 2 Tipton Town 1 *aet*

JOE McGORRIAN CUP
(League champions v League Cup holders)
(August 5th at Chasetown)
Chasetown 3 Barwell 0

MIDLAND ALLIANCE CONSTITUTION 2007-08
ALVECHURCH .... Lye Meadow, Redditch Road, Alvechurch B48 7RS 0121 445 2929
ATHERSTONE TOWN .... Sheepy Road, Sheepy, Atherstone CV9 3AD 01827 717829
BARWELL .... Kirkby Road, Barwell LE9 8FQ 01455 843067
BIDDULPH VICTORIA .... Tunstall Road, Knypersley, Stoke-On-Trent ST8 7AQ 01782 522737
BOLDMERE ST MICHAELS . Trevor Brown Mem. Ground, Church Rd, Boldmere, Sutton Coldfield B73 5RY 0121 384 7531/373 4435
CAUSEWAY UNITED .... Tividale FC, The Beeches, Packwood Road, Tividale, Warley B69 1UL 01384 211743
COALVILLE TOWN .... Owen Street Sports Ground, Owen Street, Coalville LE67 3DA 01530 833365
COVENTRY SPHINX .... Sphinx Sports & Social Club, Siddeley Ave., Stoke Aldermoor, Coventry CV3 1WA 024 7645 1361
CRADLEY TOWN .... Beeches View Avenue, Cradley, Halesowen B63 2HB 01384 569658
FRIAR LANE & EPWORTH .... Knighton Lane East, Aylestone Park, Leicester LE2 6FT 0116 283 3629
LOUGHBOROUGH DYNAMO .. Nanpantan Sports Ground, Nanpantan Road, Loughborough LE11 3YD 01509 237148
MARKET DRAYTON TOWN .... Greenfield Sports Club, Greenfield Lane, Market Drayton TF9 3SL 01630 655088
OADBY TOWN .... Topps Park, Wigston Road, Oadby LE2 5QG 0116 271 5728
OLDBURY UNITED .... The Cricketts, York Road, Oldbury, Warley B65 0RT 0121 559 5564
RACING CLUB WARWICK .... Townsend Meadow, Hampton Road, Warwick CV34 6JP 01926 495786
ROCESTER .... Hillsfield, Mill Street, Rocester, Uttoxeter ST14 5TX 01889 590463
SHIFNAL TOWN .... Phoenix Park, Coppice Green Lane, Shifal TF11 8PB 01952 463667
STAPENHILL .... Maple Grove, Stapenhill, Burton-on-Trent DE15 9NN 01283 562471
STRATFORD TOWN .... Masons Road, Stratford-on-Avon CV37 9NF 01789 297479
STUDLEY .... The Bee Hive, Abbeyfield Drive, off Birmingham Road, Studley B80 7BE 01527 853817
TIPTON TOWN .... Tipton Sports Academy, Wednesbury Oak Road, Tipton DY4 0BS 0121 502 5534/556 5067
WESTFIELDS .... Allpay Park, Widemarsh Common, Hereford HR4 9NA 07860 410548
IN: Coventry Sphinx (P – Midland Combination Premier Division), Shifnal Town (P – West Midlands (Regional) League Premier Division), Stapenhill (P – Leicestershire Senior League Premier Division)
OUT: Leamington (P – Southern League Division One Midlands), Quorn (P – Northern Premier League Division One South), Romulus (P – Southern League Division One Midlands)

MIDLAND COMBINATION

(6

	Alveston	Barnt Green Spartak	Bolehall Swifts	Brereton Social	Brocton	Cadbury Athletic	Castle Vale	Coleshill Town	Continental Star	Coventry Copsewood	Coventry Sphinx	Feckenham	Heath Hayes	Highgate United	Massey-Ferguson	Meir KA	Nuneaton Griff	Pershore Town	Pilkington XXX	Southam United	Walsall Wood
Alveston		1-1	1-2	1-1	1-3	2-2	0-3	0-11	2-3	1-2	0-4	1-1	2-2	1-1	1-1	1-6	1-4	1-0	2-3	0-3	2-0
Barnt Green Spartak	6-0		2-2	4-0	1-1	2-1	0-3	0-1	1-0	4-0	0-1	1-3	1-2	1-3	3-1	1-0	0-2	8-0	0-1	2-1	2-0
Bolehall Swifts	2-2	5-4	P	1-1	4-0	5-1	1-4	1-3	3-3	2-2	3-4	2-3	2-2	1-2	2-0	0-0	1-0	3-1	1-3	1-2	0-0
Brereton Social	1-0	1-1	0-5	R	1-1	0-3	1-2	0-3	1-2	4-1	1-1	1-2	3-2	1-4	2-0	2-4	2-1	0-1	1-0	0-1	2-0
Brocton	1-0	2-2	1-1	3-4	E	0-0	0-2	2-4	1-1	1-1	1-4	3-0	1-2	0-2	2-0	1-1	2-1	2-3	2-3	2-4	0-1
Cadbury Athletic	2-1	1-4	2-1	0-2	2-0	M	0-7	2-4	2-1	0-0	0-2	0-0	2-2	1-3	0-4	0-4	2-0	3-3	0-1	3-2	1-2
Castle Vale	4-0	3-0	0-1	7-2	2-0	2-0	I	1-0	2-1	1-1	3-3	5-2	1-2	2-0	3-0	4-1	2-2	4-3	3-0	4-0	4-2
Coleshill Town	3-0	2-0	1-2	1-0	1-0	1-0	2-2	E	1-0	1-1	0-1	2-1	4-1	1-1	1-2	5-0	1-3	3-5	1-1	4-0	3-1
Continental Star	0-0	2-3	2-2	2-2	0-2	1-2	0-2	0-2	R	0-1	3-2	4-1	3-2	1-5	3-2	2-3	1-6	2-4	3-4	2-0	1-1
Coventry Copsewood	2-1	2-1	1-3	3-6	0-1	1-3	0-4	0-1	1-0		1-3	1-0	1-1	1-1	0-3	2-0	2-7	0-4	0-0	1-2	1-2
Coventry Sphinx	4-1	1-1	3-0	1-2	4-0	4-0	6-0	2-2	8-1	3-0		3-0	1-1	2-0	5-3	2-1	1-3	3-1	5-1	2-1	1-0
Feckenham	1-0	0-3	2-3	3-0	1-3	1-1	1-3	2-2	0-3	1-3	1-1	D	4-2	0-2	1-0	1-1	2-3	1-2	1-2	1-1	0-2
Heath Hayes	3-1	2-1	0-1	3-0	2-3	0-2	1-2	0-1	1-2	3-1	2-0	3-1	I	1-0	4-3	3-1	1-2	3-3	6-1	3-3	6-1
Highgate United	0-0	1-2	0-2	4-0	2-2	2-1	4-1	0-2	4-2	3-0	1-1	2-0	4-1	V	1-0	1-0	3-2	6-1	1-1	4-2	4-1
Massey-Ferguson	2-1	0-1	0-3	3-1	3-0	5-2	0-0	2-1	1-2	4-1	0-2	1-4	3-0	0-0	I	0-4	2-5	1-0	2-0	0-1	2-2
Meir KA	1-3	2-1	3-2	1-0	1-4	6-0	4-2	1-1	4-0	0-0	0-4	1-4	4-2	0-3	2-2	S	1-0	4-3	0-0	3-1	2-1
Nuneaton Griff	3-2	1-2	3-5	4-0	0-1	2-2	3-1	4-1	2-4	1-0	0-2	1-3	4-0	0-0	0-1	0-0	O	1-4	2-3	6-4	1-3
Pershore Town	3-0	4-4	2-3	1-1	3-0	1-2	1-6	2-1	1-0	2-1	2-3	3-1	0-2	0-3	1-1	1-1	1-1	O	2-4	1-2	1-0
Pilkington XXX	1-0	3-0	3-2	2-1	5-2	1-0	0-0	1-4	3-0	3-2	2-4	1-1	1-2	0-0	0-0	1-0	2-2	1-0	N	1-1	1-1
Southam United	3-1	0-0	1-0	0-2	0-1	3-0	2-1	2-0	2-1	0-2	2-2	2-2	1-6	3-2	1-0	1-0	3-1	1-3	0-3		0-3
Walsall Wood	1-3	2-1	3-3	0-0	1-3	3-1	1-1	0-3	3-1	0-1	2-1	1-0	1-0	1-1	1-1	2-0	1-0	1-1	1-1	0-3	

WWW.NLNEWSDESK.CO.UK

Premier Division		P	W	D	L	F	A	Pts
Coventry Sphinx		40	29	7	4	110	40	94
Castle Vale		40	26	7	7	103	47	85
Highgate United	-3	40	25	9	6	90	38	81
Coleshill Town		40	23	7	10	85	43	76
Pilkington XXX		40	21	11	8	65	53	74
Southam United		40	19	7	14	64	67	64
Bolehall Swifts		40	16	12	12	81	67	60
Heath Hayes	-3	40	17	8	15	74	70	56
Barnt G. Spartak	-3	40	16	9	15	72	57	54
Meir KA		40	15	9	16	65	62	54
Nuneaton Griff		40	15	8	17	85	71	53
Walsall Wood		40	14	11	15	50	60	53
Massey-Ferguson		40	14	6	20	56	65	48
Pershore Town		40	14	6	20	66	86	48
Brocton		40	12	9	19	51	70	45
Brereton Social		40	11	9	20	49	80	42
Cadbury Athletic		40	11	9	20	48	85	42
Feckenham		40	9	10	21	50	75	37
Continental Star	-1	40	10	7	23	59	89	36
Coventry Copsewood		40	8	11	21	39	78	35
Alveston		40	4	10	26	37	96	22

TONY ALLDEN MEMORIAL CUP
(Premier Division champions v Challenge Cup holders)

(November 7th at Highgate United)
Atherstone Town 3 Feckenham 0

Reserve Division		P	W	D	L	F	A	Pts
Hinckley United Res.		30	18	4	8	66	40	58
Friar Lane & Epworth Res.		30	16	8	6	73	40	56
Oadby Town Res.		30	15	9	6	58	46	54
Quorn Res.		30	15	7	8	66	37	52
Chasetown Res.	-3	30	15	7	8	65	46	49
Barwell Res.		30	15	4	11	55	51	49
Mickleover Sports Res.		30	15	3	12	66	54	48
Halesowen Town Res.		30	12	9	9	34	28	45
Coleshill Town Res.		30	12	6	12	59	62	42
Boldmere St Michaels Res.		30	11	4	15	57	50	37
Rushall Olympic Res.		30	10	7	13	60	77	37
Rugby Town Res.		30	11	2	17	46	62	35
Loughborough Dynamo Res.	-3	30	10	4	16	62	81	31
Alvechurch Res.		30	8	7	15	37	54	31
Gresley Rovers Res.		30	7	3	20	56	90	24
Rothwell Town Res.		30	8	0	22	52	94	24

CHALLENGE TROPHY
FINAL
(May 9th at Halesowen Town)
Halesowen Town Res. 2 Quorn Res. 0

MIDLAND COMBINATION PREMIER DIVISION CONSTITUTION 2007-08

BARNT GREEN SPARTAK ...... Alvechurch FC, Lye Meadow, Redditch Road, Alvechurch B48 7RS 0121 445 2929

BARTLEY GREEN.............. Tividale FC, The Beeches, Packwood Road, Tividale, Warley B69 1UL 01384 211743

BOLEHALL SWIFTS....................... Rene Road, Bolehall, Tamworth B77 3NN............................... 01827 62637

BRERETON SOCIAL.............. Red Lion Ground, Armitage Lane, Brereton, Rugeley WS15 1ED.................... 01889 585526

BROCTON .... Heath Hayes FC, Coppice Coll., Newlands Lane, Heath Hayes, Cannock WS12 3HH............. 07791 841774

CADBURY ATHLETIC .... Triplex Sports, Eckersall Road, Kings Norton, Birmingham B38 8SR. 0121 458 4570

CASTLE VALE .... Vale Stadium, Farnborough Road, Castle Vale, Warwick, Birmingham B35 7DA 0121 747 6969

COLESHILL TOWN .... Pack Meadow, Packington Lane, Coleshill B46 3JQ 01675 463259

CONTINENTAL STAR .... Oldbury Leisure Centre, Newbury Road, Oldbury, Warley B69 1HE................. 0121 552 4497

COVENTRY COPSEWOOD .... Copsewood Sports & Social Club, Allard Way, Binley, Coventry CV3 1HQ 02476 635992

FECKENHAM............ Studley FC, The Bee Hive, Abbeyfield Drive, Birmingham Road, Studley B80 7BE 01527 853817

HEATH HAYES .... Coppice Colliery Ground, Newlands Lane, Heath Hayes, Cannock WS12 3HH 07977 239193

HEATHER ST JOHN .... St John's Park, Ravenstone Road, Heather LE67 2QJ 01530 263986

HIGHGATE UNITED .... The Coppice, Tythe Barn Lane, Shirley, Solihull B90 1PH 0121 744 4194

LOUGHBOROUGH UNIVERSITY .. Loughborough Dynamo FC, Nanpantan Road, Loughborough LE11 3YD............. 01509 237148

MASSEY-FERGUSON .... Bannerbrook Park, off Banner Lane, Tile Hill, Coventry CV5 9GF 07985 000222

MEIR KA .... Kings Park, Hilderstone Road, Meir Heath, Stoke-on-Trent ST3 7NT 07888 750532

NUNEATON GRIFF .... The Pingles Stadium, Avenue Road, Nuneaton CV11 4LX 024 7637 0688

PERSHORE TOWN .... King George V Playing Fields, King George's Way, Pershore WR10 1AA 01386 556902

PILKINGTON XXX .... Triplex Sports Ground, Eckersall Road, Kings Norton, Birmingham B38 8SR............. 0121 458 4570

SOUTHAM UNITED.................... Banbury Road, Southam, Leamington Spa CV47 2BJ..................... 01926 812091

WALSALL WOOD..................... Oak Park, Lichfield Road, Walsall Wood WS9 9NP 01543 361084

IN: Bartley Green (P), Heather St John (formerly Heather Athletic) (P), Loughborough University (N)

OUT: Alveston (R), Coventry Sphinx (P – Midland Alliance)

CHALLENGE CUP
(Premier and Division One teams)

FIRST ROUND

Cadbury Athletic 1 **Archdale** 2
Heath Hayes 3 Meir KA 0
Highgate United 0 **Castle Vale** 3
Knowle 2 Ettington 2 *aet* (4-3p)
Southam United 2 Nuneaton Griff 0
Thimblemill REC 0 **Heather Athletic** 2

SECOND ROUND

Barnt Green Spartak 0 **Pilkington XXX** 0 *aet* (3-5p)
Bartley Green 1 Pershore Town 0 *aet*
Bolehall Swifts (w/o) v Heather Athletic (scr.)
Brereton Social 1 **University of Birmingham** 2
Brocton 2 West Midlands Police 0
Burntwood Town 0 **Coventry Copsewood** 2
Castle Vale 1 **Feckenham** 1 *aet* (3-4p)
Coleshill Town 1 Heath Hayes 0
Continental Star 0 **Stockingford AA** 1
Coventry Sphinx 3 Newhall United 0
Fairfield Villa 5 Littleton 4
Kenilworth Town KH 1 **Mile Oak Rovers** 6
Leamington Hibernian 0 **Alveston** 3
Massey-Ferguson 3 Knowle 0
Northfield Town 2 Southam United 1
Walsall Wood 5 Archdale 2 *aet*

THIRD ROUND

Alveston 0 **Bartley Green** 1 *aet*
Bolehall Swifts 3 **Pilkington XXX** 3 *aet* (3-4p)
Coventry Copsewood 4 Coleshill Town 3 *aet*
Coventry Sphinx 3 Brocton 2
Fairfield Villa 3 Feckenham 1 *aet*
Massey-Ferguson 2 University of Birmingham 1
Mile Oak Rovers 1 **Northfield Town** 3
Walsall Wood 2 Stockingford AA 1

QUARTER-FINALS

Coventry Sphinx 2 **Bartley Green** 4
Fairfield Villa 0 **Pilkington XXX** 1
Massey-Ferguson 1 **Coventry Copsewood** 4
Northfield Town 0 **Walsall Wood** 2

SEMI-FINALS

(played over two legs)
Bartley Green 2 Coventry Copsewood 0,
Coventry Copsewood 2 Bartley Green 0 *aet* (5-3p)
Pilkington XXX 1 Walsall Wood 0,
Walsall Wood 1 **Pilkington XXX** 2

FINAL

(May 10th at Tamworth)
Coventry Copsewood 1 Pilkington XXX 0

Note – Kenilworth Town KH withdrew during the course of the season Their results are shown herein but are expunged from the league table	Archdale	Bartley Green	Burntwood Town	Ettington	Fairfield Villa	Heather Athletic	Kenilworth Town KH	Knowle	Leamington Hibernian	Littleton	Mile Oak Rovers	Newhall United	Northfield Town	Stockingford AA	Thimblemill REC	Univ. of Birmingham	West Midlands Police
Archdale		2-3	3-1	2-1	2-2	0-4	n/a	2-6	2-2	3-1	3-1	8-1	1-3	1-2	2-2	2-2	0-0
Bartley Green	0-1		3-2	5-1	2-1	1-2	n/a	1-2	6-0	4-0	1-1	W-L	1-3	5-0	1-2	3-1	4-1
Burntwood Town	1-6	0-3	D	0-2	1-7	0-0	n/a	2-5	0-1	1-0	0-3	1-2	0-4	1-2	1-2	0-7	1-0
Ettington	0-0	1-3	0-1	I	2-1	0-1	n/a	0-2	1-1	1-5	0-5	3-3	1-3	1-5	2-1	2-5	0-3
Fairfield Villa	2-1	0-3	3-2	4-2	V	1-3	n/a	6-0	1-0	1-3	2-1	0-5	0-4	4-3	1-1	3-1	1-1
Heather Athletic	2-0	0-1	5-2	6-2	1-2	I	n/a	3-1	3-2	0-0	2-3	2-3	0-1	0-0	1-2	0-0	1-1
Kenilworth Town KH	n/a	n/a	n/a	n/a	n/a	n/a	S	n/a	n/a	n/a	n/a	2-3	n/a	n/a	2-5	0-3	2-2
Knowle	0-1	2-3	4-0	1-0	0-1	3-0	n/a	I	0-0	2-0	1-1	2-3	1-0	0-0	1-1	1-2	3-1
Leamington Hibernian	2-1	1-2	0-0	0-1	2-3	0-4	3-0	1-1	O	1-0	3-1	0-3	1-2	0-1	1-1	1-0	1-0
Littleton	7-0	1-0	6-0	1-2	2-2	3-2	n/a	1-3	3-2	N	1-1	2-0	2-1	0-1	4-2	2-1	3-0
Mile Oak Rovers	0-1	0-3	3-0	4-1	2-2	3-5	n/a	2-1	2-1	8-2		2-1	0-1	1-1	0-1	2-0	1-3
Newhall United	3-2	3-1	1-0	0-1	2-3	1-1	n/a	1-1	1-1	0-1	0-1		0-3	2-3	2-0	3-2	3-2
Northfield Town	2-4	0-3	1-2	3-0	2-0	0-0	n/a	2-1	6-1	0-0	0-2	5-1	O	1-0	1-0	0-1	1-1
Stockingford AA	3-1	0-2	9-1	5-0	1-2	1-0	5-1	2-1	1-1	2-1	3-1	3-2	2-3	N	1-2	2-0	1-2
Thimblemill REC	3-1	1-0	2-0	4-1	1-0	2-0	n/a	1-1	1-4	1-1	2-2	0-0	1-3	1-2	E	1-1	0-2
University of Birmingham	5-1	3-1	3-1	6-1	3-0	1-2	n/a	0-1	3-0	3-1	3-0	3-3	6-0	0-0	1-1		1-1
West Midlands Police	0-1	0-5	2-1	2-3	1-5	0-3	n/a	1-3	1-1	0-2	1-4	3-2	2-4	4-0	0-2	1-1	

Division One		P	W	D	L	F	A	Pts
Bartley Green		30	20	1	9	70	31	61
Northfield Town		30	19	3	8	60	34	60
Stockingford AA		30	17	5	8	57	36	56
Fairfield Villa		30	16	4	10	61	53	52
University Birmingham		30	13	8	9	65	36	47
Heather Athletic		30	13	7	10	53	36	46
Mile Oak Rovers		30	13	6	11	56	45	45
Knowle		30	13	6	11	50	39	45
Littleton		30	13	6	11	55	45	45
Thimblemill REC	-4	30	12	9	9	43	39	41
Archdale		30	11	6	13	53	61	39
Newhall United	-3	30	11	6	13	49	58	36
Leamington Hibernian		30	7	9	14	31	51	30
West Midlands Police		30	7	7	16	36	58	28
Ettington		30	7	3	20	32	82	24
Burntwood Town		30	4	2	24	22	89	14

Kenilworth Town KH – record expunged

PRESIDENT'S CUP

FIRST ROUND
Littleton 1 **Archdale** 2
SECOND ROUND
Burntwood Town 0 **Leamington Hibernian** 3
Ettington 2 Heather Athletic 1
Knowle 2 University of Birmingham 1
Mile Oak Rovers 3 **Fairfield Villa** 4 *aet*
Newhall United 4 Kenilworth Town KH 0
Northfield Town 1 **Bartley Green** 2
Thimblemill REC 2 **Archdale** 3
West Midlands Police 1 **Stockingford** AA 3
QUARTER-FINALS
Archdale 0 Leamington Hibernian 0 *aet* (3-1p)
Bartley Green 5 Ettington 0
Knowle 0 **Fairfield Villa** 2
Stockingford AA 0 **Newhall United** 1
SEMI-FINALS
(played over two legs)
Fairfield Villa 2 Archdale 1, **Archdale** 3 Fairfield Villa 1
Newhall Utd 0 Bartley Green 1, **Bartley Green** 1 Newhall 0
FINAL
(April 30th at Bromsgrove Rovers)
Archdale 1 Bartley Green 0

WWW.NLNEWSDESK.CO.UK

MIDLAND COMBINATION DIVISION ONE CONSTITUTION 2007-08

ALVESTON . . . . Home Guard Club, Main Street, Tiddington, Stratford-upon-Avon CV37 7AY 01789 297718
ARCHDALE . . . . County Sports Ground, Claines Lane, Worcester WR3 7SS 07736 309670
BURNTWOOD TOWN . . . . Memorial Ground, Rugeley Road, Burntwood WS7 9BE 07946 269153
COTON GREEN . . . . New Mill Lane, Fazeley, Tamworth B78 3RX . . . . None
DROITWICH SPA . . . . Droitwich Spa Leisure Centre, Briar Mill, Droitwich WR9 8UE 07860 591091
EARLSWOOD TOWN . . . . The Pavilions, Malthouse Lane, Earlswood, Solihull B94 5DX 07923 415501
FAIRFIELD VILLA . . . . Recreation Ground, Stourbridge Road, Fairfield, Bromsgrove B61 9LZ 01527 877049
KNOWLE . . . . Hampton Road, Knowle, Solihull B93 0NX 01564 779807
LEAMINGTON HIBERNIAN . . . RC Warwick FC, Townsend Meadow, Harrison Road, Warwick CV34 6JP 01926 496785
LITTLETON . . . . Five Acres, Pebworth Road, North Littleton, Evesham WR11 8QL 07966 297971
MILE OAK ROVERS . . . . Mile Oak Community Ground, Price Avenue, Mile Oak, Tamworth B78 3NL 01827 289614
NEWHALL UNITED . . . . The Hadfields, St Johns Drive, Newhall, Swadlincote DE11 0SU 01283 551029
NORTHFIELD TOWN . . Shenley Lane Community Association, 472 Shenley Lane, Selly Oak, Birmingham B29 4HZ 0121 475 3870
OLDBURY ATHLETIC . . . . Oldbury Leisure Centre, Newbury Lane, Oldbury, Warley B69 1HE 0121 552 4497
STOCKINGFORD AA . . . . The Pavilion, Ansley Road, Stockingford, Nuneaton CV10 8LP 024 7638 7743
THIMBLEMILL REC . . . . Thimblemill Road, Smethwick, Warley B66 6NR 0121 429 2459
WEST MIDLANDS POLICE . . . Tally Ho! Training Centre, Pershore Road, Edgbaston, Birmingham B5 7RD 0121 626 8228
IN: Alveston (R), Coton Green (P), Droitwich Spa (P), Earlswood Town (P), Oldbury Athletic (formerly Wernley Athletic) (P)
OUT: Bartley Green (P), Ettington (W), Heather St John (formerly Heather Athletic) (P), Kenilworth Town KH (WS), University of Birmingham (W)

	Cadbury Athletic Res.	Chelmsley Town	Continental Star Res.	Coton Green	Coventry Sphinx Res.	Droitwich Spa	Earlswood Town	Enville Athletic	Feckenham Res.	Perrywood	Warwick Town	Wernley Athletic	Worcester City 'A'
Cadbury Athletic Res.	D	1-4	4-1	1-2	1-3	0-2	0-2	4-2	2-0	1-1	7-2	0-8	1-3
Chelmsley Town	1-1	I	4-1	1-3	3-6	3-1	1-3	0-2	4-2	5-1	0-1	0-4	2-1
Continental Star Res.	1-2	3-3	V	0-6	1-1	0-2	0-2	1-0	0-0	3-1	5-0	1-4	2-0
Coton Green	5-2	2-2	1-1	I	0-1	2-1	3-0	2-0	5-1	1-3	1-0	1-3	3-0
Coventry Sphinx Res.	2-3	6-0	1-0	1-2	S	1-2	3-2	2-0	2-0	3-2	7-2	2-3	1-1
Droitwich Spa	0-0	3-0	2-3	1-4	1-0	I	3-0	3-2	2-1	2-0	2-1	0-1	3-0
Earlswood Town	2-2	3-3	0-1	1-2	4-4	1-0	O	3-1	2-0	2-0	5-0	0-2	3-2
Enville Athletic	2-0	2-3	3-0	3-3	1-5	1-3	2-2	N	4-2	2-2	1-2	1-9	0-3
Feckenham Res.	1-0	1-3	3-1	0-3	1-0	0-0	1-0	1-2		1-1	1-1	1-1	6-3
Perrywood	2-2	0-1	1-3	0-3	2-3	1-2	0-2	0-7	0-1		5-2	1-8	0-5
Warwick Town	3-3	1-0	0-0	1-3	5-1	0-1	2-4	3-2	2-0	5-2	T	1-5	3-2
Wernley Athletic	4-1	1-3	4-2	2-2	6-4	5-2	1-2	2-0	6-0	9-0	3-0	W	1-3
Worcester City 'A'	4-1	5-3	0-1	1-3	1-2	0-1	0-4	5-1	0-0	0-1	1-2	3-6	O

CHALLENGE VASE

FIRST ROUND
Cadbury Res. 4 Feckenham Res. 1
Chelmsley 0 **Wernley Athletic** 3
Coton Green 3 Earlswood Town 3
aet (9-10p)
Cov. Sphinx Res. 8 Perrywood 1
Worc. City 'A' 4 Warwick Town 3
QUARTER-FINALS
Cadbury Res. 1 **Cov. Sphinx Res.** 4
Continental Star Res. 1 **Enville** 2
Droitwich Spa 2 **Earlswood Town** 3
Wernley Athletic 1 **Worcester City
'A'** 1 *aet (0-3p)*
SEMI-FINALS
(played over two legs)
Enville Athletic 1 Earlswood Town 0,
Earlswood (scr.) v **Enville** (w/o)
Worc. City 'A' 0 Cov. Sphinx Res. 1,
Coventry Sphinx Res. 2 Worcester
City 'A' 1
FINAL
(May 7th at Pilkington XXX)
Cov. Sphinx Res. 3 Enville Ath. 0

Division Two	P	W	D	L	F	A	Pts
Wernley Athletic	24	19	2	3	98	30	59
Coton Green	24	17	4	3	62	26	55
Droitwich Spa	24	15	2	7	39	26	47
Earlswood Town	24	13	4	7	49	33	43
Coventry Sphinx Res.	24	13	3	8	61	43	42
Chelmsley Town	24	10	4	10	49	54	34
Warwick Town	24	9	3	12	39	61	30
Continental Star Res.	24	8	5	11	31	44	29
Cadbury Athletic Res.	24	6	6	12	39	57	24
Feckenham Res.	24	6	6	12	24	44	24
Worcester City 'A'	24	7	2	15	43	50	23
Enville Athletic	24	6	3	15	41	60	21
Perrywood	-3	24	3	4	17	26	73	10

MIDLAND COMBINATION DIVISION TWO CONSTITUTION 2007-08
BNJS MANN & CO . . . . Warley Rugby Club, Tat Bank Road, Oldbury, Warley B69 4NH 0121 552 104
BURNTWOOD TOWN RESERVES . . . . . Memorial Ground, Rugeley Road, Burntwood WS7 9BE 07946 26915
CADBURY ATHLETIC RESERVES . . Cadbury Rec Ground, Bournville Lane, Bournville, Birmingham 0121 458 2000x3316/454 426
CASTLE VALE JKS . . . . Vale Stadium, Farnborough Road, Castle Vale, Birmingham B35 7DA 0121 747 696
CHELMSLEY TOWN . . . . The Pavilions, Coleshill Road, Marston Green, Birmingham B37 7HW 0121 779 5400
CONTINENTAL STAR RESERVES . . Holly Lane S&S, Holly Lane, Erdington, Birmingham B24 9LH 0121 373 097
DOSTHILL COLTS . . . . Bolehall Swifts FC, Rene Road, Bolehall, Tamworth B77 3NN 01827 6263
DROITWICH SPA RESERVES . . . . . . Droitwich Spa Leisure Centre, Briar Mill, Droitwich WR9 8UE 07360 56109
ENVILLE ATHLETIC . . . . Enville Athletic Club, Hall Drive, Enville, Stourbridge DY7 5HB 01384 87236
FECKENHAM RESERVES . . . . The Playing Fields, The Square, Mill Lane, Feckenham, B96 6HY 01527 89261
GREENHILL . . . . Cradley Town FC, Beeches View Avenue, Cradley, Halesowen B63 2HB 01384 569658
NORTHFIELD TOWN RESERVES . . . . Shenley Lane, Northfield, Birmingham B29 4HZ 0121 475 3870
PERRYWOOD . . . . Neel Park, Droitwich Road, Perdiswell, Worcester WR3 7SN 01905 75661
WARWICK TOWN . . . . Ajax Park, Hampton Road, Warwick CV34 6HX 01926 49629
WORCESTER CITY ACADEMY. Worcester City Football Dev. Ground, Bilford Rd, Worcester WR3 8QA. 07778 21657
IN: BNJS Mann & Co (P), Burntwood Town Reserves (P), Castle Vale JKS (P), Dosthill Colts (P), Droitwich Spa Res. (P), Greenhill (P), Northfiel
Town Res. (P)
OUT: Birmingham Academy (WN), Coventry Sphinx Res. (W), Coton Green (P), Droitwich Spa (P), Earlswood Town (P), Oldbury Athleti
(formerly Wernley Athletic) (P)
Worcester City 'A' become Worcester City Academy

JACK MOULD TROPHY *(Division Two and Three teams)*

FIRST ROUND
BNJS Mann & Co. 2 **Droitwich Spa Res.** 3
Chelmsley Town 6 Wernley Athletic 0 *(Chelmsley expelled)*
Chelmsley Town Res. 2 **Northfield Town Res.** 3 *aet*
Continental Star Res. 3 Cadbury Athletic Res. 1
Coventry Sphinx Res. 3 Burntwood Town Res. 1
Dosthill Colts 3 Ettington Res. 2
Feckenham Res. 2 Worcester City 'A' 0

Knowle Res. 2 Heather Athletic Res. 0
Perrywood 2 Shipston Excelsior 1
Studley Athletic 2 **Castle Vale JKS** 3
Warwick Town 1 Greenhill 0 *aet*
SECOND ROUND
Castle Vale JKS 1 **Warwick Town** 2
Continental Star Res. 1 Droitwich Spa 1 *aet (4-2p)*
Cov. Sphinx Res. 1 Coton Green 1 *aet*

	BNJS Mann & Co	Burntwood T. Res.	Castle Vale JKS	Chelmsley Town Res.	Dosthill Colts	Droitwich Spa Res.	Ettington Res.	Greenhill	Heather Athletic Res.	Kenilworth Town KH Res.	Knowle Res.	Northfield Town Res.	Shipston Excelsior	Studley Athletic
BNJS Mann & Co		4-2	0-0	1-2	1-2	3-0	7-0	2-3	3-0	1-0	3-1	2-1	3-1	5-0
Burntwood Town Res.	1-2		2-7	3-0	1-1	1-0	3-1	0-3	0-1	1-0	1-2	0-0	2-0	2-2
Castle Vale JKS	1-2	4-0	D	0-0	1-1	2-0	3-3	3-1	W-L	1-1	1-1	4-2	3-0	6-1
Chelmsley Town Res.	1-1	0-4	1-3	I	2-3	1-0	1-1	2-1	0-4	2-1	3-0	1-1	1-2	3-0
Dosthill Colts	4-3	3-3	1-2	2-1	V	1-1	1-1	2-0	2-0	3-0	4-5	2-2	0-2	5-2
Droitwich Spa Res.	3-1	0-0	0-0	1-1	3-2		1-0	1-1	1-1	1-1	2-2	0-0	1-1	2-1
Ettington Res.	5-4	3-1	6-2	3-2	2-1	1-1		4-1	5-2	2-0	3-2	1-3	3-1	4-0
Greenhill	1-0	2-0	0-3	4-0	3-2	2-0	2-3	T	2-1	3-0	1-0	1-4	3-1	2-0
Heather Athletic Res.	0-5	2-1	1-4	1-3	1-4	1-1	3-5	0-2	H	2-0	1-4	2-0	3-3	2-2
Kenilworth Town KH Res.	0-4	0-1	0-1	2-2	0-5	0-2	0-4	2-1	1-1	R	3-1	1-2	1-1	0-2
Knowle Res.	1-2	1-1	0-3	1-3	3-3	1-2	2-5	1-2	3-1	3-3	E		2-1	4-2
Northfield Town Res.	0-0	2-1	0-2	0-0	2-4	2-1	1-3	2-3	0-0	2-1	2-3	E	7-1	0-3
Shipston Excelsior	1-3	1-4	3-6	1-1	3-7	2-3	3-2	0-0	0-3	2-3	1-3	1-0		2-2
Studley Athletic	3-7	0-4	3-7	0-1	2-0	0-2	3-6	3-1	0-3	3-1	1-3	0-2	1-2	

Division Three	P	W	D	L	F	A	Pts
Castle Vale JKS	26	17	7	2	69	29	58
Ettington Res.	26	17	4	5	76	50	55
BNJS Mann & Co	26	16	3	7	69	33	51
Greenhill	26	15	2	9	45	36	47
Dosthill Colts	26	12	7	7	65	46	43
Droitwich Spa Res.	26	8	12	6	28	27	36
Chelmsley Town Res.	26	9	9	8	35	40	36
Burntwood Town Res.	26	9	6	11	39	41	33
Northfield Town Res.	26	8	8	10	39	39	32
Knowle Res.	26	8	7	11	49	55	31
Heather Athletic Res. -3	26	7	6	13	36	51	24
Shipston Excelsior	26	4	8	14	36	67	20
Studley Athletic	26	5	3	18	36	76	18
Kenilworth TKH Res.	26	3	6	17	21	53	15

CHALLENGE URN

FIRST ROUND
Burntwood Res. 2 **Dosthill** 3
Heather Athletic Res. 1 Droitwich Spa Res. 1 *aet* (4-3p)
Knowle Res. 1 **Castle Vale JKS** 3
Northfield Town Res. 1 **Chelmsley Town Res. 4**
Studley Athletic 4 Kenilworth Town KH Res. 0

QUARTER-FINALS
Dosthill Colts (scr.) v **Castle Vale JKS** (w/o)
Ett'gton Res. 3 Chelmsley Res. 1
Heather Ath. Res. 1 **Greenhill 4**
Shipston Excelsior 1 **Studley A. 3**

SEMI-FINALS
(played over two legs)
Ettington Res. 1 Greenhill 0, Greenhill 2 **Ettington Res.** 1 *aet* (2-4p)
Studley Ath. 2 Castle Vale JKS 1, **Castle Vale JKS** 5 Studley Ath 0

FINAL
(May 1st at Coventry Copsewood)
Castle Vale JKS 4 Ettington Res. 1

WWW.NLNEWSDESK.CO.UK

MIDLAND COMBINATION DIVISION THREE CONSTITUTION 2007-08

AUSTIN SPORTS & SOCIAL.. Austin Sports & Social Club, Tessell Lane, Longbridge, Birmingham B31 2SF............... 0121 475 1641
CASTLE VALE RESERVES .... The Glades, Lugtrout Lane, Solihull B91 2RX 0121 711 1422
CHELMSLEY TOWN RESERVES .. The Pavilions, Coleshill Road, Marston Green, Birmingham B37 7HW 0121 779 5400
EARLSWOOD TOWN RESERVES.... The Pavilions, Malthouse Lane, Earlswood, Solihull B94 5DX 07923 415501
EVESHAM UNITED 'A'............. Evesham High School, Four Pools Road, Evesham WR11 1DQ...................... 07718 990555
GSA & SMETHWICK TOWN .... Hadley Stadium, Wilson Road, Smethwick B66 4ND 0121 434 4848
HEATHER ST JOHN RESERVES .... St John's Park, Ravenstone Road, Heather LE67 2QJ 01530 263986
HENLEY FOREST .... Henley-in-Arden Sports & Social Ground, Stratford Road, Henley-in-Arden B95 6AD 01564 792022
KENILWORTH TOWN KH............. Gypsy Lane, off Rouncil Lane, Kenilworth CV8 1FQ 01926 850851
KNOWLE RESERVES .... Hampton Road, Knowle, Solihull B93 0NX 01564 779807
LITTLETON RESERVES.......... Five Acres, Pebworth Road, North Littleton, Evesham WR11 8QL 07966 297971
RACING CLUB WARWICK RESERVES .. Warks College, Stratford Rd, Henley-in-Arden B95 6AB.................... 07745 786110
SHIPSTON EXCELSIOR .... Shipston Sports Club, London Road, Shipston-on-Stour CV36 4EP 01608 661139
STUDLEY ATHLETIC .... Studley Sports & Social Club, Eldorado Close, Studley B80 7HP 01527 852671
IN: Austin Sports & Social (formerly Austin Social Select) (P – Stratford-upon-Avon Alliance Premier Division), Castle Vale Reserves (N), Earlswood Town Reserves (P – Stratford-upon-Avon Alliance Premier Division), Evesham United 'A' (N), GSA & Smethwick Town (N), Henley Forest (P – Stratford-upon-Avon Alliance Premier Division), Littleton Reserves (P – Stratford-upon-Avon Alliance Division One), Racing Club Warwick Reserves (N)
OUT: BNJS Mann & Co (P), Burntwood Town Reserves (P), Castle Vale JKS (P), Dosthill Colts (P), Droitwich Spa Res. (P), Ettington Reserves (W), Greenhill (P), Northfield Town Res. (P)
Heather Athletic Reserves become Heather St John Reserves

Droitwich Spa Res. 1 **Northfield Town Res. 2**
Enville Athletic 3 Dosthill Colts 1
Knowle Res. (w/o) v Birmingham Academy (scr.)
Perrywood 4 Feckenham Res. 1
Wernley Athletic 5 Earlswood Town 1

QUARTER-FINALS
Enville Athletic v **Cov. Sphinx Res.** 1
Knowle Res. 2 Perrywood 1
Northfield Res. 0 **Wernley Athletic** 5
Warwick Town 1 **Cont. Star Res.** 2
SEMI-FINALS
(played over two legs)
Cont. Star Res. 0 **Cov. Sphinx Res.** 2,

Coventry Sphinx Res. 2 Continental Star Res. 1
Wernley Athletic 5 Knowle Res. 0, Knowle Res. 1 **Wernley Athletic** 4
FINAL
(May 12th at Coleshill Town)
Wernley Athletic 4 Coventry Sphinx Res. 1

NORTH BERKS LEAGUE

	Ardington & Lockinge	Blewbury	Coleshill United	Drayton	East Hendred	Faringdon Town	Grove Rangers	Lambourn Sports	Marcham	Saxton Rovers	Steventon	Wallingford Athletic
Ardington & Lockinge	D	2-1	5-0	3-1	9-0	3-0	2-2	3-0	4-3	2-0	4-1	W-L
Blewbury	1-3	I	1-0	1-2	3-1	0-3	3-0	0-3	3-1	1-2	0-2	3-5
Coleshill United	2-2	0-1	V	5-0	3-1	4-1	3-0	1-4	2-2	0-5	4-0	W-L
Drayton	0-2	6-2	2-0	I	1-1	3-2	0-5	0-5	3-1	3-3	5-3	4-2
East Hendred	1-4	2-3	0-1	2-4	S	0-3	3-2	1-8	1-7	0-3	2-3	4-3
Faringdon Town	2-2	3-3	2-0	4-2	5-2	I	4-2	1-2	2-3	0-0	4-0	2-1
Grove Rangers	1-3	0-5	2-1	2-2	2-5	0-1	O	0-2	2-3	2-3	3-4	1-0
Lambourn Sports	0-3	1-1	0-2	4-1	5-0	1-1	3-1	N	2-1	1-3	0-3	2-1
Marcham	1-6	1-2	0-3	1-5	6-2	1-3	2-2	3-2		1-3	2-3	0-5
Saxton Rovers	1-1	1-0	5-2	2-1	5-2	0-3	7-0	3-2	3-1	O	2-0	1-1
Steventon	0-0	2-4	3-2	2-1	3-1	0-0	2-2	5-3	6-3	1-4	N	4-2
Wallingford Athletic	2-3	1-0	1-2	3-2	W-L	3-2	5-1	3-4	3-1	L-W	L-W	E

Division One	P	W	D	L	F	A	Pts
Ardington & Lockinge	22	17	5	0	66	19	56
Saxton Rovers	22	16	4	2	56	24	52
Steventon	22	12	3	7	47	48	39
Lambourn Sports	22	12	2	8	54	37	38
Faringdon Town	22	11	5	6	48	32	38
Coleshill United	22	10	2	10	37	37	32
Drayton	22	9	3	10	48	55	30
Blewbury	22	9	2	11	38	41	29
Wallingford Athletic	22	8	1	13	41	36	25
Marcham	22	5	2	15	44	67	17
Grove Rangers	22	3	4	15	32	63	13
East Hendred	22	3	1	18	31	83	10

NORTH BERKS LEAGUE DIVISION ONE CONSTITUTION 2007-08

ARDINGTON & LOCKINGE . . . . White Road, Ardington, Wantage . . . . None
BLEWBURY . . . . Bohams Road, Blewbury, Didcot OX11 9QF . . . . None
COLESHILL UNITED . . . . Bottom of the Hill, Coleshill . . . . None
DRAYTON . . . . Recreation Ground, Lockway, Drayton, Abingdon OX14 4LG . . . . None
FARINGDON TOWN . . . . Tucker Park, Park Road, Faringdon SN7 7BP 01367 24175
HARWELL INTERNATIONAL . . . Main Gate, Harwell International Business Centre, Didcot OX11 0RA 01235 82022
HARWELL VILLAGE . . . . Westfields Recreation Ground, Harwell, Didcot . . . . None
LAMBOURN SPORTS . . . . Bockhampton Road, Lambourn, Hungerford RG17 8PS 01488 7221
MARCHAM . . . . Moreland Road, Marcham, Abingdon OX13 6PY . . . . None
SAXTON ROVERS . . . . Recreation Ground, Caldecott Road, Abingdon OX14 5ET . . . . None
STEVENTON . . . . Steventon Green, Milton Lane, Steventon, Abingdon OX13 6SA . . . . None
WOOTTON & DRY SANDFORD . . . . Wootton & Dry Sandford CC, Besseleigh Road, Wootton . . . . None
IN: Harwell International (P), Harwell Village (P), Wootton & Dry Sandford (P)
OUT: East Hendred (R), Grove Rangers (R), Wallingford Athletic (R)

NORTH BERKS CUP

FIRST ROUND
Benson 2 **Sutton Courtenay** 5
Benson Lions 1 Crowmarsh Gifford 1 *aet* (6-5p)
Challow United 3 Didcot Casuals 1
Childrey 2 **Harwell Village** 5
Coleshill United 4 Wallingford Ath. 0
Drayton 1 **Wootton & Dry Sandford** 3
Hagbourne United 0 East Hendred 0 *aet* (4-2p)
Hanney United 1 **Botley United** 2
Harwell International 0 **Faringdon Town** 1
Kingsclere 0 Saxton Rovers 0 *aet* (7-6p)
Lambourn Sports 3 Marcham 0

Long Wittenham Athletic 1 **Uffington United** 3
Stanford-in-the-Vale 1 **Ardington & Lockinge** 3
Steventon 2 Blewbury 1
Warborough & Shillingford 0 **Grove Rangers** 4
SECOND ROUND
Appleton Abingdon 0 **Hagbourne Utd** 1
Benson Lions 2 Coleshill United 1
Botley Utd 4 Wootton & DS 4 *aet* (8-7p)
Faringdon Town 3 Challow United 2 *aet*
Grove Rangers (w/o) v Kingsclere (scr.)
Harwell Village 0 **Ardington & Lockinge** 3

Steventon 2 **Lambourn Sports** 6
Sutton Courtenay 7 Uffington United 0
QUARTER-FINALS
Botley Utd 2 **Ardington & Lockinge** 3
Faringdon Town 6 Appleton Abingdon 0
Lambourn Sports 4 Benson Lions 3
Sutton Courtenay 1 **Grove Rangers** 3
SEMI-FINALS
Ardington & Lockinge 1 Grove Rgrs 0
(at Lambourn Sports)
Lambourn Sports 2 Faringdon Town 1
(at Ardington & Lockinge)
FINAL
(May 12th at Abingdon United)
Ardington & L. 2 Lambourn 2 *aet* (4-2p)

CHARITY SHIELD

FIRST ROUND
Appleton Abingdon 3 **Blewbury** 6
Ardington & Lockinge 4 Warborough & Shillingford 1
Benson 4 Hanney United 0
Botley United 0 **Harwell International** 4
Challow Utd 6 **Sutton Courtenay** 8 *aet*
Crowmarsh Gifford 2 Wootton & DS 1
Drayton 0 **Saxton Rovers** 6
Hagbourne United 0 **Childrey** 2
Harwell Village 2 **Kingsclere** 3
Lambourn Sports 1 **Coleshill United** 2
Marcham 2 **Didcot Casuals** 3
Stanford-in-the-Vale 1 **Long Wittenham Athletic** 1 *aet (3-5p)*

Steventon 4 East Hendred 1
Uffington United 2 **Benson Lions** 3
Wallingford Athletic 3 Grove Rangers 0
SECOND ROUND
Benson 2 **Coleshill United** 4 *aet*
Benson Lions 0 **Didcot Casuals** 1
Blewbury 2 Wallingford Athletic 1
Crowmarsh Gifford 4 Childrey United 1
Harwell International 2 Steventon 1
Long Wittenham Athletic 3 Kingsclere 2
Saxton Rovers 3 Ardington & Lockinge 1
Sutton Courtenay 3 Faringdon Town 2

QUARTER-FINALS
Blewbury 2 Didcot Casuals 0
Coleshill United 4 Crowmarsh Gifford 4 *aet (4-2p)*
Saxton Rov. 0 **Harwell International** 2
Sutton Courtenay 3 Long Wittenham Athletic 1
SEMI-FINAL
Coleshill United 3 Blewbury 0 *(at Saxton Rovers)*
Sutton Courtenay 1 **Harwell International** 2 *(at Harwell Village)*
FINAL
(May 5th at Abingdon United)
Coleshill Utd 2 Harwell International 1

Division Two	P	W	D	L	F	A	Pts
Wootton & Dry Sandford	20	19	0	1	77	23	57
Harwell Village	20	14	1	5	51	21	43
Harwell International	20	10	6	4	48	29	36
Sutton Courtenay	20	9	5	6	44	39	32
AFC Benson	20	7	5	8	37	41	26
Appleton Abingdon	20	7	5	8	54	59	26
Shrivenham 'A'	20	6	4	10	38	38	22
Long Wittenham Athletic	20	6	4	10	35	60	22
Saxton Rovers Res.	20	5	4	11	44	59	19
Stanford-in-the-Vale	20	3	5	12	35	59	14
Blewbury Res.	20	2	5	13	21	56	11

Division Three	P	W	D	L	F	A	Pts
Kingsclere	22	17	4	1	65	17	55
Crowmarsh Gifford	22	14	3	5	55	24	45
Lambourn Sports Res.	22	13	3	6	75	34	42
Coleshill United Res.	22	13	2	7	56	36	41
Didcot Casuals	22	10	4	8	53	34	34
Ardington & Lock. Res.	22	10	3	9	57	44	33
Faringdon Town Res.	22	8	5	9	40	37	29
Benson Lions	22	9	1	12	42	35	28
Warborough & Shil'ford	22	6	4	12	43	72	22
Marcham Res.	22	5	5	12	41	76	20
Drayton Res.	22	6	2	14	21	65	20
East Hendred Res.	22	2	2	18	14	88	8

Division Four	P	W	D	L	F	A	Pts
Grove Rangers Res.	22	17	1	4	63	29	52
Botley United	22	15	1	6	51	24	46
Childrey	22	14	3	5	63	31	45
Challow United	22	13	4	5	55	31	43
Wootton & Dry S. Res.	22	13	3	6	58	37	42
Harwell International Res.	22	8	7	7	42	39	31
Steventon Res.	22	9	4	9	45	52	31
Uffington United	22	7	3	12	32	54	24
Long Wittenham Ath. Res.	22	6	3	13	30	53	21
Hanney United	22	4	4	14	35	59	16
Hagbourne United	22	3	4	15	22	60	13
Stanford-in-the-Vale Res.	22	3	3	16	32	59	12

Division Five	P	W	D	L	F	A	Pts
Harwell Village Res.	22	17	0	5	66	42	51
Didcot Casuals Res.	22	15	1	6	80	35	46
Harwell International 'A'	22	13	1	8	82	41	40
Kennington United Res.	22	12	3	7	65	46	39
Faringdon Town 'A'	22	11	5	6	63	46	38
Benson Lions Res.	22	11	4	7	58	44	37
Uffington United Res.	22	11	1	10	55	37	34
Coleshill United 'A'	22	10	4	8	45	57	34
Hanney United Res.	22	7	3	12	40	70	24
Hagbourne United Res.	22	4	3	15	44	92	15
Sutton Courtenay Res.	22	3	4	15	43	87	13
Challow United Res.	22	3	1	18	35	79	10

WAR MEMORIAL CUP

FINAL
(April 27th at Wantage Town)
Wootton & Dry Sandford 5 Harwell Village 1

A G KINGHAM CUP

FINAL
(April 28th at Milton United)
Shrivenham 'A' 3 Grove Rangers Res. 1

LEAGUE CUP

FINAL
(April 14th at Didcot Town)
Grove Rangers Res. 1 Wootton & Dry Sandford Res. 0

NAIRNE PAUL CUP

FINAL
(April 21st at AFC Wallingford)
Wootton & Dry Sandford Res. 5 Lambourn Sports Res. 1

NORTH DEVON LEAGUE

	Appledore Res.	Barnstaple AAC	Boca Seniors	Bradworthy United	Braunton	Clovelly	Dolton Rangers	Georgeham & Croyde	Hartland	Kilkhampton	Lovacott/J&A	Morwenstow Res.	Northam Lions	Putford	Shamwickshire Rovers	Woolacombe
Appledore Res.	P	3-0	1-4	3-1	0-2	6-0	2-2	1-2	4-2	2-1	2-0	1-0	2-1	0-1	1-0	2-1
Barnstaple AAC	1-3	R	2-2	3-4	1-1	6-2	5-2	1-2	5-5	2-3	2-0	1-2	4-1	1-1	0-3	1-2
Boca Seniors	4-1	2-1	E	4-2	3-0	7-1	5-3	6-2	7-2	6-2	7-2	3-2	1-2	3-2	1-0	5-2
Bradworthy United	W-L	1-2	1-1	M	0-4	5-0	3-0	0-1	1-1	3-1	4-2	0-2	3-4	3-1	0-1	0-0
Braunton	3-1	6-1	3-3	W-L	I	7-0	2-1	1-2	2-3	3-0	4-1	W-L	4-0	2-0	2-1	4-1
Clovelly	2-9	1-5	1-3	1-5	0-5	E	0-5	0-2	0-5	1-3	5-7	3-3	5-2	3-3	1-8	1-4
Dolton Rangers	2-2	3-4	3-5	0-2	1-6	3-0	R	1-3	5-1	1-0	2-2	11-0	0-1	1-3	2-2	W-L
Georgeham & Croyde	1-0	5-2	3-1	2-0	2-1	3-0	6-0		3-0	7-0	1-2	2-1	3-0	4-0	2-5	0-1
Hartland	0-4	3-3	0-8	4-4	1-3	3-0	2-2	1-0	D	3-1	2-0	4-1	1-4	3-4	1-1	0-4
Kilkhampton	1-3	3-4	1-8	1-0	0-5	4-1	3-1	0-3	0-5	I	1-4	1-5	1-2	0-2	W-L	0-4
Lovacott/J&A	2-4	1-2	0-8	1-3	1-5	2-1	0-5	6-4	4-4		V	2-2	3-2	0-2	1-7	0-6
Morwenstow Res.	0-6	3-2	3-13	0-4	0-6	7-0	4-1	0-10	2-1	2-1	2-3	I	3-4	0-3	2-2	1-4
Northam Lions	1-2	1-1	3-6	0-3	1-6	6-0	1-4	0-2	2-1	4-1	1-1	3-3	S	2-1	1-6	W-L
Putford	0-1	1-1	2-2	0-3	2-0	4-3	0-2	1-2	2-1	2-1	5-4			I	1-3	1-2
Shamwickshire Rovers	4-1	4-2	0-1	3-1	2-2	9-1	6-3	2-0	3-0	2-0	8-0	4-0	3-0	2-1	O	1-4
Woolacombe	2-1	4-1	L-W	2-1	1-4	9-0	7-1	4-0	0-4	5-2	1-0	11-1	5-0	0-0	L-W	N

Premier Division		P	W	D	L	F	A	Pts
Boca Seniors		30	24	4	2	129	47	76
Braunton		30	23	3	4	95	27	72
Georgeham & Croyde		30	23	0	7	80	31	69
Shamwickshire Rovers		30	19	5	6	92	33	62
Appledore Res.		30	18	2	10	68	40	56
Woolacombe	*-12*	30	19	2	9	86	31	47
Bradworthy United	*-3*	30	13	4	13	56	45	40
Putford		30	11	6	13	48	53	39
Northam Lions		30	11	3	16	53	80	36
Barnstaple AAC		30	9	7	14	66	74	34
Hartland		30	9	6	15	63	81	33
Dolton Rangers		30	8	5	17	63	79	29
Lovacott/J&A		30	8	4	18	53	100	28
Morwenstow Res.	*-3*	30	8	4	18	52	108	25
Kilkhampton		30	7	1	22	37	92	22
Clovelly		30	1	2	27	33	153	5

WWW.CHERRYRED.CO.UK

BRAYFORD CUP

FIRST ROUND
Appledore Res. 2 Clovelly 0
Braunton 5 Kilkhampton 1
Georgeham & Croyde 0 **Bradworthy United** 1
Hartland 4 Putford 0
Morwenstow Res. 0 **Boca Seniors** 10
Northam Lions 2 Dolton Rangers 1
Shamwickshire Rovers 7 Lovacott/J&A 1
Woolacombe 2 **Barnstaple AAC** 4
QUARTER-FINALS
Appledore Res. 0 **Braunton** 2
Barnstaple AAC 0 **Hartland** 1
Boca Seniors 3 Bradworthy United 0 *(at Torrington)*
Shamwickshire Rovers 4 Northam Lions 0
SEMI-FINALS
Boca Seniors 8 Hartland 1
Braunton 2 Shamwickshire Rovers 1
FINAL
(May 12th at Ilfracombe Town)
Boca Seniors 1 Braunton 0

NORTH DEVON LEAGUE PREMIER DIVISION CONSTITUTION 2007-08

APPLEDORE RESERVES . . . . Marshford, Churchill Way, Appledore EX39 1PA 01237 477099
BARNSTAPLE AAC. . . . . Pottington Road, Barnstaple EX31 1JQ. . . . . None
BOCA SENIORS . . . . Tarka Tennis Centre, Seven Brethren Bank, Barnstaple EX31 2AS 01271 377701
BRADWORTHY UNITED. . . . . North Road, Bradworthy, Holsworthy EX22 7TJ. . . . . None
BRAUNTON. Lobb Sports Field, Saunton Road, Braunton EX33 1EB. . . . . None
COMBE MARTIN . . . . Hollands Park, Chapel Lane, Combe Martin . . . . None
DOLTON RANGERS . . . . The Playing Field, Cleave Hill, Dolton EX19 8QT . . . . None
GEORGEHAM . . . . The Recreation Ground, Newberry Road, Georgeham . . . . None
GROSVENOR. . . . . Tarka Tennis Centre, Seven Brethren Bank, Barnstaple EX31 2AS 01271 377701
HARTLAND . . . . Playing Field, Hartland . . . . None
KILKHAMPTON . . . . Lamb Park, Kilkhampton, Bude . . . . None
MORWENSTOW RESERVES . . . . Playing Field, Shop, Morwenstow, Bude EX23 9SQ. . . . . None
NORTH MOLTON . . . . Rocksfield, Old Road, North Molton 01598 740563
NORTHAM LIONS . . . . Burrough Farm, Churchill Way, Northam, Bideford EX39 1SU . . . . None
PUTFORD . . . . Parkham Village Hall, Parkham, Bideford EX39 5PG. 01237 472462
SHAMWICKSHIRE ROVERS . . Pollyfield Community Centre, Avon Road, East-the-Water, Bideford EX39 4BL. . . . . None

IN: Combe Martin (P), Grosvenor (P), North Molton (P)
OUT: Clovelly (R), Lovacott J/A (W), Woolacombe (W)

Senior Division		P	W	D	L	F	A	Pts
North Molton		26	24	2	0	93	19	74
Shamwickshire Rovers Res.		26	21	1	4	109	34	64
Combe Martin		26	20	3	3	107	32	63
Torridgeside		26	18	3	5	77	34	57
Ilfracombe Town Res.		26	13	5	8	58	44	44
Braunton Res.		26	13	2	11	75	58	41
Pilton Academicals		26	10	3	13	65	64	33
Chittlehampton		26	10	3	13	56	70	33
Appledore 'A'		26	8	4	14	54	87	28
High Bickington		26	8	2	16	61	72	26
Torrington 'A'		26	6	4	16	53	95	22
South Molton		26	5	2	19	29	99	17
Northam Lions Res.	-3	26	4	3	19	43	99	12
Woolsery		26	2	3	21	25	98	9

COMBE MARTIN FINAL
(April 28th at Combe Martin)
Torridgeside 3 North Molton 2 *aet*

Intermediate Division One		P	W	D	L	F	A	Pts
Bratton Fleming		26	19	6	1	89	32	63
Barnstaple AAC Res.		26	17	4	5	79	45	55
Torrington Admirals		26	16	5	5	70	39	53
Bude Town Res.		26	16	2	8	77	59	50
Combe Martin Res.		26	14	7	5	70	45	49
North Molton Res.		26	11	7	8	68	49	40
Dolton Rangers Res.		26	12	2	12	99	78	38
Braunton 'A'		26	11	4	11	59	66	37
Equalizers		26	8	5	13	33	62	29
Georgeham/Croyde Res.		26	8	4	14	52	67	28
Sporting Barum		26	7	5	14	50	66	26
Hartland Res.		26	5	4	17	48	77	19
Lynton & Lynmouth		26	5	4	17	54	89	19
Bradworthy United Res.	-3	26	3	1	22	33	107	7

ARLINGTON CUP FINAL
(April 21st at South Molton)
Bratton Fleming 2 Dolton Rangers Res. 1

Intermediate Division Two		P	W	D	L	F	A	Pts
Grosvenor		24	20	3	1	112	23	63
Shebbear United		24	18	2	4	78	28	56
Anchor		24	16	4	4	102	54	52
South Molton Res.		24	12	6	6	64	48	42
Pilton Academicals Res.		24	12	5	7	63	58	41
Torrington 'A'		24	10	4	10	64	47	34
Buckland Brewer		24	7	8	9	45	40	29
Park United		24	7	6	11	46	47	27
Putford Res.		24	7	6	11	36	62	27
High Bickington Res.		24	7	5	12	55	84	26
Lovacott/J&A Res.		24	5	4	15	50	88	19
Chittlehampton Res.	-3	24	6	1	17	41	88	16
Woolsery Res.		24	1	2	21	23	112	5

Clovelly Res. and Lynton & Lynmouth Res. – records expunged

BIDEFORD TOOL CUP FINAL
(May 5th at Appledore)
Shebbear United 4 Grosvenor 3 *aet*

NORTH WEST COUNTIES LEAGUE

	Abbey Hey	Atherton Colls	Atherton LR	Bacup Borough	Colne	Congleton Town	Curzon Ashton	FC United	Flixton	Formby	Glossop NE	Maine Road	Nantwich Town	Nelson	Newcastle Town	Ramsbottom	Salford City	Silsden	Squires Gate	St Helens Town	Stone Dominoes	Trafford
Abbey Hey		3-3	3-1	1-1	0-1	0-3	0-2	1-5	1-1	2-1	0-1	1-1	0-3	4-3	0-0	0-1	0-4	2-2	1-0	0-3	1-0	0-2
Atherton Collieries	4-0		2-0	3-1	1-2	1-2	2-0	0-3	3-1	3-1	0-0	1-0	4-1	5-1	1-1	5-1	0-0	1-2	3-0	1-0	1-0	1-4
Atherton LR	2-3	0-0		2-4	2-1	0-2	2-2	0-7	3-1	2-0	2-5	0-0	0-2	3-0	1-0	0-2	1-2	0-2	2-1	3-4	4-2	0-2
Bacup Borough	1-0	3-3	1-1		2-0	2-0	0-0	1-2	1-3	3-1	2-3	0-1	1-4	0-3	1-1	1-3	1-1	5-0	1-1	0-0	1-1	2-2
Colne	2-2	2-2	4-0	1-1		1-0	1-3	1-5	1-1	4-1	2-2	1-3	1-4	3-0	1-1	1-3	2-2	3-3	1-2	3-2	2-0	1-2
Congleton Town	3-1	0-1	5-2	2-1	3-0	D	0-3	1-1	3-3	4-1	2-1	1-1	1-2	7-0	1-3	1-0	2-3	2-1	2-1	1-0	5-0	0-3
Curzon Ashton	2-0	7-0	7-0	4-0	4-1	1-0	I	1-3	5-0	2-1	6-1	1-2	1-0	2-0	1-5	3-0	0-0	3-0	5-0	5-0	4-1	2-0
FC United of Manchester	7-1	0-3	7-1	3-0	6-2	3-0	3-2	V	4-0	5-0	8-0	3-0	2-0	6-0	5-1	3-2	4-2	4-2	8-0	3-0	7-0	4-4
Flixton	1-1	2-2	1-1	1-2	1-1	3-0	2-2	1-1	I	3-1	2-0	2-3	0-1	3-2	2-1	2-2	3-1	1-2	2-1	5-1	4-0	0-2
Formby	2-2	2-1	2-2	0-3	1-2	2-5	1-3	0-2		S	2-3	1-0	5-0	0-1	1-1	0-1	1-4	2-1	0-2	1-0	3-4	
Glossop North End	1-0	2-1	0-3	3-1	1-0	3-4	1-4	1-3	3-0	2-1	I	0-2	0-1	2-0	0-0	2-4	1-2	1-2	1-2	4-0	3-2	0-0
Maine Road	1-0	2-1	3-2	3-1	0-3	2-0	0-0	1-2	4-1	3-0	2-0	O	2-4	5-1	2-1	4-3	2-2	0-1	2-2	0-2	7-1	2-3
Nantwich Town	4-0	2-2	7-1	2-0	1-1	2-2	1-1	1-1	2-1	5-0	3-1	1-0	N	4-0	3-3	3-1	1-0	3-1	5-2	4-2	4-0	1-2
Nelson	2-1	0-1	1-3	1-3	1-2	1-3	0-2	0-8	2-1	2-0	0-3	3-1	2-2		0-0	1-2	0-3	0-1	1-0	0-0	0-2	2-2
Newcastle Town	4-0	2-0	3-2	2-2	0-0	1-1	2-3	2-3	3-2	3-1	2-3	1-0	1-0	4-1	O	1-3	3-4	2-3	2-0	1-0	5-0	1-0
Ramsbottom United	0-1	2-2	9-1	1-0	0-3	1-0	1-3	1-2	0-1	7-1	0-1	0-2	0-0	3-2	1-0	N	2-3	2-1	3-3	3-0	3-1	1-1
Salford City	1-0	3-0	1-0	1-1	1-3	4-4	1-3	2-1	3-1	1-0	3-3	1-2	5-2	4-2	3-1		E	2-0	5-1	2-1	4-0	1-1
Silsden	1-3	1-2	1-0	2-0	0-3	2-0	0-3	2-2	1-3	1-1	3-1	1-4	1-3	1-2	4-1	3-1	1-1		2-4	1-3	1-1	3-1
Squires Gate	2-2	1-1	2-2	0-1	0-3	4-4	0-3	0-1	3-2	2-1	2-2	0-6	0-1	3-0	0-1	5-0	0-5	2-1		1-1	7-1	0-4
St Helens Town	0-2	0-2	1-5	0-1	1-3	2-1	0-1	0-2	0-3	0-3	0-4	0-4	4-4	3-1	1-3	2-6	2-3	5-0		1-1	0-4	
Stone Dominoes	0-4	3-4	1-5	1-0	3-3	1-4	1-3	0-4	0-4	1-3	2-6	2-3	2-6	1-1	0-2	1-3	1-6	2-3	0-3	2-4		0-8
Trafford	5-1	0-0	2-2	3-0	1-1	1-1	1-5	0-1	1-0	7-0	3-1	3-0	1-2	3-0	3-2	1-1	2-3	1-3	4-1	2-0	1-0	

Division One	P	W	D	L	F	A	Pts
FC United of Manchester	42	36	4	2	157	36	112
Curzon Ashton	42	31	6	5	116	38	99
Nantwich Town	42	29	8	5	108	41	95
Salford City	42	26	9	7	103	55	87
Trafford	42	24	11	7	94	46	83
Maine Road	42	22	7	13	79	58	73
Atherton Collieries	42	19	13	10	72	55	70
Ramsbottom United	42	19	7	16	78	63	64
Glossop North End	42	19	6	17	71	71	63
Congleton Town	42	18	8	16	75	62	62
Colne	42	16	13	13	75	70	61
Newcastle Town	42	16	10	16	70	63	58
Flixton	42	15	11	16	72	67	56
Silsden	42	16	6	20	66	79	54
Bacup Borough	42	11	13	18	50	65	46
Atherton LR	42	11	9	22	65	106	42
Abbey Hey	42	10	10	22	44	83	40
Squires Gate	42	10	8	24	56	97	38
St Helens Town	42	10	6	26	47	92	36
Nelson	42	7	6	29	41	113	27
Formby	42	6	4	32	43	111	22
Stone Dominoes	42	2	5	37	36	147	9

NORTH WEST COUNTIES LEAGUE DIVISION ONE CONSTITUTION 2007-08

ABBEY HEY . . . . Abbey Stadium, Goredale Avenue, Gorton M18 7HD 0161 231 7147
ATHERTON COLLIERIES . . . . Alder House, Alder Street, Atherton M46 9EY 07729 374641
ATHERTON LR . . . . Crilly Park, Spa Road, Atherton M46 9XX 01942 883950
BACUP BOROUGH . . . . West View, Cowfoot Lane, Blackthorn, Bacup OL13 8EE 01706 878655
COLNE . . . . Holt House Stadium, Harrison Drive, Colne BB8 9SE 01282 862545
CONGLETON TOWN . . . . Booth Street Ground, off Crescent Road, Congleton CW12 4DG 01260 274460
FLIXTON . . . . Valley Road, Flixton, Manchester M41 8RQ 0161 747 7757
FORMBY . . . . Altcar Road, Formby L37 8DL 01704 833505
GLOSSOP NORTH END . . . . Arthur Goldthorpe Stadium, Surrey Street, Glossop SK13 7AJ 01457 855469
MAINE ROAD . . . . Manchester County FA Ground, Branthingham Road, Chorlton-cum-Hardy M21 0TT 0161 881 0299
NELSON . . . . Victoria Park, Lomeshaye Way, Nelson BB9 7AF 01282 613820
NEWCASTLE TOWN . . Lyme Valley Parkway Stadium, Buckmaster Avenue, Clayton, Newcastle-under-Lyme ST5 3BF 01782 662351
RAMSBOTTOM UNITED . . . . Riverside Ground, Acre Bottom, Ramsbottom BL8 3JH 01706 822799
RUNCORN LINNETS . . . . . . Witton Albion FC, Wincham Park, Chapel Street, Wincham, Northwich CW9 6DA 01606 43008
SALFORD CITY . . . . Moor Lane, Kersal, Salford M7 3PZ 0161 792 6287
SILSDEN . . . . Keighley Cougars RFC, Cougar Park, Hard Ings, Keighley BD21 3RF 01535 211311
SQUIRES GATE . . . . School Road, Marton, Blackpool FY4 3DS 01253 798584
ST HELENS TOWN . . . . St Helens RLFC, Knowsley Road, Dunriding Lane, St Helens WA10 4AD 08707 565252
TRAFFORD . . . . Shawe View, Pennybridge Lane, Flixton, Urmston M41 5DL 0161 747 1727
WINSFORD UNITED . . . . Barton Stadium, Kingsway, Winsford CW7 3AE 01606 558447

IN: Runcorn Linnets (P), Winsford United (P)
OUT: Curzon Ashton (P – Northern Premier League Division One North), FC United of Manchester (P – Northern Premier League Division One North), Nantwich Town (P – Northern Premier League Division One South), Stone Dominoes (R)

	Ashton Athletic	Ashton Town	Blackpool Mechanics	Bootle	Castleton Gabriels	Chadderton	Cheadle Town	Daisy Hill	Darwen	Eccleshall	Holker Old Boys	Leek CSOB	New Mills	Norton United	Oldham Town	Padiham	Runcorn Linnets	Winsford United
Ashton Athletic		1-2	0-2	1-2	2-1	0-1	1-1	3-1	2-2	0-2	0-0	1-3	0-2	1-0	0-2	2-0	2-1	2-2
Ashton Town	2-2		1-1	0-0	2-4	0-2	3-2	3-0	1-0	2-0	7-2	1-2	0-1	1-0	2-1	1-1	0-4	0-1
Blackpool Mechanics	1-0	3-4		0-1	4-0	0-2	1-0	1-1	1-2	0-2	2-0	1-1	1-1	1-0	0-3	1-3	0-0	1-3
Bootle	4-0	1-1	2-1	D	3-1	1-2	2-2	2-1	1-0	6-2	2-0	2-0	1-2	3-2	1-1	0-1	1-1	3-4
Castleton Gabriels	1-4	1-3	0-2	0-7	I	1-1	3-1	4-2	3-2	3-2	1-2	1-2	0-4	1-2	0-3	1-4	1-3	0-4
Chadderton	1-0	3-0	1-0	1-1	3-1	V	3-0	2-2	1-2	1-0	1-1	1-1	3-1	7-0	1-0	1-0	0-1	3-2
Cheadle Town	1-1	3-3	1-1	1-2	2-1	1-0	I	2-0	2-1	1-0	3-3	1-2	0-1	0-0	2-1	1-3	0-2	0-2
Daisy Hill	3-1	1-3	1-4	1-1	3-2	1-1	0-3	S	0-4	2-1	1-1	2-1	1-3	0-1	1-2	1-6	1-2	0-3
Darwen	2-2	2-1	1-0	4-0	3-0	2-1	0-2	0-0	I	1-0	2-0	2-1	0-2	3-1	2-2	3-1	1-3	2-2
Eccleshall	3-0	1-2	4-2	1-0	2-0	1-2	1-2	2-0	1-1	O	3-1	2-2	1-0	1-1	1-4	1-1	1-0	0-1
Holker Old Boys	2-2	2-3	0-2	1-1	3-1	2-2	4-2	0-2	2-2	2-1	N	0-1	2-2	3-2	1-3	1-3	1-1	0-4
Leek CSOB	3-3	0-1	0-2	1-0	4-1	1-2	2-0	2-1	1-0	2-1	5-0		1-1	1-2	3-2	0-2	0-2	1-4
New Mills	4-0	3-0	3-2	5-3	3-0	3-2	2-0	7-1	1-2	1-1	4-1	2-2	T	2-1	1-2	2-1	2-1	2-1
Norton United	1-0	1-4	1-0	1-6	2-2	2-1	2-2	1-1	3-2	0-3	2-4	1-1	1-2	W	0-1	1-3	1-2	1-3
Oldham Town	3-2	3-0	4-1	2-1	4-1	3-2	4-1	3-1	1-1	1-4	2-2	1-2	4-2		O	0-1	2-0	1-5
Padiham	1-1	4-0	3-0	3-2	1-1	2-1	5-0	2-3	2-2	3-0	3-1	1-1	2-0	2-1	5-1		1-0	1-5
Runcorn Linnets	4-1	4-2	2-1	2-0	5-0	2-1	3-2	4-3	3-1	2-0	2-1	6-1	5-3	2-0	4-2	3-1		1-2
Winsford United	2-1	0-0	1-0	3-1	1-1	1-3	1-0	0-1	2-2	0-2	0-0	7-2	3-1	2-0	4-2	1-3	0-0	

Division Two		P	W	D	L	F	A	Pts
Winsford United		34	23	7	4	82	35	76
Runcorn Linnets		34	24	4	6	77	35	76
Padiham		34	21	6	7	75	39	69
New Mills		34	21	6	7	74	42	69
Chadderton		34	18	7	9	59	35	61
Oldham Town		34	17	5	12	69	54	56
Darwen		34	14	10	10	56	45	52
Ashton Town		34	15	7	12	55	56	52
Leek CSOB		34	14	8	12	51	52	50
Bootle	-4	34	14	8	12	63	48	46
Eccleshall		34	12	6	16	45	46	42
Cheadle Town		34	9	8	17	41	60	35
Blackpool Mechanics	-6	34	10	6	18	39	48	30
Holker Old Boys		34	6	11	17	47	81	29
Daisy Hill		34	7	8	19	38	78	29
Ashton Athletic		34	6	10	18	38	62	28
Norton United		34	6	7	21	37	73	25
Castleton Gabriels		34	5	4	25	38	95	19

Reserve Division		P	W	D	L	F	A	Pts
Winsford United Res.		34	23	7	4	82	35	76
Runcorn Linnets Res.		34	24	4	6	77	35	76
Padiham Res.		34	21	6	7	75	39	69
New Mills Res.		34	21	6	7	74	42	69
Chadderton Res.		34	18	7	9	59	35	61
Oldham Town Res.		34	17	5	12	69	54	56
Darwen Res.		34	14	10	10	56	45	52
Ashton Town Res.		34	15	7	12	55	56	52
Leek CSOB Res.		34	14	8	12	51	52	50
Bootle Res.	-4	34	14	8	12	63	48	46
Eccleshall Res.		34	12	6	16	45	46	42
Cheadle Town Res.		34	9	8	17	41	60	35
Blackpool Mechs Res.	-6	34	10	6	18	39	48	30
Holker Old Boys Res.		34	6	11	17	47	81	29
Daisy Hill Res.		34	7	8	19	38	78	29
Ashton Athletic Res.		34	6	10	18	38	62	28
Norton United Res.		34	6	7	21	37	73	25
Castleton Gabriels Res.		34	5	4	25	38	95	19

WWW.NLNEWSDESK.CO.UK

RESERVES CUP

FINAL *(May 9th at Abbey Hey)*
FC United of Manchester Res. 4 Padiham Res. 1

NORTH WEST COUNTIES LEAGUE DIVISION TWO CONSTITUTION 2007-08

ASHTON ATHLETIC .... Brocstedes Park, Farm Road, Ashton-in-Makerfield WN4 0NQ 01942 716360
ASHTON TOWN .... Edge Green Street, Ashton-in-Makerfield, Wigan WN4 8SL 01942 510677
BLACKPOOL MECHANICS.......... Jepson Way, Common Edge Road, Blackpool FY4 5DY.................... 01253 761721
BOOTLE .... New Bucks Park, Vestey Road, off Bridle Road, Bootle, Liverpool L30 4UN 07866 912625
CASTLETON GABRIELS .... Butterworth Park, Heywood Road, Castleton, Rochdale OL11 3BY 01706 527103
CHADDERTON .... Andrew Street, Chadderton, Oldham OL9 0JT 0161 624 9733
CHEADLE TOWN.................... Park Road Stadium, Park Road, Cheadle, Stockport SK8 2AN 0161 428 2510
DAISY HILL .... New Sirs, St James Street, Westhoughton, Bolton BL5 2EB 01942 818544
DARWEN.............. Anchor Ground, Anchor Road, Darwen BB3 0BB 01254 705677
ECCLESHALL.................... Pershall Park, Chester Road, Eccleshall ST21 6NE 01785 851351
HOLKER OLD BOYS .... Rakesmoor Lane, Hawcoat, Barrow-in-Furness LA14 4QB 01229 828176
KIRKHAM & WESHAM............... Birley Arms, Brynning Lane, Warton, Preston PR4 1TN .... None
LEEK CSOB............. Leek Town FC, Harrison Park, Macclesfield Road, Leek ST13 8LD 01538 399278
NEW MILLS.................... Church Lane, Church Road, New Mills SK22 4NP 01663 747435
NORTON UNITED........ Norton CC & MW Institute, Community Drive, Smallthorne, Stoke-on-Trent ST6 1QF 01782 838290
OLDHAM TOWN......... Whitebank Stadium, Whitebank Road, Hollins, Oldham OL8 3JH 0161 624 2689
PADIHAM......... Arbories Memorial Spts Ground, Well Street, Padiham BB12 8LE 01282 773742
STONE DOMINOES .... Yarnfield Lane, Yarnfield, Stone ST3 7NT 01782 761891
IN: Kirkham & Wesham (P – West Lancs League Premier Division), Stone Dominoes (R)
OUT: Great Harwood Town (WN), Runcorn Linnets (P), Winsford United (P)

LEAGUE CUP

FIRST ROUND
Ashton Athletic 1 **Eccleshall** 2
Blackpool Mechanics 3 Bootle 0
Castleton Gabriels 1 **Chadderton** 3
Cheadle Town 0 **Norton United** 2
Darwen 0 **Daisy Hill** 2 *aet*
New Mills 3 Leek CSOB 3 *aet*
Leek CSOB 1 **New Mills** 2 *replay*
Oldham Town 3 Ashton Town 1 *aet*
Padiham (w/o) v Great Harwood Town (scr.)
Runcorn Linnets 1 **Holker Old Boys** 2 *aet (at Holker OB)*
SECOND ROUND
Atherton Collieries 2 Maine Road 1
Bacup Borough 3 **St Helens Town** 5
Blackpool Mechanics 0 **Atherton LR** 1
Chadderton 2 Daisy Hill 0
Congleton Town 2 Norton United 1
Eccleshall 0 **Curzon Ashton** 2
Flixton 7 Glossop North End 2
Holker Old Boys 1 **Salford City** 6
Nantwich Town 0 **FC United of Manchester** 3
Nelson 1 **Colne** 4
Newcastle Town 2 New Mills 0
Ramsbottom United 0 **Padiham** 1
Squires Gate 4 Abbey Hey 2 *aet*
Stone Dominoes 2 **Oldham Town** 4
Trafford 4 Formby 1

Winsford United 2 Silsden 2 *aet*
Silsden 2 Winsford United 1 *replay*
THIRD ROUND
Colne 0 **FC United of Manchester** 4
Congleton Town 3 Atherton Collieries 2
Curzon Ashton 6 Squires Gate 1
Newcastle Town 0 **Flixton** 1
Oldham Town 4 Trafford 0
Salford City 3 Chadderton 1
Silsden 4 Atherton LR 3
St Helens Town 0 **Padiham** 2 *(at St Helens Town)*
QUARTER-FINALS
Congleton Town 3 Padiham 2
Oldham Town 3 Flixton 3 *aet (at Flixton)*
Flixton 4 Oldham Town 2 *replay*
Salford City 1 **Curzon Ashton** 2 *aet*
Silsden 0 **FC United of Manchester** 3
SEMI-FINALS
(played over two legs)
Congleton Town 2 FC United of Manchester 2, **FC United of Manchester** 4 Congleton Town 3
Curzon Ashton 3 Flixton 1, Flixton 1 **Curzon Ashton** 4
FINAL
(May 3rd at Curzon Ashton)
FC United of Manchester 2 Curzon Ashton 1

DIVISION TWO TROPHY

FIRST ROUND
Eccleshall 3 Padiham 1
Great Harwood Town (scr.) v **Daisy Hill** (w/o)
New Mills 3 Blackpool Mechanics 1 *aet*
SECOND ROUND
Ashton Athletic 1 **Oldham Town** 4
Ashton Town 2 Cheadle Town 0 *(at Cheadle Town)*
Bootle 4 Eccleshall 0
Chadderton 3 Darwen 2
Daisy Hill 0 **New Mills** 5
Holker Old Boys 2 Norton United 0
Leek CSOB 2 Winsford United 2 *(at Winsford United)*
Winsford United 5 Leek CSOB 2 *replay*

Runcorn Linnets 9 Castleton Gabriels 1 *(at Castleton Gabriels)*
QUARTER-FINALS
Chadderton 1 **Oldham Town** 2
New Mills 3 Holker Old Boys 1
Runcorn Linnets 1 **Bootle** 2 *(at Bootle)*
Winsford United 5 Ashton Town 3
SEMI-FINALS
(played over two legs)
Bootle 0 Oldham Town 0, **Oldham Town** 1 Bootle 0
New Mills 3 Winsford United 1, Winsford United 3 **New Mills** 3
FINAL *(April 12th at Trafford)*
New Mills 3 Oldham Town 3 *aet (4-2p) (at Trafford)*

NORTHAMPTONSHIRE COMBINATION

Note – Corby Grampian withdrew during the course of the season Their results are shown herein but are expunged from the league table	Brixworth All Saints	Corby Grampian	Corby Hellenic Fisher	Corby St Brendans	Harpole	Heyford Athletic	Kettering Nomads	Kislingbury	Milton	Moulton	Priors Marston	Roade	Rushden Rangers	Stanion United
Brixworth All Saints		n/a	0-7	1-0	0-2	2-4	2-3	0-1	4-1	2-5	2-3	0-3	6-2	3-1
Corby Grampian	n/a	P	n/a	n/a	0-3	n/a	2-0	n/a	n/a	8-0	n/a	n/a	n/a	n/a
Corby Hellenic Fisher	3-0	n/a	R	3-0	0-2	3-1	3-1	1-0	2-1	2-1	1-1	2-1	5-0	3-0
Corby St Brendans	1-2	n/a	1-3	E	1-6	0-1	2-1	1-2	2-2	1-2	2-2	1-2	4-1	3-2
Harpole	7-1	n/a	2-1	3-1	M	2-2	5-1	3-0	1-0	3-0	3-4	5-0		7-1
Heyford Athletic	4-0	n/a	1-4	2-0	1-1	I	2-1	1-1	4-1	1-1	3-3	1-4	1-0	1-0
Kettering Nomads	1-3	n/a	1-2	0-2	0-1	2-1	E	0-4	0-3	1-2	1-3	0-3	5-0	0-2
Kislingbury	4-2	n/a	2-2	6-1	0-3	1-2	2-0	R	1-3	0-0	4-1	2-1	1-0	5-2
Milton	0-1	2-2	3-3	2-1	0-0	3-0	1-0	2-1		0-2	4-2	2-2	4-1	3-1
Moulton	6-0	n/a	1-3	1-4	0-4	1-4	6-1	2-1	1-2		9-0	4-0	5-1	3-1
Priors Marston	6-4	n/a	0-5	1-2	1-4	2-7	0-0	1-4	0-3	0-2	D	2-3	4-3	2-2
Roade	3-0	n/a	2-1	3-2	1-1	0-0	4-0	2-0	2-1	2-0	2-1	I	2-1	5-2
Rushden Rangers	1-3	n/a	1-5	4-1	0-4	2-3	1-2	1-2	2-2	4-3	4-1	1-3	V	1-5
Stanion United	5-1	n/a	2-1	4-4	0-1	2-3	1-2	0-6	1-4	1-5	9-1	2-3	3-4	

Premier Division	P	W	D	L	F	A	Pts
Harpole	24	19	4	1	72	16	61
Roade	24	19	3	2	59	29	60
Corby Hellenic Fisher	24	17	3	4	65	24	54
Heyford Athletic	24	13	6	5	50	36	45
Moulton	24	13	2	9	62	36	41
Milton	24	12	5	7	48	35	41
Kislingbury	24	12	3	9	50	34	39
Brixworth All Saints	24	8	0	16	39	73	24
Corby St Brendans	24	6	3	15	37	56	21
Stanion United	24	5	2	17	49	71	17
Priors Marston	24	4	5	15	38	83	17
Kettering Nomads	24	5	1	18	23	55	16
Rushden Rangers	24	4	1	19	35	79	13

Corby Grampian – record expunged

NORTHANTS COMBINATION/ NORTHAMPTON TOWN LEAGUE CHAMPIONS CUP

(29th March at Rounds Town)
Corby Hellenic Fisher 1 **Northampton Harlequins** 1
aet (2-4p)
(Northampton Harlequins represented Town League as champions University College were unavailable)

PREMIER DIVISION CUP

FIRST ROUND
Brixworth All Saints 5 Priors Marston 4.
Corby Hellenic Fisher 7 Rushden Rangers 0
Milton 5 Kettering Nomads 3
Moulton (w/o) v Corby Grampian
Roade 2 Kislingbury 1
Stanion United 1 **Heyford Athletic** 7

QUARTER-FINALS
Corby St Brendans 2 Moulton 1
Harpole 2 Corby Hellenic Fisher 1
Heyford Athletic 1 **Roade** 3
Milton 7 Brixworth All Saints 1

SEMI-FINALS
Harpole 4 Corby St Brendans 1
Milton 0 **Roade** 3

FINAL
(May 1st at Northampton Town)
Harpole 2 Roade 2 *aet (3-2p)*

NORTHAMPTONSHIRE COMBINATION PREMIER DIVISION CONSTITUTION 2007-08

BRIXWORTH ALL SAINTS .... St Davids Close, off Froxhill Crescent, Brixworth NN6 9EA 01604 880073
CORBY MADISONS................... Corby Rugby Club, Rockingham Road, Corby NN17 1AE .... None
CORBY PEGASUS .... West Glebe South Pavilion, Cottingham Road, Corby NN17 1EL 01536 402041
HARPOLE .... Playing Field, Larkhall Lane, Harpole NN7 4DP .... None
HEYFORD ATHLETIC.............. Nether Heyford Playing Field, Nether Heyford NN7 3LL .... None
KETTERING NOMADS .... Orlingbury Road, Isham, Kettering NN14 1HY 01536 420068
KISLINGBURY .... Beech Lane, Kislingbury, Northampton NN7 4AL 01604 831225
MILTON .... Collingtree Road, Milton Malsor NN7 3AF .... None
MOULTON .... Brunting Road, Milton, Northampton NN3 7QX 01604 492675
PRIORS MARSTON .... Priors Sports Ground, Priors Marston CV47 7RR .... None
RAVENSTHORPE ATHLETIC .... Teeton Road, Ravensthorpe NN6 8EJ .... None
ROADE.............................. Connolly Way, Hyde Road, Roade NN7 2LU 01604 862814
STANION UNITED................. Village Hall, Brigstock Road, Stanion NN14 1BX..................... None
WHITEFIELD NORPOL .... Sports Hall, Wootton Hall PHQ, Mereway, Northampton NN4 0JF .... None
IN: Corby Pegasus (P), Ravensthorpe Athletic (P), Whitefield Norpol (P)
OUT: Caledonian Strip Mills (WN), Corby Grampian (WS), Rushden Rangers (having merged with United Counties League Division One side Higham Town)
Corby Hellenic Fisher have merged with Corby St Brendans to form Corby Madisons

Division One		P	W	D	L	F	A	Pts
Whitefield Norpol	-3	28	20	3	5	83	39	60
Corby Pegasus		28	18	3	7	82	53	57
Weldon United		28	16	5	7	61	41	53
Ravensthorpe Athletic		28	15	6	7	72	48	51
Medbourne		28	13	7	8	84	55	46
Queen Eleanor Great Houghton		28	13	6	9	68	68	45
Welford Victoria		28	13	5	10	56	48	44
Harborough Town Spencers		28	12	6	10	54	41	42
Earls Barton United		28	9	6	13	44	51	33
Bective Wanderers		28	9	6	13	61	78	33
Crick Athletic		28	9	6	13	57	74	33
Stanwick Rovers		28	8	7	13	59	64	31
Spratton		28	7	7	14	46	63	28
Weedon		28	5	2	21	36	92	17
Ringstead Rangers		28	4	3	21	38	86	15

Division Two		P	W	D	L	F	A	Pts
Corby Kingfisher Athletic	-3	28	22	4	2	78	31	67
Corby Phoenix		28	19	4	5	86	37	61
James King Blisworth		28	19	4	5	69	34	61
Wootton St George		28	15	1	12	53	50	46
Clipston		28	14	3	11	54	40	45
Islip United		28	12	4	12	58	64	40
Burton United		28	11	6	11	56	47	39
Wellingborough Ranelagh		28	10	5	13	64	54	35
Gretton		28	10	5	13	51	47	35
Rushden Corner Flag	-3	28	11	4	13	67	68	34
Wollaston Victoria		28	9	5	14	52	75	32
Wilbarston		28	10	2	16	56	80	32
Finedon Volta		28	9	3	16	45	81	30
Kettering Orchard Park		28	8	4	16	42	60	28
Corby Locomotives		28	3	2	23	38	101	11

DIVISION ONE CUP FINAL
(April 19th at Northampton Sileby Rangers)
Corby Pegasus 1 Ravensthorpe Athletic 1 *aet* (5-4p)

DIVISION TWO CUP FINAL
(April 18th at Cogenhoe United)
Clipston 1 James King Blisworth 1 *aet* (4-3p)

Division Three		P	W	D	L	F	A	Pts
Punjab United	-3	24	18	2	4	94	42	53
Cold Ashby Rovers		24	16	4	4	68	29	52
Dainite Sports		24	15	2	7	103	54	47
Corby Danesholme Vikings		24	15	2	7	68	47	47
Daventry Drayton Grange		24	14	2	8	75	49	44
Weavers Old Boys		24	12	2	10	50	43	38
West Haddon		24	9	6	9	47	54	33
Ristee Towers		24	8	7	9	46	49	31
Great Doddington		24	5	8	11	51	68	23
Wellingboro. Old Grammarians		24	5	8	11	33	62	23
Wilby		24	4	5	15	30	63	17
Kettering Park Rovers		24	4	2	18	33	83	14
CSV United	-6	24	4	4	16	43	98	10

Corby Flamingo – record expunged

Division Four	P	W	D	L	F	A	Pts
Wellingborough Raffertys	16	13	1	2	68	25	37
Raunds Academy	16	9	4	3	57	31	31
Wellingborough Oak Rangers	16	8	1	7	46	48	25
Northampton Sapphires	16	6	4	6	50	51	22
Weekley Vale United	16	6	2	8	41	47	20
Corby Rockingham United	16	5	3	8	39	47	18
Yardley United	16	5	3	8	29	47	18
Corby Eagles	16	4	3	9	35	49	15
Wellingborough Rising Sun	16	4	3	9	32	52	15

Harlestone Park Wanderers – record expunged

DIVISION THREE CUP FINAL
(April 12th at Raunds Town)
Cold Ashby Rovers 1 Punjab Rovers 0

DIVISION FOUR CUP FINAL
(April 17th at Wellingborough Town)
Northampton Sapphires 2 Raunds Academy 0

Reserve Division One		P	W	D	L	F	A	Pts
Corby Hellenic Fisher Res.	+2	26	18	6	2	76	26	62
Bugbrooke St Michaels 'A'		26	16	4	6	69	41	52
Harpole Res.		26	14	7	5	60	40	49
Milton Res.		26	14	4	8	70	40	46
Weldon United Res.		26	13	5	8	58	44	44
Heyford Athletic Res.		26	12	2	12	60	70	38
Roade Res.		26	10	5	11	43	50	35
Moulton Res.	-1	26	9	8	9	57	54	34
Kettering Nomads Res.		26	10	3	13	37	37	33
Corby St Brendans Res.		26	8	7	11	61	77	31
Rushden Rangers Res.		26	9	2	15	63	76	29
Corby Pegasus Res.		26	8	3	15	45	62	27
Stanion United Res.		26	4	6	16	36	86	18
Q. Eleanor Gt Houghton Res.		26	4	4	18	32	64	16

Reserve Division Two		P	W	D	L	F	A	Pts
Kislingbury Res.		26	20	2	4	77	23	62
James King Blisworth Res.		26	18	3	5	75	28	57
N'pton ON Chenecks 'A'		26	17	3	6	86	43	54
Gretton Res.	+2	26	13	7	6	58	49	48
Whitefield Norpol Res.	-4	26	14	4	8	82	49	42
Brixworth All Saints Res.		26	12	5	9	65	53	41
Harboro. Town Spen. Res.		26	13	2	11	49	49	41
Ringstead Rangers Res.		26	10	6	10	50	57	36
Harpole 'A'		26	9	2	15	49	72	29
Corby Locomotives Res.	-3	26	8	2	16	64	80	23
Bugbrooke St Michaels 'B'	-3	26	7	5	14	49	79	23
Wollaston Victoria Res.	-3	26	6	4	16	54	73	19
Finedon Volta Res.		26	4	6	16	34	80	18
Crick Athletic Res.		26	3	5	18	35	92	14

Corby Danesholme Vikings Res. – record expunged

RESERVE DIVISION ONE CUP FINAL
(April 26th at Raunds Town)
Moulton Res. 3 Milton Res. 1

RESERVE DIVISION TWO CUP FINAL
(April 5th at Bugbrooke St Michaels)
Kislingbury Res. 3 James King Blisworth 0

Reserve Division Three		P	W	D	L	F	A	Pts
Medbourne Res.	-3	28	21	1	6	93	49	61
Spratton Res.		28	15	6	7	78	53	51
Wootton St George Res.		28	15	5	8	80	41	50
Kettering Orchard Park Res.		28	15	4	9	84	46	49
Weedon Res.		28	13	7	8	75	82	46
Welford Victoria Res.		28	13	4	11	70	48	43
Islip United Res.		28	13	3	12	64	66	42
Dainite Sports Res.		28	11	6	11	80	69	39
Wellingboro. Old Gramm Res.		28	12	3	13	70	87	39
Rushden Corner Flag Res.		28	11	5	12	64	65	38
Daventry Drayton Grange Res.		28	11	3	14	52	79	36
Earls Barton United Res.		28	8	6	14	50	82	30
Weldon United 'A'	-6	28	8	7	13	71	70	25
Stanwick Rovers Res.	-3	28	6	7	15	37	59	22
West Haddon Res.		28	2	5	21	29	101	11

RESERVE DIVISION THREE CUP FINAL
(April 3rd at Rushden Rangers)
Kettering Orchard Park Res. 6
Wellingborough Old Grammarians 2

NORTHERN ALLIANCE

	Ashington Colliers	Blyth Town	Carlisle City	Easington Colliery	Harraby Catholic Club	Heaton Stannington	Heddon	Newcastle University	Northbank Carlisle	Peterlee Town	Ponteland United	Seaton Delaval Amateurs	Shankhouse	Walker Central	Wallsend
Ashington Colliers		0-0	2-1	1-0	4-7	1-2	1-3	0-0	1-3	2-0	2-1	3-1	4-2	0-2	2-2
Blyth Town	1-0	P	0-0	3-0	1-2	2-0	1-1	2-3	2-0	0-4	2-3	5-1	2-1	0-1	1-3
Carlisle City	2-1	3-3	R	0-1	1-3	1-0	2-0	2-0	3-0	7-0	1-2	3-0	0-0	2-1	1-3
Easington Colliery	5-1	0-0	4-1	E	0-2	0-3	4-0	3-1	4-0	4-0	1-4	0-4	0-7	3-1	3-1
Harraby Catholic Club	2-3	2-0	4-0	3-1	M	2-0	6-0	2-2	1-0	2-0	1-0	2-2	2-1	3-1	2-0
Heaton Stannington	2-3	3-2	2-2	0-3	2-3	I	2-0	1-1	1-2	1-3	0-3	1-1	0-1	2-2	4-5
Heddon	2-2	1-0	1-1	1-4	0-3	0-6	E	0-1	3-1	1-3	0-1	1-0	1-2	0-6	1-4
Newcastle University	4-0	0-0	1-1	1-1	1-0	3-4	2-0	R	2-0	0-0	3-1	3-0	0-3	2-1	0-1
Northbank Carlisle	3-5	2-1	1-5	4-3	1-3	2-2	1-4	0-2		1-0	0-5	0-1	2-0	3-3	1-5
Peterlee Town	2-2	0-2	0-0	0-5	2-2	0-2	0-0	0-2	2-1		0-3	0-0	0-3	2-6	1-4
Ponteland United	3-1	4-4	2-2	4-3	2-2	1-2	4-0	1-1	2-2	1-0		0-2	2-1	0-0	3-1
Seaton Delaval Amats	2-0	2-1	0-4	5-1	2-3	0-2	4-3	3-2	1-1	0-0	3-3	D	0-3	0-2	2-3
Shankhouse	0-1	2-1	1-2	2-2	1-2	3-2	4-2	2-2	3-1	2-1	0-0	6-2	I	0-0	2-3
Walker Central	1-0	2-2	3-3	1-3	1-3	1-6	2-1	1-0	1-0	0-0	0-4	2-1	2-1	V	3-1
Wallsend	1-3	3-0	2-2	6-0	1-4	4-3	5-2	1-1	1-1	3-0	1-0	3-5	3-1	3-0	

Premier Division	P	W	D	L	F	A	Pts
Harraby Catholic Club	28	22	4	2	73	29	70
Wallsend	28	17	4	7	73	47	55
Ponteland United	28	14	8	6	59	35	50
Walker Central	28	13	7	8	47	42	46
Carlisle City	28	12	9	7	54	37	45
Newcastle University	28	11	10	7	40	30	43
Shankhouse	28	12	5	11	54	37	41
Easington Colliery	28	12	3	13	56	58	39
Ashington Colliers	28	11	4	13	45	56	37
Heaton Stannington	28	10	5	13	55	51	35
Seaton Delaval Amateurs	28	9	6	13	43	57	33
Blyth Town	28	7	8	13	38	43	29
Northbank Carlisle	28	6	5	17	33	66	23
Heddon	28	6	3	19	28	72	21
Peterlee Town	28	4	7	17	20	58	19

WWW.NL.NEWSDESK.CO.UK

CHALLENGE CUP

FIRST ROUND
Alnmouth (scr.) v **Wallsend** (w/o)
Easington Colliery 9 **Ashington Colliers** 9 *aet* (2-3p)
Harraby Catholic Club 5 Blyth Town 0
Heddon 2 Carlisle City 1
Newcastle University 3 Walker Central 1
Northbank Carlisle 1 **Ponteland United** 3
Peterlee Town 2 Shankhouse 1 *aet*
Seaton Delaval Amateurs 2 **Heaton Stannington** 4
QUARTER-FINALS
Ashington Colliers 1 **Heaton Stannington** 2
Heddon 4 Newcastle University 1
Ponteland United 2 Harraby Catholic Club 1
Wallsend 3 Peterlee Town 1
SEMI-FINALS
Ponteland United 2 Heaton Stannington 2 *aet* (3-2p)
Wallsend 2 Heddon 0
FINAL
(April 25th at West Allotment Celtic)
Ponteland United 0 **Wallsend** 2

NORTHERN ALLIANCE PREMIER DIVISION CONSTITUTION 2007-08

ALNWICK TOWN.......................St James Park, Weavers Way, Alnwick NE66 1BG.........................01665 603162
ASHINGTON COLLIERS...............Hirst Welfare, Alexandra Road, Ashington NE63 9HF...........................None
BLYTH TOWN.............................South Newsham Sports Ground, Blyth..None
CARLISLE CITY..................Sheepmount Sports Complex, Sheepmount, Carlisle CA3 8XL.............01228 625599
CRAMLINGTON TOWN.........Sporting Club of Cramlington, Highburn, Cramlington NE23 6YB.........01670 591970
GATESHEAD LEAM LANE.............Leam Lane Rangers Ground, Leam Lane, Gateshead.............................None
GILLFORD PARK.............Gillford Park Railway Club, Petteril Bank Road, Carlisle CA1 3AF..........01228 526449
HARRABY CATHOLIC CLUB.......Harraby Community Centre, Edghill Road, Carlisle CA1 3SL.................None
HEATON STANNINGTON....Grounsell Park, Newton Road, High Heaton, Newcastle-upon-Tyne NE7 7HP...............None
HEDDON..........Bullockstead Sports Complex, Ponteland Rd, Kenton Bankfoot, Newcastle-upon-Tyne NE13 8AH.......0191 271 1153
NEWCASTLE UNIVERSITY......Cochrane Park, Etherstone Avenue, Newcastle-upon-Tyne NE7 7JX.......................None
NORTHBANK CARLISLE..........Sheepmount Sports Complex, Sheepmount, Carlisle CA3 8XL.................01228 625599
PETERLEE TOWN ....Eden Lane Playing Fields, Peterlee SR8 5DS 0191 586 3004
PONTELAND UNITED.........The Leisure Centre Ground, Callerton Lane, Ponteland NE20 9EG..............01661 825441
SEATON DELAVAL AMATEURS.........Wheatridge Park, Seaton Delaval, Whitley Bay.................................None
SHANKHOUSE.............Northburn Sports & Community Complex, Crawhall Lane, Cramlington NE23 3YP..............01670 714154
WALKER CENTRAL ....Monkchester Green, Walker, Newcastle-upon-Tyne NE6 5LJ...............0191 265 7230
IN: Alnwick Town (R – Northern League Division Two), Cramlington Town (P), Gillford Park (formerly Gillford Park Spartans) (P)
OUT: Alnmouth (WN), Easington Colliery (S – Wearside League)
Wallsend become Gateshead Leam Lane

	Berwick United	Chopwell TC	Cramlington T.	Gillford Park Sp.	Gosf'th Bohemian	Haydon Bridge U.	Hebburn Reyrolle	Murton	Newc. EE Rail	Penrith United	Percy Main Am.	Rutherford Newc.	Seaton Burn	Wallington	Wark	Whitley Bay 'A'
Berwick United		4-3	1-4	1-4	3-2	5-4	1-3	1-4	1-3	0-7	1-1	2-2	3-0	4-1	6-2	3-3
Chopwell TC	5-0		0-3	1-3	1-1	3-0	2-1	1-0	1-0	0-5	3-1	5-1	3-1	2-4	0-1	
Cramlington T.	3-1	5-0	*D*	0-1	3-1	2-0	4-3	1-0	2-0	3-2	0-0	2-4	3-0	2-1	3-2	2-3
Gillford Park S.	3-0	3-3	1-0	*I*	2-1	9-1	13-3	2-1	4-1	2-1	3-1	7-1	7-2	2-1	5-2	3-1
Gosforth Boh. G.	1-0	1-1	2-1	0-3	*V*	5-0	4-0	1-2	0-3	2-3	5-0	1-3	0-1	1-2	2-1	3-4
Haydon Bridge	1-5	2-2	1-2	0-2	3-3	*I*	4-3	1-2	2-4	1-3	4-2	0-3	3-1	1-4	0-2	2-3
Hebburn Reyrolle	2-3	1-3	0-3	2-2	3-2	4-1	*S*	0-9	0-2	0-1	0-1	3-2	2-1	0-0	2-3	3-2
Murton	0-1	3-0	1-2	2-3	0-1	5-3	5-0	*I*	1-3	5-2	2-0	2-1	1-1	3-1	4-1	3-0
Newc. EE Rail C.	7-3	2-1	1-3	1-2	4-2	5-1	0-2	1-3	*O*	1-2	3-1	3-2	0-3	4-1	2-2	1-1
Penrith United	7-0	11-0	0-0	1-4	2-2	9-2	2-2	5-3	0-0	*N*	5-2	2-3	5-0	3-4	1-0	3-1
Percy Main Ams	0-1	3-2	1-2	0-1	3-4	6-0	3-1	0-5	1-0	0-2		1-7	3-1	3-3	1-5	1-5
Rutherford Newc.	0-0	3-1	1-5	4-2	1-2	2-1	4-2	0-2	1-1	1-3	5-0	*O*	3-1	4-1	5-1	2-0
Seaton Burn	2-0	0-0	0-1	1-2	1-4	2-0	1-0	3-2	1-2	1-0	1-3	1-2	*N*	1-0	1-4	0-2
Wallington	5-0	0-1	4-0	3-1	1-0	8-1	2-0	1-2	4-1	2-2	1-0	1-0	3-0	*E*	1-3	3-2
Wark		0-0	0-5	6-1	3-4	7-3	4-2	2-3	0-3	1-2	2-4	0-2	4-3			4-2
Whitley Bay 'A'	3-1	1-5	2-2	4-2	2-1	5-3	4-0	1-2	1-1	1-2	2-2	1-2	1-2	1-1	3-1	

Division One

Division One		P	W	D	L	F	A	Pts
Gillford Park Spartans		30	24	3	3	101	39	75
Cramlington Town		30	20	4	6	63	33	64
Penrith United		30	18	5	7	92	41	59
Rutherford Newcastle		30	17	3	10	73	53	54
Murton		30	17	2	11	75	43	53
Wallington		30	14	4	12	63	49	46
Newcastle EE Rail.		30	12	7	11	57	51	43
Wark		30	13	2	15	72	74	41
Chopwell Top Club		30	11	8	11	53	64	41
Whitley Bay 'A'	-7	30	12	6	12	62	60	35
Gosfth Boh. Garnett		30	10	4	16	57	61	34
Berwick United		30	10	4	16	53	85	34
Seaton Burn		30	10	2	18	32	61	32
Percy Main Amateurs		30	9	4	17	46	72	31
Hebburn Reyrolle		30	7	3	20	44	92	24
Haydon Bridge Utd		30	4	3	23	47	112	15

WWW.CHERRYRED.CO.UK

COMBINATION CUP
(Division One teams)

FIRST ROUND
Berwick United 2 Whitley Bay 'A' 2 *aet* (5-4p)
Cramlington 7 Rutherford Newc. 4
Gillford Park 6 Seaton Burn 2
Gosforth Garnett Bohemian 0 **Wallington** 2
Hebburn Reyrolle 3 Chopwell TC 2
Newcastle East End Rail Club 1 **Penrith United** 2
Percy Main Amats 3 **Murton** 4 *aet*
Wark (w/o) v Haydon Bridge United (scr.)

QUARTER-FINALS
Berwick United 1 **Penrith United** 3
Cramlington Town 1 **Wallington** 2
Murton 5 Hebburn Reyrolle 2 *aet*
Wark 2 **Gillford Park Spartans** 2 *aet* (4-5p)

SEMI-FINALS
Gillford Park Spartans 3 Wallington 1
Penrith United 0 **Murton** 1

FINAL
(April 11th at Prudhoe Town)
Gillford Park Spartans 1 Murton 0

LEAGUE CUP
(All teams in league)

FIRST ROUND
Berwick United 5 Newcastle British Telecom 2
Blaydon 0 **Seaton Burn** 7
Chopwell Top Club 1 **Gillford Park Spartans** 7
Cramlington 2 **Gosforth Bohemian Garnett** 3
Haydon Bridge United 3 Cullercoats 2
Jesmond 0 **Hexham** 1
Lowick 3 Wallington 1
Morpeth Town 'A' (scr.) v **Hebburn Reyrolle** (w/o)
Murton 2 **Red Row Welfare** 3
Newcastle Chemfica 2 **Percy Main Amateurs** 4
North Shields Ath. (w/o) v Felling Fox (scr.)
Penrith United 1 Wark 2 (*Wark expelled*)
Stocksfield 3 Whitley Bay 'A' 2
Wallsend Town 1 **Rutherford Newcastle** 2
Westerhope 5 Newcastle East End Rail Club 0
Whitley Bay Town 1 Amble 1 *aet*

SECOND ROUND
Ashington Colls 2 **Easington Coll.** 2 *aet* (3-4p)
Berwick United 1 **Newcastle University** 2
Blyth Town 7 Haydon Bridge United 1
Gillford Pk Spartans 2 Hebburn Reyrolle 1 *aet*
Harraby CC 6 North Shields Athletic 0
Heddon 4 Westerhope 3
Hexham 0 **Carlisle City** 3
Penrith United 0 **Gosforth Bohemian Garnett** 2
Percy Main Amateurs 3 Seaton Burn 1
Peterlee Town 5 Lowick 2 *aet*
Rutherford Newcastle 3 **Northbank Carlisle** 4
Stocksfield 1 **Red Row Welfare** 2
Walker Central 1 Heaton Stannington 0
Wallsend 2 **Seaton Delaval Amateurs** 3
Whitley Bay Town 3 Shankhouse 2

THIRD ROUND
Carlisle City 4 Gosforth Bohemian Garnett 0

Easington Colliery 1 **Newcastle University** 2
Gillford Park Spartans 2 Blyth Town 0 *aet*
Heddon 4 Walker Central 1
Percy Main Amateurs 5 Northbank Carlisle 1
Peterlee Town 1 **Seaton Delaval Amats** 2 *aet*
Ponteland United 1 Harraby Catholic Club 1
Red Row Welfare 2 **Shankhouse** 4

QUARTER-FINALS
Heddon 1 **Carlisle City** 2
Percy Main Amats 3 **Newcastle University** 4 *aet*
Ponteland United 1 Seaton Delaval Amats 0 *aet*
Shankhouse 5 Gillford Park Spartans 2

SEMI-FINALS
Newcastle University 0 **Carlisle City** 1 *aet*
Ponteland United 0 **Shankhouse** 2
(at Shankhouse)

FINAL *(April 30th at Prudhoe Town)*
Carlisle City 2 Shankhouse 1

NORTHERN ALLIANCE DIVISION ONE CONSTITUTION 2007-08

BERWICK UNITED ..... Swan Leisure Centre, Northumberland Rd, Tweedmouth, Berwick-on-Tweed TD15 2AS 01289 330603
CHOPWELL OFFICIALS CLUB ..... Welfare Park, Chopwell, Newcastle-upon-Tyne ..... None
GOSFORTH BOHEMIAN GARNETT ..... Benson Park, Gosforth, Newcastle-upon-Tyne ..... None
HAYDON BRIDGE UNITED ..... Low Hall Park, Haydon Bridge, Hexham NE47 6AF ..... None
HEBBURN REYROLLE ..... Hebburn Sports Ground, 16 South Drive, Hebburn NE31 1UN 0191 483 5101
MURTON ..... Recreation Park, Church Lane, Murton, Seaham SR7 9RD 07814 523289
NEWCASTLE EAST END RAIL CLUB ..... Swan Hunter Recreation Ground, Stotts Road, Walkergate, Newcastle-upon-Tyne NE6 4UD ..... None
PENRITH UNITED ..... Frenchfield Sports Centre, Penrith, Penrith CA11 8UA ..... None
PERCY MAIN AMATEURS ..... Purvis Park, St John's Green, Percy Main, North Shields NE29 6HE 0191 257 4831
RED ROW WELFARE ..... Red Row Welfare Ground, Red Row, Amble NE61 5BG ..... None
RUTHERFORD NEWCASTLE .. Farnacres, Beggarswood Park, Coach Lane, Lobley Hill, Gateshead NE11 8HJ ..... None
SEATON BURN ..... Seaton Burn Welfare, Seaton Burn, Newcastle-upon-Tyne ..... None
STOCKSFIELD ..... Stocksfield Sports Field, Main Road, Stocksfield, Prudhoe NE42 5DH ..... None
WALLINGTON ..... Oakford Park, Scots Gap, Morpeth ..... None
WARK ..... Wark Sports Club, Wark, Hexham NE48 3NP 01434 230259
WESTERHOPE ..... Westerhope Institute, Westerhope, Newcastle-upon-Tyne NE5 1NE 0191 267 3757
WHITLEY BAY 'A' ..... Hillheads Park, Rink Way, Whitley Bay NE25 8HR 0191 291 3636

IN: Red Row Welfare (P), Stocksfield (P), Westerhope (P)
OUT: Cramlington Town (P), Gillford Park (formerly Gillford Park Spartans) (P)
Chopwell Top Club become Chopwell Officials Club

	Amble	Blaydon	Cullercoats	Hexham	Jesmond	Lowick	Newc. Brit. Telecom	Newcastle Chemfica	North Shields Ath.	Red Row Welfare	Stocksfield	Wallsend Town	Westerhope	Whitley Bay Town
Amble		6-0	1-1	2-0	3-0	1-1	1-4	3-1	6-3	0-4	1-1	2-1	3-1	0-2
Blaydon	2-2	D	1-9	0-4	0-3	0-3	1-6	1-2	1-1	0-5	0-8	2-2	0-2	2-0
Cullercoats	3-1	7-2	I	2-0	0-1	3-2	5-3	5-0	3-0	1-4	2-0	2-1	1-1	0-1
Hexham	2-2	5-2	2-4	V	1-0	1-4	5-1	2-2	2-2	3-1	1-4	1-4	0-4	0-3
Jesmond	2-2	4-0	1-2	3-0	I	5-0	1-0	1-0	3-0	1-2	2-2	2-1	2-1	2-1
Lowick	4-0	3-2	0-2	0-1	0-2	S	2-2	2-1	1-1	1-1	1-2	1-3	2-4	3-1
Newcastle British Telecom	1-0	5-1	0-1	1-1	1-2	0-5	I	3-0	1-1	0-4	1-6	2-5	1-4	3-4
Newcastle Chemfica	1-7	3-2	0-0	3-2	0-1	1-4	2-1	O	1-2	3-3	2-3	1-1	0-4	2-3
North Shields Athletic	3-9	3-4	1-5	3-1	2-1	2-1	0-3	6-4	N	0-4	1-7	1-2	0-3	0-6
Red Row Welfare	2-1	8-1	1-3	1-0	2-0	4-2	4-1	5-1	1-2		1-2	1-1	2-0	5-1
Stocksfield	2-0	7-1	6-3	3-2	4-0	2-1	2-3	4-1	6-1	4-1	T	5-5	2-3	1-1
Wallsend Town	2-1	4-2	1-0	0-1	4-1	4-1	3-1	9-1	2-0	4-4	W		2-3	3-2
Westerhope	8-0	6-0	3-1	2-2	3-0	3-1	4-2	5-0	6-1	0-1	0-3	3-2	O	4-1
Whitley Bay Town	1-3	4-0	0-2	7-1	5-2	3-0	3-1	3-1	3-2	0-2	2-2	2-3	2-4	

Division Two

		P	W	D	L	F	A	Pts
Westerhope		26	19	2	5	81	31	59
Stocksfield		26	16	7	3	91	40	55
Red Row Welfare		26	17	3	6	69	30	54
Cullercoats		26	17	3	6	67	33	54
Wallsend Town		26	15	5	6	72	44	50
Jesmond		26	14	2	10	42	36	44
Whitley Bay Town		26	13	2	11	61	48	41
Amble		26	10	6	10	57	52	36
Lowick	-3	26	9	5	12	49	51	29
Newc. British Telecom		26	7	3	16	47	67	24
Hexham	-3	26	6	5	15	40	62	20
North Shields Ath.	-3	26	6	3	17	39	94	18
Newcastle Chemfica		26	4	5	17	34	76	17
Blaydon		26	2	3	21	27	112	9

AMATEUR CUP

(Division Two teams)

FIRST ROUND
Amble 4 Stocksfield 1 *aet*
Cullercoats 2 Red Row Welfare 0
Felling Fox (scr.) v **Wallsend Town** (w/o)
Lowick 4 Hexham 0
Newcastle British Telecom 6 Blaydon 0
Newcastle Chemfica 0 **Jesmond** 5
Westerhope (w/o) v Morpeth Town 'A' (scr.)
Whitley Bay Town 5 North Shields Athletic 2 *aet*

QUARTER-FINALS
Amble 2 Newcastle BT 1
Lowick 1 **Cullercoats** 2 *aet*
Wallsend Town 1 Jesmond 0
Whitley Bay Town 3 **Westerhope** 6

SEMI-FINALS
Cullercoats 2 **Amble** 2 (3-4p)
Westerhope 4 **Wallsend Town** 4 *aet* (2-3p)

FINAL
(April 18th at Shankhouse)
Wallsend Town 2 Amble 1

NORTHERN ALLIANCE DIVISION TWO CONSTITUTION 2007-08

AMBLE . . . . Amble Welfare Ground, Acklington Road, Amble NE65 0NG . . . . None
AMBLE UNITED . . . . Running Track Pitch, Coquet High Sschool, Acklington Road, Amble NE65 0NG 01665 710636
CULLERCOATS . . . . Links Avenue, Farrindon Road, Cullercoats NE30 3EY . . . . None
HEXHAM. . . . . Wentworth Leisure Centre, Wentworth Park, Hexham NE46 3PD 01434 607080
JESMOND . . . . Miller's Dene, Fossway, Walkerdene, Newcastle-upon-Tyne NE6 4YA . . . . None
KILLINGWORTH SOCIAL YPC . . Miller's Dene, Fossway, Walkerdene, Newcastle-upon-Tyne NE6 4YA . . . . None
LOWICK . . . . New Barber Park, Lowick . . . . None
NEWCASTLE BRITISH TELECOM . . Burradon Welfare Ground, Front Street, Burradon NE23 7NG . . . . None
NEWCASTLE CHEMFICA . . . . Benfield School, Benfield Road, Newcastle-upon-Tyne NE6 4NQ . . . . None
NORTH SHIELDS ATHLETIC . . . . . Collingwood View PF, West Percy Road, North Shields NE29 7RQ . . . . None
SHIELDS UNITED . . . . Chuter Ede Community Centre, Galsworthy Road, South Shields NE34 9UG 0191 536 0515
TYNEMOUTH UNITED . . . . Western Community School, Rutland Road, Wallsend NE28 8QL 0191 260 5336
WALLSEND BC . . . . St Peter's Road, Wallsend NE28 7LQ . . . . None
WALLSEND TOWN . . . . . Langdale School Ground, Mitford Gardens, Wallsend, Newcastle-upon-Tyne NE28 0HG . . . . None
WHITLEY BAY TOWN . . . . Churchill Playing Fields, Hartley Drive, Monkseaton, Whitley Bay NE26 3NS . . . . None
WIDEOPEN. Lockey Park, Great North Road, Wideopen, Newcastle-upon-Tyne NE13 6LN . . . . None
WILLINGTON QUAY SAINTS . . . Wallsend Rising Sun Ground, King's North Road, Wallsend NE28 9JQ. . . . . None
IN: Amble United (P – North Northumberland League Division One), Killingworth Social YPC (P – Tyneside Amateur League Division One),
Shields United (N), Tynemouth United (N), Wallsend BC (N), Wideopen (N), Willington Quay Saints (P – Tyneside Amateur League Division One)
OUT: Blaydon (W), Felling Fox (WN), Morpeth Town 'A' (WS), Red Row Welfare (P), Stocksfield (P), Westerhope (P)

CHARITY CUP *(League Cup First Round losers)*

FIRST ROUND
Chopwell Top Club 3 Jesmond 2
Cullercoats 2 Amble 0
Newcastle British Telecom 5 Blaydon 4
Wark 4 Newcastle Chemfica 2
Whitley Bay 'A' 6 Cramlington Town 2
Wallington 2 **Murton** 3
QUARTER-FINALS
Murton 3 Cullercoats 1
Newcastle East End Rail 4 **Newcastle BT** 1
(Newcastle East End Rail Club expelled)

Wark 2 Whitley Bay 'A' 0
Wallsend Town 1 **Chopwell Top Club** 2
SEMI-FINALS
Newcastle British Telecom 0 **Chopwell Top Club** 8
Wark 1 Murton 0
FINAL
(April 23rd at Prudhoe Town)
Chopwell Top Club 0 **Wark** 2 *aet*

NORTHERN COUNTIES EAST LEAGUE

	Armthorpe Welfare	Arnold Town	Brodsworth Miners Welf.	Carlton Town	Eccleshill United	Garforth Town	Glapwell	Glasshoughton Welfare	Hallam	Liversedge	Long Eaton United	Maltby Main	Mickleover Sports	Pickering Town	Retford United	Selby Town	Sheffield	Shirebrook Town	Sutton Town	Thackley
Armthorpe Welfare		2-0	3-0	0-3	0-3	0-2	5-1	2-1	0-0	3-2	0-2	1-0	5-3	1-0	3-1	1-2	0-2	2-1	1-1	11-0
Arnold Town	4-1		4-2	0-3	2-2	1-3	2-0	5-0	2-1	1-1	1-1	1-1	0-0	1-2	3-3	3-2	0-2	6-2	1-1	3-2
Brodsworth Miners Welfare	0-2	1-4	P	0-0	1-1	0-4	0-1	2-4	0-4	1-1	2-1	0-1	1-4	2-2	0-2	0-3	2-1	1-1	0-7	1-3
Carlton Town	3-0	3-0	4-1	R	3-2	2-1	6-1	1-2	0-1	4-0	1-2	0-0	2-0	2-1	2-5	3-4	3-0	4-0	2-2	4-0
Eccleshill United	0-2	2-3	5-2	2-0	E	1-7	1-4	3-2	3-1	0-0	4-4	1-1	2-0	2-2	2-3	0-6	0-2	3-1	2-3	2-2
Garforth Town	2-1	2-1	1-0	1-2	6-0	M	2-2	2-0	4-0	3-3	3-1	1-1	1-2	0-0	2-1	1-2	0-0	5-0	0-0	3-0
Glapwell	1-0	2-0	4-0	2-1	8-2	2-3	I	0-0	0-3	1-1	2-2	5-2	3-0	1-0	1-0	2-0	1-2	1-1	1-2	1-0
Glasshoughton Welfare	3-1	1-2	4-0	2-3	1-1	2-1	1-1	E	2-2	0-1	4-1	2-1	1-3	0-3	2-2	0-1	2-2	2-4	1-0	2-1
Hallam	1-4	4-5	3-1	0-3	5-1	0-1	1-6	1-2	R	1-0	0-1	4-2	1-0	5-0	0-3	0-1	1-3	1-0	0-2	2-3
Liversedge	4-3	3-0	5-1	1-1	2-1	4-2	0-1	2-0	0-1		1-3	1-1	4-4	0-4	4-3	2-2	0-1	1-0	4-1	3-2
Long Eaton United	4-1	2-2	6-2	0-1	2-1	0-0	1-0	3-2	2-3	1-0	D	0-3	0-1	0-1	0-0	3-0	0-0	0-3	3-3	1-1
Maltby Main	3-2	4-2	3-0	1-0	3-1	0-2	0-6	0-3	1-1	3-0	0-1	I	3-1	1-2	1-4	2-3	2-2	2-1	4-2	
Mickleover Sports	1-0	3-1	4-1	2-5	2-1	4-3	1-0	3-2	1-0	2-1	2-1	1-1	V	4-0	2-2	0-2	0-0	5-1	1-1	3-2
Pickering Town	3-0	3-1	6-1	1-3	2-3	1-3	1-2	3-1	3-1	1-0	1-1	3-1	2-2	I	1-2	1-1	2-4	2-1		4-1
Retford United	3-1	6-2	8-1	2-1	8-0	3-0	1-0	1-0	3-0	3-0	2-0	2-2	5-2	1-0	S	1-2	2-0	2-0	0-0	1-0
Selby Town	1-0	2-1	5-1	1-2	3-0	3-1	5-1	2-1	2-2	2-1	5-2	0-1	1-2	0-0	1-2	I	1-3	2-0	2-1	1-3
Sheffield	3-1	5-1	5-0	0-1	2-3	3-1	1-0	1-1	1-1	1-0	5-2	1-1	2-1	1-0	1-4	2-2	O	2-0	0-0	4-0
Shirebrook Town	1-2	1-0	4-1	2-1	2-2	0-0	0-4	0-3	1-4	1-1	0-2	1-2	3-0	0-3	1-2	0-1		N	0-0	1-1
Sutton Town	1-1	1-0	3-2	2-1	6-0	3-1	1-2	2-1	0-2	1-3	1-0	1-2	0-1	1-0	1-0	1-2	1-2			5-1
Thackley	1-0	1-1	7-0	0-3	2-4	1-4	0-1	3-1	0-0	0-2	1-1	0-1	1-1	0-1	1-0	3-2	1-3	6-6	0-2	

Premier Division		P	W	D	L	F	A	Pts
Retford United		38	25	7	6	92	37	82
Sheffield		38	23	8	7	71	39	77
Carlton Town		38	23	4	11	83	41	73
Garforth Town		38	21	7	10	83	44	70
Selby Town		38	21	6	11	75	49	69
Glapwell		38	20	6	12	71	48	66
Mickleover Sports		38	18	9	11	70	62	63
Sutton Town	-3	38	16	11	11	60	42	56
Pickering Town		38	16	8	14	61	54	56
Maltby Main		38	14	10	14	56	58	52
Long Eaton United		38	13	12	13	57	60	51
Liversedge		38	13	10	15	58	60	49
Armthorpe Welfare		38	15	3	20	62	63	48
Hallam		38	14	6	18	57	63	48
Arnold Town		38	12	9	17	66	77	45
Glasshoughton Welfare		38	12	7	19	58	66	43
Eccleshill United		38	10	9	19	63	105	39
Thackley	-1	38	8	8	22	52	89	31
Shirebrook Town		38	7	9	22	44	79	30
Brodsworth Miners Welf.	-1	38	2	5	31	30	133	10

NORTHERN COUNTIES EAST LEAGUE PREMIER DIVISION CONSTITUTION 2007-08

ARMTHORPE WELFARE . . . . Church Street, Armthorpe, Doncaster DN3 3AG 07775 915503
ARNOLD TOWN . . . . King George V Playing Field, Gedling Road, Arnold NG5 6NQ 0115 926 3660
BRODSWORTH MINERS WELFARE . . . . . . Welfare Ground, Woodlands, Doncaster DN6 7PP 01302 728380
ECCLESHILL UNITED . . . . Plumpton Park, Kingsway, Wrose, Bradford BD2 1PN 01274 615739
GLAPWELL . . . . Hall Corner, Park Avenue, Glapwell, Chesterfield S44 5NJ 01623 812213
GLASSHOUGHTON WELFARE . . . . Leeds Road, Glasshoughton, Castleford WF10 4PF 01977 518981
HALLAM . . . . Sandygate Road, Crosspool, Sheffield S10 5SD 0114 230 9484
LINCOLN MOORLANDS RAILWAY . . . . . . Moorlands Sports Ground, Newark Road, Lincoln LN6 8RT 01522 520184/874111
LIVERSEDGE . . . . Clayborn Ground, Quaker Lane, Hightown Road, Cleckheaton BD19 3RJ 01274 862108
LONG EATON UNITED . . . . Grange Park, Station Road, Long Eaton NG10 2EF 0115 973 5700
MALTBY MAIN . . . . Maltby Miners Welfare, Muglet Lane, Maltby, Rotherham S66 7JQ 07941 057883
MICKLEOVER SPORTS . . . . Mickleover Sports Club, Station Road, Mickleover, Derby DE3 5FE 01332 521167
NOSTELL MINERS WELFARE . . Miners Welfare Ground, Middle Lane, New Crofton, Wakefield WF4 1LB 01924 862348
PARKGATE . . . . Roundwood Sports Complex, Green Lane, Rawmarsh, Rotherham S62 7LA 01709 826600
PICKERING TOWN . . . . Recreation Ground, off Mill Lane, Malton Road, Pickering YO18 8DR 01751 473317
SELBY TOWN . . . . Flaxley Road Ground, Richard Street, Scott Road, Selby YO8 0BS 01757 210900
SHIREBROOK TOWN . . . . BRSA Sports Ground, Langwith Road, Shirebrook NG20 8TF 01623 742535
SOUTH NORMANTON ATHLETIC . . ExChem Sports Ground, Lees Lane, South Normanton, Alfreton DE55 2AD 01773 581491
THACKLEY . . . . Dennyfield, Ainsbury Avenue, Thackley, Bradford BD10 0LL 01274 615571
WINTERTON RANGERS . . . . 54 West Street, Winterton, Scunthorpe DN15 9QF 01724 732628

IN: Lincoln Moorlands (P) (having merged with Moorlands Railway to become Lincoln Moorlands Railway), Nostell Miners Welfare (P), Parkgate (P), South Normanton Athletic (P), Winterton Rangers (P)
OUT: Carlton Town (P – Northern Premier League Division One South), Garforth Town (P – Northern Premier League Division One North), Retford United (P – Northern Premier League Division One South), Sheffield (P – Northern Premier League Division One South), Sutton Town (W – Central Midlands League Premier Division)

WWW.CHERRYRED.CO.UK

	AFC Emley	Borrowash Victoria	Dinnington Town	Gedling Town	Hall Road Rangers	Lincoln Moorlands	Nostell Miners Welfare	Parkgate	Pontefract Collieries	Rossington Main	South Normanton Athletic	Staveley Miners Welfare	Tadcaster Albion	Teversal	Winterton Rangers	Worsbrough Bridge Miners Welfare	Yorkshire Amateur
AFC Emley		4-2	5-2	3-2	3-3	2-0	5-3	2-3	2-1	0-1	1-1	0-5	2-2	3-1	4-1	0-2	0-3
Borrowash Victoria	4-1	D	6-1	3-1	1-3	1-4	2-1	1-2	n/a	0-0	1-4	2-2	0-2	0-2	7-1	2-1	3-2
Dinnington Town	1-2	4-1	I	1-5	2-1	1-2	4-0	2-0	3-1	0-1	2-0	0-3	2-0	2-5	7-1	4-2	2-3
Gedling Town	2-2	5-0	2-1	V	6-0	3-1	2-0	1-2	n/a	2-0	4-2	3-0	1-1	3-1	2-2	0-2	1-4
Hall Road Rangers	5-2	1-3	2-0	3-2	I	0-1	8-0	0-2	5-0	1-3	3-5	2-3	2-3	2-2	3-0	1-2	0-2
Lincoln Moorlands	4-3	3-3	0-2	1-3	2-1	S	7-0	2-3	5-2	2-2	2-1	2-0	3-0	1-1	2-0	3-0	1-0
Nostell Miners Welf.	0-5	0-3	0-1	1-8	1-4	0-4	I	2-5	4-0	2-1	0-2	1-3	1-1	0-7	1-3	1-1	1-5
Parkgate	1-4	0-0	0-0	1-3	2-1	2-0	2-1	O	n/a	2-2	5-4	1-1	2-1	1-0	5-0	4-0	3-1
Pontefract Collieries	n/a	1-6	0-3	0-9	4-8	0-5	1-1	2-4	N	0-7	2-1	1-5	0-6	n/a	6-3	0-2	0-3
Rossington Main	3-1	3-2	4-1	1-1	3-0	0-2	4-0	2-1	10-0		4-2	1-0	2-1	0-1	9-0	1-2	1-3
South Normanton Athletic	5-1	2-3	1-1	3-3	5-4	1-1	3-0	1-4	4-0	2-4		2-5	1-1	4-0	5-0	0-1	2-2
Staveley Miners Welfare	1-3	3-1	1-1	1-4	3-2	0-0	3-0	0-0	n/a	2-3	6-2		4-1	1-1	3-1	0-2	1-2
Tadcaster Albion	2-1	2-1	4-2	2-4	2-2	3-1	4-0	0-2	5-1	4-0	1-4	0-1		0-2	2-2	3-1	6-1
Teversal	4-0	1-0	3-2	3-1	5-0	3-3	10-1	2-2	n/a	3-0	2-0	4-0	7-0	O	7-2	1-0	2-1
Winterton Rangers	3-1	0-4	1-6	0-7	0-2	0-5	0-0	1-2	1-2	0-7	1-3	2-3	0-5	1-5	N	1-5	1-5
Worsbrough Bridge Miners Welfare	1-3	3-0	2-1	3-2	4-2	1-0	3-3	1-3	n/a	0-0	4-1	2-0	0-0	2-2	2-0	E	1-2
Yorkshire Amateur	1-1	3-1	5-1	1-3	6-2	0-0	2-0	2-0	n/a	4-0	2-1	0-1	2-1	2-4	4-0	3-2	

Division One		P	W	D	L	F	A	Pts
Parkgate		32	26	4	2	120	38	82
Winterton Rangers		32	23	2	7	90	38	71
South Normanton Athletic		32	20	5	7	76	34	65
Nostell Miners Welfare	-3	32	20	0	12	66	41	57
Lincoln Moorlands		32	17	5	10	63	42	56
Staveley Miners Welfare		32	16	3	13	57	50	51
Tadcaster Albion		32	14	7	11	60	54	49
Worsbrough Bridge Miners Welfare		32	13	9	10	53	42	48
Dinnington Town		32	12	7	13	52	46	43
Hall Road Rangers		32	12	7	13	48	51	43
Borrowash Victoria		32	10	7	15	38	52	37
Pontefract Collieries		32	10	7	15	35	61	37
AFC Emley		32	10	4	18	48	70	34
Gedling Town		32	9	4	19	45	63	31
Teversal		32	9	4	19	35	69	31
Yorkshire Amateur		32	7	1	24	33	106	22
Rossington Main		32	4	4	24	27	89	16

NORTHERN COUNTIES EAST LEAGUE DIVISION ONE CONSTITUTION 2007-08

AFC EMLEY .... Emley Welfare Sports Ground, Emley, Huddersfield HD8 9RE. 01924 848398
BARTON TOWN OLD BOYS ...... The Euronics Ground, Marsh Lane, Barton-on-Humber DN15 5HB. 07900 105204
BORROWASH VICTORIA .... Robinson Construction Bowl, Borrowash Road, Spondon, Derby DE21 7PH 01332 669688
BOTTESFORD TOWN .... Birch Park, Ontario Road, Bottesford, Scunthorpe DN17 2TQ 01724 871883
DINNINGTON TOWN .... Resource Centre, 131 Laughton Road (The Stute), Dinnington S25 2HA 01909 518555
GEDLING TOWN .... Ferryboat Ground, Stoke Lane, Stoke Bardolph, Gedling NG14 5HX 0115 940 2145
HALL ROAD RANGERS .... Dene Park, Dene Close, Beverley Road, Dunswell, Hull HU6 0AB 01482 850101
LEEDS METROPOLITAN CARNEGIE .. LMU Headingley Campus, Headingley, Leeds LS6 3QS. 0113 2833160
PONTEFRACT COLLIERIES .... Abstract Stadium, Skinner Lane, Pontefract WF8 4QE 01977 600818
RAINWORTH MINERS WELFARE .. Welfare Ground, Kirklington Rd, Rainworth, Mansfield NG21 0JY. 01623 792495
ROSSINGTON MAIN .... Welfare Ground, Oxford Street, Rossington DN11 0DU 01302 865524
SCARBOROUGH ATHLETIC. .... Bridlington Town FC, Queensgate, Queensgate, Bridlington YO16 5LN 01262 606879
STAVELEY MINERS WELFARE .... Inkersall Road, Staveley, Chesterfield S43 3JL. 01246 471441
TADCASTER ALBION .... The Park, Ings Lane, off Centre Lane, Tadcaster LS24 9AY 01937 834119
TEVERSAL............ Teversal Grange S & S Centre, Carnarvon Street, Teversal, Sutton-in-Ashfield NG17 3HJ 01623 555944
WORSBROUGH BRIDGE MW .... Park Road, Worsbrough Bridge, Barnsley S70 5LJ. 01226 284452
YORKSHIRE AMATEUR .... Bracken Edge Ground, Sycamore Avenue, Leeds LS8 4JG 0113 262 4093

IN: Barton Town Old Boys (P – Central Midlands League Supreme Division), Bottesford Town (P – Central Midlands League Supreme Division), Leeds Metropolitan Carnegie (P – West Yorkshire League Premier Division), Rainworth Miners Welfare (P – Central Midlands League Supreme Division), Scarborough Athletic (N)
OUT: Lincoln Moorlands (P) (having merged with Moorlands Railway to become Lincoln Moorlands Railway), Nostell Miners Welfare (P), Parkgate (P), South Normanton Athletic (P), Winterton Rangers (P)

LEAGUE CUP
(All sides in league)

FIRST ROUND

Dinnington Town 3 Gedling Town 1

Rossington Main 1 **Hall Road Rangers** 2

South Normanton Athletic 1 **Worsbrough Bridge MW** 2

Staveley Miners Welfare 3 AFC Emley 1

Yorkshire Amateur 2 Borrowash Victoria 0

SECOND ROUND

Arnold Town 0 **Mickleover Sports** 3

Brodsworth Welfare 2 **Hallam** 3

Carlton Town 5 Thackley 1

Dinnington Town 0 **Parkgate** 3

Garforth Town 2 Sutton Town 1

Hall Road Rangers 4 Worsbrough Bridge MW 2

Liversedge 1 **Long Eaton United** 1 *aet* (2-3p)

Maltby Main 0 **Pontefract Collieries** 2

Nostell Miners Welfare 3 Sheffield 2

Pickering Town 2 Retford United 2
aet (4-2p)

Selby Town 2 Armthorpe Welfare 1

Shirebrook Town 1 **Eccleshill United** 3

Staveley Miners Welfare 2 Glasshoughton Welfare 0

Tadcaster Albion 1 **Lincoln Moorlands** 2

Teversal 0 **Glapwell** 3

Winterton Rangers 4 Yorkshire Amateur 2

THIRD ROUND

Carlton Town 1 **Mickleover Sports** 3

Eccleshill United 0 **Staveley Miners Welfare** 3

Garforth Town 3 Lincoln Moorlands 0

Hallam 3 Hall Road Rangers 2

Long Eaton United 0 **Parkgate** 3

Nostell Miners Welfare 0 **Winterton Rangers** 1

Pickering Town 1 Selby Town 0

Pontefract Collieries 2 Glapwell 1

QUARTER-FINALS

Garforth Town 1 Parkgate 0

Pontefract Collieries 1 **Mickleover Sports** 5

Staveley Miners Welfare 3 Pickering Town 1

Winterton Rangers 3 Hallam 0

SEMI-FINALS

Garforth Town 2 Winterton Rangers 0

Mickleover Sports 3 Staveley Miners Welfare 0

FINAL
(May 5th at Sheffield)

Mickleover Sports 1 Garforth Town 1 *aet* (7-6p)

PRESIDENT'S CUP
(Top eight finishers from Premier and Division One)

FIRST ROUND
Armthorpe Welfare 1 **Gedling Town** 2
Lincoln Moorlands 2 Winterton Rangers 1
Liversedge 3 Thackley 2
Parkgate 3 Sutton Town 1
Retford United 2 Borrowash Victoria 0
Selby Town 2 Pickering Town 0
Sheffield 2 Arnold Town 1
Tadcaster Albion 1 **Carlton Town** 2

QUARTER-FINALS
Gedling Town 2 **Sheffield** 5
Lincoln Moorlands 0 **Retford United** 3
Parkgate 5 Liversedge 0
Selby Town 2 Carlton Town 0

SEMI-FINALS
Parkgate 0 **Selby Town** 2
Sheffield 0 **Retford United** 4

FINAL
(played over two legs)
(April 11th)
Retford United 4 Selby Town 1
(April 19th)
Selby Town 2 **Retford United** 1

WILKINSON SWORD SHIELD
(Division One sides)

PRELIMINARY ROUND
Rossington Main 0 **South Normanton Athletic** 3
FIRST ROUND
Borrowash Victoria 2 Nostell Miners Welfare 1
Dinnington Town 3 Winterton Rangers 1
Hall Road Rangers 3 South Normanton Athletic 1
Lincoln Moorlands 2 Gedling Town 1
Pontefract Collieries 2 Yorkshire Amateur 1
Staveley Miners Welfare 5 Tadcaster Albion 3
Teversal 2 AFC Emley 0
Worsbrough Bridge MW 0 **Parkgate** 3
QUARTER-FINALS
Borrowash Victoria 2 **Lincoln Moorlands** 2 *aet* (1-4p)
Dinnington Town 0 **Parkgate** 1
Staveley Miners Welfare 2 Hall Road Rangers 0
Teversal 3 Pontefract Collieries 2
SEMI-FINALS
Lincoln Moorlands 2 **Staveley Miners Welfare** 3
Parkgate 5 Teversal 1
FINAL
(played over two legs)
(March 13th)
Staveley Miners Welfare 3 **Parkgate** 4
(March 27th)
Parkgate 0 Staveley Miners Welfare 0

NORTHERN LEAGUE

	Ashington	Bedlington T.	Billingham S.	Billingham T.	B. Auckland	Chester-le-Str.	Consett	Darl'gton RA	Dunston FB	Durham City	Horden CW	Jarrow Rfg	Morpeth T.	Newc. Benfield	Newcastle BS	Northallerton	Shildon	Sund. Nissan	Tow Law T.	W. Allotment	W. Auckland	Whitley Bay
Ashington		1-2	0-0	3-4	0-1	1-1	0-3	5-1	0-0	0-0	5-1	1-3	2-1	1-2	2-1	0-3	0-2	0-1	3-0	0-0	1-2	0-6
Bedlington Terriers	1-1		3-3	0-3	2-2	0-1	0-3	3-1	1-1	1-2	1-1	2-5	1-4	0-2	0-3	2-0	1-7	0-2	0-1	0-0	0-4	0-3
Billingham Synthonia	3-2	1-3		0-2	3-1	0-1	1-1	2-3	1-2	1-1	3-0	2-2	4-0	1-0	2-1	3-0	0-3	0-2	3-3	5-1	1-1	4-3
Billingham Town	0-2	3-1	8-2		2-1	4-0	3-4	2-0	1-1	2-2	2-0	4-0	1-0	2-1	3-0	0-3	0-2	3-3	5-1	1-1	4-3	1-1
Bishop Auckland	3-2	2-0	2-2	1-2		2-0	1-2	1-0	2-2	1-3	4-1	4-2	1-3	0-2	1-1	1-1	1-2	1-1	2-2	2-2	1-4	1-2
Chester-le-Street Town	1-2	3-1	0-0	0-5	6-0	*D*	1-2	2-1	1-1	0-3	3-1	3-4	2-1	1-3	1-3	1-2	2-2	0-2	1-1	0-3	1-2	0-6
Consett	4-0	2-1	0-0	0-1	5-0	1-0	*I*	1-1	4-1	1-0	1-2	3-0	0-3	0-3	0-0	4-1	1-1	1-1	5-1	4-2	3-2	
Darlington Railway Ath.	4-1	0-3	1-2	0-3	1-4	2-2	1-3	*V*	1-3	4-2	1-1	1-5	0-4	0-1	1-1	1-2	0-2	1-5	0-3	2-3	0-0	0-2
Dunston Federation Brew.	1-1	3-1	2-1	3-0	5-1	1-3	1-0	2-0	*I*	0-1	1-0	4-0	0-2	0-3	3-2	2-1	1-1	0-1	1-1	1-0	1-1	0-4
Durham City	5-0	4-2	0-0	2-3	2-3	2-1	2-1	5-1	4-1	*S*	2-2	3-3	3-3	2-1	1-1	2-2	1-0	1-3	3-3	1-0	1-2	1-3
Horden Colliery Welfare	1-0	3-3	2-1	0-4	1-0	1-1	1-5	2-2	2-2	0-5	*I*	1-2	2-1	1-4	1-6	3-2	0-1	1-2	1-2	3-3	4-3	1-3
Jarrow Roofing Boldon CA	0-4	2-1	1-0	1-4	1-2	1-3	2-2	1-3	0-4	1-5	2-2	*O*	0-2	1-0	4-1	1-3	2-3	1-5	2-1	3-2	2-2	1-2
Morpeth Town	2-1	1-2	1-1	1-2	0-2	2-2	2-2	6-0	2-2	0-2	4-0	4-1	*N*	3-2	2-4	2-2	4-1	5-3	2-1	1-1	1-1	0-0
Newcastle Benfield BP	6-0	1-2	1-3	1-1	2-1	3-1	1-1	3-0	1-1	0-0	2-1	0-0	7-0		0-2	0-1	2-2	3-1	2-1	0-0	1-1	1-1
Newcastle Blue Star	2-0	4-2	1-2	1-1	0-1	3-0	2-2	4-0	1-2	1-1	1-0	2-2	1-3	1-2	*O*	2-0	2-0	0-4	2-3	4-0	0-3	0-3
Northallerton Town	3-1	1-1	0-1	2-0	4-1	1-1	0-3	8-1	0-2	0-1	3-1	3-1	0-5	2-3	4-3	*N*	0-1	3-1	0-4	1-3	2-1	1-1
Shildon	4-1	4-0	2-2	0-1	2-1	3-1	1-2	0-1	1-1	1-3	3-2	2-0	1-3	1-0		8-3	*E*	0-1	3-1	1-1	3-0	1-1
Sunderland Nissan	2-1	2-1	1-2	1-1	2-0	0-1	5-0	2-1	1-2	3-1	4-1	5-1	3-0	2-0	1-0	2-2	3-0		4-0	6-1	3-0	1-2
Tow Law Town	0-1	3-0	1-1	0-3	2-0	3-1	4-0	6-2	0-2	1-3	3-1	1-1	2-1	3-2	1-2	1-0	1-3	0-2		1-1	1-3	1-2
West Allotment Celtic	4-1	2-0	0-0	5-0	1-2	2-2	2-1	0-3	0-2	2-2	2-1	2-1	0-2	1-2	0-2	1-2	3-5	1-2	2-2		1-3	1-2
West Auckland Town	3-0	5-1	3-0	0-2	2-1	1-0	1-3	5-1	1-1	3-2	5-0	2-0	2-2	2-3	0-1	1-0	1-2	0-2	2-1	3-1		2-1
Whitley Bay	4-0	3-2	2-1	2-3	4-1	2-1	2-1	2-0	1-1	4-0	3-0	2-1	3-1	1-1	1-3	4-1	4-0	3-2	3-3	2-1	3-4	

Division One

		P	W	D	L	F	A	Pts
Whitley Bay		42	28	8	6	104	45	92
Billingham Town		42	28	8	6	98	47	92
Sunderland Nissan		42	28	6	8	96	41	90
Consett		42	23	10	9	89	51	79
Newcastle Benfield BP		42	21	11	10	79	45	74
West Auckland Town		42	22	8	12	88	61	74
Dunston Federation Brewery		42	19	16	7	67	48	73
Durham City		42	20	12	10	87	62	72
Shildon		42	21	9	12	80	57	72
Morpeth Town		42	19	9	14	87	70	66
Newcastle Blue Star		42	17	7	18	71	60	58
Tow Law Town		42	15	11	16	68	72	56
Northallerton Town		42	16	6	20	76	82	54
Billingham Synthonia		42	13	14	15	61	71	53
Jarrow Roofing Boldon CA		42	13	7	22	68	101	46
Bishop Auckland		42	11	10	21	59	86	43
Chester-le-Street Town		42	9	9	23	51	80	39
West Allotment Celtic		42	9	11	22	62	80	38
Ashington		42	9	7	26	46	87	34
Bedlington Terriers	-3	42	7	8	27	47	99	26
Horden Colliery Welfare	-3	42	6	10	26	46	107	25
Darlington Railway Athletic		42	6	5	31	41	119	23

J R CLEATOR CUP
(League champions v League Cup holders)

(August 5th at Newcastle Blue Star)
Newcastle Blue Star 0
Dunston Federation Brewery 2

NORTHERN LEAGUE DIVISION ONE CONSTITUTION 2007-08

ASHINGTON .... Portland Park, Lintonville Terrace, Ashington NE63 9XG 01670 811991
BEDLINGTON TERRIERS .... Dr Pitt Welfare Ground, Park Road, Bedlington NE22 5DP 01670 825485
BILLINGHAM SYNTHONIA .... The Stadium, Central Avenue, Billingham TS23 1LR 01642 532348
BILLINGHAM TOWN .... Bedford Terrace, Billingham TS23 4AF 01642 560043
BISHOP AUCKLAND .... Shildon FC, Dean Street, Shildon, Durham DL4 1EZ 01388 773877
CHESTER-LE-STREET TOWN .... Moor Park, Chester Moor, Chester-le-Street DH2 3RW 07729 527973
CONSETT .... Belle Vue Park, Ashdale Road, Consett DH8 5SR 01207 503788
DUNSTON FEDERATION .... Federation Park, Wellington Road, Dunston, Gateshead NE11 9EE 0191 493 2935
DURHAM CITY .... Archibald Stadium, Belmont Industrial Estate, Durham DH1 1GG 0191 386 9616
JARROW ROOFING BOLDON CA .. Boldon CA Sports Club, New Road, Boldon Colliery NE35 9DS 0191 489 9825
MORPETH TOWN .... Craik Park, Morpeth Common, Morpeth NE61 2YX 01670 513785
NEWCASTLE BENFIELD ..... Benfield School Sports Ground, Benfield Rd, Newcastle-upon-Tyne NE6 4NU 0191 265 9357
NORTHALLERTON TOWN ...... Calvert Stadium, Ainderby Road, Romanby, Northallerton DL7 8HA 01609 772418
SEAHAM RED STAR .... Seaham Town Park, Stockton Road, Seaham SR7 0JT 0191 581 1347
SHILDON .... Dean Street, Shildon DL4 1EZ 01388 773877
SPENNYMOOR TOWN .... Brewery Field, Durham Road, Spennymoor DL16 6UU 01388 811934/814100
SUNDERLAND NISSAN .... Nissan Sports Complex, Washington Road, Sunderland SR5 3NS 0191 415 2354
TOW LAW TOWN .... Ironworks Road, Tow Law, Bishop Auckland DL13 4DH 01388 731443
WASHINGTON .... Albany Park, Spout Lane, Concord, Washington NE37 2AB 0191 417 7779
WEST ALLOTMENT CELTIC .... Blue Flames, Whitley Road, Benton, Newcastle-upon-Tyne NE12 9SF 0191 270 0885
WEST AUCKLAND TOWN ...... Darlington Road Ground, Darlington Road, West Auckland DL14 9JT 07800 796630
WHITLEY BAY .... Hillheads Park, Rink Way, Whitley Bay NE25 8HR 0191 291 3636

IN: Seaham Red Star (P), Spennymoor Town (P), Washington (P)
OUT: Darlington Railway Athletic (R), Horden Colliery Welfare (R), Newcastle Blue Star (P – Northern Premier League Division One North)
Dunston Federation Brewery become Dunston Federation, Newcastle Benfield BP become Newcastle Benfield

WWW.NLNEWSDESK.CO.UK

	Alnwick Town	Brandon United	Crook Town	Esh Winning	Guisborough Town	Hebburn Town	Marske United	North Shields	Norton & Stockton	Penrith	Prudhoe Town	Ryton	Seaham Red Star	South Shields	Spennymoor Town	Stokesley Spts Club	Sunderland Ryhope	Team Northumbria	Thornaby	Washington	Whickham
Alnwick Town		4-1	2-2	2-4	4-0	0-1	0-1	1-4	3-4	0-2	0-0	1-8	0-5	1-2	2-5	1-2	3-1	0-1	2-1	1-1	4-2
Brandon United	3-1		1-1	1-1	1-3	0-3	0-1	3-1	2-6	3-1	0-1	4-3	1-4	4-3	1-0	1-1	0-1	1-1	1-0	1-1	2-0
Crook Town	2-0	2-1		2-4	5-0	2-3	1-1	0-3	0-4	0-5	7-0	4-4	3-1	1-3	0-4	5-3	2-3	1-0	1-1	0-2	2-0
Esh Winning	4-0	1-7	1-4		1-2	1-6	1-1	2-1	1-5	3-1	8-1	1-1	0-0	1-2	0-1	2-2	1-0	0-2	3-1	3-2	0-2
Guisborough Town	6-0	3-2	2-1	4-3	*D*	1-0	1-1	4-0	0-1	2-4	2-3	3-0	3-1	0-0	2-3	4-2	3-2	0-3	1-6	5-1	
Hebburn Town	1-3	2-3	3-2	1-0	4-1	*I*	2-2	1-1	1-0	1-1	2-1	1-4	2-2	1-6	3-4	3-5	4-0	4-0	1-0	3-2	1-1
Marske United	3-1	3-3	1-0	2-0	2-0	2-2	*V*	2-1	2-1	3-0	1-1	2-3	0-1	2-2	1-1	1-1	2-1	3-1	2-1	1-1	2-3
North Shields	4-1	2-0	0-3	3-1	0-1	1-3		*I*	1-4	3-1	2-1	1-2	0-3	0-2	1-4	1-2	0-1	2-4	0-2	3-2	
Norton & Stockton	5-0	5-4	2-1	1-2	3-1	3-1	4-2	2-1	*S*	2-2	3-2	4-0	0-1	4-2	0-1	0-2	4-0	0-1	0-0	1-2	2-1
Penrith	6-0	4-0	10-1	3-2	1-0	1-0	1-3	1-1	2-0	*I*	1-2	3-1	2-3	1-1	0-1	3-1	1-1	4-1	2-2	0-0	1-0
Prudhoe Town	2-2	1-2	3-0	4-3	0-2	0-3	1-2	0-1	1-4	1-4	*O*	2-0	2-7	0-3	2-1	2-4	2-0	5-1	1-3	0-4	0-3
Ryton	5-0	1-1	2-2	0-0	1-0	0-1	0-2	2-0	0-0	5-1	2-2	*N*	1-1	2-2	1-1	3-3	8-0	1-2	0-2	0-3	1-0
Seaham Red Star	4-0	4-0	4-0	4-3	3-1	2-2	2-2	1-0	3-1	2-0	1-0	2-1		2-4	2-3	0-2	2-1	3-2	4-1	3-1	4-4
South Shields	3-0	3-2	0-1	3-0	1-2	3-0	0-2	4-2	2-2	1-0	3-1	1-0	2-1		1-3	3-1	4-3	4-2	2-0	1-3	5-5
Spennymoor Town	4-1	6-1	3-0	3-2	0-0	1-0	2-0	1-0	3-1	3-0	2-0	3-2	2-0	1-0	*T*	0-1	1-0	3-1	1-0	2-1	1-2
Stokesley Sports C.	4-2	1-0	2-1	3-1	0-0	1-0	1-2	2-0	2-4	2-2	4-2	1-1	0-1	1-3	2-2	*W*	5-2	1-2	4-3	2-3	3-1
Sunderland Ryhope	2-5	2-1	2-1	1-2	1-0	0-1	0-2	2-3	0-3	0-3	2-0	2-4	3-3	2-0	0-2	1-0	*O*	5-1	0-0	1-3	0-0
Team Northumbria	0-2	1-2	1-4	4-0	0-1	4-2	2-0	0-1	3-3	2-0	2-0	2-1	1-2	3-2	1-1	2-2	2-1		2-0	0-3	2-1
Thornaby	5-0	5-4	1-1	1-3	1-1	3-1	1-0	1-3	1-2	0-2	2-0	2-2	1-6	1-1	0-1	0-2	2-3	3-1		1-4	3-2
Washington	2-1	1-0	2-3	2-0	2-1	3-0	0-0	2-0	1-0	0-1	4-0	2-0	1-4	1-0	1-1	2-1	1-0	1-2	4-0		1-1
Whickham	6-0	0-1	4-1	1-0	3-2	3-3	1-2	4-1	3-2	1-0	0-3	1-2	1-3	1-3	8-0	3-1	1-2	2-1	2-1	2-2	

Division Two		P	W	D	L	F	A	Pts
Spennymoor Town		40	29	9	2	85	33	96
Seaham Red Star		40	26	8	6	99	52	86
Washington		40	24	9	7	78	36	81
South Shields		40	23	7	10	89	58	76
Marske United		40	20	13	7	68	44	73
Norton & Stockton Ancients		40	21	5	14	86	58	68
Penrith		40	18	10	12	81	52	64
Stokesley Sports Club		40	18	8	14	83	70	62
Guisborough Town		40	17	4	19	65	71	55
Hebburn Town		40	15	9	16	68	71	54
Team Northumbria		40	16	5	19	57	70	53
Ryton		40	12	14	14	71	60	50
Thornaby		40	13	9	18	60	69	48
Crook Town		40	13	7	20	72	88	46
Whickham		40	12	9	19	71	76	45
Esh Winning		40	12	7	21	63	83	43
Brandon United		40	12	7	21	64	87	43
North Shields		40	13	4	23	49	72	43
Sunderland Ryhope	-3	40	12	4	24	50	85	37
Prudhoe Town		40	8	4	28	48	104	28
Alnwick Town		40	8	4	28	50	118	28

NORTHERN LEAGUE DIVISION TWO CONSTITUTION 2007-08

BIRTLEY TOWN . . . . Birtley Sports Complex, Durham Road, Birtley, Chester-le-Street DH3 2TB . . . . None
BRANDON UNITED . . . . Welfare Ground, Commercial Street, Brandon DH7 8PL 0191 378 1730
CROOK TOWN . . . . Millfield Ground, West Road, Crook DL15 9PW 01388 762959
DARLINGTON RAILWAY ATHLETIC . . Darlington RA Club, Brinkburn Rd, Darlington DL3 9LF 01325 468125
ESH WINNING . . . . West Terrace, Waterhouses, Esh Winning DH7 9BQ 0191 373 3872
GUISBOROUGH TOWN . . . . King George V Playing Fields, Howlbeck Road, Guisborough TS14 6LE 01287 636925
HEBBURN TOWN . . . . Hebburn Sports & Social Club, Victoria Road West, Hebburn NE31 1UN. 0191 483 5101
HORDEN COLLIERY WELFARE. . . . Welfare Park Ground, Park Road, Horden, Peterlee SR8 4LW 0191 587 3549
MARSKE UNITED . . . . Mount Pleasant, Mount Pleasant Avenue, Marske-by-Sea TS11 7BW 01642 471091
NORTH SHIELDS . . . . Ralph Gardner Park, West Percy Road, Chirton, North Shields NE29 7RG. . . . . None
NORTON & STOCKTON ANCIENTS . . Norton Spts Complex, Station Rd, Norton, Stockton-on-Tees TS20 1PE 01642 530203
PENRITH TOWN . . . . Southend Road Ground, Penrith CA11 8JH 01768 859990
PRUDHOE TOWN. . . . . Kimberley Park, Broomhouse Road, Prudhoe NE42 5EH 01661 835900
RYTON . . . . Kingsley Park, Stannerford Road, Ryton NE40 3SN 0191 413 4448
SOUTH SHIELDS . . . . Filtrona Park, Shaftsbury Avenue, Simonside Industrial Estate NE32 3UP 0191 427 9839
STOKESLEY SPORTS CLUB . . Stokesley Sports Club, Broughton Road, Stokesley, Middlesbrough TS9 5AQ. 01642 710051
SUNDERLAND RYHOPE CA . . Meadow Park, Beechbrook, off Waterworks Rd, Ryhope, Sunderland SR2 0NZ 0191 523 6555
TEAM NORTHUMBRIA . . Bullock Steads Sports Ground, Ponteland Rd, Kenton Bank Foot, Newcastle NE13 8AH . . . . None
THORNABY. . . . . Teesdale Park, Acklam Road, Thornaby, Stockton-on-Tees TS17 7JU 01642 606803
WHICKHAM . . . . Glebe Ground Sports, Rectory Lane, Whickham, Newcastle-upon-Tyne NE16 4NA. 0191 420 0186

IN: Birtley Town (P – Wearside), Darlington Railway Athletic (R), Horden Colliery Welfare (R)
OUT: Alnwick Town (R – Northern Alliance Premier Division), Seaham Red Star (P), Spennymoor Town (P), Washington (P)
Penrith become Penrith Town

LEAGUE CUP

FIRST ROUND
Alnwick Town 3 Thornaby 1
Billingham Town 2 Bishop Auckland 0
Darlington Railway Athletic 3 South Shields 2
Jarrow Roofing Boldon CA 5 Whickham 1
Newcastle Benfield BP 1 Stokesley Sports Club 1 *aet* (3-0p)
North Shields 0 **Chester-le-Street Town** 6
Northallerton Town 2 Guisborough Town 0
Shildon 3 Ashington 1
Team Northumbria 2 Crook Town 2 *aet* (5-4p)
Washington 0 **Billingham Synthonia** 1
West Allotment Celtic 0 **Tow Law Town** 3

SECOND ROUND
Alnwick Town 2 **Horden Colliery Welfare** 5
Bedlington Terriers 2 **Chester-le-Street Town** 3
Consett 6 Whitley Bay 3
Darlington Railway Athletic 0 **Newcastle Blue Star** 2
Durham City 4 Jarrow Roofing Boldon CA 0
Hebburn Town 4 Spennymoor Town 1
Marske United 1 **Brandon United** 2
Newcastle Benfield BP 1 Shildon 0
Norton & Stockton Ancients 1 **Billingham Town** 4
Penrith 1 **Northallerton Town** 2
Prudhoe Town 3 Morpeth Town 1 *aet*
Ryton 5 Esh Winning 4
Sunderland Nissan 2 Billingham Synthonia 1
Team Northumbria 2 Seaham Red Star 2 *aet* (4-3p)
Tow Law Town 2 Kennek Ryhope CA 1
West Auckland Town 1 **Dunston Federation Brewery** 4

THIRD ROUND
Brandon United 1 **Sunderland Nissan** 2
Consett 1 **Newcastle Blue Star** 2
Dunston Federation Brewery 1 **Chester-le-Street Town** 1 *aet* (0-3p)
Durham City 0 **Newcastle Benfield BP** 2
Prudhoe Town 1 Hebburn Town 0
Ryton 4 Northallerton Town 3
Team Northumbria 2 **Billingham Town** 4
Tow Law Town 4 Horden Colliery Welfare 1

QUARTER-FINALS
Billingham Town 2 **Sunderland Nissan** 4
Newcastle Benfield BP 2 Prudhoe Town 0
Ryton 0 **Chester-le-Street Town** 3
Tow Law Town 3 Newcastle Blue Star 1

SEMI-FINALS
Sunderland Nissan 2 Chester-le-Street Town 0
Tow Law Town 3 **Newcastle Benfield BP** 3 *aet* (3-4p)
FINAL *(May 7th at Dunston Federation Brewery)*
Newcastle Benfield BP 1 Sunderland Nissan 0

ERNEST ARMSTRONG MEMORIAL CUP
(Division Two clubs)

FIRST ROUND
Alnwick Town 4 Norton & Stockton Anc. 4 *aet* (4-1p)
Marske United 3 North Shields 0
Penrith 5 Prudhoe Town 1
Seaham Red Star 1 **Spennymoor Town** 2
Thornaby 0 **Esh Winning** 6

SECOND ROUND
Alnwick Town 0 **Hebburn Town** 1
Esh Winning 0 **Crook Town** 1
Penrith 6 Marske United 1
South Shields 1 Washington 0
Spennymoor Town 2 **Stokesley Sports Club** 3
Sunderland Ryhope CA 3 Brandon United 1

Team Northumbria 0 **Guisborough Town** 1
Whickham 2 Ryton 0

QUARTER-FINALS
Crook Town 1 **Stokesley Sports Club** 3
Penrith 1 Hebburn Town 1 *aet* (4-3p)
Sunderland Ryhope CA 0 **Guisborough Town** 1
Whickham 1 South Shields 1 *aet* (4-3p)

SEMI-FINALS
Penrith 2 Guisborough 3 *aet (Guisborough expelled)*
Whickham 2 Stokesley Sports Club 1

FINAL
(May 9th at Esh Winning)
Penrith 1 **Whickham** 1 *aet* (3-4p)

WWW.NLNEWSDESK.CO.UK

NORTHERN PREMIER LEAGUE

Home \ Away	AFC Telford United	Ashton United	Burscough	Fleetwood Town	Frickley Athletic	Gateshead	Grantham Town	Guiseley	Hednesford Town	Ilkeston Town	Kendal Town	Leek Town	Lincoln United	Marine	Matlock Town	Mossley	North Ferriby United	Ossett Town	Prescot Cables	Radcliffe Borough	Whitby Town	Witton Albion
AFC Telford United		0-0	1-2	2-2	4-1	4-0	1-1	3-2	0-0	1-1	2-2	5-1	1-1	1-1	3-1	0-0	2-1	4-1	2-1	1-1	1-3	5-1
Ashton United	0-5		2-1	3-0	1-0	0-3	1-0	3-0	3-4	1-1	3-3	1-4	2-0	2-4	1-1	1-0	0-3	2-3	2-1	2-1	1-2	2-1
Burscough	0-0	3-2		4-1	5-2	2-0	3-0	1-0	2-0	1-1	8-2	2-0	0-2	0-0	0-0	4-0	3-2	4-0	1-0	2-2	4-0	1-0
Fleetwood Town	3-0	1-1	1-0	P	2-2	1-0	4-1	1-2	4-1	2-1	2-1	2-0	2-3	1-1	0-1	4-1	1-0	4-0	0-3	3-1	2-0	1-2
Frickley Athletic	0-1	2-0	1-2	1-3	R	1-1	1-1	2-0	0-2	0-2	2-1	3-1	2-0	1-2	2-0	0-4	1-1	0-0	1-1	2-2	3-2	2-1
Gateshead	4-3	2-3	1-0	3-3	2-3	E	5-2	0-1	2-3	2-1	1-1	2-1	2-2	2-0	3-2	2-0	0-0	2-1	2-3	3-1	0-0	1-0
Grantham Town	0-1	1-1	0-3	0-2	0-0	0-6	M	0-1	1-2	0-4	2-1	3-1	1-2	2-1	0-2	1-2	0-5	1-3	0-1	0-0	2-3	2-3
Guiseley	0-1	2-1	1-1	1-1	5-1	1-1	2-0	I	1-1	3-3	1-2	1-1	3-1	2-1	5-1	1-1	1-2	3-1	2-1	5-0	1-3	0-1
Hednesford Town	0-1	0-0	2-2	2-1	2-1	1-1	2-0	2-2	E	3-0	2-1	1-0	2-1	0-2	1-2	0-0	1-1	1-1	1-0	0-0	3-0	0-1
Ilkeston Town	1-1	2-1	2-2	2-2	1-2	4-2	2-1	1-2	2-0	R	2-2	2-0	0-2	1-3	2-1	1-1	0-0	1-1	1-1	0-2	3-0	0-0
Kendal Town	1-1	1-0	1-3	4-1	2-0	1-1	2-0	0-3	2-3	0-3		0-1	1-3	5-1	3-1	1-0	0-3	3-3	1-1	1-0	1-5	0-2
Leek Town	0-1	1-0	1-1	1-2	0-1	0-2	4-2	1-1	2-1	0-1	0-1	D	0-1	2-1	1-0	1-2	1-0	0-3	1-1	0-0	2-2	1-2
Lincoln United	0-4	1-1	1-1	1-1	1-1	2-4	1-0	0-0	0-0	0-2	1-1	1-2	I	1-2	0-0	2-0	2-0	0-0	2-2	0-1	1-0	1-0
Marine	0-2	2-1	2-3	2-0	1-2	1-1	1-0	1-0	2-1	1-1	1-1	4-1	1-1	V	1-2	1-0	1-4	3-2	1-0	2-1	3-1	2-2
Matlock Town	2-1	0-0	1-3	1-1	3-0	0-0	3-2	0-3	0-1	0-1	5-1	1-0	2-0	1-2	I	4-1	2-0	1-0	3-0	3-2	5-1	1-1
Mossley	3-4	1-2	3-2	1-2	1-2	0-4	3-2	1-3	1-1	2-3	0-2	1-0	1-2	1-3	0-3	S	1-2	0-2	0-0	2-0	2-0	1-2
North Ferriby United	1-2	3-0	0-2	4-1	3-2	3-1	2-2	0-2	1-0	1-0	1-1	4-1	1-5	1-1	0-2	2-1	I	0-2	2-1	1-1	0-2	0-4
Ossett Town	0-0	2-1	0-0	2-4	2-0	2-2	2-2	1-0	0-1	1-2	2-1	2-0	1-3	1-1	2-1	3-2	1-2	O	2-1	4-0	2-2	1-2
Prescot Cables	0-1	1-0	1-2	3-1	1-1	1-1	2-1	2-0	0-0	1-4	2-2	2-2	3-0	2-1	1-3	2-2	0-0	2-1	N	3-0	0-1	1-1
Radcliffe Borough	1-1	2-0	1-0	0-2	1-0	0-2	2-1	0-2	1-1	1-3	0-0	3-3	1-3	1-1	1-3	0-2	0-2	1-3	0-2		2-4	0-2
Whitby Town	1-0	2-3	1-0	0-3	3-2	2-1	3-1	2-2	2-0	4-1	1-0	2-2	2-0	2-1	1-2	3-2	4-1	0-2	1-2	3-2		0-2
Witton Albion	0-1	5-1	0-0	3-1	2-0	1-1	4-4	2-2	3-0	4-1	1-3	3-4	6-0	5-2	1-0	2-1	2-0	3-1	2-1	1-0	7-2	

Premier Division

			HOME					AWAY					TOTAL					
		P	W	D	L	F	A	W	D	L	F	A	W	D	L	F	A	Pts
Burscough	-1	42	15	5	1	50	14	8	7	6	30	23	23	12	7	80	37	80
Witton Albion		42	14	4	3	57	25	10	4	7	33	23	24	8	10	90	48	80
AFC Telford United		42	9	10	2	41	23	12	5	4	31	17	21	15	6	72	40	78
Marine		42	12	5	4	36	23	10	3	8	34	30	22	8	12	70	53	74
Matlock Town		42	12	4	5	38	20	9	5	7	32	23	21	9	12	70	43	72
Guiseley		42	10	7	4	43	25	9	5	7	28	24	19	12	11	71	49	69
Hednesford Town		42	9	8	4	26	17	9	6	6	23	24	18	14	10	49	41	68
Fleetwood Town		42	13	3	5	41	21	6	7	8	30	39	19	10	13	71	60	67
Gateshead		42	11	5	5	41	30	6	9	6	34	27	17	14	11	75	57	65
Ossett Town		42	9	6	6	33	27	9	4	8	28	25	18	10	14	61	52	64
Whitby Town		42	13	3	5	39	26	5	3	13	24	52	18	6	18	63	78	60
Ilkeston Town		42	7	6	8	29	29	9	5	7	37	33	16	11	15	66	62	59
North Ferriby United		42	10	3	8	30	30	5	6	10	24	31	15	9	18	54	61	54
Prescot Cables		42	8	8	5	30	24	5	6	10	22	32	13	14	15	52	56	53
Lincoln United		42	5	10	6	18	22	7	5	9	22	36	12	15	15	40	58	51
Frickley Athletic		42	8	6	7	27	27	5	4	12	23	42	13	10	19	50	69	49
Leek Town		42	7	5	9	21	25	6	4	11	28	36	13	9	20	49	61	48
Ashton United		42	10	3	8	33	37	3	6	12	19	35	13	9	20	52	72	48
Kendal Town		42	8	4	9	28	35	4	7	10	31	44	12	11	19	59	79	47
Mossley		42	5	2	14	24	40	5	3	13	24	39	10	5	27	48	79	35
Radcliffe Borough		42	4	5	12	19	36	3	6	12	20	35	7	11	24	39	71	32
Grantham Town		42	3	3	15	16	44	0	5	16	23	50	3	8	31	39	94	17

PLAY-OFFS

SEMI-FINALS
(May 1st)
AFC Telford United 2 Marine 0 *Att* 2,657
Witton Albion 4 Matlock Town 2 *aet Att* 553
FINAL
(May 6th at Witton Albion)
Witton Albion 1 **AFC Telford United** 3 *aet Att* 2,281

DATES & GATES

WWW.NLNEWSDESK.CO.UK

	AFC Telford United	Ashton United	Burscough	Fleetwood Town	Frickley Athletic	Gateshead	Grantham Town	Guiseley	Hednesford Town	Ilkeston Town	Kendal Town	Leek Town	Lincoln United	Marine	Matlock Town	Mossley	North Ferriby United	Ossett Town	Prescot Cables	Radcliffe Borough	Whitby Town	Witton Albion
AFC Telford United	21 Aug 346	27 Jan 2,065	28 Apr 5,710	24 Mar 2,440	14 Apr 1,981	11 Nov 2,083	19 Nov 1,755	20 Jan 2,143	26 Dec 4,260	14 Nov 1,931	3 Mar 1,910	30 Sep 1,924	24 Feb 2,039	9 Apr 1,965	26 Sep 1,646	5 Sep 1,838	7 Oct 2,124	9 Sep 1,716	28 Oct 1,925	2 Dec 2,064	9 Dec 2,005	28 Aug 1,897
Ashton United	23 Sep 471		25 Sep 181	28 Apr 226	14 Oct 147	3 Mar 148	17 Feb 165	22 Aug 145	4 Sep 399	16 Dec 122	26 Aug 301	9 Sep 184	14 Apr 113	2 Apr 133	20 Jan 176	1 Jan 325	16 Oct 126	2 Dec 132	7 Oct 140	13 Nov 194	30 Dec 136	3 Mar 230
Burscough	13 Feb 837	18 Nov 367		11 Apr 429		3 Feb 298	21 Apr 452	22 Aug 308	17 Mar 410	31 Mar 403	14 Nov 274	9 Sep 203	2 Dec 282	5 Sep 379	27 Jan 328	16 Dec 268	28 Oct 252	26 Aug 207	6 Apr 477	3 Oct 243	17 Mar 307	20 Mar 355
Fleetwood Town	26 Aug 344	28 Nov 341	12 Sep 582		9 Sep 231	3 Feb 452	27 Mar 408	27 Jan 482	25 Nov 563	21 Apr 672	17 Oct 525	26 Aug 596	7 Oct 421	26 Sep 508	9 Dec 360	24 Apr 565	4 Nov 487	31 Mar 518	22 Aug 568	9 Apr 685	22 Aug 628	3 Apr 606
Frickley Athletic	26 Aug 572	31 Mar 230	6 Jan 214			12 Dec 202	10 Oct 346	24 Oct 310	23 Sep 244	21 Apr 259	21 Apr 167	14 Apr 203	6 Apr 220	27 Jan 295	24 Feb 277	30 Dec 188	16 Dec 252	6 Apr 552	4 Nov 187	25 Nov 193	22 Aug 235	5 Dec 196
Gateshead	26 Mar 521	23 Apr 201	19 Aug 197	18 Nov 158	28 Aug 203		13 Jan 239	11 Sep 183	9 Dec 205	14 Oct 209	26 Dec 215	5 Sep 217	6 Apr 385	2 Dec 160	7 Oct 209	28 Apr 335	17 Mar 162	24 Feb 175	27 Jan 214	16 Oct 159	4 Dec 181	16 Apr 236
Grantham Town	16 Dec 427	13 Jan 237	14 Oct 242	14 Apr 175	3 Feb 303	20 Mar 128		11 Nov 217	22 Aug 330	3 Oct 282	25 Nov 208	28 Apr 254	26 Dec 321	18 Nov 252	13 Mar 186	26 Aug 264	14 Nov 229	27 Jan 312	17 Mar 183	30 Sep 266	28 Apr 363	9 Sep 246
Guiseley	18 Nov 520	13 Apr 317	12 Mar 356	12 Mar 293	26 Sep 325	9 Apr 416	7 Oct 381		16 Apr 376	9 Sep 374	20 Jan 292	5 Sep 413	3 Mar 256	17 Mar 277	19 Aug 294	26 Aug 301	2 Sep 328	30 Sep 295	11 Sep 282	17 Feb 315	27 Jan 258	17 Feb 613
Hednesford Town	1 Jan 758	13 Feb 464	2 Dec 461		28 Oct 401	31 Mar 605	10 Mar 614	13 Mar 347		31 Mar 485	20 Jan 419	25 Sep 501	16 Dec 770	19 Aug 481	28 Aug 475	7 Oct 522	2 Sep 399	20 Mar 430	11 Sep 423	28 Apr 448	24 Mar 720	11 Nov 360
Ilkeston Town	6 Apr 497	6 Jan 254	2 Sep 289	3 Mar 422	17 Oct 254	9 Apr 336	12 Sep 363	9 Dec 245	14 Apr 410		28 Aug 357	28 Oct 357	26 Sep 327	9 Dec 315	26 Dec 529	18 Mar 352	22 Aug 328	23 Sep 186	26 Aug 324	28 Aug 379	28 Aug 323	27 Jan 262
Kendal Town	30 Dec 572	13 Feb 245	6 Jan 241	24 Feb 551	24 Mar 237	22 Aug 315	2 Dec 202	2 Sep 247	28 Aug 381	9 Sep 325		17 Mar 199	28 Oct 179	7 Nov 249	18 Nov 190	9 Apr 321	14 Apr 402	23 Sep 301	10 Oct 257	14 Oct 324	19 Aug 358	24 Oct 297
Leek Town	3 Oct 845	10 Oct 306	10 Mar 306	20 Mar 208	2 Feb 219	30 Dec 230	2 Dec 320	2 Sep 231	3 Feb 350	28 Aug 337	16 Dec 243		12 Sep 199	31 Mar 298	7 Apr 417	27 Jan 346	13 Jan 268	18 Nov 222	21 Apr 305	14 Oct 278	14 Oct 307	23 Sep 135
Lincoln United	4 Nov 304	19 Apr 104	9 Dec 120	17 Feb 159	9 Apr 137	9 Apr 145	28 Aug 255	17 Oct 101	3 Oct 156	13 Jan 155	31 Mar 125	20 Jan 110		21 Apr 135	7 Nov 122	6 Jan 140	26 Jan 139	5 Sep 105	18 Nov 101	9 Sep 115	14 Apr 116	24 Oct 135
Marine	25 Nov 673	6 Apr 287	17 Oct 350	31 Oct 231	2 Sep 271	26 Feb 281	21 Apr 391	31 Mar 308	26 Dec 445	23 Sep 419	13 Jan 264	20 Jan 344	11 Nov 267		17 Feb 353	22 Aug 249	28 Apr 634	4 Nov 273	14 Nov 301	16 Dec 396	14 Apr 277	3 Oct 324
Matlock Town	3 Feb 806	17 Mar 305	11 Nov 306	28 Aug 230	9 Dec 274	10 Mar 220	28 Aug 275	23 Sep 245	4 Nov 332	19 Aug 230	11 Nov 272	14 Nov 267	22 Aug 253	10 Mar 215		2 Dec 322		12 Sep 212	24 Apr 259	23 Sep 298	19 Apr 263	5 Sep 379
Mossley	13 Jan 461	26 Dec 372	28 Aug 254	6 Apr 326	9 Dec 226	14 Nov 145	26 Sep 141	23 Sep 203	14 Oct 275	11 Nov 163	20 Dec 161	6 Mar 175	2 Sep 239	3 Mar 183	12 Sep 218		17 Feb 209	20 Feb 164	3 Feb 203	30 Mar 151	17 Oct 241	19 Aug 208
North Ferriby United	21 Apr 415	3 Feb 119	24 Mar 248	19 Aug 243	18 Nov 201	30 Dec 167	28 Aug 238	25 Nov 177	11 Nov 221	18 Nov 159	26 Dec 275	9 Apr 223	24 Apr 187	10 Oct 166	28 Apr 237	28 Oct 202			31 Mar 133	14 Apr 173	9 Apr 179	9 Dec 219
Ossett Town	10 Mar 377	28 Aug 135	9 Apr 120	23 Sep 203	26 Dec 328	10 Mar 357	31 Mar 205	25 Nov 464	13 Jan 397	24 Feb 280	27 Sep 265	17 Feb 306	2 Sep 143	7 Oct 333	2 Sep 200	17 Oct 214	12 Sep 126		2 Sep 107	5 Sep 178	17 Oct 104	9 Dec 162
Prescot Cables	21 Apr 392	25 Apr 153	26 Dec 256	3 Oct 251	19 Aug 159	9 Sep 182	26 Sep 216	6 Jan 197	27 Jan 255	30 Dec 178	20 Dec 192	24 Mar 246	10 Oct 187	10 Oct 218	28 Apr 182	17 Oct 211	11 Nov 180	20 Feb 179		14 Apr 151	23 Sep 154	31 May 283
Radcliffe Borough	31 Mar 391	9 Apr 202	3 Feb 166	26 Dec 270	13 Sep 256	10 Oct 345	9 Dec 213	6 Apr 271	11 Nov 254	18 Nov 376	6 Apr 223	22 Aug 223	28 Aug 196	7 Oct 304	28 Oct 305	26 Sep 303	24 Jan 173	16 Dec 346	2 Dec 295		11 Nov 187	21 Apr 339
Whitby Town	31 Mar 464	25 Apr 198	14 Mar 248	14 Mar 256	28 Apr 520	10 Mar 278	31 Mar 441	6 Apr 464	13 Jan 340	18 Mar 311	27 Sep 268	24 Mar 401	20 Jan 223	3 Feb 304	24 Mar 397	14 Apr 376	2 Dec 278	22 Aug 220	26 Sep 215	18 Nov 354		24 Feb 412
Witton Albion	24 Apr 1,543	12 Sep 239	7 Oct 413	14 Nov 220		10 Mar 278																

NORTHERN PREMIER LEAGUE PREMIER DIVISION
CONSTITUTION 2007-08

ASHTON UNITED
Hurst Cross, Surrey Street, Ashton-under-Lyne, Lancashire OL6 8DY
Tel: 0161 339 4158   Club: 0161 330 1511   Fax: 0161 339 4158
Manager: Danny Johnson   www.ashtonutd.com   Colours: Red, white & black

BUXTON
The Silverlands, Buxton, Derbyshire SK17 6QH
Tel: 01298 23197   Fax: 01298 24733
Manager: John Reed   Colours: Blue & white

EASTWOOD TOWN
Coronation Park, Chewton Street, Eastwood, Nottinghamshire NG16 3GL
Tel: 01773 712301   Club: 01773 715823
Manager: Paul Cox   www.eastwoodtownfc.co.uk   Colours: Black & white

FLEETWOOD TOWN
Highbury Stadium, Park Avenue, Fleetwood, Lancashire FY7 6TX
Tel: 01253 770702
Manager: Tony Greenwood   www.fleetwoodtownfc.com   Colours: Red & black

FRICKLEY ATHLETIC
Westfield Lane, South Elmsall, Pontefract, West Yorkshire WF9 2EQ
Tel: 01977 642460   Fax: 01977 642460
Manager: Billy Heath   www.frickleyafc.co.uk   Colours: Blue

GATESHEAD
The International Stadium, Neilson Road, Gateshead, Tyne & Wear NE10 0EF
Tel: 0191 478 3883   Fax: 0191 477 1315
Manager: Ian Bogie   www.gateshead-fc.com   Colours: Black & white

GUISELEY
Nethermoor Park, Otley Road, Guiseley, Leeds, West Yorkshire LS20 8BT
Tel: 01943 873223   Club: 01943 872872
Manager: Terry Dolan   www.guiseleyafc.co.uk   Colours: White & navy blue

HEDNESFORD TOWN
Keys Park, Keys Park Road, Hednesford, Staffs WS12 2DZ
Tel: 01543 422870   Fax: 01543 428180
Manager: Phil Starbuck   www.hednesfordtown.com   Colours: White & black

ILKESTON TOWN
The New Manor Ground, Awsworth Road, Ilkeston, Derbyshire DE7 8JF
Tel: 0115 932 4094   Club: 0115 930 5622
Manager: Nigel Jemson   www.whiteballproject.co.uk   Colours: Red & black

KENDAL TOWN
Parkside, Parkside Road, Kendal, Cumbria LA9 7BL
Tel: 01539 727472   Club: 01539 722469   Fax: 01539 727472
Manager: Lee Ashcroft   www.kendaltownfc.co.uk   Colours: Black & white

LEEK TOWN
Harrison Park, Macclesfield Road, Leek, Staffordshire ST13 8LD
Tel: 01538 399278   Club: 01538 383734   Fax: 01538 399826
Manager: Paul Ogden   www.leektown.co.uk   Colours: Blue & white

LINCOLN UNITED
Ashby Avenue, Hartsholme, Lincoln, Lincolnshire LN6 0DY
Tel: 01522 696400   Club: 01522 690674   Fax: 01522 696400
Manager: John Ramshaw   www.comeonyouwhites.com   Colours: White

MARINE
Rossett Park Arriva Stadium, College Road, Crosby, Liverpool, Merseyside L23 3AS
Tel: 0151 924 1743   Club: 0151 924 4046   Fax: 0151 924 1743
Manager: Alvin McDonald   www.marinefc.com   Colours: White & black

MATLOCK TOWN
Causeway Lane, Matlock, Derbyshire DE4 3AR
Tel: 01629 583866   Club: 01629 553362   Fax: 01629 583866
Manager: Phil Brown/gareth Williams   www.matlocktownfc.co.uk   Colours: Royal blue

NORTH FERRIBY UNITED
Grange Lane, Church Road, North Ferriby, East Yorkshire HU14 3AA
Tel: 01482 634601   Fax: 01482 634601
Manager: Neil Parsley   www.northferribyunited.co.uk   Colours: White & green

OSSETT TOWN
Ingfield, Prospect Road, Ossett, Wakefield, West Yorkshire WF5 9HA
Tel: 01924 272960
Manager: Steve Kittrick   www.ossetttown.co.uk   Colours: Red & white

PRESCOT CABLES
Valerie Park, Hope Street, Prescot, Merseyside L34 6HD
Tel: 0151 430 0507
Manager: Andy Gray   www.prescotcablesfc.co.uk   Colours: Gold & black

STAMFORD
Vic Couzens Stadium, Kettering Road, Stamford, Lincolnshire PE9 2JR
Tel: 01780 763079
Manager: Graham Drury   www.stamfordafc.moonfruit.com   Colours: Red & white

WHITBY TOWN
Turnbull Ground, Upgang Lane, Whitby, North Yorkshire YO21 3HZ
Tel: 01947 604847   Club: 01947 603193   Fax: 01947 603779
Manager: Lee Nogan   www.whitby-town.com   Colours: Royal blue

WITTON ALBION
CMB Stadium, Wincham Park, Chapel Street, Wincham, Northwich, Cheshire CW9 6DA
Tel: 01606 43008   Club: 01606 47117   Fax: 01606 43008
Manager: Jim Vince   www.wittonalbion.co.uk   Colours: Red & white

WORKSOP TOWN
Babbage Way, Sandy Lane, Worksop, Nottinghamshire S80 1TN
Tel: 01909 501911   Fax: 01909 501911
Manager: Peter Rinkcavage   www.worksoptownfc.co.uk   Colours: Yellow & black

IN: Buxton (P), Eastwood Town (P), Stamford (S – Southern League Premier Division), Worksop Town (R – Football Conference North)
OUT: AFC Telford United (P – Football Conference North), Burscough (P – Football Conference North), Grantham Town (R – Division One South), Mossley (R – Division One North), Radcliffe Borough (R – Division One North)

WWW.NLNEWSDESK.CO.UK

	Alsager Town	Bamber Bridge	Belper Town	Bradford Park Avenue	Bridlington Town	Brigg Town	Buxton	Cammell Laird	Chorley	Clitheroe	Colwyn Bay	Eastwood Town	Goole	Gresley Rovers	Harrogate Railway	Kidsgrove Athletic	Ossett Albion	Rossendale United	Shepshed Dynamo	Skelmersdale United	Stocksbridge Park Steels	Wakefield	Warrington Town	Woodley Sports
Alsager Town		5-4	2-1	2-0	3-0	0-3	1-3	1-4	5-0	0-2	0-1	2-3	2-3	1-3	2-2	0-3	1-1	1-0	0-2	2-0	1-1	3-1	1-1	1-1
Bamber Bridge	2-2		3-4	1-1	2-0	2-3	1-3	1-1	0-3	3-1	0-1	4-3	0-2	4-1	2-0	2-1	1-3	5-0	3-0	4-1	0-3	0-1	3-0	4-3
Belper Town	2-1	1-0		1-3	2-1	2-1	1-4	1-2	3-1	0-3	1-0	1-0	1-3	1-0	2-0	5-4	2-5	1-2	2-1	0-1	0-0	2-0	0-2	2-2
Bradford Park Ave	4-1	1-0	4-0		2-0	3-1	0-0	3-1	3-0	7-3	0-0	1-3	3-1	1-2	1-0	1-0	2-2	0-0	5-0	1-1	2-1	1-0	2-1	0-3
Bridlington Town	0-4	0-3	0-2	0-1		1-1	0-5	0-3	2-0	2-2	1-1	0-5	2-2	0-3	1-2	3-2	1-1	0-2	1-2	1-2	1-9	1-1	1-2	2-1
Brigg Town	2-0	2-1	2-1	0-1	0-0		2-2	0-3	1-0	1-0	1-5	4-3	1-3	1-1	2-1	0-1	3-2	1-0	3-1	1-0	0-2	1-2	3-2	1-1
Buxton	1-0	4-1	0-2	2-0	3-0	3-1	D	3-1	4-0	1-0	2-2	1-1	3-0	2-0	5-0	0-1	2-1	2-0	0-1	1-0	1-1	1-1	3-2	1-0
Cammell Laird	1-2	2-2	2-1	3-1	2-2	1-0	2-3	I	4-1	2-0	3-2	3-3	2-3	2-0	3-0	3-1	3-1	2-0	4-2	2-2	3-1	4-0	5-1	0-0
Chorley	0-6	2-2	1-1	0-2	2-2	2-1	0-1	1-1	V	2-2	0-1	0-4	1-3	3-1	0-2	2-5	0-2	3-0	6-1	3-1	1-2	3-0	0-1	0-1
Clitheroe	1-0	1-1	3-2	1-3	3-0	3-1	2-2	2-4	3-0	I	1-3	0-3	1-2	2-0	1-2	5-1	1-0	0-2	5-0	0-1	0-5	1-1	5-1	3-1
Colwyn Bay	1-0	0-1	2-2	1-0	1-1	4-2	2-0	2-1	2-0	2-1	S	1-2	5-2	1-0	3-2	2-2	3-0	1-1	2-0	3-3	1-1	1-0	0-2	2-2
Eastwood Town	2-1	1-2	3-0	1-0	0-0	6-0	0-0	0-2	1-0	2-1	2-1	I	2-2	2-1	1-2	3-0	1-1	1-0	5-0	2-1	1-0	0-1	1-0	2-2
Goole	0-1	2-2	3-0	4-0	1-1	0-0	2-2	0-5	6-3	0-3	4-0	0-0	O	4-2	1-1	2-3	2-1	0-4	2-1	0-4	1-3	1-3	3-1	2-1
Gresley Rovers	2-0	1-2	4-0	0-1	1-1	1-1	0-0	4-1	2-1	1-0	2-2	0-5	1-4	N	1-0	2-3	1-2	1-4	2-0	1-2	1-1	2-1	3-1	4-5
Harrogate Railway	1-2	1-1	2-0	2-1	0-0	0-3	4-3	0-3	6-1	2-1	5-1	1-0	0-1	3-1		2-3	0-2	3-2	3-2	2-0	3-3	1-0	2-4	1-0
Kidsgrove Athletic	4-3	1-0	4-1	1-2	2-0	2-1	1-2	1-4	1-2	1-3	2-3	2-1	0-1	3-0	3-0	O	4-2	1-1	0-1	1-1	1-0	1-2	3-1	3-2
Ossett Albion	1-3	2-1	1-3	1-1	1-0	1-1	1-4	1-2	0-2	1-3	1-0	0-2	1-0	1-2	3-0	1-1	N	2-2	3-2	4-1	1-0	1-1	1-2	1-2
Rossendale United	0-0	0-1	2-0	0-5	2-0	1-0	1-3	0-1	3-2	0-1	4-1	1-2	2-2	3-0	1-5	2-2	2-1	E	0-1	4-1	2-1	0-1	4-2	2-0
Shepshed Dynamo	1-2	2-2	3-1	1-0	3-1	0-0	1-4	1-1	2-0	1-3	3-2	2-1	1-2	1-2	1-2	2-2	2-2	0-1		0-0	1-3	1-1	3-2	2-0
Skelmersdale Utd	6-3	3-2	2-0	2-2	4-1	3-1	0-1	3-2	2-1	2-2	0-3	0-1	3-0	1-2	1-0	3-2	0-3	0-1	1-2		1-1	1-2	3-1	1-1
Stocksbridge Pk St	0-1	0-2	2-0	0-3	2-0	1-3	1-1	1-1	3-0	4-2	0-1	1-0	3-0	1-0	4-0	1-3	1-3	3-2	6-2	0-0		2-0	2-1	1-2
Wakefield	0-1	0-1	0-2	2-2	3-0	2-1	0-1	1-2	3-1	2-0	1-2	0-4	1-3	1-0	1-3	2-2	1-1	0-0	0-2	4-2	1-1		1-2	1-3
Warrington Town	1-2	3-0	2-1	0-0	2-1	0-0	1-1	0-1	0-0	1-1	3-0	2-4	4-0	0-1	3-1	0-3	1-2	0-1	1-3	3-2	3-1	2-2		2-4
Woodley Sports	4-1	2-1	3-1	2-1	4-2	2-0	0-3	1-1	1-2	2-0	4-0	0-0	4-1	0-0	4-1	2-4	0-3	1-3	6-3	5-3	1-2	4-0	1-1	

Division One

	P	HOME					AWAY					TOTAL					Pts
		W	D	L	F	A	W	D	L	F	A	W	D	L	F	A	
Buxton	46	17	3	3	46	14	13	8	2	48	23	30	11	5	94	37	101
Cammell Laird	46	15	5	3	58	29	13	5	5	47	27	28	10	8	105	56	94
Eastwood Town	46	14	5	4	39	17	12	4	7	50	26	26	9	11	89	43	87
Bradford Park Avenue	46	15	5	3	47	20	9	5	9	30	27	24	10	12	77	47	82
Colwyn Bay	46	13	7	3	42	25	9	4	10	32	40	22	11	13	74	65	77
Stocksbridge Park Steels	46	14	3	6	41	22	8	7	8	41	27	22	10	14	82	49	76
Goole	46	9	6	8	40	41	12	3	8	40	43	21	9	16	80	84	72
Kidsgrove Athletic	46	12	2	9	42	33	9	5	9	49	47	21	7	18	91	80	70
Rossendale United	46	11	3	9	36	32	10	4	9	28	27	21	7	18	64	59	70
Woodley Sports	46	13	4	6	52	31	6	7	10	37	40	19	11	16	89	71	68
Ossett Albion	46	10	5	8	33	34	9	6	8	38	32	19	11	16	71	66	68
Harrogate Railway	46	13	3	7	44	34	8	2	13	28	44	21	5	20	72	78	68
Bamber Bridge	46	11	3	9	47	37	7	5	11	31	38	18	8	20	78	75	62
Alsager Town	46	8	5	10	36	39	10	2	11	36	36	18	7	21	72	75	61
Skelmersdale United	46	11	4	8	42	34	6	6	11	30	43	17	10	19	72	77	61
Clitheroe	46	11	2	10	44	36	7	4	12	34	39	18	6	22	78	75	60
Brigg Town	46	12	4	7	32	32	4	6	13	25	40	16	10	20	57	72	58
Gresley Rovers	46	9	5	9	37	37	7	2	14	22	38	16	7	23	59	75	55
Belper Town	46	12	2	9	33	36	5	2	16	25	50	17	4	25	58	86	55
Shepshed Dynamo	46	8	7	8	34	34	7	0	16	28	62	15	7	24	62	96	52
Wakefield	46	6	4	13	27	37	7	6	10	21	34	13	10	23	48	71	49
Warrington Town	46	7	6	10	32	33	6	2	15	32	51	13	8	25	64	84	47
Chorley	46	6	6	12	32	42	4	1	18	20	57	10	6	30	52	99	36
Bridlington Town	46	3	6	14	20	56	0	8	15	13	45	3	14	29	33	101	23

www.CHERRYRED.CO.UK

PLAY-OFFS

SEMI-FINALS

(May 1st)

Cammell Laird 3 Colwyn Bay 2 *Att* 277

Eastwood Town 3 Bradford Park Avenue 0 *Att* 355

FINAL *(May 6th at Cammell Laird)*

Cammell Laird 1 Eastwood Town 2 *Att* 327

DATES & GATES

	Woodley Sports	Warrington Town	Wakefield	Stocksbridge Park Steels	Skelmersdale United	Shepshed Dynamo	Rossendale United	Ossett Albion	Kidsgrove Athletic	Harrogate Railway	Gresley Rovers	Goole	Eastwood Town	Colwyn Bay	Clitheroe	Chorley	Cammell Laird	Buxton	Brigg Town	Bridlington Town	Bradford Park Avenue	Belper Town	Bamber Bridge	Alsager Town
Alsager Town	17 Mar /48	28 Nov /74	11 Mar /111	24 Mar /68	23 Dec /118	19 Sep /137	24 Apr /82	13 Jan /96	9 Apr /315	10 Mar /88	17 Oct /118	14 Apr /112	6 Jan /112	22 Aug /153	23 Sep /129	24 Feb /142	3 Oct /165	24 Oct /174	27 Jan /90	9 Dec /71	26 Apr /201	30 Dec /117	14 Nov /64	
Bamber Bridge	9 Sep /109	20 Mar /122	11 Nov /134	27 Jan /182	1 Jan /173	24 Mar /169	10 Oct /177	2 Dec /159	17 Oct /107	13 Mar /98	26 Aug /138	6 Apr /204	11 Nov /143	16 Sep /141	24 Oct /231	26 Dec /363	22 Aug /126	18 Nov /265	30 Sep /157	3 Mar /154	19 Sep /140	28 Apr /106		5 Feb /111
Belper Town	19 Aug /109	28 Oct /122	26 Dec /139	12 Sep /135	3 Mar /181	20 Jan /204	31 Mar /121	17 Feb /117	17 Oct /107	27 Jan /149	21 Dec /244	18 Dec /166	23 Dec /118	6 Jan /151	18 Nov /146	21 Apr /133	2 Apr /95	14 Nov /297	13 Jan /150	3 Mar /154	16 Dec /182		4 Nov /146	17 Feb /134
Bradford Park Avenue	3 Feb /228	28 Oct /199	16 Dec /182	13 Jan /248	3 Mar /237	6 Apr /372	31 Mar /349	6 Jan /125	14 Apr /265	27 Jan /149	2 Oct /260	18 Nov /166	16 Sep /208	9 Dec /246	14 Oct /232	11 Nov /288	21 Apr /201	21 Apr /475	26 Feb /199	25 Sep /206		12 Sep /153	16 Oct /229	31 Mar /276
Bridlington Town	28 Aug /151	19 Aug /204	25 Sep /206	19 Aug /248	24 Apr /237	7 Oct /143	9 Apr /139	6 Jan /125	4 Mar /95	28 Aug /258	23 Sep /148	19 Dec /208	23 Dec /118	4 Nov /112	2 Dec /119	31 Mar /151	21 Apr /218	16 Dec /178	26 Feb /199		27 Mar /378	24 Apr /151	17 Mar /111	19 Aug /168
Brigg Town	24 Dec /151	6 Apr /137	5 Dec /98	3 Oct /129	18 Nov /112	25 Oct /116	9 Apr /139	6 Jan /125	26 Aug /157	9 Sep /152	25 Nov /181	26 Dec /169	23 Dec /118	3 Mar /123	20 Jan /160	17 Mar /143	9 Sep /153	16 Dec /146		13 Apr /148	24 Apr /151	14 Oct /153	3 Feb /111	6 Apr /126
Buxton	9 Apr /504	9 Dec /128	18 Apr /115	19 Dec /139	23 Sep /144	3 Apr /296	19 Aug /171	6 Jan /115	4 Oct /464	7 Oct /173	24 Mar /487	26 Dec /471	15 Nov /123	3 Feb /488	28 Aug /468	3 Mar /462	30 Dec /610		18 Nov /105	11 Nov /146	24 Apr /474	14 Mar /385	23 Sep /456	20 Jan /478
Cammell Laird	9 Dec /95	12 Sep /434	28 Apr /439	14 Apr /720	17 Feb /484	16 Dec /142	3 Mar /205	19 Apr /133	17 Apr /155	25 Nov /491	24 Mar /194	13 Jan /269	18 Oct /656	10 Oct /155	28 Aug /118	24 Apr /108		27 Jan /444	28 Oct /152	30 Sep /108	24 Feb /474	11 Nov /168	26 Sep /123	5 Dec /90
Chorley	27 Feb /149	10 Oct /171	18 Apr /118	9 Apr /175	14 Apr /265	14 Apr /230	3 Feb /247	4 Dec /133	30 Dec /219	4 Nov /203	10 Mar /280	17 Feb /280	14 Apr /221	24 Dec /155	17 Oct /206		2 Dec /202	27 Jan /274	14 Apr /204	2 Apr /165	24 Mar /307	23 Dec /259	9 Dec /236	3 Feb /233
Clitheroe	13 Jan /169	18 Nov /224	10 Oct /181	19 Oct /202	10 Mar /268	28 Apr /250	26 Dec /262	26 Dec /184	10 Mar /268	27 Feb /163	9 Sep /246	16 Dec /172	20 Jan /221	24 Dec /292		27 Mar /279	5 Sep /214	13 Jan /422	13 Sep /95	2 Apr /95	6 Jan /307	23 Dec /259	9 Dec /236	28 Oct /251
Colwyn Bay	13 Dec /329	10 Feb /229	10 Oct /181	28 Oct /202	26 Sep /245	10 Feb /245	28 Aug /362	4 Dec /307	10 Mar /293	23 Sep /362	14 Nov /362	11 Nov /286	11 Apr /225		24 Feb /292	27 May /375	6 Apr /551	13 Jan /422	6 Apr /445	13 Mar /378	2 Dec /271	25 Nov /303	13 Sep /101	21 Apr /223
Eastwood Town	28 Oct /200	17 Oct /241	17 Feb /256	17 Mar /433	12 Dec /252	12 Sep /142	13 Jan /218	26 Dec /145	24 Feb /249	17 Oct /138	19 Sep /254	27 Feb /170		18 May /167	18 May /167	16 Dec /173	17 Dec /218	22 Aug /268	17 Dec /218	13 Mar /148	27 Mar /207	9 Apr /230	21 Apr /183	14 Oct /223
Goole	3 Mar /226	31 Mar /207	3 Feb /190	26 Aug /202	2 Dec /174	18 Nov /116	30 Sep /250	5 Dec /145	23 Dec /184	17 Oct /138	21 Apr /198		9 Dec /203	20 Jan /217	12 Sep /176	25 Nov /186	23 Dec /233	4 Nov /270	17 Apr /209	14 Oct /127	20 Feb /214	31 Oct /134	30 Jan /168	2 Dec /130
Gresley Rovers	17 Feb /211	3 Feb /211	18 Apr /171	21 Oct /202	17 Mar /205	19 Aug /182	30 Sep /177	12 Sep /186	12 Sep /186	2 Dec /275		28 Oct /255	9 Dec /203	20 Sep /217	11 Nov /203	25 Nov /259	5 Sep /214	4 Nov /270	9 Apr /202	9 Jan /226	3 Mar /214	24 Feb /265	31 Mar /130	9 Mar /136
Harrogate Railway	28 Aug /77	28 Aug /258	18 Apr /79	80	9 Apr /103	12 Sep /114	30 Oct /80	9 Apr /103	19 Dec /202		8 Nov /102	28 Oct /255	11 Apr /102	24 Oct /145	31 Mar /124	14 Oct /135	22 Aug /244	14 Oct /370	19 Aug /265	13 Jan /155	14 Mar /160	18 Apr /82	19 Aug /118	30 Sep /105
Kidsgrove Athletic	30 Jan /112	21 Apr /77	18 Apr /118	80	17 Mar /150	10 Oct /72	27 Feb /133	28 Mar /139		9 Sep /107	16 Dec /211	31 May /163	4 Nov /225	15 Nov /121	31 Mar /175	13 Feb /121	6 Apr /149	13 Jan /325	7 May /178	2 Apr /95	6 Jan /307	18 Apr /82	10 May /115	21 Apr /91
Ossett Albion	20 Sep /90	6 Dec /101	21 Apr /128	28 Aug /148	13 Jan /173	18 Nov /116	6 Apr /144		9 Sep /107	23 Sep /167	4 Nov /111	4 Oct /144	17 Jan /116	17 Mar /145	3 Mar /122	23 Sep /112	25 Oct /113	11 Oct /146	18 Nov /105	13 Apr /148	27 Feb /172	23 Aug /79	10 Mar /115	21 Apr /91
Rossendale United	17 Oct /89	27 Jan /101	18 Apr /118	28 Aug /124	26 Aug /74	23 Sep /114		26 Dec /116	9 Sep /100	28 Mar /102	4 Nov /111	26 Aug /131	17 Jan /116	24 Oct /145	3 Apr /160	3 Sep /112	26 Apr /127	11 Oct /146	18 Oct /146	14 Oct /127	7 Oct /214	2 Dec /134	30 Jan /168	2 Dec /130
Shepshed Dynamo	21 Apr /114	20 Sep /90	16 Apr /79	28 Aug /158	28 Oct /141		6 Apr /144	14 Apr /103	9 Sep /100	23 Dec /114	27 May /86	26 Jan /131	21 Aug /192	24 Oct /145	30 Sep /148	23 Sep /112	3 Apr /127	14 Oct /160	18 Nov /105	13 Jan /155	14 May /160	7 Mar /114	31 Mar /130	9 Sep /136
Skelmersdale United	5 Dec /170	17 Oct /112	18 Apr /118	18 Oct /158		23 Feb /220	14 Nov /222	25 Nov /110	19 Dec /52	14 May /52	16 Dec /211	9 Sep /162	10 May /363	10 Mar /113	31 May /203	14 Oct /181	3 Feb /115	24 Feb /174	17 Sep /126	2 Apr /178	13 Mar /258	10 Feb /222	28 Aug /250	7 Nov /228
Stocksbridge Park Steels	31 Dec /105	16 Dec /112	18 Apr /118		28 Oct /141	23 Sep /114	30 Sep /145	3 Feb /103	3 Apr /132	24 Apr /114	22 Aug /154	14 Oct /144	26 Aug /131	24 Oct /145	30 Sep /148	14 Oct /135	3 Apr /127	24 Feb /160	17 Mar /122	13 Mar /83	3 Mar /255	14 Nov /160	31 Aug /130	28 Apr /105
Wakefield	14 Nov /105	26 Dec /224		6 Jan /251	9 Feb /132	24 Feb /110	12 Sep /83	25 Nov /110	9 Apr /120	20 Mar /114	16 Dec /87	9 Sep /110	14 May /94	9 Sep /110	13 Mar /104	24 Oct /125	27 Mar /105	26 Dec /160	26 Aug /92	17 Feb /132	3 Mar /249	9 Apr /103	23 Jan /123	3 Mar /102
Warrington Town	30 Dec /105		11 Nov /120	4 Nov /142	28 Apr /72	31 Dec /101	12 Dec /94	25 Nov /104	13 Mar /95	11 Nov /82	22 Aug /87	24 Sep /145	23 Sep /110	9 Sep /110	13 Mar /104	30 Jan /125	27 Mar /105	14 Nov /160	10 Apr /122	24 Apr /83	17 Mar /162	26 Jan /103		16 Jan /80
Woodley Sports		9 Jan /109	5 Sep /100	31 Oct /105	22 Aug /101	17 Oct /110	2 Dec /110	22 Jul /101	13 May /95	11 Nov /82	20 Jan /110	14 Apr /145	23 Sep /110	26 Sep /74	3 Oct /113	4 Oct /313	25 Dec /108	26 Dec /253	26 Dec /122	10 May /87	24 Mar /162	14 Apr /76	7 Nov /85	16 Jan /80

NORTHERN PREMIER LEAGUE DIVISION ONE
NORTH CONSTITUTION 2007-08

BAMBER BRIDGE
Colours: White & black
Irongate, Brownedge Road, Bamber Bridge,
Preston, Lancashire PR5 6UX
Tel: 01772 909690/909695 Fax: 01772 909691

BRADFORD PARK AVENUE
Colours: White
Horsfall Stadium, Cemetery Road, Low Moor,
Bradford, West Yorkshire BD6 2NG
Tel: 01274 604578 Fax: 01274 691020

BRIDLINGTON TOWN
Colours: Red
Queensgate Stadium, Queensgate,
Bridlington, East Yorkshire YO16 5LN
Tel: 01262 606879

CHORLEY
Colours: Black & white
Victory Park, Duke Street,
Chorley, Lancashire PR7 3DU
Tel: 01257 263406/275662 Fax: 01257 241625

CLITHEROE
Colours: Blue
Shawbridge, off Pendle Road,
Clitheroe, Lancashire BB7 1DP
Tel: 01200 423344

CURZON ASHTON
Colours: Royal blue
The Tameside Stadium, Richmond Street,
Ashton-under-Lyne, Lancashire OL7 9HG
Tel: 0161 330 6033

FC UNITED OF MANCHESTER
Colours: Red & white
Bury FC, Gigg Lane, Bury, Lancashire BL9 9HR
Tel: 0161 764 4881 Fax: 0161 764 5521

GARFORTH TOWN
Colours: Yellow & blue
Wheatley Park Stadium, Cedar Ridge,
Garforth, Leeds, West Yorkshire LS25 2PF
Tel: 0113 286 4083

HARROGATE RAILWAY ATHLETIC
Colours: Red & green
Station View, Station View Road, Starbeck,
Harrogate, North Yorkshire HG2 7JA
Tel: 01423 883104

LANCASTER CITY
Colours: Sky blue
Giant Axe, West Road, Lancaster, Lancashire LA1 5PE
Tel: 01524 382238/843500 Fax: 01524 382238

MOSSLEY
Colours: White & black
Seel Park, Market Street, Mossley,
Ashton-under-Lyne, Lancashire OL5 0ES
Tel: 01457 835989/836104

NEWCASTLE BLUE STAR
Colours: Blue & white
Wheatsheaf Sports Ground, Woolsington Main,
Callerton, Tyne & Wear NE13 8DF
Tel: 0191 286 0425

OSSETT ALBION
Colours: Gold & black
Queens Terrace, Dimple Wells, Ossett,
Wakefield, West Yorkshire WF5 8JU
Tel: 01924 280450/273618

RADCLIFFE BOROUGH
Colours: Blue & white
Stainton Park, Pilkington Road,
Radcliffe, Manchester M26 3PE
Tel: 0161 724 8346/5937 Fax: 0161 723 3178

ROSSENDALE UNITED
Colours: Blue & white
Dark Lane, Staghills Road, Newchurch, Rossendale,
Lancashire BB4 7UA
Tel: 01706 215119/213296 Fax: 01706 230970

SKELMERSDALE UNITED
Colours: Blue
Ashley Travel Stadium, Selby Place, Stanley
Industrial Est., Skelmersdale, Lancashire WN8 8EF
Tel: 01695 722123

WAKEFIELD
Colours: Claret & blue
College Grove, Eastmore Road,
Wakefield, West Yorkshire WF1 3RR
Tel: 01924 365007

WOODLEY SPORTS
Colours: Blue, red & white
Lambeth Grove Stadium, Lambeth Grove,
Woodley, Stockport, Cheshire SK6 1QX
Tel: 0161 406 6896/494 6429

NEW DIVISION FORMED BY (all S – Northern Premier League Divison One unless otherwise stated).
Bamber Bridge, Bradford Park Avenue, Bridlington Town, Chorley, Clitheroe, Curzon Ashton (P – North West
Counties League Division One), FC United of Manchester (P – North West Counties League Division One),
Garforth Town (P – Northern Counties East League Premier Division), Harrogate Railway Athletic, Lancaster
City (R – Football Conference North), Mossley (R), Newcastle Blue Star (P – Northern League Division One)
Ossett Albion, Radcliffe Borough (R), Rossendale United, Skelmersdale United, Wakefield, Woodley Sports

NORTHERN PREMIER LEAGUE DIVISION ONE SOUTH CONSTITUTION 2007-08

ALSAGER TOWN
Colours: Black & white
The Town Ground, Woodland Court,
Alsager, Staffordshire ST7 2DP
Tel: 01270 882336

BELPER TOWN
Colours: Yellow & black
Christchurch Meadow, Bridge Street,
Belper, Derbyshire DE56 1BA
Tel: 01773 825549

BRIGG TOWN
Colours: White & black
The Hawthorns, Hawthorn Avenue,
Brigg, North Lincs DN20 8PG
Tel: 01652 651605

CAMMELL LAIRD
Colours: Royal blue
Kirklands, St Peters Road, Rock Ferry,
Birkenhead, Merseyside CH42 1PY
Tel: 0151 645 3121

CARLTON TOWN
Colours: Blue & black
Stoke Lane, Gedling, Nottingham NG4 2QS
Tel: 0115 940 2531

COLWYN BAY
Colours: Sky blue
Llanelian Road, Old Colwyn,
Colwyn Bay, Clwyd LL29 8UN
Tel: 01492 514581/513944 Fax: 01492 514581

GOOLE TOWN
Colours: Red & white
Victoria Pleasure Grounds, Marcus Street,
Goole, East Yorkshire DN14 6TW
Tel: 01405 762794

GRANTHAM TOWN
Colours: Black & white
South Kesteven Sports Stadium, Trent Road, Grantham,
Lincolnshire NG31 7XQ
Tel: 01476 402224/402225

GRESLEY ROVERS
Colours: Red & white
Moat Ground, Moat Street, Church Gresley,
Swadlincote, Derbyshire DE11 9RE
Tel: 01283 216315 Fax: 01283 221881

KIDSGROVE ATHLETIC
Colours: Blue & white
Hollinwood Stadium, Hollinwood Road, Kidsgrove,
Stoke-on-Trent, Staffordshire ST7 1BQ
Tel: 01782 782412

NANTWICH TOWN
Colours: Black & white
*Jackson Avenue, Nantwich, Cheshire CW5 6LL
Tel: 01270 621771
(due to move to Kingsley Fields, Waterlode, Nantwich during course of 2007-08 season)

QUORN
Colours: Red & white
Sutton Park, Farley Way, Quorn, Loughborough,
Leicestershire LE12 8RB
Tel: 01509 620232

RETFORD UNITED
Colours: Black & white stripes
Canon Park, Leverton Road, Retford, Notts DN22 6QF
Tel: 01777 710300

SHEFFIELD
Colours: Red & black
Coach & Horses Ground, Stubley Hollow, Sheffield
Road, Dronfield, South Yorkshire S18 2GD
Tel: 01246 413269

SHEPSHED DYNAMO
Colours: Black & white
The Dovecote, Butt Hole Lane, Shepshed,
Loughborough, Leicestershire LE12 9BN
Tel: 01509 650992

SPALDING UNITED
Colours: Tangerine & black
Sir Halley Stewart Field, Winfrey Avenue, Spalding,
Lincolnshire PE11 1DA
Tel: 01775 713328

STOCKSBRIDGE PARK STEELS
Colours: Yellow & royal blue
Bracken Moor Lane, Stocksbridge, Sheffield, South
Yorkshire S36 5AN
Tel: 0114 288 8305/2045 Fax: 0114 288 8305

WARRINGTON TOWN
Colours: Yellow & blue
Cantilever Park, Common Lane, Warrington WA4 2RS
Tel: 01925 631932 Fax: 01925 653044

WWW.NLNEWSDESK.CO.UK

NEW DIVISION FORMED BY (all S – Northern Premier League Divison One unless otherwise stated): Alsager Town, Belper Town, Brigg Town, Cammell Laird, Carlton Town (P – Northern Counties East League Premier Division), Colwyn Bay, Goole, Grantham Town (R), Gresley Rovers, Kidsgrove Athletic, Nantwich Town (P – North West Counties League Division One), Quorn (P – Midland Alliance), Retford United (P – Northern Counties East League Premier Division), Sheffield (P – Northern Counties East League Premier Division), Shepshed Dynamo, Spalding United (S – Southern League Division One Midlands), Stocksbridge Park Steels, Warrington Town

LEAGUE CUP

FIRST ROUND
Alsager Town 1 **Kidsgrove Athletic** 4
Bamber Bridge 6 Radcliffe Borough 3 *aet*
Bridlington Town 1 **Ossett Town** 3
Cammell Laird 0 **Prescot Cables** 2
Clitheroe 5 Chorley 0
Colwyn Bay 1 **Warrington Town** 3 *aet*
Gateshead 0 **Harrogate Railway Athletic** 1
Goole 2 Ossett Albion 1
Guiseley 1 **Bradford Park Avenue** 1 *aet* (3-4p)
Leek Town 2 AFC Telford United 2 *aet* (11-10)
Lincoln United 0 **Ilkeston Town** 2
Rossendale United 1 **Skelmersdale United** 4
Shepshed Dynamo 2 **Buxton** 3
Wakefield 1 Ashton United 0

SECOND ROUND
Bamber Bridge 2 Prescot Cables 1 *aet*
Belper Town 3 **Grantham Town** 3 *aet* (4-5p)
Bradford Park Avenue 1 **North Ferriby United** 4
Brigg Town 2 Stocksbridge Park Steels 1
Burscough 1 **Kendal Town** 4
Buxton 0 **Hednesford Town** 2
Eastwood Town 1 **Leek Town** 6
Fleetwood Town 2 Mossley 1
Frickley Athletic 1 **Goole** 4
Harrogate Railway Athletic 4 Wakefield 1
Ilkeston Town 3 **Kidsgrove Athletic** 4
Marine 4 Skelmersdale United 1
Matlock Town 4 Gresley Rovers 1
(at Belper Town)

Whitby Town 3 Ossett Town 3 *aet* (5-4p)
Witton Albion 8 Clitheroe 1
Woodley Sports 3 Warrington Town 0

THIRD ROUND
Bamber Bridge 2 **Witton Albion** 3
Goole 2 **Grantham Town** 3
Harrogate Railway Athletic 3 Brigg Town 0 *aet*
Hednesford Town 1 **Woodley Sports** 2
Kendal Town 1 **Fleetwood Town** 3
Marine 1 Leek Town 0
Matlock Town 3 Kidsgrove Athletic 1
North Ferriby United 1 **Whitby Town** 2

QUARTER-FINALS
Fleetwood Town 3 Grantham Town 1
Matlock Town 5 Whitby Town 4 *aet*
Witton Albion 1 Marine 0
Woodley Sports 3 Harrogate Railway Athletic 2

SEMI-FINALS
Fleetwood Town 1 Witton Albion 0
Matlock Town 3 Woodley Sports 3 *aet* (7-6p)

FINAL
(April 16th at Witton Albion)
Fleetwood Town 1 Matlock Town 0

PETER SWALES CHALLENGE CUP
(League champions v Division One champions)
(May 5th at Burscough)
Burscough 3 Buxton 1

PRESIDENT'S CUP
(League Cup Second Round losers.
Participation optional)

SEMI-FINALS
Buxton 1 Stocksbridge Park Steels 0

Gresley Rovers 1 **Wakefield** 2

FINAL
(April 23rd at Buxton)
Buxton 3 Wakefield 1

CHAIRMAN'S CUP
(League Cup First Round losers.
Participation optional)

FIRST ROUND
Alsager Town 0 **Cammell Laird** 1
Ashton United 2 Rossendale United 0
Guiseley 5 Ossett Albion 0
Shepshed Dynamo 2 **Bridlington Town** 2 *aet* (0-3p)

SEMI-FINALS
Bridlington Town 1 **Cammell Laird** 4
Guiseley 3 Ashton United 2

FINAL
(March 27th at Guiseley)
Guiseley 2 Cammell Laird 1

NOTTS SENIOR LEAGUE

	Attenboro.	Awsworth	Basford	Bestwood	Boots A.	Caribbean	Clifton	Cotgrave	G. S'bank	Keyworth	Kimberley	Linby CW	Magdala	N. Police	Rud'gton	Sandhurst	Siemens	Wollaton
Attenborough		3-2	0-2	1-0	1-1	1-1	0-4	2-3	4-3	4-3	1-3	1-2	3-4	1-1	1-1	4-1	4-1	3-1
Awsworth Villa	1-4	*S*	0-7	1-3	3-4	2-3	2-5	1-3	4-2	3-1	2-1	0-4	1-4	1-4	2-0	3-0	1-0	1-4
Basford United	4-1	6-1	*E*	2-2	2-0	0-2	1-2	3-2	1-1	3-0	1-1	1-1	3-0	1-0	1-0	6-0	5-1	1-0
Bestwood Miners Welfare	0-0	2-2	1-2	*N*	2-1	0-3	0-7	1-2	1-1	0-2	0-1	3-0	1-1	2-2	2-1	1-0	2-0	3-5
Boots Athletic	1-1	4-2	2-2	1-2	*I*	3-2	3-5	0-2	3-3	5-1	3-1	1-3	2-4	3-2	2-1	2-1	1-2	1-0
Caribbean Cavaliers	0-1	4-4	2-1	1-1	5-2	*O*	2-1	6-0	3-0	6-0	3-2	3-4	7-3	8-0	2-1	7-0	3-1	3-2
Clifton	3-7	3-1	3-1	2-2	4-0	6-3	*R*	2-4	3-2	2-1	0-1	5-4	1-3	4-0	2-1	7-0	4-1	0-3
Cotgrave Colliery Welfare Utd	3-1	4-0	1-0	4-2	3-1	2-4	1-1		2-1	2-1	2-5	2-1	3-1	1-0	5-0	4-3	3-1	
Gedling Southbank	2-0	4-2	0-0	1-3	2-1	1-2	2-2	2-2		0-5	0-4	1-2	1-1	4-2	2-3	1-1	2-0	1-4
Keyworth United	1-2	2-1	2-0	2-0	1-1	3-1	2-1	0-1	0-0	*D*	0-2	2-1	3-2	1-1	4-0	4-5	1-0	0-3
Kimberley Miners Welfare	7-3	0-1	2-1	1-1	2-4	1-2	5-0	0-1	0-1	2-6	*I*	9-2	0-2	1-0	1-2	13-0	1-1	3-1
Linby Colliery Welfare	6-1	3-1	1-4	0-4	3-1	4-0	2-2	3-0	3-0	1-0	4-0	*V*	0-0	2-0	0-1	6-0	2-3	0-1
Magdala Amateurs	1-1	3-1	2-1	3-2	2-0	1-7	2-2	2-3	0-1	2-3	1-3	1-1	*I*	0-5	0-5	5-1	7-0	1-3
Notts Police	0-1	2-1	0-3	3-1	2-2	1-0	2-1	1-4	1-0	0-1	1-3	0-5	0-5	*S*	1-4	4-0	3-4	1-6
Ruddington United	1-7	3-2	1-1	1-2	1-2	1-0	2-0	1-4	0-4	2-2	1-3	5-0	7-2	1-2	*I*	4-0	2-0	1-3
Sandhurst	2-1	1-4	0-5	1-3	2-3	1-5	0-16	0-2	1-3	2-6	0-4	0-5	0-7	0-0		*O*	1-5	0-6
Siemens	1-1	1-2	1-2	0-5	0-4	0-3	3-1	1-1	1-4	0-2	1-5	0-4	2-0	2-3	1-1	2-0	*N*	0-1
Wollaton	0-0	2-1	1-3	4-0	3-0	4-1	6-2	1-1	1-2	4-2	1-3	4-2	3-6	1-0	0-2	2-1	6-0	

Senior Division

	P	W	D	L	F	A	Pts
Cotgrave Colliery Welfare United	34	25	4	5	95	49	79
Caribbean Cavaliers	34	22	3	9	104	54	69
Basford United	34	20	7	7	78	33	67
Linby Colliery Welfare	34	20	5	9	84	50	65
Wollaton	34	19	3	12	93	51	60
Kimberley Miners Welfare	34	17	6	11	94	70	57
Clifton	34	14	6	14	62	59	48
Keyworth United	34	13	9	12	66	66	48
Attenborough	34	14	6	14	65	70	48
Boots Athletic	34	12	10	12	54	57	46
Bestwood Miners Welfare	34	11	9	14	53	61	42
Gedling Southbank	34	11	8	15	68	72	41
Magdala Amateurs	34	11	6	17	55	64	39
Ruddington United	34	11	6	17	59	85	39
Notts Police	34	12	3	19	52	80	39
Awsworth Villa	34	9	2	23	56	97	29
Siemens	34	7	4	23	39	93	25
Sandhurst	34	1	2	31	16	160	5

Division One

	P	W	D	L	F	A	Pts
Clifton Res.	32	25	4	3	95	28	79
Boots Athletic Res.	32	24	3	5	87	34	75
Wollaton Res.	32	21	5	6	94	40	68
Keyworth United Res.	32	19	8	5	87	42	65
Gedling Southbank Res.	32	18	5	9	91	49	59
Bestwood Miners Welfare Res.	32	16	5	11	75	52	53
Cotgrave Colliery Welfare U. Res.	32	16	5	11	73	55	53
Awsworth Villa Res.	32	14	7	11	70	54	49
Basford United Res.	32	13	7	12	61	63	46
Magdala Amateurs Res.	32	13	5	14	55	64	44
Caribbean Cavaliers Res.	32	12	7	13	73	58	43
Ruddington United Res.	32	11	3	18	59	85	36
Kimberley Miners Welfare Res.	32	10	3	19	72	84	33
Linby Colliery Welfare Res.	32	8	6	18	49	75	30
Siemens Res.	32	4	3	25	32	120	15
Attenborough Res.	32	2	8	22	36	89	14
Sandhurst Res.	32	3	2	27	21	138	11

SENIOR CUP

PRELIMINARY ROUND
Bestwood Miners Welfare 1 **Caribbean Cavaliers** 2
Wollaton 5 Cotgrave Colliery Welfare Utd 2

FIRST ROUND
Attenborough 1 **Caribbean Cavaliers** 2
Boots Athletic 2 **Notts Police** 3 *aet*
Gedling Southbank 1 Basford United 0
Kimberley Miners Welfare 4 Ruddington United 2 *aet*
Linby Colliery Welfare 3 Clifton 1
Magdala Amateurs 1 **Wollaton** 5
Sandhurst 3 **Awsworth Villa** 8
Siemens 1 **Keyworth United** 3

QUARTER-FINALS
Caribbean Cavaliers 2 Awsworth Villa 1
Gedling Southbank 0 **Kimberley Miners Welfare** 1
Linby Colliery Welfare 0 **Keyworth United** 2
Wollaton 2 Notts Police 1

SEMI-FINALS
Kimberley Miners Welfare 0 **Keyworth United** 4 *(at Clifton)*
Wollaton 1 **Caribbean Cavaliers** 2 *(at Linby Colliery Welfare)*

FINAL
(May 16th at Hucknall Town)
Caribbean Cavaliers 2 Keyworth United 1

JUNIOR CUP

FINAL
(May 10th at Hucknall Town)
Boots Athletic Res. 3 Wollaton Res. 0

WWW.NLNEWSDESK.CO.UK

NOTTS SENIOR LEAGUE SENIOR DIVISION CONSTITUTION 2007-08

ATTENBOROUGH . . . . Village Green, The Strand, Attenborough NG9 6AU 0115 925 7439
AWSWORTH VILLA . . . . Shilo Park, Attewell Road, Awsworth NG16 2SY 0115 849 8741
BASFORD UNITED . . . . Greenwich Avenue, Bagnall Road, Basford, Nottingham NG6 0LE 0115 942 3918
BESTWOOD MINERS WELFARE . . Bestwood Workshops, Park Road, Bestwood Village, Nottingham NG6 8TQ . . . . None
BILBOROUGH PELICAN . . . . Brian Wakefield Sports Ground, Lenton Lane, Nottingham NG7 2SA . . . . None
BOOTS ATHLETIC . . . . Trent Vale Road, Beeston, Nottingham NG9 1ND 0115 986 8255
CARIBBEAN CAVALIERS . . . . Carrington Sports Ground, Mansfield Road, Nottingham NG5 2EJ 0115 981 9201
CLIFTON . . . . Green Lane, Clifton Estate, Nottingham NG11 9AY 0115 984 4903
COTGRAVE COLLIERY WELFARE UTD . . The Woodview, Cotgrave, Nottingham NG12 3PJ 0115 989 2414
GEDLING SOUTHBANK . . . . Carlton Recreation Ground, Carlton Hill, Nottingham . . . . None
KEYWORTH UNITED . . . . Platt Lane Sports Complex, Keyworth, Nottingham NG12 5GE 0115 937 5998
KIMBERLEY MINERS WELFARE . . . . Digby Street, Kimberley, Nottingham NG16 2HP 07966 964458
LINBY COLLIERY WELFARE . . . . Church Lane, Linby Village, Nottingham NG15 8AB . . . . None
MAGDALA AMATEURS . . . . ROKO Health Club, Wilford Lane, West Bridgford, Nottingham 0115 982 7799
MATRIXGRADE . . . . Annesley Social Club, Derby Road, Annesley, Nottingham NG15 0AP . . . . None
NOTTS POLICE . . . . Rolls Royce Leisure, Watnall Road, Hucknall 0115 982 7799
UNDERWOOD VILLA . . . Bracken Park (off A608), Felley Mill Lane North, Underwood, Nottingham NG16 5FG . . . . None
RUDDINGTON UNITED . . . . The Elms Park, Loughborough Road, Ruddington NG11 6NX 0115 984 4976
SANDHURST . . . . Walesby Sports & Social Club, Retford Road, Walesby NG22 9PE 01623 860456
SIEMENS EWS . . . . Sports Ground, Trent Vale Road, Beeston Rylands NG9 1ND 0115 943 3700
WOLLATON . . . . Sports Association, Wollaton Road, Wollaton, Nottingham NG8 2AA 0115 928 3875
IN: Bilborough Pelican (W – Central Midlands League Supreme Division), Matrixgrade (P – Notts Amateur League Premier Division), Underwood Villa (P – Midland Amateur Alliance Premier Division)

OXFORDSHIRE SENIOR LEAGUE

	Adderbury Park	BCS Bardwell	Berinsfield CA	Chadlington	Charlton United	Eynsham Association	Garsington	Haddenham United	Horspath	Kennington United	Launton Sports	Oxford University Press	Rover Cowley	Watlington Town
Adderbury Park		1-3	3-3	4-0	3-2	1-1	0-0	0-5	1-1	5-2	1-3	4-0	3-5	2-0
BCS Bardwell	2-2	P	3-3	2-1	7-0	0-4	0-2	1-1	1-1	3-1	1-1	1-4	0-5	9-0
Berinsfield CA	3-1	4-2	R	6-1	5-0	0-5	1-1	0-0	3-2	4-2	1-1	3-2	1-2	3-1
Chadlington	6-0	2-1	4-1	E	2-0	0-4	0-5	2-1	0-5	2-0	1-3	5-3	1-0	4-3
Charlton United	1-1	1-4	1-4	0-1	M	1-3	L-W	0-2	2-7	2-1	0-3	2-3	0-3	1-1
Eynsham Association	0-0	1-0	1-1	3-3	3-0	I	1-2	0-3	2-0	1-1	0-1	1-1	0-1	3-4
Garsington	4-1	0-2	4-2	2-1	1-0	0-0	E	4-0	2-0	7-1	3-2	9-1	3-0	4-1
Haddenham United	3-1	2-0	1-2	W-L	2-0	3-0	2-3	R	3-0	4-2	0-1	4-1	1-1	5-0
Horspath	6-3	0-2	2-1	1-1	1-1	3-2	0-5	4-2		0-2	2-5	6-3	1-0	4-2
Kennington United	1-2	4-1	3-5	1-3	5-0	0-1	3-3	0-2	2-0		3-5	1-3	4-2	3-5
Launton Sports	2-1	2-0	3-1	1-2	6-0	5-0	3-9	1-0	1-1	9-4	D	2-0	2-0	2-2
Oxford University Press	1-5	1-1	2-0	4-1	4-0	1-3	1-4	3-4	2-2	0-2	2-2	I	2-3	1-1
Rover Cowley	2-0	W-L	1-0	3-0	1-5	0-2	1-0	4-1	6-0	2-0	2-0		V	4-2
Watlington Town	2-3	2-7	2-4	3-0	4-0	1-2	1-2	1-3	0-1	1-1	2-2	2-3	0-2	

Premier Division	P	W	D	L	F	A	Pts
Garsington	26	21	4	1	81	23	67
Rover Cowley	26	18	1	7	53	28	55
Launton Sports	26	16	6	4	68	38	54
Haddenham Utd	26	15	3	8	53	28	48
Berinsfield CA	26	12	6	8	61	52	42
Eynsham Assoc.	26	11	7	8	46	33	40
Chadlington	26	12	2	12	43	54	38
Horspath	26	10	6	10	51	52	36
BCS Bardwell	26	9	6	11	53	45	33
Adderbury Park	26	8	7	11	48	58	31
Oxford Univ. Press	26	7	5	14	48	70	26
Kennington United	26	6	3	17	49	76	21
Watlington Town	26	4	5	17	43	75	17
Charlton United	26	1	3	22	14	79	6

PRESIDENT'S CUP

FIRST ROUND
Adderbury Park 4 Oxford University Press 2
BCS Bardwell 10 Long Crendon 2
Berinsfield CA 4 **Chadlington** 4 *aet* (2-3p)
Charlton United 2 **Watlington Town** 3
Enstone Sports (w/o) v Old Salesians (scr.)
Fritwell 3 Oakley United 2
Haddenham Utd 1 **Garsington** 4
Kidlington OB 0 **Launton Spts** 1
Kings Sutton 0 **Middleton Cheney** 1
Marston Sts 1 **Middle Barton** 3
Rover Cowley 1 **Eynsham Association** 4
Wheatley '04 1 **Horspath** 6
Worcester COB/Bletchington 1 Stonesfield 0
Yarnton 4 **Kennington United** 6

SECOND ROUND
Adderbury Park 5 BCS Bardwell 3
Eynsham Association 0 **Garsington** 1
Fritwell 1 **Enstone Sports** 2
Launton Sports 0 **Middle Barton** 3
Watlington Town 1 **Horspath** 4
Middleton Cheney 3 **Worcester COB & Bletchington** 8

QUARTER-FINALS
Garsington 3 Adderbury Park 1
Horspath 1 Enstone Sports 0
Kennington United 3 **Worcester COB & Bletchington** 3 *aet* (3-4p)
Middle Barton 3 Chadlington 2

SEMI-FINALS
Garsington 3 Horspath 1
Worcester COB & Bletchington 2 **Middle Barton** 5

FINAL
(April 9th at Oxford University Press)
Garsington 3 Middle Barton 2

BEN TURNER CUP
FINAL
(April 21st at Worcester COB & Bletchington)
Berinsfield CA 2 Haddenham United 2 *aet* (5-4p)

OXFORDSHIRE SENIOR LEAGUE PREMIER DIVISION CONSTITUTION 2007-08

ADDERBURY PARK........ Adderbury Park Playing Fields, Round Close Road, Adderbury, Banbury OX17 .... None
BCS BARDWELL........................... Chaffinch Way, Mallards Way Estate, Bicester. .... None
BERINSFIELD CA .... Green Furlong, Berinsfield, Wallingford OX8 1SX 01865 340201
CHADLINGTON .... Chadlington Sports & Social, Chapel Road, Chadlington, Chipping Norton OX7 3NX 01608 676723
ENSTONE SPORTS .... Charlbury Road, Enstone, Oxford OX2 6UT 01608 677823
EYNSHAM ASSOCIATION .... Oxford Road, Eynsham, Witney OX29 4DA .... None
GARSINGTON .... Garsington Sports Club, Denton Lane, Garsington, Oxford OX44 9EL 01865 361720
HORSPATH .... Brookes University Campus, Wheatley, Oxford OX4 6LB .... None
KENNINGTON UNITED .... Playfield Road, Kennington, Oxford OX1 5RS. .... None
OXFORD UNIVERSITY PRESS................. Jordan Hill, Banbury Road, Oxford OX2 8EF .... None
ROVER COWLEY .... Pressed Steel Sports Ground, Roman Way, Beckley, Oxford OX3 9UA .... None
STONESFIELD..................... Stonesfield Playing Field, off Longmore, Stonesfield. .... None
WATLINGTON TOWN .... Shirburn Road, Watlington OX49 5BZ .... None
WORCESTER COB & BLETCHINGTON .... Rover Cowley Sports Ground, Oxford. 01865 775463

IN: Enstone Sports (P), Stonesfield (P), Worcester COB & Bletchington (P)
OUT: Charlton United (R), Haddenham United (S – Aylesbury & District League Premier Division), Launton Sports (P – Hellenic League Division One West)

	Enstone Sports	Fritwell	Kidlington Old Boys	Kings Sutton	Long Crendon	Marston Saints	Middle Barton	Middleton Cheney	Oakley United	Stonesfield	Wheatley '04	Worcester COB & Bletchington	Yarnton
Enstone Sports	D	4-1	1-1	6-1	7-0	0-0	1-0	3-3	7-1	0-1	11-2	1-2	5-0
Fritwell	2-3	I	0-2	2-1	7-0	0-4	0-0	3-2	0-3	2-6	3-0	2-3	0-2
Kidlington Old Boys	4-1	3-2	V	1-0	5-0	1-1	4-2	6-0	6-0	0-1	1-2	4-4	2-0
Kings Sutton	1-3	0-1	0-3	I	2-1	1-2	1-4	1-1	0-3	0-2	3-5	1-3	2-3
Long Crendon	0-5	0-3	0-4	2-1	S	0-3	W-L	2-3	0-4	0-4	0-8	0-2	0-5
Marston Saints	0-1	2-1	2-1	3-0	10-0	I	2-3	3-1	3-1	0-6	0-1	1-2	2-1
Middle Barton	1-2	3-1	4-2	4-2	W-L	2-1	O	W-L	3-4	0-1	3-5	L-W	2-1
Middleton Cheney	0-7	2-3	2-6	1-1	3-0	1-1	2-5	N	3-3	0-7	1-9	0-6	2-3
Oakley United	2-2	4-0	4-2	3-4	5-3	0-2	2-3	3-1		1-4	5-3	1-2	2-3
Stonesfield	2-2	4-2	8-1	W-L	W-L	4-1	4-3	W-L	5-4		6-1	3-1	0-0
Wheatley '04	1-3	2-0	1-4	1-3	3-0	1-1	W-L	4-0	1-1	0	O	2-3	2-2
Worcester COB & Bletchington	1-2	3-1	2-1	5-1	5-2	2-4	3-2	3-3	4-0	2-3	6-1	N	2-1
Yarnton	0-1	2-1	1-7	9-0	5-0	0-1	1-2	1-1	2-2	0-1	3-3	3-1	E

Division One

	P	W	D	L	F	A	Pts
Stonesfield	24	21	3	0	73	21	66
Enstone Sports	24	16	5	3	78	26	53
Worcester COB & Bletchington	24	17	2	5	67	39	53
Kidlington Old Boys	24	14	3	7	71	38	45
Marston Saints	24	14	3	7	53	31	45
Middle Barton	24	13	1	10	49	40	40
Wheatley '04	24	10	4	10	59	62	34
Yarnton	24	9	5	10	48	41	32
Oakley United	24	9	3	12	57	66	30
Fritwell	24	7	1	16	37	55	22
Kings Sutton	24	3	2	19	26	68	11
Middleton Cheney	24	1	6	17	33	84	9
Long Crendon	24	3	0	21	14	94	9

Division Two A

	P	W	D	L	F	A	Pts
Garsington Res.	18	14	2	2	52	17	44
Berinsfield CA Res.	18	13	0	5	54	22	39
Eynsham Association Res.	18	11	1	6	60	35	34
Launton Sports Res.	18	10	2	6	39	28	32
BCS Bardwell Res.	18	10	1	7	40	31	31
Marston Saints Res.	18	6	2	10	35	35	20
Chadlington Res.	18	5	5	8	19	30	20
Horspath Res.	18	6	2	10	35	52	20
Oxford University Press Res.	18	5	4	9	33	39	19
Fritwell Res.	18	0	1	17	6	84	1

Division Two B

	P	W	D	L	F	A	Pts
Yarnton Res.	14	10	4	0	40	12	34
Stonesfield Res.	14	10	1	3	33	17	31
Worc. COB & B'ton Res.	14	9	3	2	36	18	30
Haddenham United Res.	14	9	0	5	38	20	27
Oakley United Res.	14	4	4	6	29	33	16
Watlington Town Res.	14	3	5	6	24	24	14
Enstone Sports Res.	14	1	1	12	21	39	4
Kings Sutton Res.	14	1	0	13	7	65	3

Charlton United Res. – record expunged

CLARENDON CUP

FINAL

(April 9th at Oxford University Press)

Garsington Res. 4 Berinsfield CA Res. 0

IVOR GUBBINS CUP

FINAL

(April 28th at Garsington)

Worcester COB & B. Res. 0 Oakley Res. 0 *aet* (5-3p)

OXFORDSHIRE SENIOR LEAGUE DIVISION ONE CONSTITUTION 2007-08

CHARLTON UNITED . . . . Charlton PF, Oddington Road, Charlton-on-Otmoor, Kidlington OX5 2TJ. . . . . None
FRITWELL . . . . Playing Field, Fewcott Road, Fritwell OX27 7QA. . . . . None
KIDLINGTON OLD BOYS . . . . Exeter Close, Crown Road, Kidlington OX5 1AP. . . . . None
KINGS SUTTON . . . . Longburrow Park, The Lane, Kings Sutton, Banbury. . . . . None
LONG CRENDON . . . . Rec Ground, Chearsley Road, Long Crendon, Aylesbury HP18 9AP. . . . . None
MARSTON SAINTS. . . . . Boults Lane, Old Marston, Oxford OX3 0PW 01865 203970
MIDDLE BARTON . . . . Worton Road, Middle Barton, Chipping Norton OX7 7EF. 01869 347597
MIDDLETON CHENEY . . . . Astrop Road, Middleton Cheney, Banbury OX17 2PG . . . . None
OAKLEY UNITED . . . . Playfield Fields, Oxford Road, Oakley, Aylesbury HP18 9RE. . . . . None
WHEATLEY '04 . . . . Holton Playing Fields, Wheatley, Oxford. . . . . None
YARNTON. . . . . Green Lane, Yarnton 01865 842037

IN: Charlton United (R)

OUT: Enstone Sports (P), Stonesfield (P), Worcester COB & Bletchington (P)

PETERBOROUGH & DISTRICT LEAGUE

	AFC Fletton	Alconbury	Crowland Town	Hampton Athletic	Leverington Sports	Long Sutton Athletic	Moulton Harrox	Oundle Town	Parson Drove	Perkins Sports	Peterborough Sports	Pinchbeck United	Stamford Belvedere	Uppingham Town	Whittlesey United	Wimblington
AFC Fletton	P	5-1	10-2	3-0	3-1	3-2	2-3	6-2	3-2	4-0	2-3	3-2	4-3	5-0	0-2	7-0
Alconbury	7-1	R	1-0	1-2	1-3	3-1	0-3	1-1	3-2	1-1	1-2	3-0	1-2	2-5	3-2	3-0
Crowland Town	1-3	0-6	E	0-2	2-0	1-1	0-1	2-1	2-4	1-1	1-3	0-2	1-0	3-3	1-2	4-0
Hampton Athletic	0-4	2-2	3-0	M	5-3	9-1	2-1	5-3	5-1	4-4	2-2	4-1	3-0	2-1	4-0	2-3
Leverington Sports	0-1	0-2	3-2	2-1	I	0-1	0-2	1-3	3-0	0-0	1-2	3-0	4-0	0-3	1-2	1-0
Long Sutton Athletic	0-5	1-4	3-4	0-3	1-1	E	0-6	3-6	4-0	1-2	1-3	3-1	0-2	1-3	2-6	1-5
Moulton Harrox	0-2	3-0	4-1	2-1	1-0	5-1	R	1-0	3-1	4-0	0-2	4-1	4-0	3-1	3-0	2-1
Oundle Town	2-7	1-4	1-1	1-1	0-2	3-2	0-2	D	2-2	1-2	2-2	2-4	7-1	1-1	1-1	1-5
Parson Drove	0-5	0-2	1-3	0-1	1-2	4-2	0-1	0-0	D	0-4	1-5	0-1	5-4	3-3	2-4	4-0
Perkins Sports	3-2	0-3	2-1	1-3	1-2	4-0	0-2	3-1	3-0	I	0-1	3-0	3-0	3-2	1-2	3-1
Peterborough Sports	2-1	0-1	3-1	6-0	5-1	2-1	1-1	2-1	9-0	5-2	V	3-1	7-1	1-2	5-0	
Pinchbeck United	2-4	1-3	1-2	0-1	4-2	1-1	0-3	2-1	1-2	0-1	0-2	I	1-0	1-0	1-2	3-1
Stamford Belvedere	0-4	0-1	1-0	2-5	1-4	0-0	1-4	1-4	1-2	1-3	0-0	1-1	S	2-1	0-4	1-0
Uppingham Town	2-1	2-0	1-1	1-7	2-1	1-0	5-1	2-3	3-0	0-1	0-1	1-5	0-1	I	4-2	2-2
Whittlesey United	0-3	6-2	0-1	1-0	2-0	2-2	2-1	2-2	2-1	1-3	0-5	3-1	0-1	1-3	U	2-1
Wimblington	2-0	1-3	2-1	1-5	0-3	4-1	2-0	4-2	0-3	0-3	2-6	0-1	1-3	3-1	1-4	O

Premier Division	P	W	D	L	F	A	Pts
Peterborough Sports	30	25	3	2	95	27	78
Moulton Harrox	30	24	1	5	73	22	73
AFC Fletton	30	22	0	8	103	44	66
Hampton Athletic	30	19	4	7	84	47	61
Whittlesey United	30	19	3	8	61	47	60
Perkins Sports	30	17	4	9	58	42	55
Alconbury	30	17	3	10	65	47	54
Leverington Sports	30	12	2	16	44	48	38
Uppingham Town	30	9	4	17	50	74	31
Pinchbeck United	30	9	3	18	36	58	30
Crowland Town	30	8	5	17	39	65	29
Oundle Town	30	7	7	16	54	73	28
Wimblington	30	9	1	20	41	76	28
Stamford Belvedere	30	8	3	19	34	69	27
Parson Drove	30	7	2	21	40	81	23
Long Sutton Athletic	30	3	5	22	38	95	14

PETERBOROUGH SENIOR CUP

(Premier Division teams and top eight Division One first teams)

FIRST ROUND
Alconbury 4 Uppingham Town 1
Long Sutton Athletic 0 **AFC Fletton** 5
Moulton Harrox 2 Deeping S. 0
Perkins Sports 5 Rutland Rgrs 0
Pinchbeck United 3 Crowland Town 1
Stamford Belvedere 3 **Ramsey Town** 2
Whittlesey 3 Werrington Town 2
Wimblington 1 **Oundle Town** 2

SECOND ROUND
AFC Fletton 3 Perkins **Sports** 5
Alconbury 3 Gedney Hill 2
Hampton Athletic 4 **Whittlesey United** 5
Oundle Town 5 Chatteris Town 2
Parson Drove 0 **Moulton Harrox** 0 *aet* (2-3p)

Peterborough Sports 3 Kings Cliffe United 1
Pinchbeck United 0 **Netherton United** 1
Stamford Belvedere 3 Ramsey Town 2

QUARTER-FINALS
Moulton Harrox 3 Whittlesey United 1
Netherton United 1 **Alconbury** 5
Perkins Sports 3 Stamford Belvedere 0
Peterborough Sports 5 Oundle 1

SEMI-FINALS
Moulton Harrox 2 Peterborough Sports 0
Perkins Sports 0 **Alconbury** 2

FINAL
(May 7th at Peterborough Utd)
Moulton Harrox 1 **Alconbury** 2

JACK HOGG CHARITY SHIELD

(League champions v Peterborough Senior Cup holders)

(August 11th at Chestnut Avenue)
AFC Fletton 4 Deeping Sports 0

PETERBOROUGH & DISTRICT LEAGUE PREMIER DIVISION CONSTITUTION 2007-08

AFC FLETTON	Celta Road, Peterborough PE2 9JD	01733 556104
ALCONBURY	Great North Road, Alconbury, Huntingdon PE28 4EX	01480 891313
CROWLAND TOWN	Snowden Field, Thorney Road, Crowland PE6 0AL	01733 211548
DEEPING SPORTS	Outgang Road, Towngate East, Market Deeping PE6 8LQ	01778 344701
HAMPTON ATHLETIC	Woodlands Sports Centre, Splash Lane, Peterborough CB7 5AA	01733 475000
LEVERINGTON SPORTS	Church Road, Leverington, Wisbech PE13 5DE	01945 465082
MOULTON HARROX	Broad Lane, Moulton, Spalding PE12 6PN	01406 371991
OUNDLE TOWN	Station Road, Oundle, Peterborough PE8 4DE	01832 274188
PARSON DROVE	Main Road, Parson Drove, Wisbech PE13 4LF	None
PERKINS SPORTS	Perkins Sports Pavilion, Oxney Road, Peterborough PE1 5NA	01733 567835
PETERBOROUGH SPORTS	Peterborough Sports & Leisure, Lincoln Road, Peterborough PE1 3HA	01733 567835
PINCHBECK UNITED	Glebe Playing Fields, Knight Street, Pinchbeck, Spalding PE11 3RB	01775 762057
STAMFORD BELVEDERE	Queen Eleanor School, Green Lane, Stamford PE9 1HE	01780 751011
UPPINGHAM TOWN	North Street East, Uppingham LE15 9QJ	01572 821446
WHITTLESEY UNITED	Manor Leisure Centre, Station Road, Whittlesey, Peterborough PE7 1UE	01733 202298
WIMBLINGTON	Parkfield Sports & Social Club, Chapel Lane, Wimblington, March PE15 0QX	01354 741555

IN: Deeping Sports (P)
OUT: Long Sutton Athletic (R)

Division One		P	W	D	L	F	A	Pts
Deeping Sports		28	25	1	2	109	26	76
Rutland Rangers		28	24	2	2	132	25	74
Silver Jubilee		28	18	5	5	66	30	59
Netherton United		28	17	4	7	65	31	55
Griffin Park	-1	28	14	6	8	73	55	47
Chatteris Town	-2	28	14	4	10	66	46	44
Thorney		28	11	5	12	64	70	38
Ketton		28	10	7	11	49	54	37
Sutton Bridge United		28	8	4	16	51	81	28
Werrington Town		28	7	5	16	46	82	26
Ramsey Town	-3	28	6	10	12	37	51	25
Gedney Hill		28	7	4	17	43	88	25
Kings Cliffe United	-1	28	6	3	19	54	82	20
Langtoft United		28	5	4	19	41	100	19
Castor & Ailsworth	-2	28	3	6	19	36	111	13

Ryhall United – record expunged

Division Two		P	W	D	L	F	A	Pts
Coates Athletic		26	21	4	1	117	16	67
Guyhirn		26	20	5	1	106	41	65
Stilton United		26	17	4	5	90	40	55
Sawtry		26	17	2	7	92	42	53
Warboys Town		26	15	3	8	92	43	48
Doddington United		26	16	0	10	91	44	48
Manea United		26	13	2	11	58	32	41
March St Marys		26	12	2	12	78	65	38
Farcet United		26	11	2	13	62	61	35
Peterborough Rovers		26	10	0	16	51	100	30
Chatteris Fen Tigers		26	7	2	17	57	88	23
Eye Sports & Social		26	4	6	16	44	86	18
Hereward Athletic	-1	26	3	0	23	43	128	8
Benwick Athletic		26	0	0	26	32	227	0

Combination One		P	W	D	L	F	A	Pts
AFC Fletton Res.		26	21	1	4	105	26	64
Perkins Sports Res.		26	21	1	4	93	40	64
Deeping Sports Res.		26	17	5	4	69	26	56
Whittlesey United Res.		26	15	5	6	59	34	50
Chatteris Town Res.		26	15	2	9	58	43	47
Oundle Town Res.		26	11	4	11	36	45	37
Hampton Athletic Res.		26	11	3	12	52	49	36
Moulton Harrox Res.	-2	26	12	2	12	46	50	36
Stamford Belvedere Res.		26	9	7	10	43	43	34
Ramsey Town Res.		26	11	1	14	53	72	34
Leverington Sports Res.		26	5	3	18	42	85	18
Parson Drove Res.	-3	26	5	5	16	25	59	17
Long Sutton Athletic Res.		26	4	2	20	43	93	14
Werrington Town Res.		26	3	3	20	31	90	12

Combination Two		P	W	D	L	F	A	Pts
Langtoft United Res.		24	18	2	4	55	25	56
Alconbury Res.		24	16	2	6	81	43	50
Wimblington Res.		24	14	6	4	67	44	48
Netherton United Res.		24	14	3	7	79	49	45
Pinchbeck United Res.		24	14	2	8	77	39	44
Crowland Town Res.		24	11	4	9	67	63	37
Ketton Res.		24	10	5	9	63	50	35
Peterborough Sports Res.	-1	24	11	2	11	61	64	34
Kings Cliffe United Res.		24	9	2	13	62	77	29
Eye Sports & Social Res.	-3	24	8	1	15	55	68	22
Uppingham Town Res.		24	5	3	16	54	80	18
Doddington United Res.	-3	24	6	2	16	41	71	17
Leverington Sports 'A'	-2	24	3	0	21	30	119	7

Combination Three		P	W	D	L	F	A	Pts
Silver Jubilee Res.		24	16	4	4	89	31	52
Stamford Belvedere 'A'		24	16	2	6	72	43	50
Netherton United 'A'		24	15	4	5	75	44	49
Chatteris Town 'A'		24	15	1	8	83	51	46
Rutland Rangers Res.		24	13	4	7	74	43	43
Ramsey Town 'A'		24	13	3	8	60	51	42
Coates Athletic Res.	-2	24	11	4	9	48	43	35
Thorney Res.		24	9	5	10	48	52	32
Sutton Bridge United Res.		24	7	3	14	39	68	24
Manea United Res.		24	6	5	13	35	71	23
Wimblington 'A'		24	6	2	16	45	77	20
March St Marys Res.		24	3	5	16	46	73	14
Griffin Park Res.	-3	24	5	0	19	24	91	12

WWW.NLNEWSDESK.CO.UK

PETERBOROUGH CHALLENGE CUP

FINAL

(May 18th at Peterborough Northern Star)

Silver Jubilee 4 Manea United 0

PETERBOROUGH JUNIOR CUP

FINAL

(April 27th at Chestnut Avenue)

Perkins Sports Res. 2 Netherton United Res. 0

PETERBOROUGH MINOR CUP

FINAL

(April 14th at Chestnut Avenue)

Wimblington Res. 4 Eye Sports & Social Res. 1

READING LEAGUE

	Ascot United	Berks County Sports	Cookham Dean	Forest Old Boys	Highmoor/IBIS	Hurst	Mortimer	Rabson Rovers	Reading YMCA	Royal Mail	Westwood United	Woodley Town
Ascot United		7-1	2-0	5-1	2-2	4-0	5-1	1-0	2-1	2-0	2-1	3-1
Berks County Sports	1-2	S	0-4	2-0	0-3	0-2	0-3	1-2	0-2	3-3	1-2	3-2
Cookham Dean	1-2	3-1	E	2-0	1-2	5-0	1-0	2-0	0-2	5-0	6-1	1-0
Forest Old Boys	0-2	1-6	0-3	N	2-5	0-2	0-4	L-W	L-W	3-0	2-0	5-3
Highmoor/IBIS	1-3	1-0	3-1	8-2	I	5-1	2-1	4-2	1-1	2-0	3-0	3-1
Hurst	0-4	0-4	1-4	1-2	0-2	O	2-1	1-3	1-3	1-3	2-3	3-3
Mortimer	1-1	1-1	0-4	5-1	2-0	2-1	R	3-6	0-3	0-2	1-2	0-1
Rabson Rovers	0-3	8-2	1-2	8-2	4-2	1-0	3-1		2-0	5-4	2-2	1-3
Reading YMCA	6-1	1-1	0-4	3-1	0-5	3-2	3-3	2-0	D	4-1	5-2	1-0
Royal Mail	2-2	0-0	0-1	4-0	1-2	2-5	2-2	1-0	1-1	I	2-3	1-2
Westwood United	0-3	1-0	1-0	1-0	1-2	2-1	3-1	0-5	2-3	0-1	V	2-2
Woodley Town	0-2	3-3	1-2	4-1	0-4	1-1	2-2	2-2	3-1	1-3	4-2	

WWW.CHERRYRED.CO.UK

SENIOR CUP
(Senior and Premier Division teams)

FIRST ROUND
Berks County Sports 0 **Marlow United Res.** 1
Reading YMCA 3 Sonning Common 0
Royal Mail 3 Rabson Rovers 2 *aet*
Shinfield 2 **Highmoor/IBIS** 4
Tadley Calleva Res. 1 **Hurst** 2 *aet*
West Reading 2 AFC Corinthians 1
Woodcote & Stoke Row 3 Taplow United 0
SECOND ROUND
Ascot United 6 Woodley Town 1
Cookham Dean 5 Royal Mail 2
Marlow United Res. 5 Forest Old Boys 1
Newtown Henley 0 **Hurst** 3
Reading YMCA 3 Rides Dyamos 0
West Reading 3 **Highmoor/IBIS** 5
Westwood United 2 Spencers Wood 0
Woodcote & Stoke Row 0 **Mortimer** 1
QUARTER-FINALS
Ascot United 2 **Mortimer** 3 *aet*
Cookham Dean 2 **Reading YMCA** 2 *aet* (1-4p)
Hurst 1 **Highmoor/IBIS** 3
Westwood United 2 **Marlow United Res.** 3
SEMI-FINALS
Highmoor/IBIS 0 **Reading YMCA** 0 *aet* (4-5p) *(at Newbury)*
Mortimer 4 Marlow United Res. 2 *aet (at Newbury)*
FINAL
(May 8th at Reading)
Mortimer 0 **Reading YMCA** 1

Senior Division	P	W	D	L	F	A	Pts
Ascot United	22	18	3	1	60	20	57
Highmoor/IBIS	22	17	2	3	62	25	53
Cookham Dean	22	16	0	6	52	17	48
Reading YMCA	22	13	4	5	45	32	43
Rabson Rovers	22	12	2	8	54	38	38
Westwood United	22	9	2	11	31	48	29
Woodley Town	22	6	6	10	39	46	24
Mortimer	22	6	5	11	36	43	23
Royal Mail	22	6	5	11	33	44	23
Berks County Sports	22	4	5	13	30	51	17
Forest Old Boys	22	4	0	18	23	68	12
Hurst	22	3	2	17	25	58	11

INTERMEDIATE CUP
FINAL
(May 12th at Reading Town)
OLA Newbury 3 REME Arborfield 1

JUNIOR CUP
FINAL
(May 30th at Reading Town)
Wokingham Wanderers 1 Berks CS Res. 0

READING LEAGUE SENIOR DIVISION CONSTITUTION 2007-08

BERKS COUNTY SPORTS .... Berks Co. Sports & Social Club, Sonning Lane, Sonning, Reading RG4 6ST .... None
COOKHAM DEAN .... Alfred Major Rec Ground, Hillcrest Avenue, Cookham Rise, Maidenhead SL6 9NB............. 01628 819423
FOREST OLD BOYS .... Holme Park (Adwest), Sonning Lane, Sonning, Reading RG4 6ST 01734 690356
HIGHMOOR/IBIS .... Prudential IBIS Sports Club, Scours Lane, Reading RG3 6AY .... None
MORTIMER .... Alfred Palmer Memorial PF, West End Road, Mortimer, Reading RG7 3TJ .... None
NEWBURY .... Faraday Road, Newbury RG14 2AD 01635 523222
RABSON ROVERS .... Lower Whitley Rec, Basingstoke Road, Reading RG2 0JA .... None
READING YMCA................... Reading Town FC, Scours Lane, Tilehurst, Reading RG30 6AY 0118 945 3555
ROYAL MAIL .... Prospect Park, Liebenwood Road, Reading RG30 2ND .... None
WESTWOOD UNITED .... Cotswold Sports Centre, Downs Way, Tilehurst, Reading RG31 6LX .... None
WOODCOTE & STOKE ROW .... Woodcote Recreation Ground, Woodcote, Reading RG8 0QY .... None
WOODLEY TOWN .... East Park Farm, Park Lane, Charvil, Reading RG10 9TS .... None
IN: Newbury (formerly OLA Newbury) (P – Division One), Woodcote & Stoke Row (P)
OUT: Ascot United (P – Hellenic League Division One East), Hurst (R)

	AFC Corinthians	Cookham Dean Res.	Marlow United Res.	Newtown Henley	Rides Dynamos	Shinfield	Sonning Common	Spencers Wood	Tadley Calleva Res.	Taplow United	West Reading	Woodcote & Stoke Row
AFC Corinthians	P	3-1	1-1	3-2	1-1	3-3	3-1	3-2	1-4	4-0	3-2	1-5
Cookham Dean Res.	1-0	R	5-2	2-2	2-2	0-4	2-0	2-2	0-0	5-1	2-2	2-2
Marlow United Res.	2-0	0-0	E	4-2	1-4	3-3	3-1	1-0	0-0	4-2	6-1	0-6
Newtown Henley	0-1	0-3	2-6	M	1-1	1-2	2-2	2-3	2-1	2-1	4-1	0-2
Rides Dynamos	1-3	3-3	1-2	0-0	I	3-3	1-1	1-3	1-3	3-1	0-0	1-2
Shinfield	4-1	1-2	1-4	2-0	4-1	E	1-0	2-6	1-2	1-6	3-3	0-2
Sonning Common	3-3	0-1	1-3	1-1	1-1	L-W	R	0-1	L-W	1-2	1-2	0-1
Spencers Wood	2-1	3-6	1-1	1-0	2-2	1-4	2-2		2-0	4-3	2-2	0-2
Tadley Calleva Res.	2-2	3-2	2-0	4-0	0-0	1-1	2-2	2-2		1-1	3-2	1-2
Taplow United	1-1	1-5	1-3	6-2	1-2	3-2	1-1	2-0	0-2	D	2-1	0-2
West Reading	1-1	1-1	2-0	5-1	3-0	2-3	1-1	6-2	1-2	1-2	I	1-4
Woodcote & Stoke Row	5-1	1-0	1-2	3-2	7-1	3-0	5-2	6-2	6-2	1-3	3-3	V

Premier Division

	P	W	D	L	F	A	Pts
Woodcote & Stoke Row	22	17	3	2	66	23	54
Tadley Calleva Res.	22	11	8	3	38	23	41
Marlow United Res.	22	12	5	5	48	37	41
Cookham Dean Res.	22	9	9	4	47	33	36
Shinfield	22	9	4	9	43	47	31
AFC Corinthians	22	8	7	7	40	44	31
Spencers Wood	22	7	6	9	41	52	27
Taplow United	22	7	4	11	39	49	25
Rides Dynamos	22	5	9	8	33	41	24
West Reading	22	5	8	9	43	46	23
Newtown Henley	22	4	5	13	30	53	17
Sonning Common	22	0	8	14	20	40	8

READING LEAGUE PREMIER DIVISION CONSTITUTION 2007-08

AFC CORINTHIANS . . . . Civil Service Club, James Lane, Burghfield, Reading RG30 3RS. 0118 983 3423
COOKHAM DEAN RESERVES . . Alfred Major Rec Ground, Hillcrest Ave., Cookham Rise, Maidenhead SL6 9NB. 01628 819423
FRILSHAM & YATTENDON . . . . . Frilsham Playing Field, Frilsham Common, Frilsham, near Hermitage 01635 201847
HURST . . . . Cantley Park, Twyford Road, Wokingham RG40 5QT . . . . None
MARLOW UNITED RESERVES . . . . Gossmore Park, Gossmore Lane, Marlow SL7 1QF. . . . . None
NEWTOWN HENLEY . . . . Harpsden Hall, Harpsden Village, Henley-on-Thames RG9 4HH . . . . None
SHINFIELD . . . . Millworth Lane, Shinfield, Reading RG2 9EN . . . . None
SPENCERS WOOD . . . . Coley Recreation Ground, St Saviours Road, Coley, Reading RG1 6EJ . . . . None
TADLEY CALLEVA RESERVES . . . . Barlows Park, Silchester Road, Tadley RG26 3PX . . . . None
TAPLOW UNITED . . . . Berry Hill, Taplow SL6 0DA 01628 621745
UNITY . . . . Cintra Park, Cintra Avenue, Reading RG2 7AU . . . . None
WEST READING . . . . Victoria Recreation Ground, Kentwood Hill, Tilehurst, Reading RG31 6DE . . . . None
IN: Frilsham & Yattendon (P), Hurst (R), Unity (P)
OUT: Rides Dynamos (F), Sonning Common (R), Woodcote & Stoke Row (P)

Division One

	P	W	D	L	F	A	Pts
OLA Newbury	20	17	2	1	71	16	53
Unity	20	14	3	3	53	22	45
Frilsham & Yattendon	20	14	2	4	48	19	44
Ascot United Res.	20	9	5	6	40	28	32
Wokingham & Emmbrook 'A'	20	9	4	7	50	32	31
Highmoor/IBIS Res.	20	6	5	9	30	44	23
Radstock	20	6	4	10	28	46	22
SRCC	20	6	3	11	38	41	21
REME Arborfield	20	5	6	9	30	35	21
Goring United	20	3	4	13	27	83	13
Hurst Res.	20	1	2	17	18	67	5

Division Two

	P	W	D	L	F	A	Pts
South Reading	22	19	3	0	98	18	60
Park United	22	15	4	3	50	25	49
Ashridge Park	22	13	5	4	82	36	44
Theale	22	11	4	7	34	26	37
Westwood United Res.	22	10	5	7	54	42	35
Marlow United 'A'	22	8	6	8	40	37	30
Woodley Town Res.	22	7	5	10	33	55	26
Mortimer Res.	22	7	3	12	31	50	24
Woodcote & Stoke Row Res.	22	6	4	12	40	41	22
Newtown Henley Res.	22	5	6	11	29	43	21
Twyford & Ruscombe	22	6	2	14	30	67	20
Crowthorne Sports	22	1	1	20	23	104	4

Division Three

	P	W	D	L	F	A	Pts
Finchampstead 'A'	20	13	6	1	63	20	45
Taplow United Res.	20	10	5	5	52	35	35
Berks County Sports Res.	20	10	4	6	39	28	34
Wargrave	20	9	4	7	41	44	31
Highmoor/IBIS 'A'	20	8	6	6	54	46	30
Sonning	20	9	3	8	44	38	30
Wokingham Wanderers	20	9	2	9	43	53	29
Compton	20	9	2	9	44	55	29
Wokingham & Emmbrook 'B'	20	8	2	10	48	48	26
Theale Res.	20	4	1	15	37	61	13
Englefield	20	3	1	16	29	66	10

Division Four

	P	W	D	L	F	A	Pts
Earley	22	20	2	0	121	25	62
Barton Rovers	22	18	2	2	122	34	56
Linear United	22	14	5	3	78	32	47
Goring Res.	22	11	2	9	63	50	35
Woodley Town 'A'	22	10	4	8	41	41	34
Sonning Sports	22	8	4	10	43	62	28
The Hop Leaf	22	8	2	12	52	54	26
Rides United Res.	22	7	4	11	54	74	25
Hurst 'A'	22	5	7	10	33	58	22
Thames Valley Deaf Group	22	6	3	13	42	77	21
Taplow United 'A'	22	3	2	17	38	91	11
Sonning Res.	22	3	1	18	26	111	10

WWW.NLNEWSDESK.CO.UK

SHROPSHIRE COUNTY LEAGUE

	Broseley Juniors	Church Stretton Town	Clee Hill United	Hanwood United	Haughmond	Highley Welfare	Hopesgate United	JFF Telford	Meole Brace	Morda United	Shifnal United	Telford Juniors	Tibberton United	Wellington Amateurs	Wem Town
Broseley Juniors		2-1	6-0	1-2	6-2	2-2	0-0	1-0	3-2	6-2	4-1	0-0	2-3	1-0	1-1
Church Stretton Town	3-2	P	2-1	0-1	1-2	1-1	0-3	4-2	1-1	2-1	3-1	0-1	2-2	0-3	0-0
Clee Hill United	0-1	2-3	R	2-1	1-0	2-3	1-0	2-0	5-2	0-4	1-1	1-3	0-1	0-4	2-4
Hanwood United	3-0	2-1	4-1	E	3-1	2-0	3-0	6-1	6-0	1-0	1-1	2-1	1-0	4-1	4-0
Haughmond	2-2	4-3	3-0	2-2	M	2-0	4-2	5-0	2-0	3-2	0-0	2-4	1-4	0-4	0-1
Highley Welfare	0-1	2-2	1-3	1-8	0-1	I	2-0	1-2	6-2	3-3	1-3	1-3	1-4	0-2	0-3
Hopesgate United	2-3	0-4	1-1	1-2	2-6	0-4	E	2-2	2-1	2-2	1-2	1-2	2-0	4-1	2-0
JFF Telford	1-2	0-2	4-3	4-5	2-5	4-2	1-3	R	4-1	1-0	0-2	3-1	0-7	0-2	3-1
Meole Brace	1-0	0-1	0-3	0-5	1-4	1-4	1-2	1-2		0-1	2-2	4-7	1-2	0-4	1-3
Morda United	2-2	0-1	3-1	0-1	3-3	3-2	3-1	1-1	2-1		3-1	1-5	4-5	1-4	2-2
Shifnal United	3-3	2-1	4-3	2-2	2-1	1-1	3-0	3-0	6-1	0-2		2-0	1-3	3-1	2-3
Telford Juniors	1-2	1-1	1-0	2-2	3-2	3-2	4-0	3-0	7-0	7-3	3-0	D	4-1	3-3	7-0
Tibberton United	4-1	1-0	1-1	4-2	2-2	2-0	4-3	2-0	1-1	4-3	3-0	0-1	I	0-1	1-2
Wellington Amateurs	2-0	6-1	2-0	6-1	3-2	6-0	6-0	5-0	14-0	6-2	1-1	2-2	2-0	V	3-0
Wem Town	4-1	1-0	6-3	1-4	1-2	2-0	1-2	3-2	7-0	3-0	1-1	0-1	0-1	0-1	

www.CHERRYRED.co.uk

Premier Division		P	W	D	L	F	A	Pts
Hanwood United		28	21	4	3	80	33	67
Wellington Amateurs		28	21	3	4	96	26	66
Telford Juniors		28	20	4	4	83	37	64
Tibberton United		28	16	4	8	59	37	52
Broseley Juniors		28	13	7	8	51	43	46
Haughmond		28	13	6	9	63	50	45
Shifnal United		28	11	10	7	49	41	43
Wem Town		28	13	4	11	50	46	43
Church Stretton Town		28	10	6	12	40	44	36
Morda United		28	8	6	14	52	66	30
Hopesgate United		28	8	3	17	38	64	27
JFF Telford		28	8	2	18	41	77	26
Clee Hill United		28	7	3	18	39	65	24
Highley Welfare		28	5	5	18	38	66	20
Meole Brace	-3	28	1	3	24	25	109	3

PREMIER DIVISION CUP

FIRST ROUND
Hanwood United 5 JFF Telford 0
Haughmond 7 Church Stretton Town 2
Highley Welfare 1 **Shifnal United** 4
Morda United 6 Clee Hill United 1
Telford Juniors 3 Wem Town 1
Tibberton United 4 Hopesgate United 3
Wellington Amateurs 5 Meole Brace 0
QUARTER-FINALS
Broseley Juniors 3 Haughmond 2
Shifnal United 3 Morda United 0
Telford Juniors 2 **Wellington Amateurs** 3 *aet*
Tibberton United 2 **Hanwood United** 2 *aet* (2-3p)
SEMI-FINALS
Broseley Juniors 2 Shifnal United 1
Hanwood United 2 Wellington Amateurs 2 *aet* (5-4p)
FINAL
(May 9th at Bridgnorth Town)
Broseley Juniors 3 Hanwood United 1

SHROPSHIRE COUNTY LEAGUE PREMIER DIVISION CONSTITUTION 2007-08

BROSELEY JUNIORS . . . . Birchmeadow, Broseley TF12 5LP . . . . None
CHURCH STRETTON TOWN . . . . Russell's Meadow, Church Stretton SY6 6AT . . . . None
CLEE HILL UNITED . . . . Knowle Sports Ground, Tenbury Road, Clee Hill, Ludlow SY8 3NE. . . . . None
HANWOOD UNITED . . . . Hanwood Recreation Ground, Hanwood . . . . None
HAUGHMOND. . . . . Mereside Recreation Centre, Springfield, Shrewsbury SY2 6LH 01743 357793
HOPESGATE UNITED . . . . The Cotes, Snailbeach . . . . None
LUDLOW TOWN RESERVES . . . . SBS Stadium, Bromfield Road, Ludlow SY8 2BY 01584 876000
MARKET DRAYTON TOWN RESERVES . . Greenfield Sports Club, Greenfield Lane, Market Drayton TF9 3SL 01630 655088
MORDA UNITED. . . . . Weston Road, Morda, Oswestry SY10 9NS 01691 659621
SHIFNAL TOWN RESERVES . . . . Phoenix Park, Coppice Green Lane, Shifal TF11 8PB. 01952 463667
SHIFNAL UNITED. . . . . Idsall Sports Centre, Shifnal . . . . None
TELFORD JUNIORS. . . . . Ironbridge Power Station, Buildwas Road, Ironbridge TF8 7BL . . . . None
TELFORD TOWN . . . . Sutton Hill, Telford TF7 4AQ. . . . . None
TIBBERTON UNITED. Doseley Road, Dawley, Telford TF4 . . . . None
WEM TOWN . . . . Butler Sports Centre, Bowens Field, Wem SY4 5AW 01939 233287
IN: Ludlow Town Reserves (S – West Midlands (Regional) League Division One), Market Drayton Town Reserves (P), Shifnal Town Reserves (P)
OUT: Highley Welfare (W), Meole Brace (R), Wellington Amateurs (P – West Midlands (Regional) League Division Two)
JFF Telford become Telford Town

	Bobbington	Brown Clee	Craven Arms Town	Dawley Wanderers	Ellesmere Rangers Res.	Market Drayton T. Res.	Morda United Res.	Oakengates Athletic	Shifnal Town Res.	Springvale Rovers	St Martins	W'church Alport Res.	Wrockwardine Wood	Wroxeter Rovers
Bobbington		3-2	1-3	7-1	2-1	1-1	4-1	4-2	0-3	3-1	2-3	1-0	1-0	5-1
Brown Clee	2-1	D	2-2	1-2	1-1	2-0	2-0	2-1	1-6	2-0	5-0	4-0	1-0	1-1
Craven Arms Town	0-6	0-2	I	0-2	1-3	0-3	4-2	4-1	1-5	4-1	6-0	0-0	2-0	0-0
Dawley Wanderers	1-4	3-3	1-0	V	2-0	0-5	5-0	2-3	2-1	2-2	5-3	2-3	1-1	2-0
Ellesmere Rangers Res.	1-3	3-1	3-2	1-0	I	1-1	3-0	2-1	0-1	2-1	6-1	3-1	1-0	1-2
Market Drayton T. Res.	1-0	3-0	3-2	3-0	1-0	S	6-0	1-1	1-1	3-1	4-3	3-1	5-1	3-1
Morda United Res.	0-3	2-2	0-4	3-0	1-4	1-3	I	1-2	0-6	5-1	3-3	0-5	4-1	2-3
Oakengates Athletic	2-4	2-2	3-4	3-2	1-4	2-3	0-2	O	3-2	1-3	1-3	0-2	1-1	2-3
Shifnal Town Res.	4-2	3-1	3-3	6-0	5-1	0-1	9-3	2-4	N	1-0	5-3	4-1	7-1	1-0
Springvale Rovers	1-3	0-1	1-5	3-4	0-3	1-2	2-1	3-0	1-3		3-2	1-5	4-1	2-3
St Martins	1-5	1-1	1-3	2-3	1-1	2-2	3-2	1-3	0-5	6-6	O	1-3	4-1	3-2
Whitchurch Alport Res.	4-1	3-1	4-2	0-2	3-2	2-5	2-2	1-1	0-4	2-1	3-4	N	3-2	3-1
Wrockwardine Wood	3-5	1-1	3-1	2-4	2-5	1-1	2-3	2-2	1-3	0-1	2-3	1-1	E	3-3
Wroxeter Rovers	2-0	1-0	5-0	1-1	1-3	3-3	2-2	1-0	0-3	2-2	0-2	0-0	3-0	

DIV ONE CUP

FIRST ROUND
Brown Clee 3 Market Drayton Town Res. 1
Ellesmere Rangers Res. 3 Morda United Res. 0
Springvale Rovers 1 **Wroxeter Rovers** 1 *aet* (4-5p)
St Martins 1 **Shifnal Town Res.** 4
Whitchurch Alport Res. 3 Oakengates Athletic 2
Wrockwardine Wood 1 **Bobbington** 6
QUARTER-FINALS
Brown Clee 2 Ellesmere Rangers Res. 1
Craven Arms Town 0 **Shifnal Town Res.** 4
Dawley Wanderers 1 **Bobbington** 4
Wroxeter Rovers 0 **Whitchurch Alport Res.** 1
SEMI-FINALS
Bobbington 2 **Shifnal Town Res.** 3
Brown Clee 3 Whitchurch Alport Res. 1
FINAL
(May 5th at Bridgnorth Town)
Brown Clee 2 Shifnal Town Res. 1

RON JONES MEMORIAL CUP

FIRST ROUND
Bobbington 5 Telford Juniors 1
Brown Clee 2 Springvale R. 0
Craven Arms Town 1 Clee Hill United 1 *aet* (3-5p)
Dawley Wanderers 1 **Wem Town** 3
Hanwood Utd 5 Wroxeter 0
Haughmond 3 Broseley Hopesgate United 2
Whitchurch Alport Res. 5 JFF Telford 9 Morda Res. 0
Market Drayton Town Res. 0 **Highley Welfare** 2
Meole Brace 0 **Tibberton United** 1
Morda United 2 **Church Stretton Town** 2 *aet* (2-4p)
St Martins 3 **Oakengates Athletic** 4
Wrockwardine Wood 0 **Ellesmere Rangers Res.** 2
SECOND ROUND
Bobbington 0 **Wellington Amateurs** 2 *(at Wellington Ams)*
Brown Clee 2 **Craven Arms Town** 2 *aet* (6-7p)

Church Stretton Town 1 **Wem Town** 3
Haughmond (w/o) v Highley Welfare (scr.)
JFF Telford 0 **Hanwood** 1 *aet*
Oakengates Athletic 2
Ellesmere Rangers Res. 2 *aet* (3-4p)
Tibberton United 3 Shifnal Town Res. 2
Whitchurch Alport Res. 0 **Shifnal United** 4
QUARTER-FINALS
Craven Arms Town 0 **Wellington Amateurs** 4
Ellesmere Rangers Res. 0 Shifnal United 0 *aet* (4-3p)
Hanwood Utd 4 Tibberton 2
Haughmond 0 **Wem Town** 1
SEMI-FINALS
Ellesmere Rangers 0 **Wem Town** 1
Wellingham Amateurs 2 Hanwood United 1
FINAL
(May 12th at Bridgnorth Town)
Wellington Amateurs 2 Wem Town 0

Division One	P	W	D	L	F	A	Pts
Shifnal Town Res.	26	20	2	4	93	30	62
Market Drayton Res.	26	18	7	1	67	27	61
Bobbington	26	17	1	8	71	41	52
Ellesmere Rgrs Res.	26	15	3	8	55	35	48
Whitchurch A'pt Res.	26	12	5	9	52	48	41
Brown Clee	26	11	7	8	45	39	40
Dawley Wanderers	26	12	4	10	49	57	40
Wroxeter Rovers	26	9	8	9	41	43	35
Craven Arms Town	26	9	5	12	51	55	32
St Martins	26	8	5	13	56	82	29
Oakengates Athletic	26	6	5	15	41	61	23
Springvale Rovers	26	6	3	17	42	66	21
Morda United Res.	26	5	4	17	40	81	19
Wrockwardine W. -3	26	1	7	18	32	70	7

SHROPSHIRE COUNTY LEAGUE DIVISION ONE CONSTITUTION 2007-08

BOBBINGTON . . . . Crab Lane, Bobbington, Stourbridge DY7 5DZ . . . . None
BROWN CLEE. . . . . Hall Meadow, Cleobury North, Bridgnorth WV16 6RP . . . . None
CRAVEN ARMS TOWN . . . . Community Centre Playing Fields, Newington Way, Craven Arms SY7 9PS 01588 672847
DAWLEY BANK . . . . Doseley Road, Dawley, Telford TF4 3AY . . . . None
DAWLEY WANDERERS . . . . Doseley Road, Dawley, Telford TF4 3AY . . . . None
ELLESMERE RANGERS RESERVES . . . . . . Beech Grove Playing Fields, Ellesmere SY12 0BT . . . . None
MEOLE BRACE . . . . Church Road, Meole Brace, Shrewsbury SY3 9HF . . . . None
MORDA UNITED RESERVES. . . . . Weston Road, Morda, Oswestry SY10 9NS 01691 659621
OAKENGATES ATHLETIC . . . . School Road, Oakengates. . . . . None
ST MARTINS . . . . St Martins Playing Fields, Overton Road, St Martins, Oswestry SY11 3DG. . . . . None
WHITCHURCH ALPORT RESERVES . . Yockings Park, Blackpark Road, Whitchurch SY13 1PG 01948 667415
WROCKWARDINE WOOD. . . . . New Road, Wrockwardine Wood TF2 7AB 01952 613086
WROXETER ROVERS . . . . Springfield, Wroxeter . . . . None

IN: Dawley Bank *(formerly Bulls Head Dawley Bank) (P – Telford Combination),* Meole Brace *(R)*
OUT: Market Drayton Town Reserves *(P),* Shawbury United Colts *(WN),* Shifnal Town Reserves *(P),* Springvale Rovers *(W)*

SOMERSET COUNTY LEAGUE

	Bridgwater Town Res.	Burnham United	Castle Cary	Cheddar	Cleeve West Town	Frome Town Res.	Fry Club	Glastonbury Town	Ilminster Town	Mangotsfield United Res.	Nailsea United	Oldland Abbotonians	Paulton Rovers Res.	Shirehampton	Timsbury Athletic	Wells City	Welton Rovers Res.	Winscombe
Bridgwater Town Res.		0-0	1-1	3-1	0-0	4-0	6-1	1-1	6-0	1-3	3-2	1-1	2-1	1-3	5-0	0-0	4-1	3-0
Burnham United	0-0	P	3-0	2-0	2-2	1-0	2-0	2-0	2-0	3-0	1-0	4-1	1-0	0-0	2-0	1-1	4-0	4-5
Castle Cary	3-3	1-5	R	0-1	1-2	1-2	1-1	1-0	4-1	3-1	0-3	1-2	0-1	0-3	1-0	0-4	3-2	1-0
Cheddar	2-3	2-2	5-0	E	2-0	2-2	2-0	3-2	2-1	2-0	1-4	0-0	3-0	4-1	0-0	2-1	2-0	4-0
Cleeve West Town	1-3	2-2	3-1	3-1	M	3-1	1-3	1-1	3-2	1-1	1-1	1-0	4-2	1-1	1-2	1-3	2-0	1-2
Frome Town Res.	1-3	5-2	1-1	1-2	2-0	I	5-0	1-1	1-2	3-0	n/a	1-2	0-0	2-2	3-2	0-0	8-0	1-3
Fry Club	2-2	1-2	2-1	1-2	3-2	1-4	E	1-0	0-2	0-4	0-2	0-1	1-3	1-2	1-2	1-3	6-0	1-3
Glastonbury Town	1-1	3-1	1-1	2-1	1-2	1-2	2-1	R	0-3	1-1	6-6	1-1	4-1	5-0	0-0	5-0	5-0	1-2
Ilminster Town	1-6	0-3	0-2	3-0	2-3	0-2	3-1	1-2	I	1-3	1-2	1-1	2-1	1-1	2-0	0-2	1-1	0-1
Mangotsfield United Res.	3-4	1-2	3-1	1-1	1-2	0-2	4-0	1-2	3-0	D	1-2	1-1	0-1	3-3	2-2	2-0	2-2	0-1
Nailsea United	2-3	2-2	0-0	5-0	1-1	1-2	1-0	4-4	2-0	2-0	I	1-2	4-2	4-1	1-0	2-2	7-0	3-0
Oldland Abbotonians	1-0	1-0	1-0	2-0	4-0	2-2	4-1	4-1	1-2	3-0	1-1	V	1-1	2-4	2-1	3-3	6-1	1-3
Paulton Rovers Res.	1-4	0-2	1-1	0-0	0-1	0-3	0-2	0-0	1-3	0-0	1-4	1-4	I	1-1	2-1	2-1	4-0	0-0
Shirehampton	1-4	0-3	1-2	3-0	5-0	1-1	0-1	0-1	4-3	2-2	1-3	0-2	2-0	S	W-L	5-1	10-0	4-1
Timsbury Athletic	1-7	0-4	2-4	1-3	1-4	1-1	1-2	2-2	1-3	2-1	1-1	2-1	1-1	W-L	I	1-2	2-1	1-3
Wells City	1-1	3-4	3-2	5-3	0-1	3-0	1-1	3-0	2-0	2-0	0-2	1-1	1-0	4-0	3-0	O	3-0	1-1
Welton Rovers Res.	1-4	3-5	1-2	0-5	0-7	0-1	0-2	1-0	2-1	0-4	1-3	1-3	0-3	0-1	0-4	1-9	N	2-1
Winscombe	2-0	0-2	0-2	2-1	3-1	2-4	4-1	1-2	3-0	0-1	0-2	2-1	1-1	2-2	4-2	2-2	7-0	

Premier Division		P	W	D	L	F	A	Pts
Burnham United		34	22	8	4	75	33	74
Bridgwater Town Res.	-2	34	19	11	4	89	39	66
Oldland Abbotonians		34	17	12	5	64	37	63
Nailsea United	-3	33	19	8	6	80	39	62
Wells City		34	16	11	7	70	39	59
Frome Town Res.		33	16	8	9	67	43	56
Winscombe	-1	34	17	5	12	61	52	55
Cheddar		34	16	6	12	60	49	54
Shirehampton		34	14	9	11	73	51	51
Cleeve West Town	-1	34	15	7	12	54	56	51
Glastonbury Town		34	10	11	13	53	54	41
Castle Cary		34	11	7	16	42	59	40
Mangotsfield United Res.		34	10	8	16	51	52	38
Ilminster Town		34	9	4	21	41	69	31
Timsbury Athletic		34	8	6	20	37	77	30
Fry Club		34	8	4	22	38	72	28
Paulton Rovers Res.	-3	34	7	9	18	29	52	27
Welton Rovers Res.	-3	34	3	2	29	20	131	8

Frome Town Res. v Nailsea United not played

PREMIER/DIVISION ONE CUP

FIRST ROUND
Bishop Sutton Res. 3 **Nailsea United** 6
Burnham United 5 Keynsham Town Res. 3
Cutters Friday 3 Fry Club 0, **Wells City** 6 Worle 0

SECOND ROUND
Bishops Lydeard 1 **Mangotsfield United Res.** 5
Castle Cary 0 **Cleeve West Town** 1
Cheddar 1 **Backwell United Res.** 2
Churchill Club 0 **Bridgwater Town Res.** 3
Cutters Friday 2 **Winscombe** 3
Dundry Athletic 3 Odd Down Res. 3 *aet* (8-7p)
Frome Town Res. 2 **Brislington** 5
Ilminster Town 1 Stockwood Green Robinsons 0
Nailsea Town 1 **Burnham United** 2
Oldland Abbotonians 1 Glastonbury Town 0
Shepton Mallet Res. 0 **Timsbury Athletic** 2
Shirehampton 2 **Wells City** 3
St George Easton-in-Gordano 2 **Paulton Rovers Res.** 3
(Paulton Rovers Reserves expelled)
Tunley Athletic 1 **Nailsea United** 5

SOMERSET COUNTY LEAGUE PREMIER DIVISION CONSTITUTION 2007-08

BRIDGWATER TOWN RESERVES... Fairfax Park, College Way, Bath Road, Bridgwater TA6 4TZ 01278 446899
BURNHAM UNITED .... Burnham Road Playing Fields, Cassis Close, Burnham-on-Sea TA8 1NN. 01278 794615
CASTLE CARY .... Donald Pither Memorial Playing Fields, Catherines Close, Castle Cary BA7 7HP 01963 351538
CHEDDAR .... Bowdens Park, Draycott Road, Cheddar BS27 3RL. 01934 743736
CLEEVE WEST TOWN .... King George V Playing Fields, Meeting House Lane, Cleeve BS49 4PD 01934 832173
CUTTERS FRIDAY .... The Cutters Club, Stockwood Lane, Stockwood, Bristol BS14 8SJ 01275 839830
FROME TOWN RESERVES............. Badgers Hill, Berkley Road, Frome BA11 2EH. 01373 464087
FRY CLUB .... Fry Club, Somerdale, Keynsham, Bristol BS31 2AU 0117 937 6500/6501
GLASTONBURY TOWN .... Abbey Moor Stadium, Godney Road, Glastonbury BA6 9AF. 01458 831460
ILMINSTER TOWN .... Recreation Ground, Ilminster TA19 0EF 01460 54756
MANGOTSFIELD UNITED RESERVES .... Cossham Street, Mangotsfield, Bristol BS17 3EN 0117 956 0119
NAILSEA UNITED .... Grove Sports Ground, Old Church, Nailsea BS48 4ND 01275 856892
SHIREHAMPTON .... Recreation Ground, Penpole Lane, Shirehampton, Bristol BS11 0EA. 0117 923 5461
ST GEORGE EASTON-IN-GORDANO ..... Court Hay, Easton-in-Gordano, Bristol BS20 0PY 01275 374235
TAUNTON BLACKBROOK.......... Taunton Town FC, Wordsworth Drive, Taunton TA1 2HG 01823 278191
TIMSBURY ATHLETIC............. Recreation Ground, North Road, Timsbury, Bath BA2 0JH 01761 472523
WELLS CITY .... The Athletic Ground, Rowdens Road, Wells BA5 1TU 01749 679971
WINSCOMBE.............. Recreation Ground, The Lynch, Winscombe BS25 1AP.............. 01934 842720(cricket club)

IN: *Cutters Friday (P), St George Easton-in-Gordano (P), Taunton Blackbrook (P)*
OUT: *Oldland Abbotonians (P – Western League Division One), Paulton Rovers Reserves (R), Welton Rovers Reserves (R)*

	Backwell United Res.	Bishop Sutton Res.	Bishops Lydeard	Brislington Res.	Churchill Club	Cutters Friday	Dundry Athletic	Keynsham Town Res.	Nailsea Town	Odd Down Res.	Shepton Mallet Res.	St George Easton-in-Gordano	Stockwood Green Robinsons	Taunton Blackbrook	Tunley Athletic	Watchet Town	Westland United	Worle
Backwell United Res.		1-0	4-1	0-2	1-2	4-6	2-1	5-2	3-2	2-2	3-0	0-4	1-1	0-5	0-4	1-2	1-2	1-3
Bishop Sutton Res.	2-2		4-5	0-3	0-2	2-2	0-2	2-3	2-5	2-3	2-1	0-8	0-2	0-2	0-1	4-1	2-1	0-3
Bishops Lydeard	2-1	2-1		1-3	4-3	0-2	1-2	2-0	1-0	3-0	4-1	0-0	2-1	0-1	3-2	0-1	3-1	3-1
Brislington Res.	3-0	1-0	2-2	*D*	0-3	5-0	4-1	5-0	3-0	1-0	3-0	2-2	2-2	1-1	0-0	0-3	2-2	4-2
Churchill Club	3-2	3-0	3-2	3-1	*I*	4-2	3-2	5-3	0-0	1-0	3-0	2-2	2-2	1-2	1-2	0-3	3-0	0-3
Cutters Friday	3-2	6-1	3-0	2-1	4-4	*V*	2-3	7-0	1-1	4-3	9-0	1-0	3-3	1-6	4-0	0-1	5-0	4-1
Dundry Athletic	1-1	0-0	1-0	3-1	2-1	2-2	*I*	1-2	1-3	3-0	1-1	3-2	0-4	1-1	0-0	1-1	3-5	2-2
Keynsham Town Res.	3-2	1-0	1-1	2-2	2-5	1-2	0-2	*S*	0-4	5-3	1-0	2-3	0-7	3-3	2-1	0-6	2-0	3-2
Nailsea Town	1-1	6-0	2-1	1-2	3-2	3-2	0-0	7-3	*I*	1-0	1-0	0-0	0-3	4-2	2-1	4-1	3-0	4-1
Odd Down Res.	4-0	4-1	0-2	0-1	1-1	0-1	2-0	1-0	0-0	*O*	1-1	1-2	1-1	0-0	1-2	4-1	4-0	2-2
Shepton Mallet Res.	0-1	0-1	0-1	1-2	0-2	0-4	1-0	0-3	0-5	0-1	*N*	2-3	2-2	1-1	1-1	3-0	0-4	2-0
St George Easton-in-Gordano	1-0	4-0	2-0	4-2	0-0	6-2	5-2	1-0	2-0	3-0	0-1		3-1	2-0	2-0	1-0		5-0
Stockwood Green Robinsons	1-0	3-0	2-0	1-1	0-2	3-4	0-0	1-1	1-2	2-2	1-2	0-4	*O*	1-1	1-3	2-1	1-6	3-2
Taunton Blackbrook	1-2	5-0	1-2	1-1	3-0	2-1	5-3	5-1	0-2	0-0	4-0	0-0	3-1	*N*	2-0	5-0		4-1
Tunley Athletic	1-2	7-1	2-0	4-1	1-2	0-2	2-3	13-0	0-3	2-0	1-1	0-1	1-3	1-1	*E*	2-2		3-1
Watchet Town	2-1	4-1	3-1	2-2	4-2	0-3	1-0	6-1	2-1	1-2	1-2	1-0	1-1	0-0	1-2		4-0	2-6
Westland United	0-1	1-2	1-2	2-1	2-2	0-2	3-0	2-4	2-3	4-2	5-1	1-6	1-2	0-2	1-2	3-3		1-5
Worle	2-3	2-1	4-3	3-0	1-1	0-6	2-3	5-2	2-1	4-2	2-1	1-1	2-2	0-5	2-1	0-5	3-1	

Watchet Town 2 Westland United 0
Welton Rovers Res. 1 **Taunton Blackbrook** 2
THIRD ROUND
Backwell United Res. 3 Mangotsfield United Res. 1
Burnham United 1 **Oldland Abbotonians** 4
Cleeve West Town 0 **Ilminster Town** 1
Dundry Athletic 2 **Brislington Res.** 3
Nailsea United 3 Watchet Town 1
Timsbury Athletic 0 **Taunton Blackbrook** 3
Wells City 1 St George Easton-in-Gordano 1 *aet* (6-5p)
Winscombe 3 Bridgwater Town Res. 2
QUARTER-FINALS
Ilminster Town 1 Backwell United Res. 0 *aet*
Nailsea United 3 Brislington Res. 0
Oldland Abbotonians 2 Wells City 1
Taunton Blackbrook 1 Winscombe 1 *aet* (6-5p)
SEMI-FINALS
Ilminster Town 1 **Nailsea United** 2 *aet*
Oldland Abbotonians 1 **Taunton Blackbrook** 2
FINAL
(May 17th at Bishop Sutton)
Nailsea United 1 Taunton Blackbrook 0

Division One

		P	W	D	L	F	A	Pts
St George Easton-in-Gordano		34	24	6	4	81	23	78
Cutters Friday		34	20	6	8	102	60	66
Taunton Blackbrook		34	18	10	6	79	33	64
Nailsea Town		34	19	7	8	73	39	64
Churchill Club		34	18	7	9	73	51	61
Brislington Res.	-1	34	15	10	9	64	48	54
Stockwood Green Robs		34	13	12	9	61	52	51
Watchet Town		34	15	6	13	62	55	51
Bishops Lydeard		34	16	3	15	54	55	51
Tunley Athletic		34	14	6	14	65	47	48
Worle		34	14	5	15	70	81	47
Dundry Athletic	-1	34	11	10	13	49	59	42
Backwell United Res.		34	11	5	18	50	69	38
Keynsham Town Res.		34	11	4	19	53	111	37
Odd Down Res.	-2	34	9	9	16	47	55	34
Westland United		34	8	5	21	55	84	29
Shepton Mallet Res.	-1	34	5	6	23	24	75	20
Bishop Sutton Res.		34	5	3	26	31	96	18

SOMERSET COUNTY LEAGUE DIVISION ONE CONSTITUTION 2007-08
BACKWELL UNITED RESERVES .. The Playing Fields, West Town Road, Backwell Bristol BS48 3HG 01275 462612
BISHOPS LYDEARD .... Darby Way, Bishops Lydeard TA4 3BE. .... None
BRISLINGTON RESERVES .... Ironmould Lane, Brislington, Bristol BS4 5SA 0117 977 4030
BURNHAM UNITED RESERVES .. Burnham Rd Playing Fields, Cassis Close, Burnham-on-Sea TA8 1NN 01278 794615
CHURCHILL CLUB .... Ladymead Lane, Churchill, Winscombe BS25 5NH. 01934 852739
DUNDRY ATHLETIC .... Dundry Playing Field, Crabtree Lane, Dundry, Bristol BS41 8LN 01934 852739
KEYNSHAM TOWN RESERVES .... Crown Field, Charlton Road, Keynsham, Bristol BS31 2BE. 0117 964 5536
NAILSEA TOWN .... Fryth Way, Pound Lane, Nailsea BS48 2AS .... None
ODD DOWN RESERVES .... Lew Hill Memorial Ground, Combe Hay Lane, Odd Down, Bath BA2 8PH. 01225 832491
PAULTON ROVERS RESERVES .... Athletic Ground, Winterfield Road, Paulton BS39 7RF 01761 412907
PEASEDOWN ATHLETIC .... Miners Welfare Park, Peasedown St John, Bath 01761 437319
STOCKWOOD GREEN ROBINSONS .. Hursley Lane, Woolard Lane, Whitchurch, Bristol BS14 0QY 01275 891300
STREET RESERVES .... The Tannery Ground, Middlebrooks, Street BA16 0TA 01458 444987
TUNLEY ATHLETIC .... The Recreation Centre, Bath Road, Tunley BA2 0EB .... None
WATCHET TOWN .... Memorial Ground, Doniford Road, Watchet TA23 0TG. 01984 631041
WELTON ROVERS RESERVES .... West Clewes, North Road, Midsomer Norton BA3 2QD 01761 412097
WESTLAND UNITED .... Westland Sports Club, Winterstoke Road, Weston-super-Mare BS24 9AA 01934 632037
WORLE .... Worle Recreation Ground, Station Road, Worle, Weston-super-Mare BS22 6AU .... None
IN: Burnham United Reserves (P – Division Two West), Paulton Rovers Reserves (R), Peasedown Athletic (P – Division Two East), Street Reserves (P – Division Two East), Welton Rovers Reserves (R)
OUT: Bishop Sutton Reserves (R – Division Two East), Cutters Friday (P), Shepton Mallet Reserves (R – Division Two East), St George Easton-in-Gordano (P), Taunton Blackbrook (P)

	Cheddar Res.	Clutton	Frome Collegians	Fry Club Res.	Hengrove Athletic Res.	Imperial	Larkhall Athletic Res.	Long Ashton	Peasedown Athletic	Saltford	Stockwood Green Robs Res.	Street Res.	Timsbury Athletic Res.	Wells City Res.
Cheddar Res.		2-4	0-2	2-5	0-6	0-2	1-1	1-2	0-2	1-1	0-2	4-1	1-1	1-0
Clutton	2-4	D	5-3	1-5	7-1	2-2	0-3	3-2	1-2	2-1	2-2	3-3	2-0	1-2
Frome Collegians	0-2	3-3	I	1-1	0-1	3-2	0-0	4-2	1-2	2-2	2-3	1-3	0-0	1-3
Fry Club Res.	3-2	4-2	2-1	V	2-0	3-1	0-2	1-6	0-5	6-2	6-0	0-2	2-2	5-2
Hengrove Athletic Res.	2-0	2-1	2-3	2-0		0-0	2-1	1-1	0-4	0-3	3-3	4-3	2-1	0-1
Imperial	2-0	2-1	2-2	2-1	1-1	T	3-3	0-1	4-0	1-0	0-0	3-2	1-1	2-2
Larkhall Athletic Res.	4-1	2-6	2-2	1-5	6-0	2-5	W	4-1	2-1	0-3	8-1	2-4	1-0	1-3
Long Ashton	4-1	1-1	2-2	2-2	3-2	3-0	3-2	O	1-3	1-2	2-1	0-4	5-1	2-4
Peasedown Athletic	2-1	3-0	1-0	2-0	3-2	3-2	4-3	4-1		0-0	3-0	2-4	4-0	7-1
Saltford	1-1	2-3	6-0	5-5	6-2	4-1	3-0	0-2	0-2	E	3-1	2-1	2-3	5-2
Stockwood GR Res.	2-4	2-1	3-3	0-0	0-3	1-3	2-0	0-1	2-2	1-2	A	1-3	1-1	0-1
Street Res.	1-1	2-0	6-1	4-1	1-0	2-0	0-0	2-2	3-1	2-1	5-0	S	2-0	4-1
Timsbury Athletic Res.	1-0	4-3	0-5	3-1	2-2	1-2	0-1	1-2	0-1	1-1	0-1	5-0	T	0-3
Wells City Res.	6-0	1-1	5-2	1-2	0-0	2-0	0-0	4-1	4-2	2-2	2-0	2-2	3-1	

Division Two East		P	W	D	L	F	A	Pts
Peasedown Athletic		26	19	2	5	65	32	59
Street Res.		26	17	5	4	71	33	56
Wells City Res.		26	15	6	5	57	40	51
Long Ashton		26	12	5	9	53	50	41
Saltford		26	11	7	8	59	42	40
Imperial		26	10	9	7	43	38	39
Fry Club Res.		26	11	5	10	60	53	38
Hengrove Ath. Res.		26	9	5	12	40	54	32
Larkhall Ath. Res.	-2	26	9	6	11	51	50	31
Clutton		26	8	6	12	57	60	30
Frome Collegians		26	5	9	12	44	60	24
Timsbury Athletic Res.		26	5	7	14	30	52	22
Cheddar Res.	-1	26	5	5	16	30	59	19
Stockwood Green Res.		26	4	7	15	28	65	19

PROMOTION PLAY-OFF
(Division Two East runners-up v Division Two West runners-up)

(May 12th at Portishead)
Portishead Res. 2 **Street Res.** 3

DIVISION TWO/THREE CUP

FIRST ROUND
Burnham United Res. 4 Cheddar Res. 1
Creech St Michael 1 **Langford Rovers** 3
Crewkerne 0 **Imperial** 3
Hengrove Athletic Res. 1
Clevedon United Res. 2
Nailsea United Res. 1 Fry Club Res. 0
Portishead Res. 6 Larkhall Athletic Res. 3
Stockwood Green Robs Res. 1
Frome Collegians 3
Street Res. 2 **Berrow** 0
(Street expelled)
Timsbury Athletic Res. 3
Wrington-Redhill 0
Wells City Res. 3 Long Ashton 0
Weston St Johns Res. 3 Saltford 2
Yatton Athletic 1 **Combe St Nicholas** 4

SECOND ROUND
Banwell 2 Imperial 1
Berrow 1 **Portishead Res.** 1 *aet* (3-4p)

Clevedon United Res. 5 Burnham United Res. 5 *aet* (3-0p)
Clutton 1 Nailsea United Res. 0
Combe St Nicholas 1 **Wells City Res.** 2
Congresbury 4 Timsbury Athletic Res. 1
Frome Collegians 4 Weston St John Res. 1
Peasedown Athletic 2 Langford Rovers 0

QUARTER-FINALS
Banwell 1 **Clutton** 2
Congresbury 1 **Peasedown Athletic** 4
Frome Collegians 0 **Portishead Res.** 1
Wells City Res. 1 Clevedon United Res. 0

SEMI-FINALS
Clutton 1 **Peasedown Athletic** 3
Portishead Res. 4 Wells City Res. 0

FINAL
(May 15th at Cheddar)
Portishead Res. 1 Peasedown Athletic 0

SOMERSET COUNTY LEAGUE DIVISION TWO EAST CONSTITUTION 2007-08

BISHOP SUTTON RESERVES . . . . Lake View, Wick Road, Bishop Sutton, Bristol BS39 5XP 01275 333097
CHEDDAR RESERVES . . . . Bowdens Park, Draycott Road, Cheddar BS27 3RL 01934 743734
CLUTTON . . . . Warwick Fields, Upper Bristol Road (A37), Clutton, Bristol BS39 5TA . . . . None
FROME COLLEGIANS. . . . . Selwood School, Berkley Road, Frome BA11 2EF . . . . None
FRY CLUB RESERVES. . . . . Fry Club, Somerdale, Keynsham, Bristol BS31 2AU 0117 937 6500/6501
HENGROVE ATHLETIC RESERVES . . . . Norton Lane, Whitchurch, Bristol BS14 0BT 01275 832894
IMPERIAL. . . . . Bristol Imperial Sports Club, West Town Lane, Whitchurch, Brislington BS4 5DT 01275 546000
LARKHALL ATHLETIC RESERVES. . . . Plain Ham, Charlcombe Lane, Larkhall, Bath BA1 8DJ. 01225 334952
SALTFORD. . . . . Playing Fields, Norman Road, Saltford BS31 0BQ 01225 873728
SHEPTON MALLET RESERVES . . West Shepton Playing Fields, Old Wells Rd, Shepton Mallet BA4 5XN 01749 344460
STOCKWOOD GREEN ROBINSONS RESERVES . . Hursley Lane, Woolard Lane, Whitchurch, Bristol BS14 0QY 01275 891301
TIMSBURY ATHLETIC RESERVES. . . Recreation Ground, North Road, Timsbury, Bath BA2 0JH 01761 472521
WELLS CITY RESERVES . . . . The Athletic Ground, Rowdens Road, Wells BA5 1TU 01749 67997

IN: Bishop Sutton Reserves (R), Shepton Mallet Reserves (R)
OUT: Long Ashton (S – Division Two West), Peasedown Athletic (P), Street Reserves (P)

	Banwell	Berrow	Burnham United Res.	Clevedon United Res.	Combe St Nicholas	Congresbury	Creech St Michael	Crewkerne	Langford Rovers	Nailsea United Res.	Portishead Res.	Weston St Johns Res.	Wrington-Redhill	Yatton Athletic
Banwell		1-1	0-2	2-0	1-3	0-7	0-5	0-6	1-6	2-0	0-6	0-3	0-1	1-3
Berrow	4-2	D	0-3	1-4	0-1	4-2	0-1	4-2	1-2	3-1	1-0	3-2	3-0	4-2
Burnham United Res.	9-2	1-1	I	0-1	2-1	5-3	3-4	3-1	3-0	2-2	3-2	7-0	3-1	3-2
Clevedon United Res.	3-1	2-4	1-2	V	0-1	0-2	2-2	4-1	2-1	2-0	1-6	2-0	0-0	0-2
Combe St Nicholas	6-2	4-0	6-0	0-1		6-1	1-2	1-1	1-0	0-1	2-2	1-1	4-2	1-1
Congresbury	6-2	3-3	2-7	6-0	1-1	T	2-2	4-1	3-5	4-2	1-3	3-3	3-1	3-1
Creech St Michael	8-0	0-2	2-0	2-1	2-0	2-1	W	7-1	1-1	2-3	2-2	4-0	3-0	4-2
Crewkerne	1-0	1-1	0-5	2-0	0-1	1-2	2-2	O	2-1	1-2	1-1	4-1	2-3	0-2
Langford Rovers	6-2	3-1	4-1	0-2	2-2	3-1	1-3	2-0		3-1	3-1	5-3	6-0	7-0
Nailsea United Res.	4-0	2-1	0-1	3-0	1-2	1-1	0-2	3-0	3-3	W	2-3	0-2	3-0	3-0
Portishead Res.	2-0	4-0	2-2	1-0	1-0	2-1	3-1	3-1	2-0	1-1	E	7-0	2-0	3-0
Weston St Johns Res.	5-2	3-8	2-8	0-6	3-2	1-8	3-0	2-0	0-2	1-3	1-6	S	2-1	6-2
Wrington-Redhill	4-0	0-0	0-1	0-0	1-1	2-3	0-1	1-1	2-0	3-0	0-4	4-1	T	2-4
Yatton Athletic	5-2	2-0	1-4	4-3	1-4	1-3	0-1	0-8	1-5	1-1	1-1	0-2	4-1	

Division Two West final table

Team	P	W	D	L	F	A	Pts
Burnham United Res.	26	18	3	5	80	40	57
Portishead Res.	26	17	5	4	70	24	56
Creech St Michael	26	17	5	4	65	30	56
Langford Rovers	26	15	3	8	71	29	48
Combe St Nicholas	26	12	7	7	52	29	43
Congresbury	26	11	10	5	50	59	43
Berrow	26	11	5	10	37	48	38
Clevedon United Res.	26	9	6	11	39	43	33
Nailsea United Res.	26	9	5	12	47	43	32
Weston St Johns Res.	26	8	2	15	40	88	29 −1
Yatton Athletic	26	7	3	15	31	72	27
Wrington-Redhill	26	6	5	14	40	55	26
Crewkerne	26	2	5	15	23	48	23 −2
Banwell	26			23		106	5

SOMERSET COUNTY LEAGUE DIVISION TWO WEST CONSTITUTION 2007-08

IN: Long Ashton (S – Division One East)

OUT: Burnham United (P), Crewkerne (W – Perry Street & District League Premier Division)

SOUTH DEVON LEAGUE

	Bishopsteignton United	Bovey Tracey	Brixham United	Brixham Villa	Buckfastleigh Rangers	East Allington United	Galmpton United	Hele Rovers	Kingsteignton Athletic	Liverton United	Newton Abbot Res.	Newton Abbot Spurs Res.	Totnes & Dartington Res.	Upton Athletic
Bishopsteignton United		3-4	0-3	0-5	1-2	2-0	4-2	1-1	1-0	0-4	5-0	3-0	6-1	5-2
Bovey Tracey	0-0	*P*	1-0	0-3	5-3	3-4	2-1	2-0	4-0	1-2	2-0	4-0	1-1	1-4
Brixham United	2-0	0-2	*R*	1-4	2-1	3-0	1-3	4-0	3-0	0-0	5-0	3-2	6-1	3-1
Brixham Villa	1-0	1-6	3-1	*E*	4-1	5-1	2-1	3-0	7-0	6-2	6-0	6-0	5-1	1-1
Buckfastleigh Rangers	1-0	1-1	2-1	0-4	*M*	4-1	2-3	3-2	1-4	3-0	3-1	1-4	3-1	2-3
East Allington United	6-0	2-5	1-0	1-3	4-3	*I*	0-1	1-2	2-1	4-1	5-1	2-2		W-L
Galmpton United	1-0	3-2	1-3	1-3	3-3	5-3	*E*	1-5	3-3	6-1	5-1	4-3	6-2	2-0
Hele Rovers	1-3	0-6	1-1	0-0	0-2	1-3	2-1	*R*	5-1	4-1	3-0	2-0	5-2	1-2
Kingsteignton Athletic	0-6	0-3	1-3	1-2	3-2	1-4	4-3	5-2		3-1	2-3	3-2	2-0	0-4
Liverton United	1-2	1-6	1-6	2-2	1-7	0-0	0-5	4-2	0-1		2-0	0-0	11-1	2-3
Newton Abbot Res.	3-1	0-4	1-0	0-2	1-2	0-2	0-3	0-0	0-1	0-2	*D*	0-4	1-2	0-5
Newton Abbot Spurs Res.	3-4	1-3	1-0	0-3	1-3	3-2	0-1	0-3	6-4	0-0	3-0	*I*	5-0	1-2
Totnes & Dartington SC Res.	0-2	0-3	0-7	3-0	1-1	1-0	2-1	1-0	2-2	0-4	2-6	0-2	*V*	0-5
Upton Athletic	6-0	1-0	0-0	1-3	3-0	0-0	3-2	4-1	7-2	2-3	1-0	3-1	7-2	

Premier Division

		P	W	D	L	F	A	Pts
Brixham Villa		26	21	3	2	83	24	66
Bovey Tracey		26	17	3	6	71	31	54
Upton Athletic	-3	26	17	3	6	70	32	51
Brixham United		26	14	3	9	58	27	45
Galmpton United		26	14	2	10	68	51	44
Buckfastleigh Rangers		26	12	3	11	56	54	39
Bishopsteignton United		26	12	2	12	49	49	38
East Allington United		26	11	3	12	50	50	36
Liverton United		26	9	5	12	48	62	32
Hele Rovers		26	9	4	13	43	51	31
Kingsteignton Athletic		26	9	2	15	44	76	29
New. Abbot Spurs Res.		26	8	2	16	43	58	26
Totnes & D'ton SC Res.		26	5	4	17	28	93	19
Newton Abbot Res.	-3	26	4	1	21	18	71	10

BELLI CUP

FIRST ROUND
Bishopsteignton United 0 **Brixham United** 4
Bovey Tracey 2 Hele Rovers 0
Buckfastleigh Rangers 1 Liverton United 0
Galmpton United 2 Kingsteignton Athletic 1
Newton Abbot Res. 1 **Brixham Villa** 4
Totnes & Dartington SC Res. 1 **Upton Athletic** 2
QUARTER-FINALS
Bovey Tracey 2 Galmpton United 1
Brixham United 0 **Newton Abbot Spurs Res.** 3
Buckfastleigh Rangers 0 **Brixham Villa** 2
East Allington United 3 Upton Athletic 1
SEMI-FINALS
East Allington United 1 **Bovey Tracey** 3
Newton Abbot Spurs 2 **Brixham Villa** 5
FINAL
(May 11th at Newton Abbot)
Bovey Tracey 4 Brixham Villa 2

SOUTH DEVON LEAGUE PREMIER DIVISION CONSTITUTION 2007-08

BISHOPSTEIGNTON UNITED . . . . Humber Park, Lindridge, Bishopsteignton. . . . . None
BOVEY TRACEY . . . . Mill Marsh Park, Ashburton Road, Bovey Tracey TQ13 9BY . . . . None
BRIXHAM UNITED . . . . Wall Park, Wall Park Road, Brixham TQ5 9UF . . . . None
BRIXHAM VILLA . . . . St Marys Park, Brixham TQ5 9QY . . . . None
CHAGFORD . . . . War Memorial Playing Field, Manor Road, Chagford, Newton Abbot TQ13 8AS . . . . None
EAST ALLINGTON UNITED . . . . Poole Lane, East Allington, Totnes TQ9 7PZ . . . . None
HELE ROVERS . . . . Barton Downs Plaing Fields, Lummaton Cross, Torquay TQ2 8ET . . . . None
IPPLEPEN ATHLETIC . . . . Moor Road Recreation Ground, Moor Road, Ipplepen, Newton Abbot TQ12 5TT . . . . None
KINGSKERSWELL & CHELSTON . . . . Armada Park, Nutbush Lane, Chelston, Torquay TQ2 6SQ . . . . None
KINGSTEIGNTON ATHLETIC . . . . . Broadpark, Broadway, Kingsteignton, Newton Abbot TQ12 3EH . . . . None
NEWTON ABBOT SPURS RESERVES . . Recreation Ground, Marsh Rd, Newton Abbot TQ12 2AR 01626 36534
TORBAY GENTS . . . . Stoodley Knowle Playing Fields, Bishop's Walk, Torquay TQ1 2JA . . . . None
UPTON ATHLETIC . . . . Cricketfield Road, Torquay TQ2 7NP . . . . None
WALDON ATHLETIC . . . . Windmill Hill Playing Fields, Higher Audley Avenue, Torquay TQ2 7PF . . . . Non

IN: Chagford (P), Ipplepen Athletic (P), Kingskerswell & Chelston (P), Torbay Gents (P), Waldon Athletic (P)

OUT: Buckfastleigh Rangers (P – South West Peninsular League Division One East), Galmpton United (P – South West Peninsular League Division One East), Liverton United (P – South West Peninsular League Division One East), Newton Abbot Reserves (R), Totnes & Dartington Sports Club Reserves (R)

Division One

	P	W	D	L	F	A	Pts
Ipplepen Athletic	26	23	0	3	100	38	69
Kingskerswell & Chelston +2	26	18	4	4	89	32	60
Waldon Athletic -4	26	17	4	5	76	42	51
Chagford	26	15	3	8	63	45	48
Upton Athletic Res. -6	26	15	2	9	75	44	41
Torbay Gents	26	13	2	11	72	58	41
Riviera Spurs	26	11	4	11	72	59	37
Loddiswell	26	8	7	11	42	45	31
Abbotskerswell	26	10	1	15	44	64	31
Victoria Rangers	26	9	4	14	60	101	28
Newton '66 -4	26	9	4	13	62	68	27
Ashburton +2	26	6	7	13	39	53	27
Chudleigh Athletic -6	26	4	5	17	38	80	11
Kingsteignton Athletic Res. -3	26	0	3	23	26	129	0

Division Two

	P	W	D	L	F	A	Pts
Brixham Villa Res.	26	17	5	4	59	30	56
Paignton Saints	26	16	5	5	60	26	53
Moretonhampstead	26	16	4	6	56	43	52
Watts Blake Bearne	26	13	4	9	63	44	43
Dartmouth Res.	26	13	4	9	52	41	43
K'kerswell & Chelston Res.	26	10	7	9	52	41	37
East Allington United Res.	26	9	7	10	47	51	34
Harbertonford	26	11	1	14	60	65	34
Paignton Villa	26	7	10	9	44	52	31
Brixham United Res.	26	9	4	13	40	48	31
Galmpton United Res. -6	26	9	8	9	57	59	29
Stoke Gabriel Res.	26	8	5	13	55	63	29
Hele Rovers Res. -9	26	7	6	13	40	53	18
Totnes & Dartington SC 'A'	26	1	2	23	29	98	5

DARTMOUTH CUP FINAL
(May 7th at Liverton United)
Upton Athletic Res. 5 Ipplepen Athletic 1

LIDSTONE CUP FINAL
(May 4th at Brixham United)
Brixham Villa Res. 2 Paignton Saints 1

Division Three

	P	W	D	L	F	A	Pts
Staverton & Landscove +3	26	17	2	7	96	56	56
Langdon	26	14	5	7	73	41	47
Channings Wood -9	26	16	6	4	108	50	45
South Brent	26	11	8	7	72	67	41
Liverton United Res.	26	11	6	9	78	74	39
Buckfastleigh Rangers Res.	26	10	5	11	62	57	35
Brixham Town -6	26	12	5	9	63	64	35
Ilsington Villa +3	26	7	8	11	37	49	32
Newton United	26	8	7	11	45	55	31
Meadowbrook Athletic	26	9	3	14	43	48	30
Foxhole United	26	9	3	14	50	76	30
Teign Village	26	8	5	13	50	68	29
Babbacombe Corinthians	26	5	8	13	38	67	23
Dartmouth 'A' -6	26	8	3	15	39	82	21

Division Four

	P	W	D	L	F	A	Pts
Buckland Athletic Res.	22	21	1	0	111	10	64
Newton Abbot 'A' -6	22	15	3	4	74	25	42
Bovey Tracey Res.	22	13	3	6	64	40	42
Victoria Rangers Res. -6	22	13	5	4	69	43	38
Nova	22	11	5	6	58	42	38
Waldon Athletic Res.	22	12	1	9	52	35	37
Beesands	22	11	2	9	51	46	35
K'kerswell /Chelston 'A' +3	22	9	1	12	69	60	31
Newton '66 Res.	22	6	4	12	31	70	22
Totnes & D'gton SC 'B' +3	22	3	2	17	43	71	14
Chagford Res.	22	3	3	16	29	81	12
Teignmouth Res. -15	22	0	0	22	11	139	-15

RONALD CUP FINAL
(April 30th at Buckfastleigh Rangers)
South Brent 4 Meadowbrook Athletic 4 *aet (5-4p)*

LES BISHOP CUP FINAL
(Not contested)
Buckland Athletic Res. awarded Cup as both Nova and
Newton Abbot 'A' fielded ineligible players in semi-final

Division Five

	P	W	D	L	F	A	Pts
Bishopsteignton United Res.	22	18	2	2	88	29	56
Newton Abbot Spurs 'A'	22	15	5	2	73	34	50
Broadhempston United	22	13	3	6	73	51	42
Watts Blake Bearne Res.	22	12	5	5	85	49	41
Hookhills United	22	12	2	8	51	45	38
Ipplepen Athletic Res. +3	22	7	4	11	44	50	28
Malborough & Hope Cove	22	8	2	12	48	60	26
Loddiswell Res.	22	7	4	11	43	64	25
Abbotskerswell Res.	22	6	2	14	44	72	20
Ashburton Res. -3	22	6	1	15	31	70	16
Chudleigh Athletic Res. -3	22	5	2	15	56	82	14
Brixham Town Res. -6	22	5	4	13	40	70	13

Division Six

	P	W	D	L	F	A	Pts
Staverton & L'cove Res. -6	22	20	1	1	121	25	55
Stoke Fleming -6	22	20	0	2	117	20	54
Stoke Gabriel 'A' +6	22	13	2	7	61	36	47
Broadhempston Utd Res.	22	14	3	5	61	51	45
Torbay Christians	22	9	2	11	49	65	29
Babbacombe Corries Res.	22	8	4	10	46	55	28
Riviera Spurs Res.	22	7	3	12	45	53	24
Paignton Saints Res. -3	22	9	0	13	44	64	24
Paignton Villa Res. -3	22	8	1	13	39	59	22
Moretonhampstead Res. -3	22	7	1	14	33	76	19
Kingsbridge & Kellaton	22	4	3	15	41	101	15
Dittisham United -3	22	2	2	18	29	81	5

BILL TREEBY CUP FINAL
(April 27th at Totnes & Dartington SC)
Newton Abbot Spurs 'A' 2 Hookhills United 0

IVOR ANDREWS CUP FINAL
(April 20th at Liverton United)
Staverton & Landscove Res. 1 Stoke Fleming 0

Division Seven

	P	W	D	L	F	A	Pts
Buckland Athletic 'A'	20	16	1	3	79	30	49
Denbury Athletic	20	16	0	4	73	30	48
Harbertonford Res. -3	20	12	2	6	68	36	35
Dawlish United -6	20	13	1	6	70	31	34
Marldon +3	20	9	3	8	51	54	33
Torbay Rangers	20	9	2	9	67	71	29
South Brent Res.	20	7	3	10	65	74	24
Newton United Res.	20	5	3	12	46	67	18
Langdon Res. -3	20	5	2	13	30	63	14
Ipplepen Athletic 'A' -3	20	5	1	14	43	94	13
Teign Village Res.	20	3	2	15	23	65	11

CLIVE OLNEY CUP FINAL
(April 16th at Newton Abbot Spurs)
Denbury Athletic 3 **Buckland Athletic 'A'** 1
(Denbury Athletic expelled – cup awarded to Buckland 'A')

HERALD CUP

QUARTER-FINALS
Bovey Tracey 3 Hele Rovers 1
Brixham United 1 Newton Abbot Spurs Res. 0
Ipplepen Athletic 2 East Allington United 1
Kingsteignton Athletic 1 **Brixham Villa** 2

SEMI-FINALS
Brixham United 2 Bovey Tracey 1 *(at Newton Abbot Spurs)*
Brixham Villa 4 Ipplepen Athletic 1 *(at Liverton United)*

FINAL
(April 6th at Buckland Athletic)
Brixham Villa 2 Brixham United 1

SOUTH WALES AMATEUR LEAGUE

	AFC Bargoed	Aber Valley YMCA	Abercynon Athletic	Baglan Red Dragons	Blaenrhondda	Caerau United	Cardiff Draconians	Carnetown	Corus Steel	Cwmaman Institute	Llangynwyd Rangers	Llantwit Major	Pantyscallog Village Juniors	Rhydyfelin	Taffs Well Res.	Ynysddu Welfare Crusaders
AFC Bargoed		1-0	1-3	2-0	4-2	2-2	1-1	1-5	0-2	0-3	3-3	2-2	1-2	1-2	1-1	3-4
Aber Valley YMCA	4-0		1-2	2-2	5-1	4-0	6-0	1-0	1-1	0-1	3-0	1-3	1-0	2-1	3-0	2-0
Abercynon Athletic	5-3	1-3	D	3-3	8-0	3-3	7-2	3-0	1-3	1-3	5-2	0-1	1-2	3-1	4-5	4-2
Baglan Red Dragons	3-2	1-2	1-3	I	0-1	1-0	1-1	3-4	1-4	1-1	4-1	4-3	1-1	1-1	3-4	1-0
Blaenrhondda	5-2	1-3	2-2	2-2	V	0-3	3-7	0-2	0-7	0-4	3-0	5-3	4-2	0-3	4-1	0-3
Caerau United	3-2	0-2	2-6	2-0	3-3	I	3-3	3-1	0-0	0-2	1-1	4-0	1-1	2-3	2-1	2-2
Cardiff Draconians	0-2	1-1	0-4	3-1	1-2	0-4	S	1-2	1-4	2-0	2-2	1-3	1-4	2-2	0-4	2-6
Carnetown	6-0	0-2	2-3	0-2	5-1	3-1	0-1	I	3-3	2-4	6-2	5-1	1-2	4-3	0-3	0-2
Corus Steel	6-2	1-4	6-1	1-2	7-0	0-3	8-1	4-1	O	1-4	4-2	5-0	2-0	3-1	3-1	3-1
Cwmaman Institute	6-1	0-0	5-1	8-2	3-0	3-0	3-1	3-0	4-1	N	4-0	3-3	6-0	4-1	3-0	2-1
Llangynwyd Rangers	3-0	1-5	2-1	2-6	8-1	0-2	3-0	2-1	0-2	2-0	O	2-3	1-7	4-1	1-1	4-2
Llantwit Major	2-0	2-4	6-0	6-2	4-0	1-2	3-2	5-0	2-1	1-1	3-0	O	5-1	1-1	4-0	4-2
Pantyscallog Village Juniors	1-1	0-2	4-4	3-2	5-0	4-0	0-0	3-3	2-5	0-3	1-5	2-0	N	2-2	5-0	2-2
Rhydyfelin	2-0	1-3	2-2	0-3	6-1	1-5	1-1	4-3	1-2	2-2	5-0	1-2	0-2	E	0-0	2-1
Taffs Well Res.	2-1	1-2	0-2	4-0	3-3	0-4	2-2	1-2	3-4	3-1	1-1	3-4	3-1	1-1		1-1
Ynysddu Welfare Crusaders	3-1	1-3	3-3	3-1	3-3	2-4	4-2	2-2	2-4	1-0	4-2	3-2	3-3	0-1	2-0	

WWW.CHERRYRED.CO.UK

Division One		P	W	D	L	F	A	Pts
Cwmaman Institute		30	22	5	3	89	26	71
Aber Valley YMCA		30	21	4	5	70	24	67
Corus Steel		30	20	4	6	93	41	64
Llantwit Major		30	17	4	9	79	57	55
Abercynon Athletic		30	14	6	10	86	70	48
Ynysddu Welfare Crusaders		30	14	6	10	67	58	48
Caerau United		30	12	9	9	61	55	45
Pantyscallog Village Juniors		30	10	10	10	61	60	40
Rhydyfelin		30	10	9	11	55	55	39
Carnetown		30	10	4	16	61	66	34
Taffs Well Res.		30	9	7	14	51	62	34
Baglan Red Dragons		30	9	7	14	54	69	34
Llangynwyd Rangers		30	8	4	18	54	85	28
Blaenrhondda		30	7	4	19	44	109	25
Cardiff Draconians		30	4	9	17	41	86	21
AFC Bargoed	-3	30	4	6	20	40	83	15

W J JOHN OWEN CUP

FIRST ROUND

AFC Bargoed 4 Graig 1
Blaenrhondda 5 Carnetown 4 *aet*
Brynna 6 Osborne Athletic 1
Caerau United 0 **Abercynon Athletic** 1
Corus Steel 0 **Rhydyfelin** 1
Llangynwyd Rangers 2 Splott Albion 1
Llanharry 9 Cardiff Draconians 0
Llantwit Major 3 Hirwaun Welfare 1
Pantyscallog Village Juniors 3 Trefelin BGC 2
Pencoed Athletic 1 **Aber Valley YMCA** 7
Taffs Well Res. 5 Ferndale Boys Club 0
Ton & Gelli Boys Club 1 **Ynysddu Welfare Crusaders** 4
(at Ynysddu Welfare Crusaders)
Tonyrefail Welfare 2 **Kenfig Hill** 3 *aet*
Treforest 1 **Baglan Red Dragons** 3
Trelewis Welfare 0 **FC Abercwmboi** 4
Turberville Arms 2 Cwmaman Institute 1

SOUTH WALES AMATEUR LEAGUE DIVISION ONE CONSTITUTION 2007-08

AFC PORTH . . . . Dinas Park, Dinas, Rhondda 07840 294842
ABER VALLEY YMCA . . . . Abertridwr Park, Tridwr Road, Abertridwr, Caerphilly CF83 4DN . . . . None
ABERCYNON ATHLETIC. . . . . Cae Carnetown, Grovers Lane, Carnetown . . . . None
BAGLAN RED DRAGONS . . . . Evans Bevans, Baglan, Port Talbot . . . . None
CAERAU UNITED . . . . Athletic Ground, Humphries Terrace, Caerau, Bridgend CF34 0SG 01656 732471
CARNETOWN . . . . Cae Carnetown, Grovers Lane, Carnetown . . . . None
CORUS STEEL . . . . Corus Playing Fields, Margam, Port Talbot 01639 882066
LLANGYNWYD RANGERS . . . . Llangynwyd Playing Fields, Llangynwyd, Maesteg . . . . None
LLANHARRY. . . . . Recreation Ground, Llanharry . . . . None
LLANTWIT MAJOR . . . . Windmill Lane, Llantwit Major CF61 2SU . . . . None
PANTYSCALLOG VILLAGE JUNIORS. . . . . ICI Riflefields, Pant, Merthyr Tydfil . . . . None
RHYDYFELIN . . . . Upper Boat Playing Field, Hawthorn, Rhondda . . . . None
TAFFS WELL RESERVES . . . . Rhiw Dda'r, Parish Road, Taffs Well CF15 7QB 02920 811080
TREFELIN BGC. . . . . Ynys Park, Cwmavon Road, Port Talbot SA12 8RD 01639 882609
TURBERVILLE ARMS . . . . Ely Playing Fields, Penygraig, Rhondda . . . . None
YNYSDDU WELFARE CRUSADERS. . . . . Ynysddu Welfare Park, Ynysddu . . . . None

IN: AFC Porth (Welsh League Division Three), Llanharry (P), Trefelin BGC (P), Turberville Arms (P)
OUT: AFC Bargoed (R), Blaenrhondda (R), Cardiff Draconians (R), Cwmaman Institute (Welsh League Division Three)

	Brynna	FC Abercwmboi	Ferndale Boys Club	Graig	Hirwaun Welfare	Kenfig Hill	Llanharry	Osborne Athletic	Pencoed Athletic	Splott Albion	Ton & Gelli Boys Club	Tonyrefail Welfare	Trefelin BGC	Treforest	Trelewis Welfare	Turberville Arms
Brynna		7-0	5-1	4-1	5-0	3-3	1-2	3-0	6-1	4-1	5-1	6-4	2-2	4-1	3-1	4-1
FC Abercwmboi	2-4		2-1	1-4	4-1	3-2	3-4	1-0	1-2	1-4	2-2	7-1	2-2	1-2	1-0	0-3
Ferndale Boys Club	5-1	3-1	D	8-2	2-3	0-5	4-4	1-1	2-1	4-2	3-0	6-2	2-2	3-2	3-1	2-4
Graig	7-3	3-6	3-2	I	3-2	2-1	5-5	0-1	2-2	6-1	3-1	2-0	1-6	2-0	3-1	0-3
Hirwaun Welfare	2-1	3-1	5-1	1-8	V	1-4	2-4	3-4	0-6	2-2	3-1	1-1	0-7	0-3	2-2	2-2
Kenfig Hill	4-3	0-2	6-1	6-1	1-4	I	2-3	3-1	6-0	6-2	0-0	4-0	1-4	1-1	2-0	1-2
Llanharry	4-3	4-2	6-1	1-0	3-3	1-1	S	2-0	4-1	4-1	1-2	8-1	1-0	3-1	4-1	1-1
Osborne Athletic	0-5	1-0	5-1	0-2	3-0	3-0	0-4	I	1-2	1-2	1-2	0-3	2-4	1-5	0-3	
Pencoed Athletic	1-1	5-0	3-1	2-5	4-1	1-0	3-1	3-1	O	1-0	0-2	2-0	1-6	2-1	2-0	3-4
Splott Albion	2-5	2-2	2-2	1-1	3-0	4-1	2-7	0-2	1-1	N	2-4	4-1	2-3	1-1	4-0	1-2
Ton & Gelli Boys Club	3-4	3-2	0-1	3-4	1-2	3-1	1-0	4-0	1-5	1-2		1-1	0-3	2-2	1-1	2-1
Tonyrefail Welfare	0-6	1-1	3-2	4-5	1-1	2-6	2-1	5-2	1-4	0-2	0-3	T	0-6	0-1	1-2	2-4
Trefelin BGC	5-2	2-2	5-1	6-0	1-1	5-3	1-1	5-1	4-4	3-2	2-2	6-3	W	6-0	1-0	1-0
Treforest	2-1	6-0	2-2	2-2	2-2	3-2	3-3	2-2	1-4	7-2	1-2	2-1	0-1	O	4-0	3-5
Trelewis Welfare	1-5	3-2	1-3	3-3	2-0	0-5	2-4	0-0	6-1	3-2	1-1	3-0	0-4	0-3		2-2
Turberville Arms	1-1	10-0	3-2	3-1	4-1	5-1	3-1	6-0	5-1	1-4	1-1	2-0	3-4	2-1	0-1	

SECOND ROUND
Aber Valley YMCA 3 Llangynwyd Rangers 2
Baglan Red Dragons 3 Brynna 1
Kenfig Hill 2 **Pantyscallog Village Juniors** 3
Llantwit Major 2 Llanharry 0
Rhydyfelin 2 AFC Bargoed 1
Taffs Well Res. 0 **Abercynon Athletic** 2
Turberville Arms 3 FC Abercwmboi 1
Ynysddu Welfare Crusaders 7 Blaenrhondda 1

QUARTER-FINALS
Pantyscallog Village Juniors 2 **Abercynon Athletic** 4
Rhydyfelin 2 Baglan Red Dragons 0
Turberville Arms 2 **Aber Valley YMCA** 3 *aet*
Ynysddu Welfare Crusaders 0 **Llantwit Major** 4

SEMI-FINALS
Llantwit Major 0 **Aber Valley YMCA** 2
Rhydyfelin 1 **Abercynon Athletic** 3

FINAL
(May 12th at Pontypridd Town)
Aber Valley YMCA 2 Abercynon Athletic 0

Division Two		P	W	D	L	F	A	Pts
Trefelin BGC		30	21	8	1	106	37	71
Turberville Arms		30	19	5	6	86	43	62
Llanharry		30	18	7	5	91	52	61
Brynna		30	18	4	8	107	58	58
Graig		30	15	5	10	81	79	50
Pencoed Athletic		30	15	4	11	68	66	49
Treforest		30	11	8	11	63	58	41
Ton & Gelli Boys Club		30	11	8	11	50	54	41
Kenfig Hill		30	12	4	14	78	60	40
Ferndale Boys Club	-3	30	11	5	14	70	82	35
Splott Albion		30	8	7	15	58	75	31
Trelewis Welfare		30	8	6	16	42	67	30
FC Abercwmboi		30	8	5	17	52	85	29
Hirwaun Welfare		30	7	8	15	48	86	29
Osborne Athletic		30	8	4	18	35	71	28
Tonyrefail Welfare		30	4	4	22	39	101	16

SOUTH WALES AMATEUR LEAGUE DIVISION TWO CONSTITUTION 2007-08

AFC BARGOED . . . . Bargoed Park, Bargoed . . . . None
BLAENRHONDDA . . . . Blaenrhondda Park, Blaenrhondda 01443 774772
BRYNNA . . . . Brynna Welfare Ground, Heol Dewi, Brynna, Pontyclun CF72 9SP 01443 226646
CARDIFF DRACONIANS . . . . Llanidloes Road, Gabalfa, Cardiff CF14 2ST . . . . None
FC ABERCWMBOI . . . . Recreation Ground, Abercwmboi, Rhondda . . . . None
FERNDALE BOYS CLUB . . . . Recreation Ground, Ferndale, Rhondda . . . . None
GILFACH GOCH ATHLETIC . . . . Abercerdin School Field, Kenry Street, Gilfach Goch, Porth CF39 8RS 01443 672262
GRAIG . . . . Pontypridd Town FC, Ynysangharad Park, Pontypridd 01443 486571
HIRWAUN WELFARE . . . . Manchester Place, Hirwaun, Aberdare CF44 9RB 01685 811900
KENFIG HILL . . . . Central Athletic Ground, Croft Goch, Kenfig Hill, Bridgend CF33 6HA . . . . None
PENCOED ATHLETIC . . . . Recreation Ground, Felindre Road, Pencoed, Bridgend CF35 5PB . . . . None
RHOOSE . . . . Ceri Road, Rhoose, Barry CF62 3HF . . . . None
SPLOTT ALBION . . . . University Playing Field, Llanrumney, Cardiff . . . . None
TON & GELLI BOYS CLUB . . . . Ton Pentre FC, Ynys Park, Sawmill Villas, Ton Pentre CF41 7AF 01443 432813
TREFOREST . . . . White Tips Stadium, Treforest 01443 485532
TRELEWIS WELFARE . . . . Welfare Ground, Brondeg, Trelewis . . . . None

IN: AFC Bargoed (R), Blaenrhondda (R), Cardiff Draconians (R), Gilfach Goch Athletic (P – Bridgend & District League), Rhoose (P – Vale of Glamorgan League)
OUT: Llanharry (P), Osborne Athletic (R – Aberdare League), Tonyrefail Welfare (R – Rhondda League), Trefelin BGC (P), Turberville Arms (P)

SOUTH WALES SENIOR LEAGUE

	Bridgend Street	Caerphilly Town	Cogan Coronation	Cwm Welfare	Cwmbach Royal Stars	Fairwater	Fochriw	Grange Albion	Lisvane/Llanishen	Llanrumney United	Nelson Cavaliers	Pant Yr Awel	Penrhiwfer	Penydarren Boys Club	Sully Sports	Tonyrefail BGC
Bridgend Street		7-2	2-2	1-1	2-3	4-2	9-0	2-0	1-1	2-3	4-1	2-1	4-0	1-3	4-2	0-2
Caerphilly Town	0-4		1-1	3-4	3-3	0-8	2-3	1-5	4-3	4-1	1-3	1-2	15-1	2-6	1-3	0-1
Cogan Coronation	0-2	4-0	D	2-3	0-4	1-3	2-0	0-8	1-1	1-2	1-2	2-1	4-0	2-2	2-4	2-2
Cwm Welfare	2-1	4-4	3-1	I	4-1	0-1	4-3	9-2	2-1	3-4	2-1	5-3	0-0	4-0	0-1	1-1
Cwmbach Royal Stars	3-2	1-2	2-1	1-1	V	3-2	2-0	2-1	3-4	2-1	5-3	0-0	4-0	0-1	3-2	5-2
Fairwater	2-0	1-1	3-0	2-2	3-5	I	3-1	1-4	3-3	2-4	3-1	4-1	7-1	0-7	4-3	4-1
Fochriw	1-2	4-4	1-1	1-3	2-0	2-0	S	1-1	6-0	3-1	1-1	0-9	0-4	2-6	0-2	
Grange Albion	0-2	6-1	3-1	2-1	2-2	1-1	7-0	I	2-2	5-2	3-1	0-0	5-1	1-1	1-1	1-2
Lisvane/Llanishen	0-5	0-7	4-0	0-2	2-5	3-4	2-3	0-6	O	2-5	2-0	1-8	3-1	0-6	1-4	0-4
Llanrumney United	1-1	2-1	0-2	0-2	1-0	0-1	3-4	3-3	2-1	N	4-2	1-1	10-0	0-3	3-1	2-4
Nelson Cavaliers	2-0	1-2	3-2	3-3	0-1	0-5	1-5	2-2	2-5	2-1	O	3-2	2-1	10-0	0-5	0-2
Pant Yr Awel	4-1	6-0	1-1	1-1	1-7	1-0	1-0	1-1	4-0	5-3		N	6-0	0-7	0-1	4-2
Penrhiwfer	2-3	0-9	0-6	0-12	2-6	0-6	2-2	1-4	0-4	0-1	1-8	0-3	E	1-8	1-2	0-1
Penydarren Boys Club	2-2	1-1	4-3	1-2	0-0	2-1	4-1	2-0	7-2	1-1	8-1	1-2	8-1		1-2	0-1
Sully Sports	0-0	2-1	4-3	1-1	4-0	4-1	4-3	1-0	4-0	3-2	4-5	3-0	6-1	2-0		1-1
Tonyrefail BGC	5-1	2-1	0-2	2-5	3-3	4-0	0-1	1-3	5-1	1-1	3-2	2-3	3-0	2-2	0-1	

WWW.CHERRYRED.CO.UK

Division One		P	W	D	L	F	A	Pts
Sully Sports		30	21	4	5	83	41	67
Penydarren BC		30	19	7	4	95	27	64
Cwm Welfare		30	16	8	6	92	51	56
Cwmbach RS	+3	30	16	5	9	76	57	56
Grange Albion		30	14	9	7	84	40	51
Tonyrefail BGC		30	15	6	9	65	48	51
Pant Yr Awel		30	14	7	9	65	46	49
Fairwater		30	15	4	11	76	60	49
Bridgend Street		30	14	6	10	71	47	48
Llanrumney Utd		30	11	5	14	61	62	38
Nelson Cavaliers	-3	30	11	3	16	69	79	33
Fochriw	-3	30	9	8	13	53	70	32
Cogan Coronation		30	7	7	16	47	65	28
Caerphilly Town		30	7	6	17	74	89	27
Lisvane/Llanishen		30	6	4	20	46	107	22
Penrhiwfer	-3	30	0	1	29	16	186	-5

Fochriw deducted two goals

PROMOTION PLAY-OFF

(South Wales Amateur League champions v South Wales Senior League champions)

(May 15th at Maesteg Park)

Cwmaman Institute 2 Sully Sports 1

C W BRUTY CUP

FIRST ROUND

AFC Butetown 4 Lisvane/Llanishen 1
AFC Llwynypia 3 St Athan 1
AFC Whitchurch 3 Fochriw 0
Brecon Corries 8 Llanrumney 2
Bridgend Street 2 **Tonyrefail BGC** 2 aet (3-4p)
Butetown 8 Trebanog Rangers 1
Cogan Coronation 1 Cascade 3 aet
Cwmbach RS 3 Nelson Cavaliers 2
Grange Albion 3 Stanleytown 2
Hopkinstown 5 **Fairwater** 8
Mountain Ash 0 Cadoxton Cons 4
Pant Yr Awel 3 St Josephs 0
Penydarren BC 3 AFC Caerphilly 0
Sully Sports 2 Caerphilly Town 2 aet
Tongwynlais 2 Cwm Welfare 7
Ynyshir Albion 9 Penrhiwfer 0
AFC Whitchurch 5 Ynyshir 1
Butetown 2 Tongwynlais 1
Cwmbach Royal Stars 2 Brecon Corinthians 3 aet *(Brecon Corinthians expelled)*
Pant Yr Awel 2 Cadoxton Cons 1
Sully 4 Grange Albion 4 aet (4-2p)
Tonyrefail BGC (w/o) v Cascade (scr.)

SECOND ROUND

AFC Butetown 0 Penydarren BC 3
AFC Llwynypia 0 Fairwater 3

QUARTER-FINALS

AFC Whitchurch 2 Tonyrefail BGC 3
Pant Yr Awel 2 Cwmbach RS 1
Penydarren Boys Club 2 Fairwater 1
Sully Sports 2 Butetown 3

SEMI-FINALS

Pant Yr Awel 2 Butetown 0
Penydarren Boys Club 4 Tonyrefail BGC 0

FINAL

(May 13th at Grange Albion)

Penydarren BC 3 Pant Yr Awel 2

SOUTH WALES SENIOR LEAGUE DIVISION ONE CONSTITUTION 2007-08

BRIDGEND STREET . . . . Willows High School, Willows Avenue, Splott, Cardiff CF24 2YE . . . . None

BUTETOWN . . . . The Marl, Grangetown, Cardiff CF11 7NF . . . . None

COGAN CORONATION . . . . Cogan Recreation Field, Leisure Centre, Hewell Street, Penarth CF64 2JZ 02920 337588

CWM WELFARE . . . . Mount Pleasant Park, Beddau, Pontypridd . . . . None

CWMBACH ROYAL STARS . . . . Blaennant-Y-Groes Rec Ground, Cwmbach, Aberdare CF44 0EA . . . . None

FAIRWATER . . . . Poplar Park, Poplar Road, Fairwater, Cardiff CF5 3PU . . . . None

FOCHRIW . . . . Fochriw Recreation Ground, Fochriw, Bargoed . . . . None

GRANGE ALBION . . . . Coronation Park, Sloper Road, Cardiff CF11 8TB . . . . None

LLANRUMNEY UNITED . . . . Riverside Park, Hartland Road, Llanrumney, Cardiff CF3 4JL . . . . None

NELSON CAVALIERS . . . . Wern Field, Nelson, Treharris CF46 6NL . . . . None

PANT YR AWEL . . . . Lewistown, Blackmill Road, Ogmore Vale, Bridgend CF32 7HU . . . . None

PENYDARREN BOYS CLUB . . . . The Bont, Rockery Road, Penydarren, Merthyr Tydfil 01685 375241

ST ATHAN . . . . St Athan Community Centre, Glyndwr Avenue, St Athan CF64 4PP . . . . None

ST JOSEPHS . . . . Maes-Y-Coed Road, Heath, Cardiff CF14 4HH . . . . None

SULLY SPORTS . . . . Sully Sports & Leisure Club, South Road, Sully, Penarth CF64 5SP 02920 530629

TONYREFAIL BGC . . . . Tynybryn Park, Tonyrefail, Porth, Rhondda CF39 8DA . . . . None

IN: Butetown (P), St Athan (P), St Josephs (P)

OUT: Caerphilly Town (R), Lisvane/Llanishen (R), Penrhiwfer (R)

Note – Trebanog Rangers withdrew during the course of the season. Their results are shown herein but are expunged from the league table	AFC Butetown	AFC Caerphilly	AFC Llwynypia	AFC Whitchurch	Brecon Corinthians	Butetown	Cadoxton Cons	Cascade	Hopkinstown	Mountain Ash Town	St Athan	St Josephs	Stanleytown	Tongwynlais	Trebanog Rangers	Ynyshir Albion
AFC Butetown		2-3	3-1	1-3	3-1	3-4	1-1	4-3	7-1	3-0	1-3	2-3	0-2	6-0	5-1	4-1
AFC Caerphilly	2-2		1-1	0-3	5-3	7-1	2-1	2-1	3-4	7-1	1-2	2-1	3-1	5-1	4-4	2-0
AFC Llwynypia	2-3	0-0	D	3-2	2-0	1-3	2-4	3-1	1-0	7-2	2-5	0-2	2-0	3-0	3-7	0-2
AFC Whitchurch	1-3	5-3	1-2	I	1-1	1-0	2-0	4-1	0-4	2-1	3-4	1-4	2-4	3-0	3-2	3-0
Brecon Corinthians	2-2	8-2	1-3	1-3	V	2-4	1-2	5-0	3-1	2-0	2-5	2-3	3-2	1-0	n/a	0-0
Butetown	1-1	2-1	4-2	5-1	2-0	I	2-0	1-0	8-2	5-0	1-7	2-1	1-0	2-0	6-2	3-1
Cadoxton Cons	1-0	1-1	3-4	0-3	1-1	1-3	S	2-0	5-0	10-1	1-3	3-3	1-2	3-1	3-0	2-0
Cascade	1-1	0-0	1-0	0-5	2-3	2-0	2-1	I	4-0	1-0	1-4	3-5	1-1	2-3	3-2	1-2
Hopkinstown	4-6	3-3	4-3	1-3	2-1	3-1	0-7		O	2-1	0-1	2-4	3-1	3-3	2-1	1-3
Mountain Ash Town	2-6	1-6	1-6	0-5	2-3	0-8	3-2	1-4	4-3	N	0-5	0-2	1-1	1-3	3-6	0-4
St Athan	4-1	6-2	5-3	5-3	3-1	3-2	1-2	4-0	2-2	2-0		2-1	0-0	1-0	7-0	4-2
St Josephs	3-1	4-4	1-0	2-1	7-1	0-3	1-5	1-3	7-2	5-3	1-1	T	2-0	6-2	n/a	5-1
Stanleytown	2-1	2-1	1-0	3-4	1-3	0-1	1-1	2-1	2-2	1-2	5-4	1-2	W	2-3	0-3	0-3
Tongwynlais	2-8	2-1	2-1	2-4	1-2	1-1	2-2	1-1	4-5	1-0	1-1	1-4	0-0	O	1-7	1-3
Trebanog Rangers	n/a	n/a	4-2	3-4	1-2	0-6	n/a	3-3	4-0	2-1	2-3	4-1	2-1	2-4		4-3
Ynyshir Albion	3-1	2-1	1-5	2-3	1-1	1-2	1-3	5-2	1-5	5-2	1-5	2-6	1-2	1-1	4-2	

Division Two		P	W	D	L	F	A	Pts
St Athan		28	23	4	1	90	35	73
Butetown		28	20	3	5	73	40	63
St Josephs		28	19	3	6	87	50	60
AFC Whitchurch		28	17	1	10	74	51	52
AFC Caerphilly		28	11	8	9	71	60	41
Cadoxton Cons		28	11	6	11	58	46	39
AFC Llwynypia		28	12	2	14	57	53	38
Brecon Corries		28	11	4	13	56	61	37
AFC Butetown	-6	28	12	5	11	64	56	35
Cascade	+3	28	8	6	14	45	56	33
Ynyshir Albion		28	9	5	14	49	63	32
Stanleytown	-1	28	8	7	13	37	49	30
Hopkinstown		28	9	3	16	59	94	30
Tongwynlais	+3	28	5	8	15	37	72	26
Mountain Ash	-1	28	2	1	25	31	115	6

Trebanog Rangers – record expunged
Stanleytown deducted 1 goal, Cascade deducted 6 goals

SOUTH WALES SENIOR CUP
(South Wales Amateur League and South Wales Senior League teams)

FIRST ROUND
AFC Caerphilly 2 **Cwmbach RS** 3
Aber Valley YMCA 1 **Pant Yr Awel** 1 *aet* (1-4p)
Cadoxton Cons 1 **Cardiff Draconians** 2
Graig 1 Blaenrhondda 0
Hirwaun Welfare 2 **Llanrumney** 4
Hopkinstown 3 **Penydarren BC** 7
Nelson Cavaliers 1 Bridgend Street 0
Pantyscallog Village Juniors 1 **Stanleytown** 2
Splott Albion 0 **Turberville Arm**s 1
St Athans 0 **Llangynwyd Rangers** 2
Treforest 11 Tonyrefail Welfare 2

SECOND ROUND
AFC Bargoed 1 **Fairwater** 3
AFC Whitchurch 0 **Turberville** 5
Abercynon Athletic 5 Ynyshir 2
Brynna 3 Llangynwyd Rangers 1
Caerphilly Town 2 **Llanrumney** 4
Cardiff Draconians 4 Treforest 1
Cwmbach RS 2 Nelson Cavaliers 1
FC Abercwmboi 1 **Sully Sports** 5
Graig 1 **Penydarren Boys Club** 2
Grange Albion 3 Lisvane/Llanishen 2 *aet*
Osborne Athletic 0 **Cwm Welfare** 5

Pantyscallog VJ 6 Butetown 0
St Josephs 2 AFC Llwynypia 0
Trebanog Rangers 1 **Pant Yr Awel** 2
Trefelin BGC 9 Mountain Ash 0
Trelewis Welfare 1 **Rhydyfelin** 2

THIRD ROUND
Brynna 4 St Josephs 3
Cwm Welfare 1 **Sully Sports** 2
Cwmbach RS 0 **Pant Yr Awel** 1
Fairwater 1 Turberville Arms 0
Pantyscallog Village Juniors 1 Cardiff Draconians 1 *aet* (4-2p)
Penydarren Boys Club 1 **Grange Albion** 1 *aet* (6-7p)
Rhydyfelin 2 **Abercynon Athletic** 2 *aet* (3-5p)
Trefelin BGC 2 **Llanrumney Utd** 3

QUARTER-FINALS
Brynna 4 Abercynon Athletic 2
Grange Albion 5 Fairwater 0
Llanrumney 3 **Pantyscallog VJ** 4
Sully Sports (w/o) v Pant Yr Awel

SEMI-FINALS
Grange Alb. 1 Brynna 1 *aet* (4-2p)
Sully (scr.) v **Pantyscallog** (w/o)

FINAL
(May 11th at Bryntirion Athletic)
Grange Albion 0 **Pantyscallog Village Juniors** 1

WWW.NLNEWSDESK.CO.UK

IN: Caerphilly Town (R), Lisvane/Llanishen (R), Llanbradach Social (P – Taff Ely League), Penrhiwfer (R), Tonypandy Albion (P – Rhonda League)
OUT: Butetown (P), Mountain Ash Town (R – Aberdare League), St Athan (P), St Josephs (P), Trebanog Rangers (WS)

SOUTH WESTERN LEAGUE

	Bodmin Town	Callington Town	Falmouth Town	Goonhavern	Launceston	Liskeard Athletic	Millbrook	Newquay	Penryn Athletic	Penzance	Plymouth A. 'A'	Plym. Parkway	Porthleven	Saltash United	St Austell	St Blazey	Tavistock	Torpoint Athletic	Wadebridge
Bodmin Town		2-0	2-0	4-0	2-0	2-2	5-0	0-1	1-1	3-0	1-0	1-2	2-0	2-1	4-0	0-0	1-3	0-0	2-1
Callington Town	0-4		0-2	8-0	0-3	0-0	3-1	2-2	1-2	4-2	3-2	2-0	2-2	2-2	4-1	0-2	0-4	1-2	0-1
Falmouth Town	1-3	1-0		4-0	0-1	2-3	3-0	3-1	2-2	1-2	0-4	0-1	2-1	1-2	7-0	2-1	5-0	2-2	1-1
Goonhavern	1-3	3-2	1-1		1-9	0-6	2-3	1-3	0-3	1-2	1-1	0-0	0-5	1-6	1-3	0-1	0-2	2-4	1-0
Launceston	1-3	1-2	4-1	6-0		0-2	0-1	0-1	4-2	3-3	2-4	3-0	4-0	0-1	3-1	1-1	1-1	1-1	1-0
Liskeard Athletic	0-4	2-1	5-2	6-0	1-1		5-0	2-0	2-1	2-0	3-0	2-0	1-0	1-1	4-1	0-3	3-1	2-0	2-1
Millbrook	2-1	2-1	1-4	4-0	2-3	1-4		2-2	1-7	0-0	2-3	1-0	0-0	1-7	1-2	1-10	1-2	1-2	2-5
Newquay	0-4	0-1	0-1	1-4	2-4	2-4	3-1		2-2	5-3	1-3	1-5	1-4	2-1	4-1	1-2	2-1	3-0	3-3
Penryn Athletic	0-3	3-3	1-2	4-0	1-2	0-1	2-4	4-2		5-3	1-7	1-1	2-0	2-0	3-1	1-2	2-1	2-3	1-2
Penzance	0-2	2-1	0-0	9-0	3-2	0-3	1-1	1-6	3-1		2-3	1-3	1-1	0-3	0-1	2-2	0-0	0-2	1-1
Plymouth Argyle 'A'	0-0	2-1	0-0	4-0	0-0	1-1	2-0	6-0	4-1	3-0		1-2	4-2	0-1	2-3	0-4	2-0	3-0	1-0
Plymouth Parkway	1-5	1-1	2-0	12-2	1-5	1-1	3-0	2-0	3-2	3-1	1-4		1-2	0-4	4-3	2-3	4-1	3-4	1-1
Porthleven	1-5	3-3	2-2	5-2	2-1	2-1	1-0	3-2	2-0	1-0	0-7	1-1		1-3	2-1	2-0	3-0	3-2	2-0
Saltash United	1-1	1-0	2-0	14-0	2-1	2-1	3-1	3-1	5-0	0-0	2-2	3-0		2-0	0-0	1-5	2-1	2-1	
St Austell	0-7	2-4	2-6	0-4	0-4	0-6	1-1	1-6	1-2	1-1	2-4	1-8	2-2	0-2		0-3	0-4	0-6	2-0
St Blazey	1-0	2-0	4-1	4-1	0-0	2-2	4-0	5-1	3-1	3-0	2-2	2-1	2-3	3-0	1-3		3-2	5-1	1-1
Tavistock	1-1	0-0	2-1	8-0	1-1	1-4	6-3	2-0	4-0	2-2	1-1	2-3	3-1	0-1	3-0	2-7		4-0	2-1
Torpoint Athletic	0-1	0-0	1-3	3-0	3-2	2-3	1-0	0-2	0-2	5-1	0-2	1-4	1-0	1-4	1-1	0-1	0-1		0-0
Wadebridge Town	0-1	1-2	2-0	4-0	0-7	0-2	4-1	1-2	1-1	5-1	0-6	2-3	3-2	0-2	0-2	0-2	3-3	2-3	

	P	W	D	L	F	A	Pts
St Blazey	36	25	7	4	94	37	82
Liskeard Athletic	36	25	7	4	88	34	82
Saltash United	36	25	6	5	88	30	81
Bodmin Town	36	24	7	5	82	21	79
Plymouth Argyle 'A'	36	22	8	6	91	34	74
Plymouth Parkway	36	17	7	12	81	63	58
Tavistock	36	16	8	12	75	57	56
Launceston	36	16	7	13	82	48	55
Porthleven	36	16	7	13	61	64	55
Falmouth Town	36	14	7	15	63	55	49
Torpoint Athletic	36	13	6	17	52	63	45
Newquay	36	13	4	19	65	82	43
Penryn Athletic	36	12	6	18	66	74	42
Callington Town	36	10	9	17	54	60	39
Wadebridge Town	36	8	9	19	47	63	33
Penzance	36	6	10	20	47	84	28
Millbrook	36	7	5	24	41	101	26
St Austell	36	5	5	26	34	116	20
Goonhavern	36	4	3	29	29	154	15

WWW.CHERRYRED.CO.UK

THE SOUTH WESTERN LEAGUE
HAS MERGED WITH THE DEVON
COUNTY LEAGUE.
SEE OPPOSITE FOR CLUB DETAILS

LEAGUE CUP

FIRST ROUND
Falmouth Town 4 Goonhavern 1
Launceston 1 Callington Town 0
Liskeard Athletic 1 **Tavistock** 4
SECOND ROUND
Bodmin Town 0 **Falmouth Town** 1
Millbrook 1 **Launceston** 6
Penryn Athletic 4 Tavistock 1
Penzance 2 **St Austell** 3
Plymouth Argyle 'A' 3 **Newquay** 0
(Plymouth Argyle 'A' expelled)
Plymouth Parkway 1 **St Blazey** 2
Saltash United 0 **Wadebridge Town** 2

Torpoint Athletic 0 **Porthleven** 1
QUARTER-FINALS
Falmouth Town 0 **Launceston** 2
St Austell 0 **Porthleven** 3
St Blazey 7 Newquay 1
Wadebridge Town 0 **Penryn Athletic** 2
SEMI-FINALS
Launceston 0 Penryn Athletic 0 *aet* (5-4p) *(at St Blazey)*
St Blazey 2 Porthleven 1 *aet (at Penryn Athletic)*
FINAL
(May 7th at Wadebridge Town)
Launceston 2 St Blazey 1

SOUTH WEST PENINSULAR LEAGUE

SOUTH WEST PENINSULAR LEAGUE PREMIER DIVISION

BODMIN TOWN . . . . Priory Park, Bodmin PL31 2PP 01208 78165
BUCKLAND ATHLETIC . . . . Homers Heath, Kingskerswell Road, Newton Abbot TQ12 5JU 01626 362602
CLYST ROVERS . . . . Waterslade Park, Clyst Honiton EX5 2BA 01392 366424
CULLOMPTON RANGERS . . . . Speeds Meadow, Duke Street, Cullompton EX15 1DW 01884 33090
DARTMOUTH . . . . Longcross, Townstall Road, Dartmouth TQ5 9LW 01803 832902
ELBURTON VILLA . . . . Haye Road, Elburton, Plymouth PL9 8AR 01752 480025
FALMOUTH TOWN . . . . Bickland Park, Bickland Water Road, Falmouth TR11 4PB 01326 377736
HOLSWORTHY . . . . Upcott Field, North Road, Holsworthy EX22 6HF 01409 254295
IVYBRIDGE TOWN . . . . Erme Valley, Ivybridge PL21 9GX 01752 896686
LAUNCESTON . . . . Pennygillam, Pennygillam Industrial Estate, Launceston PL15 7ED 01566 773279
LISKEARD ATHLETIC . . . . Lux Park, Coldstyle Lane, Liskeard PL14 3HZ 01579 342665
NEWTON ABBOT SPURS . . . . Recreation Ground, Marsh Road, Newton Abbot TQ12 2AR 01626 365343
PLYMOUTH PARKWAY . . . . Bolitho Park, St Peters Road, Manadon, Plymouth PL5 3DL . . . . None
SALTASH UNITED . . . . Kimberley Stadium, Callington Road, Saltash PL12 6DX 01752 845746
ST BLAZEY . . . . Blaise Park, Station Road, St Blazey PL24 2ND 01726 814110
TAVISTOCK . . . . Langsford Park, Crowndale Road, Tavistock PL19 8DD 01822 614447
TORPOINT ATHLETIC . . . . The Mill, Mill Lane, Torpoint PL11 2RE 01752 812889
WITHERIDGE . . . . Sports Field, Fore Street, Witheridge, Tiverton EX16 8PS 01884 861511
*IN: Bodmin Town (P – South Western League), Buckland Athletic (P – Devon County League), Clyst Rovers (S – Western League Division One),
Cullompton Rangers (P – Devon County League), Dartmouth (P – Devon County League), Elburton Villa (P – Devon County League), Falmouth
Town (P – South Western League), Holsworthy (P – Devon County League), Ivybridge Town (P – Devon County League), Launceston (P – South
Western League), Liskeard Athletic (P – South Western League), Newton Abbot Spurs (P – Devon County League), Plymouth Parkway (P – South
Western League), Saltash United (P – South Western League), St Blazey (P – South Western League), Tavistock (P – South Western League),
Torpoint Athletic (P – South Western League), Witheridge (P – Devon County League)*

SOUTH WEST PENINSULAR LEAGUE DIVISION ONE EAST CONSTITUTION 2007-08

ALPHINGTON . . . . The Chronicles, Alphington, Exeter EX2 8SW 01392 279556
APPLEDORE . . . . Marshford, Churchill Way, Appledore EX39 1PA 01237 477099
AXMINSTER TOWN . . . . Sector Lane, Axminster EX13 5BP . . . . None
BUCKFASTLEIGH RANGERS . . . Duckspond Playing Fields, Duckspond Road, Buckfastleigh TQ11 0DJ 01364 642853
BUDLEIGH SALTERTON . . . . Greenway Lane, Budleigh Salterton EX9 6SG 01395 443850
CREDITON UNITED . . . . Lords Meadow, Commercial Road, Crediton EX17 1ER. 01363 774671
EXMOUTH TOWN . . . . King George V Ground, Southern Road, Exmouth EX8 3EE 01395 263348
GALMPTON UNITED . . . . War Memorial Playing Field, Greenway Road, Galmpton, Brixham TQ5 0LR . . . . . . None
LIVERTON UNITED . . . . Football & Sports Club, Halford, Liverton, Newton Abbot. . . . . None
NEWTON ABBOT . . . . Coach Road Stadium, Coach Road, Newton Abbot TQ12 5DS 01626 335011
OKEHAMPTON ARGYLE . . . . Simmons Park, Mill Road, Okehampton. 01837 53997
OTTERY ST MARY . . . . Washbrook Meadows, Butts Road, Ottery St Mary EX11 1EL 01404 813539
PLYMSTOCK UNITED . . . . Dean Cross, Dean Cross Road, Plymstock PL9 7AZ 01752 406776
STOKE GABRIEL . . . . C J Churchward Memorial Ground, Broadley Lane, Stoke Gabriel, Totnes TQ9 6RR 01803 782223
TEIGNMOUTH . . . . Coombe Valley, Coombe Lane, Teignmouth TQ14 9EZ 01626 776688
TOTNES & DARTINGTON SC . . . . Foxhole Sports Ground, Dartington TQ9 6EB 01803 868032
UNIVERSITY OF EXETER. . . . . University Sports Ground, Topsham EX4 4QJ. 01392 264452
*IN: Alphington (S – Devon County League), Appledore (S – Devon County League), Axminster Town (P – Devon & Exeter League Premier Division),
Buckfastleigh Rangers (P – South Devon League Premier Division), Budleigh Salterton (S – Devon County League), Crediton United (S – Devon
County League), Exmouth Town (P – Devon & Exeter League Premier Division), Galmpton United (P – South Devon League Premier Division),
Liverton United (P – South Devon League Premier Division), Newton Abbot (S – Devon County League), Okehampton Argyle (P – Devon & Exeter
League Premier Division), Ottery St Mary (S – Devon County League), Plymstock United (S – Devon County League), Stoke Gabriel (S – Devon
County League), Teignmouth (S – Devon County League), Totnes & Dartington SC (S – Devon County League), University of Exeter (S – Devon
County League)*

SOUTH WEST PENINSULAR LEAGUE DIVISION ONE WEST CONSTITUTION 2007-08

CALLINGTON TOWN . . Ginsters Marshfield Stadium, Callington Comm. College, Launceston Rd, Callington PL17 7DR 01579 382647
CAMELFORD . . . . Trefrew Park, Trefrew, Camelford PL32 9TS . . . . None
DOBWALLS . . . . Lantoom Park, Duloe Road, Dobwalls PL14 4LR. . . . . None
FOXHOLE STARS . . . . Goverseth Playing Fields, Goverseth Terrace, Foxhole PL26 7XX. 01726 824615
GOONHAVERN. . . . . Reen Manor Parc, Reen, Perranporth TR6 0AN 01872 572493
HAYLE . . . . Trevassack Park, Viaduct Hill, Hayle TR27 4HT. 01736 757157
MILLBROOK . . . . Mill Park, off Southdown Road, Millbrook, Torpoint PL11 1EN 01752 822113
MOUSEHOLE . . . . Trungle Parc, Paul, Penzance TR19 6XB . . . . None
NEWQUAY . . . . Mount Wise, Clevedon Road, Newquay TR7 2BU 01637 872935
PENRYN ATHLETIC . . . . Kernick, Kernick Road, Penryn TR10 8NT 01326 375182
PENZANCE . . . . Penlee Park, Alexandra Place, Penzance TR18 4NE 01736 361964
PORTHLEVEN . . . . Gala Parc, Mill Lane, Porthleven TR13 9LQ 01326 574754
ST AUSTELL . . . . Poltair Park, Poltair Road, St Austell PL25 4LR. 01726 66099
VOSPERS OAK VILLA . . . . The Mill, Ferndale Road, Weston Mill, Plymouth PL2 2EL 01752 363352
WADEBRIDGE TOWN . . . . Bodieve Park, Bodieve Road, Wadebridge PL27 6EA 01208 812537
WENDRON CC UNITED . . . . Underlane, Carnkie, Wendron, Helston TR13 0EH. 01209 860946
*IN: Callington Town (S – South Western League), Camelford (P – East Cornwall League Premier Division), Dobwalls (P – East Cornwall League
Premier Division), Foxhole Stars (P – East Cornwall League Premier Division), Goonhavern (S – South Western League), Hayle (P – Cornwall
Combination), Millbrook (S – South Western League), Mousehole (S – Cornwall Combination), Newquay (S – South Western League), Penryn
Athletic (S – South Western League), Penzance (S – South Western League), Porthleven (S – South Western League), St Austell (S – South Western
League), Vospers Oak Villa (S – Devon County League), Wadebridge Town (S – South Western League), Wendron CC United (P – Cornwall
Combination)*

SOUTHAMPTON LEAGUE

	AFC Target	Academicals	Botley Village	Burridge Sports	Bush Hill	Comrades	Forest Town NFC	Hamble Harriers	Malvern	Northend United	Nursling	Otterbourne Res.	Solent WTL
AFC Target		1-2	2-1	4-2	2-1	0-1	n/a	4-0	0-5	1-2	2-9	1-3	0-4
Academicals	2-3	*P*	3-8	7-1	3-5	0-1	2-2	3-0	4-4	2-3	1-4	6-0	0-3
Botley Village	2-1	1-2	*R*	6-1	2-3	1-1	1-1	5-1	2-1	2-2	1-1	5-2	2-2
Burridge Sports	2-2	0-4	2-5	*E*	0-2	1-5	n/a	1-1	W-L	1-1	1-2	2-3	0-3
Bush Hill	6-0	4-2	2-1	5-0	*M*	3-1	n/a	8-1	0-0	9-0	0-3	4-0	4-0
Comrades	3-2	3-1	0-3	10-0	2-0	*I*	n/a	5-0	4-2	3-0	1-0	1-3	4-2
Forest Town NFC	n/a	3-2	2-3	3-0	n/a	3-3	*E*	n/a	n/a	n/a	0-4	n/a	3-1
Hamble Harriers	1-2	1-4	1-3	0-1	0-3	0-5	0-0	*R*	4-2	1-1	0-4	2-4	1-2
Malvern	3-1	2-0	1-6	1-1	2-1	0-2	1-2	5-1		W-L	2-2	1-1	3-3
Northend United	1-1	0-3	1-2	2-1	1-4	0-2	n/a	3-3	3-4	*D*	2-8	2-1	2-3
Nursling	7-2	10-1	0-0	2-1	2-2	0-1	4-0	6-0	5-1	*I*		1-1	3-0
Otterbourne Res.	2-3	0-1	1-2	2-2	1-2	0-4	n/a	5-1	3-0	5-2	0-3	*V*	0-2
Solent WTL	1-1	3-0	2-2	1-1	0-0	2-2	2-1	3-2	3-0	2-1	2-3	4-1	

Premier Division

Team	P	W	D	L	F	A	Pts
Comrades	22	17	2	3	61	20	53
Nursling	22	15	5	2	75	21	50
Bush Hill	22	15	3	4	68	23	48
Botley Village	22	12	6	4	62	32	42
Solent WTL	22	11	7	4	47	57	40
Academicals	22	9	1	12	51	46	28
Malvern	22	7	6	9	39	51	27
Otterbourne Res.	22	7	3	12	38	60	24
AFC Target	22	7	3	12	35	58	24
Northend United	22	4	4	14	29	68	16
Burridge Sports	22	2	6	14	21	68	12
Hamble Harriers	22	1	3	18	21	79	6

SOUTHAMPTON LEAGUE PREMIER DIVISION CONSTITUTION 2007-08

AFC SOLENT . . . . Green Park, Wimpson Lane, Millbrook, Southampton . . . . Non
AFC TARGET . . . . Cutbush Lane, West End, Southampton SO18 2GF 023 8046 237
BTC SOUTHAMPTON . . . . BTC Sports Ground, Stoneham Lane, Eastleigh, Southampton SO16 2PA 023 8055 661
BOTLEY VILLAGE . . . . Botley Recreation Ground, High Street, Botley, Southampton SO30 2EA 01489 78044
BURRIDGE SPORTS . . . . Allotment Road, Sarisbury SO31 7AP . . . . Non
BUSH HILL . . . . Green Park, Green Lane, Millbrook, Southampton . . . . Non
CAPITAL . . . . Fryern Recreation Ground, Green Ways, Chandlers Ford, Eastleigh, Southampton . . . . Non
COMRADES . . . . BTC Sports Ground, Stoneham Lane, Eastleigh, Southampton SO16 2PA 023 8055 661
HEDGE END RANGERS . . . Norman Rodaway Recreation Ground, Heathouse Lane, Hedge End, Southampton . . . . Non
MALVERN . . . . Cutbush Lane, West End, Southampton SO18 5RY . . . . Non
NORTHEND UNITED . . . . Test Park, Porlock Road, Millbrook, Southampton SO16 9JD . . . . Non
NURSLING . . . . Nursling Rec, Nursling Street, Romsey Road, Nursling, Southampton SO16 0XW . . . . Non
SOLENT WTL . . . . Veracity Ground, Merry Oak Road, Merryoak, Southampton . . . . Non
SPARTANS . . . . Gany Warily, Newlands Road, Blackfield, Southampton SO45 1GA 023 8089360

IN: AFC Solent (P), BTC Southampton (P), Capital (P), Hedge End Rangers (P), Spartans (P)
OUT: Academicals (S – Hampshire League), Forest Town NFC (WS), Hamble Harriers (F), Otterbourne Reserves (S – Hampshire Premier League Combination)

Senior Division One

Team		P	W	D	L	F	A	Pts
Team Solent		24	18	3	3	86	30	57
Spartans		24	18	2	4	74	26	56
AFC Solent		24	14	5	5	81	35	47
Capital		24	15	2	7	66	45	47
BTC Southampton		24	13	2	9	63	46	41
AFC Hop		24	12	2	10	53	47	38
Hedge End Rangers		24	11	4	9	32	35	37
Burridge AFC		24	11	1	12	46	49	34
Hythe Aztecs		24	7	7	10	41	66	28
Bishopstoke WMC		24	7	1	16	64	69	22
Compton	-1	24	4	5	15	39	72	16
Priory Rovers	-1	24	3	3	18	28	77	11
Test Park Rangers		24	2	5	17	31	107	11

Senior Combination

Team		P	W	D	L	F	A	Pts
Comrades Res.		18	13	2	3	53	20	41
Team Solent Res.	-3	18	13	4	1	72	21	40
Durley Res.		18	9	3	6	34	28	30
Wellow Res.		18	8	3	7	47	36	27
Hythe & Dibden Res.		18	8	3	7	38	32	27
Capital Res.		18	7	4	7	57	53	25
Michelmersh &T. Res.		18	4	6	8	31	36	18
Netley C. Spts Res.	-1	18	5	4	9	24	43	18
Stoneham Res.		18	5	2	11	31	56	17
QK Southampton Res.		18	2	1	15	11	73	7

Junior Division One

Team		P	W	D	L	F	A	Pts
Sporting Wessex		20	15	3	2	65	26	48
AP Sports		20	14	3	3	70	28	45
Freemantle		20	13	4	3	57	25	42
Langley Manor		20	13	3	4	64	40	42
Inmar		20	10	5	5	51	38	35
MMS (Southampton)		20	10	3	7	41	40	33
WEB		20	7	4	9	28	38	25
Otterbourne 'A'		20	4	2	14	27	48	14
Braishfield		20	4	0	16	20	51	12
Hythe Aztec Res.		20	3	2	15	33	75	11
Stoneham 'A'	-3	20	1	4	15	31	78	4

Junior Division Two

Team	P	W	D	L	F	A	Pts
Gardeners AFC	18	16	2	0	66	16	50
Sholing Sports	18	10	3	5	49	30	33
East Boldre	18	10	2	6	52	35	32
Inter Northam	18	7	6	5	31	25	27
Lowford	18	7	4	7	36	47	25
Cadnam United	18	8	0	10	38	44	24
BTC Southampton Res.	18	5	6	7	33	28	21
London Airways	18	6	3	9	43	54	21
Beaney Park	18	5	1	12	37	58	16
Bacardi	18	2	1	15	20	64	7

Junior Division Three

Team	P	W	D	L	F	A	Pts
AFC Redbridge	16	14	0	2	41	14	42
Rownhams	16	12	1	3	38	19	37
Allbrook	16	11	2	3	53	23	35
Hedge End Town	16	8	2	6	44	30	26
Monks Brook	16	7	2	7	33	29	23
Hamble Harrier Res.	16	7	0	9	35	37	21
DMH Gleneagles	16	5	1	10	18	25	16
Gate	16	2	0	14	15	71	6
Priory Rovers Res.	16	1	2	13	22	51	5

Junior Division Four

Team		P	W	D	L	F	A	Pts
Compton Res.		18	14	3	1	61	21	45
S & B Sports		18	12	4	2	55	22	40
AFC Energy		18	12	0	6	42	41	36
Nimbin United		18	7	7	4	31	25	28
AC Sholing		18	7	4	7	34	37	25
Academicals Res.		18	6	3	9	25	31	21
Burridge Sports Res.		18	6	3	9	37	47	21
FC Flames		18	5	5	8	27	34	20
MMS (So'pton) Res.		18	3	2	13	24	46	11
Nova Foresta		18	2	1	15	24	46	7

Junior Division Five

Team		P	W	D	L	F	A	Pts
TBC	-1	20	14	2	2	75	34	45
Wheatshield Wdrs		20	14	2	4	75	36	44
Forest Town NFC Res.		20	12	5	3	59	24	41
Southside United	-2	20	11	6	3	72	31	37
Swan		20	9	4	7	59	56	31
Netley Marsh		20	9	2	9	53	50	29
B. Waltham T. Res.	-2	20	8	3	9	36	24	25
R S Southampton		20	7	2	11	51	59	23
Michelmersh & T. 'A'		20	4	4	12	34	67	16
Botley Village Res.	-1	20	2	3	15	24	91	8
East Boldre Res.		20	2	1	17	33	99	7

Junior Division Six

Team	P	W	D	L	F	A	Pts
Sparky Albion	20	14	1	5	68	25	43
AFC Aldermoor	20	13	3	4	72	39	42
Lowford Res.	20	14	0	6	62	43	42
Stoneham 'B'	20	11	2	7	47	32	35
Academicals 'A'	20	11	2	7	54	42	35
Wombles	20	11	2	7	41	35	35
Freemantle Res.	20	10	0	10	65	54	30
QK Southampton 'A'	20	7	0	13	20	50	21
Real Way	20	5	2	13	36	54	17
AFC Southampton	20	3	4	13	41	80	13
AFC Terminal	20	2	2	16	16	67	8

SENIOR CUP FINAL
(April 23rd at Hamble ASSC)
Bush Hill 4 Comrades 3

ROY WIGHTMAN JUNIOR CUP FINAL
(May 7th at Blackfield & Langley)
Forest Town NFC Res. 2 Gardeners AFC 1

ROY VALLANCE JUNIOR PLATE FINAL
(May 7th at Blackfield & Langley)
Netley Marsh 1 Wheatsfield Wanderers 0

SOUTHERN LEAGUE

	Banbury United	Bath City	Cheshunt	Chippenham Town	Cirencester Town	Clevedon Town	Corby Town	Gloucester City	Halesowen Town	Hemel Hempstead Tn	Hitchin Town	King's Lynn	Maidenhead United	Mangotsfield United	Merthyr Tydfil	Northwood	Rugby Town	Stamford	Team Bath	Tiverton Town	Wealdstone	Yate Town
Banbury United		1-1	1-1	5-0	2-0	2-0	1-0	1-2	1-1	1-3	2-3	3-3	0-2	1-2	2-2	0-2	2-3	0-0	0-2	4-3	3-1	1-2
Bath City	1-0		5-0	1-0	1-0	0-3	3-1	2-2	3-0	1-0	1-2	1-1	2-1	2-0	4-0	0-0	6-0	1-2	5-0	1-1	2-1	1-1
Cheshunt	1-2	0-2		3-0	4-0	2-1	3-1	0-3	0-0	2-0	1-2	2-2	3-2	1-3	2-1	1-2	1-2	4-2	0-2	1-0	0-0	2-3
Chippenham Town	1-1	0-1	1-0	*P*	0-0	2-0	2-1	1-0	1-1	2-2	3-0	1-3	2-1	0-0	0-1	5-1	2-3	1-1	1-0	5-3	2-0	3-1
Cirencester Town	0-2	0-1	3-3	1-3	*R*	1-1	2-3	1-3	0-2	4-2	0-0	1-6	1-0	1-1	0-0	6-3	3-1	1-0	0-1	4-1	0-3	0-0
Clevedon Town	1-1	0-2	1-3	2-3	5-1	*E*	1-1	1-2	2-0	1-0	2-2	3-1	1-1	1-0	3-1	3-0	2-3	0-1	0-2	2-2	2-4	4-0
Corby Town	0-3	0-2	3-2	3-3	0-0	1-1	*M*	2-3	0-1	0-0	2-3	3-0	1-0	0-2	3-2	0-0	1-2	1-2	1-3	0-0	2-4	4-0
Gloucester City	1-4	0-4	0-2	1-0	0-0	3-1	2-0	*I*	1-3	3-4	1-1	0-2	2-1	1-2	3-3	3-3	3-2	1-1	2-2	1-0	0-2	0-3
Halesowen Town	3-2	3-4	1-0	2-1	4-2	1-0	1-3	1-1	*E*	3-1	2-2	2-3	1-3	0-0	1-0	2-2	1-0	4-0	1-1	2-2	5-3	3-0
Hemel Hempstead Town	2-0	1-0	2-0	0-0	4-1	2-3	3-1	3-3	0-0	*R*	2-0	1-5	1-0	1-1	3-0	4-0	4-2	1-1	0-0	4-1	5-2	1-2
Hitchin Town	1-2	0-4	0-1	3-2	1-1	1-0	1-0	2-2	1-0	1-1		0-1	2-1	1-0	1-0	1-0	1-2	3-1	1-3	2-3	4-2	4-2
King's Lynn	2-0	1-1	4-1	3-0	2-0	0-0	2-1	0-1	0-2	2-1	1-0	*D*	0-1	3-0	0-2	1-2	2-1	3-1	1-0	4-1	1-0	4-0
Maidenhead United	2-0	0-2	3-0	0-0	1-0	0-5	1-3	1-0	1-0	1-1	3-0	1-1	*I*	3-0	1-1	2-0	3-0	3-0	0-2	1-1	3-0	0-1
Mangotsfield United	2-3	0-0	2-2	0-2	1-1	0-0	1-0	3-4	1-0	0-2	2-2	0-0	0-0	*V*	2-2	0-0	1-0	1-1	1-1	1-0	3-1	0-1
Merthyr Tydfil	0-0	2-1	1-0	0-1	2-0	1-0	0-0	1-1	2-3	4-1	5-1	0-0	1-1	0-0	*I*	0-2	2-1	2-1	1-2	1-0	3-0	0-0
Northwood	1-2	1-1	2-4	2-1	0-2	0-2	1-3	0-2	0-3	2-0	1-2	0-2	0-1	0-1	0-1	*S*	3-3	2-2	1-3	1-2	1-2	3-0
Rugby Town	1-2	1-4	2-1	0-1	1-3	2-3	3-0	2-4	4-3	0-3	0-0	1-0	1-1	0-2	2-0	3-0	*I*	2-6	1-0	4-1	2-0	0-1
Stamford	0-1	2-3	2-0	1-3	1-2	3-0	1-0	3-2	2-0	4-1	2-0	1-0	1-2	0-2	1-0	2-1	1-1	*O*	1-1	2-1	2-2	0-0
Team Bath	3-0	1-2	0-0	4-1	4-1	3-1	3-2	2-1	2-0	1-3	1-0	1-2	0-3	1-2	1-0	2-0	3-0	1-0	*N*	1-1	2-3	3-0
Tiverton Town	3-0	0-0	1-0	0-1	3-1	3-0	2-1	1-3	1-1	3-4	2-1	0-0	0-1	2-3	1-0	0-2	1-1	1-3	0-3		2-1	3-0
Wealdstone	4-0	0-4	5-2	3-1	2-2	3-3	2-1	0-1	1-3	2-2	4-0	1-1	0-3	1-1	1-2	1-1	2-1	2-5	2-1	2-1		0-1
Yate Town	2-2	1-2	3-0	2-3	2-0	1-4	2-2	2-2	2-2	4-1	2-5	3-0	0-0	2-2	2-2	1-0	2-3	3-1	3-0	0-1	2-4	

Premier Division

	P	HOME					AWAY					TOTAL					
		W	D	L	F	A	W	D	L	F	A	W	D	L	F	A	Pts
Bath City	42	13	5	3	43	15	14	5	2	41	14	27	10	5	84	29	91
Team Bath	42	14	3	4	39	19	9	6	6	27	23	23	9	10	66	42	78
King's Lynn	42	15	3	3	37	12	7	7	7	32	28	22	10	10	69	40	76
Maidenhead United	42	11	6	4	31	17	9	4	8	27	19	20	10	12	58	36	70
Hemel Hempstead Town	42	12	6	3	44	22	7	6	8	35	38	19	12	11	79	60	69
Halesowen Town	42	11	6	4	43	30	7	7	7	23	23	18	13	11	66	53	67
Chippenham Town	42	11	6	4	35	20	8	3	10	26	36	19	9	14	61	56	66
Stamford	42	10	4	7	31	23	6	7	8	34	39	16	11	15	65	62	59
Mangotsfield United	42	5	11	5	21	22	8	8	5	23	23	13	19	10	44	45	58
Gloucester City	42	6	6	9	28	40	9	7	5	39	30	15	13	14	67	70	58
Hitchin Town	42	11	3	7	31	28	5	6	10	24	40	16	9	17	55	68	57
Merthyr Tydfil	42	10	7	4	28	15	4	7	10	19	31	14	14	14	47	46	56
Banbury United	42	6	6	9	33	33	9	4	8	27	31	15	10	17	60	64	55
Yate Town	42	7	7	7	41	36	7	5	9	18	35	14	12	16	59	71	54
Tiverton Town	42	10	3	8	30	26	4	5	12	26	41	14	8	20	56	67	50
Cheshunt	42	10	3	8	34	29	4	4	13	22	42	14	7	21	56	71	49
Rugby Town	42	10	2	9	32	32	5	2	14	26	47	15	4	23	58	79	49
Clevedon Town	42	6	7	8	32	30	6	5	10	28	31	12	12	18	60	61	48
Wealdstone	42	8	6	7	38	36	5	3	13	31	46	13	9	20	69	82	48
Corby Town	42	5	6	10	27	33	5	3	13	25	36	10	9	23	52	69	39
Cirencester Town	42	6	6	9	29	36	3	6	12	17	40	9	12	21	46	76	39
Northwood	42	4	4	13	23	37	4	6	11	21	37	8	10	24	44	74	34

PLAY-OFFS

SEMI-FINALS
(May 1st)
King's Lynn 0 **Maidenhead United** 1 *Att* 1,154
Team Bath 3 Hemel Hempstead Town 1 *Att* 367
FINAL
(May 6th at Bath City)
Team Bath 0 **Maidenhead United** 1 *Att* 643

DATES & GATES

Each cell shows the fixture date (top) and attendance / gate (bottom). Row = home team listed at left; columns are read left-to-right as Yate Town … Banbury United.

	Yate Town	Wealdstone	Tiverton Town	Team Bath	Stamford	Rugby Town	Northwood	Merthyr Tydfil	Mangotsfield United	Maidenhead United	King's Lynn	Hitchin Town	Hemel Hempstead Tn	Halesowen Town	Gloucester City	Corby Town	Clevedon Town	Cirencester Town	Chippenham Town	Cheshunt	Bath City	Banbury United
Banbury United	5 Dec / 250	23 Dec / 436	24 Mar / 362	14 Apr / 313	7 Apr / 351	28 Dec / 464	3 Feb / 346	13 Jan / 358	9 Dec / 318	28 Apr / 455	14 Nov / 420	28 Aug / 406	3 Mar / 347	1 Jan / 460	7 Oct / 440	3 Apr / 217	19 Aug / 316	20 Jan / 351	16 Jan / 248	5 Sep / 373	9 Sep / 473	—
Bath City	14 Oct / 708	11 Nov / 669	22 Aug / 752	26 Dec / 850	2 Sep / 581	28 Apr / 1,369	26 Aug / 642	20 Mar / 692	3 Feb / 948	14 Nov / 923	23 Sep / 633	9 Dec / 609	27 Jan / 733	1 Jan / 700	10 Mar / 917	24 Mar / 801	10 Oct / 665	14 Nov / 505	9 Apr / 2,044	13 Jan / 627	—	17 Feb / 830
Cheshunt	3 Mar / 132	1 Jan / 302	23 Sep / 147	2 Dec / 90	20 Jan / 165	17 Mar / 144	22 Aug / 138	28 Apr / 239	23 Dec / 143	14 Nov / 135	17 Feb / 243	28 Oct / 185	9 Apr / 221	14 Apr / 202	26 Aug / 161	17 Apr / 152	2 Sep / 141	3 Feb / 121	16 Dec / 133	—	7 Oct / 207	18 Nov / 173
Chippenham Town	7 Apr / 572	9 Dec / 447	3 Feb / 481	14 Nov / 324	19 Aug / 491	18 Nov / 479	2 Sep / 429	7 Oct / 526	28 Oct / 566	17 Feb / 461	2 Sep / 488	20 Jan / 422	9 Sep / 455	9 Sep / 530	31 Mar / 482	31 Mar / 359	5 Dec / 325	28 Aug / 558	—	21 Apr / 441	1 Jan / 1,250	10 Mar / 478
Cirencester Town	3 Oct / 218	27 Jan / 204	11 Nov / 171	24 Mar / 197	23 Dec / 117	24 Feb / 157	13 Jan / 139	24 Feb / 210	22 Aug / 195	16 Dec / 153	2 Sep / 185	10 Mar / 142	2 Dec / 150	3 Feb / 177	9 Apr / 356	13 Mar / 341	30 Jan / 106	—	26 Dec / 320	28 Nov / 110	31 Mar / 460	21 Apr / 169
Clevedon Town	14 Nov / 237	7 Oct / 225	9 Apr / 235	22 Aug / 167	1 Jan / 277	9 Sep / 142	20 Jan / 154	2 Dec / 257	18 Nov / 354	24 Mar / 186	9 Dec / 207	21 Apr / 177	7 Nov / 178	3 Feb / 213	1 Jan / 303	26 Aug / 141	—	17 Feb / 159	13 Jan / 301	13 Jan / 264	13 Jan / 258	23 Jan / 124
Corby Town	28 Apr / 162	14 Oct / 255	2 Sep / 201	17 Oct / 145	28 Aug / 265	28 Aug / 142	6 Dec / 110	20 Jan / 201	2 Dec / 151	1 Jan / 252	20 Feb / 284	18 Nov / 329	3 Feb / 203	3 Feb / 167	23 Dec / 151	—	13 Mar / 141	27 Jan / 142	13 Jan / 342	17 Apr / 218	22 Aug / 307	3 Apr / 217
Gloucester City	30 Jan / 299	14 Apr / 392	23 Sep / 307	14 Oct / 400	28 Oct / 344	7 Apr / 373	23 Sep / 303	26 Dec / 531	14 Nov / 388	19 Aug / 406	3 Feb / 284	2 Sep / 320	13 Jan / 337	9 Dec / 234	—	16 Dec / 394	12 Dec / 693	27 Jan / 218	17 Apr / 218	11 Nov / 245	16 Feb / 282	2 Dec / 363
Halesowen Town	17 Feb / 388	24 Mar / 424	26 Aug / 307	27 Jan / 403	21 Apr / 525	5 Dec / 196	28 Oct / 110	9 Apr / 402	6 Jan / 339	9 Sep / 306	20 Feb / 308	18 Nov / 329	9 Dec / 332	—	31 Mar / 421	10 Mar / 255	13 Mar / 301	20 Feb / 141	20 Mar / 342	10 Mar / 218	23 Feb / 243	26 Dec / 429
Hemel Hempstead Town	16 Dec / 188	5 Sep / 374	2 Sep / 204	11 Nov / 245	7 Jan / 193	14 Apr / 204	17 Apr / 246	10 Mar / 316	20 Jan / 286	1 Jan / 252	3 Feb / 251	22 Aug / 184	—	9 Dec / 332	16 Dec / 282	12 Dec / 142	24 Apr / 170	28 Aug / 173	31 Mar / 234	23 Jan / 214	23 Feb / 235	6 Feb / 205
Hitchin Town	14 Apr / 200	5 Sep / 374	2 Dec / 305	13 Jan / 323	7 Nov / 287	3 Apr / 189	17 Apr / 210	24 Mar / 251	17 Feb / 320	12 Dec / 256	22 Aug / 314	—	20 Mar / 184	21 Apr / 177	3 Apr / 394	27 Jan / 313	24 Apr / 170	9 Sep / 284	27 Jan / 301	6 Feb / 183	24 Feb / 431	17 Mar / 268
King's Lynn	27 Jan / 703	28 Apr / 823	15 Apr / 855	25 Apr / 785	28 Aug / 878	1 Jan / 785	10 Mar / 924	9 Sep / 923	7 Oct / 914	23 Dec / 744	—	7 Apr / 857	26 Dec / 473	28 Aug / 488	12 Dec / 693	22 Aug / 779	13 Jan / 885	28 Aug / 558	14 Apr / 890	11 Nov / 696	18 Feb / 1,203	24 Feb / 917
Maidenhead United	18 Nov / 248	27 Mar / 261	6 Feb / 162	9 Apr / 366	17 Mar / 346	27 Jan / 204	3 Oct / 201	9 Dec / 229	21 Apr / 492	—	5 Feb / 144	31 Mar / 265	3 Mar / 247	11 Nov / 276	17 Apr / 231	13 Jan / 307	23 Sep / 885	22 Aug / 307	22 Aug / 890	26 Dec / 243	13 Feb / 258	26 Apr / 424
Mangotsfield United	26 Dec / 601	19 Aug / 316	28 Apr / 243	10 Oct / 241	24 Apr / 98	27 Jan / 204	20 Feb / 168	14 Apr / 215	—	7 Oct / 237	21 Apr / 303	23 Sep / 264	24 Feb / 238	11 Nov / 281	9 Sep / 244	12 Dec / 142	7 Apr / 246	22 Aug / 195	3 Apr / 381	27 Jan / 211	17 Apr / 1,079	2 Sep / 259
Merthyr Tydfil	17 Mar / 376	3 Mar / 409	17 Apr / 301	3 Feb / 407	20 Feb / 278	19 Aug / 410	27 Mar / 247	—	13 Mar / 304	7 Apr / 152	21 Apr / 303	6 Jan / 171	31 Mar / 375	31 Mar / 406	3 Apr / 325	24 Feb / 341	14 Apr / 416	6 Mar / 304	27 Jan / 479	11 Nov / 346	24 Feb / 551	23 Sep / 464
Northwood	19 Aug / 121	29 Aug / 355	23 Dec / 119	28 Apr / 91	14 Oct / 171	9 Dec / 111	—	9 Sep / 923	9 Sep / 152	7 Apr / 152	5 Feb / 144	12 Mar / 124	13 Nov / 166	2 Apr / 160	27 Jan / 120	7 Oct / 142	14 Apr / 100	4 Sep / 158	18 Nov / 207	24 Mar / 128	11 Apr / 403	11 Nov / 156
Rugby Town	23 Sep / 412	16 Jan / 214	20 Jan / 287	2 Sep / 222	11 Nov / 278	—	21 Apr / 266	9 Dec / 229	21 Apr / 245	7 Apr / 237	9 Apr / 326	3 Mar / 231	3 Mar / 247	3 Oct / 263	22 Aug / 231	26 Dec / 307	18 Nov / 206	20 Mar / 207	22 Aug / 149	4 Nov / 264	13 Feb / 269	31 Mar / 339
Stamford	13 Jan / 340	2 Dec / 283	14 Apr / 213	9 Dec / 205	—	5 Sep / 259	30 Dec / 257	9 Dec / 183	24 Mar / 274	7 Oct / 251	26 Dec / 504	3 Feb / 332	24 Feb / 243	23 Sep / 251	9 Sep / 244	9 Apr / 421	23 Sep / 264	21 Apr / 192	3 Apr / 381	27 Jan / 259	17 Apr / 327	22 Aug / 228
Team Bath	9 Dec / 205	24 Feb / 163	28 Oct / 158	—	9 Dec / 205	23 Sep / 103	9 Dec / 84	4 Sep / 125	3 Mar / 206	1 Jan / 108	29 Jan / 171	6 Jan / 91	21 Apr / 151	7 Apr / 175	3 Apr / 325	24 Feb / 341	28 Mar / 145	1 Jan / 87	17 Mar / 433	11 Nov / 346	23 Feb / 205	16 Dec / 248
Tiverton Town	28 Aug / 531	9 Sep / 427	—	19 Apr / 220	25 Mar / 315	7 Oct / 434	17 Mar / 361	14 Nov / 337	5 Sep / 522	14 Oct / 457	3 Mar / 450	19 Apr / 486	13 Nov / 414	23 Sep / 502	21 Apr / 388	26 Dec / 385	3 Apr / 508	21 Apr / 391	14 Oct / 571	26 Apr / 246	13 Mar / 450	27 Jan / 495
Wealdstone	2 Sep / 216	—	10 Mar / 250	26 Aug / 215	17 Feb / 245	3 Feb / 248	26 Dec / 305	22 Aug / 262	9 Apr / 374	20 Jan / 231	5 Apr / 266	5 Apr / 266	7 Oct / 201	20 Jan / 215	5 Sep / 381	24 Feb / 235	24 Feb / 204	9 Dec / 195	11 Nov / 415	9 Sep / 207	20 Feb / 308	9 Apr / 247
Yate Town	—	9 Sep / 427	11 Apr / 201	10 Mar / 181	6 Feb / 160	24 Apr / 164	31 May / 173	22 Aug / 275	9 Apr / 374	20 Jan / 180	3 Feb / 152	23 Dec / 208	23 Dec / 201	20 Jan / 215	5 Sep / 381	28 Oct / 215	24 Feb / 270	9 Dec / 195	11 Nov / 415	9 Sep / 207	21 Apr / 975	26 Aug / 203

SOUTHERN LEAGUE PREMIER DIVISION CONSTITUTION 2007-08

BANBURY UNITED
Spencer Stadium, Station Approach, Banbury, Oxfordshire OX16 5TA
Tel: 01295 263354
Club: 01295 261899
Manager: Kieran Sullivan   www.banburyunited.co.uk   Colours: Red & gold

BASHLEY
Bashley Recreation Ground, Bashley Road, New Milton, Hampshire BH25 5RY
Tel: 01425 620280
Manager: Steve Riley   www.bashleyfc.co.uk   Colours: Gold & black

BEDFORD TOWN
The New Eyrie, Meadow Lane, Cardington, Bedford, Bedfordshire MK44 3LW
Tel: 01234 838448
Fax: 01234 831990
Manager: Stuart Bimson   www.bedfordeagles.net   Colours: Blue

BRACKLEY TOWN
St James's Park, Churchill Way, Brackley, Northants NN13 7EJ
Tel: 01280 704077
Fax: 01280 704077
Manager: Roger Ashby   www.brackleytownfc.com   Colours: Red & white

BROMSGROVE ROVERS
Victoria Ground, Birmingham Road, Bromsgrove, Worcestershire B61 8DR
Tel: 01527 876949
Fax: 01527 876265
Manager: Rod Brown   www.bromsgroveroversfc.co.uk   Colours: Green & white

CHESHUNT
The Stadium, Theobalds Lane, Cheshunt, Hertfordshire EN8 8RU
Tel: 01992 633500
Fax: 01992 626752
Manager: Tom Loizou   www.cheshuntfc.com   Colours: Amber & black

CHIPPENHAM TOWN
Hardenhuish Park, Bristol Road, Chippenham, Wiltshire SN14 6LR
Tel: 01249 650400
Fax: 01249 650400
Manager: Adie Mings   www.chippenhamtownfc.co.uk   Colours: Royal blue

CIRENCESTER TOWN
Corinium Stadium, Kingshill Lane, Cirencester, Gloucestershire GL7 1HS
Tel: 01285 654543
Fax: 01285 654474
Manager: Adie Viveash   www.cirentownfc.com   Colours: Red & black

CLEVEDON TOWN
The Hand Stadium, Davis Lane, Clevedon, North Somerset BS21 6TG
Tel: 01275 341913
Club: 01275 871600
Manager: Phil Bater   www.clevedontownafc.co.uk   Colours: Blue & white

CORBY TOWN
Rockingham Triangle Stadium, Rockingham Road, Corby, Northants NN17 2AE
Tel: 01536 401007   Club: 01536 406640   Fax: 01536 406640
Manager: Kevin Wilson   www.corbytownfc.com   Colours: White & black

GLOUCESTER CITY
Meadow Park, Sudmeadow Road, Hempsted, Gloucester, Gloucestershire GL2 5HS
Tel: 01452 421400   Club: 01452 311060   Fax: 01452 301330
Manager: Tim Harris   www.t-ender.co.uk   Colours: Yellow & black

HALESOWEN TOWN
The Grove, Old Hawne Lane, Halesowen, West Midlands B63 3TB
Tel: 0121 550 2179
Club: 0121 602 2210
Manager: Martin O'Connor   www.halesowentownfc.co.uk   Colours: Blue

HEMEL HEMPSTEAD TOWN
Vauxhall Road, Adeyfield, Hemel Hempstead, Hertfordshire HP2 4HW
Tel: 01442 259777
Manager: Steve Bateman　　www.hemelhempsteadtownfc.com　　Colours: Red & white

HITCHIN TOWN
Top Field, Fishponds Road, Hitchin, Hertfordshire SG5 1NU
Tel: 01462 434483　　　　　　　　　　　　　　　Fax: 01462 482463
Manager: Darren Salton　　　www.hitchintownfc.co.uk　　Colours: Yellow & green

KING'S LYNN
The Walks Stadium, Tennyson Road, King's Lynn, Norfolk PE30 5PB
Tel: 01553 760060
Manager: Keith Webb　　　　www.thelinnets.co.uk　　　Colours: Blue & gold

MANGOTSFIELD UNITED
Cossham Street, Mangotsfield, Bristol, Gloucestershire BS17 3EN
Tel: 0117 956 0119
Manager: Frank Gregan　　　mangos.freehosting.net　　Colours: Sky blue & maroon

MERTHYR TYDFIL
Pennydarren Park, Merthyr Tydfil, Mid-Glamorgan CF47 9YE
Tel: 01685 384102　　　　　　　　　　　　　　　Fax: 01685 382882
Manager: Garry Shephard　　www.themartyrs.com　　Colours: White & black

RUGBY TOWN
Butlin Road, Rugby, Warwickshire CV21 3ST
Tel: 01788 844806　　　　Club: 01788 844806　　　Fax: 01788 540202
Manager: Billy Jeffrey　　www.rugbytownfc.co.uk　Colours: Sky blue & white

SWINDON SUPERMARINE
Hunts Copse, Highworth Road, South Marston, Swindon, Wiltshire SN3 4SY
Tel: 01793 828778
Manager: Mark Collier　　www.swindonsupermarinefc.com　　Colours: Blue & white

TEAM BATH
Bath City FC, Twerton Park, Twerton, Bath, North Somerset BA2 1DB
Tel: 01225 423087　　　　Club: 01225 313247　　　Fax: 01225 481391
Manager: Ged Roddy　　　www.teambath.com　　　Colours: Yellow & blue

TIVERTON TOWN
Ladysmead, Bolham Road, Tiverton, Devon EX16 6SG
Tel: 01884 252397　　　　　　　　　　　　　　　Fax: 01884 258840
Manager: Martyn Rogers　　www.tivertontownfc.com　　Colours: Yellow & black

YATE TOWN
Lodge Road, Yate, Bristol, South Glos BS17 5LE
Tel: Club: 01454 228103
Manager: Richard Thompson　　www.yatetownfc.com　　Colours: White & navy blue

IN: Bashley (P – Division One South), Bedford Town (R – Football Conference South), Brackley Town (P – Division One Midlands), Bromsgrove Rovers (P – Division One Midlands), Swindon Supermarine (P – Division One South)
OUT: Bath City (P – Football Conference South), Maidenhead United (P – Football Conference South), Northwood (R – Isthmian League Division One North), Stamford (S – Northern Premier League Premier Division), Wealdstone (S – Isthmian League Premier Division)

	Aylesbury United	Barton Rovers	Bedworth United	Berkhamsted Town	Bishops Cleeve	Brackley Town	Bromsgrove Rovers	Chasetown	Cinderford Town	Dunstable Town	Evesham United	Leighton Town	Malvern Town	Rothwell Town	Rushall Olympic	Solihull Borough	Spalding United	Stourbridge	Stourport Swifts	Sutton Coldfield Town	Willenhall Town	Woodford United
Aylesbury United	D	1-0	0-0	2-0	2-2	1-0	2-1	2-1	2-2	2-0	2-2	2-0	2-0	1-2	1-1	1-0	3-1	0-1	1-1	1-1	1-2	2-0
Barton Rovers	2-3	I	2-2	4-0	0-4	0-3	0-1	1-5	1-0	1-1	1-3	2-0	1-1	0-0	3-2	1-1	1-4	2-2	2-0	1-0	1-1	1-3
Bedworth United	1-3	5-1	V	2-1	0-1	2-5	1-2	0-1	3-3	2-1	2-3	4-1	0-1	2-1	1-1	1-2	2-0	2-2	0-1	4-0	0-2	1-3
Berkhamsted Town	0-1	6-1	3-1	I	1-2	1-1	1-3	1-0	0-3	0-2	1-2	1-4	2-0	2-2	3-2	2-4	1-1	2-1	2-1	1-4	3-3	0-4
Bishops Cleeve	0-4	2-2	6-2	3-0	S	0-2	1-0	0-1	1-1	2-1	1-0	0-2	2-3	2-0	3-1	0-1	2-0	1-2	0-1	2-0	1-2	0-2
Brackley Town	2-1	7-0	3-2	6-1	0-1	I	1-1	2-1	1-0	1-2	1-2	4-2	3-2	2-0	1-1	5-2	3-0	0-2	5-1	2-0	3-2	3-2
Bromsgrove Rovers	3-0	5-3	5-2	3-0	3-3	2-0	O	0-2	1-7	1-2	4-2	2-3	0-2	1-1	3-1	3-2	2-0	1-0	5-0	4-1	2-1	3-1
Chasetown	0-1	2-1	1-0	2-0	3-1	1-2	4-1	N	1-0	0-0	1-2	2-0	0-1	3-1	1-0	3-0	2-1	2-2	1-0	0-0	2-1	2-0
Cinderford Town	0-2	0-2	4-4	3-1	4-3	0-1	1-1	2-2		0-0	0-1	2-0	2-2	2-1	2-0	2-0	5-1	2-1	3-1	2-0	0-0	1-4
Dunstable Town	0-0	4-0	2-3	3-3	2-1	1-3	1-3	0-1	0-1	O	0-0	4-0	0-0	5-0	1-2	2-1	0-1	2-4	4-3	2-6	1-1	2-0
Evesham United	2-2	4-2	2-1	0-0	0-2	1-1	2-0	0-2	1-1	1-1	N	2-1	1-1	2-2	1-1	1-5	4-1	4-0	1-1	4-1	1-2	1-0
Leighton Town	0-0	1-1	1-3	4-1	3-3	2-1	1-3	1-1	2-0	0-1	1-0	E	0-1	1-2	2-0	0-1	2-1	0-2	0-0	0-0	1-1	3-0
Malvern Town	2-1	2-2	1-2	1-1	4-2	0-1	1-2	0-1	2-2	0-3	0-2	2-2		0-2	1-3	2-1	3-2	0-0	1-3	1-2	1-3	0-0
Rothwell Town	3-0	5-1	2-1	5-2	1-2	3-4	3-0	0-1	1-2	1-3	1-1	1-0	4-0	M	1-1	2-0	1-0	2-0	3-1	1-1		
Rushall Olympic	0-3	0-1	1-2	1-2	3-1	1-2	0-0	1-0	2-0	2-1	1-1	0-1	2-3	2-0	I	1-1	5-1	1-3	3-1	0-0	1-2	1-0
Solihull Borough	3-1	1-0	4-4	1-3	2-0	1-3	1-5	3-1	3-2	2-3	1-1	2-1	4-1	2-4	0-4	D	0-3	2-4	4-2	2-2	1-1	1-1
Spalding United	0-1	2-0	5-2	3-0	1-0	0-1	1-0	1-2	1-2	0-2	0-1	0-2	1-1	2-1	0-0	0-1	L		1-2	1-0	0-2	5-1
Stourbridge	1-1	2-0	1-3	2-0	2-1	6-2	3-3	2-0	1-1	2-3	1-1	2-1	1-1	4-1	2-3	2-1	0-0	A	3-0	1-1	2-5	0-0
Stourport Swifts	2-0	1-2	1-0	2-1	3-2	1-2	0-2	2-2	2-3	1-0	2-3	2-1	0-1	0-5	1-2	0-2	0-1	2-2	N	0-4	2-2	0-0
Sutton Coldfield Town	2-0	0-1	0-3	2-3	1-3	1-4	1-2	2-0	4-2	2-1	3-0	2-0	3-2	3-2	1-1	4-2	1-1	1-1	2-0	D	0-2	0-2
Willenhall Town	0-2	3-0	1-1	4-0	0-2	3-0	2-1	2-1	2-0	0-0	1-1	0-0	1-0	2-1	0-1	0-2	1-1	2-2	3-0	0-3	S	2-1
Woodford United	2-1	3-3	3-0	2-1	1-2	2-2	3-1	4-1	1-1	0-1	3-0	2-2	3-2	3-0	0-0	1-0	6-2	1-2	2-1			

Division One Midlands

	P	HOME					AWAY					TOTAL					Pts
		W	D	L	F	A	W	D	L	F	A	W	D	L	F	A	
Brackley Town	42	15	2	4	55	25	14	2	5	40	28	29	4	9	95	53	91
Bromsgrove Rovers	42	14	2	5	53	33	9	5	7	33	29	23	7	12	86	62	76
Chasetown	42	14	3	4	33	14	9	3	9	26	25	23	6	13	59	39	75
Willenhall Town	42	10	6	5	29	19	10	6	5	38	28	20	12	10	67	47	72
Evesham United	42	10	7	4	36	25	9	8	4	30	26	19	15	8	66	51	72
Aylesbury United	42	11	7	3	31	17	9	4	8	27	25	20	11	11	58	42	71
Stourbridge	42	9	7	5	39	27	8	8	5	31	26	17	15	10	70	53	66
Woodford United	42	12	6	3	46	25	6	5	10	25	29	18	11	13	71	54	65
Cinderford Town	42	10	6	5	37	27	8	4	9	33	33	18	10	14	70	60	64
Rothwell Town	42	12	3	6	41	21	6	4	11	31	40	18	7	17	72	61	61
Dunstable Town	42	7	5	9	36	33	9	7	5	28	20	16	12	14	64	53	60
Sutton Coldfield Town	42	10	3	8	35	32	6	6	9	27	31	16	9	17	62	63	57
Bishops Cleeve	42	9	2	10	30	28	8	3	10	38	38	17	5	20	68	66	56
Solihull Borough	42	8	4	9	40	47	9	1	11	32	37	17	5	20	72	84	56
Rushall Olympic	42	8	4	9	28	25	7	5	9	28	30	15	9	18	56	55	54
Bedworth United	42	7	3	11	35	35	6	5	10	38	48	13	8	21	73	83	47
Malvern Town	42	4	6	11	24	37	8	5	8	22	29	12	11	19	46	66	47
Leighton Town	42	7	6	8	25	23	5	2	14	19	37	12	8	22	44	60	44
Spalding United	42	8	1	12	23	22	4	5	12	22	40	12	6	24	45	62	42
Barton Rovers	42	6	6	9	27	37	5	3	13	24	56	11	9	22	51	93	42
Berkhamsted Town	42	7	4	10	33	42	3	3	15	20	55	10	7	25	53	97	37
Stourport Swifts	42	6	4	11	24	37	3	3	15	19	50	9	7	26	43	87	34

PLAY-OFFS

SEMI-FINALS
(May 1st)
Bromsgrove Rovers 1 Evesham United 0 *Att* 540
Chasetown 0 **Willenhall Town** 1 *Att* 612

FINAL
(May 5th at Bromsgrove Rovers)
Bromsgrove Rovers 2 Willenhall Town 1 *aet Att* 892

DATES & GATES

Each cell gives the fixture date (top) and the attendance / gate (italic, below). Rows are home clubs; columns are away clubs.

(Home \ Away)	Woodford United	Willenhall Town	Sutton Coldfield Town	Stourport Swifts	Stourbridge	Spalding United	Solihull Borough	Rushall Olympic	Rothwell Town	Malvern Town	Leighton Town	Evesham United	Dunstable Town	Cinderford Town	Chasetown	Bromsgrove Rovers	Brackley Town	Bishops Cleeve	Berkhamsted Town	Bedworth United	Barton Rovers	Aylesbury United
Aylesbury United	23 Apr / 195	23 Dec / 134	26 Feb / 142	11 Nov / 175	23 Sep / 176	9 Dec / 158	17 Feb / 153	17 Mar / 169	18 Nov / 171	14 Oct / 173	28 Aug / 297	2 Oct / 142	1 Jan / 176	19 Aug / 191	28 Oct / 171	14 Apr / 204	28 Apr / 312	11 Feb / 152	27 Nov / 141	27 Jan / 192	7 Apr / 157	
Barton Rovers	26 Dec / 96	28 Oct / 95	20 Feb / 59	30 Sep / 72	31 Mar / 104	14 Nov / 72	9 Sep / 90	7 Oct / 76	9 Apr / 120	27 Jan / 68	24 Apr / 147	21 Apr / 111	3 Mar / 124	17 Dec / 90	16 Dec / 76	2 Dec / 137	3 Mar / 85	26 Aug / 72	22 Aug / 84	4 Nov / 110		30 Dec / 124
Bedworth United	16 Dec / 118	18 Nov / 129	26 Dec / 144	26 Aug / 134	22 Aug / 154	3 Oct / 125	9 Apr / 190	24 Mar / 130	31 Mar / 150	28 Oct / 122	20 Feb / 85	13 Mar / 137	14 Oct / 158	23 Dec / 67	3 Feb / 91	10 Mar / 185	17 Mar / 154	25 Nov / 103	2 Dec / 108		23 Sep / 145	21 Apr / 187
Berkhamsted Town	24 Oct / 73	14 Apr / 95	23 Sep / 66																		9 Dec / 73	14 Nov / 180
Bishops Cleeve	4 Nov / 78	9 Dec / 84	15 Nov / 75																5 Dec / 47		28 Apr / 61	8 Nov / 90
Brackley Town	9 Apr / 406	5 Dec / 138	20 Jan / 183																30 Dec / 202		3 Oct / 167	22 Aug / 230
Bromsgrove Rovers	21 Apr / 380	3 Oct / 341	28 Nov / 309	14 Nov / 372																	3 Apr / 313	3 Feb / 415
Chasetown	18 Nov / 243	3 Mar / 405	31 Mar / 255																		18 Mar / 246	31 Mar / 301
Cinderford Town	26 Aug / 112	10 Mar / 105	31 Mar / 90																		18 Apr / 105	26 Apr / 120
Dunstable Town	22 Aug / 87	23 Sep / 110	26 Aug / 112																		12 Dec / 82	2 Dec / 201
Evesham United	27 Jan / 109	20 Mar / 68	23 Sep / 112																		3 Feb / 69	24 Feb / 216
Leighton Town	24 Feb / 101	2 Dec / 82	21 Apr / 94																		1 Jan / 126	
Malvern Town	10 Mar / 127	7 Apr / 68	3 Feb / 60																		18 Nov / 110	24 Mar / 149
Rothwell Town	13 Mar / 119	17 Apr / 116	10 Mar / 137																		17 Mar / 116	16 Dec / 72
Rushall Olympic	10 Mar / 133	27 Feb / 124	3 Oct / 95																		10 Mar / 168	13 Jan / 221
Solihull Borough	28 Feb / 63	27 Oct / 159	13 Dec / 110																		28 Nov / 88	28 Oct / 95
Spalding United	30 Dec / 123	28 Apr / 160	9 Apr / 102																		3 Feb / 161	6 Jan / 123
Stourbridge	13 Jan / 159	29 Aug / 317	14 Oct / 200																		19 Aug / 117	16 Sep / 110
Stourport Swifts	13 Feb / 61	27 Jan / 90	24 Feb / 72																		23 Dec / 92	17 Apr / 161
Sutton Coldfield Town	31 Mar / 147	16 Apr / 134																			14 Sep / 92	24 Feb / 200
Willenhall Town	19 Aug / 82																				28 Aug / 90	16 Apr / 134
Woodford United			11 Nov / 111																		28 Aug / 89	31 Mar / 108

	Abingdon United	Andover	Bashley	Beaconsfield SYCOB	Bracknell Town	Brook House	Burnham	Chesham United	Didcot Town	Hanwell Town	Hillingdon Borough	Lymington/New Milton	Marlow	Newport IOW	Oxford City	Paulton Rovers	Swindon Supermarine	Taunton Town	Thatcham Town	Uxbridge	Winchester City	Windsor & Eton
Abingdon United		1-2	0-0	2-0	0-0	2-3	2-3	1-1	4-2	2-1	1-2	3-2	1-3	3-1	3-0	2-2	1-1	3-1	4-0	0-1	2-1	2-2
Andover	1-3		0-0	3-2	2-1	5-2	2-0	1-2	2-0	2-1	2-3	1-5	2-2	6-1	1-3	1-1	2-0	2-2	2-0	3-2	1-1	1-3
Bashley	2-0	0-1	D	6-0	4-0	3-0	3-1	4-1	2-1	2-0	2-2	2-1	2-2	3-0	6-0	2-0	3-0	2-3	2-3	4-1	7-0	5-3
Beaconsfield SYCOB	0-1	1-1	1-3	I	0-1	0-2	2-0	1-2	2-3	3-1	2-3	0-5	1-3	2-2	2-0	0-1	1-4	0-3	0-3	0-1	1-2	0-1
Bracknell Town	1-1	0-2	1-1	3-0	V	2-1	2-3	3-0	2-2	3-0	3-3	3-1	0-2	1-2	1-2	3-0	0-2	1-2	1-1	1-1	1-2	1-2
Brook House	0-3	0-3	2-4	1-2	4-1	I	2-3	0-5	1-1	3-1	0-1	1-0	6-1	3-1	0-0	0-1	0-2	3-2	1-1	6-2	1-2	5-1
Burnham	4-0	1-0	0-2	1-0	0-2	4-1	S	5-2	2-0	2-1	4-3	3-1	1-2	1-0	1-1	0-2	0-0	0-1	1-0	2-1	0-1	5-1
Chesham United	3-2	3-2	5-3	1-2	1-1	2-1	5-2	I	3-2	2-0	6-4	1-2	1-1	1-0	2-0	0-5	0-2	1-0	1-3	3-4	2-1	1-3
Didcot Town	2-2	3-1	0-1	6-0	4-0	5-1	3-0	1-1	O	1-2	2-2	3-1	3-2	0-0	3-0	1-4	2-2	3-3	3-3	3-2	2-2	0-4
Hanwell Town	2-4	3-1	1-4	2-2	1-1	1-3	0-3	2-4	1-3	N	0-3	2-1	6-0	1-1	2-1	1-1	3-6	3-4	1-2	0-3	2-0	0-4
Hillingdon Borough	1-2	0-1	1-2	5-2	1-0	3-2	4-1	1-1	0-3	1-0		2-1	1-2	1-2	2-5	1-2	2-2	0-0	0-1	0-0	3-3	4-4
Lymington & New Milton	2-2	0-2	0-3	2-1	0-1	1-2	1-2	4-1	2-4	2-2	4-1	O	1-3	4-0	2-0	1-3	1-3	0-0	0-1	5-1	1-6	2-0
Marlow	2-2	1-2	1-2	2-2	0-0	4-1	1-1	2-0	5-2	2-2	2-0	2-0	N	3-0	0-1	1-0	2-0	2-1	2-1	0-0	3-1	3-5
Newport IOW	1-1	1-1	0-2	2-0	3-2	2-1	0-3	1-2	0-3	0-2	1-2	3-4	0-4	E	1-4	0-1	1-0	1-3	4-1	1-5	2-0	1-3
Oxford City	2-1	0-4	1-3	4-2	2-0	2-0	3-1	1-0	2-2	1-1	1-5	4-3	1-0	3-2		1-1	0-3	1-4	2-3	1-3	2-0	4-2
Paulton Rovers	2-0	3-0	0-1	3-1	1-2	3-3	1-0	2-1	2-1	4-3	0-2	2-1	1-1	5-0	0-0	S	3-2	2-0	1-0	2-1	5-0	0-0
Swindon Supermarine	3-0	0-0	0-0	7-0	2-1	4-1	2-1	0-0	2-0	0-0	3-5	2-3	1-0	1-2	2-1	1-1		1-2	0-1	3-0	2-0	0-0
Taunton Town	1-2	1-3	3-2	0-0	3-0	3-3	2-3	1-0	2-2	0-0	2-2	1-0	2-3	5-0	2-0	1-1	1-0	&	2-2	1-0	1-1	2-1
Thatcham Town	3-1	2-1	2-3	1-1	1-2	2-2	0-3	2-1	1-3	5-0	2-1	0-0	3-2	2-0	1-1	0-2	2-0	1-2		0-1	1-1	2-2
Uxbridge	4-0	0-0	0-4	2-1	1-1	1-1	0-2	2-1	1-2	5-0	1-1	1-3	1-1	3-1	1-0	1-4	4-1	1-2	0-1	W	3-1	3-2
Winchester City	2-0	2-1	0-1	6-0	0-0	0-1	1-0	4-0	2-1	3-1	2-2	3-0	3-1	3-2	1-1	1-1	0-1	1-1	2-1	0-1		1-1
Windsor & Eton	1-2	3-0	1-2	3-0	1-1	3-5	0-2	4-1	1-0	5-3	1-0	1-4	3-1	2-0	0-0	0-0	0-1	0-0	4-3	0-2	2-2	

Division One South & West

	P	HOME					AWAY					TOTAL					
		W	D	L	F	A	W	D	L	F	A	W	D	L	F	A	Pts
Bashley	42	17	2	2	68	16	15	4	2	43	19	32	6	4	111	35	102
Paulton Rovers	42	13	5	3	40	19	7	9	5	26	23	20	14	8	66	42	74
Burnham	42	13	2	6	37	21	10	2	9	37	39	23	4	15	74	60	73
Swindon Supermarine	42	10	6	5	36	18	10	5	6	32	22	20	11	11	68	40	71
Taunton Town	42	9	8	4	36	25	10	6	5	32	25	19	14	9	68	50	71
Thatcham Town	42	12	4	5	37	24	9	3	9	33	36	21	7	14	70	60	69
Marlow	42	10	7	4	39	22	9	5	7	35	27	19	12	11	74	49	69
Uxbridge	42	10	4	7	36	29	10	4	7	32	29	20	8	14	68	58	68
Andover	42	10	5	6	42	34	9	4	8	28	25	19	9	14	70	59	66
Didcot Town	42	10	8	3	53	31	6	5	10	33	36	16	13	13	86	67	61
Abingdon United	42	9	6	6	39	28	7	5	9	29	39	16	11	15	68	67	59
Oxford City	42	11	3	7	38	40	6	5	10	24	35	17	8	17	62	75	59
Winchester City	42	11	6	4	37	17	5	4	12	30	48	16	10	16	67	65	58
Windsor & Eton	42	9	5	7	35	29	7	5	9	41	46	16	10	16	76	75	58
Chesham United	42	12	2	7	44	40	5	4	12	24	39	17	6	19	68	79	57
Hillingdon Borough	42	6	6	9	33	36	7	7	7	47	49	13	13	16	80	85	52
Lymington & New Milton	42	7	3	11	35	38	9	0	12	46	41	16	3	22	81	79	51
Brook House	42	8	3	10	36	40	6	3	12	35	52	14	6	22	71	92	48
Bracknell Town	42	7	5	9	35	31	4	8	9	16	31	11	13	18	51	62	46
Newport IOW	42	6	2	13	25	44	3	1	17	19	62	9	3	30	44	106	30
Hanwell Town -1	42	4	3	14	33	54	2	4	15	19	48	6	7	29	52	102	24
Beaconsfield SYCOB	42	3	2	16	19	42	2	4	15	17	62	5	6	31	36	104	21

PLAY-OFFS

SEMI-FINALS

(April 30th) Paulton Rovers 1 **Taunton Town** 4 *Att* 552

(May 1st) Burnham 1 **Swindon Supermarine** 2 *Att* 213

FINAL

(May 5th at Swindon Supermarine)

Swindon Supermarine 2 Taunton Town 0 *Att* 522

DATES & GATES

Fixture grid — each cell shows the match date and gate (attendance). Rows are home teams (listed at left); columns are the opposing teams (listed across the top). The diagonal (team versus itself) is blank.

	Abingdon United	Andover	Bashley	Beaconsfield SYCOB	Bracknell Town	Brook House	Burnham	Chesham United	Didcot Town	Hanwell Town	Hillingdon Borough	Lymington & New Milton	Marlow	Newport IOW	Oxford City	Paulton Rovers	Swindon Supermarine	Taunton Town	Thatcham Town	Uxbridge	Winchester City	Windsor & Eton
Abingdon United		30 Jan 151	17 Feb 268	16 Dec 35	26 Aug 192	2 Dec 64	20 Feb 101	22 Aug 237	9 Apr 336	3 Feb 73	18 Nov 32	6 Dec 53	26 Dec 130	14 Nov 148	14 Nov 319	13 Jan 120	20 Jan 141	24 Feb 215	3 Oct 85	14 Apr 96	24 Mar 166	9 Sep 110
Andover	28 Apr 143		31 Mar 473	24 Feb 137	28 Aug 162	20 Mar 157	9 Apr 126	26 Dec 287	21 Apr 236	21 Apr 83	14 Oct 79	16 Dec 125	13 Jan 137	17 Mar 208	27 Jan 211	3 Feb 153	3 Feb 173	3 Mar 238	17 Feb 112	23 Sep 115	6 Feb 205	28 Oct 176
Bashley	17 Mar 268	4 Nov 220		21 Apr 407	23 Sep 184	20 Mar 192	1 Jan 157	27 Mar 325	10 Mar 235	11 Nov 144	13 Jan 137	28 Aug 375	23 Dec 211	3 Oct 159	11 Nov 221	1 Jan 152	9 Dec 224	20 Jan 218	7 Apr 278	21 Oct 154	1 Jan 302	19 Aug 201
Beaconsfield SYCOB	16 Dec 35	11 Nov 56	2 Dec 56		24 Mar 60	17 Oct 74	9 Sep 102	26 Dec 123	5 Dec 242	1 Jan 96	17 Nov 59	14 Oct 45	8 Apr 116	28 Apr 42	28 Oct 65	14 Apr 35	27 Jan 45	13 Jan 73	19 Aug 64	25 Nov 106	3 Feb 80	7 Apr 76
Bracknell Town	26 Aug 192	26 Dec 123	17 Feb 118	14 Nov 90		20 Mar 74	23 Sep 93	4 Nov 160	17 Oct 279	17 Nov 147	17 Mar 131	17 Apr 66	30 Jan 82	10 Mar 105	16 Dec 120	9 Sep 113	21 Apr 95	20 Feb 81	30 Sep 148	13 Mar 75	31 Mar 120	3 Feb 178
Brook House	2 Dec 64	3 Oct 73	27 Jan 67	10 Feb 117	17 Mar 75		6 Feb 54	10 Feb 313	18 Nov 213	7 Apr 47	5 Dec 54	13 Apr 44	13 Apr 61	16 Dec 64	14 Oct 63	9 Sep 87	28 Oct 75	26 Aug 94	9 Sep 90	22 Aug 135	13 Jan 84	20 Feb 58
Burnham	20 Feb 101	9 Apr 126	31 Oct 107	26 Aug 325	27 Mar 249	27 Mar 311		26 Dec 101	24 Apr 269	27 Mar 98	31 Mar 102	11 Nov 126	17 Apr 277	26 Aug 127	22 Aug 137	24 Feb 205	16 Dec 101	31 Mar 135	14 Oct 157	26 Dec 107	3 Mar 135	13 Mar 247
Chesham United	22 Aug 237	26 Aug 287	9 Sep 328	22 Aug 120	28 Nov 249	10 Oct 298	10 Oct 298		5 Dec 242	28 Apr 294	23 Jan 120	31 May 275	20 Jan 339	28 Oct 283	20 Feb 208	10 Mar 313	14 Oct 342	16 Dec 305	2 Dec 323	9 Apr 259	21 Apr 285	11 Nov 358
Didcot Town	9 Apr 336	21 Apr 236	3 Feb 354	26 Aug 216	14 Apr 216	14 Nov 279	14 Nov 137	5 Dec 242		28 Apr 294	16 Dec 263	13 Jan 267	18 Nov 317	30 Dec 262	26 Dec 363	24 Mar 269	22 Aug 323	17 Feb 254	9 Jan 240	28 Oct 252	7 Oct 267	23 Sep 257
Hanwell Town	3 Feb 73	21 Apr 83	16 Dec 115	30 Dec 117	3 Oct 74	17 Oct 147	17 Oct 93	7 Apr 102	11 Nov 126		3 Apr 47	23 Sep 77	7 Apr 102	14 Apr 52	17 Apr 51	27 Jan 70	3 Mar 112	7 Oct 78	18 Nov 106	28 Nov 104	19 Aug 155	26 Dec 89
Hillingdon Borough	18 Nov 32	14 Oct 79	27 Mar 64	20 Feb 72	11 Nov 65	20 Jan 43	28 Apr 101	28 Apr 98	19 Aug 127	17 Mar 59		23 Dec 46	9 Dec 52	23 Sep 64	20 Jan 57	15 Nov 51	30 Dec 88	3 Feb 47	9 Apr 69	30 Sep 106	17 Oct 61	28 Aug 98
Lymington & New Milton	6 Dec 53	16 Dec 125	3 Mar 76	3 Mar 101	2 Dec 102	28 Apr 101	11 Nov 126	31 Mar 262	20 Jan 275	3 Apr 77	26 Aug 120		14 Apr 102	23 Aug 103	17 Feb 89	31 Mar 118	31 Mar 149	9 Apr 106	24 Mar 105	9 Sep 128	13 Dec 113	28 Feb 77
Marlow	26 Dec 130	13 Jan 137	26 Aug 213	19 Dec 76	2 Dec 116	17 Oct 117	14 Nov 137	20 Jan 149	18 Nov 317	7 Apr 102	14 Apr 102	14 Apr 102		11 Nov 117	9 Apr 152	2 Dec 118	31 Mar 149	17 Mar 137	3 Feb 155	21 Apr 207	16 Dec 187	14 Oct 162
Newport IOW	14 Nov 148	17 Mar 208	3 Oct 159	28 Feb 115	14 Apr 100	3 Feb 187	26 Aug 176	26 Dec 211	30 Dec 262	14 Apr 170	23 Sep 136	23 Aug 103	11 Nov 163		22 Nov 110	25 Nov 251	9 Sep 241	21 Apr 184	1 Jan 214	31 Mar 127	28 Aug 295	21 Mar 110
Oxford City	14 Nov 319	27 Jan 211	28 Apr 100	18 Nov 128	19 Aug 192	24 Mar 131	3 Oct 119	7 Apr 152	26 Dec 426	17 Apr 51	3 Apr 121	26 Apr 129	1 Jan 163	26 Apr 129		17 Oct 162	13 Jan 184	23 Sep 196	28 Apr 207	3 Feb 167	23 Dec 178	13 Feb 149
Paulton Rovers	13 Jan 120	19 Feb 224	17 Aug 210	19 Dec 160	18 Nov 163	9 Dec 126	18 Nov 141	18 Nov 183	29 Jan 202	26 Aug 115	26 Aug 111	23 Sep 100	1 Jan 163	14 Oct 137	14 Oct 166		9 Apr 178	26 Dec 257	20 Jan 133	16 Dec 128	28 Oct 154	17 Feb 186
Swindon Supermarine	20 Jan 141	3 Feb 153	24 Apr 173	19 Dec 120	18 Nov 126	9 Dec 115	24 Apr 161	23 Sep 121	13 Feb 187	23 Dec 103	23 Dec 104	17 Oct 100	17 Oct 109	2 Dec 105	21 Apr 149	3 Oct 161		9 Apr 178	28 Aug 194	20 Mar 103	23 Sep 141	14 Nov 115
Taunton Town	24 Feb 215	3 Mar 173	18 Oct 293	28 Feb 292	24 Jan 116	23 Dec 213	20 Mar 254	20 Apr 246	11 Oct 242	25 Apr 160	27 Jan 223	24 Mar 207	24 Mar 208	28 Mar 145	17 Mar 226	7 Oct 334	3 Oct 161		11 Nov 307	14 Oct 281	7 Apr 303	14 Apr 232
Thatcham Town	3 Oct 85	17 Feb 112	13 Feb 131	13 Feb 50	27 Jan 86	9 Dec 78	28 Aug 91	23 Sep 121	31 Jan 165	2 Dec 77	28 Oct 106	10 Feb 136	9 Dec 134	18 Nov 108	9 Dec 130	5 Nov 102	2 Feb 105	2 Dec 101		26 Aug 120	17 Mar 122	24 Mar 134
Uxbridge	14 Apr 96	23 Sep 115	28 Apr 165	17 Oct 89	7 Apr 127	4 Nov 132	20 Mar 170	1 Jan 176	11 Oct 142	20 Jan 120	14 Nov 127	28 Apr 209	28 Apr 278	18 Nov 180	3 Mar 130	10 Feb 172	6 Feb 110	2 Dec 105	23 Dec 101		17 Mar 145	3 Oct 201
Winchester City	24 Mar 166	28 Oct 277	18 Nov 211	30 Sep 165	23 Apr 139	23 Dec 201	23 Dec 201	18 Oct 187	27 Jan 134	22 Aug 147	9 Apr 100	17 Mar 110	27 Jan 167	18 Apr 100	31 Mar 118	26 Apr 129	26 Aug 128	30 Jan 124	16 Sep 100	2 Dec 112		24 Mar 134
Windsor & Eton	9 Dec 168	6 Feb 138	19 Aug 201	7 Apr 76	3 Feb 178	20 Feb 58	13 Mar 247	11 Nov 358	23 Sep 257	26 Dec 89	28 Aug 98	28 Feb 77	14 Oct 162	21 Mar 110	21 Apr 232	21 Apr 145	14 Nov 115	14 Apr 232	24 Mar 134	3 Oct 201	2 Dec 112	

SOUTHERN LEAGUE DIVISION ONE MIDLANDS
CONSTITUTION 2007-08

AYLESBURY UNITED
Colours: Green & white
Aylesvury Vale FC, Haywood Way, Aylesbury,
Buckinghamshire HP19 9WZ
Tel: 01296 423324

BARTON ROVERS
Colours: Royal blue
Sharpenhoe Road, Barton-le-Clay, Beds MK45 4SD
Tel: 01582 707772 Fax: 01582 882398

BEDWORTH UNITED
Colours: Green & white
The Oval, Welfare Park, Coventry Road,
Bedworth, Warwickshire CV12 8NN
Tel: 024 7649 1404/7631 4302

BERKHAMSTED TOWN
Colours: White & black
Broadwater, Lower Kings Rd, Berkhamsted HP4 2AA
Tel: 01442 862815/865054 Fax: 01442 865054

BISHOPS CLEEVE
Colours: Green & black
Kayte Lane, Bishops Cleeve,
Cheltenham, Gloucestershire GL52 3PD
Tel: 07866 077291

CHASETOWN
Colours: Royal blue
The Scholars Ground, Church Street,
Chasetown, Walsall, Staffs WS7 8QL
Tel: 01543 682222

CHESHAM UNITED
Colours: Claret & sky blue
Meadow Park, Amy Lane, Amersham Road,
Chesham, Buckinghamshire HP5 1NE
Tel: 01494 783964/791057 Fax: 01494 794244

CINDERFORD TOWN
Colours: White & black
Causeway Ground, Edge Hills Road, Hilldene,
Cinderford, Gloucestershire GL14 2QH
Tel: 01594 822039/827147

DUNSTABLE TOWN
Colours: Blue & white
Creasey Park Stadium, Brewers Hill Road,
Dunstable, Bedfordshire LU6 1BB
Tel: 01582 667555

EVESHAM UNITED
Colours: Red, white & black
Worcester City FC, St George's Lane,
Barbourne, Worcester, Worcestershire WR1 1QT
Tel: 01905 23003

LEAMINGTON
Colours: Gold & black
New Windmill Ground, Harbury Lane, Whitnash,
Leamington Spa, Warwickshire CV33 9JR
Tel: 01926 334934

LEIGHTON TOWN
Colours: Red & white
Bell Close, Lake Street, Leighton Buzzard,
Bedfordshire LU7 1RX
Tel: 01525 373311 Fax: 01525 370142

MALVERN TOWN
Colours: Sky blue & claret
Langland Stadium, Langland Avenue,
Malvern, Worcestershire WR14 2EQ
Tel: 01684 574068

ROMULUS
Colours: Red & white
Sutton Coldfield Town FC, Central Ground, Coles
Lane, Sutton Coldfield, West Midlands B72 1NL
Tel: 0121 354 2997

ROTHWELL TOWN
Colours: Blue
Home Close, Cecil Street,
Rothwell, Northants NN14 2EZ
Tel: 01536 710694

RUSHALL OLYMPIC
Colours: Amber & black
Dales Lane, off Daw End Lane, Rushall,
Walsall, West Midlands WS4 1LJ
Tel: 01922 641021

STOURBRIDGE
Colours: Red & white
War Memorial Athletic Ground, High Street,
Amblecote, Stourbridge, West Midlands DY8 4HN
Tel: 01384 394040

STOURPORT SWIFTS
Colours: Yellow
Walshes Meadow, Harold Davies Drive,
Stourport-on-Severn, Worcestershire DY13 0AA
Tel: 01299 825188 Fax: 01299 825188

SUTTON COLDFIELD TOWN
Colours: Blue
Central Ground, Coles Lane,
Sutton Coldfield, West Midlands B72 1NL
Tel: 0121 354 2997

WILLENHALL TOWN
Colours: Red
Noose Lane, Willenhall, West Midlands WV13 3BB
Tel: 01902 636586

WOODFORD UNITED
Colours: Red
Byfield Road, Woodford Halse,
Daventry, Northants NN11 3PZ
Tel: 01327 263734

IN: Chesham United (S – Division One South), Leamington (P – Midland Alliance), Romulus (P – Midlan
Alliance)
OUT: Brackley Town (P), Bromsgrove Rovers (P), Solihull Borough (merged with Conference North club Moo
Green), Spalding United (S – Northern Premier League Division One South)

SOUTHERN LEAGUE DIVISION ONE SOUTH & WEST CONSTITUTION 2007-08

AFC HAYES
Colours: Blue & white
Farm Park, Kingshill Avenue, Hayes, Middx UB4 8DD
Tel: 020 8845 0110/8842 1448

ABINGDON UNITED
Colours: Yellow & blue
Northcourt Road, Abingdon, Oxfordshire OX14 1PL
Tel: 01235 203203

ANDOVER
Colours: Red & black
The Portway Stadium, West Portway Ind. Estate,
Andover, Hampshire SP10 3LF
Tel: 01264 351302

BRACKNELL TOWN
Colours: Red & white
Larges Lane, Bracknell, Berkshire RG12 9AN
Tel: 01344 300933/412305 Fax: 01344 300933

BRIDGWATER TOWN
Colours: Red & White
Fairfax Park, College Way, Bath Road,
Bridgwater, Somerset TA6 4TZ
Tel: 01278 446899

BURNHAM
Colours: Blue & white
The Gore, Wymers Wood Road,
Burnham, Slough SL1 8JG
Tel: 01628 602697/602467

DIDCOT TOWN
Colours: Red & white
Loop Meadow Stadium, Bowmont Water,
off Avon Way, Didcot, Oxfordshire OX11 7GA
Tel: 01235 813138

FARNBOROUGH
Colours: Red & white
Cherrywood Road, Farnborough, Hants GU14 8UD
Tel: 01252 541469 Fax: 01252 372640

FLEET TOWN
Colours: Navy & sky blue
Calthorpe Park, Crookham Road,
Fleet, Hampshire GU51 5FA
Tel: 01252 623804

GODALMING TOWN
Colours: Yellow & green
Wey Court, Meadrow, Godalming, Surrey GU7 3JE
Tel: 01483 417520

GOSPORT BOROUGH
Colours: Yellow & blue
Privett Park, Privett Road,
Gosport, Hampshire PO12 3SX
Tel: 023 9250 1042

HILLINGDON BOROUGH
Colours: White & royal blue
Middlesex Stadium, Breakspear Rd, Ruislip HA4 7SB
Tel: 01895 639544

MARLOW
Colours: Royal blue & white
Alfred Davis Ground, Oak Tree Road,
Marlow, Buckinghamshire SL7 3ED
Tel: 01628 483970 Fax: 01628 477032

NEWPORT IOW
Colours: Yellow & blue
St George's Park, St George's Way,
Newport, Isle of Wight PO30 2QH
Tel: 01983 525027 Fax: 01983 826077

OXFORD CITY
Colours: Blue & white
Court Place Farm, Marsh Lane, Marston,
Oxford, Oxfordshire OX3 0NQ
Tel: 01865 744493/742492

PAULTON ROVERS
Colours: Maroon & white
Athletic Ground, Winterfield Road,
Paulton, North Somerset BS39 7RF
Tel: 01761 412907

SLOUGH TOWN
Colours: Yellow & navy blue
Beaconsfield SYCOB FC, Holloway Park, Slough
Road, Beaconsfield, Buckinghamshire HP9 2SG
Tel: 01494 676868

TAUNTON TOWN
Colours: Burgundy & sky blue
Wordsworth Drive, Taunton, Somerset TA1 2HG
Tel: 01823 278191 Fax: 01823 322975

THATCHAM TOWN
Colours: Blue & white
Waterside Park, Crookham Rd, Thatcham RG19 4PA
Tel: 01635 862016/873934 Fax: 01635 873834

UXBRIDGE
Colours: Red & white
Honeycroft, Horton Rd, W. Drayton, Middx UB7 8HX
Tel: 01895 443557/445830 Fax: 01895 445830

WINCHESTER CITY
Colours: Red & black
The City Ground, Hillier Way, Abbotts Barton,
Winchester, Hampshire SO23 7EF
Tel: 01962 810200

WINDSOR & ETON
Colours: Red & green
Stag Meadow, St Leonards Road, Windsor SL4 3DR
Tel: 01753 860656 Fax: 01753 860656

WWW.NLNEWSDESK.CO.UK

IN: Bridgwater Town (P – Western League Premier Division), Farnborough (formerly Farnborough Town) (R – Football Conference South), Fleet Town (S – Isthmian League Division One South), Godalming Town (S – Isthmian League Division One South), Gosport Borough (P – Wessex League Premier Division), Slough Town (R – Isthmian League Premier Division)
OUT: Bashley (P), Beaconsfield SYCOB (R – Spartans South Midlands League Premier Division), Chesham United (S – Division One Midlands), Hanwell Town (R – Spartan South Midlands League Premier Division), New Milton Town (formerly Lymington & New Milton) (W – Wessex League Premier Division), Swindon Supermarine (P) Brook House become AFC Hayes

LEAGUE CUP

FIRST ROUND

Abingdon United 0 **Oxford City** 2
Barton Rovers 2 Aylesbury United 1
Bashley 2 **Winchester City** 3
Berkhamsted Town 1 **Dunstable Town** 2
Bishops Cleeve 0 **Taunton Town** 1
Brook House 3 Bracknell Town 2 *aet*
Chasetown 1 Bromsgrove Rovers 0
Chesham United 4 Burnham 0
Cinderford Town 0 **Malvern Town** 5
Didcot Town 3 Brackley Town 2
Hanwell Town 0 **Windsor & Eton** 1
Hillingdon Borough 4 Marlow 3 *aet*
Newport IOW 0 **Lymington & New Milton** 2
Paulton Rovers 1 **Andover** 2 *aet*
Rushall Olympic 0 **Bedworth United** 1
Solihull Borough 1 **Stourport Swifts** 3
Spalding United 4 Rothwell Town 1
Stourbridge 4 Evesham United 3
Sutton Coldfield Town 1 **Willenhall Town** 5
Thatcham Town 1 Swindon Supermarine 1 *aet* (3-2p)
Uxbridge 2 Beaconsfield SYCOB 1
Woodford United 7 Leighton Town 0

SECOND ROUND

Andover 1 **Thatcham Town** 3
Barton Rovers 1 **Uxbridge** 2
Bedworth United 0 **Stourport Swifts** 1
Chasetown 1 Malvern Town 0
Cirencester Town 0 **Didcot Town** 4
Hillingdon Borough 1 **Brook House** 3
Lymington & New Milton 1 Winchester City 0
Northwood 0 **Chesham United** 1
Stourbridge 3 Spalding United 0 *aet*
Taunton Town 1 Oxford City 0
Willenhall Town 2 Woodford United 1
Windsor & Eton 1 **Dunstable Town** 2

THIRD ROUND

Banbury United 2 Chesham United 0
Chasetown 2 Willenhall Town 1
Chippenham 1 **Lymington & New Milton** 2
Clevedon Town 0 **Bath City** 1
Gloucester City 2 **Didcot Town** 3 *aet*
Hemel Hempstead Town 3 Dunstable 0
Hitchin Town 0 **Corby Town** 1
Maidenhead United 1 **Thatcham Town** 3
Merthyr Tydfil 1 Team Bath 0
Rugby Town 2 Halesowen Town 1 *aet*
Stamford 1 **King's Lynn** 2
Stourport Swifts 0 **Stourbridge** 1
Taunton Town 2 **Mangotsfield United** 3
Tiverton Town 4 Yate Town 2
Uxbridge 1 **Brook House** 3 *aet*
Wealdstone 0 **Cheshunt** 2

FOURTH ROUND

Banbury United 1 Chasetown 0
Cheshunt 5 Brook House 0
Didcot Town 4 Merthyr Tydfil 1
King's Lynn 2 Corby Town 1
Lymington & New Milton 0 **Mangotsfield** 1
Rugby Town 2 Stourbridge 1
Thatcham 2 **Hemel Hempstead Town** 3
Tiverton Town 3 Bath City 1

QUARTER-FINALS

Didcot Town 1 **Banbury United** 3
Hemel Hempstead Town 3 Cheshunt 2
King's Lynn 0 **Rugby Town** 1
Tiverton Town 2 Mangotsfield United 0

SEMI-FINALS

Rugby Town 3 **Hemel Hempstead Town** 4
Tiverton Town 2 Banbury United 0

FINAL

(played over two legs)
(1st leg Apr 3rd)
Tiverton Town 1 Hemel Hempstead Town 0
(2nd leg Apr 24th)
Hemel Hempstead 2 **Tiverton Town** 2

SPARTAN SOUTH MIDLANDS LEAGUE

	Aylesbury Vale	Biggleswade T.	Biggleswade U.	Broxbourne B.	Chalfont St P.	Colney Heath	Edgware Town	Harefield Utd	Haringey B.	Hertford Town	Holmer Green	Kingsbury LT	Langford	Leverstock G.	London Colney	Oxhey Jets	Royston Town	Ruislip Manor	St Marg'bury	Tring Athletic	Welwyn GC
Aylesbury Vale		2-1	5-3	1-1	2-1	3-0	0-1	1-2	3-2	2-3	1-1	1-3	2-5	2-1	6-0	1-1	3-2	2-0	1-1	5-1	1-3
Biggleswade Town	3-1		2-1	1-2	1-0	1-2	3-3	0-1	0-2	0-0	0-2	1-0	5-2	3-1	1-1	0-4	1-3	1-0	1-0	1-2	1-3
Biggleswade United	3-5	2-1	P	2-2	1-7	1-1	0-3	0-3	2-2	3-3	3-2	2-5	5-2	2-1	2-2	2-3	4-0	0-0	4-0	1-3	0-2
Broxbourne Borough V & E	1-1	2-0	2-1	R	1-2	0-1	1-2	2-1	4-1	2-3	1-2	1-2	3-2	7-2	1-2	8-2	2-1	0-0	4-3	0-0	3-3
Chalfont St Peter	1-1	2-1	2-2	1-1	E	7-2	2-3	1-2	3-1	1-2	0-0	1-0	7-0	4-1	1-0	0-1	0-0	2-1	2-2	2-0	1-2
Colney Heath	1-2	1-2	1-1	1-2	4-6	M	1-3	1-1	2-5	0-1	2-1	1-4	2-4	0-0	1-0	1-1	4-0	1-0	2-0		1-3
Edgware Town	2-1	1-1	3-1	2-0	2-1	6-0	I	0-0	5-1	3-2	7-0	2-0	3-0	4-0	2-0	6-1	3-1	3-2	4-0	3-1	1-3
Harefield United	3-0	7-0	4-0	3-1	4-3	2-0	1-1	E	4-1	0-2	3-1	1-0	3-1	2-2	0-1	1-0	6-0	3-1	3-2	2-2	1-2
Haringey Borough	1-3	2-0	2-2	2-2	2-2	4-1	1-3	1-2	R	0-9	4-1	2-2	3-3	1-4	0-0	1-3	5-1	1-2	1-0	1-1	1-3
Hertford Town	3-5	2-0	1-1	2-1	1-3	0-0	1-0	2-1	1-1		1-1	3-1	4-1	2-2	4-0	2-0	0-3	7-1	6-2	3-0	1-2
Holmer Green	2-1	0-3	1-3	0-1	1-2	0-3	3-3	1-4		1-7		1-3	3-1	0-3	0-1	1-4	1-1	6-3	0-1	1-2	2-2
Kingsbury London Tigers	0-0	2-3	2-3	4-1	0-1	1-0	0-4	1-2	4-0	1-2	2-0	D	2-5	1-2	2-1	1-2	1-2	1-4	1-3	1-0	2-2
Langford	3-0	1-3	0-2	2-4	2-0	2-2	0-4	0-5	2-0	1-5	2-4	2-3	I	1-0	3-0	0-4	2-2	2-1	1-1	2-1	1-2
Leverstock Green	1-1	2-2	3-2	3-4	1-1	1-2	4-2	1-0	3-2	0-2	0-3	0-2	3-2	V	1-0	1-1	2-0	2-2	0-2	3-0	2-1
London Colney	5-2	2-0	3-1	1-3	1-1	2-0	0-1	0-2	5-0	2-3	1-1	3-2	2-2	1-1	I	1-3	7-1	2-2	2-0	3-2	0-3
Oxhey Jets	4-1	2-1	1-0	0-3	4-2	1-2	0-0	1-1	4-1	2-1	4-5	1-0	0-1	1-3	1-1	S	1-1	3-2	4-1	1-0	2-2
Royston Town	2-0	2-0	0-2	3-2	0-3	2-2	4-8	0-4	5-1	0-7	4-2	3-3	0-1	3-1	2-1	3-1	I	0-0	0-6	2-3	2-4
Ruislip Manor	4-0	1-0	1-2	1-3	1-3	1-2	1-3	1-2	1-3	1-7	1-3	2-1	3-2	4-0	2-1	6-1	0-0	O	3-2	5-1	2-1
St Margaretsbury	0-1	3-0	5-2	0-0	0-1	2-1	1-5	0-2	2-0	2-2	0-0	1-3	1-3	0-2	9-1	2-0	5-2	0-2	N	0-0	1-1
Tring Athletic	2-1	1-2	0-0	3-3	1-2	2-6	1-2	1-3	1-2	1-3	2-1	1-0	1-1	2-2	1-3	0-2	1-0	4-3	2-0		1-4
Welwyn Garden City	2-1	3-2	5-0	0-1	0-1	4-3	0-1	1-2	1-1	3-1	4-1	2-2	1-2	5-1	2-1	1-1	6-1	2-0	1-3	0-2	

Premier Division

	P	W	D	L	F	A	Pts
Edgware Town	40	32	6	2	118	35	102
Harefield United	40	29	5	6	95	35	92
Hertford Town	40	26	8	6	122	50	86
Welwyn Garden City	40	22	9	9	90	53	75
Leverstock Green	40	20	8	12	73	66	68
Chalfont St Peter	40	19	10	11	79	50	67
Oxhey Jets	40	20	7	13	73	56	67
Broxbourne Borough V & E	40	17	11	12	86	64	62
Aylesbury Vale	40	15	8	17	71	75	53
London Colney	40	13	10	17	58	72	49
Tring Athletic	40	14	7	19	53	81	49
Ruislip Manor	40	14	6	20	71	81	48
Kingsbury London Tigers	40	14	5	21	64	69	47
Biggleswade United	40	11	11	18	68	89	44
St Margaretsbury	40	10	10	20	52	64	40
Colney Heath	40	11	7	22	51	85	40
Langford	40	11	7	22	69	107	40
Biggleswade Town	40	11	6	23	47	73	39
Holmer Green	40	9	9	22	49	91	36
Royston Town	40	9	9	22	59	117	36
Haringey Borough	40	8	11	21	59	94	35

PREMIER DIVISION CUP

FIRST ROUND
Aylesbury Vale 0 **Leverstock Green** 2
Colney Heath 0 **Langford** 2
Holmer Green 1 **Broxbourne Borough V & E** 2
Kingsbury London Tigers 3 Chalfont St Peter 2 *aet*
(Kingsbury LT expelled)
Welwyn Garden City 1 **Biggleswade United** 3 *aet*

SECOND ROUND
Biggleswade T. 0 **Hertford** 2
Broxbourne Borough V & E 6 Langford 2
Edgware 2 Leverstock Green 1
Harefield Utd 5 Haringey 0
London Colney 2 Chalfont 0
Oxhey Jets 3 Royston Town 1

Ruislip Manor 0 **St Margaretsbury** 1
Tring Athletic 1 Biggleswade United 2 *aet (Biggleswade United expelled)*

QUARTER-FINALS
Broxbourne Borough V & E 3 London Colney 1
Edgware Town 3 Tring Ath. 0
Oxhey Jets 4 Hertford 3 *aet*
St Margaretsbury 1 Harefield United 1 *aet (4-3p)*

SEMI-FINALS
Edgware Town 4 Broxbourne Borough V & E 1
St Margaretsbury 2 **Oxhey** 4

FINAL
(May 1st at Harefield Utd)
Edgware Town 1 Oxhey 0 *aet*

SPARTAN SOUTH MIDLANDS LEAGUE PREMIER DIVISION CONSTITUTION 2007-08

AYLESBURY VALE............Haywood Way Aylesbury HP19 9WZ............01296 423324
BEACONSFIELD SYCOB............Holloway Park, Slough Road, Beaconsfield HP9 2SG............01494 676868
BIGGLESWADE TOWN......Bedford FC, McMullen Park, Meadow Lane, Cardington, Bedford MK44 3LW............01234 831024
............*soon to move to Waders Stadium, Langford Road, Biggleswade*............t.b.a.
BIGGLESWADE UNITED............Second Meadow, Fairfield Road, Biggleswade SG18 0AA............01767 600408
BRIMSDOWN ROVERS............Brimsdown Sports & Social, Goldsworth Road, Enfield EN3 7RP............020 8804 5491
BROXBOURNE BOROUGH V & E............The V & E Club, Goffs Lane, Cheshunt EN7 5QN............01992 624281
CHALFONT ST PETER............Mill Meadow, Gravel Hill, Amersham Road, Chalfont St Peter SL9 9QX............01753 885797
COCKFOSTERS............Chalk Lane, Cockfosters, Barnet EN4 9JG............0208 449 5833
COLNEY HEATH............The Recreation Ground, High Street, Colney Heath, St Albans AL4 0NN............01727 826188
HANWELL TOWN............Reynolds Field, Perivale Lane, Perivale, Greenford UB6 8TL............020 8998 1701
HAREFIELD UNITED............Preston Park, Breakspeare Road, Harefield UB9 6BH............01895 823474/822275
HERTFORD TOWN............Hertingfordbury Park, West Street, Hertford SG13 8EZ............01992 583716
HOLMER GREEN............Watchet Lane, Holmer Green, High Wycombe HP15 6UF............01494 711485
LANGFORD............Forde Park, Langford Road, Henlow SG16 6AF............01462 816106
LEVERSTOCK GREEN............Pancake Lane, Leverstock Green, Hemel Hempstead HP2 4BN............01442 246280
LONDON TIGERS............Silver Jubilee Park, Townsend Lane, Kingsbury NW9 7NJ............020 8205 1645/5204
LONDON COLNEY............Cotlandswick Playing Fields, London Colney AL2 1EH............01727 822132
OXHEY JETS............The Boundary Stadium, Altham Way, South Oxhey WD19 6FW............020 8421 6277
RUISLIP MANOR............Grosvenor Vale, off West End Road, Ruislip HA4 6JQ............01895 676168/637487
ST MARGARETSBURY............Station Road, Stanstead St Margarets, near Ware SG12 8EH............01920 870473
TRING ATHLETIC............Pendley Sports Centre, Cow Lane, Tring HP23 3NR............01442 828331
WELWYN GARDEN CITY............Herns Way, Welwyn Garden City AL7 1TA............01707 329358

IN: *Beaconsfield SYCOB (R – Southern League Division One South), Brimsdown Rovers (P), Cockfosters (P), Hanwell Town (R – Southern League Division One South)*
OUT: *Edgware Town (P – Isthmian League Division One North), Haringey Borough (R), Royston Town (R)*
Kingsbury London Tigers become London Tigers

	Amersham Town	Ampthill Town	Arlesey Athletic	Bedford United & Valerio	Brache Sparta	Brimsdown Rovers	Buckingham Athletic	Cockfosters	Cranfield United	Harpenden Town	Hoddesdon Town	Kentish Town	New Bradwell St Peter	Stony Stratford Town	Sun Postal Sports	Winslow United
Amersham Town		0-1	0-4	2-2	2-1	0-5	5-1	1-5	2-0	3-0	2-3	0-3	7-3	2-0	1-1	3-3
Ampthill Town	1-0		5-0	3-0	3-2	1-4	3-2	2-3	4-0	3-0	1-1	1-2	3-2	0-1	8-2	3-1
Arlesey Athletic	3-2	1-4	D	1-3	1-4	0-5	2-0	0-4	3-2	2-1	1-3	1-1	1-2	0-2	2-0	1-1
Bedford United & Valerio	2-3	1-1	4-0	I	4-1	1-1	3-3	2-1	0-3	3-2	3-0	2-5	2-3	0-5	2-4	1-4
Brache Sparta	1-0	1-1	1-3	6-1	V	1-2	2-2	2-0	4-0	4-0	3-1	3-0	1-0	1-3	3-1	1-0
Brimsdown Rovers	2-0	1-0	1-2	5-1	3-0	I	3-0	4-0	10-0	2-0	4-0	2-2	9-0	2-1	4-1	4-0
Buckingham Athletic	4-0	1-2	3-2	9-0	3-2	0-4	S	1-2	2-2	4-1	2-3	1-1	5-1	1-2	2-1	2-0
Cockfosters	3-1	1-2	3-1	2-0	2-1	1-1	1-0	I	3-1	1-0	0-0	1-0		1-2	3-0	5-0
Cranfield United	1-2	1-7	1-5	0-2	2-2	0-6	0-3	0-3	O	1-0	0-3	1-2	0-1	1-3		0-7
Harpenden Town	2-1	1-4	6-2	2-2	0-1	0-0	6-0	1-2	3-0	N	0-2	0-2	2-1	0-1	4-2	2-3
Hoddesdon Town	2-0	0-1	5-1	3-0	3-3	1-2	0-1	2-0	6-0	0-0		0-3	5-1	1-2	2-1	5-1
Kentish Town	3-1	1-4	6-1	4-0	8-2	1-5	0-2	3-1	0-2	1-2	1-0	O	2-0	1-3	6-9	4-5
New Bradwell St Peter	0-1	0-0	3-1	5-1	1-5	0-1	2-2	0-3	3-1	1-2	0-1	2-3	N	1-6	2-3	3-0
Stony Stratford Town	1-0	1-2	2-2	3-5	2-0	0-2	2-1	1-2	4-0	6-5	3-0	3-1	3-1	E	2-1	2-1
Sun Postal Sports	4-2	1-2	3-2	2-4	1-3	2-7	3-2	0-5	7-2	4-1	1-0	2-2	0-1	0-1		0-1
Winslow United	0-6	2-4	3-5	3-2	0-0	0-8	0-1	0-2	1-4	0-1	1-2	1-1	3-4	1-1	1-1	

Division One	P	W	D	L	F	A	Pts
Brimsdown Rovers	30	25	4	1	109	15	79
Cockfosters	30	22	2	6	62	25	68
Stony Stratford Town	30	22	2	6	67	33	68
Ampthill Town	30	21	4	5	76	33	67
Hoddesdon Town	30	16	4	10	55	38	52
Kentish Town	30	15	6	9	65	45	51
Brache Sparta	30	14	5	11	61	49	47
Buckingham Athletic	30	11	6	13	60	57	39
Amersham Town	30	10	3	17	49	61	33
Bedford Utd & Valerio	30	9	5	16	53	86	32
Arlesey Athletic	30	9	4	17	50	82	31
Harpenden Town	30	9	3	18	44	57	30
Sun Postal Sports	30	9	3	18	51	74	30
New Bradwell St Peter	30	9	2	19	44	76	29
Winslow United	30	5	7	18	40	76	22
Cranfield United	30	3	2	25	24	103	11

DIVISION ONE CUP

FIRST ROUND
Amersham Town 2 **Cockfosters** 3
Arlesey Athletic 1 **Brimsdown Rovers** 2
Bedford United & Valerio 4 Winslow United 0
Brache Sparta 4 Buckingham Athletic 0
Cranfield United 1 **Kentish Town** 4
Harpenden Town 1 Hoddesdon Town 0 *aet*
New Bradwell St Peter 2 **Ampthill Town** 5
Stony Stratford Town 2 Sun Postal Sports 1

QUARTER-FINALS
Ampthill Town 2 Bedford United & Valerio 2 *aet* (3-2p)
Brache Sparta 1 **Cockfosters** 2
Brimsdown Rovers 5 Kentish Town 0
Harpenden Town 3 **Stony Stratford Town** 6

SEMI-FINALS
Ampthill Town 0 **Brimsdown Rovers** 2
Stony Stratford Town 4 Cockfosters 4 *aet* (4-3p)

FINAL
(May 5th at London Colney)
Brimsdown Rovers 3 Stony Stratford Town 1

SPARTAN SOUTH MIDLANDS LEAGUE DIVISION ONE CONSTITUTION 2007-08

AMERSHAM TOWN . . . . Spratleys Meadow, School Lane, Amersham HP7 0EJ 01494 727428
AMPTHILL TOWN . . . . Ampthill Park, Woburn Road, Ampthill MK45 2HX 01525 404440
ARLESEY ATHLETIC . . . . Arlesey Town FC, Hitchin Road, Arlesey SG15 6RS 01462 734504
BEDFORD . . . . McMullen Park, Meadow Lane, Cardington, Bedford MK44 3LW 01234 831024
BEDFORD TOWN RESERVES . . . . . The New Eyrie, Meadow Lane, Cardington, Bedford MK44 3LW 01234 838448
BRACHE SPARTA . . . . Foxdell Recreation Ground, Dallow Road, Luton LU1 1TG 01582 720751
BUCKINGHAM ATHLETIC . . . . Stratfields Fields, Stratford Road, Buckingham KM18 1NY 01280 816945
CHESHUNT RESERVES . . . . The Stadium, Theobalds Lane, Cheshunt EN8 8RU 01992 633500
CRANFIELD UNITED . . . . Crawley Road, Cranfield, Bedford MK43 0AA 01234 751444
HARINGEY BOROUGH . . . . Coles Park, White Hart Lane, Wood Green, Tottenham N17 7JP 020 8889 1415
HARPENDEN TOWN . . . . Rothamsted Park, Amenbury Lane, Harpenden AL5 2EF 01582 715724
HODDESDON TOWN . . . . Lowfield, Park View, Hoddesdon EN11 8PX 01707 870816
KENTISH TOWN . . . . Copthall Stadium, Greenland Lane, Hendon, London NW4 1RL 020 8202 6478
NEW BRADWELL ST PETER . . . . Bradwell Road Rec Ground, New Bradwell, Milton Keynes 01908 313835
ROYSTON TOWN . . . . Garden Walk, Royston SG8 7HP 01763 241204
SPORT LONDON E BENFICA . . . . Hanwell Town FC, Reynolds Field, Perivale Lane, Greenford UB6 8TL 020 8998 1701
STONY STRATFORD TOWN . . . . Ostlers Lane, Stony Stratford, Milton Keynes MK11 1AR 01908 562267
SUN POSTAL SPORTS . . . . Bellmount Wood Avenue, Watford WD17 3BN 01923 227453
WINSLOW UNITED . . . . Rec. Ground, Elmfields Gate, Winslow, Buckingham MK18 3JQ 01296 713057
IN: *Bedford Town Reserves (N), Cheshunt Reserves (P – Reserve Division One), Haringey Borough (R), Royston Town (R), Sport London E Benfica (P – Middlesex County League Premier Division)*
OUT: *Brimsdown Rovers (P), Cockfosters (P)*
Bedford United & Valerio become Bedford

	AFC Dunstable	Aston Clinton	Caddington	Crawley Green	Flamstead	Kent Athletic	Kings Langley	Loughton Orient	MK Scot	Markyate	Mursley United	Old Bradwell United	Padbury United	Pitstone & Ivinghoe	Risborough Rangers	The 61 FC (Luton)	Totternhoe	Tring Corinthians
AFC Dunstable		6-1	2-0	3-1	8-2	3-0	6-0	7-1	2-0	6-0	1-5	5-0	10-0	2-0	3-0	4-1	3-1	3-1
Aston Clinton	6-0		3-2	2-2	7-2	2-1	0-3	1-1	0-1	14-0	4-3	7-0	2-1	0-1	5-0	2-6	1-2	0-3
Caddington	4-1	2-2		1-5	2-0	3-5	0-4	5-1	1-4	5-1	2-3	4-1	9-1	3-1	3-1	2-2	1-3	2-3
Crawley Green	0-4	0-0	1-0	D	8-2	1-1	1-3	3-1	1-1	5-0	2-1	7-0	2-1	3-0	2-3	2-2	1-0	4-0
Flamstead	n/a	2-7	4-0	1-6	I	n/a	1-8	n/a	1-1	5-0	1-2	2-1	1-3	2-4	3-3	n/a	1-2	2-2
Kent Athletic	4-0	1-2	2-2	0-2	10-0	V	1-6	1-1	n/a	7-0	2-1	2-2	7-0	5-1	2-1	4-1	2-0	1-1
Kings Langley	1-2	1-2	4-0	1-2	9-0	0-2	I	5-1	3-1	4-1	3-2	4-0	2-0	1-0	1-1	3-2	2-1	2-0
Loughton Orient	0-10	0-2	1-2	3-2	3-1	1-1	0-1	S	4-0	4-2	2-1	6-0	0-2	2-0	1-1	3-0	2-4	3-6
MK Scot	0-6	n/a	n/a	2-3	4-1	2-0	0-0	I	6-0	n/a	n/a	3-0	n/a	1-5	0-5	0-3	1-1	2-1
Markyate	1-8	0-6	0-7	0-5	1-1	0-12	1-1	3-2	n/a	O	0-2	2-4	1-0	0-4	0-4	0-7	1-3	1-3
Mursley United	1-4	2-2	2-2	2-3	2-2	1-1	2-4	0-0	3-1	2-0	N	10-0	4-1	1-1	6-4	0-2	0-3	0-4
Old Bradwell United	0-10	0-2	0-14	1-7	1-6	0-10	1-5	0-5	0-0	2-2	2-2		4-1	1-4	1-3	2-4	2-3	0-2
Padbury United	3-3	4-4	1-6	0-3	0-3	2-1	1-5	0-1	n/a	2-2	1-1	1-1	T	1-0	2-3	1-5	2-2	1-3
Pitstone & Ivinghoe	0-8	0-4	1-6	0-3	1-5	1-3	0-4	1-1	2-0	3-1	0-2	4-1	4-0	W	1-1	0-0	4-3	2-3
Risborough Rangers	2-1	0-4	3-2	1-2	4-0	3-1	2-2	3-1	n/a	8-0	1-3	3-0	4-1	1-0	O	1-3	2-1	2-0
The 61 FC (Luton)	2-6	2-2	1-2	3-4	8-2	2-0	3-2	3-1	n/a	7-0	2-2	1-0	5-1	3-1	0-1		3-0	2-0
Totternhoe	3-0	1-4	2-5	0-3	1-2	2-1	0-2	2-0	n/a	7-1	0-2	5-1	3-2	1-2	0-1	2-1		1-1
Tring Corinthians	0-3	5-1	5-0	0-3	3-2	1-2	0-2	2-0	n/a	4-2	3-1	9-1	1-0	5-1	3-2	3-2	0-2	

Note – Flamstead and MK Scot withdrew during the course of the season
Their results are shown above but are expunged from the league table

Division Two		P	W	D	L	F	A	Pts
AFC Dunstable		30	23	1	6	124	38	70
Kings Langley		30	21	3	6	78	34	66
Crawley Green	-6	30	21	4	5	81	33	61
Tring Corinthians		30	18	2	10	71	46	56
Aston Clinton		30	16	7	7	87	49	55
Risborough Rangers		30	16	4	10	62	51	52
Kent Athletic		30	15	6	9	82	40	51
The 61 FC (Luton)		30	15	5	10	77	51	50
Caddington		30	14	4	12	96	62	46
Totternhoe		30	14	2	14	57	52	44
Mursley United		30	9	8	13	61	56	35
Loughton Orient		30	8	6	16	45	70	30
Pitstone & Ivinghoe		30	8	4	18	37	69	28
Padbury United		30	4	5	21	33	97	17
Markyate		30	2	4	24	22	146	10
Old Bradwell United		30	2	3	25	25	144	9

Flamstead and MK Scot – records expunged

DIVISION TWO CUP

FIRST ROUND
Caddington 1 **Mursley United** 4
The 61 FC (Luton) 0 **Flamstead** 2
SECOND ROUND
Aston Clinton 2 Mursley United 0
Crawley Green 8 Risborough Rangers 0
Flamstead 1 **Tring Corinthians** 2
Kings Langley 2 Loughton Orient 0
Markyate 0 **AFC Dunstable** 9
Old Bradwell United 0 **Totternhoe** 5
Padbury United 2 **Kent Athletic** 3
Pitstone & Ivinghoe 1 **MK Scot** 4
QUARTER-FINALS
AFC Dunstable 3 Totternhoe 2 *aet*
Crawley Green 2 **MK Scot** 3
Kings Langley 0 **Kent Athletic** 0 *aet* (5-6p)
Tring Corinthians 4 Aston Clinton 1
SEMI-FINALS
Kent Athletic 4 Tring Corinthians 3
MK Scot 0 **AFC Dunstable** 5
FINAL
(May 3rd at Ampthill Town)
Kent Athletic 3 AFC Dunstable 0

SPARTAN SOUTH MIDLANDS LEAGUE DIVISION TWO CONSTITUTION 2007-08

AFC DUNSTABLE . . . . Lancot Park, Dunstable Road, Totternhoe, Dunstable LU6 1QP 01582 663735
ASTON CLINTON . . . . London Road, Aston Clinton HP22 5HL 01296 631818
CADDINGTON. . . . . Caddington Recreation Club, Manor Road, Caddington, Luton LU1 4HH 01582 450151
CRAWLEY GREEN . . . . Crawley Green Rec Ground, Crawley Green Road, Luton LU2 9HA 01582 700883
KENT ATHLETIC . . . . Kent Social Club, Tenby Drive, Leagrave, Luton LU4 9BN 01582 582723
KINGS LANGLEY. . . . . Hempstead Road, Kings Langley WD4 8BS . . . . None
MARKYATE . . . . The Playing Fields, Cavendish Road, Markyate, St Albans AL3 8PS 01582 841731
MURSLEY UNITED . . . . Station Road, Mursley, Milton Keynes MK17 0SA . . . . None
OLD BRADWELL UNITED . . . . Abbey Road, Bradwell Village, Milton Keynes MK13 9AR. 01908 312355
PADBURY UNITED . . . . Playing Fields, Springfields, Padbury MK18 2AS. . . . . None
PITSTONE & IVINGHOE . . . . Recreation Ground, Pitstone, Leighton Buzzard. 01296 661271
RISBOROUGH RANGERS . . . . Windsor, Horsenden Lane, Princes Risborough HP27 9NE 01844 274176
THE 61 FC (LUTON) . . . . Kingsway Ground, Beverley Road, Luton LU4 8EU 01582 495417
TOTTERNHOE . . . . Totternhoe Recreation Ground, Castle Hill Road, Totternhoe, Dunstable LU6 1RG 01582 606738
TRING CORINTHIANS . . . . Icknield Way, Tring HP23 5HJ 07985 726431

OUT: Flamstead (WS), Loughton Orient (W – North Bucks & District League), MK Scot (WS)

CHALLENGE TROPHY

FIRST ROUND

Ampthill Town 1 **Harefield United** 2

Arlesey Athletic 1 **Tring Athletic** 4

Aylesbury Vale 2 Harpenden Town 1

Biggleswade Town 5 Cranfield United 1

Brache Sparta 3 **Buckingham Athletic** 5

Caddington 2 **Ruislip Manor** 7

Chalfont St Peter 3 Bedford & Valerio United 0

Cockfosters 1 **Aston Clinton** 2

Colney Heath 3 Padbury United 1

Edgware Town 5 Crawley Green 1

Haringey Borough 6 Risborough Rangers 1

Holmer Green 7 Totternhoe 0

Kentish Town 2 **Biggleswade United** 3

Kings Langley 3 St Margaretsbury 2 *aet*

Kingsbury London Tigers 3 **Markyate** 0

(Kingsbury London Tigers expelled)

Leverstock Green 1 **Oxhey Jets** 3

Loughton Orient 1 **The 61 FC (Luton)** 3

MK Scot 3 Winslow United 3 *aet* (4-3p)

New Bradwell St Peter 0 **Langford** 1

Old Bradwell United 0 **Hoddesdon Town** 3

Royston Town 1 **AFC Dunstable** 4

Stony Stratford Town 5 Flamstead 3

Tring Corinthians 4 **London Colney** 5 *aet*

SECOND ROUND

Aston Clinton 2 AFC Dunstable 1

Brimsdown Rovers 1 **Ruislip Manor** 2

Broxbourne Borough V & E 2 **Stony Straford** 3 *aet*

Buckingham Athletic 0 **Hoddesdon Town** 0 *aet* (2-4p)

Chalfont St Peter 0 **Tring Athletic** 1

Edgware Town 2 Harefield United 1

Haringey Borough 3 Mursley United 0

Hertford Town 2 Welwyn Garden City 0

Holmer Green 2 Kings Langley 0 *aet*

Kent Athletic 0 **Aylesbury Vale** 2

London Colney 1 **Amersham Town** 3 *aet*

MK Scot 6 Markyate 0

Oxhey Jets 1 Biggleswade United 1 *aet* (4-1p)

Pitstone & Ivinghoe 1 **Biggleswade Town** 1 *aet* (3-4p)

Sun Postal Sports 2 **Langford** 7

The 61 FC (Luton) 3 Colney Heath 1

THIRD ROUND

Amersham Town 5 Hoddesdon Town 3

Aston Clinton 2 Biggleswade Town 0

Edgware Town 6 MK Scot 0

Haringey Borough 1 **Holmer Green** 3

(at Holmer Green)

Hertford Town 1 **Stony Stratford Town** 2 *aet*

Oxhey Jets 4 Aylesbury Vale 2 *aet*

The 61 FC (Luton) 0 **Ruislip Manor** 2

Tring Athletic 3 Langford 1

QUARTER-FINALS

Amersham Town 3 Oxhey Jets 2

Edgware Town 3 Aston Clinton 0

Ruislip Manor 7 Holmer Green 0

Stony Stratford Town 5 Tring Athletic 1

SEMI-FINALS

Edgware Town 6 Amersham Town 1

Ruislip Manor 2 **Stony Stratford Town** 4

FINAL

(May 8th at Tring Athletic)

Stony Stratford Town 1 **Edgware Town** 3

Reserve Division One	P	W	D	L	F	A	Pts
Leverstock Green Res.	34	26	4	4	102	39	82
Hertford Town Res.	34	23	4	7	88	35	73
Sawbridgeworth Town Res.	34	22	7	5	76	41	73
Cheshunt Res.	34	21	7	6	98	39	70
Welwyn Garden City Res.	34	17	7	10	99	57	58
Berkhamsted Town Res.	34	18	2	14	77	59	56
Oxhey Jets Res.	34	17	5	12	76	62	56
Colney Heath Res.	34	15	8	11	71	49	53
Hoddesdon Town Res.	34	15	7	12	52	54	52
Mursley United Res.	34	13	7	14	67	73	46
Tring Athletic Res.	34	11	8	15	61	62	41
Buckingham Athletic Res.	34	11	4	19	50	77	37
Stony Stratford Town Res.	34	10	4	20	62	78	34
St Margaretsbury Res.	34	11	1	22	69	92	34
Harpenden Town Res.	34	7	10	17	36	74	31
Holmer Green Res.	34	7	4	23	38	89	25
New Bradwell St Peter Res.	34	8	1	25	53	137	25
Sun Postal Sports Res.	34	5	8	21	50	108	23

Reserve Division Two	P	W	D	L	F	A	Pts
London Colney Res.	22	17	1	4	61	13	52
Cockfosters Res.	22	16	4	2	56	16	52
Risborough Rangers Res.	22	13	3	6	41	30	42
Royston Town Res.	22	12	2	8	47	30	38
AFC Dunstable Res.	22	11	4	7	57	32	37
Kings Langley Res.	22	10	6	6	46	36	36
Tring Corinthians Res.	22	9	2	11	42	44	29
Winslow United Res.	22	8	3	11	37	72	27
Brimsdown Rovers Res.	22	7	2	13	42	31	23
Totternhoe Res.	22	6	3	13	39	64	21
Caddington Res.	22	4	3	15	29	63	15
Loughton Orient Res.	22	2	1	19	19	85	7

RESERVES TROPHY

FINAL

(May 12th at Sun Postal Sports)

London Colney Res. 1 Welwyn Garden City

Res. 1 *aet* (4-3p)

STAFFORDSHIRE COUNTY SENIOR LEAGUE

	Abbey Hulton	Alsager T. Res.	Ashbourne Utd	Ball Haye Green	Eccleshall AFC	Florence Coll.	Foley	Goldenhill Wdrs	Hanford	Hanley Town	Newcastle Res.	Norton	Redgate Clayton	Rocester Res.	Stafford RS	Stallington	Stone Dom. Res.	Wolstanton Utd
Abbey Hulton United		2-1	1-5	4-2	1-0	0-0	1-4	0-4	5-3	0-2	3-4	0-1	1-3	2-2	1-3	3-4	5-3	1-3
Alsager Town Res.	4-1	P	1-2	3-1	2-1	6-2	0-0	8-1	1-0	1-0	3-2	0-2	2-5	5-3	0-4	1-1	6-0	2-3
Ashbourne United	3-1	3-1	R	3-1	0-1	2-0	1-1	1-1	2-1	1-5	1-1	2-1	2-0	2-1	1-2	1-1	4-0	0-3
Ball Haye Green	3-2	1-1	0-0	E	2-1	0-0	2-3	3-0	0-2	2-3	1-4	6-2	2-0	2-2	2-2	4-0	5-1	1-2
Eccleshall AFC	1-3	2-3	0-4	1-3	M	0-0	1-0	3-1	1-2	1-2	2-3	0-2	4-4	1-3	0-1	0-1	3-7	0-3
Florence Colliery	1-1	1-2	1-2	0-3	2-3	I	1-2	2-2	0-3	0-2	2-2	0-3	0-2	0-3	0-4	2-0	0-4	0-3
Foley	3-0	0-4	6-2	0-2	0-2	1-0	E	5-5	0-3	0-3	2-0	1-2	1-1	2-2	1-2	2-0	9-1	2-3
Goldenhill Wanderers	2-1	2-2	9-4	5-1	1-5	2-2	4-4	R	2-3	1-4	4-4	4-4	4-2	0-3	3-4	3-2	4-3	1-1
Hanford	1-0	2-0	1-2	5-5	2-1	6-0	0-0	0-2		2-1	2-1	2-2	2-1	2-2	4-3	4-0	4-0	2-4
Hanley Town	4-1	0-5	2-2	1-0	1-0	4-0	0-0	1-0	0-2	D	5-2	3-0	2-0	2-1	2-0	5-2	13-0	1-4
Newcastle Town Res.	3-0	2-2	1-1	2-4	2-3	4-0	3-2	3-2	0-0	0-1	I	0-0	3-1	0-2	4-2	3-0	2-1	1-4
Norton	1-2	4-1	2-1	1-0	0-4	3-2	2-0	0-3	0-1	1-4	2-0	V	3-1	3-0	2-3	0-2	2-1	3-3
Redgate Clayton	3-0	1-2	1-2	1-3	2-2	1-2	1-4	4-0	2-1	1-2	5-2	2-1	I	3-1	1-1	2-2	4-0	1-4
Rocester Res.	4-0	1-4	3-2	1-3	4-4	0-1	1-2	2-2	3-1	2-2	2-1	2-2	0-1	S	3-0	1-4	4-0	1-2
Stafford Rangers Stripes	5-1	2-0	1-0	0-0	3-1	4-2	4-3	2-0	0-0	3-4	4-1	2-0	1-0	1-0	I	3-1	6-0	1-2
Stallington	1-2	3-3	1-3	4-2	0-2	3-1	2-1	1-0	3-4	1-0	4-0	4-0	0-2	2-8	0-0	O	4-1	1-0
Stone Dominoes Res.	1-4	0-5	0-3	2-3	0-3	1-6	0-6	2-1	1-8	1-3	0-0	0-1	0-2	0-7	0-0	2-3	N	1-3
Wolstanton United	4-0	1-1	4-2	1-0	1-1	1-0	1-0	5-1	3-0	2-1	3-0	2-0	0-2	3-0	1-1	2-1	8-1	

Premier Division

	P	W	D	L	F	A	Pts
Wolstanton United	34	26	6	2	86	29	84
Hanley Town	34	26	4	4	91	34	82
Stafford Rangers Stripes	34	21	7	6	92	42	70
Ashbourne United	34	18	7	9	68	55	61
Alsager Town Res.	34	17	7	10	82	55	58
Hanford	34	17	6	11	66	46	57
Norton	34	16	4	14	55	54	52
Stallington	34	15	5	14	61	66	50
Ball Haye Green	34	14	7	13	69	59	49
Foley	34	12	8	14	67	56	44
Newcastle Town Res.	34	11	9	14	60	66	42
Rocester Res.	34	11	8	15	66	62	41
Redgate Clayton	34	11	8	15	59	60	41
Goldenhill Wanderers	34	9	10	15	76	91	37
Eccleshall Res.	34	10	5	19	54	65	35
Abbey Hulton United	34	9	3	22	49	88	30
Florence Colliery	34	4	8	22	33	80	20
Stone Dominoes Res.	34	2	2	30	29	143	8

LEAGUE CUP
(Premier and Division One teams)

FIRST ROUND
Eccleshall Res. 7 Abbey Hulton United 1
Stone D. Res. 1 **Ball Haye Green** 2

SECOND ROUND
Abbey Hulton United 2 Alsager Town Res. 0
Alsagers Bank 2 **Florence** 3
Audley & District 2 Hanley Res. 1
Ball Haye Green 1 **Hanley Town** 3
Biddulph Town 5 Newcastle Town Youth 0
Chesterton 1 **Norton** 1 aet (3-4p)
Congleton Vale 1 Wolstanton 0
Foley 5 New Penny 0
Foley Res. 3 Barlaston 1
Goldenhill Wdrs 7 Brocton Res. 1
Manor Inne 2 **Ashbourne United** 3
Newcastle Town Res. 3 Eccleshall Res. 1
Redgate Clayton 2 Holt JCB 0
Rocester Res. 0 **Red. Clayton Res.** 1
Stallington 2 **Hanford** 4
Stone Old Alleynians 1 **Stafford Rangers Stripes** 2

THIRD ROUND
Abbey Hulton United 5 Audley & District 4
Florence Colliery 1 **Hanley Town** 2
Norton 3 Foley Res. 2
Congleton Vale 0 **Redgate Clayton** 1
Goldenhill Wanderers 1 Redgate Clayton Res. 1 aet (4-2p)
Newcastle Town Res. 0 **Foley** 1
Hanford (w/o) v Biddulph Town (scr.)
Stafford Rangers Stripes 4 Ashbourne United 1

QUARTER-FINALS
Hanford 1 Abbey Hulton United 0
Hanley Town 4 Foley 2 aet
Norton 4 Goldenhill Wanderers 1
Stafford RS 0 **Red. Clayton** 3 aet

SEMI-FINALS
Norton 0 Hanford 0 aet (3-4p)
Redgate Clayton 1 **Hanley Town** 3

FINAL
(April 30th at Norton Utd)
Hanford 1 Hanley Town 0

WWW.NLNEWSDESK.CO.UK

STAFFORDSHIRE COUNTY LEAGUE PREMIER DIVISION CONSTITUTION 2007-08

ABBEY HULTON UNITED.......... Birches Head Road, Abbey Hulton, Stoke-on-Trent ST2 8DD 01782 544232
ALSAGER TOWN RESERVES.......... The Town Ground, Woodland Court, Alsager ST7 2DP.......... 01270 882336
ASHBOURNE UNITED.......... Rocester FC, Riversfield, Mill Street, Rocester, Uttoxeter ST14 5TX.......... 01889 590463
BALL HAYE GREEN.......... Ball Haye Green WMC, Ball Haye Green, Leek ST13 6BH.......... 01538 371926
BARLASTON.......... Wedgwood Sports & Social, Barlaston Park, Barlaston, Stoke-on-Trent ST12 9ES.......... 01782 373442
CONGLETON VALE.......... Back Lane Playing Fields, Congleton CW12 4RB.......... 01260 276975
ECCLESHALL AFC.......... Pershall Park, Chester Road, Eccleshall ST21 6NE.......... 01785 851351
FLORENCE.......... Florence Sports & Social, Lightwood Road, Stoke-on-Trent ST3 4JS.......... 01782 312881
FOLEY.......... Whitcombe Road, Meir, Stoke-on-Trent ST3 6NU.......... 01782 595274
GOLDENHILL WANDERERS.. Sandyford Cricket Club, Shelford Rd, Sandyford, Stoke-on-Trent ST6 5LA.......... 01782 811977
HANLEY TOWN.......... Abbey Lane, Abbey Hulton, Bucknall, Stoke-on-Trent ST8 8AJ.......... 01782 267234
NEWCASTLE TOWN RESERVES.. Lyme Valley Parkway Stadium, Clayton, Newcastle-under-Lyme ST5 3BF........ 01782 662351/622350
NORTON.......... Norton CC & MW Institute, Community Drive, Smallthorne, Stoke-on-Trent ST6 1QE.......... 01782 838290
REDGATE CLAYTON.......... Northwood Lane, Clayton, Newcastle-under-Lyme ST5 4BN.......... 01782 717409
ROCESTER RESERVES.......... Hillsfield, Mill Street, Rocester, Uttoxeter ST14 5TX.......... 01889 590463
STALLINGTON.......... Stallington Hospital, Fulford Lane, Stallington Road, Blythe Bridge ST11 9PD.......... 07785 338804
WOLSTANTON UNITED.. Bradwell Comm. Centre, Riceyman Road, Bradwell, Newcastle-under-Lyme ST5 8LF.......... 01782 660818
IN: Barlaston (P), Congleton Vale (P)
OUT: Hanford (W), Stafford Rangers Stripes (W), Stone Dominoes Reserves (W)

	Abbey Hulton United Res.	Alsagers Bank	Audley & District	Barlaston	Biddulph Town	Brocton Res.	Chesterton	Congleton Vale	Featherstone	Foley Res.	Hanley Town Res.	Holt JCB	Manor Inne	New Penny	Newcastle Town Youth	Redgate Clayton Res.	Stone Old Alleynians
Abbey Hulton U. Res.		1-5	1-5	1-0	1-2	3-2	1-4	1-2	1-3	2-0	2-4	1-0	3-2	0-1	3-0	2-1	0-2
Alsagers Bank	1-3	*D*	1-3	1-3	4-2	3-0	3-0	3-2	4-0	8-0	1-2	3-2	1-2	3-0	1-3	2-0	4-2
Audley & District	3-1	3-3	*I*	0-2	3-0	3-1	2-2	0-3	1-5	1-0	1-3	1-3	0-1	0-1	0-0	0-3	0-3
Barlaston	2-0	3-0	7-0	*V*	3-1	3-0	0-1	0-2	10-2	0-3	2-1	4-0	4-0	4-2	2-1	1-1	1-0
Biddulph Town	2-6	2-3	1-1	0-1	*I*	5-3	2-2	0-2	4-4	1-2	4-1	3-3	3-3	1-1	3-0	3-1	2-0
Brocton Res.	4-2	0-1	3-1	1-3	1-0	*S*	0-9	0-6	2-4	1-3	1-4	1-3	0-5	1-2	2-1	0-1	1-2
Chesterton	4-1	2-3	3-5	3-2	2-1	4-0	*I*	3-2	3-2	2-0	5-0	2-2	2-1	3-0	2-1	3-3	2-2
Congleton Vale	5-0	2-0	3-0	1-2	3-2	5-0	2-1	*O*	4-0	2-1	4-1	3-1	1-0	1-2	6-1	1-2	2-0
Featherstone	2-3	0-3	1-3	2-7	3-2	3-4	2-1	0-1	*N*	0-6	0-1	5-0	3-3	2-2	1-2	2-3	0-1
Foley Res.	2-1	2-0	1-1	1-3	3-0	7-0	0-1	0-1	3-2		3-4	1-2	3-3	2-0	6-1	1-5	2-2
Hanley Town Res.	3-1	1-3	6-1	4-1	6-1	8-1	1-0	3-1	2-3	4-1		2-2	4-1	3-7	3-0	2-2	3-1
Holt JCB	7-0	1-3	5-0	1-2	1-6	3-1	2-3	1-2	4-1	0-1	2-1		7-1	1-2	2-3	0-3	2-2
Manor Inne	6-3	0-3	3-1	0-2	4-3	2-3	2-3	1-3	1-3	2-3	1-0	3-2	*N*	1-2	6-3	1-2	1-0
New Penny	6-1	1-2	3-0	1-0	4-0	3-1	0-1	0-1	3-1	1-0	1-1	3-1	0-0	*O*	2-0	0-1	4-1
Newcastle Town Yth	4-2	1-4	0-0	0-6	1-1	2-1	1-2	1-3	1-0	1-1	1-1	3-0	3-7	1-2		0-1	2-2
Redgate Clayton Res.	1-1	2-1	0-0	0-4	2-2	1-0	3-4	3-3	2-0	0-2	1-1	2-1	3-2	2-2	1-3	*E*	2-2
Stone Old Alleynians	2-1	2-1	4-0	0-1	2-0	3-1	1-4	0-6	1-3	0-4	1-2	2-3	0-1	0-0	5-3	2-3	

Division One

	P	W	D	L	F	A	Pts
Congleton Vale	32	25	1	6	87	29	76
Barlaston	32	24	1	7	85	30	73
Chesterton	32	21	5	6	83	47	68
Hanley Town Res.	32	19	5	8	83	52	62
Alsagers Bank	32	19	1	12	75	48	58
New Penny	32	17	6	9	61	43	57
Redgate Clayton Res.	32	15	10	7	57	48	55
Foley Res.	32	15	4	13	65	53	49
Manor Inne	32	12	3	17	67	77	39
Holt JCB	32	10	4	18	65	70	34
Stone Old Alleynians	32	9	7	16	47	62	34
Featherstone	32	10	3	19	61	86	33
Newcastle Town Youth	32	8	7	17	44	78	31
Audley & District	32	8	7	17	39	73	31
Abbey Hulton United Res.	32	10	1	21	49	87	31
Biddulph Town	32	7	8	17	59	76	29
Brocton Res.	32	6	1	25	37	105	19

LEAGUE TROPHY
(Division One and Division Two teams

FIRST ROUND
Stallington Res. 5 MS Akademik 0
SECOND ROUND
Abbey Hulton United Res. 2 Chesterton Y & A 0
Audley & District 6 Tunstall 0
Barlaston 2 Cheadle Town OB 0
Biddulph Town 5 Screwfix 1
Brocton Res. 1 Real Macot 4
Hanley Town Res. 2 Manor Inne 1
Hawkins Sport Youth 3 Milton United 2
Lichfield Enots 3 Congleton Vale 4
New Penny 4 Holt JCB Res. 2
Newcastle Town Youth 2 Ball Green Y & A 1
Red. Clayton Res. 3 Holt JCB 1 *aet*
Stafford Rangers u-21s 3 Leek CSOB 'A' 2
Stallington Res. 0 Alsagers Bank 5
Stone Old Alleynians 4 Stone Old Alleynians Res. 1
Stretton Eagles 4 Chesterton 1
Wolstanton United Res. 2 Foley Res. 0

THIRD ROUND
Abbey Hulton United Res. 2 Newcastle Town Youth 1
Barlaston 3 Red. Clayton Res. 0
Congleton Vale 4 Hanley Res. 0
Hawkins S. Yth 2 Alsagers Bank 4
New Penny 2 Stretton Eagles 4
Real Macot 2 Stone OA 7
Stafford Rangers u-21s (w/o) v Biddulph Town (scr.)
Wolstanton United Res. 1 Audley & District 1 aet (5-4p)
QUARTER-FINALS
Alsagers Bank 5 Stafford Rangers u-21s 1
Congleton V. 2 Wolstanton Res. 1
Stone Old Alleynians 0 Barlaston 1
Stretton Eagles 4 Abbey Hulton United Res. 2 *aet*
SEMI-FINALS
Alsagers Bank 1 Barlaston 3
Stretton Eagles 3 Congleton Vale 1
FINAL
(March 12th at Newcastle Town)
Barlaston 1 Stretton Eagles 0

STAFFORDSHIRE COUNTY LEAGUE DIVISION ONE CONSTITUTION 2007-08

ALSAGERS BANK .... The Drive, Alsagers Bank, Stoke-on-Trent ST7 8BB .... None
AUDLEY & DISTRICT .... Town Fields, Old Road, Bignall, Stoke-on-Trent ST7 8QH 01782 723482
CHESTERTON .... Red Street Community Centre, Talke Road, Newcastle-under-Lyme ST5 7AH .... None
FEATHERSTONE............ HMP Featherstone, New Road, Featherstone, Wolverhampton WV10 7PU 01902 703132
FOLEY RESERVES...................... Whitcombe Road, Meir, Stoke-on-Trent ST3 6NU 01782 595274
HANLEY TOWN RESERVES ..... Abbey Lane, Abbey Hulton, Bucknall, Stoke-on-Trent ST8 8AJ 01782 267234
HAWKINS SPORTS YOUTH ..... Hawkins Sports Club, Coppice Lane, Cheslyn Hay, Walsall WS6 7EY .... None
HOLT JCB .... JCB Lakeside Club, Station Road, Rocester, Uttoxeter ST14 5LS 01889 591057
LICHFIELD ENOTS .... Brownsfield Road, off Eastern Avenue, Lichfield WS13 6SB 01543 254361
MANOR INNE .... Sandyford Cricket Club, Shelford Road, Sandyford, Stoke-on-Trent ST6 5LA .... None
NEWCASTLE TOWN 'A' ...... Lyme Valley Parkway Stadium, Clayton, Newcastle-under-Lyne ST5 3BF 01782 662351
NORTHWOOD TOWN .... Northwood Stadium, Keelings Road, Hanley, Stoke-on-Trent ST1 6PA .... None
REDGATE CLAYTON RESERVES.... Northwood Lane, Clayton, Newcastle-under-Lyme ST5 4BN 01782 717409
SANDBACH UNITED .... Legends Sports Club, Sunnybank Road, Crewe CW2 8WB 01270 656868
STRETTON EAGLES .... Hatton Sports & Social Club Playing Fields, Scropton Road, Hatton, Derby DE65 5DT ... 01283 815119

IN: Hawkins Sport Youth (P), Lichfield Enots (P), Sandbach United (P – Crewe & District League), Stretton Eagles (P)
OUT: Abbey Hulton United Reserves (R), Barlaston (P), Biddulph Town (R), Brocton Reserves (W), Congleton Vale (P), Stone Old Alleynians (S – West Midlands (Regional) League Division Two)
New Penny become Northwood Town, Newcastle Town Youth become Newcastle Town 'A'

	Ball Green Y & A	Cheadle Town Old Boys	Chesterton Youth & Adult	Hawkins Sport Youth	Holt JCB Res.	Leek CSOB 'A'	Lichfield Enots	MS Akademik	Milton United	Real Macot	Screwfix Direct	Stafford Rangers u-21s	Stallington Res.	Stone Old Alleynians Res.	Stretton Eagles	Tunstall Town	Wolstanton United Res.
Ball Green Y & A		2-3	7-2	2-6	3-1	3-5	0-1	8-0	4-1	5-2	2-2	0-5	0-0	1-1	3-8	3-0	0-3
Cheadle Town OB	0-1	D	0-0	0-3	3-2	1-0	2-0	n/a	2-0	1-1	3-0	1-0	7-0	1-0	1-2	7-0	2-3
Chesterton Youth & Adult	2-4	2-2	I	1-4	2-1	1-3	0-6	3-1	1-0	1-1	3-1	1-5	1-3	1-3	0-3	11-0	1-5
Hawkins Sport Youth	5-1	1-1	3-0	V	4-1	4-0	1-3	n/a	1-0	3-1	11-1	2-0	1-3	4-0	0-0	8-0	2-1
Holt JCB Res.	7-2	2-1	2-1	1-4	I	0-1	1-6	n/a	1-0	2-3	1-0	0-3	2-0	1-4		6-0	1-2
Leek CSOB 'A'	3-0	3-2	1-0	4-1	1-2	S	0-5	n/a	1-0	2-1	6-0	3-2	2-1	3-2	1-2	6-0	0-1
Lichfield Enots	3-0	1-0	3-1	2-5	1-0	2-0	I	n/a	3-0	2-0	10-0	5-2	3-0	1-1	0-4	9-0	0-1
MS Akademik	1-3	1-9	n/a	1-8	1-8	2-5	n/a	O	n/a	n/a	n/a	1-4	n/a	1-3	2-4	1-0	0-10
Milton United	0-0	0-1	5-2	0-5	2-3	0-5	0-3	n/a	N	0-0	5-2	1-1	1-3	3-4	0-3	7-0	4-3
Real Macot	3-2	1-4	1-1	0-4	2-3	1-1	1-4	n/a	3-1		3-1	1-0	2-4	2-1	0-6	8-1	1-1
Screwfix Direct	2-6	0-2	4-1	0-1	2-1	1-3	0-8	6-1	1-2	0-0		0-2	8-2	2-1	0-7	2-2	0-6
Stafford Rgrs u-21s	2-2	0-1	8-1	3-1	2-1	0-2	1-4	n/a	0-0	3-0	4-0		5-1	0-1	1-1	12-0	2-2
Stallington Res.	2-2	1-1	7-3	2-2	3-0	0-3	3-3	4-0	0-0	2-1	5-1	4-5		4-0	3-5	6-0	0-1
Stone Old Alleynians Res.	1-2	3-3	2-2	0-1	1-1	1-4	0-3	6-4	2-4	8-2	5-1	0-2	0-0	O	2-6	6-2	1-2
Stretton Eagles	1-1	4-1	8-0	3-1	7-2	2-3	1-0	n/a	5-1	3-1	9-0	7-0	10-0	5-3	N	10-0	1-0
Tunstall Town	0-10	0-3	1-2	0-9	0-4	0-9	1-5	3-2	0-4	0-2	1-5	0-6	0-1	0-6	0-7	E	0-10
Wolstanton United Res.	4-1	2-3	4-1	0-2	3-1	1-0	5-1	n/a	3-4	4-0	2-1	0-2	1-2	2-1	2-5	5-0	

Note – MS Akademik withdrew during the course of the season
Their results are shown above but are expunged from the league table

Division Two	P	W	D	L	F	A	Pts
Stretton Eagles	30	26	3	1	139	27	81
Hawkins Sport Youth	30	22	3	5	99	30	69
Lichfield Enots	30	22	2	6	97	30	68
Leek CSOB 'A'	30	21	1	8	75	36	64
Wolstanton United Res.	30	20	3	7	81	35	63
Cheadle Town Old Boys	30	15	7	8	58	34	52
Stafford Rangers u-21s	30	14	5	11	77	44	47
Stallington Res.	30	13	7	10	65	67	46
Ball Green Y & A	30	10	7	13	69	75	37
Holt JCB Res.	30	11	1	18	50	66	34
Real Macot	30	8	7	15	44	70	31
Milton United	30	8	5	17	44	61	29
Stone Old Alleynians Res.	30	7	6	17	56	66	27
Chesterton Youth & Adult	30	5	5	20	45	97	20
Screwfix Direct	30	5	3	22	36	116	18
Tunstall Town	30	0	1	29	8	189	1

MS Akademik – record expunged

WWW.NLNEWSDESK.CO.UK

DIVISION TWO CUP

FIRST ROUND
Ball Green Y & A 2 **Leek CSOB 'A'** 5
Cheadle Town Old Boys 0 **Real Macot** 2
Hawkins Sport Youth 2 Stallington Res. 1
Holt JCB Res. 0 **Milton United** 1
Screwfix Direct 1 **Wolstanton United Res.** 8
Stafford Rangers u-21s 9 Tunstall Town 1
Stone Old Alleynians Res. 0 **Lichfield Enots** 6
Stretton Eagles 8 MS Akademik 0

QUARTER-FINALS
Hawkins Sport Youth 1 **Milton United** 2
Real Macot 1 **Leek CSOB 'A'** 2
Stafford Rangers u-21s 1 **Stretton Eagles** 3
Wolstanton United Res. 1 **Lichfield Enots** 4

SEMI-FINALS
Leek CSOB 'A' 1 **Stretton Eagles** 2
Milton United 1 Lichfield Enots 0

FINAL
(March 26th at Newcastle Town)
Milton United 0 **Stretton Eagles** 0 *aet* (3-4p)

STAFFORDSHIRE COUNTY LEAGUE DIVISION TWO CONSTITUTION 2007-08
ABBEY HULTON UNITED RESERVES . . Birches Head Road, Abbey Hulton, Stoke-on-Trent ST2 8DD 01782 544232
BALL GREEN Y & A. . . . . Wilding Road, Ball Green, Stoke-on-Trent ST6 8BA . . . . None
BARTON UNITED . . . . Leek Road, Milton, Stoke-on-Trent ST9 9NJ . . . . None
BIDDULPH TOWN. . . . . Biddulph Victoria FC, Tunstall Road, Knypersley, Stoke-On-Trent ST8 7AQ. 01782 522737
CHEADLE TOWN OLD BOYS . . . . Cheadle Leisure Centre, Allen Street, Cheadle ST10 1HJ 01538 753331
FLORENCE RESERVES. . . . . Florence Sports & Social, Lightwood Road, Stoke-on-Trent ST3 4JS 01782 312881
REAL MACOT . . . . Watery Lane, Longton, Stoke-on-Trent ST3 4QY . . . . None
STALLINGTON RESERVES . . Stallington Hospital, Fulford Lane, Stallington Road, Blythe Bridge ST11 9PD 07785 338804
WOLSTANTON UNITED RESERVES . . Riceyman Road, Bradwell, Newcastle-under-Lyne ST5 8LF 01782 660818
IN: Abbey Hulton United Reserves (R), Biddulph Town (R), Florence Reserves (N)
OUT: Chesterton Youth & Adult (W), Hawkins Sport Youth (P), Holt JCB Reserves (W), Leek CSOB 'A' (W), Lichfield Enots (P), MS Akademik (WS), Screwfix Direct (R), Stafford Rangers u-21s (W), Stone Old Alleynians Reserves (R), Stretton Eagles (P), Tunstall Town (R)
Milton United become Barton United

STAFFORDSHIRE COUNTY LEAGUE DIVISION THREE CONSTITUTION 2007-08
New division formed by:
Ball Haye Green Reserves (N), Initial Spartans (N), Screwfix Direct (R), Stone Old Alleynians Reserves (R), Tunstall Town (R), Sandbach United u-21s (youth football), Unity United (N), Waterhayes (N)

SUFFOLK & IPSWICH LEAGUE

	Achilles	Brantham Athletic	Capel Plough	Cockfield United	Coplestonians	Crane Sports	East Bergholt United	Felixstowe United	Grundisburgh	Haughley United	Ipswich Athletic	Leiston St Margarets	Melton St Audrys	Ransomes Sports	Stowupland Falcons	Westerfield United
Achilles	S	3-1	1-3	1-2	1-1	2-3	3-1	3-1	1-3	0-2	2-3	3-1	3-1	1-1	2-2	3-0
Brantham Athletic	3-3	E	0-1	3-2	1-1	4-1	0-0	5-1	1-5	0-2	2-2	1-0	1-0	4-1	2-0	3-1
Capel Plough	2-1	4-1	N	2-0	1-0	0-1	2-0	0-0	0-3	4-2	2-1	2-2	0-3	0-1	1-0	2-1
Cockfield United	3-1	3-3	0-9	I	3-1	3-5	3-2	1-0	0-4	1-3	0-4	1-3	2-7	1-3	2-1	0-1
Coplestonians	2-1	0-2	5-1	5-0	O	2-3	1-1	0-0	1-2	0-1	0-1	0-2	0-1	4-1	1-2	3-0
Crane Sports	2-0	2-0	2-2	3-1	3-2	R	2-2	1-0	1-3	2-3	3-5	1-2	3-0	2-0	2-1	1-2
East Bergholt United	0-2	1-0	3-2	1-1	2-3	2-3		2-1	0-5	2-2	1-1	1-0	1-1	1-1	1-5	1-1
Felixstowe United	0-0	1-2	5-4	1-1	2-1	4-1	0-2		0-1	2-1	3-3	4-0	1-0	2-0	1-3	2-4
Grundisburgh	2-1	1-1	0-1	4-0	2-0	1-0	1-0	2-1	D	2-3	4-1	2-0	4-0	3-3	1-2	2-0
Haughley United	4-2	4-1	1-0	2-0	0-0	1-2	5-0	0-0	1-0	I	7-0	3-1	2-1	1-3	1-2	4-0
Ipswich Athletic	5-2	1-1	3-1	4-1	1-4	4-3	1-2	0-2	0-1	1-5	V	1-2	3-1	1-2	2-1	4-3
Leiston St Margarets	3-1	1-3	0-1	5-1	1-2	6-0	1-2	2-1	1-2	2-4	4-0	I	3-2	1-4	2-0	2-2
Melton St Audrys	4-2	0-0	2-0	4-0	0-2	1-0	2-1	1-1	0-2	0-0	2-1	1-1	S	1-1	1-1	5-0
Ransomes Sports	5-1	1-2	0-1	2-2	2-2	1-3	0-1	1-1	1-1	1-0	0-2	1-1	I		4-2	2-1
Stowupland Falcons	0-2	1-5	0-2	6-0	3-2	2-1	3-3	1-3	1-1	0-2	0-2	2-1	0-2	1-1	O	3-2
Westerfield United	5-2	1-0	0-0	3-0	0-3	0-2	2-2	1-3	1-1	0-2	3-1	2-2	1-2	3-2	3-1	N

Senior Division		P	W	D	L	F	A	Pts
Grundisburgh		30	21	5	4	65	22	68
Haughley United		30	20	5	5	69	29	65
Capel Plough		30	16	4	10	50	38	52
Crane Sports		30	15	3	12	57	57	48
Brantham Athletic		30	13	8	9	52	44	47
Melton St Audrys	-3	30	12	8	10	46	37	41
Felixstowe United		30	11	8	11	45	42	41
Leiston St Margarets		30	12	4	14	52	49	40
Coplestonians		30	11	5	14	48	38	38
Ransomes Sports		30	9	10	11	45	49	37
Ipswich Athletic	-3	30	12	4	14	56	65	37
Stowupland Falcons		30	10	5	15	46	55	35
East Bergholt United		30	8	11	11	40	56	35
Westerfield United		30	9	6	15	43	60	33
Achilles		30	8	5	17	51	65	29
Cockfield United		30	5	5	20	34	93	20

Division One		P	W	D	L	F	A	Pts
Stonham Aspal		26	17	3	6	80	28	54
BT Trimley		26	17	2	7	74	32	53
Old Newton United		26	16	5	5	69	33	53
St Johns		26	15	5	6	78	61	50
Willis		26	14	4	8	62	54	46
Bramford United		26	14	3	9	60	38	45
Framlingham Town		26	12	5	9	51	40	41
St Edmunds 65		26	10	5	11	53	57	35
Stanton		26	10	4	12	47	60	34
Mendlesham		26	7	7	12	58	78	28
Thurston		26	7	6	13	52	56	27
Woodbridge Athletic		26	6	7	13	34	60	25
Wickham Market		25	3	3	19	36	85	12
Needham Market 'A'	-6	25	2	3	20	25	97	3

Needham Market 'A' v Wickham Market not played

SUFFOLK & IPSWICH LEAGUE SENIOR DIVISION CONSTITUTION 2007-08

BT TRIMLEY . . . . Trimley Sports & Social Club, High Road, Trimley St Martin IP11 0RJ 01394 275240
BRANTHAM ATHLETIC . . . . . Athletic & Social Club, New Village, Brantham, near Manningtree CO11 1RZ 01206 392506
CAPEL PLOUGH . . . . Friars, Capel St Mary, Ipswich IP9 2XS . . . . None
COPLESTONIANS . . . . Copleston High School, Copleston Road, Ipswich IP4 5HD 01473 244178
CRANE SPORTS . . . . King George V Playing Field, Old Norwich Road, Ipswich IP1 6LE 01473 464030
EAST BERGHOLT UNITED . . . . Gandish Road, East Bergholt, Colchester CO7 6TP . . . . None
FELIXSTOWE UNITED . . . . Kirton Recreation Ground, Back Road, Kirton, Ipswich IP10 0PW . . . . None
GRUNDISBURGH . . . . The Playing Field, Ipswich Road, Grundisburgh, Woodbridge IP13 6TJ 01473 738234
HAUGHLEY UNITED . . . . King George V Playing Field, Green Road, Haughley IP14 3RA 01449 673460
IPSWICH ATHLETIC . . . . Bourne Vale Social Ground, Halifax Road, Ipswich IP2 8RE . . . . None
LEISTON ST MARGARETS . . . . Junction Meadow, Abbey Road, Leiston IP16 4RD 01728 831239
MELTON ST AUDRYS . . . . St Audrys Sports & Social Club, Lodge Farm Lane, Melton, Woodbridge IP12 1LX . . . . None
RANSOMES SPORTS . . . . Ransomes Sports & Social Club, Sidegate Avenue, Ipswich IP4 4JJ 01473 726134
STONHAM ASPAL . . . . Delsons Meadow, Three Crossways, Stonham Aspal, Stowmarket IP14 6AN 01449 711051
STOWUPLAND FALCONS . . . . The Village Hall, Church Road, Stowupland IP14 4BQ 01449 771010
WESTERFIELD UNITED . . . . Rushmere Sports Club, The Street, Rushmere St Andrew, Ipswich IP5 1DE 01473 272525

IN: BT Trimley (P), Stonham Aspal (P)

OUT: Achilles (R), Cockfield United (R)

LEAGUE CUP

THIRD ROUND

Achilles 1 Brantham Athletic 3
(Brantham Athletic expelled)
Cockfield United 2 Trimley Red Devils 1
Coplestonians 1 Willis 1 *aet* (4-1p)
Crane Sports 3 St Clements Hospital 2
Elmswell 0 Leiston St Margarets 3
Felixstowe United 3 Mendlesham 0
Grundisburgh 5 Tattingstone United 1
Haughley United 7 Bildeston Rangers 0
Ipswich Athletic 3 Ransomes Sports 2
Old Newton United 5 Needham Market 'A' 1
St Edmunds '65 2 Wenhaston United 2 *aet* (3-5p)
Stonham Aspal 4 Framlingham Town 2
(at Framlingham Town)
Stowmarket Stag 0 Westerfield United 3
Stowupland Falcons 1 BT Trimley 3
Stradbroke United 2 John Bull United 4
Thurston 0 Melton St Audrys 3

FOURTH ROUND

Crane Sports 5 Leiston St Margarets 1
Grundisburgh 5 BT Trimley 2
Haughley United 5 Felixstowe United 0
John Bull United 1 Wenhaston United 0
Melton St Audrys 4 Achilles 0
Old Newton United 3 Cockfield United 2
Stonham Aspal 0 Coplestonians 1 *(at Coplestonians)*
Westerfield United 2 Ipswich Athletic 1

QUARTER-FINALS

Crane Sports 6 John Bull United 1
Grundisburgh 2 Haughley United 1
Melton St Audrys 2 Coplestonians 1 *aet*
Westerfield United 3 Old Newton United 2

SEMI-FINALS

Crane Sports 6 Westerfield United 2 *(at Achilles)*
Melton St Audrys 3 Grundisburgh 1 *(at Ipswich Athletic)*
FINAL *(May 8th at Woodbridge Town)*
Melton St Audrys 1 Crane Sports 1 *aet* (5-4p)

Division Two		P	W	D	L	F	A	Pts
Claydon		26	18	4	4	80	35	58
Bildeston Rangers		26	16	3	7	94	52	51
Wenhaston United	-6	26	17	5	4	81	28	50
Halesworth Town		26	14	5	7	94	45	47
Bramford Road Old Boys	-4	26	14	8	4	79	47	46
Stradbroke United		26	15	0	11	69	56	45
Bacton United		26	13	4	9	83	66	43
Salvation Army		26	9	8	9	47	45	35
AFC Hoxne		26	8	7	11	59	63	31
John Bull United		26	9	3	14	56	72	30
Peasenhall United	-6	26	7	5	14	55	71	20
Ipswich Exiles		26	5	4	17	42	69	19
Coddenham		26	5	3	18	41	87	18
Dennington United		26	2	1	23	21	165	7

Division Four		P	W	D	L	F	A	Pts
Stowmarket Stag		26	19	3	4	86	26	60
St Clements Hospital		26	19	3	4	80	29	60
Ipswich Postals		26	18	2	6	88	37	56
Waterside		26	17	5	4	68	35	56
Meadlands	-6	26	18	1	7	80	36	49
Benhall St Mary		26	13	2	11	51	50	41
Great Blakenham		26	11	5	10	54	50	38
Wenhaston United Res.		25	12	2	11	50	44	38
Henley Athletic		26	8	8	10	42	49	32
Walsham-le-Willows 'A'		26	7	1	18	43	61	22
Ipswich Exiles Res.		26	5	4	17	34	84	19
East Bergholt United 'A'		26	4	4	18	39	94	16
Somersham Res.		25	3	1	21	29	106	10
Tattingstone United	-7	26	3	7	16	39	80	9

Wenhaston United Res. v Somersham Res. not played

Division Six		P	W	D	L	F	A	Pts
Albion Mills Res.		24	20	0	4	115	31	60
Saxmundham Sports Res.		24	17	6	1	85	29	57
Halesworth Town Res.		24	14	2	8	59	42	44
AFC Hoxne Res.	-3	24	13	5	6	93	51	41
Tacket Street BBOB Res.		24	12	3	9	68	61	39
Needham Market Vets		24	10	6	8	67	55	36
BT Trimley 'A'	-3	24	12	3	9	62	67	36
Benhall St Mary Res.		24	11	1	12	50	86	34
Dennington United Res.		24	8	3	13	47	67	27
Shotley		24	6	2	16	56	103	20
Peasenhall United Res.		24	5	4	15	45	74	19
Old Newton United 'A'	-3	24	5	4	15	47	65	16
Titans	-3	24	3	1	20	39	102	7

RESERVES CUP

FINAL *(May 4th at Needham Market)*
Haughley United Res. 2 Melton St Audrys Res. 1

JUNIOR CUP

FINAL *(April 27th at Framlingham Town)*
Bramford Road OB Res. 0 Wenhaston Utd Res. 0 *aet* (4-3p)

Division Three		P	W	D	L	F	A	Pts
Saxmundham Sports		26	22	3	1	91	24	69
Sporting '87		26	17	5	4	66	24	56
Martlesham Athletic		26	16	5	5	83	37	53
Elmswell		26	15	2	9	68	59	47
Albion Mills		26	13	5	8	49	28	44
Ipswich Athletic		26	12	8	6	69	57	44
Parkside United		26	12	5	9	79	52	41
Somersham		26	12	3	11	37	44	39
Coplestonians 'A'		26	8	6	12	56	72	30
Tacket Street BBOB		26	6	6	14	44	73	24
Sproughton Sports		26	7	1	18	46	78	22
Ufford Sports		26	5	4	17	44	70	19
Sizewell & Aldeburgh	-3	26	4	4	18	32	95	13
Alstons		26	3	3	20	45	96	7

Division Five		P	W	D	L	F	A	Pts
Trimley Red Devils		26	22	4	0	149	18	70
Woolverstone United		26	20	3	3	127	40	63
Henley Athletic Res.		26	19	3	4	91	42	60
Stowupland Falcons 'A'		26	13	4	9	69	56	43
Claydon Res.		26	11	6	9	59	52	39
Bramford Road OB Res.	-3	26	11	5	10	69	61	35
St Clements Hospital Res.		26	9	4	13	36	62	31
Salvation Army Res.		26	7	6	13	50	78	27
Bacton United Res.		26	9	0	17	60	90	27
Stonham Aspal 'A'		26	8	3	15	44	76	27
Stradbroke United Res.		26	8	3	15	54	117	27
Coddenham Res.		26	7	5	14	57	69	26
Elmswell Res.		26	6	5	15	43	105	23
Sproughton Sports Res.		26	5	3	18	38	80	18

Intermediate Division A		P	W	D	L	F	A	Pts
Haughley United Res.		26	21	1	4	71	21	64
Ipswich Athletic Res.	-6	26	22	2	2	91	33	62
Brantham Athletic Res.		26	18	3	5	81	40	57
Grundisburgh Res.		26	14	4	8	63	43	46
Coplestonians Res.		26	14	3	9	63	36	45
Felixstowe United Res.		26	10	4	12	42	54	34
Crane Sports Res.		26	11	1	14	48	68	34
Capel Plough Res.		26	10	2	14	46	59	32
East Bergholt United Res.		26	9	4	13	49	60	31
Westerfield United Res.	-6	26	10	3	13	70	70	27
Old Newton United Res.		26	8	3	15	54	71	27
Leiston St Margarets Res.	-3	26	8	3	15	37	55	24
Cockfield United Res.		26	4	2	20	34	99	14
Framlingham Town Res.	-3	26	5	1	20	33	73	13

Intermediate Division B		P	W	D	L	F	A	Pts
Willis Res.		28	23	3	2	123	37	72
Melton St Audrys Res.		28	21	4	3	95	27	67
Stowupland Falcons Res.		28	16	5	7	87	51	53
Ransomes Sports Res.	-6	28	19	2	7	79	49	53
Achilles Res.		28	15	6	7	78	41	51
Stonham Aspal Res.		28	11	7	10	76	52	40
Stanton Res.		28	12	4	12	61	51	40
Woodbridge Athletic Res.		28	10	8	10	69	43	38
BT Trimley Res.		28	11	4	13	53	75	37
St Johns Res.		28	11	3	14	76	77	36
St Edmunds 65 Res.		28	11	3	14	52	80	36
Bramford United Res.		28	9	4	15	69	68	31
Mendlesham Res.		28	5	1	22	54	126	16
Wickham Market Res.	-3	28	4	2	22	42	102	11
Thurston Res.	-6	28	3	2	23	29	164	1

WWW.NLNEWSDESK.CO.UK

SUSSEX COUNTY LEAGUE

	Arundel	Chichester CU	Crowborough A.	East Preston	Eastbourne Town	Eastbourne UA	Hailsham Town	Hassocks	Littlehampton T.	Oakwood	Redhill	Ringmer	Rye United	Selsey	Shoreham	Sidley United	Three Bridges	Whitehawk	Wick	Worthing United
Arundel		0-2	0-4	1-0	1-3	3-0	2-0	1-0	6-1	5-0	0-1	3-0	3-1	0-0	3-1	0-0	4-2	0-0	2-0	7-2
Chichester City United	1-2		0-3	0-2	1-2	2-4	2-0	1-0	3-1	2-2	2-1	1-2	4-0	0-0	1-1	2-2	2-1	0-1	1-0	10-3
Crowborough Athletic	2-0	0-2		5-1	3-3	1-1	0-0	4-0	1-1	6-1	3-2	0-2	3-1	1-1	3-2	2-1	2-1	1-2	2-0	5-1
East Preston	1-2	1-0	1-2		0-2	1-0	0-1	2-3	1-2	0-2	3-2	0-0	0-0	4-0	4-1	0-1	1-0	0-3	3-0	3-1
Eastbourne Town	2-0	2-2	3-0	5-1	D	2-0	0-1	1-0	7-0	2-2	3-2	3-2	3-2	1-2	7-2	2-1	1-1	0-0	4-0	3-2
Eastbourne United Association	1-3	3-0	2-0	2-0	1-2	I	3-0	2-2	2-2	0-3	3-1	1-2	2-0	5-0	3-0	0-1	1-5	1-1	2-1	1-1
Hailsham Town	3-1	1-0	0-0	2-1	3-1	1-1	V	5-0	2-1	0-0	0-0	2-2	0-0	2-1	1-1	1-1	1-1	1-1	3-1	3-1
Hassocks	2-2	2-2	2-2	2-2	4-0	3-2	1-3	I	5-0	2-0	5-1	4-0	2-1	1-2	1-6	0-0	0-2	1-3	3-0	
Littlehampton Town	1-4	1-1	1-5	0-1	1-3	1-2	2-1	1-5	S	0-3	1-5	0-1	2-2	1-2	0-1	0-2	2-3	0-4	0-0	2-5
Oakwood	0-4	3-0	0-1	1-0	1-6	1-2	0-2	0-1	1-1	I	1-5	2-1	1-4	1-3	1-3	2-1	1-1	0-1	2-1	0-0
Redhill	3-3	1-2	0-1	0-1	2-3	1-1	2-0	5-1	0-0	1-2	O	0-2	1-1	2-0	1-1	1-3	1-0	1-1	1-4	3-0
Ringmer	0-2	0-0	1-2	2-1	1-3	3-2	1-1	1-1	2-0	2-3	0-2	N	1-1	2-0	3-1	1-1	4-3	0-4	3-3	4-2
Rye United	1-3	1-0	0-1	0-3	0-1	0-4	0-0	0-3	0-2	0-1	4-0	0-3		0-2	0-3	0-0	0-0	1-1	3-2	
Selsey	2-1	1-2	0-0	0-3	1-1	0-0	1-1	0-3	2-0	4-0	2-1	3-2	2-0	O	2-1	3-0	0-1	0-0	1-1	1-1
Shoreham	0-3	1-4	1-1	0-1	0-3	1-1	2-2	1-2	0-1	3-0	3-2	3-0	5-0	2-1	N	5-2	1-2	0-1	2-1	2-2
Sidley United	1-5	2-0	0-1	0-2	1-4	1-1	0-5	0-1	2-0	2-1	2-4	1-1	0-2	1-1	4-2	E	4-4	0-2	2-3	1-1
Three Bridges	0-2	3-2	1-2	2-3	0-4	4-3	0-1	2-2	0-1	1-1	2-1	6-2	4-0	4-1	1-2	1-1		0-4	0-1	1-1
Whitehawk	1-1	3-1	3-1	3-0	1-0	1-2	1-0	1-0	2-0	4-0	2-1	2-1	3-2	1-0	1-1	7-0	0-0		1-2	3-0
Wick	1-0	2-4	1-2	1-0	1-2	0-2	1-0	0-5	4-0	4-1	1-1	2-2	2-4	0-2	2-2	1-2	0-1	1-2		2-4
Worthing United	0-3	4-2	2-1	1-0	0-3	0-2	1-3	2-2	1-3	2-1	1-5	2-2	0-0	4-4	1-3	1-1	0-2	2-3		

Division One

		P	W	D	L	F	A	Pts
Eastbourne Town		38	27	6	5	97	42	87
Whitehawk		38	25	11	2	70	17	86
Arundel		38	23	6	9	82	39	75
Crowborough Ath.		38	22	9	7	73	40	75
Hassocks		38	20	8	10	80	45	68
Hailsham Town		38	17	15	6	52	29	66
Eastbourne Utd A.		38	16	9	13	66	51	57
Selsey		38	14	14	10	46	46	56
Ringmer	+2	38	13	11	14	59	66	52
East Preston		38	16	3	19	47	49	51
Chichester City Utd		38	14	7	17	59	58	49
Three Bridges		38	11	12	15	59	60	45
Shoreham		38	11	10	17	61	71	43
Sidley United		38	11	9	18	47	76	42
Redhill		38	11	8	19	61	65	41
Wick	-1	38	11	7	20	51	69	39
Oakwood		38	11	6	21	42	79	39
Worthing United		38	7	10	21	55	100	31
Rye United		38	6	9	23	33	73	27
Littlehampton Town		38	5	8	25	30	95	23

JOHN O'HARA LEAGUE CUP
(Division One and Two teams)

FIRST ROUND
Broadbridge Heath 2 Ringmer 2
Ringmer 4 Broadbridge Heath 0 *replay*
Crawley Down 0 **Selsey** 1
Rye United 2 Wealden 1
Sidley United 3 Peacehaven & T. 0
Storrington 0 **Hailsham Town** 1 *aet*
Westfield 1 **Worthing United** 3

SECOND ROUND
Arundel 4 Steyning Town 1
Chichester City United 0 **Lingfield** 2
East Grinstead Town 0 **Crowborough** 2
Hassocks 0 **Sidley United** 1
Lancing 1 **East Preston** 3
Littlehampton Town 0 **Pagham** 4
Mile Oak 2 Redhill 1
Oakwood 4 St Francis Rangers 1
Rye 0 **Whitehawk** 4 *(at Whitehawk)*
Seaford Town 1 **Eastbourne Town** 3
Shoreham 2 Hailsham Town 1 *aet*
Sidlesham 2 Three Bridges 2 **aet**
Three Bridges 3 Sidlesham 2 *replay*
Southwick 0 **Ringmer** 1
Wick 2 Saltdean United 1
Worthing United 3 Midhurst 2

THIRD ROUND
Eastbourne Town 4 Shoreham 1
Eastbourne UA 3 **Arundel** 3 *aet* (4-5p)
Oakwood 0 **Crowborough Athletic** 2
Pagham 5 Mile Oak 0
Sidley United 1 Lingfield 0
Three Bridges 3 Worthing United 2
Whitehawk 0 **Ringmer** 0 *aet*
Ringmer 1 Whitehawk 1 (3-1p)
replay
Wick 2 East Preston 1

QUARTER-FINALS
Arundel 3 **Eastbourne Town** 4
(at Eastbourne Town)
Crowborough Athletic 1 Ringmer 0
Sidley United 3 Pagham 2 *aet*
Wick 0 **Three Bridges** 3

SEMI-FINALS
Crowborough Ath. 5 Three Bridges 3
aet (at East Grinstead Town)
Sidley United 1 Eastbourne Town 1 *aet*
(4-3p) (at Hailsham Town)

FINAL
(April 6th at Ringmer)
Crowborough Athletic 2 Sidley United 1

SUSSEX COUNTY LEAGUE DIVISION ONE CONSTITUTION 2007-08

ARUNDEL . . . . Mill Road, Arundel BN18 9PA 01903 882548
CHICHESTER CITY UNITED . . . . Portfield, Church Road, Chichester PO19 4HN 01243 779875
CROWBOROUGH ATHLETIC . . Alderbrook Recreation Ground, Fermor Road, Crowborough TN6 3BT 01892 661893
EAST PRESTON . . . . Roundstone Recreation Ground, Lashmar Road, East Preston BN16 1ES 01903 777602
EASTBOURNE UNITED ASSOCIATION . . The Oval, Channel View Road, Eastbourne BN22 7LN 01323 726987
HAILSHAM TOWN . . . . The Beaconsfield, Western Road, Hailsham BN27 3DN 01323 840446
HASSOCKS . . . . The Beacon, Brighton Road, Hassocks BN6 9LY 01273 846044
OAKWOOD . . . . Oakwood Sports & Social Club, Tinsley Lane, Three Bridges RH10 8AW 01293 515747
PAGHAM . . . . Nyetimber Lane, Pagham, Bognor Regis PO21 3JY 01243 266111
REDHILL . . . . Kiln Brow, Three Arch Road, Redhill RH1 1HL 01737 762124
RINGMER . . . . Caburn Ground, Anchor Field, Ringmer BN8 5QN 01273 812734
RYE UNITED . . . . Rye Cricket & Football Salts, Fishmarket Road, Rye TN31 7LP 01797 223858
SELSEY . . . . High Street, Selsey, Chichester PO20 0QG 01243 603428
SHOREHAM . . . . Middle Road, Shoreham BN43 6LT 01273 454254
SIDLEY UNITED . . . . Gullivers Sports Ground, Glovers Lane, North Road, Bexhill TN39 5BL 01424 217765
ST FRANCIS RANGERS . . . . Lewes Road, Haywards Heath RH16 4EX 01444 457725
THREE BRIDGES . . . . Jubilee Field, Jubilee Way, Three Bridges, Crawley RH10 1LQ 01293 442006
WHITEHAWK . . . . Enclosed Ground, East Brighton Road, Brighton BN2 5TS 01273 609734
WICK . . . . Crabtree Park, Coomes Way, Wick, Littlehampton BN17 7LS 01903 713531
WORTHING UNITED . . . . Robert Albon Memorial Ground, Lyons Way, Worthing BN14 9JF 01903 234461
IN: Pagham (P), St Francis Rangers (P)
OUT: Eastbourne Town (P – Isthmian League Division One South), Littlehampton Town (R)

	Broadbridge Heath	Crawley Down	East Grinstead Town	Lancing	Lingfield	Midhurst & Easebourne Utd	Mile Oak	Pagham	Peacehaven & Telscombe	Saltdean United	Seaford Town	Sidlesham	Southwick	St Francis Rangers	Steyning Town	Storrington	Wealden	Westfield
Broadbridge Heath		2-1	1-0	1-2	1-1	2-2	1-2	2-1	2-3	3-2	1-3	1-3	2-0	0-1	2-1	0-2	0-0	0-0
Crawley Down	3-1		0-1	1-1	0-2	3-3	0-1	1-2	0-2	2-2	3-1	0-1	0-0	1-2	3-2	3-2	1-5	0-1
East Grinstead Town	3-0	1-2		5-1	0-1	5-4	2-2	1-2	2-0	2-1	1-2	2-1	4-1	0-0	0-2	1-2	2-0	2-1
Lancing	0-1	0-3	1-0	D	1-2	3-2	2-1	1-0	1-1	1-1	5-0	0-1	1-0	1-2	2-1		0-5	0-0
Lingfield	4-0	4-2	1-0	4-1	I	1-2	0-2	1-2	2-3	0-1	2-0	0-3	3-0	0-3	1-3	1-0	1-0	3-2
Midhurst & Easebourne United	4-0	5-2	2-2	2-1	1-0	V	1-1	1-2	4-0	3-1	0-2	4-2	4-1	4-2	2-4	3-0	3-2	2-3
Mile Oak	1-1	1-0	2-3	3-1	2-0	3-1	I	0-3	3-1	2-0	2-6	1-2	0-1	2-6	2-3	0-2	4-2	2-3
Pagham	3-0	2-2	3-0	3-0	0-1	3-2	0-1	S	4-0	5-1	3-0	1-1	2-2	0-1	2-0	2-1	1-3	2-0
Peacehaven & Telscombe	1-1	1-5	2-1	0-5	1-1	2-1	3-2	3-1	I	2-0	1-1	2-0	1-1	0-4	4-0	3-1	3-0	0-0
Saltdean United	1-1	0-0	0-1	0-2	2-1	3-8	0-1	1-3	1-4	O	0-2	4-2	3-0	2-4	3-1		0-2	0-3
Seaford Town	1-0	0-1	0-0	4-1	3-1	3-1	3-3	0-2	3-3	4-1	N	1-0	3-2	0-1	2-1	1-2	3-1	0-0
Sidlesham	0-0	1-1	2-2	5-0	2-0	1-1	4-0	1-3	1-6	1-3	1-1	T	2-2	3-2	0-0	1-1	2-5	1-2
Southwick	2-1	2-1	1-0	1-1	2-1	1-4	1-1	1-3	2-2	3-0	1-1			1-1	2-3	1-4	1-0	1-1
St Francis Rangers	1-1	1-2	2-0	1-0	3-1	4-0	4-1	0-1	5-1	2-1	4-2	3-1	1-4	W	1-1	1-1	1-4	2-1
Steyning Town	2-0	2-1	1-1	1-3	0-2	0-2	0-2	1-2	1-0	2-2	0-1	1-3	3-0	3-2	O	6-2	0-1	5-1
Storrington	0-4	3-1	1-1	2-0	0-0	3-1	0-4	0-2	2-3	2-1	0-1	1-4	0-0	2-1	0-1	O	0-2	1-3
Wealden	1-0	3-2	1-1	2-0	4-1	2-2	1-4	3-1	1-2	3-0	1-2	7-3	0-2	2-2	5-3			5-0
Westfield	2-2	0-2	5-2	1-1	3-0	1-1	3-1	3-1	5-1	5-0	0-1	3-1	1-0	2-1	0-1	2-1		

Division Two		P	W	D	L	F	A	Pts
Pagham		34	22	4	8	68	35	70
St Francis Rangers	+2	34	18	4	12	64	46	60
Westfield		34	17	8	9	59	42	59
Wealden		34	18	4	12	76	49	58
Peacehaven & Telscombe		34	17	7	10	60	61	58
Seaford Town		34	16	7	11	54	46	55
Midhurst & Easebourne Utd		34	15	7	12	82	65	52
Steyning Town		34	16	4	14	60	53	52
Mile Oak		34	15	5	14	59	60	50
Lingfield		34	14	3	17	43	49	45
East Grinstead Town		34	12	8	14	48	47	44
Sidlesham		34	11	10	13	56	63	43
Southwick		34	10	11	13	43	56	41
Lancing		34	10	8	16	40	57	38
Storrington		34	11	5	18	43	63	38
Crawley Down		34	10	7	17	49	57	37
Broadbridge Heath	-1	34	8	10	16	34	53	33
Saltdean United		34	7	6	21	41	77	27

DIVISION TWO CUP

FIRST ROUND
Mile Oak 4 Saltdean United 2
Steyning Town 2 Broadbridge Heath 1
SECOND ROUND
Crawley Down 3 Midhurst & Easebourne Utd 2
East Grinstead Town 7 Southwick 2
Mile Oak 2 **Steyning Town** 4
Pagham 0 **St Francis Rgrs** 1
Peacehaven 3 **Lancing** 4
Sidlesham 1 Seaford Town 1
Seaford Town 2 **Sidlesham** 3
replay
Storrington 1 **Wealden** 5
Westfield 3 Lingfield 0

QUARTER-FINALS
Crawley Down 1 **Steyning** 2
Lancing 2 Westfield 1
Sidlesham 1 St Francis
Rangers 1 *aet*
St Francis Rangers 1
Sidlesham 2
Wealden 3 East Grinstead
Town 0 *(at East Grinstead)*
SEMI-FINALS
Steyning Town 2 Lancing 0
(at Shoreham)
Wealden 1 Sidlesham 0
(at Worthing United)
FINAL
(April 6th at East Preston)
Steyning Town 1 **Wealden** 2

WWW.NLNEWSDESK.CO.UK

IN: Littlehampton Town (R), Pease Pottage Village (P), Rustington (P)
OUT: Pagham (P), Saltdean United (R), St Francis Rangers (P)

ROY HAYDEN TROPHY
(Sussex Senior Cup holders v Div One champions)

(August 8th at Horsham YMCA)
Lewes 0 **Horsham YMCA** 0 (2-3p)

NORMAN WINGATE TROPHY
(Division One champions v John O'Hara Cup holders)

(July 29th at Shoreham)
Horsham YMCA 0 **Shoreham** 1

	Bexhill United	Bosham	Forest	Haywards Heath Town	Hurstpierpoint	Ifield Edwards	Little Common	Loxwood	Newhaven	Pease Pottage Village	Rottingdean Village	Rustington	Uckfield Town
Bexhill United		5-1	2-3	1-3	1-2	1-2	1-4	0-1	1-2	4-3	1-2	1-3	4-3
Bosham	3-3		3-7	1-2	1-3	0-4	2-3	1-2	1-0	1-4	0-1	0-5	2-2
Forest	1-3	3-1	D	1-0	1-1	0-2	1-3	4-3	1-1	0-1	0-2	0-3	2-1
Haywards Heath Town	3-0	1-2	2-3	I	2-2	3-2	1-2	2-0	3-1	1-2	2-1	0-1	2-1
Hurstpierpoint	4-1	3-1	0-3	1-0	V	2-0	3-0	0-1	0-3	0-2	1-1	0-4	1-2
Ifield Edwards	1-1	3-1	1-3	1-2	1-0		1-3	1-2	2-4	0-3	0-2	1-0	2-0
Little Common	3-2	2-1	3-0	1-0	2-1	0-1	T	2-2	4-1	0-0	1-3	5-4	2-3
Loxwood	2-0	2-2	3-2	1-2	4-2	1-3	0-1	H	0-2	3-3	1-2	1-2	1-1
Newhaven	2-7	4-1	3-1	0-0	1-0	2-1	2-2	0-2	R	1-0	1-2	2-2	1-5
Pease Pottage Village	2-2	3-1	1-1	1-1	1-0	2-1	3-1	0-2	2-0	E	5-1	1-2	2-1
Rottingdean Village	0-3	3-1	1-2	3-0	3-0	1-2	2-2	2-0	2-2	4-1	E	0-0	0-0
Rustington	5-1	2-0	0-0	0-1	4-1	4-0	2-0	4-0	3-1	2-1	4-1		6-2
Uckfield Town	0-4	3-2	1-3	2-1	4-1	1-1	3-0	0-3	3-2	2-3	5-0	2-3	

Division Three

	P	W	D	L	F	A	Pts
Rustington	24	18	3	3	65	21	57
Pease Pottage Village	24	13	5	6	46	31	44
Little Common	24	13	4	7	46	39	43
Rottingdean Village	24	12	5	7	39	34	41
Forest	24	11	4	9	42	41	37
Haywards Heath Town	24	11	3	10	34	30	36
Loxwood	24	10	4	10	37	38	34
Ifield Edwards	24	10	2	12	33	38	32
Newhaven	24	9	5	10	38	45	32
Uckfield Town	24	9	4	11	47	48	31
Bexhill United	24	7	3	14	49	55	24
Hurstpierpoint	24	7	3	14	28	43	24
Bosham	24	2	3	19	29	70	9

DIVISION THREE CUP

FIRST ROUND
Forest 2 Bosham 0
Ifield Edwards 1 **Rustington** 2
Loxwood 2 Bexhill United 0
Pease Pottage Village 1
Hurstpierpoint 1 *aet* (3-2p)
Rottingdean Village 1 Little Common 0

QUARTER-FINALS
Forest 0 **Newhaven** 2
Haywards Heath Town 1 **Pease Pottage Village** 2
Loxwood 3 Uckfield Town 1

Rustington 2 Rottingdean Village 0

SEMI-FINALS
Loxwood 0 **Pease Pottage Village** 4 *(at Steyning Town)*
Rustington 0 **Newhaven** 1 *aet (at Shoreham)*

FINAL
(April 6th at Shoreham)
Pease Pottage Village 4 Newhaven 1

SUSSEX COUNTY LEAGUE DIVISION THREE CONSTITUTION 2007-08

BEXHILL UNITED.....................Brockley Road, Bexhill-on-Sea TN39 3EX.....................01424 220732
BOSHAM.....................Recreation Ground, Walton Lane, Bosham PO18 8QF.....................01243 574011
DORKING WANDERERS.....................London Road, Westhumble, Dorking.....................None
FOREST.....................Roffey Sports & Social Club, Spooners Road, Roffey RH12 4EB.....................01403 210221
HAYWARDS HEATH TOWN.......Hanbury Park Stadium, Allen Road, Haywards Heath RH16 3PT.....................01444 412837
HURSTPIERPOINT.....................Fairfield Recreation Ground, Cuckfield Road, Hurstpierpoint BN6 9SD.....................01273 834783
IFIELD EDWARDS.........Edwards Sports & Social Club, Ifield Green, Rusper Road, Crawley RH11 0JE.....................01293 420598
LITTLE COMMON.....................Peartree Lane, Little Common, Bexhill TN39 4PH.....................01424 845861
LOXWOOD.....................Loxwood Sports Association, Sports Pavilion, Billingshurst RH14 0SX.....................01403 753185
NEWHAVEN.....................Recreation Ground, Fort Road, Newhaven BN9 9EE.....................01273 513940
ROTTINGDEAN VILLAGE......Rottingdean Field, Wilkinson Close, Rottingdean, Brighton BN2 7EG.....................None
SALTDEAN UNITED.....................Hill Park, Coombe Vale, Saltdean, Brighton BN2 8HJ.....................01273 309898
UCKFIELD TOWN.....................Victoria Pleasure Grounds, New Town, Uckfield TN22 5DJ.....................01825 769400
IN: Dorking Wanderers (P – West Sussex League Premier Division), Saltdean United (R)
OUT: Pease Pottage Village (P), Rustington (P)

Reserve Premier Division	P	W	D	L	F	A	Pts
Hailsham Town Res.	26	19	5	2	57	29	62
Horsham YMCA Res.	26	17	6	3	69	23	57
Shoreham Res.	26	15	5	6	53	33	50
Whitehawk Res.	26	15	4	7	68	39	49
Hassocks Res.	26	12	8	6	62	48	44
Hastings United Res.	26	11	7	8	55	40	40
Eastbourne Town Res.	26	12	4	10	42	38	40
Crowborough Res.	-3 26	12	3	11	44	40	36
Arundel Res.	26	9	8	9	28	27	35
Sidley United Res.	+3 26	7	6	13	27	35	30
Oakwood Res.	26	8	4	14	45	65	28
East Preston Res.	26	5	3	18	40	88	18
Ringmer Res.	26	3	6	17	34	71	15
Worthing Utd. Res.	26	1	3	22	8	56	6

Reserve Section East	P	W	D	L	F	A	Pts
Crawley Down Res.	22	17	4	1	75	15	55
Eastbourne UA Res.	+3 22	14	3	5	47	24	48
Westfield Res.	22	15	1	6	64	32	46
Peacehaven & T. Res.	22	9	3	10	29	38	30
Rye United Res.	22	9	3	10	34	46	30
Lingfield Res.	22	9	3	10	39	53	30
Redhill Res.	-3 22	10	2	10	38	17	29
Wealden Res.	22	8	4	10	37	44	28
Newhaven Res.	22	7	3	12	34	60	24
Seaford Town Res.	22	6	3	13	28	45	21
Saltdean United Res.	22	5	4	13	23	45	19
Bexhill United Res.	22	6	1	15	41	70	19

Reserve Section West	P	W	D	L	F	A	Pts
Selsey Res.	24	20	2	2	80	19	62
Midhurst & Ease. Res.	24	18	1	5	92	28	55
Pagham Res.	+2 24	16	3	5	59	31	53
Chichester CU Res.	-1 24	14	5	4	55	24	49
Lancing Res.	24	13	3	8	67	41	42
Mile Oak Res.	24	11	2	11	28	46	35
Storrington Res.	24	10	4	10	37	39	34
St Francis Rgrs Res.	24	8	3	13	30	40	27
Steyning Town Res.	+2 24	6	5	13	39	66	25
Broadb'dge H. Res.	-1 24	7	4	13	42	51	24
Wick Res.	24	5	8	11	28	58	23
Sidlesham Res.	24	3	1	20	15	60	10
Forest Res.	24	3	1	20	28	97	10

RESERVE SECTION CUP

FINAL *(April 4th at Worthing United)*
Hassocks Res. 2 Shoreham Res. 0

TEESSIDE LEAGUE

Note – Hartlepool Chester Hotel withdrew during the course of the season Their results are shown herein but are expunged from the league table	BEADS	Carlin How WMC	Darlington Rugby Club	Fishburn Park	Grangetown Boys Club	Hart'pool Chester Hotel	Hartlepool Res.	Nunthorpe Athletic	Redcar Rugby Club	Richmond Mavericks	Richmond Town	Thornaby Athletic	Thornaby Dubliners	Thornaby Res.	Whinney Banks
BEADS		5-1	5-1	1-1	3-1	1-2	6-1	9-0	2-3	4-1	7-0	3-4	2-2	3-0	3-2
Carlin How WMC	2-1	D	6-1	4-1	4-1	n/a	3-0	4-0	4-0	3-1	4-0	0-4	3-0	5-0	6-3
Darlington Rugby Club	2-3	1-3	I	0-2	0-1	n/a	2-1	1-2	0-1	1-0	2-1	0-3	0-5	4-1	2-1
Fishburn Park	0-2	1-1	4-0	V	0-1	3-1	0-1	1-1	2-2	2-0	9-0	0-0	2-1	2-0	3-1
Grangetown Boys Club	2-1	0-2	5-1	0-1	I	3-3	2-0	7-3	1-4	2-3	7-1	4-1	2-2	3-0	5-3
Hartlepool Chester Hotel	n/a	1-3	n/a	n/a	1-1	S	3-0	6-1	n/a	n/a	n/a	n/a	n/a	3-1	7-1
Hartlepool Res.	0-4	0-4	4-0	1-1	2-1	n/a	I	2-1	0-6	5-2	2-3	1-2	2-2	5-0	2-5
Nunthorpe Athletic	2-4	2-3	0-1	0-4	3-8	n/a	6-1	O	1-3	1-2	0-2	1-0	0-6	2-1	3-3
Redcar Rugby Club	1-1	4-2	7-0	0-4	5-3	4-3	1-2	5-2	N	0-1	4-0	3-0	2-2	4-2	2-3
Richmond Mavericks	2-5	0-6	6-2	1-1	3-3	3-3	3-0	1-3	4-1		2-0	1-3	1-3	2-1	3-7
Richmond Town	1-3	2-5	0-3	0-2	1-6	0-1	2-4	0-1	0-4	0-5		3-2	2-3	2-0	1-1
Thornaby Athletic	0-4	0-3	0-0	2-1	3-1	5-3	2-1	1-0	1-1	1-1	4-1	O	0-5	1-1	3-2
Thornaby Dubliners	0-2	0-2	2-4	0-1	3-1	1-1	3-2	3-2	2-1	3-1	6-0	2-1	N	3-2	3-2
Thornaby Res.	2-6	1-5	2-1	2-7	2-8	1-5	3-1	1-2	0-7	1-2	1-0	0-1	0-6	E	1-4
Whinney Banks	1-2	1-4	3-3	3-1	3-2	n/a	2-0	3-0	1-3	4-0	7-0	2-2	4-0	2-2	

Division One		P	W	D	L	F	A	Pts
Carlin How WMC		26	22	1	3	89	29	67
BEADS		26	19	3	4	91	32	60
Redcar Rugby Club		26	15	4	7	74	40	49
Thornaby Dubliners		26	15	4	7	67	41	49
Fishburn Park		26	13	7	6	53	24	46
Thornaby Athletic		26	12	6	8	41	41	42
Grangetown Boys Club		26	13	2	11	77	54	41
Whinney Banks		26	11	5	10	73	56	38
Richmond Mavericks		26	10	3	13	48	62	33
Darlington Rugby Club		26	8	2	16	32	68	26
Hartlepool Res.	-3	26	8	2	16	40	66	23
Nunthorpe Athletic		26	7	2	17	38	76	23
Richmond Town		26	4	1	21	22	94	13
Thornaby Res.		26	3	2	21	26	88	11

Hartlepool Chester Hotel – record expunged

LOU MOORE MEMORIAL SHIELD
(Division One sides)

FIRST ROUND
Carlin How WMC 2 Hartlepool Chester Hotel 1
Grangetown Boys Club 6 Fishburn Park 0
Hartlepool Res. 4 Thornaby Res. 3
Redcar Rugby Club 5 Nunthorpe Athletic 0
Richmond Mavericks 1 **Darlington Rugby Club** 3 *aet*
Richmond Town 0 **Thornaby Athletic** 5
Thornaby Dubliners 4 Whinney Banks 1

QUARTER-FINALS
Grangetown Boys Club 1 Darlington Rugby Club 0
Redcar RC 1 **Hartlepool Res.** 0
(Redcar Rugby Club expelled)
Thornaby Ath. 0 **Carlin How** 4
Thornaby Dubliners 2 BEADS 1

SEMI-FINALS
Carlin How 4 Thornaby Dub. 0
Grangetown Boys Club 1 **Hartlepool Res.** 3

FINAL
(May 9th at Guisborough Town)
Carlin How WMC 5 Hartlepool Res. 0

TEESSIDE LEAGUE DIVISION ONE CONSTITUTION 2007-08

BEADS . . . . Beechwood & Easterside SC, Marton Road, Middlesbrough TS4 3PP 01642 311304
DARLINGTON RAILWAY ATHLETIC RESERVES . . Brinkburn Road, Darlington DL3 9LF 01325 468125
DARLINGTON RUGBY CLUB . . . . Darlington Rugby Club, Grange Road, Darlington DL1 5NR. . . . . None
FISHBURN PARK. Grangetown YCC, Trunk Road, Grangetown, Middlesbrough TS6 7HP 01642 455435
GRANGETOWN BOYS CLUB . . . Grangetown YCC, Trunk Road, Grangetown, Middlesbrough TS6 7HP 01642 455435
GUISBOROUGH BLACK SWAN RESERVES . . King George V Playing Fields, Howlbeck Road, Guisborough TS14 6LE 01287 636925
GUISBOROUGH QUOIT. . . . . King George V Playing Fields, Howlbeck Road, Guisborough TS14 6LE. 01287 636925
KIRKBYMOORSIDE . . . . Kirkby Mills, Kirkbymoorside, York YO62 6NS. . . . . None
NUNTHORPE ATHLETIC . . . . Recreation Club, Guisborough Lane, Nunthorpe TS7 0LD. 01642 313251
RICHMOND MAVERICKS. . . . . Catterick Garrison, Wavell Road, Catterick DL9 3BJ. . . . . None
RICHMOND TOWN. . . . . Earls Orchard Playing Fields, Sleegill, Richmond DL10 4RH. . . . . None
STOKESLEY SPORTS CLUB RESERVES . . Stokesley Sports Club, Broughton Road, Stokesley, Middlesbrough TS9 5AQ 01642 710051
THORNABY ATHLETIC. . . . . Harold Wilson Rec Ground, Thornaby Road, Thornaby TS17 8PH . . . . None
THORNABY DUBLINERS . . Robert Atkinson Comm. Centre, Thorntree Road, Thornaby, Stockton-on-Tees TS17 8AP. 01642 393579
WHINNEY BANKS. . . . . Hall Garth School, Hall Drive, Middlesbrough TS5 7JX. . . . . None
IN: Darlington Railway Athletic Reserves (P), Guisborough Black Swan Reserves (P), Guisborough Quoit (P), Kirkbymoorside (P), Stokesley Sports Club Reserves (P)
OUT: Carlin How WMC (merged with Wearside League side New Marske Sports Club), Hartlepool Chester Hotel (WS), Hartlepool Reserves (F), Redcar Rugby Club (F), Thornaby Reserves (W)

J V MADDEN TROPHY
(League champions v McMillan Bowl holders)
(August 5th at Carlin How WMC)
Carlin How WMC 0 **Thornaby Dubliners** 0 (4-5p)

	Bedale Athletic	Billingham Wanderers	Darlington RA Res.	Darlington Simpson RM	Guisboro. Black S. Res.	Guisborough Quoit	Kirkbymoorside	North Ormesby Sports	Spraire Lads	Stokesley Spts Club Res.	Teesside Athletic Res.	Yorkshire Coble	P	W	D	L	F	A	Pts
Bedale Athletic	D	3-3	1-1	2-1	3-1	3-1	2-3	5-0	3-4	2-3	7-2	5-1	22	18	0	4	85	38	54
Billingham Wdrs	3-2	I	3-12	0-1	0-2	1-6	0-1	1-1	0-1	2-3	6-3	0-6	22	16	2	4	46	24	50
Darlington RA Res.	7-3	5-0	V	3-1	3-2	4-6	0-2	4-0	4-5	4-1	2-1	5-2	22	14	1	7	62	37	43
Darl'ton Simpson RM	5-3	2-2	2-0	I	2-0	1-2	3-1	2-5	2-4	4-0	2-1	2-3	22	11	4	7	75	49	37
Guisborough BS Res.	2-3	3-1	7-2	1-1	S	0-4	0-1	3-2	3-0	3-1	9-1	7-4	22	12	1	9	46	49	37
Guisborough Quoit	2-0	4-1	5-3	3-0	1-0	I	1-2	3-0	4-3	5-1	3-1	8-3	22	11	2	9	39	42	35
Kirkbymoorside	2-2	2-0	2-0	2-1	0-1	3-2	O	3-0	3-1	1-2	5-2	3-0	22	10	3	9	66	53	33
North Ormesby Spts	4-3	4-1	3-3	5-2	3-4	4-6	4-2	N	3-2	2-1	5-0	7-1	22	10	3	9	62	58	33
Spraire Lads	1-3	1-0	2-2	1-0	1-4	1-5	2-3	3-1		1-5	3-1	5-3	22	7	2	13	37	50	23
Stokesley SC Res.	1-0	4-1	1-1	2-1	0-3	3-1	1-1	2-1	0-1	T	3-1	0-1	22	7	1	14	59	82	22
Teesside Athletic Res.	2-5	0-1	0-4	3-1	2-4	2-5	0-2	2-2	0-2	1-2	W	0-1	22	3	4	15	27	67	13
Yorkshire Coble	4-6	1-1	0-6	7-1	2-3	2-8	0-2	5-6	0-2	5-3	8-2	O	22	1	1	20	27	82	4

TEESSIDE LEAGUE DIVISION TWO CONSTITUTION 2007-08

BEDALE ATHLETIC.........................Leyburn Road, Bedale DL8 1HA ....None
BILLINGHAM KADER.............Billingham Rugby Club, Greenwood Road, Billingham TS23 4AZ ....None
BILLINGHAM TOWN RESERVES.............Bedford Terrace, Billingham TS23 4AF.........................01642 560043
COBLE ENNIS SQUARE.................Ayton Road, Roseberry Square, Redcar TS10 4EL.........................None
COLBURN TOWN.................Central Stadium, Richmond Road, Catterick DL9 3JD.........................None
DARLINGTON CLEVELAND BRIDGE..Eastbourne Sports Complex, Bourne Avenue, Darlington DL1 1LJ.....01325 243177/243188
DARLINGTON SIMPSON RM............Longfield School, Longfield Road, Darlington DL3 0HT.........................None
GREAT AYTON UNITED...........Level Park, Easby Lane, Great Ayton, Middlesbrough TS9 6JJ.........................None
NORTH ORMESBY SPORTS.........Pallister Park, Ormesby Road, Middlesbrough TS3 7AP.........................None
SOUTH BANK ST PETERS.....St Peters School, Normanby Road, South Bank, Middlesbrough TS6 6SP.........01642 453462
SPRAIRE LADS...........Queen Elizabeth College, Abbey Road, Darlington DL3 8ND.........................None
TEESSIDE ATHLETIC RESERVES...............Green Lane, Redcar TS10 3RW.........................None
WHINNEY BANKS YCC...............Hall Garth School, Hall Drive, Middlesbrough TS5 7JX.........................None
IN: Billingham Town Reserves (N), Colburn Town (Wensleydale League), Darlington Cleveland Bridge (P – Sunday football), Great Ayton United (P – Stokesley League), South Bank St Peters (P – StokesleyLeague), Whinney Banks YCC (P – Youth football)
OUT: Darlington Railway Athletic Reserves (P), Guisborough Black Swan Reserves (P), Guisborough Quoit (P), Kirkbymoorside (P), Stokesley Sports Club Reserves (P)
Yorkshire Coble have merged with Stokesley League Club Ennis Square to form Coble Ennis Square

McMILLAN BOWL *(All teams)*

FIRST ROUND
Bedale Athletic 1 Nunthorpe Athletic 1 *aet* (4-3p)
Carlin How WMC 5 Yorkshire Coble 1
Darlington Simpson RM 1 **Darlington Rugby Club** 3
Guisborough Quoit 1 **Redcar Rugby Club** 3
Kirkbymoorside 2 Darlington RA Res. 0
North Ormesby Sports 3 **Thornaby Athletic** 6
Richmond Town 3 **Hartlepool Chester Hotel** 5
Spraire Lads 1 **Fishburn Park** 2
Stokesley Sports Club Res. 1 **Richmond Mavericks** 3
Teesside Athletic Res. 3 **Guisborough Black Swan Res.** 6
Whinney Banks (w/o) v Hartlepool Res. (scr.)
SECOND ROUND
Bedale Athletic 1 Whinney Banks 0
Billingham Wanderers 1 **Carlin How WMC** 3
Darlington Rugby Club 0 **Guisborough Black Swan Res.** 2

Fishburn Park 2 **Kirkbymoorside** 4
Hartlepool Chester Hotel 2 **Grangetown Boys Club** 5
Redcar Rugby Club 2 **BEADS** 3
Thornaby Athletic 3 **Thornaby Dubliners** 5
Thornaby Res. 2 Richmond Mavericks 1
QUARTER-FINALS
Carlin How WMC 8 Bedale Athletic 6 *aet*
Kirkbymoorside 3 BEADS 1
Thornaby Dubliners 6 Grangetown Boys Club 1
Thornaby Res. 1 **Guisborough Black Swan Res.** 3
SEMI-FINALS
Guisborough Black Swan Res. 1 **Kirkbymoorside** 3
Thornaby Dubliners 1 **Carlin How WMC** 1 *aet* (4-5p)
FINAL
(May 2nd at Guisborough Town)
Carlin How WMC 2 Kirkbymoorside 0

R T RAINE TROPHY
(Teams knocked out in 1st Round of the McMillan Bowl)

FIRST ROUND
Hartlepool Res. 3 **Nunthorpe Athletic** 5
Richmond Town 3 **Spraire** 4
Stokesley Sports Club Res. 3 Yorkshire Coble 2
QUARTER-FINALS
Guisborough Quoit 5 Stokesley Sports Club Res. 3
North Ormesby Sports 2 Darlington RA Res. 1
Nunthorpe Athletic 1 **Darlington Simpson RM** 3

Spraire Lads 3 Teesside Athletic Res. 2
SEMI-FINALS
Darlington Simpson RM 1 Guisborough Quoit 0
North Ormesby Sports 6 Spraire Lads 3 *aet*
FINAL
(April 9th at Stokesley Sports Club)
Darlington Simpson RM 2 Spaire Lads 1

ALEX BURNESS PLATE
(Division Two teams)

GROUP A QUALIFIERS
Kirkbymoorside
North Ormesby Sports

GROUP B QUALIFIER
Darlington RA Res.

GROUP C QUALIFIER
Darlington Simpson RM

SEMI-FINALS
Darlington RA Res. 0
Darlington Simpson RM 2.
Kirkbymoorside 2 North Ormesby 2 *aet* (7-6p)
FINAL
(May 7th at Stokesley SC)
Kirkbymoorside 0 **Darlington Simpson RM** 4

UNITED COUNTIES LEAGUE

	Blackstones	Boston Town	Bourne Town	Buckingham Town	Cogenhoe United	Deeping Rangers	Desborough Town	Ford Sports Dav.	Holbeach United	Long Buckby	Newport Pagnell T	Northampton Spen.	Potton United	Raunds Town	St Ives Town	St Neots Town	Stewarts & Lloyds	Stotfold	Wellingborough T.	Wootton Blue Cross	Yaxley
Blackstones		3-0	3-3	3-1	2-0	1-2	1-1	3-2	2-0	2-0	2-3	0-1	2-2	4-3	1-1	4-1	5-0	1-2	1-1	3-2	2-3
Boston Town	3-2		2-0	4-0	2-0	1-2	2-1	7-1	3-0	4-1	2-0	1-0	1-2	3-2	2-1	6-0	3-0	4-1	2-5	3-2	3-0
Bourne Town	0-5	0-4	P	0-0	0-2	0-1	1-2	2-1	2-2	1-1	1-2	3-2	2-1	0-1	0-4	3-1	4-2	4-3	3-2	2-1	
Buckingham Town	3-3	0-4	0-5	R	2-3	0-4	2-3	1-2	1-2	0-2	1-4	1-3	1-4	0-0	1-1	4-1	0-1	5-4	0-0	1-2	2-1
Cogenhoe United	0-0	3-4	0-2	12-0	E	1-2	2-0	5-1	8-1	5-2	3-1	1-0	3-0	3-0	0-2	8-0	3-1	3-2	0-1	6-3	0-1
Deeping Rangers	1-0	4-1	3-1	3-0	3-0	M	4-1	2-0	4-0	2-0	5-1	1-0	1-1	3-2	5-0	3-0	10-0	1-1	1-1	2-0	0-1
Desborough Town	4-1	1-2	4-2	3-0	2-1	3-0	I	3-2	2-1	1-1	0-2	2-5	1-6	2-1	0-1	2-1	1-2	3-1	2-3	1-2	2-1
Ford Sports Daventry	1-1	0-2	0-0	5-0	0-6	0-3	3-1	E	2-3	1-2	1-1	1-4	0-0	3-5	2-1	0-2	2-4	3-1	2-3	0-2	1-4
Holbeach United	1-0	1-1	3-0	0-1	0-3	0-1	0-3	3-1	R	2-4	3-1	2-2	2-1	0-1	1-1	1-1	1-1	1-0	1-0	1-0	3-1
Long Buckby	1-1	0-0	7-1	5-1	1-1	1-3	0-1	0-1	1-1		0-3	1-2	0-4	3-1	1-0	2-1	3-2	3-4	2-2	4-0	6-4
Newport Pagnell Town	0-2	1-2	1-0	3-2	1-0	1-0	2-0	3-3	1-2	2-3		1-0	1-1	3-1	4-0	2-0	2-0	2-0	0-5	0-3	3-3
Northampton Spencer	1-0	1-3	3-1	4-1	1-0	2-0	4-0	1-0	1-0	2-1	1-0	D	0-1	1-2	4-0	2-0	0-2	0-0	2-3	3-2	0-0
Potton United	3-2	2-0	4-2	4-1	1-2	1-1	3-3	4-1	1-0	4-2	4-0	5-0	I	5-1	1-2	3-0	7-0	1-0	1-3	0-1	3-1
Raunds Town	1-1	0-1	1-2	3-1	0-3	1-2	2-0	1-0	2-1	1-0	3-1	1-3	2-2	V	2-2	2-3	0-1	2-0	2-1	1-3	1-4
St Ives Town	1-2	3-2	1-2	5-1	2-1	2-2	2-1	2-1	1-1	4-1	0-2	1-3	1-2	1-1	I	2-0	6-0	2-1	0-2	0-0	0-0
St Neots Town	0-1	0-4	3-2	3-0	0-1	1-1	2-1	1-0	3-2	3-1	0-0	1-4	1-2	1-0	0-1	S	3-2	1-2	2-5	1-2	1-3
Stewarts & Lloyds Corby	1-6	1-5	2-3	0-0	1-2	1-5	1-1	4-1	1-0	2-1	0-2	1-3	0-2	2-1	1-1	0-0	I	7-0	1-3	3-3	1-0
Stotfold	1-3	2-3	2-2	2-1	5-1	1-1	1-1	4-0	0-1	0-2	0-2	2-0	0-4	3-3	2-1	2-3	3-2	O	1-2	2-2	0-1
Wellingborough Town	1-1	0-1	3-2	3-1	2-1	1-1	3-0	8-1	0-1	2-1	5-1	0-2	1-3	3-2	3-1	1-0	4-1	3-2	N	1-0	0-1
Wootton Blue Cross	0-0	1-4	3-2	2-2	1-2	0-2	2-0	3-1	1-0	1-1	1-1	0-0	1-0	4-2	0-1	1-0	2-2	5-0	0-1		3-0
Yaxley	0-3	4-4	5-2	4-1	0-1	1-1	4-1	2-1	0-1	1-0	1-2	1-1	0-0	2-4	0-1	0-0	1-2	0-2	2-4	0-3	

Premier Division

		P	W	D	L	F	A	Pts
Deeping Rangers		40	30	7	3	95	25	97
Boston Town		40	31	2	7	110	47	95
Wellingborough Town		40	25	7	8	87	48	82
Potton United		40	23	9	8	91	44	78
Cogenhoe United		40	23	4	13	101	53	73
Northampton Spencer		40	22	7	11	69	41	73
Newport Pagnell Town		40	19	7	14	63	67	64
Blackstones		40	17	12	11	79	51	63
Wootton Blue Cross		40	18	8	14	70	57	62
St Ives Town		40	17	8	15	56	49	59
Holbeach United		40	14	10	16	60	65	52
Long Buckby		40	14	8	18	68	67	50
Raunds Town		40	13	6	21	61	77	45
Desborough Town	-6	40	15	5	20	60	76	44
Yaxley	-3	40	12	9	19	59	69	42
Stewarts & Lloyds Corby		40	11	8	21	52	87	41
St Neots Town		40	12	5	23	47	86	41
Bourne Town		40	11	6	23	61	92	39
Stotfold		40	10	6	24	57	101	36
Ford Sports Daventry		40	6	5	29	47	103	23
Buckingham Town		40	4	7	29	39	117	19

Reserve Division One

		P	W	D	L	F	A	Pts
Cogenhoe United Res.		28	21	3	4	81	40	66
Northampton Spencer Res.	-1	28	15	8	5	72	35	52
Whitworths Res.		28	15	6	7	68	53	51
Stotfold Res.		28	14	5	9	73	42	47
Blackstones Res.		28	12	11	5	47	27	47
Yaxley Res.		28	13	4	11	54	50	43
Deeping Rangers Res.		28	13	3	12	58	42	42
Woodford United Res.		28	11	6	11	44	59	39
Raunds Town Res.		28	11	5	12	45	59	38
Stewarts/Lloyds Res.		28	11	3	14	59	58	36
Ford Sports Daventry Res.		28	10	3	15	53	68	33
Bourne Town Res.		28	9	5	14	42	56	32
N'pton Sileby Rgrs Res.		28	8	3	17	48	90	27
Desborough Town Res.	-3	28	8	2	18	56	81	23
Rothwell Corinthians Res.		28	3	5	20	44	79	14

UNITED COUNTIES LEAGUE PREMIER DIVISION CONSTITUTION 2007-08

AFC KEMPSTON ROVERS .... Hillgrounds Road, Kempston, Bedford MK42 8QU 01234 852346
BLACKSTONES .... Blackstones Sports & Social, Lincoln Road, Stamford PE9 1SH 01780 757835
BOSTON TOWN .... The Stadium, Tattershall Road, Boston PE21 9LR 01205 365470
BOURNE TOWN .... Abbey Lawn, Abbey Road, Bourne PE10 9EN 01778 422292
COGENHOE UNITED .... Compton Park, Brafield Road, Cogenhoe NN7 1ND 01604 890521
DEEPING RANGERS .... Outgang Road, Towngate East, Market Deeping PE6 8LQ 01778 344701
DESBOROUGH TOWN .... Waterworks Field, Braybrooke Road, Desborough NN14 2PT 01536 761350
HOLBEACH UNITED .... Carters Park, Park Road, Holbeach PE12 7EE 01406 424761
LONG BUCKBY .... Station Road, Long Buckby NN6 7PQ 01327 842682
NEWPORT PAGNELL TOWN .... Willen Road Sports Ground, Newport Pagnell MK16 0DF 01908 611993
NORTHAMPTON SPENCER .... Kingsthorpe Mill, Studland Road, Kingsthorpe, Northampton NN2 6NE 01604 718898
POTTON UNITED .... The Hollow, Biggleswade Road, Potton SG19 2LU 01767 261100
RAUNDS TOWN .... Kiln Park, London Road, Raunds, Wellingborough NN9 6EQ 01933 623351
SLEAFORD TOWN .... Eslaforde Park, Boston Road, Sleaford NG34 9GH .... None
ST IVES TOWN .... Westwood Road, St Ives PE27 6WU 01480 463207
ST NEOTS TOWN .... Rowley Park, Cambridge Road, St Neots PE19 6SN 01480 470012
STEWARTS & LLOYDS CORBY .... Recreation Ground, Occupation Road, Corby NN17 1EH 01536 401497
STOTFOLD .... Roker Park, The Green, Stotfold, Hitchin SG5 4BX 01462 730765
WELLINGBOROUGH TOWN ...... Dog & Duck, London Road, Wellingborough NN8 2DP 01933 441388
WOOTTON BLUE CROSS........... Weston Park, Bedford Road, Wootton MK43 9JT 01234 767662
YAXLEY .... Leading Drove, Holme Road, Yaxley, Peterborough PE7 3NA 01733 244928
IN: AFC Kempston Rovers (P), Sleaford Town (P)
OUT: Buckingham Town (R), Daventry United (formerly Ford Sports Daventry) (R)

	AFC Kempston R.	Bugbrooke St Mich.	Burton Park Wdrs	Daventry Town	Eynesbury Rovers	Higham Town	Huntingdon Town	Irchester United	N'pton ON Chenecks	N'pton Sileby Rangers	Olney Town	Peterboro. N'thern S.	Rothwell Corinthians	Sleaford Town	Thrapston Town	Whitworths
AFC Kempston		6-0	2-0	0-0	1-1	2-0	3-1	3-1	6-3	7-0	0-0	1-4	2-1	0-1	5-0	2-2
Bugbrooke St M.	0-3		4-3	0-5	4-0	0-6	5-2	4-1	1-0	0-3	3-1	1-2	2-1	1-1	0-1	1-2
Burton Park W.	1-2	0-0	D	4-2	1-1	2-1	0-3	1-1	0-0	3-2	1-1	1-0	1-0	1-3	3-4	0-4
Daventry Town	2-2	4-0	3-1	I	5-0	3-2	6-2	3-1	7-2	1-1	1-1	1-1	3-1	0-1	2-0	2-3
Eynesbury Rov.	1-6	2-3	1-1	0-1	V	1-1	2-2	3-1	2-1	1-2	0-3	1-1	1-2	3-0	2-2	1-2
Higham Town	2-4	3-0	2-3	1-0	6-1	I	1-0	2-0	5-0	2-1	0-2	2-2	4-0	0-2	1-1	1-2
Huntingdon Town	2-2	4-2	1-4	1-1	1-6	0-1	S	2-0	1-1	0-1	3-2	3-1	1-1	0-3	2-1	1-2
Irchester United	0-6	4-3	1-2	1-4	1-5	1-2	3-5	I	4-3	0-0	0-0	1-4	1-1	2-6	1-1	0-2
N'pton ON Chen.	1-3	0-2	0-0	1-5	6-0	4-1	2-0	4-0	O	3-3	2-2	1-4	1-3	1-2	2-2	1-1
N'pton Sileby R.	1-3	4-2	2-1	2-4	1-3	1-3	2-1	4-1	4-0	N	3-3	2-5	3-4	3-0	6-0	1-3
Olney Town	1-1	1-0	4-2	4-3	1-1	0-1	1-1	4-4	3-3	1-1		2-1	1-0	0-4	3-0	1-2
Peterboro. NS	1-3	1-0	4-1	1-2	3-0	1-1	4-3	4-1	4-2	2-0	3-3	O	6-0	0-2	2-2	2-3
Rothwell Corries	4-2	2-1	1-1	1-1	1-1	3-1	2-2	3-0	3-1	3-1	5-1	2-1	N	1-1	2-0	0-1
Sleaford Town	2-2	6-1	4-2	4-1	4-1	1-1	5-2	2-0	7-1	7-1	1-1	3-2	2-1	E	1-1	3-3
Thrapston Town	2-2	9-1	3-0	2-2	8-3	2-0	3-1	3-1	3-2	3-2	1-0	3-2	1-3	2-3		1-4
Whitworths	3-2	3-1	2-2	3-1	6-1	3-0	4-1	1-1	2-0	3-0	4-1	3-1	3-1	3-3	4-1	

Division One		P	W	D	L	F	A	Pts
Whitworths		30	23	7	0	87	34	76
Sleaford Town	-3	30	21	8	1	87	35	68
AFC Kempston Rov.		30	17	9	4	83	37	60
Daventry Town		30	15	8	7	75	43	53
Peterborough NS		30	13	6	11	68	51	45
Higham Town		30	13	4	13	53	44	43
Rothwell Corinthians		30	12	7	11	52	49	43
Thrapston Town		30	12	7	11	60	64	43
Olney Town		30	7	14	9	48	55	35
Eynesbury Rovers		30	9	8	13	49	73	35
Burton Park Wdrs		30	8	9	13	42	58	33
N'pton Sileby Rgrs		30	9	4	17	53	69	31
Bugbrooke St Mich.		30	9	2	19	41	82	29
Huntingdon Town	-1	30	7	8	15	49	70	28
N'pton ON Chen.		30	5	7	18	49	80	22
Irchester United		30	2	8	20	34	86	14

Reserve Division Two		P	W	D	L	F	A	Pts
St Neots Town Res.		26	19	3	4	74	27	60
Bugbrooke St M. Res.		26	18	4	4	81	34	58
Olney Town Res.		26	18	2	6	57	38	56
Wellingborough Res.		26	17	2	7	70	34	53
St Ives Town Res.		26	11	7	8	62	45	40
Eynesbury Rovers Res.		26	10	7	9	53	49	37
N'pton ON Chen. Res.		26	10	4	12	55	65	34
Higham Town Res.		26	10	4	12	43	55	34
Thrapston Town Res.		26	9	4	13	61	57	31
Huntingdon T. Res.		26	10	1	15	49	68	31
Burton Pk W. Res.	-1	26	7	5	14	35	65	25
Long Buckby Res.		26	5	6	15	28	54	21
Irchester United Res.		26	5	5	16	41	76	20
Peterboro. NS Res.		26	3	6	17	32	74	15

RESERVES CUP

FINAL

(April 23rd at Thrapston Town)

Cogenhoe United Res. 2 Deeping Rangers Res. 1

LEAGUE CUP

PRELIMINARY ROUND
Bugbrooke St Michaels 1 Rothwell Corinthians 1 *aet* (3-2p)
Daventry Town 6 AFC Kempston Rovers 4 *aet*
Desborough Town 3 St Neots 0
Irchester Utd 1 **Eynesbury Rovers** 3
Sleaford Town 3 Thrapston Town 0

FIRST ROUND
Boston Town 3 Peterborough Northern Star 2
Cogenhoe United 5 Burton PW 0
Daventry Town 2 **Bourne Town** 4
Desborough Town 5 Stotfold 4
Higham 0 **Stewarts & Lloyds** 2
Long Buckby 1 **Wellingborough Town** 2
Newport Pagnell Town 1 **Buckingham Town** 1 *aet* (0-3p)
Northampton ON Chenecks 1 **Deeping Rangers** 4
Northampton Sileby Rangers 2 Eynesbury Rovers 0
Northampton Spencer 2 Huntingdon Town 1
Olney Town 1 **Ford Sports Daventry** 4
Potton United 1 Sleaford Town 0
Raunds Town 1 Whitworths 1 *aet* (4-2p)
St Ives Town 0 **Blackstones** 1
Wootton Blue Cross 2 **Holbeach United** 4 *aet*
Yaxley 1 Bugbrooke St Michaels 0

SECOND ROUND
Boston Town 5 Buckingham T. 1
Deeping Rangers 2 Bourne Town 1
Desborough Town 4 Wellingborough Town 0
Ford Sports Daventry 1 **Northampton Sileby Rangers** 2
Holbeach United 4 Cogenhoe 1
Potton United 4 Blackstones 0
Raunds Town 0 **Northampton Spencer** 1
Stewarts & Lloyds 0 **Yaxley** 2

QUARTER-FINALS
Boston Town 3 Holbeach United 1
Deeping Rovers 1 **Desborough** 2
Northampton Sileby Rangers 1 **Northampton Spencer** 5
Potton United 4 Yaxley 2

SEMI-FINALS
Boston Town 3 Desborough Town 1
Northampton Spencer 0 **Potton** 1

FINAL
(April 18th at Blackstones)
Boston Town 2 Potton United 2
aet (4-2p)

UNITED COUNTIES LEAGUE DIVISION ONE CONSTITUTION 2007-08
BUCKINGHAM TOWN . . . . Ford Meadow, Ford Street, Buckingham MK18 1AG 01280 816257
BUGBROOKE ST MICHAELS . . . . . . Birds Close, Gayton Road, Bugbrooke, Northampton NN7 3PH 01604 830707
BURTON PARK WANDERERS . . . . Latimer Park, Polwell Lane, Burton Latimer NN15 5PS 01536 725841
DAVENTRY TOWN . . . . Elderstubbs, Browns Road, Daventry NN11 4NS 01327 706286
DAVENTRY UNITED . . . . Royal Oak Way, Daventry NN11 5NT 01327 704914
EYNESBURY ROVERS . . . . Alfred Hall Memorial Ground, Hall Road, Eynesbury, St Neots PE19 2SF 01480 477445
HUNTINGDON TOWN . . . . Jubilee Park, Kings Ripton Road, Huntingdon PE28 2NU 07929 651226
IRCHESTER UNITED . . . . Alfred Street, Irchester NN29 7DR 01933 312877
NORTHAMPTON ON CHENECKS . . . Old Northamptonians, Billing Road, Northampton NN1 5RX 01604 634045
NORTHAMPTON SILEBY RANGERS . . . . . Fernie Fields, Woodford Chase, Moulton NN3 7BD 01604 670366
OLNEY TOWN . . . . Recreation Ground, East Street, Olney MK46 4DW 01234 712227
PETERBOROUGH NORTHERN STAR . . . Chestnut Avenue, Dogsthorpe, Peterborough PE7 4NB 01733 564894
ROTHWELL CORINTHIANS . . . . Seargents Lawn, Desborough Road, Rothwell NN14 6JG 01536 418688
RUSHDEN & HIGHAM UNITED . . . . Hayden Road, Rushden NN10 0HY 01933 410030
THRAPSTON TOWN . . . . Chancery Lane, Thrapston, Kettering NN14 4JL 01832 732470
WHITWORTHS . . . . London Road, Wellingborough NN8 2DT 01933 227324
IN: *Buckingham Town (R), Daventry United (formerly Ford Sports Daventry) (R)*
OUT: *AFC Kempston Rovers (P), Sleaford Town (P)*
Higham Town have merged with Northants Combination Premier Division club Rushden Rangers to form Rushden & Higham United

WEARSIDE LEAGUE

	Annfield Plain	Birtley Town	Boldon Community Assoc.	Cleadon SC	Cleator Moor Celtic	Coxhoe Athletic	Guisborough Black Swan	Hartlepool	Harton & Westoe CW	Jarrow	New Marske Sports Club	Nissan SSC Sunderland	Ryhope Colliery Welfare	Teesside Athletic	Whitehaven Amateurs	Willington	Windscale	Wolviston
Annfield Plain		1-3	0-2	2-0	2-2	1-2	0-2	0-1	5-1	0-5	1-2	n/a	2-4	1-2	0-8	0-1	1-3	1-0
Birtley Town	5-0		4-1	4-1	3-0	2-1	3-0	2-0	2-1	2-1	7-0	n/a	2-0	3-0	2-0	3-0	4-0	0-0
Boldon Community Association	4-0	0-3		2-4	1-0	0-1	1-3	1-3	2-2	2-1	3-3	n/a	2-0	2-0	2-2	6-0	0-1	1-0
Cleadon SC	5-2	0-4	2-1		0-3	1-0	3-1	4-2	0-1	1-5	0-2	n/a	0-3	1-1	0-1	2-4	3-0	1-0
Cleator Moor Celtic	0-2	1-2	4-2	1-1		6-3	2-2	7-1	5-0	1-2	2-1	6-0	1-6	5-2	2-3	4-1	3-0	1-3
Coxhoe Athletic	2-3	0-2	1-6	1-1	2-1		4-2	5-1	1-0	1-4	2-2	n/a	1-1	6-4	1-4	2-0	1-0	1-2
Guisborough Black Swan	11-1	1-2	1-2	1-4	5-2	4-0		4-1	6-3	1-1	3-0	n/a	4-2	2-2	3-3	5-0	3-1	1-0
Hartlepool	5-2	0-2	3-5	1-2	0-2	2-0	3-2		3-1	3-1	1-0	n/a	0-0	1-1	2-3	3-0	5-1	1-4
Harton & Westoe CW	2-2	0-3	3-1	2-3	2-2	2-2	1-4	1-3		1-6	3-1	n/a	1-4	1-6	1-4	2-7	0-1	1-5
Jarrow	6-2	1-1	0-2	1-0	2-2	3-0	1-1	2-0	3-0		2-0	7-0	3-0	0-1	1-2	2-2	2-1	1-3
New Marske Sports Club	1-4	1-4	1-3	0-3	4-3	0-1	1-2	1-2	0-4	2-1		n/a	2-2	1-2	1-2	1-1	0-4	0-6
Nissan SSC Sunderland	n/a	n/a	n/a	n/a	2-6	n/a	n/a	n/a	n/a	n/a	n/a		n/a	n/a	1-8	1-6	0-6	n/a
Ryhope Colliery Welfare	3-0	0-0	1-0	1-1	3-0	3-0	0-0	5-2	0-0	1-3	3-0	n/a		2-0	1-2	0-0	0-3	2-4
Teesside Athletic	2-5	2-3	7-2	1-2	1-0	2-1	0-1	4-0	4-0	2-1	4-1	n/a	0-3		1-1	4-0	1-0	2-2
Whitehaven Amateurs	3-2	0-0	0-1	5-1	4-2	6-1	6-0	6-0	1-1	5-1	7-0	n/a	2-0	3-3		3-1	1-0	2-1
Willington	2-3	0-4	0-2	3-5	0-4	0-1	0-4	0-4	2-1	0-2		n/a	1-0	1-2	3-2		2-3	2-6
Windscale	2-2	1-0	2-3	2-1	0-2	4-0	0-3	2-1	3-3	3-1	2-0	n/a	0-3	0-2	3-0			0-1
Wolviston	3-1	0-0	4-0	0-1	1-2	1-1	3-2	1-0	3-0	2-0	3-0	8-0	0-1	3-2	1-2	2-1	1-1	

Note – Nissan SSC Sunderland withdrew during the course of the season Their results are shown above but are expunged from the league table

		P	W	D	L	F	A	Pts
Birtley Town		32	26	5	1	81	13	83
Whitehaven Amateurs		32	23	6	3	95	35	75
Wolviston		32	18	5	9	65	32	59
Guisborough Black Swan		32	17	6	9	83	52	57
Boldon Community Association		32	16	3	13	62	56	51
Ryhope Colliery Welfare		32	14	8	10	53	36	50
Cleadon Social Club		32	15	4	13	54	57	49
Teesside Athletic	-3	32	15	6	11	68	54	48
Jarrow		32	14	5	13	64	46	47
Cleator Moor Celtic		32	13	5	14	72	61	44
Windscale		32	13	3	16	43	51	42
Hartlepool	-3	32	13	2	17	54	71	38
Coxhoe Athletic		32	11	5	16	45	70	38
Annfield Plain		32	8	3	21	48	94	27
Harton & Westoe CW		32	5	7	20	44	92	22
Willington		32	6	3	23	34	88	21
New Marske Sports Club	-3	32	5	4	23	30	87	16

Nissan SSC Sunderland – record expunged

WEARSIDE LEAGUE CONSTITUTION 2007-08

ANNFIELD PLAIN......Derwent Park, West Road, Annfield Plain DH9 8PZ......None
BELFORD HOUSE......Silksworth Welfare Park, Silksworth, Sunderland......None
BOLDON COMMUNITY ASSOCIATION..Boldon Welfare, New Rd, Boldon Colliery NE35 9DS......0191 536 4180 (Cricket Club)
CLEATOR MOOR CELTIC......Celtic Club, Birks Road, Cleator Moor CA25 5HR......01946 812476
COXHOE ATHLETIC......Beechfield Park, Coxhoe DH6 4SD......None
EASINGTON COLLIERY......Welfare Park Ground, Easington Colliery, Peterlee NE32 4SH......0191 489 6930
EAST DURHAM UNITED......Murton FC, Recreation Park, Church Lane, Murton, Seaham SR7 9RD......None
GUISBOROUGH BLACK SWAN......King George V Playing Fields, Howlbeck Rd, Guisborough TS14 6LE......01287 636925
HARTLEPOOL......Grayfields Enclose, Jesmond Gardens, Hartlepool......None
JARROW......Perth Green Community Assoc., Inverness Road, Jarrow NE32 4AQ......0191 489 3743
NEW MARSKE SPORTS CLUB......Gurney Street, New Marske, Redcar TS11 8EG......01642 479808
RYHOPE COLLIERY WELFARE...Ryhope Rec. Park, Ryhope Street, Ryhope, Sunderland SR2 0AG......0191 521 2843
SILKSWORTH CC......Silksworth Welfare Park, Silksworth, Sunderland......None
SOUTH SHIELDS CLEADON SC.....Jack Clark Park, Horsley Hill Road, South Shields NE33 3HE......0191 454 2023
SOUTH SHIELDS HARTON & WESTOE..Harton CW, Boldon Lane, South Shields NE34 0NA......0191 456 6166
TEESSIDE ATHLETIC......Green Lane, Redcar TS10 3RW......None
WHITEHAVEN AMATEURS......County Sports Field, Coach Road, Whitehaven CA22 2DD......None
WILLINGTON......Hall Lane Ground, Hall Lane Estate, Willington DL15 0QF......01388 746221
WINDSCALE......Falcon Field, Smithfield, Egremont CA22 2QN......01946 820421
WOLVISTON......Metcalfe Park, Wynyard Road, Wolviston, Billingham TS22 5NE......07768 321651

IN: Belford House (formerly Ashbrooke Belford) (P – Durham Alliance), Easington Colliery (S – Northern Alliance Premier Division), East Durham United (N), Silksworth CC (P – Durham Alliance)
OUT: Birtley Town (P – Northern League Division Two), Nissan SSC Sunderland (WS)
New Marske Sports Club have merged with Teesside League Division One club Carlin How WMC

LEAGUE CUP

FIRST ROUND
New Marske Sports Club 1 **Teesside
Athletic** 10
Ryhope Colliery Welfare 0 **Wolviston** 1

SECOND ROUND
Birtley Town 2 Wolviston 1
Boldon Colliery Welfare (w/o) v Nissan SSC
Sunderland (scr.)
Cleadon Social Club 3 Annfield Plain 1
Cleator Moor Celtic 0 **Guisborough Black Swan** 3
Harton & Westoe CW 1 **Coxhoe Athletic** 3
Teesside Athletic 3 Windscale 1
Whitehaven Amateurs 2 Jarrow 0
Willington 0 **Hartlepool** 5

QUARTER-FINALS
Boldon Colliery W. 4 **Guisborough Black Swan** 5 *aet*
Cleadon Social Club 5 Coxhoe Athletic 1
Hartlepool 0 **Birtley Town** 4
Teesside Athletic 1 Whitehaven Amateurs 0

SEMI-FINALS
Birtley Town 2 Guisborough Black Swan 1
Teesside Athletic 2 Cleadon Social Club 0

FINAL
(May 25th at Birtley Town)
Birtley Town 1 **Teesside Athletic** 2

MONKWEARMOUTH CHARITY CUP

FIRST ROUND
Birtley Town 5 Willington 0

SECOND ROUND
Birtley Town 4 Jarrow 3
Cleadon Social Club 3 Boldon Community
Association 1
Cleator Moor Celtic 3 Ryhope Colliery
Welfare 1
Harton & Westoe CW 2 **Hartlepool** 3 *aet*
Teesside Athletic 3 New Marske Sports Club 1
Whitehaven Amateurs 3 Guisborough
Black Swan 0
Windscale 3 Coxhoe Athletic 1
Wolviston 2 Annfield Plain 0

QUARTER-FINALS
Birtley Town 3 Hartlepool 0 *(at Hartlepool)*
Cleadon Social Club 1 **Windscale** 3
Teesside Athletic 5 Cleator Moor Celtic 0
Whitehaven Amateurs 2 Wolviston 1

SEMI-FINALS
Birtley Town 0 **Teesside Athletic** 1
Windscale 1 **Whitehaven Amateurs** 2

FINAL
(May 12th at Teesside Athletic)
Teesside Athletic 1 **Whitehaven Amateurs** 6

SUNDERLAND SHIPOWNERS CUP

FIRST ROUND
Hartlepool 6 New Marske
Sports Club 2
Willington 0 **Wolviston** 1
SECOND ROUND
Boldon Community Association 4 Annfield
Plain 2
Cleadon Social Club 5 Hartlepool 2
Coxhoe Athletic 0 **Jarrow** 0 *aet* (2-4p)
Harton & Westoe CW 0 **Guisborough Black Swan** 2
Ryhope Colliery Welfare 3 Windscale 1
Teesside Athletic 0 **Birtley Town** 1
Whitehaven Amateurs (w/o) v Nissan SSC
Sunderland (scr.)
Wolviston 1 Cleator Moor Celtic 0

QUARTER-FINALS
Birtley Town 2 Guisborough Black Swan 1
Cleadon Social Club 0 **Wolviston** 2
Jarrow 0 **Boldon Community Association** 2
Ryhope Colliery Welfare 1 **Whitehaven Amateurs** 2

SEMI-FINALS
Birtley Town 0 **Wolviston** 1
Boldon Community Association 1 **Whitehaven
Amateurs** 2

FINAL
(May 7th at Wolviston)
Wolviston 2 Whitehaven Amateurs 1

WELSH ALLIANCE

Note – Sealand Rovers withdrew during the course of the season Their results are shown herein but are expunged from the league table	Bethesda Athletic	Caerwys	Conwy United	Denbigh Town	Glan Conwy	Halkyn United	Holywell Town	Llanberis	Llandudno Junction	Llanrug United	Llanrwst United	Nefyn United	Pwllheli	Rhydymwyn	Rhyl Res.	Sealand Rovers
Bethesda Athletic		4-2	3-2	0-1	0-0	3-1	6-3	2-1	4-0	2-2	0-1	8-0	6-6	1-1	0-6	n/a
Caerwys	1-2		3-4	1-7	3-1	1-3	1-3	1-3	3-4	1-5	2-3	1-3	0-3	0-5	1-4	5-0
Conwy United	3-2	6-2		0-1	1-2	4-2	3-3	2-1	2-3	0-3	2-1	2-7	2-2	2-3	1-2	n/a
Denbigh Town	2-1	7-0	5-1		5-1	5-0	1-0	4-0	5-0	1-3	0-1	2-0	3-1	3-2	2-0	7-0
Glan Conwy	3-1	2-1	1-2	4-1		4-0	4-2	3-1	3-3	0-0	3-0	1-0	2-0	3-1	0-3	1-2
Halkyn United	2-5	4-0	2-1	0-2	1-2		1-1	0-4	0-2	1-3	1-3	0-6	0-3	0-7		n/a
Holywell Town	1-1	9-2	5-1	1-3	3-2	1-0		0-0	4-0	0-5	1-1	2-3	5-5	2-2	1-1	n/a
Llanberis	1-4	2-6	2-2	2-6	0-1	2-0	2-3		6-1	1-2	2-1	2-2	3-0	2-3	2-3	2-0
Llandudno Junction	0-0	6-3	1-3	0-2	0-1	1-3	4-1	2-2		0-3	1-2	0-2	4-3	2-1		6-0
Llanrug United	3-3	8-0	4-4	2-4	3-3	1-1	1-2	1-1	9-0		1-3	1-2	2-5	1-1	1-2	2-0
Llanrwst United	2-1	6-1	2-0	1-1	1-1	3-0	3-1	4-0	3-2	2-0		3-1	1-4	2-4	1-2	n/a
Nefyn United	0-2	6-0	2-4	0-2	0-1	1-2	2-3	5-1	3-2	1-2	0-2		0-6	1-1	1-2	2-2
Pwllheli	2-3	6-0	0-1	1-4	1-1	4-1	4-2	0-0	1-2	1-0	1-1	0-1		6-1	2-1	n/a
Rhydymwyn	1-5	0-2	4-2	0-2	1-2	3-2	2-1	4-3	6-0	1-1	3-0	2-1	0-1		0-2	2-0
Rhyl Res.	3-0	8-1	3-0	1-1	2-1	3-0	1-1	3-1	2-2	2-2	3-1	5-0	4-3	2-1		5-0
Sealand Rovers	1-2	n/a	n/a	n/a	2-3	1-1	0-3	1-2	0-4	1-13	0-1	1-1	n/a	0-8		

	P	W	D	L	F	A	Pts
Denbigh Town	28	23	2	3	82	23	71
Rhyl Res.	28	21	5	2	81	29	68
Llanrwst United	28	17	4	7	56	36	55
Glan Conwy	28	16	6	6	52	36	54
Pwllheli	28	14	5	9	78	46	47
Bethesda Athletic	28	13	7	8	69	50	46
Llanrug United	28	10	10	8	68	45	40
Rhydymwyn	28	11	6	11	57	53	39
Conwy United	28	11	4	13	58	70	37
Holywell Town	28	8	8	12	59	63	32
Nefyn United	28	9	2	17	41	61	29
Llandudno Junction	28	7	4	17	44	80	25
Llanberis	28	5	7	16	46	68	22
Halkyn United	28	6	2	20	28	74	20
Caerwys	28	3	0	25	39	124	9

Sealand Rovers – record expunged

COOKSON CUP

FIRST ROUND
Bethesda Athletic 6 Pwllheli 3
Conwy United 6 Holywell Town 4 *aet*
Denbigh Town 1 Glan Conwy 1 *aet* (5-4p)
Llanberis 1 **Rhyl Res.** 5
Llandudno Junction 1 Halkyn United 0
Llanrug United 4 Sealand Rovers 3
Llanrwst United 4 Caerwys 2
Nefyn United 0 **Rhydymwyn** 2

QUARTER-FINALS
Llandudno Junction 3 Bethesda Athletic 1
Llanrug United 4 Conwy United 2
Rhydymwyn 1 **Denbigh Town** 3
Rhyl Res. 5 Llanrwst United 0

SEMI-FINALS
Denbigh Town 2 Llandudno Junction 1 *aet*
Llanrug United 4 Rhyl Res. 1

FINAL
(May 5th at Bangor City)
Denbigh Town 3 Llanrug United 0

WWW.NLNEWSDESK.CO.UK

WELSH ALLIANCE CONSTITUTION 2007-08

AMLWCH TOWN . . . . Lon Bach, Amlwch, Anglesey LL68 9BL . . . . None
BETHESDA ATHLETIC . . . . Parc Meurig Park, Bethesda, Bangor LL57 3NT . . . . None
CONWY UNITED . . . . The Morfa, Penmaen Road, Conwy LL32 8HA 01492 573080
GLAN CONWY . . . . Cae Ffwt, Llanrwst Road, Glan Conwy, Colwyn Bay LL28 5SP . . . . None
HALKYN UNITED . . . . Pant Newydd, Halkyn 01352 780576
HOLYWELL TOWN . . . . Halkyn Road, Holywell CH8 7SJ . . . . None
LLANBERIS . . . . Ffordd Padarn, Llanberis, Caernarfon LL55 4SU . . . . None
LLANDUDNO JUNCTION . . . . The Flyover, Victoria Drive, Llandudno Junction LL31 9PG . . . . None
LLANRUG UNITED . . . . Eithin Duon, Llanrug, Caernarfon LL55 4DA 01286 677543
LLANRWST UNITED . . . . Gwydyr Park, Llanrwst LL26 0PN. . . . . None
NANTLLE VALE . . . . Cae Emrys, Tyn Weirglodd, Penygroes LL54 6PA . . . . None
NEFYN UNITED. . . . . Caer Delyn, Nefyn, Pwllheli. . . . . None
PWLLHELI . . . . Dwyfor Leisure Centre, Recreation Road, Pwllheli LL53 5PF 01758 613437
RHYDYMWYN . . . . Vicarage Road, Rhydymwyn, Mold CH7 5HL . . . . None
RHYL RESERVES. . . . . Belle Vue, Grange Road, Rhyl LL18 4BT 01745 338327

IN: Amlwch Town (P – Welsh Alliance), Nantlle Vale (P – Welsh Alliance)
OUT: Caerwys (R – Clwyd League Division One), Denigh Town (P – Cymru Alliance), Sealand Rovers (WS)

WELSH LEAGUE

	Afan Lido	Barry Town	Bridgend Town	Bryntirion Ath.	Caerleon	Croesyceiliog	Dinas Powys	ENTO Aber'man	Ely Rangers	Goytre United	Grange Quins	Maesteg Park	Neath Athletic	Newport YMCA	Pontardawe T.	Pontypridd T.	Taffs Well	Ton Pentre	UWIC Inter
Afan Lido		6-1	1-0	0-0	3-2	3-2	2-0	2-0	2-1	0-5	3-1	0-0	0-1	3-1	0-1	3-3	1-0	1-1	2-1
Barry Town	0-7		0-3	0-3	2-0	0-2	1-3	1-1	3-4	0-2	4-1	2-1	2-4	1-4	1-1	1-4	0-5	0-3	0-1
Bridgend Town	0-2	2-2		2-2	2-2	7-0	1-3	5-0	0-2	0-1	5-2	1-3	0-3	3-1	2-2	1-3	2-3	1-2	2-3
Bryntirion Athletic	3-0	3-1	2-0	D	2-1	5-4	2-0	3-0	2-2	1-3	3-1	1-2	1-2	4-2	2-0	1-2	1-2	0-2	1-4
Caerleon	4-1	2-0	1-0	2-2	I	0-2	4-2	0-1	1-1	1-3	1-0	7-1	0-1	4-0	2-0	2-3	1-2	0-4	1-0
Croesyceiliog	2-1	2-2	2-4	3-1	1-0	V	1-1	2-0	1-2	2-1	3-3	1-2	0-1	1-1	4-0	0-2	2-2	1-1	0-2
Dinas Powys	1-2	2-0	1-3	2-1	3-1	1-0	I	2-2	0-3	0-3	0-0	0-1	2-3	2-1	3-1	1-1	0-5	2-2	1-3
ENTO Aberaman Athletic	0-2	4-0	0-4	4-0	2-0	1-0	2-1	S	1-0	0-1	2-0	0-0	2-2	2-2	1-0	4-1	2-1	2-1	1-0
Ely Rangers	2-2	1-1	0-3	0-3	1-2	0-0	3-1	1-2	I	2-2	5-2	4-0	0-4	2-3	1-2	0-4	0-1	0-2	2-2
Goytre United	0-1	5-0	3-1	1-1	0-0	3-2	4-1	1-1	7-3	O	1-1	2-1	0-1	1-0	2-0	0-0	4-2	4-3	7-0
Grange Harlequins	0-3	1-1	1-1	2-1	1-2	1-1	1-0	0-3	2-1	1-3	N	0-3	1-5	3-2	1-0	0-0	0-0	1-2	1-1
Maesteg Park	0-1	3-0	1-3	2-0	1-2	3-0	1-1	4-3	1-0	0-1	1-0		2-1	1-3	0-1	0-2	2-1	1-0	1-0
Neath Athletic	4-4	7-0	4-1	5-0	5-0	2-1	3-1	2-1	4-0	2-1	2-0	2-1		0-0	2-0	1-1	2-1	2-2	6-0
Newport YMCA	1-1	2-3	2-2	1-0	2-0	3-2	0-1	3-0	1-0	0-5	2-2	2-3	1-4	O	1-1	2-2	2-2	3-0	0-0
Pontardawe Town	1-1	4-0	1-3	0-1	2-1	0-2	2-1	1-0	1-1	0-2	2-0	2-1	1-3	0-2	N	1-2	1-2	0-1	3-1
Pontypridd Town	3-0	4-1	2-0	4-2	3-0	0-0	1-2	2-0	4-0	1-2	3-0	2-1	1-2	3-1	5-1	E	6-2	0-0	7-3
Taffs Well	1-1	3-1	1-2	4-0	0-3	1-3	1-2	1-3	4-3	1-1	0-0	1-2	3-1	2-2	2-3	1-2		1-2	0-5
Ton Pentre	2-1	3-1	3-0	1-0	4-1	0-1	4-1	0-2	3-2	1-1	4-1	2-0	0-2	2-0	0-0	0-0	6-0		0-0
UWIC	1-4	0-2	0-1	1-2	1-2	1-3	2-0	0-4	4-3	2-4	1-3	1-1	2-2	0-3	0-1	1-2	2-0	1-2	

Division One

	P	W	D	L	F	A	Pts
Neath Athletic	36	29	5	2	100	32	92
Goytre United	36	24	8	4	86	32	80
Pontypridd Town	36	24	8	4	88	37	80
Ton Pentre	36	21	9	6	68	32	72
Afan Lido	36	19	9	8	66	45	66
ENTO Aberaman Ath.	36	18	6	12	53	45	60
Maesteg Park	36	17	4	15	47	49	55
Bryntirion Athletic	36	14	5	17	56	62	47
Croesyceiliog	36	13	7	16	53	57	46
Caerleon	36	14	4	18	52	58	46
Bridgend Town	36	13	6	17	67	61	45
Taffs Well	36	12	7	17	60	68	43
Dinas Powys	36	11	7	18	45	67	40
Newport YMCA	36	10	9	17	55	69	39
Pontardawe Town	36	11	6	19	33	54	39
UWIC	36	9	6	21	46	74	33
Ely Rangers	36	7	8	21	52	77	29
Grange Harlequins -1	36	7	9	20	34	72	29
Barry Town	36	5	5	26	33	103	20

LEAGUE CUP

FIRST ROUND

Afan Lido 5 Newport YMCA 2
Ammanford 5 Chepstow Town 2
Bridgend Town 2 Barry 1 *aet*
Briton Ferry Athletic 2
Cwmamman United 0
Bryntirion Athletic 0 **Tredegar** 1
Caerau Ely 5 AFC Llwydcoed 1
Croesyceiliog 0 **Pontypridd Town** 2
Dinas Powys 0 **Pontardawe** 2
Ely Rangers 2 **Caldicot Town** 2 *aet* (3-5p)
Garw Athletic 0 **Maesteg Park** 1
Goytre United 6 Garden Village 0
Gwynfi United 1 **Abertillery Excelsiors** 4
Llangeinor 3 Ton Pentre 2
Llansawel 4 Merthyr Saints 3 *aet*
Llantwit Fardre 3 Aberbargoed Buds 1

Neath Athletic 6 Goytre 1
Penrhiwceiber Rangers 1
Cwmbran Celtic 3
Pentwyn Dynamo 0 **Bettws** 2
Risca Utd 0 **ENTO Aberaman** 1
Troedyrhiw 1 **Llanwern** 5
UWIC 1 Cardiff Corinthians 3
(Cardiff Corinthians expelled)
West End 3 Pontyclun 1
Ystradgynlais 2 Seven Sisters 1

SECOND ROUND

Abertillery Excelsiors 3 **Maesteg Park** 4 *aet*
Bettws 2 Newcastle Emlyn 1 *aet*
Bridgend Town 2 AFC Porth 2
Briton Ferry Athletic 0 **Afan Lido** 5
Caerau Ely 3 Treharris Athletic 2 *aet*
Cambrian/Clydach Vale BC 2

	AFC Llwydcoed	Ammanford	Bettws	Briton Ferry Athletic	Caerau Ely	Caldicot Town	Cambrian & Clydach VBC	Cardiff Corinthians	Garden Village	Garw Athletic	Merthyr Saints	Morriston Town	Penrhiweiber Rangers	Pontyclun	Tredegar Town	Treharris Athletic	Troedyrhiw	West End
AFC Llwydcoed		1-2	1-2	1-2	1-1	1-4	0-4	2-0	5-2	1-2	0-3	3-2	0-5	1-2	1-3	0-0	1-2	1-5
Ammanford	4-0		2-2	2-1	3-1	2-2	0-0	2-1	4-1	0-2	2-2	1-0	4-0	2-1	2-2	1-0	1-0	0-5
Bettws	0-1	2-3	D	1-0	3-0	1-0	2-1	3-1	2-1	0-1	0-0	3-0	3-0	1-0	1-0	1-1	2-0	
Briton Ferry Athletic	2-0	2-2	0-2	I	3-3	0-3	2-3	1-4	3-1	0-2	2-0	0-0	1-0	2-1	2-1	4-2	0-1	2-0
Caerau Ely	4-1	2-4	2-2	1-2	V	3-2	1-3	0-3	2-2	2-0	4-2	4-3	0-3	1-1	0-1	4-0	0-0	2-6
Caldicot Town	2-0	3-2	1-2	2-1	0-2	I	6-3	0-0	3-0	0-0	2-1	5-0	2-0	3-3	3-1	2-0	0-0	2-2
Cambrian & Clydach Vale BC	1-0	6-1	3-0	5-2	3-0	2-1	S	1-1	1-2	0-1	2-0	1-0	5-1	2-0	2-2	3-2	4-1	3-2
Cardiff Corinthians	3-2	6-0	2-1	1-0	2-0	2-3	0-1	I	1-1	1-1	0-1	2-0	3-2	3-1	1-0	0-0	1-1	2-3
Garden Village	1-0	3-1	0-2	2-2	6-2	3-3	0-3	2-2	O	1-0	4-1	4-0	4-1	5-0	1-0	2-2	0-1	1-2
Garw Athletic	9-0	3-2	1-0	2-0	5-1	2-2	2-0	2-1	2-0	N	6-0	1-1	2-1	4-0	3-0	1-0	3-1	1-1
Merthyr Saints	2-1	2-1	3-1	2-3	0-0	1-3	0-2	1-1	2-1	2-5		1-2	2-2	6-0	1-0	3-1	1-2	1-2
Morriston Town	3-0	1-0	0-1	0-3	4-3	0-4	1-1	0-2	3-3	0-1	4-4		2-4	0-5	1-3	1-0	0-2	0-2
Penrhiweiber Rangers	4-2	3-2	3-1	1-1	2-2	0-3	1-2	3-2	0-2	0-2	2-1	2-1		2-1	0-1	1-2	1-1	1-1
Pontyclun	3-0	2-3	2-0	2-1	0-2	0-0	0-4	0-1	3-0	0-0	2-1	2-6	3-2	T	1-0	1-1	1-2	1-2
Tredegar Town	1-0	2-3	0-2	1-3	1-2	1-2	2-1	2-1	2-0	0-3	2-1	4-1	1-4		W	2-0	4-1	1-4
Treharris Athletic	1-0	1-1	2-2	3-1	2-0	1-2	1-2	3-1	5-1	1-2	5-1	1-2	0-1	0-3	1-1	O	4-0	1-1
Troedyrhiw	1-0	2-2	0-3	4-2	3-2	3-3	1-4	2-1	3-3	1-1	3-0	5-2	2-4	1-1	0-0	2-0		2-1
West End	2-1	1-2	1-1	2-4	2-3	1-2	4-0	5-2	2-1	2-1	4-1	4-1	4-1	2-1	2-2	3-2	2-2	

UWIC 1
ENTO Aberaman Athletic 1
Taffs Well 0
Goytre United 3 West End 2 *aet*
Grange Harlequins 3
Ammanford 4
Llansawel 2 Cwmbran Celtic 0
Llantwit Fardre 0 **Neath Athletic** 1
Pontardawe Town 0 **Llanwern** 3
Pontypridd Town 2 **Caldicot Town** 4
Porthcawl Town 1 **Morriston Town** 2 *aet*
Tredegar Town 2 Caerleon 1 *aet*
Ystradgynlais 3 Llangeinor 1

THIRD ROUND
Afan Lido 4 Maesteg Park 0
Ammanford 2 **Bridgend Town** 4
Bettws 2 ENTO Aberaman Athletic 1
Caerau Ely 3 **Llanwern** 5
Goytre United 5 Cambrian &

Clydach Vale BC 2
Llansawel 1 **Caldicot Town** 2
Neath Athletic 4 Morriston 0
Tredegar Town 4
Ystradgynlais 4 *aet* (5-3p)

QUARTER-FINALS
Caldicot Town 0 **Bettws** 2
Goytre Utd 2 Neath Ath. 0
Llanwern 0 **Afan Lido** 2
(at Afan Lido)
Tredegar Town 2 Bridgend Town 1

SEMI-FINALS
Afan Lido 2 Tredegar Town 1
(at Ton Pentre)
Goytre United 1 Bettws 0
(at Maesteg Park)

FINAL
(May 14th at Maesteg Park)
Afan Lido 1 Goytre United 0

Division Two		P	W	D	L	F	A	Pts
Garw Athletic		34	24	7	3	73	21	79
Cambrian & Clydach Vale		34	23	4	7	78	39	73
Caldicot Town		34	19	10	5	75	40	67
Bettws		34	20	5	9	52	32	65
West End		34	18	7	9	81	53	61
Ammanford		34	15	9	10	63	63	54
Troedyrhiw		34	14	12	8	53	53	54
Briton Ferry Athletic		34	14	5	15	54	56	47
Garden Village		34	12	9	13	64	64	45
Cardiff Corinthians	-7	34	13	8	13	54	46	40
Tredegar Town	-3	34	12	6	16	46	54	39
Pontyclun		34	11	6	17	47	63	39
Caerau Ely		34	10	8	16	56	75	38
Treharris Athletic		34	9	8	17	46	52	35
Merthyr Saints		34	9	6	19	50	72	33
Penrhiweiber Rangers	-7	34	11	5	18	54	70	31
Morriston Town		34	7	5	22	41	78	26
AFC Llwydcoed		34	4	2	28	28	84	14

RESERVES CUP

FINAL *(May 15th at Taffs Well)*
Croesyceiliog Res. 2 Dinas Powys Res. 1

WWW.NLNEWSDESK.CO.UK

WELSH LEAGUE DIVISION TWO CONSTITUTION 2007-08

AMMANFORD . . . . Rice Road, Colonel Road, Betws, Ammanford SA18 2HP 01269 592407
BARRY TOWN . . . . Jenner Park Athletic Stadium, Barry Road, Barry CF62 9BG 01446 746870
BETTWS . . . . North Site, Bettws Road, Bettws, Bridgend CF32 8YD 07887 530804
BRITON FERRY ATHLETIC . . . . Old Road, Briton Ferry, Neath SA11 2HA 07817 048195
CAERAU ELY . . . . Cwrt-y-Ala, Caerau, Cardiff CF64 4HE 07790 084636
CARDIFF CORINTHIANS . . . . Riverside Ground, Through Station Road, Radyr, Cardiff CF15 8AA 02920 843407
CWMBRAN CELTIC . . . . Cwmbran Stadium, Henllys Way, Cwmbran NP44 3XL . . . . Celtic Club: 01633 774019
ELY RANGERS . . . . Station Road, Wenvoe CF5 6AG 02920 598725
GARDEN VILLAGE . . . . Stafford Common, Victoria Road, Gowerton, Swansea SA4 3AB 01792 894933
GRANGE HARLEQUINS . . . . Leckwith Stadium, Leckwith, Cardiff CF11 8AZ 02920 225345
LLANGEINOR . . . . Llangeinor Park, Bettws Road, Llangeinor, Bridgend 01656 871676
LLANWERN . . . . Newport Stadium, Spytty Park, Newport NP19 4PT 07762 013310
PONTYCLUN . . . . Ivor Park, Cowbridge Road, Pontyclun CF72 9EE 01443 222182
TREDEGAR TOWN . . . . Tredegar Leisure Complex, Stable Lane, Tredegar NP22 3BH 01495 723554
TREHARRIS ATHLETIC . . . . Athletic Ground, Commercial Terrace, Treharris CF46 5PY 07790 511985
TROEDYRHIW . . . . Troedyrhiw B&GC, The Willows, Bridge Street, Troedyrhiw, Merthyr Tydfil CF48 4DX 01443 692198
UWIC . . . . Cyncoed Road, Cardiff CF23 6XD 02920 416155
WEST END . . . . Pryderri Park, Townhill, Swansea SA1 6LD . . . . None
IN: *Barry Town (R), Cwmbran Celtic (P), Ely Rangers (R), Grange Harlequins (R), Llangeinor (P), Llanwern (P), UWIC (R)*
OUT: *AFC Llwydcoed (R), Caldicot Town (P), Cambrian & Clydach Vale BC (P), Garw Athletic (P), Merthyr Saints (R), Morriston Town (R), Penrhiweiber Rangers (R)*

Note – Gwynfi United withdrew during the course of the season Their results are shown herein but are expunged from the league table	AFC Porth	Aberbargoed Buds	Abertillery Excelsior	Chepstow Town	Cwmmaman United	Cwmbran Celtic	Goytre	Gwynfi United	Llangeinor	Llansawel	Llantwit Fardre	Llanwern	Newcastle Emlyn	Pentwyn Dynamo	Porthcawl Town	Risca United	Seven Sisters	Ystradgynlais
AFC Porth		0-4	4-1	1-1	5-2	2-2	1-3	n/a	0-0	1-2	2-1	2-4	5-1	2-2	4-1	1-2	2-0	2-2
Aberbargoed Buds	2-1		5-3	3-0	2-2	1-1	1-2	n/a	0-1	4-0	0-4	3-0	0-4	1-1	1-2	2-1	2-3	3-0
Abertillery Excelsior	4-3	4-1	*D*	1-2	3-0	0-2	3-1	8-1	2-2	2-4	0-4	0-2	6-2	1-2	1-2	0-0	3-5	2-3
Chepstow Town	2-0	2-1	0-4	*I*	0-3	1-5	2-2	3-1	0-1	0-2	1-2	1-2	2-1	3-2	1-2	2-3	1-0	4-2
Cwmmaman United	0-2	0-1	4-2	2-5	*V*	2-2	2-0	5-1	5-0	2-1	3-1	1-6	0-2	0-1	3-1	5-1	5-1	0-1
Cwmbran Celtic	4-2	3-2	3-0	3-0	4-0	*I*	2-1	n/a	2-0	3-3	1-0	0-0	1-1	1-1	1-0	4-2	2-1	3-2
Goytre	5-3	1-1	1-2	4-2	2-0	0-1	*S*	n/a	0-2	1-0	0-1	0-2	2-3	2-3	2-1	3-1	1-2	3-2
Gwynfi United	0-2	0-2	n/a	n/a	n/a	2-6	0-5	*I*	n/a	n/a	n/a	n/a	n/a	n/a	n/a	n/a	n/a	3-5
Llangeinor	2-0	3-2	3-3	4-0	4-2	1-1	2-1	2-0	*O*	6-1	2-2	2-1	2-1	2-0	4-2	1-1	2-0	3-2
Llansawel	3-1	2-2	2-2	6-2	2-2	0-1	2-2	n/a	2-4	*N*	2-0	1-1	0-0	0-3	2-2	1-2	2-0	2-3
Llantwit Fardre	3-2	0-0	2-0	1-1	2-3	1-0	0-0	3-0	1-1	2-0		1-1	2-2	0-1	3-3	3-2	1-2	1-2
Llanwern	2-1	3-0	4-0	1-0	0-0	3-1	2-2	4-2	5-2	0-1	2-0	*T*	2-2	2-2	5-0	3-2	2-1	3-2
Newcastle Emlyn	3-2	2-2	5-5	7-0	2-1	3-6	2-0	6-2	4-2	0-1	0-4	0-4	*H*	1-2	1-2	6-0	1-0	1-2
Pentwyn Dynamo	3-1	3-3	3-0	5-2	2-1	1-2	5-0	5-0	4-2	3-2	2-2	6-1	1-1	*R*	5-1	1-1	2-0	2-5
Porthcawl Town	4-0	1-3	0-2	3-3	2-3	0-1	6-2	6-0	1-3	2-2	2-3	1-0	2-1	1-2	*E*	2-1	2-2	1-2
Risca United	4-2	0-3	0-1	3-2	1-0	1-2	0-2	3-0	1-3	3-0	0-3	0-3	4-1	1-2	0-2	*E*	3-0	1-0
Seven Sisters	3-1	3-2	1-1	6-2	2-2	1-1	0-2	2-1	0-3	3-2	2-0	0-4	1-1	2-1	2-0	3-1		2-2
Ystradgynlais	3-2	0-2	11-3	2-2	2-0	2-3	3-2	n/a	3-2	3-2	1-2	1-2	1-5	3-4	1-4	2-0	1-3	

Division Three	Ded	P	W	D	L	F	A	Pts
Cwmbran Celtic		32	20	10	2	68	35	70
Llanwern		32	20	8	4	75	35	68
Llangeinor		32	19	7	6	73	52	64
Pentwyn Dynamo	-1	32	17	9	6	75	46	59
Llantwit Fardre		32	14	9	9	51	40	51
Aberbargoed Buds		32	13	8	11	60	51	47
Ystradgynlais		32	14	5	13	77	71	47
Newcastle Emlyn		32	12	8	12	76	66	44
Seven Sisters		32	11	6	15	51	61	39
Cwmmaman United		32	11	5	16	55	62	38
Goytre		32	11	5	16	49	60	38
Risca United		32	11	4	17	46	62	37
Porthcawl Town		32	10	4	18	46	62	34
Abertillery Excelsior		32	9	6	17	61	83	33
Llansawel		32	8	9	15	51	73	33
Chepstow Town		32	8	5	19	46	84	29
AFC Porth		32	7	6	19	57	74	27

Gwynfi United – record expunged

Reserve Division East	Ded	P	W	D	L	F	A	Pts
Dinas Powys Res.		30	23	3	4	92	41	72
Llantwit Fardre Res.		30	22	3	5	85	37	69
Ely Rangers Res.		30	17	9	4	83	40	60
Croesyceiliog Res.		30	19	3	8	82	52	60
Caldicot Town Res.		30	16	4	10	74	46	52
Newport YMCA Res.	-3	30	16	4	10	63	44	49
Caerleon Res.		30	13	4	13	57	50	43
Bryntirion Athletic Res.		30	13	4	13	54	59	43
Pontyclun Res.		30	12	7	11	57	65	43
Cwmbran Celtic Res.		30	10	6	14	45	65	36
Cambrian & Clydach VBC Res.		30	8	8	14	54	60	32
Risca United Res.		30	7	9	14	41	59	30
Caerau Ely Res.		30	7	5	18	54	72	26
Chepstow Town Res.		30	6	8	16	46	87	26
Porthcawl Town Res.		30	6	2	22	27	91	20
Bridgend Town Res.	-3	30	5	5	22	35	81	11

Reserve Division West	Ded	P	W	D	L	F	A	Pts
Goytre United Res.		28	23	2	3	104	40	71
Neath Athletic Res.		28	21	3	4	113	42	66
Garden Village Res.		28	21	3	4	90	40	66
Afan Lido Res.		28	19	3	6	73	41	60
Port Talbot Town Res.		28	17	2	9	88	41	53
Ammanford Res.		28	16	5	7	80	46	53
Ystradgynlais Res.		28	11	2	15	68	72	35
Pontardawe Town Res.		28	10	4	14	46	61	34
Briton Ferry Athletic Res.		28	9	0	19	60	98	27
Cwmmaman United Res.		28	6	7	15	64	97	25
Seven Sisters Res.		28	7	3	18	35	89	24
Newcastle Emlyn Res.		28	6	5	17	48	78	23
Morriston Town Res.		28	5	8	15	46	76	23
AFC Llwydcoed Res.		28	6	5	17	42	83	23
Maesteg Park Res.	-3	28	6	2	20	33	86	17

WELSH LEAGUE DIVISION THREE CONSTITUTION 2007-08

AFC LLWYDCOED .... Welfare Ground, Llwydcoed, Aberdare CF44 0UT 01685 873924
ABERBARGOED BUDS .... Recreation Ground, Aberbargoed .... None
ABERTILLERY EXCELSIOR .... Woodland Field, Cwmtillery, Abertillery NP13 1LA 01495 217839
CWMAMAN INSTITUTE .... Canolfan, Glanaman Road, Cwmaman, Aberdare CF44 6HY 01685 887100
CWMAMAN UNITED.................... Grenig Park, Glanamman, Ammanford SA18 1YU .... None
GOYTRE .... Plough Road, Penperlleni, Pontypool NP4 0AL .... None
LLANSAWEL .... Cwrt Herbert, Neath Abbey Road, Neath SA10 7BR 01639 635013
LLANTWIT FARDRE................ Tonteg Park, Church Village, Pontypridd CF31 1ND 01443 207393
MERTHYR SAINTS .... ICI Pavilion, Pant, Merthyr Tydfil 01685 386140
MONMOUTH TOWN .... Chippenham Sports Ground, Monmouth NP25 5EY 01600 772389
MORRISTON TOWN .... The Dingle, Clydach Terrace, Morriston, Swansea SA6 6QH 01792 702033
NEWCASTLE EMLYN................ Parc Emlyn, New Road, Newcastle Emlyn SA38 9BA 01239 710007
PENRHIWCEIBER RANGERS .. Glasbrook, Glasbrook Terrace, Penrhiwceiber, Mountain Ash CF45 3SY 01443 473368
PENTWYN DYNAMO .... Parc Coed-y-Nant, Pentwyn, Cardiff 02920 549211
PORTHCAWL TOWN .... Locks Lane, Porthcawl CF36 3HY 07866 545830
RISCA UNITED .... Ty Isaf Park, Pontymister Road, Risca, Newport NP11 6ND 01633 615081/615689
SEVEN SISTERS .... Welfare Ground, Seven Sisters, Neath 01639 700354
YSTRADGYNLAIS .... Recreation Ground, Ynyscedwyn Road, Ystradgynlais, Swansea SA9 1BH .... None

IN: AFC Llwydcoed (R), Cwmaman Institute (South Wales Amateur League Division One), Merthyr Saints (R), Monmouth Town (Gwent County League Division One), Morriston Town (R), Penrhiwceiber Rangers (R)
OUT: AFC Porth (R – South Wales Amateur League Division One), Chepstow Town (R – Gwent County League Division One), Cwmbran Celtic (P), Gwynfi United (WS), Llangeinor (P), Llanwern (P)

WELSH NATIONAL LEAGUE
(WREXHAM AREA)

	Acrefair	Borras Park	Brickfield	Brymbo	Brynteg V.	Castell Alun	Cefn United	Chirk AAA	Coedpoeth	Corwen A.	Hawarden	Llangollen	Llay Welf.	Mold Alex	Penycae	Rhos Aelwyd
Acrefair Youth	P	1-4	0-3	0-2	5-0	0-4	2-5	0-2	2-0	2-3	2-4	0-3	2-1	1-3	2-1	1-3
Borras Park A.	0-2	R	2-0	1-2	4-4	2-3	0-4	0-1	1-4	4-1	3-1	0-6	2-1	0-1	1-6	1-3
Brickfield Rgrs	4-1	1-1	E	0-1	2-3	4-0	0-3	1-2	1-4	3-1	2-3	2-4	1-3	2-3	2-1	1-0
Brymbo	4-0	5-2	3-0	M	10-1	4-2	0-2	7-2	2-0	8-0	3-1	3-0	3-1	1-1	3-1	1-0
Brynteg Village	1-3	2-4	0-4	0-6	I	2-2	0-1	4-1	2-0	1-9	2-7	2-3	2-4	1-4	1-5	1-4
Castell Alun Colts	6-1	1-0	2-0	2-7	2-2	E	2-2	5-1	1-2	1-2	0-3	2-2	3-1	2-3	5-2	2-4
Cefn United	7-0	6-0	2-0	0-2	5-2	3-2	R	2-2	3-0	5-0	5-2	3-1	2-1	4-3	2-0	6-1
Chirk AAA	5-1	1-2	3-1	2-1	1-1	1-1	0-0		3-0	4-2	5-0	3-3	1-0	2-3	0-1	3-1
Coedpoeth Utd	4-4	1-1	5-0	1-5	2-0	3-3	0-1	1-1	D	1-2	2-3	4-2	1-1	1-1	2-2	1-2
Corwen Amateurs	2-1	2-3	2-5	2-7	5-2	1-3	0-2	5-0	0-5	I	1-1	2-3	0-4	1-6	2-2	6-3
Hawarden Rgrs	3-2	4-1	3-0	0-4	7-1	1-0	2-1	4-3	2-1	5-0	V	8-1	4-1	1-3	3-2	0-1
Llangollen Town	4-1	1-1	2-3	2-4	1-4	3-0	0-4	1-0	3-1	1-4	1-2	I	6-1	1-4	6-1	4-3
Llay Welfare	3-2	5-5	2-6	0-3	7-1	1-1	4-4	2-0	1-2	2-1	2-5	5-2	S	0-2	2-2	1-1
Mold Alexandra	4-0	4-2	4-0	2-3	3-1	1-0	0-0	7-0	4-2	9-3	4-2	2-1	5-1	I	4-1	1-1
Penycae	8-0	7-2	3-2	0-4	16-1	5-4	0-2	3-1	4-2	1-1	1-0	3-1	4-3	3-1	O	2-0
Rhos Aelwyd	5-3	3-0	3-1	1-2	3-1	2-3	3-3	2-1	0-0	5-0	3-3	2-4	0-1	3-2	4-0	N

PREM. DIV CUP

FIRST ROUND
Acrefair Youth 0 **Mold Alexandra** 5
Borras Park Albion 3 Brynteg 2
Brickfield Rangers 1 **Penycae** 3
Castell Alun Colts 1 Hawarden 0
Coedpoeth United 0 **Brymbo** 3
Llangollen Town 1 Corwen1
Llay Welfare 1 **Cefn United** 4
Rhos Aelwyd 6 Chirk AAA 0

QUARTER-FINALS
Castell Alun Colts 2 Borras Park 1
Cefn United 5 Brymbo 2
Llangollen Town 1 **Penycae** 2
Rhos Aelwyd 1 **Mold Alexandra** 3

SEMI-FINALS
Castell Alun Colts 2 Mold Alex 1
Penycae 2 **Cefn United** 3

FINAL
(April 28th at NEWI Cefn Druids)
Castell Alun Colts 1 **Cefn United** 2

Premier Division	P	W	D	L	F	A	Pts
Brymbo	30	27	1	2	110	26	82
Cefn United	30	24	4	2	88	25	76
Mold Alexandra	30	23	4	3	94	38	73
Penycae	30	17	4	9	89	58	55
Hawarden Rangers	30	17	3	10	78	55	54
Chirk AAA	30	12	6	12	55	61	42
Rhos Aelwyd	30	11	7	12	65	60	40
Coedpoeth United	30	9	10	11	57	59	37
Castell Alun Colts	30	10	6	14	62	65	36
Llangollen Town	30	10	4	16	61	80	34
Llay Welfare	30	9	6	15	69	74	33
Corwen Amateurs	30	10	3	17	64	94	33
Borras Park Albion	30	8	5	17	49	84	29
Brickfield Rangers	30	9	1	20	50	66	28
Acrefair Youth	30	6	1	23	41	98	19
Brynteg Village -3	30	4	3	23	45	131	12

DIV ONE CUP
FINAL
(May 5th at Rhos Aelwyd)
Overton Rec 2 Bala Town Res. 1

DIV TWO CUP
FINAL *(May 9th at Mold Alex)*
Buckley Res. 2 Ruthin Res. 2
aet (3-2p)

DIV THREE CUP
FINAL *(May 12th at Castell Alun)*
Hawarden Res. 3 Brymbo Res. 2

HORACE WYNNE CUP
FINAL *(May 11th)*
Penyfford 3 Penley 0
(May 21st at Llangollen Town)
Brymbo 3 Cefn United 1

PRESIDENT'S CUP
(Champs v Prem Div Cup winners)

WWW.NLNEWSDESK.CO.UK

WELSH NATIONAL LEAGUE (WREXHAM AREA) PREMIER DIVISION CONSTITUTION 2007-08

ACREFAIR YOUTH . . . . The Bont Playing Field, Froncysyllte, Wrexham . . . . None
BORRAS PARK ALBION . . . . Dean Road, Wrexham LL13 9EF . . . . None
BRICKFIELD RANGERS . . . . Court Road, Wrexham LL13 7SN . . . . None
BRYMBO . . . . Brymbo Sports Complex, College Hill, Tanyfron, Wrexham LL11 5TF 01978 752577
CASTELL ALUN COLTS . . . . Castell Alun Sports Centre, Fagl Lane, Hope, Wrexham LL12 9PY . . . . None
CEFN UNITED . . . . Church Field, Rhosymedre, Wrexham LL14 3EF . . . . None
CHIRK AAA . . . . Holyhead Road, Chirk, Wrexham LL14 5NA 01691 773676
COEDPOETH UNITED . . . . Pengelli Playing Fields, Coedpoeth, Wrexham . . . . None
CORWEN AMATEURS . . . . War Memorial Park, Green Lane, Corwen LL21 0DN . . . . None
HAWARDEN RANGERS . . . . Gladstone Playing Fields, Hawarden . . . . None
LLANGOLLEN TOWN . . . . Tower Field, Dinbren Road, Llangollen LL20 8TF . . . . None
LLAY WELFARE . . . . The Ring, Llay, Wrexham LL12 0TN 01978 852286
MOLD ALEXANDRA . . . . Alyn Park, Denbigh Road, Mold CH7 1SW . . . . None
OVERTON RECREATION . . . . Recreation Ground, Overton-on-Dee, Wrexham . . . . None
PENYCAE . . . . Afoneitha Road, Penycae, Wrexham LL14 2PF . . . . None
RHOS AELWYD . . . . Ponciau Park, Clarke Street, Ponciau, Wrexham LL14 1RT . . . . None

IN: Overton Recreation (P)
OUT: Brynteg Village (R)

Division One	P	W	D	L	F	A	Pts
Bala Town Res.	24	19	2	3	60	27	59
Overton Recreation	24	16	3	5	65	38	51
Penley	24	14	5	5	57	33	47
Gresford Athletic Res.	24	13	3	8	56	38	42
Penyffordd	24	13	3	8	68	68	42
Airbus UK Res.	24	12	4	8	57	44	40
Ruthin Town Res.	24	11	4	9	54	42	37
Cefn United Res.	24	11	2	11	53	42	35
New Brighton Villa	24	9	5	10	60	63	32
Penycae Res.	24	6	3	15	37	66	21
Rhos Aelwyd Res.	24	5	1	18	33	71	16
Llanuwchllyn	24	4	3	17	41	72	15
Glyn Ceiriog	24	3	2	19	46	83	11

Division Two	P	W	D	L	F	A	Pts
Venture	26	19	4	3	104	40	61
Johnstown Youth	26	17	5	4	76	39	56
Llangollen Town Res.	26	14	5	7	70	49	47
Buckley Town Res.	26	15	2	9	67	54	47
Ruthin Town Colts	26	12	6	8	53	40	42
Holt Nomads	26	12	6	8	56	46	42
Mold Alexandra Res.	26	11	7	8	65	54	40
Mold Juniors	26	9	7	10	69	66	34
Garden Village	26	7	8	11	55	59	29
Borras Park Alb. Res.	26	7	5	14	53	43	73
Llay Welfare Res. -3	26	8	6	12	70	82	27
Brickfield Rgrs Res.	26	5	6	15	57	101	21
Corwen Ams Res.	26	4	4	18	49	96	16
Acrefair Yth Res. -12	26	4	4	18	45	80	4

Division Three	P	W	D	L	F	A	Pts
Brymbo Res.	24	17	3	4	70	22	54
Hawarden Rgrs Res.	24	16	2	6	86	36	50
Gresford Ath. Colts	24	13	6	5	59	38	45
Coedpoeth United Res.	24	13	3	8	63	54	42
Chirk AAA Res.	24	13	1	10	70	65	40
Penyffordd Res.	24	12	4	8	56	54	40
New Brighton V.a Res.	24	10	5	9	58	63	35
Overton Rec. Res.	24	9	6	9	46	44	33
Caergwrle Castle -3	24	9	1	14	52	65	25
Glyn Ceiriog Res.	24	8	1	15	37	69	25
Borras Park A. Colts	24	7	3	14	44	61	24
Penley Res.	24	5	4	15	47	69	19
Brickfield Rgrs Colts	24	3	3	18	35	83	12

Brynteg Village Res. – record expunged

WELSH PREMIER LEAGUE

	Aberystwyth Town	Airbus UK	Bangor City	Caernarfon Town	Caersws FC	Carmarthen Town	Connah's Quay Nomads	Cwmbran Town	Haverfordwest County	Llanelli AFC	NEWI Cefn Druids	Newtown AFC	Port Talbot Town	Porthmadog FC	Rhyl FC	The New Saints	Welshpool Town
Aberystwyth Town		1-1	0-2	2-0	1-0	4-2	1-1	3-1	2-2	1-1	3-0	4-2	0-2	0-1	2-3	0-0	0-0
Airbus UK	0-0		4-1	2-3	0-3	2-2	2-3	3-0	2-0	1-4	0-1	1-2	3-0	1-1	0-1	0-1	1-4
Bangor City	1-4	3-1		0-0	1-2	1-3	3-1	1-1	4-1	4-0	6-0	5-2	0-0	2-1	1-3	0-2	1-3
Caernarfon Town	1-3	0-2	0-1		2-2	3-5	0-2	0-1	1-4	2-6	1-1	1-0	1-2	2-2	2-6	1-3	2-0
Caersws FC	0-1	0-0	0-1	1-1		1-7	2-1	3-3	3-3	0-3	2-1	0-1	1-4	0-1	1-1	0-2	1-3
Carmarthen Town	1-0	2-1	2-2	4-1	2-0		1-3	1-0	1-3	0-2	4-0	2-0	1-0	1-1	1-1	0-0	2-4
Connah's Quay Nomads	1-0	1-2	3-0	2-2	4-3	4-1		2-2	5-3	0-1	1-0	2-1	2-1	1-0	0-2	0-0	1-3
Cwmbran Town	2-0	2-2	0-1	0-3	2-5	4-5	0-1		0-0	2-2	3-2	0-2	1-2	2-3	2-3	0-5	1-4
Haverfordwest County	1-1	5-1	2-0	2-1	1-0	0-1	0-0	2-0		1-1	0-1	3-2	1-2	1-1	0-1	0-3	0-1
Llanelli AFC	1-3	4-0	3-0	4-2	0-0	1-1	1-1	5-1	3-2		3-1	3-2	0-0	5-0	6-0	1-2	2-3
NEWI Cefn Druids	1-2	3-1	0-3	3-2	2-2	1-2	2-2	3-0	2-2	0-1		1-1	0-3	3-0	2-3	2-3	1-3
Newtown AFC	1-1	1-1	2-1	0-1	0-1	1-1	0-1	2-3	1-0	0-2	0-2		1-2	0-0	0-6	0-4	0-4
Port Talbot Town	1-3	0-2	0-5	7-1	0-0	1-0	0-1	2-0	1-4	1-0	1-1	2-1		1-2	3-2	2-1	0-0
Porthmadog FC	0-4	1-1	1-1	2-2	4-0	3-0	1-2	2-2	0-3	1-1	3-0	2-3	1-1		1-2	1-2	2-1
Rhyl FC	3-0	4-0	3-1	0-0	4-0	1-0	2-1	1-0	3-2	2-2	2-2	2-0	2-1	1-2		0-0	0-0
The New Saints	4-1	7-0	5-2	1-3	2-1	4-1	4-0	4-0	2-1	0-2	3-1	4-0	2-0	3-0	2-0		6-0
Welshpool Town	1-0	6-3	1-1	3-0	1-0	1-1	0-0	1-1	0-0	0-2	4-2	1-0	0-1	3-1	1-1	1-0	

	P	W	D	L	F	A	W	D	L	F	A	W	D	L	F	A	Pts
The New Saints	32	14	0	2	53	12	10	4	2	28	8	24	4	4	81	20	76
Rhyl FC	32	10	6	0	31	11	10	3	3	36	24	20	9	3	67	35	69
Llanelli AFC	32	9	4	3	42	18	9	5	2	30	15	18	9	5	72	33	63
Welshpool Town	32	8	6	2	24	13	9	3	4	30	20	17	9	6	54	33	60
Connah's Quay Nomads	32	9	3	4	29	21	7	5	4	20	19	16	8	8	49	40	56
Port Talbot Town	32	7	3	6	22	23	8	3	5	20	16	15	6	11	42	39	51
Carmarthen Town	32	8	4	4	25	18	6	4	6	32	32	14	8	10	57	50	50
Aberystwyth Town	32	6	6	4	24	18	7	3	6	23	19	13	9	10	47	37	48
Bangor City	32	8	3	5	33	21	6	3	7	22	26	14	6	12	55	47	48
Haverfordwest County	32	6	4	6	19	16	4	5	7	30	30	10	9	13	49	46	39
Porthmadog FC	32	4	6	6	25	25	4	5	7	15	27	8	11	13	40	52	35
Airbus UK	32	4	3	9	22	27	3	5	8	18	40	7	8	17	40	67	29
NEWI Cefn Druids	32	4	4	8	26	30	3	3	10	15	36	7	7	18	41	66	28
Caersws FC	32	2	5	9	15	33	4	4	8	19	26	6	9	17	34	59	27
Caernarfon Town	32	2	3	11	19	40	4	5	7	22	33	6	8	18	41	73	26
Newtown AFC	32	2	4	10	9	30	4	2	10	21	33	6	6	20	30	63	24
Cwmbran Town	32	2	3	11	21	40	2	5	9	15	35	4	8	20	36	75	20

WWW.CHERRYRED.CO.UK

DATES & GATES

	Aberystwyth Town	Airbus UK	Bangor City	Caernarfon Town	Caersws	Carmarthen Town	Connah's Quay Nomads	Cwmbran Town	Haverfordwest County	Llanelli	NEWI Cefn Druids	Newtown	Port Talbot Town	Porthmadog	Rhyl	The New Saints	Welshpool Town
Welshpool Town	21 Apr / 238	25 Aug / 152	8 Sep / 455	7 Apr / 251	14 Oct / 310	23 Sep / 309	28 Oct / 122	18 Nov / 286	24 Mar / 201	13 Jan / 242	13 Apr / 215	10 Mar / 230	2 Dec / 243	19 Aug / 185	17 Feb / 511	26 Dec / 479	—
The New Saints	24 Feb / 351	18 Aug / 217	6 Jan / 554	8 Dec / 184	20 Jan / 270	1 Sep / 360	27 Jan / 380	11 Apr / 141	9 Apr / 231	17 Mar / 322	21 Apr / 260	14 Feb / 275	8 Oct / 478	21 Oct / 307	31 Mar / 876	—	17 Apr / 458
Rhyl	2 Sep / 384	6 Apr / 260	2 Dec / 701	28 Oct / 263	16 Dec / 205	14 Apr / 301	27 Apr / 430	19 Aug / 214	10 Mar / 171	16 Sep / 491	23 Mar / 282	14 Oct / 275	6 Jan / 235	20 Jan / 302	—	19 Nov / 637	8 Oct / 320
Porthmadog	26 Dec / 652	28 Oct / 83	23 Mar / 562	17 Feb / 307	7 Apr / 182	18 Nov / 318	1 Dec / 252	14 Apr / 105	23 Sep / 203	28 Apr / 404	13 Oct / 104	27 Jan / 205	16 Dec / 128	—	9 Sep / 490	10 Mar / 278	30 Dec / 228
Port Talbot Town	3 Apr / 191	14 Oct / 101	10 Mar / 371	27 Jan / 87	23 Mar / 112	27 Oct / 423	18 Nov / 154	7 Apr / 150	8 Sep / 223	26 Dec / 420	23 Sep / 110	13 Jan / 265	—	21 Apr / 178	26 Aug / 325	17 Feb / 227	9 Apr / 750
Newtown	19 Jan / 347	2 Dec / 103	14 Apr / 406	24 Mar / 167	1 Jan / 380	16 Dec / 241	19 Aug / 165	6 Jan / 145	28 Oct / 172	20 Mar / 180	17 Nov / 255	—	2 Sep / 210	16 Sep / 198	24 Feb / 394	6 Apr / 424	21 Oct / 188
NEWI Cefn Druids	6 Oct / 476	1 Jan / 176	19 Aug / 316	9 Apr / 267	2 Sep / 208	6 Jan / 253	20 Mar / 177	16 Sep / 183	26 Nov / 232	21 Oct / 279	—	31 Mar / 150	28 Apr / 130	24 Feb / 167	10 Nov / 481	3 Apr / 246	8 Dec / 228
Llanelli	18 Aug / 650	24 Mar / 105	18 Nov / 413	14 Oct / 248	2 Dec / 225	6 Apr / 462	14 Apr / 224	15 Dec / 263	16 Feb / 391	—	27 Mar / 160	23 Sep / 220	1 Jan / 351	6 Jan / 188	24 Apr / 333	28 Oct / 393	2 Sep / 148
Haverfordwest County	15 Sep / 402	28 Apr / 97	16 Nov / 358	18 Nov / 119	19 Aug / 210	1 Jan / 376	6 Jan / 149	1 Sep / 166	—	6 Oct / 341	7 Apr / 115	3 Mar / 175	19 Jan / 222	17 Apr / 157	21 Oct / 515	11 Nov / 140	16 Dec / 156
Cwmbran Town	9 Apr / 227	17 Feb / 98	14 Oct / 417	9 Sep / 217	28 Oct / 115	24 Mar / 342	21 Apr / 131	—	12 Jan / 229	21 Apr / 210	27 Jan / 101	26 Aug / 155	27 Jan / 413	24 Mar / 122	8 Sep / 205	28 Apr / 156	9 Dec / 211
Connah's Quay Nomads	25 Nov / 340	22 Sep / 251	17 Feb / 355	13 Jan / 146	17 Apr / 179	14 Oct / 285	—	11 Nov / 103	26 Aug / 293	9 Dec / 238	8 Sep / 205	13 Mar / 150	31 Mar / 128	3 Apr / 162	26 Dec / 707	15 Sep / 302	17 Mar / 166
Carmarthen Town	23 Mar / 404	9 Sep / 85	23 Sep / 467	27 Jan / 420	28 Apr / 169	—	6 Oct / 225	24 Mar / 122	26 Dec / 382	21 Oct / 230	11 Nov / 161	23 Jan / 321	27 Aug / 155	21 Apr / 247	9 Dec / 424	24 Apr / 256	27 Mar / 322
Caersws	18 Nov / 185	16 Sep / 168	26 Aug / 287	10 Mar / 107	—	17 Feb / 246	21 Oct / 130	3 Mar / 115	30 Dec / 214	11 Nov / 161	21 Oct / 184	25 Nov / 184	9 Apr / 242	21 Apr / 390	9 Sep / 283	23 Feb / 382	23 Sep / 382
Caernarfon Town	23 Sep / 128	2 Feb / 207	1 Jan / 618	—	10 Mar / 107	1 Sep / 237	17 Apr / 111	17 Mar / 115	31 Mar / 168	24 Feb / 209	1 Dec / 224	11 Nov / 205	16 Sep / 170	8 Oct / 312	3 Mar / 383	14 Apr / 247	25 Nov / 186
Bangor City	3 Mar / 251	12 Jan / 212	—	26 Dec / 1,007	16 Sep / 313	6 Oct / 351	3 Apr / 107	9 Dec / 275	21 Oct / 315	17 Apr / 220	11 Nov / 324	9 Apr / 291	21 Oct / 212	24 Feb / 127	9 Nov / 275	20 Jan / 758	5 Jan / 208
Airbus UK	21 Oct / 382	—	2 Sep / 284	21 Apr / 157	16 Sep / 168	20 Aug / 245	20 Feb / 133	8 Oct / 147	9 Apr / 230	24 Feb / 120	11 Nov / 131	26 Dec / 131	26 Feb / 147	20 Feb / 162	25 Nov / 411	9 Apr / 324	5 Jan / 261
Aberystwyth Town	—	10 Mar / 114	23 Sep / 128	18 Nov / 185	23 Mar / 404	7 Apr / 158	1 Dec / 210	26 Jan / 217	13 Mar / 269	20 Feb / 101	9 Sep / 252	14 Apr / 161	26 Aug / 337	13 Jan / 101	9 Sep / 252	13 Dec / 342	16 Dec / 270

WELSH PREMIER LEAGUE
CONSTITUTION 2008-09

ABERYSTWYTH TOWN
Park Avenue, Maesgogerddan, Aberystwyth, Ceredigion SY23 2EY
Tel: 01970 617939   Fax: 01970 617939
Manager: Bryan Coyne   www.atfc.org.uk   Colours: Green, black & white

AIRBUS UK
The Airfield, Broughton, Chester, Cheshire CH4 0BA
Tel: 01244 522356
Manager: Gareth Owen   www.airbusfc.co.uk   Colours: White & navy blue

BANGOR CITY
The Stadium, Farrar Road, Bangor, Gwynedd LL57 3HU
Tel: 01248 355852   Fax: 01248 716873
Manager: Neville Powell   www.bangorcityfc.com   Colours: Blue

CAERNARFON TOWN
The Oval, Marcus Street, Caernarfon, Gwynedd LL55 2RT
Tel: 01286 676885   Club: 01286 674620   Fax: 01286 675002
Manager: Steve O'Shaughnessy www.caernarfontown.net   Colours: Yellow & green

CAERSWS
Recreation Ground, Bridge Street, Caersws, Powys SY17 5DT
Tel: 01686 688753
Manager: Mike Barton   www.caersws-fc.com   Colours: Blue & white

CARMARTHEN TOWN
Richmond Park, Priory Street, Carmarthen, Carmarthenshire SA31 1LR
Tel: 01267 232101   Fax: 01267 222851
Manager: Deryn Brace   www.carmarthentownafc.net   Colours: Old gold & black

CONNAH'S QUAY NOMADS
Flint Town United FC, Cae-y-Castell, Marsh Lane, Flint, Flintshire CH6 5PJ
Tel: 01352 730982   Club: 01352 762804
Manager: Jim Hackett   www.sportnetwork.net/main/s493.htm   Colours: White & black

HAVERFORDWEST COUNTY
New Bridge Meadow, Bridge Meadow Lane, Haverfordwest, Pembrokeshire SA61 2EX
Tel: 01437 769048   Fax: 01437 769048
Manager: Derek Brazil   www.haverfordwestcounty.com   Colours: Royal blue

LLANELLI
Stebonheath Park, Penallt Road, Stebonheath, Llanelli, Carmarthenshire SA15 1EY
Tel: 01554 772973   Club: 01554 773847   Fax: 01554 772973
Manager: Peter Nicholas   www.llanelliafc.org   Colours: Red

LLANGEFNI TOWN
Cae Bob Parry, Talwrn Road, Llangefni, Anglesey LL77 7LP
Tel: 01248 724999
Manager: Adrian Jones   www.llangefnifc.co.uk   Colours: Yellow & black

NEWI CEFN DRUIDS
Plas Kynaston Lane, Plas Kynaston, Cefn Mawr, Wrexham, Denbighshire LL14 3PY
Tel: 01978 824332   Club: 01978 824279   Fax: 01978 824332
Manager: Lee Jones/Wayne Phillips   Colours: Black & white
www.cefndruidsafc.co.uk

NEATH ATHLETIC
Llandarcy Park, Llandarcy, Neath, West Glamorgan SA10 6JD
Tel: 01792 812036
Manager: Andrew Dyer   www.neathathletic.ik.com   Colours: Yellow & blue

NEWTOWN
Latham Park, Park Lane, Newtown, Powys SY1 6XX
Tel: 01686 623120/622666   Club: 01686 626159   Fax: 01686 623813
Manager: Darren Ryan   www.newtownafc.co.uk   Colours: Red

PORT TALBOT TOWN
The Remax Stadium, Victoria Road, Aberavon, Port Talbot, West Glamorgan SA12 6AD
Tel: 01639 882465   Fax: 01639 886991
Manager: Tony Pennock   www.porttalbottown.co.uk   Colours: Blue

PORTHMADOG
Y Traeth, Porthmadog, Gwynedd LL49 9PP
Tel: 01766 514687
Manager: Clayton Blackmore   www.porthmadogfc.com   Colours: Red & black

RHYL
Belle Vue, Grange Road, Rhyl, Clwyd LL18 4BT
Tel: 01745 338327   Fax: 01745 338327
Manager: John Hulse   www.rhylfc.com   Colours: White & black

THE NEW SAINTS
Recreation Park, Treflan, Llansantffraid, Powys SY22 6AE
Tel: 01691 828112   Fax: 01691 828862
Manager: Ken McKenna   www.saints-alive.co.uk   Colours: Green & white

WELSHPOOL TOWN
Maesydre Recreation Grounds, Howells Drive, Welshpool, Powys SY21 7SU
Tel: 01938 553027
Manager: Tomi Morgan   www.welshpooltownfc.co.uk   Colours: White & black

IN: Llangefni Town (P – Cymru Alliance, Neath Athletic (P – Welsh League Division One)
OUT: Cwmbran Town (R – Welsh League Division One)

WWW.NLNEWSDESK.CO.UK

WELSH PREMIER TEAMS IN EUROPE

CHAMPIONS LEAGUE
FIRST QUALIFYING ROUND
MyPa-47 1 THE NEW SAINTS 0, THE NEW SAINTS 0 MyPa-47 1 *(at Newtown)*

U E F A CUP
FIRST QUALIFYING ROUND
Gefle IF 1 LLANELLI 2,
LLANELLI 0 Gefli IF 0
RHYL 0 FK Suduva 0, FK Suduva 2 RHYL 1
SECOND QUALIFYING ROUND
Odenske 1 Llanelli 0, LLANELLI 1 Odenske 5 *(at Swansea City)*

INTERTOTO CUP
FIRST ROUND
Tampere United 5 CARMARTHEN TOWN 0, CARMARTHEN TOWN 1 Tampere United 3 *(at Newtown)*

LEAGUE CUP

GROUP A

	P	W	D	L	F	A	Pts
Rhyl	6	4	1	1	13	4	13
Porthmadog	6	2	2	2	8	7	8
Bangor City	6	2	1	3	11	16	7
Caernarfon Town	6	2	0	4	10	15	6

Bangor City 2 Porthmadog 2
Caernarfon Town 2 Rhyl 1
Porthmadog 3 Caernarfon Town 1
Rhyl 4 Bangor City 0
Bangor City 3 Caernarfon Town 1
Rhyl 1 Porthmadog 0
Porthmadog 0 Rhyl 0
Caernarfon Town 4 Bangor City 3
Porthmadog 1 Bangor City 2
Rhyl 3 Caernarfon Town 1
Bangor City 1 Rhyl 4
Caernarfon Town 1 Porthmadog 2

GROUP B

	P	W	D	L	F	A	Pts
The New Saints	6	5	0	1	32	7	15
Connah's Quay Nomads	6	5	0	1	22	9	15
NEWI Cefn Druids	6	2	0	4	7	14	6
Airbus UK	6	0	0	6	6	33	0

The New Saints 3 NEWI Cefn Druids 0
Airbus UK 1 Connah's Quay Nomads 6
Connah's Quay Nomads 2 The New Saints 1
NEWI Cefn Druids 3 Airbus UK 0
Connah's Quay Nomads 3 NEWI Cefn Druids 0
The New Saints 11 Airbus UK 0
NEWI Cefn Druids 0 Connah's Quay Nomads 1
Airbus UK 1 The New Saints 5
Connah's Quay Nomads 7 Airbus UK 2
NEWI Cefn Druids 1 The New Saints 5
The New Saints 5 Connah's Quay Nomads 3
Airbus UK 2 NEWI Cefn Druids 3

GROUP C

	P	W	D	L	F	A	Pts
Caersws	6	3	1	2	11	9	10
Aberystwyth Town	6	3	1	2	8	7	10
Welshpool Town	6	2	2	2	7	6	8
Newtown	6	2	0	4	9	13	6

Aberystwyth Town 3 Caersws 1
Newtown 2 Welshpool Town 1
Caersws 4 Newtown 3
Welshpool Town 2 Aberystwyth Town 1
Aberystwyth Town 2 Newtown 1
Welshpool Town 0 Caersws 1
Caersws 1 Welshpool Town 1
Newtown 0 Aberystwyth Town 2
Caersws 3 Aberystwyth Town 0
Welshpool Town 3 Newtown 1
Aberystwyth Town 0 Welshpool Town 0
Newtown 2 Caersws 1

GROUP D

	P	W	D	L	F	A	Pts
Llanelli	7	7	0	0	24	8	21
Carmarthen Town	8	5	1	2	21	13	16
Port Talbot Town	8	2	1	5	15	22	7
Haverfordwest County	7	2	1	4	10	17	7
Cwmbran Town	9	1	1	6	13	23	4

Carmarthen Town 4 Port Talbot Town 2
Haverfordwest County 2 Cwmbran Town 1
Port Talbot Town 3 Haverfordwest County 1
Cwmbran Town 0 Carmarthen Town 3
Llanelli 3 Port Talbot Town 1
Cwmbran Town 7 Haverfordwest County 2
Llanelli 4 Carmarthen Town 3
Port Talbot Town 3 Cwmbran Town 1
Carmarthen Town 3 Haverfordwest County 1
Cwmbran Town 0 Llanelli 3
Carmarthen Town 4 Cwmbran Town 0
Haverfordwest County 2 Port Talbot Town 0
Port Talbot Town 1 Llanelli 4
Carmarthen Town 0 Llanelli 4
Cwmbran Town 3 Port Talbot Town 3
Haverfordwest County 0 Carmarthen Town 0
Llanelli 3 Cwmbran Town 1
Haverfordwest County 2 Llanelli 3
Port Talbot Town 2 Carmarthen Town 4
Llanelli 5 Haverfordwest County 2

Top two teams from each group qualify for knockout stage

SECOND ROUND

Caersws 2 Carmarthen Town 1
Rhyl 2 Connah's Quay Nomads 0
The New Saints 1 **Porthmadog** 2
Llanelli 1 **Aberystwyth Town** 2

SEMI-FINALS

(played over two legs)
Aberystwyth Town 1 Caersws 2,
Caersws 3 Aberystwyth Town 3
Porthmadog 0 Rhyl 0,
Rhyl 4 Porthmadog 0

FINAL

(March 18th at Aberystwyth Town)
Caersws 1 Rhyl 1 *aet* (3-0p)

WESSEX LEAGUE

	AFC Totton	Alton Town	Bemerton Heath H.	Bournemouth	Brading Town	Brockenhurst	Christchurch	Cowes Sports	Downton	Fareham Town	Gosport Borough	Hamble ASSC	Hamworthy Utd	Horndean	Lymington Town	Moneyfields	Poole Town	Ringwood Town	VTFC	Wimborne Town
AFC Totton		3-0	1-0	1-0	3-2	4-0	3-1	2-2	5-1	3-3	1-0	5-1	4-0	5-0	1-1	1-2	3-1	2-0	3-1	0-3
Alton Town	1-2		1-1	1-3	5-1	1-2	1-1	2-1	5-2	4-0	1-2	2-2	0-2	0-1	0-4	2-4	6-0	1-5	1-2	
Bemerton Heath Harlequins	0-2	2-2	P	1-0	1-1	2-2	2-1	2-2	2-1	0-8	3-4	3-0	1-2	1-0	0-1	0-1	2-4	3-1	2-1	2-4
Bournemouth	2-0	0-0	3-0	R	3-0	3-1	1-0	0-0	1-0	5-2	1-0	4-2	3-0	4-2	1-1	1-3	0-1	1-1	1-2	2-2
Brading Town	0-1	3-1	5-2	0-2	E	2-0	4-1	1-2	6-1	2-1	3-3	3-0	2-2	1-4	0-4	3-4	1-1	2-0	1-2	1-1
Brockenhurst	1-1	2-3	1-3	0-5	2-3	M	1-1	1-1	1-1	1-2	1-2	0-1	2-2	4-0	1-0	0-2	1-3	1-2	2-3	2-5
Christchurch	0-5	3-1	1-1	2-0	2-2	0-1	I	1-0	2-3	2-3	1-2	3-1	2-2	2-3	2-0	1-3	0-4	1-1	2-2	1-2
Cowes Sports	1-3	2-4	3-0	2-2	2-4	1-6	2-0	E	5-2	1-1	1-2	2-0	2-0	4-2	5-0	3-0	0-1	3-1	0-0	2-1
Downton	0-2	3-1	0-0	2-2	2-0	1-1	2-1	1-2	R	1-1	1-1	1-2	2-2	1-2	0-2	3-1	4-1	0-1	0-1	2-2
Fareham Town	3-3	4-1	3-0	1-1	1-2	3-0	1-1	3-0	2-1		0-2	6-1	3-0	5-0	3-2	1-2	3-4	7-0	1-1	1-1
Gosport Borough	0-0	4-1	4-1	2-0	2-0	0-0	1-1	1-1	6-0	3-0	D	3-1	6-0	2-0	1-0	2-1	2-0	4-1	2-2	4-0
Hamble ASSC	1-1	1-0	0-3	1-5	0-3	0-2	0-3	0-1	2-1	0-3	2-3	I	0-5	0-2	0-0	0-1	1-3	0-4	1-3	2-8
Hamworthy United	0-4	0-0	0-0	1-2	1-2	1-3	0-0	0-1	5-1	2-3	0-2	6-2	V	1-0	0-2	0-0	2-1	3-1	2-2	0-1
Horndean	1-5	1-2	2-6	1-2	5-4	1-1	1-5	1-2	1-3	1-2	0-6	2-0	0-2	I	2-1	0-3	1-4	5-2	0-5	3-1
Lymington Town	0-1	3-3	1-1	0-1	2-2	1-0	0-1	0-1	3-2	1-5	0-0	2-0	3-0	5-0	S	2-3	3-0	2-0	0-1	1-2
Moneyfields	0-1	4-0	4-0	0-2	1-2	2-3	0-1	2-0	7-1	1-2	0-2	3-0	1-0	1-2	4-1	I	0-4	0-0	2-0	1-2
Poole Town	0-2	8-1	4-0	1-0	10-1	0-1	1-0	1-1	2-2	0-1	0-2	3-0	2-1	3-1	2-1	0-1	O	2-0	1-2	1-0
Ringwood Town	1-2	3-0	0-3	2-2	0-3	0-1	2-1	0-2	1-2	4-4	0-2	1-0	0-2	2-0	0-1	1-2	0-6	N	0-2	0-2
VTFC	0-2	2-1	2-3	2-2	1-0	2-1	0-2	2-1	2-0	2-2	3-1	5-0	4-2	3-1	1-0	1-1	3-2	3-0		1-0
Wimborne Town	2-2	4-2	1-2	1-2	5-2	2-2	3-0	1-0	3-1	1-1	0-2	1-2	3-1	4-2	2-2	4-2	0-0	2-2	4-0	

Premier Division		P	W	D	L	F	A	Pts
Gosport Borough		38	27	8	3	87	27	89
AFC Totton		38	27	8	3	89	31	89
VTFC		38	24	8	6	76	44	80
Poole Town		38	23	4	11	88	41	73
Bournemouth		38	20	10	8	69	38	70
Wimborne Town		38	19	10	9	82	54	67
Moneyfields		38	21	3	14	69	46	66
Fareham Town	-1	38	18	12	8	95	57	65
Cowes Sports		38	17	9	12	61	50	60
Brading Town		38	15	7	16	74	80	52
Bemerton Heath Harlequins		38	13	9	16	55	73	48
Lymington Town		38	13	8	17	49	48	47
Brockenhurst		38	10	11	17	52	66	41
Christchurch		38	9	10	19	47	63	37
Hamworthy United		38	9	10	19	49	70	37
Horndean		38	11	4	23	51	104	37
Alton Town	-1	38	9	7	22	59	87	33
Downton		38	7	10	21	48	89	31
Ringwood Town		38	5	8	25	34	85	23
Hamble ASSC		38	5	3	30	24	105	18

WESSEX LEAGUE PREMIER DIVISION CONSTITUTION 2007-08

FC TOTTON . . . . Testwood Park, Testwood Place, Totton, Southampton SO40 3BE 023 8086 8981
LRESFORD TOWN . . . . Alrebury Park, The Avenue, Alresford SO24 9EP 01962 735100
LTON TOWN . . . . Bass Sports Ground, Anstey Road, Alton GU34 2LS 01420 82465
EMERTON HEATH HARLEQUINS . . Westwood Rec Ground, Western Way, Bemerton Heath, Salisbury SP2 9DR 01722 331925
OURNEMOUTH . . . . Victoria Park, Namu Road, Winton, Bournemouth BH9 2RA 01202 515123
RADING TOWN . . . . Vicarage Lane, Brading PO36 0AR 01983 405217
ROCKENHURST . . . . Grigg Lane, Brockenhurst SO42 7RE 01590 623544
HRISTCHURCH . . . . Hurn Bridge Sports Club, Avon Causeway, Christchurch BH23 6DY 01202 473792
OWES SPORTS . . . . Westwood Park, Reynolds Close, off Park Road, Cowes PO31 7NT 01983 293793
OWNTON . . . . Brian Whitehead Sports Centre, Wick Lane, Downton, Salisbury SP5 3NF 01725 512162
AREHAM TOWN . . . . Cams Alders Sports Stadium, Highfield Avenue, Fareham PO15 5NL 01329 231151
AMBLE ASSC . . . . Folland Park, Kings Avenue, Hamble-le-Rice, Southampton SO31 4NF 023 8045 2173
AMWORTHY UNITED . . . . The County Ground, Blandford Close, Hamworthy, Poole BH15 4BF 01202 674974
AYLING UNITED . . . . Hayling Sports Centre, Mengham Park, Hayling Island PO11 9BG 023 9263 7758
ORNDEAN . . . . Five Heads Park, Five Heads Road, Horndean PO8 9NZ 023 9259 1363
YMINGTON TOWN . . . . Sports Ground, Southampton Road, Lymington SO41 0UU 01590 671305
IONEYFIELDS . . . . Moneyfields Sports & Social Club, Moneyfields Avenue, Copnor, Portsmouth PO3 6LA 023 9266 5260
EW MILTON TOWN . . . . Fawcetts Field, Christchurch Road, New Milton BH25 6QB 01425 628191
OOLE TOWN . . . . Tatnam Farm, School Road, off Stanley Green/Palmer Road, Poole BH15 3AT 07771 604289
INGWOOD TOWN . . . . The Clubhouse, Long Lane, Ringwood BH24 3BX 01425 473448
OMSEY TOWN . . . . The By-Pass Ground, South Front, Romsey SO51 4GJ 01794 512003
TFC . . . . VT Sports Ground, Portsmouth Road, Sholing SO19 9PW 023 8040 3829
IMBORNE TOWN . . . . The Cuthbury, Cowgrove Road, Wimborne BH21 2EL 01202 884821

V: Alresford Town (P), Hayling United (P), New Milton Town (formerly Lymington & New Milton) (R – Southern League Division One South),
omsey Town (P)
UT: Gosport Borough (P – Southern League Division One South)

WWW.CHERRYRED.CO.UK

Home \ Away	Alresford Town	Amesbury Town	Andover New Street	Blackfield & Langley	East Cowes Victoria Athletic	Farnborough North End	Fawley	Hayling United	Hythe & Dibden	Laverstock & Ford	Liss Athletic	Locks Heath	Petersfield Town	Romsey Town	Shaftesbury	Stockbridge	United Services Portsmouth	Verwood Town	Warminster Town
Alresford Town		2-1	2-1	2-1	6-1	2-0	1-0	0-0	1-0	1-2	0-0	0-4	2-1	0-1	0-0	2-2	1-0	1-0	0-2
Amesbury Town	1-4		3-1	3-3	1-2	1-2	0-2	1-3	3-1	0-0	0-1	1-2	1-1	1-1	3-4	1-2	1-2	1-3	1-2
Andover New Street	0-1	0-5		3-1	1-2	0-0	1-4	0-4	2-1	3-3	0-1	2-3	0-2	2-3	0-1	0-2	0-2	0-3	1-3
Blackfield & Langley	0-2	2-0	4-2	D	4-1	2-3	1-2	1-5	0-2	5-1	3-3	3-1	1-1	2-5	2-4	2-1	1-8	0-1	1-3
East Cowes Victoria Athletic	0-2	2-2	2-2		I	2-2	1-4	1-3	3-2	2-1	1-3	0-4	1-1	0-2	2-0	1-2	5-3	0-1	0-1
Farnborough North End	1-1	3-2	0-4	0-3	4-0	V	4-3	0-1	1-3	1-1	3-0	1-1	1-0	1-1	2-2	0-5	2-2	1-2	1-0
Fawley	0-0	2-4	3-2	3-2	6-6	2-0	I	4-3	3-0	3-1	3-0	5-3	4-1	0-1	5-2	2-2	3-3	3-1	0-3
Hayling United	0-1	3-1	1-0	10-0	9-0	7-0	1-1	S	2-2	6-1	3-2	3-1	7-1	2-1	1-3	6-1	5-2	4-1	3-2
Hythe & Dibden	1-4	1-1	2-2	3-2	5-2	4-0	1-6	0-5	I	2-0	1-1	0-1	8-5	2-2	0-0	0-1	0-4	3-2	1-2
Laverstock & Ford	1-2	3-2	6-2	1-0	3-0	0-2	0-0	0-3	3-0	O	2-5	2-2	4-1	2-0	0-0	0-2	2-2	1-1	2-0
Liss Athletic	2-3	6-2	1-2	3-2	3-0	1-1	3-1	0-4	2-4	1-3	N	0-2	2-1	0-0	1-1	2-3	1-1	1-1	1-6
Locks Heath	0-1	2-3	1-0	4-2	3-0	1-1	3-0	1-0	4-0	2-0	4-1		4-3	0-2	1-0	1-2	4-1	1-1	2-0
Petersfield Town	0-1	4-4	3-1	4-1	0-1	2-4	3-2	1-4	3-1	2-1	1-4	2-2		2-0	1-3	0-3	0-1	1-3	1-1
Romsey Town	0-2	3-0	3-1	1-2	3-0	0-0	2-0	1-0	2-2	4-1	6-1	1-0	2-0	O	2-0	1-0	3-1	1-2	1-2
Shaftesbury	1-2	0-0	2-0	0-1	5-1	2-0	1-2	1-3	2-0	0-2	1-1	7-0	1-3	1-3	N	1-2	3-3	1-0	1-0
Stockbridge	1-2	1-1	0-0	4-3	2-4	0-0	0-1	1-3	4-0	4-1	3-0	0-5	6-0	2-5	0-0	E	1-1	1-5	1-0
United Services Portsmouth	3-1	2-1	0-1	8-2	1-1	1-2	1-1	0-0	2-2	1-2	1-4	1-4	3-0	0-1	0-2	2-3		0-4	4-0
Verwood Town	0-0	4-3	1-1	5-2	9-0	0-0	2-1	0-1	4-0	1-1	1-1	1-4	4-0	3-1	1-4	2-0	3-4		0-2
Warminster Town	1-1	1-2	7-2	3-3	1-3	1-0	0-1	0-0	3-0	2-2	0-0	4-2	2-3	4-0	0-0	2-6	1-1		

Division One	P	W	D	L	F	A	Pts
Hayling United	36	27	4	5	116	32	85
Alresford Town	36	23	8	5	53	28	77
Romsey Town	36	22	6	8	68	36	72
Locks Heath	36	21	7	8	78	40	70
Fawley	36	18	7	11	57	61	61
Verwood Town	36	17	9	10	73	46	60
Stockbridge	36	17	8	11	64	54	59
Warminster Town	36	16	9	11	63	48	57
Shaftesbury	36	15	9	12	58	47	54
United Services Portsmouth	36	12	10	14	76	68	46
Farnborough North End	36	11	13	12	40	56	46
Laverstock & Ford	36	12	9	15	55	65	45
Liss Athletic -1	36	11	10	15	59	73	42
Hythe & Dibden	36	9	9	18	54	81	36
East Cowes Victoria Athletic	36	10	6	20	49	101	36
Blackfield & Langley	36	9	5	22	66	104	32
Petersfield Town	36	7	6	23	50	98	27
Amesbury Town	36	5	10	21	57	78	25
Andover New Street	36	5	5	26	37	82	20

WESSEX LEAGUE DIVISION ONE CONSTITUTION 2007-08

AFC ALDERMASTON .. Aldermaston Rec Society, Atomic Weapons Establishment, Aldermaston, Reading RG7 4PR 0118 982 454
AFC PORTCHESTER .... Portchester Community School, White Hart Lane, Fareham PO16 9BD .... 023 9236 43#
AMESBURY TOWN .... Amesbury Recreation Ground, Recreation Road, Amesbury SP4 7BB .... 01980 6234#
ANDOVER NEW STREET .... Foxcotte Park, Hatherton Road, Charlton, Andover SP11 0HS .... 01264 35835#
BLACKFIELD & LANGLEY .... Gang Warily Community Centre, Newlands Road, Blackfield SO45 1GA .... 023 8089 36#
EAST COWES VICTORIA ATHLETIC .. Beatrice Avenue, Whippingham, East Cowes PO32 6PA .... 01983 2971#
FARNBOROUGH NORTH END ... Cody S&S Club, Old Iveley Road, Pyestock, Farnborough GU14 0LS .... Non#
FAWLEY .... Waterside Sports & Social, Long Lane, Holbury, Southampton SO45 2PA .... 023 8089 37#
FLEET SPURS .... Kennels Lane, Southwood, Farnborough GU14 0LT .... Non#
HYTHE & DIBDEN .... Ewart Recreation Ground, Jones Lane, Hythe, Southampton SO45 6DG .... 023 8084 52#
LAVERSTOCK & FORD ... The Dell, Laverstock & Ford SC, 23 Church Road, Laverstock, Salisbury SP1 1QX ... 01722 32740#
LISS ATHLETIC .... Newman Collard Ground, Hill Brow Road, Liss GU33 7NS .... 01730 89402#
PETERSFIELD TOWN .... Love Lane, Petersfield GU31 4BW .... 01730 23341#
SHAFTESBURY .... Cockrams, Coppice Street, Shaftesbury SP7 8PD .... 01747 85399#
STOCKBRIDGE .... Recreation Ground, High Street, Stockbridge SO20 6HG .... Non#
TADLEY CALLEVA .... Barlows Park, Silchester Road, Tadley RG26 3PX .... Non#
TOTTON & ELING .... BAT Sports Ground, Southern Gardens, Ringwood Road, Totton SO40 8RW .... 023 8086 21#
UNITED SERVICES PORTSMOUTH .... Victory Stadium, Burnaby Road, Portsmouth PO1 2EJ .... 023 9272 531#
VERWOOD TOWN .... Potterne Park, Potterne Way, Verwood BH21 6RS .... Non#
WARMINSTER TOWN .... Weymouth Street, Warminster BA12 9NS .... 01985 21782#
WHITCHURCH UNITED .... Longmeadow, Winchester Road, Whitchurch RG28 7RB .... 01256 89249#

IN: AFC Aldermaston (P), AFC Portchester (P), Fleet Spurs (P), Tadley Calleva (P), Totton & Eling (formerly BAT Sports) (P), Whitchurch United (P)

OUT: Alresford Town (P), Hayling United (P), Locks Heath (R – Hampshire Premier League), Romsey Town (P)

Note – AFC Newbury and Bishops Waltham Town withdrew during the course of the season Their results are shown herein but are expunged from the league table	AFC Aldermaston	AFC Newbury	AFC Portchester	BAT Sports	Bishops Waltham T.	Clanfield	Colden Common	Fleet Spurs	Fleetlands	Hamble Club	Otterbourne	Overton United	Paulsgrove	QK Southampton	Stoneham	Tadley Calleva	Wellow	Whitchurch United
AFC Aldermaston		n/a	0-1	2-5	6-0	4-2	2-5	0-3	2-6	3-1	0-2	6-4	2-2	5-1	4-1	0-1	0-2	5-4
AFC Newbury	n/a		n/a	n/a	n/a	n/a	n/a	n/a	n/a	n/a	0-1	n/a	n/a	n/a	0-6	n/a	n/a	n/a
AFC Portchester	4-0	n/a		0-0	3-0	2-4	3-1	3-1	1-2	3-2	1-2	0-1	1-2	7-1	1-2	2-4	3-0	1-0
BAT Sports	4-3	n/a	3-2	D	6-1	1-1	2-0	3-1	3-1	8-1	0-3	3-1	2-2	4-0	2-1	0-3	3-3	1-2
Bishops Waltham Town	n/a	0-1	n/a	n/a	I	n/a	0-9	n/a	n/a	1-3	n/a	n/a	n/a	n/a	n/a	n/a	n/a	2-0
Clanfield	3-1	4-2	1-0	3-1	n/a	V	1-1	2-1	0-6	4-1	2-2	2-4	2-3	8-1	1-1	2-3	1-1	2-3
Colden Common	5-2	n/a	1-3	1-1	n/a	3-0	I	2-3	0-3	8-2	2-4	2-3	3-1	8-1	1-1	2-3	1-1	4-2
Fleet Spurs	2-1	n/a	2-3	1-2	n/a	1-1	4-1	S	0-2	8-0	0-1	1-0	2-1	1-1	1-2	4-4	3-1	5-1
Fleetlands	6-2	n/a	4-0	3-1	n/a	2-0	7-1	4-0	I	5-0	1-3	2-0	2-0	8-0	0-0	3-0	0-0	4-0
Hamble Club	1-1	1-3	3-6	1-2	n/a	0-5	1-5	1-2	1-5	O	2-3	0-3	1-6	1-0	1-3	0-4	0-5	2-5
Otterbourne	2-2	1-1	0-2	2-1	n/a	3-0	2-5	3-3	0-1	4-0	N	2-1	2-0	3-0	2-2	1-2	1-1	0-2
Overton United	2-2	n/a	1-1	2-2	n/a	3-3	2-0	2-1	0-6	4-0	2-0		2-4	4-0	0-1	2-2	3-2	2-0
Paulsgrove	2-4	n/a	0-3	1-3	n/a	1-0	0-2	5-2	0-4	1-1	1-1	0-2	T	6-1	6-2	1-2	1-3	3-2
QK Southampton	0-1	n/a	1-3	0-2	n/a	1-3	1-5	1-1	0-7	2-2	0-7	1-4	1-3	W	0-2	1-3	0-1	1-1
Stoneham	2-4	n/a	3-6	2-0	n/a	1-4	1-4	3-2	0-2	3-3	4-1	3-3	2-6	1-1	O	0-1	0-3	1-2
Tadley Calleva	2-1	n/a	2-2	4-0	n/a	3-0	5-0	1-0	2-1	9-0	8-2	3-4	6-0	6-1	9-2		3-0	5-0
Wellow	3-1	n/a	3-0	2-0	n/a	4-3	1-1	4-0	2-3	5-1	5-1	4-3	4-1	2-0	4-1	1-1		3-0
Whitchurch United	0-1	10-0	0-0	2-3	n/a	1-0	6-1	3-0	1-3	2-2	0-1	1-3	1-3	2-0	2-1	1-1	2-3	

Division Two	P	W	D	L	F	A	Pts
Fleetlands	30	25	2	3	101	18	77
Tadley Calleva	30	23	5	2	103	33	74
Wellow	30	19	6	5	77	36	63
AFC Portchester	30	16	4	10	68	45	52
BAT Sports	30	15	6	9	61	49	51
Otterbourne	30	15	6	9	60	50	51
Overton United	30	14	6	10	66	55	48
Paulsgrove	30	14	3	13	69	63	45
Clanfield	30	10	7	13	60	59	37
Colden Common	30	11	3	16	66	76	36
Fleet Spurs	30	10	5	15	55	58	35
Whitchurch United	30	10	4	16	48	61	34
AFC Aldermaston	30	10	4	16	61	78	34
Stoneham	30	9	6	15	51	76	33
Hamble Club	30	1	4	25	29	130	7
QK Southampton	30	0	5	25	18	106	5

AFC Newbury and Bishops Waltham Town – records expunged

THE DIVISION HAS BROKEN AWAY FROM THE WESSEX LEAGUE AND NOW OPERATES AS THE HAMPSHIRE PREMIER LEAGUE

HAMPSHIRE PREMIER LEAGUE CONSTITUTION 2007-08

AFC STONEHAM . . . . Stoneham Park, Stoneham Lane, Eastleigh, Southampton SO50 9HT . . . . None
BISHOPS WALTHAM TOWN . . . Priory Park, Elizabeth Way, Bishops Waltham, Southampton SO32 1SQ 01489 894269
CLANFIELD . . . . Peel Park, Chalton Lane, Clanfield, Waterlooville PO8 0RJ . . . . None
COLDEN COMMON . . . . Colden Common Rec., Main Road, Colden Common, Winchester SO21 1RP 01962 712365
FLEETLANDS . . . . DARA Fleetlands, Fareham Road, Gosport PO13 0AA 01329 239723
HAMBLE CLUB . . . . Shell Mex Ground, Hamble Lane, Hamble-le-Rice, Southampton SO31 4QJ 07881 766085
HEADLEY UNITED . . . . Headley Pavilion, Mill Lane, Headley. . . . . None
LOCKS HEATH . . . . Locksheath Rec, Warsash Road, Titchfield Common, Fareham PO14 4JX 01489 600932
LUDWIG LEISURE BASINGSTOKE . . Basingstoke Cricket Club, Mays Bounty, Fairfields, Basingstoke RG21 3DR . . . . None
LYNDHURST STJS . . . . Wellands Road, Lyndhurst SO43 7AB . . . . None
OTTERBOURNE . . . . Oakwood Park, Oakwood Avenue, Otterbourne SO21 2ED 01962 714681
OVERTON UNITED . . . . Overton Recreation Centre, Bridge Street, Overton RG25 3EW 01256 770561
QK SOUTHAMPTON . . . . Lordshill Recreation Centre, Redbridge Lane, Southampton SO16 9BP. 023 8073 2531
PAULSGROVE . . . . The Grove Club, Marsden Road, off Allaway Avenue, Paulsgrove, Portsmouth PO6 4JB 023 9232 4102
SPORTING BTC . . . . Itchen College Sports & PA Centre, Middle Road, Bitterne, Southampton SO19 7TB 023 8044 8787
TEAM SOLENT . . . . Hardmoor Sports Ground, Stoneham Lane, Eastleigh, Southampton SO50 9HY 023 8061 7574
WELLOW . . . . Hatches Farm, Romsey Road, West Wellow, Romsey SO51 6EA . . . . None
WINCHESTER CASTLE . . . Hants County Council Sports Ground, Petersfield Rd (A31), Chilcomb, Winchester . . . . None

IN: Headley United (P – Aldershot & District League Senior Division), Locks Heath (R – Wessex League Division One), Ludwig Leisure Basingstoke (P – Hampshire League), Lyndhurst STJs (P – Hampshire League), Sporting BTC (P – Hampshire League), Team Solent (P – Southampton League Senior Division One), Winchester Castle (P – Hampshire League)
OUT: AFC Aldermaston (P), AFC Newbury (WS), AFC Portchester (P), Fleet Spurs (P), Tadley Calleva (P), Totton & Eling (formerly BAT Sports) (P), Whitchurch United (P)
Stoneham become AFC Stoneham

LEAGUE CUP

FIRST ROUND
AFC Totton 5 Colden Common 1
Alresford Town 2 AFC Newbury 0
Alton Town 7 Bishops Waltham Town 0
Amesbury Town 6 Wellow 3
Andover New St. 2 Utd Services Portsmouth 1
BAT Sports 0 **East Cowes Victoria Athletic** 3
Bemerton Heath Quins 2 **Wimborne Town** 3 *aet*
Blackfield & Langley 3 Ringwood Town 2
Brading Town 1 **VTFC** 2
Fareham Town 4 Fleetlands 1
Farnborough North End 2 Overton United 1
Fawley 0 **Downton** 3
Hamble ASSC 2 Hamble Club 0
Horndean 3 Clanfield 2
Hythe & Dibden 2 Otterbourne 1 *aet*
Laverstock & Ford 1 **Christchurch** 5
Liss Athletic 6 AFC Portchester 4 *aet*
Locks Heath 8 Paulsgrove 2
Lymington Town 2 Hamworthy United 1
Moneyfields 3 Hayling United 0
Petersfield Town 1 **Fleet Spurs** 5
Poole Town 3 Verwood Town 0
Romsey Town 4 **QK Southampton** 0
(Romsey Town expelled)
Warminster Town 1 **Bournemouth** 3
Whitchurch United 0 **Stoneham** 2

SECOND ROUND
AFC Aldermaston 4 Fleet Spurs 1
AFC Totton 2 **Lymington Town** 3
Alton Town 3 Tadley Calleva 2
Andover New Street 1 **Alresford Town** 5
Bournemouth 11 QK Southampton 0
Brockenhurst 0 **Farnborough North End** 2
Christchurch 4 Hythe & Dibden 1
Cowes Sports 4 Blackfield & Langley 2

East Cowes Victoria Athletic 1 Fareham 3
(Fareham Town expelled)
Gosport Borough 3 Liss Athletic 2
Hamble ASSC 0 **Downton** 2
Moneyfields 4 Horndean 0
Shaftesbury 4 Poole Town 1
Stockbridge 2 Stoneham 2 *aet* (5-4p)
VTFC 2 Locks Heath 0
Wimborne Town 5 Amesbury Town 0

THIRD ROUND
Alton Town 1 **VTFC** 3
Christchurch 3 Alresford Town 2
Downton 1 Stockbridge 0
Farnborough North End 4 AFC Aldermaston 0
Gosport Borough 0 **Bournemouth** 2
Lymington Town 3 East Cowes Vics 0
Moneyfields 1 Shaftesbury 0
Wimborne Town 4 Cowes Sports 0

QUARTER-FINALS
Downton 0 **Lymington Town** 1
Farnborough North End 0 **Bournemouth** 3
Moneyfields 0 **VTFC** 2
Wimborne Town 3 Christchurch 0

SEMI-FINALS
(played over two legs)
Bournemouth 1 Wimborne Town 0,
Wimborne Town 1 **Bournemouth** 0 *aet* (4-5p)
Lymington Town 1 VTFC 1,
VTFC 3 Lymington Town 3
(Lymington Town win on away goals rule)

FINAL
(May 7th at Christchurch)
Lymington Town 1 **Bournemouth** 1 *aet* (6-7p)

Combination One	P	W	D	L	F	A	Pts
Gosport Borough Res.	38	32	2	4	155	39	98
VTFC Res.	38	28	5	5	105	35	89
Bemerton Heath Quins Res.	38	25	4	9	100	52	79
Moneyfields Res.	38	21	7	10	77	54	70
AFC Totton Res.	38	19	6	13	105	70	63
Wimborne Town Res.	38	18	7	13	91	73	61
Lymington Town Res.	38	18	5	15	71	72	59
Cowes Sports Res.	38	18	4	16	84	82	58
Bashley Res.	38	16	6	16	77	72	54
Brockenhurst Res.	38	16	4	18	91	84	52
Locks Heath Res.	38	13	7	18	68	84	46
Hamble ASSC Res.	38	13	7	18	60	80	46
Horndean Res.	38	13	7	18	60	100	46
Poole Town Res.	38	14	3	21	73	98	45
Winchester City Res.	38	12	6	20	57	79	42
Ringwood Town Res.	38	11	7	20	54	105	40
Laverstock & Ford Res.	38	12	3	23	56	89	39
Downton Res.	38	10	6	22	49	80	36
Christchurch Res.	38	11	3	24	72	108	36
Alton Town Res.	38	8	5	25	49	98	29

Combination Two		P	W	D	L	F	A	Pts
Hayling United Res.		32	26	3	3	112	29	81
Fleetlands Res.		32	21	4	7	95	54	67
Alresford Town Res.		32	20	5	7	88	41	65
Paulsgrove Res.		32	18	3	11	80	73	57
Clanfield Res.		32	14	10	8	65	51	52
AFC Portchester Res.		32	16	4	12	69	61	52
AFC Aldermaston Res.		32	16	4	12	73	69	52
Utd Services Portsmouth Res.		32	14	3	15	79	67	45
Fawley Res.		32	13	6	13	80	70	45
Colden Common Res.		32	11	6	15	60	67	39
Romsey Town Res.		32	11	5	16	52	80	38
Liss Athletic Res.		32	10	4	18	60	89	34
Andover New Street Res.		32	8	9	15	57	72	33
Blackfield & Langley Res.	-1	32	10	4	18	57	102	33
Fleet Spurs Res.		32	7	6	19	59	88	27
Overton United Res.		32	7	5	20	44	75	26
Petersfield Town Res.		32	6	7	19	40	82	25

COMBINATION CUP

FINAL
(May 4th at Brockenhurst)
AFC Totton Res. 2 Cowes Sports Res. 0

WEST CHESHIRE LEAGUE

	Aintree Villa	Ashville	Blacon YC	Cam. Ld Res.	Castrol Social	Christleton	Ellesmere Port	Heswall	Maghull	Marine Res.	M. Police	New Brighton	Newton	Poulton Vics	Upton AA	Vauxhall Res.	West Kirby
Aintree Villa		0-0	0-5	5-3	2-0	3-2	1-2	1-0	1-4	1-1	3-2	0-2	0-0	1-3	1-5	2-1	0-8
Ashville	0-2	D	2-2	1-0	2-3	3-0	1-1	0-0	0-1	2-1	1-2	2-1	2-2	0-4	1-1	0-3	0-1
Blacon Youth Club	1-1	1-1	I	1-1	0-1	3-2	1-1	0-2	1-1	1-3	3-1	0-2	2-2	0-1	3-1	1-1	1-4
Cammell Laird Res.	0-3	0-2	3-0	V	3-1	0-3	2-1	1-1	1-2	1-1	2-1	1-1	3-2	1-2	4-4	1-2	0-3
Castrol Social	6-0	4-2	1-0	0-2	I	2-0	1-1	1-1	3-3	0-1	3-3	1-1	0-4	0-1	2-0	2-1	2-3
Christleton	1-1	1-3	5-2	3-1	0-1	S	1-0	1-2	0-0	5-1	4-1	1-1	0-4	2-0	1-1		0-2
Ellesmere Port	1-2	2-0	1-1	1-0	2-2	1-0	I	2-1	1-4	2-1	2-0	2-1	0-1	0-0	2-1	0-0	0-1
Heswall	2-2	1-1	1-1	1-0	3-1	1-3	2-1	O	2-1	2-0	1-2	1-1	3-0	4-1	0-2	4-1	0-2
Maghull	1-0	4-1	0-1	1-0	0-1	0-2	1-1		N	1-0	2-1	1-0	5-1	0-0	5-0	2-0	2-1
Marine Res.	3-5	2-0	2-1	1-1	2-0	2-1	0-2	2-3	1-1		3-1	0-0	5-1	1-0	0-4	2-0	2-3
Merseyside Police	3-2	1-6	2-1	0-2	2-3	2-2	2-2	1-2	0-1	1-1		3-3	1-0	0-4	1-2	3-4	2-7
New Brighton	1-4	3-2	1-1	2-0	4-0	2-2	4-1	1-2	2-2	0-0	2-0		1-1	2-1	3-2	1-0	1-3
Newton	0-0	2-2	1-2	5-2	2-2	1-2	1-1	1-0	1-1	1-2	5-2	0-2		1-2	0-2	1-1	1-2
Poulton Victoria	1-3	2-1	2-1	2-0	1-1	3-4	0-2	0-0	0-3	2-2	4-1	4-0	3-1	O	1-1	0-0	1-4
Upton Athletic Association	3-0	0-2	1-1	2-1	5-3	1-1	3-0	2-1	6-1	3-2	1-3	3-4	2-0	1-2	N	3-2	0-5
Vauxhall Motors Res.	2-2	4-2	0-1	4-1	1-0	2-1	0-3	0-2	0-0	3-0	1-0	1-1	0-3	4-3		E	1-2
West Kirby	4-1	3-3	10-0	4-1	2-0	0-1	3-4	1-0	1-2	3-0	7-2	3-2	3-2	2-0	1-1	5-1	

Division One

	P	W	D	L	F	A	Pts
West Kirby	32	26	2	4	103	33	80
Maghull	32	19	7	6	57	34	64
Poulton Victoria	32	15	8	9	55	41	53
Heswall	32	14	9	9	47	33	51
Upton Athletic Association	32	15	5	12	65	56	50
Ellesmere Port	32	13	10	9	40	37	49
Christleton	32	13	6	13	51	48	45
New Brighton	32	11	11	10	51	50	44
Aintree Villa	32	12	8	12	49	67	44
Marine Res.	32	10	11	11	41	43	41
Castrol Social	32	10	8	14	46	55	38
Ashville	32	8	10	14	45	54	34
Newton	32	8	9	15	43	54	33
Vauxhall Motors Res.	32	9	6	17	42	54	33
Blacon Youth Club	32	7	12	13	41	58	33
Cammell Laird Res.	32	9	6	17	43	61	33
Merseyside Police	32	6	6	20	48	89	24

PYKE CUP

PRELIMINARY ROUND
Vauxhall Motors Res. 0 **Merseyside Police** 4
FIRST ROUND
Ashville 1 Christleton 1 *aet*
Christleton 1 **Ashville** 2 *replay*
Cammell Laird Res. 0 **Poulton Victoria** 4
Ellesmere Port 2 **Merseyside Police** 3
Heswall 3 Aintree Villa 2
Maghull 2 Castrol Social 0
Marine Res. 1 **West Kirby** 2 *aet*
West Kirby 2 Marine Res. 1 *replay*
New Brighton 4 Blacon Youth Club 2
Newton 0 **Upton Athletic Association** 2
QUARTER-FINALS
Ashville 4 New Brighton 1
Poulton Victoria 1 Maghull 0
Upton Athletic Association 1 **Heswall** 3
West Kirby 3 Merseyside Police 0
SEMI-FINALS
Heswall 3 Ashville 1 *(at Cammell Laird)*
West Kirby 0 **Poulton Victoria** 2 *(at Ashville)*
FINAL
(April 6th at Vauxhall Motors)
Heswall 0 **Poulton Victoria** 0 *aet* (7-8p)

WWW.NLNEWSDESK.CO.UK

WEST CHESHIRE LEAGUE DIVISION ONE CONSTITUTION 2007-08

AINTREE VILLA . . . . Aintree Racecourse, Melling Road, Aintree L9 5AS. . . . . None
ASHVILLE. . . . . Villa Park, Cross Lane, Wallasey Village, Wallasey CH45 8RH 0151 638 2127
BLACON YOUTH CLUB . . . . Cairns Crescent Playing Fields, Blacon, Chester CF1 5JF . . . . None
CAMMELL LAIRD RESERVES . . . . . Kirklands, St Peters Road, Rock Ferry, Birkenhead CH42 1PY 0151 645 3121
CASTROL SOCIAL. . . . . Castrol Sports & Social Club, Chester Road, Whitby, Ellesmere Port CH66 2NZ. 0151 357 3712
CHRISTLETON. . . . . Little Heath Road, Christleton, Chester CH3 7AH 01244 332153
ELLESMERE PORT . . . . Whitby Sports & Social Club, Chester Road, Whitby, Ellesmere Port CH66 1QF 0151 200 7080/7050
HESWALL. . . . . Gayton Park, Brimstage Road, Heswall CH60 1XG 0151 342 8172
MAGHULL. . . . . Old Hall Field, Hall Lane, Maghull LE31 7BB 0151 526 7320
MARINE RESERVES. . . . . Rossett Park Arriva Stadium, College Road, Crosby, Liverpool L23 3AS 0151 924 1743/4046
NEW BRIGHTON . . . . Harrison Drive, Wallasey Village, Wallasey CH45 3HL . . . . None
NEWTON . . . . Millcroft, Frankby Road, Greasby CH47 0NB 0151 677 8282
POULTON VICTORIA . . . . Victoria Park, Clayton Lane, Wallasey CH44 5SR. 0151 638 3559
RUNCORN TOWN. . . . . Pavilions Club, Sandy Lane, Weston Point, Runcorn WA7 4EX 01928 590508/07734 558 8795
UPTON ATHLETIC ASSOCIATION . . Cheshire Co. S & S Club, Plas Newton Lane, Chester CH2 1PR. 01244 318167
VAUXHALL MOTORS RESERVES . . . . . . Rivacre Road, Hooton, Ellesmere Port CH66 1NJ. 0151 328 1114/327 2294
WEST KIRBY . . . . Marine Park, Greenbank Road, West Kirby CH48 5HL . . . . None

IN: Runcorn Town (P)
OUT: Merseyside Police (R)

	Ashville Res.	Capenhurst Villa	Chester Nomads	Christleton Res.	FC Pensby	Halton	Helsby	Heswall Res.	MANWEB	Maghull Res.	Mallaby	New Brighton Res.	Poulton Vics Res.	Runcorn Town	West Kirby Res.	Willaston
Ashville Res.		1-6	0-1	2-0	3-1	1-1	0-3	1-1	2-1	0-0	2-1	0-3	1-0	1-1	1-1	1-1
Capenhurst Villa	3-0		1-0	1-1	1-1	4-1	1-1	0-2	1-0	1-2	3-0	1-0	4-1	3-2	3-0	0-1
Chester Nomads	3-2	3-2	D	2-0	2-1	1-1	2-4	2-0	4-0	0-0	3-2	3-4	0-6	3-4	4-5	6-2
Christleton Res.	2-2	2-2	0-1	I	3-1	2-1	0-0	2-4	1-0	1-2	2-3	2-1	2-2	1-1	2-1	1-1
FC Pensby	3-1	1-2	4-2	0-1	V	3-1	0-1	1-1	4-2	1-3	2-0	0-1	0-6	1-5	1-1	4-1
Halton	3-0	5-1	4-2	5-3	3-2	I	1-1	1-2	2-4	3-2	2-1	1-2	3-1	0-4	4-4	
Helsby	1-2	1-3	1-5	2-3	4-1	2-1	S	0-2	3-3	0-0	2-3	1-4	2-1	2-3	1-1	3-2
Heswall Res.	1-2	3-0	3-2	3-1	3-1	2-0	1-0	I	6-2	0-0	0-1	0-2	2-0	0-0	3-2	0-0
MANWEB	4-3	1-1	3-2	1-3	5-3	1-3	0-7	2-5	O	1-2	3-3	0-2		0-8	1-2	2-3
Maghull Res.	1-1	2-1	1-1	3-0	2-2	1-2	1-6	0-2	0-1	N	0-1	5-0	0-3	0-2	0-0	6-1
Mallaby	0-1	0-0	1-0	1-1	1-3	1-1	2-2	0-0	4-0	3-0		1-0	0-0	0-2	1-4	1-1
New Brighton Res.	2-3	2-2	5-2	4-3	0-0	1-5	3-1	1-0	2-6	2-0	2-1	T	2-2	1-1	1-3	3-2
Poulton Victoria Res.	1-0	3-1	0-2	5-0	3-1	2-1	3-1	2-2	2-1	4-2	0-0	1-2	W	1-5	3-2	4-1
Runcorn Town	4-0	4-2	7-0	6-1	4-2	0-0	3-2	1-0	3-2	3-1	1-2	6-1	3-0	O	4-0	3-1
West Kirby Res.	1-1	3-3	2-1	4-3	5-1	2-1	3-0	1-1	4-1	1-1	3-2	3-0	4-1	3-2		0-2
Willaston	2-6	4-3	4-2	1-0	1-2	5-0	1-1	3-2	2-0	1-3	0-1	1-1	2-3	0-3	1-6	

WWW.CHERRYRED.CO.UK

Division Two	P	W	D	L	F	A	Pts
Runcorn Town	30	21	5	4	92	33	68
West Kirby Res.	30	16	8	6	71	46	56
Heswall Res.	30	15	9	6	54	26	54
Poulton Victoria Res.	30	16	5	9	63	44	53
New Brighton Res.	30	13	6	11	54	60	45
Capenhurst Villa	30	12	8	10	56	47	44
Mallaby	30	11	9	10	37	38	42
Halton	30	10	10	10	59	59	40
Ashville Res.	30	10	9	11	40	52	39
Maghull Res.	30	9	9	12	44	46	36
Chester Nomads	30	11	3	16	59	71	36
Helsby	30	9	8	13	51	56	35
Willaston	30	9	7	14	51	71	34
Christleton Res.	30	8	8	14	43	62	32
FC Pensby	30	8	5	17	48	68	29
MANWEB	30	5	5	20	48	91	20

WEST CHESHIRE BOWL

FIRST ROUND
Capenhurst Villa 2 **Christleton Res.** 3
Chester Nomads 3 Heswall Res. 0
Halton 6 FC Pensby 1
Maghull Res. 2 Helsby 1
(at Helsby)
New Brighton Res. 2 Runcorn Town 1
Poulton Victoria Res. 1 Mallaby 0
West Kirby Res. 1 **MANWEB** 2
Willaston 1 **Ashville Res.** 2

QUARTER-FINALS
Ashville Res. 4 **New Brighton Res.** 3
(at New Brighton) (Ashville Res. expelled)
Chester Nomads 7 MANWEB 2
Halton 2 Poulton Victoria Res. 1
Maghull Res. 3 Christleton Res. 1

SEMI-FINALS
Halton 2 Chester Nomads 1
(at Ashville)
Maghull Res. 3 New Brighton Res. 2
(at Poulton Victoria)

FINAL
(May 3rd at MANWEB)
Maghull Res. 2 **Halton** 2 *aet* (3-4p)

BILL WEIGHT MEMORIAL CUP
(Divisional champions and Pyke Cup holders)

SEMI-FINALS
New Brighton 1 **Poulton Victoria** 2
West Kirby 2 Upton Athletic Association 1

FINAL
(September 19th at Cammell Laird)
West Kirby 1 Poulton Victoria 0

WEST CHESHIRE LEAGUE DIVISION TWO CONSTITUTION 2007-08
AFC BEBINGTON ATHLETIC .... Unilever Sports Ground, Bromborough CH62 3PU ...... None
ASHVILLE RESERVES .... Villa Park, Cross Lane, Wallasey Village, Wallasey CH45 8RH 0151 638 2127
CAPENHURST VILLA .... Capenhurst Sports Ground, Capenhurst Lane, Capenhurst CH1 6ER ...... None
CHESTER NOMADS .... Boughton Hall Cricket Club, Boughton, Chester CH3 5EL 01244 326072
CHRISTLETON RESERVES .... Little Heath Road, Christleton, Chester CH3 7AH 01244 332153
GRANGE ATHLETIC .... West Cheshire College, Sutton Way, Ellesmere Port CH65 7BF ...... None
HALTON .... Picow Farm Road, Runcorn WA7 4TS ...... None
HELSBY .... Helsby Sports & Social Club, Chester Road, Helsby WA6 0DL 01928 722267
HESWALL RESERVES .... Gayton Park, Brimstage Road, Heswall CH60 1XG 0151 342 8172
MAGHULL RESERVES .... Old Hall Field, Hall Lane, Maghull LE31 7BB 0151 526 7320
MALLABY .... Unilever Sports Ground, Bromborough CH62 3PU ...... None
MERSEYSIDE POLICE .... Police Club, Fairfield, Prescot Road, Liverpool L7 0JD. 0151 228 2352
NEW BRIGHTON RESERVES .... Harrison Drive, Wallasey Village, Wallasey CH45 3HL ...... None
POULTON VICTORIA RESERVES .... Victoria Park, Clayton Lane, Wallasey CH44 5SR. 0151 638 3555
WEST KIRBY RESERVES .... Marine Park, Greenbank Road, West Kirby CH48 5HL. ...... None
WILLASTON .... Johnston Recreation Ground, Neston Road, Willaston CH64 2TL. ...... None
IN: *AFC Bebington Athletic (P), Grange Athletic (P), Merseyside Police (R)*
OUT: *FC Pensby (R), MANWEB (W), Runcorn Town (P)*

Note – MANWEB Reserves withdrew during the course of the season. Their results are shown herein but are expunged from the league table

	AFC Bebington Athletic	Blacon Youth Club Res.	Bronze Social	Capenhurst Villa Res.	Ellesmere Port Res.	FOCUS	Grange Athletic	MANWEB Res.	Manor Athletic	Mersey Royal	Merseyside Police Res.	Runcorn Town Res.	Shaftesbury	St Werburghs	Upton AA Res.	Willaston Res.
AFC Bebington Athletic		2-1	0-0	1-0	2-1	4-1	3-1	2-0	0-4	1-0	3-1	3-1	2-0	2-1	4-0	1-1
Blacon Youth Club Res.	0-3	D	2-3	2-1	3-0	1-6	1-3	4-0	2-0	4-4	3-2	0-4	1-4	2-2	1-3	0-3
Bronze Social	2-4	2-1	I	6-1	2-2	3-1	0-1	n/a	1-3	2-1	2-3	3-0	5-1	2-1	2-1	1-0
Capenhurst Villa Res.	4-4	0-2	0-2	V	0-0	0-0	3-1	n/a	2-2	4-0	1-4	3-2	1-0	4-1	2-3	1-1
Ellesmere Port Res.	0-2	0-1	3-5	4-2	I	3-1	0-4	n/a	0-3	1-2	0-0	4-2	1-1	3-1	2-3	1-1
FOCUS	2-3	3-3	1-4	2-1	3-1	S	1-1	n/a	4-2	5-1	3-2	3-1	6-2	0-2	0-1	
Grange Athletic	0-0	3-2	4-2	2-1	2-1	1-3	I	n/a	1-3	1-3	8-0	1-1	4-1	10-0	1-1	1-3
MANWEB Res.	n/a	n/a	n/a	n/a	0-3	3-1	n/a	O	n/a	1-1	1-4	n/a	1-2	n/a	n/a	n/a
Manor Athletic	1-0	1-1	2-3	1-2	2-1	2-1	1-1	6-1	N	1-1	3-1	0-1	4-3	3-0	1-2	5-3
Mersey Royal	0-2	1-1	5-4	3-0	2-1	1-0	1-3	n/a	1-1		1-0	1-5	1-0	5-2	1-5	1-0
Merseyside Police Res.	1-4	7-1	3-0	3-1	4-1	2-2	0-2	2-2	1-2	0-2	T	3-1	3-3	7-3	4-2	1-2
Runcorn Town Res.	2-1	0-0	1-0	1-3	1-2	1-0	0-4	n/a	0-0	4-1	1-2	H	2-0	7-1	5-0	2-2
Shaftesbury	3-2	3-3	6-4	2-1	2-3	1-2	1-3	n/a	4-5	1-2	2-0	2-2	R	3-4	2-1	1-1
St Werburghs	1-11	3-3	0-8	0-3	1-7	2-6	1-6	5-4	0-1	2-4	1-2	3-3	3-2	E	0-0	2-1
Upton AA Res.	0-3	2-2	3-1	4-4	1-2	2-2	0-2	4-0	1-1	5-1	1-5	1-3	3-0	12-0	E	2-0
Willaston Res.	1-1	2-1	2-1	2-2	3-2	0-1	4-2	n/a	0-2	3-3	1-0	1-3	3-1	4-6	4-1	

Division Three	P	W	D	L	F	A	Pts
AFC Bebington Athletic	28	19	5	4	68	29	62
Grange Athletic	28	17	4	7	73	36	55
Manor Athletic	28	15	5	8	54	38	50
Bronze Social	28	15	2	11	70	52	47
Mersey Royal	28	14	4	10	50	56	46
Runcorn Town Res.	28	12	6	10	57	44	42
FOCUS	28	12	5	11	60	49	41
Willaston Res.	28	11	8	9	49	45	41
Merseyside Police Res.	28	12	3	13	60	58	39
Upton Athletic A. Res.	28	11	5	12	60	55	38
Ellesmere Port Res.	28	9	5	14	49	55	32
Capenhurst Villa Res.	28	8	7	13	47	55	31
Blacon Youth Club Res.	28	7	8	13	45	67	29
Shaftesbury	28	6	5	17	50	69	23
St Werburghs	28	4	4	20	43	127	16

MANWEB Res. – record expunged

WEST CHESHIRE SHIELD

FIRST ROUND
Bronze Social 2 Blacon Youth Club Res. 1
Capenhurst Villa Res. 0 **AFC Bebington Athletic** 4
Grange Athletic 2 Merseyside Police Res. 1 *aet*
Manor Athletic 0 **FOCUS** 2
Shaftesbury 8 MANWEB Res. 1
St Werburghs 1 **Mersey Royal** 5
Upton AA Res. 5 Runcorn Town Res. 1
Willaston 2 **Ellesmere Port Res.** 3 *aet*

QUARTER-FINALS
AFC Bebington Athletic 4 Ellesmere Port Res. 1
Grange Athletic 2 Bronze Social 2 *aet*
Bronze Social 4 Grange Athletic 1 *replay*
Mersey Royal 1 **FOCUS** 2
Shaftesbury 4 Upton AA Res. 3 *aet*

SEMI-FINALS
Bronze Social 6 AFC Bebington Athletic 3 *(at Ashville)*
Shaftesbury 2 FOCUS 0 *(at Poulton Victoria)*

FINAL
(May 1st at Ashville)
Shaftesbury 0 **Bronze Social** 4

WWW.NLNEWSDESK.CO.UK

WEST CHESHIRE LEAGUE DIVISION THREE CONSTITUTION 2007-08
BLACON YOUTH CLUB RESERVES . . . Cairns Crescent Playing Fields, Blacon, Chester CF1 5JF . . . . None
BRONZE SOCIAL. Unilever Sports Ground, Bromborough CH62 3PU. . . . . None
CAPENHURST VILLA RESERVES . . . . Capenhurst Lane, Capenhurst CH1 6ER . . . . None
ELLESMERE PORT RESERVES . . . . Whitby S&S, Chester Road, Whitby, Ellesmere Port CH66 1QF 0151 200 7080/7050
FC PENSBY . . . . Ridgewood Park, Fishers Lane, Pensby CH61 5YQ. . . . . None
FOCUS. . . . . Riversdale Police Ground, Aigburth, Liverpool L19 3QN. 0151 724 5214
HALE. . . . . Hale Park, The High Street, Hale Village, Liverpool L24 4AF . . . . None
MANOR ATHLETIC . . . . Octel Sports & Social Club, 28 Bridle Road, Bromborough CH62 6AR 0151 3566159
MERSEY ROYAL . . . . Unilever Sports Ground, Bromborough CH62 3PU. . . . . None
MERSEYSIDE POLICE RESERVES . . . . . Police Club, Fairfield, Prescot Road, Liverpool L7 0JD. 0151 228 2352
MOSSLEY HILL ATHLETIC . . . . . . Mossley Hill Athletic Club, Mossley Hill Road, Liverpool L18 8DX. 0151 724 4377
RICHMOND RAITH ROVERS . . . . Ridgewood Park, Fishers Lane, Pensby CH61 5YP . . . . None
RUNCORN TOWN RESERVES . . . . . Pavilions Club, Sandy Lane, Weston Point, Runcorn WA7 4EX 01928 590508/07734 558 8795
SHAFTESBURY . . . . Memorial Ground, Borough Road, Birkenhead CH42 8NU 0151 608 7165
ST WERBURGHS . . . . Kings School, Wrexham Road (A483), Chester CH4 7QL . . . . None
UPTON A.A. RESERVES. . . . . Cheshire County S & S Club, Plas Newton Lane, Chester CH2 1PR. 01244 318167
IN: FC Pensby (R), Hale (P – West Cheshire League Youth Division), Mossley Hill Athletic (S – Liverpool County Premier League), Richmond Raith Rovers (P – West Cheshire League Youth Division)
OUT: AFC Bebington Athletic (P), Grange Athletic (P), MANWEB Res. (WS), Willaston Reserves (F)

WEST LANCS LEAGUE

	Barnoldswick Town	Blackpool Wren Rov.	Blackrod Town	Burnley United	Charnock Richard	Coppull United	Dalton United	Eagley	Euxton Villa	Fleetwood Hesketh	Freckleton	Fulwood Amateurs	Haslingden St Mary's	Kirkham & Wesham	Turton	Wyre Villa
Barnoldswick Town	P	1-6	3-3	3-2	3-5	2-1	2-1	2-1	2-1	2-3	0-1	4-1	0-4	0-5	2-2	4-1
Blackpool Wren Rovers	1-1	R	3-0	4-1	2-2	3-2	4-2	1-1	1-3	1-0	1-1	2-1	3-3	0-1	1-0	3-0
Blackrod Town	0-2	1-4	E	3-3	0-3	0-5	0-1	1-2	1-4	2-0	2-3	0-8	2-2	1-1	1-0	0-2
Burnley United	4-3	0-1	3-1	M	3-4	2-1	3-4	1-3	2-1	1-1	0-2	0-0	2-6	0-3	1-1	2-3
Charnock Richard	3-2	1-3	0-0	0-2	I	3-0	4-2	1-4	2-1	3-0	2-1	3-4	1-2	1-1	3-1	2-0
Coppull United	6-6	1-1	1-0	2-2	0-1	E	2-2	0-1	2-2	3-0	0-2	1-2	2-1	1-1	0-1	1-1
Dalton United	1-3	6-1	3-0	2-2	1-5	2-1	R	1-3	3-1	3-3	2-0	5-1	2-5	0-2	1-2	2-2
Eagley	1-3	4-3	6-0	3-2	1-0	1-2	2-2		2-2	3-3	0-4	3-4	1-3	1-4	0-2	2-3
Euxton Villa	2-1	0-2	2-2	1-3	2-1	1-1	5-1	1-5	D	3-0	1-1	1-1	2-0	0-1	3-2	2-2
Fleetwood Hesketh	3-2	0-2	3-3	2-2	3-2	1-2	3-2	2-2	0-1	I	0-1	1-4	6-3	1-5	0-2	5-3
Freckleton	3-2	3-3	4-1	1-1	0-0	1-0	0-0	1-1	1-3	0-1	V	2-2	2-1	0-1	1-1	4-0
Fulwood Amateurs	4-1	1-3	2-1	3-1	1-1	3-2	2-4	4-1	3-0	1-2	2-2	I	0-1	0-0	4-2	3-2
Haslingden St Mary's	0-0	2-2	4-1	1-1	0-0	3-0	5-0	3-2	3-0	5-1	1-1	3-2	S	1-1	3-1	3-1
Kirkham & Wesham	1-0	3-1	5-0	2-0	0-1	2-1	1-0	3-2	2-0	0-1	5-3	1-1	1-1	I	3-1	1-0
Turton	0-0	0-0	6-0	1-1	0-1	3-2	2-2	2-1	1-1	1-1	0-1	3-1	4-0	0-1	O	0-0
Wyre Villa	0-1	2-2	3-0	2-0	0-0	0-0	0-1	1-4	1-0	1-3	0-2	0-2	0-1	1-3	1-3	N

Premier Division		P	W	D	L	F	A	Pts
Kirkham & Wesham		30	22	6	2	62	19	72
Haslingden St Mary's		30	16	9	5	70	41	57
Freckleton		30	16	9	5	49	27	57
Blackpool Wren Rovers		30	15	10	5	64	43	55
Charnock Richard		30	15	7	8	55	39	52
Fulwood Amateurs		30	14	6	10	69	56	48
Turton		30	11	9	10	46	36	42
Eagley		30	12	5	13	62	60	41
Euxton Villa		30	9	9	12	46	50	36
Dalton United		30	10	6	14	58	67	36
Barnoldswick Town	-3	30	11	6	13	57	66	36
Fleetwood Hesketh		30	8	7	15	47	70	31
Burnley United		30	6	10	14	47	64	28
Coppull United		30	6	9	15	42	50	27
Wyre Villa		30	6	7	17	32	56	25
Blackrod Town		30	2	7	21	26	88	13

RICHARDSON CUP

FIRST ROUND
Barnoldswick Town 5 Haslingden St Mary's 3
Blackpool Wren Rovers 0 **Freckleton** 3
Burnley United 1 Dalton United 0
Charnock Richard 1 Blackrod Town 0
Eagley 3 Kirkham & Wesham 1
Fulwood Amateurs 0 **Euxton Villa** 1
Turton 6 Fleetwood Hesketh 2
Wyre Villa 2 Coppull United 1
QUARTER-FINALS
Euxton Villa 2 Barnoldswick Town 0
Freckleton 2 **Eagley** 3
Turton 1 **Charnock Richard** 4 *(at Charnock Richard)*
Wyre Villa 1 **Burnley United** 2
SEMI-FINALS
Burnley United 0 **Euxton Villa** 2 *(at Stonelough)*
Charnock Richard 3 Eagley 0 *(at Croston Sports)*
FINAL
(April 13th at LCFA, Leyland)
Euxton Villa 7 Charnock Richard 3

	BAE Barrow Sports Club	Crooklands Casuals	Crosshills	Croston Sports	Furness Rovers	Garstang	Hesketh Bank	Millom	Norcross & Warbreck	Poulton Town	Stoneclough	Tempest United	Trimpell	Whinney Hill
BAE Barrow Sports Club		2-2	0-2	2-2	1-2	2-1	2-1	2-1	1-1	1-2	2-3	4-3	1-2	1-0
Crooklands Casuals	1-1	D	0-2	1-1	1-0	1-3	0-6	2-1	1-3	1-10	1-2	1-2	1-7	0-3
Crosshills	4-2	3-4	I	2-0	2-4	0-5	3-2	5-4	2-0	1-2	3-4	0-1	2-1	4-0
Croston Sports	3-0	1-1	1-3	V	4-1	0-2	2-0	3-2	1-2	2-2	0-0	3-0	1-0	1-1
Furness Rovers	0-1	2-1	1-3	0-0	I	0-0	2-2	1-0	1-3	1-0	1-2	0-4	0-0	2-0
Garstang	1-3	2-1	6-4	3-0	4-0	S	1-0	3-3	3-0	1-1	0-3	2-3	0-0	1-0
Hesketh Bank	6-4	2-0	2-2	2-2	1-1	0-2	I	3-1	2-2	1-6	0-2	2-1	1-2	0-2
Millom	6-0	1-0	2-1	4-0	0-1	1-1	4-1	O	2-3	4-4	5-1	3-1	2-4	0-2
Norcross & Warbreck	3-1	0-4	4-0	2-1	0-0	1-2	2-2	1-1	N	1-9	1-1	0-3	1-0	2-4
Poulton Town	3-1	3-0	2-0	1-0	5-1	1-3	5-4	5-3	1-1		2-2	3-3	2-2	2-1
Stoneclough	3-2	2-1	2-2	2-0	2-4	0-2	3-1	2-1	3-3	2-3	O	2-1	2-1	1-4
Tempest United	1-1	0-1	6-1	1-1	3-2	1-1	1-3	0-1	2-2	1-3	2-3	N	3-2	0-4
Trimpell	3-1	3-1	4-3	4-1	7-0	0-2	4-1	2-1	2-1	3-1	0-0	1-1	E	3-1
Whinney Hill	0-3	5-1	0-1	0-4	0-2	1-4	4-1	0-2	0-5	1-3	1-1	1-3	3-0	

Division One		P	W	D	L	F	A	Pts
Poulton Town		26	17	7	2	84	41	58
Garstang		26	17	6	3	56	25	57
Trimpell		26	15	4	7	61	33	49
Stoneclough		26	13	7	6	48	43	46
Norcross & Warbreck		26	9	9	8	42	48	36
Crosshills	-3	26	12	2	12	55	59	35
Tempest United		26	9	6	11	45	48	33
Croston Sports		26	8	8	10	34	36	32
Whinney Hill		26	9	3	14	38	45	30
Furness Rovers		26	7	7	12	27	48	28
BAE Barrow Spts Club		26	7	5	14	39	57	26
Millom	-6	26	9	4	13	55	48	25
Hesketh Bank		26	6	6	14	46	60	24
Crooklands Casuals		26	5	4	17	28	67	19

PRESIDENT'S CUP

FIRST ROUND
Crosshills 2 BAE Barrow Sports Club 0
Hesketh Bank 2 **Croston Sports** 3
Poulton Town 6 Crooklands Casuals 3
Stoneclough 3 Trimpell 1
Tempest United 2 **Norcross & Warbreck** 3
Whinney Hill 4 Furness Rovers 0

QUARTER-FINALS
Crosshills 3 **Norcross & Warbreck** 3 *aet* (3-5p)
Croston Sports 1 **Poulton Town** 2 *aet*
Garstang 1 Stoneclough 0 *aet*
Whinney Hill 1 Millom 0 *aet*

SEMI-FINALS
Norcross & Warbreck 0 **Whinney Hill** 2
(at Fulwood Amateurs)
Poulton Town 3 Garstang 0 *(at Kirkham & Wesham)*

FINAL
(April 11th at Lancaster City)
Poulton Town 0 Whinney Hill 0 *aet* (3-2p)

WWW.NLNEWSDESK.CO.UK

WEST LANCASHIRE LEAGUE DIVISION ONE CONSTITUTION 2007-08

BAE BARROW SPORTS CLUB .... Vickers Sports Club, Hawcoat Lane, Barrow-in-Furness LA14 4HF 01229 825296
BLACKROD TOWN .... Blackrod Community Centre, Vicarage Road, Blackrod, Bolton BL6 5DD 01204 692614
CROSSHILLS .... Holme Lane, Crosshills, Keighley BD20 7RL .... None
CROSTON SPORTS .... Old Emmanuel School, Westhead Road, Croston, Leyland PR26 9RR 01772 600261
FURNESS ROVERS .... Wilkie Road, Barrow-in-Furness LA14 5UQ .... None
HESKETH BANK .... Hesketh Sports Field, Station Road, Hesketh Bank PR4 6SR .... None
LOSTOCK ST GERARDS .... Wateringpool Lane, Lostock Hall PR5 5UA .... None
MILLOM .... Millom RL Club, Devonshire Road, Millom LA18 4PG 01229 772030
NORCROSS & WARBRECK .... Anchorsholme Lane, Thornton Cleveleys, near Blackpool FY5 .... 01253 859836
STONECLOUGH .... Brook Street, opposite Europa Business Park, Stoneclough, Kearsley, Bolton....................... None
TEMPEST UNITED .... Tempest Road, Chew Moor Village, Lostock, near Bolton BL6 4EL 01942 811938
TRIMPELL .... Trimpell Sports & Social Club, Out Moss Lane, Morecambe LA4 4UP 01524 412984
VICKERSTOWN .... Park Vale, Mill Lane, Walney, Barrow-in-Furness LA14 3ND .... None
WHINNEY HILL .... Clayton-le-Moors, Accrington. .... None

IN: Blackrod Town (R), Lostock St Gerards (P), Vickerstown (P)
OUT: Crooklands Casuals (R), Garstang (P), Poulton Town (P)

	Askam United	BAE Canberra	Bolton County	Burnley Belvedere	Furness Cavaliers	Glaxo Ulverston Rangers	Lancs Constabulary	Lostock St Gerards	Mill Hill St Peters	Milnthorpe Corinthians	Springfield BAC/EE	Thornton Cleveleys	Todmorden Borough	Vickerstown
Askam United		2-0	1-2	1-3	2-2	1-1	3-0	2-2	2-2	2-3	1-1	0-2	1-0	0-0
BAE Canberra	1-2	D	2-1	1-2	2-3	4-3	1-1	1-3	1-4	2-1	3-2	0-2	0-1	1-1
Bolton County	3-2	4-0	I	0-1	1-3	3-2	2-1	1-3	1-1	3-2	0-2	3-2	1-1	3-3
Burnley Belvedere	2-6	0-0	1-2	V	4-0	3-2	0-1	1-2	0-2	2-0	0-2	0-1	2-1	1-2
Furness Cavaliers	0-2	3-1	2-0	4-2	I	2-2	4-0	2-2	1-1	1-3	1-3	4-2	1-2	2-5
Glaxo Ulverston Rgrs	1-4	0-3	0-1	3-1	1-2	S	0-0	1-1	4-0	1-1	4-1	0-4	3-2	0-3
Lancs Constabulary	1-3	3-3	0-2	2-3	2-2	0-4	I	1-0	3-2	1-3	2-0	0-1	2-1	2-4
Lostock St Gerards	5-1	4-1	4-0	1-0	6-3	2-1	5-1	O	1-1	2-1	2-1	1-1	1-4	2-1
Mill Hill St Peters	5-1	0-2	3-1	0-0	3-4	2-0	1-0	0-1	N	0-2	5-0	0-0	2-1	2-4
Milnthorpe Corinthians	3-1	5-1	4-0	1-2	3-1	3-4	4-1	0-4	2-3		3-6	1-2	3-2	0-0
Springfield BAC/EE	5-0	2-1	3-2	1-1	3-2	3-1	3-3	1-2	2-3	1-0	T	1-1	2-1	0-4
Thornton Cleveleys	2-0	4-1	3-0	2-0	5-4	3-3	4-0	4-1	1-1	1-1	5-0	W	2-0	3-3
Todmorden Borough	3-1	0-2	0-2	1-2	3-0	0-1	3-0	0-1	1-1	2-3	1-1	0-3	O	1-4
Vickerstown	3-1	6-2	5-3	4-1	2-2	2-2	6-0	2-0	2-2	5-0	1-1	6-1	2-0	

CHALLENGE CUP

FIRST ROUND

Askam 4 Thornton Cleveleys 1

Lancashire Constabulary 2 **Burnley Belvedere** 2 *aet* (4-5p)

Mill Hill SP 1 Glaxo Ulverston 0

Milnthorpe Cor. 4 Bolton Co. 2

Springfield BAC/EE 1 **Vickerstown** 1 *aet* (4-5p)

Todmorden 1 **Lostock St G.** 3

QUARTER-FINALS

Askam United 3 Vickerstown 2

BAE Canberra 5 Furness Cav. 4

Burnley Belvedere 3 Mill Hill 0

Lostock St G. 5 Milnthorpe 2

SEMI-FINALS

Askam United 0 **BAE Canberra** 2
(at Poulton Town)

Lostock St Gerards 2 Burnley Belvedere 1 *(at Mill Hill St Peters)*

FINAL *(April 11th at Squires Gate)*

BAE Canberra 5 Lostock St G. 0

Division Two

	P	W	D	L	F	A	Pts
Vickerstown	26	16	9	1	80	32	57
Lostock St Gerards	26	17	5	4	58	32	56
Thornton Cleveleys	26	16	7	3	61	30	55
Mill Hill St Peters	26	10	9	7	46	37	39
Springfield BAC/EE	26	11	6	9	47	49	39
Milnthorpe Corinthians	26	11	3	12	52	50	36
Bolton County	26	11	3	12	41	51	36
Furness Cavaliers	26	9	6	11	55	62	33
Burnley Belvedere	26	10	3	13	34	42	33
Askam United	26	8	6	12	42	52	30
Glaxo Ulverston Rangers	26	7	7	12	44	51	28
BAE Canberra	26	7	4	15	36	59	25
Todmorden Borough	26	6	3	17	31	43	21
Lancashire Constabulary	26	5	5	16	27	64	20

Reserve Division One

		P	W	D	L	F	A	Pts
Poulton Town Res.		28	22	3	3	90	28	69
Euxton Villa Res.	-3	28	17	4	7	73	45	52
Kirkham & Wesham Res.		28	16	4	8	70	45	52
Fulwood Amateurs Res.		28	14	7	7	72	58	49
Eagley Res.		28	15	2	11	67	58	47
Charnock Richard Res.		28	12	5	11	61	42	41
Blackpool Wren Rovers Res.		28	11	6	11	60	55	39
Freckleton Res.		28	11	4	13	50	53	37
Norcross & Warbreck Res.		28	10	7	11	56	67	37
Burnley United Res.		28	10	4	14	42	61	34
Tempest United Res.		28	9	4	15	68	78	31
Fleetwood Hesketh Res.		28	9	4	15	48	75	31
Turton Res.		28	8	5	15	48	65	29
Thornton Cleveleys Res.		28	7	6	15	30	50	27
Blackrod Town Res.	-6	28	5	3	20	47	103	12

Reserve Division Two

		P	W	D	L	F	A	Pts
Springfield BAC EE Res.		28	20	5	3	97	32	65
Barnoldswick Town Res.		28	19	4	5	73	34	61
Garstang Res.		28	18	4	6	83	27	58
Haslingden St Mary's Res.		28	13	9	6	71	46	48
Whinney Hill Res.		28	14	4	10	79	53	46
Stoneclough Res.		28	10	11	7	56	58	41
Milnthorpe Corinthians Res.		28	11	7	10	58	56	40
Hesketh Bank Res.	-6	28	11	7	10	60	64	34
Todmorden Borough Res.		28	9	6	13	48	63	33
Crosshills Res.	-3	28	9	5	14	56	106	29
Coppull United Res.	-6	28	8	6	14	49	68	24
Burnley Belvedere Res.	-3	28	6	6	16	55	79	21
Mill Hill St Peters Res.	-6	28	7	4	17	54	90	19
Wyre Villa Res.	-6	28	7	3	18	50	79	18
Bolton County Res.	-3	28	6	3	19	50	79	18

HOUSTON CUP

FINAL

(April 26th at Blackpool Wren Rovers)

Fulwood Amateurs Res. 4 Poulton Town Res. 1

WEST LANCASHIRE LEAGUE DIVISION TWO CONSTITUTION 2007-08

ASKAM UNITED . . . . Duddon Road, James Street, Askam-in-Furness LA16 7AH 01229 46457

BAC/EE SPRINGFIELD . . . . BAC Sports Ground, South Meadow Lane, Preston PR1 8JP. 01772 46435

BOLTON COUNTY . . . . Radcliffe Road, Darcy Lever, Bolton BL3 1RU. . . . . None

BURNLEY BELVEDERE. . . . . Belvedere & Caldervale SC, Holden Road, Burnley BL10 2LE 01282 43317

CROOKLANDS CASUALS. . . . . Longlands Park, Greystone Lane, Dalton-in-Furness LA15 8PX 01229 46501

FURNESS CAVALIERS . . . . Rampside Road, Barrow-in-Furness LA13 0HN . . . . Non

GSK ULVERSTON RANGERS . . . . off North Lonsdale Road, Ulverston LA12 9DZ 01229 58226

LANCASHIRE CONSTABULARY. . . . . Police HQ, Saunders Lane, Hutton, Preston PR4 5SG. 01772 41059

LYTHAM TOWN. . . . . Lytham Cricket Club, Church Road, Lytham St Annes 01253 73413

MILL HILL ST PETERS. . . . . . Opposite Mill Hill Hotel, Bridge Street, off Buncer Lane, Blackburn BB2 2QY 01254 67555

MILNTHORPE CORINTHIANS . . . . Strands Lane, Milnthorpe LA7 7AE 01539 56213

THORNTON CLEVELEYS . . . . Bourne Road, Cleveleys, Thornton Cleveleys FY5 4AB 01253 86966

TODMORDEN BOROUGH . . . . Bellholme, Walsden Road (off A6033), Todmorden . . . . Non

IN: Crooklands Casuals (R), Lytham Town (P – Preston & District League Division Three)

OUT: BAE Canberra (W), Lostock St Gerards (P), Vickerstown (P)

Springfield BAC/EE become BAC/EE Springfield

WEST MIDLANDS (REGIONAL) LEAGUE

Note – Great Wyrley withdrew during the course of the season Their results are shown herein but are expunged from the league table

	Bewdley Town	Bridgnorth Town	Brierley & Hagley	Bromyard Town	Bustleholme	Dudley Sports	Dudley Town	Ellesmere Rangers	Goodrich	Gornal Athletic	Great Wyrley	Ledbury Town	Ludlow Town	Lye Town	Pelsall Villa	Shawbury United	Shifnal Town	Tividale	Wednesfield	Wellington	Wolv'pton Casuals	Wyrley Rangers
Bewdley Town		2-1	4-3	2-2	4-0	5-1	1-1	3-0	1-1	1-0	n/a	2-2	3-1	1-1	5-3	2-0	1-4	2-2	3-1	1-1	1-1	3-1
Bridgnorth Town	1-1		2-1	3-0	1-0	0-0	3-3	1-2	4-0	2-1	n/a	5-2	3-0	2-0	5-2	1-1	0-1	0-0	5-0	1-2	2-2	1-0
Brierley & Hagley	0-0	2-1		5-1	2-1	0-2	0-2	1-4	1-4	2-2	n/a	1-2	1-1	1-1	1-0	3-2	0-4	0-3	0-1	3-1	3-2	1-2
Bromyard Town	0-1	2-5	1-2	*P*	1-0	1-3	0-3	4-1	2-3	0-2	n/a	1-3	1-3	0-1	4-4	4-1	1-6	1-1	2-2	0-1	2-1	3-1
Bustleholme	4-4	4-1	5-1	1-3	*R*	3-1	1-2	1-0	0-1	1-3	n/a	3-0	0-1	1-3	2-0	0-1	0-2	0-3	2-1	2-3	2-2	1-1
Dudley Sports	1-2	2-3	1-1	0-0	2-2	*E*	0-1	0-1	0-2	4-3	n/a	0-1	3-1	1-3	4-1	1-2	0-4	0-1	0-1	3-1	1-0	0-1
Dudley Town	1-2	3-2	2-0	1-2	1-0	0-1	*M*	1-2	1-2	1-2	n/a	5-1	2-0	1-3	2-1	3-0	2-1	3-4	4-0	2-0	1-1	4-0
Ellesmere Rangers	1-2	0-0	2-2	3-1	1-4	4-2	0-1	*I*	1-2	1-3	n/a	2-0	1-0	1-2	1-3	0-3	0-3	2-3	2-0	1-2	1-0	0-1
Goodrich	4-2	0-4	5-0	4-2	3-0	1-3	1-2	1-0	*E*	4-1	3-1	3-1	4-1	3-3	1-4	1-1	0-2	0-1	2-0	3-1	3-1	1-3
Gornal Athletic	1-5	1-0	2-1	1-2	1-0	0-0	0-0	1-0	2-1	*R*	n/a	1-1	2-1	2-0	2-0	1-0	1-0	1-1	3-0	4-2	1-1	1-1
Great Wyrley	n/a	n/a	n/a	n/a	n/a	n/a	n/a	n/a	n/a	n/a		n/a	n/a	n/a	n/a	n/a	n/a	n/a	n/a	n/a	n/a	n/a
Ledbury Town	0-3	1-3	2-2	1-1	1-0	1-3	1-2	1-2	4-2	0-3	n/a	*D*	1-3	0-7	0-4	3-2	0-1	0-3	2-3	3-1	3-0	1-4
Ludlow Town	0-6	0-0	0-1	1-1	0-2	1-2	1-3	2-3	3-6	1-1	n/a	4-0	*I*	3-0	1-0	1-0	0-0	1-0	3-2	2-1	0-4	2-3
Lye Town	4-2	3-4	1-1	1-2	1-0	0-0	3-1	4-3	2-1	0-1	5-0	4-1	4-1	*V*	6-0	6-2	0-3	1-3	1-1	3-1	3-0	5-0
Pelsall Villa	2-1	2-1	0-1	0-3	3-1	2-2	2-2	1-1	2-1	1-4	n/a	0-1	3-2	2-0	*I*	2-1	1-0	0-2	2-2	2-2	1-1	2-2
Shawbury United	1-6	2-5	5-2	4-0	1-1	1-1	0-1	1-2	0-2	2-1	n/a	0-1	1-2	0-0	1-4	*S*	1-0	1-2	2-0	5-3	4-1	2-2
Shifnal Town	1-1	5-3	2-1	2-3	3-1	4-0	3-2	4-4	3-1	0-1	8-1	10-0	0-0	2-1	6-0		*I*	6-0	6-1	1-0		
Tividale	2-2	0-4	3-2	4-2	3-3	1-0	0-0	3-1	4-0	1-1	n/a	1-4	3-2	5-1	2-2	3-0	0-2	*O*	3-0	2-2	2-2	0-2
Wednesfield	0-1	2-1	0-2	1-0	4-2	0-6	2-0	1-1	2-1	1-1	n/a	2-4	3-3	1-1	2-1	1-1	0-2	0-7	*N*	0-0	0-0	3-0
Wellington	1-1	0-0	2-1	2-1	4-1	0-0	3-2	0-3	1-3	n/a	n/a	4-0	2-3	3-3	4-4	2-0	3-1	4-1			3-1	2-0
Wolverhampton Casuals	3-1	0-1	3-2	1-2	1-1	3-1	3-0	1-2	3-3	1-2	n/a	2-1	2-0	2-0	1-1	1-5	0-3	2-2	0-0	1-1		3-0
Wyrley Rangers	2-2	0-2	2-1	2-1	2-2	2-3	1-0	1-2	2-3	1-2	n/a	1-1	0-3	1-1	2-0	1-0	1-1	0-1	2-3	0-1	4-2	

Premier Division		P	W	D	L	F	A	Pts
Shifnal Town		40	27	7	6	100	27	88
Tividale		40	22	12	6	84	49	78
Bewdley Town		40	20	15	5	92	55	75
Gornal Athletic		40	20	10	10	61	47	70
Dudley Town		40	20	7	13	67	46	67
Goodrich		40	21	4	15	83	69	67
Bridgnorth Town	-3	40	20	9	11	83	49	66
Lye Town		40	19	9	12	83	57	66
Pelsall Villa		40	15	12	13	70	69	57
Wellington		40	15	10	15	66	73	55
Dudley Sports		40	14	9	17	56	58	51
Ellesmere Rangers		40	15	5	20	57	68	50
Wednesfield		40	13	9	18	46	76	48
Wyrley Rangers	-1	40	12	10	18	50	68	45
Brierley & Hagley		40	12	7	21	55	80	43
Ledbury Town		40	12	5	23	51	97	41
Wolverhampton Casuals		40	9	13	18	53	72	40
Bromyard Town		40	11	7	22	56	83	40
Ludlow Town		40	11	7	22	49	78	40
Bustleholme		40	10	9	21	55	69	39
Shawbury United		40	10	8	22	55	82	38

Great Wyrley – record expunged

PREMIER DIVISION CUP

FIRST ROUND
Bewdley Town 5 Ellesmere Rovers 1
Bridgnorth Town 3 Bustleholme 1
Pelsall Villa 3 Wellington 0
Shawbury United 6 Ledbury Town 1
Wolverhampton Casuals 0 Ludlow Town 3

SECOND ROUND
Bewdley Town 2 Wyrley Rangers 0
Brierley & Hagley 0 Tividale 2
Bromyard Town 2 Shawbury United 2 *aet* (4-2p)
Dudley Sports 1 Bridgnorth Town 4
Goodrich 3 Dudley Town 5
Ludlow Town 1 Lye Town 3
Pelsall Villa 5 Wednesfield 3
Shifnal Town 2 Gornal Athletic 4

QUARTER-FINALS
Bewdley Town 1 Tividale 4
Bridgnorth Town 3 Bromyard Town 1
Dudley Town 2 Pelsall Villa 1 *aet*
Shifnal Town 3 Lye Town 1

SEMI-FINALS
(played over two legs)
Bridgnorth Town 0 Dudley Town 3, Dudley Town 0 Bridgnorth Town 0
Tividale 0 Shifnal Town 1, Shifnal Town 2 Tividale 2

FINAL
(May 7th at Tividale)
Shifnal Town 1 Dudley Town 0

WWW.NLNEWSDESK.CO.UK

WEST MIDLANDS (REGIONAL) LEAGUE PREMIER DIVISION CONSTITUTION 2007-08

AFC WULFRUNIANS . . . Wolverhampton Casuals FC, Brinsford Lane, Coven Heath, Wolverhampton WV10 7PR 01902 783214
BEWDLEY TOWN . . . . Ribbesford Meadows, Ribbesford, Bewdley 01299 405837
BRIDGNORTH TOWN . . . . Crown Meadow, Innage Lane, Bridgnorth WV16 4HS 01746 762747
BRIERLEY & WITHYMOOR . . . Halesowen Town FC, The Grove, Old Hawne Lane, Halesowen B63 3TB 0121 550 2179
BROMYARD TOWN . . . . Delahay Meadow, Stourport Road, Bromyard HR7 4NT 01885 483974
BUSTLEHOLME . . . . Tipton Town FC, Wednesbury Oak Road, Tipton DY4 0BS 0121 502 5534/556 5067
DARLASTON TOWN . . . . City Ground, Waverley Road, Darlaston WS10 8ED 0121 526 4423
DUDLEY SPORTS . . . . Dudley Employees S&S, Hillcrest Avenue, Brierley Hill DY5 3QH 01384 826420
DUDLEY TOWN . . . . Dell Stadium, Bryce Road, Brierley Hill DY5 4NE 01384 812943
ELLESMERE RANGERS . . . . Beech Grove Playing Fields, Ellesmere SY12 0BT . . . . None
GOODRICH . . . . Goodrich Sports Ground, Stafford Road, Fordhouses, Wolverhampton WV10 7EH . . . . None
GORNAL ATHLETIC . . . . Garden Walk Stadium, Garden Walk, Lower Gornal, Dudley DY3 2NH 01384 358398
LEDBURY TOWN . . . . New Street Ground, New Street, Ledbury HR8 2EL 07879 268205
LUDLOW TOWN . . . . SBS Stadium, Bromfield Road, Ludlow SY8 2BY 01584 876000
LYE TOWN . . . . Sports Ground, Stourbridge Road, Lye, Stourbridge DY9 7DH 01384 422672
PELSALL VILLA . . . . The Bush Ground, Walsall Road, Heath End, Pelsall WS3 4ET 01922 692748/682018
SHAWBURY UNITED . . . . Butlers Sports Centre, Bowens Field, Wem SY4 5AW 01939 233287
TIVIDALE . . . . The Beeches, Packwood Road, Tividale, Oldbury B69 1UL 01384 211743
WEDNESFIELD . . . . Cottage Ground, Amos Lane, Wednesfield WV11 1ND 01902 735506
WELLINGTON . . . . Wellington Playing Fields, Wellington, Hereford HR4 8AZ . . . . None
WOLVERHAMPTON CASUALS . . . . Brinsford Lane, Coven Heath, WV10 7PR 01902 783214

IN: AFC Wulfrunians (P), Darlaston Town (P)
OUT: Great Wyrley (WS), Shifnal Town (P – Midland Alliance), Wyrley Rangers (W)
Brierley & Hagley have merged with Withymoor Colts to become Brierley & Withymoor

	AFC Wulfrunians	Bilbrook	Bilston Town	Blackheath Town	Bridgnorth Town Res.	Cresswell Wanderers	Darlaston Town	Hinton	Ludlow Town Res.	Malvern Town Res.	Parkfield Leisure	Riverway	Sporting Khalsa	Stafford Town	Tenbury United	Wolverhampton United
AFC Wulfrunians		7-1	1-3	2-0	3-0	0-1	3-1	2-2	1-0	1-1	10-0	0-1	7-1	2-4	3-0	3-0
Bilbrook	2-3		1-2	1-2	1-2	0-2	0-5	1-3	4-2	2-0	6-0	3-1	3-2	0-2	0-2	3-2
Bilston Town	0-4	3-0	D	1-2	2-1	1-1	5-3	6-1	2-1	4-0	3-3	5-1	2-2	4-2	3-2	
Blackheath Town	0-2	5-2	2-1	I	3-0	0-2	1-0	1-2	6-0	3-1	3-0	1-3	2-1	2-5	6-1	2-3
Bridgnorth Town Res.	1-2	1-1	1-0	4-0	V	2-0	0-2	4-0	2-0	0-3	4-1	1-1	4-0	1-3	1-1	2-3
Cresswell Wanderers	2-0	1-1	1-1	3-1	2-1	I	0-5	0-2	4-2	1-0	2-1	3-2	2-2	1-1	1-0	
Darlaston Town	1-0	5-0	3-1	5-0	3-1	3-0	S	3-0	4-0	1-0	3-0	1-1	7-1	3-0	3-0	1-0
Hinton	0-3	4-0	1-2	1-1	0-2	2-5	1-2	I	4-1	1-2	4-0	1-3	5-0	1-4	4-0	3-1
Ludlow Town Res.	0-3	3-0	0-4	1-3	2-0	3-2	0-2	2-1	O	1-2	4-0	2-1	3-2	2-4	3-1	2-0
Malvern Town Res.	0-3	2-3	3-1	2-1	1-1	1-0	0-2	0-2	1-2	N	4-0	6-3	1-2	0-0	3-4	3-1
Parkfield Leisure	0-1	1-4	0-0	0-5	0-2	1-1	0-2	1-3	1-0	3-3		1-2	0-3	1-1	0-1	1-3
Riverway	0-2	3-1	1-0	0-3	0-1	4-2	2-2	14-0	8-2	1-0	4-0	O	1-1	5-2		4-0
Sporting Khalsa	1-2	1-3	1-1	0-4	1-0	0-1	0-1	1-3	0-2	3-1	1-1		N	2-4	3-2	2-1
Stafford Town	0-3	3-1	3-4	1-2	1-1	0-4	1-1	4-1	0-1	4-2	11-0	1-0	2-2	E	3-2	3-1
Tenbury United	1-2	3-3	3-1	0-4	1-0	3-1	0-6	3-2	2-1	1-3	7-1	2-2	3-1	1-2		0-3
Wolverhampton United	0-6	3-4	0-0	4-4	2-3	1-3	2-1	0-0	0-1	4-2	1-1	2-0	1-3	4-1		

(vertical left margin: WWW.CHERRYRED.CO.UK)

Division One	P	W	D	L	F	A	Pts
Darlaston Town	30	24	4	2	82	14	76
AFC Wulfrunians	30	22	2	6	81	23	68
Cresswell Wanderers	30	18	4	8	52	38	58
Stafford Town	30	16	8	6	74	47	56
Riverway	30	15	8	7	75	42	53
Blackheath Town	30	17	2	11	69	48	53
Bilston Town	30	15	7	8	63	44	52
Bridgnorth Town Res.	30	12	5	13	41	37	41
Malvern Town Res.	30	11	5	14	50	50	38
Hinton	30	11	2	17	55	72	35
Bilbrook	30	10	3	17	51	75	33
Tenbury United	30	10	3	17	49	75	33
Ludlow Town Res.	30	10	3	17	40	69	33
Wolverhampton United	30	8	4	18	44	63	28
Sporting Khalsa	30	6	4	20	37	80	22
Parkfield Leisure	30	1	4	25	17	103	7

DIVISION ONE CUP

FIRST ROUND
AFC Wulfrunians 3 Malvern Town Res. 1
Bilbrook 0 Wolverhampton United 0 *aet* (5-6p)
Blackheath Town 2 Riverway 1
Bridgnorth Town Res. 1 Tenbury United 0
Darlaston Town 2 Stafford Town 2 *aet* (4-3p)
Hinton 1 **Bilston Town** 2 *aet*
Ludlow Town Res. 3 **Cresswell Wanderers** 4 *aet*
Sporting Khalsa 2 Parkfield Leisure 1
QUARTER-FINALS
AFC Wulfrunians 3 Bridgnorth Town Res. 0
Cresswell Wanderers 3 Bilston Town 3 *aet* (5-3p)
Sporting Khalsa 2 **Blackheath Town** 3 *aet*
Wolverhampton United 1 **Darlaston Town** 2
(at Bilston Town)
SEMI-FINALS
(played over two legs)
Cresswell Wanderers 1 AFC Wulfrunians 1,
AFC Wulfrunians 3 Cresswell Wanderers 0
Darlaston Town 7 Blackheath Town 0,
Blackheath Town 2 **Darlaston Town** 1
FINAL
(May 12th at Gornal Athletic)
Darlaston Town 1 AFC Wulfrunians 0

WEST MIDLANDS (REGIONAL) LEAGUE DIVISION ONE CONSTITUTION 2007-08

AFC WOMBOURNE UNITED .... Mile Flat Sports Ground, Mile Flat, Wall Heath, Kingswinford. .... Non
BILBROOK .... Pendeford Lane, Wolverhampton WV9 5HQ .... Non
BIRCHILLS UNITED .... Grosvenor Park, Somerfield Road, Bloxwich. .... Non
BLACKHEATH TOWN ...... York Road Social & Sports Club, York Road, Oldbury, Rowley Regis B65 0RR 0121 559 556
BRIDGNORTH TOWN RESERVES ...... Crown Meadow, Innage Lane, Bridgnorth WV16 4HS 01746 76274
CRESSWELL WANDERERS . Sporting Khalsa FC, Abbey Park, Glastonbury Crescent, Mossley, Bloxwich, Walsall ST17 9XX. 01785 25106
DUDLEY UNITED .... Mile Flat Sports Ground, Mile Flat, Wall Heath, Kingswinford DY6 0AU .... Non
GORNAL ATHLETIC RESERVES ... Garden Walk, Garden Walk, Lower Gornal, Dudley DY3 2NH. 01384 35839
HEATH TOWN RANGERS ...... Wednesfield FC, Cottage Ground, Amos Lane, Wednesfield WV11 1ND. 01902 73550
HINTON. .... Broomy Hill, Hereford HR4 0LH .... Non
MALVERN TOWN RESERVES .... Langland Stadium, Langland Avenue, Malvern WR14 2EQ 01684 57406
PENNCROFT .... Aldersley Leisure Village, Aldersley Road, Wolverhampton WV6 9NW 01902 55620
RIVERWAY .... Long Lane Park, Long Lane, Essington WV11 2AA 01922 40660
SHENSTONE PATHFINDER .. Shenstone PF (Pavilion Club), Birmingham Rd, Shenstone, Lichfield WS14 0LR 01543 48165
SPORTING KHALSA .... Abbey Park, Glastonbury Crescent, Mossley, Bloxwich WS3 2RQ. 01922 47764
STAFFORD TOWN .... Rowley Park Stadium, Averill Road, West Road, Stafford ST17 9YA 01785 25106
WARSTONE WANDERERS .... Parkfields Stadium, Rooker Avenue, Parkfield, Wolverhampton WV2 2DT .... Non
WEDNESBURY TOWN ...... Darlaston Town FC, City Ground, Waverley Road, Darlaston WS10 8ED. 0121 526 442
WOLVERHAMPTON DEVELOPMENT ... Four Ashes, Stafford Road, Wolverhampton. .... Non
WOLVERHAMPTON UNITED ...... Prestwood Road West, Wednesfield, Wolverhampton WV11 1HL. 01902 73088
IN: *AFC Wombourne United (formerly Orton Vale) (P – Wolverhampton Combination), Birchills United (P – Wolverhampton Combination), Dudley United (P), Gornal Athletic Reserves (P), Heath Town Rangers (P), Penncroft (P – Birmingham AFA Premier Division), Shenstone Pathfinder (P), Warstone Wanderers (P), Wednesbury Town (P), Wolverhampton Development (P)*
OUT: *AFC Wulfrunians (P), Bilston Town (R), Darlaston Town (P), Ludlow Town Reserves (S – Shropshire County League Premier Division), Parkfield United (formerly Parkfield Leisure) (R), Tenbury United (R)*

	Bewdley Town Res.	Brereton Town	Bustleholme Res.	Chaddesley Corbett	Dudley United	Gornal Athletic Res.	Heath Town Rangers	Mahal	Penkridge Town	Penn Colts	Shenstone Pathfinder	Warstone Wanderers	Wednesbury Town	Wolverhampton Development	Wyrley Juniors
Bewdley Town Res.		3-4	1-5	1-4	1-4	1-3	0-0	1-2	2-2	2-1	2-2	4-2	1-4	1-1	0-2
Brereton Town	1-3	D	3-4	2-2	1-1	3-5	1-4	0-1	1-1	3-3	0-1	5-6	0-6	1-5	4-4
Bustleholme Res.	0-3	6-1	I	8-1	0-1	1-3	0-3	2-2	2-1	3-1	1-3	0-6	3-3	3-4	0-2
Chaddesley Corbett	3-1	6-0	2-4	V	4-2	1-3	1-2	3-3	3-2	1-3	2-2	2-3	2-1	2-1	2-2
Dudley United	0-0	3-2	4-4	1-1	I	0-2	1-2	0-1	1-1	3-1	5-4	2-7	0-3	1-1	0-0
Gornal Athletic Res.	1-0	1-1	3-1	0-2	3-1	S	0-5	3-3	1-1	1-1	0-0	2-2	5-2	2-3	9-2
Heath Town Rangers	3-4	5-1	4-3	1-1	1-2	2-1	I	3-1	3-0	2-4	3-0	0-0	2-3	2-1	3-1
Mahal	3-1	1-1	2-4	0-2	3-1	1-1	0-0	O	1-1	3-0	2-3	5-0	1-1	0-1	2-2
Penkridge Town	3-0	2-1	2-2	1-0	3-2	0-0	0-2	3-4	N	1-4	0-2	1-0	2-1	1-1	1-3
Penn Colts	1-2	1-1	6-2	4-2	0-4	1-2	1-2	7-1	2-4		5-1	3-3	3-1	1-0	1-0
Shenstone Pathfinder	5-1	6-3	3-1	2-0	3-1	1-0	1-3	6-1	3-0	4-2		2-1	3-3	3-1	1-1
Warstone Wanderers	5-2	2-0	0-0	2-1	0-2	2-3	1-1	0-2	3-2	1-5	1-2	T	0-1	1-0	5-2
Wednesbury Town	4-2	3-1	5-0	2-1	4-3	1-1	0-1	2-0	3-2	0-2	2-3	3-3	W	0-1	1-2
Wolv'pton Development	2-2	3-1	4-0	4-0	0-2	4-1	1-2	0-0	2-2	2-2	3-1	2-0	3-3	O	4-2
Wyrley Juniors	4-2	1-2	5-2	4-1	2-4	1-3	1-4	1-3	3-2	3-4	1-2	4-4	2-1	0-3	

Division One		P	W	D	L	F	A	Pts
Heath Town Rangers		28	19	5	4	65	30	62
Shenstone Pathfinder		28	18	5	5	69	45	59
Gornal Athletic Res.		28	13	9	6	59	43	48
Wolv'pton Development		28	13	8	7	57	36	47
Penn Colts		28	14	5	9	73	54	47
Wednesbury Town		28	12	6	10	63	49	42
Warstone Wanderers		28	10	7	11	60	58	37
Dudley United	-1	28	10	7	11	51	54	36
Mahal		28	9	9	10	47	53	36
Chaddesley Corbett		28	9	6	13	52	61	33
Wyrley Juniors		28	9	6	13	57	70	33
Bustleholme Res.		28	9	4	15	61	77	31
Penkridge Town		28	7	9	12	41	52	30
Bewdley Town Res.		28	6	6	16	43	71	24
Brereton Town		28	2	8	18	44	89	14

DIVISION ONE CUP

FIRST ROUND
Bewdley Town Res. 0 **Warstone Wanderers** 1
Brereton Town 3 Mahal 2
Bustleholme Res. 3 **Wednesbury Town** 4
Chaddesley Corbett (scr.) v **Heath Town Rangers** (w/o)
Gornal Athletic Res. 0 **Penn Colts** 1
Penkridge Town 6 Wyrley Juniors 0
Wolverhampton Development 2 **Shenstone Pathfinder** 3
QUARTER-FINALS
Dudley United 2 Warstone Wanderers 1
Penkridge Town 2 Heath Town Rangers 0
Penn Colts 1 **Wednesbury Town** 2
Shenstone Pathfinder 2 Brereton Town 0
SEMI-FINALS
(played over two legs)
Penkridge Town 1 Wednesbury Town 4,
Wednesbury Town 4 Penkridge Town 0
Shenstone Pathfinder 2 Dudley United 0,
Dudley United 4 **Shenstone Pathfinder** 4 *aet*
FINAL
(May 12th at Wednesfield)
Wednesbury Town 3 Shenstone Pathfinder 2

WEST MIDLANDS (REGIONAL) LEAGUE DIVISION TWO CONSTITUTION 2007-08
BENTLEY YOUTH . . . . Bentley Road South, Darlaston, West Midlands WS10 8LN 07737 296751
BILSTON TOWN . . . . Queen Street, Bilston WV14 7EX 01902 491498
BLACK COUNTRY RANGERS . . . . Willenhall Town FC, Noose Lane, Willenhall, WV13 2BB 01902 636586
BRERETON TOWN . . . . Ravenhill Park, Brereton, Rugeley WS15 1DF 01889 578255
BUSTLEHOLME RESERVES . . . . . Great Barr Club, Ray Hall Lane, Great Barr, Birmingham B43 6JF. 07836 765300
HEATH TOWN RANGERS RESERVES . . Bilbrook FC, Pendeford Lane, Wobaston Road, Wolverhampton WV9 5HG . . . . None
MAHAL . . . . Hadley Stadium, Wilson Road, Smethwick, Warley B68 9JW 0121 434 4848
PARKFIELD UNITED . . . . Parkfields Stadium, Rooker Avenue, Parkfields, Wolverhampton WV2 2DT 07723 640511
PENKRIDGE TOWN . . . . Monkton Recreation Centre, Pinfold Lane, Penkridge, Stafford ST19 5QP. . . . . None
PENN COLTS . . . . The Pavilion, Stafford Road, Wolverhampton WV10 6DH . . . . None
POWICK . . . . Victoria Park Playing Fields, Malvern Link WR14 2JX . . . . None
PUNJAB UNITED SPORTS . . Wolverhampton United FC, Prestwood Road West, Wolverhampton WV11 1HN. 01902 730881
STONE OLD ALLEYNIANS . . . . Springbank Park, Yarnfield Road, Yarnfield, Stone ST15 0NF 01785 761891
TENBURY UNITED . . . . Palmers Meadow, Burford, Tenbury Wells WR15 8AP . . . . None
WELLINGTON AMATEURS . . . . School Grove, Oakengates, Telford, Shropshire TF2 6BQ . . . . None
WYRLEY JUNIORS . . . . Yates Sports & Social Club, Lime Lane, Pelsall, Walsall WS3 5AS 01543 373458
IN: Bentley Youth (youth football), Bilston Town (R), Black Country Rangers (youth football), Heath Town Rangers Reserves (N), Parkfield United (formerly Parkfield Leisure) (R), Powick (Worcester & District League), Punjab United Sports (P – Wolverhampton Combination), Stone Old Alleynians (S – Staffordshire County Senior League Division One), Tenbury United (R), Wellington Amateurs (P – Shropshire County League Premier Division)
OUT: Bewdley Town Reserves (W), Chaddesley Corbett (W – Kidderminster & District League Premier Division), Dudley United (P), Gornal Athletic Reserves (P), Heath Town Rangers (P), Shenstone Pathfinder (P), Warstone Wanderers (P), Wednesbury Town (P), Wolverhampton Development (P)

WEST RIDING COUNTY AMATEUR LEAGUE

	Ardsley Celtic	Bay Athletic	Brighouse Town	Campion	Eastmoor	Golcar United	Halifax Irish Club	Hall Green United	Hemsworth Miners Welfare	Lower Hopton	Ovenden West Riding	Storthes Hall	Tyersal	Wibsey
Ardsley Celtic		2-1	1-1	3-4	3-3	2-1	3-4	2-1	1-2	1-1	3-5	0-1	1-1	3-1
Bay Athletic	4-0	*P*	1-2	6-0	4-2	5-0	5-0	1-1	0-5	2-2	2-0	2-0	3-2	3-1
Brighouse Town	2-0	0-2	*R*	2-1	3-1	1-1	1-0	3-1	0-0	3-2	2-1	1-0	4-0	2-3
Campion	2-1	2-2	2-0	*E*	3-1	2-0	3-1	5-2	3-1	1-1	1-1	3-2	1-3	4-2
Eastmoor	1-3	1-3	2-1	0-2	*M*	2-2	0-1	1-2	2-1	0-4	0-1	1-3	1-2	2-4
Golcar United	5-1	0-2	0-2	2-2	5-2	*I*	1-0	2-2	0-2	4-4	4-0	0-2	0-1	1-2
Halifax Irish Club	2-1	1-4	0-4	2-4	3-1	2-3	*E*	3-4	1-0	0-4	0-1	2-1	4-1	1-9
Hall Green United	1-3	0-3	0-2	1-1	1-1	2-2	1-1	*R*	4-1	2-3	1-2	1-1	3-2	1-2
Hemsworth Miners Welfare	2-2	1-3	1-1	1-1	0-0	3-2	0-4	2-2		1-0	4-1	2-1	5-2	0-2
Lower Hopton	0-0	1-5	2-2	2-2	1-1	4-2	3-2	1-1	2-2		4-1	6-3	3-2	3-3
Ovenden West Riding	1-6	1-0	2-0	2-6	4-0	0-1	3-0	2-2	4-2	3-3	*D*	1-3	2-1	0-5
Storthes Hall	4-0	1-1	2-1	0-2	5-1	4-4	2-2	2-0	3-2	5-0	4-2	*I*	4-0	2-5
Tyersal	1-0	3-3	2-2	2-1	1-2	4-3	3-0	2-2	2-2	2-0	1-3	0-1	*V*	0-3
Wibsey	1-3	5-5	1-1	3-1	10-1	2-0	3-3	7-1	4-2	5-0	5-2	2-1	2-0	

Premier Division	P	W	D	L	F	A	Pts
Wibsey	26	18	4	4	92	42	58
Bay Athletic	26	16	6	4	72	33	54
Campion	26	14	7	5	59	43	49
Brighouse Town	26	13	7	6	43	28	46
Storthes Hall	26	13	4	9	57	41	43
Lower Hopton	26	8	12	6	56	55	36
Ovenden West Riding	26	11	3	12	45	60	36
Hemsworth Miners Welfare	26	8	8	10	44	47	32
Ardsley Celtic	26	8	6	12	45	52	30
Tyersal	26	8	5	13	40	55	29
Halifax Irish Club	26	9	2	15	40	65	29
Golcar United	26	6	7	13	45	55	25
Hall Green United	26	4	10	12	39	58	22
Eastmoor	26	3	5	18	29	72	14

PREMIER DIVISION CUP

FIRST ROUND
Bay Athletic 6 Eastmoor 0
Golcar United 2 Halifax Irish Club 1
Hall Green United 3 **Campion** 4
Ovenden West Riding 2 **Storthes Hall** 1
Tyersal 0 **Brighouse Town** 2
Wibsey 4 Hemsworth Miners Welfare 2
QUARTER-FINALS
Ardsley Celtic 0 **Brighouse Town** 2
Bay Athletic 3 Ovenden West Riding 0
Campion 3 Lower Hopton 3 *aet* (4-3p)
Golcar United 2 Wibsey 0
SEMI-FINALS
Campion 2 Bay Athletic 1
(at Brighouse Town)
Golcar United 1 Brighouse Town 0
(at Halifax Irish Club)
FINAL
(May 7th at Littletown)
Campion 4 Golcar United 0

	Dudley Hill Rangers	Farnley	Heckmondwike Town	Keighley Shamrocks	Kirkburton	Littletown	Marsden	Meltham Athletic	Overthorpe Sports	Salts	South Bradford	Steeton	Ventus & Yeadon Celtic	Wakefield City
Dudley Hill Rangers		4-0	3-2	4-4	3-2	4-4	1-1	1-1	0-0	1-0	1-1	3-2	2-1	1-1
Farnley	1-2	D	2-2	2-3	2-0	4-1	2-3	3-4	2-2	1-1	4-0	1-1	5-0	3-2
Heckmondwike Town	3-1	2-4	I	2-3	1-3	2-2	2-4	2-2	1-5	2-2	3-2	2-0	2-5	3-3
Keighley Shamrocks	2-0	2-1	4-2	V	1-0	5-1	3-0	4-0	1-4	2-1	0-1	4-0	6-1	1-1
Kirkburton	2-1	2-2	0-0	3-2	I	2-6	2-2	0-3	4-1	0-1	1-1	1-1	1-0	1-3
Littletown	2-1	0-4	0-2	0-1	2-0	S	2-0	2-4	1-2	1-1	2-0	2-2	3-3	1-4
Marsden	3-1	3-4	4-2	1-0	2-5	1-2	I	0-9	0-4	0-0	5-3	3-1	3-1	0-4
Meltham Athletic	2-1	4-2	1-0	5-0	3-3	1-0	4-0	O	3-4	1-2	3-1	5-2	1-0	6-0
Overthorpe Sports	2-1	3-3	3-0	1-1	0-0	3-3	1-3	4-1	N	1-0	2-1	0-0	8-3	1-6
Salts	3-1	0-2	2-1	2-3	1-2	0-0	1-0	0-1	3-1		0-1	2-2	5-4	1-2
South Bradford	2-2	2-3	3-1	1-1	2-0	4-0	1-5	1-3	1-5	3-1	O	1-5	1-2	2-1
Steeton	4-0	2-1	1-3	5-0	2-1	2-2	1-3	4-2	2-0	2-3	1-3	N	5-1	0-1
Ventus & Yeadon C.	4-0	2-2	3-0	2-4	0-6	5-2	0-2	1-5	2-5	1-4	5-2	4-1	E	3-2
Wakefield City	2-0	0-4	4-2	1-1	0-2	1-1	2-0	1-1	0-1	1-0	0-0	2-3	6-0	

DIV ONE CUP

FIRST ROUND
Heckmondwike 1 **Meltham Athletic 4**
Littletown 3 Ventus/Yeadon Celtic 1
Marsden 4 **Keighley S. 4** aet (3-4p)
Overthorpe Sports 4 Farnley 0
Salts 0 **Dudley Hill Rangers 2**
South Bradford 2 Steeton 1
QUARTER-FINALS
Dudley Hill Rangers 1 **Littletown 2**
Keighley S. 1 Meltham A. 1 *aet* (4-3p)
Kirkburton 7 Overthorpe Sports 1
Wakefield City 2 **South Bradford 3**
SEMI-FINALS
Keighley Shamrocks 0 **Littletown 1**
(at Campion)
Kirkburton 2 South Bradford 2
(at Heckmondwike Town)
South Bradford 1 **Kirkburton 3**
(at Lower Hopton) replay
FINAL
(May 19th at Brighouse Town)
Littletown 1 **Kirkburton 2**

Division One	P	W	D	L	F	A	Pts
Meltham Athletic	26	17	4	5	75	38	55
Keighley Shamrocks	26	15	5	6	58	41	50
Overthorpe Sports	26	14	7	5	63	42	49
Farnley	26	11	7	8	64	47	40
Wakefield City	26	11	7	8	50	38	40
Marsden	26	12	3	11	48	58	39
Kirkburton	26	9	7	10	43	42	34
Steeton	26	9	6	11	51	50	33
Salts	26	9	6	11	36	36	33
Dudley Hill Rangers	26	7	8	11	39	51	29
South Bradford	26	8	5	13	40	56	29
Littletown	26	6	9	11	42	58	27
Ventus & Yeadon Celtic	26	8	2	16	53	83	26
Heckmondwike Town	26	5	6	15	44	66	21

Reserves Division	P	W	D	L	F	A	Pts
Farnley Res.	24	21	2	1	102	29	65
Golcar United Res.	24	15	3	6	77	44	48
Keighley Shamrocks Res.	24	14	3	7	72	44	45
Ovenden West Riding Res.	24	13	3	8	57	55	42
Bay Athletic Res.	24	12	4	8	61	41	40
Dudley Hill Rangers Res.	24	11	3	10	54	63	36
Ardsley Celtic Res.	24	9	3	12	55	59	30
Wakefield City Res.	24	8	4	12	52	66	28
Salts Res.	24	7	5	12	40	55	26
Littletown Res.	24	5	9	10	36	43	24
Steeton Res.	24	6	5	13	38	61	23
Kirkburton Res.	24	6	3	15	42	66	21
Hunsworth Res.	24	3	5	16	25	85	14

Barclays Res. – record expunged

RESERVES CUP

FINAL
(May 2nd at Golcar United)
Bay Athletic Res. 1 Kirkburton Res. 1 *aet* (4-3p)

WEST RIDING COUNTY AMATEUR LEAGUE DIVISION ONE CONSTITUTION 2007-08

BRONTE WANDERERS . . . . Marley Stadium, Keighley BD21 4DB 01535 609910
CRAG ROAD UNITED . . . . Apperley Road, Greengates, Bradford BD10 0PX 07781 808212
DUDLEY HILL RANGERS . . . . Newhall Park School, Newhall Road, Bierley, Bradford BD4 6AF 07967 359883
EASTMOOR . . . . King George V Playing Fields, Woodhouse Road, Eastmoor, Wakefield WF1 4RD 01924 375367
FARNLEY . . . . Farnley Cricket Club, Church Lane, Farnley 0113 253 5950
HECKMONDWIKE TOWN . . . . Cemetery Road, Heckmondwike WF16 9ED 01924 442907
KIRKBURTON . . . . Gregory Playing Fields, Kirkburton, Huddersfield HD8 0XH . . . . None
LITTLETOWN . . . . Beck Lane, Heckmondwike WF16 0JZ 07930 852796
MARSDEN . . . . Fell Lane, Marsden, Huddersfield 01484 844191
RAWDON OLD BOYS . . . . Hanson Field, Rawdon, Leeds . . . . None
SALTS . . . . Salts Playing Fields, Hirst Lane, Saltaire, Shipley BD18 4DD 01274 583427
SOUTH BRADFORD . . . . Broadstone Way, Holmewood, Bradford BD4 9BU 01274 751160
STEETON . . . . Summer Hill Lane, Steeton BD20 6RX 01585 683387
WAKEFIELD CITY . . . . West Yorks Sports & Social, Walton Lane, Sandal, Wakefield WF2 6NG 01924 258760

IN: Bronte Wanderers (P), Crag Road United (P), Eastmoor (R), Rawdon Old Boys (P)
OUT: Keighley Shamrocks (P), Meltham Athletic (P), Overthorpe Sports (P), Ventus & Yeadon Celtic (R)

	Barclays	Brighouse Town Res.	Bronte Wanderers	Campion Res.	Crag Road United	Dudley Hill Athletic	Dynamoes	Hall Green United Res.	Hemsworth Miners Welfare Res.	Hunsworth	Lower Hopton Res.	Morley Town	Rawdon Old Boys	Storthes Hall Res.	Tyersal Res.	Wibsey Res.
Barclays		0-2	0-9	1-3	0-3	2-5	2-4	2-1	1-1	1-4	1-3	1-2	0-0	1-1	0-6	2-3
Brighouse Town Res.	4-1		1-1	3-1	0-2	10-1	8-0	4-1	3-0	6-1	4-2	5-1	2-0	3-0	1-1	7-1
Bronte Wanderers	5-0	5-2	D	7-1	2-0	3-1	2-1	4-2	4-1	6-1	4-2	6-1	1-1	2-1	5-4	2-1
Campion Res.	6-0	1-3	1-1	I	2-1	2-2	1-2	4-0	4-2	2-0	1-0	1-5	0-2	0-5	1-5	1-0
Crag Road United	1-3	3-2	2-2	3-1	V	6-3	6-2	4-1	2-0	3-2	3-2	2-2	2-1	0-2		8-4
Dudley Hill Athletic	5-0	0-1	2-3	3-3	0-6	I	1-2	1-2	3-1	1-4	0-2	1-0	1-3	1-1	1-2	3-5
Dynamoes	5-0	1-1	1-4	1-3	2-6	3-1	S	0-2	2-4	3-3	1-4	1-1	2-1	0-3	0-2	0-1
Hall Green United Res.	4-0	1-4	1-3	6-2	1-0	3-3	3-1	I	2-3	1-1	3-3	0-0	0-0	2-2	3-4	4-3
Hemsworth Miners Welfare Res.	6-0	1-2	0-1	1-1	2-1	4-3	3-1	5-5	O	4-2	2-1	4-0	4-0	1-5	2-5	3-2
Hunsworth	4-0	0-2	0-2	1-4	2-3	5-1	4-2	3-1	3-1	N	0-2	0-2	1-2	1-2	2-2	1-5
Lower Hopton Res.	3-0	1-5	2-3	1-4	2-4	2-4	4-1	3-3	2-1	2-1		3-1	1-5	0-7	1-1	1-2
Morley Town	1-3	2-5	1-3	3-2	0-3	2-2	5-4	2-1	3-2	2-3	3-2	T	1-4	1-5	2-3	2-0
Rawdon Old Boys	4-1	1-2	2-0	4-2	2-0	3-1	5-0	1-2	5-1	3-1	1-1	5-1	W	0-2	4-2	2-1
Storthes Hall Res.	3-3	0-0	2-2	2-3	4-1	0-1	0-0	3-1	3-0	2-2	2-3	2-4		O	1-4	0-1
Tyersal Res.	3-0	0-3	2-1	1-3	6-1	4-7	3-1	1-0	3-2	2-2	7-2	4-1	3-1	1-1		3-2
Wibsey Res.	7-0	1-0	4-7	1-2	3-4	2-0	4-2	1-1	3-7	1-3	2-1	1-1	1-3	0-2	0-2	

Division Two	P	W	D	L	F	A	Pts
Bronte Wanderers	30	23	5	2	100	40	74
Brighouse Town Res.	30	22	4	4	95	30	70
Tyersal Res.	30	22	4	4	89	42	70
Rawdon Old Boys	30	18	5	7	70	38	59
Crag Road United	30	18	2	10	79	55	56
Storthes Hall Res.	30	12	10	8	65	40	46
Campion Res.	30	14	4	12	62	66	46
Hemsworth Miners Welfare Res.	30	12	3	15	68	72	39
Hall Green United Res.	30	9	8	13	56	65	35
Hunsworth	30	10	5	15	55	66	35
Wibsey Res.	30	11	2	17	62	74	35
Morley Town	30	9	5	16	51	80	32
Lower Hopton Res.	30	8	4	18	55	77	28
Dudley Hill Athletic	30	6	5	19	52	89	23
Dynamoes	30	6	4	20	45	87	22
Barclays	30	3	4	23	25	108	13

DIVISION TWO CUP

FIRST ROUND
Barclays 1 **Morley Town** 3
Campion Res. 2 **Crag Road United** 5
Hall Green United Res. 3 **Hunsworth** 4
Hemsworth Miners Welfare Res. 6 Dynamoes 1
Lower Hopton Res. 3 Dudley Hill Athletic 0
Rawdon Old Boys 1 **Brighouse Town Res.** 2 *aet*
Storthes Hall Res. 4 Bronte Wanderers 2
Wibsey Res. 4 **Tyersal Res.** 5 *aet*

QUARTER-FINALS
Hunsworth 2 Hemsworth Miners Welfare Res. 0
Lower Hopton Res. 3 Morley Town 1 *aet*
Storthes Hall Res. 2 Brighouse Town Res. 1 *aet*
Tyersal Res. 5 Crag Road United 1

SEMI-FINALS
Lower Hopton Res. 1 **Storthes Hall Res.** 2 *aet*
(at Golcar United)
Tyersal Res. 4 Hunsworth 2
(at Dudley Hill Athletic)

FINAL
(May 9th at Lower Hopton)
Storthes Hall Res. 4 Tyersal Res. 3 *aet*

WEST RIDING COUNTY AMATEUR LEAGUE DIVISION TWO CONSTITUTION 2007-08

BARCLAYS . . . . Crawshaw Street, Ravensthorpe, Dewsbury WF13 3ER 01924 49702
BRIGHOUSE TOWN RESERVES . . . . St Giles Road, Hove Edge, Brighouse HD6 2RX . . . . Non
CAMPION RESERVES . . Manningham Mills Sports Ground, Scotchman Road, Manningham, Bradford BD9 4SH 01274 54672
DUDLEY HILL ATHLETIC . . . . Hunsworth Lane, East Bierley BD4 6RN . . . . Non
DYNAMOES . . . . Dudley Hill Athletic FC, Hunsworth Lane, East Bierley BD4 6RN. 01274 82357
GOLCAR UNITED RESERVES . . . . . . Longfield Recreation Ground, Golcar, Huddersfield HD7 4AZ 07779 70009
HALL GREEN UNITED RESERVES . . Crigglestone Sports Club, Painthorpe Lane, Crigglestone, Wakefield WF4 3JU 01924 25454
HEMSWORTH M.W. RESERVES . . Fitzwilliam Sports Complex, Wakefield Road, Fitzwilliam, Pontefract WF9 5BP 01977 61044
HUNSWORTH . . . . Birkenshaw Middle School, Bradford Road, Gomersal, Cleckheaton BD19 4BE 07711 19774
MORLEY TOWN . . . . Glen Road, Morley, Leeds LS27 9HG 07709 72708
STORTHES HALL RESERVES . . Police Sports Ground, Woodfield Park, Lockwood Scar, Huddersfield HD4 6BW 07957 69118
TYERSAL RESERVES . . . . Arkwright Street, off Dick Lane, Tyersal, Bradford BD4 8JL 07710 00624
U SAVE ALBION . . . . Seymour Street Recreation Ground, Upper Seymour Street, Bradford BD3 9LJ 01274 66175
VENTUS & YEADON CELTIC . . . . Dam Lane, Yeadon, Leeds 07721 46896
WEST HORTON . . . . Avenue Road, Bradford BD5 8DB 07974 17698
WIBSEY RESERVES . . . . Westwood Park, Cooper Lane, Bradford BD6 3NN . . . . Non
IN: Golcar United Reserves (P – Reserves Division), U Save Albion (P – Bradford League), Ventus & Yeadon Celtic (R), West Horton (P – Bradford League)
OUT: Bronte Wanderers (P), Crag Road United (P), Lower Hopton Reserves (R – Reserves Division), Rawdon Old Boys (P)

WEST YORKSHIRE LEAGUE

	Aberford Albion	Bardsey	Beeston St Anthony's	Boroughbridge	Carlton Athletic	Horsforth St Margaret's	Howden Clough	Knaresborough Town	Leeds Met. Carnegie	Ossett Common Rovers	Pontefract Sports & S.	Rothwell Athletic	Sherburn White Rose	Street Work Soccer	Wetherby Athletic	Whitkirk Wanderers
Aberford Albion	P	2-3	0-4	1-2	1-3	1-3	1-1	1-2	1-1	1-0	2-1	3-3	1-0	2-2	2-0	1-4
Bardsey	2-2	R	3-1	2-0	5-1	8-0	0-0	4-2	3-2	1-2	5-2	3-0	1-2	6-3	0-4	0-0
Beeston St Anthony's	2-1	0-2	E	2-3	2-4	7-3	3-5	2-1	2-1	4-0	2-1	1-5	4-1	1-1	4-0	
Boroughbridge	3-4	2-4	0-1	M	1-3	2-0	0-1	0-0	1-1	1-1	2-1	2-4	3-1	4-0	2-2	0-1
Carlton Athletic	0-0	2-3	0-1	1-1	I	0-0	0-3	3-1	1-4	1-1	2-1	4-2	1-1	5-0	3-2	5-1
Horsforth St Margaret's	0-4	1-1	1-3	3-2	3-3	E	2-1	0-1	2-3	1-1	0-1	3-0	1-4	1-2	1-1	2-3
Howden Clough	0-0	2-4	1-5	1-1	0-2	0-0	R	0-1	3-2	1-1	3-1	3-1	5-2	6-1	4-1	3-0
Knaresborough Town	0-0	2-3	0-2	0-1	0-1	1-2	1-4		2-2	0-1	2-0	1-0	1-0	2-0	2-2	1-1
Leeds Metropolitan Carnegie	2-1	1-2	4-4	0-1	4-5	8-1	0-1	2-0	D	6-0	6-1	5-1	2-0	2-0	2-3	7-2
Ossett Common Rovers	0-2	0-1	2-7	2-4	0-0	3-1	1-2	3-1	0-5	I	0-1	2-2	1-1	1-0	2-2	1-2
Pontefract Sports & Social	0-2	2-1	0-2	4-3	1-2	2-3	2-0	1-3	1-7	1-1	V	3-1	0-3	3-3	2-1	0-1
Rothwell Athletic	1-1	0-5	0-2	1-2	2-2	0-1	4-1	1-2	1-1	3-1	4-1	I	2-1	0-1	1-1	3-2
Sherburn White Rose	4-1	2-0	0-0	1-0	2-1	2-1	1-2	2-0	1-2	1-2	1-0	1-0	S	1-2	1-2	1-0
Street Work Soccer	0-2	1-3	0-2	1-1	2-2	1-1	1-3	0-0	1-2	2-0	4-1	0-0	1-1	I	4-1	3-3
Wetherby Athletic	4-2	2-6	1-3	1-1	3-1	2-2	1-4	1-1	0-2	0-1	1-1	0-3	1-3	1-4	O	2-0
Whitkirk Wanderers	2-1	2-4	1-2	3-5	2-0	1-1	0-1	4-0	4-3	4-2	2-4	0-3	2-5	3-1	4-2	N

Premier Division

Premier Division		P	W	D	L	F	A	Pts
Bardsey		30	21	4	5	85	42	67
Beeston St Anthony's		30	21	3	6	80	42	66
Howden Clough		30	17	6	7	61	39	57
Leeds Met. Carnegie		30	16	5	9	89	45	53
Carlton Athletic		30	13	9	8	58	49	48
Sherburn White Rose		30	14	4	12	46	40	46
Boroughbridge		30	11	8	11	50	47	41
Aberford Albion	+3	30	9	9	12	43	49	39
Rothwell Athletic		30	9	7	14	48	55	34
Whitkirk Wdrs	-6	30	12	4	14	54	67	34
Knaresborough Town		30	9	7	14	30	43	34
Street Work Soccer		30	8	8	14	42	63	32
Horsforth St Marg.	+3	30	7	8	15	40	49	32
Ossett Common Rov.		30	7	9	14	32	58	30
Wetherby Athletic		30	6	10	14	45	65	28
Pontefract Spts & S.		30	8	3	19	39	69	27

Alliance Division One

	P	W	D	L	F	A	Pts
Beeston St Anthony's Res.	22	18	4	0	76	19	58
Whitkirk Wanderers Res.	22	12	5	5	52	27	41
Rothwell Athletic Res.	22	11	7	4	53	33	40
Boroughbridge Res.	22	12	3	7	52	29	39
Ripon City Magnets Res.	22	9	6	7	66	39	33
Sherburn White Rose Res.	22	10	3	9	46	38	33
Knaresborough Town Res.	22	8	4	10	49	55	28
Bardsey Res.	22	7	7	8	44	50	28
Aberford Albion Res.	22	8	4	10	35	54	28
Ossett Common Rovers Res.	22	5	5	12	31	42	20
Wetherby Athletic Res.	22	3	3	16	23	82	12
Tadcaster Magnet Sports Res.	22	3	1	18	23	82	10

Churwell Lions Res. – record expunged

Alliance Division Two

		P	W	D	L	F	A	Pts
Robin Hood Athletic Res.		28	21	1	6	100	35	64
Hartshead Res.		28	19	1	8	69	46	58
Altofts Res.		28	16	6	6	83	46	54
Kippax Athletic Res.		28	16	3	9	84	57	51
Old Headingley Res.		28	14	6	8	67	47	48
Otley Town Res.		28	14	3	11	58	61	45
Field Res.		28	13	5	10	69	50	44
Horbury Town Res.		28	11	6	11	64	75	39
Woodhouse Hill WMC Res.		28	10	8	10	65	69	38
Ilkley Res.		28	10	3	15	58	55	33
Rothwell Town Res.	-3	28	10	3	15	52	58	30
Baildon Trinity Athletic Res.		28	7	9	12	31	52	30
Kippax Welfare Res.		28	6	6	16	41	82	24
Barwick Res.		28	6	5	17	50	110	23
Sandy Lane Res.		28	2	5	21	26	74	11

WEST YORKSHIRE LEAGUE PREMIER DIVISION CONSTITUTION 2007-08

ABERFORD ALBION.................Bunkers Hill, Main Street (South), Aberford LS25 3DE.................None
BARDSEY.................The Sportsfield, Keswick Lane, Bardsey LS17 9AQ.................01937 574286
BEESTON ST ANTHONY'S.........Beggars Hill, Sunnyview Gdns, Beeston Road, Beeston, Leeds.........0113 270 7223
BOROUGHBRIDGE.................Aldborough Road, Boroughbridge, York YO51 9EA.................01423 324206
CARLTON ATHLETIC.........Carlton Cricket Club, Town Street, Carlton, Wakefield WF3 3QU.........0113 282 1114
FIELD SPORTS & SOCIAL.....Field Sports Ground, Hollingwood Lane, Lidget Green, Bradford BD7 2RQ.....01274 546726
HORSFORTH ST MARGARET'S..Cragg Hill Rec Ground, off Ring Road, Horsforth, Leeds LS18 4NT.................None
HOWDEN CLOUGH.................Batley Sports Centre, Windmill Lane, Batley WF17 0QD.................01924 326181
KNARESBOROUGH TOWN.................Manse Lane, Knaresborough HG5 8LF.................07773 679971
OSSETT COMMON ROVERS.........Illingworth Park, Manor Road, Ossett WF5 0LH.................None
POOL.................Arthington Lane, Pool-in-Wharfedale, Otley LS21.................0113 284 3932
ROTHWELL ATHLETIC.........Royds Lane, Rothwell, Leeds.........Club HQ: 0113 282 0723
SHERBURN WHITE ROSE.......Recreation Ground, Finkle Hill, Sherburn-in-Elmet, Leeds LS25 6EB.................None
STREET WORK SOCCER.........Buslingthorpe Rec Ground, Saville Drive, Chapeltown, Leeds LS7 3EJ.................None
WETHERBY ATHLETIC......Wetherby Sports Association, The Ings, Boston Road, Wetherby LS22 5HA.................01937 585699
WHITKIRK WANDERERS......Whitkirk Sports & Social Club, Selby Road, Whitkirk, Leeds LS15 0AA.................0113 264 6623
IN: Field Sports & Social (P), Pool (P)
OUT: Leeds Metropolitan Carnegie (P – Northern Counties East League Division One), Pontefract Sports & Social (R)

	Altofts	Barwick	Churwell Lions	Field Sports & Social	Hartshead	Ilkley	Kellingley Welfare	Kippax Athletic	Old Headingley	Otley Town	Pool	Ripon City Magnets	Robin Hood Athletic	Sandy Lane	Tadcaster Magnet S.	Woodhouse Hill
Altofts		3-0	2-2	1-2	2-0	3-1	2-2	0-1	0-2	1-2	3-0	1-2	3-1	6-2	1-0	4-4
Barwick	0-4		1-2	0-8	0-5	0-2	0-6	3-2	3-4	3-5	1-2	1-2	3-5	0-2	1-0	2-4
Churwell Lions	1-3	7-1	D	3-3	2-0	0-4	0-3	2-0	3-0	3-5	1-4	2-2	2-0	4-3	3-1	3-1
Field Sports & Social	6-1	4-0	5-6	I	1-1	2-3	2-1	4-0	1-0	0-0	2-0	5-0	4-1	3-1	3-1	2-0
Hartshead	4-1	5-1	1-0	1-4	V	6-0	1-0	2-4	1-3	1-2	1-1	2-3	5-1	6-0	3-1	2-1
Ilkley	1-3	5-0	3-2	1-3	3-0	I	4-3	1-4	3-1	2-4	0-2	0-1	1-1	4-2	3-0	4-2
Kellingley Welfare	6-2	5-1	2-1	0-2	0-1	1-1	S	1-6	0-2	2-3	1-5	1-2	2-4	4-2	2-1	2-0
Kippax Athletic	0-2	13-0	4-1	0-3	2-4	0-0	5-2	I	2-0	4-2	3-2	3-3	2-2	2-2	5-0	5-1
Old Headingley	1-1	4-4	3-0	4-2	3-1	1-0	2-4	1-2	O	2-1	0-1	2-0	6-2	3-1	0-1	1-0
Otley Town	6-0	4-0	4-2	2-2	2-1	1-1	3-1	5-3	0-1	N	0-3	2-1	3-1	2-1	2-0	0-0
Pool	2-1	5-3	2-2	1-5	5-2	1-0	2-1	1-0	5-1	3-2		3-2	3-1	0-2	5-3	6-0
Ripon City Magnets	2-0	10-0	2-0	3-2	2-0	1-1	2-0	1-2	2-3	2-0	0-2	O	8-0	5-1	5-2	3-1
Robin Hood Athletic	7-4	3-2	2-1	2-1	4-1	1-1	3-1	3-4	3-4	2-1	1-2	1-1	N	1-1	4-1	2-1
Sandy Lane	5-2	4-2	0-5	0-5	5-3	2-3	2-5	0-7	1-2	2-2	1-2	2-3	2-1	E	2-0	4-2
Tadcaster Magnet Sports	1-1	6-1	0-6	0-1	0-2	1-6	0-2	2-1	1-2	0-1	2-4	1-4	2-0	4-3		5-0
Woodhouse Hill WMC	2-2	7-1	1-1	2-5	2-1	1-1	2-3	1-2	0-3	0-2	1-3	1-2	4-3	3-1	3-3	

Division One	P	W	D	L	F	A	Pts
Pool	30	23	3	4	77	40	72
Field Sports & Social	30	21	5	4	92	33	68
Ripon City Magnets	30	19	5	6	77	38	62
Old Headingley	30	19	2	9	61	48	59
Otley Town	30	17	5	8	68	46	56
Kippax Athletic	30	17	4	9	89	49	55
Ilkley	30	12	8	10	58	49	44
Hartshead	30	13	2	15	63	55	41
Churwell Lions	30	12	5	13	67	62	41
Robin Hood Athletic	30	12	4	14	63	77	40
Altofts	30	11	6	13	59	65	39
Kellingley Welfare	30	12	2	16	62	64	38
Sandy Lane	30	8	2	20	56	94	26
Woodhouse Hill WMC	30	5	6	19	47	78	21
Tadcaster Magnet Spts	30	6	2	22	39	76	20
Barwick	30	2	1	27	34	138	7

WWW.CHERRYRED.CO.UK

LEAGUE CUP

FIRST ROUND
Bardsey 4 Robin Hood Athletic 2
Barwick 1 **Pontefract Sports & Social** 2
Boston Spartans 3 Nostell Miners Welfare 1
Carlton Athletic 2 Knaresborough Town 1
Horsforth St Margaret's 1 **Field Sports & Social** 3
Ilkley 4 Wyke Wanderers 1
Kippax Athletic 3 **Boroughbridge** 4
Old Headingley 0 **Whitkirk Wanderers** 1
Ossett Common Rovers 2 Mount St Mary's 0
Otley Town 1 **Horbury Town** 2
Rothwell Athletic 1 **Beeston St Anthony's** 4
Rothwell Town 3 Great Preston 0
Sandy Lane 2 **Stanley United** 3
Sherburn White Rose 4 East End Park WMC 0
Swillington Saints 2 **Baildon Trinity Athletic** 3
Tadcaster Magnet Sports 0 **Featherstone Colliery** 2
SECOND ROUND
Bardsey 4 Ossett Common Rovers 2
Beeston St Anthony's 2 Carlton Athletic 1
Boroughbridge 5 Horbury Town 1
Boston Spartans 0 **Aberford Albion** 4
Featherstone Colliery 6 Upper Armley Old Boys 0
Field Sports & Social 4 Sherburn White Rose 0
Hartshead 2 **Leeds City** 4
Kippax Welfare 0 **Leeds Metropoitan Carnegie** 8
Pool (w/o) v Altofts (scr.)

WEST YORKSHIRE LEAGUE DIVISION ONE CONSTITUTION 2007-08
ALTOFTS . . . . Altofts Sports Club, Lock Lane, Altofts, Normanton WF6 2QJ 01924 892708
CHURWELL LIONS . . . . Bruntcliffe High School, Bruntcliffe Lane, Morley, Leeds LS27 0LZ . . . . None
HARTSHEAD . . . . Littletown Recreation Ground, Hartshead 01274 873368
HORBURY TOWN . . . . Slazengers Sports Complex, Engine Lane, Horbury, Wakefield WF4 5NH 01924 274228
ILKLEY TOWN . . . . Denton Road, Ilkley LS29 0AA . . . . None
KELLINGLEY WELFARE . . Kellingley (Knottingley) Social Centre, Marine Villa Road, Knottingley, Wakefield WF11 8ER 01977 673113
KIPPAX ATHLETIC . . . . Rear of Swillington Miners Welfare, Wakefield Road, Swillington LS26 8DT . . . . None
LEEDS CITY . . . . Adel WMA, Church Lane, Adel, Leeds LS16 8DE. 0113 293 0528
NOSTELL MINERS WELFARE RESERVES . . Miners Welfare Ground, Middle Lane, New Crofton, Wakefield WF4 1LB 01924 862340
OLD HEADINGLEY . . . . Collington & Linton SA, Harewood Road, Collingham, Wetherby L22 5BL . . . . None
OTLEY TOWN. . . . . Old Show Ground, Pool Road, Otley LS20 1DY 01943 451029
PONTEFRACT SPORTS & SOCIAL . . Willow Park School, Harewood Avenue, Pontefract WF8 2ER . . . . None
RIPON CITY. . . . . Mallorie Park Drive, Ripon HG4 2QD 01765 60054
ROBIN HOOD ATHLETIC. . . . . Behind Coach & Horses, Rothwell Haigh, Leeds LS26 0SF 0113 282 102
SANDY LANE. . . . . Marley Stadium, Marley Road, Keighley, West Yorkshire BD21 4LY . . . . None
WOODHOUSE HILL WMC . . . . . Woodlands School Playing Field, Wakefield Road, Normanton WF6 1BB 01924 89346
IN: Horbury Town (P), Leeds City (P), Nostell Miners Welfare Reserves (P), Pontefract Sports & Social (P)
OUT: Barwick (R), Field Sports & Social (P), Pool (P), Tadcaster Magnet Sports (R)
Ripon City Magnets become Ripon City

Note – Upper Armley Old Boys withdrew during the course of the season

Their results are shown herein but are expunged from the league table

	Baildon Trinity Athletic	Boston Spartans	East End Park WMC	Featherstone Colliery	Great Preston	Horbury Town	Hunslet	Kippax Welfare	Leeds City	Mount St Mary's	Nostell Miners W. Res.	Rothwell Town	Stanley United	Swillington Saints	Upper Armley Old Boys	Wyke Wanderers
Baildon Trinity Athletic		0-1	1-1	2-2	7-0	2-4	0-1	5-0	0-3	2-2	3-1	2-3	1-2	2-2	4-1	5-0
Boston Spartans	0-2		3-1	4-2	3-3	1-1	2-1	7-2	0-6	2-2	1-2	1-0	4-2	4-0	2-1	1-2
East End Park WMC	3-1	0-2	D	4-0	3-1	1-2	1-1	5-2	2-1	4-1	3-3	5-2	1-1	4-0	5-0	2-2
Featherstone Colliery	1-2	1-2	2-4	I	5-3	0-3	1-3	2-0	3-2	3-2	0-3	1-1	4-5	5-2	n/a	4-2
Great Preston	0-5	0-1	3-4	0-1	V	1-6	2-4	1-2	2-4	0-1	0-2	1-1	1-3	1-2	1-2	1-1
Horbury Town	4-1	5-2	4-3	2-1	5-2	I	4-0	4-4	5-3	3-3	4-2	4-1	4-3	5-2	n/a	2-0
Hunslet	1-2	1-2	2-1	1-3	6-2	2-3	S	3-0	3-2	1-2	1-5	2-2	2-2	2-0	n/a	2-0
Kippax Welfare	1-7	1-2	3-4	0-1	0-2	2-3	2-0	I	1-2	0-3	1-3	2-3	3-3	0-2	n/a	2-1
Leeds City	5-0	6-0	5-2	7-0	3-1	2-0	1-1	8-1	O	7-3	3-1	1-3	1-3	4-1	7-1	0-1
Mount St Mary's	4-3	0-3	2-1	1-2	3-0	0-3	3-4	3-2	3-3	N	2-5	3-1	0-1	1-5	5-0	0-1
Nostell Miners Welfare Res.	4-0	6-2	3-0	1-1	6-2	7-3	4-2	3-2	3-1	2-2		0-1	4-1	1-1	n/a	1-1
Rothwell Town	0-1	0-5	1-2	0-5	5-1	0-3	2-2	2-2	0-0	0-4	2-2	T	2-6	3-2	n/a	0-3
Stanley United	2-2	1-2	1-1	6-1	1-1	1-3	0-1	8-0	0-2	2-2	5-6	4-1	W	1-2	n/a	4-0
Swillington Saints	1-2	0-1	2-3	0-1	0-1	2-5	4-7	2-0	0-7	0-2	4-4	3-3	2-3	O	4-0	1-0
Upper Armley Old Boys	n/a	n/a	n/a	n/a	n/a	n/a	1-4	1-1	0-3	n/a	1-4	1-4	0-6	n/a		1-4
Wyke Wanderers	0-2	3-3	0-3	0-0	3-2	2-2	1-3	2-1	3-2	1-2	3-3	4-1	1-5	1-2	n/a	

Pontefract Sports & Social 1 Ilkley 3
Ripon City Magnets 3 **Wetherby Athletic** 4
Rothwell Town 5 Hunslet 2
Stanley United 1 **Baildon Trinity Athletic** 3
Street Works Soccer 0 **Howden Clough** 3
Woodhouse Hill WMC 1 **Kellingley Welfare** 6
Whitkirk Wanderers 5 Churwell Lions 1

THIRD ROUND
Featherstone Colliery 1 **Boroughbridge** 3
Field Sports & Social 1 Leeds Metropolitan Carnegie 1 *aet* (7-6p)
Ilkley 1 **Pool** 5
Kellingley Welfare 2 **Beeston St Anthony's** 4
Leeds City 7 Baildon Trinity Athletic 1
Rothwell Town 1 **Aberford Albion** 2
Wetherby Athletic 0 **Bardsey** 3
Whitkirk Wanderers 4 Howden Clough 2

QUARTER-FINALS
Bardsey 6 Aberford Albion 1
Boroughbridge 2 **Leeds City** 4
Field Sports & Social 2 Pool 1 *aet*
Whitkirk Wanderers 0 **Beeston St Anthony's** 1

SEMI-FINALS
Beeston St Anthony's 5 Field Sports & Social 0 (at Nostell MW)
Leeds City 2 **Bardsey** 5 (at Nostell Miners Welfare)

FINAL
(May 5th at Wetherby Athletic)
Bardsey 1 Beeston St Anthony's 1 *aet* (5-4p)

Division Two	P	W	D	L	F	A	Pts
Horbury Town	28	22	4	2	95	50	70
Leeds City	28	18	4	6	98	38	58
Nostell Miners Welfare Res.	28	17	7	4	88	50	58
Boston Spartans	28	17	4	7	61	50	55
East End Park WMC	28	14	6	8	68	49	48
Hunslet	28	14	4	10	62	54	46
Stanley United	28	13	6	9	75	54	45
Baildon Trinity Athletic	28	12	5	11	62	48	41
Featherstone Colliery	28	12	4	12	50	62	40
Mount St Mary's	28	10	8	10	54	60	38
Wyke Wanderers	28	6	7	15	37	59	25
Rothwell Town	28	6	7	15	41	70	25
Swillington Saints	28	6	5	17	42	74	23
Kippax Welfare	28	3	2	23	32	93	11
Great Preston	28	2	3	23	34	88	9

Upper Armley Old Boys – record expunged

LEAGUE TROPHY

FINAL
(April 27th at Altofts)
Whitkirk Wanderers Res. 3 Aberford Albion Res. 1

WWW.NLNEWSDESK.CO.UK

WEST YORKSHIRE LEAGUE DIVISION TWO CONSTITUTION 2007-08

BAILDON TRINITY ATHLETIC........The Dell, Cliffe Lane, West Baildon, Shipley BD17 5LB .... None
BARWICK.................... Back of Village Hall, Chapel Lane, Barwick-in-Elmet, Leeds LS15 4HL......... Club HQ: 0113 281 3065
BOSTON SPARTANS .... Stables Lane, Boston Spa, Wetherby LS23 6BX .... None
BRIGHOUSE OLD BOYS..... Lightcliffe & Hipperholme School, Stoney Lane, Lightcliffe, Halifax HX3 8TL 01422 201028
EAST END PARK WMC .... Skelton Road, Leeds LS9 9EP .... None
FEATHERSTONE COLLIERY .. Featherstones MW, Cresseys Corner, Green Lane, Featherstone WF7 6EH .... None
GREAT PRESTON......................... Berry Lane, Great Preston LS25 8AX .... None
HUNSLET .... Community Sports Club, Anchor Street, Hunslet Green, Leeds LS10 2AT.................. 0113 270 6851
MOUNT ST MARY'S............ David Young Academy, off North Parkway, Seacroft, Leeds LS14 6NU ..... None
OLD CENTRALIANS........... West Park Playing Fields, North Parade, West Park, Leeds LS16 5AY......................... None
ROTHWELL TOWN.................. off Fifth Avenue, Leeds Road, Rothwell, Leeds LS26 0HG .... None
STANLEY UNITED............... Welfare Sports Ground, Saville Road, Methley, Leeds LS26 0DT .... None
SWILLINGTON SAINTS .... Welfare Sports Ground, Wakefield Road, Swillington, Leeds LS26 8DT .... None
TADCASTER MAGNET SPORTS .. Magnet Sports & Social Club, Queens Gardens, Tadcaster LS24 9HD 01937 833435
WYKE WANDERERS .. The Albert Morton Playing Fields, New Popplewell Lane, Scholes, Cleckheaton BD19 6NN................. None
IN: Barwick (R), Brighouse Old Boys (P – Halifax & District League Premier Division), Old Centralians (P – Yorkshire Old Boys League Senior Division B), Tadcaster Magnet Sports (R)
OUT: Horbury Town (P), Kippax Welfare (W), Leeds City (P), Nostell Miners Welfare Reserves (P), Upper Armley Old Boys (WS)

WESTERN LEAGUE

	Barnstaple T.	Bideford	Bishop Sutton	Bitton	Bridgwater T.	Brislington	Bristol MF	Calne Town	Chard Town	Corsham Town	Dawlish Town	Devizes Town	Frome Town	Hallen	Keynsham T.	Melksham T.	Odd Down	Radstock T.	Street	Torrington	Welton Rovers	Willand Rov.
Barnstaple Town		0-3	2-1	3-0	2-3	2-1	3-2	0-2	3-2	1-1	3-3	2-2	2-4	1-3	2-0	0-0	1-0	4-2	4-3	2-0	5-3	2-3
Bideford	1-1		3-0	2-1	1-2	2-0	3-2	3-1	4-2	2-2	3-0	1-0	0-1	1-2	2-3	2-2	0-2	1-0	3-0	3-0	6-2	4-2
Bishop Sutton	0-3	0-4		1-0	0-5	1-1	1-0	0-2	0-2	3-3	1-3	2-1	2-3	2-5	2-0	1-0	3-1	0-5	1-2	2-0	0-4	1-2
Bitton	2-1	1-4	2-1	P	1-2	5-0	1-1	1-2	1-0	1-1	6-1	2-1	0-2	1-1	2-1	1-1	1-0	3-1	0-0	6-0	1-0	1-1
Bridgwater Town	3-3	1-1	2-0	1-1	R	5-0	3-0	5-1	7-0	0-0	2-1	3-1	0-2	4-2	3-0	1-0	2-0	2-0	0-0	1-0	1-0	2-0
Brislington	0-1	0-5	1-0	1-2	1-0	E	0-0	1-1	1-0	0-1	2-1	1-1	2-5	1-2	1-1	0-1	1-1	1-5	3-0	0-1	0-2	0-2
Bristol Manor Farm	1-1	0-0	1-0	1-1	1-1	1-1	M	2-0	3-2	0-1	0-1	0-0	1-2	1-2	2-0	2-0	0-1	3-0	2-1	4-1	1-1	2-2
Calne Town	1-3	0-0	4-0	2-3	2-3	1-1	2-3	I	2-1	0-1	0-0	1-2	1-1	2-1	2-0	2-2	0-1	2-1	2-0	4-2	0-1	1-2
Chard Town	1-2	1-2	1-0	2-3	2-0	0-5	2-2	1-1	E	1-0	1-0	1-2	0-2	1-2	2-2	3-3	2-0	0-0	3-3	5-1	1-1	2-1
Corsham Town	1-0	0-2	1-0	2-1	0-0	2-0	2-0	1-0	3-1	R	3-1	1-0	1-0	2-0	4-0	1-0	3-0	1-0	2-0	4-0	0-6	1-2
Dawlish Town	0-1	3-0	2-2	3-2	1-2	0-3	1-1	3-1	1-1	1-6		4-1	0-2	4-0	0-0	0-1	1-1	0-1	3-1	0-3	3-1	3-0
Devizes Town	5-0	2-0	4-1	0-0	3-0	1-1	0-1	0-3	2-0	1-5	0-0	D	1-0	1-1	2-1	0-1	0-5	2-2	1-0	2-4	0-0	0-2
Frome Town	3-0	1-0	2-0	2-1	0-2	2-2	2-0	2-1	4-0	2-2	3-1	3-1	I	2-3	4-2	1-2	0-0	3-2	2-0	3-2	0-0	2-2
Hallen	2-0	5-0	3-2	0-1	0-1	0-0	0-1	1-0	3-1	1-1	1-2	1-4	1-0	V	4-1	7-2	3-0	1-2	1-3	1-3	2-2	0-4
Keynsham Town	0-1	2-6	2-2	1-4	1-2	0-1	2-1	1-0	1-2	0-5	0-4	1-3	1-6	0-3	I	2-0	0-5	4-1	4-1	0-0	0-4	0-1
Melksham Town	8-1	0-0	1-0	1-0	0-5	1-1	4-0	2-4	1-0	2-0	3-1	8-3	1-3	1-2	5-0	S	2-3	2-0	5-1	7-0	0-0	1-1
Odd Down	1-1	0-0	1-0	2-0	4-2	0-1	1-2	2-0	0-3	3-4	0-1	3-2	1-0	2-0	1-0	1-0	I	1-1	1-0	1-3	2-0	0-4
Radstock Town	0-1	3-2	1-1	2-1	2-4	1-4	2-1	0-6	1-4	1-1	0-1	2-1	0-2	1-0	1-0	2-3	4-2	O	2-3	4-2	0-2	0-0
Street	1-2	0-3	3-1	0-3	0-3	1-0	0-2	3-1	2-2	0-1	0-4	5-2	1-1	0-2	2-2	1-3	3-1	3-3	N	3-3	0-2	0-0
Torrington	1-3	1-6	0-2	1-2	0-4	2-4	2-1	2-1	1-0	1-2	2-7	2-1	0-3	1-2	1-1	0-3	1-1	1-1	1-3		1-1	0-1
Welton Rovers	1-2	1-2	0-1	0-1	1-0	0-0	2-0	1-1	1-1	1-3	0-1	1-2	1-1	3-0	0-1	1-2	1-3	3-0	0-1	1-1		0-1
Willand Rovers	1-1	2-1	5-0	2-0	0-2	2-0	2-0	0-1	2-0	1-1	0-1	2-1	3-1	0-1	1-1	5-1	0-4	3-1	1-2	1-2	2-2	

Premier Division	P	W	D	L	F	A	Pts
Corsham Town	42	29	9	4	81	30	96
Bridgwater Town	42	29	7	6	91	34	94
Frome Town	42	28	7	7	86	41	91
Bideford	42	23	8	11	88	48	77
Melksham Town	42	21	10	11	84	48	73
Willand Rovers	42	21	10	11	69	46	73
Barnstaple Town	42	21	9	12	72	71	72
Bitton	42	19	10	13	66	49	67
Hallen	42	20	7	15	72	60	67
Dawlish Town	42	17	8	17	73	66	59
Odd Down	42	17	7	18	50	53	58
Bristol Manor Farm	42	14	12	16	50	51	54
Calne Town	42	15	7	20	57	58	52
Devizes Town	42	14	10	18	58	70	52
Welton Rovers	42	12	15	15	54	47	51
Radstock Town	42	14	5	23	58	78	47
Brislington	42	11	13	18	44	61	46
Chard Town	42	9	11	22	51	78	38
Street	42	9	11	22	50	83	38
Torrington	42	9	6	27	46	105	33
Bishop Sutton	42	9	4	29	38	89	31
Keynsham Town	42	4	8	30	35	107	20

LES PHILLIPS CUP

PRELIMINARY ROUND

Barnstaple 3 Clyst Rovers 2
Bradford Town 2 **Weston St Johns** 3
Bridgwater Town 4 Larkhall Athletic 0
Cadbury Heath 3 Dawlish 1
Devizes Town (w/o) v Backwell United (scr.)
Elmore 1 **Calne Town** 4
Frome Town 4 Truro City 3
Melksham Town 5 Shepton Mallet 0
Odd Down 0 **Keynsham Town** 1
Portishead 2 **Bridport** 3
Torrington 5 Minehead Town 1

Westbury Utd 3 Ilfracombe Tn 1

FIRST ROUND

Barnstaple 1 **Frome Town** 6
Bideford 1 Biddestone 0
Bitton 0 **Bridgwater Town** 2
Bridport 0 **Chard Town** 3
Bristol Manor Farm 4 Street 2
Cadbury Heath 0 **Bishop Sutton** 2
Calne Town 2 Weston St Johns 1
Keynsham Town 0 **Hallen** 2
Melksham Town 2 Corsham Town 2 *aet* (3-1p)
Radstock Town 2 **Longwell Green Sports** 5
Sherborne Town 2 Almondsbury 1 *aet*

WESTERN LEAGUE PREMIER DIVISION CONSTITUTION 2007-08

BARNSTAPLE TOWN . . . . Mill Road, Barnstaple EX31 1JQ 01271 34346
BIDEFORD . . . . The Sports Ground, Kingsley Road, Bideford EX39 2LH 01237 47497
BISHOP SUTTON . . . . Lake View, Wick Road, Bishop Sutton, Bristol BS39 5XP 01275 33309
BITTON . . . . Recreation Ground, Bath Road, Bitton, Bristol BS30 6HX 0117 932 322
BRISLINGTON . . . . Ironmould Lane, Brislington, Bristol BS4 5SA 0117 977 403
BRISTOL MANOR FARM . . . . The Creek, Portway, Sea Mills, Bristol BS9 2HS 0117 968 491
CALNE TOWN . . . . Lickhill Road, Bremhill View, Calne SN11 8AE 01249 81918
CHARD TOWN . . . . Denning Sports Field, Zembard Lane, Chard TA20 1JL . . . . 01460 6140?
CORSHAM TOWN . . . . Southbank Ground, Lacock Road, Corsham SN13 9HS . . . . 01249 71560?
DAWLISH TOWN . . . . Playing Fields, Sandy Lane, Exeter Road, Dawlish EX7 0AF . . . . 01626 86311?
DEVIZES TOWN . . . . Nursteed Road, Devizes SN10 3EJ 01380 72281
FROME TOWN . . . . Badgers Hill, Berkley Road, Frome BA11 2EH. . . . . 01373 46408?
HALLEN . . . . Hallen Centre, Moorhouse Lane, Hallen, Bristol BS10 7RU 0117 950 555
ILFRACOMBE TOWN . . . . Marlborough Park, Marlborough Road, Ilfracombe EX34 8JB . . . . 01271 86593?
MELKSHAM TOWN . . . . The Conigre, Market Place, Melksham SN12 6ES 01225 70284
ODD DOWN . . . . Lew Hill Memorial Ground, Combe Hay Lane, Odd Down, Bath BA2 8PH 01225 83249
RADSTOCK TOWN . . . . Southfield Recreation Ground, Frome Hill, Radstock BA3 3NZ 01761 43500
STREET . . . . The Tannery Ground, Middlebrooks, Street BA16 0TA 01458 44498
TRURO CITY . . . . Treyew Road, Truro TR1 2TH 01872 27885
WELTON ROVERS . . . . West Clewes, North Road, Midsomer Norton BA3 2QD . . . . 01761 41209?
WILLAND ROVERS . . . . Silver Street, Willand, Cullompton EX15 2SL 01884 3388

IN: Ilfracombe Town (P), Truro City (P)
OUT: Bridgwater Town (P – Southern League Division One South), Keynsham Town (R), Torrington (W)

	Almondsbury	Backwell United	Biddestone	Bradford Town	Bridport	Cadbury Heath	Clevedon United	Clyst Rovers	Elmore	Hengrove Athletic	Ilfracombe Town	Larkhall Athletic	Longwell Green Sports	Minehead Town	Portishead	Shepton Mallet	Sherborne Town	Shrewton United	Truro City	Wellington Town	Westbury United	Weston St Johns
Almondsbury		2-1	0-2	3-2	0-3	2-1	3-0	0-0	0-1	0-2	0-4	1-0	1-1	0-2	0-0	0-2	1-3	0-1	0-1	2-3	2-0	
Backwell United	1-1		1-1	2-3	2-4	1-4	0-2	2-1	4-3	0-2	4-1	0-2	1-4	2-1	0-2	1-1	0-2	0-8	3-2	1-1		2-2
Biddestone	1-1	3-0		2-0	1-4	2-1	1-2	8-0	2-2	1-0	3-2	0-4	1-1	1-0	0-3	1-0	2-4	2-0	1-4	1-2	2-1	2-0
Bradford Town	2-0	0-1	2-0		1-3	2-3	1-2	1-1	2-1	2-0	0-3	1-2	0-1	1-1	1-7	0-2	1-2	3-1	0-3	1-3	0-1	2-0
Bridport	2-0	4-1	0-1	1-2		0-3	3-0	5-0	1-1	1-3	2-3	0-1	5-2	1-1	2-2	0-1	1-4	1-2	1-3			5-2
Cadbury Heath	0-4	0-1	2-2	3-0	1-2	D	5-0	1-1	1-2	2-1	2-3	1-1	0-0	3-2	1-0	0-0	3-1	3-2	0-4	0-0	2-1	5-0
Clevedon United	2-2	0-0	2-1	2-1	4-2	2-0	I	2-1	0-0	1-1	2-5	0-3	1-0	2-0	0-3	1-1	1-1	3-1	0-1	2-2	0-1	5-0
Clyst Rovers	1-2	3-3	2-1	6-0	2-3	0-4	0-3	V	2-2	3-3	1-2	1-1	4-1	0-2	1-3	0-2	1-5	0-0	1-2	1-1	5-3	
Elmore	1-0	1-1	0-3	0-2	3-3	4-4	3-1	1-6	I	2-1	3-3	1-1	3-1	2-3	0-3	2-2	0-3	3-2	1-10	0-2	1-2	3-1
Hengrove Athletic	2-1	0-1	4-2	2-0	1-0	2-0	2-2	1-0	1-2	S	0-0	3-3	4-2	2-1	3-2	2-0	2-3	0-0	2-3	2-0	1-1	2-0
Ilfracombe Town	4-2	4-3	3-0	3-1	4-3	5-2	3-2	2-0	5-0	3-0	I	0-2	5-0	3-1	0-1	1-2	1-2	3-0	3-0	3-0		
Larkhall Athletic	1-2	4-0	4-2	3-0	1-2	3-2	2-0	4-0	1-1	2-0	1-2	O	1-0	4-1	0-0	8-0	0-1	2-2	3-0	0-0	2-1	1-0
Longwell Green Sports	1-1	1-2	2-1	0-2	3-2	4-1	0-0	1-0	0-0	2-0	0-1	0-0	N	1-1	1-1	0-1	1-1	2-0	0-3	2-0	2-2	4-0
Minehead Town	2-2	1-1	1-1	0-1	2-4	4-2	2-1	2-3	0-2	1-2	0-2	0-3	0-2		0-3	0-1	0-2	1-1	0-3	0-1	2-1	3-1
Portishead	6-0	2-0	3-2	4-0	4-0	1-0	4-1	3-2	1-0	3-1	1-2	1-0	2-0	1-1	O	4-2	1-0	2-1	0-1	1-0	1-0	5-2
Shepton Mallet	0-5	0-3	0-0	2-0	0-5	0-2	0-2	2-3	3-3	1-0	0-1	0-3	1-2	0-1	0-1	N	1-1	1-1	0-4	1-1	2-0	0-1
Sherborne Town	5-0	4-1	1-1	3-1	2-0	3-1	2-1	5-1	2-1	1-0	5-2	4-0	1-2	3-1	2-0		E	1-2	0-2	3-1	1-1	2-2
Shrewton United	3-1	3-0	0-0	2-2	1-3	3-3	0-0	1-0	4-2	2-2	0-2	1-3	0-2	6-0	1-1	3-1	1-5		0-2	1-2	1-1	1-1
Truro City	7-1	15-0	7-3	8-0	6-0	3-1	3-0	11-2	2-0	3-2	5-1	1-2	3-0	12-0	3-0	8-0	1-1	8-1		6-0	7-0	4-0
Wellington Town	1-1	2-1	1-3	1-2	2-2	0-1	4-0	0-2	4-1	4-0	2-1	1-1	3-1	4-1	2-2	2-0	2-1	5-0	1-1		0-2	0-2
Westbury United	1-1	4-1	5-3	1-0	3-0	2-2	0-3	5-0	6-0	1-1	3-1	1-3	4-1	1-3	1-3	0-2	2-1	1-2	0-3	4-1		0-1
Weston St Johns	1-1	3-1	0-5	3-1	1-2	0-3	3-3	2-2	2-4	2-1	0-2	0-1	3-1	1-3	3-1	1-1	4-3	2-4	0-2	0-0	0-2	

Shrewton United 1 **Clevedon United 2**

Torrington 1 **Hengrove Athletic** 3

Wellington Town 2 Devizes 1

Welton Rovers 5 Brislington 0

Willand Rovers 2 Westbury 1

SECOND ROUND

Bishop Sutton 3 Clevedon United 1

Bristol Manor Farm 1 **Willand Rovers** 2

Calne Town 1 **Hallen** 1 *aet* (4-5p)

Chard Town 1 Bideford 0

Frome 1 **Melksham Town** 2

Hengrove Athletic 1 **Longwell Green Sports** 4

Sherborne Town 1 **Bridgwater Town** 2

Wellington 0 **Welton Rovers** 2

QUARTER-FINALS

Bishop Sutton 1 Longwell Green Sports 0

Bridgwater Town 0 **Willand Rovers** 0 *aet* (6-7p)

Chard Town 0 **Hallen** 3

Melksham Town 0 **Welton Rovers** 4 *aet* (4-5p)

SEMI-FINALS

Hallen 0 **Welton Rovers** 1

Willand Rovers 3 Bishop Sutton 0

FINAL

(May 20th at Shepton Mallet)

Willand Rovers 2 Welton Rovers 0

Division One

	P	W	D	L	F	A	Pts
Truro City	42	37	4	1	185	23	115
Portishead	42	29	6	7	88	33	93
Ilfracombe Town	42	29	5	8	98	51	92
Sherborne Town	42	25	8	9	87	44	83
Larkhall Athletic	42	24	8	10	88	41	80
Westbury United	42	19	10	13	71	57	67
Wellington Town	42	18	9	15	63	60	63
Longwell Green Spts	42	17	11	14	51	44	62
Cadbury Heath	42	17	9	16	78	69	60
Hengrove Athletic	42	17	7	18	58	64	58
Bridport	42	17	6	19	84	81	57
Shrewton United	42	15	11	16	65	71	56
Biddestone	42	15	9	18	69	73	54
Clevedon United	42	14	12	16	54	69	54
Almondsbury	42	11	11	20	47	73	44
Elmore	42	10	14	18	62	94	44
Bradford Town	42	12	4	26	42	86	40
Backwell United	42	10	8	24	48	105	38
Weston St Johns	42	8	10	24	47	93	34
Shepton Mallet	42	8	10	24	34	83	34
Clyst Rovers	42	8	9	25	61	108	34
Minehead Town	42	7	9	26	42	100	30

WWW.NLNEWSDESK.CO.UK

WESTERN LEAGUE DIVISION ONE CONSTITUTION 2007-08

ALMONDSBURY .... Almondsbury S & S Centre, Gloucester Road, Almondsbury BS34 4AA 01454 612240
BACKWELL UNITED .... The Playing Fields, West Town Road, Backwell, Bristol BS48 3HG 01275 462612
BRADFORD TOWN .... Avon Sports Ground, Trowbridge Road, Bradford-on-Avon BA15 1EE 01225 866649
BRIDPORT .... St Marys Field, Skilling Hill Road, Bridport DT6 5LN 01308 423834
CADBURY HEATH .... Springfield, Cadbury Heath Road, Warmley, Bristol BS30 8BX 0117 967 5731
CLEVEDON UNITED ...... Clevedon Town FC, The Hand Stadium, Davis Way, Clevedon BS21 6TG 01275 341913
ELMORE .... Horsdon Park, Heathcoat Way, Tiverton EX16 4DB 01884 252341
HENGROVE ATHLETIC .... Norton Lane, Whitchurch, Bristol BS14 0BT 01275 832894
KEYNSHAM TOWN .... Crown Field, Bristol Road, Keynsham, Bristol BS31 2BE 0117 986 5876
LARKHALL ATHLETIC .... Plain Ham, Charlcombe Lane, Larkhall, Bath BA1 8DJ 01225 334952
LONGWELL GREEN SPORTS .. Longwell Green Comm. Centre, Shellards Rd, Longwell Green BS30 9DU .. 0117 932 5111
MINEHEAD TOWN .... Recreation Ground, Irnham Road, Minehead TA24 5DP 01643 704989
OLDLAND ABBOTONIANS .... Aitchinson Playing Field, Castle Road, Oldland Common BS30 9SZ 0117 932 8263
PORTISHEAD .... Bristol Road Playing Fields, Portishead, Bristol BS20 6QB 01275 847156
ROMAN GLASS ST GEORGE .... Bell Hill, Whiteway Road, St George, Bristol BS5 7RW 0117 983 7707
SHEPTON MALLET .... West Shepton Playing Fields, Old Wells Road, Shepton Mallet BA4 5XN 01749 344609
SHERBORNE TOWN .... Raleigh Grove, The Terrace Playing Fields, Sherborne DT9 5NS 01935 816110
SHREWTON UNITED .... Recreation Ground, Mill Lane, Shrewton, Salisbury SP3 4JU 07796 098122
WELLINGTON TOWN .... Wellington Playing Field, North Street, Wellington TA1 8NA 01823 664810
WESTBURY UNITED .... Meadow Lane, Westbury BA13 3AF 01373 823409
WESTON ST JOHNS .... Coleridge Road, Bournville Estate, Weston-super-Mare BS23 3UP 01934 612862
IN: Keynsham Town (R), Oldland Abbotonians (P – Somerset County League Premier Division), Roman Glass St George (P – Gloucestershire County League)
OUT: Biddestone (W), Clyst Rovers (S – South West Peninsular League Premier Division), Ilfracombe Town (P), Truro City (P)

WESTMORLAND LEAGUE

Note – Kendal Town Reserves withdrew during the course of the season

Their results are shown herein but are expunged from the league table

	Appleby	Burnside	Coniston	Greystoke	Ibis	Kendal County	Kendal Town Res.	Keswick	Lunesdale United	N'bank Carlisle Res.	Sedbergh Wanderers	Wetheriggs United	Windermere SC
Appleby		1-1	1-0	0-0	3-2	2-5	0-1	1-4	4-3	0-1	2-2	0-5	3-2
Burnside	1-0		5-0	4-3	3-0	2-3	3-2	1-4	3-0	1-0	5-1	0-0	1-2
Coniston	3-1	2-0	D	2-2	2-2	0-6	1-3	2-2	4-6	5-0	1-0	1-2	1-1
Greystoke	3-0	1-3	3-2	I	6-1	0-4	1-0	2-4	5-3	1-2	2-2	2-1	1-7
Ibis	0-2	2-1	0-1	3-3	V	1-3	1-1	1-1	3-3	2-3	3-2	3-7	0-3
Kendal County	8-1	4-1	3-0	4-0	5-1		5-0	3-1	8-1	4-1	5-0	3-2	4-1
Kendal Town Res.	0-2	0-0	7-0	0-1	1-1	0-0		n/a	2-5	4-0	3-2	0-3	n/a
Keswick	4-0	2-1	3-1	5-2	0-2	0-2			4-2	3-0	1-0	0-2	4-0
Lunesdale United	3-1	3-5	0-4	1-3	3-3	2-5	2-5	0-3	O	2-1	5-1	2-5	2-5
Northbank Carlisle Res.	3-1	2-0	1-3	2-5	4-1	0-4	2-0	1-2	6-6	N	1-3	5-2	0-2
Sedbergh Wanderers	0-3	3-5	1-4	1-4	1-0	1-3	n/a	0-7	3-5	2-1	E	1-2	1-5
Wetheriggs United	2-2	2-1	1-1	5-0	1-0	3-3	3-1	3-2	3-1	3-0	3-0		2-0
Windermere SC	6-0	0-0	0-1	4-0	4-2	0-4	5-1	0-0	5-3	1-1	4-0	2-0	

Division One

	P	W	D	L	F	A	Pts
Kendal County	22	21	1	0	93	20	64
Keswick	22	14	4	4	57	25	46
Wetheriggs United	22	14	4	4	56	29	46
Windermere SC	22	12	4	6	54	30	40
Burnside	22	10	3	9	44	35	33
Coniston	22	9	6	7	40	38	33
Greystoke	22	8	4	10	47	58	28
Northbank Carlisle Res.	22	7	2	13	35	53	23
Appleby	22	6	4	12	28	58	22
Lunesdale United	22	5	3	14	56	84	18
Ibis	22	2	5	15	32	66	11
Sedbergh Wanderers	22	3	2	17	25	71	11

Kendal Town Res. – record expunged

HIGH SHERIFF'S CUP

FIRST ROUND

Appleby 0 **Windermere SC** 4
Coniston 2 **Lunesdale United** 3
Kendal County 1 Greystoke 0
Northbank Carlisle Res. 4
Wetheriggs United 1
Sedbergh Wanderers 1 Kendal Town Res. 0 *(at Kendal Town)*

Sedbergh Wanderers 4 **Burnside** 4 *aet* (5-6p)
Windermere SC 1 **Kendal County** 2

QUARTER-FINALS

Keswick 3 Ibis 0
Lunesdale United 0 **Northbank Carlisle Res.** 1

SEMI-FINALS

Burnside 1 **Kendal County** 2
Keswick 3 Northbank Carlisle Res. 1

FINAL
(May 10th at Coniston)
Keswick 3 **Kendal County** 4

WESTMORLAND LEAGUE DIVISION ONE CONSTITUTION 2007-08

AMBLESIDE UNITED . . . . Hilliard Park, Millers Field, Ambleside LA22 9DH . . . . None
APPLEBY . . . . The Board Close, Chapel Street, Bolton, Appleby-in-Westmorland CA16 6QR . . . . None
BURNSIDE . . . . Cricket Pavilion, Hollins Lane, Burnside, Kendal LA9 6QL . . . . None
CARVETII UNITED . . . . Parrot Park, Hartley Road, Kirkby Stephen . . . . None
CONISTON . . . . Shepherds Bridge, Coniston LA21 8AL . . . . None
GREYSTOKE . . . . Greystoke Playing Field, Greystoke . . . . None
IBIS . . . . Millennium Field, Kendal . . . . None
KENDAL COUNTY . . . . Netherfield Cricket Club, Parkside Road, Kendal LA9 7BL 01539 724051
KESWICK . . . . Walker Park, Keswick . . . . None
LUNESDALE UNITED . . . . Recreation Ground, Orton Road, Tebay, Penrith CA10 3TL . . . . None
NORTHBANK CARLISLE RESERVES . . Sheepmount Sports Complex, Sheepmount, Carlisle CA3 8XL 01228 625599
SEDBERGH WANDERERS . . . . Havera Playing Field, Sedbergh LA10 5HD . . . . None
WETHERIGGS UNITED . . . . Gilwilly Recreation Ground, Castletown, Penrith . . . . None
WINDERMERE SC . . . . Queen's Park, Windermere . . . . None

IN: Ambleside United (P), Carvetii United (P)
OUT: Kendal Town Res. (WS)

Division Two

	P	W	D	L	F	A	Pts
Carvetii United	24	20	3	1	96	28	63
Ambleside United	24	16	6	2	85	28	54
Penrith Rangers	24	16	5	3	106	31	53
Kendal County Res.	24	14	2	8	62	34	44
Wetheriggs Utd Res.	24	13	2	9	52	33	41
Kirkoswald	24	11	5	8	49	34	38
Kendal Celtic	24	11	4	9	62	52	37
Keswick Res.	24	10	2	12	51	59	32
Windermere SC Res.	24	9	2	13	33	57	29
Staveley United	24	5	4	15	32	71	19
Ibis Res.	24	5	2	17	22	72	17
Sedbergh Wdrs Res. -6	24	5	3	16	27	84	12
Ullswater United	24	2	2	20	11	105	2

Division Three

	P	W	D	L	F	A	Pts
Shap	22	15	5	2	66	26	50
Dent	22	15	4	3	75	38	49
Carvetii United Res.	22	12	3	7	53	42	39
Wetheriggs Utd 'A'	22	10	3	9	57	46	33
Penrith United Res. -3	22	11	3	8	44	41	33
Burnside Res.	22	10	3	9	48	52	33
Lunesdale Utd Res.	22	8	6	8	57	47	30
Ambleside Utd Res. -3	22	10	2	10	37	57	29
Appleby Res.	22	8	4	10	37	36	28
Endmoor KGR	22	5	7	10	41	43	22
Penrith Rangers Res.	22	5	2	15	42	54	17
Braithwaite -3	22	0	2	20	22	97	-1

Division Four

	P	W	D	L	F	A	Pts
Shap Res.	18	16	0	2	65	16	48
Kendal United	18	15	1	2	68	25	46
Greystoke Res.	18	11	5	2	57	22	38
Kendal Celtic Res.	18	10	4	4	53	31	34
Endmoor KGR Res.	18	6	3	9	46	58	21
Windermere SC 'A'	18	5	3	10	47	49	18
Burnside 'A'	18	4	2	12	48	52	14
Staveley United Res.	18	3	1	14	27	71	10
Dent Res. -3	18	4	1	13	23	67	10
Coniston Res. -9	18	5	2	11	24	52	8

MASON & FREEMAN CUP
(May 8th at Kendal Town)
Ambleside Utd 1 **Carvetii United** 1 *aet* (5-6p)

PETER DAWS MEMORIAL SHIELD
(May 11th at Penrith)
Carvetii United Res. 4 Lunesdale United Res. 1

AUSTIN WREN CUP
(April 4th at Burnside)
Shap Res. 4 Kendal County Res. 1

WILTSHIRE LEAGUE

	AFC Trowbridge Town Youth	Blueprint Chiseldon	Bradford Town Res.	Bromham	Calne Town Res.	Corsham Town Res.	Devizes Town Res.	Malmesbury Victoria Res.	Marlborough Town	Melksham Town Res.	New College	Pewsey Vale Res.	Purton Res.	Shrewton United Res.	Westbury United Res.	Westside	Wroughton
AFC Trowbridge Town Youth	P	0-0	2-1	3-0	2-1	3-2	3-1	2-0	2-0	1-2	0-1	2-1	6-0	1-0	0-1	1-2	0-1
Blueprint Chiseldon	0-3	R	3-3	11-1	1-2	3-2	2-2	1-4	1-0	0-0	0-2	2-1	5-0	1-2	2-5	0-2	0-2
Bradford Town Res.	0-3	2-5	E	1-2	1-2	0-4	5-0	2-0	2-1	2-3	0-3	1-1	1-0	1-1	1-2	1-2	2-2
Bromham	1-2	1-4	2-2	M	1-6	1-3	0-1	1-2	4-2	0-2	0-4	2-7	5-2	1-1	1-2	0-3	0-5
Calne Town Res.	0-0	1-1	2-1	4-0	I	2-4	0-3	3-0	1-1	1-1	1-2	2-3	1-0	1-1	1-2	1-1	1-1
Corsham Town Res.	2-0	3-1	4-2	5-2	4-0	E	0-2	2-1	2-0	2-2	2-3	2-0	9-0	6-1	3-0	2-0	3-0
Devizes Town Res.	0-0	W-L	4-0	5-0	7-2	1-2	R	6-1	3-1	3-1	3-4	7-3	6-1	16-1	0-1	1-0	1-2
Malmesbury Victoria Res.	0-0	2-0	0-1	2-1	1-0	0-3	1-2		0-0	2-1	0-2	2-2	0-3	0-1	2-0		1-3
Marlborough Town	1-5	0-2	1-0	3-0	0-2	1-6	2-3	0-3		1-3	1-2	3-1	3-0	6-0	2-3	1-0	1-3
Melksham Town Res.	1-3	4-5	3-2	6-1	1-1	2-1	3-4	1-0	0-0	D	5-6	8-3	5-2	3-1	2-2	1-0	2-3
New College	0-1	0-3	0-1	11-1	7-0	1-2	0-3	2-4	1-2	0-1	I	2-1	7-0	10-1	1-1	5-2	1-0
Pewsey Vale Res.	1-1	1-2	3-3	0-1	1-2	0-2	1-0	1-1	2-2	3-5	2-1	V	2-0	1-2	3-0	2-0	1-3
Purton Res.	0-3	2-0	0-0	0-2	2-1	0-3	2-4	0-0	0-1	1-2	0-2	0-2	I	1-7	1-5	1-0	0-4
Shrewton United Res.	0-2	2-3	0-4	1-1	0-4	0-2	0-3	0-1	2-0	2-3	0-5	1-0	4-1	S	0-2	2-1	0-3
Westbury United Res.	2-0	0-0	1-1	1-0	0-2	1-1	1-0	4-0	3-0	2-0	1-1	3-0	5-1	5-1	I	2-0	0-3
Westside	3-0	3-1	5-1	2-2	1-0	1-3	0-4	0-1	2-3	0-3	0-2	2-2	3-0	2-0	1-0	O	1-3
Wroughton	1-0	1-0	2-0	3-0	1-3	0-1	2-2	7-0	3-0	0-3	3-0	0-0	1-1	10-1	0-0	3-0	N

Premier Division		P	W	D	L	F	A	Pts
Corsham Town Res.	-1	32	25	2	5	92	30	76
Wroughton		32	21	6	5	73	25	69
New College		32	21	4	7	90	35	67
Devizes Town Res.		32	21	3	8	97	41	66
Westbury United Res.	-6	32	20	7	5	55	26	61
Melksham Town Res.		32	18	5	9	82	57	59
AFC Trowbridge Youth	-3	32	18	5	9	51	25	56
Calne Town Res.		32	12	9	11	50	50	45
Blueprint Chiseldon	-1	32	12	6	14	60	55	41
Pewsey Vale Res.		32	10	7	15	52	60	37
Westside		32	11	3	18	42	52	36
Malmesbury Victoria Res.		32	10	5	17	27	53	35
Bradford Town Res.		32	7	8	17	44	63	29
Marlborough Town		32	8	4	20	38	63	28
Shrewton United Res.	-5	32	7	4	21	35	104	20
Bromham		32	5	4	23	34	106	19
Purton Res.	-1	32	3	4	25	21	98	12

WILTSHIRE LEAGUE PREMIER DIVISION CONSTITUTION 2007-08

AFC TROWBRIDGE TOWN YOUTH ..... Woodmarsh, North Bradley, Trowbridge BA14 0SA .... None
ALDBOURNE.................... Farm Lane, Aldbourne, Marlborough SN8 2DS .... None
BLUEPRINT CHISELDON..... Chiseldon Recreation Ground, Norris Close, Chiseldon, Swindon SN4 0LP. .... None
BRADFORD TOWN RESERVES .. Avon Sports Ground, Trowbridge Road, Bradford-on-Avon BA15 1EE 01225 866649
BROMHAM .... Jubilee Field, Bromham, Chippenham.......................... 01380 850671
CALNE TOWN RESERVES............... Lickhill Road, Bremhill View, Calne SN11 8AE 01249 819186
CORSHAM TOWN RESERVES .... Southbank Ground, Lacock Road, Corsham SN13 9HS 01249 715609
DEVIZES TOWN RESERVES..................... Nursteed Road, Devizes SN10 3EJ............................. 01380 722817
MALMESBURY VICTORIA RESERVES .. Flying Monk Ground, Gloucester Road, Malmesbury SN16 0AJ 01666 822141
MARLBOROUGH TOWN .... Elcot Lane, Marlborough SN8 2BG 01672 513340
MELKSHAM TOWN RESERVES .... The Conigre, Market Place, Melksham SN12 6ES 01225 702843
NEW COLLEGE............ Swindon Supermarine FC, Highworth Road, South Marston, Swindon SN3 4SF 01793 828778
PEWSEY VALE RESERVES .... Recreation Ground, Kings Corner, Ball Road, Pewsey SN9 5GF 01672 562990
PURTON RESERVES...................... The Red House, Church Street, Purton SN5 4DT.................. 01793 770262
SHREWTON UNITED RESERVES .... Recreation Ground, Mill Lane, Shrewton, Salisbury SP3 4JU 07796 098122
WESTBURY UNITED RESERVES.............. Meadow Lane, Westbury BA13 3AF............................. 01373 823409
WESTSIDE .... Southbrook Recreation Ground, Pinehurst Road, Swindon............... None
WROUGHTON .... The Weir Field, Wroughton WMC, Devizes Road, Wroughton SN4 0SA................ 01793 812319

IN: Aldbourne (Re-instated)
OUT: Aldbourne (WN)

SENIOR CUP
(Premier Division teams)

FIRST ROUND
Aldbourne (scr.) v **Pewsey Vale Res.** (w/o).
Shrewton United Res. 1 **Melksham Town Res.** 5
SECOND ROUND
Blueprint Chiseldon 1 **Westside** 2
Bromham 2 **Malmesbury Victoria Res.** 3
Corsham Town Res. 4 Pewsey Vale Res. 1
Devizes Town Res. 4 Bradford Town Res. 2
Marlborough Town 2 AFC Trowbridge Town Youth 4
(AFC Trowbridge Town Youth expelled)
Melksham Town Res. 3 Calne Town Res. 0
New College 0 **Purton Res.** 2
Westbury United Res. 0 **Wroughton** 2
QUARTER-FINALS
Corsham Town Res. 4 Westside 3
Marlborough Town 2 Malmesbury Victoria Res. 0
Melksham Town Res. 6 Purton Res. 1
Wroughton 0 **Devizes Town Res.** 2
SEMI-FINALS
Corsham Town Res. 2 Devizes Town Res. 0
Marlborough Town 2 **Melksham Town Res.** 2 *aet* (3-4p)
FINAL
(April 28th at Corsham Town)
Corsham Town Res. 4 Melksham Town Res. 2

Division One		P	W	D	L	F	A	Pts
AFC Castrol		26	20	3	3	93	37	63
Pinehurst Old Boys		26	17	6	3	75	40	57
Minety	-3	26	18	3	5	86	40	54
AFC Stratton		26	15	6	5	76	41	51
Stratton Rovers		24	13	4	7	68	43	43
AFC Abbey Rodbourne	-2	26	15	0	11	62	61	43
SKS Blyskawica	-3	26	13	1	12	64	65	37
Aldbourne Res.		26	8	3	15	48	61	27
Biddestone Res.	-4	24	9	3	12	69	56	26
AFC Rodbourne		26	8	1	17	73	105	25
Blunsdon United		26	7	2	17	41	69	23
Westlecot United		26	6	3	17	45	74	21
Castle Combe		26	3	10	13	38	69	19
Marlborough Town Res.	-1	26	4	3	19	33	110	14

Biddestone Res. v Stratton Rovers and Stratton Rovers v Biddestone Res. not played

Division Two		P	W	D	L	F	A	Pts
Lower Stratton		20	15	2	3	52	25	47
Stratton Juniors	-1	20	14	3	3	56	22	44
Wroughton Res.		20	13	1	6	54	29	40
Stratton Rovers Res.		20	11	1	8	52	36	34
Westlecot United Res.	-1	20	7	5	8	38	48	25
CHQ United.	-1	20	7	4	9	47	47	24
FC Chippenham		20	6	6	8	35	41	24
Bromham Res.	-1	20	6	4	10	23	49	21
Dynamo CDR	-2	20	6	2	12	36	48	18
Blunsdon United Res.	-1	20	4	4	12	28	47	15
Westside Res.	-1	20	4	2	14	26	55	13

JUNIOR CUP
(Division One and Two teams)

FINAL
(April 28th at Corsham Town)
SKS Blyskawica 3 Pinehurst Old Boys 1

OTHER LEAGUES

All league tables in this section are final.
It is the policy of some competitions to leave some oft postponed matches as unplayed if they do not affect end of season issues.

ABERYSTWYTH & DISTRICT LEAGUE

Division One	P	W	D	L	F	A	Pts
Bow Street	22	17	2	3	75	34	53
Tregaron Turfs	22	16	3	3	75	25	51
Penparcau	22	15	2	5	71	32	47
Bont	22	12	2	8	60	44	38
Dolgellau	22	9	6	7	49	39	33
P'rhyncoch Res. *-15*	22	14	3	5	60	28	30
Talybont	22	7	4	11	41	67	25
Llanrhystud	22	5	4	13	48	70	19
Llanilar	22	6	1	15	30	57	19
UW A'wyth Res.	22	5	4	13	35	65	19
Aberdyfi	22	5	2	15	40	87	17
Padarn United	22	4	1	17	26	62	13

Division Two	P	W	D	L	F	A	Pts
Aberystwyth T. 'A'	24	21	3	0	116	14	66
Tywyn/B'crug Res.	24	21	1	2	110	24	64
Penrhyncoch 'A'	24	13	7	4	63	34	46
Bow Street Res.	24	12	6	6	64	41	42
UW Aber'wyth 'A'	24	10	2	12	61	53	32
Machynlleth *-9*	24	12	1	11	57	61	28
Dolgellau Res.	24	8	3	13	45	56	27
Penparcau Res.	24	8	3	13	53	66	27
Trawsgoed	24	6	4	14	41	96	22
Llanon *-6*	24	7	6	11	39	67	21
Corris United	24	6	2	16	34	68	20
Talybont Res.	24	5	4	15	43	83	19
Llanilar Res.	24	5	2	17	33	96	17

ACCRINGTON & DISTRICT LEAGUE

Division One	P	W	D	L	F	A	Pts
Bridge Inn	18	18	0	0	86	17	54
Church Town *-4*	18	12	1	5	62	30	33
Brittania Padiham	18	8	3	7	30	29	27
Wellington *-6*	18	10	1	7	45	41	25
Baileys	18	7	4	7	46	45	25
Crown Rovers	18	6	3	9	33	36	21
Foxhill Falcons *-3*	18	6	1	11	39	59	16
Whinney Hill 'A'	18	4	3	11	26	71	15
Bold Street *-6*	18	6	1	11	37	40	13
Oswaldtwistle St M Res.	18	3	3	12	18	54	12

Division Two	P	W	D	L	F	A	Pts
Royal Hotel	22	19	1	2	111	36	58
Edenfield	22	19	1	2	102	31	58
King Street	22	16	2	4	109	36	50
Woolpack	22	13	2	7	81	53	41
Ramsbottom T. *-7*	22	14	2	6	66	43	37
Black Horse	22	10	1	11	60	60	31
Baxenden	22	7	4	11	52	59	25
Crown Rov. Res. *-3*	22	7	1	14	54	71	19
Acc. Loyal A. 'B' *-3*	22	6	3	13	63	83	18
Sydney Str. WMC	22	6	0	16	33	73	18
Churchtown Res. *-3*	22	5	2	15	32	91	14
NSD	22	0	1	21	16	143	1

✔ALTRINCHAM & DISTRICT LEAGUE

Division One	P	W	D	L	F	A	Pts
Broadh'th C. 'A' *-3*	18	14	2	2	71	26	41
King George	18	10	6	2	53	32	36
Knutsford Res.	18	11	2	5	66	33	35
Stretford Victoria	18	8	6	4	67	44	30
Quarry Bank	18	8	3	7	34	30	27
Atlantic	18	7	4	7	53	57	25
Trafford 'A'	18	7	3	8	42	46	24
Kartel Sports	18	4	1	13	29	59	13
Wyth'shawe Am 'A'	18	4	1	13	32	74	13
Brooklands	18	2	2	14	20	66	8

AFC Sale – record expunged

Division Two	P	W	D	L	F	A	Pts
Old York	22	16	2	4	92	42	50
Northenden Village	22	13	3	6	58	35	42
Northenden Victoria	22	13	3	6	54	38	42
Sale Rovers	22	13	2	7	66	34	41
Styal 'A'	22	12	2	8	57	40	38
Timperley Wdrs	22	9	4	9	44	35	31
Sale Amateurs	22	9	4	9	58	54	31
Salford AFC	22	7	2	13	49	73	23
Old Altrinchamians	22	6	4	12	34	71	22
Trafford United *-3*	22	7	2	13	50	65	20
Northern Moor	22	5	4	13	52	83	19
NCC Group *-3*	22	5	2	15	39	83	14

AMATEUR COMBINATION

Higher divisions on page 12

Int. Division North	P	W	D	L	F	A	Pts
Enfield OG Res.	18	12	2	4	61	33	38
Old Edmontonians	18	11	2	5	40	29	35
Old Buckwellians	18	10	2	6	39	35	32
William Fitt	18	9	3	6	57	30	30
Egbertian	18	8	4	6	45	40	28
Old Magdalenians	18	7	5	6	37	35	26
Bealonians Res.	18	6	3	9	38	47	21
Old Woodhouseians	18	6	2	10	31	46	20
Old Camdenians	18	6	2	10	22	47	20
O. Parmiterians Res.	18	2	1	15	25	53	7

Int. Division South	P	W	D	L	F	A	Pts
Centymca	22	18	2	2	77	30	56
Economicals Res.	22	13	3	6	57	36	42
Witan	22	12	3	7	57	47	39
Kings OB Res.	22	10	5	7	62	41	35
Chislehurst Sports	22	10	5	7	45	44	35
Old Thorntonians *-4*	22	9	9	4	62	38	32
Old Josephians	22	9	4	9	64	55	31
Mickleham Old Box.	22	7	3	12	31	54	24
Old Sedcopians	22	8	0	14	45	74	24
Reigatians	22	6	4	12	30	51	22
Queen Mary COB	22	5	1	16	31	68	16
Old Suttonians Res.	22	4	3	15	27	50	15

Int. Division West	P	W	D	L	F	A	Pts
O. Hamptonians 'A'	20	13	4	3	63	44	43
Old Kolsassians	20	13	1	6	57	33	40
Ful. Compton OB	20	12	3	5	50	31	39
Old Challoners Res.	20	9	3	8	46	52	30
Old Uffingtonians	20	8	5	7	53	46	29
Old Manorians Res.	20	8	5	7	42	49	29
O. Vaughanians Res.	20	6	6	8	54	54	24
Pegasus	20	6	6	8	46	52	24
Card. Manning OB	20	7	2	11	46	58	23
London Welsh	20	3	6	11	39	54	15
Parkfield 'A' *-3*	20	3	3	14	30	53	9

Division One North	P	W	D	L	F	A	Pts
Leyton County OB	18	12	4	2	59	21	40
Egbertian Res.	18	13	1	4	54	30	40
Old Aloysians 'A'	18	11	3	4	41	28	36
Old Ed'tonians Res.	18	9	2	7	40	37	29
UCL Acad'cals 'A'	18	7	4	7	30	31	25
O. Parmiterians 'A'	18	6	4	8	34	36	22
Old Ignatian Res. *-3*	18	6	3	9	27	38	18
Wood G. OB Res.	18	5	1	12	18	42	16
Old Tollingtonians	18	3	6	9	26	39	15
Univ. of Herts	18	3	2	13	22	49	11

Division One South	P	W	D	L	F	A	Pts
Royal Bank of Scot.	20	11	6	3	49	37	39
Old Bromleians	20	12	2	6	54	39	38
Credit Suisse	20	11	4	5	53	34	37
Old Wokingians	20	10	6	4	44	29	36
Old St Marys	20	7	7	6	40	37	28
Clapham OX Res.	20	8	4	8	50	48	28
Old Suttonians 'A'	20	8	3	9	54	49	27
O. Tenisonians Res.	20	8	2	10	47	49	26
Sinjuns Gram. Res.	20	5	3	12	29	52	18
Reigatians Res.	20	4	4	12	22	40	16
Valley Park Rgrs *-4*	20	4	3	13	26	54	11

Division One West	P	W	D	L	F	A	Pts
Parkfield 'B'	20	15	2	3	61	33	47
Chert. Old Salesians	20	14	2	4	74	30	44
Old Kingsburians	20	13	3	4	73	41	42
Old Meadonians 'B'	20	10	4	6	42	28	34
O. Salvatorians 'A'	20	7	3	10	43	43	24
O. Uff'tonians Res.	19	7	3	9	61	67	24
Phoenix Old Boys	20	6	4	10	35	48	22
Old Uxonians	20	5	5	10	45	62	20
Old Manorians 'A'	20	5	3	12	32	64	18
O. Vaughanians 'A'	20	4	4	12	40	63	16
Old Islew'th. Res. *-3*	19	5	3	11	35	62	15

Division Two North	P	W	D	L	F	A	Pts
Bealonians 'A'	16	11	4	1	43	27	37
Enfield Old G. 'A'	16	6	5	5	36	30	23
Old Aloysians 'B'	16	5	8	3	27	31	23
Q. Mary COB Res.	16	5	7	4	32	32	22
Mill Hill Co. OB *-6*	16	8	3	5	49	41	21
Egbertian 'A'	16	6	3	7	48	42	21
Albanian 'A'	16	6	1	9	34	38	19
Latymer OB Res.	16	3	6	7	31	46	15
L'don Hosp. OB *-3*	16	1	5	10	34	47	5

Ravenscroft Old Boys – record expunged

Division Two South	P	W	D	L	F	A	Pts
City of London	20	15	2	3	60	19	47
Glyn Old Boys Res.	20	11	5	4	41	20	38
Old Tenisonians 'A'	20	11	5	4	41	26	38
Old Whitgiftians	20	11	4	5	41	32	37
Natwest Bank Res.	20	10	4	6	34	26	34
Chislehurst Spts Res.	20	8	6	6	56	48	30
Pegasus Res.	20	6	4	10	30	31	22
Clapham Old X. 'A'	20	7	1	12	33	47	22
The Comets	19	5	2	12	27	60	17
Sinjuns Gramm. 'A'	20	5	1	14	31	49	16
Coutts Co. *-1*	19	2	2	15	20	56	7

Division Two West	P	W	D	L	F	A	Pts
Old Challoners 'A'	20	16	1	3	65	30	49
Old Manorians 'B'	20	15	2	3	77	28	47
Old K'burians Res.	20	12	3	5	56	39	39
Old Uxonians Res.	19	8	3	8	29	28	27
Brent Res.	20	8	3	9	41	55	27
Hampstead H. Res.	20	8	1	11	36	59	25
O. Salvatorians 'B'	20	7	2	11	47	53	23
Phoenix OB Res. *-3*	19	8	1	10	51	39	22
Old Meadonians 'C'	20	5	3	12	55	77	18
Parkfield 'C'	20	5	2	13	33	53	17
O. Vaughanians 'B'	20	4	5	11	57	86	17

Division Three North	P	W	D	L	F	A	Pts
Southgate Co. 'A'	18	13	4	1	71	25	43
Old M'denians Res.	18	13	2	3	62	26	41
Leyton Co. OB Res.	18	11	2	5	83	51	35
Hale End Ath. 'A'	18	7	5	6	51	60	26
Albanian 'B'	18	7	2	9	52	60	23
Old Edmont. 'A'	18	7	2	9	37	52	23
Old Ignatian 'A'	18	6	1	11	36	59	19
Davenant Wdrs OB	18	6	0	12	34	51	18
O. W'houseians Res.	18	5	3	10	38	60	18
O. Parmiterians 'B'	18	3	3	12	33	53	12

Division Three South	P	W	D	L	F	A	Pts
Old Strandians	18	15	1	2	65	22	46
Zurich Eagle Star	18	13	2	3	63	33	41
Old Paulines Res.	18	11	0	7	51	31	33
Centymca Res. *-3*	18	10	3	5	46	32	30
Sinjuns Gram. 'B'	18	8	4	6	39	39	28
Witan Res.	18	8	2	8	42	50	26
Marsh Res.	18	5	3	10	35	47	18
Old Dorkinians Res.	18	4	5	9	43	55	17
O. Wokingians Res.	18	2	2	14	30	64	8
Old Tiffinians Res.	18	2	2	14	20	61	8

Division Three West	P	W	D	L	F	A	Pts
Old Manorians 'C'	16	11	4	1	51	32	37
Shene Old G. Res.	16	10	4	2	50	18	34
Chertsey OS Res.	16	7	1	8	37	49	22
Birkbeck College *-3*	16	7	3	6	49	44	21
Card. M. OB Res. *-3*	16	7	2	7	34	49	20
O. Salvatorians 'C'	16	5	3	8	41	37	18
Fulham COB Res.	16	4	4	8	40	40	16
Old Isleworth. 'A'	16	3	7	6	33	49	16
O. Meadonians 'D'	16	1	6	9	23	40	9

London Airways – record expunged

Division Four North	P	W	D	L	F	A	Pts
Mill Hill COB Res.	18	15	3	0	77	27	48
Old Buckwell. Res.	18	11	2	5	50	28	35
Mayfield Athletic	18	9	4	5	51	32	31
Mill Hill V. Res.	18	9	2	7	54	42	29
Old C'denians Res.	18	9	2	7	57	46	29
Old Parmiterians 'C'	18	7	5	6	41	47	26
Bealonians 'B'	18	6	4	8	45	48	22
Old Aloysians 'C'	18	5	2	11	39	69	17
Latymer OB 'A'	18	4	2	12	38	58	14
Wood G. OB 'A'	18	1	2	15	19	74	5

Division Four South	P	W	D	L	F	A	Pts
Old Josephians Res.	18	16	1	1	55	17	49
Old Suttonians 'B'	18	9	4	5	29	18	31
Economicals 'A'	18	10	1	7	39	29	31
Old Guildford. Res.	18	9	2	7	36	27	29
Royal Bk of S. Res.	18	7	4	7	34	38	25
Old Tiffinians 'A'	18	6	2	10	20	34	20
Wand. Bor. Res. -3	18	7	1	10	35	41	19
BBC	18	5	1	12	36	50	16
Old Sedcopians Res.	16	4	1	11	22	39	13
Natwest Bank 'A' -9	16	5	3	8	24	37	9

Division Four West	P	W	D	L	F	A	Pts
Old K'burians 'A'	18	12	2	4	65	31	38
Ealing Assoc. -6	18	14	0	4	63	32	36
Phoenix OB 'A'	18	11	0	7	69	41	33
O. M'dalenians Res.	18	10	3	5	45	31	33
Holland Park OB	18	10	1	7	51	39	31
O. Salvatorians 'D'	18	9	0	9	56	48	27
Brent 'A'	18	7	1	10	40	60	22
O. Kolsassians Res.	18	6	1	11	34	46	19
Old Challoners 'B'	18	5	3	10	33	45	18
O. Vaughanians 'C'	18	0	1	17	19	102	1

Division Five North	P	W	D	L	F	A	Pts
William Fitt Res.	20	17	2	1	109	24	53
Enfield Old G. 'B'	20	13	3	4	84	54	42
UCL Academ. 'B'	20	10	4	6	47	44	34
Old Aloysians 'D'	20	9	6	5	68	51	33
Southgate Co. 'B'	20	11	0	9	59	49	33
Bealonians 'C'	20	7	7	6	40	35	28
Wood G. OB 'B'	20	7	4	9	55	69	25
Old Buckwell. 'A'	20	7	3	10	51	59	24
O. Camdenians 'A'	20	6	2	12	49	86	20
Hale End Ath. 'B'	20	4	4	12	30	57	16
Old Ignatians 'B'	20	0	3	17	30	94	3

Division Five South	P	W	D	L	F	A	Pts
Clapham Old X. 'B'	18	16	0	2	72	22	48
O. Josephians 'A' -6	18	14	2	2	64	28	38
Old Wokingians 'A'	16	10	1	5	41	31	31
JP Morgan Chase	17	8	4	5	41	32	28
Natwest Bank 'B'	15	7	2	6	32	22	23
Witan 'A'	18	6	2	10	35	51	20
Old Suttonians 'C'	18	5	3	10	35	45	18
Sinjuns Gram. 'C'	18	5	2	11	35	62	17
Old St Marys Res. -3	18	3	4	11	28	55	10
Reigatians 'A'	18	2	2	14	32	67	8

Division Five West	P	W	D	L	F	A	Pts
Phoenix OB 'B'	18	17	1	0	91	21	52
Holland Pk OB Res.	18	12	0	6	64	38	36
Cardinal M. OB 'A'	18	11	1	6	92	47	34
Ealing Assoc. Res.	18	8	5	5	52	38	29
Old Islew'thians 'B'	18	8	4	6	56	48	28
O. Uff'tonians 'A' -3	18	9	2	7	67	74	26
Old K'burians 'B'	18	5	3	10	40	63	18
Old Manorians 'D'	18	4	2	12	27	68	14
O. Vaughanians 'D'	18	2	4	12	33	96	10
London Welsh Res.	18	2	2	14	46	75	8

Division Six North	P	W	D	L	F	A	Pts
Albanian 'C'	18	15	3	0	75	20	48
Old Tollington Res.	18	13	2	3	65	28	41
Old Gladstonians	18	11	1	6	66	39	34
Mill Hill COB 'A'	18	7	5	6	59	50	26
Leyton COB 'A'	18	8	2	8	45	50	26
O. Woodhouse. 'A'	18	6	4	8	49	80	22
Mill Hill Vill. 'A'	18	6	3	9	42	58	21
Old M'denians 'A'	18	4	5	9	42	53	17
Egbertian 'B'	18	3	2	13	45	72	11
Old Edmont. 'B'	18	2	3	13	23	61	9

Division Six South	P	W	D	L	F	A	Pts
Citigroup	18	14	2	2	60	20	44
Royal Sun Alliance	18	10	6	2	66	24	36
Glyn Old Boys 'A'	18	10	4	4	64	32	34
Temple Bar	16	9	3	4	46	30	30
Old Thornton. Res.	18	9	1	8	37	62	28
British Council	16	6	4	6	29	34	22
John Fisher OB Res.	18	6	2	10	45	57	20
Old Wokingians 'B'	18	5	1	12	31	55	16
Sinjuns Gramm. 'D'	18	2	4	12	23	77	10
Old Dorkinians 'A'	18	2	3	13	36	46	9

Division Seven North	P	W	D	L	F	A	Pts
Old Parmiterians 'D'	16	15	0	1	72	22	45
Mill Hill COB 'B'	16	13	0	3	72	19	39
UCL Academ. 'C'	16	8	2	6	42	35	26
Old Woodh'se. 'B'	16	7	2	7	42	38	23
Wood G. OB 'C'	16	7	0	9	40	64	21
Lon. Hosp. OB Res.	16	6	2	8	34	42	20
Leyton Co. OB 'B'	16	5	2	9	32	34	17
Q. Mary COB 'A'	16	5	2	9	38	44	17
Old M'denians 'B'	16	1	0	15	18	92	3

Ravenscroft Old Boys Res. – record expunged

Division Seven South	P	W	D	L	F	A	Pts
Old Meadonians 'E'	18	15	2	1	69	17	47
Clapham Old X. 'C'	18	10	4	4	52	26	34
Old Paulines 'A'	18	8	4	6	37	42	28
O. Suttonians 'D' -3	18	8	4	6	43	34	25
Sinjuns Gram. 'E'	18	6	5	7	45	46	23
Glyn Old Boys 'B'	18	7	2	9	36	41	23
Old Josephians 'B'	18	6	3	9	42	50	21
Old Tiffinians 'B'	18	6	2	10	24	48	20
Heathrow Seniors	18	5	3	10	39	42	18
John Fisher OB 'A'	18	3	3	12	26	67	12

Division Eight North	P	W	D	L	F	A	Pts
Latymer OB 'B'	14	11	2	1	68	22	35
Mill Hill COB 'C'	14	9	3	2	48	21	30
Davenant WOB Res.	13	5	4	4	38	38	19
O. Parmiterians 'E'	14	6	1	7	33	33	19
Southgate Co. 'C'	13	5	1	7	27	41	16
Bealonians 'D'	14	4	2	8	38	48	14
Albanian 'D'	14	4	1	9	31	49	13
Mayfield Ath. Res.	14	4	0	10	27	58	12

Ravenscroft Old Boys 'A' – record expunged

Division Eight South	P	W	D	L	F	A	Pts
Old Meadonians 'F'	18	13	2	3	58	32	41
O. Thorntonians 'A'	18	12	1	5	63	18	37
City of London Res.	18	10	3	5	41	27	33
O. Bromleians Res.	18	10	3	5	41	33	33
O. Suttonians 'E' -3	18	8	3	7	44	47	24
Centymca 'A'	18	7	2	9	48	42	23
Old Wokingians 'C'	18	7	2	9	28	43	23
Old Guildford. 'A'	18	6	3	9	42	51	21
BBC Res.	18	4	0	14	30	76	12
Old Sedcopians 'A'	18	3	1	14	27	53	10

Division Nine North	P	W	D	L	F	A	Pts
Egbertian 'C'	14	11	2	1	61	16	35
Mayfield Ath. 'A'	14	7	4	3	65	35	25
Old Edmont. 'C'	14	7	4	3	44	37	25
Enfield Old G. 'C'	14	6	4	4	28	28	22
Bealonians 'E'	14	4	4	6	34	51	16
Old Ignatian 'C'	14	3	4	7	27	33	13
UCL Acad'cals 'D'	14	4	0	10	26	46	12
O. Camden. 'B' -3	14	2	2	10	23	62	5

Ravenscroft Old Boys 'B' – record expunged

Division Nine South	P	W	D	L	F	A	Pts
Royal Sun All. Res.	18	12	4	2	57	27	40
Economicals 'B'	18	11	4	3	65	30	37
O. Guildf'dians 'B'	18	11	2	5	56	32	35
Kings Old Boys 'A'	18	8	4	6	41	42	28
Glyn Old Boys 'C'	18	8	3	7	39	39	27
Fulham COB 'A'	18	8	2	8	51	41	26
Reigatians 'B'	18	8	2	8	45	54	26
Mick.O Box. Res. -1	18	6	1	11	38	49	18
Old Dorkinians 'B'	18	4	3	11	47	74	15
Wandswth B. 'A' -4	18	1	1	16	20	71	0

Division Ten South	P	W	D	L	F	A	Pts
Old Tenisonians 'B'	16	15	1	0	60	15	46
John Fisher OB 'B'	16	10	2	4	55	34	32
O. Whitgiftians Res.	16	9	2	5	42	24	29
Old Sedcopians 'B'	16	8	2	6	33	33	26
Reigatians 'C'	16	8	1	7	34	29	25
Old Bromleians 'A'	16	8	1	7	43	45	25
Old Wokingians 'D'	16	5	1	10	38	45	16
O. Meadonians 'G'	16	3	0	13	31	56	9
Old St Marys 'A' -3	16	1	0	15	12	67	0

Div. Eleven South	P	W	D	L	F	A	Pts
Fulham COB 'B'	16	14	2	0	54	17	44
Shene Old G. 'A'	16	13	0	3	62	21	39
Old Guildford. 'C'	16	12	0	4	74	16	36
Old Tenison. 'C' -1	16	6	4	6	55	34	21
Sinjuns Gram. 'F'	16	5	4	7	27	36	19
Old Wokingians 'E'	16	4	2	10	24	75	14
Reigatians 'D'	16	3	3	10	23	59	12
Old Tiffinians 'C'	16	3	1	12	34	62	10
Old Paulines 'B' -1	16	3	2	11	38	71	10

Div. Twelve South	P	W	D	L	F	A	Pts
Clapham Old X. 'D'	16	13	2	1	94	16	41
Glyn Old Boys 'D'	16	11	2	3	54	30	35
City of London 'A'	16	10	2	4	55	24	32
Old Sedcopians 'C'	16	7	5	4	47	44	26
Fulham COB 'C'	16	5	3	8	28	44	18
O. Meadonians 'H'	16	5	1	10	25	63	16
Reigatians 'E'	16	5	0	11	32	56	15
Old Suttonians 'F'	16	3	4	9	27	42	13
Old Guildford. 'D'	16	2	3	11	25	68	9

ANDOVER & DISTRICT LEAGUE

	P	W	D	L	F	A	Pts
ABC United	18	15	2	1	70	14	47
Wherwell	18	13	2	3	103	34	41
Burghclere	18	12	2	4	91	46	38
AFC Wol'dene Res.	18	10	3	5	60	34	33
Stannah	18	10	0	8	52	39	30
Borough Arms	18	10	0	8	56	45	30
Whitchurch Utd Res.	18	7	0	11	48	58	21
Picket Piece S&S	18	3	1	14	20	94	10
King's Somborne	18	3	0	15	25	100	9
AFC St M. Bourne	18	2	0	16	28	89	6

ANGLESEY LEAGUE

(Stena Line)

	P	W	D	L	F	A	Pts
H'hd Gwelfor Ath.	18	15	1	2	64	29	46
Bodedern Res.	18	12	2	4	40	15	38
Bro Goronwy	18	10	3	5	46	26	33
Pentraeth	18	10	3	5	53	39	33
Llanerchymedd -3	18	10	4	4	40	23	31
L'dudno Junc. Res.	18	8	2	8	46	28	26
Llanfairpwll Res.	18	3	7	8	28	38	16
Gwalchmai	18	4	3	11	26	53	15
Llandegfan	18	3	3	12	30	65	12
Llangoed & Dist.	18	0	2	16	15	72	2

AYLESBURY & DISTRICT LEAGUE

(Perrys Peugeot)

Premier Division	P	W	D	L	F	A	Pts
Aston Park	24	16	6	2	89	34	54
Aylesbury V. Res.	24	15	2	7	67	34	47
St Johns	24	14	5	5	64	40	47
Bucks CC	24	13	4	7	53	39	43
Bierton	24	12	5	7	61	43	41
Aston Clinton Res.	24	12	3	9	54	38	39
Bedgrove United	24	10	5	9	59	41	35
Bedgrove Dynamos	24	10	4	10	67	67	34
Long Marston	24	10	3	11	43	65	33
Elmhurst	24	7	4	13	42	85	25
Wingrave	24	7	2	15	32	62	23
Mandeville OB	24	3	3	18	29	72	12
Wendover	24	3	2	19	25	65	11

Division One	P	W	D	L	F	A	Pts
Walton Court Wdrs	26	21	3	2	129	33	66
Bedgrove Dyn. Res.	26	17	4	5	84	56	55
Black Horse	26	16	4	6	70	36	52
Jakemans Sports	26	17	1	8	77	50	52
Cheddington	26	13	3	10	69	65	42
Fairford Leys	26	13	3	10	69	66	42
Dairy Maid	26	12	4	10	80	70	40
Thame Snooker C.	26	9	8	9	57	61	35
Bedgrove Utd Res.	26	10	4	12	60	60	34
Oving	26	10	4	12	64	71	34
Bucks CC Res.	26	8	4	14	50	57	28
Waddesdon	26	5	1	20	38	86	16
Aston Clinton 'A'	26	3	4	19	52	111	13
Bierton Res.	26	4	1	21	52	129	13

Division Two	P	W	D	L	F	A	Pts
New Zealand	24	20	2	2	102	34	62
Quainton	24	19	2	3	93	31	59
Cheddington Res.	24	17	3	4	81	40	54
Cross Keys	24	14	3	7	82	35	45
St Johns Res.	24	12	1	11	103	60	37
Wendover Res.	24	11	4	9	73	68	37
Long Marston Res.	24	9	7	8	57	69	34
Wingrave Res.	24	10	0	14	62	74	30
Fairford Leys Res.	24	8	2	14	42	80	26
Hobgoblin	24	7	3	14	56	91	24
Ludgershall	24	6	4	14	67	77	22
Black Horse Res.	24	6	0	18	43	136	18
AC Meadowcroft	24	1	1	22	26	92	4

BANBURY & LORD JERSEY FA

Premier Division	P	W	D	L	F	A	Pts
Broughton & NN	22	18	3	1	78	22	57
Bishops Itchington	22	17	2	3	89	32	53
Hethe	22	16	1	5	98	41	49
Cropredy	22	13	1	8	64	36	40
Kineton SSC	22	10	3	9	41	38	33
Steeple Aston	22	9	3	10	42	41	30
Bodicote Sports	22	9	1	12	30	40	28
Finmere	22	9	0	13	35	49	27
Arncott	22	8	1	13	38	76	25
Hornton	22	6	5	11	36	52	23
Deddington Town	22	1	6	15	28	74	9
Wroxton Sports	22	2	2	18	22	100	8

WWW.CHERRYRED.CO.UK

Division One	P	W	D	L	F	A	Pts
Drayton Village	22	17	2	3	60	30	53
Barford United	22	16	2	4	81	29	50
Ruscote	22	16	1	5	73	28	49
Heyford Ath. 'A'	22	13	4	5	67	35	43
Fenny Compton	22	10	7	5	54	31	37
Bish. Itch'gton Res.	22	11	2	9	40	48	35
Heyford United	22	8	4	10	57	51	28
St Johns	22	6	5	11	27	30	23
Decoma Sybex	22	6	5	11	31	37	23
Cropredy Res.	22	3	7	12	39	72	16
Souldern	22	2	5	15	37	85	11
Merton Mustangs	22	1	2	19	24	114	5

Division Two	P	W	D	L	F	A	Pts
Slade Farm	18	14	2	2	50	11	44
KEA	18	14	2	2	60	28	44
ABK Sports	18	12	2	4	68	26	38
Real Islip	18	9	3	6	67	42	30
Adderbury Pk Res.	18	7	3	8	35	56	24
Abba Athletic	18	6	5	7	41	50	23
Bloxham	18	5	4	9	32	63	19
Heyford Park	18	5	1	12	30	68	16
Duke of Wellington	18	4	2	12	35	38	14
Wroxton Spts Res.	18	1	2	15	22	58	5

Division Three	P	W	D	L	F	A	Pts
B'ton/N. N'ton Res.	22	18	2	2	72	20	56
Hethe Res.	22	17	1	4	91	45	52
Ruscote Res.	22	12	3	7	73	46	39
Finmere Res.	22	12	1	9	68	43	37
KEA Res.	22	11	3	8	81	45	36
Real Islip Res.	22	11	1	10	67	58	34
Steeple Aston Res.	22	9	5	8	49	44	32
Cropredy 'A'	22	10	2	10	45	51	32
Deddington T. Res.	22	8	2	12	31	45	26
Heyford Ath. 'B'	22	5	1	16	32	95	16
Heyford Utd Res.	22	5	0	17	22	94	15
Bodicote Spts Res.	22	3	1	18	26	71	10

BASINGSTOKE & DISTRICT LEAGUE

Premier Division	P	W	D	L	F	A	Pts
New Inn FC	16	13	0	3	63	10	39
R & B Sports	16	11	2	3	54	17	35
AFC A'maston 'A'	16	11	1	4	53	21	34
Bramley United	16	8	1	7	33	31	25
Rangers	16	7	4	5	25	28	25
Hook	16	6	4	6	36	25	22
Oakley Athletic	16	5	4	7	28	34	19
Preston Candover	16	3	0	13	18	62	9
B'stoke Lab. Club	16	0	0	16	7	89	0

Division One	P	W	D	L	F	A	Pts
Tadley Calleva 'A'	18	15	2	1	59	14	47
Bramley Utd Res.	18	14	3	1	29	15	45
R & B Sports Res.	18	12	0	6	53	34	36
Hook Res.	18	11	0	7	41	30	33
New Inn FC Res.	18	10	1	7	38	26	31
Sherborne	18	5	3	10	38	38	18
Oakley Ath. Res.	18	5	2	11	36	53	17
AFC A'rmaston 'B'	18	4	2	12	20	34	14
RG Select	18	4	2	12	35	50	14
AFC Berg	18	1	3	14	25	80	6

Division Two	P	W	D	L	F	A	Pts
Silchester United	18	15	1	2	65	29	46
AFC Sleepers	18	14	1	3	80	26	43
Sherborne St John	18	13	2	3	54	24	41
Sherfield	18	12	1	5	50	27	37
Rangers Res.	18	7	3	8	42	46	24
Overton United 'A'	18	7	0	11	34	45	21
Herriard Sports	18	6	1	11	31	59	19
Heathpark	18	5	1	12	31	55	16
Headley Athletic	18	3	2	13	20	51	11
Chineham	18	2	0	16	23	68	6

BATH & DISTRICT LEAGUE

(Roper Rhodes Bathrooms)

Division One	P	W	D	L	F	A	Pts
University of Bath	20	16	1	3	48	15	49
Odd Down 'A'	20	15	3	2	72	30	48
Crown Sports	20	15	1	4	57	19	46
Saltford Res.	20	14	2	4	51	21	44
WESA	20	9	1	10	48	47	28
Aces SSJ	20	8	3	9	40	40	27
Sportzcoach Utd	20	7	0	13	39	45	21
Cutters Friday Res.	20	5	3	12	25	51	18
Bath Spa University	20	5	0	15	23	53	15
CCB United -3	20	6	0	14	34	66	15
Keynsham T. 'A'	20	3	0	17	17	67	9

Division Two	P	W	D	L	F	A	Pts
Civil Service Filos	20	13	4	3	45	21	43
Fry Club Old Boys	20	13	3	4	61	24	42
Oldfield Sports	20	10	6	4	55	33	36
Chew Valley Snrs	20	11	2	7	45	26	35
Bath Arsenal	20	9	3	8	41	41	30
Stothert & Pitt	20	8	2	10	46	48	26
Univ. Bath Res. -3	20	8	3	9	43	35	24
Freshford Sports	20	6	2	12	35	66	20
Fairfield Park Rgrs	20	5	4	11	24	54	19
Timsbury Ath. 'A'	20	4	6	10	24	40	18
Oval Sports	20	5	1	14	23	54	16

Division Three	P	W	D	L	F	A	Pts
Civil Serv. Filos 'A'	22	17	3	2	82	29	54
AFC Bath Rangers	22	14	2	6	68	25	44
Aces SSJ Res.	22	13	2	7	63	38	41
Rising Sun	22	11	5	6	55	40	38
WESA Res.	22	12	1	9	68	49	37
Golden Oldies	22	11	3	8	58	55	36
Wesco United	22	10	5	7	63	52	35
Fry Club OB Res.	22	10	2	10	62	74	32
Cutters Friday 'A'	22	7	3	12	35	56	24
Westfield 'A'	22	6	5	11	47	67	23
Wansdyke	22	3	2	17	35	92	11
Crown/Anc. Weston	22	1	1	20	36	95	4

Westwood United – record expunged

BIRMINGHAM AFA

Premier Division	P	W	D	L	F	A	Pts
Sutton United	26	19	3	4	68	25	60
B'mere Falcon Snrs	26	17	3	6	69	34	54
AFC Lakin	26	17	1	8	67	50	52
Shirley Athletic	26	14	6	6	56	50	48
Ajax United	26	12	7	7	58	29	43
Village	26	12	5	9	48	37	41
Wake Green Amats	26	10	5	11	44	39	35
Cresconians	26	9	5	12	50	46	32
Woodbourne Sports	26	10	2	14	38	64	32
Handsworth GSOB	26	7	7	12	49	62	28
Sillhill	26	7	6	13	40	50	27
Colinthians	26	7	4	15	40	67	25
Penncroft	26	6	4	16	39	58	22
CPA H & N	26	4	4	18	22	77	16

Division One	P	W	D	L	F	A	Pts
Billesley United	22	15	3	4	64	31	48
Village Res.	22	14	3	5	57	29	45
AFC Somers	22	13	4	5	59	28	43
Walsall Phoenix	22	13	3	6	49	30	42
Resolution	22	12	4	6	47	33	40
Kynoch	22	11	5	6	47	30	38
Kings Norton Celtic	22	8	4	10	46	52	28
Old Wulfrunians	22	6	7	9	36	40	25
Sutton United Res.	22	6	5	11	29	40	23
Solihull Gas	22	5	2	15	24	59	17
Parkfield Amateurs	22	5	0	17	22	68	15
West Mids Travel	22	3	2	17	27	67	11

Division Two	P	W	D	L	F	A	Pts
Erin Go Bragh	24	19	1	4	90	37	58
Flamengo	24	16	5	3	73	31	53
Old Nortonians	24	15	3	6	72	48	48
H'wth GSOB Res.	24	10	4	10	52	51	34
John Rose	24	10	2	12	67	66	32
Wake Green Res.	24	8	8	8	50	56	32
Village 'A'	24	8	6	10	39	41	30
Silhill Res.	24	8	5	11	49	61	29
Acocks Green	24	7	7	10	46	48	28
Old Wulfs Res.	24	8	4	12	46	64	28
West Hagley	24	6	9	9	48	51	27
Airmark	24	7	6	11	31	46	27
Britannia Old Boys	24	3	2	19	36	99	11

Division Three	P	W	D	L	F	A	Pts
St Francis	22	16	5	1	66	13	53
Aston Detached	22	16	3	3	75	21	51
Wake Green A. 'A'	22	15	2	5	50	31	47
Cresconians Res.	22	12	3	7	64	41	39
Aston Youth F & N	22	10	2	10	48	52	32
Shirley Ath. Res.	22	8	5	9	41	42	29
W'sall Phoenix Res.	22	8	5	9	48	55	29
Malremo Rangers	22	8	2	12	39	52	26
Sutton United 'A'	22	6	7	9	36	46	25
Silhill 'A'	22	6	2	14	43	71	20
Dosthill Old Boys	22	2	5	15	31	67	11
Colinthians Res.	22	2	5	15	34	84	11

Division Four	P	W	D	L	F	A	Pts
Shere Punjab	24	17	3	4	71	29	54
DESI 2	24	17	0	7	82	33	51
Resolution Res.	24	16	3	5	74	30	51
Inter Vaughans	24	14	5	5	40	33	47
Great Barr	24	14	3	7	59	37	45
CPA H&N Res.	24	12	3	9	55	42	39
Crusaders	24	10	5	9	49	36	35
MG Star	24	8	5	11	42	52	29
Welwyn	24	7	6	11	42	50	27
Castle Brom. Alb.	24	8	3	13	24	39	27
Village 'B'	24	8	0	16	39	67	24
Old W'lfrunians 'A'	24	3	1	20	28	82	10
Parkfield Ams Res.	24	2	3	19	18	93	9

Division Five	P	W	D	L	F	A	Pts
Athletic Sparkhill	24	21	1	2	108	35	64
Pathfinder	24	12	6	6	67	35	42
Halesowen Alliance	24	13	2	9	78	72	41
Bearwood Athletic	24	12	3	9	54	38	39
IDQ	24	12	3	9	61	57	39
Old Nortonians Res.	24	12	2	10	63	41	38
Shirley Athletic 'A'	24	11	3	10	72	58	36
Wood Wanderers	24	7	7	10	36	53	28
Bustleholme Ath.	24	9	1	14	48	86	28
Inter Quinton	24	8	3	13	53	81	27
Birmingham Citadel	24	8	2	14	53	65	26
Sutton United 'B'	24	7	3	14	35	55	24
Manchester Wdrs	24	6	0	18	40	92	18

Division Six	P	W	D	L	F	A	Pts
Elmdon Heath	20	16	2	2	88	34	50
Rubery -3	20	13	0	7	69	43	36
Wylde Green Wdrs	20	11	3	6	50	39	36
Phoenix	20	10	4	6	63	54	34
Acocks Green Ath.	20	10	4	6	37	28	34
Cable & Wireless	20	9	2	9	56	50	29
Handsworth Rec.	20	8	1	11	39	55	25
Silhill 'B'	20	5	5	10	32	56	20
H'worth GSOB 'A'	20	5	2	13	31	54	17
Colinthians 'A'	20	5	2	13	29	61	17
Cresconians 'A'	20	4	3	13	32	52	15

Maypole Youth Project – record expunged

Division Seven	P	W	D	L	F	A	Pts
Schofield United	24	17	4	3	80	28	55
Alcoa Europe	24	18	1	5	68	33	55
Bromsgrove Town	24	16	1	7	76	40	49
Asgard Rovers	24	14	5	5	53	33	47
Coton Green Res.	24	11	2	11	61	55	35
H'worth GSOB 'B'	24	9	6	9	55	52	33
Wythall Athletic	24	10	2	12	68	66	32
Royal Heath Rovers	24	8	4	12	53	63	28
Aston '76	24	8	3	13	57	78	27
Walsall Phoenix 'A'	24	8	3	13	36	77	27
Tamworth QEOB	24	6	3	15	49	76	21
Sutton United 'C'	24	6	2	16	40	64	20
Kinghurst Phoenix	24	6	2	16	35	66	20

Division Eight	P	W	D	L	F	A	Pts
AFC Hayes HA	24	16	5	3	77	26	53
King Edward Lions	24	16	4	4	80	44	52
Meriden Athletic	24	15	4	5	68	50	49
Crusaders Res.	24	12	3	9	57	42	39
Village 'C'	24	11	6	7	56	50	39
St Pauls FC	24	11	5	8	53	48	38
AFC Meadway	24	8	7	9	64	61	31
Wake Green A. 'B'	24	9	4	11	56	59	31
Maple Leaf Rovers	24	6	6	12	41	66	24
Aston Yth F&N Res.	24	6	6	12	47	73	24
Old W'frunians 'B'	24	7	2	15	42	75	23
Wylde Green Res.	24	6	1	17	50	76	19
Sutton United 'D'	24	4	5	15	60	81	17

Division Nine	P	W	D	L	F	A	Pts
St Georges Warriors	20	18	1	1	81	19	55
BCS Social	20	17	0	3	104	25	51
Four Oaks	20	12	3	5	63	39	39
Balsalorna	20	12	0	8	61	46	36
Cresconians 'B'	20	9	3	8	54	48	30
Elmdon Heath Res.	20	9	3	8	42	43	30
Maypole	20	9	2	9	37	41	29
Real Riverside	20	5	5	10	30	52	20
Wulfrun Invicta	20	4	0	16	30	89	12
Wake Green A. 'C'	20	3	1	16	24	66	10
Bournville Colts	20	2	2	16	25	83	8

BOSTON & DISTRICT LEAGUE
(Cropley's Suzuki)

Premier Division	P	W	D	L	F	A	Pts
Croft United	20	13	4	3	75	24	43
Billinghay Ath. -1	20	12	4	4	40	21	39
Spilsby Town	20	12	2	6	51	36	38
Wyberton	20	11	1	8	34	36	34
Sleaford T. Res. -3	20	11	3	6	44	33	33
Swineshead Inst.	20	11	0	9	53	44	33
Skegness T. Res.	20	9	6	5	40	39	33
Coningsby	20	8	2	10	47	46	26
Gedney Drove End	20	5	1	14	34	62	16
Wrangle United	20	3	2	15	33	59	11
Kirton Town	20	2	1	17	26	77	7

Division One	P	W	D	L	F	A	Pts
West End Tigers	20	13	4	3	71	32	43
Westside Rangers	20	11	5	4	54	30	38
Swineshead I. Res.	20	10	7	3	47	27	37
North Sea United	20	11	2	7	56	46	35
Old Leake	20	9	5	6	52	39	32
Fishtoft	20	8	6	6	59	39	30
Holbeach Bank	20	5	6	9	40	47	21
Spilsby T. Res. -3	20	7	2	11	37	52	20
Old Doningtonians	20	4	7	9	39	66	19
Spalding Town	20	4	6	10	20	50	18
Tydd St Mary	20	1	4	15	20	67	7

Division Two	P	W	D	L	F	A	Pts
Freiston	22	17	2	3	79	28	53
Coningsby Res.	22	13	6	3	58	33	45
Wainfleet United	22	11	6	5	59	45	39
Woodhall Spa Utd	22	10	5	7	62	36	35
Black Bull United	22	11	1	10	47	56	34
Kirton Town Res.	22	9	5	8	45	32	32
Spalding Harriers	22	9	3	10	45	49	30
Sutterton	22	9	2	11	34	52	29
Mareham United	22	6	7	9	45	50	25
Park Road Old Boys	22	7	4	11	47	58	25
Fosdyke	22	6	5	11	50	68	23
Park United	22	1	0	21	35	99	3

Division Three	P	W	D	L	F	A	Pts
Marshalls	20	18	0	2	118	24	54
Wrangle Utd Res.	20	13	3	4	89	51	42
Nortoft United	20	13	2	5	56	36	41
Friskney	20	10	3	7	56	43	33
Billinghay Res.	20	10	3	7	53	44	33
Freiston Res. -3	20	11	0	9	60	54	30
Westside Rgrs Res.	20	8	1	11	39	52	25
Holbeach Utd SC	20	6	4	10	38	55	22
Old Dons Res.	20	3	6	11	35	58	15
Park United Res.	20	4	1	15	29	82	13
Mareham Utd Res.	20	1	3	16	21	95	6

BOURNEMOUTH LEAGUE
(Hayward)

Division One	P	W	D	L	F	A	Pts
Suttoners Civil	22	17	5	0	59	20	56
Sway	22	12	6	4	51	22	42
West Moors	22	11	2	9	47	38	35
H'worthy Rec. Res.	22	10	4	8	47	45	34
Southbourne -3	22	11	2	9	43	38	32
Lym. & Pennington	22	8	3	11	41	56	27
Redlynch & WU	22	7	5	10	34	42	26
Westover B'mouth	22	7	4	11	43	48	25
Bournemouth Res.	22	5	9	8	28	29	24
Redhill Rangers	22	6	5	11	29	51	23
Trinidad	22	5	7	10	30	47	22
B'mouth Electric	22	5	4	13	36	52	19

Division Two	P	W	D	L	F	A	Pts
Old Oakmeadians	22	14	4	4	58	25	46
Verwood T. Res.	22	14	2	6	57	28	44
Westover B. Res.	22	12	6	4	59	27	42
Suttoners Civil Res.	22	12	5	5	65	40	41
Ferndown Town	22	10	6	6	42	34	36
Bmth Electric Res.	22	11	2	9	53	39	35
All Stars United	22	10	3	9	50	40	33
Mploy	22	10	1	11	52	59	31
AFC Highcliffe	22	9	2	11	33	44	29
Fordingbdge Turks	22	8	2	12	48	62	26
Allendale Res.	22	4	2	16	25	65	14
AFC Burton	22	0	1	21	13	92	1

Division Three	P	W	D	L	F	A	Pts
Mudef'd Mens Club	22	18	2	2	69	24	56
Urban Bournemouth	22	13	4	5	65	33	43
Parley Sports	22	12	5	5	52	40	41
Harrington United	22	12	3	7	49	37	39
St Mary's	22	11	5	6	46	26	38
JP Morgan	22	10	2	10	51	55	32
Sway Res.	22	9	3	10	52	43	30
Slades Farm	22	8	3	11	43	68	27
Bisterne United	22	7	5	10	36	56	26
New Milton Linnets	22	5	4	13	35	56	19
Redlynch/W. Res.	22	4	2	16	27	55	14
Malt n' Hops Utd	22	3	2	17	26	58	11

Division Four	P	W	D	L	F	A	Pts
AFC Branksome	20	17	1	2	82	28	52
Westover Bmth 'A'	20	14	5	1	73	28	47
St Andrews	20	14	4	2	64	33	46
Twynham Rangers	20	12	2	6	69	41	38
Portcastrian	20	8	2	10	38	45	26
Stourvale	20	7	3	10	31	41	24
O Oakmeadians Res.	20	7	1	12	36	49	22
Magpies/Woolsbdge	20	6	4	10	32	45	22
Woodman	20	5	3	12	35	66	18
Fencing Centre	20	4	1	15	34	75	13
Queens Park Ath.	20	2	2	16	26	69	8

Division Five	P	W	D	L	F	A	Pts
Alderholt Res.	20	16	2	2	67	16	50
Walkford Stores	20	13	4	3	60	32	43
Wessex Lions	20	12	2	6	68	42	38
Winton CC	20	11	5	4	53	29	38
Parkside Wanderers	20	10	4	6	64	37	34
Winton United	20	9	3	8	58	51	30
Griffin	20	7	3	10	39	47	24
Burley	20	6	3	11	31	39	21
Phoenix	20	6	0	14	32	53	18
Boscombe Celtic	20	3	4	13	29	94	13
Duke of Wellington	20	1	2	17	22	83	5

Division Six	P	W	D	L	F	A	Pts
Bearwood SC	24	19	3	2	81	29	60
New Milton Eagles	24	18	4	2	80	27	58
Bisterne Utd Res.	24	15	2	7	66	37	47
ELE	24	12	4	8	42	37	40
AFC Highcliffe Res.	24	11	4	9	50	51	37
Pilot Sports Flyers	24	11	3	10	57	51	36
Magpies & W. Res.	24	10	3	11	37	36	33
St Andrews Res.	24	9	4	11	41	49	31
Fifa Standards	24	9	3	12	62	42	30
Southbourne Res.	24	5	7	12	40	64	22
Fordingbridge Res.	24	6	2	16	26	60	20
Walker Scott Wdrs	24	6	1	17	36	72	19
Redlynch & W. 'A'	24	4	2	18	22	85	14

BRIGHTON, HOVE & DISTRICT LEAGUE

Premier Division	P	W	D	L	F	A	Pts
Hanover	18	12	2	4	59	26	38
Montpelier Villa	18	11	2	5	53	28	35
Master Tiles	18	11	2	5	45	31	35
Brighton Rangers	18	9	4	5	36	33	31
American Express	18	8	3	7	61	30	27
O & G United	18	8	2	8	39	39	26
Brighton Electricity	18	6	4	8	39	37	22
AFC St Georges	18	5	5	8	31	45	20
Ovingdean	18	5	2	11	40	59	17
Alpha Sports	18	2	0	16	15	90	6

Division One	P	W	D	L	F	A	Pts
Real Brunswick	20	15	3	2	65	28	48
Portslade Athletic	20	14	2	4	51	31	44
Rottingdean V. Res.	20	13	2	5	58	29	41
AFC Stadium	20	9	6	5	60	48	33
Coversure Athletic	20	10	1	9	46	46	31
Montpelier V. Res.	20	8	4	8	48	42	28
Southern Rgrs OB	20	8	3	9	36	35	27
Midway	20	6	2	12	38	51	20
Harbour View	20	5	4	11	35	54	19
Brighton BBOB	20	5	2	13	45	72	17
Chailey	20	2	1	17	29	75	7

Division Two	P	W	D	L	F	A	Pts
CCK	18	14	2	2	80	19	44
Ampito	18	13	3	2	57	34	42
Portslade Rangers	18	12	4	2	58	26	40
Autopaints Brighton	18	10	2	6	43	35	32
Midway Res.	18	6	4	8	42	57	22
Lectern Sports	18	6	3	9	30	51	21
AFC Stanley	18	6	2	10	43	43	20
R'dean Village Vets	18	5	4	9	36	51	19
Whitehawk 'A'	18	4	1	13	26	57	13
Kings Head	18	1	1	16	18	60	4

Division Three	P	W	D	L	F	A	Pts
Teamstats.net	16	12	2	2	51	26	38
The Windmill	16	11	3	2	58	29	36
American Ex. Res.	16	8	3	5	36	22	27
Ricardo	16	8	3	5	46	35	27
Rottingdean V. 'A'	16	9	0	7	42	41	27
R'gdean Dynamos	16	6	2	8	34	26	20
AFC Cosmos	16	6	1	9	42	46	19
APS Wanderers	16	3	2	11	29	56	11
Portslade Ath. Res.	16	1	0	15	15	72	3

Division Four	P	W	D	L	F	A	Pts
Buckingham Arms	20	16	0	4	96	33	48
Spanish Lady	20	16	0	4	74	33	48
Hikers Rest Vets	20	15	1	4	99	30	46
Stoneham Park	20	10	5	5	66	33	35
Adur Athletic 'A'	20	11	1	8	65	51	34
Legal & Gen. Res.	20	9	3	8	43	49	30
Brighton BBOB Res.	20	8	2	10	44	50	26
Brighton A & E	20	7	1	12	45	47	22
Montpelier V. 'A'	20	6	2	12	34	47	20
Chailey Res.	20	3	0	17	23	82	9
Southwick Dyn.	20	1	1	18	30	164	4

BRISTOL DOWNS LEAGUE

Division One	P	W	D	L	F	A	Pts
Sneyd Park	26	18	4	4	52	19	58
Lawes Juniors	26	16	6	4	64	28	54
Retainers	26	16	5	5	67	37	53
Ashley	26	12	10	4	60	34	46
Cotswool Old Boys	26	11	5	10	49	49	38
Easton Cowboys	26	9	6	11	58	54	33
Portland Old Boys	26	8	9	9	56	54	33
Bristol Juve	26	7	9	10	32	41	30
Clifton St Vincents	26	7	9	10	40	53	30
Hare-on-the Hill -3	26	8	7	11	32	42	28
Bristol Barcelona	26	7	7	12	39	52	28
Durdham Down AS	26	5	11	10	34	53	26
Sporting Greyh'nd	26	5	8	13	34	49	23
Clifton Rockets	26	2	6	18	20	72	12

Division Two	P	W	D	L	F	A	Pts
Torpedo	26	23	1	2	88	18	70
Cabot Asset Finance	26	18	5	3	65	32	59
AFC Bohemia	26	17	5	4	96	39	56
Saints Old Boys	26	15	9	2	66	38	54
Jamaica Bell	26	13	3	10	74	50	42
Red Lion	26	11	6	9	58	57	39
Sneyd Park Res.	26	12	3	11	47	64	39
Hydez	26	10	5	11	54	57	35
Luccombe Garage	26	8	4	14	51	66	28
Portland OB Res.	26	8	4	14	43	58	28
St Andrews	26	6	8	12	33	51	26
Clifton St V. Res.	26	7	4	15	40	60	25
Bristol Dynamos	26	2	2	22	22	85	8
Tebby	26	2	1	23	25	87	7

Division Three	P	W	D	L	F	A	Pts
Cotswool OB Res.	26	21	2	3	76	30	65
Retainers Res.	26	18	4	4	74	35	58
Torpedo Res.	26	15	6	5	70	29	51
Easton C'boys Res.	26	12	5	9	58	50	41
Sneyd Park 'A'	26	11	5	10	61	51	38
AFC Bohemia Res.	26	11	4	11	72	70	37
Ashley Res.	26	10	6	10	52	46	36
Clifton St Vinc. 'A'	26	11	3	12	58	59	36
LA Cricketers	26	9	5	12	52	54	32
Clifton Rkts Res.	26	8	4	14	41	65	28
Sporting Grey. Res.	26	8	3	15	44	61	27
Evergreen -3	26	6	7	13	43	57	22
Jersey Rangers	26	6	3	17	41	85	21
Cotham Old Boys	26	6	3	17	32	82	21

Division Four	P	W	D	L	F	A	Pts
Torpedo 'A'	30	21	3	6	99	36	66
L'combe G. Res. -3	30	19	6	5	97	45	60
Blackboy Inn	30	17	7	6	108	56	58
Beachcroft LLP	30	16	6	8	77	48	54
Hare-on-the H. Res.	30	16	6	8	69	60	54
Retainers 'A'	30	16	4	10	73	70	52
West Town United	30	15	2	13	57	62	47
Durdham DAS Res.	30	14	3	13	74	61	45
Penpole Inn	30	10	11	9	69	60	41
Hydez Res.	30	13	2	15	73	93	41
Red Lion Res.	30	12	2	16	68	63	38
Sneyd Park 'B'	30	11	3	16	73	90	36
Conham Rangers	30	10	5	15	67	68	35
Clifton St Vinc. 'B'	30	8	2	20	64	106	26
Bengal Tigers	30	4	4	22	43	128	16
Tebby AFC Res.	30	3	4	23	29	94	13

BRISTOL PREMIER COMBINATION

Premier Division

	P	W	D	L	F	A	Pts
Nicholas Wanderers	24	16	5	3	46	19	53
Bitton Res.	24	14	2	8	41	20	44
Hartcliffe	24	12	8	4	48	28	44
RG St George Res.	24	13	4	7	49	31	43
Highridge Utd Res.	24	12	2	10	28	30	38
Shaftesb'y Crusade	24	10	5	9	35	35	35
Chipping Sod. T. *-3*	24	10	7	7	43	28	34
Hallen Res.	24	9	7	8	35	28	34
Wick	24	6	12	6	26	31	30
Brimsham Green	24	5	9	10	27	43	24
Totterdown United	24	5	8	11	22	36	23
Longshore	24	2	8	14	17	40	14
AEK Boco	24	1	5	18	25	73	8

Division One

	P	W	D	L	F	A	Pts
Winterbourne Res.	26	19	1	6	63	26	58
Talbot Knowle	26	17	5	4	70	35	56
St Philips Marsh AS	26	17	4	5	74	36	55
Frampton Ath Rgrs	26	16	2	8	54	36	50
South Bristol Cent.	26	12	6	8	59	39	42
Olveston United	26	11	4	11	39	37	37
Seymour United	26	10	5	11	34	45	35
Fishponds Athletic	26	9	3	14	41	64	30
Henbury OB Res.	26	8	5	13	30	42	29
Greyfriars Athletic	26	8	4	14	43	55	28
Hillfields Old Boys	26	7	7	12	37	57	28
Patchway T. Res.	26	7	5	14	28	50	26
Warmley Saints	26	6	4	16	38	59	22
Iron Acton	26	5	5	16	33	62	20

BRISTOL & AVON LEAGUE

	P	W	D	L	F	A	Pts
Broadwalk	28	22	5	1	118	25	71
Long Ashton Res.	28	22	3	3	106	45	69
Crown Parkway *-3*	28	24	0	4	79	22	69
Hartwood Fathers	28	16	5	7	76	45	53
Mendip United Res.	28	17	1	10	100	64	52
Eagle House Elite	28	15	4	9	89	54	49
Stockwood W. Res.	28	12	5	11	80	46	41
Lawrence Rov. Res.	28	12	4	12	64	69	40
Brad. Stoke T. Res.	28	12	2	14	52	69	38
Bideford OB *-3*	28	11	3	14	49	44	33
Sev. Beach Fusion	28	10	1	17	58	75	31
Henleaze Rovers	28	9	2	17	70	77	29
Greyfriars Ath. 'B'	28	4	1	23	34	102	13
YMCA Cricketers	28	3	2	23	51	128	11
Wessex Wdrs 'A'	28	2	0	26	27	188	6

BRISTOL & DISTRICT LEAGUE

Senior Division

	P	W	D	L	F	A	Pts
Avonmouth Village	24	14	7	3	51	30	49
Mendip United	24	15	3	6	51	30	48
Oldland Abb. Res.	24	14	3	7	59	43	45
Longwell G. S. Res.	24	13	4	7	53	26	43
Nicholas Wdrs Res.	24	12	4	8	48	33	40
Hanham Ath. Res.	24	12	3	9	33	29	39
AXA Res.	24	11	4	9	53	40	37
Knowle United	24	11	1	12	48	52	34
Shirehampton Res.	24	9	4	11	35	39	31
Pucklechurch Res.	24	7	2	15	34	53	23
Westerleigh Sports	24	6	4	14	43	65	22
Crosscourt United	24	5	4	15	37	76	19
Sea Mills Park Res.	24	4	3	17	28	57	15

Division One

	P	W	D	L	F	A	Pts
Soundwell Victoria	26	19	5	2	96	46	62
Wick Res.	26	19	4	3	78	33	61
Hartcliffe Com. Cte	26	19	3	4	85	35	60
Lawrence Rovers	26	15	4	7	83	38	49
Bitton 'A'	26	13	5	8	69	56	44
Hallen 'A'	25	12	2	11	57	51	38
Bendix	26	11	3	12	59	58	36
Coalpit Heath	26	10	4	12	66	54	34
Made for Ever	26	10	3	13	50	66	33
FM Sports	26	8	5	13	48	64	29
Hartcliffe Res.	26	7	7	12	41	59	28
Highridge Utd 'A'	25	7	2	16	40	67	23
Iron Acton Res.	26	5	5	16	32	65	20
DRG Stapleton Res.	26	0	0	26	14	126	0

Division Two

	P	W	D	L	F	A	Pts
RG St George 'A'	26	18	4	4	57	28	58
Chipping Sod. Res.	26	17	4	5	71	38	55
St Pancras	26	16	7	3	70	41	55
Shaftesbury C. Res.	26	16	3	7	56	32	51
Hillfields OB Res.	26	12	5	9	50	48	41
Henbury OB 'A'	26	11	3	12	62	53	36
Hambrook	26	10	3	13	51	54	33
Patchway Town 'A'	26	9	6	11	41	58	33
AEK Boco Res.	26	8	7	11	49	55	31
S. Bristol Cent. Res.	26	8	5	13	45	66	29
Greyfriars Ath. Res.	26	7	6	13	46	59	27
Seymour Utd Res.	26	8	2	16	45	55	26
Nicholas Wdrs 'A'	26	7	5	14	36	59	26
Stockw'd B'kaways	26	2	6	18	23	56	12

Division Three

	P	W	D	L	F	A	Pts
Old Sodbury	26	24	2	0	134	26	74
Miners Rangers	26	21	1	4	77	26	64
Longwell Green 'A'	26	15	4	7	57	26	49
Shirehampton 'A'	26	15	4	7	69	56	49
Rangeworthy	26	13	2	11	64	49	41
Fry Club 'A'	26	13	2	11	52	64	41
Winterbourne 'A'	26	12	4	10	61	46	40
Totterdown U. Res.	26	9	4	13	43	54	31
Hallen 'B'	26	9	3	14	53	59	30
Frampton AR Res.	26	9	1	16	57	74	28
Fishponds Ath. Res.	26	6	6	14	38	63	24
Tilly Rangers	26	7	0	19	43	105	21
Olveston Utd Res.	26	5	5	16	35	70	20
Brimsham G. Res.	26	3	4	19	23	88	13

Division Four

	P	W	D	L	F	A	Pts
Brisl'ton Cricketers	26	23	1	2	124	40	70
Frampton AR 'A'	26	19	2	5	86	23	59
Oakland	26	17	2	7	61	42	53
Chipping Sod. 'A'	26	15	5	6	78	41	50
Eden Grove *-3*	26	15	3	8	59	43	45
Hanham Ath. 'A'	26	13	3	10	71	46	42
Warmley Sts Res.	26	9	4	13	57	75	31
Stockwood Wdrs	26	8	6	12	42	56	30
AXA 'A'	26	8	5	13	37	68	29
Made for Ever Res.	26	7	6	13	46	75	27
Fry Club 'B'	26	6	8	12	50	58	26
Westerleigh S. Res.	26	7	2	17	38	66	23
Hartcliffe 'A'	26	6	4	16	35	72	22
Pucklechurch 'A'	26	2	3	21	22	101	9

Division Five

	P	W	D	L	F	A	Pts
Shaftesb'y Crus. 'A'	22	18	0	4	82	38	54
St Nicholas	22	17	2	3	52	30	53
Oldland Abbs 'A'	22	14	3	5	47	30	45
Wick 'A'	22	11	5	6	55	42	38
St Pancras Res.	22	11	4	7	60	46	37
Talbot Knowle Res.	22	10	2	10	62	46	32
Soundwell V. Res.	22	10	0	12	49	60	30
Air	22	9	2	11	46	48	29
Henbury OB 'B'	22	8	1	13	38	54	25
Longwell Green 'B'	22	7	2	13	51	51	23
AEK Boco 'A'	22	4	1	17	26	67	13
Bendix Res.	22	0	4	18	26	82	4

Division Six

	P	W	D	L	F	A	Pts
Bradley Stoke T.	26	22	1	3	124	32	67
Inter The Bloomf'ld	26	22	1	3	121	36	67
Shireway Sports	25	20	1	4	96	31	61
Impact Squad	26	17	5	4	102	52	56
St Philips MAS Res.	26	14	2	10	87	73	44
Coalpit Heath Res.	26	14	2	10	62	53	44
Portville Warriors	26	11	2	13	76	68	35
Greyfriars Ath. 'A'	26	9	2	15	50	70	29
Little Thatch	26	9	2	15	53	83	29
Fishponds Ath. 'A'	26	7	4	15	42	103	25
S. Bristol Cent. 'A'	26	5	5	16	34	102	20
Crosscourt Utd Res.	25	5	3	17	42	78	18
Seymour United 'A'	26	4	4	18	36	83	16
AXA 'B'	26	4	2	20	21	82	14

BRISTOL & SUBURBAN LEAGUE

Premier Div One

	P	W	D	L	F	A	Pts
Avonmouth	28	22	0	6	94	45	66
Broad Plain Hse OB	28	21	2	5	87	38	65
Potterswood	28	15	6	7	90	67	51
Teyfant Athletic	28	14	5	9	79	44	47
Glenside Five	28	14	5	9	53	41	47
St Aldhelms	28	12	9	7	70	48	45
Stoke Gifford	28	13	3	12	59	63	42
Almondsb'y T. Res.	28	11	8	9	54	50	41
Almondsbury Res.	28	10	6	12	58	65	36
B & W Avonside	28	8	10	10	48	50	34
De Veys	28	8	4	16	55	73	28
Fishponds Old Boys	28	8	3	17	55	79	27
Ashton United	28	8	3	17	54	81	27
Ridings High	28	8	3	17	38	66	27
Bristol Telephones	28	3	3	22	26	110	12

Premier Div Two

	P	W	D	L	F	A	Pts
Winford PH	28	23	2	3	97	33	71
Old Georgians	28	22	2	4	102	29	68
Brist. Builders Supp.	28	21	5	2	102	37	68
Cadbury Heath Res.	28	18	4	6	73	33	58
St Aldhelms Res.	28	15	5	8	65	42	50
Whitchurch	28	16	2	10	69	51	50
Golden Hill	28	11	1	16	57	73	34
Brislington 'A'	28	10	1	17	54	77	31
Old Cothamians	28	10	1	17	41	79	31
Little Stoke	28	9	3	16	41	64	30
Ashton Rangers	28	9	1	18	56	64	28
Glenside Five Res.	28	8	2	18	32	88	26
Filton Athletic	28	7	4	17	61	80	25
Totterdown PB Res.	28	6	5	17	40	80	23
Hartcliffe Old Boys	28	5	2	21	31	91	17

Division One

	P	W	D	L	F	A	Pts
TC Sports	28	22	4	2	101	31	70
Astra Zeneca	28	20	5	3	88	29	65
CTK Southside	28	20	3	5	85	39	63
S. Glos (Hambrook)	28	18	3	7	84	39	57
Lockleaze	28	17	2	9	86	47	53
Broad Plain H. Res.	28	17	2	9	78	59	53
Bristol North West	28	12	7	9	68	55	43
Ashton United Res.	28	10	4	14	36	63	34
Ridings High Res.	28	10	3	15	41	64	33
Corinthian Sports	28	9	3	16	53	94	30
Hengrove BC	28	8	3	17	38	69	27
Stoke Gifford Res.	28	7	4	17	47	61	25
B&W Avonside Res.	28	5	4	19	41	74	19
Tyndalls Park Rgrs	28	4	5	19	40	62	17
Brist. Phones Res.	28	4	2	22	30	130	14

Division Two

	P	W	D	L	F	A	Pts
Southmead Athletic	28	27	0	1	112	31	81
Tytherington Res.	28	22	2	4	100	28	68
Avonmouth Res.	28	19	3	6	74	34	60
Lawrence Weston	28	15	7	6	76	63	52
Totterdown PoB 'A'	28	14	5	9	79	69	47
St Aldhelms 'A'	28	12	5	11	58	57	41
Rolls Royce	28	12	4	12	74	68	40
Almondsbury 'A'	28	13	0	15	58	56	39
Fishponds OB Res.	28	12	3	13	58	61	39
Cadbury Heath 'A'	28	11	4	13	66	89	37
Hengrove Old Boys	28	7	4	17	56	66	25
Oldbury Crusaders	28	5	7	16	44	85	22
Sefton Park	28	6	2	20	35	74	20
O. Cothamians Res.	28	5	5	18	44	92	20
Imperial Saints	28	2	5	21	33	94	11

Division Three

	P	W	D	L	F	A	Pts
Ashton Old Boys	20	17	2	1	79	15	53
Wessex Wanderers	20	14	2	4	57	18	44
Little Stoke Res.	20	13	3	4	52	36	42
Ingleside	20	12	1	7	52	32	37
Parson Street OB	20	9	1	10	47	54	28
Brandon TT Sports	20	7	4	9	46	53	25
Unathletico	20	6	3	11	23	36	21
Ashton United 'A'	20	5	3	12	35	64	18
Teyfant Ath. Res.	20	5	2	13	29	55	17
Thrissells Nomads	20	5	2	13	25	65	17
Ridings High 'A'	20	5	1	14	49	66	16

Division Four

	P	W	D	L	F	A	Pts
Avonmouth Rgrs	22	18	1	3	89	35	55
Glenside Five 'A'	22	12	6	4	52	35	42
Southmead A. Res.	22	12	5	5	64	48	41
Broad Plain Hse 'A'	22	11	6	5	49	36	39
Astra Zeneca Res.	22	11	5	6	60	33	38
St Annes Town	22	11	2	9	60	72	35
Old Georgians Res.	22	9	5	8	57	47	32
Fishponds OB 'A'	22	8	6	8	54	42	30
Bristol Phones 'A'	22	6	2	14	35	43	20
Wanderers AFC	22	5	4	13	36	62	19
Lockleaze Res.	22	5	4	13	37	66	19
Oldbury Crus. Res.	22	1	0	21	22	96	3

Division Five

	P	W	D	L	F	A	Pts
TC Sports Res.	18	16	0	2	68	27	48
Avonmouth 'A'	18	14	3	1	58	22	45
Winford PH Res.	18	12	2	4	58	40	38
Whitchurch Res.	18	10	2	6	50	48	32
Fishponds OB 'B'	18	7	2	9	45	34	23
Parson Str. OB Res.	18	5	5	8	32	51	20
Stoke Gifford 'A'	18	5	2	11	34	44	17
Filton Athletic Res.	18	4	3	11	30	42	15
Wessex Wdrs Res.	18	3	6	9	27	51	15
LK Sports	18	1	1	16	25	68	4

BROMLEY & DISTRICT LEAGUE

Premier Division

	P	W	D	L	F	A	Pts
Blackheath United	18	15	2	1	53	12	47
Caribb	18	10	3	5	41	28	33
Old Addeyans Res.	18	9	6	3	37	25	33
Univ. of Greenwich	18	9	3	6	53	32	30
South East Athletic	18	10	0	8	53	51	30
Unity Res.	17	6	4	7	26	25	22
Phoenix Sp. Res. *+3*	18	6	1	11	35	40	22
Rotherhithe	18	6	4	8	42	49	22
Seven Acre Sp. Res.	17	2	2	13	29	77	8
O. Colfeians Res. *-3*	18	3	1	14	25	55	7

Hollington YPC – record expunged

Division One	P	W	D	L	F	A	Pts
OPK Infero	18	14	2	2	54	19	44
Cray W & NB Res.	18	13	2	3	63	26	41
AFC Mottingham	18	11	4	3	60	31	37
South East Four	18	9	3	6	54	50	30
Erith '147 Res.	18	7	2	9	35	46	23
Gold Hawks	18	6	2	10	43	43	20
Dulwich Town	18	5	5	8	50	52	20
Chislehurst D'moes	18	5	4	9	28	52	19
Barnet Wood	18	5	0	13	30	69	15
AFC Bromley	18	2	2	14	33	62	8

Ex-Blues – record expunged

Division Two	P	W	D	L	F	A	Pts
Biggin Hill	22	17	2	3	78	24	53
South Star	22	17	1	4	63	28	52
Highfield Rovers	22	15	3	4	67	32	48
Iron Tugboat City	22	14	3	5	57	33	45
Welling Park	22	13	3	6	71	34	42
Crofton Albion 'A'	22	9	0	13	62	60	27
Charlton Ath. Deaf	22	8	2	12	50	69	26
Heathfield	22	7	2	13	36	51	23
Farnboro. OBG 'B'	22	6	3	13	32	52	21
Latter-Day Sts *+2*	22	4	4	14	46	77	18
Penhill S'dard Res.	22	5	1	16	28	87	16
O. Colfeians 'B' *-3*	22	5	0	17	46	89	12

Ex-Blues Res. – record expunged

BURY & DISTRICT LEAGUE
(Glasswells)

Division One	P	W	D	L	F	A	Pts
Black Eagles	24	20	0	4	84	33	60
Barons	24	14	2	8	52	51	44
Westbury United	24	12	6	6	56	41	42
Rising Sun	24	13	2	9	54	36	41
Bushel	24	11	4	9	64	51	37
Lawshall Swan	24	10	3	11	60	56	33
Macebearer	24	8	1	15	38	69	25
Jubilee '96	24	5	4	15	54	84	19
Pot Black '06	24	2	4	18	38	79	10

Division Two	P	W	D	L	F	A	Pts
Priors Inn	21	17	1	3	75	24	52
Studlands Park	21	12	3	6	54	30	39
Sporting '87 Res.	21	11	5	5	49	32	38
Ixworth Pykkerell	21	11	3	7	65	51	36
Bartons	21	7	5	9	30	41	26
AFC Norton	21	5	3	13	43	51	18
Elveden Phoenix	21	4	5	12	29	62	17
RF Saints	21	4	1	16	25	79	13

WWW.CHERRYRED.CO.UK

CAERNARFON &DISTRICT LEAGUE

	P	W	D	L	F	A	Pts
Llanystumdwy	26	24	1	1	100	35	73
Talysarn Celts	26	16	5	5	71	40	53
Y Felinheli *-3*	26	17	3	6	87	50	51
Llanrug Utd Res.	26	15	2	9	65	43	47
Caernarfon Boro.	26	11	6	9	66	49	39
Pwllheli Res.	26	12	2	12	66	66	38
Rhiwlas	26	9	8	9	60	57	35
Trefor	26	9	5	12	46	47	32
Blaenau FA Res. *-3*	26	9	5	12	60	80	29
Nefyn United Res.	26	6	10	10	44	50	28
Penrhyndeudraeth	26	8	3	15	49	76	27
Llanrwst Res. *-3*	26	10	2	14	44	63	29
Machno United	26	6	4	16	57	88	22
Myn'd Llandegai *-3*	26	2	0	24	30	101	3

CARDIFF COMBINATION

Premier Division	P	W	D	L	F	A	Pts
Avenue Hotspur	22	19	0	3	99	40	57
Baybridge	22	18	2	2	75	26	56
Thornhill United	22	13	2	7	62	31	41
Heath Park United	22	10	5	7	53	44	35
Cardiff Hibernians	22	9	3	10	55	67	30
Butetown United	22	8	4	10	36	49	28
Fairwater Hotel	22	7	4	11	32	55	25
Cdf Inter Churches	22	6	6	10	57	58	24
Park Lawn	22	6	4	12	42	63	22
Cathays United	22	5	6	11	42	56	21
Highcroft	22	6	3	13	35	66	21
Fairoak	22	3	5	14	33	66	14

Division One	P	W	D	L	F	A	Pts
Heath Park Utd Res.	22	17	3	2	71	32	54
AC Central	22	14	3	5	84	48	45
South Park Athletic	22	14	3	5	60	34	45
AFC W'church Res.	22	12	4	6	65	59	40
Thornhill Utd Res.	22	10	3	9	57	49	33
Royal Exchange	22	8	1	13	40	61	25
Thornhill	22	8	1	13	44	70	25
Cardiff Hibs Res.	22	7	3	12	57	66	24
AFC Highcroft	22	6	5	11	61	59	23
BTD Stars	22	6	5	11	49	68	23
Baybridge Res.	22	6	5	11	41	62	23
Cathays Cons	22	5	2	15	35	56	17

Division Two	P	W	D	L	F	A	Pts
Park Villa	18	16	1	1	107	24	49
Llanedeyrn Bulldogs	18	12	3	3	71	23	39
Fairoak Res.	18	8	6	4	51	42	30
AC Central Res.	18	6	5	7	37	37	23
Pontprennau Pumas	18	6	4	8	37	48	22
Ely Rangers 'A'	18	6	3	9	33	58	21
Avenue H'spur Res.	18	6	2	10	48	50	20
Greenway	18	5	5	8	34	59	20
Cathays Park Rgrs	18	4	4	10	31	66	16
Park Lawn Res.	18	2	5	11	35	77	11

CENTRAL & SOUTH NORFOLK LEAGUE
(Crown Fire)

Division One	P	W	D	L	F	A	Pts
Toftwood United	24	18	1	5	83	36	55
Redgrave Rangers	24	15	5	4	66	41	50
Hingham Athletic	24	15	5	4	58	42	50
North Elmham	24	17	1	6	78	50	49
Yaxham	24	11	5	8	65	52	38
Saham Toney	24	11	4	9	57	36	37
Swaffham T. 'A'	24	9	4	11	52	54	31
Mulbarton Wdrs	24	9	3	12	51	57	30
Stoke Ferry	24	8	3	13	53	78	27
Gressenhall	24	7	5	12	48	70	26
Feltwell United	24	7	2	15	44	67	23
Rockland United	24	3	5	16	35	66	17
Tacolneston	24	1	7	16	29	70	10

Division Two	P	W	D	L	F	A	Pts
Dereham Posties	22	20	2	0	105	11	62
East Harling Res.	22	16	4	2	88	32	52
Shipdham	22	16	2	4	73	31	50
Wymondham T. 'A'	22	14	0	8	72	37	42
Bridgham United	22	10	4	8	58	49	34
Attleborough T. 'A'	22	9	2	11	66	76	29
Morley Village Res.	22	8	1	13	47	75	25
Saham Toney Res.	22	8	0	14	45	71	24
Necton SSC Res.	22	6	3	13	46	80	21
Dickleburgh	22	4	4	14	51	98	16
Yaxham Res.	22	5	0	17	37	70	15
Wendling	22	4	2	16	32	90	14

Division Three	P	W	D	L	F	A	Pts
Thetford Athletic	22	17	2	3	76	24	53
Mattishall 'A'	22	14	5	3	64	34	47
North Elmham Res.	22	10	4	8	60	43	34
Bunwell	22	10	1	11	44	45	31
Watton United 'A'	22	9	4	9	48	49	31
Foulsham Res	22	9	2	11	44	38	29
Toftwood Utd Res.	22	9	2	11	55	63	29
Hingham Ath. Res.	22	8	4	10	48	54	28
Rockland Utd Res.	22	8	4	10	44	50	28
West End	22	9	1	12	39	59	28
Bawdeswell	22	7	1	14	42	70	22
Shipdham Res	22	6	2	14	40	75	20

Division Four	P	W	D	L	F	A	Pts
Cockers	22	19	1	2	86	25	58
Brandon Town 'A'	22	18	2	2	73	27	56
Swanton Morley	22	15	1	6	82	35	46
Gressenhall Res.	22	14	1	7	69	42	43
Bintree	22	12	5	5	55	36	41
Thurton & Ashby	22	10	1	11	53	55	31
Great Cressingham	22	7	4	11	42	49	25
Bunwell Res	22	7	2	13	39	74	23
Beetley	22	5	4	13	41	66	19
Colkirk	22	6	0	16	33	73	18
Garboldisham	22	3	5	14	34	76	14
Splitz United	22	2	2	18	27	76	8

CHELTENHAM ASSOCIATION LEAGUE

Division One	P	W	D	L	F	A	Pts
Hatherley Rangers	26	21	2	3	92	34	65
Winchcombe Town	26	19	4	3	65	25	61
Andoversford Nmds	26	16	4	6	71	45	52
Endsleigh *-3*	26	14	6	6	66	41	45
Shipton Oliffe	26	11	5	10	47	43	38
Newton FC	26	11	4	11	47	41	37
Bishops Cleeve 'A'	26	9	7	10	40	47	34
Kings AFC	26	6	9	11	43	44	27
Chelt. Civil S. Res.	26	7	6	13	33	59	27
Naunton Park *-3*	26	7	8	11	50	67	26
Northway *-3*	26	7	6	13	44	58	24
Prestbury Rovers	26	4	8	14	30	66	20
Dynamos	26	4	7	15	35	69	19
Belmore Jags *-7*	26	6	4	16	39	63	15

Division Two	P	W	D	L	F	A	Pts
Finlay Rovers	22	18	2	2	77	21	56
Moreton Rangers	22	18	1	3	79	33	55
Woodmancote	22	13	5	4	68	38	44
FC Barometrics	22	13	2	7	47	35	41
Star Res.	22	12	2	8	44	45	38
Brockw'th Alb. Res.	22	9	3	10	53	49	30
Northleach Town	22	9	2	11	48	50	29
High Tech Rangers	22	7	4	11	45	57	25
Gala Wilton Res.	22	8	1	13	43	60	25
Chelt. Saras 'A' *-4*	22	5	5	12	34	56	16
Bredon Res.	22	4	2	16	47	69	14
Bourton Rov. Res.	22	1	1	20	23	95	4

Tewkesbury YMCA – record expunged

Division Three	P	W	D	L	F	A	Pts
Whaddon United	24	22	0	2	108	20	66
AC Olympia	24	16	3	5	66	31	51
Tewkesbury Dyn.	24	11	4	9	56	37	37
Charlton Rovers	24	10	7	7	42	40	37
Winchcombe Res.	24	10	6	8	52	49	36
Broadway Utd *-3*	24	11	5	8	66	44	35
Smiths Athletic Res.	24	8	9	7	57	55	33
Bishops Cleeve 'B'	24	7	8	9	51	48	29
Falcons	24	9	1	14	39	72	28
Phoenix United	24	9	0	15	36	69	27
FC Electrics	24	7	5	12	53	74	26
Belmore J. Res. *-3*	24	8	4	12	50	62	25
Andoversford Res.	24	2	0	22	23	98	6

Northway Res. – record expunged

Division Four	P	W	D	L	F	A	Pts
Tewkesbury Town	22	15	4	3	61	29	49
Tivoli Rovers	22	15	2	5	67	33	47
Charlton Rov. Res.	22	13	4	5	72	40	43
Whaddon Utd Res.	22	9	8	5	49	37	35
Kings AFC Res.	22	9	5	8	40	43	32
Gaffers *-3*	22	9	7	6	53	49	31
Chelt'ham CS 'A'	22	5	9	8	35	43	24
Brockworth A. 'A'	22	6	4	12	42	55	22
Elmbridge OB	22	5	7	10	50	71	22
Chelt. Saracens 'B'	22	5	3	14	56	81	18
Charlton Kings *-3*	22	4	7	11	36	56	16
Smiths Ath. 'A' *-3*	22	5	4	13	36	60	16

Division Five	P	W	D	L	F	A	Pts
Churchdown Panth.	26	18	5	3	94	40	59
Gala Wilton 'A'	26	18	4	4	64	42	58
Finlay Rovers Res.	26	18	3	5	82	48	57
Bredon 'A'	26	15	4	7	94	56	49
Tewkesbury D. Res.	26	15	4	7	63	46	49
FC Electrics Res.	26	14	4	8	70	54	46
Southside	26	11	4	11	73	61	37
Northleach T.Res.	26	8	4	14	52	76	28
Star 'A'	26	7	6	13	35	58	27
Cleevonians	26	6	8	12	50	72	26
Charlton Rov. 'A'	26	7	3	16	59	78	24
Cheltenham CS 'B'	26	5	5	16	26	72	20
Sherborne Harr. *-3*	26	6	4	16	67	74	19
Gaffers Res.	26	3	4	19	36	88	13

CHESTER & DISTRICT LEAGUE

Premier Division	P	W	D	L	F	A	Pts
Castrol Social Res.	22	19	2	1	99	22	59
Kydds Athletic	22	14	3	5	69	45	45
Waggon & Horses	22	12	4	6	67	52	40
Highfield Athletic	22	10	7	5	58	40	37
Hoole Rangers	22	11	2	9	49	46	35
Tarvin Athletic *-2*	22	9	5	8	46	36	30
Duddon United	22	8	6	8	34	44	30
Frodsham United	22	7	4	11	39	45	25
Chester Nmds Res.	22	7	4	11	45	62	25
Blacon YC 'A'	22	6	3	13	34	65	21
Newton Celtic	22	4	3	15	48	78	15
Team Highfield	22	3	1	18	43	96	10

Division One	P	W	D	L	F	A	Pts
Kelsall	16	11	2	3	48	32	35
Crossway	16	10	3	3	56	30	33
Cestrian Alexandra	16	10	2	4	59	39	32
AFC Bebington Res.	16	9	1	6	56	41	28
Ashton Lions	16	7	3	6	47	32	24
Bank of Scotland	16	5	2	9	36	49	17
Blacon YC Colts	16	4	2	10	26	50	14
Chester Nmds 'A'	16	3	3	10	32	52	12
Barrow Athletic	16	4	0	12	26	61	12

Division Two	P	W	D	L	F	A	Pts
Sutton Way Villa	16	13	1	2	61	17	40
City Bar *-4*	16	13	2	1	66	16	37
Parkgate	16	10	3	3	59	18	33
Helsby Res.	16	7	3	6	40	35	24
Robin Hood	16	6	2	8	26	45	20
Rangers Breaks	16	4	4	8	26	39	16
Barrow Ath. Res.	16	3	3	10	33	55	12
Runcorn Albion 'A'	16	3	3	10	27	52	12
Boughton Athletic	16	1	3	12	18	79	6

CIRENCESTER & DISTRICT LEAGUE

Division One	P	W	D	L	F	A	Pts
Siddington	24	19	2	3	107	30	59
Beeches	24	18	4	2	95	35	58
Bibury	24	18	2	4	69	31	56
South Cerney	24	14	4	6	68	39	46
Real Fairford	24	12	6	6	68	49	42
Taverners Res.	24	12	5	7	52	38	41
Oaksey	24	9	5	10	53	52	32
Kingshill SC	24	9	2	13	55	54	29
Avonvale United	24	8	4	12	52	47	28
Poulton	24	8	2	14	50	81	26
Golden Farm	24	4	1	19	33	86	13
Bees Knees *-3*	24	3	2	19	37	92	8
Tetbury T. 'A' *-1*	24	2	1	21	25	130	6

Division Two	P	W	D	L	F	A	Pts
South Cerney Res.	30	21	3	6	93	27	66
Down Ampney	30	22	0	8	96	45	66
Lechlade	30	20	5	5	85	38	65
Beeches Res.	30	17	8	5	103	51	59
Stratton United	30	14	5	11	74	85	47
Oakridge	30	13	7	10	91	68	46
Bibury Res.	30	13	4	13	74	81	43
Taverners 'A'	30	16	4	10	97	68	40
Corinium Sports	30	11	7	12	66	79	40
Ashton Keynes Res.	30	10	8	12	67	64	38
Minety Res.	30	11	4	15	74	79	37
Avonvale Utd Res.	30	9	6	15	59	80	33
Kingshill SC Res.	30	8	4	18	74	138	28
CHQ United Res.	30	6	6	18	63	99	24
Chalford 'A'	30	7	6	17	48	77	22
Oaksey Res.	30	2	3	25	57	142	9

COVENTRY ALLIANCE

Premier Division	P	W	D	L	F	A	Pts
Witherley United	28	19	5	4	47	26	62
Christ The King	28	16	4	8	66	36	52
Bedworth Ex-Serv.	28	13	8	7	51	31	47
Woodlands WMC	28	14	5	9	49	31	47
Alvis	28	14	4	10	49	36	46
Mount Nod H'way	28	14	4	10	54	49	46
Brooklands-Jaguar	28	11	8	9	36	45	41
Stockton	28	12	2	14	50	42	38
Bulkington S&S	28	9	8	11	37	44	35
Folly Lane BCOB	28	9	7	12	50	46	34
Stock'ford AA Pav.	28	9	7	12	38	47	34
Dunlop	28	9	3	16	36	51	30
Peugeot	28	8	6	14	49	65	30
Copsew'd Coventry	28	7	5	16	43	67	26
Coundon Court OB	28	5	6	17	33	72	21

Division One	P	W	D	L	F	A	Pts
AEI Rugby	22	15	7	0	57	21	52
Hawkes Mill Sports	22	14	6	2	65	31	48
Triumph Athletic	22	14	2	6	56	29	44
Coventry University	22	11	2	9	63	40	35
Potters Green	22	10	5	7	45	29	35
Ambleside Sports	22	9	4	9	51	38	31
Coventry Colliery	22	8	6	8	34	41	30
Folly Lane Res.	22	7	4	11	27	41	25
Nun. Griff & Coton	22	6	4	12	36	60	22
Brooklands-J. Res.	22	5	5	12	30	62	20
Bourton/Frankton	22	3	7	12	30	51	16
Kenilworth Wdns	22	4	0	18	22	73	12

Division Two	P	W	D	L	F	A	Pts
Collycroft Sports	22	16	4	2	62	30	52
Alvis Res.	22	13	6	3	58	36	45
Christ The K. Res.	22	13	5	4	53	19	44
Shilton	22	12	4	6	57	44	40
Triumph Ath. Res.	22	11	2	9	46	43	35
Fillongley	22	8	3	11	39	42	27
Copsew'd Cov. Res.	22	6	6	10	36	48	24
Balsall & Berkswell	22	7	3	12	38	62	24
Folly Lane 'A'	22	6	5	11	39	41	23
Peugeot Res.	22	7	2	13	57	64	23
Dunlop Res.	22	3	7	12	24	52	16
Mount Nod Res. *-3*	22	5	3	14	32	60	15

Division Thtree	P	W	D	L	F	A	Pts
Stockton Res.	22	14	4	4	78	34	46
Potters Green Res.	22	14	3	5	50	57	45
Spting Club (GNP)	22	13	2	7	57	50	41
Christ The King 'A'	22	11	4	7	47	39	37
Witherley Utd Res.	22	10	5	7	44	38	35
Brinklow	22	9	4	9	58	49	31
Cov. Univ. Res. *-3*	22	10	2	10	50	41	29
Coundon Court Res.	22	7	5	10	52	58	26
Bulkington SS Res.	22	5	8	9	34	46	23
Bedw'th Ex-S. Res.	22	7	1	14	38	53	22
AEI Rugby Res.	22	5	5	12	40	60	20
Hillmorton *-3*	22	4	3	15	36	59	12

Division Four	P	W	D	L	F	A	Pts
Woodlands Res.	20	16	2	2	68	17	50
Hub	20	14	3	3	69	38	45
Heart Athletic	20	14	2	4	56	29	44
Cov. Colliery Res.	20	9	1	10	43	35	28
Hawkes Mill Res.	20	8	3	9	40	46	27
Bermuda WMC	20	8	3	9	36	45	27
Ambleside S. Res.	20	8	3	9	30	43	27
Bilton Social	20	8	1	11	30	52	25
Collycroft Spts Res.	20	5	3	12	39	59	18
Kenilworth W. Res.	20	4	3	13	37	51	15
AEI Rugby 'A'	20	2	4	14	24	57	10

Division Five	P	W	D	L	F	A	Pts
Hartshill	18	14	3	1	82	21	45
Cherry Tree	18	14	3	1	69	31	45
Balsall/B'well Res.	18	11	2	5	49	25	35
Bourton & F. Res.	18	10	1	7	49	48	31
Church Lawford	18	7	3	8	62	59	24
Cov. University 'A'	18	6	4	8	47	45	22
Shilton Res.	18	6	2	10	30	58	20
Fillongley Res.	18	3	5	10	32	57	14
Peugeot 'A'	18	3	1	14	30	61	10
Bermuda Res.	18	2	4	12	18	63	10

CRAVEN & DISTRICT FA

Premier Division	P	W	D	L	F	A	Pts
Oxenhope Rec.	22	19	2	1	78	24	59
Waddington	22	13	3	6	65	46	42
WFC Clitheroe	22	12	3	7	69	70	39
Embsay	22	12	0	10	56	45	36
Skipton LMS	22	11	3	8	56	45	36
Grassington United	22	10	5	7	69	51	35
Cononley Sports	22	9	1	12	71	63	28
Gargrave *-6*	22	8	3	11	39	58	21
Hellifield Sports	22	7	4	11	60	73	25
Bradley	22	6	5	11	54	59	23
Carleton	22	5	4	13	49	73	19
Bronte Wdrs Res.	22	2	3	17	27	86	9

Division One	P	W	D	L	F	A	Pts
Oxenhope Rec. Res.	22	15	3	4	66	32	48
Skipton Town	22	15	2	5	75	47	47
Clitheroe Lions	22	13	5	4	66	44	44
Grindleton *-3*	22	13	5	4	62	44	41
Pendle Athletic	22	12	1	9	53	56	37
Long Lee Juniors	22	8	6	8	49	40	30
Keighley	22	9	2	11	50	58	29
Intake	22	7	3	12	43	55	24
Rolls Royce	22	7	2	13	41	51	23
Cowling	22	6	3	13	45	66	21
Embsay Res.	22	3	5	14	36	59	14
Trawden Celtic	22	3	5	14	31	65	14

Division Two	P	W	D	L	F	A	Pts
Gargrave Res.	20	17	3	0	115	31	54
Oakworth	20	14	5	1	63	24	47
Barrowford United	20	12	4	4	62	33	40
Cononley Spts Res.	20	10	2	8	68	64	32
Grassington Res. *-3*	20	9	2	9	52	53	26
Chatburn	20	8	2	10	55	68	26
Skipton LMS Res.	20	7	2	11	53	69	23
Rolls Royce Res.	20	6	3	11	41	52	21
Horton	20	6	3	11	46	70	21
Barn'wick Barons	20	5	3	12	34	66	18
Waddington Res.	20	0	3	17	42	101	3

Intake Res. – record expunged

Division Three	P	W	D	L	F	A	Pts
Pendle Renegades	19	16	2	1	73	30	50
Earby Town	20	15	3	2	98	40	48
Oakworth Res.	20	12	2	6	71	55	38
Silsden White Star	19	11	1	7	67	39	34
Hellifield Spts Res.	20	9	2	9	43	53	29
Bradley Res.	20	8	3	9	58	77	27
Grindleton Res.	20	8	0	12	62	68	24
B'wick Barons Res.	20	6	3	11	57	64	21
Skipton Town Res.	20	6	2	12	50	66	20
Carleton Res.	20	5	1	14	44	86	16
Cowling Res.	20	3	1	16	44	89	10

Ingleton 'B' – record expunged

CRAWLEY & DISTRICT LEAGUE

Premier Division	P	W	D	L	F	A	Pts
GSK Phoenix	18	11	5	2	52	19	38
Merstham Newton	18	11	3	4	46	21	36
Holland Sports	18	11	1	6	58	36	34
Three Bridges 'A'	18	10	3	5	55	34	33
Ifield Edwards Res.	18	10	3	5	38	30	33
Trumpton Town	18	6	5	7	34	30	23
Horley Albion	18	6	2	10	26	49	20
Bletchingley	18	4	4	10	21	35	16
Oakwood 'A'	18	5	1	12	26	49	16
Cent. Sussex College	18	2	1	15	12	65	7

Division One	P	W	D	L	F	A	Pts
Northgate Athletic	18	15	2	1	55	14	47
St Francis Flyers	18	12	4	2	62	18	40
Maidenbower Vill.	18	12	3	3	52	24	39
County Oak	18	9	2	7	49	34	29
Broadfield *-3*	18	9	2	7	46	43	26
Ifield Edw'ds 'A' *+3*	18	5	1	12	37	67	19
Real Hydraquip	18	4	6	8	39	48	18
GSK Phoenix Res.	18	6	0	12	37	54	18
Sporting Crawley	18	5	1	12	39	59	16
Worth Park Rangers	18	2	1	15	30	85	7

Division Two	P	W	D	L	F	A	Pts
Crawley Elite	18	16	0	2	66	22	48
St Francis F. Res. *+3*	18	14	1	3	61	23	46
Sussex Elite	18	13	0	5	74	30	39
Stone Brite *-3*	18	13	0	5	68	40	36
Ifield Edwards 'B'	18	8	1	9	69	47	25
GSK Phoenix 'A' *+3*	18	7	1	10	48	64	25
Holland Sports Res.	18	5	3	10	35	58	18
M'nbwr D'moes *-3*	18	5	2	11	33	70	14
Horley Albion Res.	18	2	3	13	21	57	9
Wingspan	18	0	3	15	25	89	3

Division Three	P	W	D	L	F	A	Pts
Real Hyd'quip Res.	14	13	0	1	65	12	39
Seebrook Rovers	14	10	1	3	43	24	31
Pelham Wanderers	14	8	1	5	43	23	25
Rowfant Village	14	6	3	5	31	23	21
Stones	14	6	2	6	27	28	20
Border Wanderers	14	3	3	8	18	43	12
Sptng Crawley Res.	14	2	3	9	24	50	9
M'bwr Village Res.	14	0	3	11	17	65	3

DONCASTER & DIST. SENIOR LEAGUE

Premier Division	P	W	D	L	F	A	Pts
Kinsley Boys	28	24	2	2	135	24	74
Hemsworth Alpha	28	23	2	3	127	46	71
Thorne Town	28	19	1	8	79	50	58
Upton & Harewood	28	15	4	9	82	59	49
Retford Town	28	15	4	9	63	49	49
Mexborough Ath.	28	13	5	10	71	64	44
Moorland	28	11	5	12	57	70	38
Pontefract C. Res.	28	11	4	13	37	48	37
Sth Kirkby C. Res.	28	10	3	15	58	81	33
Rossington M. Res.	28	10	0	18	60	80	30
Askern Welf. Res.	28	9	3	16	61	88	30
Bawtry Town	28	9	3	16	52	81	30
Swinton Station	28	8	3	17	56	85	27
Ackworth United	28	6	2	20	43	93	20
Eden Grove	28	4	5	19	37	100	17

Division One	P	W	D	L	F	A	Pts
Maltby Sheppey	26	24	2	0	111	34	74
Edlington Rangers	26	17	4	5	100	63	55
Donc. College Deaf	26	17	3	6	87	51	54
Armthorpe W. Res.	26	15	6	5	82	41	51
TPS	26	15	2	9	66	49	47
Adwick Park Rgrs	26	13	2	11	80	57	41
Kinsley Boys Res.	26	11	7	8	42	48	40
Hemsworth Tavern	26	10	5	11	78	63	35
Hemswth Alpha Res.	26	9	2	15	56	86	29
Edlington/Wadw'rth	26	6	6	14	56	89	24
AFC Beeches	26	6	3	17	53	79	21
Wickersley OB Res.	26	6	3	17	44	70	21
Cooplands United	26	4	4	18	48	121	16
Sutton Rovers	26	0	9	17	35	87	9

DRIFFIELD & DISTRICT LEAGUE

Premier Division	P	W	D	L	F	A	Pts
Bridlington Sports C.	16	14	1	1	75	15	43
Yorkies	15	10	4	1	44	10	34
Driffield Rangers	15	8	3	4	34	23	27
Driffield Recreation	12	7	1	4	29	22	22
Driffield EI	15	7	1	7	35	40	22
Brid'ton Excelsior	16	5	4	7	29	35	19
Hutton Cran. SRA	16	2	6	8	20	40	12
Foresters Athletic	16	3	3	10	26	70	12
Bull & Sun Rangers	15	0	1	14	21	58	1

Burton Agnes – record expunged

Division One	P	W	D	L	F	A	Pts
Bridge Cafe United	18	11	4	3	51	28	37
Poachers Res.	18	10	4	4	53	30	34
Brid'ton Excel. Res.	18	8	7	3	37	27	31
Globe	18	7	6	5	41	46	27
Stirling Castle	18	7	5	6	42	36	26
Rose/Crown Driff'd	18	6	5	7	30	34	23
Flamborough	18	5	5	8	34	39	20
Hutton Cran. U. 'A'	18	6	2	10	39	44	20
Brid'gton Seabirds	18	4	6	8	37	54	18
Bridlington Rovers	18	3	2	13	27	53	11

Division Two	P	W	D	L	F	A	Pts
Yorkies Extra	18	14	3	1	62	24	45
Bridlington SC Res.	18	11	4	3	64	36	37
Hutton CSRA OB	18	11	4	3	62	36	37
Flamborough Res.	18	8	3	7	46	34	27
Burton Agnes Res.	18	8	3	7	47	49	27
Middleton Rovers	18	5	6	7	48	50	21
North Frodingham	18	5	4	9	44	56	19
Nafferton CK	18	4	2	12	43	67	14
North Burton	18	4	2	12	28	55	14
Driffield Wdrs	18	2	5	11	33	70	11

Division Three	P	W	D	L	F	A	Pts
Nafferton SRA	18	18	0	0	111	25	54
Little Driffield	18	14	1	3	76	44	43
Langtoft	18	12	0	6	45	31	36
Pocklington T 'B'	18	11	2	5	69	41	35
Forester Ath. Res.	18	11	1	6	60	49	34
Driffield Star	18	7	1	10	59	64	22
Spiders	18	3	4	11	43	67	13
Red Star Parade *-3*	18	3	2	13	39	73	8
Poachers 'A'	18	2	2	14	33	86	8
AFC United	18	2	1	15	26	81	7

WWW.CHERRYRED.CO.UK

DUCHY LEAGUE
(Bodmin Sports Trophies)

Premier Division	P	W	D	L	F	A	Pts
Bere Alston United	26	18	3	5	98	35	57
Polperro	26	17	2	7	71	32	53
St Dominick	26	16	4	6	86	33	52
Lamerton	26	16	3	7	80	38	51
St Newlyn East	26	14	5	7	71	29	47
Gunnislake	26	12	6	8	60	39	42
St Dennis Res.	26	12	5	9	54	45	41
Pensilva	26	11	5	10	46	41	38
Dobwalls Res.	26	9	4	13	67	67	31
St Mawgan	26	9	4	13	66	69	31
St Merryn	26	8	3	15	40	64	27
Sticker Res. *-3*	26	8	3	15	44	64	24
Boscastle	26	6	5	15	47	72	23
St Minver *-3*	26	0	0	26	12	214	-3

Division One	P	W	D	L	F	A	Pts
St Stephens Boro.	24	18	4	2	62	15	58
Edgcumbe	24	18	3	3	91	29	57
Launceston United	24	15	3	6	55	35	48
Torpoint Ath. 'A'	24	15	2	7	81	46	47
Roseland *-3*	24	15	2	7	51	29	44
Altarnun	24	11	4	9	71	66	37
St Anns Chapel	24	11	4	9	60	56	37
St Teath *+3*	24	9	3	12	48	41	33
Maker With Rame	24	6	5	13	43	57	23
Tywardreath RBL	24	5	4	15	45	62	19
Mevagissey	24	5	2	17	25	78	17
St Stephen Res.	24	4	2	18	28	88	14
St Columb Minor	24	3	4	17	37	95	13

Division Two	P	W	D	L	F	A	Pts
Looe	26	20	4	2	101	21	64
Lanivet	26	20	0	6	96	36	60
Godolphin A. Res. *-1*	26	15	7	4	71	36	51
Menheniot	26	14	5	7	75	61	47
Foxhole S. Res. *+2*	26	13	3	10	70	46	44
St Dominick Res.	26	11	7	8	55	44	40
Delabole United	26	9	9	8	57	51	36
St Cleer Res.	26	11	1	14	65	78	34
Pelynt	26	8	9	9	64	76	33
Camelford Res.	26	7	7	12	44	84	28
Polperro Res.	26	6	8	12	55	75	26
Callington T. 'A' *-3*	26	6	4	16	40	81	19
Gerrans	26	3	6	17	39	91	15
Newmoor Rov. *-9*	26	3	2	21	36	88	2

Division Thtree	P	W	D	L	F	A	Pts
Holywell B./Cubert	26	19	4	3	74	29	61
Fowey United	26	15	5	6	85	46	50
Saltash United 'A'	26	15	5	6	82	52	50
Probus Res. *+3*	26	13	5	8	62	39	47
St Breward	26	13	6	7	74	61	45
Grampound	26	13	5	8	52	38	44
Wadebridge T. 'A'	26	12	4	10	48	42	40
Roche Res.	26	11	5	10	41	43	38
Calstock	26	11	2	13	63	73	35
Biscovey Res. *-3*	26	8	5	13	46	58	26
Lewdown Rovers *-3*	26	8	5	13	50	71	26
Queens Rangers *-3*	26	7	6	13	45	69	24
Garrison Club *+3*	26	3	3	20	31	74	15
North Hill	26	3	2	21	35	93	11

Division Four	P	W	D	L	F	A	Pts
Lostwithiel	28	23	3	2	88	21	72
Bere Alston Res.	28	20	4	4	133	49	64
Week St Mary	28	20	2	6	105	36	62
Bodmin Saints	28	18	2	8	85	54	56
Lanreath Res. *-3*	28	18	4	6	76	55	55
Padstow Utd Res.	28	14	5	9	86	74	47
Pensilva Res.	28	11	3	14	45	57	36
Nanpean R. Res. *-6*	28	11	6	11	36	47	33
St New. East Res. *+2*	28	6	9	13	50	71	29
Boscastle Res.	28	8	4	16	51	96	28
St Mawgan Res. *+2*	28	6	7	15	36	62	27
Gorran	28	8	2	18	61	85	26
St Merryn Res.	28	7	3	18	67	104	24
Newmoor R. Res.	28	6	4	18	44	82	22
Lifton Res. *+3*	28	4	2	22	33	103	17

Division Five	P	W	D	L	F	A	Pts
Stratton United	24	18	1	5	91	39	55
Gunnislake Res. *+2*	24	15	4	5	77	40	51
Dynamo St Dennis	24	14	3	7	71	42	45
Looe Res.	24	14	3	7	60	42	45
Tintagel	24	12	2	10	59	55	38
St Teath Res.	24	11	4	9	38	34	37
St Austell Res.	24	11	3	10	86	53	36
Biscovey 'A' *-1*	24	11	3	10	52	53	35
Delabole Utd Res.	24	9	3	12	56	79	30
Altarnun Res.	24	8	3	13	54	67	27
Pelynt Res. *-3*	24	8	3	13	37	66	24
Grampound Res.	24	5	3	16	41	57	18
Stoke Climsland	24	2	1	21	31	126	7

St Columb Major Res. – record expunged

EAST BERKSHIRE LEAGUE

Premier Division	P	W	D	L	F	A	Pts
Waltham	24	17	4	3	56	27	55
Slough Heating	23	15	3	5	53	33	48
Spital Old Boys	24	14	5	5	70	41	47
Burnham Swan *-1*	24	14	5	5	54	39	46
FC Beaconsfield	23	12	3	8	55	46	39
Chalvey (WMC) S.	24	11	5	8	54	40	38
Orchard Park Rgrs	24	11	5	8	40	38	38
Old Windsor	24	11	4	9	41	41	37
Bracknell Town 'A'	24	7	4	13	34	35	25
FC Wraysbury	24	6	3	15	28	60	21
New W'sor OB *+2*	24	5	3	16	41	75	20
Burnham Beeches	24	4	5	15	31	51	17
Datchet	24	3	1	20	24	55	10

Division One	P	W	D	L	F	A	Pts
Holland Park	20	16	3	1	59	20	51
Iver Heath Rovers	20	14	4	2	65	23	46
Slough Laurencians	20	9	3	8	57	46	30
Maidenhead Town	20	8	4	8	49	41	28
Running Horse	20	8	4	8	50	57	28
Cippenham Sports	20	8	3	9	44	35	27
Chalvey Res.	20	7	5	8	37	37	26
Iver	20	7	4	9	45	51	25
Frontline	20	7	4	9	30	49	25
Burnham Athletic	20	5	1	14	28	70	16
ICI (Slough)	20	2	3	15	31	66	9

Division Two	P	W	D	L	F	A	Pts
Windsor Great Park	18	15	1	2	65	22	46
Foxes	18	10	3	5	43	27	33
Burnham United	18	10	2	6	41	27	32
Stoke Green	18	8	7	3	38	25	31
Stoke Poges	18	8	4	6	38	32	28
Burn. Beeches Res.	18	6	5	7	26	31	23
Orchard Park Res.	18	5	4	9	36	31	19
Slough Heating Res.	18	5	1	12	28	52	16
Boyne Hill	18	5	1	12	41	69	16
Falcons	18	4	0	14	23	63	12

Division Thtree	P	W	D	L	F	A	Pts
Bagshot	20	18	2	0	81	16	56
New Hanford	20	17	1	2	75	26	52
Burnham Swan Res.	20	11	2	7	51	39	35
Braybrooke	20	11	1	8	64	48	34
Slough Lauren. Res.	20	10	1	9	51	52	31
E'cote/Richings Pk	20	10	1	9	70	29	31
Englef'd Green 'A'	20	9	1	10	56	42	28
Holland Park Res.	20	7	3	10	29	57	24
Langley Athletic	20	6	1	13	42	64	19
Chalvey WMC 'A'	19	1	2	16	25	100	5
GNSSS Maidenh'd	19	1	1	17	13	84	4

Division Four	P	W	D	L	F	A	Pts
Barnhill Social	22	15	6	1	94	24	51
Bracknell Athletic	22	16	0	6	58	25	48
Running Horse Res.	22	14	4	4	75	29	46
Campion United	22	13	3	6	65	39	42
Hayes Villa OB	22	12	4	6	60	39	40
AFC Lady Haig	22	11	2	9	68	60	35
Win. Gt Park Res.	22	9	4	9	43	46	31
Mercian United	22	8	3	11	58	58	27
Willow Wanderers	22	7	6	9	40	46	27
SA Stainash	22	4	2	16	29	91	14
Crowthorne Royals	22	2	5	15	34	80	11
KS Gryf	22	1	1	20	32	119	4

EAST GWENT LEAGUE

Division One	P	W	D	L	F	A	Pts
Tintern Abbey	21	18	0	3	79	25	54
Monmouth T. Res.	21	15	2	4	74	26	47
Caldicot Town 'A'	21	12	1	8	57	50	37
Undy Athletic Res.	21	11	3	7	47	50	36
Rockfield Rovers	21	10	0	11	58	56	30
Portskewett/Sudb'k	21	8	2	11	45	39	26
Chepstow Athletic	21	3	3	15	39	67	12
Chepstow Town 'A'	21	1	1	19	23	109	4

Division Two	P	W	D	L	F	A	Pts
Monm'th Town 'A'	21	16	0	5	51	19	48
Underwood S. Res.	21	12	2	7	58	51	38
Sudbrook CC Res.	21	10	4	7	42	35	34
Thornwell RW Res.	21	8	5	8	58	50	29
Rogiet & Tippling	21	7	5	9	44	46	26
Caldicot Castle Res.	21	8	1	12	42	55	25
Mathern Wdrs *-3*	21	6	5	10	35	42	20
P'skewett & S. Res.	21	5	2	14	36	68	17

Division Three	P	W	D	L	F	A	Pts
Undy Athletic 'A'	24	19	1	4	91	38	58
Devauden Green	24	18	1	5	100	37	55
Rogiet	24	16	4	4	99	45	52
C'stow Ath. Res. *-3*	24	11	2	11	63	57	32
Bulwark	24	10	0	14	63	72	30
Rockfield R. Res. *-4*	24	10	3	11	58	52	29
Sudbrook CC 'A' *-7*	24	9	1	14	57	80	21
Mathern W. Res. *-6*	24	6	2	16	52	96	14
C'cot Castle 'A' *-3*	24	2	0	22	26	132	3

EAST LANCASHIRE LEAGUE

Division One	P	W	D	L	F	A	Pts
Hurst Green	26	21	2	3	73	28	65
Rimington	26	17	4	5	72	29	55
Stacksteads St Jos.	26	15	3	8	75	36	48
Langho	26	15	1	10	67	51	46
Goodshaw United	26	14	3	9	59	46	45
Rock Rovers	26	13	4	9	56	49	43
Worsthorne	26	12	3	11	58	52	39
Enfield	26	11	5	10	45	53	38
Silsden Res.	26	10	6	10	64	54	36
Colne United	26	9	4	13	52	60	31
Settle United	26	8	4	14	38	64	28
Kelbrook United	26	7	3	16	44	75	24
Peel Park	26	4	2	20	39	83	14
Witton Albion	26	3	2	21	35	97	11

Division Two	P	W	D	L	F	A	Pts
Mill Hill St P. 'A' *-3*	28	22	4	2	121	37	67
Borrowdale United	28	21	1	6	115	48	64
Barrowford YCW	28	17	3	8	77	38	54
Burnley Belv. 'A' *-3*	28	17	4	7	94	48	52
Bacup CC	28	14	7	7	73	62	49
Burnley GSOB	28	14	3	11	82	62	45
Oswaldtwistle St M	28	12	6	10	74	53	42
Padiham 'A'	28	11	6	11	67	69	39
Read United	28	12	3	13	98	104	39
Rawtenstall	28	12	2	14	69	68	38
Clitheroe RBL	28	11	3	14	81	72	36
Barrowford Celtic	28	11	1	16	72	106	34
Barnoldswick T. 'A'	28	6	1	21	45	125	19
Sabden	28	4	1	23	42	136	13
Burnley Boys Club	28	2	3	23	38	120	9

Reserve Division	P	W	D	L	F	A	Pts
Rimington Res.	28	19	2	7	129	55	59
Colne United Res.	28	16	8	4	86	43	56
Langho Res.	28	16	8	4	80	47	56
Burnley GSOB Res.	28	17	3	8	100	68	54
Hurst Green Res.	28	15	5	8	87	53	50
Rock Rovers Res.	28	14	7	7	67	64	49
Enfield Res.	28	14	5	9	81	59	47
Goodshaw Utd Res.	28	12	7	9	69	59	43
Peel Park Res.	28	11	4	13	61	71	37
Worsthorne Res.	28	10	6	12	65	78	36
Rawtenstall Res.	28	10	1	17	54	89	31
Stacksteads SJ Res.	28	5	8	15	52	92	23
Read United Res.	28	5	7	16	55	87	22
Kelbrook Utd Res.	28	5	2	21	46	103	17
Settle Utd Res. *+3*	28	2	5	21	36	100	14

EAST RIDING AMATEUR LEAGUE

Premier Division	P	W	D	L	F	A	Pts
Kinnersley	20	17	3	0	71	23	54
Pinefleet Wolf. Res.	20	15	1	4	67	36	46
Crown	20	13	4	3	60	45	43
Orchard Park Tigers	20	10	2	8	62	37	32
Kingburn Athletic	20	9	1	10	44	43	28
Eddie Beedle	20	9	1	10	38	42	28
AFC Preston	20	7	2	11	46	41	23
Hessle Sp'ting Club	20	5	4	11	28	46	19
Hull Athletic	20	5	2	13	30	55	17
Spring Bank Tigers	20	3	5	12	35	63	14
Hallgate Tavern	20	4	1	15	15	65	13

Division One	P	W	D	L	F	A	Pts
Hessle Sptng Res.	22	17	3	2	99	36	54
Mainbrace	22	16	2	4	76	37	50
Inter Charter	22	15	3	4	78	32	48
Anlaby Park	22	14	1	7	50	39	43
Orchard Pk T. Res.	22	13	2	7	96	38	41
Raine	22	12	2	8	80	43	38
Kingburn Ath. Res.	22	11	2	9	47	47	35
Blackburn Leisure	22	8	2	12	52	54	26
Cavalier Wanderers	22	7	0	15	44	66	21
Paull Wanderers	22	5	3	14	52	63	18
Priory Inn	22	3	1	18	31	109	10
Hull Hawks	22	0	1	21	20	161	1

Division Two	P	W	D	L	F	A	Pts
Bridges	22	17	4	1	92	30	55
Cross Keys Tigers	22	16	1	5	115	34	49
SC Electrical	22	15	4	3	84	35	49
Tenyas	22	12	4	6	57	42	40
Malt Shovel	22	11	4	7	59	43	37
AFC Preston Res.	22	10	2	10	68	54	32
Jenko Sporting	22	10	2	10	58	57	32
Hull Grass Roots	22	7	0	15	66	95	21
Hessle Sporting 'A'	22	7	0	15	51	99	21
Mainbrace Res.	22	6	2	14	49	83	20
Hallgate Tav. Res.	22	5	4	13	39	90	19
Greatfield Old Boys	22	1	3	18	36	112	6

EAST RIDING COUNTY LEAGUE

Premier Division	P	W	D	L	F	A	Pts
Old George	22	16	6	0	56	22	54
Howden Amateurs	22	16	5	1	79	46	53
Viking Raiders	22	12	3	7	64	37	39
Skidby Millers	22	10	5	7	55	54	35
Poachers	22	9	5	8	49	51	32
Northfield Athletic	22	10	1	11	47	36	31
Boothferry Rangers	22	8	5	9	35	49	29
Easington Utd Res.	22	8	3	11	45	64	27
Sculcoates A. Res.	22	8	2	12	43	41	26
Holme Rovers	22	6	5	11	37	41	23
Reckitts Res.	22	5	3	14	35	52	18
C Ridings	22	2	1	19	27	79	7

Division One	P	W	D	L	F	A	Pts
North Ferriby Ath.	18	12	2	4	58	30	38
Beverley Town Res.	18	10	6	2	39	21	36
Dales Tigers YC	18	9	6	3	45	32	33
Westella & W. Res.	18	8	6	4	40	35	30
Hutton C'wick Res.	18	7	4	7	33	32	25
C Swallow	18	7	3	8	37	33	24
Brandesburton Res.	18	7	2	9	43	47	23
Lord Nelson (Bev.)	18	6	3	9	40	41	21
Aldbrough United	18	4	3	11	26	52	15
Hornsea Town Res.	18	2	1	15	24	62	7

Division Two	P	W	D	L	F	A	Pts
Patrington Stan. U.	22	18	2	2	78	20	56
Beaver	22	16	3	3	75	32	51
South Cave United	22	15	3	4	64	31	48
Hodgsons	22	13	3	6	60	41	42
Leven M. Club *+3*	22	10	2	10	64	60	35
Hedon United Res.	22	9	5	8	38	42	32
Gilberdyke	22	6	8	8	53	53	26
Howden Ams Res.	22	8	2	12	42	72	26
Pavillion *-3*	22	7	1	14	38	52	19
N. Frodingham Res.	22	4	4	14	36	60	16
Withernsea Res.	22	4	3	15	32	72	15
North Newbald	22	3	2	17	29	74	11

Division Three	P	W	D	L	F	A	Pts
Haltemprice OB	20	16	1	3	47	23	49
Market Weighton U.	20	13	3	4	52	26	42
North Cave Res.	20	12	3	5	56	31	39
West Hull Amateurs	20	12	1	7	63	51	37
Molescroft Rangers	20	8	7	5	44	37	31
FC Robin	20	10	1	9	50	49	31
Plexus Networking	20	7	4	9	38	38	25
Boothferry R. Res.	20	6	2	12	47	46	20
Total Sign Solutions	20	6	1	13	40	58	19
Roos	20	5	3	12	27	53	18
Hedon Rangers Res.	20	1	2	17	22	74	5

Division Four	P	W	D	L	F	A	Pts
Long Riston Res. *+3*	22	15	4	3	73	45	52
DADS	22	15	3	4	71	34	48
Skidby Millers Res.	22	15	2	5	86	37	47
Howden Town	22	14	4	4	92	48	46
Skirlaugh	22	12	4	6	78	66	40
Leven Memb. Res.	22	10	1	11	58	61	31
Patrington SU Res.	22	9	3	10	49	49	30
Holme Rovers Res.	22	8	1	13	40	72	25
Brandesburton 'A' *-3*	22	7	6	9	39	40	24
Easington Utd Cas.	22	5	1	16	36	90	16
Molescroft R. Res.	22	4	2	16	37	69	14
Withernsea 'A'	22	2	1	19	25	73	7

Division Five	P	W	D	L	F	A	Pts
Westella/W. Juniors	22	15	4	3	67	24	49
Eastrington Village	22	15	4	3	68	32	49
Darleys Old Boys	22	14	3	5	57	28	45
Shiptonthorpe Utd	22	11	4	7	56	38	37
Mkt Weighton Res.	22	9	8	5	61	43	35
Gilberdyke Res.	22	8	5	9	48	61	29
Howden Town Res.	22	8	3	11	38	45	27
Hornsea Town 'A'	22	8	3	11	47	58	27
South Cave U. Res.	22	6	5	11	36	53	23
Haltemprice Rgrs	22	5	2	15	27	53	17
West Hull Ams Res.	22	3	7	12	38	66	16
Skirlaugh Res.	22	3	6	13	40	82	15

EAST SUSSEX LEAGUE

Premier Division	P	W	D	L	F	A	Pts
Hawkhurst United	22	20	2	0	75	18	62
Heathfield Hot. *+3*	22	14	2	6	47	29	47
Hollington United	22	13	2	7	81	41	41
St Leonards Social	22	12	2	8	45	40	38
Rock-a-Nore	22	12	2	8	38	51	38
Bodiam	22	10	2	10	37	53	32
Peche Hill Select	22	9	4	9	47	43	31
Peasmarsh & Iden	22	6	7	9	46	45	25
Ridge W. Garage *-3*	22	7	4	11	35	41	22
Eastbourne WMC	22	5	2	15	26	50	17
Ticehurst	22	4	2	16	34	64	14
Mountfield United	22	4	1	17	30	66	13

Division One	P	W	D	L	F	A	Pts
Punnetts Town	20	14	2	4	55	26	44
Hooe Sports	20	13	4	3	63	28	43
Jnr Club Tackleway	20	13	4	3	48	19	43
Icklesham Casuals	20	10	5	5	54	48	35
Bexhill AAC	20	9	5	6	52	35	32
Sedlescombe	20	8	5	7	33	31	29
Hollington Utd Res.	20	7	4	9	41	52	25
Ninfield United	20	6	5	9	30	38	23
Sandhurst	20	5	3	12	34	44	18
Northiam	20	3	1	16	33	65	10
Firehills Seniors	20	3	0	17	40	97	9

Division Two	P	W	D	L	F	A	Pts
Hastings Rangers	20	13	4	3	65	35	43
Crowhurst	20	14	0	6	78	25	42
Athletico	20	13	3	4	77	46	42
Little Common Res.	20	10	3	7	52	38	33
Herstmonceux	20	8	5	7	48	40	29
White Knight	20	8	5	7	34	46	29
Old Hastonians	20	6	7	7	34	44	25
Wheatsheaf	20	7	3	10	54	57	24
P'marsh/Iden Res.	20	6	3	11	33	70	21
Wadhurst United	20	5	3	12	36	48	18
JC Tackleway Res.	20	2	0	18	23	85	6

Division Three	P	W	D	L	F	A	Pts
Little Common 'A'	22	15	1	6	49	35	46
Catsfield	22	13	6	3	90	38	45
Magham Down	22	11	6	5	63	41	39
Mayfield	22	12	3	7	62	68	39
Battle Baptists	22	12	2	8	45	52	38
Hastings Rgrs Res.	22	11	4	7	63	45	37
Beulah Baptists	22	9	9	4	60	50	36
Red Lion *-1*	22	9	4	9	35	43	30
E'bourne Dynamos	22	6	4	12	45	59	22
Wittersham *+2*	22	3	4	15	51	70	15
Burwash	22	4	3	15	36	64	15
Cranbrook Town	22	2	4	16	32	66	10

Division Four	P	W	D	L	F	A	Pts
Robertsbridge Utd	22	15	4	3	67	31	49
Battle Rangers	22	12	5	5	50	29	41
E'bourne Fishermen	22	9	10	3	46	27	37
Pebsham Sibex	22	10	7	5	42	24	37
Benbow	22	11	3	8	57	18	36
Hawkhurst U. Res.	22	9	2	11	37	50	29
St Helens *-3*	22	9	3	10	38	48	27
Bodiam Res.	22	7	6	9	32	46	27
Victoria Baptists	22	7	5	10	39	55	26
Punnetts T. Res. *+2*	22	6	5	11	32	50	25
Westfield 'A' *+2*	22	5	4	13	30	67	21
Northiam Res.	22	3	4	15	28	53	13

Division Five	P	W	D	L	F	A	Pts
Cinque Ports	22	16	1	5	75	47	49
Panako *+3*	22	13	4	5	76	38	46
Hollington 'A' *-3*	22	14	3	5	75	41	42
Peasmarsh & I. 'A'	22	13	1	8	38	40	40
Bexhill AAC Res.	22	10	5	7	47	44	35
Travaux	22	9	5	8	55	61	32
Icklesham C. Res.	22	8	5	9	52	55	29
Heathfield H. Res.	22	9	1	12	32	71	28
Mountfield Res. *-3*	22	9	2	11	41	45	26
O. C'modians Res.	22	7	0	15	33	42	21
Sedlescombe Res.	22	6	2	14	39	48	20
Sandhurst Res. *+3*	22	2	3	17	32	63	12

Division Six	P	W	D	L	F	A	Pts
Pelham *-3*	22	17	2	3	77	39	50
Wadhurst Utd Res.	22	14	5	3	68	34	47
Peche Hill S. Res.	22	13	5	4	61	34	44
Orington	22	10	4	8	63	58	34
Hastings R. 'A' *+3*	22	9	4	9	56	56	34
White Knight Res.	22	8	3	11	43	57	27
Belmont United	22	7	4	11	49	54	25
Magham Down Res.	22	7	4	11	48	61	25
Battle Baptists Res.	22	7	4	11	62	77	25
Hastings Elite	22	7	3	12	52	64	24
Herstmonceux Res.	22	6	5	11	46	54	23
Beulah Bapt. Res.	22	3	5	14	40	77	14

ESSEX BUSINESS HOUSES LEAGUE

Premier Division	P	W	D	L	F	A	Pts
Sungate	22	15	6	1	67	28	51
Newham United	22	13	2	7	62	40	41
Euro Dagenham	22	12	4	6	54	37	40
Toby	22	13	1	8	50	40	40
Old Barkabbeyans	22	11	5	6	50	33	38
Flanders	22	10	5	7	54	37	35
Bancroft	22	8	6	8	38	41	30
Brampton Park	22	8	6	8	46	52	30
West Essex	22	6	7	9	32	42	25
Rainham Athletic	22	5	4	13	32	60	19
Heath Park	22	4	3	15	22	49	15
Globe Rangers	22	2	1	19	28	76	7

Division One	P	W	D	L	F	A	Pts
Platinium	22	17	4	1	79	35	55
Rainham WMC	22	12	5	5	68	40	41
Melbourne Sports	22	12	3	7	49	40	39
PLA Vets	22	10	6	6	55	44	36
West Green	22	10	4	8	60	39	34
Newham Borough	22	9	4	9	43	36	31
Barking Borough	22	9	3	10	43	46	30
Sungate Res.	22	7	4	11	35	58	25
Romford Town	22	7	4	11	45	73	25
Fairbairn House	22	5	6	11	43	57	21
Snaresbrook	22	5	4	13	31	57	19
Old Barks Res.	22	5	1	16	35	61	16

Division Two	P	W	D	L	F	A	Pts
Stags Head	24	20	1	3	97	26	61
Old Barks 'A'	24	17	4	3	59	20	55
Barking Boro. Res.	24	13	4	7	57	33	43
Newham Res. *-1*	24	12	6	6	50	32	41
Clockwork	24	13	2	9	58	41	41
Dodd'ghurst Olym.	24	10	9	5	52	30	39
Harold Park	24	10	3	11	55	56	33
West Essex Res.	24	7	6	11	40	64	27
Westhamians Res.	24	8	2	14	52	65	26
PLA Res.	24	6	5	13	43	64	23
Forest Glade	24	6	4	14	23	56	22
Ford Athletic	24	4	5	15	36	73	17
Newark Youth *-1*	24	3	3	18	21	83	11

Division Three	P	W	D	L	F	A	Pts
Loass *-1*	26	21	2	3	101	32	64
Frenford Snr ‘C’ *-1*	26	18	6	2	84	39	59
Singh Sabha Bark.	26	13	3	10	60	50	42
Old Barks ‘B’	26	12	5	9	53	50	41
Lord Morpeth	26	11	7	8	58	51	40
Denmark Arms	26	11	6	9	59	45	39
Major Park	26	11	4	11	52	57	37
Clarendon	26	10	5	11	63	53	35
Sungate ‘A’	26	9	7	10	54	52	34
Heath Park Res.	26	8	6	12	48	54	30
Bancroft Res.	26	8	4	14	43	67	28
Globe Rangers Res.	26	6	5	15	45	82	23
Newham Utd ‘A’	26	7	2	17	47	92	23
Barking Boro. ‘A’	26	5	2	19	46	89	17

ESSEX & HERTS BORDER COMBINATION

	P	W	D	L	F	A	Pts
Heybridge S. Res.	34	27	1	6	105	37	82
Dagenham/R. Res.	34	24	5	5	107	30	77
Brentwood T. Res.	34	23	5	6	80	33	74
Romford Res.	34	23	2	9	83	59	71
East Thurrock Res.	34	19	4	11	62	45	61
Harlow Town Res.	34	15	8	11	77	59	53
Bowers/Pitsea Res.	34	16	5	13	70	58	53
Barking Res.	34	13	13	8	77	59	52
Billericay T. Res.	34	15	3	16	57	66	48
Waltham Abbey Res.	34	12	9	13	66	68	45
Concord Rgrs Res.	34	14	2	18	58	62	44
Maldon Town Res.	34	13	4	17	64	84	43
Gt Wakering Res.	34	11	8	15	82	78	41
Ilford Res. *-3*	34	14	1	19	54	78	40
Canvey Island Res.	34	10	6	18	59	76	36
Burnham R. Res.	34	11	2	21	52	81	35
Basildon Utd Res.	34	4	1	29	30	99	13
Stansted Res.	34	1	3	30	31	142	6

FALMOUTH-HELSTON LEAGUE

Division One	P	W	D	L	F	A	Pts
Porthleven Res.	30	25	1	4	110	32	76
Mawnan	30	20	6	4	66	31	66
Hayle Res.	30	20	2	8	73	40	62
Falmouth Albion	30	15	5	10	55	37	50
Falmouth Athletic	30	14	6	10	64	59	48
Wendron CCU Res.	30	13	5	12	58	53	44
St Agnes Res.	30	13	4	13	59	59	43
Chacewater	30	12	5	13	57	59	41
Holmans SC Res.	30	10	8	12	55	67	38
Lizard Argyle	30	9	10	11	55	49	37
Stithians	30	12	1	17	44	66	37
Mousehole Res.	30	10	6	14	47	59	36
Penryn Athletic ‘A’	30	9	7	14	44	57	34
Truro City ‘A’ *-5*	30	10	7	13	48	59	32
Helston Ath. Res.	30	9	3	18	48	76	30
Trispen *+3*	30	0	2	28	24	104	5

Division Two	P	W	D	L	F	A	Pts
Falmouth Town ‘A’	30	25	2	3	121	47	77
Mawnan Res.	30	21	5	4	77	27	68
St Keverne	30	18	5	7	91	42	59
St Day Res. *+3*	30	16	4	10	76	51	55
Mawgan *-6*	30	17	5	8	75	43	50
Pendeen Rovers	30	14	6	10	68	51	48
Constantine	30	12	6	12	74	77	42
Hayle ‘A’	30	10	8	12	54	64	38
Perranporth Res.	30	10	8	12	47	65	38
Rosudgeon-Kenn.	30	10	7	13	50	68	37
Perranwell Res.	30	9	6	15	47	59	33
Carharrack	30	10	3	17	59	70	33
Marazion Blues	30	7	9	14	64	78	30
Wendron CCU ‘A’	30	8	4	18	46	78	28
Helston Athletic ‘A’	30	5	4	21	51	88	19
Penryn Athletic ‘B’	30	5	4	21	36	128	19

Division Three	P	W	D	L	F	A	Pts
RNAS C’rose Res.	30	23	5	2	86	35	74
Frogpool-Cusgarne	30	22	5	3	86	29	71
Falmouth Alb. Res.	30	20	3	7	99	42	63
Ruan Minor	30	18	5	7	99	38	59
Falmouth Ath. Res.	30	17	5	8	94	80	56
Camborne Park	30	14	11	5	89	41	53
Mullion Res.	30	13	6	11	79	44	45
Porthleven Rgrs *-3*	30	15	3	12	74	81	45
Hayle ‘B’	30	9	5	16	61	93	32
Troon *-3*	30	10	5	15	61	74	32
Lanner	30	9	5	16	62	73	32
Lizard Argyle Res.	30	9	4	17	63	89	31
Stithians Res.	30	9	3	18	59	90	30
Trevenson	30	8	3	19	53	68	27
Cury *+3*	30	4	2	24	52	161	17
Carharrack Res.	30	4	2	24	39	118	14

FURNESS PREMIER LEAGUE

Premier Division	P	W	D	L	F	A	Pts
Vickerstown Res.	28	20	5	3	91	33	65
Walney Island	28	15	7	6	77	47	52
Bootle	28	15	5	8	61	39	50
BAE Barrow Res.	28	16	1	11	57	53	49
Furness Rovers Res.	28	14	6	8	53	34	48
Askam United Res.	28	14	2	12	69	53	44
Haverigg United *-3*	28	14	3	11	61	55	42
Dalton United Res.	28	11	7	10	66	61	40
Barrow Island	28	11	4	13	71	88	37
Millom Res.	28	9	7	12	64	54	34
Crooklands C. Res.	28	10	4	14	51	71	34
Barrow Celtic	28	9	5	14	54	52	32
Glaxo Ulv’ston Res.	28	8	4	16	58	89	28
Holker OB ‘A’	28	6	5	17	34	73	23
Furness Cav. Res. *-3*	28	4	3	21	29	94	12

Division One	P	W	D	L	F	A	Pts
Furness Hotel	24	17	4	3	78	21	55
Furness Seniors	24	17	3	4	71	27	54
Barrow Wanderers	24	15	5	4	70	34	50
Kirkby United	24	12	5	7	65	43	41
Furness Rovers ‘A’	24	12	4	8	55	39	40
Walney Island Res.	24	11	6	7	55	45	39
Vickerstown Snrs	24	11	6	7	62	57	39
Millom ‘A’	24	10	3	11	44	54	33
Holker OB ‘B’ *-6*	24	8	3	13	47	56	21
Haverigg Utd Res.	24	6	2	16	31	71	20
BAE Barrow SC ‘A’	24	4	5	15	40	90	17
Barrow C. Res. *-3*	24	5	4	15	31	59	16
Dalton United ‘A’	24	1	4	19	32	85	7

GAINSBOROUGH & DISTRICT LEAGUE

Division One	P	W	D	L	F	A	Pts
AFC Friendship	16	14	0	2	49	11	42
Harworth CI Res.	16	11	2	3	44	25	35
Sun Inn Tuxford	16	11	1	4	46	30	34
Rampton Hospital	16	6	3	7	33	40	21
Masons Arms	16	6	3	7	33	46	21
Eaton Hall College	16	5	2	9	26	35	17
Misterton United	16	5	1	10	24	40	16
Half Moon Retford	16	4	2	10	20	31	14
Epworth Town Res.	16	2	2	12	16	33	8

Division Two	P	W	D	L	F	A	Pts
Harworth CI Colts	24	21	0	3	118	29	63
Retford Town Res.	24	20	2	2	95	27	62
Wroot	24	14	4	6	75	56	46
East Drayton	24	13	2	9	56	41	41
Bridon	24	13	1	10	53	47	40
Elm Cottage	24	10	6	8	46	43	36
Crooked Billet	24	10	4	10	64	69	34
Eaton Hall C. Res.	24	8	3	13	50	65	27
Saxilby Athletic	24	8	2	14	37	67	26
Castle Hills	24	6	3	15	62	91	21
Peacock	24	6	3	15	40	84	21
Marshalls Sports	24	5	5	14	46	78	20
Cons Club	24	3	3	18	32	77	12

GRAVESEND LEAGUE

Premier Division	P	W	D	L	F	A	Pts
Viewpoint	16	13	3	0	55	15	42
The O. Pce Orange	16	10	0	6	53	29	30
Craggs Farm	16	9	2	5	53	35	29
Lullingstone Castle	16	8	2	6	37	37	26
Ace of Clubs	16	6	2	8	29	37	20
Horton Kirby	16	6	1	9	48	56	19
South Darenth	16	5	4	7	26	40	19
Istead Rise	16	4	4	8	39	47	16
Woodlands Athletic	16	1	2	13	13	57	5

Division One	P	W	D	L	F	A	Pts
FC Istead	18	15	1	2	49	17	46
Real Man of Kent	18	11	4	3	55	24	37
Craggs Farm Res.	18	12	1	5	61	31	37
Swan Valley	18	10	0	8	43	43	30
Peacock Celtic	18	8	3	7	31	40	27
Duke of Wellington	18	8	2	8	47	48	26
Stone Club & Inst.	18	7	1	10	38	52	22
Borough United ‘A’	18	5	3	10	40	46	18
Horns Cross United	18	4	0	14	28	65	12
Guru Nanak Res.	18	2	1	15	23	49	7

Division Two	P	W	D	L	F	A	Pts
The Rising Eagles	22	18	2	2	83	26	[illegible]
Ace of Clubs Res.	22	17	3	2	73	30	[illegible]
Viewpoint Res.	22	15	4	3	76	40	[illegible]
Stone C & I Res.	22	11	6	5	72	36	[illegible]
Earl Grey	22	11	3	8	58	53	[illegible]
Waterloo	22	10	5	7	70	57	[illegible]
Meopham	22	8	5	9	69	49	[illegible]
AZ ’82	22	5	6	11	40	57	[illegible]
Fleetway Printers	22	6	2	14	50	73	[illegible]
Oakfield	22	5	2	15	45	92	[illegible]
The Red Lion	22	4	1	17	33	88	[illegible]
Beausports	22	2	1	19	26	94	[illegible]

GREAT YARMOUTH & DISTRICT LEAGUE

Division One	P	W	D	L	F	A	Pts
Catfield	20	18	2	0	107	18	[illegible]
Gapton Car Hire	20	17	2	1	95	32	[illegible]
MK United	20	14	1	5	90	41	[illegible]
Gorleston Rangers	20	11	2	7	51	62	[illegible]
Gt Yarm. Town Hall	20	7	3	10	32	47	[illegible]
Caister United ‘A’	20	7	3	10	53	78	[illegible]
Arches	20	6	4	10	45	48	[illegible]
Golfers Arms	20	5	3	12	41	62	[illegible]
Gt Yarm’th Peelers	20	5	2	13	43	78	[illegible]
Burgh Hall	20	2	5	13	38	81	[illegible]
Star & Garter *-2*	20	3	3	14	37	85	[illegible]

GUERNSEY LEAGUE
(Cable & Wireless)

Priaulx League	P	W	D	L	F	A	Pts
Northerners AC	24	19	3	2	83	29	[illegible]
Belgrave Wanderers	24	14	2	8	63	39	[illegible]
Sylvans	24	13	1	10	58	33	[illegible]
Vale Recreation	24	11	6	7	48	35	[illegible]
St Martins AC	24	11	5	8	57	39	[illegible]
Guernsey Rangers	24	3	3	18	29	86	[illegible]
Rovers	24	1	4	19	17	94	[illegible]

Jackson League	P	W	D	L	F	A	Pts
Northerners AC Res.	18	12	2	4	53	43	[illegible]
Belgrave Wdrs Res.	18	12	1	5	57	23	[illegible]
St Martins AC Res.	18	11	3	4	61	33	[illegible]
Sylvans Res.	18	9	5	4	55	29	[illegible]
Guernsey Rgrs Res.	18	5	4	9	33	69	[illegible]
Vale Recreation Res.	18	4	3	11	36	49	[illegible]
Rovers Res.	18	1	0	17	18	67	[illegible]

Railway League	P	W	D	L	F	A	Pts
St Martins AC ‘A’	18	16	1	1	78	27	[illegible]
Port City	18	10	2	6	55	47	[illegible]
Guernsey Rgrs ‘A’	18	9	1	8	47	41	[illegible]
Sylvans ‘A’	18	8	4	6	48	42	[illegible]
Bavaria Nomads	18	8	3	7	47	43	[illegible]
Belgrave Wdrs ‘A’	18	8	2	8	52	45	[illegible]
Rovers ‘A’	18	7	3	8	41	48	[illegible]
Northerners ‘A’	18	5	5	8	45	41	[illegible]
Vale Recreation ‘A’	18	5	1	12	34	46	[illegible]
Island Police	18	3	0	15	27	94	[illegible]

GUILDFORD & WOKING ALLIANCE

Premier Division	P	W	D	L	F	A	Pts
University of Surrey	20	13	4	3	51	22	[illegible]
Addlestone Town	20	13	1	6	42	26	[illegible]
Hersham	20	12	2	6	52	28	[illegible]
Holmbury St Mary	20	11	4	5	55	36	[illegible]
Burpham	20	11	4	5	52	36	[illegible]
Bedfont Green ‘A’	20	11	0	9	35	34	[illegible]
Hambledon	20	8	3	9	31	23	[illegible]
Lightwater United	20	8	2	10	38	37	[illegible]
Milford/Witley ‘A’	20	7	1	12	29	45	[illegible]
Shalford ‘A’	20	2	2	16	20	56	[illegible]
Weybrook Wdrs	20	2	1	17	17	79	[illegible]

Division One	P	W	D	L	F	A	Pts
Abbey Rangers	18	14	1	3	45	18	[illegible]
AFC Bourne	18	13	2	3	54	29	[illegible]
Millmead	18	12	2	4	72	38	[illegible]
West Byfleet Alb.	18	8	3	7	37	31	[illegible]
Emmanuel	18	7	4	7	37	42	[illegible]
Univ. of Surrey Res.	18	6	3	9	36	40	[illegible]
New Haw Wdrs	18	4	5	9	32	42	[illegible]
Surrey Athletic	18	4	4	10	31	43	[illegible]
Guild. City Wey. ‘A’	18	4	4	10	30	56	[illegible]
AFC Chilworth	18	2	4	12	14	49	[illegible]

Division Two	P	W	D	L	F	A	Pts
Border & Hth End	22	17	3	2	79	28	54
Pirbright Sports	22	15	5	2	65	26	50
Shepperton FB	22	14	4	4	59	21	46
Oatlands	22	12	1	9	53	52	37
Shottermill/H. 'A'	22	10	2	10	35	51	32
Univ. of Surrey 'A'	22	8	5	9	42	42	29
Lightwater Utd Res.	22	8	3	11	24	43	27
Mytchett Rangers	22	8	3	11	40	68	27
Staines Lammas 'A'	22	7	5	10	45	23	26
Milford/Witley 'B'	22	8	1	13	44	47	25
Guild. City W. 'B'	22	7	3	12	42	52	24
Merrow 'A'	22	0	1	21	15	90	1

Division Three	P	W	D	L	F	A	Pts
Hersham Res.	26	20	3	3	99	29	63
Abbey Rangers Res.	26	19	6	1	92	32	63
Bedfont Green 'B'	26	19	2	5	108	40	59
Farncombe	26	16	2	8	91	34	50
Staines Lammas 'B'	26	15	2	9	68	41	47
Burpham Res.	26	14	4	8	70	45	46
Guildford Park	26	12	3	11	71	68	39
Christch'ch Woking	26	10	4	12	39	60	34
Emmanuel Res.	26	10	3	13	64	60	33
Queen Street Rgrs	26	7	2	17	45	118	23
Knaphill 'A'	26	6	3	17	43	71	21
Elstead	26	6	2	18	41	91	20
Worplesdon 'A'	26	4	3	19	32	114	15
Surrey Athletic Res.	26	3	3	20	47	107	12

Division Four	P	W	D	L	F	A	Pts
Bedfont Green 'C'	26	22	2	2	125	25	68
Hersham 'A'	26	17	4	5	94	45	55
Cranleigh 'A'	26	15	3	8	63	41	48
Park Barn United	26	13	7	6	78	42	46
Holmbury SM Res.	26	13	7	6	78	54	46
Shalford 'B'	26	12	7	7	62	54	43
Woking Park/H. 'A'	26	12	6	8	59	44	42
Elstead Res.	26	12	6	8	69	55	42
New Haw W. Res.	26	8	3	15	38	84	27
Milford/Witley 'C'	26	7	5	14	56	82	26
Hambledon Res.	26	6	3	17	56	96	21
Horsley 'A'	26	4	5	17	39	93	17
Weybrook W. Res.	26	3	7	16	44	102	16
Byfleet	26	4	3	19	38	82	15

GWENT CENTRAL LEAGUE

(Knauf)

Division One	P	W	D	L	F	A	Pts
Govilon	28	25	1	2	128	25	76
Pandy	28	19	5	4	97	57	62
Clydach Wasps Res.	28	17	6	5	84	43	57
Cwmffrwdoer Res.	28	17	5	6	90	54	56
Goytre Res.	28	13	7	8	73	59	46
Pontypool Town	28	11	6	11	89	76	39
Race Res.	28	10	8	10	56	63	38
Gilwern & District	28	12	2	14	70	78	38
Blaenavon B. Res.	28	9	4	15	54	56	31
Llanarth	28	8	6	14	72	72	30
Usk Town -3	28	9	5	14	77	82	29
Mardy Res. -3	28	8	7	13	55	93	28
Tranch Res. -3	28	8	5	15	50	109	26
Panteg Res.	28	5	1	22	46	99	16
Lower New Inn	28	3	4	21	54	129	13

Division Two	P	W	D	L	F	A	Pts
Pontypool T. Res.	26	20	3	3	84	31	63
Fairfield Utd Res.	26	17	5	4	91	32	56
New Inn Res.	26	17	2	7	83	40	53
Prescoed	26	14	4	8	85	65	46
Usk Town Res.	26	14	2	10	86	59	44
Abergavenny Res.	26	12	4	10	61	49	40
PILCS Res. -3	26	12	5	9	75	64	38
Clydach Wasps 'A'	26	9	6	11	48	53	33
Gilwern & D. Res.	26	9	6	11	53	83	33
Llanfoist	26	8	8	10	72	78	32
Govilon Res.	26	9	2	15	62	68	29
Sebastopol Res. -3	26	6	2	18	48	82	17
Llanarth Res. +3	26	3	2	21	43	128	14
Crickhowell Res. -6	26	6	1	19	60	119	13

HALIFAX & DISTRICT LEAGUE

Premier Division	P	W	D	L	F	A	Pts
Stainland United	24	21	1	2	111	31	64
Hebden Royd RS	24	15	5	4	81	37	50
Brighouse Old Boys	24	14	4	6	70	50	46
Halifax Irish Centre	24	13	4	7	62	45	43
Holmfield	24	11	2	11	78	85	35
Sowerby United	24	10	4	10	84	72	34
Midgley United	24	10	3	11	71	71	33
Siddal Athletic	24	9	6	9	62	65	33
Elland United	24	9	5	10	60	63	32
Shelf United	24	10	1	13	61	66	31
Ryburn United	24	5	7	12	39	61	22
Denholme United	24	4	2	18	46	107	14
St Andrews	24	3	0	21	47	119	9

Division One	P	W	D	L	F	A	Pts
Warley Rangers	20	15	1	4	54	20	46
Calder '76	20	12	2	6	47	31	38
Stump Cross	20	12	2	6	55	39	38
Martins Nest	20	10	3	7	43	36	33
Salem	20	9	2	9	46	54	29
Northowram	20	7	6	7	39	45	27
Greetland CC	20	8	1	11	40	46	25
Mixenden United	20	6	7	7	26	34	25
Brighouse OB Res.	20	6	3	11	44	48	21
Friendly	20	4	5	11	33	52	17
Sowerby Bridge	20	3	4	13	41	63	13

FC Fold – record expunged

Division Two	P	W	D	L	F	A	Pts
Luddendenfoot	22	18	3	1	117	31	57
Stainland Utd Res.	22	15	4	3	63	43	49
Junction	22	13	5	4	71	37	44
Copley United	22	12	4	6	65	46	40
Shelf United Res.	22	9	4	9	70	70	31
Pellon United	22	8	4	10	61	55	28
Ryburn United Res.	22	8	3	11	53	69	27
Volunteer Arms	22	7	5	10	58	83	26
H'fax Irish Cte Res.	22	7	4	11	51	63	25
Sowerby Bdge Res.	22	7	2	13	52	72	23
Warley Rgrs Res.	22	2	9	11	45	71	15
Denholme Utd Res.	22	1	3	18	25	91	6

Division Three	P	W	D	L	F	A	Pts
Kingston	20	16	3	1	88	29	51
Bowling Green	20	14	3	3	82	44	45
Hebden RRS Res.	20	13	3	4	68	25	42
Elland Allstars	20	10	4	6	66	51	34
Hipperholme Ath.	20	9	5	6	63	41	32
Siddal Athletic Res.	20	8	7	5	57	45	31
Midgley Utd Res.	20	6	4	10	51	54	22
Sowerby Utd Res.	20	5	3	12	41	82	18
Wadsworth United	20	4	3	13	33	56	15
Calder '76 Res.	20	5	0	15	37	80	15
Salem Res.	20	0	5	15	31	110	5

Stafford – record expunged

HARROGATE & DISTRICT LEAGUE

Premier Division	P	W	D	L	F	A	Pts
Sherwood	26	19	4	3	67	31	61
Thirsk Falcons	26	18	6	2	97	28	60
Thackley Res.	26	14	3	9	77	46	45
Kirk Deighton Rgrs	26	11	9	6	49	37	42
Eccleshill Utd Res.	26	10	8	8	59	51	38
Spa Athletic	26	11	5	10	47	53	38
Otley Town 'A'	26	10	4	12	41	53	34
Kirkby Malzeard	26	9	5	12	50	57	32
Harlow Hill	26	8	5	13	48	61	29
Burley Trojans	26	7	7	12	42	70	28
Bramhope	26	8	3	15	41	57	27
Pannal Sports	26	7	6	13	47	68	27
Pateley Bridge	26	6	7	13	40	63	25
Beckwithshaw Sts	26	7	2	17	32	62	23

Division One	P	W	D	L	F	A	Pts
Bramham	26	18	4	4	71	35	58
Albert	26	17	4	5	69	34	55
Bedale Town	26	17	2	7	77	49	53
Knaresboro. Celtic	26	14	2	10	62	43	44
Addingham	26	13	4	9	61	60	43
Masham	26	14	0	12	81	70	42
Thirsk Falcons Res.	26	11	6	9	61	61	39
Dalton Athletic	26	11	5	10	55	61	38
Pool Res.	26	10	7	9	62	46	37
Otley Rovers	26	10	6	10	68	59	36
Harold Styans	26	10	4	12	58	65	34
Pannal Sports Res.	26	5	2	19	43	95	17
Kirk Deight. R. Res.	26	3	4	19	40	83	13
Spa Athletic Res.	26	3	2	21	35	82	11

Division Two	P	W	D	L	F	A	Pts
H'forth St M. Res.	24	15	4	5	61	31	49
Killinghall Nomads	24	15	3	6	53	44	48
Kirkby M'zd Res.	24	13	6	5	77	57	45
Sherwood Res.	24	12	3	9	66	51	39
Clifford	24	11	5	8	63	50	38
Beckwithshaw Res.	24	9	10	5	47	41	37
Half Moon	24	10	3	11	50	45	33
Ripon C. Mag. 'A'	24	8	7	9	43	49	31
Boroughbridge 'A'	24	8	5	11	69	54	29
Harlow Hill Res.	24	8	5	11	55	56	29
Burley Trojans Res.	24	7	5	12	38	58	26
Otley Town 'B'	24	7	2	15	45	68	23
Helperby United	24	3	2	19	28	91	11

Empress – record expunged

Division Three	P	W	D	L	F	A	Pts
Yorks Amateur Res.	26	24	2	0	130	23	74
Harold Styans Res.	26	17	3	6	80	48	54
Ripon Red Arrows	26	15	4	7	76	58	49
Pannal Sports 'A'	26	15	0	11	62	44	45
Bramham Res.	26	14	3	9	53	48	45
Catterick Village	26	12	5	9	67	53	41
Wetherby Ath. 'A'	26	13	1	12	71	64	40
Brafferton Rangers	26	12	4	10	54	49	40
Pateley Bridge Res.	26	12	1	13	43	64	37
Pool 'A'	26	10	1	15	52	70	31
Hampsthwaite Utd	26	7	3	16	44	78	24
Thirsk Falcons 'A'	26	6	2	18	48	75	20
Addingham Res.	26	6	2	18	37	78	20
Otley Rovers Res.	26	1	5	20	24	89	8

HEREFORDSHIRE LEAGUE

(Hereford Times)

Premier Division	P	W	D	L	F	A	Pts
Wellington Rangers	30	23	4	3	84	26	73
Sutton United	30	22	6	2	106	27	72
Westfields Res.	30	21	4	5	81	33	67
Ewyas Harold	30	21	1	8	90	37	64
Woofferton	30	19	4	7	94	42	61
Colwall Rangers	30	16	4	10	81	61	52
Pegasus Jnrs Res.	30	14	6	10	91	61	48
Ledbury Town Res.	30	13	5	12	56	75	44
Kington Town	30	10	6	14	58	72	36
Bromyard T. Res.	30	10	5	15	43	61	35
Hereford Lads Club	30	9	5	16	58	78	32
Bartestree	30	7	5	18	50	74	26
Hinton Res.	30	7	5	18	39	88	26
Leominster Town	30	5	7	18	47	77	22
Fownhope	30	2	10	18	46	91	16
Weston	30	1	3	26	23	144	6

Division One	P	W	D	L	F	A	Pts
Widemarsh Rangers	16	12	3	1	46	21	39
Ewyas Harold Res.	16	10	3	3	41	23	33
Shobdon	16	8	3	5	35	32	27
Orcop Juniors	16	7	5	4	46	28	26
Well'gton Rgrs Colts	16	7	2	7	42	37	23
Kington Town Res.	16	6	3	7	30	49	21
Holme Lacy	16	5	5	6	38	34	20
Ross Town Res.	16	3	3	10	21	36	12
Woofferton Res.	16	0	1	15	21	60	1

Division Two	P	W	D	L	F	A	Pts
Fownhope Res.	18	15	0	3	57	32	45
Stoke Prior	18	14	1	3	62	20	43
Burghill	18	11	2	5	60	29	35
Bartestree Res.	18	9	2	7	33	33	29
Weobley	18	8	1	9	28	29	25
Hereford LC Colts	18	8	1	9	40	52	25
Orleton	18	7	1	10	43	46	22
Hereford Civil Serv.	18	5	1	12	23	48	16
Leintwardine Colts	18	4	2	12	26	39	14
Pencombe	18	3	1	14	19	63	10

Division Three	P	W	D	L	F	A	Pts
Bartonsham	16	12	1	3	71	22	37
Pegasus Jnrs Colts	16	11	4	1	43	18	37
Ross	16	10	3	3	51	19	33
Dore Valley	16	8	3	5	49	35	27
Holme Lacy Res.	16	4	4	8	32	47	16
Presteigne SA 'A'	16	4	3	9	31	46	15
Bartestree Colts -3	16	5	3	8	34	52	15
Kingstone Rovers	16	4	3	9	23	52	15
Eardisley	16	2	0	14	15	58	6

HERTFORD & DISTRICT LEAGUE

(McMullen)

Premier Division	P	W	D	L	F	A	Pts
Harlow Link	16	11	2	3	42	18	24
Hertford Heath Res.	16	11	2	3	40	19	24
Bengeo Trinity	16	8	3	5	31	24	19
Greenbury United	16	8	3	5	32	28	19
Westmill	16	5	4	7	35	33	14
Waltham Abbey 'A'	16	4	4	8	21	37	12
John Warner	16	5	1	10	23	26	11
Inter	16	4	3	9	22	40	11
County Hall Rgrs	16	4	2	10	20	41	10

Division One	P	W	D	L	F	A	Pts
Ware Lions	22	19	2	1	93	26	40
Thundridge United	22	17	1	4	61	35	35
Elizabeth Allen OB	22	15	2	5	79	38	32
Wodson Park Res.	22	11	5	6	53	45	27
Cottered	22	9	7	6	47	33	25
Broxb'rne Badgers	22	12	0	10	62	60	24
Westmill Res.	22	9	4	9	55	50	22
Watton-at-Stone	22	6	4	12	43	53	16
Kings Sports 'A'	22	5	3	14	33	53	13
Bengeo Trinity Res.	22	3	6	13	36	70	12
Buntingford T. 'A'	22	3	3	16	30	74	9
Mangrove	22	3	3	16	27	82	9

Division Two	P	W	D	L	F	A	Pts
Baldock Cannon	24	20	0	4	90	27	40
Bury Rangers	24	15	2	7	68	35	32
Saracens	24	14	4	6	52	36	32
Inter Res.	24	11	5	8	44	35	27
Eliz. Allen OB Res.	24	10	3	11	65	70	23
County Hall R. Res.	24	7	3	14	46	53	17
Parklands	24	5	6	13	44	85	16
Wodson Park 'A'	24	6	3	15	47	89	15
Much Hadham Res.	24	6	2	16	37	63	14

Division Three	P	W	D	L	F	A	Pts
Royston Town 'A'	22	16	3	3	95	36	35
Braughing Rovers	22	14	3	5	71	38	31
Brox. Badgers Res.	22	13	4	5	77	44	30
North Met Vets	22	12	3	7	61	37	27
Watton-at-Stone Res.	22	13	1	8	81	64	27
Harlow Link Res.	22	11	5	6	62	53	27
Eliz. Allen OB 'A'	22	8	2	12	42	63	18
Buntingford T. 'B'	22	8	2	12	44	71	18
Bury Rangers Res.	22	6	5	11	45	53	17
Mangrove Res.	22	6	4	12	45	63	16
Cottered Res.	22	4	3	15	22	71	11
E-Trade Deaconsf'd	22	3	1	18	28	80	7

HUDDERSFIELD WORKS & COMBINATION LEAGUE

	P	W	D	L	F	A	Pts
Syngenta	30	26	4	0	163	47	82
Uppermill 'A'	30	21	6	3	114	43	69
Sovereign Spts Res.	30	20	5	5	99	50	65
Warren House	30	20	1	9	96	73	61
Lindley Libs 'A'	30	16	3	11	84	83	51
Berry Brow WLT	30	12	6	12	69	80	42
Heywood Spts 'A'	30	13	3	14	88	104	42
Hepworth Utd Res.	30	12	5	13	66	79	41
Kirkburton 'A'	30	12	4	14	100	99	40
Crossland Moor	30	11	3	16	76	94	36
Moldgreen Cons	30	10	5	15	89	71	35
Bay Athletic 'A'	30	8	7	15	66	88	31
Railway	30	6	10	14	79	88	28
Grange Moor Res.	30	7	4	19	46	85	25
The Stag Res.	30	5	5	20	54	142	20
Clothiers Arms	30	3	5	22	59	122	14

HUDDERSFIELD & DISTRICT LEAGUE

Division One	P	W	D	L	F	A	Pts
Newsome WMC	22	17	1	4	84	38	52
Diggle	22	14	5	3	62	30	47
Heywood Sports	22	14	5	3	67	44	47
New Mill	22	13	2	7	46	34	41
Wooldale Wdrs	22	8	5	9	61	62	29
Meltham Ath. Res.	22	8	5	9	44	51	29
Lepton Highlanders	22	8	2	12	32	47	26
Aimbry	22	7	3	12	50	57	24
Shepley	22	6	6	10	33	43	24
Uppermill	22	5	5	12	43	52	20
Sovereign Sports	22	5	5	12	31	47	20
Honley	22	4	2	16	38	86	14

Division Two	P	W	D	L	F	A	Pts
Britannia Sports	26	22	2	2	86	12	68
Slaithwaite United	26	19	4	3	75	33	61
Netherton	26	15	3	8	52	37	48
KKS Ashbrow	26	13	4	9	62	51	43
Moldgreen	26	13	3	10	59	43	42
Hepworth United	26	10	8	8	52	45	38
Scholes	26	9	10	7	53	55	37
Berry Brow Libs	26	10	6	10	59	47	36
Lindley Liberals	26	10	6	10	61	55	36
Kirkheaton Rovers	26	11	2	13	62	61	35
Mount	26	8	4	14	44	74	28
Linthwaite Athletic	26	6	2	18	47	83	20
Holmbridge	26	4	5	17	50	82	17
Grange Moor	26	2	1	23	25	109	7

Division Three	P	W	D	L	F	A	Pts
Westend	20	16	2	2	96	19	50
Shelley	20	12	2	6	59	53	38
Scisset	20	11	4	5	46	34	37
Cumberworth	20	11	2	7	56	34	35
Sikh Leisure Centre	20	10	4	6	60	40	34
Heyside	20	8	5	7	55	54	29
HV Academicals	20	9	2	9	43	36	29
Paddock Rangers	20	7	3	10	43	53	24
The Stag	20	4	4	12	34	68	16
Lindley	20	4	1	15	25	70	13
Skelmanthorpe	20	3	1	16	28	84	10

Cravens and Space – records expunged

Division Four	P	W	D	L	F	A	Pts
SC Cowlersley	24	19	1	4	103	34	58
Upperthong	24	14	4	6	74	40	46
Coach & Horses	24	14	4	6	65	35	46
Farnley Terriers	24	14	2	8	53	38	44
Hade Edge	24	14	1	9	56	32	43
Flockton	24	12	4	8	53	40	40
Brook Motors	24	9	5	10	49	49	32
Dalton Crusaders	23	10	0	13	74	63	30
Marsden Res.	24	8	5	11	58	74	29
Fenay Bridge *-3*	23	10	0	13	60	58	27
Cartworth Moor	24	8	3	13	45	60	27
Royal Dolphins	24	6	4	14	57	71	22
Ireti Athletic	24	0	1	23	36	189	1

YMCA – record expunged

Reserve Division One	P	W	D	L	F	A	Pts
Diggle Res.	24	20	1	3	92	25	61
Uppermill Res.	23	18	1	4	90	36	55
Kirkheaton R. Res.	24	17	2	5	71	43	53
Newsome Res.	24	14	5	5	83	47	47
Heywood Spts Res.	23	15	2	6	56	40	47
Honley Res.	24	12	2	10	53	52	38
New Mill Res.	24	9	2	13	54	60	29
Lep. H'landers Res.	24	9	1	14	45	56	28
Meltham Ath. 'A'	24	8	3	13	40	60	27
Berry Brow L. Res.	24	7	4	13	60	64	25
Shepley Res.	24	8	1	15	55	59	25
Slaithwaite U. Res.	24	6	0	18	40	89	18
Mount Res.	24	0	0	24	25	133	0

Reserve Division Two	P	W	D	L	F	A	Pts
Lindley Libs Res.	20	15	1	4	67	24	46
Aimbry Res.	20	14	3	3	58	36	45
Britannia Spts Res.	20	10	5	5	59	32	35
Netherton Res.	20	10	5	5	50	37	35
Diggle 'A'	20	9	4	7	47	45	31
Cumberworth Res.	20	9	0	11	33	46	27
Uppermill 'B'	20	7	3	10	38	45	24
Scholes Res.	20	7	3	10	39	51	24
Wooldale W. Res.	20	6	4	10	31	42	22
Linthwaite A. Res.	20	4	3	13	35	53	15
Honley 'A'	20	3	1	16	18	64	10

Reserve Div. Three	P	W	D	L	F	A	Pts
Scisset Res.	20	15	1	4	54	25	46
Heyside Res.	20	13	3	4	69	38	42
Paddock Rgrs Res.	20	12	1	7	58	46	37
Kirkheaton R. 'A'	20	10	3	7	44	44	33
Holmbridge Res.	20	9	4	7	58	44	31
Brook Motors Res.	20	8	5	7	50	47	29
Shelley Res.	20	8	4	8	55	48	28
Netherton 'A'	20	6	6	8	60	57	24
HV Acad. Res.	20	5	5	10	44	62	20
Cartw'th Moor Res.	20	4	1	15	25	86	13
Meltham Ath. 'B'	20	2	3	15	27	47	9

Cravens Res. – record expunged

Reserve Div. Four	P	W	D	L	F	A	Pts
Westend Res.	20	17	0	3	88	27	51
Upperthong Res.	20	14	3	3	74	30	45
KKS Ashbrow Res.	20	14	2	4	66	27	44
Cumberworth 'A'	20	14	1	5	75	46	43
Lindley Res.	20	10	4	6	63	45	34
Britannia Sports 'A'	20	9	4	7	55	40	31
New Mill 'A'	20	6	3	11	46	72	21
Scholes 'A'	20	6	2	12	46	72	20
Mount 'A'	20	3	3	14	27	71	12
Hade Edge Res.	20	2	3	15	27	87	9
Flockton Res.	20	2	1	17	21	71	7

I ZINGARI COMBINATION

Division One	P	W	D	L	F	A	Pts
Sth Liverpool Res.	20	17	1	2	47	15	52
Sacre Coeur FP Res.	20	14	3	3	51	24	45
NELTC Res.	20	12	4	4	40	18	40
Old Xaverians Res.	20	8	6	6	33	28	30
Warbreck Res.	20	8	5	7	43	41	29
Collegiate OB Res.	20	8	3	9	35	29	27
Birchfield Res. *-3*	20	7	5	8	32	35	23
Edge H. BCOB Res.	20	6	4	10	35	47	22
Leyfield Res.	20	5	1	14	30	60	16
Aintree V. Res. *+3*	20	3	3	14	20	44	15
Alsop OB Res.	20	3	3	14	28	53	12

Division Two	P	W	D	L	F	A	Pts
Old Xaverians 'A'	20	15	3	2	60	20	48
Stoneycroft Res.	20	14	5	1	68	18	47
Mossley Hill Res.	20	13	3	4	46	25	42
BRNESC Res.	20	11	4	5	57	27	37
L'pool NALGO Res.	20	10	3	7	54	39	33
Mexoc	20	8	3	9	40	39	27
Birchfield 'A'	20	6	3	11	31	37	21
Chatsworth	20	5	3	12	32	64	18
Essemmay OB Res.	20	5	2	13	31	76	17
Quarry Bk OB Res.	20	4	2	14	34	57	14
Rockville W. Res.	20	1	5	14	15	66	8

ILFORD & DISTRICT LEAGUE

Premier Division	P	W	D	L	F	A	Pts
Galatasaray UK	14	10	1	3	37	25	31
Prostar	14	8	3	3	34	15	27
St Vincents	14	8	3	3	27	16	27
East Barking Utd *+3*	14	5	2	7	26	30	20
Debden Sports *-3*	14	7	1	6	32	37	19
AFC Kings	14	5	3	6	28	22	18
St Francis	14	3	2	9	22	37	11
Border Rangers	14	2	1	11	18	42	7

London APSA Res. and Yalova – records expunged

Division One	P	W	D	L	F	A	Pts
Titans United	18	13	4	1	61	19	43
Baronsmere	18	14	1	3	64	38	43
London & Essex	18	12	3	3	52	23	39
E. Thames Win. Pk	18	9	3	6	51	30	30
East London Celtic	18	8	1	9	58	55	25
Forest United	18	7	4	7	49	47	25
Westill	18	6	4	8	38	44	22
Ryan 'A'	18	3	5	10	29	46	14
St Francis Res.	18	3	3	12	29	76	12
St Vincents Res.	18	0	2	16	25	78	2

Division Two	P	W	D	L	F	A	Pts
Castle United	16	12	1	3	63	23	37
Melbourne S. Res.	18	11	3	4	37	30	36
Avondale Rangers	18	10	4	4	43	32	34
May & Baker	18	9	3	5	37	37	30
Cowley Leyton *-3*	17	9	3	6	37	31	27
Lotus Sports	18	6	5	7	35	40	23
Debden Colts	18	6	4	8	39	34	22
Trelawny	18	4	2	12	40	52	14
Ryan 'B'	17	4	2	11	35	55	14
Alliance United	18	2	3	13	26	58	9

Division Three	P	W	D	L	F	A	Pts
Glendale	20	18	1	1	80	20	55
Puma 2000 Res.	20	15	0	5	58	36	45
East Ham Inter	20	14	1	5	102	37	43
Ascot United	20	9	1	10	32	47	28
Ludlows *-6*	20	11	0	9	49	26	27
Newham Royals	20	9	0	11	53	72	27
Midland	20	7	2	11	43	66	23
Renegades	20	6	1	13	39	73	19
Durning	20	5	2	13	38	55	17
Forest United Res.	20	5	2	13	30	69	17
E. Bark. Utd Res. *-4*	20	5	2	13	47	70	13

JERSEY COMBINATION

Division One	P	W	D	L	F	A	Pts
Jersey Scottish	16	12	2	2	67	16	38
Grouville	16	10	1	5	52	18	31
St Peter	16	9	2	5	39	16	29
Trinity	16	9	1	6	41	30	28
St Pauls	16	7	5	4	39	23	26
Rozel Rovers	16	8	1	7	21	31	25
First Tower United	16	5	0	11	32	40	15
St Ouen	16	4	2	10	30	40	14
Magpies	16	1	0	15	8	115	3

Division Two	P	W	D	L	F	A	Pts
Portuguese	18	16	0	2	77	30	48
Jersey Wanderers	18	14	1	3	62	21	43
Jersey Nomads	18	11	1	6	49	34	34
St Clement	18	10	3	5	55	32	33
Sporting Academics	18	10	0	8	72	51	30
St Brelade	18	6	5	7	33	38	23
Beeches	18	5	2	11	31	62	17
St Martin/SCF	18	4	4	10	32	39	16
St Lawrence	18	3	0	15	21	62	9
St John	18	3	0	15	19	82	9

WWW.CHERRYRED.CO.UK

eserve Division One	P	W	D	L	F	A	Pts
rouville Res.	16	10	1	5	45	19	31
irst Tower Utd Res.	16	8	3	5	33	23	27
t Peter Res.	16	8	3	5	36	29	27
ersey Scottish Res.	16	8	1	7	35	25	25
t Brelade Res.	16	7	3	6	32	39	24
ozel Rovers Res.	16	7	1	8	29	40	22
ersey Wdrs Res.	16	6	3	7	31	31	21
p. Academics Res.	16	5	1	10	21	42	16

eserve Division Two	P	W	D	L	F	A	Pts
t Ouen Res.	18	15	2	1	99	18	47
t Pauls Res.	18	14	1	3	74	35	43
t Clement Res.	18	14	1	3	57	26	43
t Martin/SCF Res.	18	10	3	5	48	37	33
ortuguese Res.	18	7	1	10	40	40	22
ersey Nomads Res.	18	7	0	11	37	59	21
lagpies Res.	18	6	2	10	34	48	20
t John Res.	18	5	2	11	32	70	17
eeches Res.	18	4	1	13	21	48	13
t Lawrence Res.	18	1	1	16	17	78	4

ivision C	P	W	D	L	F	A	Pts
rouville 'A'	18	13	4	1	91	17	43
t Peter 'A'	18	13	3	2	59	30	42
ersey Wdrs 'A'	18	12	3	3	76	36	39
t Brelade 'A'	18	12	3	3	63	37	39
t Ouen 'A'	18	7	0	11	55	58	21
ozel Rovers 'A'	18	5	4	9	40	64	19
porting Acad. 'A'	18	5	2	11	48	62	17
t Martin/SCF 'A'	18	4	3	11	29	73	15
t Clement 'A'	18	4	2	12	37	69	14
t Lawrence 'A'	18	2	2	14	32	84	8

KINGSLEY LEAGUE

	P	W	D	L	F	A	Pts
orth Petherwin	22	16	2	4	109	38	50
ideford Res.	22	15	3	4	93	29	48
andkey	22	15	3	4	73	33	48
outh Petherwin -3	22	14	5	3	86	26	44
olsworthy 'A'	22	12	3	7	52	41	39
ilkhampton Res. +3	22	7	4	11	48	70	28
ierton	22	8	2	12	47	58	26
lack Torrington	22	6	6	10	49	66	24
ridgerule	22	7	3	12	38	75	24
Veek St Mary Res.	22	6	5	11	31	48	23
tratton United Res.	22	5	2	15	51	92	17
artland 'A'	22	1	2	19	28	129	5

KINGSTON & DISTRICT LEAGUE

Premier Division	P	W	D	L	F	A	Pts
laori Park	16	13	2	1	57	16	41
Vestminster Cas.	16	13	1	2	43	17	40
hessington KC	16	10	1	5	43	27	31
Iolesey Villa	16	7	1	8	36	32	22
obin Hood	16	6	4	6	29	27	22
look Venturers	16	5	2	9	23	40	17
lbert Royals	16	4	1	11	23	43	13
'ston Academicals	16	4	0	12	20	45	12
ynamo Pimlico	16	3	2	11	14	41	11

ivision One	P	W	D	L	F	A	Pts
ummerstown	18	15	1	2	85	18	46
nternational FC	18	12	2	4	38	26	38
Vest End Esher	18	11	3	4	69	35	36
Vandsworth Cor.	18	9	3	6	31	29	30
hornton Heath	18	9	2	7	46	40	29
Vestside Res.	18	9	1	8	39	37	28
epton	18	6	0	12	34	43	18
partak Molesey	18	3	6	9	23	38	15
sher Athletic Res.	18	4	3	11	25	68	15
Ierton Social	18	1	1	16	20	76	4

ivision Two	P	W	D	L	F	A	Pts
Vandsworth Town	18	14	2	2	47	18	44
sher United	18	12	2	4	38	27	38
ulham Deaf	18	10	3	5	45	30	33
HFC London	18	10	3	5	51	37	33
Iaori Park Res.	18	7	5	6	37	40	26
C Malden	18	7	1	10	47	47	22
ld Rutlishians 'A'	18	5	6	7	36	45	21
iverdale	18	5	3	10	31	37	18
outhfields	18	4	4	10	40	58	16
IMB	18	0	3	15	12	45	3

Division Three	P	W	D	L	F	A	Pts
Kingston Alb. Res.	18	13	2	3	42	19	41
Lower Green	18	12	3	3	63	22	39
Wandle AFC	18	11	2	5	56	31	35
Surrey Fire	18	9	2	7	36	25	29
Barnslake	18	8	4	6	44	43	28
Chess'gton KC Res.	18	7	4	7	28	39	25
Oxshott Royals	18	6	6	6	39	40	24
Jolly Coopers	18	5	2	11	33	41	17
NPL 'A'	18	4	5	9	36	50	17
Red Star	18	0	0	18	20	87	0

Division Four	P	W	D	L	F	A	Pts
Claygate Royals	20	17	2	1	67	22	53
Claygate Swans	20	17	1	2	83	12	52
Darkside	20	12	1	7	59	31	37
NPL 'B'	20	11	1	8	47	50	34
Surbiton Eagles	20	9	3	8	40	43	30
Hersham RBL 'A'	20	8	0	12	43	53	24
Merton Social Res.	20	6	5	9	30	55	23
Lower Green Res.	20	6	2	12	39	58	20
Westside 'A'	20	5	4	11	31	57	19
Hook Vent. Res.	20	4	4	12	36	62	16
AFC Hampton	20	2	3	15	30	62	9

LANCASHIRE AMATEUR LEAGUE
(Redrow)

Premier Division	P	W	D	L	F	A	Pts
R'dale St Clements	26	16	3	7	53	33	51
Bury GSOB	26	16	3	7	43	33	51
Old Boltonians	26	14	3	9	53	41	45
Old Mancunians	26	11	9	6	49	38	42
Chaddertonians	26	11	7	8	55	36	40
Little Lever SC	26	11	7	8	49	39	40
Bury Amateurs	26	11	4	11	54	52	37
Rossendale Amats	26	9	8	9	43	48	35
Mostonians	26	9	4	13	37	49	31
Radcliffe Town	26	7	8	11	36	44	29
Lymm	26	8	4	14	33	46	28
Bolton Lads Club	26	8	3	15	47	59	27
Hindley Juniors *-8*	26	10	4	12	40	36	26
Prairie United	26	5	5	16	34	72	20

Division One	P	W	D	L	F	A	Pts
Old Blackburnians	24	21	1	2	93	27	64
Horwich RMI	24	18	3	3	67	22	57
Tyldesley United	24	15	5	4	65	36	50
Thornleigh	24	12	3	9	59	50	39
Bolton Wyresdale	24	11	3	10	55	53	36
Spotland Methodists	24	9	5	10	67	66	32
Hesketh Casuals	24	10	2	12	46	61	32
Tonge United	24	9	2	13	58	71	29
Little Lever SC Res.	24	8	2	14	55	57	26
Chad'tonians Res.	24	8	2	14	41	61	26
Bolt. Ambassadors	24	6	4	14	41	67	22
Broughton Amatrs	24	5	3	16	51	80	18
Oldham Hulmeians	24	5	3	16	45	92	18

Division Two	P	W	D	L	F	A	Pts
Failsw'th Dynamos	24	18	6	0	79	17	60
Old B'burnians Res.	24	17	4	3	75	32	55
Howe Bridge Mills	24	16	5	3	75	30	53
Horwich Victoria	24	15	6	3	67	27	51
Bromley Cross *-3*	24	12	5	7	68	48	38
Rossendale A. Res.	24	10	3	11	64	54	33
Rochdale St C. Res.	24	9	5	10	54	57	32
Old Boltonians Res.	24	7	5	12	35	56	26
Acc. Loyal Amats	24	6	4	14	50	70	22
Radcliffe Boys	24	6	4	14	51	97	22
Bacup United	24	6	3	15	29	66	21
Ashtonians	24	4	1	19	36	77	13
Lymm Res.	24	3	3	18	33	85	12

Division Three	P	W	D	L	F	A	Pts
Rochdale St C. 'A'	24	15	5	4	50	34	50
Old B'burnians 'A'	24	14	6	4	58	41	48
O. Mancunians Res.	24	14	6	4	47	30	48
Hesketh Cas. Res.	23	14	1	8	57	40	43
Broughton A. Res.	24	10	3	11	60	50	33
Bolton W'dale Res.	24	8	7	9	48	51	31
Ainsworth	23	9	3	11	46	43	30
Acc. Lyl Ams Res.	24	7	8	9	39	36	29
Radcliffe T. Res.	24	8	5	11	42	50	29
Tottington United	24	7	5	12	47	60	26
Bury GSOB Res.	24	7	4	13	30	45	25
Mostonians Res.	24	6	6	12	36	49	24
Prairie United Res.	24	5	3	16	31	62	18

Division Four	P	W	D	L	F	A	Pts
Bury Amateurs Res.	22	14	6	2	54	24	48
Little Lever SC 'A'	22	14	6	2	55	31	48
Tonge United Res.	22	15	2	5	56	28	47
Spotland Meth. Res.	22	12	3	7	50	39	39
Hesketh Cas. 'A'	22	12	2	8	56	43	38
Old B'burnians 'B'	22	8	6	8	54	45	30
Chaddertonians 'A'	22	8	4	10	37	41	28
Horwich RMI Res.	22	8	3	11	40	50	27
Thornleigh Res.	22	8	0	14	52	70	24
Old Boltonians 'A'	22	5	4	13	27	53	19
Oldham Hulm. Res.	22	5	2	15	36	58	17
Radcliffe Boys Res.	22	2	4	16	35	70	10

Division Five	P	W	D	L	F	A	Pts
Rossendale A. 'A'	20	13	3	4	66	31	42
Little Lever SC 'B'	20	11	4	5	42	34	37
Rochdale St C. 'B'	20	11	2	7	51	42	35
O. Mancunians 'A'	20	9	8	3	39	23	35
Acc. Loyal Ams 'A'	20	10	4	6	48	36	34
Ashtonians Res.	20	9	5	6	55	51	32
Thornleigh 'A'	20	9	1	10	54	63	28
Bolton Amb. Res.	20	7	1	12	42	57	22
Old Boltonians 'B'	20	5	5	10	45	47	20
Mostonians 'A'	20	5	2	13	31	59	17
Ainsworth Res.	20	2	3	15	27	57	9

Division Six	P	W	D	L	F	A	Pts
Bury Amateurs 'A'	22	19	3	0	79	20	60
Rossendale A. 'B'	22	13	3	6	59	34	42
Bury GSOB 'A'	22	13	3	6	45	33	42
Hesketh Casuals 'B'	22	11	6	5	50	33	39
Oldham Hulme. 'A'	22	10	3	9	62	61	33
Broughton Ams 'A'	22	8	7	7	52	48	31
Lymm 'A'	22	8	7	7	54	53	31
Old Mancunians 'B'	22	8	3	11	49	50	27
Bolton W'sdale 'A'	22	8	1	13	44	64	25
Radcliffe Town 'A'	22	4	6	12	47	78	18
Horwich RMI 'A'	22	3	5	14	39	61	14
Thornleigh 'B'	22	2	3	17	36	81	9

Division Seven	P	W	D	L	F	A	Pts
Mostonians 'B' *-4*	22	17	3	2	79	21	50
Bury Amateurs 'B'	22	14	4	4	80	39	46
Lymm 'B'	22	14	4	4	56	36	46
O. B'kburnians 'C'	22	13	3	6	72	54	42
Broughton Ams 'B'	22	11	3	8	77	53	36
Chaddertonians 'B'	22	8	6	8	38	55	30
Spotland Meth. 'A'	22	8	5	9	48	49	29
Spotland Meth. 'B'	22	8	3	11	78	68	27
Bolton W'sdale 'B'	22	7	3	12	41	54	24
Rossendale A. 'C'	22	5	2	15	46	98	17
Bury GSOB 'B'	22	4	3	15	34	78	15
Oldham Hulme. 'B'	22	3	1	18	39	83	10

LANCASHIRE LEAGUE
(Lancit Haulage)

East Division	P	W	D	L	F	A	Pts
Farsley Celtic Res.	18	14	2	2	52	19	44
Altrincham Res.	18	12	3	3	53	26	39
Guiseley Res.	18	10	3	5	46	39	33
Wakefield Res.	18	10	0	8	36	35	30
Hyde United Res.	18	8	3	7	34	33	27
Rossendale U. Res.	18	6	5	7	34	38	23
Woodley Sports 'A'	18	5	5	8	27	29	20
Bradford PA Res.	18	6	2	10	35	59	20
Ossett Town Res.	18	4	2	12	24	36	14
Ossett Albion Res.	18	2	1	15	22	49	7

West Division	P	W	D	L	F	A	Pts
Morecambe Res.	18	16	1	1	61	12	49
Fleetwood T. Res.	18	9	5	4	39	28	32
Lancaster City Res.	18	9	3	6	33	31	30
Leigh RMI Res.	18	8	4	6	35	27	28
Bamber Bridge Res.	18	8	4	6	36	29	28
Skelmersdale Res.	18	8	3	7	44	46	27
Workinton Res.	18	6	0	12	35	40	18
Atherton Colls Res.	18	4	4	10	28	46	16
Burscough Res.	18	4	2	12	25	45	14
Barrow Res.	18	3	4	11	22	54	13

CHAMPIONSHIP PLAY-OFF

1st leg: Morecambe Res. 4 Farsley Celtic Res. 3

2nd leg: Farsley Celtic Res. 3 Morecambe Res. 1

LANCASHIRE & CHESHIRE AMATEUR LEAGUE

Premier Division	P	W	D	L	F	A	Pts
Denton Town	26	21	5	0	90	26	68
Hooley Bdge Celtic	26	14	7	5	70	49	49
Rochdalians	26	13	7	6	62	30	46
Abacus Media	26	11	6	9	64	53	39
Heaton Mersey	26	12	3	11	46	54	39
South Manchester	26	10	8	8	60	58	38
Norris Villa	26	9	7	10	54	61	34
Mellor	26	10	3	13	44	56	33
Bedians	26	9	4	13	63	71	31
Old Ashtonians	26	9	4	13	52	60	31
Beechfield United	26	9	3	14	54	68	30
Hazel Grove	26	7	7	12	49	57	28
Newton Heath	26	7	3	16	38	69	24
Burnage Metro	26	6	3	17	46	80	21

Division One	P	W	D	L	F	A	Pts
Old Trafford	26	21	1	4	105	40	64
Old Standians	26	16	4	6	82	50	52
Newton	26	15	4	7	81	47	49
Parrswood Celtic	26	15	3	8	59	41	48
Old Stretfordians	26	12	7	7	58	47	43
Stoconians	26	12	6	8	59	45	42
Hollingworth OB	26	12	4	10	42	42	40
Irlam Steel	26	9	8	9	64	69	35
Spurley Hey	26	10	5	11	53	68	35
Moston Brook OB	26	10	2	14	60	43	32
Gatley	26	6	6	14	48	64	24
Old Chorltonians	26	5	6	15	46	91	21
Oldham Victoria	26	4	5	17	31	85	17
Aldermere	26	3	3	20	42	98	12

Division Two	P	W	D	L	F	A	Pts
Whalley Range	24	18	3	3	67	22	57
Eagle	24	18	2	4	81	36	56
Offerton Villa	24	18	2	4	70	31	56
Govan Athletic	24	17	3	4	83	29	54
Droylsden Amats	24	14	6	4	73	41	48
Alkrington D'moes	24	11	3	10	70	48	36
AFC Oldham	24	12	0	12	58	46	36
New East Manch.	24	8	5	11	69	59	29
Manchester Albion	24	7	2	15	38	81	23
Deans	24	5	4	15	36	64	19
St Margaret Marys	24	5	1	18	38	68	16
Moorside Rangers	24	5	0	19	32	89	15
Lime Street SC	24	2	1	21	22	123	7

Division A	P	W	D	L	F	A	Pts
Rochdalians Res.	26	19	1	6	71	31	58
South Manch. Res.	26	18	3	5	90	45	57
Beechfield Utd Res.	26	15	6	5	68	40	51
Denton Town Res.	26	14	3	9	69	55	45
Newton Heath Res.	26	13	5	8	67	52	44
Mellor Res.	26	13	4	9	91	52	43
Hazel Grove Res.	26	12	5	9	77	77	41
Hooley Bridge Res.	26	10	6	10	70	64	36
Old Ashtonians Res.	26	10	5	11	59	59	35
Burnage Metro Res.	26	9	4	13	61	74	31
Stoconians Res.	26	8	6	12	52	68	30
Bedians Res.	26	8	1	17	59	77	25
Old Stretford. Res.	26	6	2	18	45	80	20
Spurley Hey Res.	26	1	1	24	29	134	4

Division B	P	W	D	L	F	A	Pts
Norris Villa Res.	26	18	5	3	106	33	59
Whalley Range Res.	26	18	5	3	71	33	59
Moston Brook Res.	26	19	2	5	73	42	59
Newton Res.	26	13	3	10	60	56	42
Abacus Media Res.	26	12	3	11	58	57	39
Stoconians 'A'	26	10	6	10	49	50	36
Old Trafford Res.	26	11	2	13	60	57	35
Heaton Mersey Res.	26	9	5	12	58	66	32
Gatley Res.	26	8	8	10	50	59	32
Hollingwth OB Res.	26	8	7	11	50	66	31
Cheadle Hulme	26	9	3	14	59	76	30
Irlam Steel Res.	26	7	7	12	39	41	28
Old Standians Res.	26	7	3	16	49	76	24
Old Chorlton. Res.	26	1	5	20	40	110	8

Division C	P	W	D	L	F	A	Pts
Burnage Metro 'A'	24	21	0	3	98	30	63
Aldermere Res.	24	19	1	4	99	38	58
Stoconians 'B'	24	15	4	5	71	46	49
Old Stretford. 'A'	24	14	5	5	67	41	47
Parrswood C. Res.	24	10	5	9	60	42	35
St Marg. Marys Res.	24	10	4	10	67	69	34
Govan Athletic Res.	24	9	6	9	49	49	33
Mellor 'A'	24	9	3	12	50	56	30
Whalley Range 'A'	24	8	3	13	73	75	27
Bedians 'A'	24	7	6	11	36	60	27
AFC Oldham Res.	24	6	2	16	39	95	20
Oldham Vics Res.	24	3	3	18	31	94	12
Lime Street SC Res.	24	3	2	19	37	82	11

Division D	P	W	D	L	F	A	Pts
Bedians 'B'	22	14	5	3	82	35	47
Hooley Bridge 'A'	22	14	4	4	79	36	46
Beechfield Utd 'A'	22	14	1	7	62	58	43
Irlam Steel 'A'	22	11	5	6	59	42	38
Burnage Metro 'B'	22	11	5	6	54	42	38
O. Chorltonians 'A'	22	9	8	5	67	51	35
Mellor 'B'	22	10	5	7	54	41	35
Old Ashtonians 'A'	22	9	3	10	55	48	30
Aldermere 'A'	22	8	1	13	45	63	25
Whalley Range 'B'	22	4	4	14	53	95	16
Stoconians 'C'	22	4	1	17	41	78	13
O. Stretfordians 'B'	22	1	4	17	26	88	7

Division E	P	W	D	L	F	A	Pts
Beechfield Uied 'B'	22	17	5	0	105	33	56
Burnage Metro 'C'	22	17	2	3	91	43	53
Mellor 'C'	22	14	4	4	85	41	46
AFC Oldham 'A'	22	12	2	8	76	58	38
Old Ashtonians 'B'	22	10	2	10	74	63	32
Newton 'A'	22	9	2	11	84	88	29
Newton Heath 'A'	22	9	2	11	60	69	29
Stoconians 'D'	22	8	4	10	66	59	28
Bedians 'C'	22	7	1	14	40	78	22
Moston Brook 'A'	22	5	4	13	38	71	19
Old Stretford. 'C'	22	5	2	15	52	85	17
Old Chorlton. 'B'	22	3	2	17	26	109	11

LEEDS RED TRIANGLE LEAGUE

Premier Division	P	W	D	L	F	A	Pts
East Leeds	22	18	2	2	86	26	56
Wykebeck Arms U.	22	17	1	4	85	34	52
Halton Moor.	22	14	3	5	57	43	45
Farnley Nags Head	22	13	3	6	76	33	42
Churwell New Inn	22	13	3	6	77	58	42
Seacroft WMC	22	10	2	10	52	56	32
Yew Tree E. Leeds	21	9	4	8	97	55	31
Amaranth	22	8	3	11	69	81	27
Rowland Rd WMC	22	7	1	14	46	77	22
Ekhaya African S.	21	4	3	14	46	83	15
Merlins	22	4	3	15	45	94	15
Middleton Park	22	0	0	22	35	131	0

Harehills Labour Club, Middleton Arms, Swinnow Athletic and Queens – records expunged

Division One	P	W	D	L	F	A	Pts
Gate	24	20	2	2	98	37	62
Bainbridge United	24	20	0	4	78	35	60
Skinners Arms	24	15	2	7	63	44	47
Leodis	24	14	3	7	51	41	45
Drigh'ton Adwalton	24	13	4	7	62	39	43
Farnley Sports	24	12	3	9	65	49	39
New Farnley CC	24	10	5	9	61	43	35
Super Eagles	24	10	4	10	72	60	34
Farsley Bay Horse	24	9	5	10	59	45	32
Churwell NI Res.	24	6	0	18	45	65	18
Dynamo Turbot	24	4	6	14	28	51	18
Leeds Deaf	24	3	0	21	33	77	9
Middleton Park Res.	24	3	0	21	41	170	9

Shadwell Town – record expunged

LEICESTER CITY LEAGUE

Premier Division	P	W	D	L	F	A	Pts
FC Khalsa	12	8	3	1	57	21	27
FC Belgrave	12	6	1	5	54	48	19
Parva Wayfarers	12	4	3	5	41	44	15
Sporting United	12	4	2	6	23	29	14
Park End	12	3	1	8	30	63	10

Division One	P	W	D	L	F	A	Pts
FC Rowlatts	15	10	3	2	46	27	33
FC Khalsa Res.	15	7	3	5	45	26	24
Sth Wigston Wdrs	15	7	3	5	41	39	24
Mayflower	15	7	2	6	38	41	23
Aylestone/DWMC	15	3	3	9	28	41	12
Brock Design	15	2	4	9	26	50	10

Division Two	P	W	D	L	F	A	Pts
Tele Link Taxis	20	16	3	1	82	30	51
Netherhall Rgrs *-6*	20	16	1	3	98	36	43
AFC Aylestone	20	11	6	3	64	35	39
Kirkland *+3*	20	10	4	6	52	33	37
Cosby Victory	20	8	2	10	37	55	26
Generous Briton	20	8	1	11	71	70	25
Park End Res.	20	7	4	9	57	65	25
FC Khalsa 'A'	20	7	3	10	49	52	24
FC GNG	20	7	2	11	49	83	23
FC Cricks	20	3	4	13	34	69	13
Brock Design Res.	20	1	2	17	27	92	5

LINCOLN LEAGUE

	P	W	D	L	F	A	Pts
Moorlands Railway	30	23	2	5	70	22	71
AFC Victory	30	21	4	5	84	23	67
Heckington	30	19	5	6	75	33	62
Plough Skell'thorpe	30	17	5	8	82	46	56
Ivy Tavern	30	17	4	9	80	37	55
RMSC Athletic	30	15	7	8	63	49	52
AFC Bull & Chain	30	14	6	10	77	55	48
FC Rustons United	30	15	2	13	63	45	47
Fulbeck United	30	11	9	10	56	52	42
Horncastle T. Res.	30	12	6	12	51	53	42
Market Rasen Town	30	11	6	13	56	73	39
Ruston Sports Res.	30	8	5	17	54	89	29
Metheringham	30	9	1	20	43	84	28
Cherry Knights	30	7	4	19	38	55	25
Metheringham Wed.	30	2	5	23	19	77	11
Harby	30	2	3	25	16	134	9

✓LIVERPOOL OLD BOYS AMATEUR LEAGUE

Division One	P	W	D	L	F	A	Pts
Bankfield Old Boys	22	20	2	0	75	19	62
Naylorsfield	22	17	4	1	75	31	55
Old Bootleians	22	16	3	3	73	39	51
FC Salle	22	13	1	8	54	50	40
Old Instonians	22	10	5	7	48	37	35
Old Xaverians 'B'	22	9	3	10	40	42	30
L'pool NALGO 'A'	22	7	4	11	43	47	25
De La Salle OB	22	6	4	12	43	53	22
Wavertree WDOB	22	5	7	10	30	47	22
Hope Park	22	4	3	15	34	69	15
Collegiate OB 'A'	22	2	5	15	27	65	11
Business School *-1*	22	1	3	18	29	72	5

Division Two	P	W	D	L	F	A	Pts
Alumni	22	18	2	2	74	26	56
Old Bootleians Res.	22	15	3	4	71	41	48
Cardinal Newman	22	15	1	6	54	39	46
Sacre Coeur FP 'A'	22	12	5	5	56	33	41
Waterloo GSOB	22	9	6	7	51	45	33
Old Xaverians 'C'	22	10	3	9	38	41	33
Alsop Old Boys 'A'	22	6	7	9	50	46	25
Corinthian *-1*	22	6	6	10	36	47	23
Mossley Hill A. 'A'	22	6	3	13	44	52	21
Quarry Bk OB 'A'	22	5	3	14	48	70	18
Bankfield OB Res.	22	4	3	15	32	90	15
Collegiate OB 'B'	22	3	4	15	38	62	13

Division Three	P	W	D	L	F	A	Pts
Bootech Old Boys	20	14	3	3	55	29	45
W'loo GSOB Res.	20	14	2	4	59	27	44
Oaks Institute OB	20	10	5	5	60	33	35
Quarry Bank OB 'B'	20	8	6	6	55	44	30
Alsop OB 'B' *+3*	20	7	5	7	36	38	29
Gateacre *-6*	20	9	5	6	47	45	26
Blue Coat OB	20	7	3	9	36	49	24
Convocation	20	6	5	9	32	42	23
Old Cathinians *-3*	20	7	4	9	43	52	22
Essemmay OB 'A'	20	3	3	14	47	76	12
Old Bootleians 'A'	20	2	3	15	27	62	9

Division Four	P	W	D	L	F	A	Pts
St Mary's Coll. OB	22	18	3	1	90	27	57
St Benedicts OB *+3*	22	15	4	3	66	21	52
South Mersey	22	16	3	3	65	28	51
Cardinal New. Res.	22	12	3	7	61	36	39
Ercanil Old Boys	22	11	3	8	56	51	36
Liobians Res.	22	9	3	10	51	67	30
Alsop Old Boys 'C'	22	8	1	13	42	48	25
Old Cathinians Res.	22	6	4	12	38	61	22
Old Xaverians 'D'	22	5	5	12	42	68	20
Business Sc. Res. *-1*	22	5	3	14	49	63	17
Richmond *-3*	22	7	2	13	35	58	17
Collegiate OB 'C'	22	2	2	18	30	97	8

Division Five	P	W	D	L	F	A	Pts
Quarry Bk OB 'C'	22	18	2	2	87	20	53
Old Holts Res.	22	16	2	4	74	36	50
Old Cathinians 'A'	22	15	4	3	58	26	49
Collegiate OB 'D'	22	12	3	7	73	40	39
W'loo GSOB 'A'	22	10	6	6	63	42	36
Rhein	22	11	2	9	50	39	35
De La Salle OB Res.	22	8	4	10	38	52	28
Old Bootleians 'B'	22	7	4	11	58	70	25
Kingsford	22	6	3	13	44	61	24
Wv. WDOB Res. *-6*	22	7	1	14	32	65	16
St Mary's COB Res.	22	3	1	18	30	89	10
Liobians 'A'	22	1	4	17	27	94	7

LOWESTOFT & DISTRICT LEAGUE

ivision One	P	W	D	L	F	A	Pts
earts of Oak	22	21	1	0	84	17	64
pexhall	22	13	1	8	46	30	40
irkley 'A' -3	22	13	3	6	52	30	39
/aveney Youth	22	12	3	7	44	48	39
/rentham	22	10	2	10	62	48	32
orton Athletic	22	8	6	8	50	48	30
owestoft T. 'A'	22	8	3	11	42	48	27
orton Res.	22	8	2	12	33	52	26
xford Arms	22	6	4	12	45	53	22
ot Black	22	6	3	13	32	53	21
DS Waveney	22	6	2	14	27	52	20
lundeston M. -16	22	5	2	15	25	63	1

ivision Two	P	W	D	L	F	A	Pts
outhwold T. Res.	26	20	4	2	91	29	64
earts of Oak Res.	26	18	3	5	103	58	57
arlton Rangers	26	16	4	6	75	55	52
ulton Bd/N. Res.	26	14	5	7	72	54	47
uffolk Punch	26	13	4	9	91	68	43
axton Res.	26	12	4	10	66	57	40
llingham	26	12	3	11	72	68	39
/esthall	26	11	4	11	54	66	37
acon Arms	26	10	2	14	64	57	32
arsham	26	8	6	12	52	65	30
orton Ath. Res.	26	7	5	14	44	62	26
oyal Standard	26	5	3	18	62	89	18
pexhall Res.	26	4	4	18	28	76	16
lun. Mags Res. -3	26	5	3	18	40	110	15

ivision Three	P	W	D	L	F	A	Pts
rusaders	26	21	5	0	124	49	68
akefield Re-United	26	18	4	4	90	33	58
/hite Horse Celtic	26	18	3	5	107	32	57
/aveney Gunners	26	16	4	6	72	50	52
le Frank	26	13	3	10	84	46	42
'stoft International	26	11	3	12	55	50	36
arsham	26	10	6	10	56	60	36
opton White Hart	26	11	3	12	68	82	36
DS Waveney Res.	26	11	2	13	80	74	35
xf'd Arms Res. -3	26	12	2	12	71	92	35
larquis of Lorne	26	9	2	15	58	77	29
ungay T. 'A' -3	26	5	7	14	56	86	19
outhwold T. 'A'	26	2	4	20	38	114	10
C Edgebar	26	0	2	24	38	152	2

LUTON & SOUTH BEDS LEAGUE

remier Division	P	W	D	L	F	A	Pts
unstable United	16	11	3	2	51	28	36
lub Lewsey	16	11	2	3	58	23	35
we & Lamb	16	11	1	4	36	20	34
oater	16	8	2	6	31	28	26
ewsey Park	16	6	7	3	28	24	25
hristians in Sport	16	7	3	6	35	30	24
t Josephs	16	3	2	11	34	55	11
C Bellini	16	2	1	13	18	36	7
aton Bray	16	2	1	13	23	70	7

ivision One	P	W	D	L	F	A	Pts
topsley Common	21	15	4	2	52	22	49
t Josephs Res.	21	13	5	3	66	38	44
hrist. in Sport Res.	21	13	3	5	62	28	42
he 61 FC 'A'	21	8	5	8	45	58	29
FC Offley Social	21	7	1	13	37	53	22
uton Eagles	21	5	5	11	37	53	20
uton Leagrave	21	4	6	11	37	49	18
rown Sundon	21	3	3	15	31	66	12

MATLOCK & DISTRICT LEAGUE

remier Division	P	W	D	L	F	A	Pts
otes Park	16	15	0	1	68	16	45
ive & Let Live	16	12	1	3	54	29	37
latlock Utd Res.	16	10	1	5	54	28	31
aburnum Saints	16	9	3	4	45	35	30
romford Greyh'nd	16	6	2	8	26	35	20
omerlea	16	6	0	10	32	46	18
ings Arms	16	3	5	8	26	45	14
latlock Youth	16	2	2	12	16	45	8
hirland Miners W.	16	1	2	13	16	58	5

ivision One	P	W	D	L	F	A	Pts
arley Dale Lions	18	16	2	0	66	18	50
eak United	18	13	0	5	59	30	39
ibshelf	18	10	2	6	43	22	32
agle Tavern	18	10	1	7	66	40	31
achells	18	6	1	11	24	57	19
FC Lea Holloway	18	3	2	13	25	68	11
uke William	18	0	2	16	15	63	2

MIDLAND AMATEUR ALLIANCE

Premier Division	P	W	D	L	F	A	Pts
Woodborough Utd	24	20	1	3	86	40	61
Ashland Rovers	24	19	2	3	74	26	59
Old Elizabethans	24	17	2	5	93	32	53
FC05	24	13	5	6	73	36	44
Underwood Villa	24	14	1	9	63	46	43
Steelers	24	10	4	10	65	57	34
Monty Hind OB	24	9	5	10	47	43	32
Wollaton 'A'	24	7	7	10	57	71	28
County NALGO	24	7	4	13	48	56	25
Brunts Old Boys	24	6	4	14	42	73	22
Beeston OB Assoc.	24	4	5	15	29	60	17
Lady Bay	24	5	1	18	33	104	16
Bassingfield	24	4	1	19	31	97	13

Division One	P	W	D	L	F	A	Pts
Heanor Colliers -1	28	24	3	1	118	28	74
Pinxton Sun Inn	28	20	2	6	99	53	62
Southwell Amats	28	17	3	8	84	65	54
Wollaton 'B'	28	17	1	10	107	64	52
Notting'shire Res.	28	14	4	10	59	37	46
Top Club -1	28	13	7	8	59	56	45
Keyworth U. 'A' -2	28	13	7	8	81	59	44
Radcliffe Olym. 'A'	28	11	7	10	68	66	40
PASE -4	28	11	6	11	57	54	35
Sherwood Forest -1	28	9	5	14	49	60	31
O. E'bethans Res. -1	28	8	5	15	60	71	28
Acorn Athletic	28	8	4	16	63	101	28
Derbys Amats Res.	28	6	4	18	51	93	22
Old Bemrosians	28	5	5	18	48	95	20
Clinphone	28	2	1	25	42	143	7

Division Two	P	W	D	L	F	A	Pts
Calverton MW 'A'	30	26	0	4	156	39	78
West Bridgford Utd	30	23	5	2	88	39	74
Ashland Rov. Res.	30	17	7	6	117	58	58
TVFC	30	18	4	8	114	61	58
Bassingfield Res.	30	15	6	9	96	62	51
Hickling	30	16	2	12	88	77	50
EMTEC	30	14	4	12	87	72	46
Cambridge Knights	30	14	4	12	67	77	46
Broadmeadows	30	14	2	14	67	68	44
Notting'shire 'A'	30	12	5	13	80	83	41
Tibshelf Old Boys	30	11	2	17	62	107	35
Beeston AFC Res.	30	9	6	15	53	69	33
Town Mill	30	7	4	19	39	83	25
Derbyshire Ams 'A'	30	6	5	19	57	107	23
O. Bemrosians Res.	30	3	5	22	35	116	14
Ashfield Athletic	30	2	5	23	45	133	11

MIDLAND REGIONAL ALLIANCE

Premier Division	P	W	D	L	F	A	Pts
Ashover	32	20	8	4	97	56	68
Derby Rolls R. Leis.	32	19	6	7	82	34	63
Carlton Town Res.	32	19	6	7	77	44	63
Wirksworth Town	32	16	5	11	74	46	53
Holbrook St Mich.	32	15	7	10	61	41	52
Ilkeston Town Res.	32	15	7	10	49	42	52
Rowsley	32	15	4	13	74	61	49
Cromford	32	14	7	11	62	61	49
Allestree	32	12	8	12	45	59	44
Belper United	32	12	7	13	49	55	43
Melbourne Dyn.	32	13	3	16	58	65	42
Borrowash V. Res.	32	13	3	16	65	76	42
Shirebrook T. Res.	32	12	4	16	59	69	40
Belper Town Res.	32	9	7	16	60	69	34
Eastwood T. Res.	32	10	4	18	55	85	34
Chesterfield Ath.	32	5	9	18	45	90	24
Long Eaton Utd Res.	32	4	3	25	39	98	15

Division One	P	W	D	L	F	A	Pts
Dronfield Town	32	28	1	3	130	21	85
Newmount	32	20	8	4	96	33	68
Castle Donington T.	32	20	2	10	98	47	62
Ripley -1	32	18	7	7	79	47	60
Pastures	32	16	7	9	74	46	55
Swanwick Pent. Rd	32	16	7	9	62	46	55
Dovedale L. Eaton	32	14	9	9	56	58	51
Derbyshire Amats	32	13	9	10	58	63	48
Sutton Town Res.	32	12	6	14	50	65	42
Shirebrook T. 'A'	32	11	8	13	58	62	41
Holbrook St M. Res.	32	11	5	16	50	70	38
Little Eaton -1	32	10	5	17	52	72	34
Derby RR Leis.Res.	32	7	8	17	49	76	29
Bargate Rovers	32	8	5	19	53	85	29
Woolley Moor Utd	32	7	7	18	45	77	28
Beeston AFC	32	7	5	20	48	106	26
Rowsley Res.	32	2	5	25	33	117	11

Division Two	P	W	D	L	F	A	Pts
Parkhouse +3	30	26	3	1	139	17	84
Wirksworth Sports	30	22	4	4	96	34	70
Belper United Res.	30	21	3	6	78	25	66
Findern	30	19	3	8	94	46	60
Chellaston	30	18	5	7	88	31	59
Wirksworth Athletic	30	19	1	10	89	56	58
Mickleover RBL	30	18	3	9	77	50	57
Ripley Res.	30	14	3	13	69	58	45
Pastures Res.	30	12	1	17	60	85	37
Kingsway	30	11	3	16	51	85	36
Melbourne D. Res.	30	9	4	17	56	90	31
Wirksworth Ivanhoe	30	8	5	17	53	93	29
Allestree Res. -3	30	8	3	19	45	88	24
Little Eaton Res.	30	5	2	23	38	116	17
Swanwick PR Res.	30	3	3	24	35	94	12
Bargate Rovers Res.	30	3	2	25	32	132	11

MID-ESSEX LEAGUE

Premier Division	P	W	D	L	F	A	Pts
S'minster St Leo. +2	20	13	2	5	44	22	43
Harold Wood 'A'	20	12	5	3	65	34	41
Bradwell United	19	12	3	4	51	23	39
Ravens	20	9	3	8	39	31	30
Beacon Hill Rovers	20	8	6	6	40	34	30
Frenford Senior 'A'	20	8	4	8	44	43	28
Sporting Stones	20	8	1	11	36	48	25
Mundon Victoria	19	6	4	9	43	45	22
Gidea Park Rgrs -1	20	5	7	8	32	37	21
Shelley Royals	20	4	6	10	27	64	18
Old C'fordians 'A'	20	3	1	16	36	76	10

Division One	P	W	D	L	F	A	Pts
Scotia Billericay	24	17	3	4	83	38	54
Welcome	24	15	7	2	77	21	52
Outwood Common	23	15	3	5	63	35	48
Silver End United	24	13	3	8	53	33	42
Manford Way 'A'	24	13	3	8	66	51	42
Boreham	24	10	7	7	53	43	37
S'thminster SL Res.	24	9	5	10	54	78	32
Springfield Rouge	24	7	8	9	59	60	29
Utd Christ. Churches	24	7	6	11	50	55	27
Boundary	24	6	7	11	41	61	25
LWSC Gallabright	23	5	8	10	47	55	23
Essex Police	24	3	2	19	36	87	11
Stock United	24	3	2	19	30	95	11

Division Two	P	W	D	L	F	A	Pts
Braintree/Bocking	22	16	3	3	68	22	51
Dunmow	22	13	3	6	65	44	42
Ferrers Athletic	22	13	3	6	53	43	42
Tillingham	22	12	5	5	45	43	41
Focus Ferrers	22	11	6	5	46	29	39
Ravens Res.	22	9	7	6	42	36	34
Manford Way 'B'	22	9	6	7	62	37	33
Marconi	22	9	3	10	55	53	30
Harold Wood A. 'B'	22	6	3	13	43	69	21
Latchingdon	22	5	4	13	41	75	19
Outwood Cmn Res.	22	2	8	12	18	33	14
Shenfield Ass. 'A'	22	1	1	20	30	84	4

Division Three	P	W	D	L	F	A	Pts
Rayleigh Town 'A'	24	19	2	3	99	24	59
Epping 'A'	24	17	3	4	74	31	54
Byfleet Rangers +2	24	15	6	3	72	28	53
Focus Ferrers Res.	24	13	4	7	69	57	43
O. C'fordians 'B' +3	24	12	4	8	51	48	43
Writtle Manor -7	24	13	4	7	62	40	36
St Margarets	24	8	4	12	45	64	28
City Colts	24	6	8	10	56	56	26
E2V Technologies	24	7	5	12	40	53	26
Crays Hill +3	24	6	3	15	31	63	24
Marconi Res.	24	7	2	15	34	57	23
Springfield Res. +3	24	5	1	18	25	77	19
Burnham R. 'A' -3	24	4	2	18	22	82	11

Division Four	P	W	D	L	F	A	Pts
Gt Baddow Res. +2	24	17	2	5	64	45	55
Brendans	24	17	3	4	65	41	54
Scotia Bill'cay Res.	24	16	3	5	65	32	51
Cricketers Horndon	24	15	2	7	61	33	47
Bradwell Utd Res.	24	10	5	9	45	52	35
Wickham Royals	24	10	3	11	62	49	33
Hutton 'A' -3	24	8	4	12	53	66	31
Shelley Ryls Res. -3	24	10	3	11	44	59	30
Felsted	24	9	2	13	49	56	29
Mundon Vics Res.	24	8	4	12	62	76	28
Boreham Res.	24	8	2	14	49	66	26
Woodham Radars	24	5	4	15	29	37	19
Silver End Res. -1	24	2	5	17	33	69	10

Division Five	P	W	D	L	F	A	Pts
Frenford Senior 'B'	26	20	0	6	119	31	60
Braintree & B. Res.	26	18	3	5	78	34	57
Runwell H. 'A' *+9*	26	14	3	9	68	56	54
Marks Farm *+3*	26	17	0	9	74	65	54
Boormans *-9*	25	20	0	5	90	25	51
Burnham Ramb. 'B'	26	14	3	9	58	56	45
Beacon Hill R. Res.	26	13	4	9	62	40	43
Writtle Mnr Res. *-3*	26	12	3	11	66	61	42
Springfield 'A'	26	7	4	15	39	76	25
Old C'fordians 'C'	26	6	4	16	42	90	22
Dunmow Res.	26	6	3	17	39	64	21
Shelley Royals 'A'	26	6	3	17	48	86	21
Focus Ferrers 'A' *-6*	25	8	2	15	39	58	20
Real Firmans	26	3	2	21	33	113	11

MID-SOMERSET LEAGUE

Premier Division	P	W	D	L	F	A	Pts
Purnell Sports	20	14	1	5	61	25	43
Meadow Rangers	20	14	1	5	54	20	43
Coleford Athletic	20	14	0	6	58	36	42
Mells & Vobster U.	20	11	5	4	55	31	38
Westfield	20	10	2	8	35	44	32
Radstock T. Res.	20	10	1	9	47	41	31
Belrose	20	7	5	8	48	43	26
Littleton Sports	20	6	4	10	29	48	22
Chew Magna	20	6	3	11	34	50	21
Wookey	20	4	1	15	27	63	13
Chilcompton	20	2	1	17	29	76	7

Division One	P	W	D	L	F	A	Pts
Pensford	20	14	4	2	92	20	46
Norton Hill Rangers	20	15	1	4	63	35	46
Glastonbury T. Res.	20	15	0	5	86	31	45
Stoke Rovers	20	11	3	6	29	21	36
Farrington Gurney	20	9	5	6	56	43	32
Temple Cloud *-2*	20	10	2	8	51	48	30
Frome Colls Res.	20	8	1	11	54	49	25
Evercreech Rovers	20	6	2	12	35	62	20
Littleton Sports Res.	20	6	0	14	29	51	18
Welton Arsenal	20	5	1	14	27	62	16
Welton Rovers 'A'	20	1	1	18	10	110	4

Division Two	P	W	D	L	F	A	Pts
Purnell Sports Res.	22	15	4	3	60	36	49
Frome Town S. Res.	22	13	4	5	57	37	43
Mells/Vobster Res.	22	13	3	6	56	36	42
Westfield Res.	22	13	2	7	67	39	41
Wells City 'A'	22	11	3	8	46	41	36
Oakhill	22	9	5	8	48	44	32
Farmborough	22	9	3	10	50	49	30
Clutton Res.	22	8	3	11	53	55	27
Interhound	22	6	7	9	54	65	25
Chilcompton Res.	22	6	2	14	34	63	20
Pilton United	22	5	3	14	40	62	18
Tunley Ath. Res.	22	3	3	16	29	67	12

Division Three	P	W	D	L	F	A	Pts
Coleford Ath. Res.	26	20	1	5	113	25	61
Mells & Vobster 'A'	26	19	3	4	88	39	60
Frome Colls 'A'	26	17	3	6	83	52	54
Belrose Res.	26	14	7	5	68	49	49
Wookey Res.	26	14	5	7	89	53	47
Radstock Town 'A'	26	11	4	11	60	64	37
Chew Magna Res.	26	12	1	13	57	64	37
Meadow Rgrs Res.	26	11	2	13	44	71	35
Pensford Res.	26	9	6	11	83	65	33
Westfield 'B'	26	9	4	13	73	61	31
Far'ton Gurney Res.	26	9	4	13	54	68	31
Evercreech R. Res.	26	7	1	18	55	100	22
Chilcompton United	26	5	2	19	33	111	17
Stoke Rovers Res.	26	1	5	20	27	105	8

MID-SUSSEX LEAGUE

(Gray Hooper Holt LLP)

Note – the regular season was abandoned due to bad weather. Each division was split into two groups with points carried forward from regular season, and champions decided by a play-off. Eventual champion clubs are asterisked.

Premier Division	P	W	D	L	F	A	Pts
*Old Varndeanians	14	8	4	2	29	14	28
Jarvis Brook	13	8	4	1	29	18	28
Lewes Bridgeview	12	7	3	2	33	18	24
Felbridge	15	7	3	5	38	34	24
Lindfield	14	7	2	5	25	25	23
East Grinstead Utd	11	5	3	3	26	14	18
Willingdon Athletic	10	4	5	1	22	10	17
Hassocks 'A'	15	5	2	8	30	32	17
Wisdom Sports	12	4	4	4	28	22	16
Balcombe	14	4	4	6	20	23	16
Maresfield Village	16	4	4	8	30	34	16
Plumpton Athletic	14	1	3	10	18	41	6
Cuckfield Town	14	1	3	10	13	56	6

Division One	P	W	D	L	F	A	Pts
*Hartfield	13	9	1	3	25	22	28
Sporting Lindfield	15	7	3	5	27	22	24
Rotherfield	16	7	3	6	30	26	24
Forest Row	11	7	2	2	28	15	23
O. V'deanians Res.	11	6	3	2	25	16	21
Heath Pilgrims	17	6	2	9	33	37	20
Wisdom Sports Res.	13	5	4	4	27	22	19
Village of Ditchling	12	5	2	5	25	25	17
Hurstpierpoint Res.	17	3	6	8	20	28	15
Wivelsfield Green	10	3	4	3	15	17	13
Turners Hill	13	3	4	6	25	29	13
Horsted Keynes	11	3	3	5	23	31	12
Buxted	15	3	3	9	18	31	12

Division Two	P	W	D	L	F	A	Pts
Franklands Village	16	11	2	3	50	32	35
*Uckfield T. Res.	10	10	0	0	42	9	30
Crawley Down 'A'	11	7	1	3	36	18	22
Ashurst Wood	12	6	4	2	29	18	22
Willingdon A. Res.	14	5	7	2	31	22	22
Handcross Village	14	6	1	7	38	36	19
Burgess Hill Albion	13	4	4	5	24	27	16
Cuckfld Wheatsheaf	14	4	3	7	28	39	15
Peacehaven United	18	4	1	13	33	58	13
Ardingly	10	3	2	5	17	24	11
E. Grinstead U. Res.	13	2	4	7	25	41	10
Pease Pottage Res.	15	3	1	11	24	53	10

Division Three	P	W	D	L	F	A	Pts
Horley Athletico	14	10	2	2	44	23	32
*AFC Ringmer	11	9	1	1	32	14	28
East Court	12	7	4	1	50	20	25
Scaynes Hill	11	8	1	2	33	18	25
Maresf'd V. Res. *+3*	16	6	3	7	27	31	24
E. Grin. Mariners *-3*	13	6	4	3	33	29	19
Cuckfield T. Res.	15	6	0	9	22	42	18
Roffey	11	4	3	4	25	21	15
East Grinst'd T. 'A'	15	3	2	10	16	34	11
Lindfield Res.	12	3	1	8	25	31	10
Fletching	11	3	0	8	16	32	9
West Hoathly	15	1	3	11	16	44	6

Division Four	P	W	D	L	F	A	Pts
*Keymer/Hassocks	14	10	4	0	56	19	34
Nutley	15	9	2	4	46	28	29
Ardingly Res.	14	8	0	6	40	33	24
Dormansland Rckts	9	7	1	1	27	13	22
Uckfield Town 'A'	14	6	1	7	32	36	19
O Varndeanians 'A'	13	6	1	6	31	40	19
Crowborough 'A'	15	5	3	7	37	43	18
Roffey Res.	12	4	4	4	30	20	16
Framfld/Blackboys	10	4	2	4	23	16	14
Lewes B'view Res.	15	4	2	9	27	41	14
Danehill	15	3	1	11	29	70	10
Plumpton A. Res.	12	2	1	9	20	39	7

Division Five	P	W	D	L	F	A	Pts
Turners Hill Res.	14	11	1	2	43	22	34
Scaynes Hill Res.	17	9	2	6	46	41	29
Fairwarp	12	8	1	3	37	23	25
Barcombe	12	7	1	4	40	20	22
Wisdom Sports 'A'	14	7	0	7	31	21	21
Burg. Hill Alb. Res.	15	6	3	6	31	30	21
*Lingfield 'A'	10	5	3	2	15	11	18
Handcross V. Res.	15	4	4	7	36	45	16
Fairfield	13	4	0	9	17	32	12
Buxted Res.	13	3	3	7	17	42	12
Newick Res.	15	2	5	8	28	40	11
Willingdon Ath. 'A'	12	3	1	8	22	36	10

Division Six	P	W	D	L	F	A	Pts
Copthorne Rovers	16	11	2	3	88	18	35
Heath Pilgrims Res.	15	9	2	4	58	35	29
Wivelsfield G. Res.	14	8	2	4	45	27	26
*Ansty Sports & S.	9	8	1	0	41	5	25
V. of Ditchling Res.	10	8	1	1	34	17	25
Jarvis Brook Res.	12	7	2	3	32	23	23
Horsted K. Res.	12	5	3	4	23	23	18
Rotherfield Res.	16	4	2	10	33	51	14
E. Grin. Mar. Res.	16	3	2	11	31	65	11
Bolney Rovers	16	3	1	12	20	67	10
East Grin. Utd 'A'	10	2	2	6	14	43	8
Ashurst Wood Res.	12	1	0	11	10	55	3

Division Seven	P	W	D	L	F	A	Pts
*Copthorne R. Res.	13	12	0	1	84	14	36
Hartfield Res.	15	11	1	3	43	21	34
Balcombe Res.	15	9	1	5	37	34	28
Maresfield V. 'A'	14	6	3	5	36	32	21
Felbridge Res.	10	5	2	3	15	12	17
Dormansland Res.	13	5	2	6	22	28	17
Lindfield 'A'	13	4	2	7	24	35	14
Fletching Res.	10	3	2	5	11	17	11
Cuckfield Town 'A'	14	3	2	9	18	30	11
Ansty S & S Res.	13	3	2	8	23	46	11
Uckfield Town 'B'	11	3	2	6	19	43	11
Cuckfield W. Res.	13	3	1	9	19	39	10

Division Eight	P	W	D	L	F	A	Pts
Forest Row Res.	13	10	3	0	53	11	[illegible]
*Scaynes Hill 'A'	15	10	2	3	56	21	[illegible]
Burg. Hill Alb. 'A'	16	8	5	3	47	32	[illegible]
Lindfield 'B'	17	6	3	8	29	38	[illegible]
V. of Ditchling 'A'	13	5	3	5	28	23	[illegible]
Maresfield V. 'B'	15	5	3	7	27	35	[illegible]
Framfield & B. Res.	10	5	0	5	22	26	[illegible]
Wivelsfield G. 'A'	10	5	0	5	21	25	[illegible]
Handcross V. 'A'	16	4	2	10	30	48	[illegible]
Danehill Res.	13	4	1	8	17	54	[illegible]
Fairwarp Res.	10	0	2	8	10	27	[illegible]

Division Nine	P	W	D	L	F	A	Pts
West Hoathly Res.	16	13	2	1	77	17	[illegible]
*Copthorne *+3*	12	10	1	1	75	18	[illegible]
Cowden Mavericks	15	11	1	3	63	29	[illegible]
Halsford Lions	17	11	0	6	74	29	[illegible]
Lindfield 'C'	17	9	2	6	40	33	[illegible]
Franklands V. Res.	17	9	0	8	36	35	[illegible]
Plumpton A. 'A'	16	5	5	6	39	44	[illegible]
Ardingly 'A' *-3*	18	7	2	9	33	46	[illegible]
Buxted 'A'	17	6	1	10	46	54	[illegible]
Scaynes Hill 'B'	16	3	3	10	25	69	[illegible]
Maresfield V. 'C'	14	2	0	12	17	65	[illegible]
Heath Rangers	15	0	1	14	16	102	[illegible]

MID-WALES (SOUTH) LEAGUE

(Watson Associates)

Premier Division	P	W	D	L	F	A	Pts
Hay-on-Wye	22	20	2	0	99	17	[illegible]
Rhosgoch Rangers	22	17	2	3	74	21	[illegible]
Llandrindod Wells	22	14	3	5	71	24	[illegible]
Builth Wells	22	14	1	7	68	39	[illegible]
Newcastle	22	11	3	8	49	40	[illegible]
St Harmon	22	9	4	9	35	38	[illegible]
Penybont	22	8	4	10	57	64	[illegible]
Sennybridge	22	5	8	9	38	66	[illegible]
Presteigne SA Res.	22	6	4	12	34	48	[illegible]
Gwernyfed	22	5	4	13	47	72	[illegible]
Knighton T. Res. *-3*	22	3	2	17	20	84	[illegible]
Radnor Valley	22	0	3	19	18	97	[illegible]

Brecon – record expunged

MINING LEAGUE

Division One	P	W	D	L	F	A	Pts
Portreath	28	21	2	5	99	36	[illegible]
Praze-an-Beeble	28	19	5	4	92	22	[illegible]
Threemilestone SC	28	17	5	6	70	34	[illegible]
Illogan RBL Res. *-3*	28	16	8	4	74	35	[illegible]
Gulval	28	16	3	9	81	41	[illegible]
Robartes Arms	28	16	2	10	73	58	[illegible]
Storm	28	13	5	10	66	66	[illegible]
Spice of Life	28	12	7	9	69	68	[illegible]
Halsetown	28	11	4	13	65	88	[illegible]
Gwinear *-3*	28	9	3	16	58	78	[illegible]
Trevenson Res.	28	7	5	16	48	87	[illegible]
St Just Res.	28	7	4	17	46	81	[illegible]
St Ives T. Res. *-3*	28	7	3	18	56	81	[illegible]
Goonhavern Res. *-1*	28	3	6	19	36	84	[illegible]
Holmans SC 'A' *-1*	28	3	4	21	41	115	[illegible]

Division Two	P	W	D	L	F	A	Pts
Troon Res. *-6*	30	28	0	2	133	23	[illegible]
Redruth United	30	19	7	4	102	42	[illegible]
Illogan RBL 'A'	30	19	5	6	108	47	[illegible]
New Park Rangers	30	17	6	7	81	42	[illegible]
St Buryan	30	18	2	10	75	58	[illegible]
Four Lanes *-6*	30	18	3	9	92	49	[illegible]
Mousehole 'A' *-1*	30	15	5	10	64	65	[illegible]
Trispen *-3*	30	12	8	10	77	62	[illegible]
School of Mines	30	9	8	13	80	78	[illegible]
St Agnes 'A'	30	8	5	17	70	93	[illegible]
Newlyn Non-Ath'co	30	9	2	19	71	98	[illegible]
Ludgvan Res.	30	9	1	20	62	106	[illegible]
Madron	30	8	2	20	42	89	[illegible]
Marazion B. Res.	30	7	3	20	45	111	[illegible]
Mount Ambrose	30	7	2	21	65	123	[illegible]
Goonhavern 'A'	30	7	1	22	43	124	[illegible]

Division Three	P	W	D	L	F	A	Pts
Halsetown Res.	28	21	4	3	90	25	[illegible]
Sennen	28	20	4	4	94	44	[illegible]
Crown Inn Glory	28	19	4	5	96	38	[illegible]
T'milestone Res.	28	17	5	6	76	40	[illegible]
Chacewater Res.	27	17	3	7	87	54	[illegible]
Gulval Res.	28	16	6	6	93	65	[illegible]
Portreath Res.	28	17	3	8	80	66	[illegible]
Wendron CCU 'B'	28	13	3	12	60	67	[illegible]
St Ives Mariners	28	8	3	17	64	71	[illegible]
Storm Res. *-3*	28	9	3	16	55	68	[illegible]
St Buryan Res.	28	7	3	18	26	83	[illegible]
Frogpool-C. Res.	28	7	2	19	75	146	[illegible]
Pendeen R. Res. *-1*	27	6	4	17	38	72	[illegible]
Madron Res. *-6*	28	5	1	22	42	77	[illegible]
First & Last	28	2	2	24	29	89	[illegible]

MONTGOMERYSHIRE & DISTRICT LEAGUE

(J T Hughes)

Premier Division	P	W	D	L	F	A	Pts
Bishops Castle	20	19	0	1	89	19	57
Waterloo Rov. Res.	20	14	0	6	43	36	42
Meifod	20	11	1	8	34	38	34
Bettws	20	10	3	7	40	36	33
Dyffryn Banw	20	10	2	8	54	42	32
Guilsfield Res.	20	9	4	7	47	40	31
Abermule	20	8	1	11	42	46	25
Llangedwyn	20	6	4	10	40	49	22
Llanfyllin T. Res.	20	6	4	10	37	48	22
Llanfair United	20	4	2	14	35	59	14
Severn Valley *-3*	20	2	1	17	22	70	4

NEATH & DISTRICT LEAGUE

Premier Division	P	W	D	L	F	A	Pts
Onllwyn	22	18	3	1	61	19	57
Giants Grave	22	18	2	2	70	35	56
Bryn Rovers	22	13	2	7	50	33	41
Glynneath Town	22	11	6	5	60	45	39
Sunnybank WMC	22	9	6	7	38	25	33
Caewern	22	8	8	6	36	35	32
Ynysygerwen	22	7	5	10	39	44	26
Cwm Wanderers	22	5	5	12	52	62	20
Park Travellers	22	6	2	14	43	59	20
Cilfrew Rovers	22	5	4	13	44	76	19
Rhos	22	4	6	12	47	71	18
Resolven	22	1	5	16	22	58	8

NEWPORT & DISTRICT LEAGUE

Premier Division X	P	W	D	L	F	A	Pts
Pioneer *-3*	22	20	1	1	99	22	58
Ship & Pilot	22	14	3	5	94	55	45
Pill	22	12	6	4	43	32	42
Llanwern Sports	22	12	3	7	53	42	39
Pontnewydd Utd	22	10	3	9	50	48	33
Merry Miller	22	9	4	9	56	54	31
Duffryn	22	8	5	9	57	47	29
Pill Hibernians *-3*	22	9	3	10	48	59	27
Malpas	22	7	1	14	47	68	22
Henllys Rangers	22	6	1	15	45	84	19
Caerleon Town	22	5	2	15	25	50	17
New Lysaghts Club	22	4	0	18	32	88	12

Premier Division Y	P	W	D	L	F	A	Pts
C'bran Celtic 'A'	26	17	4	5	91	41	55
Lliswerry Res.	26	15	7	4	80	43	52
Albion Rovers Res.	26	14	5	8	68	46	47
Rogerstone W. Res.	26	14	2	10	70	59	44
Malpas Glad. Res.	26	14	2	10	57	57	44
Trethomas B. Res.	26	13	4	9	63	52	43
AC Pontymister Res.	26	12	6	8	53	38	42
Cromwell Yth Res.	26	8	7	11	54	62	31
Newport CS Res.	26	9	3	14	57	81	30
West P'newydd Res.	26	8	4	14	48	74	28
Spencer YB Res.	26	7	6	13	43	56	27
C'church Ham. Res.	26	7	5	13	51	67	26
Coed Eva Ath. Res.	26	6	5	15	59	77	23
Newport Cor. Res.	26	7	2	17	49	90	23

Division One	P	W	D	L	F	A	Pts
St Julians Youth	22	19	1	2	93	33	58
Marshfield	22	19	0	3	76	21	57
Oakfield	22	18	1	3	100	30	55
Shaftesbury Youth	22	14	2	6	70	42	44
Lucas C'bran Res.	22	11	2	9	62	43	35
Spencer Old Boys	22	10	4	8	42	45	34
Lliswerry 'A'	22	10	2	10	46	43	32
Croesyceiliog 'A'	22	7	1	14	51	62	22
Albion Rovers 'A'	22	5	2	15	32	81	17
Christchurch H. 'A'	22	5	1	16	31	72	16
Six in Hand	22	3	2	17	29	83	11
Caerleon Town Res.	22	2	0	20	19	96	6

NORTH BUCKS & DISTRICT LEAGUE

Premier Division	P	W	D	L	F	A	Pts
PB (MK)	30	29	0	1	157	30	87
Potterspury	30	20	4	6	79	34	64
Brackley Sports	30	20	2	8	66	52	62
Emberton Athletic	30	19	1	10	100	66	58
Steeple Claydon *-6*	30	17	9	4	91	48	54
Heath United RBL	30	16	6	8	70	62	54
Kingfisher Titans *-3*	29	14	2	13	76	70	41
Hanslope	30	12	5	13	65	71	41
Bletchley Trees	30	11	4	15	55	79	37
Grendon Rangers	30	10	2	18	68	89	32
Deanshanger Ath.	30	9	3	18	48	70	30
Wing Village	30	9	2	19	61	76	29
Southcott Vill. RA	30	7	5	18	54	76	26
Wicken Sports	30	7	2	21	34	89	23
Castlethorpe	30	6	4	20	36	87	22
Silverstone	29	6	3	20	42	103	21

Intermediate Division	P	W	D	L	F	A	Pts
Thornborough Ath.	30	24	3	3	87	40	75
Lavendon Sports	30	22	3	5	139	45	69
Bletchley Manor	30	19	5	6	79	49	62
AFC Brickhill Rgrs	30	17	6	7	105	56	57
Stewkley	30	16	9	5	73	36	57
Syresham *-3*	30	15	9	6	82	43	51
Abbey	30	15	1	14	77	65	46
Bletch. Trees Res.	30	14	2	14	85	91	44
Woughton	30	12	3	15	75	75	39
Marsh Gibbon	30	11	3	16	78	93	36
Great Horwood	30	10	3	17	60	86	33
Yardley Gobion	30	9	4	17	75	100	31
Twyford United	30	9	2	19	55	90	29
Sherington	30	8	4	18	52	98	28
Silverstone Res.	30	4	3	23	48	126	15
Southcott VRA Res.	30	4	2	24	33	110	14

Division One	P	W	D	L	F	A	Pts
Brackley Spts Res.	28	23	3	2	115	38	72
Workplace Wdrs	28	21	3	4	128	40	66
Bletchley Town	28	19	3	6	83	35	60
Wolverton Town *-9*	28	22	2	4	104	44	59
Great Linford	28	17	4	7	82	48	55
Potterspury Res.	28	16	7	5	74	47	55
MK Wanderers *-6*	28	13	4	11	63	66	37
Steeple Clay. Res.	27	11	3	13	65	63	36
Twyford Utd Res.	28	9	3	16	48	97	30
Heath Utd RBL Res.	27	8	4	15	59	69	28
Yardley Gob. Res.	28	6	4	18	39	95	22
Denbigh S & S *-3*	28	4	6	18	46	85	15
Wing Village Res.	28	3	6	19	32	95	15
Westbury	28	3	5	20	48	95	14
Grendon Rgrs Res.	28	3	5	20	58	127	14

Division Two	P	W	D	L	F	A	Pts
Lavendon Spts Res.	24	20	2	2	88	29	62
Linslade	24	18	2	4	70	27	56
K'fisher Titans Res.	24	18	2	4	60	26	56
Stewkley Res.	24	15	3	6	70	39	48
Hanslope Res.	24	11	3	10	48	44	36
Bletch. Town Res.	24	8	8	8	49	48	32
Wicken Sports Res.	24	9	3	12	48	64	29
Deanshanger Res.	24	7	5	12	40	51	26
Syresham Res.	24	7	5	12	35	49	26
Great Linford Res.	24	7	5	12	45	59	26
Sherington Res.	24	4	7	13	36	61	19
Marsh Gibbon Res.	24	4	2	18	32	71	14
Great Horwood Res.	24	3	3	18	21	74	12

NORTH GWENT LEAGUE

Premier Division	P	W	D	L	F	A	Pts
Abertillery B. Res.	30	25	2	3	129	46	77
Southend Athletic	30	24	2	4	100	47	74
The Woodlands	30	22	4	4	130	34	70
Brynmawr Athletic	30	19	0	11	103	69	57
Rhymney	30	17	4	9	74	56	55
Castle United	30	17	1	12	104	78	52
Pantside	30	15	4	11	100	78	49
Drysiog Inn	30	15	1	14	95	93	46
Aberbargoed Res.	30	13	2	15	82	79	41
Brynmawr Town	29	12	2	15	98	106	38
Cefn Fforest Res.	30	10	5	15	70	78	35
Pentwynmawr Res.	30	8	3	19	50	106	27
Abertillery Res.	30	7	3	20	51	109	24
Trinant Res.	30	8	0	22	62	124	24
Abercarn Utd Res.	30	6	4	20	66	94	22
Tafarn-y-Werin	29	2	1	26	29	146	7

Division One	P	W	D	L	F	A	Pts
Treowen Stars Res.	32	29	2	1	160	30	89
Cwm Sports	32	29	0	3	134	40	87
Tredegar Athletic	32	25	2	5	96	30	77
Phoenix United	32	25	0	7	138	46	75
Tredegar Arms	32	22	2	8	106	41	68
Fleur-de-Lys	31	16	3	12	92	71	51
Red Lion	32	16	3	13	63	68	51
Abertillery B. 'A'	32	13	6	13	68	77	45
Abertillery Ex. Res.	32	12	3	17	73	94	39
Llanhilleth A. Res.	32	11	2	19	58	112	35
RTB Ebbw V. Res.	32	9	3	20	66	107	30
Crusaders Res.	32	9	2	21	71	111	29
Cefn Fforest 'A'	32	8	4	20	62	108	28
Abertillery B. 'B'	32	6	7	19	49	77	25
Blaenau Gwent Utd	32	5	6	21	39	98	21
FC Dugout Res.	31	4	7	20	54	122	19
Rhymney Res.	32	4	4	24	35	132	16

NORTH LANCASHIRE & DISTRICT LEAGUE

Premier Division	P	W	D	L	F	A	Pts
Marsh United	26	23	2	1	90	21	71
Storeys	26	20	3	3	90	35	63
Highgrove	26	17	3	6	75	32	54
TIC Dynamos	26	15	3	8	58	38	48
Cartmel & Dist. *-6*	26	16	5	5	81	40	47
Ingleton	26	12	7	7	56	45	43
Morecambe Royals	26	12	5	9	55	43	41
Kirkby Lonsdale	26	11	4	11	49	44	37
Galgate	26	7	4	15	30	48	25
Caton United	26	7	4	15	51	78	25
Slyne with Hest	26	5	5	16	37	65	20
Torrisholme	26	5	3	18	36	90	18
Westgate Wdrs	26	4	0	22	17	115	12
Boys Club	26	2	4	20	26	57	10

Division One	P	W	D	L	F	A	Pts
Swarthmoor Soc. C.	28	23	2	3	107	38	71
Carnforth Rangers	28	22	4	2	85	20	70
Bentham	28	19	4	5	80	49	61
Storeys Res.	28	15	7	6	87	61	52
Cartmel & D. Res.	28	12	4	12	75	61	40
Community Sports	28	11	4	13	54	64	37
Grange	28	10	4	14	54	64	34
Marsh United Res.	28	10	4	14	61	83	34
Vine FC	28	9	5	14	54	81	32
M'cambe Ryls Res.	28	9	4	15	63	73	31
Ingleton Res.	28	8	5	15	58	78	29
Millhead *-3*	28	9	4	15	60	83	28
Lanc. City Council	28	5	9	14	31	60	24
Burton Thistle *-3*	28	6	8	14	56	73	23
Slyne with H. Res.	28	5	6	17	49	86	21

Division Two	P	W	D	L	F	A	Pts
Halton Rangers	22	21	0	1	102	16	63
Morecambe Hoops	22	19	1	2	86	33	58
Middleton	22	14	3	5	84	34	45
Arnside	22	12	5	5	48	28	41
M'cambe Ckt Club	22	13	0	9	63	51	39
Bolton-le-Sands	22	11	3	8	56	41	36
Caton Utd Res. *-6*	22	9	2	11	40	50	23
Swarthmoor Res.	22	6	2	14	32	67	20
Kirkby Lon. Rgrs	22	5	2	15	25	69	17
Torrisholme Res.	22	4	1	17	24	72	13
Freehold *-3*	22	5	0	17	37	83	12
Millhead Res. *-3*	22	3	1	18	27	80	7

Division Three	P	W	D	L	F	A	Pts
Highgrove Res.	22	18	3	1	76	17	57
Central Pier	22	15	3	4	97	42	48
Furness Rovers 'B'	22	15	2	5	70	23	47
Bowerham	22	15	2	5	72	27	47
Gregson	22	13	4	5	55	30	43
Allithwaite Rangers	22	10	3	9	59	66	33
Boys Club Res.	22	8	5	9	43	48	29
Galgate Res.	22	8	3	11	47	44	27
Arnside Res.	22	2	7	13	22	66	13
Grange Res.	22	3	4	15	33	78	13
AFC Moorlands	22	3	1	18	26	87	10
Burton Thistle Res.	22	2	3	17	24	96	9

Division Four	P	W	D	L	F	A	Pts
Heysham	16	10	3	3	57	32	33
Bolton-le-S. Res.	16	9	4	3	41	28	31
Carnforth R. Res. *-3*	16	9	3	4	46	26	27
Overton	16	7	4	5	39	28	25
Middleton Res. *-3*	16	8	2	6	38	31	23
Bentham Res.	16	6	2	8	29	39	20
Ingleton 'A'	16	5	3	8	29	37	18
Villa Royals	16	5	2	9	20	34	17
Gregson Res.	16	1	1	14	13	57	4

NORTH NORTHUMBERLAND LEAGUE

Division One	P	W	D	L	F	A	Pts
Amble United	18	16	1	1	89	18	49
Berwick Harrow	18	13	2	3	82	34	41
North Sunderland	18	10	3	5	38	32	33
Rothbury	18	8	6	4	61	52	30
Lynemouth MW	18	8	3	7	72	41	27
Shilbottle CW	18	7	5	6	48	47	26
Stobswood Welfare	18	5	5	8	34	46	20
Belford	18	4	2	12	25	56	14
Acklington Athletic	18	3	2	13	29	96	11
Alnmouth United	18	1	1	16	18	74	4

Division Two	P	W	D	L	F	A	Pts
Hedgeley Rovers	20	18	1	1	78	25	55
Craster Rovers	20	15	2	3	60	20	47
Swarland	20	12	4	4	85	45	40
Springhill	20	13	1	6	67	37	40
Berwick Utd Res.	20	11	2	7	61	42	35
Embleton	20	10	0	10	44	51	30
B'wck Harrow Res.	20	7	2	11	43	45	23
Bamburgh Castle	20	4	5	11	37	70	17
Wooler	20	5	1	14	35	57	16
Rothbury Res.	20	2	2	16	23	79	8
Poachers Rest	20	2	2	16	31	93	8

NORTH WEST NORFOLK LEAGUE

Division One	P	W	D	L	F	A	Pts
Ingoldisthorpe	22	19	3	0	88	19	60
King's Lynn 'A'	22	17	4	1	100	29	55
Terrington	22	15	3	4	35	25	48
Wiggenhall	22	11	5	6	48	30	38
West Winch	22	11	3	8	71	46	36
Heacham	22	10	4	8	55	60	34
Millfleet	22	8	1	13	29	40	25
Gaywood	22	7	2	13	59	66	23
Woottons	22	6	3	13	43	55	21
Great Massingham	22	5	6	11	31	47	21
Watlington	22	6	0	16	30	67	18
Snettisham	22	0	0	22	18	123	0

Division Two	P	W	D	L	F	A	Pts
Ingoldisthorpe Res.	26	19	3	4	69	29	60
Marham Wanderers	26	18	3	5	88	43	57
Lynn Napier	26	18	2	6	62	37	56
Narborough	26	16	2	8	36	23	50
Hunstanton	26	15	1	10	44	42	46
Bircham Newton	26	14	3	9	53	40	45
Lynn Docklands	26	13	4	9	63	42	43
Sandringham	26	10	4	12	49	44	34
Gt Mass'gham Res.	26	10	4	12	55	52	34
Flitcham	26	9	3	14	38	63	30
Terrington Res.	26	7	3	16	49	64	24
Wiggenhall Res.	26	5	2	19	26	53	17
West Winch Res.	26	5	2	19	41	75	17
Stanhoe	26	5	0	21	45	111	15

Division Three	P	W	D	L	F	A	Pts
Castle Rising	26	19	3	4	93	38	60
Gaywood Res.	26	18	5	3	107	31	59
Docking	26	17	4	5	106	65	55
Old Hunstanton	26	16	3	7	83	46	51
William Burt	26	13	7	6	90	49	46
Dersingham R. 'A'	26	14	2	10	51	53	44
Castle Acre	26	13	0	13	62	69	39
Ashill	26	10	5	11	51	63	35
Burnham Market	26	11	1	14	66	82	34
Heacham Res.	26	8	4	14	51	93	28
Walsingham	26	8	3	15	65	69	27
Millfleet Res.	26	7	3	16	70	68	24
Narborough Ship	26	7	2	17	67	103	23
Snettisham Res.	26	0	0	26	15	148	0

Division Four	P	W	D	L	F	A	Pts
Dersingham R. 'B'	20	16	1	3	72	24	49
Denver Bell	20	13	4	3	68	29	43
Fakenham T. 'A'	20	12	6	2	48	26	42
FC Walpole	20	10	1	9	41	42	31
Queensway	20	8	3	9	42	53	27
Sporle	20	7	5	8	35	30	26
Lynn Fern	20	6	4	10	45	53	22
Greyfriars	20	6	3	11	31	48	21
South Creake	20	6	2	12	28	46	20
Smithdon	20	5	2	13	43	69	17
Lynn Napier Res.	20	5	1	14	26	59	16

NORTH & MID HERTS LEAGUE

Premier Division	P	W	D	L	F	A	Pts
St Ippolyts	18	15	1	2	72	20	46
Clannad Celtic	18	13	2	3	55	24	41
Baldock Town	18	13	2	3	38	18	41
Woolmer Green	18	11	2	5	50	36	35
Colney Heath 'A'	18	7	3	8	53	37	24
Whitwell Village	18	5	3	10	47	54	18
London Colney 'A'	18	5	2	11	28	49	17
Redbourn	18	5	1	12	37	57	16
Kings Sports 'B'	18	2	5	11	31	68	11
Magnum	18	3	1	14	37	85	10

Division One Mid	P	W	D	L	F	A	Pts
RCD Harpenden	20	14	3	3	64	19	45
New Greens	20	12	3	5	62	48	39
Park Street V. Res.	20	10	5	5	46	35	35
Kimpton Rovers	20	9	4	7	56	40	31
Harpenden Rov. 'A'	20	9	4	7	38	44	31
St Albans North	20	6	9	5	48	40	27
Inn on the Green	20	7	5	8	27	27	26
St Albans Wdrs	20	6	6	8	48	64	24
Global	20	5	7	8	37	39	22
London Colney V.	20	5	2	13	41	76	17
IFK Buttles	20	1	4	15	30	65	7

Division One North	P	W	D	L	F	A	Pts
Woolmer G. Res.	20	18	0	2	72	24	54
Wilbury Wanderers	20	13	4	3	74	26	43
Fairlands	20	12	5	3	77	35	41
AFC Santos	20	11	3	6	43	34	36
Baldock Town Res.	20	10	5	5	59	45	35
City Hearts	20	10	3	7	69	49	33
Codicote 'A'	19	8	4	7	44	43	28
Bedwell Rangers	19	4	2	13	48	67	14
Kimpton Rov. Res.	20	3	4	13	40	40	13
Westwell	20	2	1	17	11	81	7
Benington	20	1	3	16	27	120	6

NORTHAMPTON TOWN LEAGUE

(Peter Smith Recruitment)

Premier Division	P	W	D	L	F	A	Pts
Duston United	21	16	3	2	79	15	51
Univ. of N'hampton	21	14	2	5	54	18	44
Airflow	21	12	2	7	65	46	38
N'pton Harlequins	21	10	4	7	79	38	34
Birchfield Rovers	21	10	1	10	59	21	31
TACT	21	7	2	12	31	75	23
Thorpland United	21	6	3	12	38	74	21
Ashley Rovers	21	0	1	20	15	133	1

Division One	P	W	D	L	F	A	Pts
Asda George	26	22	1	3	129	32	67
Blufish	26	20	2	4	108	46	62
Double Four	26	20	1	5	99	44	61
Delapre Old Boys	26	20	0	6	75	42	60
Northampton Exiles	26	13	2	11	77	61	41
Airflow Res.	26	12	4	10	89	74	40
FC Crispin	26	11	4	11	81	65	37
Obelisk United	26	11	1	14	72	103	34
Denton	26	10	2	14	48	54	32
N'pton Diamonds	26	10	1	15	57	75	31
Ashley Rovers Res.	26	6	6	14	44	67	24
Northants Police	26	5	3	18	41	100	18
Thorpland Utd Res.	26	5	2	19	55	117	17
Kingsthorpe Wdrs	26	2	1	23	34	129	7

NOTTS AMATEUR ALLIANCE

Premier Division	P	W	D	L	F	A	Pts
Bulwell	24	16	4	4	85	33	52
Matrixgrade	24	15	3	6	77	39	48
Stanton Ilkeston	24	14	4	6	77	41	46
Vernon Villa	24	13	5	6	73	36	44
Beacon	24	12	5	7	71	56	41
Lime Kiln	24	11	7	6	49	33	40
Burton Joyce -3	24	12	7	5	52	44	40
Nottinghamshire	24	10	6	8	49	37	36
Netherfield Albion	24	8	3	13	58	80	27
Boots Athletic 'A'	24	8	1	15	43	68	25
Premium	24	4	4	16	24	69	16
Trident -3	24	4	5	15	43	80	14
Bottesford	24	1	2	21	25	110	5

Division One	P	W	D	L	F	A	Pts
Premium Res.	26	19	3	4	112	38	60
United	26	18	4	4	106	51	58
Winning Post	26	15	4	7	78	55	49
Greygoose	26	15	4	7	95	76	49
Kirton Brickworks	26	14	4	8	68	52	46
Leen Athletic	26	13	3	10	82	52	42
Maid Marion	26	10	7	9	63	47	37
Gedling S'bank 'A'	26	12	1	13	60	52	37
Vernon Villa Res.	26	11	4	11	53	56	37
FC Samba	26	10	6	10	78	54	36
Sherwood	26	10	3	13	56	81	33
Ruddington Village	26	5	6	15	54	78	21
Bunny United	26	3	0	23	36	142	9
Durham Ox Wellow	26	2	1	23	21	128	7

Division Two	P	W	D	L	F	A	Pts
Kimberley MWOB	24	17	4	3	64	36	55
Clifton 'A'	24	17	2	5	66	35	53
Mach One	24	12	6	6	65	44	42
Nottm Sikh Lions	24	13	2	9	63	55	41
AFC Bridgford	24	12	4	8	59	45	40
Mansf'd Woodhouse	24	11	4	9	56	42	37
Vernon Villa 'A'	24	10	3	11	42	47	33
Nuthall	24	8	6	10	45	45	30
Premium 'A'	24	8	3	13	57	85	27
Hoofers	24	6	6	12	37	47	24
Sherwood Casuals	24	6	4	14	47	72	22
Gedling S'bank 'B'	24	4	6	14	39	57	18
AFC Acad. OB -3	24	6	2	16	34	64	17

Division Three	P	W	D	L	F	A	Pts
FC Gunthorpe	30	23	2	5	130	31	71
East Valley United	30	20	3	7	111	47	63
United Res.	30	18	6	6	87	59	60
Pegasus	30	17	4	9	96	72	55
Basford	30	16	6	8	82	59	54
Bulwell Rangers	30	15	6	9	110	80	51
Chrom Alloy	30	15	5	10	58	49	50
Engine House	30	14	2	14	115	80	44
Ali I	30	12	6	12	80	79	42
The Mill	30	11	7	12	68	80	40
East Bridgford	30	11	4	15	58	86	37
Clifton United	30	11	1	18	53	67	34
Nott'ghamshire 'B'	30	10	3	17	68	99	33
Jackson United	30	6	2	22	60	104	20
R. Hood/Little John	30	5	4	21	41	99	19
Notts Metropolis	30	3	5	22	33	159	14

PERRY STREET & DISTRICT LEAGUE

Premier Division	P	W	D	L	F	A	Pts
South Petherton	22	17	3	2	71	17	54
Lyme Regis	22	17	2	3	60	23	53
Merriott Rovers	22	13	5	4	48	35	44
W. Hse Symondsb'y	22	10	4	8	65	45	34
Perry Street & YH	22	8	5	9	40	41	29
Ilminster Town Res.	22	8	3	11	46	57	27
Combe St N. Res.	22	7	5	10	35	39	26
Farway United	22	6	7	9	38	56	25
Chard Town Res.	22	5	8	9	28	44	23
Barrington	22	5	5	12	34	52	20
Forton Rangers	22	4	5	13	30	62	17
Beaminster -1	22	3	6	13	31	55	14

Division One	P	W	D	L	F	A	Pts
Winsham	22	17	3	2	93	28	54
Crewkerne Res.	22	14	5	3	41	19	47
Merriott Rov. Res.	22	10	7	5	65	45	37
Charmouth	22	11	3	8	54	47	36
Lyme Regis Res.	22	10	4	8	33	35	34
Hinton St George	22	10	3	9	56	54	33
Netherbury	22	10	0	12	53	57	30
Thorncombe	22	8	1	13	38	47	25
Pymore -1	22	8	2	12	55	67	25
Chard Rangers	22	6	6	10	40	63	24
Uplyme	22	4	5	13	51	68	17
Chard United	22	3	3	16	42	91	12

Division Two	P	W	D	L	F	A	Pts
Misterton	20	15	4	1	75	17	49
Sth Petherton Res.	20	14	3	3	68	37	45
Drimpton	20	11	4	5	55	41	37
Combe St Nich. 'A'	20	9	3	8	60	58	30
Dowlish & Donyatt	20	7	4	9	54	56	2[illegible]
Hawkchurch	20	7	4	9	36	46	25
Millwey Rise	20	6	5	9	38	41	23
Shepton Beauchamp	20	7	1	12	31	57	2[illegible]
Haselbury	20	6	3	11	40	60	21
Norton Athletic	20	5	3	12	49	65	1[illegible]
Forton Rangers Res.	20	4	4	12	29	57	1[illegible]

Division Three	P	W	D	L	F	A	Pts
Chard Town Colts	20	16	1	3	79	25	4[illegible]
Ilminster T. Colts	20	14	2	4	68	36	4[illegible]
Perry St & YH Res.	20	14	1	5	70	40	4[illegible]
Fivehead United -5	20	12	4	4	69	40	3[illegible]
White Horse S. Res.	20	10	4	6	64	27	3[illegible]
Shep. B'champ Res.	20	9	1	10	43	46	2[illegible]
Combe St Nich. 'B'	20	9	1	10	49	64	2[illegible]
Barrington Res. -3	20	8	0	12	38	77	2[illegible]
Hinton St G. Res.	20	6	2	12	35	62	2[illegible]
L. Regis Bantams	20	2	0	18	31	82	[illegible]
Chard Rgrs Res. -1	20	2	0	18	33	80	[illegible]

Division Four	P	W	D	L	F	A	Pts
Beaminster Res.	20	17	1	2	91	18	52
Luso-Chard -3	20	17	2	1	112	23	50
Netherbury Res.	20	12	5	3	86	36	41
Farway United Res.	20	10	5	5	62	47	35
Misterton Res. -1	20	8	3	9	48	58	26
Winsham Res.	20	7	4	9	44	47	25
Millwey Rise Res.	20	6	3	11	34	54	21
Hawkchurch Res.	20	5	4	11	33	52	19
Charmouth Res. -1	20	6	2	12	34	68	19
Chard United Res.	20	3	2	15	28	119	11
Thorncombe Res.	20	3	1	16	24	74	10

PORTSMOUTH & DISTRICT LEAGUE

Premier Division	P	W	D	L	F	A	Pts
Wymering	14	10	1	3	46	29	31
Kingston Arrows	14	8	4	2	67	37	28
Old Portmuthians	14	7	5	2	44	34	26
Prospect	14	6	5	3	44	33	23
Co-op	14	4	2	8	33	36	14
Waterlooville SC	14	3	4	7	44	55	13
Segensworth	14	3	4	7	31	47	13
St Helena Bobs	14	2	1	11	25	63	7

Division One	P	W	D	L	F	A	Pts
Horndean United	18	13	3	2	74	26	42
Tardis Music	18	12	4	2	68	28	40
AFC Ventora	18	12	3	3	60	31	39
Fleur-de-Lys	18	8	3	7	57	29	27
Purbrook Sports	18	7	5	6	70	54	26
Southside	18	8	2	8	53	47	26
Cosham Blues	18	7	3	8	51	54	24
Portchester	18	6	1	11	49	63	19
SL Southsea	18	3	2	13	31	74	11
Jamocha	18	1	0	17	14	121	3

Division Two	P	W	D	L	F	A	Pts
Hayling Billy	18	13	3	2	82	36	42
Fleet Support Ltd	18	13	2	3	57	30	41
Farefield Sports	18	10	2	6	60	34	32
Wymering Res. -3	18	11	1	6	53	35	31
Carberry	18	9	2	7	48	44	29
Purbrook Spts Res.	18	7	3	8	59	52	24
Castle United	18	7	2	9	47	59	23
Tardis Music Res.	18	5	1	12	30	64	16
Harchester United	18	4	2	12	38	64	14
Westover Rangers	18	1	2	15	34	90	5

PRESTON & DISTRICT LEAGUE

Premier Division	P	W	D	L	F	A	Pts
Southport Trinity	24	20	2	2	95	26	62
Burscough R'mond	24	19	0	5	73	20	57
Longridge Town	24	18	2	4	82	38	56
Preston Wanderers	24	13	4	7	69	50	43
Southport Amateurs	24	10	4	10	49	48	34
Leyland Red Rose	24	9	6	9	44	55	33
Eccleston/Heskin U.	24	9	4	11	46	53	31
Hoghton West End	24	8	4	12	53	60	28
Town Green	24	8	2	14	38	61	26
Baxters	24	5	6	13	49	84	21
Appley Bridge -3	24	6	5	13	46	60	20
Tarleton Corries	24	4	4	16	39	72	16
Croston Sports Res.	24	3	5	16	33	89	14

Division One	P	W	D	L	F	A	Pts
Leyland St Marys	22	17	1	4	55	28	52
Burscough Bridge	22	11	6	5	44	33	39
CCA	22	11	4	7	44	41	37
New Longton Rov.	22	10	4	8	43	38	34
Blessed Sacrement	22	11	0	11	56	60	33
Southport Trin. Res.	22	9	5	8	34	28	32
Walmer Bridge	22	9	5	8	46	46	32
Preston GSA	22	9	2	11	39	41	29
Top Spinners	22	8	3	11	50	55	27
Royal Garrison	22	6	7	9	37	48	25
Bur. Richmond Res.	22	6	2	14	46	50	20
Newman College	22	5	1	16	31	57	16

Division Two East	P	W	D	L	F	A	Pts
Lostock St G. Res.	22	18	3	1	65	27	57
Halsall	22	14	4	4	71	46	46
Chipping	22	11	2	9	57	43	35
Heath Charnock	22	9	8	5	50	45	35
Leyland RR Res.	22	10	4	8	66	57	34
CCA Res.	22	10	2	10	61	61	32
Tarleton Cor. Res.	22	10	2	10	51	51	32
Walton-le-Dale	22	8	4	10	51	57	28
Walmer Bridge Res.	22	8	2	12	47	58	26
Southport Ams Res.	22	6	3	13	50	75	21
Longridge T. Res.	22	3	5	14	44	75	14
Hoghton WE Res. -3	22	4	3	15	44	62	12

Division Two West	P	W	D	L	F	A	Pts
Hoole United	22	15	5	2	63	30	50
Charnock Rich. 'A'	22	15	2	5	55	32	47
Farington Villa -3	22	14	1	7	61	38	40
Preston United	22	10	6	6	62	45	36
Mawdesley	22	10	4	8	53	43	34
Southp't Trin. 'A' -3	22	10	6	6	52	36	33
Highcross -3	22	10	4	8	48	41	31
Muldoons	22	7	4	11	41	50	25
Catforth	22	5	5	12	43	68	20
Preston GSA Res.	22	6	2	14	36	61	20
N. Longton Res. -3	22	5	2	15	27	55	14
Hesketh Bank 'A'	22	3	3	16	30	72	12

Division Three	P	W	D	L	F	A	Pts
Lytham Town	24	20	2	2	113	26	62
Ainsdale United	24	19	4	1	98	35	61
Chorley Res.	24	16	3	5	88	31	51
Ley. St Marys Res.	24	15	4	5	83	50	49
Eccleston/HU Res.	24	13	4	7	67	44	43
Greenlands	24	12	0	12	57	60	36
Leyland Red R. 'A'	24	11	0	13	69	75	33
Newman Coll. Res.	24	9	2	13	65	83	29
Deepdale	24	8	3	13	54	82	27
New Longton 'A'	24	7	1	16	38	71	22
Tarleton Corries 'A'	24	4	2	18	44	101	14
Halsall Res.	24	3	4	17	48	101	13
Hoole United Res.	24	3	3	18	27	92	12

REDHILL & DISTRICT LEAGUE

Premier Division	P	W	D	L	F	A	Pts
Reigate Priory	20	16	2	2	50	20	50
South Godstone	20	14	3	3	69	27	45
Limpsfield Blues	20	13	1	6	67	44	40
Smallfield	20	12	3	5	43	17	39
Frenches Athletic	20	11	5	4	54	32	38
Charlwood	20	8	1	11	32	38	25
Horley Town 'A'	20	5	6	9	41	47	21
Marlpit United	20	6	2	12	39	45	20
Woodland Albion	20	6	0	14	38	68	18
Kenley	20	4	3	13	29	72	15
Reigate Sala	20	1	2	17	21	73	5

Division One	P	W	D	L	F	A	Pts
South Park Res.	18	14	4	0	65	22	46
Brockham	18	14	2	2	79	18	44
Caterham Old Boys	18	14	1	3	77	26	43
Bookham 'A'	18	10	2	6	56	44	32
Reigate Priory Res.	18	10	1	7	62	38	31
Walton Heath	18	7	1	10	41	44	22
Reed	18	5	2	11	30	53	17
Smallfield Res.	18	3	2	13	29	63	11
Nutfield Res.	18	2	2	14	25	74	8
Duke of York	18	2	1	15	20	102	7

Division Two	P	W	D	L	F	A	Pts
Real Holmesdale	20	16	2	2	90	33	50
RH123 Athletic	20	16	2	2	78	38	50
Warlingham 'A'	20	13	1	6	72	25	40
Mer. Newton Res.	20	10	2	8	49	44	32
Horley Wanderers	20	10	2	8	47	48	32
Reigate Hill	20	10	1	9	54	52	31
Cheam Village Res.	20	6	4	10	46	58	22
Caterham OB Res.	20	5	5	10	39	53	20
Oxted & Dist. 'A'	20	6	0	14	33	54	18
Paynes Sports	20	5	0	15	41	87	15
Westcott	20	2	3	15	34	91	9

Division Three	P	W	D	L	F	A	Pts
Nork Social	20	18	1	1	107	34	55
Park Lane	20	12	3	5	67	44	39
Tatsfield Rov. Res	20	11	2	7	57	49	35
Sth Godstone Res.	20	10	3	7	50	44	33
South Park 'A'	20	9	5	6	63	53	32
Alma Tavern Res.	20	9	1	10	64	61	28
Warlingham 'B'	20	7	4	9	45	38	25
Reigate Priory 'A'	20	7	3	10	52	70	24
RH123 Ath. Res.	20	6	4	10	46	68	22
Godstone	20	3	5	12	36	79	14
Limpsfield B. Res.	20	2	1	17	24	71	7

Division Four	P	W	D	L	F	A	Pts
Wal'gtn New Forest.	22	16	5	1	90	33	53
Reigate Hill Res.	22	17	2	3	82	38	53
Bletchingley Res.	22	14	3	5	64	34	45
R. Holmesdale Res.	22	10	5	7	41	24	35
Reigate Priory 'B'	22	9	4	9	43	46	31
Frenches Ath. Res.	22	8	4	10	41	41	28
Cheam Village 'B'	22	7	7	8	34	44	28
Racing Epsom	22	8	3	11	43	54	27
Park Lane Res.	22	6	6	10	53	58	24
Walton Heath Res.	22	7	2	13	29	63	23
Nutfield 'A'	22	3	5	14	37	59	14
Merstham New. 'A'	22	2	4	16	27	90	10

Division Five	P	W	D	L	F	A	Pts
Sutton Churches	20	16	1	3	75	18	49
Heath Old Boys	20	13	3	4	79	31	42
Brockham Res.	20	13	2	5	83	32	41
Trinity AFC	20	11	4	5	61	44	37
Court Lodge	20	8	3	9	61	54	27
RH123 Athletic 'A'	20	8	3	9	55	63	27
Sagemaster	20	8	2	10	49	69	26
Park Lane 'A'	20	7	4	9	43	54	25
Reigate Hill 'A'	20	6	2	12	51	63	20
Horley Elite	20	3	2	15	24	100	11
Frenches Ath. 'A'	20	2	4	14	38	91	10

ROCHESTER & DISTRICT LEAGUE

Premier Division	P	W	D	L	F	A	Pts
Wayfield Athletic	24	19	1	4	90	33	58
Gillingham Green	24	18	3	3	75	30	57
Lordswood Athletic	24	15	1	8	55	36	46
Sheerness East Res.	24	13	5	6	56	39	44
Medway City	24	11	7	6	51	52	40
Cliffe Woods	24	10	2	12	51	62	32
Emerald Star	24	8	6	10	36	65	30
Roch. Pce of Wales	24	8	4	12	44	56	28
Horsted	24	7	5	12	37	46	26
Hollands/Blair Res.	24	6	4	14	30	42	22
Medway Queen	24	5	6	13	43	51	21
Greenwich Thistle	24	5	6	13	30	53	21
Plough/Chequers Sp.	24	4	4	16	33	66	16

Division One	P	W	D	L	F	A	Pts
FC Quayside	22	16	3	3	70	26	51
Bredhurst	22	16	2	4	66	31	50
The Waggon	22	15	3	4	83	41	48
Medway Knights	22	14	4	4	64	36	46
Upchurch	22	11	4	7	47	40	37
Cliffe Woods Res.	22	10	3	9	60	43	33
Three Sisters	22	8	2	12	53	68	26
Evolution	22	6	3	13	44	73	21
O'Connell's	22	6	3	13	23	63	21
Grain Athletic	22	4	8	10	37	57	20
Pegasus	22	2	7	13	38	62	13
Poachers	22	1	4	17	31	76	7

Division Two	P	W	D	L	F	A	Pts
Cannon '24	24	21	3	0	134	32	66
Stockbury Athletic	24	17	3	4	69	33	54
BAE Systems	24	16	3	5	98	57	51
Medway Ports	24	12	3	9	56	58	39
Anchorians	24	10	6	8	65	62	36
Isle of Grain	24	9	3	12	67	79	30
M'way Galvanising	24	9	2	13	55	68	29
General at Sea	24	9	2	13	51	73	29
Pegasus Res.	24	8	3	13	60	65	27
Plough/C. Spts Res.	24	6	7	11	50	57	25
Eurobars	24	6	7	11	42	76	25
Luton Athletic	24	6	4	14	60	86	22
Emerald Star Res.	24	3	2	19	29	90	11

Division Three	P	W	D	L	F	A	Pts
Evolution Res.	26	23	1	2	125	34	70
FC Cobras	26	19	4	3	99	36	61
Cliffe Woods 'A'	26	19	1	6	86	45	58
Breach Rovers	26	16	7	3	68	33	55
Victoria Taverns	26	13	4	9	74	63	43
Burnhill	26	13	3	10	71	60	42
AMBS Sports	26	11	4	11	71	64	37
Park Regis	26	9	2	15	71	83	29
Collyers	26	7	7	12	44	72	28
Bredhurst Juniors	26	7	6	13	51	45	27
Horsted Reserves	26	7	5	14	51	62	26
Beechwood '76	26	6	3	17	43	73	21
Swaleside	26	3	4	19	50	120	13
UK Paper Res.	26	3	1	22	25	139	10

Division Four	P	W	D	L	F	A	Pts
Strood	26	23	1	2	113	27	70
The Good Intent	26	19	2	5	111	54	59
Insanity	26	16	1	9	79	47	49
Star Sports	26	14	6	6	88	53	48
Woodcoombe S & S	26	14	4	8	83	52	46
Outer Fenn	26	14	3	9	88	59	45
Bredhurst Res.	26	13	4	9	65	59	43
The Rising Sun	26	13	1	12	47	49	40
Emerald S. Classics	26	12	3	11	59	60	39
Lycos	26	11	2	13	58	69	35
Valley Colts	26	8	3	15	57	64	27
Elm Windows Star	26	5	1	20	54	99	16
Sturdee	26	2	2	22	38	110	8
AFC Medway	26	1	1	24	20	158	4

Division Five	P	W	D	L	F	A	Pts
Park Regis Res.	26	23	0	3	137	29	69
Riverside	26	18	2	6	85	40	56
Royalside	26	17	4	5	91	53	55
Bleakwood Rangers	26	15	5	6	70	51	50
The H'shoe Strood	26	15	4	7	116	69	49
Rainham '84	26	13	4	9	82	93	43
AFC Phoenix	26	13	2	11	75	68	41
Stockbury Ath. Res.	26	11	4	11	82	72	37
Slade '05	26	9	2	15	59	91	29
Southern Belle	26	7	2	17	63	107	23
Bowaters	26	5	6	15	51	89	21
Lloyds	26	6	3	17	60	113	21
Medway Ports Res.	26	4	4	18	50	91	16
Roofing Care	26	4	2	20	48	103	14

SALISBURY & DISTRICT LEAGUE

Premier Division	P	W	D	L	F	A	Pts
Chalke Valley	20	14	3	3	61	27	45
Friends Provident	20	12	3	5	41	26	39
Stockton & Codford	20	10	4	6	50	41	34
Tisbury	20	9	6	5	33	26	33
Bemerton HH 'A'	20	10	1	9	35	34	31
Whiteparish	20	9	3	8	42	39	30
Castle Street Club	20	7	5	8	38	39	26
Alderbury	20	7	4	9	36	40	25
West Harnham	20	5	4	11	27	61	19
Plough	20	5	1	14	26	33	16
Damerham	20	4	2	14	28	51	14

Division One	P	W	D	L	F	A	Pts
New Inn (Amesb'y)	22	18	2	2	95	19	56
St Pauls Club	22	16	2	4	73	33	50
Porton Sports	22	13	3	6	79	43	42
Nomansland	22	13	3	6	77	45	42
S. Newton /Wishf'd	22	14	0	8	68	53	42
Enford	22	11	4	7	59	51	37
James Hay	22	9	3	10	53	60	30
Winterslow Lions	22	7	1	14	43	74	22
West Harnham Res.	22	5	5	12	38	66	20
Rouge Raiders	22	6	1	15	25	60	19
Boscombe Down	22	4	2	16	32	80	14
Beacon Sports	22	1	4	17	30	88	7

Division Two	P	W	D	L	F	A	Pts
SN & Wishford Res.	20	17	2	1	89	20	53
Greyhound (Wilton)	20	16	1	3	60	19	49
Bosc. Down Rec C.	20	14	0	6	70	34	42
Alderbury Res.	20	10	5	5	51	37	35
Stockton & C. Res.	20	10	3	7	45	33	33
Tisbury Res.	20	9	4	7	47	33	31
Duck Inn	20	6	3	11	42	72	21
Victoria Hotel	20	6	2	12	37	55	20
Hi-Flex Sports	20	4	3	13	27	71	15
Porton Sports Res.	20	3	1	16	40	80	10
Devizes Inn	20	2	2	16	28	82	8

Division Three	P	W	D	L	F	A	Pts
Five Bells	20	14	2	4	85	36	44
Chalke Valley Res.	20	12	4	4	54	41	40
Castle St Club Res.	20	11	4	5	61	42	37
Langford	20	11	3	6	54	42	36
Alderholt	20	8	4	8	34	48	28
Woodisbury	20	7	4	9	51	60	25
Phil Small Sports	20	7	3	10	27	58	24
Winterslow L. Res.	20	7	2	11	52	56	23
Figheldean Rangers	20	5	4	11	40	55	19
Devizes Inn Res.	20	5	4	11	49	67	19
Damerham Res.	20	3	6	11	32	34	15

SCUNTHORPE & DISTRICT LEAGUE
(Fallen Hero)

Division One	P	W	D	L	F	A	Pts
BBM	22	20	0	2	85	24	60
AFC Brumby	22	19	1	2	79	13	58
Scunthonians	22	15	1	6	80	32	46
Crowle Colts	22	12	2	8	52	48	38
Ashby Cons	22	9	3	10	46	42	30
Epworth Town	22	8	4	10	39	36	28
Smiffy's *-1*	22	7	7	8	37	38	27
Appleby F. Colts *+2*	22	7	4	11	44	55	27
Scawby	22	7	5	10	37	55	26
Sherpa	22	6	1	15	40	91	19
Crosby Colts	22	5	3	14	47	63	18
Barnetby United	22	0	3	19	26	115	3

Division Two	P	W	D	L	F	A	Pts
Swinefleet Juniors	24	20	1	3	66	24	61
Scotter United	24	17	3	4	82	28	54
BBM Res.	24	16	2	6	76	45	50
AFC Brumby Res.	24	15	4	5	59	43	49
Haxey Town	24	14	1	9	67	49	43
New Holland Villa	24	12	3	9	65	45	39
Barton United Colts	24	11	4	9	56	49	37
Messingham Trin. J.	24	10	2	12	54	52	32
Scunthonians Res.	24	9	2	13	45	50	29
Limestone Rangers	24	9	2	13	51	65	29
Luddington	24	4	3	17	41	95	15
Crosby Colts Res.	24	2	2	20	44	89	8
Deltron	24	1	3	20	18	90	6

Division Three	P	W	D	L	F	A	Pts
Crosby Colts Junior	22	15	5	2	83	33	50
Briggensians	22	15	4	3	72	31	49
Barrow Wanderers	22	13	5	4	60	33	44
College Wanderers	22	13	4	5	62	37	43
Limestone R. Res.	22	9	4	9	45	44	31
Epworth Town Res.	22	7	9	6	61	46	30
Crowle Colts Res.	22	8	4	10	41	44	28
Winterton Town	22	7	5	10	47	58	26
Epworth T. Colts	22	6	6	10	48	54	24
Scotter United Res.	22	5	5	12	54	50	20
Scawby Hotshots	22	3	8	11	38	74	17
Santon	22	1	1	20	31	138	4

SELBY & DISTRICT LEAGUE

Division One	P	W	D	L	F	A	Pts
Pollington	22	17	5	0	105	43	56
Rileys	22	13	5	4	71	47	44
Knottingley	22	14	2	6	69	47	44
Bird In Hand	21	9	5	7	49	43	32
New Airedale	21	8	8	5	43	37	32
Hensall Athletic *+3*	21	7	6	8	43	49	30
Pontefract Town	21	8	4	9	58	64	28
Riccall	22	7	6	9	63	65	27
South Milford	22	8	3	11	59	64	27
Garforth WMC	22	5	5	12	43	63	20
Kellington	22	6	2	14	60	82	20
Yorkshire Penny	22	1	3	18	28	87	6

Division Two	P	W	D	L	F	A	Pts
Fairburn	26	22	3	1	116	31	69
Moorends	26	18	3	5	146	47	57
Pontefract S&S Res.	26	18	2	6	92	50	56
Rileys Rangers	26	16	4	6	80	45	52
New Airedale Res.	26	13	4	9	72	58	43
Snaith	26	11	5	10	87	62	38
Garforth Rangers	25	11	5	9	57	57	38
Garforth WMC Res.	25	11	5	9	67	80	38
Yorkshire Rose	26	11	2	13	53	69	35
Garforth AFC	26	7	4	15	59	80	25
Monk Fryston	26	5	5	16	41	89	20
Selby RSSC Res.	26	6	2	18	48	101	20
North Duffield	26	6	2	18	44	108	20
Drax	26	3	0	23	32	117	9

SHEFFIELD & HALLAMSHIRE SENIOR LEAGUE
(Windsor Food Service)

Premier Division	P	W	D	L	F	A	Pts
Athersley Rec.	26	21	3	2	74	21	66
Stocksbdge PS Res.	26	17	4	5	72	25	55
Wombwell Main	26	15	6	5	73	34	51
Mexborough MS	26	14	3	9	61	39	45
Hollinsend Amats	26	10	6	10	36	45	36
HSBC	26	10	4	12	58	67	34
Outo Kumpu S&SC	26	9	6	11	56	76	33
Sheffield Lane Top	26	9	5	12	56	45	32
Oughtibdge WMSC	26	9	5	12	50	59	32
Thorpe Hesley *-3*	26	11	2	13	46	58	32
Dinnington T. Res.	26	9	4	13	47	50	31
Houghton Main	26	7	5	14	29	51	26
Penistone Church	26	6	4	16	33	65	22
Edlington WMC	26	5	3	18	27	83	18

Division One	P	W	D	L	F	A	Pts
Springwood Davy	26	19	4	3	65	29	61
Dearne Coll. MW *-6*	26	21	2	3	84	31	59
Parkgate Res.	26	15	4	7	73	33	49
Worsbro Common	26	14	3	9	58	45	45
Frecheville CA	26	11	6	9	64	44	39
Handsworth *-6*	26	14	3	9	57	44	39
ADS Precision	26	12	3	11	49	46	39
Dodworth MW *-4*	26	11	2	13	53	55	31
Silkstone United	26	8	6	12	41	55	30
Ecclesfield R. Rose	26	8	5	13	40	46	29
South Kirkby Coll.	26	7	7	12	32	42	28
Wickersley OB	26	6	4	16	33	57	22
Parramore Sports	26	6	3	17	37	76	21
Elm Tree	26	2	4	20	26	109	10

Division Two	P	W	D	L	F	A	P
Worsbro. BMW Res.	24	16	3	5	64	37	[illegible]
Everest	24	14	4	6	47	28	[illegible]
Sheffield Athletic	24	12	7	5	67	44	[illegible]
Sheffield Bankers	24	13	3	8	49	39	[illegible]
Sheff. Centralians	24	12	4	8	42	38	[illegible]
Caribbean Sports *-6*	24	14	2	8	60	45	[illegible]
Millmoor Juniors	24	10	4	10	62	55	[illegible]
Thorncliffe	24	9	4	11	42	53	[illegible]
Bramley S'side Jnrs	24	8	6	10	57	52	[illegible]
De La Salle OB	24	7	8	9	47	57	[illegible]
Frickley Ath. Res.	24	4	6	14	35	57	[illegible]
Penistone Ch. Res.	24	3	5	16	29	66	[illegible]
High Green Villa *-3*	24	4	4	16	25	55	[illegible]

Phoenix Sports & Social – record expunged

SHEFFIELD SPORTS & ATH. LEAGUE

	P	W	D	L	F	A	P
Wybourn	12	8	2	2	45	17	[illegible]
Boynton Sports	12	7	2	3	30	16	[illegible]
Penguin	12	7	1	4	42	20	[illegible]
Sheffield Medics	12	5	3	4	33	35	[illegible]
Millmoor Jnrs Res.	12	5	1	6	34	47	[illegible]
Fairways Inn	12	2	1	9	28	63	[illegible]
Tsunami	12	1	4	7	25	39	[illegible]

SOUTH LONDON ALLIANCE

Premier Division	P	W	D	L	F	A	P
Kingfisher	20	13	4	3	68	26	[illegible]
Forest Hill Park	20	12	2	6	48	32	[illegible]
Johnson & Phillips	20	9	6	5	33	27	[illegible]
Drummond Athletic	20	7	7	6	27	26	[illegible]
Metrogas Res.	20	8	4	8	38	40	[illegible]
Long Lane	20	7	5	8	38	29	[illegible]
Cray Vall. PM Res.	20	8	2	10	35	36	[illegible]
Old Roan Res.	20	8	2	10	35	40	[illegible]
Middle Park	20	7	2	11	36	50	[illegible]
Tudor Spts Res. *+2*	20	6	2	12	31	49	[illegible]
Dresdner K'wort *-1*	20	6	2	12	29	63	[illegible]

Division One	P	W	D	L	F	A	P
Wilmington	20	13	5	2	46	21	[illegible]
Crofton Albion	20	12	3	5	57	29	[illegible]
Blackheath Wdrs	20	9	7	4	42	27	[illegible]
Seven Acre Sports	20	7	10	3	44	37	[illegible]
Beaverwood	20	9	2	9	41	35	[illegible]
Eltham Town	20	8	5	7	31	31	[illegible]
Bridon Ropes Res.	20	7	6	7	37	32	[illegible]
Farnbor. OBG Res.	20	5	6	9	43	50	[illegible]
Penhill Standard	20	5	6	9	34	54	[illegible]
Eltham Royals	20	3	6	11	28	58	[illegible]
Cray Valley PM 'A'	20	2	4	14	23	52	[illegible]

Division Two	P	W	D	L	F	A	P
AFC Sydenham	22	16	5	1	71	24	[illegible]
Bexlians *+2*	22	16	2	4	75	28	[illegible]
Parkhurst Rgrs *-3*	22	15	5	2	71	24	[illegible]
Lewisham Athletic	22	12	4	6	60	34	[illegible]
Wickham Wdrs *-1*	22	12	5	5	59	42	[illegible]
Johnson & P. Res. *+3*	22	8	3	11	38	55	[illegible]
Oakdale Athletic	22	8	4	10	27	41	[illegible]
Old Roan 'A'	22	8	1	13	43	68	[illegible]
Catford Exiles	22	7	1	14	49	62	[illegible]
Beckenham Royals	22	6	1	15	27	66	[illegible]
Avery Hill College	22	3	2	17	23	55	[illegible]
Bexley	22	2	5	15	26	70	[illegible]

Division Three	P	W	D	L	F	A	P
Elite	22	18	1	3	76	25	[illegible]
New Park	22	17	2	3	67	23	[illegible]
Metrogas 'A'	22	15	2	5	65	41	[illegible]
Old Town New Boys	22	13	2	7	39	29	[illegible]
Ravens	22	10	4	8	46	41	[illegible]
Old Colfeians	22	10	2	10	42	46	[illegible]
Long Lane Res.	22	9	4	9	50	44	[illegible]
Longlands Athletic	22	9	4	9	52	52	[illegible]
Crockenhill Res.	22	7	2	13	41	63	[illegible]
Old Roan 'B'	22	5	1	16	41	58	[illegible]
Catford Exiles Res.	22	5	1	16	35	71	[illegible]
Crayford Arrows	22	1	1	20	20	81	[illegible]

Tudor Sports 'A' – record expunged

Division Four	P	W	D	L	F	A	P
Crofton Alb. Res. *+3*	24	18	1	5	71	42	[illegible]
Eltham Palace Res.	24	18	2	4	81	33	[illegible]
Charterh'se-S'wk *-3*	24	16	5	3	78	32	[illegible]
Bridon Ropes 'A'	24	14	4	6	55	41	[illegible]
Blackheath W. Res.	24	12	4	8	49	44	[illegible]
F'boro OBG 'A' *+3*	24	9	4	11	49	56	[illegible]
Elite Res. *-3*	24	10	3	11	44	71	[illegible]
Old Colfeians 'A' *-3*	24	9	3	12	48	49	[illegible]
Wickham Park 'A'	24	8	2	14	58	75	[illegible]
Beaverwood Res. *+3*	24	6	2	16	51	80	[illegible]
Salmon	24	6	3	15	55	72	[illegible]
Bexley Park	24	5	5	14	35	55	[illegible]
Heath	24	4	4	16	43	67	[illegible]

SOUTH YORKSHIRE AMATEUR LEAGUE

remier Division	P	W	D	L	F	A	Pts
rimethorpe Ath.	22	21	1	0	84	16	64
thersley Rec. Res.	22	18	2	2	103	25	56
ross Scythes	22	14	3	5	95	32	45
ıbilee Sports	22	13	3	6	74	41	42
ew Tree	22	13	2	7	79	48	41
hoenix	22	10	5	7	53	36	35
& Ts	22	11	2	9	57	57	35
xspring United	22	6	2	14	57	66	20
ivil Service -3	22	6	0	16	42	61	15
radway	22	4	3	15	22	93	15
e La Salle OB Res.	22	2	1	19	23	114	7
orwich Union	22	2	0	20	18	118	6

ivision One	P	W	D	L	F	A	Pts
iveton Pk Res. -3	24	20	3	1	94	21	60
ale Tavern	24	16	3	5	80	53	51
ston	24	15	3	6	88	44	48
ırm Road S & S.	24	13	6	5	64	42	45
leadless	24	13	3	8	77	40	42
ughtibridge Res.	24	12	5	7	75	42	41
odworth MW Res.	24	13	2	9	62	57	41
ıeffield West End	24	10	0	14	50	64	30
ew Bohemians	24	9	2	13	48	69	29
onnie Rovers	24	7	2	15	44	70	23
ıeff. Bankers Res.	24	6	2	16	31	67	20
hurgoland Welfare	24	4	1	19	35	84	13
astle	24	1	2	21	22	117	5

SOUTHEND BOROUGH COMBINATION

remier Division	P	W	D	L	F	A	Pts
xhibition United	22	18	2	2	86	20	38
orough Rovers	22	14	4	4	55	23	32
atholic United	22	15	1	6	58	32	31
eigh Town	22	14	3	5	63	47	31
ıoebury Town	22	13	4	5	43	30	30
ld Southendian	22	11	3	8	52	43	25
ssendon	22	5	7	10	33	47	17
rit Academicals	22	5	6	11	44	51	16
ıoebury Old Boys	22	5	2	15	35	66	12
ebra Sports	22	4	3	15	39	65	11
xco/Thames Park	22	4	3	15	40	93	11
ısign	22	4	2	16	43	74	10

ivision One	P	W	D	L	F	A	Pts
ochford Town	20	18	0	2	89	24	36
xco/Thames Res.	20	13	5	2	61	32	31
lackgate Gunners	20	12	2	6	47	27	26
'estcliff Amateur	20	10	3	7	48	52	23
'eir Sports	20	8	5	7	47	35	21
thend Collegians	20	10	0	10	45	51	20
ırborne United	20	8	0	12	47	73	16
ourne Athletic	20	6	3	11	43	52	15
ıorpe Athletic	20	6	3	11	49	71	15
ternational PMS	20	3	4	13	34	58	10
ıttlesbridge	20	3	1	16	25	60	7

ivision Two	P	W	D	L	F	A	Pts
outhchurch HOS	20	18	0	2	77	15	36
KS Sports	20	15	0	5	55	31	30
orough Rov. Res.	20	14	1	5	74	36	29
outhbury	20	9	4	7	48	29	22
iddleway	20	11	0	9	55	46	22
ısign Res.	20	8	3	9	37	49	19
ıstoms & Excise	20	7	4	9	45	48	18
ld S'thendian Res.	20	6	5	9	38	45	17
ttle Theatre Club	20	5	4	11	34	47	14
ıpids Country C.	20	4	2	14	35	75	10
thend Colls Res.	20	1	1	18	22	99	3

ivision Three	P	W	D	L	F	A	Pts
nstar United	22	19	2	1	71	24	40
orinthians	22	15	3	4	58	30	33
shingdon Boys	22	13	5	4	71	28	31
xco/Thames P. 'A'	22	13	1	8	84	42	27
eigh Town Res.	22	12	2	8	51	42	26
it Acad. Res.	21	12	1	8	64	49	25
ıttlesbridge Res.	22	9	3	10	43	33	21
ırls Hall United	22	9	1	12	54	58	19
ıllbridge Spts 'A'	22	6	3	13	36	48	15
atholic Utd Res.	21	6	1	14	28	58	13
ackback	22	3	1	18	25	90	7
igh Ramblers 'A'	22	2	1	19	21	104	5

Division Four	P	W	D	L	F	A	Pts
Shoebury T. Res.	20	18	1	1	83	29	37
Thundersley United	20	15	2	3	92	31	32
Cupids Co. C. Res.	20	13	2	5	66	41	28
Smith's Sports	20	12	2	6	84	53	26
Rayford Athletic	20	12	2	6	57	39	26
S'church HOS Res.	20	8	1	11	52	50	17
O. Southendian 'A'	20	7	3	10	50	50	17
Earls Hall Utd Res.	20	6	1	13	28	66	13
Highbank	20	4	4	12	37	44	12
Southend Rangers	20	3	2	15	29	88	8
Southend Colls 'A'	20	1	2	17	24	111	4

Division Five	P	W	D	L	F	A	Pts
Parkway Sports	22	19	0	3	82	27	38
Ashingdon B. Res.	22	16	3	3	75	33	35
Trinity (S)	22	14	3	5	70	37	31
White Horse Rgrs	22	11	3	8	62	36	25
Heathfield	22	11	1	10	48	48	23
Battlesbridge 'A'	22	11	0	11	48	48	22
S'church HOS 'A'	22	7	5	10	60	64	19
Elmwood Old Boys	22	7	3	12	63	82	17
Barnsf'd Hurricanes	22	8	1	13	50	78	17
Hullbridge Athletic	22	7	2	13	47	83	16
Landwick	22	6	3	13	39	55	15
O. Southendian 'B'	22	2	2	18	44	97	6

Division Six	P	W	D	L	F	A	Pts
Weir Sports Res.	15	12	2	1	78	20	26
S'thend Police SU	15	8	5	2	52	31	21
Leigh Ramblers 'B'	15	8	2	5	39	37	18
Rayford Ath. Res.	15	6	3	6	40	40	15
Catholic United 'A'	15	3	0	12	30	64	6
Trinity (S) Res.	15	2	0	13	26	73	4

Division Seven	P	W	D	L	F	A	Pts
Weir Sports 'A'	18	17	1	0	89	28	35
Leigh Town 'A'	18	7	5	6	56	46	19
Castle Point Gas	18	8	2	8	45	38	18
Southend Colls 'B'	18	7	3	8	52	55	17
Elmwood OB Res.	18	7	1	10	50	56	15
Rayford Ath. 'A'	18	4	4	10	28	58	12
Thundersley Res.	18	4	2	12	34	73	10

SOUTHEND & DISTRICT LEAGUE

Premier Division	P	W	D	L	F	A	Pts
Forest Rangers	16	11	4	1	50	18	37
Runnymede	16	10	3	3	41	24	33
Rochford T. Res.	16	9	1	6	37	37	28
Chase	16	7	6	3	50	35	27
Stambridge	16	7	2	7	30	27	23
Rhodesia United	16	6	3	7	34	28	21
Signet United	16	6	1	9	40	49	19
Sparco	16	3	2	11	20	43	11
Hockley/Hawkwell	16	2	0	14	15	56	6

Division One	P	W	D	L	F	A	Pts
AFC Horndon	18	14	2	2	85	26	44
Club Sirrus	18	11	3	4	63	39	36
Wickford Rangers	18	11	3	4	43	30	36
Sparkbridge	18	8	3	7	54	35	27
Rochford Town 'A'	18	8	3	7	48	46	27
Eversley	18	8	2	8	52	35	26
Hockley & H. Res.	18	7	5	6	43	34	26
Thundersley Rovers	18	6	5	7	24	49	23
Chalkwell Park	18	2	2	14	17	62	8
Weir	18	0	2	16	14	87	2

SOUTHERN AMATEUR LEAGUE

Higher divisions on page 14

Junior Division One	P	W	D	L	F	A	Pts
Nottsborough 'A'	20	11	5	4	54	27	38
Winchmore Hill 'A'	20	10	5	5	58	42	35
Old Owens 'A'	20	10	4	6	56	35	34
Civil Service 'A'	20	8	7	5	32	24	31
O. Esthameians 'A'	20	9	3	8	33	35	30
Norsemen 'A'	20	8	3	9	49	51	27
O. Actonians A. 'A'	20	7	3	10	45	47	24
Old Stationers 'A'	20	7	3	10	50	54	24
Weirside Rgrs 'A'	20	6	5	9	30	49	23
Polytechnic 'A'	20	7	2	11	43	68	23
Old Finchleians 'A'	20	6	2	12	38	56	20

Junior Division Two	P	W	D	L	F	A	Pts
Alleyn OB 'A'	20	13	2	5	62	27	41
East Barnet OG 'A'	20	11	3	6	64	37	36
Carshalton 'A'	20	11	3	6	70	45	36
West Wickham 'A'	20	10	5	5	49	32	35
HSBC 'A'	20	9	5	6	41	39	32
Old Salesians 'A'	20	7	9	4	67	48	30
O. Westminster 'A'	20	7	2	11	41	60	23
Crouch End V. 'A'	20	6	4	10	39	59	22
Bank of Eng. 'A'	20	5	4	11	46	65	19
Ibis 'A'	20	5	2	13	43	68	17
Southgate O. 'A' -3	20	4	5	11	34	76	14

Junior Division Three	P	W	D	L	F	A	Pts
Kew Assoc. 'A'	20	14	6	0	68	29	48
Broomfield 'A'	20	13	2	5	60	46	41
Old Wilsonians 'A'	20	11	6	3	53	25	39
Merton 'A'	20	11	4	5	60	32	37
Sth Bank Cuaco 'A'	20	9	5	6	41	32	32
Old Parkonians 'A'	20	8	2	10	34	46	26
Alexandra Park 'A'	20	5	9	6	45	52	24
BB Eagles 'A'	20	5	3	12	35	57	18
O. Latymerians 'A'	20	5	2	13	30	50	17
Old Lyonians 'A'	20	2	7	11	27	47	13
Lloyds TSB Bk 'A'	20	3	2	15	21	58	11

Minor Division One	P	W	D	L	F	A	Pts
Civil Service 'C'	20	14	3	3	55	18	45
Old Owens 'B'	20	12	4	4	51	29	40
O. Actonians A. 'B'	20	12	1	7	48	27	37
Winchmore Hill 'B'	20	11	4	5	55	44	37
Nottsborough 'B'	20	10	3	7	57	36	33
Alexandra Park 'B'	20	8	5	7	42	37	29
West Wickham 'B'	20	8	4	8	35	53	28
Winchmore Hill 'C'	20	7	4	9	43	51	25
Civil Service 'B'	20	6	4	10	40	38	22
Old Finchleians 'B'	20	3	2	15	32	55	11
Old Stationers 'B'	20	1	2	17	16	86	5

Minor Div Two North	P	W	D	L	F	A	Pts
Crouch End V. 'B'	18	13	2	3	62	36	41
Old Owens 'C'	18	9	2	7	45	43	29
Old Owens 'D'	18	8	2	8	43	33	26
Crouch End V. 'C'	18	8	1	9	45	44	25
Winchmore Hill 'D'	18	7	4	7	54	54	25
East Barnet OG 'B'	18	7	4	7	38	38	25
East Barnet OG 'C'	18	6	7	5	39	45	25
Norsemen 'B'	18	5	8	5	42	40	23
Norsemen 'C'	18	6	5	7	45	47	23
Polytechnic 'C'	18	2	3	13	31	64	9

Minor Div Two South	P	W	D	L	F	A	Pts
O. Actonians A. 'C'	20	14	6	0	59	27	48
Civil Service 'D'	20	9	4	7	50	45	31
West Wickham 'C'	20	8	6	6	48	38	30
Carshalton 'B'	20	8	6	6	56	47	30
Kew Assoc. 'B'	20	8	5	7	35	43	29
O. Westminster 'B'	20	7	6	7	36	39	27
Old Wilsonians 'B'	20	6	6	8	46	37	24
HSBC 'B'	20	6	5	9	47	46	23
BB Eagles 'B'	20	6	5	9	45	48	23
Polytechnic 'B'	20	6	4	10	29	48	22
Ibis 'B'	20	3	5	12	24	57	14

Minor Div Three Nth	P	W	D	L	F	A	Pts
Old Parkonians 'B'	18	12	0	6	56	36	36
Southgate O. 'B'	18	10	6	2	46	34	36
Norsemen 'D'	18	10	3	5	70	33	33
Old Finchleians 'C'	18	8	4	6	50	52	28
Crouch End V. 'D'	18	8	3	7	50	38	27
Broomfield 'B'	18	8	3	7	30	31	27
O. Esthameians 'B'	18	6	5	7	36	58	23
Norsemen 'E'	18	6	4	8	41	44	22
Winchmore Hill 'E'	18	4	1	13	33	52	13
Alexandra Park 'C'	18	3	1	14	24	58	10

Minor Div Three Sth	P	W	D	L	F	A	Pts
HSBC 'C'	18	13	2	3	56	27	41
Merton 'B'	18	12	4	2	48	14	40
Polytechnic 'D'	18	9	3	6	42	30	30
Sth Bank Cuaco 'B'	18	9	2	7	48	32	29
Old Actonians 'D'	18	8	4	6	35	29	28
Old Actonians 'E'	18	6	5	7	43	62	23
Old Wilsonians 'C'	18	6	4	8	37	42	22
Carshalton 'C'	18	7	1	10	26	36	22
Kew Assoc. 'C'	18	5	3	10	47	41	18
S. Bank Cuaco 'C'	18	0	2	16	19	88	2

Minor Div Four Nth	P	W	D	L	F	A	Pts
Old Stationers 'C'	20	15	2	3	64	37	47
Southgate O. 'C'	20	13	6	1	69	27	45
Old Parkonians 'C'	20	12	3	5	55	29	39
Alexandra Park 'D'	20	10	6	4	63	31	36
Winchmore Hill 'F'	20	10	4	6	61	41	34
Broomfield 'C'	20	9	4	7	41	49	31
Crouch End V. 'E'	20	7	6	7	54	47	27
Norsemen 'F'	20	5	3	12	37	60	18
Old Finchleians 'D'	20	4	3	13	36	64	15
Winchmore Hill 'G'	20	3	4	13	30	60	13
East Barnet OG 'D'	20	0	3	17	30	95	3

Minor Div Four Sth	P	W	D	L	F	A	Pts
Weirside Rgrs 'B'	20	13	5	2	59	33	44
BB Eagles 'C'	20	11	3	6	50	36	36
Alleyn OB 'B'	20	10	4	6	50	39	34
Lloyds TSB Bk 'B'	20	10	3	7	57	50	33
Weirside Rgrs 'C'	20	9	5	6	54	37	32
Old Salesians 'B'	20	9	4	7	54	35	31
Alleyn OB 'C'	20	8	5	7	55	41	29
Bank of England 'B'	20	7	5	8	32	48	26
HSBC 'D'	20	4	4	12	27	45	16
Carshalton 'D' *-2*	20	5	1	14	49	74	14
Old Wilsonians 'D'	20	4	1	15	27	76	13

Minor Div Five Nth	P	W	D	L	F	A	Pts
Winchmore Hill 'H'	20	18	2	0	118	23	56
Old Finchleians 'E'	20	15	4	1	92	41	49
Broomfield 'D'	20	12	2	6	64	48	38
Norsemen 'G'	20	10	2	8	50	55	32
East Barnet OG 'E'	20	9	2	9	70	60	29
Old Stationers 'D'	20	8	2	10	65	55	26
Alexandra Park 'E'	20	8	2	10	45	59	26
Old Parkonians 'D'	20	6	4	10	48	63	22
Southgate O. 'D'	20	7	0	13	45	82	21
Alexandra Park 'F'	20	6	2	12	51	70	20
East Barnet OG 'F'	20	0	0	20	26	118	0

Minor Div Five Sth	P	W	D	L	F	A	Pts
Old Lyonians 'B'	20	11	6	3	67	42	39
Carshalton 'E'	20	12	3	5	56	36	39
HSBC 'E'	20	11	5	4	57	34	38
Merton 'C'	20	9	6	5	51	33	33
Lloyds TSB Bk 'C'	20	10	1	9	28	46	31
Kew Assoc. 'D'	20	9	3	8	50	43	30
Old Actonians 'F'	20	8	3	9	41	49	27
O. Westminster 'C'	20	8	2	10	46	42	26
Polytechnic 'F'	20	7	5	8	31	35	26
Polytechnic 'E'	20	5	2	13	28	49	17
Old Wilsonians 'E'	20	1	2	17	19	65	5

Minor Div Six South	P	W	D	L	F	A	Pts
Old Westminster 'D'	20	16	3	1	81	25	51
Kew Assoc. 'E'	20	15	4	1	78	31	49
Civil Service 'E'	20	14	1	5	67	35	43
West Wickham 'D'	20	11	2	7	50	48	35
Merton 'D'	20	10	3	7	69	44	33
Sth Bank Cuaco 'D'	20	8	4	8	52	55	28
O. Latymerians 'B'	20	6	1	13	50	61	19
BB Eagles 'D'	20	4	7	9	45	58	19
HSBC 'F'	20	5	3	12	31	64	18
Lloyds TSB Bk 'E'	20	5	2	13	34	56	17
Lloyds TSB Bk 'D'	20	1	0	19	21	101	3

Minor Div Six Seven	P	W	D	L	F	A	Pts
Civil Service 'F'	22	19	1	2	117	42	58
Old Actonians 'G'	22	18	1	3	86	33	55
Old Actonians 'H'	22	17	1	4	98	39	52
Kew Assoc. 'F'	22	13	2	7	72	55	41
Old Wilsonians 'F'	22	11	1	10	52	65	34
Polytechnic 'G'	22	9	0	13	57	66	27
Sth Bank Cuaco 'E'	22	8	2	12	58	73	26
Kew Assoc. 'G'	22	8	1	13	54	73	25
Bank of England 'C'	22	6	5	11	32	55	23
Carshalton 'F'	22	5	3	14	58	82	18
Lloyds TSB Bk 'F'	22	4	2	16	32	81	14
Merton 'E'	22	3	3	16	45	97	12

SOUTHPORT & DISTRICT LEAGUE

	P	W	D	L	F	A	Pts
Formby Dons	24	19	1	4	87	39	58
The Dales	24	14	4	6	83	58	46
Poulton Wanderers	24	14	3	7	84	54	45
Blundell Arms *-3*	24	13	2	9	78	60	38
St Pauls	24	11	3	10	62	60	36
Christ The King OB	24	10	4	10	60	60	34
Massams	24	5	5	14	49	68	20
Banks	24	5	2	17	39	76	17
Sporting Dynamo	24	4	2	18	21	88	14

SPEN VALLEY LEAGUE

Premier Division	P	W	D	L	F	A	Pts
Soothill	16	11	1	4	59	37	34
Old Bank WMC	16	9	4	3	52	30	31
Hare & Hounds	16	10	1	5	54	40	31
Bosnia	16	9	2	5	57	37	29
Wellington Wdrs	16	7	3	6	32	34	24
Dewsbury W. Side	16	6	3	7	48	39	21
Howden Clough Res.	16	4	3	9	28	63	15
Bank Top	15	3	1	11	29	48	10
Old Magnet	15	0	6	9	24	55	6

Division One	P	W	D	L	F	A	Pts
Shooters	18	13	2	3	59	35	41
Youth 2000	18	12	3	3	65	32	39
Barfield	18	11	3	4	75	33	36
Savile Youth	18	9	6	3	48	34	33
Marsh	18	8	3	7	55	47	27
Wellington W. Res.	18	6	4	8	55	46	22
Queensbury	18	5	3	10	66	59	18
Norfolk	18	5	3	10	39	57	18
Inter Batley	18	4	3	11	24	73	15
Cleckheaton OB	18	1	2	15	25	95	5

ST HELENS COMBINATION

Premier Division	P	W	D	L	F	A	Pts
Knowsley South	22	15	3	4	55	27	48
Dentons Green	22	14	4	4	54	29	46
East Villa Res.	22	11	7	4	56	38	40
Clock Face Miners	22	12	3	7	47	34	39
Top Nogs	22	11	4	7	42	29	37
Old Congs	22	10	3	9	40	47	33
Rainford North End	22	8	3	11	33	38	27
Stars	22	8	3	11	40	53	27
York	22	6	8	8	34	33	26
Prescot Leisure	22	4	6	12	35	54	18
Shoe	22	3	8	11	24	47	17
The Flagship	22	2	4	16	27	58	10

Division One	P	W	D	L	F	A	Pts
Old Xaverians 'E'	20	14	4	2	63	24	46
Pilkington 'A'	20	14	1	5	51	31	43
Boilermakers	20	12	3	5	48	37	39
Gerard Arms	20	8	7	5	36	33	31
Rainford NE Res.	20	9	3	8	42	47	30
Farnworth	20	8	3	9	28	33	27
Greenfields	20	7	3	10	48	38	24
Knowsley Sth Res.	20	7	1	12	29	36	22
Eccleston United	20	6	2	12	41	56	20
Sidac Social Res.	20	5	5	10	39	57	20
Junction	20	3	2	15	29	62	11

Wastelbridge Park – record expunged

Division Two	P	W	D	L	F	A	Pts
Fleetcar	16	14	2	0	72	16	44
Top Nogs Res.	16	10	2	4	55	31	32
New Street	16	8	5	3	62	23	29
Care Trust	16	7	3	6	42	36	24
Sony	16	7	3	6	38	35	24
Sidac Social 'A'	16	7	3	6	29	29	24
Oddfellows	16	2	4	10	33	64	10
Carborundum Eagles	16	1	4	11	23	70	7
Official Club Speed	16	1	4	11	18	68	7

The Glassblower – record expunged

Division Three	P	W	D	L	F	A	Pts
Bold Rangers	16	14	0	2	63	25	42
Thatto Heath	16	12	2	2	64	25	38
Prescot Leisure Res.	16	11	2	3	72	27	35
Penlake Sen Res.	16	8	1	7	41	39	25
Clock Face M. Res.	16	8	1	7	36	47	25
Lingholme	16	4	3	9	31	54	15
The Griffin Inn	16	4	2	10	26	50	14
Globe	16	2	5	9	27	46	11
Assembly	16	1	0	15	18	65	3

STOKESLEY LEAGUE

Premier Division	P	W	D	L	F	A	Pts
S. Bank St Peters *-6*	22	21	1	0	109	20	58
Rudds Arms	22	19	0	3	128	19	57
Grangetown YCC	22	14	1	7	80	56	43
The Smithy	22	12	5	5	68	55	41
Ennis Square	22	12	3	7	118	65	39
St Marys Coll.OB	22	12	2	8	76	47	38
Coulby Newham	22	11	1	10	76	50	34
Acklam Steelworks	22	7	2	13	40	68	23
Stokesley SC 'A'	22	5	2	15	39	78	17
Great Ayton United	22	4	1	17	45	81	13
NS Bulls Head	22	3	0	19	30	118	9
Asda Teesport	22	3	0	19	31	183	9

STRATFORD-ON-AVON ALLIANCE

Acquaid Division	P	W	D	L	F	A
Earlswood T. Res.	16	12	0	4	34	21
Henley Forest	16	11	2	3	39	22
Austin Social Select	16	9	3	4	35	17
Ilm'gton Revolution	16	9	1	6	42	19
Halfords Athletic	16	8	4	4	43	21
Quinton	16	6	1	9	25	35
Inkberrow	16	4	4	8	24	26
FISSC	16	5	0	11	27	46
Badsey United	16	0	1	15	12	74

Division One	P	W	D	L	F	A
Henley Forest Res.	20	14	2	4	58	27
Welford	20	12	4	4	64	40
Littleton Res.	20	12	0	8	56	35
Badsey Rangers	20	11	3	6	50	47
S. Redditch Sp. *-12*	20	15	1	4	69	31
Bidford Boys Club	20	10	2	8	40	35
Seven Stars	20	10	1	9	38	39
Cubbington Albion	20	6	5	9	47	47
Studley Nags Head	20	7	2	11	33	44
Ilmington Rev. Res.	20	2	0	18	27	73
FISSC Res.	20	0	2	18	16	80

Division Two	P	W	D	L	F	A
Henley Forest 'A'	20	16	2	2	73	26
Welford Res.	20	12	2	6	47	48
Ship. Excelsior Res.	20	11	4	5	62	37
Wellesbourne Utd	20	11	2	7	60	46
Quinton Res.	20	9	4	7	57	48
Blockley Sports	20	9	3	8	68	40
Tysoe United	20	7	2	11	39	65
Snitterfield Snipers	20	6	3	11	29	43
Inkberrow Res.	20	5	3	12	38	56
Red Alert! Stratford	20	5	3	12	35	63
Badsey United Res.	20	3	4	13	41	77

STROUD & DISTRICT LEAGUE

Division One	P	W	D	L	F	A
Ramblers	26	24	0	2	74	24
Whitminster	26	18	2	6	66	31
Frampton United	26	18	2	6	61	30
Barnwood United	26	15	6	5	78	29
M'chinhampton RDS	26	14	3	9	46	41
Leonard Stanley	26	13	5	8	47	34
Kings Stanley Res.	26	11	4	11	51	44
Longlevens Res.	26	9	7	10	47	52
Tuffley Rovers Res.	26	9	4	13	41	47
Gloucester Civil S.	26	6	7	13	35	47
Shurdington Rovers	26	6	3	17	31	71
Coaley Rovers	26	5	3	18	36	68
Horsley United	26	4	4	18	25	72
Thornbury T. Res.	26	3	4	19	26	74

Division Two	P	W	D	L	F	A
Matson	22	17	2	3	89	27
Marshall Langston	22	17	2	3	74	21
Abbeymead Rovers	22	15	3	4	65	32
Hardwicke Res.	22	13	2	7	42	33
Randwick	22	10	4	8	55	56
Cashes Green	22	8	6	8	47	37
Whiteshill United	22	7	6	9	34	35
Wotton Rovers Res.	22	7	6	9	37	43
Brimscombe/T. Res.	22	6	6	10	38	45
Stonehouse F. Res.	22	4	5	13	34	75
Longford Res.	22	2	4	16	29	76
Shipton Moyne	22	2	2	18	20	84

Division Three	P	W	D	L	F	A
Ebley Omega	24	19	0	5	83	26
Tibberton United	24	15	4	5	61	33
Uley	24	13	7	4	76	48
Wickwar Wdrs	24	12	4	8	55	54
Cam Bulldogs Res.	24	11	4	9	63	47
Hawkesbury Upton	24	11	4	9	59	47
Quedgeley Wdrs	24	11	4	9	51	39
Trident	24	11	2	11	65	56
Dursley Town Res.	24	10	3	11	44	48
Tetbury Town Res.	24	9	5	10	50	47
Sharpness Res.	24	5	5	14	59	91
M'pton RDS Res.	24	3	2	19	28	85
Chalford Res.	24	2	3	19	28	101

Division Four	P	W	D	L	F	A
Kingswood Res.	24	20	1	3	100	24
Berkeley Town Res.	24	16	4	4	52	21
Eastcombe	24	15	2	7	47	31
Alkerton Rangers	24	13	3	8	57	44
Charfield Res.	24	12	3	9	52	48
Frampton Utd Res.	24	9	5	10	48	46
Stonehouse F. 'A'	24	9	4	11	38	42
Longlevens 'A'	24	8	3	13	42	57
Thornbury T. 'A'	24	8	3	13	47	63
Uley Res.	24	6	6	12	38	58
Nympsfield	24	6	6	12	32	59
North Nibley	24	5	4	15	43	68
Glevum United	24	4	6	14	26	61

Division Five	P	W	D	L	F	A	Pts
Barnwood Utd Res.	20	15	2	3	67	26	47
Ramblers Res.	20	13	3	4	46	19	42
Upton St Leonards.	20	11	3	6	61	37	36
Gloucester CS Res.	20	11	3	6	48	35	36
Randwick Res.	20	10	3	7	42	29	33
Quedgeley W. Res.	20	9	1	10	41	36	28
Dursley Town 'A'	20	7	5	8	35	45	26
Leonard Stan. Res.	20	7	3	10	37	54	24
Arlingham	20	6	3	11	49	63	21
M'chinhampton 'A'	20	2	6	12	25	71	12
Longlevens 'B'	20	3	0	17	22	58	9

Division Six	P	W	D	L	F	A	Pts
AFC Phoenix	22	19	1	2	89	27	58
BA Rangers	22	19	0	3	83	27	57
AC Royals	22	15	2	5	72	39	47
Matchplay Reeves	22	13	3	6	68	37	42
Victoria Celtic *+2*	22	10	3	9	66	49	35
Stroud Harriers	22	9	2	11	46	69	29
Ebley Omega Res.	22	8	4	10	52	53	28
Wotton Rovers 'A'	22	5	6	11	42	58	21
Eastcombe Res.	22	6	1	15	31	82	19
Coaley Rovers Res.	22	5	3	14	43	82	18
Brockw'th Alb. 'B'	22	4	2	16	32	61	14
Charfield 'A'	22	3	5	14	37	77	14

Division Seven	P	W	D	L	F	A	Pts
Whitminster Res.	24	19	4	1	95	24	61
Didmarton	24	15	5	4	71	37	50
Abbeymead R. Res.	24	14	6	4	83	45	48
Cam Bulldogs 'A'	24	14	5	5	67	31	47
Cashes Green Res.	24	14	4	6	87	42	46
NSSC	24	13	2	9	65	55	41
Trident Res.	24	10	3	11	42	62	33
Shurdington R. Res.	24	7	5	12	37	52	26
Wickwar Wdrs Res.	24	8	2	14	51	67	26
BA Rangers Res.	24	8	2	14	56	73	26
Uley 'A'	24	6	1	17	39	89	19
Whiteshill Utd Res.	24	4	2	18	34	87	14
Stonehouse F. 'B'	24	2	3	19	28	91	9

Division Eight	P	W	D	L	F	A	Pts
Ramblers 'A'	22	21	0	1	88	18	63
Alkerton Rgrs Res.	22	15	2	5	64	41	47
NSSC Res.	22	14	2	6	81	42	44
Randwick 'A'	22	13	3	6	62	47	42
Upton St Leo. Res.	22	11	3	8	57	50	36
Quedgeley W. 'A'	22	10	4	8	75	57	34
Essilor	22	9	4	9	62	43	31
Woodchester	22	6	2	14	62	85	20
North Nibley Res.	22	6	2	14	48	71	20
M'play Reeves Res.	22	6	2	14	61	98	20
Stroud Imperial	22	5	2	15	37	77	17
Avondale 'A'	22	2	2	18	38	106	8

SUBURBAN LEAGUE

Premier Division	P	W	D	L	F	A	Pts
Basingstoke T. Res.	34	22	7	5	67	30	73
Hayes Res.	34	21	7	6	81	33	70
Sutton United Res.	34	20	9	5	75	33	69
Carshalton A. Res.	34	17	12	5	67	37	63
Eastleigh Res.	34	17	5	12	60	44	56
Met Police Res.	34	15	7	12	60	71	52
Harefield Utd Res.	34	13	11	10	57	45	50
Ashford (Mx) Res.	34	15	5	14	72	64	50
Whyteleafe Res.	34	14	7	13	65	53	49
Uxbridge Res.	34	13	9	12	59	58	48
Beaconsfield Res.	34	12	7	15	54	59	43
Burnham Res.	34	12	6	16	55	62	42
Wealdstone Res.	34	13	3	18	50	63	42
Corinthian C. Res.	34	11	8	15	59	70	41
Three Bridges Res.	34	10	6	18	47	68	36
Waltham F. Res.	34	10	0	24	54	104	30
Hemel Town Res. *-1*	34	8	6	20	41	75	29
Walton & Her. Res.	34	4	3	27	46	100	15

Northern Division	P	W	D	L	F	A	Pts
Hillingdon B. Res.	26	19	3	4	59	25	60
Fleet Town Res.	26	17	4	5	68	24	55
Potters Bar T. Res.	26	16	5	5	65	34	53
Edgware Town Res.	26	15	4	7	55	37	49
N'port Pagnell Res.	26	12	4	10	45	43	40
Nth Greenford Res.	26	11	5	10	42	34	38
Leighton Town Res.	26	10	6	10	47	52	36
Chalfont St P. Res.	26	10	5	11	55	51	35
Dunstable T. Res.	26	10	4	12	50	50	34
Brook House Res.	26	6	11	9	31	46	29
Ruislip Manor Res.	26	8	3	15	45	71	27
Sandhurst T. Res.	26	7	4	15	26	60	25
Boreham W. Res.	26	5	6	15	49	65	21
Bedfont Res.	26	2	4	20	24	69	10

Southern Division	P	W	D	L	F	A	Pts
Burgess Hill T. Res.	30	23	2	5	66	31	71
AFC Wimb'don Res.	30	22	3	5	103	19	69
Tooting & MU Res.	30	22	3	5	86	26	69
Tonbridge A. Res.	30	17	7	6	73	29	58
Merstham Res.	30	14	4	12	55	53	46
Lewes Res.	30	12	8	10	51	30	44
Walton Cas. Res.	30	11	10	9	54	52	43
Raynes PV Res.	30	12	6	12	43	42	42
Chipstead Res.	30	12	4	14	35	48	40
Molesey Res.	30	9	9	12	45	49	36
Camberley T. Res.	30	10	6	14	39	49	36
Haywards Hth Res.	30	9	6	15	44	84	33
Horley Town Res.	30	8	5	17	34	70	29
Godalming T. Res.	30	5	8	17	36	60	23
Epsom/Ewell Res.	30	4	10	16	37	85	22
East Grinstead Res.	30	3	3	24	24	98	12

SURREY INT. LEAGUE (WEST)

Premier Division	P	W	D	L	F	A	Pts
Knaphill	26	15	6	5	61	38	51
Woking & Horsell	26	13	8	5	56	22	47
Shalford	26	14	5	7	50	32	47
Old Rutlishians	26	12	8	6	50	35	44
Milford & Witley	26	13	5	8	41	29	44
Ripley Village	26	11	8	7	52	51	41
Eversley Social	26	10	10	6	52	34	40
Virginia Water	26	11	2	13	43	50	35
Yateley	26	9	7	10	60	49	34
Shottermill/H. Res.	26	9	7	10	41	47	34
Horsley	26	9	6	11	51	55	33
Chiddingfold	26	6	5	15	39	66	23
Pyrford	26	4	5	17	33	69	17
Ockham	26	2	6	18	31	83	12

Division One	P	W	D	L	F	A	Pts
Liphook	26	19	5	2	80	27	62
Elm Grove	26	19	2	5	81	24	59
Worplesdon	26	17	5	4	83	34	56
Old Salesians	26	17	3	6	69	26	54
Godalming/F'combe	26	14	2	10	57	48	44
Windlesham United	26	11	5	10	43	52	38
Hammer United	26	10	6	10	45	42	36
Royal Holloway OB	26	10	6	10	61	68	36
Ewhurst	26	10	4	12	50	48	34
Fairlands Wdrs	26	9	5	12	57	68	32
Gfd City Weysiders	26	7	4	15	35	63	25
Unis Old Boys	26	6	3	17	34	60	21
Burymead	26	5	2	19	32	74	17
Dunsfold	26	1	2	23	27	120	5

Reserve Prem Div	P	W	D	L	F	A	Pts
Yateley Res.	26	22	2	2	81	13	68
Shalford Res.	26	19	4	3	63	24	61
Woking & H. Res.	26	18	3	5	68	29	57
Old Rutlish. Res. *-3*	26	16	2	8	70	39	47
Milford & W. Res.	26	14	4	8	57	41	46
Ripley Village Res.	26	12	7	7	40	29	43
Eversley S. Res. *-3*	26	10	7	9	50	49	34
Pyrford Res.	26	8	4	14	30	42	28
Shottermill/H. 'A'	26	7	7	12	28	51	28
Horsley Res.	26	6	8	12	33	61	26
Virginia Water Res.	26	7	4	15	42	50	25
Knaphill Res.	26	5	7	14	29	61	22
Ockham Res.	26	3	3	20	22	85	12
Chiddingfold Res.	26	3	2	21	28	67	11

Reserve Div One	P	W	D	L	F	A	Pts
Worplesdon Res.	26	22	2	2	143	34	68
Elm Grove Res.	26	19	1	6	98	39	58
Liphook Res. *-3*	26	17	4	5	73	34	52
Ryl Holloway Res.	26	14	4	8	60	55	46
Windlesham Res.	26	14	3	9	74	63	45
Unis Old Boys Res.	26	13	4	9	53	51	43
God. & Farn.c Res.	26	13	2	11	75	54	41
Old Salesians Res.	26	12	3	11	48	61	39
Burymead Res.	26	9	3	14	54	65	30
GC Weysiders Res.	26	7	5	14	68	76	26
Fairlands Wdrs Res.	26	7	5	14	51	73	26
Hammer Utd Res.	26	6	3	17	53	80	21
Ewhurst Res.	26	6	3	17	34	74	21
Dunsfold Res.	26	1	2	23	16	141	5

SURREY SOUTH EASTERN COMB.

Intermediate Div One	P	W	D	L	F	A	Pts
Battersea Ironsides	26	18	4	4	74	28	58
Epsom Athletic	26	19	1	6	75	40	58
Sutton Cmn Rovers	26	18	4	4	73	39	58
Greenside *+2*	26	14	5	7	61	38	49
Tadworth	26	14	3	9	57	39	45
Continental Stars	26	11	6	9	48	48	39
Old Bristolians *+3*	26	9	5	12	50	60	35
St Andrews	26	10	4	12	45	46	34
Battersea *-5*	26	12	2	12	62	53	33
NPL *-3*	26	8	6	12	57	69	27
Old Plym'thians *+3*	26	6	3	17	45	72	24
Esher Athletic *-3*	26	7	4	15	42	63	22
Nutfield	26	6	3	17	36	94	21
Hersham RBL *-1*	26	3	4	19	31	67	12

Intermediate Div Two	P	W	D	L	F	A	Pts
Epsom Eagles	26	20	3	3	78	26	63
Sporting Bahia	26	15	4	7	62	48	49
W'mansterne Hyde	26	15	2	9	71	51	47
Cranleigh	26	14	2	10	66	62	44
Westside	26	13	2	11	48	38	41
Tooting Bec	26	12	4	10	63	54	40
Merton NDTC	26	10	4	12	47	60	34
Thornton Heath Rov.	26	10	4	12	48	72	34
Oxted & District	26	10	3	13	43	40	33
Alma Tavern *-1*	26	11	0	15	43	38	32
Ashtead	26	9	5	12	46	61	32
Croydon Postal *-3*	26	9	7	10	58	59	31
AFC Ewell	26	5	4	17	43	72	19
Wandgas Sports	26	5	4	17	35	70	19

Junior Division One	P	W	D	L	F	A	Pts
FC Triangle	20	14	3	3	55	29	45
Puretown	20	12	5	3	48	23	41
Athletico	20	12	4	4	49	25	40
Sutton High	20	9	5	6	37	23	32
Wandgas S. Res. *-3*	20	10	3	7	33	28	30
B'sea Iron. Res. *+3*	20	7	5	8	39	36	29
Trinity	20	9	1	10	38	40	28
New Life	20	6	2	12	27	36	20
Clapham Town	20	6	2	12	25	49	20
Your Story All Stars	20	3	5	12	35	60	14
Cheam Village W.	20	2	5	13	27	64	11

Junior Division Two	P	W	D	L	F	A	Pts
Inter Class	22	18	2	2	86	33	56
Lambeth Acad. *-1*	22	18	1	3	85	27	54
St Andrews Res.	22	14	3	5	69	33	45
Weston Green Spts	22	12	2	8	60	35	38
NPL Res.	22	11	3	8	59	57	36
Worcester Pk 'A' *-1*	22	10	2	10	47	59	31
Tadworth Res.	22	9	2	11	41	63	29
Cont. Stars Res. *+2*	22	6	6	10	39	43	26
Old P'mthians Res.	22	6	1	15	45	63	19
Battersea Res. *-5*	22	8	0	14	41	67	19
Wilf Kroucher	22	4	3	15	50	99	15
Crescent Rovers 'A'	22	3	1	18	35	78	10

Junior Division Three	P	W	D	L	F	A	Pts
Supercala	24	16	8	0	96	23	56
Fetcham	24	16	4	4	76	44	52
Epsom Athletic Res.	24	13	5	6	63	52	44
Norton	24	14	1	9	66	56	43
Oakhill United	24	11	5	8	54	48	38
Sutton Cmn R. Res.	24	10	7	7	48	34	37
Greenside Res.	24	8	7	9	50	50	31
Ashtead Res.	24	9	3	12	56	64	30
Battersea Iron. 'A'	24	8	2	14	44	74	26
Oxted & Dist. Res.	24	6	8	10	32	68	26
FC Maurice *-6*	24	8	5	11	52	54	23
Alexander Forbes *-1*	24	4	6	14	39	73	17
Sutton High Res. *+3*	24	2	1	21	18	54	10

Junior Division Four	P	W	D	L	F	A	Pts
Trinity Res.	24	19	1	4	102	39	58
Cheam VW 'A' *-1*	24	15	4	5	85	44	48
Crescent Rovers 'B'	24	15	2	7	88	56	47
Oakhill Utd Res. *+2*	24	13	4	7	55	65	45
O. Plym'thians 'A'	24	13	3	8	69	45	42
Tooting Bec Res.	24	10	3	11	58	51	33
Fetcham Res. *+3*	24	8	4	12	65	96	31
Old Bristolians Res	23	10	0	13	63	49	30
Croydon Ath. 'A'	23	9	2	12	68	60	29
Norton Res.	24	9	2	13	61	75	29
W'sterne Hyde 'A' *-3*	24	9	3	12	60	68	27
Ashtead 'A'	24	7	2	15	45	71	23
FC Maurice Res.	24	2	2	20	27	127	8

SWINDON & DISTRICT LEAGUE

Premier Division	P	W	D	L	F	A	Pts
Queensfield	18	14	2	2	61	20	44
Running Horse	18	11	5	2	66	24	38
Zurich	18	12	2	4	67	31	38
Jesters	18	12	2	4	48	35	38
Southbrook	18	8	3	7	41	31	27
Shield & Dagger	18	7	2	9	35	36	23
Iron Horse	18	6	4	8	37	38	22
Eastville	18	4	4	10	32	51	16
The Messenger	18	2	2	14	23	62	8
Lower Stratton Res.	18	0	2	16	11	93	2

Regent – record expunged

Division One	P	W	D	L	F	A	Pts
Fratellos	20	18	0	2	93	17	54
Rodbourne Arms	20	15	0	5	81	41	45
The Messenger Res.	20	12	1	7	69	57	37
Spectrum	20	12	0	8	64	40	36
Ramsbury	20	11	0	9	61	56	33
Trailers	20	9	1	10	60	52	28
PSS HiLo	20	8	1	11	63	54	25
Walcot	20	7	2	11	46	42	23
Wason & Webb	20	7	2	11	54	80	23
Pembroke	20	6	3	11	42	71	21
Goan Rodbourne	20	0	0	20	13	136	0

AFC Abbey – record expunged

TAUNTON & DISTRICT LEAGUE

(Silver Street Volkswagon)

Division One	P	W	D	L	F	A	Pts
Porlock	24	20	3	1	91	25	63
Bridgwater Sports	24	16	2	6	86	43	50
Wyvern	24	13	5	6	77	40	44
Staplegrove	24	14	2	8	73	44	44
Middlezoy Rovers	24	12	8	4	54	33	44
Taverners	24	13	0	11	75	67	39
Cossington	24	10	4	10	74	55	34
Highbridge Town	24	10	4	10	54	45	34
Locomotives	24	9	7	8	58	62	34
Norton Fitzwarren	24	6	2	16	65	120	20
Alcombe Rovers	24	6	1	17	45	83	19
B. Lydeard Res. *-6*	24	4	5	15	33	91	11
Sampford Blues	24	1	1	22	31	108	4

Division Two	P	W	D	L	F	A	Pts
Staplegrove Res.	24	16	5	3	71	31	53
Marketeers	24	16	4	4	77	36	52
Wellworthy Saints	24	14	3	7	78	50	45
Hulan	24	14	3	7	64	49	45
Dulverton Town	24	11	6	7	72	53	39
Spaxton	24	12	3	9	65	55	39
Wellington T. 'A'	24	12	2	10	69	43	38
Civil Service	24	9	6	9	49	42	33
Hamilton Hawks	24	9	1	14	54	59	28
Minehead T. Res. *-6*	24	9	3	12	49	60	24
Westonzoyland *-3*	24	7	3	14	51	64	21
Sydenham Rangers	24	4	0	20	39	84	12
Norton Fitz. Res.	24	3	1	20	32	144	10

Division Three	P	W	D	L	F	A	Pts
Wyvern Res.	22	14	3	5	72	40	45
Nether Stowey	22	13	2	7	46	32	41
B'water Spts Res.	22	11	4	7	56	52	37
Milverton Rangers	22	11	3	8	60	41	36
North Petherton	22	9	4	9	46	54	31
Predators	22	9	3	10	45	55	30
White Hart Rangers	22	8	5	9	49	46	29
Staplegrove Colts	22	8	4	10	62	60	28
Redgate	22	8	4	10	49	49	28
Alcombe Rov. Res.	22	8	3	11	68	64	27
Watchet Town Res.	22	8	3	11	44	48	27
Highbridge T. Res.	22	4	4	14	21	77	16

Division Four	P	W	D	L	F	A	Pts
Hemyock	24	19	4	1	94	21	61
Wembdon	24	18	1	5	94	30	55
Williton *-3*	24	17	0	7	77	50	48
Porlock Res.	24	13	4	7	82	47	43
Stogursey G'hounds	24	14	0	10	67	55	42
Exmoor Rangers	24	11	4	9	64	45	37
Hamilton H. Res.	24	9	5	10	49	53	32
Norton Dragons *-3*	24	11	2	11	57	66	32
W'zoyland Res. *-3*	24	8	2	14	47	79	23
Dulverton T. Res.	24	6	3	15	47	83	21
Wyvern Foxes	24	6	3	15	52	98	21
Old Inn All Stars	24	4	5	15	47	88	17
Swallowfields	24	3	1	20	22	84	10

TELFORD COMBINATION

	P	W	D	L	F	A	Pts
Bulls Head DB	20	17	1	2	101	36	35
Impact United	20	13	1	6	74	46	27
Pigeon Box	20	12	2	6	46	39	26
Red Lion Dawley	20	11	1	8	60	52	23
Much Wenlock	20	9	5	6	45	46	23
Shifnal United Res.	20	8	5	7	38	31	21
Norton	20	9	2	9	51	38	20
Play & Party	20	7	1	12	48	61	15
Claverley	20	5	1	14	45	76	11
Atlas	20	4	2	14	33	84	10
Royal Oak	20	3	3	14	35	67	9

THANET & DISTRICT LEAGUE

Division One	P	W	D	L	F	A	Pts
Flying Horse	14	13	1	0	55	19	40
Tara Plumbing	14	10	3	1	48	19	33
Feeneys	14	9	1	4	32	26	28
AFC Aussie	14	5	1	8	29	32	16
Minster	14	5	1	8	23	37	16
S. Eastern Tavern	14	4	3	7	22	34	15
AFC Margate	14	4	1	9	23	35	13
The Bedford Inn	14	0	1	13	15	45	1

Division Two	P	W	D	L	F	A	Pts
Westcliff United	12	9	3	0	37	15	30
Hugin Vikings Ath.	12	9	2	1	43	6	29
Ambrosetti UK	12	6	3	3	50	19	21
Barnaby Rudge	12	6	2	4	39	20	20
Milton Ashbury	12	3	2	7	24	39	11
Hugin Hammers	12	1	1	10	14	59	4
KTFC	12	1	1	10	9	58	4

TROWBRIDGE & DISTRICT LEAGUE

(Revolutions)

Division One	P	W	D	L	F	A	Pts
Nth Bradley Saints	18	15	0	3	52	28	45
Frome Town Sports	18	12	3	3	69	35	39
Seend United	18	10	4	4	40	15	34
Bradford United	18	9	2	7	29	27	29
Freshford United	18	7	4	7	44	36	25
Blue Circle	18	6	6	6	42	38	24
FC Northbridge	18	6	1	11	36	53	19
The Deverills	18	5	2	11	29	50	17
Warminster T. Res.	18	4	4	10	20	32	16
Heytesbury	18	1	4	13	27	74	7

Division Two	P	W	D	L	F	A	Pts
AFC Trow. Yth Res.	20	16	4	0	72	20	52
Steeple Ashton	20	12	3	5	52	37	39
Westbury Utd 'A'	20	10	6	4	50	29	36
Lavington *-2*	20	10	2	8	58	51	30
Semington Magpies	20	8	6	6	43	38	30
Bratton	20	7	5	8	38	38	26
St Andrews FC	20	7	5	8	42	45	26
AFC Trow. Wdrs *-1*	20	5	6	9	46	52	20
Hilperton United	20	5	5	10	46	69	20
Lamb FC *-1*	20	4	2	14	39	69	13
Frome T. Spts 'A'	20	3	2	15	35	73	11

TYNESIDE AMATEUR LEAGUE

Division One	P	W	D	L	F	A	Pts
Winlaton Vulcan Inn	22	17	3	2	64	22	54
Willington Quay Sts	22	15	1	6	63	28	46
Bellingham	22	13	6	3	74	31	45
Blyth Town Res.	22	13	5	4	56	29	44
Wardley Dur. Rgrs	22	12	3	7	44	45	39
Gos. B. Garnett Res.	22	10	3	9	60	44	33
Cullercoats Piper	22	9	5	8	48	51	32
Newcastle Medicals	22	7	2	13	46	66	23
West Jesmond	22	6	2	14	36	47	20
Lindisfarne Athletic	22	5	1	16	32	69	16
Killingworth SYPC	22	4	3	15	36	81	15
Cramlington T. Res.	22	3	2	17	17	63	11

Division Two	P	W	D	L	F	A	Pts
Forest Hall	20	15	2	3	62	20	47
Blyth Waterloo *-6*	20	15	1	4	76	28	40
Wallsend T. Res.	20	12	3	5	55	33	39
Newcastle City	20	11	2	7	45	42	35
G'head Three Tuns	20	9	4	7	34	32	31
New York	20	9	2	9	48	50	29
Red Star Benwell	20	9	1	10	51	49	28
Blyth Spartans 'A'	20	8	4	8	29	31	28
Newcastle RVI	20	5	6	9	35	52	21
MDT Newcastle	20	2	2	16	24	65	8
Newc. IJLW Brazil	20	1	1	18	15	72	4

WAKEFIELD & DISTRICT LEAGUE

Premier Division	P	W	D	L	F	A	Pts
Airedale Celtic	20	17	3	0	85	20	54
Horb'y Cherry Tree	20	17	2	1	81	26	53
Snydale Athletic	20	10	3	7	64	38	33
White Bear Kexboro.	20	9	3	8	44	41	30
Mitres Well	20	8	4	8	40	52	28
Crofton Sports	20	6	5	9	38	42	23
Fieldhead Hosp. *-3*	20	8	2	10	54	65	23
Smiths Arms	20	6	5	9	38	50	23
Walton *-3*	20	7	4	9	38	53	22
Snydale Sports	20	3	2	15	45	91	11
Eastmoor Res. *-3*	20	1	3	16	23	72	3

Silcoates – record expunged

Division One	P	W	D	L	F	A	Pts
Thornhill *-3*	23	20	1	2	129	19	58
Ryecroft Sports	24	15	5	4	86	32	50
Ferrybridge Ams	24	16	2	6	67	32	50
Royal Oak	24	14	3	7	66	49	45
Wrenthorpe *-3*	24	15	2	7	77	49	44
Shepherds Arms	24	12	3	9	57	61	39
Nostell MW 'A'	24	11	5	8	45	33	38
K'stone UWMC *-13*	23	12	5	6	55	53	28
Knottingley W'side	24	6	3	15	41	71	21
Wakefield City 'A'	24	4	5	15	34	71	17
Waterloo	24	5	2	17	46	94	17
AFC Thornhill	24	3	3	18	34	106	12
AFC Foresters	24	2	1	21	34	101	7

Division Two	P	W	D	L	F	A
Stanley Arms	24	23	1	0	125	22
Smawthorne *-3*	24	17	2	5	90	46
Stanley United Res.	24	14	5	5	81	59
White Rose	24	15	0	9	91	64
Cross Keys	24	12	5	7	64	56
Jolly Miller	24	11	4	9	68	56
Two Brewers	24	10	2	12	64	76
Snydale Ath. Res.	24	7	3	14	29	71
Wakefield United	24	7	2	15	38	65
Gawthorpe Shoulder	24	7	2	15	51	96
Horbury CT Res. *-3*	24	8	1	15	54	75
Crofton Sports Res.	24	5	2	17	45	76
Morley C & SC	24	5	1	18	37	75

Westgate Common – record expunged

Division Three	P	W	D	L	F	A
Cliffe Tree	24	19	4	1	129	43
Alverthorpe WMC	24	17	4	3	95	24
Featherstone C. Res.	24	16	3	5	86	29
Ossett Athletic	24	14	5	5	73	41
Little Bull *-10*	24	12	6	6	75	41
Two Brewers Utd	24	7	6	11	52	77
Scissett	24	7	2	15	40	100
Duke of Wel'ton *-3*	24	6	6	12	40	64
Ossett Panthers *-12*	24	9	5	10	70	58
Snydale Spts Res. *-3*	24	7	2	15	60	95
Inns of Court	24	4	6	14	37	89
Weavers Arms	24	4	4	16	49	119
Altofts 'A' *-6*	24	6	3	15	34	60

✓WARRINGTON & DISTRICT LEAGUE

Premier Division	P	W	D	L	F	A
Rainhill Town	22	19	1	2	57	16
Moore United	22	15	3	4	51	32
Halebank	22	15	0	7	62	34
St Michaels DH	22	12	2	8	54	48
Haydock	22	10	4	8	41	36
Penlake Res.	22	7	7	8	37	33
Moorfield	22	7	5	10	34	43
Beeches	22	8	2	12	28	52
Vulcan	22	7	3	12	42	43
Cronton Villa	22	7	3	12	47	51
Blackbrook	22	4	5	13	55	68
Downall Green Utd	22	3	1	18	34	86

Division One	P	W	D	L	F	A
Whiston Cross	18	13	3	2	57	25
Grappenhall Sports	18	13	2	3	43	24
Act R Sports	18	11	1	6	57	29
Sidac Social	18	9	6	3	43	22
Ford Motors Res.	18	7	3	8	33	39
Runcorn Albion	18	8	0	10	32	45
Halton Borough	18	6	4	8	29	37
Greenalls PSO 'A'	18	4	6	8	27	37
Beechwood	18	2	3	13	26	55
Croft	18	3	0	15	35	69

Division Two	P	W	D	L	F	A
Orford B'bne Arms	20	14	2	4	59	33
Grange SC	20	14	0	6	54	33
Rainhill Town Res.	20	12	5	3	64	23
Whiston Cross Res.	20	10	5	5	35	33
Windle Lab. Club	20	11	1	8	44	41
Halebank Res.	20	9	5	6	51	39
Vulcan Res.	20	8	2	10	37	32
Culcheth SC	20	7	3	10	31	42
Cronton Villa Res.	20	4	3	13	31	54
Winwick United	20	4	0	16	33	67
Avon Athletic	20	2	4	14	30	72

Division Three	P	W	D	L	F	A
Burtonwood Albion	22	16	5	1	85	31
Fife Rangers	22	16	4	2	76	35
Rainhill Town 'A'	22	12	2	8	60	36
Newton-le-Will. *-3*	22	10	4	8	58	56
Culcheth SC Res.	22	9	4	9	74	73
St Mich. DH Res.	22	9	3	10	53	38
Widnes Bayer	22	9	3	10	46	52
Village Social	22	9	2	11	45	67
Monks Sports Res.	22	8	2	12	40	50
Lomax	22	7	4	11	44	44
Whiston Cross 'A'	22	7	4	11	51	79
Penketh United	22	1	1	20	23	94

ivision Four	P	W	D	L	F	A	Pts
t Michaels DH 'A'	22	14	5	3	62	31	47
uncorn Alb. Res.	22	15	1	6	54	34	46
loorfield Res.	22	14	3	5	57	34	45
ife Rangers Res.	22	11	5	6	61	54	38
rford B. Arms Res	22	11	3	8	54	46	36
loore United Res.	22	8	5	9	45	51	29
range SC Res.	22	8	5	9	39	47	29
lackbrook Res.	22	8	3	11	50	61	27
lalton Boro. Res.	22	7	5	10	41	48	26
partak	22	6	6	10	44	51	24
Vidnes Bayer Res.	22	7	2	13	41	67	23
earnhead Res.	22	1	1	20	8	32	4

ivision Five	P	W	D	L	F	A	Pts
ane Ends Athletic	20	18	1	1	79	14	55
rappenhall Res.	20	14	5	1	65	19	47
laydock Res.	20	9	4	7	40	38	31
lewton-le-W. Res.	20	9	3	8	39	51	30
tockton Lane	20	9	1	10	52	57	28
loorfield 'A'	20	7	5	8	35	38	26
von Athletic Res.	20	7	2	11	62	60	23
Vaterloo Wdrs	20	6	4	10	44	50	22
t Maries Widnes	20	6	2	12	46	57	20
urtonwood A. Res.	20	6	2	12	37	58	20
ronton Villa 'A'	20	3	3	14	31	88	12

WENSLEYDALE LEAGUE

	P	W	D	L	F	A	Pts
eyburn United	26	24	0	2	140	31	72
iwes	26	22	2	2	128	28	68
liddleham Town	26	22	1	3	99	40	67
'mond Mav. Res.	26	18	2	6	95	43	56
arperby Rovers	26	18	2	6	76	37	56
lawes United	26	14	1	11	55	54	43
olburn Town	26	10	2	14	50	56	32
eeth & District AC	26	9	5	12	56	84	32
uck Inn United	26	8	2	16	42	60	26
uck Inn Broncos	26	8	2	16	47	83	26
lawes	26	6	4	16	31	84	22
edmire United	26	6	0	20	35	80	18
skrigg United	26	2	2	22	27	122	8
pennithorne Harm.	26	2	1	23	31	110	7

WEST HERTS LEAGUE

(Arlon Printers)

remier Division	P	W	D	L	F	A	Pts
lemel H'std Rovers	16	14	0	2	66	27	42
ings Sports	16	13	1	2	71	18	40
erkhamsted Sports	16	10	1	5	62	26	31
larpenden Rovers	16	8	1	7	30	36	25
Vellington Arms	16	7	1	8	39	36	22
)xhey Jets 'A'	16	5	3	8	32	34	18
nter Hemel	16	5	3	8	37	60	18
'Artista	16	2	2	12	25	85	8
omarth C'struction	16	1	2	13	22	62	5

ivision One	P	W	D	L	F	A	Pts
ladley 'A'	20	18	2	0	61	6	56
ed Lion Rovers	20	13	3	4	45	24	42
lemel Rovers Res.	20	11	4	5	49	44	37
)xhey	20	9	5	6	50	41	32
)xhey Wanderers	20	8	6	6	37	33	30
larp. Rovers Res.	20	8	4	8	32	41	28
ings Sports Res.	20	6	6	8	31	36	24
ifle Volunteer	20	6	3	11	39	48	21
Tring Athletic 'A'	20	6	2	12	43	44	20
Metpol Bushey 'A'	20	3	3	14	35	67	12
lenn Sports	20	1	4	15	20	58	7

ivision Two	P	W	D	L	F	A	Pts
un Postal Rovers	16	12	2	2	64	24	38
Metpol Bushey 'B'	16	12	2	2	56	17	38
WR Garage Doors	16	10	3	3	61	26	33
ovingdon 'A'	16	9	3	4	50	34	30
lunton Bridge	16	7	1	8	28	44	22
ldenham	16	4	2	10	22	37	14
)xhey Jets 'B'	16	4	1	11	26	38	13
otten End	16	3	3	10	27	52	12
roxley Guild 'A'	16	2	1	13	20	82	7

Division Three	P	W	D	L	F	A	Pts
Hadley 'B'	20	15	3	2	57	22	48
Croxley Guild 'B'	20	14	3	3	55	27	45
Langleybury CC	20	12	3	5	67	34	39
Bovingdon 'B'	20	11	2	7	63	34	35
Old Parmiterians 'A'	20	8	5	7	41	26	29
Hemel Rovers 'A'	20	9	2	9	56	42	29
Tring Athletic 'B'	20	8	3	9	42	62	27
AFC Levy	20	6	1	13	37	61	19
Oxhey Reserves	20	4	5	11	20	59	17
Rick. St George	20	4	3	13	33	68	15
Harpenden Rov. 'A'	20	2	4	14	39	75	10

WEST SUSSEX LEAGUE

(Covers)

Premier Division	P	W	D	L	F	A	Pts
Dorking Wanderers	22	16	3	3	65	34	51
Univ. of Chichester	22	14	5	3	49	25	47
TD Shipley	22	14	2	6	55	24	44
Barnham	22	12	4	6	67	32	40
South Bersted	22	10	2	10	41	39	32
Rogate	22	9	3	10	43	46	30
Clymping	22	9	3	10	41	49	30
Predators	22	8	5	9	37	33	29
Eastergate United	22	8	1	13	32	44	25
East Dean	22	6	5	11	33	49	23
Henfield	22	6	1	15	34	69	19
Upper Beeding	22	2	2	18	15	68	8

Division One	P	W	D	L	F	A	Pts
Newtown Villa	22	17	1	4	55	25	52
Wittering United	22	16	2	4	61	23	50
West Chiltington	22	12	3	7	53	38	39
Fittleworth	22	11	4	7	50	43	37
Lancing United	22	10	4	8	62	51	34
Southwater	22	11	1	10	46	46	34
Lower Beeding	22	9	3	10	36	40	30
TD Shipley Res.	22	8	4	10	38	45	28
Angmering	22	9	0	13	61	68	27
Holbrook	22	8	3	11	41	49	27
Partridge Green	22	4	3	15	38	65	15
Yapton	22	2	2	18	22	70	8

Division Two North	P	W	D	L	F	A	Pts
Billingshurst	22	16	3	3	66	24	51
Cowfold	22	15	3	4	57	25	48
Ashington Rovers	22	14	4	4	41	22	46
Faygate United	22	13	3	6	49	34	42
Wisborough Green	22	10	5	7	56	38	35
Ockley	22	8	4	10	59	54	28
Rudgwick	22	7	4	11	42	49	25
Horsham Olympic	22	7	3	12	41	56	24
Alfold	22	6	5	11	44	64	23
Pulborough	22	6	3	13	48	55	21
Dorking Wdrs Res.	22	6	2	14	45	80	20
Slinfold	22	3	3	16	27	74	12

Division Two South	P	W	D	L	F	A	Pts
Rustington Res.	22	17	1	4	51	23	52
Petworth	22	13	4	5	45	23	43
Chichester Hosps	22	13	2	7	56	27	41
Stedham United	22	12	4	6	46	25	40
Wittering Utd Res.	22	11	4	7	39	27	37
Clymping Res.	22	8	6	8	30	38	30
Worthing BCOB	22	9	2	11	48	41	29
Eastergate Utd Res.	22	8	5	9	40	45	29
Lancing United Res.	22	6	5	11	38	70	23
Lavant	22	6	4	12	32	44	22
Predators Res.	22	5	2	15	29	58	17
Lodsworth	22	3	3	16	22	55	12

Division Three North	P	W	D	L	F	A	Pts
Newdigate	22	17	1	4	56	20	52
Capel	22	15	2	5	56	30	47
Watersfield	22	14	4	4	62	35	46
Barns Green	22	11	3	8	37	31	36
Friends Provident	22	10	5	7	46	38	35
Horsham Trinity	22	9	3	10	41	41	30
Horsham Baptists	22	8	3	11	46	54	27
Billingshurst Res.	22	8	2	12	38	49	26
Holbrook Res.	22	7	3	12	38	50	24
Faygate United Res.	22	4	9	9	41	54	21
Southwater Res.	22	5	3	14	40	64	18
Ockley Res.	22	3	4	15	28	63	13

Division Three South	P	W	D	L	F	A	Pts
Middleton-on-Sea	20	16	0	4	81	32	48
Hunston CC	20	13	1	6	57	32	40
Milland	20	12	2	6	43	36	38
Newtown Villa Res.	20	11	3	6	76	46	36
Ambassadors	20	11	3	6	57	43	36
Square Deal	20	11	3	6	40	30	36
Angmering Res.	20	9	4	7	53	45	31
Pulborough Res.	20	6	4	10	27	52	22
Petworth Res.	20	3	3	14	34	62	12
Yapton Res.	20	3	2	15	25	74	11
Boxgrove	20	2	1	17	35	76	7

Division Four North	P	W	D	L	F	A	Pts
Storrington 'A'	24	20	1	3	115	37	61
Barnham 'A'	24	18	1	5	93	36	55
Warnham	24	15	4	5	78	42	49
TD Shipley 'A'	24	14	5	5	54	28	47
Cowfold Res.	24	10	2	12	41	54	32
W. Chiltington Res.	24	8	7	9	41	41	31
W'boro. Green Res.	24	8	6	10	49	54	30
Alfold Res.	24	8	4	12	47	51	28
Fittleworth Res.	24	8	4	12	47	70	28
Horsham O. Res.	24	8	1	15	29	74	25
Holbrook 'A'	24	7	2	15	41	71	23
Loxwood Res.	24	6	2	16	33	77	20
Henfield Res.	24	5	3	16	50	83	18

Division Four South	P	W	D	L	F	A	Pts
Selsey Town	20	19	0	1	95	15	57
General Henry	20	15	2	3	85	21	47
Barnham Res.	20	14	2	4	79	25	44
The Wheatsheaf	20	13	2	5	68	43	41
Fernhurst	20	10	3	7	63	55	33
Coal Exchange	20	7	2	11	35	58	23
The Sportsman	20	7	1	12	29	53	22
Bosham Res.	20	5	6	9	37	44	21
Graffham	20	6	2	12	45	78	20
Amberley	20	1	2	17	16	79	5
Regis Veterans	20	1	2	17	20	101	5

Division Five North	P	W	D	L	F	A	Pts
AFC Roffey	18	16	0	2	124	18	48
Horsham Trin. Res.	18	16	0	2	62	25	48
Capel Res.	18	8	3	7	40	40	27
Horsham Bapt. Res.	18	7	4	7	39	55	25
Rudgwick Res. *-1*	18	7	4	7	39	38	24
Norfolk Arms	18	8	0	10	43	62	24
B52's *-3*	18	8	1	9	34	38	22
Newdigate Res.	18	4	3	11	33	62	15
Holbrook 'B'	18	3	3	12	23	61	12
Slinfold Res.	18	2	4	12	22	60	10

Division Five Central	P	W	D	L	F	A	Pts
Ashington R. Res.	18	13	3	2	58	19	42
Plaistow	18	13	3	2	45	16	42
Barns Green Res.	18	11	4	3	34	26	37
Upper Beeding Res.	18	9	5	4	42	26	32
Billingshurst 'A'	18	6	5	7	33	39	23
Henfield 'A'	18	6	2	10	32	40	20
Partridge G. Res.	18	5	5	8	31	45	20
Watersfield Res.	18	5	5	8	26	43	20
Southwater 'A'	18	2	4	12	27	46	10
Chapel	18	2	0	16	23	51	6

Division Five South	P	W	D	L	F	A	Pts
Predators 'A'	18	15	1	2	66	25	46
Stedham Utd Res.	18	12	2	4	63	32	38
Ambassadors Res.	18	7	7	4	44	34	28
Rustington Pk Snrs	18	8	3	7	42	50	27
Harting	18	7	5	6	35	36	26
Lavant Res.	18	7	2	9	42	34	23
Tangmere	18	7	2	9	49	52	23
Graffham Res.	18	5	4	9	37	50	19
Lodsworth Res.	18	4	4	10	30	58	16
Fernhurst Res.	18	3	0	15	21	58	9

WESTON & DISTRICT LEAGUE

Division One	P	W	D	L	F	A	Pts
Worlebury Spartans	22	18	2	2	75	33	56
Winscombe Res.	22	14	3	5	76	40	45
East Worle	22	14	1	7	59	35	43
Hutton	22	13	3	6	46	37	42
Bournville Rovers	22	10	1	11	43	52	31
Kewstoke Lions	22	9	4	9	46	55	31
Portishead 'A'	22	9	3	10	43	41	30
Draycott	22	8	4	10	40	39	28
Cleeve West T. Res.	22	7	6	9	35	39	27
Nailsea United 'A'	22	7	5	10	46	50	26
Blagdon	22	4	1	17	21	57	13
Clevedon Utd 'A'	22	2	1	19	34	86	7

Division Two	P	W	D	L	F	A	Pts
Churchill Club Res.	22	16	3	3	59	23	51
St George EG Res.	22	16	2	4	46	19	50
Congresbury Res.	22	14	4	4	57	30	46
Portishead 'B'	22	11	7	4	49	31	40
Burnham United 'A'	22	12	2	8	63	48	38
Portishead WMC	22	8	5	9	38	46	29
KVFC	22	7	5	10	45	47	26
Milton Crusaders *-4*	22	9	3	10	47	56	26
Selkirk United	22	6	4	12	36	43	22
Westland Utd Res.	22	5	4	13	43	57	19
Hutton Res.	22	5	3	14	59	75	18
Worle Res. *-1*	22	1	2	19	23	90	4

WWW.NLNEWSDESK.CO.UK

Division Three	P	W	D	L	F	A	Pts
Nailsea Town Res.	22	13	5	4	49	37	44
Clarence Park	22	12	5	5	74	38	41
Swiss Valley Rov.	22	12	4	6	67	26	40
Kewstoke L. Res.	22	13	1	8	64	50	40
South Park Rangers	22	10	7	5	53	49	37
Clevedon Utd 'B'	22	9	5	8	57	61	32
Locking Park	22	9	4	9	42	54	31
Yatton Athletic Res.	22	8	2	12	42	54	26
Nailsea United 'B'	22	8	1	13	53	57	25
Banwell Res.	22	7	3	12	46	59	24
Cheddar 'A'	22	6	2	14	39	58	20
Wring.-Redhill Res.	22	5	1	16	26	69	16

Division Four	P	W	D	L	F	A	Pts
Weston SJ Sp. Bar	22	21	1	0	94	26	64
Winscombe 'A'	22	13	5	4	56	34	44
Cleeve West T. 'A'	22	13	2	7	52	30	41
Westend	22	10	3	9	62	51	33
King Alfred SC	22	10	3	9	60	57	33
Draycott Res.	22	9	5	8	56	44	32
Locking Villa	22	8	8	6	54	45	32
Wedmore	22	8	4	10	45	44	28
KVFC Res.	22	8	1	13	45	68	25
Berrow Res. *-1*	22	6	2	14	40	56	19
Blagdon Res.	22	5	4	13	28	54	19
Congresbury 'A'	22	1	2	19	24	107	5

Division Five	P	W	D	L	F	A	Pts
Nailsea Utd Colts	26	22	1	3	96	31	67
Stotties Rovers	26	19	0	7	110	50	57
Portishead Colts	26	15	6	5	70	39	51
Worlebury S. Res.	26	12	4	10	65	70	40
Burnham Utd 'B'	26	11	3	12	73	57	36
P'head WMC Res.	26	10	6	10	70	68	36
AFC Nailsea	26	10	5	11	64	62	35
Hutton 'A'	26	9	5	12	69	80	32
Bournville R. Res.	26	9	5	12	57	81	32
Kewstoke Lions 'A'	26	9	4	13	54	65	31
Cheddar 'B'	26	8	7	11	43	60	31
St George EG 'A'	26	8	4	14	55	73	28
Yatton Athletic 'A'	26	8	1	17	51	83	25
Athletico Wrington	26	5	3	18	46	104	18

Division Six	P	W	D	L	F	A	Pts
Weston United	20	18	0	2	108	32	54
Axbridge Town	20	16	1	3	91	36	49
East Worle Res.	20	14	3	3	85	31	45
Clevedon Dons	20	12	3	5	64	41	39
Dolphin Athletic	20	8	6	6	46	44	30
St George EG 'B'	20	8	4	8	53	49	28
Westend Res.	20	7	3	10	40	67	24
Weston Athletic	20	5	0	15	35	91	15
Selkirk United Res.	20	4	2	14	27	63	14
Wedmore Res.	20	3	3	14	23	68	12
Berrow 'A'	20	1	3	16	23	73	6

WIMBLEDON & DISTRICT LEAGUE

Premier Division	P	W	D	L	F	A	Pts
Brentnal *+2*	20	16	2	2	50	16	52
Real Phoenix	20	13	4	3	68	17	43
AFC Cubo	20	14	1	5	44	23	43
Partizan Wandsw'th	20	13	2	5	28	23	41
Duet	20	9	3	8	45	37	30
London Lionh'rts *+3*	20	7	5	8	46	48	29
Wandle	20	6	3	11	34	47	21
Leamington	20	6	1	13	33	59	19
Ocean *-4*	20	5	5	10	28	45	16
PWCA	20	4	3	13	32	53	15
Union	20	2	1	17	15	55	7

Division One	P	W	D	L	F	A	Pts
AFC Battersea	20	15	2	3	83	33	47
Lancaster Youth	20	15	1	4	56	26	46
Brompton Spts Cas.	20	11	2	7	37	43	35
Spartak Clapham	20	10	4	6	66	39	34
Rivelino City	20	7	5	8	35	46	26
Claremont	20	8	2	10	28	41	26
Brentside	20	7	4	9	33	38	25
Shaftesbury Exiles	20	7	3	10	36	53	24
Cosmos United	20	6	2	12	43	59	20
Hyde Pk Thursday	20	5	1	14	32	56	16
Brentnal Res.	20	3	6	11	37	52	15

Division Two	P	W	D	L	F	A	Pts
Wadham COB *-3*	12	10	0	2	46	18	27
Los Boca Gunners	12	8	2	2	35	27	26
Kiwi	12	8	1	3	36	21	25
FC Centaur *+5*	12	4	2	6	17	27	19
Boca Seniors	12	3	2	7	21	44	11
Agricola	12	3	0	9	23	39	9
Buca Juniors *-3*	12	2	1	9	24	26	4

Division Three	P	W	D	L	F	A	Pts
Goldfingers	16	12	4	0	47	24	40
Sth East Londoners	16	9	2	5	69	39	29
Sporting Brixton	16	8	4	4	43	27	28
Sth West Eleven *+3*	16	6	4	6	45	42	25
Nottingham OB	16	7	3	6	55	26	24
Wandsworth *-3*	16	7	3	6	31	32	21
L. Lionhearts Res.	16	4	4	8	32	58	16
South Lodge	16	4	3	9	30	55	15
Brentnal 'A'	16	0	3	13	12	61	3

WINCHESTER & DISTRICT LEAGUE

	P	W	D	L	F	A	Pts
Crusaders	20	17	2	1	76	23	53
Twyford	20	15	3	2	47	19	48
Sutton Scotney	20	13	3	4	45	18	42
Sth Wonston Swifts	20	10	7	3	51	32	37
Winch. Castle Res.	20	8	4	8	42	42	28
Castel De Sangro	20	6	6	8	35	42	24
Infinity	20	6	5	9	36	39	23
Sparsholt	20	6	4	10	26	39	22
Ropley	20	6	1	13	38	50	19
Eastleigh Town	20	1	4	15	19	48	7
Upham Res.	20	1	3	16	21	84	6

WITNEY & DISTRICT FA

Premier Division	P	W	D	L	F	A	Pts
Freeland	24	18	4	2	76	30	58
Hailey	24	18	2	4	63	30	56
Ducklington	24	17	3	4	75	29	54
Charlbury Town	24	16	4	4	48	30	52
Brize Norton	24	9	4	11	61	54	31
West Witney	24	9	4	11	56	58	31
Hanborough	24	8	7	9	48	54	31
Spartan Rangers	24	9	3	12	43	48	30
Carterton 'A'	24	8	4	12	42	62	28
Millpark	24	9	0	15	41	69	27
North Leigh 'A'	24	7	1	16	51	67	22
FC Nomads	24	4	7	13	25	44	19
Aston	24	2	1	21	28	82	7

Division One	P	W	D	L	F	A	Pts
Bampton	24	21	3	0	82	17	66
Cassington	24	17	6	1	72	22	57
Carterton 'B'	24	15	5	4	83	33	50
Witney Royals	24	14	1	9	59	54	43
FC Mills	24	12	3	9	32	36	39
Ducklington Res.	24	12	2	10	55	45	38
Minster Lovell	24	9	4	11	43	46	31
Witney Wdrs *+3*	24	8	4	12	48	60	31
Milton	24	8	3	13	58	65	27
Eynsham A. 'A'	24	4	4	16	48	72	16
Hanborough Res.	24	4	4	16	31	72	16
North Leigh 'B'	24	5	0	19	33	65	15
W. Witney Res. *-6*	24	6	3	15	22	79	15

Division Two	P	W	D	L	F	A	Pts
Brize Norton Res.	26	23	1	2	125	28	70
Spartan Rgrs Res.	26	17	3	6	91	40	54
Kingham All Blacks	25	16	5	4	93	51	53
Combe	26	16	2	8	90	41	50
Tackley	25	15	2	8	87	50	47
Chippy Swifts	26	14	4	8	60	55	46
Freeland Res.	26	11	4	11	55	64	37
Wootton Sports	26	11	2	13	48	71	35
AC Finstock	26	8	3	15	41	55	27
Charlbury T. Res.	26	7	4	15	47	86	25
Wychwood Forest	26	7	1	18	38	87	22
Fieldtown	26	5	5	16	34	69	20
FC Nomads Res.	26	5	3	18	34	114	18
Minster Lovell Res.	26	3	7	16	48	80	16

Division Three	P	W	D	L	F	A	Pts
Combe	24	20	3	1	108	20	63
Kingham AB Res.	24	15	3	6	50	30	48
Fieldtown Res.	24	13	3	8	77	44	42
Freeland Res.	24	11	9	4	66	39	42
Charlbury T. Res.	24	12	5	7	65	50	41
Ducklington 'A'	24	12	5	7	58	43	41
FC Mills Res. *-3*	24	13	3	8	52	38	39
Witney Royals Res.	24	9	3	12	47	69	30
Aston Res. *+3*	24	6	4	14	38	46	25
Two Rivers	24	7	4	13	32	60	25
Southrop *+3*	24	6	2	16	52	84	23
AC Finstock Res.	24	6	2	16	34	87	20
Burford Utd Res. *-6*	24	3	0	21	26	95	3

WORCESTER & DISTRICT LEAGUE

Premier Division	P	W	D	L	F	A	Pts
Martley Spurs	18	14	2	2	75	32	44
Powick	18	11	3	4	47	26	36
Talbot FC	18	11	2	5	55	34	35
Hanley Swan	18	8	6	4	48	36	30
Upton Town	18	9	3	6	39	30	30
West Malvern	18	6	3	9	51	54	21
Pershore MR	18	5	3	10	41	65	18
Hallow WMC	18	4	4	10	34	48	16
UOW	18	2	7	9	27	42	13
VBL Sports	18	2	3	13	39	89	9

WORTHING & DISTRICT LEAGUE

Premier Division	P	W	D	L	F	A	Pts
L & S Athletic	20	16	3	1	85	26	51
Warren Sports	20	13	2	5	55	24	41
Tabernacle	20	12	5	3	53	26	41
Sompting	20	13	2	5	62	42	41
Worthing Athletic	20	12	2	6	56	50	38
GSK Sports	20	8	4	8	59	47	28
Worthing Wdrs	20	8	2	10	52	34	26
AFC Broadwater	20	5	4	11	30	47	19
Revenue	20	5	1	14	25	58	16
Adur Athletic	20	3	2	15	27	75	11
Northbrook	20	1	1	18	16	91	4

Division One	P	W	D	L	F	A	Pts
Jolly Brewers	18	13	5	0	66	28	44
Worthing Mitsubishi	18	13	1	4	43	21	40
Durrington RAFA	18	12	3	3	68	23	39
L & S Athletic Res.	18	9	3	6	55	39	30
Adur Athletic Res.	18	10	0	8	53	38	30
Goring St Theresas	18	9	3	6	49	36	30
Worthing Albion	18	5	2	11	27	44	17
GSK Sports Res.	18	5	1	12	30	59	16
Sompting Res.	18	3	0	15	20	75	9
St Marys	18	1	2	15	20	68	5

Division Two	P	W	D	L	F	A	Pts
Shoreham RBL	18	18	0	0	83	14	54
Woodside	18	12	1	5	69	27	37
TMG	18	11	2	5	65	31	35
Edge	18	10	4	4	42	29	34
Lancing United 'B'	18	8	3	7	34	34	27
Hill Barn Rangers	18	8	1	9	57	56	25
Worth. BCOB Res.	18	7	1	10	24	38	22
The Globe	18	6	2	10	39	37	20
Ath. Wenban Smith	18	3	0	15	20	58	9
W. Worthing WMC	18	0	0	18	7	116	0

Division Three	P	W	D	L	F	A	Pts
Worthing Wdrs Res.	14	12	1	1	46	11	37
Highdown Rovers	14	11	1	2	50	15	34
Fern Estates	14	9	2	3	36	21	29
Northbrook Res.	14	6	2	6	30	25	20
West Tarring WMC	14	4	4	6	31	33	16
AFC Phoenix	14	4	2	8	38	42	14
GSK Sports 'B'	14	3	0	11	24	72	9
Lancing United 'C'	14	0	2	12	10	46	2

WYCOMBE & DISTRICT LEAGUE

(Walters Group)

Senior Division	P	W	D	L	F	A	Pts
Wycombe Judo	18	12	4	2	40	19	40
Winchmore Hill	18	8	6	4	38	28	30
Downley Albion	18	8	4	6	34	21	28
AFC Spartans	18	8	2	8	45	47	26
Lane End	18	5	4	9	30	41	19
AC Marlow	18	4	5	9	34	39	17
Hambleden	18	4	3	11	34	60	15

Premier Division	P	W	D	L	F	A	Pts
Holmer Green OB	18	18	0	0	55	15	54
R. Lion (Wooburn)	18	11	3	4	60	27	36
AFC Amersham	18	11	2	5	53	39	35
Walters Group	18	7	2	9	45	51	23
Great Missenden	18	6	5	7	37	44	23
Penn/Tylers G. 'A'	18	5	5	8	44	42	20
AC Marlow Res.	18	6	2	10	39	43	20
Lane End Res.	18	6	2	10	34	49	20
Wooburn Athletic	18	4	2	12	25	51	14
Downley Alb. Res.	18	2	3	13	25	56	[illegible]

ivision One	P	W	D	L	F	A	Pts
otteridge Wdrs	22	19	3	0	74	26	60
: Titans	22	16	1	5	80	30	49
ix	22	15	2	5	98	23	47
innor 'A'	22	12	4	6	64	45	40
ycombe Athletic	22	12	1	9	63	50	37
inchmore H. Res.	22	10	3	9	51	51	33
olywell Mead Ath.	22	9	1	12	65	73	28
: Missenden Res.	22	8	3	11	54	57	27
/Horses (Marlow)	22	7	2	13	26	52	23
ueens Head Sports	22	5	4	13	46	76	19
of Wales Rgrs	22	3	1	18	27	91	10
alters Group Res.	22	3	1	18	32	106	10

YEOVIL & DISTRICT LEAGUE

remier Division	P	W	D	L	F	A	Pts
oke-sub-Hamdon	16	13	0	3	48	20	39
estland Spts Res.	16	11	2	3	45	17	35
ormalair RSL	16	10	0	6	42	26	30
ilborne Port	16	7	2	7	44	34	23
nsford Rovers	16	7	2	7	41	42	23
enstridge United	16	6	2	8	33	31	20
artock United	16	6	1	9	34	42	19
einton Mandeville	16	5	3	8	37	47	18
ictoria Sports	16	0	2	14	15	80	2

ivision One	P	W	D	L	F	A	Pts
en Mill	18	13	4	1	56	20	43
or	18	13	2	3	60	28	41
astle Cary Res.	18	12	2	4	49	21	38
altonsborough	18	9	3	6	48	30	30
oyal Oak Rangers	18	9	2	7	37	37	29
ormalair RSL Res.	18	5	4	9	37	43	19
dcombe	18	5	2	11	24	52	17
oke-sub-H. Res.	18	4	4	10	29	48	16
oopers Mill	18	4	0	14	20	47	12
ilborne Port Res.	18	3	3	12	26	60	12

ivision Two		P	W	D	L	F	A	Pts
omerton Sports		20	18	1	1	105	14	55
emplecombe Rov.		20	17	1	2	83	17	52
itney		20	12	3	5	42	19	39
artock Utd Res.		20	11	4	5	42	52	37
en Mill Res.		20	9	2	9	48	46	29
harlton United		20	7	3	10	34	40	24
yde United		20	7	1	12	37	52	22
ilborne Pt 'A'	*-1*	20	6	1	13	39	67	18
Iontacute		20	5	2	13	31	55	17
nsford R. Res.	*-2*	20	5	1	14	29	68	14
Iermaid United		20	2	3	15	25	85	9

ivision Three		P	W	D	L	F	A	Pts
arwick & Stoford		20	19	1	0	86	18	58
outh Cheriton Utd		20	18	1	1	130	19	55
yde United Res.		20	12	3	5	63	42	39
chester		20	12	3	5	57	44	39
ingsbury		20	7	3	10	36	70	24
angport Town		20	7	1	12	42	44	22
ruton United		20	7	0	13	43	66	21
emplecombe Res.		20	7	0	13	35	66	21
shwood		20	6	1	13	62	84	19
dcombe Res.		20	5	0	15	44	87	15
altonsboro. Res.	*-1*	20	3	1	16	36	94	9

YORK LEAGUE
(Leeper Hare)

remier Division	P	W	D	L	F	A	Pts
untington Rovers	28	20	1	7	66	38	61
ringhouses	28	18	6	4	89	37	60
artiers (Selby)	28	15	9	4	56	29	54
ld Malton St M.	28	13	5	10	44	45	44
opmanthorpe	28	12	5	11	62	44	41
unnington	28	12	5	11	63	51	41
ockwith	28	10	10	8	51	44	40
Vigg'ton G'hoppers	28	13	1	14	65	72	40
ate & Lyle Selby	28	11	5	12	58	67	38
Ialton & Norton	28	11	4	13	49	58	37
Iestle Rowntree	28	9	8	11	44	50	35
horpe United	28	11	1	16	46	73	34
ork St Johns Coll.	28	8	3	17	42	60	27
Ieslington	28	7	6	15	49	73	27
ocklington T. Res.	28	3	5	20	26	69	14

ivision One	P	W	D	L	F	A	Pts
Iaxby United	24	19	3	2	95	27	60
Iamilton Panthers	24	16	4	4	75	29	52
Vilberfoss	24	16	4	4	55	27	52
iccall United	24	12	3	9	50	48	39
oppleton United	24	9	10	5	46	37	37
Amotherby/Swinton	24	11	3	10	51	49	36
ishopthorpe Utd	24	9	5	10	57	56	32
Iorwich Union	24	5	9	10	32	45	24
useburn United	24	6	5	13	35	64	23
asingwold Town	24	5	6	13	29	50	21
tamford Bridge	24	6	3	15	32	69	21
lvington Harriers	24	4	7	13	26	46	19
ufforth United	24	5	4	15	30	66	19

Division Two		P	W	D	L	F	A	Pts
Osbaldwick		22	19	1	2	105	38	58
Tadcaster Alb. Res.		22	16	3	3	75	25	51
Post Office		22	14	4	4	64	48	46
York Railway Inst.		22	13	2	7	87	40	41
Fulford United		22	11	5	6	56	37	38
Hemingbrough Utd		22	10	3	9	48	37	33
Selby RSSC		22	8	4	10	53	45	28
WH Church Fenton		22	8	2	12	38	55	26
Huby United		22	6	5	11	38	70	23
Moor Lane		22	5	2	15	44	70	17
New Earswick		22	3	6	13	40	53	15
Civil Service	*-3*	22	0	1	21	26	156	-2

Division Three		P	W	D	L	F	A	Pts
St Clements		24	20	4	0	112	41	64
Strensall		24	17	4	3	93	39	55
Stillington		24	18	0	6	80	36	54
Rawcliffe Rangers		24	14	7	3	94	43	49
Barmby Moor		24	12	3	9	67	40	39
Cawood		24	12	2	10	70	56	38
Melbourne		24	11	2	11	46	64	35
Norton United	*-3*	24	8	5	11	67	63	26
Heworth		24	8	2	14	43	55	26
LNER Builders		24	7	4	13	42	73	25
Bishop Wilton		24	4	5	15	41	89	17
Wheldrake		24	2	2	20	29	91	8
N. Duffield Res.	*-3*	24	2	2	20	25	119	5

Reserve Division A		P	W	D	L	F	A	Pts
Dunnington Res.		22	16	4	2	45	20	52
York St JC Res.	*-3*	22	15	4	3	60	23	46
Dringhouses Res.		22	14	2	6	60	28	44
Copmanthorpe Res.		22	11	6	5	46	25	39
Huntington R. Res.		22	7	8	7	35	31	29
Kartiers (Sel.) Res.		22	7	7	8	42	49	28
Rufforth Utd Res.		22	8	2	12	43	59	26
Nestle R'tree Res.		22	7	2	13	54	57	23
Old Malton SM Res.		22	6	4	12	35	52	22
Thorpe United Res.		22	5	7	10	31	49	22
New Earswick Res.		22	5	4	13	27	54	19
Pocklington T. 'A'		22	5	2	15	32	63	17

Reserve Division B		P	W	D	L	F	A	Pts
Wigginton G. Res.		22	17	0	5	91	35	51
Heworth Res.		22	15	5	2	69	18	50
Bishopthorpe Res.		22	14	5	3	75	25	47
Haxby United Res.		22	14	1	7	63	50	43
Easingwold Res.	*-3*	22	11	1	10	36	42	31
Stamford Bdge Res.		22	9	3	10	49	47	30
Malton/Norton Res.		22	7	4	11	38	56	25
Poppleton Res.	*-3*	22	8	2	12	51	62	23
Hamilton P. Res.		22	6	2	14	31	61	20
Wilberfoss Res.		22	6	2	14	26	62	20
Tockwith Res.		22	5	4	13	36	61	19
Amotherby/S. Res.		22	4	3	15	29	75	15

Reserve Division B	P	W	D	L	F	A	Pts
York Rail. I. Res.	22	19	2	1	88	26	59
Riccall United Res.	22	16	2	4	64	22	50
Heslington Res.	22	16	1	5	89	44	49
Hemingbrough Res.	22	12	4	6	57	41	40
Ouseburn Utd Res.	22	11	4	7	65	48	37
Norwich Union Res.	22	10	3	9	70	52	33
Stillington Res.	22	6	3	13	53	61	21
LNER Builders Res.	22	6	3	13	40	66	21
Huby United Res.	22	5	6	11	35	79	21
Fulford United Res.	22	6	2	14	36	55	20
Civil Service Res.	22	4	2	16	32	103	14
WH Ch. Fenton Res.	22	3	4	15	32	64	13

YORKSHIRE OLD BOYS LEAGUE

Senior Division A	P	W	D	L	F	A	Pts
Yorkshire Bank	22	15	4	3	60	23	49
Leeds Medics & D.	22	13	5	4	59	26	44
St Nicholas	22	13	4	5	50	33	43
Trinity/All Sts OB	22	13	3	6	56	24	42
H'mondwike GSOB	22	11	7	4	62	35	40
Stanningley OB	22	10	3	9	49	48	33
Huddersfield Ams	22	8	2	12	32	37	26
Old Rovers	22	7	4	11	39	49	25
Old Collegians	22	7	4	11	41	62	25
Leeds Univ. OB	22	6	5	11	44	56	23
Western Juniors OB	22	3	3	16	38	91	12
Roundhegians	22	3	2	17	28	74	11

Senior Division B	P	W	D	L	F	A	Pts
Old Centralians	22	18	1	3	60	30	55
FC Headingley	22	14	1	7	67	46	43
Ealandians	22	12	3	7	56	50	39
Gildersome Spurs	22	11	4	7	75	55	37
Leeds M/D'tists Res.	22	10	4	8	56	38	34
Bramley Juniors OB	22	11	1	10	66	55	34
Old Modernians	22	9	3	10	57	50	30
Leeds City Old B.	22	9	3	10	47	52	30
Wortley	22	7	4	11	38	63	25
Calverley	22	7	2	13	44	66	23
Old Batelians	22	6	4	12	44	51	22
East Ardsley Wdrs	22	2	2	18	30	84	8

Division One	P	W	D	L	F	A	Pts
Sandal Athletic	22	17	3	2	76	27	54
South Leeds Saints	22	16	2	4	70	40	50
St Bedes Old Boys	22	12	4	6	53	42	40
Shire Academics	22	11	5	6	66	47	38
Alwoodley	22	10	4	8	62	46	34
Leeds City OB Res.	22	10	3	9	50	36	33
Leeds M/D'tists 'A'	22	8	7	7	55	44	31
Old Thornesians	22	8	3	11	38	57	27
W'hse Moor Meth.	22	7	5	10	35	45	26
Sandal Wanderers	22	5	4	13	49	64	19
Colton Academicals	22	2	5	15	39	78	11
Roundhegians Res.	22	2	3	17	25	92	9

Division Two	P	W	D	L	F	A	Pts
Gildersome S. Res.	24	16	7	1	71	29	55
Wortley Res.	24	17	3	4	69	30	54
Wheelwright OB	24	14	7	3	96	45	49
Leeds Independent	24	14	7	3	66	45	49
Commonside OB	24	11	8	5	77	61	41
Trinity/ASOB Res.	24	9	8	7	49	42	35
Agnes Stewart OB	24	8	5	11	42	58	29
O. Modernians Res.	24	7	7	10	50	52	28
Carlton Ath. Res.	24	7	7	10	40	49	28
O. Centralians Res.	24	6	4	14	36	59	22
Almondburians	24	6	3	15	35	54	21
Leeds City OB 'A'	24	4	2	18	36	79	14
Old Modernians 'A'	24	2	2	20	33	97	8

Division Three	P	W	D	L	F	A	Pts
East Leeds Trin. OB	24	19	1	4	97	36	58
Horbury Town OB	24	18	2	4	79	46	56
Hudd'fld Ams Res.	24	16	3	5	76	29	51
Moortown OB	24	16	2	6	98	52	50
H'wike GSOB Res.	24	13	4	7	54	46	43
Grangefield OB	24	8	5	11	45	50	29
Old Batelians Res.	24	8	5	11	62	87	29
St Bedes OB Res.	24	8	3	13	46	54	27
Gildersome S. 'A'	24	8	3	13	57	70	27
Old Modernians 'B'	24	8	2	14	46	72	26
Colton Acad. Res.	24	5	6	13	43	65	21
Roundhegians 'A'	24	4	5	15	30	93	17
O Thornesians Res.	24	3	3	18	32	65	12

Division Four	P	W	D	L	F	A	Pts
Old Collegians Res.	26	20	2	4	98	35	62
Ealandians Res.	26	17	3	6	71	41	54
W'wright OB Res.	26	17	3	6	82	55	54
E. Ardsley W. Res.	26	13	4	9	74	64	43
Colton Acad. 'A'	26	13	3	10	80	74	42
Leeds City OB 'B'	26	11	6	9	67	60	39
Old Batelians 'A'	26	12	3	11	77	81	39
Old Centralians 'A'	26	9	5	12	48	64	32
Hudd. Amateurs 'A'	26	9	2	15	45	67	29
Sandal Wdrs Res.	26	8	5	13	43	68	29
Leeds City OB 'C'	26	8	5	13	54	81	29
Leeds M. & D. 'B'	26	8	4	14	60	63	28
Sandal Athletic Res.	26	7	3	16	58	71	24
W'house MM Res.	26	5	2	19	46	79	17

Division Five	P	W	D	L	F	A	Pts
Bramley Jnrs Res.	26	23	1	2	102	19	70
Alwoodley OB Res	26	20	2	4	77	31	62
Heckmondwike 'A'	26	17	2	7	65	37	53
St Bedes OB 'A'	26	15	3	8	70	49	48
Alwoodley OB 'A'	26	14	4	8	72	47	46
Old Modernians 'C'	26	13	3	10	49	51	42
Collegians 'A'	26	11	5	10	53	45	38
Leeds City OB 'D'	26	9	3	14	43	59	30
Thornesians 'A'	26	7	7	12	31	48	28
Old Centralians 'B'	26	8	4	14	41	68	28
Wheelwright 'A'	26	6	3	17	44	70	21
Hudd. Amateurs 'B'	26	6	3	17	46	82	21
Roundhegians 'B'	26	6	3	17	33	70	21
Old Modernians 'D'	26	3	5	18	40	90	14

WWW.NLNEWSDESK.CO.UK

WEBSITES OF FEATURED LEAGUES

AMATEUR FOOTBALL ALLIANCE
www.amateur-fa.com

ANGLIAN COMBINATION
www.angliancombination.org.uk

CLWYD LEAGUE
clwydfootballleague.co.uk

COMBINED COUNTIES LEAGUE
www.combinedcountiesleague.co.uk

CYMRU ALLIANCE
www.cymru-alliance.co.uk

DORSET PREMIER LEAGUE
www.the-dpl.co.uk

DURHAM ALLIANCE
www.durhamalliance.co.uk

EASTERN COUNTIES LEAGUE
www.ridgeonsleague.co.uk

ESSEX OLYMPIAN LEAGUE
www.eofl.co.uk

ESSEX SENIOR FOOTBALL LEAGUE
essexseniorfootballleague.moonfruit.com

ESSEX & SUFFOLK BORDER LEAGUE
www.essexsuffolkborderleague.freeserve.co.uk

FOOTBALL CONFERENCE
www.footballconference.co.uk

GLOUCESTERSHIRE COUNTY LEAGUE
www.countyleague.co.uk

GWENT COUNTY LEAGUE
www.gwentfa.co.uk

GWYNEDD LEAGUE
www.cynghrair-gwynedd-league.co.uk

HAMPSHIRE LEAGUE
www.thehampshireleague2004.com

HAMPSHIRE PREMIER LEAGUE
www.hpfl.co.uk

HELLENIC LEAGUE
www.hellenicleague.co.uk

HERTS SENIOR COUNTY LEAGUE
www.hsc.leaguemanager.biz

HUMBER PREMIER LEAGUE
www.humberprem.com

ISTHMIAN LEAGUE
www.isthmian.co.uk

KENT COUNTY LEAGUE
www.kentcountyleague.co.uk

KENT LEAGUE
www.kentleague.com

LINCOLNSHIRE LEAGUE
www.lincolnshirefootballleague.co.uk

MANCHESTER LEAGUE
www.manchester-league.co.uk

MID-CHESHIRE LEAGUE
www.mcfl.co.uk

MIDLAND ALLIANCE
www.midlandfootballalliance.co.uk

MIDLAND COMBINATION
www.midcomb.com

NORTH BERKS LEAGUE
www.nbfl.co.uk

NORTH DEVON LEAGUE
www.northdevonfootballleague.org.uk

NORTH WEST COUNTIES LEAGUE
www.nwcfl.co.uk

NORTHAMPTONSHIRE COMBINATION
www.northantscombination.co.uk

NORHTERN ALLIANCE
northernfootballalliance.org.uk

NORTHERN COUNTIES EAST LEAGUE
www.ncel.org.uk

NORTHERN LEAGUE
www.northernleague.org

NORTHERN PREMIER LEAGUE
www.unibondleague.com

NOTTS SENIOR LEAGUE
www.nottsseniorleague.co.uk

PETERBOROUGH & DISTRICT LEAGUE
www.pdfl.org

READING LEAGUE
www.rdgleague.co.uk

SHROPSHIRE COUNTY LEAGUE
www.scpfl.co.uk

SOUTH WALES AMATEUR LEAGUE
www.southwalesamateurleague.co.uk

SOUTH WEST PENINSULAR LEAGUE
www.swpleague.co.uk

SOUTHERN LEAGUE
www.southern-football-league.co.uk

SPARTAN SOUTH MIDLANDS LEAGUE
www.ssmfl.org

STAFFORDSHIRE COUNTY SENIOR LEAGUE
www.staffordshirecountyseniorleague.co.uk

SUFFOLK & IPSWICH LEAGUE
www.suffolkandipswichleague.co.uk

SUSSEX COUNTY LEAGUE
www.scfl.org.uk

UNITED COUNTIES LEAGUE
www.ebucl.com

WEARSIDE LEAGUE
www.wearside-football-league.org.uk

WELSH ALLIANCE
www.welshallianceleague.co.uk

WELSH LEAGUE
www.welshleague.org.uk

WELSH NATIONAL LEAGUE (WREXHAM AREA)
www.wnl.org.uk

WELSH PREMIER LEAGUE
www.welsh-premier.com

WESSEX LEAGUE
www.wessexleague.co.uk

WEST CHESHIRE LEAGUE
www.west-cheshire.org.uk

WEST RIDING COUNTY AMATEUR LEAGUE
www.wrc.leaguemanager.biz

WEST YORKSHIRE LEAGUE
www.wya.leaguemanager.biz

WESTERN LEAGUE
www.toolstationleague.com

WESTMORLAND LEAGUE
www.westmorlandfootball.co.uk

WILTSHIRE LEAGUE
www.wiltshirefootballleague.com

F A CHALLENGE CUP

EXTRA-PRELIMINARY ROUND
(£500 to each winning club)

New Mills 2 Atherton Collieries 1 *(at Atherton Colls)*	Att: 71
Sunderland Nissan 5 Darlington Railway Athletic 0	Att: 50
Glasshoughton Welfare 2 Bacup Borough 0	Att: 29
Hall Road Rangers 0 **Durham City** 1	Att: 127
Atherton LR 5 Parkgate 1	Att: 17
Congleton Town 1 Winsford United 0	Att: 153
Dunston Federation Brewery 4 Holker Old Boys 0	Att: 119
Cheadle Town 3 Crook Town 1	Att: 142
Whickham 1 Marske United 2	Att: 150
Jarrow Roofing BCA 5 Billingham Synthonia 2	Att: 67
Whitley Bay 2 Northallerton Town 1	Att: 139
Hebburn Town 3 Alnwick Town 1	Att: 69
Selby Town 3 Morpeth Town 3	Att: 58
Replay: Morpeth Town 3 Selby Town 1 *aet*	Att: 84
Salford City 0 Shildon 1	Att: 75
Billingham Town 5 Borrowash Victoria 2	Att: 110
Bishop Auckland 3 Squires Gate 1	Att: 84
Thackley 1 Ramsbottom United 1	Att: 77
Replay: Ramsbottom United 0 **Thackley** 1	Att: 94
Prudhoe Town 0 Consett 5	Att: 55
Blackpool Mechanics 2 **Armthorpe Welfare** 0	Att: 60
(Blackpool Mechanics expelled)	
Ashington 0 Thornaby 0	Att: 146
Replay: Thornaby 3 Ashington 2	Att: 60
Daisy Hill 1 Winterton Rangers 1	Att: 52
Replay: **Winterton Rangers** 3 Daisy Hill 0	Att: 91
West Allotment Celtic 1 Norton/Stockton Ancients 1	Att: 44
Replay: Norton/Stockton Anc. 6 West Allotment 1	Att: 42
Brandon United 3 Seaham Red Star 5	Att: 65
Liversedge 2 Nelson 0	Att: 105
Oldham Town 1 Trafford 3	Att: 75
Pickering Town 4 Formby 0	Att: 131
Chadderton 2 Rossington Main 1	Att: 30
Retford United 6 Tadcaster Albion 0	Att: 157
Garforth Town 2 Penrith 0	Att: 86
Silsden 1 Hallam 1	Att: 101
Replay: **Hallam** 3 Silsden 2	Att: 75
Tow Law Town 1 St Helens Town 1	Att: 93
Replay: **St Helens Town** 2 Tow Law Town 1	Att: 92
Glossop North End 2 North Shields 0	Att: 102
Norton United 1 Colne 5	Att: 30
Newcastle Blue Star 3 South Shields 1	Att: 97
Teversal 0 Loughborough Dynamo 3	Att: 73
Blackstones 1 Oadby Town 1	Att: 88
Replay: Oadby Town 3 Blackstones 2	Att: 145
Quorn 6 Arnold Town 0	Att: 163
Mickleover Sports 1 Glapwell 0	Att: 167
Staveley Miners Welfare 1 **Boston Town** 5	Att: 75
Atherstone Town 3 Carlton Town 2	Att: 222
Eccleshall 1 Pegasus Juniors 1	Att: 59
Replay: Pegasus Juniors 0 **Eccleshall** 3	Att: 91
Ford Sports Daventry 2 Racing Club Warwick 2	Att: 71
Replay: **RC Warwick** 4 Ford Sports Daventry 1	Att: 96
Deeping Rangers 5 Lincoln Moorlands 4	Att: 114
Coalville Town 4 Studley 0	Att: 94
St Margaretsbury 1 Eton Manor 1	Att: 50
Replay: Eton Manor 1 St Margaretsbury 1 *aet* (4-1p)	Att: 22
Dereham Town 3 Brentwood Town 1	Att: 139
Sawbridgeworth Town 1 **St Neots Town** 2	Att: 101
Haverhill Rovers 2 Welwyn Garden City 0	Att: 119
Felixstowe & Walton United 0 **Potton United** 1	Att: 96
Holmer Green 1 **Wootton Blue Cross** 3	Att: 42
Halstead Town 0 Harefield United 0	Att: 92
Replay: **Harefield United** 3 Halstead Town 1	Att: 115
Broxbourne Borough V & E 1 Colney Heath 0	Att: 30
Fakenham Town 4 Norwich United 0	Att: 86
Stanway Rovers 0 **Leverstock Green** 1	Att: 70
Wembley 3 Thame United 0	Att: 174
Hertford Town 1 Stotfold 2	Att: 67

Cogenhoe United 2 Saffron Walden Town 2	Att: 85
Replay: **Saffron Walden Town** 6 Cogenhoe United 2	Att: 127
Needham Market 2 Desborough Town 1	Att: 102
Bowers & Pitsea 2 Haringey Borough 0	Att: 66
Ruislip Manor 3 Aylesbury Vale 1	Att: 76
Mildenhall Town 8 Kirkley 2	Att: 115
Lowestoft Town 3 Stansted 1	Att: 228
Barkingside 2 Clacton Town 1	Att: 140
Biggleswade Town 4 Clapton 2	Att: 34
Chalfont St Peter 0 **Hullbridge Sports** 1	Att: 63
Langford 2 **Ely City** 4 *(at Biggleswade United)*	Att: 70
Gorleston 0 **Tiptree United** 1	Att: 69
March Town United 3 St Ives Town 3	Att: 185
Replay: **St Ives Town** 2 March Town United 1	Att: 195
Stowmarket Town 1 Soham Town Rangers 1	Att: 99
Replay: Soham Town Rangers 1 **Stowmarket Town** 4	Att: 110
Walsham-le-Willows 1 **Leiston** 4	Att: 202
Long Melford 1 **Cornard United** 3	Att: 84
Long Buckby 2 London APSA 1	Att: 70
Tring Athletic 2 Diss Town 1 *aet*	Att: 105
Royston Town 2 Harwich & Parkeston 2	
Replay: **Harwich & Parkeston** 4 Royston Town 1	Att: 135
Newport Pagnell Town 0 **Romford** 1	Att: 133
Oxhey Jets 3 Concord Rangers 0	Att: 97
Ipswich Wanderers 2 Woodbridge Town 2	Att: 127
Replay: Woodbridge Town 1 **Ipswich Wanderers** 3	Att: 179
London Colney 0 **Raunds Town** 1	Att: 53
Newmarket Town 4 Southend Manor 1	Att: 111
Arundel 5 Dorking 1	Att: 84
Farnham Town 0 **Three Bridges** 1	Att: 55
Moneyfields 2 Oakwood 1	Att: 64
Croydon 0 **Sandhurst Town** 2	Att: 79
Wick 1 Westfield 1	Att: 57
Replay: **Westfield** 0 Wick 0 *aet* (5-3p)	
East Preston 3 Milton United 1	Att: 79
Ash United 5 Deal Town 0	Att: 80
Chessington & Hook United 3 Mile Oak 1	Att: 151
Saltdean United 0 **Lancing** 1	Att: 49
Brockenhurst 1 **Hamble ASSC** 2	Att: 48
Guildford City 0 **Whitstable Town** 1	Att: 95
Reading Town 3 **Thamesmead Town** 4	Att: 44
Egham Town 2 Hungerford Town 3	Att: 49
Rye United 0 **Bedfont Green** 2 *(at Yeading)*	Att: 140
Hassocks 1 Wantage Town 0	Att: 91
Frimley Green 1 **VTFC** 5	Att: 30
Lymington Town 0 **Sidley United** 4 *(at Bashley)*	Att: 122
Sporting Bengal United 0 **Slade Green** 2	Att: 155
Selsey 0 **AFC Totton** 5	Att: 135
Redhill 1 **Cowes Sports** 2	Att: 112
Eastbourne United Association 0 Cobham 0	Att: 84
Replay: **Cobham** 2 Eastbourne United Association 1	Att: 245
Abingdon Town 3 Camberley Town 0	Att: 60
Raynes Park Vale 1 **Shoreham** 6	Att: 61
Hythe Town 2 Lordswood 2	Att: 147
Replay: Lordswood 0 **Hythe Town** 6	Att: 49
Herne Bay 1 **Erith & Belvedere** 6	Att: 125
Erith Town 0 Hailsham Town 2	Att: 52
Banstead Athletic 1 **Worthing United** 2	Att: 49
Carterton 1 Gosport Borough 0	Att: 81
Devizes Town 3 Calne Town 0	Att: 79
Almondsbury Town 0 **Odd Down** 1	Att: 76
Christchurch 3 Bitton 1	Att: 63
Shortwood United 4 Backwell United 2	Att: 65
Fairford Town 2 Harrow Hill 0	Att: 83
Westbury United 2 **Slimbridge** 3	Att: 55
Welton Rovers 2 Wimborne Town 0	Att: 70
St Blazey 1 Bodmin Town 0	Att: 82
Corsham Town 4 Shepton Mallet 0	Att: 82
Melksham Town 2 Torrington 1	Att: 42
Bemerton Heath Harlequins 1 **Downton** 3	Att: 145
Bristol Manor Farm 0 Barnstaple Town 0	Att: 55

WWW.NLNEWSDESK.CO.UK

Replay: **Barnstaple Town** 5 Bristol Manor Farm 3	Att: 160
Liskeard Athletic 4 Sherborne Town 1	Att: 88
Witney United 2 Highworth Town 1	Att: 145
Bournemouth 2 Minehead Town 0	Att: 70
Wadebridge Town 1 Elmore 1 *(at Bodmin Town)*	
Replay: **Elmore** 3 Wadebridge Town 2	Att: 57
Brislington 0 **Dawlish Town** 1	Att: 40
Hamworthy United 1 **Hallen** 2	Att: 100
Penzance 1 **Clevedon United** 2	Att: 105
Porthleven 0 **Newquay** 1	Att: 118

PRELIMINARY ROUND

(£1,000 to each winning club)

Pontefract Collieries 0 **Woodley Sports** 3	Att: 56
Spennymoor Town 3 Bamber Bridge 1	Att: 159
Trafford 4 Brodsworth Miners Welfare 1	Att: 121
Bridlington Town 1 **Bishop Auckland** 2	Att: 144
Cammell Laird 2 Morpeth Town 0	Att: 135
Norton & Stockton Ancients 5 Darwen 1	Att: 40
Consett 1 Rossendale United 1	Att: 161
Replay: **Rossendale United** 2 Consett 1	Att: 132
Eccleshill United 2 Glasshoughton Welfare 1	Att: 74
Garforth Town 1 **Chorley** 2	Att: 124
Guisborough Town 0 **Hallam** 3	Att: 130
Goole 5 Bradford Park Avenue 3	Att: 276
Pickering Town 0 **New Mills** 1	Att: 105
Atherton LR 0 **Clitheroe** 3	Att: 94
Glossop North End 2 Seaham Red Star 1	Att: 97
Shildon 0 **Harrogate Railway Athletic** 3	Att: 199
Bedlington Terriers 1 **Curzon Ashton** 4	Att: 188
St Helens Town 0 **Skelmersdale United** 3	Att: 141
Alsager Town 6 Cheadle Town 0	Att: 120
Sheffield 0 Retford United 0	Att: 264
Replay: Retford United 1 **Sheffield** 1 *aet* (0-3p)	Att: 272
Liversedge 2 Newcastle Blue Star 2	Att: 152
Replay: **Newcastle Blue Star** 3 Liversedge 2	Att: 163
Yorkshire Amateur 1 **Warrington Town** 5	Att: 41
Abbey Hey 1 **Chadderton** 2	Att: 55
Thornaby 0 **Chester-le-Street Town** 2	Att: 63
Jarrow Roofing Boldon CA 5 Thackley 4	Att: 57
Colwyn Bay 1 Ossett Albion 1	Att: 207
Replay: **Ossett Albion** 4 Colwyn Bay 2	Att: 99
Whitley Bay 1 Stocksbridge Park Steels 0	Att: 138
Maine Road 1 **Armthorpe Welfare** 2	Att: 74
Sunderland Nissan 3 Horden Colliery Welfare 2	Att: 29
Winterton Rangers 3 West Auckland Town 0	Att: 101
Marske United 3 Brigg Town 1	Att: 149
Hebburn Town 3 Flixton 3	Att: 102
Replay: **Flixton** 3 Hebburn Town 0	Att: 80
Padiham 3 Colne 2	Att: 158
Billingham Town 4 Congleton Town 0	Att: 140
Long Eaton United 1 Washington 0	Att: 86
Wakefield 3 **Dunston Federation Brewery** 2	Att: 126
Newcastle Benfield BP 3 Ryton 3	Att: 69
Replay: Ryton 0 **Newcastle Benfield BP** 2	Att: 174
Esh Winning 3 **Durham City** 5	Att: 91
Rocester 1 Oldbury United 0	Att: 101
Eccleshall 0 **Shepshed Dynamo** 2	Att: 110
Kidsgrove Athletic 2 Spalding United 0	Att: 128
Tipton Town 1 Rushall Olympic 0	Att: 137
Coalville Town 0 Chasetown 0	Att: 180
Replay: **Coalville Town** 3 Chasetown 1	Att: 34
Nantwich Town 1 **Deeping Rangers** 2	Att: 165
Gresley Rovers 1 South Normanton Athletic 1	Att: 223
Replay: South Normanton 1 **Gresley R.** 1 *aet* (3-5p)	Att: 145
Stratford Town 2 Bourne Town 2	Att: 125
Replay: Bourne Town 2 **Stratford Town** 3	Att: 148
Buxton 4 Atherstone Town 1	Att: 418
Eastwood Town 5 Bromsgrove Rovers 5	Att: 178
Replay: **Bromsgrove Rovers** 2 Eastwood Town 0	Att: 221
Gedling Town 4 Holbeach United 0	Att: 50
Newcastle Town 2 Stourbridge 1	Att: 108
Sutton Coldfield Town 3 Leek CSOB 0	Att: 88

Alvechurch 1 **Bedworth United** 2	Att: 168
Solihull Borough 6 Sutton Town 2	Att: 119
Belper Town 2 Boston Town 2	Att: 164
Replay: Boston Town 1 **Belper Town** 2	Att: 84
Shirebrook Town 3 Barwell 1	Att: 90
Westfields 3 Racing Club Warwick 0	Att: 71
Quorn 3 Malvern Town 0	Att: 103
Romulus 0 Stourport Swifts 0	Att: 147
Replay: Stourport Swifts 0 **Romulus** 5	Att: 70
Oadby Town 7 Cradley Town 0	Att: 136
Loughborough Dynamo 1 **Willenhall Town** 2	Att: 174
Biddulph Victoria 2 Boldmere St Michaels 2	Att: 94
Replay: **Boldmere St Michaels** 7 Biddulph Victoria 0	Att: 69
Leamington 6 Stone Dominoes 0	Att: 527
Causeway United 3 Mickleover Sports 2	Att: 50
Great Yarmouth Town 0 **Needham Market** 2	Att: 109
Tilbury 0 **Romford** 2	Att: 102
Cornard United 1 **St Ives Town** 3	Att: 50
Wroxham 1 Aylesbury United 1	Att: 193
Replay: Aylesbury United 1 **Wroxham** 2	Att: 286
Arlesey Town 2 Ilford 2	Att: 161
Replay: Ilford 1 **Arlesey Town** 2 *aet*	Att: 74
Harefield United 1 **Wivenhoe Town** 4	Att: 121
Broxbourne Borough V & E 1 Stotfold 1	Att: 25
Replay: Stotfold 0 **Broxbourne Borough V & E** 4	Att: 54
Long Buckby 3 Flackwell Heath 2	Att: 87
Harwich & Parkeston 0 **Leiston** 4	Att: 133
Marlow 0 **Waltham Forest** 2	Att: 116
Barkingside 0 **Maldon Town** 2	Att: 11
Haverhill Rovers 3 Wootton Blue Cross 0	Att: 132
Uxbridge 0 **Potton United** 2	Att: 79
Wisbech Town 4 Mildenhall Town 1	Att: 202
Biggleswade United 2 **AFC Hornchurch** 4	Att: 155
Raunds Town 1 Enfield 1	Att: 109
Replay: Enfield 1 **Raunds Town** 2	Att: 83
Bowers & Pitsea 0 **Dunstable Town** 1	Att: 72
Leverstock Green 1 **Beaconsfield SYCOB** 2	Att: 79
Stowmarket Town 0 **Dereham Town** 2	Att: 67
Northampton Spencer 2 **Chesham United** 3	Att: 138
St Neots Town 2 Brackley Town 2	Att: 148
Replay: **Brackley Town** 4 St Neots Town 0	Att: 164
Hadleigh United 2 **Rothwell Town** 3	Att: 125
Great Wakering Rovers 4 Newmarket Town 1	Att: 108
Hullbridge Sports 0 **Yaxley** 2	Att: 5
Tiptree United 2 Ipswich Wanderers 1	Att: 107
Lowestoft Town 2 Witham Town 0	Att: 298
Barton Rovers 0 **Barking** 1	Att: 92
Biggleswade Town 0 Leighton Town 0	Att: 5
Replay: **Leighton Town** 2 Biggleswade Town 0	Att: 110
Potters Bar Town 2 Waltham Abbey 2	Att: 94
Replay: Waltham Abbey 1 **Potters Bar Town** 2	Att: 152
Ruislip Manor 2 Enfield Town 1	Att: 174
Hanwell Town 2 Buckingham Town 2	Att: 116
Replay: **Buckingham Town** 3 Hanwell Town 2	Att: 116
Ely City 0 **Woodford United** 3	Att: 118
Bury Town 6 Brook House 1	Att: 16
Berkhamsted Town 2 **AFC Sudbury** 6	Att: 17
Eton Manor 0 **Wingate & Finchley** 2	Att: 3
Hillingdon Borough 1 **Tring Athletic** 2	Att: 6
Burnham Ramblers 0 Ware 0	Att: 9
Replay: Ware 1 **Burnham Ramblers** 2	Att: 9
Harlow Town 0 **Saffron Walden Town** 1	Att: 18
Aveley 0 **Oxhey Jets** 1	Att: 6
Canvey Island 4 Fakenham Town 1	Att: 34
Wembley 0 **Redbridge** 3	Att: 7
Hailsham Town 0 **AFC Totton** 1	Att: 9
Kingstonian 3 Pagham 1	Att: 30
Hungerford Town 1 Littlehampton Town 0	Att: 5
Croydon Athletic 4 Arundel 2	Att: 9
Fareham Town 2 **Carterton** 2	Att: 10
Cowes Sports 1 Sandhurst Town 0	Att: 10
Dover Athletic 3 Bracknell Town 0	Att: 51
Whyteleafe 3 Ash United 2	Att: 9

Fleet Town 1 Thatcham Town 0 — Att: 128
Walton Casuals 2 **Cray Wanderers** 3 — Att: 75
Sevenoaks Town 1 **Moneyfields** 3 — Att: 83
Dulwich Hamlet 3 Three Bridges 0 — Att: 244
Colliers Wood United 1 Chipstead 1 — Att: 77
Replay: Chipstead 1 **Colliers Wood United** 2 — Att: 86
AFC Wallingford 1 Burnham 0 — Att: 55
Peacehaven & Telscombe 0 **Whitehawk** 1 — Att: 112
Ashford Town 7 Bedfont Green 0 — Att: 147
Epsom & Ewell 0 **Leatherhead** 2 — Att: 205
Bedfont 0 **Whitstable Town** 1 — Att: 81
Maidstone United 2 Burgess Hill Town 1 — Att: 400
Godalming Town 1 North Greenford United 1 — Att: 71
Replay: **North Greenford United** 4 Godalming 2 *aet* — Att: 110
Slade Green 2 Cobham 2 — Att: 74
Replay: **Cobham** 2 Slade Green 0 *aet* — Att: 67
Sittingbourne 3 Thamesmead Town 1 — Att: 167
Eastbourne Town 2 VCD Athletic 2 — Att: 259
Replay: **VCD Athletic** 1 Eastbourne Town 0 — Att: 154
Hassocks 2 Newport IOW 0 — Att: 154
Ardley United 3 Ringmer 0 — Att: 128
Hythe Town 1 **VTFC** 3 — Att: 162
Lymington & New Milton 4 Shoreham 2 — Att: 108
Cove 0 **Tooting & Mitcham United** 6 — Att: 110
Oxford City 2 Abingdon United 2 — Att: 160
Replay: Abingdon United 3 **Oxford City** 4 *aet* — Att: 303
Hastings United 0 Merstham 0 — Att: 281
Replay: Merstham 2 **Hastings United** 4 *aet* — Att: 147
Sidley United 0 **Worthing United** 1 — Att: 195
Winchester City 4 Chatham Town 3 — Att: 151
Horsham YMCA 1 **Molesey** 2 — Att: 122
Lancing 3 North Leigh 1 — Att: 84
East Preston (w/o) v Horley Town (scr.)
Andover 1 Corinthian Casuals 1 — Att: 135
Replay: Corinthian Casuals 3 **Andover** 4 *aet* — Att: 129
Windsor & Eton 1 **Bashley** 2 — Att: 104
Metropolitan Police 7 Chessington & Hook 0 — Att: 108
Chertsey Town 3 Abingdon Town 2 — Att: 130
Hamble ASSC 1 East Grinstead Town 1 — Att: 77
Replay: East Grinstead Town 1 **Hamble ASSC** 3 — Att: 130
Tunbridge Wells 0 **Dartford** 5 — Att: 280
Westfield 2 **Alton Town** 5 — Att: 70
Didcot Town 2 Erith & Belvedere 1 — Att: 206
Penryn Athletic 2 **Slimbridge** 3 — Att: 72
Liskeard Athletic 1 Welton Rovers 0 — Att: 68
Saltash United 3 Barnstaple Town 3 — Att: 108
Replay: Barnstaple Town 0 **Saltash United** 1 — Att: 159
Odd Down 0 **Bridgwater Town** 1 — Att: 64
Downton 2 Christchurch 1 — Att: 75
Radstock Town 3 Elmore 1 — Att: 46
Melksham Town 1 **Cinderford Town** 2 — Att: 98
Street 0 **Bishops Cleeve** 1 — Att: 61
Tavistock 4 Bridport 2 — Att: 120
Fairford Town 3 Bournemouth 0 — Att: 64
Poole Town 0 **Taunton Town** 1 — Att: 184
Evesham United 6 Clevedon United 0 — Att: 128
Bideford 2 Hallen 1 — Att: 192
Falmouth Town 1 **Bishop Sutton** 2 — Att: 110
Paulton Rovers 1 Witney United 1 — Att: 102
Replay: Witney United 1 **Paulton Rovers** 2 — Att: 146
Devizes Town 1 Swindon Supermarine 1 — Att: 141
Replay: **Swindon Supermarine** 3 Devizes Town 0 — Att: 149
Chard Town 0 **Willand Rovers** 4 — Att: 87
Shortwood United 0 **Truro City** 5 — Att: 89
Corsham Town 3 Dawlish Town 1 — Att: 103
Newquay 1 St Blazey 1 — Att: 250
Replay: **St Blazey** 3 Newquay 1 — Att: 289

FIRST QUALIFYING ROUND
(£2,250 to each winning club)

Chorley 1 **North Ferriby United** 3 — Att: 242
Durham City 2 Alsager Town 0 *(at Spennymoor)* — Att: 125
Eccleshill United 1 **Flixton** 2 — Att: 76

Witton Albion 3 Sheffield 2 — Att: 231
Armthorpe Welfare 1 **Burscough** 3 — Att: 113
Cammell Laird 0 **Newcastle Benfield BP** 2 — Att: 181
Fleetwood Town 3 Jarrow Roofing Boldon CA 0 — Att: 377
Guiseley 2 **Mossley** 1 — Att: 253
Long Eaton United 1 **Warrington Town** 3 — Att: 79
Glossop North End 3 New Mills 1 — Att: 430
Chadderton 1 Trafford 1 — Att: 123
Replay: **Trafford** 3 Chadderton 1 — Att: 151
Winterton Rangers 0 **Kendal Town** 5 — Att: 106
Hallam 2 Sunderland Nissan 1 — Att: 102
Clitheroe 0 **Marine** 2 — Att: 345
Radcliffe Borough 1 **Skelmersdale United** 2 — Att: 217
Whitby Town 2 **Frickley Athletic** 4 — Att: 293
Harrogate Railway 3 **Marske United** 4 — Att: 182
Gateshead 3 Rossendale United 1 — Att: 166
Whitley Bay 3 Norton & Stockton Ancients 2 — Att: 218
Newcastle Blue Star 0 **Prescot Cables** 4 — Att: 103
Chester-le-Street Town 0 **Wakefield** 1 — Att: 92
Woodley Sports 4 Bishop Auckland 0 *(at Cheadle T.)* — Att: 103
Ossett Town 1 **Ossett Albion** 2 — Att: 356
Curzon Ashton 4 Billingham Town 2 — Att: 120
Goole 4 Spennymoor Town 1 — Att: 252
Ashton United 4 Padiham 2 — Att: 115
Sutton Coldfield Town 3 Newcastle Town 0 — Att: 85
Oadby Town 4 Grantham Town 2 — Att: 277
Bedworth United 1 **Matlock Town** 3 — Att: 254
AFC Telford United 2 **Halesowen Town** 4 — Att: 1,472
Gresley Rovers 0 **Quorn** 1 — Att: 208
Rugby Town 4 Deeping Rangers 1 — Att: 202
Kidsgrove Athletic 0 Leek Town 0 — Att: 395
Replay: Leek Town 1 **Kidsgrove Athletic** 1 — Att: 412
Romulus 6 Shirebrook Town 0 — Att: 83
Hednesford Town 1 Gedling Town 1 — Att: 367
Replay: **Gedling Town** 1 Hednesford Town 0 — Att: 150
Shepshed Dynamo 0 **Chasetown** 2 — Att: 218
Causeway United 2 Boldmere St Michaels 0 — Att: 110
Tipton Town 1 Buxton 1 — Att: 191
Replay: **Buxton** 2 Tipton Town 1 — Att: 491
Belper Town 4 Westfields 0 — Att: 142
Rocester 1 Leamington 0 — Att: 267
Ilkeston Town 1 Bromsgrove Rovers 1 — Att: 433
Replay: Bromsgrove Rovers 0 **Ilkeston Town** 1 — Att: 374
Corby Town 1 **Solihull Borough** 3 — Att: 236
Lincoln United 2 Stamford 2 — Att: 107
Replay: Lincoln United 1 **Stamford** 2 — Att: 258
Willenhall Town 2 **Stratford Town** 3 — Att: 137
Canvey Island 1 **Lowestoft Town** 3 — Att: 464
Boreham Wood 8 St Ives Town 2 — Att: 201
Hendon 4 Arlesey Town 0 — Att: 132
Potters Bar Town 2 Wealdstone 1 — Att: 234
Hitchin Town 1 Saffron Walden Town 1 — Att: 351
Replay: Saffron Walden 1 **Hitchin Town** 1 *aet* (1-4p) — Att: 517
Hemel Hempstead Town 6 Leyton 3 — Att: 189
AFC Sudbury 1 Waltham Forest 0 — Att: 278
Woodford United 3 Wroxham 1 — Att: 102
Great Wakering Rovers 2 Burnham Ramblers 1 — Att: 164
Redbridge 1 **AFC Hornchurch** 2 — Att: 251
Heybridge Swifts 6 Potton United 1 — Att: 209
Buckingham Town 1 **Raunds Town** 4 — Att: 137
Hampton & Richmond Borough 1 Billericay 1 — Att: 331
Replay: Billericay 0 Hampton & RB 0 *aet* (4-1p) — Att: 314
Dunstable Town 3 Leiston 2 — Att: 132
Haverhill Rovers 3 Broxbourne Borough V & E 1 — Att: 176
Banbury United 5 Beaconsfield SYCOB 1 — Att: 382
Wingate & Finchley 1 **East Thurrock United** 2 — Att: 77
Tiptree United 0 **Brackley Town** 4 — Att: 86
Maldon Town 2 Staines Town 1 — Att: 76
Tring Athletic 1 **King's Lynn** 5 — Att: 301
Wivenhoe Town 1 **Yaxley** 2 — Att: 83
Long Buckby 1 **Rothwell Town** 2 — Att: 145
Bury Town 0 **Wisbech Town** 2 — Att: 284
Oxhey Jets 2 Ruislip Manor 0 — Att: 98

Harrow Borough 2 Northwood 0 — Att: 225
Romford 3 Leighton Town 0 — Att: 156
Chesham United 2 **Cheshunt** 3 — Att: 338
Barking 1 **Chelmsford City** 4 — Att: 269
Needham Market 3 **Dereham Town** 4 — Att: 156
Worthing 3 Colliers Wood United 0 — Att: 275
Ashford Town 1 **Tonbridge Angels** 3 — Att: 394
Cobham 1 **Slough Town** 2 — Att: 200
Sittingbourne 3 Hassocks 0 — Att: 183
Margate 0 Fleet Town 0 — Att: 535
Replay: Fleet Town 0 **Margate** 1 — Att: 171
Maidenhead United 1 Carterton 1 — Att: 197
Replay: Carterton 2 **Maidenhead United** 3 — Att; 120
Dover Athletic 6 Alton Town 1 — Att: 559
Dartford 0 **Hastings United** 2 — Att: 274
Whyteleafe 1 **Folkestone Invicta** 2 — Att: 190
Ashford Town (Middx) 4 Maidstone United 0 — Att: 401
Molesey 1 Leatherhead 1 — Att: 198
Replay: **Leatherhead** 3 Molesey 0 — Att: 209
Hungerford Town 3 Ardley United 0 — Att: 61
Tooting & Mitcham United 6 Lancing 0 — Att: 282
Bromley 4 AFC Totton 0 — Att: 610
Cowes Sports 1 **Lymington & New Milton** 2 — Att: 179
Oxford City 5 Chertsey Town 0 — Att: 134
North Greenford United 0 **VTFC** 1 — Att: 68
Kingstonian 1 **Ramsgate** 2 — Att: 317
Andover 0 **Carshalton Athletic** 2 — Att: 197
Walton & Hersham 3 Dulwich Hamlet 0 — Att: 141
Whitstable Town 1 Croydon Athletic 0 — Att: 330
Winchester City 2 Cray Wanderers 2 — Att: 193
Replay: **Cray Wdrs** 2 Winchester City 2 *aet* (5-4p) — Att: 168
Bashley 5 VCD Athletic 0 — Att: 196
AFC Wimbledon 1 Horsham 0 — Att: 1,966
Worthing United 3 Hamble ASSC 2 — Att: 62
Didcot Town 6 Whitehawk 1 — Att: 228
Moneyfields 3 AFC Wallingford 1 — Att: 93
East Preston 1 **Metropolitan Police** 3 — Att: 81
Fairford Town 0 **Cinderford Town** 3 — Att: 94
Downton 0 **Team Bath** 7 — Att: 160
St Blazey 3 Saltash United 1 — Att: 255
Cirencester Town 2 **Merthyr Tydfil** 3 — Att: 228
Bishop Sutton 0 Bishops Cleeve 0 — Att: 58
Replay: **Bishops Cleeve** 5 Bishop Sutton 1 — Att: 158
Radstock Town 1 **Evesham United** 6 — Att: 88
Mangotsfield United 1 Paulton Rovers 0 — Att: 255
Taunton Town 2 Swindon Supermarine 2 — Att: 264
Replay: Swindon Supermarine 2 **Taunton Town** 3 — Att: 176
Bath City 0 Tiverton Town 0 — Att: 567
Replay: Tiverton Town 1 **Bath City** 3 — Att: 500
Bideford 2 Bridgwater Town 2 — Att: 372
Replay: Bridgwater Town 0 **Bideford** 2 — Att: 440
Willand Rovers 4 Tavistock 0 — Att: 102
Clevedon Town 1 Truro City 1 — Att: 231
Replay: Truro City 0 **Clevedon Town** 1 — Att: 580
Gloucester City 0 Liskeard Athletic 0 — Att: 344
Replay: Liskeard Athletic 0 **Gloucester City** 3 — Att: 200
Yate Town 1 **Slimbridge** 2 — Att: 190
Chippenham Town 2 Corsham Town 0 — Att: 671

SECOND QUALIFYING ROUND
(£3,750 to each winning club)

North Ferriby United 0 **Whitley Bay** 2 — Att: 174
Leigh RMI 0 **Woodley Sports** 2 — Att: 130
Droylsden 2 Worksop Town 0 — Att: 474
Burscough 3 Blyth Spartans 2 — Att: 334
Trafford 5 Glossop North End 0 — Att: 169
Marske United 0 **Skelmersdale United** 2 — Att: 349
Farsley Celtic 3 Wakefield 0 — Att: 280
Witton Albion 3 Vauxhall Motors 0 — Att: 308
Prescot Cables 1 **Marine** 2 — Att: 332
Hyde United 0 **Newcastle Benfield BP** 2 — Att: 268
Scarborough 1 Lancaster City 1 — Att: 667
Replay: Scarborough 1 **Lancaster City** 2 — Att: 248

Ashton United 0 **Gainsborough Trinity** 2 — Att: 153
Durham City 5 Hallam 1 *(at Esh Winning)* — Att: 125
Flixton 1 **Barrow** 0 — Att: 222
Ossett Albion 2 Workington 1 — Att: 210
Curzon Ashton 0 **Harrogate Town** 2 — Att: 173
Guiseley 1 Gateshead 0 — Att: 402
Fleetwood Town 4 Goole 2 — Att: 427
Stalybridge Celtic 1 Frickley Athletic 1 — Att: 449
Replay: Frickley Athletic 0 **Stalybridge Celtic** 1 — Att: 338
Kendal Town 1 Warrington Town 1 — Att: 245
Replay: **Warrington Town** 3 Kendal Town 2 *ae* — Att: 132
Raunds Town 1 **Stratford Town** 2 — Att: 126
Halesowen Town 3 Chasetown 1 — Att: 598
Sutton Coldfield Town 0 **Cambridge City** 2 — Att: 163
Worcester City 2 Romulus 0 — Att: 692
Replay: Romulus 1 **Worcester City** 3 — Att: 344
Solihull Borough 1 Alfreton Town 1 — Att: 265
Replay: Solihull Borough 1 **Alfreton Town** 3 *aet* — Att: 229
Histon 0 **Matlock Town** 1 — Att: 524
Lincoln United 0 **Hucknall Town** 2 — Att: 158
Redditch United 2 **Wisbech Town** 3 — Att: 387
Oadby Town 0 **Nuneaton Borough** 6 — Att: 714
Kidsgrove Athletic 6 Rothwell Town 0 — Att: 200
Gedling Town 0 **Rocester** 2 — Att: 79
Belper Town 1 Quorn 1 — Att: 209
Replay: **Quorn** 3 Belper Town 1 — Att: 317
King's Lynn 3 Causeway United 1 — Att: 843
Ilkeston Town 1 **Rugby Town** 3 — Att: 393
Kettering Town 5 Yaxley 1 — Att: 1,066
Moor Green 4 Hinckley United 2 — Att: 302
Buxton 0 **Woodford United** 1 — Att: 542
East Thurrock United 1 **Maidenhead United** 2 — Att: 122
Cray Wanderers 1 Leatherhead 1 — Att: 116
Replay: **Leatherhead** 4 Cray Wanderers 2 — Att: 227
Ramsgate 0 **Yeading** 1 — Att: 316
Heybridge Swifts 2 Didcot Town 2 — Att: 270
Replay: Didcot Town 1 **Heybridge Swifts** 3 — Att: 344
Braintree Town 0 **Brackley Town** 2 — Att: 365
Hemel Hempstead Town 4 Harrow Borough 2 — Att: 265
AFC Wimbledon 3 Oxhey Jets 0 — Att: 1,747
Worthing United 4 Romford 2 — Att: 165
Hastings United 1 Metropolitan Police 1 — Att: 351
Replay: **Metropolitan Police** 5 Hastings United 1 — Att: 134
Hendon 0 **Lewes** 2 — Att: 210
Fisher Athletic 7 Sittingbourne 1 — Att: 204
Maldon Town 0 Potters Bar Town 0 — Att: 149
Replay: **Potters Bar Town** 3 Maldon Town 2 *aet* — Att: 102
Sutton United 1 **Bishop's Stortford** 3 — Att: 449
Haverhill Rovers 1 Eastbourne Borough 0 — Att: 504
Farnborough Town 2 Slough Town 0 — Att: 525
Worthing 0 Cheshunt 0 — Att: 326
Replay: **Cheshunt** 1 Worthing 0 — Att: 130
Great Wakering Rovers 0 **Carshalton Athletic** 1 — Att: 165
Lowestoft Town 0 **Bromley** 1 — Att: 651
Tooting & Mitcham United 2 **AFC Sudbury** 3 — Att: 392
Folkestone Invicta 1 Welling United 1 — Att: 508
Replay: **Welling United** 3 Folkestone Invicta 2 — Att: 548
Whitstable Town 1 **Margate** 2 — Att: 1,144
Walton & Hersham 2 Ashford Town (Middx) 2 — Att: 202
Replay: **Ashford (Middx)** 3 Walton & Hersham 1 *aet* — Att: 247
Billericay Town 0 Hayes 0 — Att: 468
Replay: **Hayes** 2 Billericay Town 1 — Att: 193
Thurrock 0 **Dover Athletic** 3 — Att: 274
Tonbridge Angels 1 Banbury United 1 — Att: 596
Replay: Tonbridge Angels 1 **Banbury United** 2 — Att: 518
Bedford Town 3 Dunstable Town 2 — Att: 616
Hitchin Town 0 Bognor Regis Town 0 — Att: 356
Replay: Bognor Regis Town 0 **Hitchin Town** 1 — Att: 340
Boreham Wood 0 **AFC Hornchurch** 2 — Att: 311
Dereham Town 2 Chelmsford City 2 — Att: 472
Replay: **Chelmsford City** 4 Dereham Town 0 — Att: 646
Dorchester Town 3 Cinderford Town 0 — Att: 308
Bishops Cleeve 3 Oxford City 1 — Att: 203

Eastleigh 3 Gloucester City 2 — Att: 418
Clevedon Town 3 Willand Rovers 1 — Att: 186
Slimbridge 3 Chippenham Town 1 — Att: 375
Lymington & New Milton 0 Basingstoke Town 0 — Att: 202
Replay: **Basingstoke Town** 1 Lymington & NM 0 — Att: 324
Bideford 0 **Newport County** 3 — Att: 680
Bashley 3 Taunton Town 1 — Att: 279
Moneyfields 1 **Evesham United** 4 — Att: 157
Bath City 0 Merthyr Tydfil 0 — Att: 645
Replay: **Merthyr Tydfil** 3 Bath City 2 — Att: 553
Havant & Waterlooville 3 Team Bath 1 — Att: 400
VTFC 0 **Salisbury City** 3 — Att: 370
Weston-super-Mare 1 **Hungerford Town** 2 — Att: 247
Mangotsfield United 3 St Blazey 1 — Att: 302

THIRD QUALIFYING ROUND
(£5,000 to each winning club)

Ossett Albion 1 Scarborough 1 — Att: 582
Replay: **Scarborough** 2 Ossett Albion 0 — Att: 804
Durham City 0 **Barrow** 1 *(at Esh Winning)* — Att: 287
Woodley Sports 0 **Gainsborough Trinity** 2 — Att: 435
(at Gainsborough Trinity)
Droylsden 3 Skelmersdale United 2 — Att: 490
Whitley Bay 2 Blyth Spartans 2 — Att: 2,023
Replay: Blyth Spartans 1 **Whitley Bay** 2 — Att: 1,697
Trafford 0 **Harrogate Town** 1 — Att: 284
Guiseley 0 **Newcastle Benfield BP** 1 — Att: 429
Marine 3 Stalybridge Celtic 2 — Att: 511
Witton Albion 1 Farsley Celtic 1 — Att: 343
Replay: **Farsley Celtic** 1 Witton Albion 0 *aet* — Att: 224
Fleetwood Town 2 Warrington Town 0 — Att: 567
Halesowen Town 1 **King's Lynn** 2 — Att: 632
Nuneaton Borough 0 **Hucknall Town** 1 — Att: 1,090
Bedford Town 0 **Moor Green** 2 — Att: 632
Solihull Borough 1 **Wisbech Town** 2 — Att: 274
Cambridge City 0 Matlock Town 0 — Att: 414
Replay: Matlock Town 2 **Cambridge City** 3 *aet* — Att: 504
Woodford United 1 **AFC Sudbury** 3 — Att: 309
Kettering Town 2 Rocester 1 — Att: 1,057
Worcester City 1 Hemel Hempstead Town 1 — Att: 767
Replay: Hemel Hempstead Town 0 **Worcester City** 2 — Att: 366
Bishop's Stortford 2 Stratford Town 1 — Att: 489
Rugby Town 1 **Chelmsford City** 3 — Att: 546
Haverhill Rovers 2 Kidsgrove Athletic 1 — Att: 669
Quorn 0 Brackley Town 0 — Att: 300
Replay: **Brackley Town** 2 Quorn 1 — Att: 230
Mangotsfield United 1 Leatherhead 1 — Att: 410
Replay: **Leatherhead** 4 Mangotsfield United 1 — Att: 282
Bashley 1 **Hungerford Town** 2 — Att: 320
Maidenhead United 3 Worthing United 1 — Att: 304
Dorchester Town 0 **Lewes** 4 — Att: 425
Heybridge Swifts 0 **Dover Athletic** 3 — Att: 424
Hayes 1 **Bromley** 3 — Att: 261
Margate 1 **Potters Bar Town** 2 — Att: 725
AFC Hornchurch 1 Welling United 1 — Att: 1,002
Replay: **Welling United** 3 AFC Hornchurch 1 — Att: 712
Clevedon Town 1 Hitchin Town 1 — Att: 203
Replay: Hitchin Town 2 **Clevedon Town** 2 *aet* (3-4p) — Att: 286
Fisher Athletic 6 Metropolitan Police 1 — Att: 237
Cheshunt 1 **Tonbridge Angels** 2 — Att: 265
Eastleigh 0 **Salisbury City** 1 — Att: 1,402
Newport County 4 Bishops Cleeve 2 — Att: 809
AFC Wimbledon 2 Evesham United 1 — Att: 1,935
Merthyr Tydfil 2 Slimbridge 0 — Att: 511
Havant & Waterlooville 2 Carshalton Athletic 0 — Att: 241
Farnborough Town 1 Yeading 1 — Att: 564
Replay: **Yeading** 3 Farnborough Town 0 — Att: 206
Basingstoke Town 3 Ashford Town (Middx) 0 — Att: 626

FOURTH QUALIFYING ROUND
(£10,000 to each winning club)

Barrow 3 Marine 2 — Att: 1,078
Stafford Rangers 3 Scarborough 0 — Att: 1,043

Tamworth 3 Harrogate Town 1 — Att: 719
Gainsborough Trinity 2 Whitley Bay 0 — Att: 780
King's Lynn 3 Hucknall Town 0 — Att: 1,371
Newcastle Benfield BP 0 **York City** 1 — Att: 926
Fleetwood Town 3 Wisbech Town 0 — Att: 1,005
Rushden & Diamonds 3 Altrincham 0 — Att: 1,509
Burton Albion 1 Halifax Town 0 — Att: 1,938
Northwich Victoria 2 Cambridge United 0 — Att: 1,039
Farsley Celtic 2 Cambridge City 1 — Att: 494
Southport 0 **Kettering Town** 1 — Att: 943
Kidderminster Harriers 5 Droylsden 1 — Att: 1,424
Moor Green 1 **Morecambe** 2 — Att: 550
Worcester City 1 Basingstoke Town 1 — Att: 1,128
Replay: **Basingstoke Town** 1 Worcester 1 *aet* (7-6p) — Att: 681
Crawley Town 2 **Lewes** 3 — Att: 1,646
Dover Athletic 0 Bishop's Stortford 0 — Att: 1,322
Replay: **Bishop's Stortford** 3 Dover Athletic 2 — Att: 767
Hungerford Town 0 **Weymouth** 3 — Att: 839
Woking 3 Potters Bar Town 2 — Att: 1,443
Maidenhead United 1 Merthyr Tydfil 0 — Att: 711
Welling United 0 **Clevedon Town** 3 — Att: 802
Stevenage Borough 4 Forest Green Rovers 1 — Att: 1,190
Tonbridge Angels 0 **Newport County** 1 — Att: 1,549
Dagenham & Redbridge 0 **Oxford United** 1 — Att: 2,605
Yeading 2 St Albans City 1 — Att: 376
Haverhill Rovers 0 **Aldershot Town** 4 — Att: 1,710
Exeter City 2 AFC Wimbledon 1 — Att: 4,562
AFC Sudbury 1 **Leatherhead** 2 — Att: 815
Chelmsford City 1 Gravesend & Northfleet 0 — Att: 1,609
Grays Athletic 1 **Bromley** 2 — Att: 820
Fisher Athletic 0 **Salisbury City** 1 — Att: 432
Brackley Town 0 **Havant & Waterlooville** 2 — Att: 505

FIRST ROUND
(£16,000 to each winning club)

AFC Bournemouth 4 Boston United 0 — Att: 4,263
Wycombe Wanderers 2 Oxford United 1 — Att: 6,279
Peterborough United 3 Rotherham United 0 — Att: 4,281
Torquay United 2 Leatherhead 1 — Att: 2,218
Morecambe 2 Kidderminster Harriers 1 — Att: 1,673
Tranmere Rovers 4 Woking 2 — Att: 4,591
Salisbury City 3 Fleetwood Town 0 — Att: 2,684
Chelmsford City 1 Aldershot Town 1 — Att: 2,838
Replay: **Aldershot Town** 2 Chelmsford City 0 — Att: 2,731
Weymouth 2 Bury 2 — Att: 2,503
Replay: **Bury** 4 Weymouth 3 — Att: 2,231
Nottingham Forest 5 Yeading 0 — Att: 7,704
Stafford Rangers 1 Maidenhead United 1 — Att: 1,526
Replay: Maidenhead United 0 **Stafford Rangers** 2 — Att: 1,934
Shrewsbury Town 0 Hereford United 0 — Att: 5,574
Replay: **Hereford United** 2 Shrewsbury Town 0 — Att: 4,224
Northampton Town 0 Grimsby Town 0 — Att: 4,092
Replay: Grimsby Town 0 **Northampton Town** 2 — Att: 2,657
Wrexham 1 Stevenage Borough 0 — Att: 2,863
Chesterfield 0 **Basingstoke Town** 1 — Att: 3,539
Gainsborough Trinity 1 **Barnet** 3 — Att: 1,914
Lewes 1 **Darlington** 4 — Att: 1,500
Clevedon Town 1 **Chester City** 4 — Att: 2,261
Barrow 2 **Bristol Rovers** 3 — Att: 2,939
Rushden & Diamonds 3 Yeovil Town 1 — Att: 2,530
Burton Albion 1 **Tamworth** 2 — Att: 4,150
Farsley Celtic 0 Milton Keynes Dons 0 — Att: 2,365
Replay: **Milton Keynes Dons** 2 Farsley Celtic 0 — Att: 2,676
Brentford 0 **Doncaster Rovers** 1 — Att: 3,607
Gillingham 4 Bromley 1 — Att: 5,547
York City 0 **Bristol City** 1 — Att: 3,525
Bishop's Stortford 3 **King's Lynn** 5 — Att: 1,750
Exeter City 1 **Stockport County** 2 — Att: 4,454
Newport County 1 **Swansea City** 3 — Att: 4,660
Kettering Town 3 **Oldham Athletic** 4 — Att: 3,481
Rochdale 1 Hartlepool United 1 — Att: 2,098
Replay: **Hartlepool Utd** 0 Rochdale 0 *aet* (4-2p) — Att: 2,788
Brighton & Hove Albion 8 Northwich Victoria 0 — Att: 4,487

Mansfield Town 1 Accrington Stanley 0 — Att: 3,909
Cheltenham Town 0 Scunthorpe United 0 — Att: 2,721
Replay: **Scunthorpe United** 2 Cheltenham Town 0 — Att: 3,074
Macclesfield Town 0 Walsall 0 — Att: 2,018
Replay: Walsall 0 **Macclesfield Town** 1 — Att: 3,114
Bradford City 4 Crewe Alexandra 0 — Att: 3,483
Leyton Orient 2 Notts County 1 — Att: 3,011
Swindon Town 3 Carlisle United 1 — Att: 4,938
Huddersfield Town 0 **Blackpool** 1 — Att: 6,597
Havant/Waterlooville 1 **Millwall** 2 *(at Portsmouth)* — Att: 5,793
Port Vale 2 Lincoln City 1 — Att: 3,884

SECOND ROUND
(£24,000 to each winning club)

Milton Keynes Dons 0 **Blackpool** 2 — Att: 3,837
Scunthorpe United 0 **Wrexham** 2 — Att: 5,054
Brighton & Hove Albion 3 Stafford Rangers 0 — Att: 5,741
Bristol City 4 Gillingham 3 — Att: 5,663
Hereford United 4 Port Vale 0 — Att: 4,076
Macclesfield Town 2 Hartlepool United 1 — Att: 1,992
Stockport County 2 Wycombe Wanderers 1 — Att: 3,821
Bury 2 Chester City 2 — Att: 3,428
Replay: Chester City 1 **Bury** 3 — Att: 2,810
(Bury expelled)
Barnet 4 Northampton Town 1 — Att: 2,786
Tranmere Rovers 1 **Peterborough United** 2 — Att: 6,308
King's Lynn 0 **Oldham Athletic** 2 — Att: 5,444
Darlington 1 **Swansea City** 3 — Att: 4,183
Salisbury City 1 Nottingham Forest 1 — Att: 3,100
Replay: **Nottingham Forest** 2 Salisbury City 0 — Att: 6,177
Torquay United 1 Leyton Orient 1 — Att: 2,392
Replay: Leyton Orient 1 **Torquay United** 2 — Att: 2,384
Bristol Rovers 1 AFC Bournemouth 1 — Att: 6,252
Replay: AFC Bournemouth 0 **Bristol Rovers** 1 — Att: 4,153
Bradford City 0 Millwall 0 — Att: 4,346
Replay: **Millwall** 1 Bradford City 0 *aet* — Att: 3,220
Swindon Town 1 Morecambe 0 — Att: 5,942
Mansfield Town 1 Doncaster Rovers 1 — Att: 4,837
Replay: **Doncaster Rovers** 2 Mansfield Town 0 — Att: 5,338
Aldershot Town 1 Basingstoke Town 1 — Att: 4,525
Replay: Basingstoke Town 1 **Aldershot Town** 3 — Att: 3,010
Rushden & Diamonds 1 **Tamworth** 2 — Att: 2,815

THIRD ROUND
(£40,000 to each winning club)

Blackpool 4 Aldershot Town 2 — Att: 6,355
Barnet 2 Colchester United 1 — Att: 3,075
Sheffield United 0 **Swansea City** 3 — Att: 15,896
Reading 3 Burnley 2 — Att: 11,514
Portsmouth 2 Wigan Athletic 1 — Att: 14,336
Doncaster Rovers 0 **Bolton Wanderers** 4 — Att: 14,297
West Ham United 3 Brighton & Hove Albion 0 — Att: 32,874
Leicester City 2 Fulham 2 — Att: 15,499
Replay: **Fulham** 4 Leicester City 3 — Att: 11,222
Derby County 3 Wrexham 1 — Att: 15,609
Wolverhampton Wanderers 2 Oldham Athletic 2 — Att: 14,524
Replay: Oldham Athletic 0 **Wolverhampton W.** 2 — Att: 9,628
Chester City 0 Ipswich Town 0 — Att: 4,330
Replay: **Ipswich Town** 1 Chester City 0 — Att: 11,732
Manchester United 2 Aston Villa 1 — Att: 74,924
Sheffield Wednesday 1 Manchester City 1 — Att: 28,487
Replay: **Manchester City** 2 Sheffield Wednesday 1 — Att: 25,621
Tamworth 1 **Norwich City** 4 — Att: 3,165
Nottingham Forest 2 Charlton Athletic 0 — Att: 19,017
Cardiff City 0 Tottenham Hotspur 0 — Att: 20,376
Replay: **Tottenham Hotspur** 4 Cardiff City 0 — Att: 27,641
Preston North End 1 Sunderland 0 — Att: 10,318
Liverpool 1 **Arsenal** 3 — Att: 43,617
Bristol Rovers 1 Hereford United 0 — Att: 8,978
Watford 4 Stockport County 1 — Att: 11,475
Crystal Palace 2 Swindon Town 1 — Att: 10,238
Bristol City 3 Coventry City 3 — Att: 13,336
Replay: Coventry City 0 **Bristol City** 2 — Att: 13,055

Peterborough United 1 Plymouth Argyle 1 — Att: 6,2..
Replay: **Plymouth Argyle** 2 Peterborough United 1 — Att: 9,9.
Queens Park Rangers 2 Luton Town 2 — Att: 10,0.
Replay: **Luton Town** 1 Queens Park Rangers 0 — Att: 7,4.
Southend United 1 Barnsley 1 — Att: 5,4.
Replay: Barnsley 0 **Southend United** 2 — Att: 4,9.
West Bromwich Albion 3 Leeds United 1 — Att: 16,9.
Hull City 1 Middlesbrough 1 — Att: 17,5.
Replay: **Middlesbrough** 4 Hull City 3 — Att: 16,7.
Birmingham City 2 Newcastle United 1 — Att: 26,0.
Replay: Newcastle United 1 **Birmingham City** 5 — Att: 26,0.
Torquay United 0 **Southampton** 2 — Att: 5,3.
Everton 1 **Blackburn Rovers** 4 — Att: 24,4.
Chelsea 6 Macclesfield Town 1 — Att: 41,3.
Stoke City 2 Millwall 0 — Att: 8,0.

FOURTH ROUND
(£60,000 to each winning club)

Arsenal 1 Bolton Wanderers 1 — Att: 59,7.
Replay: Bolton Wanderers 1 **Arsenal** 3 — Att: 21,08.
West Ham United 0 **Watford** 1 — Att: 31,1.
Bristol City 2 Middlesbrough 2 — Att: 19,0.
Replay: **Middlesbrough** 2 Bristol City 2 *aet* (5-4p) — Att: 26,3.
Chelsea 3 Nottingham Forest 0 — Att: 41,5.
Ipswich Town 1 Swansea City 0 — Att: 16,6.
Tottenham Hotspur 3 Southend United 1 — Att: 33,4.
Barnet 0 **Plymouth Argyle** 2 — Att: 5,2.
Birmingham City 2 **Reading** 3 — Att: 20,04.
Derby County 1 Bristol Rovers 0 — Att: 25,0.
Manchester City 3 Southampton 1 — Att: 26,4.
Crystal Palace 0 **Preston North End** 2 — Att: 8,4.
Manchester United 2 Portsmouth 1 — Att: 71,1.
Blackpool 1 Norwich City 1 — Att: 9,4.
Replay: **Norwich City** 3 Blackpool 2 *aet* — Att: 19,1.
Luton Town 0 **Blackburn Rovers** 4 — Att: 5,88.
Wolverhampton Wdrs 0 **West Bromwich Albion** 3 — Att: 28,1.
Fulham 3 Stoke City 0 — Att: 11,05.

FIFTH ROUND
(£120,000 to each winning club)

Chelsea 4 Norwich City 0 — Att: 41,5.
Watford 1 Ipswich Town 0 — Att: 17,01.
Preston North End 1 **Manchester City** 3 — Att: 18,89.
Plymouth Argyle 2 Derby County 0 — Att: 18,02.
Manchester United 1 Reading 1 — Att: 70,60.
Replay: Reading 2 **Manchester United** 3 — Att: 23,82.
Arsenal 0 Blackburn Rovers 0 — Att: 56,76.
Replay: **Blackburn Rovers** 1 Arsenal 0 — Att: 18,88.
Middlesbrough 2 West Bromwich Albion 2 — Att: 31,49.
Replay: West Brom. 2 **Middlesbrough** 2 *aet* (4-5p) — Att: 24,92.
Fulham 0 **Tottenham Hotspur** 4 — Att: 18,65.

QUARTER-FINALS
(£300,000 to each winning club)

Middlesbrough 2 Manchester United 2 — Att: 33,30.
Replay: **Manchester United** 1 Middlesbrough 0 — Att: 61,32.
Blackburn Rovers 2 Manchester City 0 — Att: 27,74.
Chelsea 3 Tottenham Hotspur 3 — Att: 41,51.
Replay: Tottenham Hotspur 1 **Chelsea** 2 — Att: 35,51.
Plymouth Argyle 0 **Watford** 1 — Att: 20,65.

SEMI-FINALS
(£900,000 to each winning club)

Chelsea 2 Blackburn Rovers 1 *aet* — Att: 50,55.
(at Manchester United)
Manchester United 4 Watford 1 — Att: 37,42.
(at Aston Villa)

FINAL
(£1,000,000 to winning club)
(May 19th at Wembley Stadium)

Chelsea 1 Manchester United 0 *aet* — Att: 89,82.

F A CHALLENGE TROPHY

PRELIMINARY ROUND
(£1,000 to each winning club)

Warrington Town 3 Wakefield 2 — Att: 104
Willenhall Town 3 Gresley Rovers 1 — Att: 152
Belper Town 0 Skelmersdale United 0 — Att: 143
Replay: **Skelmersdale United** 2 Belper Town 1 — Att: 204
Alsager Town 2 Stocksbridge Park Steels 0 — Att: 114
Clitheroe 3 Bamber Bridge 2 — Att: 244
Goole 0 Kidsgrove Athletic 0 — Att: 165
Replay: **Kidsgrove Athletic** 3 Goole 2 — Att: 144
Cammell Laird 2 Rossendale United 0 — Att: 151
Enfield Town 0 **Rothwell Town** 2 — Att: 207
Dartford 4 Ilford 2 — Att: 227
Canvey Island 0 **Maldon Town** 3 — Att: 338
Horsham YMCA 3 Aveley 1 — Att: 143
Maidstone United 2 Bury Town 0 — Att: 307
Enfield 1 Corinthian Casuals 1 — Att: 76
Replay: Corinthian Casuals 0 **Enfield** 1 — Att: 84
Godalming Town 1 **Dunstable Town** 2 — Att: 102
Tooting & Mitcham United 2 Dulwich Hamlet 2 — Att: 322
Replay: Dulwich Hamlet 6 **Tooting & Mitcham** 7 *aet* — Att: 288
Chatham Town 1 **AFC Sudbury** 2 — Att: 230
Waltham Forest 1 Ashford Town 1 — Att: 45
Replay: Ashford Town 1 **Waltham F.** 1 *aet* (4-5p) — Att: 101
Waltham Abbey 1 Burgess Hill Town 0 — Att: 103
Redbridge 2 **Sittingbourne** 3 — Att: 74
Leatherhead 1 Berkhamsted Town 1 — Att: 191
Replay: Berkhamsted Town 2 **Leatherhead** 4 — Att: 84
Molesey 3 Metropolitan Police 0 — Att: 110
Leighton Town 2 Woodford United 1 — Att: 97
AFC Hornchurch 2 Fleet Town 1 — Att: 464
Hastings United 2 Croydon Athletic 1 — Att: 246
Arlesey Town 0 Flackwell Heath 0 — Att: 112
Replay: Flackwell Heath 1 **Arlesey Town** 2 — Att: 39
Oxford City 1 Bashley 1 — Att: 91
Replay: Bashley 1 **Oxford City** 3 — Att: 150
Bromsgrove Rovers 1 Abingdon United 1 — Att: 242
Replay: **Abingdon United** 3 Bromsgrove Rovers 2 *aet* — Att: 165
Andover 3 Chesham United 1 — Att: 159
Bishops Cleeve 1 Newport IOW 0 — Att: 134
Uxbridge 1 Marlow 1 — Att: 118
Replay: **Marlow** 3 Uxbridge 3 *aet* (5-4p) — Att: 102
Lymington & New Milton 1 **Brook House** 4 — Att: 113
Bracknell Town 2 Beaconsfield SYCOB 1 — Att: 104
Cinderford Town 2 **Windsor & Eton** 3 — Att: 124
Malvern Town 0 **Stourbridge** 4 — Att: 127

FIRST QUALIFYING ROUND
(£1,350 to each winning club)

Witton Albion 2 Fleetwood Town 1 — Att: 284
Alsager Town 3 Brigg Town 0 — Att: 97
Skelmersdale United 3 Prescot Cables 0 — Att: 244
Guiseley 5 Grantham Town 4 — Att: 282
Sutton Coldfield Town 2 Gateshead 2 — Att: 102
Replay: **Gateshead** 3 Sutton Coldfield Town 0 — Att: 119
Spalding United 1 **Ilkeston Town** 4 — Att: 145
Burscough 2 Matlock Town 1 — Att: 260
Radcliffe Borough 3 Leek Town 2 — Att: 163
Rushall Olympic 3 Colwyn Bay 0 — Att: 140
Warrington Town 1 **Clitheroe** 1 — Att: 132
Bridlington Town 2 **Stamford** 4 — Att: 199
Mossley 5 Lincoln United 1 — Att: 276
Kendal Town 4 Buxton 2 — Att: 239
Woodley Sports 6 Marine 1 — Att: 142
Kidsgrove Athletic 2 Harrogate Railway Athletic 1 — Att: 111
Ossett Albion 2 Willenhall Town 2 — Att: 129

Replay: **Willenhall Town** 2 Ossett Albion 1 — Att: 101
Hednesford Town 2 Halesowen Town 2 — Att: 613
Replay: **Halesowen Town** 2 Hednesford Town 1 — Att: 362
North Ferriby United 1 Bradford Park Avenue 2 — Att: 235
Replay: **Bradford Park Ave.** 3 North Ferriby Utd 2 — Att: 188
Whitby Town 3 Shepshed Dynamo 0 — Att: 356
Frickley Athletic 0 **Cammell Laird** 4 — Att: 205
Ossett Town 2 **Ashton United** 3 — Att: 142
Chasetown 3 Chorley 1 — Att: 320
AFC Telford United 1 Eastwood Town 1 — Att: 1,485
Replay: **Eastwood Town** 1 AFC Telford United 0 — Att: 325
Hampton & Richmond Borough 5 Hitchin Town 3 — Att: 229
Worthing 0 **King's Lynn** 1 — Att: 278
AFC Wimbledon 2 Dunstable Town 1 — Att: 1,344
Staines Town 0 **Folkestone Invicta** 1 — Att: 215
Boreham Wood 1 **Tooting & Mitcham United** 1 — Att: 194
Replay: **Tooting & Mitcham** 2 Boreham Wood 0 — Att: 205
Wivenhoe Town 1 **Margate** 3 — Att: 182
Ware 0 **Enfield** 1 — Att: 151
Wingate & Finchley 0 **Northwood** 1 — Att: 77
Maidenhead United 3 Dover Athletic 1 — Att: 290
Hastings United 0 **Waltham Forest** 1 — Att: 250
Wealdstone 2 Witham Town 0 — Att: 179
Corby Town 2 **Hemel Hempstead Town** 4 — Att: 189
Dartford 6 Horsham YMCA 0 — Att: 235
Bromley 6 East Thurrock United 3 — Att: 555
Carshalton Athletic 4 Potters Bar Town 1 — Att: 216
Cheshunt 0 **Cray Wanderers** 1 — Att: 105
Waltham Abbey 1 Heybridge Swifts 1 — Att: 103
Replay: **Heybridge Swifts** 8 Waltham Abbey 0 — Att: 176
Billericay Town 2 Aylesbury United 2 — Att: 388
Replay: Aylesbury United 1 **Billericay Town** 4 — Att: 165
Leatherhead 1 Rothwell Town 0 — Att: 151
Maldon Town 0 Leyton 0 — Att: 92
Replay: **Leyton** 3 Maldon Town 1 — Att: 52
Hendon 1 **Ramsgate** 2 — Att: 128
Tonbridge Angels 3 Harlow Town 1 — Att: 478
Leighton Town 4 Slough Town 1 — Att: 179
Molesey 3 Barton Rovers 1 — Att: 80
Chelmsford City 1 **Maidstone United** 2 — Att: 859
Walton & Hersham 0 **Great Wakering Rovers** 1 — Att: 66
AFC Sudbury 2 Kingstonian 2 — Att: 406
Replay: Kingstonian 2 **AFC Sudbury** 3 — Att: 307
Ashford Town (Middx) 2 Brackley Town 1 — Att: 103
Sittingbourne 0 Arlesey Town 0 — Att: 209
Replay: Arlesey Town 1 **Sittingbourne** 2 — Att: 146
Whyteleafe 0 Walton Casuals 0 — Att: 101
Replay: **Walton Casuals** 5 Whyteleafe 0 — Att:
Tilbury 0 **Horsham** 1 — Att: 91
AFC Hornchurch 1 Harrow Borough 0 — Att: 440
Bedworth United 0 Solihull Borough 0 — Att: 176
Replay: **Solihull Borough** 5 Bedworth United 1 — Att: 129
Thatcham Town 1 **Didcot Town** 3 — Att: 205
Evesham United 2 Brook House 0 — Att: 92
Stourport Swifts 1 **Mangotsfield United** 5 — Att: 107
Clevedon Town 1 **Windsor & Eton** 3 — Att: 174
Hanwell Town 1 Rugby Town 0 — Att: 86
Burnham 0 **Team Bath** 5 — Att: 78
Bath City 2 Bishops Cleeve 1 — Att: 363
Taunton Town 0 Banbury United 0 — Att: 319
Replay: **Banbury United** 5 Taunton Town 1 — Att: 319
Paulton Rovers 0 **Cirencester Town** 3 — Att: 110
Tiverton Town 2 Gloucester City 2 — Att: 479
Replay: **Gloucester City** 2 Tiverton T. 2 *aet* (4-2p) — Att: 372
Merthyr Tydfil 2 Stourbridge 0 — Att: 373
Abingdon United 4 Bracknell Town 2 — Att: 140

Winchester City 1 Oxford City 0 — Att: 167
Marlow 0 Andover 0 — Att: 152
Replay: Andover 1 **Marlow** 2 — Att: 187
Swindon Supermarine 2 Yate Town 1 — Att: 164
Hillingdon Borough 2 Chippenham Town 2 — Att: 140
Replay: **Chippenham Town** 3 Hillingdon Boro. 0 *aet* — Att: 337

SECOND QUALIFYING ROUND
(£2,000 to each winning club)

Cammell Laird 2 Mossley 1 — Att: 190
Skelmersdale United 4 Kendal Town 2 — Att: 177
Burscough 3 Eastwood Town 0 — Att: 233
Woodley Sports 3 Whitby Town 2 — Att: 80
Ashton United 0 **Gateshead** 1 — Att: 126
Halesowen Town 1 Clitheroe 1 — Att: 324
Replay: **Clitheroe** 1 Halesowen Town 0 — Att: 229
Witton Albion 2 Alsager Town 0 — Att: 233
Ilkeston Town 2 Guiseley 0 — Att: 275
Willenhall Town 1 Rushall Olympic 1 — Att: 132
Replay: **Rushall Olympic** 2 Willenhall Town 0 — Att: 212
Bradford Park Avenue 2 Solihull Borough 0 — Att: 250
Kidsgrove Athletic 0 Chasetown 0 — Att: 193
Replay: **Chasetown** 1 Kidsgrove Athletic 1 *aet* (3-2p) — Att: 302
Radcliffe Borough 1 **Stamford** 2 — Att: 156
Maidstone United 2 **Ashford Town (Middx)** 3 — Att: 321
Enfield 1 Walton Casuals 1 — Att: 126
Replay: Walton Casuals 2 **Enfield Town** 2 *aet* (4-5p) — Att: 73
Sittingbourne 0 Bath City 0 — Att: 310
Replay: **Bath City** 4 Sittingbourne 0 — Att: 317
Folkestone Invicta 1 **Billericay Town** 3 — Att: 344
Hanwell Town 2 **Cirencester Town** 3 — Att: 101
Hemel Hempstead Town 1 Abingdon United 4 — Att: 155
Chippenham Town 3 Didcot Town 3 — Att: 455
Replay: **Didcot Town** 3 Chippenham Town 1 *aet* — Att: 396
Carshalton Athletic 0 **Heybridge Swifts** 1 — Att: 223
Leyton 1 **King's Lynn** 2 — Att: 154
AFC Wimbledon 3 Tonbridge Angels 2 — Att: 1,347
Tooting & Mitcham United 1 Bromley 1 — Att: 467
Replay: Bromley 0 **Tooting & Mitcham United** 1 — Att: 482
Leatherhead 0 **Team Bath** 3 — Att: 254
Dartford 0 **Evesham United** 1 — Att: 274
Leighton Town 2 Wealdstone 2 — Att: 223
Replay: **Wealdstone** 3 Leighton Town 0 — Att: 159
Gloucester City 1 Margate 0 — Att: 428
AFC Hornchurch 1 **Mangotsfield United** 3 — Att: 484
Molesey 1 Swindon Supermarine 0 — Att: 133
Windsor & Eton 2 Hampton & Richmond 0 — Att: 291
AFC Sudbury 2 Ramsgate 0 — Att: 329
Maidenhead United 2 Horsham 1 — Att: 322
Northwood 0 Winchester City 0 — Att: 131
Replay: Winchester City 1 **Northwood** 4 — Att: 147
Great Wakering Rovers 0 **Merthyr Tydfil** 1 — Att: 127
Waltham Forest 1 **Cray Wanderers** 2 — Att: 100
Marlow 0 **Banbury United** 2 — Att: 255

THIRD QUALIFYING ROUND
(£3,000 to each winning club)

Lancaster City 0 **Redditch United** 1 — Att: 209
Skelmersdale United 1 **Farsley Celtic** 2 — Att: 216
Hinckley United 1 Ilkeston Town 0 — Att: 507
Chasetown 0 **Hyde United** 3 — Att: 418
Droylsden 3 Rushall Olympic 1 — Att: 332
Kettering Town 10 Clitheroe 1 — Att: 761
Leigh RMI 1 Cammell Laird 0 — Att: 130
Alfreton Town 0 **Harrogate Town** 1 — Att: 273
Stamford 0 **Witton Albion** 3 — Att: 306
Blyth Spartans 1 Worcester City 1 — Att: 707
Replay: **Worcester City** 1 Blyth Spartans 1 *aet* (5-4p) — Att: 754
Hucknall Town 1 Barrow 1 — Att: 369
Replay: **Barrow** 2 Hucknall Town 1 — Att: 713
Gainsborough Trinity 1 Stalybridge Celtic 1 — Att: 448
Replay: **Stalybridge Celtic** 2 Gainsborough Trinity 1 — Att: 249
Moor Green 0 **Woodley Sports** 3 — Att: 180

Bradford Park Avenue 1 **Nuneaton Borough** 2 — Att: 218
Workington 2 **Gateshead** 4 — Att: 454
Burscough 1 **Scarborough** 2 — Att: 409
Vauxhall Motors 2 Worksop Town 2 — Att: 176
Replay: Worksop Town 0 **Vauxhall Motors** 1 — Att: 355
Banbury United 2 **Lewes** 3 — Att: 461
Windsor & Eton 1 **King's Lynn** 2 — Att: 151
Cambridge City 0 **AFC Sudbury** 1 — Att: 523
Havant & Waterlooville 3 Team Bath 0 — Att: 174
Ashford Town (Middx) 2 Thurrock 1 — Att: 171
AFC Wimbledon 1 Eastleigh 1 — Att: 1,346
Replay: Eastleigh 2 **AFC Wimbledon** 2 *aet* (2-4p) — Att: 631
Bishop's Stortford 2 Molesey 1 — Att: 271
Basingstoke Town 2 Bedford Town 0 — Att: 405
Northwood 1 **Histon** 2 — Att: 142
Merthyr Tydfil 2 Wealdstone 1 — Att: 353
Heybridge Swifts 2 Bognor Regis Town 0 — Att: 227
Weston-super-Mare 1 Cirencester Town 0 — Att: 241
Hemel Hempstead 2 Evesham United 2 — Att: 233
Evesham United 3 Hemel Hempstead 3 *aet* (4-2p) — Att: 87
Didcot Town 0 **Newport County** 3 — Att: 632
Gloucester City 2 **Eastbourne Borough** 5 — Att: 273
Cray Wanderers 1 Yeading 1 — Att: 169
Replay: **Yeading** 7 Cray Wanderers 1 — Att: 58
Sutton United 2 **Braintree Town** 3 — Att: 385
Salisbury City 2 Enfield 1 — Att: 1,452
Billericay Town 1 **Mangotsfield United** 2 — Att: 373
Welling United 3 Dorchester Town 0 — Att: 404
Hayes 0 **Fisher Athletic** 5 — Att: 194
Bath City 1 Tooting & Mitcham United 1 — Att: 541
Replay: Tooting & Mitcham United 0 **Bath City** 1 — Att: 263
Farnborough Town 1 Maidenhead United 1 — Att: 344
Replay: Maidenhead United 0 **Farnborough Town** 3 — Att: 217

FIRST ROUND
(£4,000 to each winning club)

Lancaster City 0 **Redditch United** 1 — Att: 209
Skelmersdale United 1 **Farsley Celtic** 2 — Att: 216
Hinckley United 1 Ilkeston Town 0 — Att: 507
Chasetown 0 **Hyde United** 3 — Att: 418
Droylsden 3 Rushall Olympic 1 — Att: 332
Kettering Town 10 Clitheroe 1 — Att: 761
Leigh RMI 1 Cammell Laird 0 — Att: 130
Alfreton Town 0 **Harrogate Town** 1 — Att: 273
Stamford 0 **Witton Albion** 3 — Att: 306
Blyth Spartans 1 Worcester City 1 — Att: 707
Replay: **Worcester City** 1 Blyth Spartans 1 *aet* (5-4p) — Att: 754
Hucknall Town 1 Barrow 1 — Att: 369
Replay: **Barrow** 2 Hucknall Town 1 — Att: 713
Gainsborough Trinity 1 Stalybridge Celtic 1 — Att: 448
Replay: **Stalybridge Celtic** 2 Gainsborough Trinity 1 — Att: 249
Moor Green 0 **Woodley Sports** 3 — Att: 180
Bradford Park Avenue 1 **Nuneaton Borough** 2 — Att: 218
Workington 2 **Gateshead** 4 — Att: 454
Burscough 1 **Scarborough** 2 — Att: 409
Vauxhall Motors 2 Worksop Town 2 — Att: 176
Replay: Worksop Town 0 **Vauxhall Motors** 1 — Att: 355
Banbury United 2 **Lewes** 3 — Att: 461
Windsor & Eton 1 **King's Lynn** 2 — Att: 151
Cambridge City 0 **AFC Sudbury** 1 — Att: 523
Havant & Waterlooville 3 Team Bath 0 — Att: 174
Ashford Town (Middx) 2 Thurrock 1 — Att: 171
AFC Wimbledon 1 Eastleigh 1 — Att: 1,346
Replay: Eastleigh 2 **AFC Wimbledon** 2 *aet* (2-4p) — Att: 631
Bishop's Stortford 2 Molesey 1 — Att: 271
Basingstoke Town 2 Bedford Town 0 — Att: 405
Northwood 1 **Histon** 2 — Att: 142
Merthyr Tydfil 2 Wealdstone 1 — Att: 353
Heybridge Swifts 2 Bognor Regis Town 0 — Att: 227
Weston-super-Mare 1 Cirencester Town 0 — Att: 241
Hemel Hempstead 2 Evesham United 2 *aet* (2-4p) — Att: 233
Didcot Town 0 **Newport County** 3 — Att: 632
Gloucester City 2 **Eastbourne Borough** 5 — Att: 273

Cray Wanderers 1 Yeading 1 — Att: 169
Replay: **Yeading** 7 Cray Wanderers 1 — Att: 58
Sutton United 2 **Braintree Town** 3 — Att: 385
Salisbury City 2 Enfield 1 — Att: 1,452
Billericay Town 1 **Mangotsfield United** 2 — Att: 373
Welling United 3 Dorchester Town 0 — Att: 404
Hayes 0 **Fisher Athletic** 5 — Att: 194
Bath City 1 Tooting & Mitcham United 1 — Att: 541
Replay: Tooting & Mitcham United 0 **Bath City** 1 — Att: 263
Farnborough Town 1 Maidenhead United 1 — Att: 344
Replay: Maidenhead United 0 **Farnborough Town** 3 — Att: 217

SECOND ROUND
(£4,000 to each winning club)

Stalybridge Celtic 1 Kettering Town 1 — Att: 526
Replay: **Kettering Town** 3 Stalybridge Celtic 1 — Att: 938
Oxford United 2 Halifax Town 2 — Att: 2,631
Replay: **Halifax Town** 2 Oxford United 1 — Att: 1,330
Morecambe 5 Mangotsfield United 0 — Att: 859
Tamworth 1 Welling United 1 — Att: 372
Replay: **Welling United** 2 Tamworth 1 — Att: 331
Newport County 0 Histon 0 — Att: 752
Replay: **Histon** 3 Newport County 1 — Att: 485
Eastbourne Borough 0 **Northwich Victoria** 1 — Att: 287
Exeter City 0 **Kidderminster Harriers** 1 — Att: 2,418
Salisbury City 2 Southport 1 — Att: 1,183
Redditch United 3 Dagenham & Redbridge 2 — Att: 762
Worcester City 2 Burton Albion 1 — Att: 1,499
Witton Albion 0 **Rushden & Diamonds** 1 — Att: 602
Weston-super-Mare 0 **Grays Athletic** 4 — Att: 354
Farnborough Town 0 **Braintree Town** 2 — Att: 675
Stevenage Borough 3 Leigh RMI 1 — Att: 1,184
Yeading 2 Bishop's Stortford 0 — Att: 235
Gravesend & Northfleet 0 **AFC Wimbledon** 1 — Att: 2,106
(AFC Wimbledon expelled)

THIRD ROUND
(£6,000 to each winning club)

Histon 1 **Northwich Victoria** 2 — Att: 717
Welling United 2 Worcester City 1 — Att: 606
Kettering Town 0 **Salisbury City** 2 — Att: 1,795
Morecambe 1 Stevenage Borough 1 — Att: 1,131
Replay: **Stevenage Borough** 3 Morecambe 0 *aet* — Att: 1,056
Halifax Town 3 Redditch United 1 — Att: 1,592
Kidderminster Harriers 0 Braintree Town 0 — Att: 1,543
Replay: Braintree Town 1 **Kidderminster Harriers** 3 — Att: 508
Gravesend & Northfleet 2 Rushden & Diamonds 1 — Att: 1,127
Grays Athletic 2 Yeading 1 — Att: 649

QUARTER-FINALS
(£7,000 to each winning club)

Welling United 1 **Grays Athletic** 4 — Att: 1,163
Stevenage Borough 3 Salisbury City 0 — Att: 2,148
Northwich Victoria 3 Gravesend & Northfleet 0 — Att: 810
Kidderminster Harriers 3 Halifax Town 1 — Att: 1,580

SEMI-FINALS
(£16,000 to each winning club)
1st leg

Grays Athletic 0 **Stevenage Borough** 1 — Att: 1,918
Kidderminster Harriers 2 Northwich Victoria 0 — Att: 2,383
1st leg
Northwich Victoria 3 Kidderminster Harriers 2 — Att: 2,125
Stevenage Borough 2 Grays Athletic 0 — Att: 3,008

FINAL
(£50,000 to winning club)
(May 12th at Wembley Stadium)
Stevenage Borough 3 Kidderminster Harriers 2 — Att: 53,262

THE FOOTBALL TRAVELLER

The magazine is published weekly throughout the season and includes up-to-date fixtures from around a hundred different leagues in England, Wales, Ireland and Scotland.......

Plus, all the latest news from around the clubs, programme reviews, club focuses and maps, cup draws, and much, much more.......

All for around a pound a week (including first class postage).

Subscription rates for the 2007/2008 season are:-

£50-00 (full season), £26-00 (half-year to Christmas 2007)

Please write to:

The Football Traveller
Top o' the Bank
Evesham Road
Broadway
Worcs WR12 7DG
Phone:- 01386 853289 Fax:- 01386 858036
E-Mail:- bill.berry@talk21.com

F A CHALLENGE VASE

FIRST QUALIFYING ROUND
(£500 to each winning club)

Esh Winning 0 **Whitley Bay** 4	Att: 91
Darlington Railway Athletic 2 Thornaby 2	Att: 114
Replay: Thornaby 0 **Darlington Railway Athletic** 2	Att: 88
West Allotment Celtic 4 Horden CW 2 *aet*	Att: 132
Prudhoe Town 0 **Norton & Stockton Ancients** 3	Att: 17
Marske United 1 **Sunderland Nissan** 3	Att: 128
Consett 3 Armthorpe Welfare 1	Att: 123
Pontefract Collieries 3 Washington 2	Att: 55
Curzon Ashton 2 Oldham Town 1	Att: 84
Salford City 6 Bootle 2	Att: 82
Atherton LR 3 Ramsbottom United 2 *aet*	Att: 61
Hallam 0 **Flixton** 4 *(at Flixton)*	Att: 63
Anstey Nomads 2 Leek CSOB 1	Att: 58
Newark Town 3 Pilkington XXX 2 *aet*	Att: 44
Ibstock United 0 **Newcastle Town** 1	Att: 77
Blidworth Welfare 0 **Rocester** 2	Att: 31
Highgate United 3 Stone Dominoes 0	Att: 57
Pelsall Villa 0 **Dunkirk** 5	Att: 44
Brocton 2 Kirby Muxloe SC 1	Att: 42
Stratford Town 3 Highfield Rangers 1	Att: 123
Cradley Town 0 **Barnt Green Spartak** 2	Att: 32
Ratby Sports (scr.) v **Market Drayton Town** (w/o)	
Staveley Miners Welafre 0 **Coleshill Town** 5	Att: 58
Alvechurch 3 Shirebrook Town 1	Att: 90
Shifnal Town 4 Eccleshall 0	Att: 70
Carlton Town 2 Westfields 0	Att: 50
Castle Vale 2 Ellistown 0	Att: 49
Oldbury United 2 Stapenhill 1 *aet*	Att: 53
Bridgnorth Town 2 Glapwell 1	Att: 59
Graham Street Prims 0 **Racing Club Warwick** 5	Att: 108
Thurnby Rangers 2 **Clipstone Welfare** 3	Att: 75
Teversal 2 Southam United 1	Att: 58
Radford 2 **Cadbury Athletic** 3 *aet*	Att: 51
Blackwell MW 1 Blaby & Whetstone Athletic 0	Att: 45
Kimberley Town 0 **Barwell** 5	Att: 29
Barrow Town 6 Greenwood Meadows 0	Att: 80
Pershore Town 0 **Sutton Town** 4	Att: 77
Ely City 6 Cornard United 1	Att: 58
Norwich United 0 **Ipswich Wanderers** 2	Att: 44
Felixstowe & Walton 2 **Kirkley** 3	Att: 86
Holbeach United 2 **Diss Town** 3	Att: 129
Arlesey Athletic 0 **Wootton Blue Cross** 2	Att: 92
Bedfont Green 4 Desborough Town 2	Att: 85
Sawbridgeworth Town 2 North Greenford United 1	Att: 60
Haringey Borough 1 **Halstead Town** 4	Att: 61
Edgware Town 3 Hertford Town 0	Att: 71
Sileby Rangers 3 **Harpenden Town** 4	Att: 61
Cogenhoe United 4 Basildon United 2	Att: 42
Romford 3 Bugbrooke St Michael 0	Att: 108
Brimsdown Rovers 2 Sun Postal Sports 0	
Stotfold 1 **Wellingborough Town** 3	Att: 54
Raunds Town 7 Stansted 1	Att: 68
London APSA 3 Colney Heath 1 *(at Colney Heath)*	Att: 56
Tunbridge Wells 3 East Grinstead Town 2	Att: 102
Selsey 2 Rye United 1	Att: 118
Lingfield 2 East Preston 0	Att: 69
Shoreham 0 **Whitstable Town** 2	Att: 80
Guildford City 4 Redhill 2 *aet*	Att: 67
Egham Town 4 Saltdean United 1	Att: 87
Worthing United 1 **Peacehaven & Telscombe** 3	Att: 35
Deal Town 0 **Eastbourne Town** 2	Att: 106
Eastbourne United Association 4 Faversham Town 0	Att: 92
Bicester Town 2 **Abingdon Town** 4	Att: 46
Shrewton United 1 Wootton Bassett Town 1	Att: 71
Replay: Wootton Bassett Town 2 **Shrewton Utd** 3 *aet*	Att: 70
Holmer Green 1 United Services Portsmouth 0	Att: 54

Highworth Town 3 Westbury United 2	Att: 119
Melksham Town 2 Hungerford Town 0	Att: 62
Kidlington 0 **Witney United** 4	Att: 92
Gosport Borough 4 Downton 0	Att: 133
VTFC 0 **Chalfont St Peter** 2	Att: 86
Marlow United 2 Bournemouth 1	Att: 161
Bishop Sutton 2 Penzance 1	Att: 56
Fairford Town 4 Cullompton Rangers 4 *aet* (4-3p)	Att: 68
Clevedon United 2 Shaftesbury 0	Att: 48
Hamworthy United 2 Shepton Mallet 0	Att: 91
Street 2 Ottery St Mary 2	Att: 60
Replay: Ottery St Mary 1 **Street** 5	Att: 28
Odd Down 2 Larkhall Athletic 1	Att: 78
Willand Rovers 4 Newquay 2	Att: 97
Brislington 1 **Hallen** 1	Att: 60
Replay: **Hallen** 3 Brislington 1	Att: 84
Plymouth Parkway 5 Elmore 1	Att: 110
Wadebridge Town 3 Saltash United 2 *(at Newquay)*	Att: 51
Almondsbury Town 2 **Barnstaple Town** 3	Att: 70
Chard Town 3 Wellington Town 1	Att: 68

SECOND QUALIFYING ROUND
(£600 to each winning club)

Northallerton Town 0 **Ashington** 1	Att: 72
Team Northumbria 2 Bottesford Town 1	Att: 108
Billingham Synthonia 1 Spennymoor Town 0	Att: 106
Jarrow Roofing Boldon CA 4 Pontefract Collieries 1	Att: 108
Glasshoughton Welfare 2 West Allotment Celtic 0	Att: 49
Hall Road Rangers 4 Sunderland Ryhope CA 1	Att: 59
Eccleshill United 4 Whickham 0	Att: 79
North Shields 3 Hebburn Town 2	Att: 122
Darlington Railway Athletic 0 **Silsden** 2	Att: 81
Winterton Rangers 2 Alnwick Town 0	Att: 62
Chester-le-Street Town 0 **South Shields** 2	Att: 113
Durham City 2 Seaham Red Star 1 *(at Esh Winning)*	Att: 92
Tadcaster Albion 2 **Easington Colliery** 3	Att: 65
Peterlee Town 1 **Norton & Stockton Ancients** 2	Att: 49
Garforth Town 2 Selby Town 0	Att: 91
Morpeth Town 2 **Whitley Bay** 3	Att: 124
Tow Law Town 3 **Shildon** 5	Att: 135
Consett 7 Brandon United 0	Att: 171
Ryton 5 Yorkshire Amateur 1	Att: 86
West Auckland Town 8 Willington 0	Att: 63
Sunderland Nissan 4 Guisborough Town 0	Att: 38
Winsford United 3 Holker Old Boys 1	Att: 91
Darwen 1 **Curzon Ashton** 3	Att: 86
Daisy Hill 0 **Congleton Town** 5	Att: 55
Abbey Hey 4 St Helens Town 3	Att: 40
Dinnington Town 2 Bacup Borough 1	Att: 85
Maine Road 2 **Salford City** 3	Att: 71
Padiham 1 Cheadle Town 0	Att: 94
Brodsworth MW 1 **FC United of Manchester** 3	Att: 1,251
Poulton Victoria 2 AFC Emley 0	Att: 56
Ashton Town 1 **Blackpool Mechanics** 2	Att: 42
Worsborough Bridge MW 2 Rossington Main 1	Att: 35
Colne 4 Maltby Main 1	Att: 116
Castleton Gabriels 0 **Nelson** 6	Att: 58
Trafford 2 Formby 1 *aet*	Att: 88
Flixton 2 Chadderton 1	Att: 62
Atherton LR 1 **Parkgate** 2	Att: 41
Atherton Collieries 2 Penrith 1	Att: 52
Gedling MW 0 **Coalville Town** 4 *(at Coalville Town)*	Att: 39
Bromyard Town 0 **Causeway United** 4	Att: 55
Clipstone Welfare 0 **Carlton Town** 1	Att: 57
Atherstone Town 2 Norton United 1	Att: 187
Barwell 0 Oadby Town 1	Att: 133
Replay: Oadby Town 0 **Barwell** 2	Att: 157
Market Drayton Town 7 Dunkirk 2	Att: 107

Wyrley Rangers 0 **Downes Sports** 1	
Wellington 0 **New Mills** 2	Att: 75
Anstey Nomads 0 **Brierley & Hagley** 1	Att: 68
Teversal 3 **Barnt Green Spartak** 6 *aet*	Att: 43
Blackwell Miners Welfare 2 Birstall United 2 *aet*	Att: 53
Replay: **Birstall United** 2 Blackwell Miners Welfare 0	Att: 67
Studley 1 **Holwell Sports** 2	Att: 39
Ledbury Town 0 **Shifnal Town** 2 *aet*	Att: 55
Rainworth MW 1 Racing Club Warwick 0	Att: 100
Cadbury Athletic 2 **Tipton Town** 3 *aet*	Att: 32
Rocester 0 **Friar Lane & Epworth** 1	Att: 114
Sutton Town 9 Barrow Town 1	Att: 133
Mickleover Sports 2 Newark Town 0	Att: 74
Retford United 3 Sandiacre Town 0	Att: 148
Quorn 5 Heather Athletic 0	Att: 101
Borrowash Victoria 2 Meir KA 1	Att: 59
Boldmere St Michaels 4 Pegasus Juniors 0	Att: 60
St Andrews SC 0 **Stratford Town** 4	Att: 52
Oldbury United 2 Bridgnorth Town 1	Att: 61
Heanor Town 0 **Calverton Miners Welfare** 1	Att: 106
Holbrook Miners Welfare 2 Rothley Imperial 0	Att: 48
Long Eaton United 0 **Bolehall Swifts** 1	Att: 72
Alvechurch 5 Coventry Sphinx 1	Att: 105
Biddulph Victoria 2 Glossop North End 1	Att: 53
Newcastle Town 1 Brocton 0	Att: 112
Nuneaton Griff 4 **Tividale** 5 *aet*	Att: 32
Loughborough Dynamo 2 Dudley Town 1	Att: 74
Coventry Copsewood 0 **Shawbury United** 2	Att: 27
South Normanton Athletic 2 Gornal Athletic 0	Att: 59
Highgate United 0 **Castle Vale** 3	Att: 42
Radcliffe Olympic 1 Lye Town 1 *aet*	Att: 97
Replay: Lye Town 1 **Radcliffe Borough** 3	Att: 81
Coleshill Town 4 Wolverhampton Casuals 1	Att: 49
Blackstones 4 Downham Town 1	Att: 55
Bourne Town 4 Diss Town 4 *aet*	Att: 111
Replay: Diss Town 2 **Bourne Town** 5	Att: 154
Kirkley 2 St Ives Town 0	Att: 123
Lincoln Moorlands 2 March Town United 1	Att: 55
Godmanchester Rovers 1 Huntingdon Town 0	Att: 100
Leiston 2 Great Yarmouth Town 0	Att: 93
Ipswich Wanderers 11 Long Melford 0	Att: 59
Soham Town Rangers 5 Whitton United 0	Att: 98
Boston Town 3 Haverhill Rovers 2 *aet*	Att: 67
Woodbridge Town 5 Hadleigh United 0	Att: 51
Dereham Town 0 **Wroxham** 3	Att: 257
Deeping Rangers 3 Yaxley 1	Att: 122
Stowmarket Town 0 **Ely City** 1	Att: 57
Walsham-le-Willows 0 **Fakenham Town** 2	Att: 57
Thetford Town 2 Debenham Leisure Centre 1	Att: 65
Eynesbury Rovers 1 **Gorleston** 2	Att: 69
Bowers & Pitsea 1 Sawbridgeworth Town 0	Att: 52
Bedfont Green 3 Cranfield United 0	Att: 22
Biggleswade United 2 **Leverstock Green** 3	Att: 48
Tring Athletic 0 **Wellingborough Town** 1	Att: 110
Edgware Town 3 Long Buckby 0	Att: 44
Clapton 3 London APSA 2 *aet*	
Rothwell Corinthians 1 **Eton Manor** 2 *aet*	
Hullbridge Sports 1 **Stanway Rovers** 2	Att: 35
Feltham 3 Ford Sports Daventry 2 *aet*	Att: 94
Cogenhoe United 3 Biggleswade Town 1 *aet*	Att: 40
Langford 1 **Hounslow Borough** 3	Att: 68
Bedford United & Valerio 3 Hoddesdon Town 2	Att: 45
Clacton Town 0 Wembley 0 *aet*	Att: 81
Replay: **Wembley** 4 Clacton Town 2	Att: 61
Romford 3 St Margaretsbury 1	Att: 104
Royston Town 0 **Ruislip Manor** 2	Att: 43
AFC Kempston 0 **Saffron Walden Town** 3	Att: 44
Bedfont 1 **Erith Town** 3	Att: 49
Oxhey Jets 2 Raunds Town 1	Att: 39
Concord Rangers 2 **Brimsdown Rovers** 4	Att: 48
London Colney 1 **Burnham Ramblers** 2	Att: 49

Tiptree United 5 Harwich & Parkeston 0	Att: 68
Cockfosters 2 Stewarts & Lloyds Corby 0	Att: 60
Southend Manor 0 **Brentwood Town** 1	Att: 38
Harpenden Town 2 Wootton Blue Cross 1	Att: 31
Sporting Bengal United 0 **Halstead Town** 4	Att: 72
Wealden 4 Chertsey Town 2	Att: 90
Frimley Green 0 **Arundel** 3	Att: 54
Lingfield 1 **Three Bridges** 4	Att: 90
Chipstead 8 Sidlesham 2	Att: 40
Camberley Town 0 **Haywards Heath Town** 2	Att: 49
Epsom & Ewell 0 **Sevenoaks Town** 1 *aet*	Att: 44
Oakwood 1 Whitstable Town 0	Att: 55
Eastbourne Town 3 Hassocks 1	Att: 102
Herne Bay 1 **Selsey** 2	Att: 106
Crowborough Athletic 2 Broadbridge Heath 1	Att: 34
Guildford City 2 Raynes Park Vale 0	Att: 51
Horley Town 3 Bookham 1 *aet*	Att: 75
Croydon 2 Eastbourne United Association 1	Att: 70
Pagham 2 Slade Green 2 *aet*	Att: 63
Replay: Slade Green 0 **Pagham** 4	Att: 38
Wick 3 Lancing 1 *aet*	Att: 60
Mile Oak 1 **Hailsham Town** 2	Att: 132
Lordswood 2 **Cobham** 3 *aet*	Att: 47
Tunbridge Wells 6 Farnham Town 1	Att: 98
Egham Town 2 Peacehaven & Telscombe 1 *aet*	Att: 46
Westfield 1 **Sidley United** 3 *(at Sidley United)*	Att: 83
Moneyfields 1 Carterton 1 *aet*	Att: 69
Replay: Carterton 0 **Moneyfields** 3	Att: 85
Henley Town 1 **Hamble ASSC** 2	Att: 45
Gosport Borough 5 Alton Town 1	Att: 148
Buckingham Town 1 **Witney United** 7	Att: 102
Calne Town 3 Holmer Green 2	Att: 53
Fareham Town 4 Andover New Street 1	Att: 113
Amesbury Town 1 Cove 1 *aet*	Att: 52
Replay: Cove 0 **Amesbury Town** 2	Att: 55
Clanfield 1 Buckingham Athletic 0	Att: 43
Shrewton United 3 Malmesbury Victoria 0	Att: 85
Hartley Wintney 0 **Ardley United** 3	Att: 45
Marlow United 1 **Wantage Town** 2	Att: 81
AFC Wallingford 1 **Sandhurst Town** 5	Att: 50
Pewsey Vale 1 Aylesbury Vale 0	Att: 47
Milton United 3 Highworth Town 0	Att: 40
Bemerton Heath Harlequins 2 Devizes Town 0	Att: 86
Chipping Norton Town 2 Abingdon Town 1	Att: 37
Blackfield & Langley 0 **Shrivenham** 1	Att: 72
Newport Pagnell Town 0 **Chalfont St Peter** 3 *aet*	Att: 38
Reading Town 3 Ringwood Town 2 *aet*	Att: 21
Christchurch 0 **Cowes Sports** 2	Att: 58
Melksham Town 0 **Lymington Town** 3	Att: 52
Bridport 1 Harrow Hill 1 *aet*	Att: 105
Replay: Harrow Hill 0 **Bridport** 1 *aet*	Att: 70
Penryn Athletic 3 Plymouth Parkway 1	Att: 72
Hallen 3 Newton Abbot 0	Att: 39
Dawlish Town 1 **Frome Town** 2	Att: 87
Sherborne Town 4 Minehead 2	Att: 68
Radstock Town 0 **Bodmin Town** 4	Att: 67
Liskeard Athletic 5 Clevedon United 1	Att: 83
Odd Down 1 Shortwood United 0	Att: 38
Bitton 2 Backwell United 1	Att: 66
Truro City 5 Wadebridge Town 2	Att: 254
Budleigh Salterton 3 Poole Town 3 *aet*	Att: 93
Replay: **Poole Town** 5 Budleigh Salterton 0	Att: 173
Willand Rovers 2 Chard Town 0	Att: 95
Gillingham Town 1 **Bishop Sutton** 2	Att: 101
Bridgwater Town 0 **Slimbridge** 3	Att: 200
Porthleven 2 Falmouth Town 1	Att: 130
Fairford Town 2 **Launceston** 4	Att: 43
Barnstaple Town 2 Torrington 1 *aet*	Att: 166
Hamworthy United 1 Ilfracombe Town 1 *aet*	Att: 110
Replay: **Ilfracombe Town** 4 Hamworthy United 2	Att: 85
Street 2 Keynsham Town 0	Att: 59

FIRST ROUND
(£700 to each winning club)

Glasshoughton Welfare 3 Easington Colliery 1	Att: 51
Liversedge 1 Norton & Stockton Ancients 0	Att: 118
Team Northumbria 0 **West Auckland Town** 3	Att: 98
North Shields 1 **Consett** 4	Att: 135
Sunderland Nissan 3 **Shildon** 4	Att: 62
South Shields 2 Jarrow Roofing Boldon CA 1	Att: 257
Ashington 1 **Durham City** 3	Att: 174
Hall Road Rangers 1 **Winterton Rangers** 2	Att: 87
Garforth Town 3 Silsden 0	Att: 118
Ryton 0 **Billingham Synthonia** 2	Att: 76
Billingham Town 0 **Whitley Bay** 1	Att: 170
Eccleshill United 0 **Newcastle Blue Star** 3	Att: 80
Bishop Auckland 1 **Dunston Federation Brewery** 2	Att: 132
Worsborough Bridge MW 2 **Colne** 4	Att: 72
Padiham 0 **FC United of Manchester** 3	Att: 1,371
Salford City 2 Blackpool Mechanics 1	Att: 142
Flixton 3 Abbey Hey 1	Att: 62
Congleton Town 4 Dinnington Town 0	Att: 147
Trafford 3 Parkgate 3 *aet*	Att: 93
Replay: **Parkgate** 2 Trafford 1	Att: 118
Nelson 0 **Sheffield** 1	Att: 129
Atherton Collieries 4 Winsford United 0	Att: 63
Poulton Victoria 2 Curzon Ashton 2 *aet*	Att: 37
Replay: **Curzon Ashton** 3 Poulton Victoria 1	Att: 126
Calverton Miners Welfare 0 **Newcastle Town** 7	Att: 116
Sutton Town 2 Brierley & Hagley 2 *aet*	Att: 107
Replay: Brierley & Hagley 0 **Sutton Town** 3	Att: 108
New Mills 2 Stratford Town 2 *aet*	Att: 195
Replay: **Stony Stratford Town** 2 New Mills 1 *aet*	Att: 153
Borrowash Victoria 0 **Castle Vale** 3	Att: 51
Alvechurch 1 Coleshill Town 0	Att: 92
Romulus 1 Shifnal Town 0	Att: 98
Friar Lane & Epworth 0 **Carlton Town** 4	Att: 72
Market Drayton Town 1 **Quorn** 2	Att: 74
Biddulph Victoria 4 Shawbury United 1	Att: 65
Tividale 2 Barnt Green Spartak 1	Att: 96
Retford United 2 Bolehall Swifts 2 *aet*	Att: 189
Replay: Retford United 0 **Bolehall Swifts** 8	Att: 40
Downes Sports 0 **Holwell Sports** 2	Att: 25
Holbrook Miners Welfare 2 **Coalville Town** 6	Att: 71
South Normanton Ath. 4 Loughborough Dynamo 1	Att: 62
Radcliffe Olympic 0 **Rainworth Miners Welfare** 1	Att: 97
Causeway United 3 Tipton Town 2 *aet*	Att: 111
Birstall United 0 **Oldbury United** 1	Att: 77
Atherstone Town 0 **Boldmere St Michaels** 1	Att: 225
Barwell 2 Mickleover Sports 0	Att: 74
Wroxham 4 Deeping Rangers 1	Att: 193
Ipswich Wanderers 4 Soham Town Rangers 0	Att: 102
Leiston 0 **Woodbridge Town** 1	Att: 152
Thetford Town 3 Lincoln Moorlands 2	Att: 75
Kirkley 3 Godmanchester Rovers 0	Att: 126
Fakenham Town 5 Gorleston 0	Att: 79
Ely City 0 Wisbech Town 0 *aet*	Att: 178
Replay: **Wisbech Town** 2 Ely City 1 *aet*	Att: 220
St Neots Town 2 Blackstones 1	Att: 82
Boston Town 6 Bourne Town 0	Att: 68
Feltham 0 **Brimsdown Rovers** 4	Att: 36
Wembley 1 Northampton Spencer 1 *aet*	Att: 62
Replay: **Northampton Spencer** 1 Wembley 0	Att: 105
Bedford United & Valerio 2 Cockfosters 1	Att: 33
Stanway Rovers 2 Burnham Ramblers 2 *aet*	Att: 91
Replay: **Burnham Ramblers** 0 Stanway 0 *aet* (4-2p)	Att: 78
Oxhey Jets 3 Bedfont Green 2	Att: 51
Edgware Town 3 Brentwood Town 1	Att: 87
Cogenhoe United 3 Bowers & Pitsea 1	Att: 35
Tiptree United 1 **Ruislip Manor** 3 *aet*	Att: 73
Barking 0 **Hounslow Borough** 4	Att: 64
Eton Manor (w/o) v Clapton (scr.)	
Harpenden Town 2 **Halstead Town** 3 *aet*	Att: 40

Wellingborough Town 0 **Leverstock Green** 4	Att: 188
Erith Town 2 **Romford** 3	Att: 84
Potton United 2 Barkingside 1	Att: 101
Saffron Walden Town 2 Thamesmead Town 1	Att: 143
Erith & Belvedere 4 Cobham 1	Att: 78
Guildford City 0 **Three Bridges** 2	Att: 70
Wick 2 Oakwood 1	Att: 76
Hailsham Town 4 Haywards Heath Town 1	Att: 103
Ringmer 0 **Selsey** 1 *aet*	Att: 85
Eastbourne Town 3 Merstham 2 *aet*	Att: 176
Banstead Athletic 3 Wealden 0	Att: 55
Colliers Wood United 2 Crowborough Athletic 1	Att: 45
Sidley United 3 Arundel 2	Att: 100
Tunbridge Wells 6 Pagham 1	Att: 110
Egham Town 0 **Whitehawk** 2	Att: 68
Chipstead 0 **Ash United** 1	Att: 58
Croydon 4 Littlehampton Town 0	Att: 55
Horley Town 1 **Sevenoaks Town** 2	Att: 65
Calne Town 4 Pewsey Vale 3 *aet*	Att: 46
North Leigh 2 Milton United 1 *aet*	Att: 55
Hamble ASSC 0 **Cowes Sports** 5	Att: 71
Clanfield 0 **Chalfont St Peter** 5	Att: 45
Lymington Town 0 Shrivenham 0 *aet*	Att: 97
Replay: Shrivenham 1 **Lymington Town** 2	Att: 284
Wantage Town 2 Witney United 1	Att: 81
Moneyfields 2 Sandhurst Town 2 *aet*	Att: 77
Replay: Sandhurst Town 0 **Moneyfields** 1	Att: 78
Fareham Town 4 Ardley United 0	Att: 128
Bemerton Heath Harlequins 4 Shrewton United 1	Att: 100
Reading Town 0 Gosport Borough 0 *aet*	Att: 84
Replay: **Gosport Borough** 5 Reading Town 0	Att: 141
AFC Totton 4 Chipping Norton Town 0	Att: 120
Amesbury Town 4 Thame United 2	Att: 81
Corsham Town 1 Harefield United 0	Att: 81
Sherborne Town 2 Bishop Sutton 0	Att: 110
Porthleven 1 Bodmin Town 0	Att: 143
Willand Rovers 1 **Odd Down** 2	Att: 51
Slimbridge 4 Barnstaple Town 0	Att: 103
Bideford 1 Welton Rovers 0	Att: 194
Launceston 2 Liskeard Athletic 1	Att: 103
Street 5 Penryn Athletic 2	Att: 78
Bristol Manor Farm 2 Bridport 0	Att: 64
Poole Town 1 **Frome Town** 3	Att: 243
Truro City 2 Bitton 1	Att: 285
Ilfracombe Town 2 Hallen 1	Att: 85

SECOND ROUND
(£1,000 to each winning club)

Glasshoughton Welfare 2 Atherton Collieries 1	Att: 65
Flixton 4 Pickering Town 0	Att: 84
Winterton Rangers 3 Ashville 1	Att: 77
Dunston Federation 1 **Newcastle Benfield BP** 6	Att: 168
South Shields 5 Crook Town 4 *aet*	Att: 187
Congleton Town 1 **Whitley Bay** 3	Att: 176
Thackley 3 Squires Gate 2	Att: 70
Nantwich Town 3 **Shildon** 4 *aet*	Att: 353
Curzon Ashton 7 Parkgate 1	Att: 102
Durham City 1 Sheffield 0 *(at Esh Winning)*	Att: 135
Bedlington Terriers 0 **West Auckland Town** 6	Att: 110
Billingham Synthonia 3 Colne 2	Att: 89
Consett 3 Garforth Town 0	Att: 194
Newcastle Blue Star 2 Liversedge 0	Att: 63
Salford City 2 **FC United of M.** 3 *(at Salford RLFC)*	Att: 2,799
Stratford Town 2 Tividale 0 *aet*	Att: 119
Barwell 2 Arnold Town 1	Att: 89
Causeway United 1 Holwell Sports 1 *aet*	Att: 72
Replay: Holwell Sports 0 **Causeway United** 3	Att: 110
Retford United 2 Rainworth Miners Welfare 1	Att: 281
Romulus 3 Oldbury United 1	Att: 97
Leamington 4 Sutton Town 0	Att: 62
Newcastle Town 0 **Gedling Town** 2	Att: 71

Biddulph Victoria 1 **Alvechurch** 3 — Att: 64
Carlton Town 1 **Coalville Town** 2 — Att: 86
Castle Vale 3 South Normanton Athletic 0 — Att: 107
Boldmere St Michaels 0 **Quorn** 1 — Att: 62
Northampton Spencer 5 Thetford Town 2 — Att: 115
Romford 4 Oxhey Jets 4 *aet* — Att: 138
Replay: **Oxhey Jets** 3 Romford 1 — Att: 102
Wisbech Town 4 Boston Town 0 — Att: 312
Leverstock Green 1 Woodbridge Town 0 *aet* — Att: 105
Halstead Town 5 Eton Manor 0 — Att: 121
Potton United 3 Ruislip Manor 3 *aet* — Att: 104
Replay: Ruislip Manor 1 **Potton United** 2 — Att: 60
St Neots Town 1 **Lowestoft Town** 6 — Att: 134
Fakenham Town 1 Newmarket Town 0 — Att: 93
Brimsdown Rovers 2 **Ipswich Wanderers** 3 — Att: 110
Wroxham 2 Needham Market 1 — Att: 201
Bedford United & Valerio 1 **Welwyn Garden City** 5 — Att: 78
Edgware Town 3 Saffron Walden Town 0 — Att: 101
Burnham Ramblers 3 Hounslow Borough 2 — Att: 70
Broxbourne Borough V & E 1 **Mildenhall Town** 3 — Att: 66
Kirkley 1 **Cogenhoe United** 2 — Att: 212
North Leigh 2 **Eastbourne Town** 3 *aet* — Att: 126
Dorking 1 **Wick** 2 — Att: 101
Chessington & Hook United 3 Erith & Belvedere 1 — Att: 116
Three Bridges 2 Sevenoaks Town 0 — Att: 121
Croydon 3 Sidley United 1 — Att: 83
Moneyfields 1 Cowes Sports 0 — Att: 73
AFC Totton 4 Gosport Borough 1 — Att: 226
Banstead Athletic 1 **Colliers Wood United** *aet* 2 — Att: 48
Selsey 3 Wantage Town 0 — Att: 138
Chalfont St Peter (w/o) v Fareham Town (scr.)
Whitehawk 3 Ash United 0 *aet* — Att: 113
VCD Athletic 3 Tunbridge Wells 0 — Att: 149
Hailsham Town 2 Hythe Town 0 — Att: 145
Bideford 2 Tavistock 0 — Att: 183
Bemerton Heath Harlequins 2 Porthleven 1 — Att: 74
Amesbury Town 2 **Corsham Town** 3 — Att: 146
Brockenhurst 1 Sherborne Town 3 — Att: 62
Bristol Manor Farm 0 **Slimbridge** 5 — Att: 65
Street 3 Launceston 3 *aet* — Att: 107
Replay: Launceston 4 **Street** 4 *aet* (4-5p) — Att: 164
Ilfracombe Town 2 **Wimborne Town** 3 — Att: 147
Lymington Town 1 Frome Town 0 — Att: 152
Calne Town 2 Odd Down 1 *aet* — Att: 41
Truro City 3 St Blazey 2 — Att: 886

THIRD ROUND
(£1,200 to each winning club)

Barwell 4 Thackley 2 — Att: 121
Gedling Town 0 **West Auckland Town** 2 — Att: 61
Consett 2 **Causeway United** 3 — Att: 144
Whitley Bay 1 Coalville Town 0 — Att: 173
Newcastle Benfield BP 2 Castle Vale 0
Newcastle Blue Star 3 Alvechurch 2 — Att: 79
Durham City 1 **Flixton** 4 (at Eppleton Colliery W.) — Att: 98
Retford United 4 Shildon 3 — Att: 409
South Shields 3 **Curzon Ashton** 4 — Att: 235
Glasshoughton Welfare 4 Winterton Rangers 3 — Att: 75
Billingham Synthonia 5 Romulus 3 — Att: 87
FC United of Manchester 2 **Quorn** 3 *aet* — Att: 1,858
Stratford Town 2 Colliers Wood United 1 *aet* — Att: 149
Burnham Ramblers 3 Wroxham 1 — Att: 99
Fakenham Town 1 **Cogenhoe United** 5 — Att: 111
Wisbech Town 1 **VCD Athletic** 2 — Att: 308
Leverstock Green 0 **Potton United** 1 — Att: 130
Halstead Town 0 **Edgware Town** 1 — Att: 126
Croydon 0 **Leamington** 1 — Att: 279
Ipswich Wanderers 4 Oxhey Jets 0 — Att: 158
Mildenhall Town 2 Northampton Spencer 1 — Att: 189
Lowestoft Town 5 Welwyn Garden City 0 — Att: 337
Hailsham Town 2 **Sherborne Town** 4 *aet* — Att: 118

Lymington Town 0 **Truro City** 1 — Att: 178
Whitehawk 2 Selsey 0 — Att: 70
Chalfont St Peter 0 **Wimborne Town** 2 *aet* — Att: 90
Wick 0 **Eastbourne Town** 1 — Att: 99
Chessington & Hook United 0 **Street** 4
Calne Town 1 **Slimbridge** 4 — Att: 88
Three Bridges 1 Bemerton Heath Harlequins 1 *aet* — Att: 115
Replay: **Bemerton Heath Quins** 3 Three Bridges 0 — Att: 64
AFC Totton 3 Moneyfields 0 — Att: 103
Bideford 3 Corsham Town 1 — Att: 221

FOURTH ROUND
(£1,500 to each winning club)

Mildenhall Town 2 Sherborne Town 1 — Att: 243
Truro City 3 Newcastle Benfield BP 1 — Att: 765
Wimborne Town 4 Glasshoughton Welfare 2 *aet* — Att: 596
Bideford 7 Barwell 0 — Att: 378
VCD Athletic 2 West Auckland Town 1 — Att: 281
Quorn 2 Stratford Town 1 — Att: 291
Eastbourne Town 0 **Curzon Ashton** 3 — Att: 404
Leamington 4 Bemerton Heath Harlequins 1 — Att: 1,045
Billingham Synthonia 2 Newcastle Blue Star 0 — Att: 133
Flixton 2 **Retford United** 5 — Att: 220
Whitehawk 1 Edgware Town 1 — Att: 190
Replay: Edgware Town 0 **Whitehawk** 1 — Att: 116
Slimbridge 1 Whitley Bay 0 — Att: 219
Lowestoft Town 1 **Ipswich Wanderers** 2 *aet* — Att: 482
Burnham Ramblers 1 **Street** 2 — Att: 123
Potton United 1 **AFC Totton** 2 — Att: 390
Causeway United 2 Cogenhoe United 1 *aet* — Att: 153

FIFTH ROUND
(£2,000 to each winning club)

Wimborne Town 4 Street 0 — Att: 738
Causeway United 0 **Curzon Ashton** 5 — Att: 220
Slimbridge 0 **Truro City** 3 — Att: 433
Ipswich Wanderers 1 **AFC Totton** 2 — Att: 191
VCD Athletic 2 **Bideford** 3 — Att: 414
Whitehawk 2 Quorn 1 — Att: 376
Leamington 5 Retford United 1 — Att: 1,380
Billingham Synthonia 4 Mildenhall Town 0 — Att: 246

QUARTER-FINALS
(£4,000 to each winning club)

Curzon Ashton 4 Leamington 1 — Att: 898
Whitehawk 0 **Truro City** 1 — Att: 1,009
AFC Totton 2 Wimborne Town 1 — Att: 1,309
Billingham Synthonia 1 Bideford 0 — Att: 423

SEMI-FINALS
(£6,000 to each winning club)

1st leg
AFC Totton 1 Billingham Synthonia 2 — Att: 1,332
Curzon Ashton 1 Truro City 0 — Att: 875

2nd leg
Billingham Synthonia 1 **AFC Totton** 2 *aet* (4-5p) — Att: 2,386
Truro City 3 Curzon Ashton 1 — Att: 2,637

FINAL
(£15,000 to winning club)
(May 13h at Wembley Stadium)

Truro City 3 AFC Totton 1 — Att: 27,754

WELSH CUP COMPETITIONS

WELSH CUP

PRELIMINARY ROUND
Aberbargoed Buds 2 Ystradgynlais 1
Conwy United 2 Glan Conwy 1
Corwen Amateurs 0 **Rhydymwyn** 2
Cwmbran Celtic 2 Newcastle Emlyn 1
Four Crosses 2 Carno 2 *aet* (4-2p)
Llangollen Town 0 **Ruthin Town** 1
Llanidloes Town 2 Knighton Town 1
Llansawel 0 **Goytre** 1
Llantwit Fardre 3 Chepstow Town 2
Llanwern 4 Abertillery Excelsiors 1
Pentwyn Dynamo 5 Cwmamman United 1
Penycae 4 Caerwys 0
Risca United 1 **AFC Porth** 3
Sealand Rovers 2 **Cefn United** 4

FIRST ROUND
Afan Lido 3 Penrhiwceiber Rangers 1
AFC Porth 2 **West End** 4
Ammanford 1 Pontyclun 1 *aet* (4-1p)
Barry Town 3 Croesyceiliog 2
Bridgend Town 2 Taffs Well 0
Briton Ferry Athletic 0 **Bettws** 1
Buckley Town 3 Castell Alun Colts 1
Caerleon 2 Garw Athletic 1
Caldicot Town 0 **Cwmbran Celtic** 1
Cambrian & Clydach Vale BGC 1 **Morriston Town** 3
Cardiff Corinthians 3 **Maesteg Park** 1 *(Cardiff Cor. expelled)*
Chirk AAA 1 **Conwy United** 3
Coedpoeth United 0 **Bethesda Athletic** 3
Denbigh Town 6 Glyn Ceiriog 1
Dinas Powys 1 Bryntirion Athletic 0
ENTO Aberaman Athletic 1 **Neath Athletic** 2
Flint Town United 4 Nefyn United 0
Garden Village 6 AFC Llwydcoed 0
Glantraeth 3 **Bodedern** 3 *aet* (4-5p)
Goytre 0 **UWIC Inter Cardiff** 0 *aet* (2-3p)
Gresford Athletic 6 Halkyn United 3
Guilsfield 3 Four Crosses 2
Hawarden Rangers 0 **Llanrwst United** 1
Holyhead Hotspur 2 Lex XI 1
Holywell Town 1 **Brickfield Rangers** 1 *aet* (3-5p)
Llanberis 0 **Mynydd Isa** 3
Llandudno Junction 3 **Llanrug United** 4
Llandudno Town 4 Ruthin Town 0
Llanrhaedr 3 **Penryhncoch** 4
Llantwit Fardre 0 **Newport YMCA** 1
Llanwern 7 Aberbargoed Buds 2
Llanyfyllin Town 3 Llanidloes Town 2
Mold Alexandra 1 **Llanfairpwll** 2
Pentwyn Dynamo 3 **Caerau Ely** 4
Pontardawe Town 4 Porthcawl Town 1
Pontypridd Town 4 Treharris Athletic 0
Prestatyn Town 5 Llandrynog United 0
Presteigne St Andrews 4 Kerry 0
Pwllheli 2 Cefn United 1
Queens Park 3 **Brymbo** 7
Rhos Aelwyd 2 **Bala Town** 4
Rhydymwyn 1 **Penycae** 3
Ton Pentre 1 Merthyr Saints 0
Tredegar Town 0 **Llangeinor** 1
Troedyrhiw 1 **Ely Rangers** 2

SECOND ROUND
Barry Town 0 **Afan Lido** 4
Bodedern 3 Bethesda Athletic 3 *aet* (4-3p)
Brickfield Rangers 1 **Airbus UK** 4
Bridgend Town 5 Garden Village 2
Brymbo 2 NEWI Cefn Druids 2 *aet* (5-3p)
Buckley Town 2 Llanfyllin Town 1

Caerleon 2 UWIC Inter Cardiff 1
Connah's Quay Nomads 2 Aberystwyth Town 1
Cwmbran Celtic 2 **Maesteg Park** 3
Cwmbran Town 1 **Carmarthen Town** 7
Denbigh Town 2 **Newtown** 4
Dinas Powys 3 Morriston Town 0
Ely Rangers 2 Caerau Ely 2 *aet* (4-2p)
Goytre United 1 **West End** 2
Guilsfield 0 **Bala Town** 5
Llandudno Town 3 Flint Town United 0
Llanegfni Town 0 **Holyhead Hotspur** 2
Llanelli 5 Bettws 0
Llanfairpwll 0 **Rhyl** 6
Llanrug United 0 **Bangor City** 2
Mynydd Isa 0 **Caersws** 5
Neath Athletic 2 Llanwern 0
Newport YMCA 2 Ammanford 1
Penrhyncoch 2 Conwy United 0
Pontardawe Town 1 **Pontypridd Town** 2
Port Talbot Town 3 Haverfordwest County 2
Prestatyn Town 2 **Porthmadog** 4
Presteigne St Andrews 1 Penycae 1 *aet* (4-3p)
Pwllheli 2 Gresford Athletic 0
The New Saints 3 Llanrwst United 1
Ton Pentre 6 Llangeinor 0
Welshpool Town 4 Caernarfon Town 1

THIRD ROUND
Afan Lido 3 Bodedern 0
Bridgend Town 1 Airbus UK 1 *aet* (5-4p)
Caerleon 2 **Ely Rangers** 1 *aet* (2-4p)
Caersws 3 Buckley Town 0
Carmarthen Town 2 West End 0
Holyhead Hotspur 2 Presteigne St Andrews 0 *aet*
Maesteg Park 0 **Llandudno Town** 1
Neath Athletic 3 Brymbo 2
Newport YMCA 1 **Connah's Quay Nomads** 3
Newtown 2 Dinas Powys 0
Penrhyncoch 0 **Llanelli** 2
Port Talbot Town 3 Bala Town 0
Porthmadog 2 Bangor City 0
Pwllheli 1 **The New Saints** 2
Ton Pentre 1 Rhyl 0
Welshpool Town 2 Pontypridd Town 1 *aet*

FOURTH ROUND
Carmarthen Town 0 Caersws 0 *aet* (5-4p)
Connah's Quay Nomads 3 Llandudno Town 1
Ely Rangers 1 **Afan Lido** 2
Holyhead Hotspur 2 Bridgend Town 1 *aet*
Llanelli 7 Newtown 0
Port Talbot Town 3 Ton Pentre 1
Porthmadog 2 The New Saints 2 *aet* (3-2p)
Welshpool Town 3 Neath Athletic 0

QUARTER-FINALS
Carmarthen Town 1 Porthmadog 1 *aet* (4-3p)
Holyhead Hotspur 1 **Welshpool Town** 5
Port Talbot Town 0 **Afan Lido** 1
Llanelli 6 Connah's Quay Nomads 2

SEMI-FINALS
Afan Lido 1 Welshpool 1 *aet* (7-6p) *(at Aberystwyth)*
Carmarthen Town 1 Llanelli 0 *(at Haverfordwest County)*

FINAL
(May 6th at Llanelli)
Carmarthen Town 3 Afan Lido 2 *aet*

F A W PREMIER CUP

(Top ten placed clubs from the Welsh Premier League along with the best placed 'exiled' club (Newport County), the Welsh Cup winners plus the three English League clubs (Cardiff City, Swansea City and Wrexham); Porthmadog qualified despite finishing 11th in the Welsh Premier as Rhyl finished in the top ten and won the Welsh Cup)

FIRST ROUND

Bangor City 3 Caersws 1

Haverfordwest County 1 **Port Talbot Town** 2

NEWI Cefn Druids 3 Welshpool Town 2

Porthmadog 1 Aberystwyth Town 0

SECOND ROUND

Carmarthen Town 3 Bangor City 1

NEWI Cefn Druids 1 **Newport County** 2 *aet*

Port Talbot Town 2 Rhyl 1

Porthmadog 2 Llanelli 1

QUARTER-FINALS

Carmarthen Town 2 **Cardiff City** 3 *aet*

Newport County 2 Wrexham 1

Port Talbot Town 2 Swansea City 1

Porthmadog 1 **The New Saints** 3

SEMI-FINALS

Cardiff City 0 **The New Saints** 1

Newport County 2 Port Talbot Town 1

FINAL
(23rd March at Newport County)

The New Saints 1 Newport County 0

WELSH TROPHY

PRELIMINARY ROUND
North End 4 AFC Whitchurch 1
FIRST ROUND
AFC Llwynypia 0 **Llanharry** 7
Barry 0 **Ragged School** 1
Blaengwawr Inn 1 **South Gower** 6
Blaenrhondda 5 Trelewis Welfare 2
Bonymaen Colts 1 Corus Steel 0
Brymbo 3 Llandudno Junction 1
Caerwys 0 **Llanrug United** 3
Carnetown 4 **Maltsters Sports** 4 *aet* (3-4p)
Carno 0 **Llanrhaeadr** 1
Clydach Wasps 2 Baglan Red Dragons 0
Coedpoeth United 0 Penmaenmawr Phoenix 0 *aet* (3-2p)
Cogan Coronation 4 Llanrumney United 1
Conwy United 5 Penycae 1
Corwen Amateurs 2 Brickfield Rangers 1
Cwmbach Royal Stars 1 **Cwmaman Institute** 5
Denbigh Town 3 Rhos Aelwyd 1
Four Crosses 0 **Presteigne St Andrews** 1
Kerry 3 Llanidloes Town 0
Llandrindod Wells 0 **Berriew** 1
Llanfyllin Town 5 Knighton Town 1
Llangollen Town 3 Sealand Rovers 2
Llanrwst United 0 **Mold Alexandra** 3
Llay Welfare 2 Hawarden Rangers 1
Monmouth Town 4 AFC Bargoed 2
Nefyn United 4 Holywell Town 4 *aet* (4-3p)
North End 0 **Sully Sports** 1
Rhydymwyn 3 Chirk AAA 0
Ton & Gelli Boys Club 4 Osborne Athletic 0
Tongwynlais 2 **FC Abercwmboi** 3
Venture Community 3 **Cefn United** 4
Y Felinheli 2 **Glan Conwy** 3
Ynysddu Welfare Crusaders 1 **Kenfig Hill** 3

SECOND ROUND
Bonymaen Colts 2 Kenfig Hill 0

Brymbo 5 Kerry 0
Cefn United 2 **Corwen Amateurs** 2 *aet* (5-6p)
Conwy United 3 **Coedpoeth United** 3 *aet* (3-4p)
Cwmaman Institute 0 **Clydach Wasps** 1
FC Abercwmboi 2 **Monmouth Town** 4
Glan Conwy 3 Llanrug United 1
Llanfyllin Town 2 **Rhydymwyn** 4
Llangollen Town 5 Nefyn United 2
Llanharry 3 Ton & Gelli Boys Club 1
Llay Welfare 0 **Denbigh Town** 4
Maltsters Sports 3 Blaenrhondda 1
Mold Alexandra 1 **Berriew** 3
Presteigne St Andrews 1 Llanrhaeadr 0
Ragged School 3 South Gower 2
Sully Sports 2 Cogan Coronation 0

THIRD ROUND
Bonymaen Colts 1 **Presteigne St Andrews** 2
Coedpoeth United 5 Corwen Amateurs 1
Denbigh Town 1 **Brymbo** 2
Llangollen Town 3 Berriew 0
Llanharry 2 **Sully Sports** 4
Maltsters Sports 1 **Clydach Wasps** 3
Monmouth Town 1 **Ragged School** 2 *aet*
Rhydymwyn 1 **Glan Conwy** 3

QUARTER-FINALS
Clydach Wasps 4 Ragged School 1
Coedpoeth United 1 **Glan Conwy** 2
Presteigne St Andrews 1 **Brymbo** 2
Sully Sports 5 **Llangollen Town** 0
(Sully Sports expelled)

SEMI-FINALS
Glan Conwy 3 Clydach Wasps 2
Llangollen Town 1 **Brymbo** 7

FINAL
(14th April at Airbus UK)
Glan Conwy 2 **Brymbo** 6

MAJOR COUNTY CUP FINALS

BEDFORDSHIRE PREMIER CUP
(August 1st at Biggleswade United)
Biggleswade United 1 **Luton Town** 5
BERKS & BUCKS SENIOR CUP
(May 7th at Wycombe Wanderers)
Maidenhead United 1 **Milton Keynes Dons** 2
BIRMINGHAM SENIOR CUP
(May 1st at Walsall)
Coventry City 3 Walsall 2
CAMBRIDGESHIRE PROFESSIONAL CUP
(July 11th at Histon)
Histon 0 **Cambridge United** 0 (3-4p)
CHESHIRE SENIOR CUP
(March 13th at Witton Albion)
Northwich Victoria 1 **Cammell Laird** 3
CORNWALL SENIOR CUP
(April 9th at Bodmin Town)
Truro City 1 Liskeard Athletic 0
CUMBERLAND SENIOR CUP
(May 8th at Carlisle United)
Carlisle United 1 **Workington** 2
DERBYSHIRE SENIOR CUP
1st leg *(April 3rd):*
Ilkeston Town 1 Matlock Town 2
2nd leg *(April 26th):*
Matlock Town 0 **Ilkeston Town** 2
DEVON St LUKES COLLEGE BOWL
(May 11th at Exeter City)
Exeter City 0 **Torquay United** 2
DORSET SENIOR CUP
(April 17th at Hamworthy United)
Dorchester Town 2 Sherborne Town 1
DURHAM CHALLENGE CUP
(April 6th at Sunderland Nissan)
Chester-le-Street Town 2 **Consett** 3
EAST RIDING SENIOR CUP
(May 8th at Hull City)
North Ferriby United 1 Bridlington Town 0 *aet*
ESSEX SENIOR CUP
(March 27th at Southend United)
AFC Hornchurch 2 Great Wakering Rovers 1
GLOUCESTERSHIRE SENIOR CUP
(to be played in pre-seaon)
HAMPSHIRE SENIOR CUP
(May 5th at AFC Bournemouth)
Fleet Town 1 **Aldershot Town** 2
HEREFORDSHIRE SENIOR CUP
(April 17th at Hereford United)
Hereford United 3 Ledbury Town 0
HERTFORDSHIRE SENIOR CUP
(April 17th at HCFA, Letchworth)
Barnet 4 Hemel Hempstead Town 2
HUNTINGDONSHIRE SENIOR CUP
(May 7th at Huntingdon Town)
St Ives Town 2 Hampton Athletic 0
KENT SENIOR CUP
(April 24th at Bromley)
Bromley 3 Tonbridge Angels 1
LANCASHIRE TROPHY
(April 26th at LCFA, Leyland)
Marine 1 **Burscough** 2
LEICESTERSHIRE CHALLENGE CUP
(May 8th at Leicester City)
Hinckley United 4 Barwell 3
LINCOLNSHIRE SHIELD
(April 18th at Lincoln City)
Brigg Town 0 **Stamford** 1

LIVERPOOL SENIOR CUP
(May 8th at Tranmere Rovers)
Tranmere Rovers 1 **Everton** 2
LONDON SENIOR CUP
(April 26th at Tooting & Mitcham United)
Tooting & Mitcham United 4 Bromley 2
MANCHESTER PREMIER CUP
(April 18th at Curzon Ashton)
Flixton 0 **Droylsden** 3
MIDDLESEX SENIOR CUP
(April 9th at Hayes)
Hayes 1 **Northwood** 1 *aet* (2-4p)
NORFOLK SENIOR CUP
(March 27th at Norwich City)
Dereham Town 1 Wroxham 0
NORTH RIDING SENIOR CUP
(April 24th at Billingham Synthonia)
Northallerton Town 0 **Middlesbrough** 5
NORTHAMPTONSHIRE SENIOR CUP
(March 20th at Woodford United)
Woodford United 1 **Rushden & Diamonds** 4
NORTHUMBERLAND SENIOR CUP
(May 8th at Newcastle United)
Blyth Spartans 2 **Morpeth Town** 3
NOTTINGHAMSHIRE SENIOR CUP
(April 26th at Notts County)
Eastwood Town 0 Arnold Town 0 *aet* (4-3p)
OXFORDSHIRE SENIOR CUP
(April 24th at Oxford United)
Banbury United 0 Oxford City 1
SHEFFIELD & HALLAMSHIRE SENIOR CUP
(May 1st at Sheffield Wednesday)
Stocksbridge Park Steels 2 Worksop Town 1
SHROPSHIRE SENIOR CUP
(July 25th at AFC Telford United)
Shrewsbury Town 1 AFC Telford United 1 *aet* (4-1p)
SOMERSET PREMIER CUP
(April 24th at Paulton Rovers)
Team Bath 3 Bitton 1 *aet*
STAFFORDSHIRE SENIOR CUP
(April 25th at Port Vale)
Rushall Olympic 1 **Kidsgrove Athletic** 6
SUFFOLK PREMIER CUP
(April 17th at Ipswich Town)
Ipswich Town Res. 8 Leiston 0
SURREY SENIOR CUP
(April 24th at Tooting & Mitcham United)
Tooting & Mitcham Utd 4 Metropolitan Police 1 *aet*
SUSSEX SENIOR CUP
(May 7th at Eastbourne Borough)
Brighton & Hove Albion 2 Worthing 0
WEST RIDING COUNTY CUP
(April 11th at WRCFA, Woodlesford)
Guiseley 1 **Goole** 3
WESTMORLAND SENIOR CUP
(April 21st at Kendal Town)
Wetheriggs United 3 Milnthorpe Corinthians 0
WILTSHIRE PREMIER SHIELD
(May 9th at Swindon Supermarine)
Swindon Supermarine 2 Swindon Town 1
WORCESTERSHIRE SENIOR CUP
1st leg *(April 24th)*
Stourbridge 0 Evesham United 0
2nd leg *(May 7th)*
Evesham United 2 Stourbridge 1 *aet*

OTHER COUNTY AND DISTRICT CUP FINALS

ALDERSHOT SENIOR CUP
(May 3rd at Aldershot Town)
Badshot Lea 3 **Camberley Town** 3 *aet* (4-5p)

ANCASTER CUP
(May 7th at Bourne Town)
Sleaford Town Res. 5 Deeping Sports 1

ANDOVER OPEN CUP
(April 30th at Andover)
Stockbridge 2 Alresford Town 1

ATHERTON COLLIERIES CHARITY CUP
(May 17th at Ashton Town)
Ashton Town 0 **Ashton Athletic** 1

AXMINSTER HOSPITAL CUP
(May 16th at Axminster Town)
Cullompton Rangers 5 **Chard Town** 9

BARKESTON ASH BURTON CUP
(April 9th at Tadcaster Albion)
Old Headingley 2 Sherbur White Rose 0

BARRITT CUP
(May 5th at Bangor City)
Rhyl Res. 3 Prestatyn Town Res. 2

BASINGSTOKE SENIOR CUP
(May 12th at Fleet Town)
Fleet Town 0 **Thatcham Town** 3

BEDFORDSHIRE SENIOR CUP
(May 8th at Arlesey Town)
Dunstable Town 2 Biggleswade United 0

BEDFORDSHIRE SENIOR TROPHY
(April 3rd at Leighton Town)
AFC Dunstable 4 Bedford United & Valerio 1

BEDFORDSHIRE INTERMEDIATE CUP
(April 20th at AFC Kempston Rovers)
Heath United RBL 1 **Bedford Town Res.** 3

BEDFORDSHIRE JUNIOR CUP
(April 27th at Potton United)
Sandy Res. 0 **Meltis Corinthians** 2

BEDWORTH NURSING CUP
(April 6th at Bedworth United)
Bedworth United Res. 2 Woodlands WMC 0

BERKS & BUCKS TROPHY
(April 25th at Marlow Town)
Milton United 1 **Sandhurst Town** 1 *aet* (5-6p)

BERKS & BUCKS INTERMEDIATE CUP
(March 31st at Buckingham Town)
Chalfont Wasps 3 Kintbury Rangers 2

BERKS & BUCKS JUNIOR CUP
(April 14th at Burnham)
Shrivenham 'A' 3 Walton Court Wanderers 0

BIGGLESWADE CUP
(May 10th at Langford)
Stotfold Res. 1 Sandy Town 1 *aet* (10-9p)

BILL SPURGEON CUP
(May 1st at Witham Town)
Ramsden 2 Ongar Town 2 *aet* (5-4p)

BIRMINGHAM FLOODLIGHT CUP
(April 18th at Solihull Borough)
Dudley Town 2 **Coventry Sphinx** 4 *aet*

BIRMINGHAM VASE
(April 21st at BCFA, Great Barr)
AFC Wulfrunians 3 Stockingford AA 1

BIRMINGHAM JUNIOR CUP
(March 31st at BCFA, Great Barr)
Colinthians 4 Boldmere Falcons Seniors 0

BOLTON HOSPITAL CUP
(May 4th at Bolton Wanderers)
Ramsbottom United 5 Tempest United 1

BRADFORD & DISTRICT SENIOR CUP
(May 10th at Bradford City)
Bradford Park Avenue 2 Wibsey 1

BRAUNTON CUP
(May 13th at Barnstaple Town)
Pilton Academicals 3 Barnstaple AAC 1 *aet*

BRIGHTON CHARITY CUP
(April 24th at Horsham)
Horsham 5 Chichester City United 2

BUCKINGHAM CHARITY CUP
(May 7th at Buckingham Athletic)
Leighton Town 3 Bicester Town 0

CAMBRIDGESHIRE INVITATION CUP
(April 24th at Cambridge United)
Soham Town Rangers 0 **Cambridge City** 1

CAMBRIDGESHIRE CHALLENGE CUP
(April 9th at Histon)
Sawston United 3 Waterbeach 2

CAMBRIDGESHIRE JUNIOR INVITATION CUP
(May 2n at Cambridge City)
Cambridge University Press Res. 3 Sutton United 1

CAMBRIDGESHIRE LOWER JUNIOR CUP
(May 3rd at Cambridge City)
Chatteris Res. 3 **Cambridge University Press 'A'** 5 *aet*

CENTRAL WALES CUP
(May 22nd at The New Saints)
Llanfyllin Town 2 Guilsfield 0

CEREDIGION CUP
(May 7th at Aberystwyth Town)
St Dogmaels 4 Lampeter Town 3

CHESHIRE AMATEUR CUP
(April 13th at Vauxhall Motors)
Heswall 0 **New Brighton** 3

CHESTER SENIOR CUP
(April 27th at Christleton)
Upton AA 4 Chester Noamds 1

CHESTER CHALLENGE CUP
(April 20th at Christleton)
Highfield 2 Wagon & Horses 1

COMMANDER ETHELSTON CUP
(May 7th at Whitchurch Alport)
Wem Town 2 Wellington Amateurs 0

CORNWALL CHARITY CUP
(May 15th at Wadebridge Town)
Bodmin Town 2 **St Blazey** 2 *aet* (9-10p)

CORNWALL JUNIOR CUP
(April 9th at Bodmin Town)
St Dennis Res. 0 Mawgan 0
(Replay April 12th at Bodmin Town)
Mawnan 1 St Dennis Res. 1 *aet* (4-2p)

COVENTRY CHARITY CUP
(March 27th at Coventry City)
Coventry Sphinx 3 Dunlop Sports 0

WWW.NLNEWSDESK.CO.UK

COVENTRY EVENING TELEGRAPH CUP
(April 30th at Coventry City)
Christ The King 1 Highgate United 1
(Replay May 11th at Coventry Copsewood)
Highgate United 0 Christ The King 0 aet (8-7p)
CRAVEN CHALLENGE CUP
(May 3rd at Settle United)
Barnoldswick Town 3 Ingleton 2
CRAVEN MORRISON CUP
(April 27th at Settle United)
Gargrave 3 Skipton Town 1
DERBYSHIRE DIVISIONAL CUP NORTH
(April 27th at Tideswell United)
Dove Holes 1 Wirksworth Town 0
DERBYSHIRE DIVISIONAL CUP SOUTH
(April 12th at Long Eaton United)
Melbourne Dynamo 1 Holbrook St Michaels 0
DERBYSHIRE JUNIOR CUP NORTH
(April 19th at Shirebrook Town)
Brampton 2 Dronfield United 1
DERBYSHIRE JUNIOR CUP SOUTH
(April 19th at Long Eaton United)
Heanor Colliers 2 Newmount 1
DEVON PREMIER CUP
(May 8th at Tiverton Town)
Tavistock 6 Upton Athletic 0
DEVON SENIOR CUP
(April 23rd at Bideford)
Combe Martin 3 Lamerton 1
DEVON INTERMEDIATE CUP
(April 12th at Tavistock)
Shebbear United 0 **Sidbury United Res.** 1
DIDCOT FESTIVAL CUP
(September 2nd at Didcot Town)
Didcot Town Res. 5 Blewbury 0
DORSET TROPHY
(April 26th at Dorchester Town)
Chickerell United Res. **1 Poole Borough Res. 2**
DORSET INTERMEDIATE CUP
(April 12th at Shaftesbury)
Stourpaine Res. 3 West Moors 2
DORSET JUNIOR CUP
(April 10th at Weymouth)
Railway Tavern, Weymouth 1 **Upwey & Broadwey** 1
DORSET MINOR CUP
(April 3rd at Hamworthy United)
Kingston Lacy 4 Harbour View Developments 2
DURHAM TROPHY
(April 16th at Durham City)
Chopwell TC 2 **Rutherford Newcastle** 2 aet (7-8p)
EAST ANGLIAN CUP
(May 11th at Great Wakering Rovers)
Needham Market 2 Concord Rangers 1
EAST HAM MEMORIAL CUP
(May 8th at Cave Road, Plaistow)
Newham United 4 Ryan 1
EAST RIDING SENIOR COUNTRY CUP
(May 12th at Bridlington Town)
Dunnington 3 Howden Amateurs 1
EAST RIDING INTERMEDIATE CUP
(April 26th at Hall Road Rangers)
Smith & Nephew 2 Discount Carpets 1
EAST RIDING INTERMEDIATE COUNTRY CUP
(April 24th at Pocklington Town)
Bridlington Sports Club 2 Stamford Bridge 1

EAST RIDING JUNIOR COUNTRY CUP
(April 1st at Pocklington Town)
Long Riston Res. 5 Dunnington Res. 0
EMRYS MORGAN CUP
(April 6th at Rhayader Town)
Rhosgoch Rangers 0 **Tregaron Turfs** 1
ESSEX PREMIER CUP
(April 18th at Thurrock)
Takeley 1 Ongar Town 0
ESSEX THAMESSIDE TROPHY
(May 7th at Tilbury)
Tilbury 1 **Aveley** 3
ESSEX JUNIOR CUP
(April 11th at Harlow Town)
Shell Club Corringham Res. 5
Scotia Billericay 2
ESSEX JUNIOR TROPHY
(April 4th at Billericay Town)
Baronsmere 3 Dunmow 0
FARINGDON THURSDAY MEMORIAL CUP
(May 3rd at Faringdon Town)
CHQ 2 Letcombe 1
FAZELEY CHARITY CUP
(May 6th at Coton Green)
Tamworth Youth 5 Chelmsley Town 4 aet
FIELD CHARITY CUP
(April 6th at Aylesbury Vale)
Walton Court Wanderers 5 Haddenham United 4
GLOUCESTERSHIRE TROPHY
(May 1st at GCFA, Oaklands Park)
Slimbridge 3 Almondsbury Town 1
GOLDLINE TROPHY
(March 12th at Bolton Wanderers)
Prestwich Heys 1 Charnock Richard 1
aet (2-0p)
GOLESWORTHY CUP
(May 22nd at Ottery St Mary)
Axminster Town Res. 2 Farway United 1
GRANDISSON CUP
(May 24th at Ottery St Mary)
Lympstone 2 Broadclyst Social Club 1
GWENT SENIOR CUP
(May 5th at Abergavenny Thursdays)
Croesyceiliog 3 Cwmbran Town 1
GWENT AMATEUR CUP
(May 12th at Abergavenny Thursdays)
AC Pontymister 0 **Abertillery Bluebirds** 1
HAMPSHIRE RUSSELL COTES CUP
(May 9th at Gosport Borough)
Gosport Borough 0 **Fleet Town** 2
HAMPSHIRE INTERMEDIATE CUP
(May 2nd at Christchurch)
Fleetlands 2 Suttoners Civil 1
HAMPSHIRE JUNIOR A CUP
(April 14th at Andover New Street)
R & B Sports 3 Bramley United 1
HAMPSHIRE JUNIOR B CUP
(April 14th at Andover New Street)
Twyford 3 Kyngs Towyne 1
HANSEN CUP
(May 7th at Torrington)
Torrington Admirals 1 **Dolton Rangers Res.** 4
HEREFORDSHIRE CHALLENGE CUP
(April 9th at Hereford United)
Ledbury Town 1 Wellington 0

HEREFORDSHIRE BOWL
(March 14th at Wellington)
Codicote 2 Hoddesdon Town 0
HEREFORDSHIRE JUNIOR SHIELD
(April 21st at Westfields)
Widemarsh Rangers 2 Ewyas Harold Res. 1
HERTFORDSHIRE CHARITY CUP
(May 9th at HCFA, Letchworth)
Potters Bar Town 3 Hemel Hempstead Town 0
HERTFORDSHIRE CENTENARY TROPHY
(March 27th at HCFA, Letchworth)
London Lions 4 Metropolitan Police Bushey 0
HERTFORDSHIRE CHARITY SHIELD
(May 2nd at HCFA, Letchworth)
St Margaretsbury 2 **Leverstock Green** 2 *aet* (3-4p)
HERTFORDSHIRE INTERMEDIATE CUP
(March 20th at HCFA, Letchworth)
Kings Langley 3 London Colney Res. 2 *aet*
HERTFORDSHIRE JUNIOR CUP
(April 6th at HCFA, Letchworth)
Kings Sports 5 Baldock Town 4 *aet*
HINCHINGBROOKE CUP
(May 11th at St Neots Town)
St Ives Town 2 Deeping Rangers 0
HOLMAN CUP
(April 9th at Lynmouth & Lynton)
Torridgeside 4 Shamwickshire Rovers 2
HUNTINGDONSHIRE PREMIER CUP
(May 9th at St Neots Town)
St Ives Town 2 Biggleswade United 0
HUNTINGDONSHIRE SCOTT GATTY CUP
(March 28th at Somersham Town)
St Neots Town Res. 3 AFC Fletton Res. 1
HUNTINGDONSHIRE BENEVOLENT CUP
(April 25th at Huntingdon Town)
Ramsey Town Res. 1 **Huntingdon United RGE** 2
HUNTINGDONSHIRE JUNIOR CUP
(April 18th at Huntingdon Town)
Godmanchester Rovers Res. 4 St Ives
Rangers 3 *aet*
ISLE OF WIGHT SENIOR (GOLD) CUP
(May 3rd at East Cowes Victoria Athletic)
Newport IOW 1 **Cowes Sports** 2
ISLE OF WIGHT MEMORIAL CUP
(May 7th at Newport IOW)
Shanklin 2 Sandown 0
J W HUNT CUP
(May 15th at Wolverhampton Wanderers)
Wyrley Rangers 3 Darlaston Town 0
JIM NEWMAN CUP
(August 6th at Clanfield)
Carterton 5 Abingdon Town 3
KEIGHLEY & DISTRICT CUP
(May 11th at Silsden)
Bronte Wanderers 2 Keighley Shamrocks 1
KENT SENIOR TROPHY
(April 15th at Dartford)
Whitstable Town 1 Bearsted 0
**KENT INTERMEDIATE
CHALLENGE SHIELD**
(April 7th at Thamesmead Town)
Greenways 0 **Stansfeld O & B Club** 1
KENT INTERMEDIATE CUP
(May 12th at Deal Town)
Deal Town Res. 4 Thamesmead Town Res. 0

KENT JUNIOR A CUP
(May 5th at Ashford Town)
Whitstable Town 1 Bearsted 0
KENT JUNIOR B CUP
(April 28th at Lordswood)
Sutton Athletic Res. 3 Cliff Woods Res. 0
KENT JUNIOR C CUP
(April 21st at Sevenoaks Town)
Yalding 2 Wickham Wanderers 1
LANCASHIRE AMATEUR SHIELD
(March 28th at LCFA, Leyland)
Charnock Richard 3 Coppull United 1
LANCASHIRE AMATEUR CUP
(April 2nd at LCFA, Leyland)
Poulton Town 2 **Vickerstown** 3
LEEK & DISTRICT CUP
(March 30th at Ball Haye Green)
Hanley Town 2 Redgate Clayton 0
LEICESTERSHIRE SENIOR CUP
(April 24th at LCFA, Holmes Park)
Ibstock United 2 **Kirby Muxloe SC** 3
LEICESTERSHIRE JUNIOR CUP
(April 9th at LCFA, Holmes Park)
Barlestone St Giles 5 Queniborough 0
LINCOLNSHIRE SENIOR TROPHY
(April 25th at Lincoln City)
Lincoln Moorlands 3 Deeping Rangers 1
LINCOLNSHIRE JUNIOR CUP
(April 28th at Brigg Town)
AFC Brumby 3 Croft United 0
LIVERPOOL CHALLENGE CUP
(April 8th at LCFA, Walton Hall Avenue)
Waterloo Dock 1 Marine Res. 0
LIVERPOOL INTERMEDIATE CUP
(April 24th at LCFA, Walton Hall Avenue)
Collegiate Old Boys 4 Bankfield 1
LIVERPOOL JUNIOR CUP
(May 1st at LCFA, Walton Hall Avenue)
Rainhill Town 3 Penlake 0
LONDON INTERMEDIATE CUP
(March 31st at Metropolitan Police)
Corinthian Casuals Res. 2 Metrogas 2
aet (5-4p)
LONDON JUNIOR CUP
(March 17th at Hendon)
Tornados 2 Battersea 1
LONDON OLD BOYS CUP
(March 31st at Old Dorkinians)
Centymca 3 Old Wokingians 1
LONDON OLD BOYS SENIOR CUP
(April 17th at Wingate & Finchley)
Old Minchendenians 2 Old Meadonians 1
MIDDLESEX CHARITY CUP
(April 25th at Yeading)
Harrow Borough 0 Brook House 0 *aet* (5-4p)
MIDDLESEX PREMIER CUP
(March 21st at Uxbridge)
Ashford Town (Middlesex) Res. 1
Hillingdon Borough Res. 1 *aet* (3-1p)
MIDDLESEX INTERMEDIATE CUP
(March 28th at Hanwell Town)
Rayners Lane 2 Hanworth Villa 2 *aet* (5-4p)
MIDDLESEX JUNIOR CUP
(April 18th at Yeading)
North Hayes Academicals 2 British Airways Res. 0

WWW.NLNEWSDESK.CO.UK

MIDDLESEX JUNIOR TROPHY
(April 4th at Hillingdon Borough)
British Airways 'A' 3 Broadfields
United Vets 2

MID-CHESHIRE SENIOR CUP
(March 27th at Witton Albion)
Witton Albion 0 **Congleton Town** 3

MID-SOMERSET CHARITY CUP
(May 12th at Shepton Mallet)
Westfield 2 Belrose 0

MID-SUSSEX SENIOR CHARITY CUP
(May 10th at Haywards Heath Town)
Pease Pottage Village 1 Holland Sports 0

MORRISON BELL CUP
(May 25th at Ottery St Mary)
Budleigh Salterton 4 Sidmouth Town 0

NORFOLK JUNIOR CUP
(March 20th at Norwich City)
Catfield 0 **Norwich United Res.** 2

NORTH BEDFORDSHIRE CHARITY CUP
(May 7th at Langford)
Biggleswade Town 2 Potton United 1 *aet*

NORTH CAMBRIDGESHIRE JUNIOR CUP
(April 18th at Wisbech Town)
Doddington United 2 Coates Athletic 1

NORTH EAST WALES CUP
(May 8th at Wrexham)
Bala Town 2 Gresford Athletic 1

NORTH RIDING CHALLENGE CUP
(April 4th at Stokesley Sports Club)
Guisborough Quoit 2 **Rudds Arms** 3 aet

NORTH RIDING COUNTY CUP
(March 7th at Stokesley Sports Club)
Thornaby Athletic 0 **BEADS** 2

NORTH WALES COAST CUP
(May 9th at Colwyn Bay)
Flint Town United 1 Prestatyn Town 0

NORTH WALES COAST JUNIOR CUP
(May 16th at Colwyn Bay)
Beaumaris Town 4 Rhuddlan Town 0

NORTHAMPTONSHIRE JUNIOR CUP
(March 28th at Rushden & Diamonds)
Peterborough Sports 3 Kislingbury 1

NORTHAMPTONSHIRE LOWER JUNIOR CUP
(April 11th at Wellingborough Town)
Silver Jubilee 2 Clipston 0

NORTHAMPTONSHIRE AMATEUR CUP
(March 21st at Raunds Town)
Perkins Sports Res. 2
Northampton ON Chenecks 'A' 1

NORTHUMBERLAND BENEVOLENT BOWL
(May 11th at Whitley Park, Benton)
Wallsend 1 Whitley Bay 'A' 0

NORTHUMBERLAND MINOR CUP
(May 2nd at Whitley Park, Benton)
Amble United 1 Willington Quay Saints 0

NOTTS INTERMEDIATE CUP
(April 18th at Hucknall Town)
Blidworth Welfare 2 Bulwell 0

OKEHAMPTON CUP
(May 26th at Okehampton Argyle)
Okehampton Argyle 3 Heavitree Social United 1

OLD BOYS SENIOR INVITATION CUP
(March 24th at Old Parkonians)
Old Esthameians 1 Bealonians 0

OXFORDSHIRE CHARITY CUP
(April 28th at Kidlington)
Eynsham Association 4 Freeland 3

OXFORDSHIRE INTERMEDIATE CUP
(April 25th at Oxford City)
Stonesfield Sports 3 Kidlington Res. 1

OXFORDSHIRE JUNIOR SHIELD
(May 12th at Witney United)
Hailey 3 Spartan Rangers 2

PAULTON HOSPITAL CUP
(April 6th at Paulton Rovers)
Radstock Town Res. 2 Coleford Athletic 0

PORTSMOUTH SENIOR CUP
(April 4th at Havant & Waterlooville)
Gosport Borough Res. 2 Fleetlands 0

POTTERS BAR CHARITY CUP
(May 2nd at Potters Bar Town)
Potters Bar Town 5 London Lions 0

POWELL CHARITY CUP
(May 6th at Wem Town)
Shawbury United 0 **Ellesmere Rangers** 3

READING SENIOR CUP
(May 10th at Reading)
Highmoor/IBIS 5 Marlow United 1

ROLLESTON CHARITY CUP
(May 7th at LCFA, Holmes Park)
Oadby Town 2 Barwell 1

ROMFORD CHARITY CUP
(April 30th at Aveley)
Faces 3 Harold Wood Athletic 1

SACRISTON AGED MINERS CUP
(May 7th at Sacriston Welfare)
Brandon Prince Bishop 4 Whitehill 1

SEATON CUP
(May 17th at Seaton Town)
Seaton Town 1 East Budleigh 0

SHEFFIELD & HALLAMSHIRE ASSOCIATION CUP
(April 17th at Rotherham United)
Stocksbridge Park Steels Res. 3
Hemsworth Miners Welfare Res. 1

SHEFFIELD & HALLAMSHIRE JUNIOR CUP
(April 26th at Stocksbridge Park Steels)
Kinsley Boys 2 Hepworth United 0

SHROPSHIRE CHALLENGE CUP
(May 22nd at Shrewsbury Town)
Telford Juniors 1 Shifnal Town 0

SHROPSHIRE JUNIOR CUP
(May 15th at Shrewsbury Town)
Market Drayton Town Res. 1
Ludlow Town Res. 0

SMEDLEY CROOKE MEMORIAL CHARITY CUP
(April 19th at Bromsgrove Rovers)
Barnt Green Spartak 5 Wernley Athletic 2

SOMERSET SENIOR CUP
(May 7th at Weston-super-Mare)
Wells City 2 Burnham United 1

SOMERSET JUNIOR CUP
(May 8th at Shepton Mallet)
Normalair RSL 3 Merriott Rovers 0

SOMERSET INTERMEDIATE CUP
(May 1st at Taunton Town)
Dulverton Town 3 Weston St Johns 'B' 2

SOUTHAMPTON A CUP
(April 9th at Blackfield & Langley)
Gardeners 1 **East Boldre** 2

SOUTHAMPTON B CUP
(April 9th at Blackfield & Langley)
Bishops Waltham Town Res. 5 S & B Sports 0

SOUTH MIDLANDS FLOODLIGHT CUP
(May 16th at Saffron Walden Town)
Saffron Walden Town 2 Eynesbury Rovers 1

SOUTH MIDLANDS RESERVES FLOODLIGHT CUP
(May 10th at Cockfosters)
Cockfosters Res. 0 **Hertford Town Res.** 1

SOUTH WALES INTERMEDIATE CUP
(May 9th at Taffs Well)
Glyncorrwg Hall 4 FC Martyrs 3

SOUTHEND CHARITY A CUP
(May 9th at Great Wakering Rovers)
Shell Club Corringham 3 Rochford Town 0

SOUTHEND CHARITY B CUP
(April 19st at White Ensign)
White Ensign Res. 5 Basildon Town 5 *aet* (4-3p)

SOUTHEND CHARITY C CUP
(April 5th at White Ensign)
Galleywood Res. 2 Forest Rangers 0

SOUTHERN COMBINATION CUP
(August 4th at Merstham (provisional))
Merstham v Staines Lammas

STAFFORDSHIRE VASE
(April 2nd at Stafford Rangers)
Wolstanton United 2 Pelsall Villa 1

STAFFORDSHIRE CHALLENGE CUP
(April 16th at Eccleshall)
Foley Res. 3 Rushall Olympic Res. 0

STAFFORDSHIRE PRESIDENT'S CUP
(March 21st at Rushall Olympic)
Silverdale Globe 3 Lichfield Enots 0

SUFFOLK SENIOR CUP
(March 27th at Ipswich Town)
Stowmarket Town 2 Grundisburgh 1

SUFFOLK JUNIOR CUP
(April 19th at Ipswich Town)
Stonham Aspal 3 Hundon 0

SURREY PREMIER CUP
(April 11th at Metropolitan Police)
Carshalton Athletic Res. 1
Tooting & Mitcham United Res. 1 *aet* (3-4p)

SURREY INTERMEDIATE CUP
(May 8th at Molesey)
Epsom Eagles 2 Shottermill & Haslemere 0

SURREY JUNIOR CUP
(May 3rd at Leatherhead)
Molesey Villa 3 Frensham 2

SURREY LOWER JUNIOR CUP
(May 9th at Leatherhead)
Athletico 3 Kingston Albion Res. 0

SUSSEX R U R CHARITY CUP
(March 27th at Lancing)
Chichester City United 2 Whitehawk 1

SUSSEX INTERMEDIATE CUP
(May 1st at Lancing)
Pease Pottage Village 3 Uckfield Town 1 *aet*

SUSSEX JUNIOR CUP
(April 3rd at Eastbourne Town)
Polegate Town 0 **Athletico** 2 *aet*

TOLLSHUNT D'ARCY CUP
(May 14th at Witham Town)
Witham Town Res. 1 **Heybridge Swifts Res.** 3

TORRIDGE CUP
(May 3rd at Torrington)
Morwenstow 5 Boca Seniors 2 *aet*

VERNON WENTWORTH CUP
(May 14th at Worthing)
Rustington 1 Horsham YMCA Res. 1 *aet* (3-1p)

WALSALL SENIOR CUP
(May 8th at Walsall)
Boldmere St Michaels 3 Goodrich 1

WEDNESBURY CHARITY CUP
(May 15th at Walsall Wood)
Brereton Social 4 Shenstone Pathfinder 1

WEST HERTS ST MARYS CUP
(May 7th at Hemel Hempstead)
Hemel Hempstead Town 3 Berkhamsted Town 2

WEST RIDING CHALLENGE CUP
(April 4th at WRCFA, Woodlesford)
Campion 2 Golcar United 1

WEST RIDING CHALLENGE TROPHY
(April 27th at WRCFA, Woodlesford)
Beeston St Anthony's Res. 0 **Otley Town Res.** 1

WEST WALES SENIOR CUP
(May 16th at Neath Athletic)
Neath Athletic 2 Garden Village 1

WESTMORLAND BENEVOLENT TROPHY
(April 11th at Kendal Town)
Wetheriggs United 3
Kendal County 3 *aet* (6-5p)

WESTMORLAND JUNIOR CUP
(April 18th at Kendal Town)
Penrith Rangers 3 Kirkoswald 2

WESTWARD HO! CUP
(May 6th at Barnstaple Town)
Boca Seniors 1 Braunton 0

WILTSHIRE SENIOR CUP
(April 25th at Chippenham Town)
Corsham Town 1 Melksham Town 0

WILTSHIRE JUNIOR CUP
(April 21st at Laverstock & Ford)
Redlynch & Woodfalls United 3
North Bradley Saints 2

WIRRAL SENIOR CUP
(May 10th at Tranmere Rovers)
Ashville 2 **West Kirby** 4

WIRRAL AMATEUR CUP
(April 9th at Ashville)
Manor Athletic 0 **Poulton Victoria Res.** 2

WORCESTER ROYAL INFIRMARY CUP
(May 10th at Malvern Town)
Alvechurch 3 Redditch United 1

WORCESTERSHIRE URN
(May 2nd at Kidderminster Harriers)
Alvechurch 1 **Barnt Green Spartak** 2 *aet*

WORCESTERSHIRE JUNIOR CUP
(March 28th at Worcester City)
Littleton 4 Tenbury United 0

WYCOMBE SENIOR CUP
(May 15th at Wycombe Wanderers)
Chalfont St Peter 7 Downley Albion 0

Y M C A CUP
(May 19th at South Molton)
Landkey 3 North Molton 1

INDEX

Page numbers point to league table
If a team's 2007-08 directory entry is on a different page, this precedes in round brackets
Clubs subject to name changes and mergers are asterisked
Both new and old names are included in the index, and a full listing follows the index

WWW.CHERRYRED.CO.UK

WWW.CHERRYRED.CO.UK

WWW.CHERRYRED.CO.UK

WWW.CHERRYRED.CO.UK

WWW.NLNEWSDESK.CO.UK

*NAME CHANGES AND MERGERS

Ashbrooke Belford become **Belford House**
Austin Social Select become **Austin Sports & Social**
BAT Sports become **Totton & Eling**
Bedford United & Valerio become **Bedford**
Billingham Wanderers become **Billingam Kader**
Blackhall become **Blackhall Hardwick**
Brandon Prince Bishop become **Brandon British Legion**
Brierley & Withymoor are an amalgamation of **Brierley & Hagley** and **Withymoor Colts**
Brook House become **AFC Hayes**
Bulls Head Dawley Bank become **Dawley Bank**
Caister United become **Caister**
Chopwell Top Club become **Chopwell Officials Club**
Clacton Town become **FC Clacton**
Coble Ennis Square are an amalgamation of **Yorkshire Coble** and **Ennis Square**
Corby Madisons are an amalgamation of **Corby Hellenic Fisher** and **Corby St Brendans**
Coulsdon United are an amalgamation of **Coulsdon Town** and **Salfords**
Croxteth Red Rum become **Red Rum**
Downes Sports become **Hinckley Downes**
Dunston Federation Brewery become **Dunston Federation**
Farnborough Town become **Farnborough**
Ford Sports Daventry become **Daventry United**
Gillford Park Spartans become **Gillford Park**
Gravesend & Northfleet become **Ebbsfleet United**
Hayes & Yeading United are an amalgamation of **Hayes** and **Yeading**
Heather Athletic become **Heather St John**
Hill Athletic become **North Sefton**
JFF Telford become **Telford Town**
Kingsbury London Tigers become **London Tigers**
Kirkley become **Kirkley & Pakefield**
Lincoln Moorlands Railway are an amalgamation of **Lincoln Moorlands** and **Moorlands Railway**
Liverpool NALGO become **Alder**
Louth United become **Louth Town**
Louth United Reserves become **Louth United**
Lymington & New Milton become **New Milton Town**
Mackets become **Mackets Grenadier**
Mauritius Sports & Pennant are an amalgamation of **Mauritius Sports (CMB)** and **Walthamstow Avenue & Pennant**
Milton United (Staffs) become **Barton United**
New Marske Sports Club are an amalgamation of **Carlin How WMC** and **New Marske Sports Club**
New Penny become **Northwood Town**
Newcastle Benfield BP become **Newcastle Benfield**
Newcastle Town Youth become **Newcastle Town 'A'**
OLA Newbury become **Newbury**
Orton Vale become **AFC Wombourne United**
Oxford Quarry Nomads become **Oxford City Nomads**
Parkfield Leisure become **Parkfield United**
Penrith become **Penrith Town**
Ripon City Magnets become **Ripon City**
Rolls Royce become **Telecoms**
Rushden & Higham United are an amalgamation of **Rushden Rangers** and **Higham United**
Solihull Moors are an amalgamation of **Moor Green** and **Solihull Borough**
Southwold Town become **Sole Bay**
Springfield BAC/EE become **BAC/EE Springfield**
Stoneham become **AFC Stoneham**
Stonehouse Freeway become **Stonehouse Town**
Vision become **Angus Village**
Wallsend become **Gateshead Leam Lane**
Wernley Athletic become **Oldbury Athletic**
West Didsbury & Chorlton become **West Didsbury**
West Suffolk College become **Team Bury**
Worcester City 'A' become **Worcester City Academy**

WWW.NLNEWSDESK.CO.UK

CHERRY RED RECORDS
THE *VERY* BEST OF FOOTBALL MUSIC ON CD

ARSENAL
Highbury Anthems

ASTON VILLA
Come On You Villa

BIRMINGHAM
Keep Right On

CELTIC
The Songs Of Celtic
Vol 2

CHARLTON
The Red Red Robin

CHELSEA
Blue Flag

EVERTON
Forever Everton

FULHAM
Viva El Fulham

LIVERPOOL
This Is Anfield

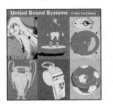

MAN. UTD.
United Sound Systems

MIDDLESBROUGH
Boro Songs

RANGERS
Follow! Follow!

SUNDERLAND
Mackem Music

TOTTENHAM
We Are Tottenham

WEST BROM.
Boing Boing Baggies

WEST HAM
Forever Blowing
Bubbles

All club releases are full length albums. Each one contains between 13 and 24 tracks. Clubs also available in this series include **Aberdeen**, **Arsenal** *Good Old Arsenal*, **Burnley**, **Cardiff**, **Celtic** *Hail Hail Celtic* and *The Songs of Celtic*, **Coventry**, **Crystal Palace**, **Derby**, **Hearts**, **Hibernian**, **Ipswich**, **Kilmarnock**, **Leicester**, **Liverpool** *Kop Choir*, **Middlesbrough** *Up The 'Boro*, **Norwich**, **Nottingham Forest**, **Portsmouth**, **QPR**, **Rangers** *The Famous Glasgow Rangers*, *Blue Anthems*, *Ibrox Anthems* and *Didn't You Know*, **Republic of Ireland**, **Scotland**, **Sheffield Wednesday**, **Southampton**, **Tottenham** *The Cup Kings*, **Stoke City**, **Sunderland** *Roker Roar*, **Wales** and **Wolverhampton Wanderers**.

ALL CD'S £9.95 including postage. Add 50p for Europe and £1.00 Rest Of The World.
(Selected titles also available on cassette.)
CREDIT CARD HOTLINE 020 8740 4110 E-Mail infonet@cherryred.co.uk

Make cheques payable to: **CHERRY RED RECORDS LTD** and send to:
Cherry Red Records, Unit 3A, Long Island House, Warple Way, London W3 ORG

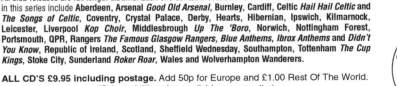

www.cherryred.co.uk